LEGENDS IN THEIR OWN TIME

Coral Amende

Prentice Hall General Reference

New York   London   Toronto   Sydney   Tokyo   Singapore

PRENTICE HALL GENERAL REFERENCE
15 Columbus Circle
New York, New York 10023

Library of Congress Cataloging in Publication Data

Amende, Coral.
    Legends in their own time / Coral Amende.
       p.   cm.
    Includes bibliographical references.
    ISBN 0-671-88052-7—ISBN 0-671-88053-5
    1. Celebrities—Biography—Dictionaries.   I. Title.
CT103.A64   1994
920'.003—dc20   93-47630
[B]

Designed by Irving Perkins Associates, Inc.

Manufactured in the United States of America

First Edition

CONTENTS

☆

ACKNOWLEDGMENTS

☆

Many thanks to the Los Angeles Public Library, Jim and Norma Amende, Hal Belden, Dave Dutton and Dutton's Books, Dave Frishberg, Scott Malick, Deirdre Mullane, David Rosner, Teressa Rowell, and Nancy Yost.

How to Use This Book

☆

This volume was designed to include a great deal of basic biographical information about a wide variety of famous figures in a minimum amount of space. It contains eminent names from the annals of history as well as from the present day, drawn from the fields of entertainment, sports, politics, science, and the arts, with an emphasis on contemporary popular figures not found in standard biographical dictionaries.

There are more than 10,000 individuals included in the Index of Last Names. For each, dates of birth and death, as well as alternate names, nicknames, and pen names are given. For most entries, especially those of entertainers and writers, the most well-known works or creations are included, and important awards like the Nobel Prize, Pulitzer Prize, Oscar, Emmy, Tony, and Grammy are also noted.

When you know a person's first name but can't remember the last, the second part of the book, an Index of First Names, will be helpful. A list of individuals with that first name follows, with their general occupational categories noted. Once you have found the name, refer to the Index of Last Names for more detailed biographical information.

Other useful ready-reference features include an Index of Nicknames, a list of Famous Marriages, and a Subject Index.

Whether you're a student or writer needing quick biographical information, a crossword puzzle enthusiast stumped by a clue, or just want to know when your favorite celebrity was born, *Legends in Their Own Time* will prove to be an indispensable, one-stop resource.

GUIDE TO ABBREVIATIONS

ACLU—American Civil Liberties Union
AFL; AF OF L—American Federation of Labor
AFR.—African
AFR.-AM.—African-American
A/K/A—also known as
ALB.—Albanian
AM.—American
ARAB.—Arabian
ARG.—Argentinian
ARM.—Armenian
ASSYR.—Assyrian
ATH.—Athenian
AUS.—Austrian
AUSTRAL.—Australian
BAB.—Babylonian
BARB.—Barbadian
BELG.—Belgian
BOHEM.—Bohemian
BRAZ.—Brazilian
BULG.—Bulgarian
BUR.—Burmese
C—contemporary
CAM.—Cameroonian
CAMBOD.—Cambodian
CAN.—Canadian
CARTH.—Carthagenian
CEO—Chief Executive Officer
CHIL.—Chilean
CHIN.—Chinese
COL.—Colombian
CONT.—continued
CUB.—Cuban
CZ.—Czechoslovakian
DAN.—Danish
DOM.—Dominican
E—Emmy winner
ECUA.—Ecuadoran
EGYPT.—Egyptian
ENG.—English
ETH.—Ethiopian
FINN.—Finnish
FL.—flourished
FLEM.—Flemish
FLOR.—Florentine
FR.—French
FR. W. IND.—French West Indian
G—Grammy winner
GER.—German
GHAN.—Ghanaian

GOV.—governor
GR.—Greek
GUAT.—Guatemalan
GUI.—Gianan
GUIN.—Guinean
GUY.—Guyanese
HEB.—Hebrew
H.H.—His/Her Highness
HUNG.—Hungarian
ICEL.—Icelandic
IND.—Indian
INDON.—Indonesian
IR.—Irish
IRAN.—Iranian
ISL.—Islamic
ISR.—Israeli
ITAL.—Italian
JAM.—Jamaican
JAP.—Japanese
JEW.—Jewish
JORD.—Jordanian
LAT.—Latvian
LIB.—Libyan
LITH.—Lithuanian
MET, THE MET—Metropolitan Opera (New York City)
MEX.—Mexican
MGM—Metro-Goldwyn-Mayer
MIL.—military
MIT—Massachusetts Institute of Technology
MONG.—Mongolian
MOR.—Moroccan
MPAA—Motion Picture Association of America
N—Nobel Prize winner
NAACP—National Association for the Advancement of Colored People
NATO—North Atlantic Treaty Organization
NEP.—Nepalese
NFL—National Football League
NIC.—Nicaraguan
NIGER.—Nigerian
NORW.—Norwegian
N.Z.—New Zealand
O—Oscar winner
ORIG.—originally
P—Pulitzer Prize winner
PAL.—Palestinian

PAN.—Panamanian
PERS.—Persian
PERUV.—Peruvian
PHIL.—Philippine
PLO—Palestine Liberation Organization
POL.—Polish
PORT.—Portugese
P.R.—Puerto Rican
PROV.—Provençal
PSEUD.—pseudonym
REV.—Reverend
ROM.—Romanian
RUSS.—Russian
S. AFR.—South African
SAUD. ARAB.—Saudi Arabian
SCAND.—Scandinavian
SCOT.—Scottish
SEN.—Senegalese
SERBO-CR.—Serbo-Croatian
S. KOR.—South Korean
S.L.—Sierra Leonean
SPAN.—Spanish
SPART.—Spartan
SWED.—Swedish
SWI.—Swiss
SYR.—Syrian
T—Tony winner
TANZ.—Tanzanian
TAS.—Tasmanian
TRIN.—Trinidadian
TURK.—Turkish
UG.—Ugandan
U.N.—United Nations
URUG.—Uruguayan
VEN.—Venetian
VENEZ.—Venezuelan
VIET.—Vietnamese
W—Wimbledon winner
WEL.—Welsh
W. IND.—West Indian
WWI—World War I
WWII—World War II
YUG.—Yugoslav

INDEX OF LAST NAMES

☆

Information about the more than 10,000 people included in this list is presented as follows:

★ Entries are listed alphabetically by last name and include titles—Sir, Dame, Lord, etc.—when applicable.
★ Following each name in parentheses are birth name, where known; pseudonyms and aliases (preceded by *a/k/a*); and nicknames in quotation marks.
★ Years of birth and death are enclosed within parentheses. Accuracy of birth years, particularly for those individuals within the entertainment field, is notoriously unreliable (and in fact it is not uncommon to find a different year given in each available source). I have tried in each case to verify questionable years, but when this was not possible, the earliest year found was used. Where no information was available, a question mark or a capital letter *C* was used. "C" denotes "Contemporary," that is, known to be living or to have lived in the twentieth century.
★ Nationality (see "Guide to Abbreviations" at the beginning of the book) and occupation(s).
★ Familial relationship to others included in this book, excluding marriages, which are listed in the "Famous Marriages" chapter.
★ Examples of best-known work or works.
★ Notable awards and prizes (and year received), abbreviated as follows:

N — Nobel prize
O — Oscar (Academy Award for Best Actor/Actress, Best Supporting Actor/Actress, and Best Director only) and title of winning film
P — Pulitzer prize (and title of winning work if applicable)
W — Wimbledon (men's and women's singles only)
G — Grammy
E — Emmy
T — Tony

1

Aaker, Lee (1943–) Am. child actor (Rusty in "The Adventures of Rin Tin Tin" TV series)

Aalto, Alvar (Hugo Alvar Henrik Aalto) (1898–1976) Finn. architect/furniture designer/educator (at M.I.T.)

Aames, Willie (William Upton) (1960–) Am. actor ("Eight Is Enough" TV series)

Aaron (c. 14th century B.C.) Heb. priest (brother of Moses)

Aaron, Hank (Henry Louis Aaron; "Bad Henry"; "The Hammer"; "The New Sultan of Swat") (1934–) Am. baseball Hall-of-Famer

Abbado, Claudio (1933–) Ital. orchestra conductor (London Symphony)

Abbey, Edward (1927–) Am. naturalist/writer (*Desert Solitaire*)

Abbey, Edwin (Edwin Austin Abbey) (1852–1911) Am. illustrator (*Harper's Weekly*)/muralist

Abbott, Berenice (1898–) Am. photographer (apprentice of Man Ray)

Abbott, Bud (William Alexander Abbott) (1895–1974) Am. comedian (with Abbott and Costello)

Abbott, George (George Francis Abbott) (1887–) Am. theatrical producer/director/playwright (P—1960—*Fiorello*)

Abbott, John (1905–) Eng.-Am. actor (*Gigi; The Greatest Story Ever Told*)

Abdul, Paula (Paula Julie Abdul) (1961–) Am. pop singer ("Forever Your Girl"; "Straight Up")

Abdul-Jabbar, Kareem (Ferdinand Lewis Alcindor, Jr.; "The Franchise") (1947–) Am. basketball player

Abe, Kōbō (1924–1993) Jap. novelist (*The Woman in the Dunes*)

Abel, Sid (Sidney Gerald Abel; "Bootnose") (1918–) Can. hockey player

Abélard, Pierre or **Peter** (1079–1142) Fr. philosopher/theologian

Abercrombie, James (1706–1781) Scot.-Eng. general

Abernathy, Ralph (Ralph David Abernathy) (1926–1990) Am. clergyman/civil rights leader (president of the Southern Christian Leadership Conference, succeeding Martin Luther King, Jr.)

Abington, Fanny (née Frances Barton) (1737–1815) Eng. actress (created Lady Teazle)

Abraham (fl. c. 1800 B.C.) Heb. patriarch

Abraham, F. Murray (Fahrid Murray Abraham) (1939–) Am. actor (*All the President's Men; The Bonfire of the Vanities*; O—1984—*Amadeus*)

Abramowitz, Max (1908–) Am. architect (Lincoln Center's Avery Fisher Hall)

Absalom (fl. c. 1020 B.C.) Heb. son of King David

Abzug, Bella (née Savitsky; "Battling Bella") (1920–) Am. congresswoman

Ace, Goodman (1899–1982) Am. humorist/radio comedian ("Easy Aces")

Ace, Jane (née Sherwood) (1905–1974) Am. humorist/radio comedienne ("Easy Aces")

Ace, Johnny (John Marshall Alexander, Jr.) (1929–1954) Am. rhythm and blues singer ("Pledging My Love")

Achebe, Chinua (Albert Chinualumogu) (1930–) Niger. writer (*Things Fall Apart*)

Acheson, Dean (Dean Gooderham Acheson) (1893–1971) Am. secretary of state/writer (P—1970—*Present at the Creation: My Years in the State Department*)

Ackland, Joss (1928–) Eng. actor (*The Hunt for Red October*)

Acord, Art (1890–1931) Am. cowboy actor (*The Squaw Man; The Arizona Kid*)

Acton, John (John Emerich Edward Dalberg Acton) (1834–1902) Eng. historian/editor (*Cambridge Modern History*)

Acuff, Eddie (1902–1956) Am. actor (*Blondie* postman)

Acuff, Roy (Roy Claxton Acuff; "The Smokey Mountain Boy"; "King of Country Music") (1903–1992) Am. country singer ("Wabash Cannonball")

Adam, Robert (1728–1792) Scot. architect/furniture designer/decorator

Adams, Abigail (née Smith; "Mrs. President") (1744–1818) Am. first lady (John)/letter-writer

Adams, Alice (1926–) Am. writer (*Second Chances; Almost Perfect*)

Adams, Ansel (Ansel Easton Adams) (1902–1984) Am. wilderness photographer

Adams, Babe (Charles Benjamin Adams) (1882–1968) Am. baseball player

Adams, Brooke (1949–) Am. actress (*The Dead Zone; Days of Heaven; Gas, Food, Lodging*)

Adams, Bryan (1959–) Can. rock singer ("Heaven"; "Lonely Nights")

Adams, Catlin (1950–) Am. actress ("Square Pegs" TV series)

Adams, Don (Donald James Yarmy) (1926–) Am. comedian (Maxwell Smart in "Get Smart" TV series; E—1966/67, 1967/68, 1968/69)

Adams, Edie (Elizabeth Edith Enke) (1927–) Am. actress/singer ("The Jack Paar Show" and "The Ernie Kovacs Show" TV series)

Adams, Franklin P. (Franklin Pierce Adams; "FPA") (1881–1960) Am. humorist/columnist ("The Conning Tower")

Adams, Henry (Henry Brooks Adams) (1838–1918) Am. historian (P—1919— *The Education of Henry Adams*)

Adams, Joey (Joseph Abramowitz) (1911–) Am. comedian

Adams, John ("The Atlas of Independence") (1735–1826) 2nd Am. pres. (1797–1801)

Adams, John Quincy ("The Accidental President"; "Old Man Eloquent"; "Publicola"; "The Second John") (1767–1848) 6th Am. pres. (1825–1829)

Adams, Julie (Betty May Adams) (1926–) Am. actress (*The Creature from the Black Lagoon; Hollywood Story*)

Adams, Louise (Louise or Louisa Catherine Johnson) (1775–1852) Am. first lady (John Quincy)

Adams, Maud (Maud Solveig Christina Wikstrom; a/k/a Maude Adams) (1945–) Am. actress (*Octopussy; Rollerball*)

Adams, Maude (Maude Ewing Adams née Kiskaden) (1872–1953) Am. stage actress/drama teacher

Adams, Nick (Nicholas Aloysius Adamshock) (1931–1968) Am. actor ("The Rebel" TV series; *Twilight of Honor*)

Adams, Oleta (C) Am. pop singer ("Get Here")

Adams, Richard (Richard George Adams) (1920–) Eng. novelist (*Watership Down; The Plague Dogs*)

Adams, Samuel ("Father of the American Revolution") (1722–1802) Am. revolutionary leader/gov. of Massachusetts

Adams, Sarah (née Flower) (1805–1848) Eng. poet/hymn writer (Nearer, My God, to Thee)

Adams, Sherman (Sherman Llewellyn Adams) (1899–1966) Am. congressman/gov. (New Hampshire)/chief of staff

Adamson, Joy (Joy Friederieke Victoria Gessner) (1910–1980) Eng. naturalist/writer (*Born Free*)

Addams, Charles (Charles Samuel Addams) (1912–1988) Am. cartoonist (*The Addams Family*)

Addams, Dawn (1930–1985) Eng. actress (*The Robe*; Chaplin's *A King in New York*)

Addams, Jane (1860–1935) Am. social reformer (helped found the ACLU)/writer (*Twenty Years at Hull-House*; N—1931)

Adderley, Cannonball (Julian Edwin Adderley) (1928–1975) Am. jazz saxophonist/composer ("Jive Samba")

Adderley, Herb (Herbert Anthony Adderley) (1939–) Am. football Hall-of-Famer

Addison, Joseph ("Atticus"; "Clio"; "The English Atticus"; "A Literary Machiavel") (1672–1719) Eng. poet/essayist (*The Campaign; Rosamond; Cato*)

Addy, Wesley (1913–) Am. actor (*Whatever Happened to Baby Jane?*; *Network*)

Ade, George (1866–1944) Am. humorist/playwright (*Fables in Slang*)

Adenauer, Konrad (1876–1967) Ger. statesman/chancellor (1949–1963)

Ader, Clément (1841–1926) Fr. inventor (microphone)

Adjani, Isabelle (1955–) Fr.-Ger. actress (*The Story of Adele H.; Camille Claudel*)

Adler, Alfred (1870–1937) Aus. psychiatrist (a follower of Freud; coined the term *inferiority complex*)

Adler, Luther (Lutha Adler) (1903–1984) Am. actor (brother of Stella; *The Brotherhood; The Last Angry Man*)

Adler, Mortimer (Mortimer Jerome Adler) (1902–) Am. philosopher/writer (*How to Read a Book*)

Adler, Stella (a/k/a Stella Ardler) (1902–1993) Am. stage/film actress/acting teacher (helped found New York's Group Theater)

Adlon, Percy (1935–) Ger. film director (*Sugarbaby; Bagdad Cafe*)

Adonis, Joe (Joseph Doto) (1902–1972) Am. crime boss

Adorée, Renée (Jeanne de la Fonte) (1898–1933) Fr. actress (*The Big Parade*)

Adrian (Adrian Adolph Greenberg; a/k/a Gilbert A. Adrian) (1903–1959) Am. fashion designer

Adrian, Iris (Iris Adrian Hostetter) (1912–) Am. actress ("The Abbott and Costello Show" TV series; *The Love Bug*)

Aelfric (a/k/a Grammaticus) (c. 955–c. 1010) Eng. writer (*Lives of the Saints*)

Aeschylus ("The Father of Greek Tragedy") (c. 525–456 B.C.) Gr. dramatist (*Prometheus Bound*)

Aesop (?620–?560 B.C.) Gr. fabulist, probably legendary (*Aesop's Fables*)

Aga Khan (Aga Khan IV; H. H. Prince Karim Khan) (1936–) Muslim leader 1957–

Agar, Herbert (Herbert Sebastian Agar) (1897–1980) Am. journalist/writer (*Bread and Circuses*; P—1934—*The People's Choice*)

Agassi, Andre (1970–) Am. tennis player (W—1992)

Agassiz, Louis (Jean Louis Rodolphe Agassiz) (1807–1873) Am. zoologist/geologist/writer (*Lake Superior*)

Agee, James (James Rufus Agee) (1909–1955) Am. writer (P—1958—*Let Us Now Praise Famous Men; A Death in the Family;*)/screenwriter (Night of the Hunter)

Ager, Milton (1893–1979) Am. songwriter ("Ain't She Sweet"; "Happy Days Are Here Again")

Agnew, Spiro T. (Spiro Theodore Agnew) (1918–) Am. v.p. (R. Nixon)

Agnon, Shmuel (Shmuel Yosef Agnon; orig. Samuel Josef Czaczkes) (1888–1970) Isr. novelist/short story writer (N—1966; *Twenty-One Stories*)

Agrippa (Marcus Vipsanius Agrippa) (c. 63–12 B.C.) Roman statesman/general

Agrippina (c. 14 B.C.–A.D. 33) Roman mother of Caligula, wife of Agrippa

Agronsky, Martin (Martin Zama Agronsky) (1915–) Am. journalist/newscaster ("Agronsky and Company")

Aguilera, Rick (Richard Warren Aguilera) (1961–) Am. baseball pitcher

Agutter, Jenny (1952–) Eng. actress (*The Eagle Has Landed; Walkabout; Equus*)

Ahab 7th king of Israel (c. 874–c. 853 B.C.)

Aherne, Brian (Brian Delacy Aherne) (1902–1986) Eng.-Am. actor (*Sylvia Scarlett; Juarez*)

Ahn, Philip (1911–1978) Am. actor ("Kung Fu" TV series; *Blood on the Sun*)

Aiello, Danny (Danny Louis Aiello, Jr.) (1933–) Am. actor (*Bang the Drum Slowly; The Purple Rose of Cairo; Do the Right Thing*)

Aiken, Conrad (Conrad Potter Aiken; a/k/a Samuel Leake, Jr.) (1889–1973) Am. poet/writer (*Conversation; or, Pilgrim's Progress*; P—1930—*Selected Poems*)

Aiken, Joan (Joan Delano Aiken; a/k/a Nicholas Dee and Rosie Lee) (1924–) Eng. mystery writer/novelist (*The Wolves of Willoughby Chase*)

Ailey, Alvin (Alvin Ailey, Jr.) (1931–1989) Am. choreographer (*Blues Suite; Revelations*)

Aimée, Anouk (François Sorya Dreyfus) (1932–) Fr. actress (*A Man and a Woman; La Dolce Vita*)

Ainsworth, William Harrison (1805–1882) Eng. novelist (*Tower of London; Guy Fawkes*)

Aitken, Robert Ingersoll (1878–1949) Am. sculptor (McKinley monuments)

Aitken, Spottiswoode (Frank Spottiswoode Aitken) (1869–1933) Am. actor (*Intolerance; The Birth of a Nation*)

Aitken, William Maxwell, Lord Beaverbrook (1879–1964) Can.-Eng. politician/newspaper magnate (*Daily Express, Evening Standard*)

Akers, Karen (c. 1946–) Am. cabaret singer/actress (*Heartburn*)

Akhenaton (a/k/a Amenhotep IV, Amenophis IV) Egypt. king 1379–1362 B.C. (married to Nefertiti)

Akhmatova, Anna (Anna Andreyevna Gorenko) (1889–1966) Russ. poet (*Poem without a Hero*)

Akihito (1933–) Jap. emperor 1989– (son of Hirohito, father of Naruhito)

Akins, Zoë (1886–1958) Am. playwright (P—1935—*The Old Maid*)/poet/screenwriter (*How to Marry a Millionaire; Stagestruck*)

Akiyoshi, Toshiko (1929–) Am. jazz keyboardist/composer

Aladdin (Aladdin Abdullah Achmed Anthony Pallante) (1917–) Am. violinist (in the Lawrence Welk orchestra)

Alban, Saint (died c. 304 A.D.) Eng. soldier/martyr

Albanese, Licia (1913–) Ital. opera singer (soprano)

Albee, Edward (Edward Franklin Albee) (1928–) Am. playwright (Who's Afraid of Virginia Woolf? P—1967—*A Delicate Balance*; P—1975—*Seascape*)

Albéniz, Isaac (Isaac Manuel Francisco Albéniz) (1860–1909) Span. composer (*Iberia*)

Alberghetti, Anna Maria (1936–) Ital.-Am. singer/actress (*Cinderfella*); T—1962

Albers, Josef (1888–1976) Ger.-Am. painter (Bauhaus)

Albert (Albert Alexandre Louis Pierre Grimaldi; "The Sun King") (1958–) prince of Monaco

Albert, Prince (Francis Charles Augustus Albert Emmanuel) (1819–1861) Eng. husband of Queen Victoria

Albert, Carl (Carl Bert Albert) (1908–) Am. politician (speaker of the house)

Albert, Eddie (Edward Albert Heimberger) (1908–) Am. actor ("Green Acres" TV series; Roman Holiday)

Albert, Morris (Morris Albert Kaisermann) (1951–) Braz. pop singer ("Feelings")

Albertson, Jack (1907–1981) Am. actor (Days of Wine and Roses; O—1968— The Subject Was Roses; E—1975/76)

Albright, Hardie (Hardy Albrecht) (1903–1971) Am. actor (Three Cornered Moon; Angel on My Shoulder)

Albright, Lola (Lola Jean Albright) (1924–) Am. actress ("Peyton Place" and "Peter Gunn" TV series)

Albright, Tenley (Tenley Emma Albright) (1935–) Am. figure skater

Alcaeus (c. 620–580 B.C.) Gr. poet (possible inventor of the alcaic stanza)

Alcott, Amy (Amy Strum Alcott) (1956–) Am. golfer

Alcott, Bronson (Amos Bronson Alcott) (1799–1888) Am. poet/philosopher/educator (Tablets)

Alcott, Louisa May (1832–1888) Am. novelist (Little Women; Little Men)

Alda, Alan (Alphonso D'Abruzzo) (1936–) Am. actor (son of Robert; Crimes and Misdemeanors; "M*A*S*H" TV series; E—1973/74, 1981/82)

Alda, Robert (Alphonso Giovanni Giuseppe Roberto d'Abruzzo) (1914–1986) Am. stage actor (father of Alan; Guys and Dolls; What Makes Sammy Run; T—1951)

Alden, John (c. 1599–1687) Eng. Mayflower pilgrim/colonist

Aldiss, Brian W. (Brian Wilson Aldiss; a/k/a Jael Cracken, Arch Mendicant, Peter Pica, and C. C. Shackleton) (1925–) Eng. science fiction writer (Frankenstein Unbound; Billion Year Spree)

Aldrich, Nelson (Nelson Wilmarth Aldrich) (1841–1915) Am. senator

Aldrich, Robert (1918–1983) Am. film director (Whatever Happened to Baby Jane?; The Dirty Dozen; Hush . . . Hush Sweet Charlotte)

Aldrin, Buzz (Edwin Eugene Aldrin, Jr.) (1930–) Am. astronaut (second man on the moon)

Aleichem, Sholom or Sholem (Sholem Yakov Rabinowitz; "The Yiddish Mark Twain") (1859–1916) Russ.-Jew. humorist (Tevye's Daughter [staged and filmed as Fiddler on the Roof])

Alexander I (Aleksandr Pavlovich) (1777–1825) Russ. emperor 1801–1825

Alexander II (Aleksandr Nikolayevich; "The Emancipator") (1818–1881) Russ. emperor 1855–1881

Alexander III (Aleksandr Aleksandrovich) (1845–1894) Russ. emperor 1881–1894

Alexander The Great (Alexander III; "Conqueror of the World"; "Madman of Macedonia") (356–323 B.C.) Gr. warrior/king of Macedonia 336–323 B.C.

Alexander, Doyle (Doyle Lafayette Alexander) (1950–) Am. baseball pitcher

Alexander, Erika (c. 1969–) Am. actress ("The Cosby Show" TV series)

Alexander, Grover Cleveland ("Alex the Great"; "Pete"; "Old Pete"; "Old Low-And-Away") (1887–1950) Am. baseball Hall-of-Famer

Alexander, Jane (Jane Quigley) (1939–) Am. actress (The Great White Hope; Testament; Kramer vs. Kramer)

Alexander, Shana (née Ager) (1925–) Am. journalist/crime writer (Nutcracker: Money, Madness, Murder)

Alexander, Terence (1923–) Eng. actor (The League of Gentlemen; The Day of the Jackal)

Alexis I (Alexis I Mikhaylovich) (1629–1676) Russ. czar 1645–1676

Alexis, Kim (1960–) Am. model

Alfonso XIII (1886–1941) Span. king 1886–1931

Alfred The Great (849–899) Saxon king of Wessex (871–899)/soldier/scholar

Alger, Horatio (Horatio Alger, Jr.) (1832–1899) Am. writer of more than 100 books for boys ("rags to riches" stories; Luck and Pluck; Sink or Swim)

Algren, Nelson (Nelson Algren Abraham; "Poet of the Chicago Slums") (1909–1981) Am. novelist/short story writer (A Walk on the Wild Side; The Man with the Golden Arm)

Ali, Muhammed or Muhammad (Cassius Marcellus Clay, Jr.; "The Greatest";

"Cassius the Brashest"; "Gaseous Cassius"; "The Louisville Lip") (1942–) Am. boxer

Alicia, Ana (Ana Alicia Ortiz) (1956–) Am. actress ("Falcon Crest" TV series)

Alighieri, Dante see Dante

Alioto, Joseph (Joseph Lawrence Alioto) (1916–) Am. govt. official (mayor of San Francisco)

Allanson, Andy (Andrew Neal Allanson) (1961–) Am. baseball player

Allégret, Marc (1900–1973) Fr. film director (brother of Yves; *Lady Chatterley's Lover*; *Fanny*)

Allégret, Yves (a/k/a Yves Champlain) (1907–1987) Fr. film director/screenwriter (brother of Marc; *Dedee*; *The Cheat*)

Allen, Barbara Jo (a/k/a Vera Vague) (1905–1974) Am. radio/TV comedienne

Allen, Byron (1961–) Am. TV host/comedian ("Real People" TV series)

Allen, Dayton (1919–) Am. comedian (on "The Steve Allen Show" TV series)

Allen, Debbie (Deborah Allen) (1950–) Am. dancer/choreographer/actress ("Fame" TV series)

Allen, Deborah (Deborah Lynn Thurmond) (1953–) Am. country singer ("Baby I Lied"; "If You're Not Gonna Love Me")

Allen, Elizabeth (Elizabeth Ellen Gillease) (1934–) Am. actress ("The Jackie Gleason Show" TV series; *Donovan's Reef*)

Allen, Ethan (1738–1789) Am. Revolutionary soldier/leader of the Green Mountain Boys

Allen, Fred (John Florence Sullivan) (1894–1956) Am. comedian ("What's My Line?" TV series)

Allen, George (George Herbert Allen; "Ice Cream") (1922–1990) Am. football coach

Allen, Gracie (Gracie Ethel Cecile Rosalie Allen) (1902 or 1906–1964) Am. comedienne (with George Burns)

Allen, Hervey (William Hervey Allen, Jr.) (1889–1949) Am. poet/historical novelist (*Anthony Adverse*)

Allen, Irwin (1916–1991) Am. film director/producer (*The Towering Inferno*; *The Poseidon Adventure*)

Allen, Karen (Karen Jane Allen) (1951–) Am. actress (*Raiders of the Lost Ark*; *Animal House*; *Scrooged*)

Allen, Mel (Melvin Allen Israel) (1913–) Am. sportscaster

Allen, Nancy (1950–) Am. actress (*Dressed to Kill*; *Blow Out*; *Robocop*)

Allen, Peter (Peter Woolnough Allen) (1944–1992) Austral. songwriter (theme from *Arthur*)/singer

Allen, Red (Henry James Allen, Jr.) (1900–1967) Am. jazz trumpeter

Allen, Rex (Rex E. Allen; "Mister Cowboy") (1922–) Am. cowboy actor/singer (and narrator of many Disney films)

Allen, Rex, Jr. (1947–) Am. country singer ("Arizona" [became that state's anthem])

Allen, Steve (Stephen Valentine Patrick William Allen; "Stevereeno") (1921–) Am. comedian ("The Steve Allen Show" TV series)/TV host ("The Tonight Show")

Allen, Tim (Timothy Allen Dick) (1953–) Am. comedian/actor ("Home Improvement" TV series)

Allen, Woody (Allen Stewart Konigsberg) (1935–) Am. actor/film director (*Bananas*; *Sleeper*; *Love and Death*; O—1977—*Annie Hall*)

Allende, Isabelle (1942–) Chil. writer (*The House of Spirits*)

Allende, Salvador (Salvador Allende Gossens) (1908–1973) Chil. pres. 1970–1973

Alley, Kirstie (1955–) Am. actress (*Look Who's Talking*; "Cheers" TV series; E—1990/91)

Allingham, Margery (Margery Louise Allingham Carter) (1904–1966) Eng. mystery writer (created Albert Campion)

Allison, Bobby (Robert Arthur Allison) (1937–) Am. auto racer

Allison, Fran (Frances Allison) (1907–1989) Am. actress ("Kukla, Fran & Ollie")

Allison, Mose (1927–) Am. jazz pianist/songwriter

Allman, Duane (Howard Duane Allman) (1946–1971) Am. rock musician (with The Allman Brothers)

Allman, Gregg (Gregory Lenoir Allman) (1947–) Am. rock singer ("I'm No Angel"; "Midnight Rider"; formerly with The Allman Brothers)

Allston, Washington (1779–1843) Am. landscape painter (*Belshazzar's Feast*)

Allyson, June (Ella Geisman) (1917–) Am. actress (*Till the Clouds Roll By*; *The Glenn Miller Story*)

Almendros, Nestor (a/k/a John Nestor) (1930–1992) Span.-Am. cinematographer/director (*New York Stories*)

Almodóvar, Pedro (a/k/a Patti Diphusa) (1949–) Span. film director (*Tie Me Up! Tie Me Down!*; *Women on the Verge of a Nervous Breakdown*)

Almond, Marc (Peter Marc Almond) (1957–) Eng. pop singer (with Soft Cell; "Tainted Love")

Alonso, Alicia (Alicia Ernestina de la Caridad del Cobre Martínez Hoyo) (1921–) Cub. ballerina/choreographer

Alonso, Maria Conchita (1957–) Cub.-Am. actress (*Moscow on the Hudson*; *Colors*)

Alpert, Herb (1935–) Am. trumpeter ("Rise")/bandleader (Tijuana Brass)/cofounder of A&M Records

Alsop, Joseph W. (Joseph Wright Alsop, Jr.) (1910–1989) Am. journalist/writer (*From the Silent Earth*)

Alston, Walter (Walter Emmons Alston; "Smokey") (1911–1984) Am. baseball Hall-of-Famer

Alt, Carol (1960–) Am. model

Altman, Robert (Robert B. Altman) (1925–) Am. film director (*M*A*S*H*; *The Player*; *Short Cuts*)

Alvarez, Luis (Luis Walter Alvarez) (1911–1988) Am. physicist (discovered transient resonance particles; N—1968)

Alworth, Lance (Lance Dwight Alworth; "Bambi") (1940–) Am. football Hall-of-Famer

Alzado, Lyle (Lyle Martin Alzado) (1949–1992) Am. football player

Amado, Jorge ("The Brazilian Boccaccio") (1912–) Braz. novelist (*The Violent Land*; *Doña Flor and Her Two Husbands*)

Amati, Nicolò (1596–1684) Ital. violin maker (taught Stradivarius)

Ambler, Eric (a/k/a Eliot Reed) (1909–) Eng. novelist (*Epitaph for a Spy*; *Journey into Fear*)

Ambrose, Saint (339–397) Rom. bishop of Milan

Ameche, Don (Dominic Felix Amici) (1908–1993) Am. actor (*The Story of Alexander Graham Bell* [title role]; *Trading Places*; O—1985—*Cocoon*)

Amenhotep (Amenhotep III) (1417–1379 B.C.) Egypt. king

Ames, Ed (Edmund Dantes Urick) (1927–) Am. singer (with The Ames Brothers)/actor ("Daniel Boone" TV series)

Ames, Leon (Leon Waycoff; a/k/a Leon Wycoff) (1903–1993) Am. actor ("Mr. Ed" TV series; *The Count of Monte Cristo*)

Amherst, Jeffrey (1717–1797) Eng. soldier/gov. of British North America 1760–1763

Amin, Idi (Idi Amin Dada Oumee; "Big Daddy"; "The Wild Man of Africa") (1925–) Ug. dictator 1971–1979

Amis, Kingsley (Kingsley William Amis; a/k/a Robert Markham; "Angry Young Man") (1922–) Eng. novelist/poet (*Lucky Jim*)

Amis, Martin (Martin Louis Amis) (1949–) Eng. novelist/short story writer (son of Kingsley; *The Rachel Papers*; *London Fields*; *Time's Arrow*)

Ammann, Othmar Hermann (1897–1965) Am. bridge designer (the George Washington; the Golden Gate)/architectural planner (Dulles airport)

Amory, Cleveland (1917–) Am. historian/conservationist/writer (*The Cat Who Came for Christmas*)

Amos (born 750 B.C.) Heb. prophet

Amos, Tori (c. 1963–) Am. pop singer ("Little Earthquakes")

Ampère, André (André Marie Ampère) (1775–1836) Fr. physicist/inventor (astatic needle)

Amsterdam, Morey (1914–) Am. comedian ("The Dick Van Dyke Show" TV series)

Amundsen, Roald (Roald Engelbregt Amundsen) (1872–1928) Norw. explorer (first man to reach the South Pole [December 14, 1911])

Anacreon ("The Teian Muse") (c. 582–c. 485 B.C.) Gr. lyric poet

Anastasia (Anastasia Nikolayevna) (1901–1918) Russ. daughter of Czar Nicholas II

Anastasia, Albert ("The Lord High Executioner of Murder, Inc.") (1903–1957) Am. crime boss (partnered in Murder, Inc. with Lepke Buchalter)

Anaxagoras (c. 500–428 B.C.) Gr. philosopher (teacher of Pericles, Euripides, and possibly Socrates)

Anaximander (611–657 B.C.) Gr. philosopher/astronomer (possible inventor of the sundial)

Andersen, Hans Christian (a/k/a Villiam Christian Walter; "The Danish La Fontaine") (1805–1875) Dan. poet/

playwright/novelist/fairy tale writer (*The Ugly Duckling*; *The Emperor's New Clothes*)

Anderson, Barbara (1945–) Am. actress ("Mission: Impossible" TV series; E— 1967/68)

Anderson, Bill (James William Anderson III; "Whisperin' Bill") (1937–) Am. country singer ("Still")

Anderson, Brad (1924–) Am. cartoonist (*Marmaduke*)

Anderson, Eddie "Rochester" (1905– 1977) Am. actor (Jack Benny's butler, Rochester, on TV)

Anderson, Gilbert (Gilbert Max Aronson; "Broncho Billy") (1882–1972) Am. actor (*The Great Train Robbery*)

Anderson, Harry (1952–) Am. comedian/ magician/actor ("Night Court" and "Dave's World" TV series)

Anderson, Ian (1947–) Eng. rock singer/ musician (flutist with Jethro Tull)

Anderson, Jack (Jack Northman Anderson) (1922–) Am. journalist ("Washington Merry-Go-Round" column)/war correspondent (P—1972)

Anderson, John (1922–1992) Am. actor ("The Rifleman" TV series; *Cotton Comes to Harlem*)

Anderson, Jon (1944–) Eng. rock singer (with Yes)

Anderson, Dame Judith (Frances Margaret Anderson) (1898–1992) Austral.-Eng. actress (*Rebecca*; *The Ten Commandments*; T—1948)

Anderson, Kevin (1960–) Am. actor (*Sleeping with the Enemy*)

Anderson, Laurie (1947–) Am. rock singer/performance artist

Anderson, Leroy (Franklin Leroy Anderson) (1908–1975) Am. orchestra conductor/composer ("The Syncopated Clock")

Anderson, Lindsay (1923–) Scot.-Eng. film director (*The Whales of August*; *This Sporting Life*)

Anderson, Loni (a/k/a Loni K. Reynolds) (1945–) Am. actress ("WKRP in Cincinnati" TV series)

Anderson, Louie (C) Am. comedian

Anderson, Lynn (Lynn Rene Anderson) (1947–) Am. country singer ("Rose Garden")

Anderson, Marian ("The Philadelphia Lady") (1902–1993) Am. opera singer (contralto; first Afr.-Am. to perform at the Met)

Anderson, Maxwell (1888–1959) Am. playwright (P–1933—*Both Your Houses*; *What Price Glory?* [with Laurence Stallings]; *Key Largo*)

Anderson, Melissa Sue (1962–) Am. actress ("Little House on the Prairie" TV series)

Anderson, Michael (1920–) Eng. film director (*Around the World in Eighty Days*; *The Shoes of the Fisherman*)

Anderson, Pamela (Pamela Denise Anderson) (1966–) Can.-Am. actress ("Home Improvement" and "Baywatch" TV series)

Anderson, Philip W. (Philip Warren Anderson) (1923–) Am. physicist (N—1977)

Anderson, Poul (Poul William Anderson) (1926–) Am. science fiction writer (*The Shields of Time*; *Brain Wave*)

Anderson, Richard Dean (1950–) Am. actor ("MacGyver" TV series)

Anderson, Robert (Robert Woodruff Anderson) (1917–) Am. playwright (*Tea and Sympathy*)

Anderson, Sherwood (1876–1941) Am. novelist/short story writer (*Winesburg, Ohio*; *Beyond Desire*)

Anderson, Sparky (George Lee Anderson; "Captain Hook") (1934–) Am. baseball manager

Andersson, Bibi (Birgitta Andersson) (1935–) Swed. actress (*Wild Strawberries*; *The Seventh Seal*)

Andress, Ursula ("The Ice Maiden") (1936–) Swi. actress (*What's New, Pussycat?*)

Andretti, Mario (Mario Gabriele Andretti) (1940–) Am. auto racer

Andrew (Andrew Albert Christian Edward; "Randy Andy") (1960–) Eng. prince

Andrews, Anthony (1948–) Eng. actor ("Brideshead Revisited" TV series)

Andrews, Dana (Carver Daniel Andrews) (1909–1992) Am. actor (brother of Steve Forrest; *Laura*; *The Best Years of Our Lives*; *The Ox-Bow Incident*)

Andrews, Julie (Julia Elizabeth Wells; a/k/a Julia Edwards) (1935–) Eng.-Am. actress (*Thoroughly Modern Millie*; O— 1964—*Mary Poppins*; *The Sound of Music*)

Andrews, Laverne (1913–1967) Am. pop singer (with The Andrews Sisters; "In Apple Blossom Time")

Andrews, Maxene (1916–) Am. pop singer (with The Andrews Sisters)

Andrews, Patty (1918–) Am. pop singer (with The Andrews Sisters)

Andrews, Stanley (1892–1969) Am. western actor ("Death Valley Days" TV series narrator)

Andrews, Tige (Tiger Andrawaous) (1923–) Am. actor ("The Mod Squad" TV series)

Andrews, V. C. (Virginia Cleo Andrews) (1924–1986) Am. writer (*Flowers in the Attic*; *Petals in the Wind*)

Andreyev, Leonid (Leonid Nikolayevich Andreyev; a/k/a James Lynch; "The Edgar Allan Poe of Russian Literature") (1871–1919) Russ. writer (*The Red Laugh*)

Andrić, Ivo (1892–1975) Serbo-Cr. novelist/short story writer (*The Bridge on the Drina*; N—1961)

Andropov, Yuri (Yuri Vladimirovich Andropov) (1914–1984) Russ. communist political leader

Anfinsen, Christian (Christian Boehmer Anfinsen) (1916–) Am. biochemist (N—1972)

Angel, Heather (Heather Grace Angel) (1909–1986) Eng.-Am. actress ("Family Affair" and "Peyton Place" TV series)

Angeli, Pier (Anna Maria Pierangeli) (1932–1971) Ital. actress (twin sister of Marisa Pavan; *Somebody Up There Likes Me*)

Angelico, Fra (Guido di Pietro; a/k/a Fra Giovanni da Fiesole) (c. 1400–1455) Flor. Renaissance painter

Angell, Sir Norman (Ralph Norman Angell Lane) (1872–1967) Eng. economist/writer (*The Great Illusion*; N—1933)

Angelou, Maya (Marguerite Johnson) (1928–) Am. writer/poet (*I Know Why the Caged Bird Sings*)

Anger, Kenneth (1929–) Am. filmmaker (*Lucifer Rising*)/writer (*Hollywood Babylon*)

Anka, Paul (Paul Albert Anka) (1941–) Can. pop singer ("Diana")/songwriter ("My Way")

Ankers, Evelyn ("Queen of the Horror Movies"; "The Screamer") (1918–1985) Eng. actress (*The Wolf Man*)

Anna (Anna Ivanovna) (1693–1740) Russ. empress 1730–1740

Annakin, Ken (Kenneth Annakin) (1914–) Eng. film director (*The Swiss Family Robinson*; *Battle of the Bulge*)

Anne ("Brandy Nan") (1665–1714) queen of England and Ireland 1702–1714

Anne (Anne Elizabeth Alice Louise Mountbatten) (1950–) Eng. princess

Annenberg, Walter Hubert (1908–) Am. magazine publisher (founded *Seventeen* and *TV Guide*)

Anne of Cleves ("The Mare of Flounders") (1515–1557) Eng. wife of Henry VIII

Ann-Margret (Ann-Margret Olsson) (1941–) Am. actress (*Carnal Knowledge*; *Tommy*; *52 Pick-Up*)

Anouilh, Jean (Jean Marie Lucien Pierre Anouilh) (1910–1987) Fr. playwright (*Becket*; *The Waltz of the Toreadors*)

Anselm, Saint (1033–1109) Ital. archbishop of Canterbury/philosopher (*Monologian*)

Ansermet, Ernest (Ernest Alexandre Ansermet) (1883–1969) Swi. conductor (for Ballet Russe)

Anson, Cap (Adrian Constantine Anson; "Pop") (1882–1922) Am. baseball Hall-of-Famer

Anspach, Susan (1939–) Am. actress (*Five Easy Pieces*; *Montenegro*)

Ant, Adam (Stuart Goddard) (1954–) Eng. pop/rock singer ("Goody Two Shoes"; formerly with Adam and The Ants)

Antheil, George (Georg Johann Carl Antheil) (1900–1959) Am. composer (*Volpone*; *Ballet Mécanique*)

Anthony, Michael (1955–) Am. rock bassist (with Van Halen)

Anthony, Ray (Raymond Antonini) (1922–) Am. jazz trumpeter/bandleader ("Worried Mind")

Anthony, Susan B. (Susan Brownell Anthony) (1820–1906) Am. suffragist

Antisthenes (c. 445–c. 365 B.C.) Ath. philosopher (founder of the Cynic school)

Antoinette, Marie (Josephe-Jeanne-Marie-Antoinette) (1755–1793) Fr. queen of Louis XVI

Anton, Susan (1950–) Am. singer/actress ("Stop Susan Williams" TV series)

Antonescu, Ion (1882–1946) Rom. general/dictator 1940–1944 (executed for war crimes)

Antonioni, Michelangelo (1912–) Ital. filmmaker (*The Red Desert*; *Blow-Up*)

Antony, Marc (Marcus Antonius) (c. 81–30 B.C.) Rom. general/ruler

Anwar, Gabrielle (c. 1969–) Eng. actress (*Scent of a Woman*; *For Love or Money*; *Body Snatchers*)

Anza, Juan Batista de (1735–1788) Span. explorer (founded San Francisco)

Aparicio, Luis (Luis Ernesto Monteil Aparicio; "Little Looie") (1934–) Am. baseball Hall-of-Famer

Apollinaire, Guillaume (Wilhelm Apollinaris de Kostrowitzky) (1880–1918) Fr. poet (coined the term *surrealism*)

Appice, Carmen (1946–) Am. rock drummer (with Vanilla Fudge and Cactus)

Applegate, Christina (1972–) Am. actress (*Don't Tell Mom the Babysitter's Dead*; "Married . . . With Children" TV series)

Appleseed, Johnny (John Chapman) (1774–1845) Am. pioneer/apple tree planter

Appling, Luke (Lucius Benjamin Apling; "Old Aches and Pains") (1907–1991) Am. baseball Hall-of-Famer

Appolonia (Patricia Kotero) (1959–) Am. pop singer/actress (protégée of Prince; *Purple Rain*)

Apted, Michael (1941–) Eng. film director (*Coal Miner's Daughter*; *Gorillas in the Mist*)

Aquinas, Saint **Thomas** ("Angelic Doctor"; "Doctor of the School") (1225–1274) Ital. Catholic theologian/philosopher (*Summa Theologica*)

Aquino, Corazon (Maria Corazon Cojuangco; "Cory") (1933–) Phil. pres. 1986–1992

Arafat, Yasir or **Yasser** (Mohammed Abed Ar'ouf Arafat) (1929–) Pal. politician/guerilla leader/PLO head

Aragon, Louis (Louis Marie Antoine Alfred Aragon) (1897–1982) Fr. poet/novelist/critic (*Holy Week*)

Arbuckle, Fatty (Roscoe Conkling Arbuckle; a/k/a William B. Goodrich) (1887–1933) Am. comedian/actor/director (*Fatty and the Heiress*; *Fatty's Debut*; *Fatty's Gift*)

Arbus, Diane (Diane Nemerov) (1923–1971) Am. photographer

Arcaro, Eddie (George Edward Arcaro; "Big A"; "King of Little Men"; "King of the Stakes Riders"; "Banana Nose"; "The Master") (1916–) Am. jockey (the only jockey to win the Triple Crown twice [1941, 1948])

Archer, Anne (1947–) Am. actress (daughter of Marjorie Lord and John Archer; *Fatal Attraction*; *Patriot Games*)

Archer, Jeffrey Howard (1940–) Eng. politician/novelist (*Kane and Abel*; *First Among Equals*)

Archer, John (Ralph Shipworth Bowman) (1915–) Am. actor (father of Anne; *Guadalcanal Diary*; *Blue Hawaii*)

Archerd, Army (Armand Archerd) (1919–) Am. (Hollywood) gossip columnist

Archimedes (c. 287–212 B.C.) Gr. mathemetician/inventor (Archimedian screw for raising water)

Archipenko, Aleksandr (Aleksandr Porfiryevich Archipenko) (1887–1964) Am. painter/sculptor (introduced "sculpto-painting")

Ardant, Fanny (1949–) Fr. actress (in Truffaut films)

Arden, Elizabeth (Florence Nightingale Graham) (1884–1966) Can.-Am. cosmetics entrepreneur

Arden, Eve (Eunice Quedens) (1912–1990) Am. actress ("Our Miss Brooks" TV series; *Mildred Pierce*; E—1953, 1966/67)

Arendt, Hannah (1906–1975) Ger.-Am. political philosopher (*Eichmann in Jerusalem*; *The Origins of Totalitarianism*)

Argento, Dario (1943–) Ital. film director (*The Bird with the Crystal Plumage*; *Once Upon a Time in the West*)

Ariosto, Lodovico or **Ludovico** (1474–1533) Ital. poet (*Orlando Furioso*)

Aristides ("The Just") (c. 530–c. 468 B.C.) Ath. statesman/general

Aristophanes (c. 450–c. 388 B.C.) Ath. playwright/satirist (*The Frogs*; *The Clouds*)

Aristotle (384–322 B.C.) Gr. philosopher (*Physics*; *Politics*; *Nicomachean Ethics*; *Poetics*)

Arkin, Alan (Alan Wolf Arkin) (1934–) Am. actor (*The Seven Per-Cent Solution*; *The Heart Is a Lonely Hunter*)

Arkush, Allan (1948–) Am. film director (*Rock 'n' Roll High School*)

Arledge, Roone (Roone Pinckney Arledge, Jr.) (1931–) Am. TV executive (pres. of ABC Sports and ABC News)

Arlen, Harold (Hyman Arluck; a/k/a Harold Arluck) (1905–1986) Am. composer ("Stormy Weather"; "Over the Rainbow"; "It's Only a Paper Moon")

Arlen, Richard (Richard Cornelius van Mattimore) (1898–1976) Am. actor (*The Virginian*; *Wings*)

Arletty (Arlette-Léonie Bathiat) (1898–1992) Fr. stage/film actress (*Les Enfants du Paradis*)

Arliss, George (George Augustus Andrews) (1868–1946) Eng. actor (*Alexander Hamilton*; O—1929/30—*Disraeli*)

Armani, Giorgio (1934–) Ital. fashion designer

Armas, Tony (Antonio Rafael Armas Machado) (1953–) Am. baseball player

Armatrading, Joan (1950–) W. Ind.-Eng. folk/pop singer/guitarist/pianist/songwriter

Armendariz, Pedro (1912–1963) Mex. actor (*The Fugitive*; *From Russia, with Love*)

Armour, Richard (Richard Willard Armour) (1906–) Am. humorist ("It All Started With . . ." series)

Armstrong, Bess (Elizabeth Key Armstrong) (1953–) Am. actress (*Nothing in Common*)

Armstrong, Charlotte (1905–1969) Am. poet/playwright/short story writer/mystery writer (*A Dram of Poison*)

Armstrong, Edwin (Edwin Howard Armstrong) (1890–1954) Am. inventor/engineer (perfected FM radio)

Armstrong, Gillian (1950–) Austral. film director (*My Brilliant Career*; *Mrs. Soffel*)

Armstrong, Harry (Henry Worthington Armstrong) (1879–1951) Am. composer ("Sweet Adeline")

Armstrong, Henry (Henry Jackson Armstrong, Jr.; "Homicide Hank"; "The Human Buzzsaw"; "Hurricane Henry") (1912–1988) Am. boxer

Armstrong, Louis (Louis Daniel or Daniel Louis Armstrong; "Satchmo"; "Pops") (1900–1971) Am. jazz trumpeter/bandleader ("Hello, Dolly!"; G—1964)

Armstrong, Neil (Neil Alden Armstrong) (1930–) Am. astronaut (first man on the moon)

Arnaz, Desi (Desiderio Alberto Arnaz y de Acha, III) (1917–1986) Cub. singer/musician/actor ("I Love Lucy" TV series)

Arnaz, Desi, Jr. (1953–) Am. actor (son of Desi Arnaz and Lucille Ball; *The Mambo Kings*)

Arnaz, Lucie (Lucie Desiree Arnaz) (1951–) Am. actress (daughter of Desi Arnaz and Lucille Ball; "Here's Lucy" TV series)

Arne, Thomas Augustine (1710–1778) Eng. composer (*Rule Brittania*)

Arness, James (James King Aurness) (1923–) Am. actor (brother of Peter Graves; *The Farmer's Daughter*; "Gunsmoke" TV series)

Arngrim, Alison (1962–) Am. actress ("Little House on the Prairie" TV series)

Arno, Peter (Curtis Arnoux Peters, Jr.) (1904–1968) Am. cartoonist (*New Yorker*)

Arno, Sig (Siegfried Aron) (1895–1975) Ger. comedian/actor (*The Palm Beach Story*)

Arnold, Benedict ("The Traitorous Hero") (1741–1801) Am. army general/traitor (plotted to surrender West Point to the British)

Arnold, Eddy (Richard Edward Arnold; "The Tennessee Plowboy") (1918–) Am. country singer ("Make the World Go Away")

Arnold, Edward (Gunter Edward Arnold Schneider) (1890–1956) Am. actor (*Mr. Smith Goes to Washington*; *You Can't Take It with You*)

Arnold, Matthew (1822–1888) Eng. critic/poet (*Dover Beach*)

Arnold, Roseanne (Roseanne Barr; "Rosie") (1952–) Am. actress/comedienne ("Roseanne" TV series)

Arnold, Tom (1959–) Am. comedian/actor ("The Jackie Thomas Show" TV series)

Arp, Jean (Hans Arp) (1887–1966) Fr. artist/poet (cofounder of Dada; *Word-Dreams and Black Stars*)

Arpel, Adrien (1941–) Am. fashion designer

Arquette, Cliff (a/k/a Charlie Weaver) (1905–1974) Am. radio/TV comedian/actor (grandfather of Patricia and Rosanna)

Arquette, Patricia (1968–) Am. actress (sister of Rosanna; *True Romance*; *Ethan Frome*; *The Indian Runner*)

Arquette, Rosanna (1959–) Am. actress (granddaughter of Cliff; *The Executioner's Song*; *Desperately Seeking Susan*)

Arrau, Claudio (1903–1991) Chil.-Am. concert pianist

Arroyo, Martina (1937–) Am. opera singer (soprano)

Artaud, Antonin (1896–1948) Fr. drama critic/writer/actor (*The Theater and Its Double*)

Arthur, Bea or **Beatrice** (Bernice Frankel) (1923–) Am. actress ("Maude" and "The Golden Girls" TV series; E—1987/88)

Arthur, Chester (Chester Alan Arthur) (1829–1886) 21st Am. pres. (1881–1885)
Arthur, Ellen (Ellen Lewis Herndon) (1837–1880) Am. first lady (Chester)
Arthur, Jean (Gladys Georgianna Greene) (1901 or 1905 or 1908–1991) Am. actress (*You Can't Take It with You*; *Shane*)
Arzner, Dorothy (1900–1979) Am. film director (*Christopher Strong*; *Nana*)
Asa (10th–9th century B.C.) 3rd king of Judea (c. 913–c. 873 B.C.)
Asch, Sholem or Shalom (1880–1957) Pol. novelist/playwright (*The Nazarene*)
Ascoli, Max (1898–1978) Am. newspaper editor/publisher/writer (*The Fall of Mussolini*)
Ash, Mary Kay Wagner (C) Am. businesswoman (Mary Kay Cosmetics)
Ashbery, John (John Lawrence Ashbery) (1927–) Am. poet (P—1976—*Self-Portrait in a Convex Mirror*)
Ashby, Alan (Alan Dean Ashby) (1951–) Am. baseball player
Ashby, Hal (1929–1988) Am. film director (*Shampoo*; *Harold and Maude*; *Being There*)
Ashcroft, Dame Peggy (Edith Margaret Emily Hutchinson) (1907–1991) Eng. actress (*Sunday, Bloody Sunday*; O— 1984—*A Passage to India*)
Ashe, Arthur (Arthur Robert Ashe, Jr.) (1943–1993) Am. tennis player (W— 1975)
Ashford, Daisy (Margaret Mary Julia Ashford) (1881–1972) Eng. novelist (*The Young Visitors*)
Ashford, Nickolas (1942–) Am. pop musician/singer (with Ashford & Simpson; "Solid")
Ashkenazy, Vladimir (1937–) Russ. concert pianist
Ashley, Elizabeth (Elizabeth Ann Cole) (1939–) Am. actress (*Ship of Fools*; *The Carpetbaggers*)
Ashley, Laura (Laura Mountney) (1925–1985) Wel. fashion designer
Asimov, Isaac (a/k/a Dr. A. Paul French; "The Writer of the Universe"; "The Father of Modern Science Fiction") (1920–1992) Russ.-Am. scientist/science fiction writer (*Foundation* trilogy)
Askew, Luke (1937–) Am. westerns actor (*Cool Hand Luke*)
Asner, Ed (Yitzak Edward Asner) (1929–) Am. actor ("Lou Grant" TV series; *Roots*; E—1970/71, 1971/72, 1974/75, 1977/78, 1979/80)

Aspin, Les (Leslie Aspin, Jr.) (1938–) Am. congressman/govt. official (secretary of defense)
Asquith, Anthony (a/k/a "Puffin") (1902–1968) Eng. film director (*The Importance of Being Earnest*; *Pygmalion*)
Asquith, Herbert (Herbert Henry Asquith, 1st Earl of Oxford and Asquith) (1852–1928) Eng. prime minister 1908–1916
Asquith, Countess Margot (Emma Alice Margaret Tennant) (1864–1945) Eng. society figure/writer (*Octavia*)
Assad, Hafez or Hafiz Al- (1928–) Syr. pres. 1971–
Assante, Armand (1949–) Am. actor (*The Mambo Kings*; *Q & A*; *Hoffa*)
Astaire, Adele (Adele Marie Austerlitz) (1898–1981) Am. dancer (early partner of her brother Fred)
Astaire, Fred (Frederick Austerlitz) (1899–1987) Am. dancer/singer/actor (*Top Hat*; *Swing Time*; *Shall We Dance*)
Astin, John (John Allen Astin) (1930–) Am. actor ("The Addams Family" TV series)
Astin, Sean (1971–) Am. actor (son of John Astin and Patty Duke; *Encino Man*; *Rudy* [title role])
Astley, Rick (1966–) Eng. pop singer ("Cry for Help"; "Together Forever"; "Never Gonna Give You Up")
Astor, Brooke (Brooke Marshall Astor; born Roberta B. Russell) (1902–) Am. philanthropist
Astor, Gertrude (1887–1977) Am. actress (*The Man Who Shot Liberty Valance*; *Around the World in Eighty Days*)
Astor, John Jacob (1763–1848) Am. fur trader/capitalist
Astor, Mary (Lucille Vasconcellos Langehanke) (1906–1987) Am. actress (*Beau Brummel*; *The Maltese Falcon*; O— 1941—*The Great Lie*)
Astor, Viscountess Nancy (Nancy Witcher Langhorne Astor) (1879–1964) Eng. politician (first woman member of Parliament)
Asturias, Miguel Angel (1899–1974) Guat. novelist/short story writer (N—1967; *El Señor President*)
Atahuallpa (c. 1502–1533) Peruv. king of the Incas 1530–1533
Atatürk, Kemal (Mustafa) (1881–1938) Turk. pres. 1923–1938
Ates, Roscoe (1892–1962) Am. actor (*Gone with the Wind*; *Freaks*)

Atkins, Chet (Chester Burton Atkins; "Mr. Guitar") (1924–) Am. country guitarist (with the Grand Ole Opry)

Atkins, Christopher (1961–) Am. actor (*The Blue Lagoon*)

Atkins, Doug (Douglas L. Atkins) (1930–) Am. football Hall-of-Famer

Atkinson, Brooks (Justin Brooks Atkinson "The Autocrat of the Aisle") (1894–1984) Am. drama critic (P—1947)

Atlas, Charles (Angelo Siciliano) (1894–1972) Am. bodybuilder/physical culturist (invented "dynamic tension")

Attenborough, Sir Richard (Richard Samuel Attenborough) (1923–) Eng. film director (*The Sand Pebbles*; O—1982—*Gandhi*)

Attila The Hun ("Scourge of God") (c. 406–453) king of the Huns 434–453

Attlee, Clement (Clement Richard Attlee) (1883–1967) Eng. prime minister 1945–1951

Attucks, Crispus ("The First Black American Martyr") (c. 1723–1770) Am. patriot (first to die in the Boston Massacre)

Atwill, Lionel (Lionel Alfred William Atwill) (1885–1946) Eng. actor (*The Hound of the Baskervilles*; *Captain Blood*)

Atwood, Margaret (Margaret Eleanor Atwood) (1939–) Can. novelist/poet (*The Handmaid's Tale*; *Cat's Eye*)

Auberjonois, René (René Murat Auberjonois) (1940–) Am. actor ("Benson" TV series; *Eyes of Laura Mars*)

Auchincloss, Louis (Louis Stanton Auchincloss; a/k/a Andrew Lee) (1917–) Am. novelist (*Portrait in Brownstone*; *Diary of a Yuppie*)

Auden, W. H. (Wystan Hugh Auden) (1907–1973) Am. poet/playwright (P—1948—*The Age of Anxiety*)

Audran, Stéphane (Colette Suzanne Dacheville) (1939–) Fr. actress (*Babette's Feast*; *The Prisoner of Zenda*)

Audubon, John (John James Leforest Audubon) (1785–1851) Am. ornithologist/artist/writer (*The Birds of America*)

Auel, Jean M. (Jean Marie Auel) (1936–) Am. historical novelist (*Clan of the Cave Bear*)

Auerbach, Artie (1928–) Am. comedian

Auerbach, Red (Arnold James Auerbach) (1917–) Am. basketball coach (with most wins in NBA history)

Augustine, Saint (Aurelius Augustinus; Saint Augustine of Hippo; "The Hammer of the Heretics") (354–430) Tunisian philosopher/church father

Aumont, Jean-Pierre (Jean-Pierre Salomons) (1909–) Fr. actor (*Day for Night*; *Mahogany*)

Aurelius, Marcus (Marcus Aurelius Antonius; born Marcus Annius Verus) (121–180) Roman philosopher/emperor 161–180

Austen, Jane (1775–1817) Eng. novelist (*Pride and Prejudice*; *Sense and Sensibility*)

Austin, Herbert, 1st Baron Austin (1866–1941) Eng. automobile manufacturer

Austin, Patti (1948–) Am. pop singer ("Baby, Come to Me" duet with James Ingram)

Austin, Stephen (Stephen Fuller Austin) (1793–1836) Am. (Texas) pioneer/statesman

Austin, Teri (1959–) Am. actress ("Knots Landing" TV series)

Austin, Tracy (Tracy Ann Austin) (1962–) Am. tennis player

Austin-Green, Brian (1973–) Am. actor ("Beverly Hills, 90210" TV series)

Autry, Alan (c. 1952–) Am. football player/actor ("In the Heat of the Night" TV series)

Autry, Gene (Orvon Gene Autry; "The Singing Cowboy") (1907–) Am. cowboy actor (*In Old Santa Fe*)/singer ("Back In The Saddle Again")/songwriter ("Here Comes Santa Claus")

Avakian, Aram (1926–1987) Am. film director (*Lad: A Dog*; *11 Harrowhouse*)

Avalon, Frankie (Francis Thomas Avallone) (1939–) Am. pop singer ("Venus"; "Why")/actor

Avedon, Richard (1923–) Am. fashion photographer

Averill, Earl (Earl Douglas Averill) (1931–) Am. baseball player (son of Earl)

Averill, Earl (Howard Earl Averill; "The Rock"; "Earl of Snohomish") (1902–1983) Am. baseball Hall-of-Famer

Averroës (Ibn Rushd; in full, Abu al-Walid Muhammad Ibn Ahmad Ibn Muhammad Ibn Rushd) (1126–1198) Span. Isl. philosopher

Avery, Tex (Frederick Bean Avery) (1907–1980) Am. animator/cartoonist for MGM (created Droopy)

Avicenna (Ibn Sina; in full, Abu Ali Al-Husayn ibn Abd Allah ibn Sina) (980–1037) Arab. physician/philosopher/scientist/writer (*Canon of Medicine*)

Avildsen, John (John G. Avildsen) (1936–) Am. film director (*The Karate Kid*; O— 1976—*Rocky*)

Ax, Emanuel (1949–) Am. classical pianist

Axelrod, Julius (1912–) Am. biochemist (N—1970)

Axton, Hoyt (Hoyt Wayne Axton) (1938–) Am. country singer/songwriter

Ayckbourn, Alan (Roland Allen Ayckbourn) (1939–) Eng. playwright (*Absurd Person Singular*)/theatrical director (*How the Other Half Lives*)

Ayer, Sir A. J. (Alfred Jules Ayer) (1910–1989) Eng. philosopher (logical positivism)/writer (*Language, Truth and Logic*)

Aykroyd, Dan (Daniel Edward Aykroyd; a/k/a Elwood Blues) (1952–) Can.-Am. actor/comedian (The *Coneheads*; "Saturday Night Live" TV series)

Ayres, Lew (Lewis Frederick Ayer III) (1908–) Am. actor (*All Quiet on the Western Front*; *Holiday*)

Aznavour, Charles (Shahnour Varenagh Aznavourian; a/k/a Charles Aznavourian) (1924–) Fr.-Arm. singer/actor (*Shoot the Piano Player*; *The Tin Drum*)

Baader, Andreas (Bernd Andreas Baader) (1943–1977) Ger. terrorist (with Ulrike Meinhoff)

Babenco, Hector (1946–) Arg. film director (*Kiss of the Spider Woman*)

Babilonia, Tai (Tai Reina Babilonia) (1960–) Am. ice skater

Bacall, Lauren (Betty Joan Perske; "Betty") (1924–) Am. actress (*To Have and Have Not*; *The Big Sleep*; *Key Largo*; T—1970, 1981)

Bach, Barbara (Barbara Goldbach) (1951–) Am. actress (*The Spy Who Loved Me*)

Bach, Catherine (Catherine Bachman) (1954–) Am. actress ("The Dukes of Hazzard" TV series)

Bach, Johann Sebastian (1685–1750) Ger. composer (*The Well-Tempered Clavier*)

Bach, Richard (Richard David Bach) (1936–) Am. writer (*Jonathan Livingston Seagull*)

Bacharach, Burt (1928–) Am. pop pianist/songwriter ("Raindrops Keep Fallin' on My Head"; "What the World Needs Now Is Love"; "Walk On By"; "Do You Know the Way to San Jose?")

Backman, Wally (Walter Wayne Backman) (1959–) Am. baseball player

Backus, Jim (James Gilmore Backus) (1913–1989) Am. actor ("I Married Joan" and "Gilligan's Island" TV series)

Baclanova, Olga (1899–1974) Russ. dancer/actress (*Freaks*; *Street of Sin*)

Bacon, Sir Francis, 1st Baron Verulam and Viscount St. Albans (1561–1626) Eng. philosopher/essayist (*Advancement of Learning*)

Bacon, Francis (1909–1992) Eng. painter

Bacon, Henry (1866–1924) Am. architect (Lincoln Memorial)

Bacon, Kevin (1958–) Am. actor (*Diner*; *Footloose*; *Flatliners*)

Bacon, Nathaniel (1647–1676) Am. colonial political leader (led Bacon's Rebellion in Virginia in 1676)

Bacon, Roger ("The Father of Philosophy") (1214–1294) Eng. philosopher/scientist/writer (*Opus Majus*)

Baddeley, Angela (Madeleine Angela Clinton-Baddeley) (1900–1976) Eng. actress ("Upstairs Downstairs" TV series)

Baddeley, Hermione (Hermione Clinton-Baddeley) (1906–1986) Eng. actress ("Maude" TV series; *Room at the Top*)

Badger, Clarence (Clarence G. Badger) (1880–1964) Am. film director (*No No Nanette* [1931]; *It*)

Badham, John (1939–) Eng.-Am. film director (*Bird on a Wire*; *The Hard Way*; *Stakeout*; *Point of No Return*)

Baedeker, Karl (1801–1859) Ger. travel guide writer/publisher

Baekeland, Leo (Leo Hendrik Baekeland) (1863–1944) Am. chemist/inventor (Bakelite)

Baer, Arthur ("Bugs") (1886–1969) Am. journalist/sports columnist

Baer, Max (Maximilian Adelbert Baer; "The Merry Madcap") (1909–1959) Am. boxer/actor (*The Prizefighter and the Lady*)

Baer, Max, Jr. (Maximilian Adelbert Baer, Jr.) (1937–) Am. actor (son of Max; "The Beverly Hillbillies" TV series)

Baer, Parley (C) Am. actor ("The Adventures of Ozzie and Harriet" and "The Andy Griffith Show" TV series)

Baeyer, Adolf von (Johann Friedrich Wilhelm Adolf von Baeyer) (1835–1917) Ger. chemist (N—1905)

Baez, Joan (Joan Chandos Baez) (1941–) Am. folk/pop singer ("We Shall Overcome")

Bagnold, Enid (Enid Algerine Bagnold)

(1889–1981) Eng. playwright/novelist (*National Velvet*)

Bailey, F. Lee (Francis Lee Bailey) (1933–) Am. lawyer (criminal defense: Patty Hearst, the Boston Strangler)

Bailey, Gamaliel (1807–1859) Am. abolitionist editor (first published *Uncle Tom's Cabin* in the *National Era* newspaper 1851–1852)

Bailey, H. C. (Henry Christopher Bailey) (1878–1961) Eng. detective story writer (created Reggie Fortune)

Bailey, James Anthony (1847–1906) Am. circus owner (Barnum & Bailey)

Bailey, Pearl (Pearl Mae Bailey; "Pearlie May") (1918–1990) Am. jazz singer (with Count Basie and Cootie Williams)/ actress (*Porgy and Bess*; *Hello, Dolly!*)/ U.N. delegate

Bailey, Philip (1951–) Am. pop singer/percussionist/songwriter ("Easy Lover"; formerly with Earth, Wind & Fire)

Bailey, Razzy (Rasie Michael Bailey) (1939–) Am. country singer ("She Left Love All Over Me")/songwriter ("9,999,999 Tears")

Bain, Barbara (Millie Fogel) (1931–) Am. actress ("Mission: Impossible" TV series; E—1966/67, 1967/68, 1968/69)

Bain, Conrad (Conrad Stafford Bain) (1923–) Can. actor ("Diff'rent Strokes" TV series)

Bainbridge, Beryl (Beryl Margaret Bainbridge) (1934–) Eng. novelist (*Young Adolf*; *A Quiet Life*)

Bainter, Fay (Fay Okell Bainter) (1891–1968) Am. actress (*A Bill of Divorcement*; O—1938—*Jezebel*)

Baio, Jimmy (1963–) Am. actor (cousin of Scott; "Soap" TV series)

Baio, Scott (Scott Vincent Baio) (1961–) Am. actor ("Charles in Charge" TV series)

Baird, Bil (William Britton Baird) (1904–1987) Am. puppeteer

Baird, Cora (née Eisenberg) (1912–1967) Am. puppeteer

Baird, John Logie (1888–1946) Scot.-Am. inventor of TV

Bajer, Fredrik (1837–1922) Dan. writer/ statesman (N—1908)

Baker, Anita (1958–) Am. pop singer ("Rapture"; "Giving You the Best That I Got")

Baker, Carroll (1931–) Am. actress (*Baby Doll*; *Giant*)

Baker, Chet (1929–1988) Am. jazz trumpeter (*Let's Get Lost*)

Baker, Diane (1938–) Am. actress (*Marnie*; *The Diary of Anne Frank*)

Baker, Dusty (Johnnie B. Baker) (1949–) Am. baseball player

Baker, Frank (John Franklin Baker; "Bye-Bye"; "Home Run Baker") (1886–1963) Am. baseball Hall-of-Famer

Baker, George (1915–1975) Am. cartoonist (*The Sad Sack*)

Baker, Ginger (Peter Baker) (1939–) Eng. jazz/rock drummer (with Cream, Ginger Baker's Air Force, and Blind Faith)

Baker, James (James Addison Baker III) (1930–) Am. govt. official (secretary of the treasury, chief of staff)

Baker, Joe Don (1936–) Am. actor (*Walking Tall*; *Cool Hand Luke*)

Baker, Josephine (Freda Josephine MacDonald) (1906–1975) Am. dancer/ entertainer

Baker, Kathy (Kathy Whitton Baker) (1950–) Am. actress (*Clean and Sober*; *Mad Dog and Glory*)

Baker, Lavern (Delores Williams) (1929–) Am. blues singer ("I Cried a Tear")

Baker, Ray Stannard (a/k/a David Grayson) (1870–1946) Am. journalist/writer (P—1940—*Woodrow Wilson: Life and Letters*)

Baker, Russell (Russell Wayne Baker) (1925–) Am. journalist (P—1979)/writer (P—1983—*Growing Up*)

Bakker, Jim (James Orsen Bakker) (1939–) Am. TV evangelist

Bakker, Tammy Faye (1942–) Am. TV evangelist

Bakshi, Ralph (1938–) Pal.-Am. animation film director (*Fritz the Cat*; *Wizards*)

Bakst, Léon (Lev Samoylovich Rosenberg) (1866–1924) Russ. painter/scenic designer (for Pavlova, the Paris Opera, and Ballet Russe)

Bakula, Scott (1955–) Am. actor ("Quantum Leap" TV series)

Balanchine, George (Georgy Melitonovich Balanchivadze; "Mr. B") (1904–1983) Am. ballet dancer/choreographer

Balboa, Vasco Núñez De (1475–1519) Span. explorer (discovered the Pacific Ocean)

Baldridge, Letitia (Letitia Katherine Baldridge; "Tish") (1927–) Am. etiquette expert/columnist

Baldridge, Malcolm (Howard Malcolm

Baldridge, Jr.; "Mac") (1922–) Am. politician (secretary of commerce)
Baldry, Long John (1941–) Eng.-Can. rock/blues singer/guitarist (with Steampacket and Bluesology)
Baldwin, Adam (1962–) Am. actor (brother of Alec, Billy, Daniel, and Stephen; *Radio Flyer*)
Baldwin, Alec (1958–) Am. actor (*Prelude to a Kiss*; *The Hunt for Red October*; *The Marrying Man*; *Glengarry Glen Ross*)
Baldwin, Billy or **William** (1963–) Am. actor (brother of Adam, Alec, Daniel, and Stephen; *Sliver*; *Backdraft*)
Baldwin, Daniel (c. 1959–) Am. actor (brother of Adam, Alec, Billy, and Stephen; "Homicide" TV series)
Baldwin, James (James Arthur Baldwin) (1924–1987) Am. novelist/essayist (*The Fire Next Time*; *Notes of a Native Son*)
Baldwin, Roger (Roger Nash Baldwin) (1884–1981) Am. lawyer/social reformer (founded the ACLU)
Baldwin, Stanley (1867–1947) Eng. prime minister 1923–1924, 1924–1929, 1935–1937
Baldwin, Stephen (1967–) Am. actor (brother of Adam, Alec, Billy, and Daniel; "The Young Riders" TV series; *Posse*)
Balenciaga, Cristóbal ("Prophet of Silhouette") (1895–1972) Span. fashion designer
Balfe, Michael (Michael William Balfe) (1808–1870) Ir. composer (*The Bohemian Girl*; *Falstaff*)
Balfour, Arthur James, 1st Earl of Balfour (1848–1930) Eng. prime minister 1902–1905
Balin, Ina (Ina Sandra Rosenberg) (1937–1990) Am. actress (*Compulsion*; *The Greatest Story Ever Told*)
Balin, Marty (Martyn Jerel Buchwald) (1942–) Am. rock musician/singer ("Hearts"; formerly with Jefferson Airplane)
Ball, Ernest (1878–1927) Am. composer ("When Irish Eyes Are Smiling")
Ball, Hugo (1886–1927) Ger. actor/writer (founder of Dada)
Ball, John (John Dudley Ball, Jr.) (1911–1988) Am. mystery writer (created Virgil Tibbs; *In the Heat of the Night*)
Ball, Lucille (Lucille Désirée Ball) (1911–1989) Am. actress/comedienne (mother of Lucie Arnaz and Desi Arnaz, Jr.; "I

Love Lucy" TV series; *Mame*; E—1952, 1955, 1966/67, 1967/68)
Ballantine, Ian (Ian Keith Ballantine) (1916–) Am. publisher (founded Ballantine Books)
Ballard, Carroll (1937–) Am. film director (*The Black Stallion*; *Never Cry Wolf*)
Ballard, Florence (1943–1976) Am. pop singer (with The Supremes)
Ballard, Hank (John Kendricks) (1936–) Am. blues singer/bandleader ("Let's Go, Let's Go, Let's Go"; with The Midnighters)
Ballard, J. G. (James Graham Ballard) (1930–) Eng. writer (*Empire of the Sun*)
Ballard, Kaye (Catherine Gloria Balotta) (1926–) Am. singer/actress ("The Steve Allen Comedy Hour" TV series)
Ballesteros, Seve (Severiano Ballesteros Sota; "The Car Park Golfer") (1957–) Span. golfer
Balmain, Pierre (Pierre Alexandre Balmain) (1914–1982) Fr. fashion designer
Balsam, Martin (Martin Henry Balsam) (1919–) Am. actor (*Twelve Angry Men*; *On the Waterfront*; O—1965—*A Thousand Clowns*; T—1968)
Balzac, Honoré de (Honoré de Balsa) (1799–1850) Fr. novelist (*The Human Comedy*; *Eugenie Grandet*)
Bancroft, Anne (Anna Maria Luisa Italiano; a/k/a Anne Marno) (1931–) Am. actress (*The Graduate*; *The Turning Point*; O—1962—*The Miracle Worker*; T—1960)
Banderas, Antonio (1960–) Span. actor (*Tie Me Up! Tie Me Down!*; *The Mambo Kings*)
Bandy, Moe (Marion Bandy; "King of Honky Tonk") (1944–) Am. country singer ("I Cheated Me Right Out of You")
Bankhead, Tallulah (Tallulah Brockman Bankhead; "Tallu") (1903–1968) Am. actress (*Stage Door Canteen*; *Lifeboat*)
Banks, Ernie (Ernest Banks; "Mr. Cub"; "Mr. Sunshine") (1931–) Am. baseball Hall-of-Famer
Banks, Russell (1940–) Am. writer (*Continental Drift*; *The Sweet Hereafter*)
Banks, Tony (1950–) Eng. rock keyboardist (with Genesis)
Banky, Vilma (Vilma Lonchit; "The Hungarian Rhapsody") (1898–1991) Hung.-Am. actress (*The Son of the Sheik*)
Banneker, Benjamin (1731–1806) Am. astronomer/mathemetician

Bannen, Ian (1928–) Scot. actor (*The Flight of the Phoenix*; *Hope and Glory*)
Bannister, Sir Roger (1929–) Eng. runner (first to run a mile in under 4:00)
Bannon, Jim (1911–1986) Am. radio/film actor (Red Ryder in films)
Bara, Theda (Theodosia Goodman; "The Vamp") (1885–1955) Am. actress (*Cleopatra* [1917]; *Romeo and Juliet*)
Baraka, Imamu Amiri (LeRoi Jones) (1934–) Am. playwright/poet/essayist (*Dutchman*; *The Slave*)
Barbarossa (Redbeard) (died 1546) Barbary pirate
Barbeau, Adrienne (1945–) Am. actress ("Maude" TV series)
Barber, Red (Walter Lanier Barber; "Voice of the Dodgers") (1908–1992) Am. sportscaster
Barber, Samuel (1910–1981) Am. composer (*Medea*; *Dover Beach*; *Antony And Cleopatra*; P—1958—*Vanessa*; P—1963—*Piano Concerto No. 1*)
Barbera, Joseph (Joseph Roland Barbera) 1911–) Am. cartoonist/animator (with William Hanna; *The Flintstones*; *Yogi Bear*)
Barbie, Klaus (a/k/a Klaus Altmann; "The Butcher of Lyons") (1914–) Ger. Nazi gestapo chief/war criminal
Barbieri, Gato (Leandro Barbieri) (1934–) Arg. jazz saxophonist (part of Lalo Schifrin's orchestra in the early 1960s)
Barbirolli, Sir John (Giovanni Battista Barbirolli) (1899–1970) Eng. orchestra conductor
Bardeen, John (1908–1991) Am. physicist (helped develop the transistor; N—1956, 1972)
Bardette, Trevor (1902–1977) Am. actor ("The Life and Legend of Wyatt Earp" TV series; *The Big Sleep*)
Bardot, Brigitte (Camille Javal) (1934–) Fr. actress (*And God Created Woman*; *Contempt*)
Bare, Bobby (Robert Joseph Bare; "Hit Picker") (1935–) Am. country singer/ songwriter/guitarist ("The All American Boy"; "Detroit City")
Barents, Willem (c. 1550–1597) Dutch navigator/explorer
Barfield, Jesse (Jesse Lee Barfield) (1959–) Am. baseball player
Bari, Lynn (Marjorie Schuyler Fisher; a/k/a Marjorie Bitzer) (1911–1989) Am. actress (*The Bridge of San Luis Rey*; *Tampico*)

Barker, Bob (Robert William Barker) (1923–) Am. TV host ("Truth or Consequences")
Barker, Clive (1952–) Eng. horror novelist (*Books of Blood* series)
Barker, Francine (Francine Hurd) (1947–) Am. pop singer (with Peaches & Herb; "Reunited"; "Shake Your Groove Thing")
Barker, Lex (Alexander Crichlow Barker, Jr.) (1919–1973) Am. actor (Tarzan in films)
Barker, Ma (Kate Barker; born Arizona Donnie Clark) (1880–1935) Am. outlaw
Barkin, Ellen (1955–) Am. actress (*Sea of Love*; *Siesta*; *Switch*; *This Boy's Life*)
Barkley, Alben W. (Alben William Barkley) 1877–1956) Am. v.p. (H. Truman)/ politician
Barkley, Charles ("Sir Charles") (1963–) Am. basketball player
Barnard, Christiaan (Christiaan Neethling Barnard) (1922–) S. Afr. surgeon (performed the first human-heart transplant)
Barnard, George (George Grey Barnard) (1863–1938) Am. sculptor
Barnes, Binnie (Gertrude Maude Barnes) (1905–1983) Eng. actress (*The Private Life of Henry VIII*; *The Divorce of Lady X*)
Barnes, Clive (Clive Alexander Barnes) (1927–) Am. journalist/dance and drama critic
Barnes, Djuna (a/k/a Lydia Steptoe) (1892–1982) Am. painter/novelist/short story writer (*Nightwood*)
Barnes, Joanna (1934–) Am. actress (*Spartacus*; *The Parent Trap*)/writer
Barnes, Priscilla (1955–) Am. actress ("Three's Company" TV series)
Barnet, Charlie (Charles Daly Barnet) (1913–1991) Am. jazz saxophonist/ bandleader
Barnum, P. T. (Phineas Taylor Barnum) (1810–1891) Am. circus impresario
Barr, Roseanne see Arnold, Roseanne
Barrault, Jean-Louis (1910–) Fr. actor (*The Longest Day*; *Les Enfants Du Paradis*)
Barrett, Majel (1939–) Am. actress ("Star Trek" TV series)
Barrett, Rona (Rona Burstein) (1934–) Am. (Hollywood) gossip columnist
Barrett, Syd (Roger Barrett) (1946–) Eng. rock guitarist/singer (with Pink Floyd)

Barrie, Barbara (Barbara Ann Berman) (1931–) Am. actress ("Barney Miller" TV series)

Barrie, Sir J. M. (James Matthew Barrie) (1860–1937) Scot. novelist/playwright (*Peter Pan*; *The Admirable Crichton*)

Barrie, Wendy (Marguerite Wendy Jenkins) (1912–1978) Eng. actress (*The Private Life of Henry VIII*; *It Should Happen to You*)

Barris, Chuck (1928–) Am. TV host ("The Gong Show")

Barrow, Clyde ("Public Enemy Number One of the Southwest") (1909–1934) Am. outlaw (with Bonnie Parker)

Barrow, Ed (Edward Grant Barrow; "Cousin Ed") (1868–1953) Am. baseball manager/Hall-of-Famer

Barry, Dave (1947–) Am. humorist/ journalist (P—1988)/writer (*Dave Barry Turns 40*; *Dave Barry Slept Here*)

Barry, Gene (Eugene Klass) (1921–) Am. actor (TV's "Bat Masterson")

Barry, Jeanne Bécu (Madame du Barry Comtesse) (1743–1793) Fr. mistress of Louis XV of France

Barry, Jeff (1938–) Am. pop songwriter (with wife Ellie Greenwich, "Be My Baby"; "Da Doo Ron Ron"; "Chapel of Love")

Barry, John (1933–) Eng.-Am. film composer (*The Lion in Winter*; James Bond films)

Barry, Philip (Philip James Quinn Barry) (1896–1949) Am. playwright (*The Philadelphia Story*; *Holiday*)

Barry, Rick (Richard Francis Barry III) (1944–) Am. basketball player/ sportscaster

Barrymore, Drew (1975–) Am. actress (daughter of John Jr.; granddaughter of John Sr.; *Poison Ivy*; *E.T.: The Extra-Terrestrial*)

Barrymore, Ethel (Ethel Mae Blythe; "First Lady of the American Theater") (1879–1959) Am. actress (sister of John and Lionel; *The Spiral Staircase*; *The Paradine Case*; O—1944—*None but the Lonely Heart*)

Barrymore, Georgiana (Georgianna Emma Drew) (1854–1893) Am. stage actress (mother of Lionel, Ethel, and John)

Barrymore, John (John Sidney Blythe; "The Great Profile") (1882–1942) Am. actor (*Twentieth Century*; *Grand Hotel*)

Barrymore, John, Jr. (John Blythe Barrymore, Jr.; a/k/a John Drew Barrymore)

(1932–) Am. actor (son of John; *War of the Zombies*)

Barrymore, Lionel (Lionel Blythe) (1878–1954) Am. film director/actor (*Decameron Nights*; O—1931—*Free Soul*)

Bartel, Paul (1938–) Am. actor/film director (*Scenes from the Class Struggle in Beverly Hills*; *Eating Raoul*)

Barth, John (John Simmons Barth) (1930–) Am. novelist/short story writer (*Giles Goat-Boy*; *Chimera*)

Barth, Karl (1886–1968) Swi. theologian/ writer (*Credo*; *Church Dogmatics*)

Barthelme, Donald (1931–1989) Am. novelist/short story writer (*Snow White*; *City Life*; *The Dead Father*)

Barthelmess, Richard (1895–1963) Am. actor (*Broken Blossoms*; *The Noose*)

Bartholdi, Frederic (Frederic-Auguste Bartholdi) (1834–1904) Fr. sculptor (Statue of Liberty)

Bartholomew, Freddie (Frederick Llewellyn Bartholomew) (1924–1992) Eng. child actor (*David Copperfield*; *Little Lord Fauntleroy*)

Bartlett, Bonnie (1935–) Am. actress ("St. Elsewhere" TV series; E—1985/86, 1986/87)

Bartlett, Jennifer (Jennifer Losch Bartlett) (1941–) Am. painter/artist

Bartlett, John (1820–1905) Am. editor/ bookseller (compiled *Familiar Quotations*)

Bartlett, Josiah (1729–1795) Am. Revolutionary leader

Bartók, Béla (1881–1945) Hung. composer ("Duke Bluebeard's Castle")

Bartok, Eva (Eva Martha Szöke) (1926–) Hung. actress (*Front Page Story*)

Bartoli, Cecelia (c. 1966–) Ital. opera singer (mezzo-soprano)

Bartolommeo, Fra (Bartolommeo di Pagolo del Fattorino; a/k/a Baccio della Porta) (1475–1517) Flor. painter

Barton, Charles (Charles T. Barton) (1902–1981) Am. film director (*Africa Screams*; *The Shaggy Dog*)

Barton, Clara (Clarissa Harlowe Barton; "Angel of the Battlefield") (1821–1912) Am. Red Cross founder

Barty, Billy (1924–) Am. actor (*Life Stinks*)

Baruch, Bernard M. (Bernard Mannes Baruch) (1870–1965) Am. statesman (advised presidents from Woodrow Wilson to JFK)/financier

Baryshnikov, Mikhail (Mikhail

Nikolayevich Baryshnikov; "Misha") (1948–) Russ.-Am. ballet dancer

Barzun, Jacques (Jacques Martin Barzun) (1907–) Fr.-Am. educator/writer (*The House of Intellect*)

Basehart, Richard (1914–1984) Am. actor (*La Strada; Being There*)

Basho (Matsuo Munefusa; a/k/a Matsuo Basho) (1644–1694) Jap. poet (developed Haiku)

Basia (Basia Trzetrzelewska) (C) Pol. pop singer ("Cruising for Bruising")

Basie, Count (William James Basie, Jr.) (1904–1984) Am. jazz pianist/ bandleader/composer ("One O'Clock Jump"; "April in Paris")

Basil, Toni (1950–) Am. choreographer/ dancer/pop singer ("Mickey")

Basilio, Carmen (1927–) Am. boxer

Basinger, Kim (Kimila Ann Basinger) (1953–) Am. actress (*Batman; 9½ Weeks; Nadine*)

Basquette, Lina (Lena Baskette) (1907–) Am. actress (*The Godless Girl*)/dancer (Ziegfeld Follies)

Bass, Alfie (Alfred Bass) (1920–1987) Eng. actor/comedian (*The Lavender Hill Mob; The Millionairess*)

Bassani, Georgio (1916–) Ital. poet/ novelist/screenwriter (*The Garden of the Finzi-Continis*)

Bassett, Angela (1959–) Am. actress (*What's Love Got to Do With It; Malcolm X*)

Bassey, Shirley (1937–) Eng. singer (*Goldfinger; Diamonds Are Forever*)

Bataille, Georges (1897–1962) Fr. novelist/ philosopher (*Blue of Noon*)

Bataille, Henry (Félix Henry Bataille) (1872–1922) Fr. playwright (*Poliche*)

Bateman, Jason (1969–) Am. actor (brother of Justine; "The Hogan Family" TV series)

Bateman, Justine (1966–) Am. actress (sister of Jason; "Family Ties" TV series)

Bates, Alan (Alan Arthur Bates) (1934–) Eng. actor (*The Fixer; The Entertainer*)

Bates, Kathy (1948–) Am. actress (*Shadows and Fog; Fried Green Tomatoes*; O—1990—*Misery*; T—1973)

Bateson, William ("The Father of Genetics") (1861–1926) Eng. genetecist (coined the word *genetics*)

Bathsheba (1040–1015 B.C.) Heb. mother of Solomon/wife of Uriah the Hittite

Batista, Fulgencio (Fulgencio Batista y

Zaldívar) (1901–1973) Cub. dictator (overthrown by Castro)

Battle, Kathleen (1948–) Am. opera singer (soprano)

Battles, Cliff (Clifford Franklin Battles) (1910–1981) Am. football Hall-of-Famer

Baudelaire, Charles (Charles-Pierre Baudelaire) (1821–1867) Fr. poet (*Les Fleurs du Mal*)

Bauer, Hank (Henry Albert Bauer) (1922–) Am. baseball player/manager

Bauer, Jaime Lyn (1949–) Am. actress ("The Young and the Restless" soap opera)

Bauer, Steven (Steven Echevarria) (1956–) Cub.-Am. actor (*Scarface* [1983])

Baugh, Sammy (Samuel Adrian Baugh; "Slingin' Sam"; "Texas Cowboy") (1914–) Am. football Hall-of-Famer

Baum, L. Frank (Lyman Frank Baum; a/k/a Edith Van Dyne) (1856–1919) Am. journalist/playwright/children's book writer (*The Wonderful Wizard of Oz*)

Baum, Vicki (Hedvig Baum) (1888–1960) Am. novelist (*Grand Hotel*)

Bauman, Jon "Bowser" (1947–) Am. TV host/singer ("Sha Na Na")

Bax, Sir Arnold (Arnold Edward Trevor Bax; a/k/a Dermont O'Byrne) (1883–1953) Eng. composer ("November Woods")

Baxley, Barbara (1925–1990) Am. actress (*Norma Rae*)/stage star (*Period of Adjustment*)

Baxter, Anne (1923–1985) Am. actress (granddaughter of Frank Lloyd Wright; *The Magnificent Ambersons; All About Eve*; O—1946—*The Razor's Edge*)

Baxter, Les (1922–) Am. orchestra leader/ composer ("Unchained Melody")

Baxter, Warner (1889–1951) Am. actor (*The Squaw Man*; O—1928/29—*In Old Arizona*)

Baxter, Meredith (a/k/a Meredith Baxter-Birney) (1947–) Am. actress ("Family Ties" TV series)

Bayes, Nora (Dora Goldberg) (1880–1928) Am. vaudeville singer ("Shine On, Harvest Moon," which she cowrote)

Baylor, Don (Don Edward Baylor) (1949–) Am. baseball player

Baylor, Elgin (Elgin Gay Baylor; "The Man of a Thousand Moves") (1934–) Am. basketball player

Bazin, André (1918–1958) Fr. film critic (cofounded *Cahiers du Cinéma* magazine)

Beacham, Stephanie (1947–) Eng. actress ("Dynasty" and "Beverly Hills, 90210" TV series)

Beadle, George (George Wells Beadle) (1903–1989) Am. geneticist (N—1958)

Beal, John (John Alexander Bliedung) (1909–) Am. actor (*The Little Minister*; *Madame X*)

Beals, Jennifer (1963–) Am. actress (*Flashdance*)

Bean, L. L. (Leon Leonwood Bean) (1872–1967) Am. sportswear merchant

Bean, Orson (Dallas Frederick Burroughs) (1928–) Am. actor/game show panelist/wit

Bean, Judge Roy ("The Law West of the Pecos") (c. 1825–1903) Am. frontier judge

Beard, James (James Andrews Beard) (1903–1985) Am. cookbook writer

Beardsley, Aubrey (Aubrey Vincent Beardsley) (1872–1898) Eng. illustrator (grotesque)

Bearse, Amanda (1958–) Am. actress ("Married . . . With Children" TV series)

Beasley, Allyce (Allyce Tannenberg) (1951–) Am. actress ("Moonlighting" TV series)

Beaton, Sir Cecil (Cecil Walter Hardy Beaton) (1904–1980) Eng. fashion photographer/costume designer (*Gigi*; *My Fair Lady*)

Beatrix (Beatrix Wilhelmina Armgard) (1938–) Dutch queen 1980–

Beattie, Ann (1947–) Am. novelist/short story writer (*Falling in Place*; *Picturing Will*; *Chilly Scenes of Winter*)

Beatty, Ned (1937–) Am. actor (*Deliverance*; *Switching Channels*)

Beatty, Warren (Henry Warren Beaty) (1937–) Am. actor/film director (brother of Shirley MacLaine; *Dick Tracy*; *Shampoo*; O[director]—1981—*Reds*)

Beaufort, Sir Francis (1774–1857) Eng. navy admiral/inventor (Beaufort's scale)

Beauregard, Pierre (Pierre Gustave Toutant de Beauregard) (1818–1893) Am. Civil War Confederate general

Beaverbrook, Lord *see* Aitken, William Maxwell

Beavers, Louise (1902–1962) Am. actress ("Beulah" TV series; *Imitation of Life*)

Bechet, Sidney (1897–1959) Am. jazz saxophonist

Beck, C. C. (Charles Clarence Beck) (1910–1989) Am. cartoonist (*Captain Marvel*)

Beck, Jeff (1944–) Eng. rock guitarist/musician (formerly with The Yardbirds; currently with The Honeydrippers)

Beck, Martin (1867–1940) Hung.-Am. theatrical producer (discovered Houdini)

Becker, Boris (1967–) Ger. tennis player (W—1985, 1986, 1989)

Becker, Walter (1950–) Am. rock musician/singer (with Steely Dan; "Rikki Don't Lose That Number")

Becket, St. Thomas À (c. 1118–1170) Eng. archbishop of Canterbury

Beckett, Samuel (Samuel Barclay Beckett) (1906–1989) Ir. novelist/playwright/poet (*Waiting for Godot*; N—1969)

Beckett, Scotty (1929–1968) Am. child actor ("Our Gang" TV series; *The Jolson Story*)

Beckmann, Max (1884–1950) Ger.-Am. expressionist painter (*Sinking of the Titanic*)

Beckwith, Reginald (1908–1965) Eng. actor (*The Thirty-Nine Steps*; *A Shot in the Dark*)

Bede, The Venerable (672 or 673–735) Eng. historian/scholar (*Eccliastical History of the English Nation*)

Bedelia, Bonnie (Bonnie Culkin) (1946–) Am. actress (*Presumed Innocent*; *Heart Like a Wheel*; *Die Hard*)

Bednarik, Chuck (Charles Philip Bednarik) (1925–) Am. football Hall-of-Famer

Bedrosian, Steve (Stephen Wayne Bedrosian) (1957–) Am. baseball pitcher

Beebe, William (Charles William Beebe) (1877–1962) Am. naturalist/explorer/writer (*Jungle Peace*)

Beech, Keyes (1913–) Am. journalist (P—1951)

Beecham, Sir Thomas (1879–1961) Eng. conductor (founded the London and Royal Philharmonic orchestras)

Beecher, Lyman (1775–1863) Am. preacher/writer (father of Harriet Beecher Stowe)

Beene, Geoffrey (1927–) Am. fashion designer

Beerbohm, Sir Max (Henry Maximilian Beerbohm; "The Incomparable Max") (1872–1956) Eng. caricaturist/essayist/novelist (*Zuleika Dobson*)

Beery, Noah (1884–1946) Am. actor (brother of Wallace, father of Noah, Jr.; *Zorro Rides Again*; *The Sea Wolf*; *Beau Geste*)

Beery, Noah, Jr. (1916–) Am. actor ("The

Rockford Files" TV series; *Walking Tall*)

Beery, Wallace (1885–1949) Am. actor (*Dinner at Eight*; *Grand Hotel*; O—1931/32—*The Champ*)

Beethoven, Ludwig Van (1770–1827) Ger. composer (*Eroica*; *Pathetique*; *Fifth Symphony*)

Begin, Menachem (Menachem Wolfovitch Begin) (1913–1992) Isr. prime minister 1977–1983 (N—1978)

Begley, Ed (Edward James Begley) (1901–1970) Am. actor (*Twelve Angry Men*; O—1962—*Sweet Bird of Youth*)

Begley, Ed, Jr. (Edward James Begley, Jr.) (1949–) Am. actor ("St. Elsewhere" TV series; *She-Devil*)

Behan, Brendan (Brendan Francis Behan) (1923–1964) Ir. playwright (*Borstal Boy*)

Behn, Aphra (née Johnson) (1640–1689) Eng. novelist/playwright (*Oroonoko*; *The Rover*)

Behrens, Hildegard (1937–) Ger. opera singer (soprano)

Behrman, S. N. (Samuel Nathaniel Behrman) (1893–1973) Am. biographer/playwright (*No Time for Comedy*; *Rain from Heaven*)

Beiderbecke, Bix (Leon Bismarck Beiderbecke) (1903–1931) Am. jazz cornetist/pianist

Béjart, Maurice (Maurice Jean Berger) (1927–) Fr. ballet dancer/choreographer

Belafonte, Harry (Harold George Belafonte, Jr.) (1927–) Am. singer ("Banana Boat [Day-O]")

Belafonte-Harper, Shari (1954–) Am. actress (daughter of Harry; "Hotel" TV series)

Belasco, David (1853–1931) Am. playwright/theatrical producer (*The Girl of the Golden West*; *Madame Butterfly*)

Bel Geddes, Barbara (Barbara Geddes Lewis) (1922–) Am. actress ("Dallas" TV series; *I Remember Mama*; E—1979/80)

Beliveau, Jean ("Le Gros Bill") (1931–) Can. hockey player

Bell, Alexander Graham (1847–1922) Am. inventor (telephone)

Bell, Andy (1956–) Eng. rock singer (with Erasure; "A Little Respect")

Bell, Archie (1944–) Am. pop singer/musician (with Archie Bell and The Drells; "Tighten Up")

Bell, Bobby (Robert L. Bell) (1940–) Am. football Hall-of-Famer

Bell, Buddy (David Gus Bell) (1951–) Am. baseball player

Bell, Clive (Arthur Clive Howard Bell) (1881–1964) Eng. art critic/writer (*Since Cézanne*)

Bell, Rex (George Francis Beldam) 1905–1962) Am. actor (*True to the Navy*)

Bell, Vanessa (1879–1961) Eng. artist (member of the Bloomsbury Group)

Bellamy, David (1950–) Am. country singer (with The Bellamy Brothers; "Let Your Love Flow")

Bellamy, Edward (1850–1898) Am. writer (*Looking Backward: 2000–1877*)

Bellamy, Howard (1946–) Am. country singer (with The Bellamy Brothers)

Bellamy, Ralph (Ralph Rexford Bellamy) (1904–1991) Am. actor (*His Girl Friday*; *The Awful Truth*; T—1958)

Belli, Melvin (Melvin Mouron Belli; "The King of Torts") (1907–) Am. attorney (defended Jack Ruby)/writer (*Dallas Justice*)

Bellini, Gentile (c. 1429–1507) Ven. painter

Bellini, Giovanni (1428–1516) Ven. painter

Bellini, Vincenzo (1801–1835) Ital. composer (*La Somnambula*)

Belloc, Hilary or **Hilaire** (Joseph Hilary Pierre Rene Belloc) (1870–1953) Eng. poet/essayist/historian (*The Bad Child's Book of Beasts*)

Bellow, Saul (1915–) Am. novelist (*The Adventures of Augie March*; *Herzog*; N—1976; P—1976—*Humboldt's Gift*)

Bellson, Louis (Louis Balassoni) (1924–) Am. jazz drummer

Belmondo, Jean-Paul (1933–) Fr. actor (*Breathless*)

Belushi, Jim or **James** (James Belushi) (1954–) Am. actor (brother of John; *Red Heat*; *K-9*)

Belushi, John ("The Black Rhino" a/k/a Joliet Jake Blues) (1949–1982) Am. comedian/actor ("Saturday Night Live" TV series; *Animal House*)

Belzer, Richard (1944–) Am. comedian

Bemelmans, Ludwig (1898–1962) Am. painter/writer (*My War with the United States*)

Benaderet, Bea (1906–1968) Am. actress ("Petticoat Junction" TV series)

Benatar, Pat (Patricia Andrzejewski) (1952–) Am. rock singer ("Hit Me with Your Best Shot"; "Love Is a Battlefield")

Benavente, Jacinto (Jacinto Benavente y

Martínez) (1866–1954) Span. playwright (*Bonds of Interest*; N—1922)

Bench, Johnny (Johnny Lee Bench; "Hands") (1947–) Am. baseball Hall-of-Famer

Benchley, Nathaniel (Nathaniel Goddard Benchley; a/k/a Guy Fawkes) (1915–1981) Am. editor/journalist/novelist (*Lassiter's Folly*)

Benchley, Peter (Peter Bradford Benchley) (1940–) Am. novelist (*Jaws*; *The Deep*)

Benchley, Robert (Robert Charles Benchley; a/k/a Guy Fawkes) (1889–1945) Am. drama critic/essayist/humorist (*From Bed to Worse*; *My Ten Years in a Quandary*)

Bender, Chief (Charles Albert Bender) (1884–1954) Am. baseball Hall-of-Famer

Bendix, William (1906–1964) Am. actor ("The Life of Riley" radio and TV series; *The Babe Ruth Story*)

Benedict, Billy (William Benedict) (1906–) Am. actor (one of the Bowery Boys; *The Ox-Bow Incident*)

Benedict, Dirk (Dirk Niewoehner) (1944–) Am. actor ("The A-Team" TV series)

Benedict, Saint (a/k/a Benedict of Nursia) (c. 480–547) Ital. monk

Beneke, Tex (Gordon Beneke) (1914–) Am. jazz saxophonist/vocalist (with Glenn Miller's band)

Beneš, Eduard (1884–1948) Cz. pres. 1935–1938, 1940–1948

Benét, Stephen Vincent (1898–1943) Am. novelist/short story writer/poet (brother of William Rose; *The Devil and Daniel Webster*; P—1929—*John Brown's Body*; P—1944—*Western Star*)

Benét, William Rose (1886–1950) Am. poet/editor (P—1942—*The Dust Which Is God*)

Ben-Gurion, David (David Gruen) (1886–1973) Isr. prime minister 1949–1953, 1955–1963

Bening, Annette (1958–) Am. actress (*Bugsy*; *The Grifters*)

Benitez, Jellybean (John Benitez) (1957–) Am. pop music producer (Madonna, Sting, Michael Jackson)

Benjamin, Richard (1938–) Am. actor (*Catch-22*)/film director (*Mermaids*)

Bennett, Arnold (Enoch Arnold Bennett) (1867–1931) Eng. novelist/journalist/playwright (*The Old Wives' Tale*)

Bennett, Compton (Robert Compton-Bennett) (1900–1974) Eng. film director (*King Solomon's Mines*; *The Seventh Veil*)

Bennett, Constance (Constance Campbell Bennett) (1904–1965) Am. actress (*Topper*; *Madame X*)

Bennett, Joan (1910–1990) Am. actress ("Dark Shadows" TV series; *Bulldog Drummond*)

Bennett, Tony (Antonio Dominick Benedetto; "The Singer's Singer") (1926–) Am. singer ("I Left My Heart in San Francisco"; G—1962)

Benny, Jack (Joseph Benjamin Kubelsky; "The Meanest Man in the World") (1894–1974) Am. comedian/actor (*George Washington Slept Here*; signature phrase: "Well!"; E—1958/59)

Benoit, Joan (1957–) Am. marathon runner

Benson, George (1943–) Am. pop singer ("This Masquerade"; "On Broadway")/jazz guitarist

Benson, Robby (Robert Segal) (1955–) Am. actor (*Ode to Billy Joe*; *Ice Castles*)

Benson, Sally (Sara Mahala Redway Smith) (1900–1972) Am. novelist/short story writer (*Junior Miss*; *Meet Me in St. Louis*)

Bentham, Jeremy (1748–1832) Eng. philosopher (utilitarianism)/jurist

Bentley, E. C. (Edmund Clerihew Bentley) (1875–1956) Eng. detective story writer (*Trent's Last Case*)

Benton, Barbi (Barbara Klein) (1950–) Am. actress/singer ("Hee Haw" TV series)

Benton, Brook (Benjamin Franklin Peay) (1931–1988) Am. pop singer ("It's Just a Matter of Time")

Benton, Robert (1932–) Am. film director/screenwriter (*Places in the Heart*; O—1979—*Kramer vs. Kramer*)

Benton, Thomas Hart ("Old Bullion Benton") (1782–1858) Am. senator/statesman

Benton, Thomas Hart (1889–1975) Am. painter/muralist

Bentsen, Lloyd (Lloyd Millard Bentsen, Jr.) (1921–) Am. senator/govt. official (treasury secretary)

Benz, Karl Friedrich (1844–1929) Ger. engineer/automobile manufacturer

Berenger, Tom (Thomas Berenger) (1950–) Am. actor (*Platoon*; *The Field*)

Berenson, Marisa (1946–) Am. model/actress (granddaughter of Elsa Schiaparelli; *White Hunter, Black Heart*)

Beresford, Bruce (1940–) Austral. film director (*Crimes of the Heart; Driving Miss Daisy*)

Berg, Alban (Alban Maria Johannes Berg) (1885–1935) Aus. composer (*Lulu; Wozzeck*)

Berg, Gertrude (Gertrude Edelstein) (1899–1966) Am. TV/radio actress ("Fibber McGee and Molly"; E—1950; T—1959)

Berg, Moe (Morris Berg; "The Intellectual of Baseball") (1902–1972) Am. baseball player/WWII intelligence agent

Bergen, Candice (1946–) Am. actress (daughter of Edgar; "Murphy Brown" TV series; *Carnal Knowledge*; E—1988/89, 1989/90)

Bergen, Edgar (Edgar John Bergren) (1903–1978) Am. ventriloquist (dummy: Charlie McCarthy)/entertainer

Bergen, Polly (Nellie Paulina Burgin) (1929–) Am. actress (*The Winds of War; The Helen Morgan Story*)

Berger, Hans (1873–1941) Ger. psychiatrist/inventor (electroencephalograph)

Berger, Helmut (Helmut Steinberger) (1944–) Aus. actor (*The Damned; The Garden of the Finzi-Continis*)

Berger, Thomas (Thomas Louis Berger) (1924–) Am. novelist (*Little Big Man*)

Bergerac, Cyrano de (Savinien de Cyrano de Bergerac) (1619–1655) Fr. poet/soldier

Bergerac, Jacques (1927–) Fr. actor (*Gigi*)/cosmetics executive (Revlon)

Bergey, Bill (1945–) Am. football player

Bergin, Patrick (c. 1954–) Am. actor (*Sleeping with the Enemy; Robin Hood*)

Bergman, Alan (1925–) Am. pop songwriter ("How Do You Keep the Music Playing?"; "The Way We Were")

Bergman, Ingmar (Ernst Ingmar Bergman) (1918–) Swed. film director (*Wild Strawberries; The Seventh Seal*)

Bergman, Ingrid (1915–1982) Swed. actress (O—1944—*Gaslight*; O—1956—*Anastasia*; O—1974—*Murder on the Orient Express*; T—1947)

Bergman, Marilyn (Marilyn Keith) (1929–) Am. pop songwriter ("How Do You Keep the Music Playing?"; "The Way We Were")

Bergson, Henri (Henri-Louis Bergson) (1859–1941) Fr. philosopher/writer (*Time and Free Will; Creative Evolution*; N—1927)

Berigan, Bunny (Rowland Bernart Berigan) (1908–1942) Am. jazz trumpeter

Bering, Vitus (Vitus Jonassen Bering) (1681–1741) Dan. navigator/explorer (discovered the Bering Strait and Alaska)

Berkeley, Busby (William Berkeley Enos) (1895–1976) Am. choreographer/film director (*Forty-Second Street; Stage Struck*)

Berkowitz, David ("Son of Sam") (1953–) Am. murderer (killed six in New York City 1976–1977)

Berle, Milton (Mendel Berlinger; "Uncle Miltie"; "Mr. Television") (1908–) Am. comedian (E—1949)

Berlin, Irving (Israel Isidore Baline) (1888–1989) Russ.-Am. songwriter ("God Bless America"; "White Christmas"; "Alexander's Ragtime Band")

Berlin, Sir Isaiah (1909–) Eng. philosopher/writer (*The Hedgehog and the Fox*)

Berliner, Emile (1851–1929) Ger.-Am. inventor (phonograph record)

Berlioz, Hector (Louis-Hector Berlioz) (1803–1869) Fr. composer (*Symphonie Fantastique; Romeo and Juliet*)

Berlitz, Charles (Charles Frambach Berliner) (1914–) Am. languages educator

Berman, Shelley (Sheldon Leonard Berman) (1924–) Am. comedian ("Mary Hartman, Mary Hartman" TV series)

Bernanos, Georges (1888–1948) Fr. novelist/political writer (*Diary of a Country Priest*)

Bernard, Crystal (1963–) Am. actress ("It's a Living" and "Wings" TV series)

Bernardi, Herschel (1923–1986) Am. actor ("Peter Gunn" TV series)

Bernhard, Sandra (1955–) Am. comedienne/actress (*The King of Comedy*)

Bernhardt, Sarah (Henriette Rosine Bernard; "The Divine Sarah") (1844–1923) Fr. stage actress

Berning, Susie (née) **Maxwell** (1941–) Am. golfer

Bernini, Gian, or **Giovanni Lorenzo** (1598–1680) Ital. painter/sculptor/architect

Bernsen, Corbin (1954–) Am. actor ("L.A. Law" TV series)

Bernstein, Carl (1944–) Am. journalist (Watergate)/writer (with Bob Woodward, *All the President's Men*)

Bernstein, Elmer ("Bernstein West") (1922–) Am. film composer (*Thoroughly Modern Millie*)

Bernstein, Leonard (1918–1990) Am. composer/conductor/pianist (*West Side Story; Candide*)

Berra, Yogi (Lawrence Peter Berra) (1925–) Am. baseball Hall-of-Famer

Berry, Chuck (Charles Edward Anderson Berry) (1926–) Am. rock singer/musician ("Maybellene"; "Johnny B. Goode")

Berry, Halle (1965–) Am. actress (*Boomerang; Strictly Business; The Flintstones*)

Berry, Jan (1941–) Am. pop singer (with Jan and Dean; "Surf City")

Berry, Ken (1933–) Am. actor ("Mayberry R.F.D." TV series)

Berry, Raymond (Raymond Emmett Berry) (1933–) Am. football Hall-of-Famer

Berry, Wendell (1934–) Am. poet ("Gift of Good Land")

Berryman, John (1914–1972) Am. poet (*Homage to Mistress Bradstreet*; P— 1965—77 *Dream Songs*)

Bertinelli, Valerie (Valerie Anne Bertinelli) (1960–) Am. actress ("One Day at a Time" and "Cafe Americain" TV series)

Bertolucci, Bernardo (1940–) Ital. film director (*Last Tango in Paris; The Sheltering Sky*; O—1987—*The Last Emperor*)

Bessell, Ted (1935–) Am. actor ("That Girl" TV series)

Bessemer, Sir Henry (1813–1898) Eng. engineer/inventor (the Bessemer process for manufacturing steel)

Besson, Luc (1959–) Fr. film director (*La Femme Nikita*)

Best, Charles Herbert (1899–1978) Am.-Can. scientist (discovered insulin)

Best, Edna (1900–1974) Eng. actress (*The Man Who Knew Too Much; The Swiss Family Robinson*)

Bester, Alfred (1913–) Am. science fiction writer (*The Demolished Man*)

Bethune, Mary McLeod (1875–1955) Am. educator/civil rights advocate

Betjeman, Sir John (1906–1984) Eng. Poet Laureate (*New Bats in Old Belfries*)

Bettelheim, Bruno (1903–1990) Aus.-Am. psychologist/educator

Bettger, Lyle (1915–) Am. actor (*Gunfight at the OK Corral; The Lone Ranger*)

Betts, Dickey (Richard Betts) (1943–) Am. rock musician/songwriter ("Ramblin' Man"; with The Allman Brothers)

Betz, Carl (1920–1978) Am. actor ("The Donna Reed Show" TV series; "Love of Life" soap opera; E—1968/69)

Betz, Pauline (1919–) Am. tennis player (W—1946)

Bevans, Clem (Clement Bevans) (1879–1963) Am. actor (*Saboteur; The Yearling*)

Bevens, Bill (Floyd Clifford Bevens) (1916–1991) Am. baseball pitcher

Bey, Turhan (Turhan Selahettin Saultavey Bey) (1920–) Turk. actor (*Ali Baba and the Forty Thieves; The Mummy's Tomb*)

Bhutto, Benazir (1953–) Pak. prime minister 1988–1990

Bialik, Mayim (1975–) Am. actress (TV's "Blossom")

Bickford, Charles (Charles Ambrose Bickford) (1889–1967) Am. actor (*The Farmer's Daughter; The Song of Bernadette; Johnny Belinda*)

Biddle, Nicholas (1786–1844) Am. financier

Biddle Barrows, Sydney (a/k/a Sheila Devin; "The Mayflower Madam") (1952–) Am. socialite/madam

Biden, Joseph R. (Joseph Robinette Biden, Jr.) (1942–) Am. senator

Biehn, Michael (1956–) Am. actor (*The Terminator; The Abyss; Aliens*)

Bierce, Ambrose (Ambrose Gwinnett Bierce; a/k/a Dod Grile) (1842–1914) Am. poet/journalist/short story writer (*The Devil's Dictionary*)

Big Bopper, The (Jiles Perry Richardson) (1930–1959) Am. disc jockey (signature phrase: "Oh baby, that's what I like!")/ pop singer ("Chantilly Lace")

Bigelow, Kathryn (1951–) Am. film director (*Blue Steel*)

Biggers, Earl Derr (1884–1933) Am. detective story writer (created Charlie Chan)

Biggs, E. Power (Edward George Power Biggs) (1906–1977) Eng.-Am. concert organist

Bikel, Theodore (Theodore Meir Bikel) (1924–) Am. singer/actor (*The African Queen*)

Biko, Steve (1946–1977) S. Afr. political leader (led "black consciousness" movement)

Biletnikoff, Fred (Frederick Biletnikoff) (1943–) Am. football Hall-of-Famer
Bill, Tony (1940–) Am. actor (*Ice Station Zebra*)/film producer/director (*Crazy People*)
Billings, Josh (Henry Wheeler Shaw; "Uncle Esek") (1818–1885) Am. humorist/writer (*Josh Billings, His Sayings*)
Billingsley, Barbara (1922–) Am. actress (June Cleaver in "Leave It to Beaver" TV series)
Billy The Kid (William Henry Bonney) (1859–1881) Am. western outlaw
Binet, Alfred (1857–1911) Fr. psychologist (developed intelligence testing)
Bing, Dave (David Bing) (1943–) Am. basketball player
Bing, Sir Rudolf (Rudolf Franz Josef Bing) (1902–) Aus.-Eng.-Am. opera impresario/manager
Bingham, George (George Caleb Bingham) (1811–1879) Am. frontier painter
Binoche, Juliette (c. 1964–) Fr.-Am. actress (*The Unbearable Lightness of Being*; *Damage*)
Binyon, Claude (1905–1978) Am. film director (*North to Alaska*)/journalist (*Variety*)
Biondi, Matt (1965–) Am. swimmer
Birch, John (John Morrison Birch) (1918–1945) Am. missionary/soldier/spy (killed by the communist Chinese)
Bird, Larry (Larry Joe Bird) (1956–) Am. basketball player
Birdseye, Clarence (Clarence Frank Birdseye) (1886–1956) Am. industrialist/inventor (quick-freezing and dehydrating food; founded General Foods)
Birkin, Jane (1946–) Eng. actress (*Blow-Up*; *Death on the Nile*)
Birney, David (David Edwin Birney) (1939–) Am. actor ("St. Elsewhere" TV series)
Bishop, Elizabeth (1911–1979) Am. poet (P—1956—*Poems, North and South*)
Bishop, Elvin (1942–) Am. rock musician ("Fooled Around and Fell in Love"; formerly with the Paul Butterfield Blues Band)
Bishop, Jim (James Alonzo Bishop) (1907–1987) Am. journalist/writer (*The Day Lincoln Was Shot*; *The Day Christ Died*)
Bishop, Joey (Joseph Abraham Gottlieb) (1918–) Am. comedian/entertainer/TV personality

Bishop, Julie (Jacqueline Brown; a/k/a Jacqueline Wells) (1914–) Am. actress (*The High and the Mighty*; *Sands of Iwo Jima*)
Bishop, Stephen (1951–) Am. pop/rock singer ("On and On")
Bismarck, Otto von (Otto Eduard Leopold von Bismarck-Schonhausen; "The Iron Chancellor"; "The Man of Blood and Iron") (1815–1898) Ger. soldier/chancellor 1871–1890
Bisoglio, Val (1926–) Am. actor ("Quincy" TV series)
Bissell, Whit (Whitner Bissell) (1909–1981) Am. actor ("The Time Tunnel" TV series; *The Caine Mutiny*)
Bisset, Jacqueline (Jacqueline Fraser Bisset) (1944–) Eng.-Am. actress (*Day for Night*; *Scenes from the Class Struggle in Beverly Hills*)
Bixby, Bill (Wilfrid Bailey Bixby) (1934–1993) Am. actor ("My Favorite Martian" and "The Courtship of Eddie's Father" TV series)
Bizet, Georges (Alexandre-César-Léopold Bizet) (1838–1875) Fr. composer (*Carmen*)
Biz Markie (Marcel Hall) (1964–) Am. rapper ("Just a Friend")
Björk, Anita (1923–) Swed. actress (*Miss Julie*; *Secrets of Women*)
Bjorling or **Bjoerling, Jüssi** (Johan Jonaton Bjorling) (1911–1960) Swed. opera singer (tenor)
Bjørnson, Bjørnstjerne (Bjørnstjerne Martinius Bjørnson) (1832–1910) Norw. poet/novelist/playwright (*Trust and Trial*; *A Happy Boy*; N—1903)
Black, Cilla (Priscilla Maria Veronica White) (1943–) Eng. pop singer ("You're My World")
Blackbeard (Edward Teach) (died 1718) Eng. pirate
Black, Clint (Clint Patrick Black; "C. B.") (1962–) Am. country singer ("Killin' Time"; "Better Man"; "Nobody's Home")
Black Hawk (Indian name Ma-ka-ta-i-me-she-kia-kiak) (1767–1838) Am. Indian chief
Black, Hugo (Hugo LaFayette Black) (1886–1971) Am. Supreme Court jurist (1937–1971)/senator/civil rights advocate
Black, Karen (Karen Blanche Ziegler) (1942–) Am. actress (*Five Easy Pieces*; *Airport 75*)

Black, Shirley Temple see Temple, Shirley

Blackman, Honor (1926–) Eng. actress (*Goldfinger*; *A Night to Remember*; "The Avengers" TV series)

Blackmer, Sidney (Sidney Alderman Blackmer) (1895–1973) Am. actor (*High Society*; *Rosemary's Baby*; T—1950)

Blackmore, Ritchie (1945–) Eng. rock guitarist (with Deep Purple and Rainbow)

Blackmun, Harry A. (Harry Andrew Blackmun) (1908–) Am. Supreme Court jurist (1970–1993)

Blackstone, Harry (Henri Bouton) (1885–1965) Am. magician

Blackstone, Harry, Jr. (1934–) Am. magician (son of Harry)

Blackwell, Earl, Jr. (Samuel Earl Blackwell, Jr.; a/k/a Mr. Blackwell) (1913–) Am. publisher/fashion critic

Blackwell, Ewell ("The Whip") (1922–) Am. baseball pitcher

Blackwood, Algernon (Algernon Henry Blackwood) (1869–1951) Eng. novelist/short story writer (*Jimbo*)

Blades, Rubén (1948–) Pan. singer/actor (*The Milagro Beanfield War*; *The Lemon Sisters*)

Blair, Betsy (Elizabeth Boger) (1923–) Am. actress (*Another Part of the Forest*; *Marty*)

Blair, Linda (Linda Denise Blair) (1959–) Am. actress (*The Exorcist* and sequels)

Blake, Amanda (Beverly Louise Neill) (1929–1989) Am. actress ("Gunsmoke" [as Miss Kitty] TV series)

Blake, Eubie (James Hubert Blake) (1883–1983) Am. jazz pianist/composer ("I'm Just Wild About Harry")

Blake, Robert (Michael James Vijencio Gubitosi) (1933–) Am. actor (TV's "Baretta"; *In Cold Blood*; E—1974/75)

Blake, Toe (Hector Blake) (1912–) Can. hockey player

Blake, William (1757–1827) Eng. poet/artist/mystic (*Songs of Innocence*; *The Marriage of Heaven and Hell*)

Blakely, Colin (Colin George Edward Blakely) (1930–1987) Ir. actor (*The Private Life of Sherlock Holmes*; *Equus*)

Blakely, Susan (1948–) Am. model/actress (*The Lords of Flatbush*; *The Towering Inferno*)

Blakey, Art (Muslim name Abdullah Ibn Buhaina) (1919–1990) Am. jazz drummer/bandleader (with Art Blakey and The Jazz Messengers)

Blakley, Ronee (1946–) Am. country singer/actress (*A Nightmare on Elm Street*; *Nashville*)

Blanc, Mel (Melvin Jerome Blanc) (1908–1989) Am. actor/cartoon character voice actor (Bugs Bunny; Porky Pig; Daffy Duck; the Flintstones)

Bland, Bobby "Blue" (Robert Calvin Bland) (1930–) Am. pop singer ("Call on Me"; "Ain't Nothing You Can Do")

Blanda, George (George Frederick Blanda) (1927–) Am. football Hall-of-Famer

Blane, Sally (Elizabeth Jane Young) (1910–) Am. actress (sister of Loretta Young; *Silver Streak*)

Blanton, Jimmy (1918–1942) Am. jazz bassist (with Duke Ellington)

Blasco Ibañez, Vicente (1867–1928) Span. novelist (*Blood and Sand*; *The Four Horsemen of the Apocalypse*)

Blass, Bill (William Ralph Blass) (1922–) Am. fashion designer

Blass, Steve (Stephen Robert Blass) (1942–) Am. baseball pitcher

Blatty, William Peter (1928–) Am. horror novelist (*The Exorcist*)/screenwriter (*A Shot in the Dark*)

Bledsoe, Tempestt (Tempestt Kenieth Bledsoe) (1973–) Am. actress ("The Cosby Show" TV series)

Bleyer, Archie (1909–1989) Am. orchestra leader/music impresario ("The Naughty Lady of Shady Lane"; "Hernando's Hideaway")

Blier, Bernard (1916–1989) Fr. actor (*Buffet Froid*; *The Cheat*)

Blier, Bertrand (1939–) Fr. film director (son of Bernard; *Get Out Your Handkerchiefs*)

Blige, Mary J. (c. 1971–) Am. pop singer ("Real Love")

Bligh, Captain William (1754–1817) Eng. naval officer (commander of the Bounty)

Blish, James (James Benjamin Blish) (1921–1975) Am. science fiction writer (*Cities in Flight*; *Star Trek* novels)

Bliss, Sir Arthur (Arthur Edward Drummond Bliss) (1891–1975) Eng. composer (*Lady of Shallott*)

Blitzstein, Marc (1905–1964) Am. composer (*The Cradle Will Rock*)

Bloch, Ernest (1880–1959) Am. composer (*Voice in the Wilderness*; *Sacred Service*)

Bloch, Ernst (1885–1977) Ger. philosopher/writer (*The Principle of Hope*)

Bloch, Felix (1905–1983) Am. physicist (with E. M. Purcell, discovered nuclear magnetic resonance; N—1952)

Bloch, Ray (Raymond A. Bloch) (1902–1982) Am. orchestra conductor (for Ed Sullivan)

Bloch, Robert (Robert Albert Bloch; a/k/a Tarleton Fiske, Nathan Hindin, and Collier Young) (1917–) Am. suspense writer (*Psycho*)/screenwriter (for "Alfred Hitchcock Presents" TV series)

Block, Lawrence (1938–) Am. mystery writer (*Eight Million Ways to Die; A Ticket to the Boneyard*)

Blocker, Dan (1927–1972) Am. actor ("Bonanza" TV series)

Blondell, Joan (1909–1979) Am. actress (*Nightmare Alley; A Tree Grows in Brooklyn*)

Blondie *see* Harry, Deborah

Bloody Mary *see* Mary I

Bloom, Allan (1930–1992) Am. educator/writer (*The Closing of the American Mind*)

Bloom, Claire (Patricia Claire Blume) (1931–) Eng. actress (*Crimes and Misdemeanors; Limelight*)

Bloomfield, Mike (Michael Bloomfield) (1944–1981) Am. rock singer/guitarist/songwriter (formerly with The Paul Butterfield Blues Band)

Bloor, Mother (Ella Reeve Bloor) (1862–1951) Am. communist agitator

Blow, Kurtis (1960–) Am. rapper ("The Breaks")

Blue, Ben (Benjamin Bernstein) (1901–1975) Can.-Am. vaudeville/film actor (*The Russians Are Coming, The Russians Are Coming*)

Blue, Vida (Vida Rochelle Blue) (1949–) Am. baseball pitcher

Bluebeard (Henri-Désiré Landru) (1869–1922) Fr. murderer (killed ten women in five years; executed)

Blume, Judy (Judy Sussman Blume) (1938–) Am. children's book writer (*Are You There, God? It's Me, Margaret; Forever*)

Bluth, Don (1938–) Am. animation film director (*All Dogs Go to Heaven; An American Tail*)

Bly, Nellie (Elizabeth Seaman née Cochrane) (1867–1922) Am. journalist/writer (*Ten Days in a Madhouse*)

Bly, Robert (Robert Elwood Bly) (1926–) Am. poet (*Silence in the Snowy Fields*)/translator

Blyleven, Bert (Rik Aalbert Blyleven) (1951–) Am. baseball pitcher

Blyth, Ann (Ann Marie Blyth) (1928–) Am. singer/actress (*Mildred Pierce; The Great Caruso*)

Blyth, Harry (1852–1898) Eng. mystery writer (created Sexton Blake)

Blyton, Enid (Enid Mary Blyton; a/k/a Mary Pollock) (1897–1968) Eng. children's book writer (created The Secret Seven, The Famous Five, and Mr. Meddle)

Boas, Franz (1858–1942) Am. anthropologist/writer (*The Mind of Primitive Man*)

Bob & Ray *see* Elliott, Bob, and Goulding, Ray

Boccaccio, Giovanni (1313–1375) Ital. poet/writer (*The Decameron*)

Bochco, Steven (1943–) Am. TV writer/series creator ("Hill Street Blues"; "L.A. Law"; "NYPD Blue")

Bochner, Hart (1956–) Can.-Am. actor (son of Lloyd; *War and Remembrance; Die Hard*)

Bochner, Lloyd (1924–) Can. actor ("Dynasty" TV series)

Bock, Jerry (Jerrold Lewis Bock) (1928–) Am. composer (*Fiddler on the Roof* with Sheldon Harnick; P—1960—*Fiorello*)

Boddicker, Mike (Michael James Boddicker) (1957–) Am. baseball pitcher

Bodenheim, Maxwell (1893–1954) Am. novelist/poet (*Sixty Seconds*)

Boeing, William (William Edward Boeing) (1881–1956) Am. aircraft manufacturer (founded the Boeing Airplane Company)

Boesky, Ivan (1937–) Am. banker/criminal (jailed for insider trading)

Boethius (Anicius Manlius Torquatus Severinus Boethius) (475–524) Roman philosopher (*On the Consolation of Philosophy*)

Bofill, Angela (1954–) Am. pop singer (performed with Dizzy Gillespie and Cannonball Adderley; "This Time I'll Be Sweeter")

Bogan, Louise (1897–1970) Am. poet/poetry editor (*Dark Summer*)

Bogarde, Dirk (Derek Niven van den Bogaerde) (1920–) Eng. actor (*The Damned; The Servant; Death in Venice*)

Bogart, Humphrey (Humphrey De Forest Bogart; "Bogie") (1899–1957) Am. actor (*Casablanca; The Big Sleep*; O—1951—*The African Queen*)

Bogdanovich, Peter (a/k/a Derek Thomas) (1939–) Am. film director (*The Last Picture Show*; *What's Up, Doc?*; *Paper Moon*)

Boggs, Wade (Wade Anthony Boggs) (1958–) Am. baseball player

Bogguss, Suzy (Susan Kay Bogguss) (1956–) Am. country singer ("Drive South"; "Aces")

Bogosian, Eric (1953–) Am. actor/comedian (*Talk Radio*; *Sex, Drugs, Rock & Roll*)

Bohay, Heidi (1959–) Am. actress ("Hotel" TV series)

Bohr, Niels (Niels Henrik David Bohr) (1885–1962) Dan. physicist (developed quantum physics N—1922)

Boiardo, Matteo (Matteo Maria Boiardo; Conte di Scandiano) (c. 1441–1494) Ital. poet (*Orlando Innamorato*)

Boitano, Brian (1963–) Am. figure skater

Boito, Arrigo (Enrico Giuseppe Giovanni Boito) (1842–1918) Ital. poet/composer (*Mefistofele*)/librettist (*La Gioconda*; *Otello*; *Falstaff*)

Bok, Derek (Derek Curtis Bok) (1930–) Am. educator (pres. of Harvard University)

Bok, Sissela (1934–) Am. philosopher/writer (*Lying: Moral Choice in Public and Private Life*)

Bolan, Marc (Mark Feld) (1948–1977) Eng. rock singer/musician (with T. Rex; "Bang a Gong [Get It On]")

Bolden, Buddy (Charles Joseph Bolden) (1868–1931) Am. jazz cornetist

Boleyn, Anne ("Anne of the Thousand Days") (c. 1507–1536) Fr. queen (Henry VIII's second wife; mother of Elizabeth I)

Bolger, Ray (Raymond Wallace Bolger) (1904–1987) Am. dancer/actor (scarecrow in *The Wizard of Oz*; T—1949)

Bolívar, Simon ("El Libertador") (1783–1830) Venez. liberator of South America

Böll, Heinrich (Heinrich Theodor Boll) (1917–1985) Ger. novelist/short story writer (*Traveler, If You Come to Spa*; *The Clown*; N—1972)

Bolling, Claude (1930–) Fr. pianist/composer

Bologna, Giovanni Da (a/k/a Giambologna) (1529–1608) Flem. sculptor

Bologna, Joseph (1936–) Am. actor (*My Favorite Year*)/screenwriter (*It Had to Be You*)

Bolt, Robert (Robert Oxton Bolt) (1924–) Eng. playwright (*A Man for All Seasons*)/screenwriter (*Lawrence of Arabia*; *Doctor Zhivago*)

Bolt, Tommy (Thomas Bolt) (1918–) Am. golfer

Bolton, Michael (Michael Bolotin) (1954–) Am. pop singer ("Soul Provider"; "How Am I Supposed to Live without You"; G—1989, 1991)

Bombeck, Erma (Erma Louise Fiste) (1927–) Am. columnist ("At Wit's End")/humorist/writer (*The Grass Is Always Greener Over the Septic Tank*)

Bonaduce, Danny (1959–) Am. actor ("The Partridge Family" TV series)

Bonanno, Joseph ("Joe Bananas") (1904–) Am. gangster

Bonaparte, Napoléon (Napoléon I) (1769–1821) Fr. soldier/emperor 1804–1814

Bonaventura, Saint (Giovanni DiFidenza; "The Seraphic Doctor") (c. 1217–1274) Ital. theologian/philosopher

Bond, Johnny (Cyrus Whitfield Bond) (1915–1978) Am. country singer ("Hot Rod Lincoln")

Bond, Julian (1940–) Am. senator/civil rights advocate

Bond, Sudie (1923–1984) Am. actress ("Flo" TV series)

Bond, Ward (1903–1960) Am. actor ("Wagon Train" TV series; *Drums Along the Mohawk*; *The Grapes of Wrath*)

Bondi, Beulah (Beulah Bondy) (1889–1981) Am. actress (*It's a Wonderful Life*; *Street Scene*)

Bonds, Gary "U.S." (Gary Anderson) (1939–) Am. pop singer ("Quarter to Three")

Bonerz, Peter (1938–) Am. actor ("The Bob Newhart Show" TV series)

Bonet, Lisa (1967–) Am. actress ("The Cosby Show" TV series)

Bonham, John ("Bonzo") (1947–1979) Eng. rock drummer (with Led Zeppelin)

Bonham Carter, Helena (1966–) Eng. actress (*A Room with a View*; *Howard's End*; *Much Ado About Nothing*)

Bonheur, Rosa (Marie-Rosalie Bonheur) (1822–1899) Fr. painter (*The Horse Fair*)

Bonhoeffer, Dietrich (1906–1945) Ger. theologian (*Ethik*; executed for plotting to assassinate Hitler)

Boniface, Saint (Wynfrid or Wynfrith; "Apostle of Germany") (c. 675–754) Eng. missionary

Bonilla, Bobby (Roberto Martin Antonio Bonilla) (1964–) Am. baseball player
Bon Jovi, Jon (Jon Bongiovi) (1961–) Am. rock singer ("Livin' on a Prayer"; "You Give Love a Bad Name")
Bonnard, Pierre (1867–1947) Fr. painter (*The Breakfast Room*)
Bonnie and Clyde *see* Parker, Bonnie, and Barrow, Clyde
Bono (Bono Vox; born Paul Hewson) (1960–) Ir. rock singer (with U2)
Bono, Chastity (1969–) Am. actress/singer (daughter of Sonny Bono and Cher)
Bono, Sonny (Salvatore Phillip Bono) (1935–) Am. actor/singer/politician (mayor of Palm Springs)
Bonoff, Karla (1952–) Am. pop singer ("Personally")/songwriter ("Someone to Lay Down Beside Me")
Bontemps, Arna (Arna Wendell Bontemps) (1902–1973) Am. writer/leader of the Harlem Renaissance (*Drums at Dusk*; *One Hundred Years of Negro Freedom*)
Boone, Daniel (c. 1734–1820) Am. frontiersman/pioneer
Boone, Debby (Deborah Ann Boone) (1956–) Am. pop singer (daughter of Pat; "You Light Up My Life"; G—1977)
Boone, Pat (Charles Eugene Boone) (1934–) Am. singer ("Ain't That a Shame")
Boorman, John (1933–) Eng. film director (*Deliverance*)
Boorstin, Daniel (Daniel Joseph Boorstin) (1914–) Am. historian/writer (*The Discoverers*; P—1974—*The Americans: The Democratic Experience*)
Boosler, Elayne (c. 1952–) Am. comedienne
Booth, Edwin (Edwin Thomas Booth) (1833–1893) Am. stage actor
Booth, John Wilkes (1838–1865) Am. actor/assassin of Pres. Lincoln
Booth, Shirley (Thelma Booth Ford) (1907–1992) Am. actress ("Hazel" [title role] TV series; O—1952—*Come Back Little Sheba*; E—1961/62, 1962/63; T—1950, 1953)
Boothe, Powers (1949–) Am. actor (Rev. Jim Jones in *The Guyana Tragedy*)
Borden, Gail (1801–1874) Am. inventor (evaporated milk)
Borden, Lizzie (Lizzie Andrew Borden) (1860–1927) Am. alleged murderess (of her parents)
Borden, Lizzie (Linda Elizabeth Borden) (1954–) Am. film director (*Love Crimes*)

Borg, Bjorn (Bjorn Rune Bork) (1956–) Swed. tennis player (W—1976 through 1980)
Borg, Veda Ann (1915–1973) Am. actress ("The Abbott and Costello Show" TV series; *Love Me or Leave Me*)
Borge, Victor (Borge Rosenbaum) (1909–) Am. pianist/comedian
Borges, Jorge (Luis) (1899–1986) Arg. short story writer/poet/essayist (*Labyrinths*)
Borgia, Cesare (1475 or 1476–1507) Span.-Ital. Renaissance ruler/soldier
Borgia, Lucrezia (1480–1519) Span.-Ital. duchess of Ferrara (sister of Cesare)
Borglum, Gutzon (John Gutzon de la Mothe Borglum) (1867–1941) Am. sculptor (Mt. Rushmore)
Borgnine, Ernest (Ermes Effron Borgnino) (1917–) Am. actor ("McHale's Navy" TV series; *The Poseidon Adventure*; O—1955—*Marty*)
Bori, Lucrezia (Lucrecia Borja y Gonzalez de Riancho) (1887–1960) Span.-Ital. opera singer
Bork, Robert (Robert Heron Bork) (1927–) Am. lawyer/federal judge (Supreme Court nominee)/writer (*The Tempting of America*)
Borman, Frank (1928–) Am. astronaut
Bormann, Martin (Martin Ludwig Bormann) (1900–1945) Ger. Nazi leader
Borodin, Aleksandr (Aleksandr Porfiryevich Borodin) (1833–1887) Russ. composer (*Prince Igor*)/chemist
Borzage, Frank (1893–1962) Am. film director (*A Farewell to Arms*; O—1927/28—*Seventh Heaven*; O—1931/32—*Bad Girl*)
Bosch, Hieronymus (Jeroen van Aeken or Aken) (1450–1516) Dutch painter (*Garden of Earthly Delights*)
Bosco, Philip (1930–) Am. actor (*True Colors*; *The Pope of Greenwich Village*; *Children of a Lesser God*; T—1989)
Bosley, Tom (Thomas Edward Bosley) (1927–) Am. actor ("Happy Days" TV series)
Boss Tweed *see* Tweed, William Marcy
Bosson, Barbara (1939–) Am. actress ("Hill Street Blues" TV series)
Bossy, Mike ("Boss") (1957–) Can. hockey player
Bostock, Lyman (Lyman Wesley Bostock) (1950–1978) Am. baseball player
Bostwick, Barry (1945–) Am. actor (*The

Rocky Horror Picture Show; Movie Movie; T—1977)
Boswell, Connee (1907–1976) Am. singer (with The Boswell Sisters)
Boswell, James (1740–1795) Scot. biographer (*Life of Samuel Johnson*)
Boswell, Martha (1905–1958) Am. singer (with The Boswell Sisters)
Boswell, Vet (Helvetia Boswell) (1911–1988) Am. singer (with The Boswell Sisters)
Bosworth, Brian ("Boz") (1965–) Am. football player/actor
Botha, Pieter (Pieter Willem Botha) (1916–) S. Afr. prime minister 1978–1984/pres. 1984–1989
Botticelli, Sandro (Alessandro di Mariano Filipepi) (1445–1510) Ital. painter (*The Birth of Venus*)
Bottoms, Joseph (1954–) Am. actor (brother of Sam and Timothy; *Holocaust*)
Bottoms, Sam (1955–) Am. actor ("Santa Barbara" soap opera)
Bottoms, Timothy (1951–) Am. actor (*The Paper Chase; The Last Picture Show; East of Eden* TV movie)
Boucher, Anthony (William Anthony Parker White) (1911–1968) Am. science fiction writer/crime novelist/critic/anthologist/editor (for *Ellery Queen's Mystery Magazine*)
Boucher, François (1703–1770) Fr. rococo painter
Boudreau, Lou (Louis Boudreau) (1917–) Am. baseball Hall-of-Famer
Boulanger, Nadia (Nadia-Juliette Boulanger) (1887–1979) Fr. music teacher (Aaron Copland, Darius Milhaud, Walter Piston)/conductor
Boulez, Pierre ("20th-Century Limited") (1925–) Fr. composer/conductor (New York Philharmonic)
Boulle, Pierre (Pierre Francois Marie-Louis Boulle) (1912–1994) Fr. novelist (*Planet of the Apes; The Bridge on the River Kwai*)
Boult, Sir **Adrian** (Adrian Cedric Boult) (1899–1983) Eng. orchestra conductor
Bourke-White, Margaret (Margaret White) (1906–1971) Am. photographer/war correspondent
Bouton, Jim (James Alan Bouton; "Bulldog") (1939–) Am. baseball pitcher/writer (*Ball Four*)
Boutros-Ghali, Boutros (1922–) Egypt. United Nations secretary general

Bova, Ben (Benjamin William Bova) (1932–) Am. science fiction writer (*Kinsman*)
Bow, Clara (Clara Gordon Bow; "The 'It' Girl") (1901–1965) Am. actress (*Wings; It*)
Bowa, Larry (Lawrence Robert Bowa) (1945–) Am. baseball player
Bowe, Riddick (Riddick Lamont Bowe) (c. 1967—) Am. boxer
Bowes, Major (Edward Bowes) (1874–1946) Am. radio personality
Bowie, David (David Robert Jones) (1947–) Eng. rock singer ("Fame"; "Golden Years"; "Let's Dance")/actor (*The Man Who Fell to Earth*)
Bowie, Jim (James Bowie) (1796–1836) Am. soldier (hero of the Texas revolution)/inventor (Bowie knife)
Bowles, Paul (1910–) Am. writer (*The Sheltering Sky*)
Boxcar Willie (Lecil Travis Martin; "The Singing Hobo") (1931–) Am. country singer ("Train Medley")
Boxer, Barbara (1940–) Am. senator
Boxleitner, Bruce (1950–) Am. actor ("Scarecrow and Mrs. King" TV series)
Boy George (George Alan O'Dowd) (1961–) Eng. pop singer ("Do You Really Want to Hurt Me")
Boyd, Oil Can (Dennis Ray Boyd) (1959—) Am. baseball pitcher
Boyd, William (1898–1972) Am. actor ("Hopalong Cassidy" films; *King of Kings*)
Boyer, Charles (1899–1978) Fr.-Am. actor (*Gaslight; Algiers; Barefoot in the Park*)
Boyer, Clete (Cletis Leroy Boyer) (1937–) Am. baseball player
Boyington, Pappy (Gregory Boyington) (1912–1988) Am. aviator/WWII hero/autobiographer (*Baa Baa Black Sheep*)
Boyle, Kay (1903–1992) Am. short story writer/novelist/poet (*Plagued by the Nightingale; The Underground Woman*)
Boyle, Lara Flynn (1970–) Am. actress ("Twin Peaks" TV series; *The Temp*)
Boyle, Peter (1933–) Am. actor (*The Candidate; Taxi Driver; Young Frankenstein*)
Bracco, Lorraine (1955–) Am. actress (*Medicine Man; Switch; Traces of Red*)
Bracken, Eddie (Edward Vincent Bracken) (1920–) Am. actor (*The Miracle of Morgan's Creek; Hail the Conquering Hero*)
Brackenridge, Hugh (Hugh Henry Brackenridge) (1748–1816) Am. novelist/poet (*The Battle of Bunker Hill*)

Bradbury, Malcolm (Malcolm Stanley Bradbury) (1932–) Eng. novelist/literary critic (*Eating People Is Wrong*)

Bradbury, Ray (Raymond Douglas Bradbury) (1920–) Am. science fiction novelist/short story writer (*The Illustrated Man*; *The Martian Chronicles*; *Fahrenheit 451*; *Something Wicked This Way Comes*)

Braddock, Jim (James Joseph Braddock; "Cinderella Man") (1905–1974) Am. boxer

Bradford, Barbara Taylor (1933–) Eng.-Am. romance novelist (*A Woman of Substance*)

Bradford, William ("The Father of American History") (1590–1657) Am. pilgrim father/early politician (governed the Plymouth Colony)/writer (*History of Plimmoth Plantation*)

Bradlee, Ben (Benjamin Crowninshield Bradlee) (1921–) Am. journalist/editor (*Washington Post*)

Bradley, Bill (William Warren Bradley; "Dollar Bill"; "Mr. Knickerbocker") (1943–) Am. basketball player/senator

Bradley, Ed (Edward R. Bradley, Jr.) (1941–) Am. TV newscaster ("60 Minutes")

Bradley, Marion Zimmer (1941–) Am. science fiction/fantasy writer (*The Colors of Space*; *Firebrand*)

Bradley, Omar (Omar Nelson Bradley; "The GI's General") (1893–1981) Am. army general/chief of staff

Bradley, Tom (Thomas Bradley) (1917–) Am. mayor of Los Angeles 1973–1993

Bradshaw, Terry (Terry Paxton Bradshaw; "Ozark Ike") (1948–) Am. football Hall-of-Famer/sportscaster

Bradstreet, Anne (née Dudley) (c. 1612–1672) Am. poet (*The Tenth Muse Lately Sprung Up in America*)

Brady, Alice (1892–1939) Am. actress (*My Man Godfrey*; O—1937—*In Old Chicago*)

Brady, "Diamond" Jim (James Buchanan Brady) (1856–1917) Am. railroad tycoon/philanthropist

Brady, James (James Scott Brady; "The Bear") (1940–) Am. press secretary (shot by John Hinckley, Jr.)/ gun control advocate ("the Brady Bill")

Brady, Matthew (Matthew B. Brady; "Mr. Lincoln's Cameraman") (1823–1896) Am. Civil War photographer

Brady, Nicholas (Nicholas Frederick Brady) (1930–) Am. govt. official (treasury secretary)

Braga, Sonia ("Brazilian Bombshell") (1951–) Braz. actress (*Doña Flora and Her Two Husbands*; *Kiss of the Spider Woman*)

Bragg, Braxton (1817–1876) Am. Confederate Army general

Brahe, Tycho (1546–1601) Dan. astronomer

Brahms, Johannes (1833–1897) Ger. composer (*Hungarian Dances*)

Braille, Louis (1809–1852) Fr. teacher of the blind/inventor of Braille

Braine, John (John Gerard Braine) (1922–1986) Eng. novelist (*Room at the Top*)

Bramlett, Bonnie (Bonnie Lynn Bramlett; born Bonnie Lynn O'Farrell) (1944–) Am. pop singer ("Never Ending Song of Love"; with Delaney & Bonnie)

Bramlett, Delaney (1939–) Am. pop singer (with Delaney & Bonnie)

Branagh, Kenneth (1960–) Ir.-Eng. actor/film director (*Much Ado About Nothing*; *Peter's Friends*)

Branca, Ralph (Ralph Theodore Joseph Branca; "Hawk") (1926–) Am. baseball pitcher

Brancusi, Constantin (1876–1957) Rom. sculptor (*Bird in Space*)

Brand, Max (Frederick Schiller Faust; "King of the Pulp Writers") (1892–1944) Am. westerns writer (*Destry Rides Again*)

Brand, Neville (1921–1992) Am. actor (TV's "Laredo"; *The George Raft Story*)

Brandauer, Klaus Maria (1944–) Aus. actor (*Mephisto*; *The Russia House*)

Brandeis, Louis (Louis Dembitz Brandeis; "The People's Attorney") (1856–1941) Am. Supreme Court jurist 1916–1939/writer (*Other People's Money*)

Brando, Marlon (Marlon Brando, Jr.; "Buddy") (1924–) Am. actor (*Last Tango in Paris*; *Apocalypse Now*; O—1954—*On the Waterfront*; O—1972—*The Godfather* [refused])

Brandt, Willy (Herbert Ernst Karl Frahm) (1913–1992) Ger. politician/chancellor 1969–1974 (N—1971)

Branigan, Laura (1957–) Am. pop singer ("Gloria"; "Solitaire")

Branson, Richard (1951–) Eng. businessman/entrepreneur (Virgin Records/Airlines; one-time richest man in the U.K.)

Brant, Sebastian (c. 1458–1521) Ger. poet (*Ship of Fools*)

Braque, Georges (1882–1963) Fr. painter (developed cubism with Picasso)

Brasselle, Keefe (John J. Brasselli) (1923–1981) Am. actor (*The Eddie Cantor Story*)/TV producer

Brattain, Walter (Walter Houser Brattain) (1902–1987) Am. physicist (helped develop the transistor; N—1956)

Braun, Eva (1912–1945) Ger. mistress of Adolf Hitler (they married a few days before their suicides)

Braun, Wernher Von (1912–1977) Ger.-Am. rocket scientist/engineer (developed the Saturn V rocket)

Brautigan, Richard (1933–1984) Am. poet/novelist (*Trout Fishing in America*)

Braverman, Bart (1946–) Am. actor ("Vega$" TV series)

Braxton, Toni (c. 1968–) Am. pop singer ("Love Shoulda Brought You Home")

Brazzi, Rossano (1916–) Ital. actor (*Little Women; The Barefoot Contessa*)

Bream, Sid (Sidney Eugene Bream) (1960–) Am. baseball player

Breathed, Berke (1957–) Am. cartoonist (*Bloom County*; P—1987)

Brecheen, Harry (Harry David Brecheen; "The Cat") (1914–) Am. baseball pitcher

Brecht, Bertolt (Eugen Berthold Friedrich Brecht) (1898–1956) Ger. poet/playwright (*The Threepenny Opera; Mother Courage; The Seven Deadly Sins*)

Breckinridge, John C. (John Cabell Breckinridge) (1760–1806) Am. v.p. (J. Buchanan)

Brel, Jacques (1929–1978) Belg. composer/singer

Brendel, El (Elmer G. Brendel) (1890–1964) Am. vaudeville/film actor (*The Beautiful Blonde from Bashful Bend*)

Brenly, Bob (Robert Earl Brenly) (1954–) Am. baseball player

Brennan, Eileen (Verla Eileen Brennan or Eileen Regina Brennan) (1935–) Am. actress (*Private Benjamin; Murder by Death*; E—1980/81)

Brennan, Walter (Walter Andrew Brennan) (1894–1974) Am. actor (O—1936—*Come and Get It*; O—1938—*Kentucky*; O—1940—*The Westerner*)

Brennan, William J., Jr. (William Joseph Brennan, Jr.) (1906–) Am. Supreme Court jurist (1956–1990)

Brenner, David (1945–) Am. comedian

Brent, George (George Brendan Nolan) (1904–1979) Ir.-Am. actor (*Dark Victory; Jezebel*)

Brentano, Clemens Maria (1778–1842) Ger. poet (*Lorelai*)

Breslin, Jimmy (1930–) Am. sports columnist (P—1986)

Bresnahan, Roger (Roger Philip Bresnahan; "The Duke of Tralee") (1879–1944) Am. baseball Hall-of-Famer

Bresson, Robert (1901–) Fr. film director/screenwriter (*The Trial of Joan of Arc; Diary of a Country Priest*)

Brest, Martin (1951–) Am. film director (*Beverly Hills Cop; Midnight Run*)

Breton, André (1896–1966) Fr. artist/poet/novelist (founder of surrealism; *What Is Surrealism?*)

Brett, George (George Howard Brett; "Mullethead") (1953–) Am. baseball player

Brett, Jeremy (Jeremy Huggins) (1935–) Eng. actor (TV's "Sherlock Holmes")

Breuer, Marcel (Marcel Lajos Breuer) (1902–1981) Am. architect (UNESCO headquarters in Paris)

Brewer, Gay (Gay Brewer, Jr.) (1932–) Am. golfer

Brewer, Teresa (Theresa Breuer) (1931–) Am. pop singer ("Till I Waltz with You Again")

Brewster, William (1567–1644) Eng.-Am. pilgrim father

Brezhnev, Leonid (Leonid Ilyich Brezhnev) (1906–1982) Russ. political leader 1964–1982

Briand, Aristide (1862–1932) Fr. statesman (N—1926)

Brice, Fanny (Frances Borach; "Baby Snooks") (1891–1951) Am. singer/entertainer (in the Ziegfeld Follies; subject of *Funny Girl*)

Brickell, Edie (1966–) Am. pop/rock singer ("What I Am"; with Edie Brickell and The New Bohemians)

Bridges, Beau (Lloyd Vernet Bridges III) (1941–) Am. actor (brother of Jeff, son of Lloyd; *The Fabulous Baker Boys*; "Harts of the West" TV series)

Bridges, James (1936–1993) Am. film director/writer (*The China Syndrome; Bright Lights, Big City*)

Bridges, Jeff (1949–) Am. actor (brother of Beau, son of Lloyd; *The Fabulous Baker Boys; The Fisher King*)

Bridges, Lloyd (Lloyd Vernet Bridges II)

(1913–) Am. actor (father of Beau and Jeff; "Sea Hunt" TV series; *High Noon*)

Bridges, Robert (Robert Seymour Bridges) (1844–1930) Eng. poet laureate (*The Testament of Beauty*)

Bridges, Todd (1965–) Am. actor ("Diff'rent Strokes" TV series)

Bridgman, Percy (Percy Williams Bridgman) (1882–1961) Am. physicist (N—1946)

Brigit, Saint (a/k/a Brigit of Kildare; Brigit of Ireland) (died c. 524–528) patron saint of Ireland

Brimley, Wilford (1934–) Am. actor (*The China Syndrome*; *Absence of Malice*; *Tender Mercies*)

Brinkley, Christie (1953–) Am. model/artist

Brinkley, David (David McClure Brinkley) (1920–) Am. newscaster ("The Huntley-Brinkley Report")

Brisebois, Danielle (1969–) Am. actress ("Knots Landing" TV series)

Britt, May (Maybritt Wilkins) (1933–) Swed. actress (*The Young Lions*; *The Blue Angel*)

Brittain, Vera (Vera Mary Brittain) (1893–1970) Eng. novelist (*Testament of Youth*)

Brittany, Morgan (Suzanne Cupito) (1951–) Am. actress ("Dallas" TV series)

Britten, Baron Benjamin (Edward Benjamin Britten) (1913–1976) Eng. composer (*Billy Budd*; *Death in Venice*)

Britton, Barbara (Barbara Brantingham Czukor) (1920–1980) Am. actress ("Mr. and Mrs. North" TV series)

Britton, Pamela (1923–1974) Am. actress (TV's "Blondie")

Britz, Jerilyn (1943–) Am. golfer

Brock, Greg (Gregory Allen Brock) (1957–) Am. baseball player

Brock, Lou (Louis Clark Brock; "The Base Burglar"; "The Franchise") (1939–) Am. baseball Hall-of-Famer

Broderick, Helen (1890–1959) Am. singer/comedienne/actress (*Top Hat*; *Swing Time*)

Broderick, James (James Joseph Broderick) (1927–1982) Am. actor (father of Matthew; "Family" TV series)

Broderick, Matthew (1962–) Am. actor (son of James; *Biloxi Blues*; *Ferris Bueller's Day Off*; *The Freshman*)

Brodie, Steve (Walter Scott Brodie) (1868–1935) Am. baseball player

Brodsky, Joseph (Iosif Aleksandrovich

Brodsky) (1940–) Russ. poet (*History of the Twentieth Century*; N—1987)

Brody, Jane (Jane Ellen Brody) (1941–) Am. writer/journalist/nutritionist (*Jane Brody's Nutrition Book*)

Brokaw, Tom (Thomas John Brokaw) (1940–) Am. newscaster

Brolin, James (James Brunderlin) (1940–) Am. actor ("Marcus Welby, M.D." TV series; E—1969/70)

Bromfield, Louis (Louis Brucker Bromfield) (1896–1956) Am. novelist (*The Rains Came*; P—1927—*Early Autumn*)

Bromwich, Jack (John Edward Bromwich) (1918–) Austral. tennis player

Bronowski, Jacob (1908–1974) Am. scientist/philosopher/historian (*The Ascent of Man*)

Bronson, Charles (Charles Dennis Bunchinsky) (1921–) Am. actor (*Machine Gun Kelly* [title role]; *Death Wish*; *Once Upon a Time in the West*)

Brontë, Anne (a/k/a Acton Bell, Lady Geralda, Olivia Vernon and Alexandria Zenobia) (1820–1849) Eng. writer (*Agnes Grey*)

Brontë, Branwell (Patrick Branwell Brontë) (1817–1848) Eng. painter (brother of Anne, Charlotte, and Emily)

Brontë, Charlotte (a/k/a Carter Bell) (1816–1855) Eng. novelist/poet (sister of Emily, Anne, and Branwell; *Jane Eyre*)

Brontë, Emily (Emily Jane Brontë; a/k/a Ellis Bell and R. Alcon) (1818–1848) Eng. novelist/poet (sister of Charlotte, Anne, and Branwell; *Wuthering Heights*)

Brook, Clive (Clifford Hardman Brook) (1887–1974) Eng. actor (*Shanghai Express*; *Underworld*)

Brook, Sir Peter (Peter Stephen Paul Brook) (1925–) Eng. theatrical/film director (*The Beggar's Opera*; *Lord of the Flies*)

Brooke, Rupert (Rupert Chawner Brooke) (1887–1915) Eng. poet (*Heaven*; *Dust*)

Brookner, Anita (1938–) Eng. novelist (*Providence*; *Hotel Du Lac*)

Brooks, Albert (Albert Einstein) (1947–) Am. film director/actor/screenwriter (*Lost in America*; *Modern Romance*; *Defending Your Life*)

Brooks, Avery (C) Am. actor ("Spenser: For Hire" TV series)

Brooks, Foster (Foster Murrell Brooks;

"The Lovable Lush") (1912–) Am. comedian/actor ("The Dean Martin Show" TV series)

Brooks, Garth (Troyal Garth Brooks) (1962–) Am. country singer/guitarist ("Friends in Low Places"; "The Dance"; "Rodeo")

Brooks, Geraldine (Geraldine Stroock) (1925–1977) Am. actress (*Possessed; Volcano*)

Brooks, Gwendolyn (Gwendolyn Elizabeth Brooks) (1917–) Am. poet (P—1950—*Annie Allen*; first Afr.-Am. woman to win a Pulitzer Prize)

Brooks, Hubie (Hubert Brooks, Jr.) (1956–) Am. baseball player

Brooks, James L. (1940–) Am. film producer/director/screenwriter (*Broadcast News*; O—1983—*Terms of Endearment*)

Brooks, Kix (Leon Eric Brooks) (1958–) Am. country singer (with Brooks & Dunn; "Boot Scootin' Boogie"; "Brand New Man")

Brooks, Louise (1905–1985) Am. actress (*Ziegfeld Follies; Diaries of a Lost Girl*)

Brooks, Mel (Melvin Kaminsky) (1926–) Am. film director/comedian (*Blazing Saddles; High Anxiety; Young Frankenstein*)/TV series creator ("Get Smart")

Brooks, Phyllis (Phyllis Steiller) (1914–) Am. actress (*Rebecca of Sunnybrook Farm; Dangerous Passage*)

Brooks, Richard (1912–1992) Am. film director (*The Blackboard Jungle; Looking for Mr. Goodbar*)

Brooks, Van Wyck (1886–1963) Am. biographer/critic (*America's Coming of Age*; P—1937—*The Flowering of New England*)

Broonzy, Big Bill (William Lee Conley Broonzy) (1893–1958) Am. blues singer/guitarist

Brophy, Brigid (Antonia Brigid Brophy) (1929–) Eng.-Ir. novelist/playwright (*Flesh*)

Brosnan, Pierce (1952–) Ir.-Am. actor (TV's "Remington Steele")

Brothers, Joyce (Joyce Diane Bauer; a/k/a Dr. Joyce Brothers) (1928–) Am. psychologist/writer

Brough, Louise (Louise Althea Brough) (1923–) Am. tennis player (W—1948, 1949, 1950, 1955)

Broun, Heywood (Matthew Heywood Campbell Broun) (1888–1939) Am. journalist/columnist ("It Seems to Me")

Brouthers, Dan (Dennis Joseph Brouthers; "Big Dan") (1858–1932) Am. baseball Hall-of-Famer

Browder, Earl (Earl Russell Browder) (1891–1973) Am. Communist party leader

Brown, Blair (1948–) Am. actress ("The Days and Nights of Molly Dodd" TV series)

Brown, Bobby (1969–) Am. pop singer ("Don't Be Cruel"; "My Prerogative"; formerly with New Edition)

Brown, Bryan (1947–) Austral. actor (*F/X; The Thorn Birds*)

Brown, Clancy (1959–) Am. actor (*The Bride; Blue Steel*)

Brown, Clarence (1890–1987) Am. film director (*Anna Karenina; The Yearling*)

Brown, Claude (1937–) Am. novelist/autobiographer (*Manchild in the Promised Land*)

Brown, Dee Alexander (1908–) Am. writer (*Bury My Heart at Wounded Knee*)

Brown, Ford Madox (1821–1893) Eng. painter

Brown, Fredric (1906–1972) Am. science fiction/mystery writer (*The Screaming Mimi; His Name Was Death*)

Brown, Georg Sanford (1943–) Am. actor ("The Rookies" TV series)

Brown, Georgia (Lillian Claire Laizer Getel Klot) (1933–1992) Eng. singer/actress (*The Seven Per-Cent Solution*)

Brown, Helen Gurley (1922–) Am. magazine editor (*Cosmopolitan*)/writer (*Sex and the Single Girl*)

Brown, H. Rap (Hubert Geroid Brown; a/k/a Jamil Abdullah al-Amin) (1943–) Am. political activist

Brown, James ("The King of Soul Music"; "The Hardest Working Man in Show Business"; "Mister Dynamite"; "Soul Brother Number One"; "The Godfather of Soul") (1928–) Am. rock singer ("I Got You [I Feel Good]")

Brown, Jerry (Edmund Gerald Brown, Jr.; "Governor Moonbeam") (1938–) Am. gov. of California

Brown, Jim (James Nathaniel Brown) (1936–) Am. football Hall-of-Famer/actor

Brown, Jim Ed (1934–) Am. country singer ("Morning")

Brown, Joe E. (Joe Evans Brown) (1892–1973) Am. comedian (*Some Like It Hot*; *Show Boat*)

Brown, John ("Old Brown of Osawatomie") (1800–1859) Am. abolitionist (hanged for attack on Harper's Ferry)

Brown, Julie ("West Coast") (c. 1958–) Am. comedienne/actress (*Earth Girls Are Easy*)

Brown, Lancelot ("Capability Brown") (1715–1783) Eng. landscape gardener (Kew and Blenheim gardens)

Brown, Les (Lester Raymond Brown) (1912–) Am. bandleader ("Sentimental Journey"; with Les Brown and His Band of Renown)

Brown, Marty (1965–) Am. country singer ("Every Now and Then"; "Wildest Dreams")

Brown, Nacio Herb (1896–1964) Am. composer ("Singin' in the Rain")

Brown, Paul (1908–1991) Am. football coach/executive

Brown, Rita Mae (1944–) Am. novelist (*Rubyfruit Jungle*; *Southern Discomfort*)

Brown, Roosevelt (1932–) Am. football Hall-of-Famer

Brown, T. Graham (Anthony Graham Brown; "His T-Ness") (1954–) Am. country singer ("Don't Go to Strangers")

Brown, Three Finger (Mordecai Peter Centinnial Brown; "Miner") (1876–1948) Am. baseball Hall-of-Famer

Brown, Three-Finger (Lucchese Gaetano) (1900–1967) Am. mobster

Brown, William Wells (1815–1884) Am. social reformer/writer (first Afr.-Am. to publish a novel; *Clotel*)

Brown, Willie (William F. Brown) (1940–) Am. football Hall-of-Famer

Browne, Coral (Coral Edith Browne) (1913–1991) Austral. actress (*Auntie Mame*; *The Drowning Pool*)

Browne, Dik (1917–1989) Am. cartoonist (*Hi and Lois*; *Hagar the Horrible*)

Browne, Jackson (1948–) Am. rock singer/songwriter/musician ("Doctor My Eyes"; "Running on Empty")

Browne, Roscoe Lee (1925–) Am. actor ("Falcon Crest" TV series; *Logan's Run*)

Browning, Elizabeth Barrett (Elizabeth Moulton; later Barrett) (1806–1861) Eng. poet (*Sonnets from the Portugese*)

Browning, Pete (Louis Rogers Browning; "The Gladiator") (1861–1905) Am. base-ball player (his custom-made bat became the "Louisville Slugger")

Browning, Robert (1812–1889) Eng. poet (*The Ring and the Book*; *Bells and Pomegranates*)

Browning, Tod (Charles Albert Browning) (1882–1962) Am. film director (*Freaks*)

Browning, Tom (Thomas Leo Browning) (1960–) Am. baseball pitcher

Brubeck, Dave (David Warren Brubeck) (1920–) Am. jazz pianist/composer ("Take Five")

Bruce, Lenny (Leonard Alfred Schneider) (1926–1966) Am. comedian/writer (*How to Talk Dirty and Influence People*)

Bruce, Nigel (William Nigel Bruce) (1895–1953) Eng. actor (*Rebecca*; radio's "Sherlock Holmes")

Bruce, Virginia (Helen Virginia Briggs) (1910–1982) Am. actress (*Jane Eyre*; *Strangers When We Meet*)

Bruch, Max (Max Karl August Bruch) (1838–1920) Ger. composer (*Hermione*)

Bruckheimer, Jerry (C) Am. film producer (with Don Simpson, *Top Gun*; *Beverly Hills Cop*)

Bruckner, Anton (Josef Anton Bruckner) (1824–1896) Aus. composer (*Requiem*; *Te Deum*)

Bruegel, Pieter (the Younger) (1564–1638) Flem. painter

Bruegel, Pieter (the Elder; "Peasant Bruegel"; "The Droll") (c. 1525–1569) Flem. painter

Brummell, Beau (George Bryan Brummell) (1778–1840) Eng. court (of George IV) dandy

Brundage, Avery (1887–1975) Am. Olympics executive

Brunelleschi or **Brunellescho, Filippo** (1377–1446) Flor. architect

Brunhoff, Jean de (1899–1937) Fr. children's book writer/illustrator (created Babar the Elephant)

Brüning, Heinrich (1885–1970) Ger. politician/chancellor 1930–1932/educator (at Harvard)

Brush, Charles (Charles Francis Brush) (1849–1929) Am. inventor (arc light)

Brutus, Marcus Junius (a/k/a Quintus Caepio Brutus) (85–42 B.C.) Roman politician (one of Caesar's assassins)

Bryan, William Jennings ("The Commoner") (1860–1925) Am. politician/secretary of state

Bryant, Anita (Anita Jane Bryant) (1940–)

Am. pop singer ("Paper Roses")/
conservative activist
Bryant, Bear (Paul William Bryant; "The
Great Rehabilitator"; "The Man")
(1913–1983) Am. football coach
Bryant, William Cullen (1794–1878) Am.
editor/poet (*Thanatopsis*)
Bryher (Annie Winifred Ellerman Mac-
Pherson) (1894–1983) Eng. historical
novelist (*The Coin of Carthage; Roman
Wall*)
Brynner, Yul (Taidje Khan, Jr.; a/k/a Youl
Brynner) (1915–1985) Am. actor (*The
Magnificent Seven; Westworld; O—
1956—The King and I*)
Bryson, Peabo (Robert Peabo Bryson)
(1951–) Am. soul/pop singer ("If Ever
You're in My Arms Again")
Brzezinski, Zbigniew (Zbigniew Ka-
zimierz Brzezinski) (1928–) Pol.-Am.
statesman/political scientist/national se-
curity advisor
Bubbles, John (John William Sublett)
(1902–1986) Am. dancer
Buber, Martin (1878–1965) Ger.-Jew.
scholar/Hassidic philosopher (*I and
Thou*)
Buchalter, Lepke (Louis Buchalter)
(1897–1944) Am. mobster (partnered
with Jacob Shapiro in Murder, Inc.)
Buchan, Sir John, 1st Baron Tweedsmuir
(1875–1940) Scot.-Can. writer (*The
Thirty-Nine Steps*)/Canadian gov.-
general 1935–1940
Buchanan, Edna (Edna Rydzik
Buchanan) (c. 1939–) Am. journalist
(P—1986)/writer (*The Corpse Had a Fa-
miliar Face*)
Buchanan, Jack (1891–1957) Eng.
entertainer/actor (*Brewster's Millions*)
Buchanan, James ("The Bachelor Presi-
dent") (1791–1868) 15th Am. pres.
(1857–1861)
Buchanan, Pat (Patrick Buchanan) (1938–)
Am. political commentator
Buchanan, Roy (1940–1988) Am. blues/
rock guitarist
Buchholz, Horst (Horst Werner
Buchholz) (1933–) Ger. actor (*The Mag-
nificent Seven*)
Buchwald, Art (Arthur Buchwald) (1925–)
Am. humorist/journalist (P—1982)
Buck, Pearl S. (Pearl Comfort née Syd-
enstricker) (1892–1973) Am. novelist
(P—1932—*The Good Earth*; N—1938)
Buckingham, Lindsey (1947–) Am. rock

musician ("Trouble"; a founder of Fleet-
wood Mac)
Buckley, Betty (Betty Lynn Buckley)
(1947–) Am. cabaret singer/actress
("Eight Is Enough" TV series)
Buckley, William F., Jr. (William Frank
Buckley, Jr.; "Scourge of American Lib-
eralism") (1925–) Am. magazine editor
(founded *National Review*)/TV host
("Firing Line")/novelist (*Mongoose,
R.I.P.*)
Buddha (Siddhartha Gautama; "Bud-
dha"="The Enlightened One") (c. 563–
c. 483 B.C.) Nep. philosopher/founder of
Buddhism
Budge, Don (John Donald Budge; "The
California Comet") (1915–) Am. tennis
player (W—1937, 1938)
Buell, Marjorie H. (Marjorie Henderson
Buell; born Marjorie Lyman Hender-
son) (1904–1993) Am. cartoonist (*Little
Lulu*)
Bueno, Maria (Maria Ester Audion
Bueno) (1939–) Braz. tennis player
(W—1959, 1960, 1964)
Buffalo Bill (William Frederick Cody)
(1846–1917) Am. frontiersman/scout
Buffett, Jimmy (1946–) Am. rock
musician/singer ("Margaritaville")/
writer (*Where Is Joe Merchant?*)
Bugatti, Ettore (Ettore Arco Isidoro Bug-
atti) (1881–1947) Ital. automobile manu-
facturer
Bugliosi, Vincent (Vincent T. Bugliosi)
(1934–) Am. lawyer/writer (*Helter Skel-
ter*)
Bujold, Geneviève (1942–) Fr.-Can. actress (*Dead Ringers; Anne of the Thousand Days; Coma; Tightrope*)
Bukharin, Nikolay (Nikolay Ivanovich
Bukharin) (1888–1938) Russ. communist political leader/editor (*Pravda*)
Bukowski, Charles (1920–) Am. "beat"
poet/novelist (*Tales of Ordinary Madness*)
Bulfinch, Charles (1763–1844) Am. architect (introduced the Adam style in
America; designed the Capitol in Washington, D.C.)
Bulfinch, Thomas (1796–1867) Am.
teacher/writer (*Bulfinch's Mythology*
a/k/a *The Age of Fable*)
Bullock, Sandra (c. 1967–) Am. actress
(*Demolition Man; The Thing Called
Love; Wrestling Ernest Hemingway*)
Bulwer-Lytton, Edward (Edward George

Earle Lytton Bulwer-Lytton) (1803–1873) Eng. novelist/playwright (*The Last Days of Pompeii*)

Bumbry, Grace (Grace Ann Jaeckel) (1937–) Am. opera singer (mezzo-soprano)

Bumpers, Dale (Dale Leon Bumpers) (1925–) Am. lawyer/senator

Bunche, Ralph (Ralph Johnson Bunche) (1904–1971) Am. diplomat/U.N. under-secretary (N—1950)

Bundy, Ted (Theodore Robert Cowell; later Bundy) (1946–1989) Am. serial killer (executed)

Bunin, Ivan (Ivan Alekseyevich Bunin) (1870–1953) Russ. novelist/short story writer/poet (*The Gentleman from San Francisco*; N—1933)

Bunning, Jim (James Paul David Bunning) (1931–) Am. baseball pitcher

Bunsen, Robert (Robert Wilhelm Eberhard Bunsen) (1811–1899) Ger. chemist/inventor (Bunsen cell, Bunsen burner)

Buntline, Ned (pseud. of E(dward). Z(ane). C(arroll). Judson) (1823–1886) Am. novelist/adventurer (*The Scouts of the Plains*)

Buñuel, Luis (1900–1983) Span. film director (*The Discreet Charm of the Bourgeoisie*; *That Obscure Object of Desire*)

Bunyan, John (1628–1688) Eng. preacher/writer (*Pilgrim's Progress*)

Buono, Victor (Charles Victor Buono) (1938–1982) Am. actor (*Whatever Happened to Baby Jane?*; *The Greatest Story Ever Told*)

Burchfield, Charles (Charles Ephraim Burchfield) (1893–1967) Am. painter

Burdette, Lew (Selva Lewis Burdette, Jr.) (1926–) Am. baseball pitcher

Burdick, Eugene (Eugene Leonard Burdick) (1918–1965) Am. novelist/political theorist/writer (with William Lederer, *The Ugly American*)

Burdon, Eric (1941–) Eng. rock singer (with Eric Burdon and The Animals; "House of the Rising Sun")

Burger, Warren E. (Warren Earl Burger) (1907–) Am. Supreme Court chief justice (1969–1986)

Burgess, Anthony (John Anthony Burgess Wilson; a/k/a Joseph Kell) (1917–1993) Eng. novelist/critic (*A Clockwork Orange*)

Burgess, Thornton Waldo (1874–1965)

Am. columnist/children's book writer (*Peter Rabbit*)

Burghoff, Gary (1940–) Am. actor (Radar O'Reilly in "M*A*S*H" TV series; E—1976/77)

Burgoyne, John ("Gentleman Johnny") (1722–1792) Eng. army general/playwright (*The Heiress*)

Burke, Billie (Mary William Ethelbert Appleton Burke) (1884–1970) Am. actress (*The Wizard of Oz*; *Topper* films)

Burke, Delta (1956–) Am. actress ("Designing Women" and "Delta" TV series)

Burke, Johnny (1908–1964) Am. lyricist (collaborations with Jimmy Van Heusen; "Personality"; "Swinging on a Star"; "Misty"; "Polka Dots and Moonbeams")

Burke, Solomon (1935–) Am. soul singer ("Got to Get You Off My Mind")

Burkett, Jesse (Jesse Cail Burkett; "The Crab") (1868–1953) Am. baseball Hall-of-Famer

Burks, Ellis (Ellis Rena Burks) (1964–) Am. baseball player

Burne-Jones, Sir Edward Coley (Edward Coley Jones) (1833–1898) Eng. painter/designer (a pioneer of the Arts and Crafts movement)

Burnett, Carol (Carol Creighton Burnett) (1933–) Am. comedienne (mother of Carrie Hamilton; "The Carol Burnett Show")

Burnett, Frances Hodgson (Frances Eliza Hodgson) (1849–1924) Am. children's book writer (*Little Lord Fauntleroy*; *The Secret Garden*)

Burnett, T-Bone (John Henry Burnett) (1948–) Am. rock musician/producer

Burnett, W. R. (William Riley Burnett; a/k/a James Updyke) (1899–1982) Am. novelist (*Little Caesar*; *High Sierra*; *The Asphalt Jungle*)

Burnette, Dorsey (1933–1979) Am. country singer/songwriter (brother of Johnny; "Tall Oak Tree")

Burnette, Johnny (1934–1964) Am. pop singer/songwriter (brother of Dorsey; "You're Sixteen")

Burney, Fanny (Frances Burney; a/k/a Madame d'Arblay) (1752–1840) Eng. novelist/diarist (*Evelina*)

Burnham, Daniel (Daniel Hudson Burnham) (1846–1912) Am. architect (Union Station in Washington, D.C.; Flatiron Building in New York City)

Burns, George (Nathan Birnbaum; a/k/a

Eddie DeLight and Jed Jackson) (1896–) Am. actor/comedian (*Oh God!*; O— 1975—*The Sunshine Boys*; signature phrase: "Say goodnight, Gracie")

Burns, Jere (c. 1956–) Am. actor (*Wired*; "Dear John" TV series)

Burns, Robert (1759–1796) Scot. poet (*Auld Lang Syne*; *Tam O'Shanter*)

Burns, Ronnie (1935–) Am. actor (adopted son of George Burns and Gracie Allen; appeared on their TV show)

Burnside, Ambrose (Ambrose Everett Burnside) (1824–1881) Am. army general/senator/gov. of Rhode Island

Burr, Aaron (1756–1836) Am. v.p. (T. Jefferson; killed Alexander Hamilton in a duel)

Burr, Raymond (Raymond William Stacey Burr) (1917–1993) Can. actor (TV's "Perry Mason" and "Ironside"; E— 1958/59, 1960/61)

Burroughs, Edgar Rice (1875–1950) Am. fantasy writer (*Tarzan of the Apes*)

Burroughs, William S. (William Seward Burroughs; a/k/a William Lee) (1914–) Am. novelist (*Naked Lunch*)

Burrows, Abe (Abram Solman Borowitz) (1910–1985) Am. playwright/composer/ conductor (P—1962—*How to Succeed in Business without Really Trying*)

Burstyn, Ellen (Edna Rae Gilhooley; a/k/a Edna Rae, Keri Flynn, Erica Dean, and Ellen McRae) (1932–) Am. actress (*The Exorcist*; O—1974—*Alice Doesn't Live Here Anymore*; T—1975)

Burton, Levar (Levardis Robert Martyn Burton, Jr.) (1957–) Am. actor (*Roots*)

Burton, Richard (Richard Walter Jenkins, Jr.) (1925–1984) Wel. actor (*Equus*; *The Robe*; *Becket*; T—1961)

Burton, Sir Richard Francis (1821–1890) Eng. explorer/writer (translated *Arabian Nights*)

Burton, Tim (1959–) Am. film director (*Edward Scissorhands*; *Batman*; *Beetlejuice*)

Buscaglia, Leo (Felice Leonardo Buscaglia; "Dr. Hug"; "Dr. Love") (1925–) Am. writer/educator (*Living, Loving, Learning*)

Buscemi, Steve (C) Am. actor (*Reservoir Dogs*; *Even Cowgirls Get the Blues*)

Busch, Mae (1897–1946) Austral. actress (*Foolish Wives*; Laurel and Hardy's *The Bohemian Girl*)

Busch, Niven (1903–) Am. journalist/ novelist (*Duel in the Sun*)/screenwriter (*The Postman Always Rings Twice*)

Busey, Gary (a/k/a Teddy Jack Eddy) (1944–) Am. actor (*The Buddy Holly Story* [title role]; *Under Siege*)

Busfield, Timothy (1957–) Am. actor ("thirtysomething" TV series; E— 1990/91)

Bush, Barbara (Barbara Pierce) (1925–) Am. first lady (George)

Bush, George (George Herbert Walker Bush) (1924–) 41st Am. pres. (1988–1992)

Bush, Kate (Katherine Bush) (1958–) Eng. rock singer ("Running Up That Hill")

Bush, Vannevar (1890–1974) Am. electrical engineer (built first analog computer)

Bushman, Francis X. (Francis Xavier Bushman) (1883–1966) Am. actor (*Ben Hur*; *David and Bathsheba*)

Bushmiller, Ernie (Ernest Paul Bushmiller) (1905–1982) Am. cartoonist (*Nancy*)

Busoni, Ferruccio (Ferruccio Benevenuto Busoni) (1866–1924) Ital. composer (*Turandot*; *Doktor Faust*)

Butkus, Dick (Richard Butkus; "Animal"; "The Enforcer"; "The Maestro of Mayhem"; "Paddles") (1942–) Am. football Hall-of-Famer/actor

Butler, Brett (c. 1958–) Am. comedienne/ actress ("Grace Under Fire" TV series)

Butler, Brett (Brett Morgan Butler) (1957–) Am. baseball player

Butler, Geezer (Terry Butler) (1949–) Eng. rock bassist (with Black Sabbath)

Butler, Jerry ("The Ice Man") (1939–) Am. gospel/pop singer ("For Your Precious Love"; "Moon River")

Butler, Samuel (1612–1680) Eng. poet (*Hudibras*)

Butler, Samuel (1835–1902) Eng. novelist/ satirist (*Erewhon*; *The Way of All Flesh*)

Butler, Yancy (C) Am. actress (*Hard Target*)

Buttafuoco, Joey (c. 1954–) Am. auto mechanic (convicted of statutory rape of 16-year-old Amy Fisher, who shot his wife Mary Jo)

Butterfield, Billy (1917–1988) Am. jazz trumpeter

Butterfield, Paul (1942–1987) Am. blues musician/singer/bandleader (with the Paul Butterfield Blues Band; "Born Under a Bad Sign")

Butterworth, Charles (1896–1946) Am. actor (*Ruggles of Red Gap*; *Magnificent Obsession*)

Button, Dick (Richard Totten Button) (1929–) Am. figure skater/sportscaster

Buttons, Red (Aaron Chwatt) (1919–) Am. actor (*Stagecoach*; O—1957—*Sayonara*)

Buttram, Pat (1917–1994) Am. actor ("Green Acres" TV series)

Butz, Earl (Earl Lauer Butz) (1909–) Am. agriculturist/govt. official (secretary of agriculture)

Buzzi, Ruth (Ruth Ann Buzzi) (1936–) Am. comedienne ("Rowan & Martin's Laugh-In" TV series)

Byner, John (c. 1937–) Am. actor/comedian

Byrd, Charlie (Charles Lee Byrd) (1925–) Am. jazz guitarist ("Desafinado")

Byrd, Richard (Richard Evelyn Byrd) (1888–1957) Am. navy admiral/polar explorer/writer (*Alone*)

Byrd, William (1543–1623) Eng. organist/composer (*Psalms, Songs and Sonnets*)

Byrd, William (a/k/a William Byrd of Westover) (1674–1744) Am. planter/Virginia Colony historian

Byrne, David (1952–) Scot. rock singer/songwriter (with The Talking Heads)/filmmaker (*True Stories*)

Byrne, Gabriel (1950–) Ir. actor (*Siesta*; *Miller's Crossing*; *Cool World*)

Byrnes, Edd "Kookie" (Edward Breitenberger) (1933–) Am. actor ("77 Sunset Strip" TV series)

Byron, Lord (George Gordon Noel Byron) (1788–1824) Eng. poet (*Don Juan*)

Caan, James ("The Jewish Cowboy") (1939–) Am. actor (*Misery*; *Brian's Song*; *Honeymoon in Vegas*)

Cabell, James Branch (1879–1958) Am. novelist/essayist (*Jurgen*)

Cable, George Washington (1844–1925) Am. novelist (*Old Creole Days*)

Cabot, Bruce (Etienne Pelissier Jacques de Bujac) (1904–1972) Am. actor (*The Green Berets*; *King Kong*)

Cabot, John (Giovanni Caboto) (c. 1450–c. 1499) Ven. explorer/navigator (possibly first European to reach North America)

Cabot, Sebastian (Charles Sebastian Thomas Cabot) (1918–1977) Eng. actor (Mr. French in "Family Affair" TV series)

Cabot, Sebastian (c. 1476–1557) Eng. map maker/navigator/explorer (son of John)

Cabral, Pedro (Pedro Álvarez Cabral) (1467 or 1468–1520) Port. navigator/explorer (discovered Brazil)

Cabrillo, Juan (João Rodrígues Cabrilho) (1520–1543) Span. explorer (discovered California)

Cabrini, Francesca (Frances Xavier Cabrini; born Maria Francesca Cabrini) (1850–1917) first canonized Am. saint

Cadore, Leon (Leon Joseph Cadore) (1890–1958) Am. baseball pitcher

Caen, Herb (1916–) Am. columnist (*San Francisco Chronicle*)

Caesar, Julius (Gaius Julius Caesar) (100–44 B.C.) Roman general/statesman

Caesar, Sid (Isaac Sidney Caesar) (1922–) Am. comedian ("Your Show of Shows" TV series; E—1951, 1956)

Caffey, Charlotte (1953–) Am. pop singer/guitarist (with the Go-Go's)

Cage, John (John Milton Cage, Jr.) (1912–1992) Am. composer (*Music of Changes*; *Speech*)

Cage, Nicolas (Nicolas Coppola) (1964–) Am. actor (*Wild at Heart*; *Moonstruck*; *Honeymoon in Vegas*)

Cagney, James (James Francis Cagney, Jr.) (1899–1986) Am. actor (*The Public Enemy*; *Angels with Dirty Faces*; O—1942—*Yankee Doodle Dandy*)

Cahn, Sammy (Samuel Cohen) (1913–1993) Am. lyricist ("High Hopes"; "Love and Marriage"; "Call Me Irresponsible")

Cain, Dean (c. 1966–) Am. actor ("Beverly Hills, 90210" and "Lois and Clark: The New Adventures of Superman" TV series)

Cain, James M. (James Mallahan Cain) (1892–1977) Am. novelist (*The Postman Always Rings Twice*; *Double Indemnity*; *Mildred Pierce*)

Caine, Michael (Maurice Joseph Micklewhite) (1933–) Eng. actor (*Alfie*; *Sleuth*; *Educating Rita*; O—1986—*Hannah and Her Sisters*)

Calamity Jane (Martha Jane Burk née Canary) (c. 1852–1903) Am. frontierswoman

Calder, Alexander (Alexander Milne Calder) (1846–1923) Am. sculptor/painter

Caldwell, Bobby (1951–) Am. pop singer/composer ("What You Won't Do for Love")

Caldwell, Erskine (Erskine Preston Caldwell) (1903–1987) Am. novelist/short story writer (*God's Little Acre*; *Tobacco Road*)

Caldwell, Sarah (1924–) Am. orchestra conductor/opera producer (first woman to conduct at the Met)

Caldwell, Taylor (Janet Miriam Taylor Holland Caldwell) (1900–1985) Am.

novelist (*Dynasty of Death*; *Captains and the Kings*)
Caldwell, Zoe (Zoe Ada Caldwell) (1933–) Austral. stage actress (*Medea*); T—1968, 1982
Cale, J. J. (Jean Jacques Cale) (1938–) Am. rock singer/musician ("Lies"; "Crazy Mama")
Cale, John (1940–) Wel.-Am. rock musician (with The Velvet Underground)
Calhern, Louis (Carl Henry Vogt) (1895–1956) Am. actor (*Julius Caesar* [1953]; *The Asphalt Jungle*)
Calhoun, John C. (John Caldwell Calhoun) (1782–1850) Am. v.p. (A. Jackson/J. Q. Adams)/statesman
Calhoun, Rory (Francis Timothy Durgin) (1922–) Am. actor (*How to Marry a Millionaire*; "The Texan" TV series)
Califano, Joseph (Joseph Anthony Califano, Jr.) (1931–) Am. lawyer/writer (*The Media and the Law*)
Caligula (Gaius Caesar Germanicus) (12–41) Roman emperor 37–41
Calisher, Hortense (1911–) Am. novelist/short story writer (*The New Yorkers*)
Calisthenes (c. 360–328 B.C.) Gr. philosopher/historian
Calkins, Richard (1895–1962) Am. cartoonist (with Philip Nowlan, created Buck Rogers)
Callas, Maria (Maria Anna Sofia Cecilia Kalogeropoulos) (1923–1977) Am. opera singer (soprano)
Callicrates (5th century B.C.) Gr. architect (with Ictinus, designed the Parthenon)
Calloway, Cab (Cabell Calloway III; "King of Hi De Ho") (1907–) Am. bandleader/singer ("Minnie the Moocher")
Calvé, Emma (Rosa-Noémie-Emma Calvet de Roquer) (1858–1942) Fr. opera singer (soprano)
Calvin, John (Jean Chauvin or Cauvin) (1509–1564) Fr. Protestant reformer/writer (*Institutes of the Christian Religion*)
Calvin, Melvin (1911–) Am. biochemist (N—1961)
Calvino, Italo (1923–1985) Ital. novelist/short story writer (*If on a Winter's Night a Traveler . . .*)
Camarata, Tutti (Savador Camarata; "Toots") (1913–) Am. orchestra leader/arranger
Cambridge, Godfrey (Godfrey Mac-

Arthur Cambridge) (1929–1976) Am. actor/comedian (*The Watermelon Man*)
Cameron, James (1954–) Can.-Am. film director (*The Terminator*; *Aliens*)
Cameron, Kirk (1970–) Am. actor ("Growing Pains" TV series)
Camiletti, Rob ("Bagel Boy") (1964–) Am. actor (romantically involved with Cher)
Camilli, Dolf (Adolf Louis Camilli) (1908–) Am. baseball player
Camp, Walter Chauncey ("Father of American Football") (1859–1925) Am. football player/coach
Campanella, Roy ("Campy"; "The Good Humor Man") (1921–1993) Am. baseball Hall-of-Famer
Campaneris, Bert (Blanco Dagoberto Campaneria; "Campy") (1942–) Am. baseball player
Campbell, Archie ("Mayor of Bulls Gap") (1914–1987) Am. country singer ("The Men in My Little Girl's Life")
Campbell, Bill (c. 1959–) Am. actor (*The Rocketeer*; "Moon over Miami" TV series)
Campbell, Bruce (c. 1958–) Am. actor ("The Adventures of Brisco County, Jr." TV series [title role])
Campbell, Earl (Earl Christian Campbell) (1955–) Am. football Hall-of-Famer
Campbell, Glen (Glen Travis Campbell) (1935–) Am. country/pop singer ("Galveston"; "Rhinestone Cowboy"; G—1967)
Campbell, Joseph (1904–1987) Am. writer/philosopher/scholar (*The Masks of God*; *The Power of Myth*)
Campbell, Kim (c. 1946–) Can. politician (first woman prime minister of Canada, 1993–)
Campbell, Naomi (1970–) Am. model
Campbell, Mrs. Patrick (Beatrice Stella Tanner) (1865–1940) Eng. actress/wit (George Bernard Shaw wrote *Pygmalion* for her)
Campin, Robert ("Master of Flemalle"; "Master of Merode") (c. 1378–1444) Flem. painter
Campion, Jane (c. 1954–) N.Z. film director (*Sweetie*; *The Piano*)
Campion, Thomas (1567–1620) Eng. poet/composer (*A Book of Airs*)
Camus, Albert (a/k/a Bauchart and Albert Mathe) (1913–1960) Fr. novelist/playwright/philosopher (*The Plague*; *Caligula*; N—1957)

Camus, Marcel (1912–1982) Fr. film director (*Black Orpheus*)

Canadeo, Tony (Anthony Canadeo; "The Gray Ghost of Gonzaga") (1919–) Am. football Hall-of-Famer

Canaletto (Giovanni Antonio Canal) (1697–1768) Ven. painter

Canby, Vincent (1924–) Am. film critic/columnist

Candelaria, John (John Robert Candelaria; "The Candy Man") (1953–) Am. baseball pitcher

Candy, John (John Franklin Candy) (1950–1994) Can.-Am. comedian/actor (*Uncle Buck; Only the Lonely*)

Canetti, Elias (1905–) Bulg.-Eng. writer (*Crowds and Power; Auto-Da-Fé; N—* 1981)

Canfield, Cass (1897–1986) Am. publisher (with Harper & Row)

Caniff, Milton (Milton Arthur Caniff) (1907–1988) Am. cartoonist (*Terry and the Pirates; Steve Canyon*)

Cannell, Stephen J. (Stephen Joseph Cannell) (1942–) Am. TV writer/producer (created "The Rockford Files")

Canning, Victor (1911–) Eng. detective story writer (*A Forest of Eyes; The Whip Hand*)

Cannon, Annie Jump (1863–1941) Am. astronomer/educator (at Harvard Observatory)

Cannon, Dyan (Samille Diane Friesen; a/k/a Dianne Cannon; "Frosty") (1937–) Am. actress (mother of Jennifer Grant; *Honeysuckle Rose; Bob & Carol & Ted & Alice*)/film director (*The End of Innocence*)

Cannon, Freddy (Frederick Anthony Picariello) (1939–) Am. singer/musician/bandleader ("Tallahassee Lassie")

Canova, Antonio (1757–1822) Ital. sculptor (*Cupid and Psyche*)

Canova, Diana (Diana Canova Rivero) (1953–) Am. actress ("Soap" TV series)

Canova, Judy (Juliet Canova) (1916–1983) Am. actress (*The Adventures of Huckleberry Finn; True to the Army*)

Canseco, José (1964–) Cub. baseball player

Cantinflas (Mario Moreno Reyes) (1911–1993) Mex. clown/acrobat/actor (*Neither Blood nor Sand*)

Cantor, Eddie (Edward Israel Iskowitz; "Izzie") (1892–1964) Am. comedian

Canute (also Cnut, Knud, Knut; a/k/a Can-ute the Great) (died 1035) King of Denmark (1018–1035) and England (1016–1035)

Capaldi, Jim (1944–) Eng. rock drummer (with Traffic)/singer ("Oh Lord, Why Lord")

Čapek, Karel (1890–1938) Cz. novelist/journalist/playwright (*R.U.R. [Rossum's Universal Robots]*)

Capet, Hugh (c. 938–996) Fr. king 987–996

Capone, Al (Alphonse Capone; "Scarface"; "Scarface Al"; "Big Al") (1899–1947) Am. gangster

Capote, Truman (Truman Streckfus Persons; "Tru") (1924–1984) Am. novelist/short story writer (*In Cold Blood; Breakfast at Tiffany's*)/actor (*Murder by Death*)

Capp, Al (Alfred Gerald Caplin) (1909–1979) Am. cartoonist (*Li'l Abner*)

Capra, Frank (Frank R. Capra) (1897–1991) Am. film director (O—1934—*It Happened One Night*; O—1936—*Mr. Deeds Goes to Town*; O—1938—*You Can't Take It with You*)

Capriati, Jennifer (1976–) Am. tennis player

Capshaw, Kate (Kathleen Sue Nail) (1953–) Am. actress (*Indiana Jones and the Temple of Doom; Black Rain*)

Captain Beefheart (Don Van Vliet) (1941–) Am. rock singer (with Captain Beefheart & The Magic Band)

Captain Kangaroo *see* Keeshan, Bob

Capucine (Germaine Lefebvre) (1933–1990) Fr. actress (*Pink Panther* films)

Cara, Irene (Irene Escalera) (1959–) Am. pop singer ("Flashdance . . . What a Feeling"; G—1983)/actress ("Fame" TV series and film)

Caracalla (Marcus Aurelius Antoninus) (188–217) Roman emperor 211–217

Caravaggio (Michelangelo Merisi da Caravaggio; "The Master of Light and Violence") (1573–1610) Ital. naturalistic painter

Caraway, Hattie (Hattie Ophelia Caraway née Wyatt) (1878–1950) Am. politician (first woman senator)/teacher

Card, Orson Scott (1951–) Am. science fiction writer (*Lost Boys; Folk of the Fringe*)

Cardin, Pierre (1922–) Fr. fashion designer

Cardinale, Claudia (1938–) Ital. actress (*The Pink Panther*; 8½)

Cardozo, Benjamin (Benjamin Nathan Cardozo) (1870–1938) Am. Supreme Court jurist 1932–1938/writer (*Nature of the Judicial Process*)

Carew, Rod (Rodney Cline Scott Carew) (1945–) Am. baseball Hall-of-Famer

Carew, Thomas (1595–1639) Eng. poet (*Mediocrity in Love Rejected*)

Carey, Ernestine (Ernestine Moller Carey née Gilbreth) (1908–) Am. writer (*Cheaper by the Dozen*)

Carey, Harry (Henry DeWitt Carey II) (1878–1947) Am. actor (*Mr. Smith Goes to Washington*; *Trader Horn*)

Carey, Harry, Jr. (1921–) Am. actor (son of Harry; *The Whales of August*; *Mask*)

Carey, MacDonald (Edward MacDonald Carey) (1913–) Am. actor ("Days of Our Lives" soap opera; *Shadow of a Doubt*)

Carey, Mariah (1970–) Am. pop singer ("Vision of Love"; "Love Takes Time"; G—1990)

Carey, Max (Maximilian Carnarius; "Scoops") (1890–1976) Am. baseball Hall-of-Famer

Carlin, George (George Denis Carlin) (1937–) Am. comedian

Carlisle, Belinda (1958–) Am. pop singer ("Heaven Is a Place on Earth"; "Mad About You"; formerly with the Go-Go's)

Carlisle, Kitty (Katherine Conn or Catherine Holzman; a/k/a Kitty Carlisle-Hart) (1914–) Am. actress (*A Night at the Opera*)/game show panelist ("To Tell the Truth")

Carlos, Walter (and, after sex-change operation) **Wendy** (1939–) Am. musician (*Switched-on Bach* album)

Carlota (Marie-Charlotte-Amélie-Augustine-Victoire-Clémentine-Léopoldine) (1840–1927) Mex. empress 1864–1867

Carlton, Steve (Stephen Norman Carlton; "Lefty") (1944–) Am. baseball pitcher

Carlyle, Thomas (1795–1881) Scot. writer/historian (*French Revolution*)

Carmen, Eric (1949–) Am. pop singer ("All by Myself")

Carmichael, Hoagy (Hoagland Howard Carmichael) (1899–1981) Am. singer/songwriter/pianist ("Stardust"; "Georgia on my Mind"; "Anything Goes")

Carmichael, Ian (1920–) Eng. actor (*Private's Progress*; TV's Lord Peter Wimsey)

Carmichael, Stokely (Kwame Toure) (1941–) Trin.-Am. civil rights leader (coined the term *black power*)

Carne, Judy (Joyce A. Botterill) (1939–) Eng. comedienne ("Rowan & Martin's Laugh-In" TV series)

Carnegie, Andrew ("The Steel King"; "The Prince of Peace") (1835–1919) Am. steel manufacturer/humanitarian/philanthropist

Carnegie, Dale (Dale Carnagey) (1888–1955) Am. writer (*How to Win Friends and Influence People*)

Carnegie, Hattie (Henriette Kannengiser) (1889–1956) Am. fashion designer

Carner, Joanne (née) **Gunderson** ("The Great Gundy"; "Big Momma") (1939–) Am. golfer

Carnera, Primo ("The Ambling Alp"; "The Preem"; "Ponderous Primo"; "The Vast Venetian") (1906–1967) Am. boxer

Carnes, Kim (1945–) Am. pop singer ("Bette Davis Eyes"; "More Love")

Carney, Art (Arthur William Matthew Carney) (1918–) Am. actor (O—1974—*Harry and Tonto*; "The Jackie Gleason Show" TV series; Ed Norton in "The Honeymooners" TV series; E—1953, 1954, 1955)

Carnovsky, Morris (1897–1992) Am. actor (*Rhapsody in Blue*; *Cyrano de Bergerac* [1950])

Caroline (1957–) princess of Monaco (sister of Stephanie and Albert; daughter of Grace Kelly and Rainier III)

Caron, Leslie (Leslie Clare Margaret Caron) (1931–) Fr. actress (*An American in Paris*; *Father Goose*)

Carothers, Wallace Hume (1896–1937) Am. chemist (developed nylon and neoprene)

Carpaccio, Vittore (c. 1460–1525 or 1526) Ven. painter

Carpenter, John (John Howard Carpenter) (1948–) Am. film director (*Escape from New York*; *Christine*; *Halloween*)

Carpenter, John Alden (1876–1951) Am. composer (*Krazy Kat* ballet; *Skyscrapers*)

Carpenter, Karen (Karen Anne Carpenter) (1950–1983) Am. pop singer (sister of Richard; "Close to You"; G—1970)

Carpenter, Mary-Chapin (1958–) Am. country singer ("Passionate Kisses"; "I Feel Lucky")

Carpenter, Richard (Richard Lynn Carpenter) (1945–) Am. pop musician (brother of Karen; with The Carpenters; G—1970)

Carpenter, Scott (Malcolm Scott Carpenter) (1925–) Am. astronaut

Carr, Darleen (Darleen Farnon) (1950–) Am. actress ("The Streets of San Francisco" TV series)

Carr, John Dickson (a/k/a Carter Dixon) (1905–1977) Am. mystery writer (created Dr. Gideon Fell)

Carr, Vikki (Florencia Bisenta de Casillas Martinez Cardona) (1941–) Am. pop singer ("It Must Be Him")

Carrack, Paul (1951–) Eng. pop singer ("Don't Shed a Tear"; with Ace, Squeeze, Roxy Music, and Mike + The Mechanics)

Carradine, David (John Arthur Carradine) (1936–) Am. actor (father of Martha Plimpton; *The Long Riders*; "Kung Fu" TV series)

Carradine, John (Richmond Reed Carradine; a/k/a John Peter Richmond; "Bard of the Boulevard") (1906–1988) Am. actor (father of David and Keith; *Stagecoach*)

Carradine, Keith (Keith Ian Carradine) (1949–) Am. actor (*The Long Riders*; *Choose Me*)/pop singer ("I'm Easy")

Carrera, Barbara (1945–) Nic.-Am. model/actress ("Dallas" TV series)

Carreras, José (1947–) Span. opera singer (tenor)

Carrere, Tia (c. 1967–) Am. actress (*Wayne's World*; *Rising Sun*)

Carrey, Jim (James Carrey) (c. 1962–) Am. comedian/actor ("In Living Color" TV series)

Carrillo, Leo (1880–1961) Am. actor (Pancho in "The Cisco Kid" TV series)

Carroll, Diahann (Carol Diahann Johnson) (1935–) Am. singer/actress ("Julia" TV series; *Carmen Jones*; T—1962)

Carroll, Jim (1950–) Am. rock singer ("People Who Died")/writer (*The Basketball Diaries*)

Carroll, Leo G. (1892–1972) Eng. actor (*Spellbound*; TV's "Topper")

Carroll, Lewis (Charles Lutwidge Dodgson) (1832–1898) Eng. mathematician/photographer/writer (created *Alice in Wonderland*)

Carroll, Madeleine (Marie-Madeleine Bernadette O'Carroll) (1906–1987) Eng. actress (*The Prisoner of Zenda*; *The Thirty-Nine Steps*; *Secret Agent*)

Carruth, Hayden (1921–) Am. poet/editor (*The Voice That Is within Us: American Poetry of the Twentieth Century*)

Carruthers, Kitty (Caitlin Carruthers) (1962–) Am. figure skater

Carsey, Marcy (c. 1945–) Am. TV producer (with Tom Werner, "The Cosby Show"; "Roseanne"; "Grace under Fire")

Carson, Jack (John Elmer Carson) (1910–1963) Can.-Am. actor/comedian (*A Star Is Born* [1954])

Carson, Johnny (John William Carson; "The Prince of Darkness") (1925–) Am. talk show host/comedian ("The Tonight Show")

Carson, Kit (Christopher Carson) (1809–1868) Am. soldier/scout/frontiersman

Carson, Rachel (Rachel Louise Carson) (1907–1964) Am. scientist/writer (*Silent Spring*)

Carstens, Karl (Karl Walter Carstens) (1914–) Ger. pres. (1979–1984)

Carte, D'oyly (Richard D'oyly Carte) (1844–1901) Eng. entertainment impresario (partnered with Gilbert & Sullivan; built the Savoy Theatre)

Carter, Angela (1940–) Eng. novelist/short story writer (*The Magic Toyshop*)

Carter, Benny (Bennett Lester Carter) (1907–) Am. jazz saxophonist/composer

Carter, Betty (Lillie Mae Jones) (1930–) Am. jazz/pop singer

Carter, Billy (William Alton Carter III) (1937–1988) Am. peanut farmer (brother of Jimmy)

Carter, Boake (1898–1947) Am. radio newscaster

Carter, Carlene (1955–) Am. country singer (daughter of June Carter and Carl Smith; "Every Little Thing")

Carter, Dixie (1939–) Am. actress ("Designing Women" TV series)

Carter, Helena Bonham *see* Bonham Carter, Helena

Carter, Hodding Jr. ("The Spokesman for the New South") (1907–1972) Am. social reformer/publisher/editor (P—1946)

Carter, Jack (John Chakrin) (1923–) Am. comedian/actor (*Viva Las Vegas*)

Carter, Jimmy (James Earl Carter, Jr.) (1924–) 39th Am. pres. (1977–1981)

Carter, June (Valerie June Carter; a/k/a June Carter Cash) (1929–) Am. country singer (mother of Carlene; with The Carter Family; "Wildwood Flower")

Carter, Lynda (Lynda Jean Carter) (1951–) Am. model/actress (TV's "Wonder Woman")

Carter, Nell (Nell Hardy) (1948–) Am. actress ("Gimme a Break" TV series)

Carter, Rosalynn (Eleanor Rosalynn Smith; "The Iron Magnolia") (1927–) Am. first lady (Jimmy)

Carteris, Gabrielle (1960–) Am. actress ("Beverly Hills, 90210" TV series)

Cartier, Jacques (1491–1557) Fr. explorer of Canada (discovered the St. Lawrence River)

Cartier-Bresson, Henri (1908–) Fr. photographer (*The Decisive Moment*)

Cartland, Dame Barbara (Barbara Hamilton Cartland; a/k/a Barbara Hamilton McCorquodale; "The Queen of Romance") (1901–) Eng. writer (300+ romance novels)

Cartwright, Angela (1952–) Am. actress (sister of Veronica; "Lost in Space" TV series)

Cartwright, Veronica (1949–) Am. actress ("Daniel Boone" TV series)

Caruso, David (1956–) Am. actor (*Mad Dog and Glory*; "NYPD Blue" TV series)

Caruso, Enrico (Errico Caruso; "The World's Greatest Tenor") (1873–1921) Ital. opera singer (tenor)

Carver, George Washington ("The Peanut Man"; "The Sweet-Potato Man"; "Wizard of Tuskegee") (1861–1943) Am. botanist/educator

Carver, John (1576–1621) Eng. Mayflower pilgrim/Plymouth Colony leader

Carver, Raymond (Raymond Clevie Carver, Jr.) (1938–1988) Am. short story writer (*Will You Be Quiet, Please?*)

Carvey, Dana (1955–) Am. comedian/actor ("Saturday Night Live" TV series; *Wayne's World*)

Carville, James ("The Ragin' Cajun") (c. 1944–) Am. political strategist (for Bill Clinton)

Cary, Joyce (Arthur Joyce Lunel Cary) (1888–1957) Eng. novelist (*Mister Johnson*)

Cary, Phoebe (1824–1871) Am. poet (hymns)

Casady, Jack (1944–) Am. rock musician (with Jefferson Airplane)

Casals, Pablo (Pablo Pau Carlos Salvador Defillo de Casals) (1876–1973) Span. cellist/conductor

Casals, Rosemary (1948–) Am. tennis player

Casanova, Giacomo (Giovanni Giacomo Casanova de Seingalt, Chevalier de Seingalt) (1725–1798) Ital. adventurer/writer (*Histoire de ma Vie*)

Casey, Harry ("KC") (1951–) Am. disco singer (with KC and The Sunshine Band; "Get Down Tonight"; "That's the Way [I Like It]")

Casey, William (1913–1987) Am. head of the CIA

Cash, Johnny (John Ray Cash; "The Man in Black") (1932–) Am. country singer (father of Rosanne; "I Walk the Line"; "A Boy Named Sue")

Cash, Norm (Norman Dalton Cash; "Stormin' Norman") (1934–1986) Am. baseball player/sportscaster

Cash, Pat (Patric Cash) (1965–) Austral. tennis player (W—1987)

Cash, Rosanne (1955–) Am. country singer (daughter of Johnny; "Seven Year Ache")

Caspary, Vera (1899 or 1904–1987) Am. crime novelist (*Laura*)/screenwriter (*A Letter to Three Wives*)

Casper, Billy (William Earl Casper, Jr.) (1931–) Am. golfer

Casper, Dave (1951–) Am. football player

Cass, Peggy (Mary Margaret Cass) (1924–) Am. actress/comedienne ("The Jack Paar Show" TV series)

Cassatt, Mary (Mary Stevenson Cassatt) (1844–1926) Am. impressionist painter

Cassavetes, John (1929–1989) Am. actor/film director (*Rosemary's Baby*; *The Dirty Dozen*; *A Woman Under the Influence*)

Cassidy, Butch (Robert Leroy Parker) (1867–1912) Am. train robber/outlaw

Cassidy, David (David Bruce Cassidy) (1950–) Am. actor/singer (son of Evelyn Ward and Jack Cassidy; "The Partridge Family" TV series)

Cassidy, Hopalong see Boyd, William

Cassidy, Jack (John Edward Joseph Cassidy) (1927–1976) Am. actor (father of Shaun and David; *The Eiger Sanction*)

Cassidy, Joanna (Joanna Virginia Caskey) (1944–) Am. actress ("Buffalo Bill" TV series; *Bullitt*; *Blade Runner*)

Cassidy, Shaun (Shaun Paul Cassidy) (1958–) Am. actor ("The Hardy Boys Mysteries" TV series)/pop singer (son of Shirley Jones and Jack Cassidy)

Cassidy, Ted (1932–1979) Am. actor (Lurch in "The Addams Family" TV series)

Cassini, Oleg (Oleg Lolewski-Cassini) (1913–) Fr. fashion designer

Cassius (Gaius Cassius Longinus; "The Last of the Romans") (died 42 B.C.) Roman politician/general/conspirator (against Julius Caesar)

Castagno, Andrea Del (Andrea di Bartolo de Simone) (1423–1457) Flor. painter (*Last Supper*)

Castaneda, Carlos (Carlos Araña Castaneda) (1931–) Braz.-Am. metaphysician/writer (*The Teachings of Don Juan*)

Castellano, Richard (1933–) Am. actor (*The Godfather*; *Lovers and Other Strangers*)

Castle, Irene (née Foote; "The Best-Dressed Woman in the World") (1893–1969) Eng. dancer (created the One-Step and the Turkey Trot)

Castle, Peggie (Peggie Thomas Blair) (1927–1973) Am. actress ("Lawman" and "The Outlaws" TV series)

Castle, Vernon (Vernon Castle Blythe) (1887–1918) Eng. dancer

Castro, Fidel (Fidel Castro Ruiz) (1927–) Cub. communist political leader 1959–

Catalani, Angelica ("The Italian Nightingale") (1780–1849) Ital. opera singer (soprano)

Cates, Phoebe (Phoebe Katz) (1963–) Am. actress (*Fast Times at Ridgemont High*; *Bodies, Rest and Motion*)

Cather, Willa (Willa Sibert Cather) (1873–1947) Am. novelist (*My Antonia*; *O Pioneers!*; P—1923—*One Of Ours*)

Catherine I (Yekaterina Alekseyevna; born Marta Skowronska) (1684–1727) Russ. empress 1725–1727

Catherine II (Sophie Friederike Auguste von Anhalt-Zerbst; Catherine the Great) (1729–1796) Russ. empress 1762–1796

Catherine of Aragon (1485–1536) Span. princess/first wife of King Henry VIII

Catlett, Sid (Sidney Catlett; "Big Sid") (1910–1951) Am. jazz drummer

Catlin, George (1796–1872) Am. writer/artist (primarily of American Indians)

Cato (Marcus Porcius Cato; "The Elder"; "The Censor") (234–149 B.C.) Roman statesman

Cattrall, Kim (1956–) Am. actress (*Mannequin*; *The Bonfire of the Vanities*)

Catullus, Gaius Valerius (c. 84–c. 54 B.C.) Roman lyric poet

Caulfield, Joan (Beatrice Joan Caulfield) (1922–1991) Am. actress ("My Favorite Husband" TV series)

Caulfield, Maxwell (1959–) Eng. actor

("The Colbys" TV series; *The Boys Next Door*)

Caulkins, Tracy (1963–) Am. swimmer

Cauthen, Steve (Stephen Mark Cauthen; "The Kid") (1960–) Am. jockey

Cavallaro, Carmen (1913–) Am. bandleader/composer

Cavendish, Margaret, Duchess of Newcastle (c. 1624–1674) Eng. novelist (*Sociable Letters*)

Cavett, Dick (Richard Alva Cavett) (1936–) Am. TV host

Caxton, William (1422–1491) Eng. printer/publisher of the first book printed in English

Cayce, Edgar (1877–1945) Am. mystic/psychic/writer (*Edgar Cayce on Reincarnation*)

Ceauşescu, Nicolae (1918–1989) Rum. communist dictator 1965–1989 (executed)

Cecilia, Saint (2nd or 3rd century A.D.) Roman martyr/patron saint of the blind and of music

Cela, Camilo (Camilo José Cela Trulock) (1916–) Span. novelist/essayist/publisher (*San Camilo*; N—1989)

Cellini, Benvenuto (1500–1571) Flor. sculptor/goldsmith

Celsius, Anders (1701–1744) Swed. astronomer (developed the centigrade [celsius] thermometer)

Cendrars, Blaise (Frederic-Louis Sauser) (1887–1961) Swi. poet/novelist (*Sutter's Gold*)

Cepeda, Orlando (Orlando Manuel Cepeda; "Cha-Cha"; "The Baby Bull") (1937–) Am. baseball player

Cerf, Bennett (Bennett Alfred Cerf) (1898–1971) Am. publisher/founder of Random House/columnist ("Cerfboard")

Cerf, Christopher (Christopher Bennett Cerf) (1941–)Am. writer (son of Bennett; *Experts Speak*)

Cerone, Rick (Richard Aldo Cerone) (1954–) Am. baseball player

Cervantes, Miguel de (Miguel de Cervantes Saavedra) (1547–1616) Span. novelist/poet/playwright (*Don Quixote de la Mancha*)

Césaire, Aimé (Aimé Fernand Césaire) (1913–) W. Ind. poet/playwright/essayist (*Return to My Native Land*)

Cetera, Peter (1944–) Am. pop singer ("Glory of Love"; formerly with Chicago)

Cézanne, Paul ("The Father of Modernism") (1839–1906) Fr. impressionist painter

Chabrol, Claude (1930–) Fr. film director (*Story of Women; This Man Must Die*)

Chad and Jeremy *see* Stuart, Chad, and Clyde, Jeremy

Chadwick, Florence (Florence May Chadwick) (1918–) Am. distance swimmer (first woman to swim the English Channel in both directions)

Chadwick, George W. (George Whitefield Chadwick) (1854–1931) Am. composer (*Rip Van Winkle*)

Chaffee, Suzy (1946–) Am. skier/Chapstick pitchwoman

Chagall, Marc (1887–1985) Russ.-Fr. "naive" painter

Chakiris, George (1933–) Am. actor/dancer (*Gentlemen Prefer Blondes; Brigadoon*; O—1961—*West Side Story*)

Chaliapin, Fyodor (Fyodor Ivanovich Chaliapin) (1873–1938) Russ. opera singer (basso)

Chalke, Sarah (c. 1976–) Am. actress ("Roseanne" TV series)

Chamberlain, Neville (Arthur Neville Chamberlain) (1869–1940) Eng. prime minister 1937–1940

Chamberlain, Owen (1920–) Am. physicist (worked on the Manhattan Project; N—1959)

Chamberlain, Richard (George Richard Chamberlain; "King of the Mini-Series") (1935–) Am. actor (TV's "Dr. Kildare"; *The Thorn Birds*)

Chamberlain, Wilt (Wilton Norman Chamberlain; "Wilt the Stilt"; "The Big Dipper") (1936–) Am. basketball player

Chambers, Marilyn (1952–) Am. model (for Ivory soap)/actress in porn films

Chambers, Whittaker (Jay David Whittaker Chambers) (1901–1961) Am. journalist/editor (*Time*; accused Alger Hiss of spying, in the "pumpkin papers")

Champion, Gower (1919–1981) Am. choreographer/dancer/actor (*Show Boat; Till the Clouds Roll By*)

Champion, Marge (Marjorie Celeste Belcher) (1923–) Am. dancer/choreographer/actress (*The Party; The Swimmer*)

Champlain, Samuel de (c. 1567–1635) Fr. explorer (founded Quebec)/gov. of French Canada

Champollion, Jean-François (a/k/a

Champollion-Figeac "The Father of Egyptology") (1790–1832) Fr. Egyptologist (translated the Rosetta Stone)

Chance, Frank (Frank Leroy Chance; "Husk"; "The Peerless Leader") (1887–1924) Am. baseball Hall-of-Famer

Chancellor, John (John William Chancellor) (1927–) Am. newscaster

Chandler, Gene (Eugene Chandler; born Eugene Dixon; "The Duke of Earl") (1937–) Am. pop singer ("Duke of Earl")

Chandler, Happy (Albert Benjamin Chandler) (1898–1991) Am. baseball Hall-of-Famer/govt. official (gov. of Kentucky)

Chandler, Harry (1864–1944) Am. newspaper publisher (*Los Angeles Times*)

Chandler, Otis (1927–) Am. newspaper publisher (*Los Angeles Times*)

Chandler, Raymond (Raymond Thornton Chandler; "The Poet of Violence") (1888–1959) Am. mystery writer (created Philip Marlowe; *The Big Sleep; The Long Goodbye*)/screenwriter (*The Blue Dahlia; Double Indemnity*)

Chandler, Spud (Spurgeon Ferdinand Chandler) (1907–) Am. baseball pitcher

Chanel, Coco (Gabrielle Bonheur) (1883–1971) Fr. fashion designer

Chaney, Lon (Alonso Chaney; "Man of a Thousand Faces") (1883–1930) Am. actor (*The Phantom of the Opera; The Hunchback of Notre Dame*)

Chaney, Lon, Jr. (Creighton Tull Chaney) (1905–1973) Am. actor (son of Lon; *High Noon*)

Channing, Carol (Carol Elaine Channing) (1921–) Am. singer/actress (*Thoroughly Modern Millie*; T—1964)

Channing, Stockard (Susan Williams Antonia Stockard Channing Smith) (1944–) Am. actress (*Grease; Heartburn; Married to It*; T— 1985)

Chapin, Harry (Harry Forster Chapin) (1942–1981) Am. rock singer/musician/songwriter ("Cat's in the Cradle")

Chaplin, Sir Charlie (Charles Spencer Chaplin; "The Little Tramp") (1889–1977) Eng.-Am. comedian/actor/film director (*The Kid; City Lights; Modern Times*)

Chaplin, Geraldine (1944–) Am. actress (daughter of Charlie and Oona; granddaughter of Eugene O'Neill; *Nashville; Doctor Zhivago*)

Chaplin, Oona (Oona O'Neill) (c. 1921–

1991) Am. actress (daughter of Eugene O'Neill; wife of Charlie Chaplin)

Chapman, Graham (1940–1989) Eng. actor/comedian (*Monty Python's Flying Circus*)

Chapman, Mark David (1955–) Am. obsessed fan/murderer (killed John Lennon)

Chapman, Tracy (1964–) Am. pop singer ("Fast Car"; G—1988)

Chardin, Jean-Baptiste-Siméon (1699–1779) Fr. painter (*Le Buffet*)

Charisse, Cyd (Tula Ellice Finklea; a/k/a Lily Norwood) (1923–) Am. dancer/actress (*Singin' in the Rain; The Band Wagon*)

Charlemagne (a/k/a Charles the Great; Karl der Grosse; Carolus Magnus) (742–814) Frankish mil. leader/political ruler

Charles (Charles Philip Arthur George Mountbatten) (1948–) Eng. prince of Wales

Charles I (1600–1649) king of England and Ireland 1625–1649

Charles II (1630–1685) king of England and Ireland 1660–1685 (son of Charles I)

Charles IV (Charles the Fair) (1294–1328) Fr. king 1322–1328

Charles V (Charles the Wise) (1337–1380) Fr. king 1364–1380

Charles VI (The Well-Beloved; The Mad) (1368–1422) Fr. king 1380–1422

Charles VII (1403–1461) Fr. king 1422–1461

Charles VIII (1470–1498) Fr. king 1483–1498

Charles IX (1550–1574) Fr. king 1560–1574

Charles X (1757–1836) Fr. king 1824–1830

Charles, Ezzard (Ezzard Mack Charles; "The Hawk") (1921–1975) Am. boxer

Charles, Ray (Ray Charles Robinson; "The Genius of Soul") (1930–) Am. singer/pianist ("What'd I Say"; "Georgia on My Mind"; "Hit the Road Jack"; G—1960)

Charleson, Ian (1949–1990) Scot.-Eng. actor (*Chariots of Fire*)

Charleston, Oscar (Oscar McKinley Charleston; "Charlie"; "The Hoosier Comet") (1896–1954) Am. baseball Hall-of-Famer

Charo (Maria Rosario Pilar Martinez Molina Baeza) (1951–) Span. singer/actress/guitarist

Charteris, Leslie (Leslie Charles Bowyer

Yin) (1907–1993) Eng.-Am. crime novelist (created *The Saint* [Simon Templar])

Charvet, David (1971–) Am. model/actor ("Baywatch" TV series)

Chase, Chevy (Cornelius Crane Chase) (1943–) Am. comedian/actor ("Saturday Night Live" TV series; *Fletch; Foul Play*)

Chase, Hal (Harold Homer Chase; "Prince Hal"; "The Peerless Hal") (1883–1947) Am. baseball player/manager

Chase, Ilka (1900–1978) Am. columnist/actress (*Now, Voyager*)

Chase, Mary (née) Coyle (1907–1981) Am. playwright (P—1945—*Harvey*)

Chase, Salmon P. (Salmon Portland Chase) (1808–1873) Am. Supreme Court chief justice (1864–1873)

Chase, Samuel (1741–1811) Am. Supreme Court jurist (1796–1811)/lawyer (signed the Declaration of Independence)

Chast, Roz (1954–) Am. cartoonist ("bonfire of the banalities" in the *New Yorker*)

Chatterton, Ruth (1893–1961) Am. novelist/actress (*Dodsworth; Madame X*)

Chatterton, Thomas (1752–1770) Eng. poet (*The Revenge*)

Chaucer, Geoffrey (1340–1400) Eng. poet (*The Canterbury Tales*)

Chávez, Carlos (Carlos Antonio de Padua Chávez) (1899–1978) Mex. composer (*Sinfonia Romantica*)

Chavez, Cesar (Cesar Chavez Estrada) (1927–1993) Am. farm labor leader

Chayefsky or **Chayevsky, Paddy** (Sidney Aaron Chayefsky; a/k/a Sidney Aaron) (1923–1981) Am. playwright/screenwriter (*Marty; Network*)

Checker, Chubby (Ernest Evans) (1941–) Am. rock singer ("The Twist")

Cheever, John (1912–1982) Am. novelist/short story writer (*The Wapshot Scandal*; P—1979—*The Stories of John Cheever*)

Chekhov, Anton (Anton Pavlovich Chekhov) (1860–1904) Russ. playwright/short story writer (*Uncle Vanya; The Cherry Orchard*)

Chen, Joan (1961–) Am. actress ("Twin Peaks" TV series)

Cheney, Richard B. (Richard Bruce Cheney) (1941–) Am. govt. official (secretary of defense)

Chénier, André (André-Marie de Chénier) (1762–1794) Fr. poet (*Bucoliques*)

Chennault, Claire (Claire Lee Chennault) (1890–1958) Am. general/founder of WWII's Flying Tigers

Cheops (a/k/a Khufu) (26th century B.C.) Egypt. king

Cher (Cherilyn Lapierre Sarkisian; a/k/a Bonnie Jo Mason and Cherilyn) (1946–) Am. singer ("Gypsies, Tramps and Thieves")/actress (O—1987—*Moonstruck*)

Chernenko, Konstantin (Konstantin Ustinovich Chernenko) (1911–1985) Russ. political leader (general secretary of the Communist party; chairman of the Presidium of Supreme Soviet)

Cherry, Neneh (1964–) W. Afr.-Swed. pop singer ("Buffalo Stance")

Cherubini, Luigi (Luigi Carlo Zenobio Salvadore Maria Cherubini) (1760–1842) Ital. composer (*Medea*)

Chesbro, Jack (John Dwight Chesbro; "Happy Jack") (1874–1931) Am. baseball Hall-of-Famer

Chesnutt, Charles W. (Charles Waddell Chesnutt) (1858–1932) Am. writer (*The Conjure Woman*)

Chesnutt, Mark (1963–) Am. country singer ("Bubba Shot the Jukebox"; "It Sure Is Monday")

Chessman, Caryl (Caryl Whittier Chessman; "The Red Light Bandit") (1921–1960) Am. criminal (executed for robberies, kidnappings, rapes)/writer (*Cell 2455, Death Row*)

Chesterton, G. K. (Gilbert Keith Chesterton) (1874–1936) Eng. novelist/poet/essayist (created Father Brown)

Chevalier, Maurice (Maurice-Auguste Chevalier) (1888–1972) Fr. actor/dancer/singer (*Gigi*; *The Love Parade*; *The Merry Widow*)

Chevrolet, Louis (Louis Joseph Chevrolet) (1878–1941) Swi.-Am. auto racer/manufacturer

Chiang Kai-Shek (Chiang Chung-cheng) (1887–1975) Chin. army general/pres. 1943–1949, 1950–1975

Chicago, Judy (Judy Cohen) (1939–) Am. artist (*The Dinner Party*)

Chilkis, Michael (c. 1963–) Am. actor (TV's "The Commish"; *Wired* [as John Belushi])

Child, Julia (née McWilliams) (1912–) Am. chef/TV host ("The French Chef")/writer (*Mastering the Art of French Cooking*)

Childs, Lucinda (1940–) Am. choreographer

Childs, Marquis (Marquis William Childs) (1903–1990) Am. journalist

Chiles, Lawton (Lawton Mainor Chiles, Jr.) (1930–) Am. senator/gov. of Florida

Chin, Tiffany (c. 1968–) Am. figure skater

Chippendale, Thomas (1718–1779) Eng. cabinetmaker (English Rococo style)

Chirico, Giorgio de (1888–1978) Ital. painter (metaphysical subjects)

Chisolm, Shirley (Shirley Anita St. Hill) (1924–) Am. politician (first Afr.-Am. congresswoman)/educator/lecturer

Chomsky, Marvin (Marvin J. Chomsky) (1929–) Am. TV/film director (*Holocaust*)

Chomsky, Noam (Avram Noam Chomsky) (1928–) Am. linguist/writer/radical political activist (*Syntactic Structures*)

Chong, Rae Dawn (1961–) Can.-Am. actress (daughter of Tommy; *Soul Man*; *Choose Me*)

Chong, Tommy (Thomas Chong) (1938–) Can.-Am. comedian/actor (father of Rae Dawn; with Cheech & Chong; *Born in East L. A.*)

Chopin, Frédéric (Frédéric-François Chopin) (1810–1849) Pol. pianist/composer (polonaises, etudes, sonatas)

Chopin, Kate (Katherine Chopin née O'Flaherty) (1851–1904) Am. novelist/short story writer (*The Awakening*)

Chou En-Lai (1898–1976) Chin. revolutionary leader/premier 1949–1976

Chow, Tina (c. 1951–1992) Am. model/restauranteur/jewelry designer

Christ *see* Jesus Christ

Christian, Charlie (Charles Christian) (1919–1942) Am. jazz guitarist (with Benny Goodman)

Christian, Fletcher (Fl. 1789) Eng. naval officer/mutineer (the *Bounty*)

Christian, Linda (Blanca Rosa Welter) (1923–) Mex.-Am. actress (*The VIPs*; *Green Dolphin Street*)

Christiansen, Jack (Jack L. Christiansen; "Chris") (1928–1986) Am. football Hall-of-Famer

Christie, Dame Agatha (Agatha Mary Clarissa Miller; a/k/a Mary Westmacott and Agatha Christie Mallowen; "Queen of Crime") (1891–1976) Eng. mystery writer (created Miss Jane Marple and Hercule Poirot; *And Then There Were None*)

Christie, Julie (Julie Frances Christie) (1940–) Eng. actress (*Doctor Zhivago*; O—1965—*Darling*)

Christie, Lou (Lugee Geno Sacco) (1943–) Am. pop musician/singer/songwriter ("Lightnin' Strikes")

Christina (1626–1689) queen of Sweden 1632–1654

Christo (Christo Javacheff) (1935–) Bulg.-Am. sculptor/artist (wrapped works)

Christopher, Warren (Warren Miner Christopher) (1925–) Am. govt. official (secretary of state; negotiated with Iran for release of American hostages in 1980–1981)

Christy, June (1925–1990) Am. jazz singer

Chrysler, Walter (Walter Percy Chrysler) (1875–1940) Am. automobile manufacturer

Chung, Connie (Constance Yu-Hwa Chung) (1946–) Am. TV newscaster ("Eye to Eye")

Church, Frederick (Frederick Edwin Church) (1826–1900) Am. landscape painter

Churchill, Marguerite (1909–) Am. actress (*Charlie Chan Carries On*; *Riders of the Purple Sage*)

Churchill, Sir Winston (Winston Leonard Spencer Churchill; "Winnie") (1874–1965) Eng. prime minister 1940–1945/writer (N—1953)

Cicciolina (Ilona Staller) (C) Ital. porn actress/member of Italian parliament

Ciccolini, Aldo (1925–) Ital. concert pianist

Cicero (Marcus Tullius Cicero) (106–43 B.C.) Roman statesman/orator/writer/philosopher (*Philippics*)

Cilento, Diane (1933–) Austral. actress (*Tom Jones*; *The Agony and the Ecstasy*)

Cimabue, Giovanni (Bencivieni di Pepo; "The Father of Italian Painting") (c. 1240–1302) Ital. painter (Byzantine style)

Cimino, Michael (1943–) Am. film director (*Thunderbolt and Lightfoot*; *Heaven's Gate*; O—1978—*The Deer Hunter*)

Cincinnatus, Lucius Quinctius (born c. 519 B.C.) Roman general/statesman

Citroën, André Gustav ("The French Henry Ford") (1878–1935) Fr. automobile manufacturer

Claiborne, Craig (1920–) Am. food editor/writer

Claiborne, Liz (Elisabeth Claiborne) (1929–) Am. fashion designer

Clair, René (René-Lucien Chomette) (1898–1981) Fr. film director (*A Nous la Liberté*; *And Then There Were None*)

Claire, Ina (Ina Fagan) (1892–1985) Am. actress/comedienne (*The Awful Truth*; *Ninotchka*)

Clancy, Tom (Thomas L. Clancy, Jr.) (1947–) Am. novelist (techno-thrillers; *The Hunt for Red October*; *A Clear and Present Danger*; *Patriot Games*)

Clapton, Eric (Eric Clapp) (1945–) Eng. rock guitarist/singer ("Tears in Heaven"; "Layla"; "Lay Down Sally"; formerly with Cream, Blind Faith, and Derek & The Dominoes; G—1992)

Clark, Candy (1947–) Am. actress (*American Grafitti*; *The Man Who Fell to Earth*)

Clark, Dave (1942–) Eng. rock musician ("Glad All Over"; with The Dave Clark Five)

Clark, Dick (Richard Wagstaff Clark) (1929–) Am. TV host ("American Bandstand")

Clark, Dutch (Earl Harry Clark) (1906–1978) Am. football Hall-of-Famer

Clark, Jim (James Clark; "The Flying Scot") (1936–1968) Scot.-Eng. auto racer

Clark, Mary Higgins (1931–) Am. suspense writer (*Loves Music, Loves to Dance*)

Clark, Petula (Petula Sally Olwen) (1932–) Eng. pop singer ("Downtown")/actress (*Goodbye, Mr. Chips*)

Clark, Ramsey (William Ramsey Clark) (1927–) Am. govt. official (attorney general)

Clark, Roy (Roy Linwood Clark; "Superpicker") (1933–) Am. country musician/singer/TV host ("Hee Haw")

Clark, Susan (1940–) Can.-Am. actress ("Webster" TV series)

Clark, Walter (Walter van Tilberg Clark) (1909–1971) Am. novelist/short story writer (*The Ox-Bow Incident*)

Clark, Will (William Nuschler Clark) (1964–) Am. baseball player

Clark, William (1770–1838) Am. explorer (with Meriwether Lewis)

Clarke, Arthur C. (Arthur Charles Clarke) (1917–) Eng. science/science fiction writer (*Childhood's End*; *2001: A Space Odyssey*)

Clarke, Bobby (Robert Earl Clarke) (1949–) Can. hockey player

Clarke, Mae (Mary Klotz) (1910–1992) Am. actress (*The Public Enemy*; *The Front Page*)

Clarke, Martha (1944–) Am. dancer/choreographer

Clarke, Stanley (Stanley Marvin Clarke) (1951–) Am. jazz guitarist (former member of Chick Corea's band and Animal Logic)

Claudel, Paul (Paul-Louis-Charles-Marie Claudel) (1868–1955) Fr. poet/playwright (*The Satin Slipper*)

Claudius I (Tiberius Claudius Drusus Nero Germanicus) (10 B.C.–A.D. 54) Roman emperor 41–54

Claudius II (Marcus Aurelius Claudius Gothicus) (214–270) Roman emperor 268–270

Clavell, James (James duMaresq Clavell; born Charles Edmond DuMaresq de Clavelle) (1924–) Eng.-Am. historical novelist (*Tai-Pan*; *Shōgun*; *Noble House*)

Clay, Andrew "Dice" (Andrew Clay Silverstein) (c. 1958–) Am. comedian/actor (*The Adventures of Ford Fairlane*)

Clay, Henry ("The Great Compromiser"; "The Great Pacificator") (1777–1852) Am. senator/govt. official (secretary of state)/orator

Clayburgh, Jill (1944–) Am. actress (*An Unmarried Woman*; *Semi-Tough*)

Clayderman, Richard (Phillipe Pages; "The Prince of Romance") (1953–) Fr. pianist

Clayton, Adam (1960–) Ir. rock bassist (with U2)

Clayton, Jan (Jane Byral Clayton) (1917–1983) Am. actress ("Lassie" TV series)

Cleanthes (331 or 330–232 or 231 B.C.) Gr. Stoic philosopher

Clearchus (5th century B.C.) Spart. soldier/gov. of Byzantium 408 B.C.

Cleary, Beverly (Atlee Bunn Cleary) (1916–) Am. children's book writer (*Beezus and Ramona*)

Cleaver, Eldridge (Leroy Eldridge Cleaver) (1935–) Am. civil rights radical (with the Black Panthers)/writer (*Soul on Ice*)

Cleese, John (John Marwood Cleese) (1939–) Eng. film director/actor/writer (*A Fish Called Wanda*; "Fawlty Towers" TV series)

Cleland, John (1709–1789) Eng. novelist (*Fanny Hill or Memories of a Woman of Pleasure*)

Clemenceau, Georges (Georges Eugene Benjamin Clemenceau; "The Tiger") (1841–1929) Fr. premier 1906–1909, 1917–1920/writer/newspaper publisher (*La Justice*)

Clemens, Roger (William Roger Clemens; "Rocket Man") (1962–) Am. baseball pitcher

Clément, René (1913–) Fr. film director (*Is Paris Burning?*; *Knave of Hearts*)

Clemente, Roberto (Roberto Walker Clemente; "Arriba"; "The Great One") (1934–1972) P.R. baseball Hall-of-Famer

Clemons, Clarence (1942–) Am. saxophonist (with Bruce Springsteen and The E Street Band)

Cleopatra (a/k/a Cleopatra VII) (69–30 B.C.) Egypt. queen 51–30 B.C.

Cleveland, Frances (Frances Folsom) (1864–1947) Am. first lady (Grover)

Cleveland, Grover (Stephen Grover Cleveland) (1837–1908) 22nd and 24th Am. pres. (1885–1889, 1893–1897)

Cleveland, Reverend James ("The Crown Prince of Gospel"; "King of Gospel Music") (1931–1991) Am. clergyman/gospel singer

Cliburn, Van (Harvey Lavan Cliburn, Jr.) (1934–) Am. concert pianist

Cliff, Jimmy (James Chambers) (1948–) Jam. reggae singer/musician ("Wonderful World, Beautiful People")

Clift, Montgomery (Edward Montgomery Clift) (1920–1966) Am. actor (*A Place in the Sun*; *From Here to Eternity*)

Cline, Eddie (Edward F. Cline) (1892–1961) Am. film director (*The Bank Dick*; *My Little Chickadee*)

Cline, Patsy (Virginia Patterson Hensley) (1932–1963) Am. country singer ("I Fall to Pieces"; "Crazy")

Clinton, Bill (William Jefferson Blythe IV; "Slick Willie") (1946–) 42nd Am. pres. (1993–)

Clinton, Chelsea (1981–) Am. daughter of Pres. Clinton

Clinton, De Witt (1769–1828) Am. mayor and gov. of New York/senator

Clinton, George (1739–1812) Am. v.p. (T. Jefferson/J. Madison)

Clinton, George (1940–) Am. pop/funk singer ("One Nation Under A Groove")/musician/producer (Parliament, Funkadelic)

Clinton, Hillary Rodham (1948–) Am. first lady (Bill)/attorney

Clive, Colin (Clive Greig) (1898–1937) Eng.-Am. actor (*Frankenstein* [title role]; *Jane Eyre*)

Clooney, Rosemary (1928–) Am. singer ("Come-on-a-My House")/actress (*White Christmas*)

Close, Glenn (1945–) Am. actress (*Fatal Attraction*; *Reversal of Fortune*; T— 1984)

Clower, Jerry ("Mouth of the South") (1926–) Am. country singer/TV host ("Nashville on the Road")

Clyde, Andy (1892–1967) Scot. actor ("Lassie" TV series; *Abe Lincoln in Illinois*)

Clyde, Jeremy (1944–) Eng. pop singer (with Chad and Jeremy)

Cobain, Curt (c. 1965–) Am. rock singer (with Nirvana)

Cobb, Irvin S. (Irvin Shrewsbury Cobb) (1876–1944) Am. writer/humorist/columnist (created Judge Priest)

Cobb, Lee J. (Leo Jacoby) (1911–1976) Am. actor ("The Virginian" TV series; *The Song of Bernadette*)

Cobb, Ty (Tyrus Raymond Cobb; "The Georgia Peach") (1886–1961) Am. baseball Hall-of-Famer

Cobham, Billy (1944–) Am. rock/jazz drummer (for Miles Davis, James Brown, Roberta Flack, Carly Simon, etc.)

Coburn, Charles (Charles Douville Cobb) (1877–1961) Am. actor (*The Lady Eve*; *The Devil and Miss Jones*; O—1943— *The More the Merrier*)

Coburn, James (1928–) Am. actor (*Our Man Flint*; *In Like Flint*; *The Magnificent Seven*)

Coca, Imogene (Imogene Fernandez y Coca) (1908–) Am. comedienne/actress ("Your Show of Shows" TV series; E— 1951)

Cochise (c. 1812–1874) Am. Apache chief

Cochran, Eddie (Edward Ray Cochrane) (1938–1960) Am. rock singer/guitarist ("Summertime Blues")

Cochran, Jacqueline (1912–1980) Am. aviatrix (first woman to fly faster than sound)

Cochrane, Mickey (Gordon Stanley Cochrane; "Black Mike") (1903–1962) Am. baseball Hall-of-Famer

Cocker, Joe (John Robert Cocker) (1944–) Eng. rock singer ("You Are So Beautiful")

Coco, James (James Emil Coco) (1928–1987) Am. actor (*Only When I Laugh*; *Murder by Death*; E—1982/83)

Cocteau, Jean (Jean Maurice Eugene Clement Cocteau) (1889–1963) Fr. poet/playwright/essayist/film director-writer (*Les Enfants Terribles*; *Beauty and the Beast*)

Coe, David Allan ("The Mysterious Rhinestone Cowboy") (1939–) Am. country singer ("Mona Lisa Lost Her Smile")/songwriter ("Take This Job and Shove It")

Coe, Sebastian (Sebastian Newbold Coe) (1956–) Eng. runner

Coen, Ethan (1958–) Am. screenwriter/producer (brother of Joel; *Barton Fink*; *Raising Arizona*; *Blood Simple*; *The Hudsucker Proxy*)

Coen, Joel (1955–) Am. film director (with brother, Ethan)

Coffin, Tristam (Robert Peter Tristam Coffin) (1892–1955) Am. writer/poet (P—1936—*Strange Holiness*)

Cohan, George M. (George Michael Cohan) (1878–1942) Am. songwriter ("Give My Regards to Broadway"; "Yankee Doodle Dandy"; "Over There"; "You're a Grand Old Flag")

Cohen, Leonard (Leonard Norman Cohen) (1934–) Can. singer/composer ("Suzanne"; "Famous Blue Raincoat")/poet/novelist (*Beautiful Losers*)

Cohen, Mickey ("Snow White") (1913–1976) Am. (California) gangster

Cohen, Myron (1902–1986) Am. comedian

Cohn, Al (1925–1988) Am. jazz saxophonist/composer

Cohn, Harry (1891–1958) Am. movie pioneer/Columbia Pictures founder

Cohn, Marc (C) Am. rock singer/songwriter ("Walking in Memphis"; G—1991)

Cohn, Mindy (1966–) Am. actress ("The Facts of Life" TV series)

Colbert, Claudette (Lily Claudette Chauchoin) (1903–) Fr.-Am. actress (*The Palm Beach Story*; O—1934—*It Happened One Night*)

Cole, Cozy (William Randolph Cole) (1909–1981) Am. jazz drummer

Cole, Gary (1957–) Am. actor ("Midnight Caller" TV series)

Cole, Lloyd (1961–) Can. rock musician/singer (with Lloyd Cole and The Commotions)

Cole, Nat "King" (Nathaniel Adams Coles) (1919–1965) Am. singer (father of Natalie; "Unforgettable")

Cole, Natalie (Stephanie Natalie Maria Cole) (1950–) Am. pop singer (daughter of Nat; "This Will Be"; "Miss You Like Crazy"; G—1991, 1994)

Cole, Thomas (1801–1848) Am. painter (founded the Hudson River School)

Coleman, Cy (Seymour Kaufman) (1929–) Am. composer/pianist/orchestra leader (*Witchcraft*)

Coleman, Dabney (1932–) Am. actor ("Mary Hartman, Mary Hartman" TV series; *Tootsie*)

Coleman, Gary (1968–) Am. actor ("Diff'rent Strokes" TV series)

Coleman, Ornette (1930–) Am. jazz saxophonist (originated "free jazz")

Coleman, Vince (Vincent Maurice Coleman) (1961–) Am. baseball player

Coleridge, Hartley (David Hartley Coleridge) (1796–1849) Eng. writer (*Worthies of Yorkshire*)

Coleridge, Samuel Taylor (1772–1834) Eng. poet/essayist/critic (*The Rime of the Ancient Mariner*; *Kubla Khan*)

Coles, Cyril Henry (1899–1965) Eng. mystery writer (with Adelaide Manning, known as Manning Coles)

Coles, Robert (1929–) Am. child psychiatrist/educator/writer (*Still Hungry in America*; *Teachers and the Children of Poverty*)

Colette (Sidonie-Gabrielle Colette) (1873–1954) Fr. novelist (*Gigi*)

Coley, John Ford (1948–) Am. pop singer/musician ("I'd Really Love to See You Tonight"; with England Dan & John Ford Coley)

Colfax, Schuyler (1823–1885) Am. v.p. (U.S. Grant)

Collie, Mark (1956–) Am. country singer

Collier, Constance (Laura Constance Hardie) (1880–1955) Am. actress (*Stage Door*; *Shadow of a Doubt*)

Collier, John (1901–1980) Am. novelist/short story writer (*His Monkey Wife*)

Collins, Dorothy (Marjorie Chandler) (1926–) Can.-Am. singer ("My Boy-Flat Top")/entertainer ("Candid Camera" TV series)

Collins, Eddie (Edward Trowbridge Collins, Sr.; "Cocky") (1887–1951) Am. baseball Hall-of-Famer

Collins, Gary (1938–) Am. TV host/actor

Collins, Jackie (Jacqueline Jill Collins) (1939–) Eng. novelist (sister of Joan; *Hollywood Wives*)

Collins, Joan (Joan Henrietta Collins) (1933–) Eng. actress (sister of Jackie; "Dynasty" TV series)

Collins, Judy (Judith Marjorie Collins) (1939–) Am. folk singer ("Both Sides Now")

Collins, Michael (1930–) Am. astronaut

Collins, Pauline (1940–) Eng. actress (*Shirley Valentine*; T—1989)

Collins, Phil (1951–) Eng. rock/pop singer/musician/actor ("One More Night"; formerly with Genesis and Brand X; G—1984, 1985)

Collins, Wilkie (William Wilkie Collins) (1824–1889) Eng. detective story writer (*The Woman in White*; *The Moonstone*)

Collodi, Carlo (Carlo Lorenzini) (1826–1890) Ital. children's story writer (*The Adventures of Pinocchio*)

Collyer, Bud (Clayton Collyer) (1908–1969) Am. TV host (brother of June; "To Tell the Truth")

Collyer, June (Dorothea Heermance) (1907–1968) Am. actress (sister of Bud; "The Stu Erwin Show" and "The Trouble with Father" TV series)

Colman, Ronald (Ronald Charles Colman) (1891–1958) Eng.-Am. actor (*Dark Angel*; *Beau Geste*; O—1947—*A Double Life*)

Colonna, Jerry (Gerald Colonna) (1903–1986) Am. comedian/actor (Bob Hope's sidekick on radio and TV)

Colson, Charles W. ("Chuck") (1919–) Am. presidential aide (Nixon)/Watergate participant

Colt, Samuel (1814–1862) Am. inventor (Colt revolver)

Colter, Jessi (Miriam Johnson) (1945–) Am. country/pop singer ("I'm Not Lisa")

Coltrane, Chi (1948–) Am. pop musician/singer ("Thunder and Lightning")

Coltrane, John (John William Coltrane; "Trane") (1926–1967) Am. jazz saxophonist

Columbo, Russ (Ruggiero de Rudolpho Columbo) (1908–1934) Am. violinist/bandleader

Columbus, Chris (Christopher Columbus)

(1959–) Am. film director (*Home Alone*; *Adventures in Babysitting*)

Columbus, Christopher (Cristoforo Colombo; a/k/a Cristóbal Colón) (1451–1506) Span. explorer (discovered Dominica, Guadeloupe, Puerto Rico, Jamaica, Trinidad, Martinique, Honduras)

Colvig, Vance (1892–1967) Am. voice actor (Pluto and Goofy)

Comaneci, Nadia (1961–) Rom. gymnast

Combs, Earle (Earle Bryan Combs; "The Kentucky Colonel"; "The Mail Carrier") (1899–1976) Am. baseball Hall-of-Famer

Comden, Betty (Elizabeth Cohen) (1916–) Am. singer/playwright/lyricist ("Singin' in the Rain")

Comfort, Alex (Alexander Comfort) (1920–) Am. writer (*The Joy of Sex*)

Comiskey, Charlie (Charles Albert Comiskey; "Commy"; "The Old Roman") (1859–1931) Am. baseball Hall-of-Famer

Como, Perry (Pierino Roland Como; a/k/a Nick Perido) (1912–) Am. singer ("Some Enchanted Evening"; G—1958)

Compton, Arthur (Arthur Holly Compton) (1892–1962) Am. physicist (discovered the Compton effect; N—1927)

Compton, Forrest (1925–) Am. actor ("Gomer Pyle, U.S.M.C." TV series)

Compton-Burnett, Dame Ivy (1884–1969) Eng. novelist (*Men and Wives*)

Comte, Auguste (Isidore-Auguste-Marie-François-Xavier Comte) (1798–1857) Fr. positivist philosopher (*Philosophie Positive*; coined the word *sociology*)

Conaway, Jeff (1950–) Am. actor ("Taxi" TV series)

Concepcion, Dave (David Ismael Benitez Concepcion) (1948–) Am. baseball player

Condon, Eddie (Albert Edwin Condon) (1904–1973) Am. jazz bandleader/guitarist

Condon, Richard (Richard Thomas Condon) (1915–) Am. novelist (*The Manchurian Candidate*)

Confucius (K'ung Ch'iu) (551–479 B.C.) Chin. philosopher (*The Analects of Confucius*)

Conklin, Chester (Jules Cowles) (1888–1971) Am. comedian (one of the Keystone Kops)

Conkling, Roscoe (1829–1888) Am. senator

Conlan, Jocko (John Bertrand Conlan) (1899–1989) Am. baseball Hall-of-Famer

Conlee, John (1946–) Am. country singer ("Back Side of Thirty")

Conley, Earl Thomas (1941–) Am. country singer ("Fire and Smoke")

Conn, Billy (William David Conn; "The Pittsburgh Kid") (1917–1993) Am. boxer

Conn, Didi (Didi Bernstein) (1951–) Am. comedienne/actress ("Benson" TV series)

Connell, Evan S., Jr. (Evan Shelby Connell, Jr.) (1924–) Am. novelist (*The Patriot*; *Mrs. Bridge*; *Mr. Bridge*)

Connelly, Jennifer (c. 1971–) Am. actress (*The Rocketeer*; *Career Opportunities*)

Connelly, Marc (Marcus Cook Connelly) (1890–1980) Am. playwright (*The Farmer Takes a Wife*; P—1930—*The Green Pastures*)

Connery, Sean (Thomas Sean Connery) (1930–) Scot. actor (James Bond in many films; *Rising Sun*; *The Hunt for Red October*; O—1987—*The Untouchables*)

Connick, Harry, Jr. (1967–) Am. jazz/pop singer/pianist (*When Harry Met Sally. . .* soundtrack)

Conniff, Ray (1916–) Am. singer ("Somewhere, My Love [Lara's Theme]")

Connolly, Maureen (Maureen Catherine Connolly; "Little Mo") (1934–1969) Am. tennis player (W—1952, 1953, 1954)

Connolly, Tommy (Thomas Henry Connolly) (1870–1961) Am. baseball umpire

Connor, George (1925–) Am. football Hall-of-Famer

Connors, Chuck (Kevin Joseph Connors) (1921–1992) Am. actor ("The Rifleman" TV series; *Geronimo* [title role])

Connors, Jimmy (James Scott Connors) (1952–) Am. tennis player (W—1974, 1982)

Connors, Mike or **Michael** (Krekor Ohanian; a/k/a Touch Connors) (1925–) Am. actor (TV's "Mannix")

Conrad, Con (Conrad K. Dober) (1893–1938) Am. film songwriter (*The Gay Divorcee*; *The Great Ziegfeld*)

Conrad, Joseph (Jozef Teodor Konrad Nalecz Korzeniowski) (1857–1924) Eng. novelist (*Heart of Darkness*; *Lord Jim*)

Conrad, Robert (Conrad Robert Falk) (1935–) Am. actor ("The Wild, Wild West" and "Hawaiian Eye" TV series)

Conrad, William (1920–1994) Am. actor

("Jake and the Fatman" and "Cannon" TV series)

Conreid, Hans (Frank Foster Conreid) (1915–1982) Am. actor ("The Danny Thomas Show" TV series; *The 5,000 Fingers of Dr. T*)

Conroy, Frank (1936–) Am. writer (*Stop-Time*; *Body & Soul*)

Conroy, Pat (1945–) Am. novelist (*The Great Santini*; *The Prince of Tides*; *The Lords of Discipline*)

Constable, John (1776–1837) Eng. landscape painter

Constantine the Great (Flavius Valerius Aurelius Constantinus) (c. 280–337) Roman emperor 306–337

Conti, Bill (1942–) Am. film composer/conductor ("Gonna Fly Now [Theme from Rocky]")

Conti, Tom (Thomas Antonio Conti) (1941–) Scot.-Eng. actor (*Reuben, Reuben*; *Shirley Valentine*; T—1979)

Convy, Bert (Bernard Whalen Patrick Convy) (1934–1991) Am. game show host ("Password")

Conway, Jack (1887–1952) Am. film director (*Libeled Lady*; *A Tale of Two Cities*)

Conway, Morgan (1900–1981) Am. actor (Dick Tracy in films)

Conway, Shirl (Shirley Conway Larson or Shirley Elizabeth Crosman) (1916–) Am. actress ("The Nurses" TV series)

Conway, Tim (Thomas Daniel Conway) (1933–) Am. comedian ("McHale's Navy" and "The Carol Burnett Show" TV series)

Cooder, Ry (Ryland Peter Cooder) (1947–) Am. rock musician/film composer (*The Long Riders*; *Paris, Texas*)

Coogan, Jackie (John Leslie Coogan, Jr.; "The Youngest Millionaire") (1914–1984) Am. actor (*The Kid*; *Tom Sawyer*; Uncle Fester in "The Addams Family" TV series)

Cook, Elisha, Jr. (1902–) Am. actor (*The Maltese Falcon*; *Phantom Lady*)

Cook, Captain James (1728–1779) Eng. navigator/explorer (discovered the Sandwich Islands)

Cook, Robin (1940–) Am. suspense novelist (*Coma*)

Cooke, Alistair (Alfred Alistair Cooke) (1908–) Eng.-Am. TV host ("Masterpiece Theatre")/writer (*Alistair Cook's America*)

Cooke, Sam (a/k/a Dale Cook) (1935–1964) Am. rock singer ("You Send Me")

Coolbrith, Ina (Ina Donna Coolbrith; born Josephine Donna Smith) (1841–1928) Am. poet (*A Perfect Day*; *Songs from the Golden Gate*)

Cooley, Spade (1910–1969) Am. country singer ("Shame on You")

Coolidge, Calvin (John Calvin Coolidge; "Silent Cal") (1872–1933) 30th Am. pres. (1923–1929)

Coolidge, Grace (Grace Anne Goodhue) (1879–1957) Am. first lady (Calvin)

Coolidge, Martha (1946–) Am. film director (*Valley Girl*; *Rambling Rose*)

Coolidge, Rita (1944–) Am. pop singer ("[Your Love Has Lifted Me] Higher and Higher"; "We're All Alone")

Coombs, Jack (John Wesley Coombs; "Colby Jack") (1882–1957) Am. baseball player

Cooney, Gerry (Gerald Arthur Cooney; "The Great White Hope") (1956–) Am. boxer

Cooper, Alice (Vincent Damon Furnier) (1948–) Am. rock singer ("School's Out"; "I Never Cry")

Cooper, Gary (Frank James Cooper) (1901–1961) Am. actor (*Mr. Deeds Goes to Town*; O—1941—*Sergeant York*; O—1952—*High Noon*)

Cooper, Dame Gladys (Gladys Constance Cooper) (1888–1971) Eng. actress (*My Fair Lady*; *Now, Voyager*; *The Song of Bernadette*)

Cooper, Jackie (John Cooper, Jr.) (1921–) Am. actor ("The People's Choice" TV series; *Skippy*; *Treasure Island*)

Cooper, James Fenimore (1789–1851) Am. novelist (*The Leather-Stocking Tales*; *The Last of the Mohicans*; *The Deer-Slayer*)

Cooper, Melville (1896–1973) Eng. actor (*Pride and Prejudice*; *Father of the Bride*)

Cooper, Mort (Morton Cecil Cooper) (1913–1958) Am. baseball player

Cooper, Walker (William Walker Cooper) (1915–1991) Am. baseball player

Copeland, Stewart (1952–) Am. rock musician (with The Police and Animal Logic)/film composer

Copernicus, Nicolaus (Mikolaj Kopernik) (1791–1883) Pol. astronomer (discovered that planets orbit the sun)

Copland, Aaron (1900–1990) Am. composer (P—1945—*Appalachian Spring*; *Billy the Kid*)

Copley, John (John Singleton Copley) (1738–1815) Am. portrait painter

Copley, Teri (1961–) Am. actress ("We Got It Made" TV series)

Copperfield, David (David Seth Kotkin) (1957–) Am. magician

Coppola, Carmine (1910–1991) Am. composer (father of Francis Ford; *The Godfather* films)

Coppola, Francis Ford (1939–) Am. film director (father of Sofia, brother of Talia Shire; *Apocalypse Now*; *The Godfather*; *The Conversation*; O—1974—*The Godfather, Part II*)

Coppola, Sofia (c. 1971–) Am. actress (daughter of Francis Ford Coppola; *The Godfather, Part III*)

Corbett, James J. (James John Corbett; "Gentleman Jim") (1866–1933) Am. boxer

Corbett, John (1962–) Am. actor ("Northern Exposure" TV series)

Corbin, Barry (1940–) Am. actor ("Northern Exposure" TV series)

Corby, Ellen (Ellen Hansen) (1913–) Am. actress (*I Remember Mama*; "The Waltons" TV series; E—1972/73, 1974/75, 1975/76)

Cord, Alex (Alexander Viespi) (1931–) Am. actor ("Airwolf" TV series)

Cordero, Angel, Jr. (Angel Tomas Cordero, Jr.) (1942–) P.R. jockey

Cordobés, El (Manuel Benítez Pérez) (1936–) Span. bullfighter

Corea, Chick (Armando Anthony Corea) (1942–) Am. jazz pianist/composer (cofounded Return to Forever with Stanley Clarke)

Corelli, Franco (Dario Franco Corelli) (1921 or 1923–) Ital. opera singer (tenor)

Corelli, Marie (Mary Mackay) (1855–1924) Eng. novelist (*Barabbas*)

Corey, Irwin ("Professor") (1912–) Am. comedian/actor ("The Andy Williams Show" TV series)

Corey, Wendell (Wendell Reid Corey) (1914–1968) Am. actor (*The Great Missouri Raid*; *Rear Window*)/film executive

Cori, Carl (Carl Ferdinand Cori) (1896–1984) Cz.-Am. biochemist (husband of Gerty; discovered the Cori ester with wife; N—1947)

Cori, Gerty (Gerty Theresa Cori née Radnitz) (1896–1957) Cz.-Am. biochemist (N—1947)

Corman, Roger (Roger William Corman) (1926–) Am. film director (*Not of This Earth*; *Bloody Mama*; *Frankenstein Unbound*)

Corneille, Pierre ("The Father of French Tragedy") (1606–1684) Fr. playwright (*Horace*; *Le Cid*)

Cornelius, Helen (Helen Lorene Johnson) (1941–) Am. country singer ("Nashville on the Road" TV series)

Cornell, Ezra (1807–1874) Am. financier/university founder/founder of the Western Union Telegraph Company

Cornell, Katharine ("First Lady of the American Theater") (1893–1974) Am. stage actress (*A Bill of Divorcement*; T—1948)

Cornwell, Patricia D. (Patricia Daniels Cornwell) (1956–) Am. mystery writer (created Dr. Kay Scarpetta; *Cruel & Unusual*)

Coronado, Francisco de (Francisco Vásquez de Coronado; "El Dorado") (c. 1510–1554) Span. explorer (discovered the Grand Canyon)

Corot, Jean (Jean-Baptiste-Camille Corot; "Papa") (1796–1875) Fr. painter

Correggio, Antonio (Antonio Allegri) (1494–1534) Ital. painter

Corri, Adrienne (Adrienne Riccoboni) (1930–) Scot.-Eng. actress (*A Clockwork Orange*; *Doctor Zhivago*)

Corrigan, Crash (Raymond Bernard Corrigan) (1907–1976) Am. cowboy actor (*The Three Mesquiteers*)

Corrigan, Wrong Way (Douglas Corrigan) (1907–) Am. aviator

Corso, Gregory (Nunzio Gregory Corso) (1930–) Am. "beat" poet (*Gasoline*; *Happy Birthday of Death*)

Cort, Bud (Walter Edward Cox) (1950–) Am. actor (*Harold and Maude*)

Cortázar, Julio (1914–1984) Arg. novelist/short story writer (*The Winners*; *Hopscotch*; *Blow-Up*)

Cortés, Hernándo or Hernán (1485–1547) Span. conqueror of Mexico/explorer (founded Veracruz; discovered lower California)

Cortesa (in America) or Cortese, Valentina (1924–) Ital. actress (*The Barefoot Contessa*; *Day for Night*)

Cortez, Ricardo (Jacob Kranz) (1899–1977) Aus.-Am. actor (*Blackmail*; *The Maltese Falcon* [1931; as Sam Spade])

Coryell, John R. (John Russell Coryell) (1848–1924) Am. mystery writer (created Nick Carter)

Cosby, Bill (William Henry Cosby, Jr.) (1937–) Am. comedian/actor

("The Cosby Show" TV series; E—1965/66; 1966/67, 1967/68)/writer (*Fatherhood*)

Cosell, Howard (Henry William Cohen; "The Mouth") (1920–) Am. sportscaster

Costa-Gavras (Henri Konstantinos Costa-Gavras) (1933–) Gr.-Fr. film director (*Z*; *Betrayed*; *Music Box*)

Costain, Thomas (Thomas Bertram Costain) (1885–1965) Can. editor/novelist (*The Black Rose*; *The Silver Chalice*)

Costas, Bob (Robert Quinlan Costas) (1952–) Am. sportscaster/talk show host

Costello, Dolores (1905–1979) Am. actress (sister of Helene; *The Magnificent Ambersons*; *Little Lord Fauntleroy*)

Costello, Elvis (Declan Patrick Aloysius MacManus) (1954–) Eng. rock/pop singer ("Alison"; band: The Attractions)

Costello, Frank (Francesco Castiglia; "Prime Minister of the Underworld") (1891–1973) Ital.-Am. racketeer

Costello, Helene (1904–1957) Am. actress (sister of Dolores; *Lights of New York*; *In Old Kentucky*)

Costello, Lou (Louis Francis Cristillo) (1906–1959) Am. comedian (with Bud Abbott)

Costner, Kevin (Kevin Michael Costner) (1955–) Am. actor/film director (*The Untouchables*; *Bull Durham*; O[director]—1990—*Dances with Wolves*)

Cotler, Kami (1965–) Am. child actress ("The Waltons" TV series)

Cotten, Joseph (Joseph Cheshire Cotten) (1905–1994) Am. actor (*The Third Man*; *Citizen Kane*; *Shadow of a Doubt*)

Cougar, John see Mellencamp, John Cougar

Coulier, Dave (c. 1960–) Am. actor ("Full House" TV series)

Couperin, François ("Le Grand") (1668–1733) Fr. organist/composer

Courbet, Gustave (Jean-Désiré-Gustave Courbet) (1819–1877) Fr. painter

Couric, Katie (1957–) Am. newscaster ("Today")

Courrèges, André (1923–) Fr. fashion designer (credited with the invention of the mini-skirt)

Court, Margaret (née) Smith ("Amazin' Amazon") (1942–) Austral. tennis player (W—1963, 1965, 1970)

Courtneidge, Dame Cicely (1893–1980) Eng. actress (*The Wrong Box*; *The Magnificent Men in Their Flying Machines*)

Cousin, Victor (1792–1867) Fr. philosopher (founded eclecticism)

Cousins, Norman (1915–1990) Am. editor (the *Saturday Review*)/writer (*Anatomy of an Illness*)

Cousteau, Jacques (Jacques-Yves Cousteau) (1910–) Fr. sea explorer/oceanographer/documentarist (*The Silent World*)

Cousy, Bob (Robert Joseph Cousy; "Cooz"; "The Houdini of the Hardwood") (1928–) Am. basketball player/coach

Covarrubias, Miguel (1904–1957) Mex. artist/writer (*Island of Bali*)

Coveleski, Harry (Harry Frank Coveleski; "The Giant Killer"; "The Silent Pole") (1886–1950) Am. baseball pitcher (brother of Stan)

Coveleski, Stan (Stanley Anthony Coveleski, born Stanislaus Kowalewski) (1889–1984) Am. baseball Hall-of-Famer

Coward, Sir Noël (Noël Peirce Coward) (1899–1973) Eng. playwright/actor (*Mad Dogs and Englishmen*; *Blithe Spirit*)

Cowley, Hannah (née Parkhouse) (1743–1809) Eng. playwright (*The Belle's Stratagem*)

Cox, Alex (1954–) Eng. film director (*Repo Man*; *Sid and Nancy*)

Cox, Anthony Berkeley (a/k/a Anthony Berkeley, Francis Iles and A. B. Cox) (1893–1970) Eng. mystery writer/journalist (*Malice Aforethought*)

Cox, Archibald (1912–) Am. Watergate prosecutor (fired by Robert Bork)

Cox, Courteney (1964–) Am. actress ("Family Ties" TV series)

Cox, Danny (Danny Bradford Cox) (1959–) Am. baseball pitcher

Cox, Ronny (1938–) Am. actor ("St. Elsewhere" TV series; *Beverly Hills Cop*; *Total Recall*)

Cox, Wally (Wallace Maynard Cox) (1924–1973) Am. actor (TV's "Mr. Peepers")

Coyote, Peter (Peter Cohon) (1942–) Am. actor (*Outrageous Fortune*; *Jagged Edge*)

Cozzens, James Gould (1903–1978) Am. writer (*By Love Possessed*; P—1949—*Guard of Honor*)

Crabbe, Buster (Clarence Linden Crabbe) (1907–1983) Am. swimmer/actor (played Tarzan in the 1930s)

Craddock, Crash (Billy Craddock; "Mr.

Country Rock") (1939–) Am. country singer ("Rub It In"; "Ruby, Baby")

Craig, Roger (Roger Timothy Craig) (1962–) Am. football player

Crain, Jeanne (1925–) Am. actress (*State Fair*; *Pinky*)

Cramer, Floyd (1933–) Am. country musician (with Elvis Presley, Johnny Cash, and Chet Atkins)

Crane, Bob (1929–1978) Am. actor ("The Donna Reed Show" and "Hogan's Heroes" TV series)

Crane, Hart (Harold Hart Crane) (1899–1932) Am. poet (*The Bridge*; *Praise for an Urn*)

Crane, Stephen (1871–1900) Am. novelist/short story writer/poet (*The Red Badge of Courage*)

Cranston, Alan (Alan MacGregor Cranston) (1914–) Am. senator

Craven, Wes (Wesley Earl Craven) (1939–) Am. horror film director (the *Nightmare on Elm Street* series)

Crawford, Broderick (William Broderick Crawford) (1911–1986) Am. actor (*Born Yesterday*; O—1949—*All the King's Men*)

Crawford, Cindy (1966–) Am. model

Crawford, Joan (Lucille Fay LeSueur; a/k/a Billie Cassin) (1908–1973) Am. actress (*Whatever Happened to Baby Jane?*; *The Women*; O—1945—*Mildred Pierce*)

Crawford, Michael (Michael Patrick Dumble-Smith) (1942–) Eng. stage actor/singer (*The Phantom of the Opera*; T—1988)

Crawford, Sam (Samuel Earl Drawford; "Wahoo Sam"; "The Wahoo Barber") (1880–1968) Am. baseball Hall-of-Famer

Crazy Horse (1842–1877) Am. Sioux chief

Cray, Robert (1953–) Am. blues singer/musician ("Smoking Gun"; "Right Next Door [Because of Me]")

Cray, Seymour R. (1925–) Am. computer pioneer (developed the world's fastest computer)

Creasey, John (some pseuds.: Jeremy York, Kyle Hunt, Anthony Morton, Michael Halliday, Norman Deane, J. J. Marric, Gordon Ashe, Robert Caine Frazier) (1908–1973) Eng. mystery writer (wrote almost 600 books using 28 pseudonyms; created George Gideon and The Toff)

Cregar, Laird (Laird Samuel Cregar) (1916–1944) Am. actor (*I Wake Up Screaming*; *The Lodger*)

Creme, Lol (1947–) Eng. pop singer/musician ("Cry"; with Godley & Creme; formerly with 10CC)

Crenna, Richard (1927–) Am. actor (*The Sand Pebbles*; "Our Miss Brooks" and "The Real McCoys" TV series)

Crenshaw, Marshall (1954–) Am. pop singer ("Someday, Someway")

Creston, Paul (1906–1985) Am. orchestral composer

Crichton, Charles (1910–) Eng. film director (*The Lavender Hill Mob*; *A Fish Called Wanda*)

Crichton, James ("The Admirable Crichton") (1560–1582) Scot. writer/prodigy

Crichton, Michael (John Michael Crichton; a/k/a Jeffrey Hudson and John Lange) (1942–) Am. novelist (*The Andromeda Strain*; *Jurassic Park*)/film director (*Westworld*; *Physical Evidence*)

Crick, Francis (Francis Harry Compton Crick) (1916–) Eng. biologist (discovered DNA with James Watson; N—1962)

Crisp, Donald (1880–1974) Scot.-Eng. actor (O—1941—*How Green Was My Valley*; *Lassie* films)

Crisp, Quentin (Dennis Pratt) (1908–) Eng. autobiographer (*The Naked Civil Servant*)

Crispin, Edmund (Robert Bruce Montgomery) (1921–1978) Eng. mystery writer (created Gervase Fen)

Criss, Peter (Peter Crisscoula) (1947–) Am. rock drummer (with Kiss)

Crist, Judith (Judith Klein) (1922–) Am. film critic/writer

Cristofer, Michael (Michael Anthony Procaccino) (1945–) Am. actor/playwright (P—1977—*The Shadow Box*)

Croce, Jim (1942–1973) Am. rock/pop singer ("Bad, Bad Leroy Brown"; "Time in a Bottle")

Crockett, Davy (David Crockett; "King of the Wild Frontier") (1786–1836) Am. frontiersman/statesman (killed at the Alamo)

Croesus (died c. 546 B.C.) last king of Lydia c. 560–546 B.C.

Crofts, Dash (1940–) Am. pop singer/musician ("Summer Breeze"; with Seals and Crofts)

Crofts, Freeman (Freeman Wills Crofts) (1879–1957) Ir. detective story writer (created Inspector French)

Cromwell, John (Elwood Dagger Cromwell) (1888–1979) Am. film director (*Of Human Bondage*; *The Prisoner of Zenda*; *Anna and the King of Siam*)

Cromwell, Oliver ("Old Noll") (1599–1658) Eng. mil. leader/statesman

Cromwell, Thomas, Earl of Essex (1485–1540) Eng. statesman (worked for Henry VIII)

Cronenberg, David (1943–) Can. horror film director (*The Fly* [1986]; *The Dead Zone*; *Videodrome*; *Naked Lunch*)

Cronin, A. J. (Archibald Joseph Cronin) (1896–1981) Eng. physician/novelist (*The Keys to the Kingdom*)

Cronin, Joe (Joseph Edward Cronin) (1906–1984) Am. baseball Hall-of-Famer

Cronin, Kevin (1951–) Am. rock singer (with REO Speedwagon)

Cronkite, Walter (Walter Leland Cronkite, Jr.; "Uncle Walter") (1916–) Am. newscaster (signature phrase: "And that's the way it is")

Cronyn, Hume (Hume Blake) (1911–) Can.-Am. actor (*Cocoon*; *Shadow of a Doubt*)

Crosby, Bing (Harry Lillis Crosby) (1904–1977) Am. singer ("White Christmas")/actor (*The Country Girl*; O—1944—*Going My Way*)

Crosby, Bob (George Robert Crosby) (1913–1993) Am. bandleader (brother of Bing)

Crosby, Cathy Lee (1948–) Am. TV host ("That's Incredible")

Crosby, David (David Van Cortland) (1941–) Am. rock musician (with Crosby, Stills, Nash & Young and The Byrds)

Crosby, Mary (Mary Frances Crosby) (1959–) Am. actress (daughter of Bing; "Dallas" TV series)

Crosby, Norm (Norman Lawrence Crosby) (1927–) Am. comedian

Crosetti, Frank (Frank Peter Crosetti; "The Crow") (1910–) Am. baseball player

Cross, Christopher (Christopher Geppert) (1951–) Am. pop singer ("Sailing"; "Ride Like the Wind"; G—1980)

Crothers, Scatman (Benjamin Sherman Crothers) (1910–1986) Am. actor ("Chico and the Man" TV series)

Crouch, Andrae (1942–) Am. gospel singer/songwriter

Crouse, Lindsay (Lindsay Ann Crouse) (1948–) Am. actress (daughter of Russel; *House of Games*; *The Verdict*)

Crouse, Russel M. (1893–1966) Am. playwright (*The Sound of Music*; with Howard Lindsay, P—1946—*State of the Union*)

Crowe, Cameron (1957–) Am. film director/screenwriter (*Fast Times at Ridgemont High*; *Singles*; *Say Anything . . .*)

Crowell, Rodney (1950–) Am. country singer ("Ashes by Now"; "It's Such a Small World" [duet with Rosanne Cash])

Crowley, Aleister (Edward Alexander Crowley; "The Great Beast") (1875–1947) Eng. poet/occultist

Crowther, Bosley (Francis Bosley Crowther) (1905–1981) Am. film critic (*New York Times*)

Cruise, Tom (Thomas Cruise Mapother IV) (1962–) Am. actor (*Top Gun*; *A Few Good Men*; *The Firm*)

Crumb, R. (Robert Crumb) (1943–) Am. "underground" cartoonist (created Fritz the Cat and the Truckin' Man ["Keep on truckin' "])

Cruz, Brandon (1962–) Am. child actor ("The Courtship of Eddie's Father" TV series)

Cruze, James (Jens Cruze Bosen) (1884–1942) Am. film director (*Sutter's Gold*; *The Covered Wagon*)

Cryer, Jon (1965–) Am. actor (*Pretty in Pink*; *Hotshots*)

Crystal, Billy (William Crystal) (1947–) Am. comedian/actor (*When Harry Met Sally . . .*; *City Slickers*; *Mr. Saturday Night*)/host of the Academy Awards

Csonka, Larry (Lawrence Richard Csonka; "Zonk") (1946–) Am. football Hall-of-Famer

Cugat, Xavier (Francisco de Asis Javier Cugat Mingall de Bru y Deulofeo; "Rhumba King") (1900–1990) Span. bandleader ("Brazil")

Cukor, George (George Dewey Cukor) (1899–1983) Am. film director (*Holiday*; *The Philadelphia Story*; *Adam's Rib*; *Dinner at Eight*; O—1964—*My Fair Lady*)

Culbertson, Ely (1891–1955) Am. bridge (card game) expert

Culkin, Macaulay (1980–) Am. child actor (*Home Alone*; *My Girl*; *The Good Son*)

Cullen, Bill (William Lawrence Cullen) (1920–1990) Am. game show host ("The Price Is Right")

Cullen, Countee (1903–1946) Am. poet (*Heritage*; *Color*)

Culliford, Pierre (Peyo) (1928–1993) Belg. cartoonist (created The Smurfs)

Cullum, John (1930–) Am. singer/stage actor/director (T—1975, 1978)

Culp, Curley (1946–) Am. football player

Culp, Robert (1930–) Am. actor ("I Spy" TV series; *Bob & Carol & Ted & Alice*)

Cummings, Bob or Robert (Charles Clarence Robert Orville Cummings; a/k/a Blade Stanhope Conway and Brice Hutchens) (1908–1991) Am. actor (*Dial M for Murder*; *Twelve Angry Men*)

Cummings, Constance (Constance Halverstadt) (1910–) Am. actress (*Blithe Spirit*; T—1979)

cummings, e. e. (Edward Estlin Cummings) (1894–1962) Am. poet (*Tulips and Chimneys*)

Cummings, Candy (William Arthur Cummings; "The Father of the Curveball") (1848–1924) Am. baseball Hall-of-Famer

Cummings, Quinn (1967–) Am. actress (*The Goodbye Girl*)

Cunningham, Glenn (Glenn Clarence Cunningham; "The Kansas Ironman"; "Kansas Flyer") (1909–1988) Am. runner

Cunningham, Imogen (1883–1976) Am. photographer (plants, flowers)

Cunningham, Merce (1919–) Am. dancer/choreographer

Cuomo, Mario (Mario Matthew Cuomo) (1932–) Am. gov. of New York

Cuppy, Will (William Jacob Cuppy) (1884–1949) Am. critic/humorist/writer (*The Decline and Fall of Practically Everybody*)

Curie, Eve (1904–) Fr. journalist/biographer (daughter of Marie and Pierre; *Madame Curie*)

Curie, Marie (Manya Sklodowska; "Madame Curie") (1867–1934) Fr. scientist (discovered radium; N—1903, 1911)

Curie, Pierre (1859–1906) Fr. scientist (husband of Marie; N—1903)

Curran, Kevin (1958–) S. Afr. tennis player

Currie, Cherie (1960–) Am. rock musician (with The Runaways)

Currier, Nathaniel (1813–1888) Am. lithographer (with James Ives)

Curry, Tim (1946–) Eng. pop singer/actor (*The Rocky Horror Picture Show*)

Curtin, Jane (Jane Therese Curtin) (1947–) Am. actress ("Saturday Night Live" and "Kate & Allie" TV series; E—1983/84, 1984/85)

Curtis, Charles (1860–1936) Am. v.p. (H. Hoover)

Curtis, Cyrus H. K. (Cyrus Hermann Kotszchmar Curtis) (1850–1933) Am. magazine publisher (*Saturday Evening Post*; *Ladies' Home Journal*; *New York Evening Post*)/philanthropist

Curtis, Jamie Lee (1958–) Am. actress (daughter of Tony Curtis and Janet Leigh; *A Fish Called Wanda*; *Blue Steel*; *Mother's Boys*)

Curtis, Ken (Curtis Gates) (1916–1991) Am. actor ("Gunsmoke" TV series)

Curtis, Tony (Bernard Schwartz) (1925–) Am. actor (father of Jamie Lee; *Some Like It Hot*; *The Defiant Ones*)

Curtiss, Glenn (Glenn Hammond Curtiss) (1878–1930) Am. aviator/inventor (hydroplane)

Curtiz, Michael (Mihaly Kertész) (1888–1962) Hung.-Am. film director (*Mildred Pierce*; O—1943—*Casablanca*)

Cusack, Cyril (Cyril James Cusack) (1910–1993) Ir. actor (father of Sinead; *Fahrenheit 451*; *My Left Foot*)

Cusack, Joan (1962–) Am. actress (sister of John; *Broadcast News*; *Working Girl*; *Say Anything . . .*)

Cusack, John (1966–) Am. actor (brother of Joan; *Say Anything . . .*; *The Grifters*; *Shadows and Fog*; *Money for Nothing*)

Cusack, Sinead (1948–) Ir. actress (daughter of Cyril; *David Copperfield*)

Cushing, Caleb (1800–1879) Am. lawyer/diplomat/govt. official (attorney general)

Cushing, Cardinal (Richard James Cushing) (1895–1970) Am. Roman-Catholic cardinal

Cushing, Peter (1913–) Eng. actor (*Dracula*; *Hamlet*)

Cussler, Clive (Clive Eric Cussler) (1931–) Am. novelist (*Deep Six*; *Raise the Titanic*; *Sahara*)

Custer, George A. (George Armstrong Custer; "Yellow Hair") (1839–1876) Am. army officer/mil. leader (killed in the Battle of Little Big Horn)

Cuyler, Kiki (Hazen Shirley Cuyler) (1899–1950) Am. baseball Hall-of-Famer

Cuyp, Albert (1620–1691) Dutch landscape painter

Cynewulf (9th century) Anglo-Saxon poet (*The Fates of the Apostles*)

Cyrus (Cyrus II; Cyrus The Great) (c. 585–c. 529 B.C.) Pers. king

Cyrus, Billy Ray (1961–) Am. country singer ("Achy Breaky Heart")

Czerny, Karl (1791–1857) Aus. pianist/composer (*The School of Fingering*)

D'abo, Maryam (1961–) Am. actress (sister of Olivia; *The Living Daylights*)

D'abo, Olivia (1967–) Am. actress ("The Wonder Years" TV series)

Da Costa, Morton (Morton Tecosky) (1914–) Am. stage/film director (*The Music Man*; *Auntie Mame*)

Dafoe, Willem (William Dafoe) (1955–) Am. actor (*Platoon*; *The Last Temptation of Christ*; *Wild at Heart*)

Da Gama, Vasco (c. 1460–1524) Port. explorer (first voyage from Europe to Asia via Africa)

Dagmar (Virginia Ruth Egnor; a/k/a Jennie Lewis) (1926–) Am. TV host ("Masquerade Party")

Dagover, Lil (Marta Maria Liletta Dagover) (1897–1980) Ger. actress (*The Cabinet of Dr. Caligari* [1919]; *Harakiri*)

Daguerre, Louis (Louis-Jacques-Mandé Daguerre) (1789–1851) Fr. painter/inventor (daguerrotype)

Dahl, Arlene (Arlene Carol Dahl) (1924–) Am. actress ("One Life to Live" soap opera; *Journey to the Center of the Earth*)

Dahl, Roald (1916–1990) Eng. short story writer/children's book writer (*Charlie and the Chocolate Factory*; *Chitty Chitty Bang Bang*)

Dahmer, Jeffrey (1960–) Am. serial killer

Dailey, Dan (1914–1978) Am. dancer/actor (*Give My Regards to Broadway*; *When My Baby Smiles at Me*)

Dailey, Janet (1944–) Am. romance novelist (*Calder Born; Calder Bred*)

Daily, Bill (1928–) Am. actor ("I Dream of Jeannie" TV series)

Daimler, Gottlieb (Gottlieb Wilhelm Daimler) (1834–1900) Ger. engineer/automobile manufacturer (Mercedes)/inventor (carburetor)

Dalai Lama, 14th (Gejong Tenzin Gyatsho) (1935–) Tibetan religious leader (N—1989)

Daley, Richard (Richard Joseph Daley) (1902–1976) Am. govt. official (mayor of Chicago)

Dalhart, Vernon (Marion Try Slaughter) (1883–1948) Am. country music pioneer ("The Prisoner's Song")

Dali, Salvador (Salvador Felipe Jacinto Dali) (1904–1989) Span. surrealist painter

Dallas, George M. (George Mifflin Dallas) (1792–1864) Am. v.p. (J. Polk)

Dallesandro, Joe (1948–) Am. film director/actor (Warhol films)

Dalton, Abby (Marlene Wasden) (1932–) Am. actress ("Falcon Crest" TV series)

Dalton, Lacy J. (Jill Croston; born Jill Byrem) (1946–) Am. country singer ("Can't Make a Rock from a Rolling Stone")

Dalton, Timothy (1946–) Wel. actor (plays James Bond; *The Living Daylights*)

Daltrey, Roger (1944–) Eng. rock singer (with The Who)

Daly, Chuck (Charles Joseph Daly; "Prince of Pessimism") (1930–) Am. basketball coach

Daly, Elizabeth (1879–1967) Am. mystery writer (created Henry Gamadge; *Unexpected Night*)

Daly, James (James Firman Daly) (1918–1978) Am. actor ("Medical Center" TV series; *Planet of the Apes*)

Daly, Timothy (1956–) Am. actor (brother of Tyne; *Spellbinder*; *In the Line of Duty: Ambush in Waco* [as David Koresh])

Daly, Tyne (Ellen Tyne Daly) (1945–) Am. actress (sister of Timothy; "Cagney & Lacey" TV series; E—1982/83, 1983/84, 1984/85, 1987/88; T—1990)

D'Amato, Alfonse (Alfonse Marcello D'Amato) (1937–) Am. senator

D'Amboise, Jacques (Jacques Joseph D'Amboise Ahearn) (1934–) Am. ballet dancer

Damian, Michael (Michael Damian Weir) (1962–) Am. actor ("The Young and the Restless" soap opera)/singer ("Rock On")

Damita, Lili (Liliane-Marie-Madeleine Carré; a/k/a Damita del Rojo and Lily Seslys) (1901–) Fr. actress (*The Bridge of San Luis Rey*; *Brewster's Millions*)

Damon, Cathryn (1930–1987) Am. actress ("Soap" TV series; E—1979/80)

Damone, Vic (Vito Farinola) (1928–) Am. singer ("On the Street Where You Live")

Damrosch, Walter (Walter Johannes Damrosch) (1862–1950) Am. musician/conductor

Dana, Bill (William Szathmary) (1924–) Am. comedian/actor (created and played Jose Jimenez)

Dana, Leora (1923–1983) Am. actress (*Pollyanna*; *The Boston Strangler*)

Dana, Richard Henry (Richard Henry Dana, Jr.) (1815–1882) Am. novelist/social reformer (*Two Years Before the Mast*)

Dana, Vic (1942–) Am. pop singer ("Red Roses for a Blue Lady")

Dando, Evan (c. 1967–) Am. pop singer (with the Lemonheads)

Dandridge, Dorothy (1923–1965) Am. actress (sister of Ray; "Beulah" radio and TV series; *Porgy and Bess*; *Carmen Jones*)

Dandridge, Ray (Raymond Dandridge; "Hooks") (1913–) Am. baseball Hall-of-Famer (brother of Dorothy)

D'Angelo, Beverly (1952–) Am. actress (*Coal Miner's Daughter*; *Hair*; *Annie Hall*)

Dangerfield, Rodney (Jacob Cohen; a/k/a Jack Roy) (1921–) Am. comedian (signature phrase: "I don't get no respect")

Daniel, Glyn E. (Glyn Edmund Daniel) (1914–1986) Wel. archaeologist/writer (*Ancient Peoples and Places* series)

Daniels, Bebe (Virginia [or Phyllis] Daniels) (1901–1971) Scot.-Am. actress (*The Maltese Falcon*; *Rio Rita*)

Daniels, Charlie (1936–) Am. country/pop singer/musician ("The Devil Went Down to Georgia")

Daniels, Faith (1957–) Am. talk show host

Daniels, Jeff (1955–) Am. actor (*The Purple Rose of Cairo*; *Arachnophobia*; *The Butcher's Wife*; *Radio Days*)

Danko, Rick (1942–) Can.-Am. rock bassist (with The Band)

Dannay, Fred (Frederic Dannay; born Daniel Nathan; with Manfred Lee, a/k/a Ellery Queen and Barnaby Ross) (1905–1982) Am. detective story writer

Danner, Blythe (Blythe Katherine Danner) (1943–) Am. actress (mother of Gwyneth Paltrow; *The Great Santini*)

Danning, Sybil ("Queen of the Killer B's") (C) Aus.-Am. B-movie actress (*Hercules*; *Chained Heat*; *Warrior Queen*)

Dano, Linda (1943–) Am. actress ("Another World" soap opera)

Dano, Royal (Royal Edward Dano) (1922–) Am. actor (*The Red Badge of Courage*; *King of Kings*)

Danson, Ted (Edward Bridge Danson III) (1947–) Am. actor ("Cheers" TV series; *Cousins*; *The Onion Field*; *Three Men and a Baby*; E—1989/90)

Dante (Dante Alighieri) (1265–1321) Ital. poet (*The Divine Comedy*; *Inferno*)

Dantine, Helmut (1917–1982) Aus. actor (*Mrs. Miniver*; *Casablanca*)

Dantley, Adrian (1956–) Am. basketball player

Danton, Ray (Raymond Danton) (1931–1992) Am. actor (*The George Raft Story*; *The Longest Day*)

Danza, Tony (Anthony Iadanza) (1950–) Am. actor ("Who's the Boss?" and "Taxi" TV series)

D'Arblay, Madame see Burney, Fanny

Darby, Kim (Deborah Elias Zerby) (1947–) Am. actress (*True Grit*)

D'Arby, Terence Trent (Terence Trent Darby) (1962–) Am.-Eng. pop singer ("Wishing Well"; "Sign Your Name")

Darden, Severn (1929–) Am. actor ("Mary Hartman, Mary Hartman" TV series)

Dare, Virginia (1587) first child born in America of English parents

Darin, Bobby (Walden Robert Cassotto) (1936–1973) Am. rock/pop singer ("Mack the Knife"; "Splish Splash")

Darío, Rubén (Felix Rubén Garcia Sarmiento) (1867–1916) Nic. "modernismo" poet (*Profane Hymns*)

Darius the Great (Darius I) (550–486 B.C.) king of Persia 522–486 B.C.

Dark, Al or Alvin (Alvin Ralph Dark; "The Swamp Fox"; "Blackie") (1922–) Am. baseball player/manager

Darling, Ron (Ronald Maurice Darling, Jr.) (1960–) Am. baseball pitcher

Darman, Richard (Richard Gordon Darman) (1943–) Am. politician/govt. official

Darnell, Linda (Monetta Eloyse Darnell) (1921–1965) Am. actress (*A Letter to Three Wives*; *Blood and Sand*)

Darren, James (James William Ercolani) (1936–) Am. actor ("Time Tunnel" and "T. J. Hooker" TV series)

Darrieux, Danielle (1917–) Fr. actress (*The Rage of Paris*; *Alexander the Great*)

Darrow, Clarence (Clarence Seward Darrow; "Defender of the Damned") (1857–1938) Am. lawyer (defense attorney)

Darwell, Jane (Patti Woodward) (1879–1967) Am. actress (*The Ox-Bow Incident*; *O—1940—The Grapes of Wrath*)

Darwin, Charles (Charles Robert Darwin) (1809–1882) Eng. naturalist/evolutionist (*Origin of Species*)

Darwin, Danny (Danny Wayne Darwin) (1955–) Am. baseball pitcher

Da Silva, Howard (Harold Silverblatt) (1909–1986) Am. actor/theatrical director

Dassin, Jules (Julius Dassin; a/k/a Perlo Vita) (1911–) Am. film director (Rififi; Never on Sunday)

Daudet, Alphonse (Alphonse Marie Leon Daudet) (1840–1897) Fr. novelist/playwright (La Dernière Idole)

Daumier, Honoré (1808–1879) Fr. painter/sculptor/caricaturist

Dauphin, Claude (Claude Franc Nohain) (1903–1978) Fr. actor (Phantom of the Rue Morgue; Is Paris Burning?)

Davenport, Nigel (Arthur Nigel Davenport) (1928–) Eng. actor (A Man for All Seasons; Look Back in Anger)

Daves, Delmer (1904–1977) Am. film director (Destination Tokyo; The Petrified Forest)

Davi, Robert (c. 1953–) Am. actor (License to Kill; Action Jackson)

David (died 962 B.C.) second king of Israel and Judea (c. 1000–c. 962 B.C.)

David, Gerard (c. 1460–1523) Dutch religious painter

David, Hal (1921–) Am. lyricist ("What the World Needs Now Is Love"; "Close to You")

David, Louis (Jacques-Louis David) (1748–1825) Fr. painter (founded the French Neoclassical school of painting)

Davidovich, Lolita ("Lolly") (1961–) Am. actress (Blaze; Leap of Faith; Intersection)

Davidson, Jo (1883–1952) Am. sculptor (busts of Woodrow Wilson, Anatole France, Gertrude Stein)

Davidson, John (John Hamilton Davidson) (1941–) Am. actor/singer/TV host ("That's Incredible"; "Hollywood Squares")

Davidtz, Embeth (c. 1966–) Am. actress (Army of Darkness; Schindler's List)

Davies, Marion (Marion Cecilia Douras) (1897–1961) Am. actress (protégée of W. R. Hearst)

Davies, Sir Peter (Peter Maxwell Davies) (1934–) Eng. composer (Eight Songs for a Mad King)

Davies, Ray (1944–) Eng. rock singer (with The Kinks; "Lola")

Davies, Robertson (William Robertson Davies) (1913–) Can. writer (The Depford Trilogy; What's Bred in the Bone)

Davies, Rupert (1916–1976) Eng. actor (TV's Inspector Maigret)

Da Vinci, Leonardo (1452–1519) Ital. painter/sculptor/architect/engineer

Davis, Adelle (Daisie Adelle Davis) (1904–1974) Am. nutritionist/writer (Let's Eat Right to Keep Fit)

Davis, Angela (Angela Yvonne Davis) (1944–) Am. civil rights leader/writer (Women, Race and Class)

Davis, Ann B. (Ann Bradford Davis) (1926–) Am. actress ("The Brady Bunch" TV series; E—1957, 1958/59)

Davis, Bette (Ruth Elizabeth Davis) (1908–1989) Am. actress (Hush . . . Hush, Sweet Charlotte; Now Voyager; O—1935—Dangerous; O—1938—Jezebel)

Davis, Billy, Jr. (1940–) Am. pop/soul singer (formerly with The Fifth Dimension)

Davis, Brad (Robert Davis) (1949–1991) Am. actor (Midnight Express; The Player)

Davis, Chili (Charles Theodore Davis) (1960–) Am. baseball player

Davis, Clifton (1945–) Am. actor ("Amen" TV series)

Davis, Geena (Virginia Davis) (1957–) Am. actress (O—1988—The Accidental Tourist; Thelma and Louise; A League of Their Own)

Davis, Jefferson (1808–1889) Am. statesman/Confederate pres.

Davis, Jim (1915–1981) Am. actor ("Dallas" TV series)

Davis, Jim (James Robert Davis) (1945–) Am. cartoonist (Garfield)

Davis, Joan (Madonna Josephine Davis) (1907–1961) Am. actress ("I Married Joan" TV series)

Davis, Jody (Jody Richard Davis) (1956–) Am. baseball player

Davis, Judy (1956–) Austral. actress (My Brilliant Career; A Passage to India; Husbands and Wives)

Davis, Mac (Morris Mac Davis) (1942–) Am. country/pop singer ("Baby Don't Get Hooked on Me")

Davis, Martha (1951–) Am. rock singer (with The Motels; "Suddenly Last Summer")

Davis, Miles (Miles Dewey Davis, III) (1926–1991) Am. jazz trumpeter

Davis, Ossie (1917–) Am. actor (Jungle Fever; "Evening Shade" TV series)/film director (Cotton Comes to Harlem)

Davis, Owen (Owen Gould Davis) (1874–

1956) Am. playwright (P—1923— *Icebound*)

Davis, Patti (1952–) Am. writer (daughter of Ronald and Nancy Reagan; *Home Front*; *The Way I See It*)

Davis, Sammi (1964–) Eng. actress (*Mona Lisa*; *Hope and Glory*; "Homefront" TV series)

Davis, Sammy, Jr. (1925–1990) Am. entertainer/singer ("The Candy Man")

Davis, Skeeter (Mary Frances Penick) (1931–) Am. country singer ("The End of the World")

Davis, Spencer (1942–) Wel.-Eng. rock musician ("I'm a Man"; "Gimme Some Lovin'")

Davis, Tommy (Herman Thomas Davis; "Uncle Tired") (1939–) Am. baseball player

Davis, Willie (William Henry Davis; "Comet") (1934–) Am. football Hall-of-Famer

Davison, Bruce (1946–) Am. actor (*Long-time Companion*; *Short Cuts*)

Davisson, Clinton (Clinton Joseph Davisson) (1881–1958) Am. physicist (N—1937)

Dawber, Pam (1951–) Am. actress ("Mork & Mindy" and "My Sister Sam" TV series)

Dawes, Charles G. (Charles Gates Dawes) (1865–1951) Am. v.p. (C. Coolidge) (N—1925)

Dawkins, Daryl (1957–) Am. basketball player

Dawson, Len (Leonard Ray Dawson) (1935–) Am. football Hall-of-Famer

Dawson, Richard (1932–) Am. game show host ("Family Feud")

Day, Bobby (Robert Byrd) (1934–) Am. pop singer ("Rockin' Robin")

Day, Clarence (Clarence Shepard Day, Jr.) (1874–1935) Am. playwright/writer (*Life with Father*)

Day, Doris (Doris von Kappelhoff) (1924–) Am. singer ("Que Sera, Sera")/actress (*Pillow Talk*; *Love Me or Leave Me*)

Day, Laraine (La Raine Johnson) (1917–) Am. actress (*Foreign Correspondent*; *Dr. Kildare* films)

Day, Morris (C) Am. soul/pop singer (with Morris Day and the Time; "Fishnet")

Dayan, Moshe (1915–1981) Isr. mil./political leader/writer (*Diary of the Sinai Campaign*)

Day Lewis, C. (Cecil Day Lewis; a/k/a Nicholas Blake) (1904–1972) Eng. mystery writer (as Blake)/poet laureate (*The Magnetic Mountain*)

Day-Lewis, Daniel (1958–) Eng. actor (O—1989—*My Left Foot*; *My Beautiful Laundrette*; *The Last of the Mohicans*; *The Age of Innocence*)

Dayne, Taylor (Leslie Wonderman) (1962–) Am. pop singer ("I'll Always Love You"; "Love Will Lead You Back")

Dean, Billy (1962–) Am. country singer ("Only the Wind"; "Somewhere in My Broken Heart")

Dean, Dizzy (Jay Hanna Dean) (1911–1974) Am. baseball Hall-of-Famer

Dean, James (James Byron Dean) (1931–1955) Am. actor (*Rebel without a Cause*; *East of Eden*; *Giant*)

Dean, Jimmy (Jimmy Ray Dean; born Seth Ward) (1928–) Am. country singer ("Big Bad John")/sausage merchant

Dean, John (John Wesley Dean III) (1938–) Am. lawyer/presidential adviser (Nixon)/Watergate participant/writer (*Blind Ambition*)

Deane, Silas (1737–1789) Am. diplomat/lawyer

Dearden, Basil (Basil Dear) (1911–1971) Eng. film director (father of James; *The League of Gentlemen*; *Man in the Moon*)

Dearden, James (1949–) Eng.-Am. film writer/director (*Fatal Attraction*; *A Kiss Before Dying*)

Dearie, Blossom (1926–) Am. singer

Debakey, Michael Ellis (1908–) Am. surgeon (first successful human artificial heart transplant, 1966)/writer (*The Living Heart*)

DeBarge, Bunny (1955–) Am. pop musician (with DeBarge; "Rhythm of the Night"; "Who's Holding Donna Now")

DeBarge, El (Eldra DeBarge) (1961–) Am. pop singer (with DeBarge)

DeBarge, James (1963–) Am. pop musician (with DeBarge)

DeBarge, Mark (1959–) Am. pop musician (with DeBarge)

DeBarge, Randy (1958–) Am. pop musician (with DeBarge)

De Beauvoir, Simone (Simone Lucie Ernestine Marie Bertrand de Beauvoir) (1908–1986) Fr. novelist/essayist (*The Second Sex*)

Debeck, Billy (1890–1942) Am. cartoonist (*Barney Google*)

De Broca, Phillipe (Phillipe Claude Alex De Broca) (1933–) Fr. film director (*King of Hearts*)

Debs, Eugene V. (Eugene Victor Debs) (1855–1926) Am. socialist/labor organizer

Deburgh, Chris (Christopher John Davidson) (1948–) Ir. pop singer ("The Lady in Red")

DeBusschere, Dave ("The Buffalo") (1940–) Am. basketball player/executive

Debussy, Claude (Achille-Claude Debussy) (1862–1918) Fr. composer (*Clair de Lune*)

Debye, Peter (Peter Joseph William Debye; orig. Petrus Josephus Wilhelmus Debije) (1884–1966) Am. chemist (N— 1936)

De Camp, L. Sprague (Lyon Sprague De Camp) (1907–) Am. science fiction writer (*The Ancient Engineers*)

De Camp, Rosemary (1910–) Am. actress ("The Bob Cummings Show" and "That Girl" TV series)

De Carlo, Yvonne (Peggy Yvonne Middleton) (1924–) Can.-Am. actress ("The Munsters" TV series)

Decinces, Doug (Douglas Vernon Decinces) (1950–) Am. baseball player

Decker, Mary (Mary Teresa Decker; a/k/a Mary Decker-Slaney; "Little Mary") (1958–) Am. runner

De Concini, Dennis (Dennis Webster De Concini) (1937–) Am. senator

Dee, Frances (Jean Dee) (1907–) Am. actress (*Playboy of Paris*; *Little Women*)

Dee, Joey (1940–) Am. pop singer/musician ("Peppermint Twist"; with Joey Dee and The Starlighters)

Dee, Kiki (Pauline Matthews) (1947–) Eng. pop singer ("Don't Go Breaking My Heart" duet with Elton John)

Dee, Ruby (Ruth Ann Wallace) (1923–) Am. actress (*A Raisin in the Sun*; *The Jackie Robinson Story*)

Dee, Sandra (Alexandra Zuck) (1942–) Am. actress (*Imitation of Life*; *A Summer Place*)

Deer, Rob (Robert George Deer) (1960–) Am. baseball player

Deere, John (1804–1886) Am. industrialist/manufacturer of steel plows

Dees, Rick (Rigdon Osmond Dees III) (1950–) Am. disc jockey/TV host/pop singer ("Disco Duck")

Defoe, Daniel (Daniel Foe) (1660–1731) Eng. novelist (*Robinson Crusoe*; *Moll Flanders*)

DeFore, Don (1917–1994) Am. actor ("The Adventures of Ozzie and Harriet" and "Hazel" TV series)

De Forest, Lee ("Father of Radio") (1873–1961) Am. inventor (triode; dubbing systems; camera blimp)

De Franco, Buddy (Boniface Ferdinand Leonardo De Franco) (1933–) Am. jazz clarinetist

Degas, Edgar (Hilaire-Germain-Edgar Degas) (1834–1917) Fr. impressionist painter

De Gaulle, Charles (Charles-André-Marie-Joseph De Gaulle) (1890–1970) Fr. soldier/statesman (pres.)

De Haven, Gloria (Gloria Mildred De Haven) (1924–) Am. actress (*The Thin Man Goes Home*; *Broadway Rhythm*; "Ryan's Hope" soap opera)

De Havilland, Olivia (Olivia Mary De Havilland) (1916–) Am. actress (sister of Joan Fontaine; Melanie in *Gone With the Wind*; O—1946—*To Each His Own*; O—1949—*The Heiress*)

Deighton, Len (Leonard Cyril Deighton) (1929–) Eng. spy novelist (*The Ipcress File*; *Funeral in Berlin*)

De Klerk, F. W. (Frederik Willem de Klerk) (1936–) S. Afr. pres. 1989–

De Kooning, Willem (1904–) Am. abstract expressionist painter

Delacroix, Eugène (Ferdinand-Victor-Eugène Delacroix) (1798–1863) Fr. "romantic" painter/muralist

Delahanty, Ed (Edward James Delahanty; "Big Ed"; "The Only Del") (1867–1903) Am. baseball Hall-of-Famer

De La Mare, Walter (Walter John De La Mare; a/k/a Walter Ramal) (1873–1956) Eng. poet/novelist (*Memoirs of a Midget*)

Delaney & Bonnie see Bramlett, Delaney, and Bramlett, Bonnie

Delaney, Shelagh (1939–) Eng. playwright (*A Taste of Honey*; *The House That Jack Built*)

Delany, Dana (1956–) Am. actress ("China Beach" TV series; *Wild Palms*)

Delany, Martin (Martin Robinson Delany) (1812–1885) Am. orator/writer/mil. officer (first Afr.-Am. to receive a commission [major] in the U.S. Army)

Delany, Samuel (Samuel Ray Delany) (1942–) Am. science fiction writer (*The Bridge of Lost Desire*; *Nova*)

De La Renta, Oscar (1932–) Am. fashion designer

Delaroche, Paul (Hippolyte-Paul Delaroche) (1797–1856) Fr. painter/muralist

De Laurentiis, Dino (Agostino Dino De Laurentiis) (1919–) Ital. film producer (*Barbarella*; *Blue Velvet*)

Delbrück, Max (1906–1981) Am. biologist/physicist (N—1969)

Deledda, Grazia (Grazia Madesani) (1875–1936) Ital. novelist (N—1926)

De León, Ponce (Juan Ponce De León) (1460–1521) Span. explorer (founded San Juan, Puerto Rico; discovered Florida)

Delibes, Léo (Clément-Philibert-Léo Delibes) (1836–1891) Fr. composer (*Lakme*; *Coppelia*)

Delibes, Miguel (Miguel Delibes Setién) (1920–) Span. novelist/essayist/short story writer (*The Path*)

Delillo, Don (1936–) Am. novelist (*The Day Room*; *White Noise*)

Delius, Frederick (Frederick Theodore Albert Delius) (1862–1934) Eng. composer (*Appalachia*)

Dell, Gabriel (Gabriel del Vecchio) (1919–) Am. actor (one of the Dead End Kids)

Della Robbia, Luca (Luca di Simone di Marco della Robbia) (1400–1482) Ital. sculptor

Dello Joio, Norman (Norman Joseph Dello Joio) (1913–) Am. composer (*The Triumph of St. Joan*; P—1957—*Meditations on Ecclesiastes*)

Delon, Alain (1935–) Fr. actor (*Borsalino*; *Is Paris Burning?*)

De Lorean, John (John Zachary De Lorean) (1925–) Am. automobile manufacturer (arrested on drug charges in 1982; acquitted)

Del Rey, Lester (Lester Ramon Alvarez Del Rey) (1915–) Am. science fiction writer/anthologist

Del Rio, Dolores (Lolita Dolores Martinez Asunsolo Lopez Negrette) (1905–1983) Mex. actress (*Journey into Fear*)

De Luca, Giuseppe (1876–1950) Ital. opera singer (baritone)

Delucia, Paco (Francisco Sanchez Gomez) (1947–) Span. classical guitarist

Delugg, Milton (1918–) Am. orchestra leader

Deluise, Dom (a/k/a The Great Dominick) (1933–) Am. actor (*Loose Cannons*; *The Cannonball Run*)/magician/comedian (father of Peter)

Deluise, Peter (c. 1967–) Am. actor (son of Dom; "21 Jump Street" TV series)

Demarest, William (1892–1983) Am. actor ("My Three Sons" TV series)

Demaris, Ovid (1919–) Am. writer (*The Boardwalk Jungle*; *The Last Mafioso*)

De Mille, Agnes (Agnes George De Mille) (1905–1993) Am. theatrical choreographer (niece of Cecil B.; *Oklahoma!*; *Brigadoon*; *Carousel*)

De Mille, Cecil B. (Cecil Blount De Mille) (1881–1959) Am. film director/producer (*The Ten Commandments*; *Cleopatra*)

Demille, Nelson (1943–) Am. novelist (*The Charm School*)

Demme, Jonathan (1944–) Am. film director (*Swing Shift*; *Married to the Mob*; O—1991—*The Silence of the Lambs*)

Democritus ("The Laughing Philosopher"; "The Aberdite") (c. 460–c. 370 B.C.) Gr. philosopher

De Mornay, Rebecca (1961–) Am. actress (*Risky Business*; *The Hand That Rocks the Cradle*)

Demosthenes (384–322 B.C.) Ath. orator/statesman (*Philippics*)

Dempsey, Jack (William Harrison Dempsey; "The Manassa Mauler") (1895–1983) Am. boxer/restauranteur

Dempsey, Patrick (1966–) Am. actor (*Coupe De Ville*; *Can't Buy Me Love*)

Dench, Dame Judi (Judith Olivia Dench) (1934–) Eng. stage/film actress (*84 Charing Cross Road*)

Deneuve, Catherine (Catherine Dorléac) (1943–) Fr. actress (*Indochine*; *Repulsion*; *Belle de Jour*)

Deng Xiaoping (1904–) Chin. political leader

De Niro, Robert (1943–) Am. actor (*Mean Streets*; *Taxi Driver*; O—1974—*The Godfather, Part II*; O—1980—*Raging Bull*)

Denis, Saint (died c. 258) patron saint of France

Dennehy, Brian (1939–) Am. actor (*The Belly of an Architect*; *Presumed Innocent*)

Denning, Richard (Louis Albert Denninger) (1914–) Am. actor ("Hawaii Five-O" TV series)

Dennis, Cathy (1970–) Eng. pop singer ("Moments of Love"; "Too Many Walls"; formerly with D-Mob)

Dennis, Patrick (Edward Everett Tanner III; a/k/a Virginia Rowens) (1921–1976) Am. novelist (*Auntie Mame*)

Dennis, Sandy (Sandra Dale Dennis) (1937–1992) Am. actress (*Up the Down Staircase*; O—1966—*Who's Afraid of Virginia Woolf?*; T—1964)

Denny, Reginald (Reginald Leigh Daymore) (1891–1967) Eng. actor (*Mr. Blandings Builds His Dream House*; *Anna Karenina*)

Densmore, John (1945–) Am. rock musician (with The Doors)

Dent, Bucky (Russell Earl O'Dey) (1951–) Am. baseball player

Denver, Bob (1935–) Am. actor ("Gilligan's Island" [title role] TV series)

Denver, John (Henry John Deutschendorf, Jr.) (1943–) Am. pop singer ("Rocky Mountain High")/songwriter ("Leaving on a Jet Plane")

Deodato (Eumir Deodato Almeida) (1942–) Braz. musician (*Also* "Sprach Zarathustra" [*2001*])

DePalma, Brian (Brian Russell DePalma) (1940–) Am. film director (*Dressed to Kill*; *Body Double*; *The Untouchables*; *Carrie*)

Depardieu, Gérard (1948–) Fr. actor (*Cyrano De Bergerac*; *Green Card*)

Depp, Johnny (John Christopher Depp, Jr.) (1963–) Am. actor (*Edward Scissorhands*; *Benny & Joon*; "21 Jump Street" TV series)

De Quincey, Thomas (1785–1859) Eng. essayist/critic (*Confessions of an English Opium Eater*)

Derain, André (1880–1954) Fr. Fauvist painter/illustrator/theatrical designer

Derek, Bo (Mary Cathleen Collins) (1956–) Am. actress (*10*)

Derek, John (Derek Harris) (1926–) Am. actor/film director (*Bolero*)

Derleth, August (August William Derleth) (1909–1971) Am. novelist/poet (*Sac Prairie Saga*)

Dern, Bruce (Bruce MacLeish Dern) (1936–) Am. actor (*Coming Home*; *After Dark, My Sweet*; *Wild at Heart*)

Dern, Laura (Laura Elizabeth Dern) (1966–) Am. actress (daughter of Bruce; *Rambling Rose*; *Jurassic Park*)

Derringer, Rick (Rick Zehringer) (1947 or 1949–) Am. rock singer/musician ("Rock and Roll, Hoochie Koo")

Dershowitz, Alan (Alan Morton Dershowitz) (1938–) Am. lawyer/writer (*Reversal of Fortune*)

De Sade, Marquis (Donatien-Alphonse-François de Sade) (1740–1814) Fr. soldier/writer (*Justine*; *Juliette*)

Desai, Anita (1937–) Ind. novelist (*Bye-Bye Blackbird*; *Clear Light of Day*)

Descartes, René (1596–1650) Fr. philosopher ("I think, therefore I am")

Deshannon, Jackie (1944–) Am. pop singer ("What the World Needs Now Is Love")

De Sica, Vittorio (1901–1974) Ital. film actor/director (*The Bicycle Thief*; *The Garden of the Finzi-Continis*)

Desmond, Paul (Paul Breitenfield) (1924–1977) Am. jazz saxophonist

Desmond, William (William Mannion) (1878–1949) Ir.-Am. cowboy actor (*Arizona Days*)

De Soto, Hernando (c. 1496–1542) Span. explorer (discovered the Mississippi River)

Desylva, Buddy (George Gard Desylva) (1895–1950) Am. lyricist ("April Showers"; "Look for the Silver Lining")

Detaille, Édouard (Jean-Baptiste-Édouard Detaille) (1848–1912) Fr. painter (battle scenes)

De Valera, Eamon (1882–1975) Ir. prime minister 1937–1948, 1951–1954, 1957–1959/pres. 1959–1973

Devane, William (1939–) Am. actor ("Knots Landing" TV series; *Family Plot*; *Marathon Man*)

Devine, Andy (Jeremiah Schwartz) (1905–1977) Am. actor ("The Adventures of Wild Bill Hickok" and "Andy's Gang" TV series)

Devine, Dan (Daniel John Devine) (1924–) Am. football coach

Devito, Danny (Daniel Michael Devito) (1944–) Am. actor ("Taxi" TV series)/film director (*The War of the Roses*)

Devito, Karla (c. 1953–) Am. actress (*Modern Love*)

Devries, Peter (1910–1993) Am. novelist (*Sauce for the Goose*; *Slouching Towards Kalamazoo*; *The Prick of Noon*)

Dewar, Thomas Robert, 1st Baron Dewar of Homestall (1864–1930) Eng. distiller/sportsman

Dewey, George (1837–1917) Am. navy admiral

Dewey, John (1859–1952) Am. philosopher (developed Pragmatism)/educator/writer (*The Quest for Certainty*)

Dewey, Melvil (1851–1931) Am. librarian (created the Dewey Decimal System)

Dewey, Thomas E. (Thomas Edmund Dewey; "Gangbuster"; "The Boy Scout") (1902–1971) Am. gov. (of New York)/pres. candidate 1944, 1948

Dewhurst, Colleen (1924–1992) Can.-Am. actress (*Annie Hall*; *The Dead Zone*; also noted for stage performances: *Desire Under the Elms*; T—1974)

De Wilde, Brandon (Andre Brandon De Wilde) (1942–1972) Am. actor (*Shane*; *Hud*)

Dewitt, Joyce (1949–) Am. actress ("Three's Company" TV series)

De Wolfe, Billy (William Andrew Jones) (1907–1974) Am. comedian/actor ("The Doris Day Show" TV series)

Dey, Susan (Susan Hallock Dey; born Susan Smith) (1952–) Am. actress ("The Partridge Family" and "L.A. Law" TV series)

Deyoung, Cliff (1945–) Am. actor (*Harry and Tonto*)

Dheigh, Khigh (1910–1991) Am. actor (Wo-Fat [the villain] in "Hawaii Five-O" TV series)

Diaghilev, Sergey (Sergey Pavlovich Diaghilev) (1872–1929) Russ. ballet/art/ music impresario (founded Ballet Russe)

Diamond, David (1915–) Am. composer (symphonies)

Diamond, Legs (John Thomas Nolan) (1896–1931) Am. mobster

Diamond, Neil (Neil Leslie Diamond) (1941–) Am. pop singer/songwriter ("Sweet Caroline"; "Song Sung Blue"; "I Am . . . I Said")/actor (*The Jazz Singer*)

Diana, Princess of Wales *see* Spencer, Diana

Dias, Bartolomeu (c. 1450–1500) Port. explorer of Africa (first to sail around the Cape of Good Hope)

Díaz, Porfirio (José de la Cruz Porfirio Díaz) (1830–1915) Mex. general/dictator (pres. 1877–1880, 1884–1911)

Di Caprio, Leonardo (1974–) Am. actor (*This Boy's Life*; *What's Eating Gilbert Grape*)

Dick, A. B. (Albert Blake Dick) (1856–1934) Am. inventor (mimeograph)

Dick, Philip K. (Philip Kendrick Dick; a/k/a Richard Phillips) (1928–1982) Am. science fiction writer (*Do Androids Dream of Electric Sheep?* [filmed as *Blade Runner*])

Dickens, Charles (Charles John Huffam

Dickens; "Boz") (1812–1870) Eng. novelist (*Oliver Twist*; *Great Expectations*; *David Copperfield*; *Bleak House*; *A Tale of Two Cities*)

Dickens, Little Jimmy (James Cecil Dickens) (1920–) Am. country singer ("May the Bird of Paradise Fly Up Your Nose")

Dickey, Bill (William Malcolm Dickey; "Baseball's Quiet Man") (1907–1993) Am. baseball Hall-of-Famer

Dickey, James (James Lafayette Dickey) (1923–) Am. poet/novelist (*Deliverance*)

Dickinson, Angie (Angeline Brown) (1931–) Am. actress (*Dressed to Kill*; "Police Woman" TV series)

Dickinson, Bruce (Paul Bruce Dickinson) (1958–) Eng. rock singer (with Iron Maiden)

Dickinson, Emily (Emily Elizabeth Dickinson; "The Belle of Amherst") (1830–1886) Am. poet

Dickson, Gordon (Gordon Rupert Dickson) (1923–) Can. science fiction writer (*The Forever Man*; *None but Man*)

Diddley, Bo (Otha Elias Bates McDaniel) (1928–) Am. blues guitarist/singer/ songwriter ("Who Do You Love")

Diderot, Denis (a/k/a Pantophile Diderot) (1713–1784) Fr. philosopher (*Encyclopédie*)

Didion, Joan (1934–) Am. novelist/ essayist/journalist (*Slouching Towards Bethlehem*; *Play It As It Lays*)

Didrikson, Babe (Mildred Ella Didrikson; married name Zaharias) (1914–1956) Am. golfer/athlete

Diefenbaker, John (John George Diefenbaker) (1895–1979) Can. prime minister 1957–1963

Diesel, Rudolf (Rudolf Christian Karl Diesel) (1858–1913) Ger. mechanical engineer (built first diesel engine)

Dietrich, Marlene (born Maria Magdalene Dietrich; a/k/a Maria Magdalena Von Losch) (1901–1992) Ger.-Am. actress (*The Blue Angel*; *Blonde Venus*)

Dietz, Howard (Howard M. Dietz) (1896–1983) Am. lyricist ("That's Entertainment")/librettist (*The Band Wagon*)

Diffie, Joe (1960–) Am. country singer ("Ships That Don't Come In"; "New Way to Light Up an Old Flame")

Difford, Chris (1954–) Eng. pop singer/ musician (with Squeeze and Difford & Tilbrook)

Dillard, Annie (1945–) Am. writer (P— 1975—*Pilgrim at Tinker Creek*)

Diller, Barry (Barry Charles Diller) (1942–) Am. film executive (CEO of Fox network; owner of QVC shopping channel)

Diller, Phyllis (Phyllis Driver) (1917–) Am. comedienne

Dillinger, John (John Herbert Dillinger) (1902–1934) Am. outlaw (bank robberies, jail escapes)

Dillman, Bradford (1930–) Am. actor (*Compulsion*; "Falcon Crest" TV series)

Dillon, Kevin (1965–) Am. actor (brother of Matt; *Immediate Family*; *The Doors*)

Dillon, Matt (1964–) Am. actor (brother of Kevin; *Drugstore Cowboy*; *A Kiss before Dying*; *Singles*)

Dillon, Melinda (1939–) Am. actress (*Close Encounters of the Third Kind*; *The Prince of Tides*)

DiMaggio, Joe (Joseph Paul DiMaggio; "Joe D"; "Joltin' Joe"; "The Yankee Clipper") (1914–) Am. baseball Hall-of-Famer

Di Meola, Al (1954–) Am. jazz guitarist (formerly with Return to Forever)

D'Indy, Vincent (Paul-Marie-Théodore-Vincent d'Indy) (1851–1931) Fr. composer (*L'Etranger*)

Dinesen, Isak (Karen Christence Blixen-Finecke; a/k/a Pierre Andrezel) (1885–1962) Dan. short story writer/autobiographer (*Out of Africa*; *Shadows on the Grass*)

Dinkins, David (David Norman Dinkins) (1927–) Am. mayor of New York 1990–1993

Dio, Ronnie James (c. 1950–) Am. rock singer (with Black Sabbath and Rainbow)

Diogenes (died c. 320 B.C.) Gr. philosopher (founded the Cynics school)

Dion (Dion Di Mucci) (1939–) Am. pop singer ("Runaround Sue"; "The Wanderer")

Dion, Celine (1968–) Can. pop singer ("Where Does My Heart Beat Now"; "Beauty and the Beast")

Dionysius (c. 430–367 B.C.) Gr. mil. leader/tyrant

Dior, Christian (1905–1957) Fr. fashion designer

Dirks, Rudolph (1877–1968) Am. cartoonist (*The Katzenjammer Kids*)

Disney, Walt (Walter Elias Disney) (1901–1966) Am. pioneering animator/film producer/entertainment executive

Disraeli, Benjamin, 1st Earl of Beaconsfield (Benjamin D'Israeli; "Dizzy") (1804–1881) Eng. prime minister (1868, 1874–1880)

Ditka, Mike (Michael Keller Ditka; "Hammer") (1939–) Am. football coach/Hall-of-Famer

Ditko, Steve (1927–) Am. cartoonist (*Spider Man*)

Divine (Harris Glenn Milstead; a/k/a Glenn Divine) (1946–1989) Am. transvestite actor (in John Waters films)

Divine, Father (George Baker; a/k/a Major M. J. Divine) (c. 1880–1965) Am. evangelist (founded the Peace Mission movement)

Dix, Dorothea (Dorothea Lynde Dix) (1802–1887) Am. philanthropist/educator/social reformer

Dix, Dorothy (Elizabeth Seaman née Meriwether) (1870–1951) Am. journalist/advice columnist/writer (*How to Win and Hold a Husband*)

Dix, Otto (1891–1961) Ger. painter (developed "new realism")

Dixon, Donna (1957–) Am. actress ("Bosom Buddies" TV series)

Dixon, Ivan (Ivan N. Dixon III) (1931–) Am. actor ("Hogan's Heroes" TV series)

Dixon, Jeane (Jeane Pinckert Dixon) (1918–) Am. astrologer/columnist

Dixon, Willie (1915–1992) Am. blues singer/musician/songwriter

D. J. Jazzy Jeff (Jeff Townes) (C) Am. rapper ("Summertime")/actor ("The Fresh Prince of Bel Air" TV series)

Dmytryk, Edward (1908–) Can.-Am. film director (*Murder, My Sweet*; *Hitler's Children*; *The Caine Mutiny*)

Döblin, Alfred (1878–1957) Ger. writer (*Alexanderplatz, Berlin*)

Dobson, Kevin (1943–) Am. actor ("Knots Landing" TV series)

Dr. John (Malcolm John Creaux "Mac" Rebennack) (1940–) Am. rock/jazz pianist/singer ("Right Place Wrong Time")

Doctorow, E. L. (Edgar Lawrence Doctorow) (1931–) Am. novelist (*Ragtime*; *Billy Bathgate*; *Loon Lake*)

Dodge, Mary Elizabeth (Mary Elizabeth Mapes; a/k/a Mary Mapes Dodge) (1831–1905) Am. editor/children's book writer (*Hans Brinker, or the Silver Skates*)

Doerr, Bobby (Robert Pershing Doerr) (1918–) Am. baseball Hall-of-Famer

Doherty, Shannen (1971–) Am. actress (*Heathers*; "Beverly Hills, 90210" TV series)

Dohrn, Bernadine (Bernadine Rae Dohrn) (1942–) Am. radical activist (leader of the Weathermen)

Dolby, Thomas (Thomas Morgan Dolby Robertson) (1958–) Eng. rock singer/musician ("She Blinded Me with Science")

Dole, Bob (Robert Joseph Dole) (1923–) Am. senator

Dole, Elizabeth (Elizabeth Hanford Dole; "Liddy") (1936–) Am. politician (secretary of labor)

Dole, James Drummond ("The Pineapple King") (1877–1958) Am. businessman/pineapple exporter

Dolenz, Ami (1970–) Am. actress (daughter of Mickey; *She's Out of Control*)

Dolenz, Mickey (George Michael Dolenz) (1945–) Am. singer/actor (former drummer for The Monkees)

Dolly, Jenny (Janszieka Deutsch) (1892–1941) Hung.-Am. dancer (with The Dolly Sisters)

Dolly, Rosie (Roszika Deutsch) (1892–1970) Hung.-Am. dancer (with The Dolly Sisters)

Domenichino (Domenico Zampieri) (1581–1641) Ital. painter/architect

Domingo, Plácido (1941–) Span. opera singer (tenor)

Dominic, Saint (Domingo de Guzman) (c. 1170–1221) Span. founder of the Dominican order

Domino, Fats (Antoine Domino) (1928–) Am. jazz pianist ("Ain't That a Shame"; "Blueberry Hill")

Domitian (Titus Flavius Domitianus) (51–96) Roman emperor 81–96

Donahue, Phil (Philip John Donahue) (1935–) Am. talk show host

Donahue, Troy (Merle Johnson, Jr.) (1936–) Am. actor (*The Godfather, Part II*; *Imitation of Life*; "Hawaiian Eye" TV series)

Donaldson, Roger (1945–) Austral.-Am. film director (*No Way Out*; *White Sands*)

Donaldson, Sam (Samuel Andrew Donaldson, Jr.) (1934–) Am. newscaster ("Prime Time Live")

Donat, Robert (1905–1958) Eng. actor (*The Private Life of Henry VIII*; *The Count of Monte Cristo*; *O—1939—Goodbye, Mr. Chips*)

Donatello (Donato de Betto di Bardi)

(1386–1466) Flor. sculptor (*St. George Slaying the Dragon*)

Donegan, Lonnie (Anthony Donegan; "King of Skiffle") (1931–) Scot. jazz/rock singer/musician ("Does Your Chewing Gum Lose Its Flavor [On the Bedpost Overnight]")

Donen, Stanley (1924–) Am. film director (*Indiscreet*; *On the Town*; *Charade*)

Donizetti, Gaetano (Domenico Gaetano Maria Donizetti) (1797–1848) Ital. operatic composer (*Don Pasquale*)

Donleavy, J. P. (James Patrick Donleavy) (1926–) Ir. novelist/playwright/short story writer (*The Ginger Man*)

Donlevy, Brian (Grosson Brian Boru Donlevy) (1899–1972) Ir. actor (*The Great McGinty*; *Beau Geste*)

Donne, John (1572–1631) Eng. poet (*Songs and Sonnets*)

Donner, Clive (1926–) Eng. film director (*What's New, Pussycat?*)

Donner, Richard (1939–) Am. film director (*The Omen*; *Lethal Weapon*; *Radio Flyer*)

D'Onofrio, Vincent (Vincent Phillip D'Onofrio) (c. 1959–) Am. actor (*Mystic Pizza*; *Full Metal Jacket*; *Dying Young*)

Donohoe, Amanda (1962–) Eng. actress ("L.A. Law" TV series)

Donovan (Donovan Philip Leitch) (1943–) Am. rock singer ("Sunshine Superman"; "Mellow Yellow"; father of Ione Skye)

Donovan, Art (Arthur Donovan, Jr.) (1925–) Am. football Hall-of-Famer

Doohan, James (James Montgomery Doohan) (1920–) Can. actor (Scotty in *Star Trek* TV series and films)

Doppler, Christian (Christian Johann Doppler) (1803–1853) Aus. physicist (discovered the Doppler effect)

Doré, Gustave (Paul-Gustave Doré) (1832–1883) Fr. illustrator/painter

Doria, Andrea ("Father of Peace"; "Liberator of Genoa") (1466–1560) Ital. soldier/statesman

Dors, Diana (Diana Fluck) (1931–1984) Eng. actress (*Oliver Twist*)

Dorsett, Tony (Anthony Drew Dorsett; "Hawk"; "TD") (1954–) Am. football player

Dorsey, Jimmy (James Frances Dorsey) (1904–1957) Am. saxophonist/bandleader (brother of Tommy; "Besame Mucho")

Dorsey, Lee (Irving Lee Dorsey; a/k/a Kid Chocolate [in a short boxing career])

(1924–1986) Am. pop singer ("Working in the Coal Mine")

Dorsey, Tommy (Thomas Francis Dorsey; "Sentimental Gentleman of Swing") (1905–1956) Am. trombonist/bandleader (brother of Jimmy; "I'll Never Smile Again")

Dos Passos, John (John Roderigo Dos Passos) (1896–1970) Am. novelist (*U.S.A.* trilogy; *The Manhattan Transfer*)

Dostoyevsky, Fyodor (Fyodor Mikhaylovich Dostoyevsky) (1821–1881) Russ. novelist (*Crime and Punishment*; *The Brothers Karamazov*)

Doubleday, Abner ("The Father of Baseball") (1819–1893) Am. army officer (credited with inventing baseball)

Doubleday, Nelson (Frank Nelson Doubleday; "Effendi") (1862–1934) Am. publisher (founded Doubleday & Co.)

Douglas, Donald Wills (1892–1981) Am. aircraft designer/manufacturer (founded Douglas Aircraft; DC-1, DC-3)

Douglas, Helen (Helen Mary Douglas née Gahagan) (1900–1980) Am. politician/actress

Douglas, Kirk (Issur Danielovich Demsky; a/k/a Isidore Demsky) (1916–) Am. actor (father of Michael; *Lust for Life*; *Spartacus*)

Douglas, Lloyd C. (Lloyd Cassel Douglas) (1877–1951) Am. clergyman/novelist (*Magnificent Obsession*; *The Robe*)

Douglas, Melvyn (Melvyn Edouard Hesselberg) (1901–1981) Am. actor (*Ninotchka*; O—1963—*Hud*; O—1979—*Being There*; T—1960)

Douglas, Michael (Michael Kirk Douglas) (1944–) Am. actor (son of Kirk; *Fatal Attraction*; *Basic Instinct*; O—1987—*Wall Street*)/film producer ("One Flew Over the Cuckoo's Nest")

Douglas, Mike (Michael Delaney Dowd, Jr.) (1925–) Am. talk show host

Douglas, Norman (George Norman Douglas) (1868–1952) Eng. novelist (*South Wind*; *Siren Land*)

Douglas, Paul (1907–1959) Am. actor (*A Letter to Three Wives*; *Executive Suite*)

Douglas, Stephen A. (Stephen Arnold Douglas; "Little Giant") (1813–1861) Am. statesman/senator

Douglas, William O. (William Orville Douglas) (1898–1980) Am. Supreme Court jurist (1939–1975)/writer (*Go East, Young Man*)

Douglass, Frederick (Frederick Augustus Washington Bailey) (1817–1895) Am. abolitionist/writer (*Narrative of the Life of Frederick Douglass*)

Dourif, Brad (Brad C. Dourif) (1950–) Am. actor (*One Flew Over the Cuckoo's Nest*; *Dune*; *Jungle Fever*)

Dove, Ronnie (1940–) Am. country singer ("Right or Wrong"; "One Kiss for Old Time's Sake")

Dow, Peggy (Peggy Josephine Varnadow) (1928–) Am. actress (*Harvey*; *Bright Victory*)

Down, Lesley-Anne (1954–) Eng. actress ("Dallas" and "Upstairs, Downstairs" TV series; *The Pink Panther Strikes Again*)

Downey, Morton, Jr. (1932–) Am. talk show host

Downey, Robert, Jr. (1965–) Am. actor (*The Pick-Up Artist*; *Less Than Zero*; *Chaplin*)

Downs, Hugh (Hugh Malcolm Downs) (1921–) Am. newscaster ("20/20" TV series)

Doyle, Sir Arthur Conan (1859–1930) Scot.-Eng. novelist (created Sherlock Holmes)

Dozier, Lamont (a/k/a Lamont Anthony) (1941–) Am. pop songwriter (with Brian and Eddie Holland, "Heat Wave"; "Stop! In the Name of Love"; "Baby Love")

Drabble, Margaret (1939–) Eng. novelist (*The Millstone*)

Drabek, Doug (Douglas Dean Drabek) (1962–) Am. baseball pitcher

Drabowsky, Moe (Myron Walter Drabowsky; "The Snake Man") (1935–) Am. baseball pitcher

Draco or **Dracon** (died 650 B.C.) Ath. lawgiver

Dragon, Daryl (1942–) Am. pop musician (with The Captain and Tennille)

Drake, Alfred (Alfredo Capurro) (1914–1992) Ital.-Am. stage actor/singer (T—1954)

Drake, Betsy (1923–) Am. actress (*Every Girl Should Be Married*; *Will Success Spoil Rock Hunter?*)

Drake, Dona (Rita Novella; a/k/a Rita Rio) (1920–) Mex.-Am. actress/singer/dancer (*Road to Morocco*; *Valentino*)

Drake, Sir Francis ("The Terror of the Spanish Main"; "The Dragon") (1540 or 1543–1596) Eng. admiral/explorer (first Englishman to sail around the world)

Drake, Larry (C) Am. actor (Benny in "L.A. Law" TV series; *Dr. Giggles*; E—1987/88, 1988/89)
Draper, Polly (C) Am. actress ("thirtysomething" TV series)
Draper, Rusty (Farrell H. Draper) (1925–) Am. pop singer ("The Shifting, Whispering Sands")
Dravecky, Dave (David Francis Dravecky) (1956–) Am. baseball pitcher
Dreiser, Theodore (Theodore Herman Albert Dreiser) (1871–1945) Am. novelist (*Sister Carrie; An American Tragedy*)
Dresser, Davis (a/k/a Brett Halliday and Asa Baker) (1904–1977) Am. detective story writer (created Mike Shayne)
Dressler, Marie (Leila Maria Von Koerber) (1869–1934) Can.-Am. actress (*Dinner at Eight; Tugboat Annie*; O—1930/31—*Min and Bill*)
Drew, Ellen (Terry Ray) (1915–) Am. actress (*Christmas in July; Sing You Sinners*)
Drew, John (1954–) Am. basketball player
Drexler, Clyde ("The Glide") (1962–) Am. basketball player
Dreyer, Carl (Carl Theodor Dreyer) (1889–1968) Dan. film director (*Vampyr; The Passion of Joan of Arc*)
Dreyfus, Alfred (1859–1935) Court-martialed French mil. officer (treason charges investigated and dropped)
Dreyfuss, Richard (Richard Stephan Dreyfuss) (1947–) Am. actor (*Jaws; Close Encounters of the Third Kind*; O—1977—*The Goodbye Girl*)
Driscoll, Bobby (1937–1968) Am. child actor (*Song of the South; Treasure Island*)
Driscoll, Paddy (John L. Driscoll) (1896–1968) Am. football Hall-of-Famer
Dru, Joanne (Joanne Letitia La Cock) (1923–) Am. actress (sister of Peter Marshall; *All the King's Men; Red River*)
Drucker, Mort (1929–) Am. cartoonist (*Mad* magazine)
Drury, Allen (Allen Stuart Drury) (1918–) Am. journalist/novelist (P—1960—*Advise and Consent*)
Dryden, John (1631–1700) Eng. poet/playwright (*Absalom and Achitopel*)
Dryden, Spencer (1943–) Am. rock musician (with Jefferson Airplane)
Dryer, Fred (1946–) Am. actor (TV's "Hunter")
Drysdale, Don (Donald Scott Drysdale;

"Big D"; "Double D") (1936–1993) Am. baseball Hall-of-Famer
Duarte, José Napoléon (1926–1990) Salvadoran pres. 1984–1989
Dubois, Théodore (François-Clément-Théodore Dubois) (1837–1924) Fr. organist/composer (*Les Sept Paroles de Christ*)
Dubois, W. E. B. (William Edward Burghardt Dubois) (1868–1963) Am. civil rights leader/writer (*The Souls of Black Folk*)
Dubos, René (René Julius Dubos) (1901–1982) Fr.-Am. microbiologist/writer (P—1969—*So Human an Animal*)
Dubuffet, Jean (1901–1985) Fr. "art brut" painter/sculptor/lithographer
Duchamp, Marcel (1887–1968) Fr. avant-garde painter/artist (*Nude Descending a Staircase*)
Duchin, Eddy or Eddie (Edwin Frank Duchin; "Magic Fingers of Radio") (1909–1951) Am. pianist/bandleader
Duchin, Peter (Peter Oelrichs Duchin) (1937–) Am. orchestra leader/pianist (son of Eddy)
Duchovny, David (c. 1960–) Am. actor (*The Rapture; Kalifornia*; "The X Files" TV series)
Ducommun, Elie (1833–1906) Swi. journalist (N—1902)
Dudek, Les (C) Am. rock guitarist/producer
Dudley, Bill (William M. Dudley; "Bullet Bill"; "The Bullet") (1921–) Am. football Hall-of-Famer
Duesenberg, Samuel (Samuel Frederick Duesenberg) (1877–1932) Ger.-Am. automobile manufacturer
Duff *see* Duffy, Karen
Duff, Howard (1913–1990) Am. actor ("Dallas" and "Knots Landing" TV series)
Duff-Gordon, Lady Lucie (née Austin) (1821–1869) Eng. writer (*Letters from the Cape; Letters from Egypt*)
Duffy, Hugh (1866–1954) Am. baseball Hall-of-Famer
Duffy, Julia (1951–) Am. actress ("Newhart" and "Designing Women" TV series)
Duffy, Karen ("Duff") (c. 1962–) Am. "veejay" (MTV)
Duffy, Patrick (Patrick Garfield Duffy) (1949–) Am. actor ("Dallas" TV series)
Dufy, Raoul (Raoul Ernest Joseph Dufy) (1877–1953) Fr. Fauvist painter/designer

Dugan, Dennis (1948–) Am. actor (*Harry and Walter Go to New York*; "Moonlighting" TV series)

Dukakis, Kitty (Katherine Dickson) (1936–) Am. political wife of Michael/autobiographer (*Now You Know*)

Dukakis, Michael (Michael Stanley Dukakis) (1933–) Am. gov. of Massachusetts/pres. candidate 1988

Dukakis, Olympia (1931–) Am. actress (*Steel Magnolias*; O—1987—*Moonstruck*)

Dukas, Paul (Paul-Abraham Dukas) (1865–1935) Fr. composer (*The Sorcerer's Apprentice*)

Duke, Doris (1912–1993) Am. philanthropist/socialite

Duke, James Buchanan (1856–1925) Am. tobacco magnate/philanthropist (Duke University)

Duke, Vernon (Vladimir Dukelsky) (1903–1969) Am. film composer/songwriter ("April In Paris")

Duke, Patty (Anna Marie Patricia Duke; a/k/a Patty Duke-Astin) (1946–) Am. actress ("The Patty Duke Show" TV series; O—1962—*The Miracle Worker*)

Dulbecco, Renato (1914–) Am. molecular biologist/virologist (N—1975)

Dullea, Keir (1936–) Am. actor (*2001: A Space Odyssey*; *David and Lisa*)

Dulles, John Foster (1888–1959) Am. govt. official (secretary of state)/statesman

Dumas, Alexandre (a/k/a Dumas fils) (1824–1895) Fr. novelist/playwright (*Camille*)

Dumas, Sir Alexandre (a/k/a Dumas père; Davy de la Pailleterie) (1802–1870) Fr. novelist/playwright (*The Three Musketeers*; *The Count of Monte-Cristo*)

Dumaurier, Dame Daphne (a/k/a Lady Browning) (1907–1989) Eng. short story writer/suspense novelist (*The Birds*; *Rebecca*)

Dumbrille, Douglas (1890–1974) Can.-Am. actor ("The Life of Riley" TV series; *The Ten Commandments*)

Dumont, Margaret (Margaret Baker) (1889–1965) Am. comedienne (Marx Brothers movies)

Dunaway, Faye (Dorothy Faye Dunaway) (1941–) Am. actress (*Bonnie and Clyde*; *Chinatown*; O—1976—*Network*; "It Had to Be You" TV series)

Dunbar, Dixie (Christina Elizabeth Dunbar) (1915–) Am. dancer/actress (*Alexander's Ragtime Band*; *Rebecca of Sunnybrook Farm*)

Dunbar, Paul (Paul Laurence Dunbar) (1872–1906) Am. poet/short story writer/novelist (*Lyrics of Lowly Life*)

Duncan, Isadora (1878–1927) Am. dancer/modern dance pioneer

Duncan, Johnny (1938–) Am. country singer ("She Can Put Her Shoes Under My Bed Anytime")

Duncan, Mariano (Mariano Duncan Nalasco) (1963–) Am. baseball player

Duncan, Sandy (1946–) Am. actress ("The Hogan Family" TV series)

Dunham, Katherine (1910–) Am. dancer/choreographer

Dunn, Holly (1957–) Am. country singer/songwriter ("You Really Had Me Going")

Dunn, James (1905–1967) Am. actor (*Stand Up and Cheer*; O—1945—*A Tree Grows in Brooklyn*)

Dunn, Nora (1951–) Am. comedienne ("Saturday Night Live" TV series)

Dunn, Ronnie (Ronnie Gene Dunn) (1953–) Am. country singer (with Brooks & Dunn; "Boot Scootin' Boogie"; "Brand New Man")

Dunne, Dominick (1921–) Am. journalist/novelist (*An Inconvenient Woman*; *The Two Mrs. Grenvilles*)

Dunne, Finley Peter (1867–1936) Am. humorist (created Mr. Dooley; *Mr. Dooley in Peace and War*)

Dunne, Griffin (1955–) Am. actor (*Who's That Girl*; *My Girl*)

Dunne, Irene (Irene Marie Dunn) (1898–1990) Am. actress (*The Awful Truth*; *I Remember Mama*; *Cimarron*)

Dunne, John (John Gregory Dunne) (1932–) Am. novelist (*Delano*; *The Red, White and Blue*)

Dunne, Philip (1908–1992) Am. screenwriter/film director (*How Green Was My Valley*; *The Agony and the Ecstasy*)

Dunning, Debbe (c. 1966–) Am. actress (Tool Time girl in "Home Improvement" TV series)

Dunnock, Mildred (Mildred Dorothy Dunnock) (1904–1991) Am. actress (*Death of a Salesman*)

Dunston, Shawon (Shawon Donnell Dunston) (1963–) Am. baseball player

Dupont, F. I. (Francis Irenee Dupont) (1873–1942) Am. chemist/financier

Dupree, Robbie (Robert Dupuis) (1947–) Am. pop singer ("Steal Away")

Duran, Roberto ("Hands of Stone") (1951–) Pan. boxer

Durand, Asher B. (Asher Brown Durand) (1796–1886) Am. painter (*The Signing of the Declaration of Independence*)

Durant, Ariel (Ida Kaufman) (1898–1981) Am. historian (with husband Will; *The Story of Civilization*; P—1968— *Rousseau and the Revolution*)

Durant, Will (William James Durant) (1885–1981) Am. historian (with wife Ariel: P—1968—*Rousseau and the Revolution*)

Durante, Jimmy (James Francis Durante; "The Schnoz"; "Ol' Schnozzola") (1893– 1980) Am. comedian (signature phrase: "Goodnight, Mrs. Calabash, wherever you are"; theme song: "Inka Dinka Doo"; E—1952)

Duras, Marguerite (Marguerite Donnadieu) (1914–) Fr. writer (*Hiroshima, Mon Amour*; *The Lover*)

Durbin, Deanna (Edna Mae Durbin) (1921–) Can.-Am. actress (*Can't Help Singing*; *Three Smart Girls*)

Dürer, Albrecht (1471–1528) Ger. painter/ engraver

Durfee, Minta (1897–1975) Am. comedienne (Chaplin and Arbuckle films)

Durkin, Junior (Trent Durkin) (1915– 1935) Am. child actor (*Tom Sawyer*; *Huckleberry Finn*)

Durning, Charles (1933–) Am. actor ("Evening Shade" TV series; *Dog Day Afternoon*)

Durocher, Leo (Leo Ernest Durocher; "The Lip") (1905–1991) Am. baseball coach (coined the phrase "Nice guys finish last")

Durrell, Lawrence (Lawrence George Durrell; a/k/a Charles Norden) (1912–) Eng. novelist/poet/playwright (*The Alexandria Quartet*)

Dürrenmatt, Friedrich (Friedrich Duerrenmatt) (1921–) Swi. playwright/ novelist (*The Visit*)

Dury, Ian (1942–) Eng. rock/"new wave" singer/musician (with Ian Dury and The Blockheads; "Hit Me with Your Rythm Stick")

Duryea, Dan (Daniel Edward Duryea) (1907–1968) Am. actor (*Ministry of Fear*; *Scarlet Street*)

Duse, Eleonora ("Duse the God") (1858– 1924) Ital. stage actress

Dussault, Nancy (Nancy Elizabeth Dussault) (1936–) Am. actress ("Too Close

for Comfort" TV series)/TV host ("Good Morning, America")

Dutra, Olin (1901–1983) Am. golfer

Duvalier, François ("Papa Doc") (1907– 1971) Haitian pres. 1957–1971

Duvall, Robert (Robert Selden Duvall) (1931–) Am. actor (*The Great Santini*; *The Godfather*; O—1983—*Tender Mercies*)

Duvall, Shelley (1949–) Am. actress (*The Shining*; *Popeye*)/TV producer

Duveneck, Frank (Frank Decker) (1848– 1919) Am. painter/sculptor/educator

Du Vigneaud, Vincent (1901–1978) Am. biochemist (synthesized penicillin; N— 1955)

Duvivier, Julien (1896–1967) Fr. film director (*Flesh and Fantasy*; *Marie Chapdelaine*)

Dvorak, Ann (Ann McKim) (1912–1979) Am. actress (*Scarface* [1932]; *G-Men*)

Dvořák, Antonín (Antonín Leopold Dvořák) (1841–1904) Bohem. composer ("Humoresque")

Dwan, Allan (Joseph Aloysius Dwan) (1885–1981) Am. film director (*Sands of Iwo Jima*; *Heidi*; *Rebecca of Sunnybrook Farm*)

Dykstra, Lenny (Lenny Kyle Dykstra; "Nails") (1963–) Am. baseball player

Dylan, Bob (Robert Allen Zimmerman) (1941–) Am. rock singer/songwriter ("Blowin' in the Wind"; "Like a Rolling Stone" with The Traveling Wilburys)

Dysart, Richard (Richard Allan Dysart) (1929–) Am. actor ("L.A. Law" TV series)

Dzundza, George (1945–) Am. actor (*The Butcher's Wife*; *No Mercy*; *White Hunter, Black Heart*)

Eakins, Thomas (1844–1916) Am. painter/ sculptor

Eames, Charles (1907–1978) Am. furniture designer

Earhart, Amelia (Amelia Mary Earhart; "Lady Lindy") (1897–1937) Am. aviatrix (first solo flight from Hawaii to mainland America; vanished on her last flight)

Earle, Merie (c. 1889–1984) Am. actress ("The Waltons" TV series)

Earle, Steve (1955–) Am. country singer ("Copperhead Road")

Early, Jubal (Jubal Anderson Early; "Old Jube"; "Old Jubilee") (1816–1894) Am. Confederate army general

Earp, Wyatt (Wyatt Berry Stappe Earp)

(1848–1929) Am. frontiersman/lawman (participated in the gunfight at the O.K. Corral)

Eastman, George (1854–1932) Am. industrialist/inventor (roll film, Kodak camera)

Eastman, Max (Max Forrester Eastman) (1883–1969) Am. editor (*Reader's Digest*)/writer (*Heroes I Have Known*)

Easton, Elliot (Elliot Shapiro) (1953–) Am. rock guitarist (with The Cars)

Easton, Sheena (Sheena Shirley Orr) (1959–) Scot. pop singer ("Morning Train"; "For Your Eyes Only"; "Strut"; G—1981)

Eastwood, Clint (Clinton Eastwood, Jr.) (1930–) Am. actor (*In the Line of Fire*; *Dirty Harry*)/film director (*A Perfect World*; O—1993—*Unforgiven*)

Eazy-E (Eric Wright) (1973–) Am. rapper (with N.W.A.)

Ebb, Fred (1933–) Am. lyricist (*Cabaret*)

Eberhart, Mignon G. (Mignon Good Eberhart) (1899–) Am. detective story writer (created sleuth Nurse Sarah Keate)

* **Eberhart, Richard** (Richard Ghormley Eberhart) (1904–) Am. poet (P—1966—*Selected Poems*)

Eberle, Ray (1919–1979) Am. singer (with Glenn Miller's band)/bandleader

Ebert, Roger (Roger Joseph Ebert) (1942–) Am. film critic (P—1975)

Ebsen, Buddy (Christian Rudolf Ebsen, Jr.) (1908–) Am. actor ("The Beverly Hillbillies" and "Barnaby Jones" TV series)

Eckstine, Billy (William Clarence Eckstine; "The Fabulous Mr. B") (1914–1993) Am. singer/bandleader ("Body and Soul")

Eco, Umberto (1932–) Ital. novelist (*The Name of the Rose*)

Edberg, Stefan (1966–) Am. tennis player (W—1988, 1990)

Eddy, Duane (1938–) Am. country guitarist/songwriter ("Rebel-'Rouser"; "Because They're Young")

Eddy, Mary Baker (Mary Morse Eddy née Baker) (1821–1910) Am. founder of Christian Science

Eddy, Nelson (1901–1967) Am. singer ("Indian Love Call"; duets with Jeanette MacDonald)/actor (*The Phantom of the Opera*)

Edel, Leon (Joseph Leon Edel) (1907–) Can.-Am. biographer (*The Conquest of London*; P—1963—*Henry James: Vols. II and III*)

Edelman, Gerald (Gerald Maurice Edelman) (1929–) Am. biochemist (N—1972)

Edelman, Herb (Herbert Edelman) (1930–) Am. actor ("The Golden Girls" TV series)

Eden, Sir Anthony (Robert Anthony Eden, Earl of Avon) (1897–1977) Eng. prime minister 1955–1957

Eden, Barbara (Barbara Huffman) (1934–) Am. actress ("I Dream of Jeannie" TV series)

Ederle, Gertrude (Gertrude Caroline Ederle) (1906–) Am. swimmer (first woman to swim the English Channel [1926])

Edge, The (David Evans) (1961–) Ir. rock guitarist (with U2)

Edison, Thomas (Thomas Alva Edison; "The Wizard of Menlo Park") (1847–1931) Am. inventor (phonograph, microphone; stock ticker, incandescent lamp, alkaline battery, carbon filament, light bulb [with J. W. Swan])

Edmonds, Walter D. (Walter Dumaux Edmonds) (1903–) Am. novelist (*Drums Along the Mohawk*)

Edmunds, Dave (1944–) Wel. rock singer/musician ("Slipping Away"; formerly with Rockpile)

Edward (Edward Antony Richard Louis) (1964–) Eng. prince

Edward I (1239–1307) Eng. king 1272–1307

Edward II (Edward of Caernarvon) (1284–1327) Eng. king 1307–1327

Edward III (Edward III of Windsor) (1312–1377) Eng. king 1327–1377

Edward IV (1442–1483) Eng. king 1461–1483

Edward V (1470–1483) Eng. king 1483

Edward VI (1537–1553) king of England and Ireland 1547–1553

Edward VII (Albert Edward) (1841–1910) Eng. king 1901–1910

Edward VIII (Edward Albert Christian George Andrew Patrick David; a/k/a Duke of Windsor) (1894–1972) Eng. king 1936

Edwards, Anthony (1962–) Am. actor (*Top Gun*; *Fast Times At Ridgemont High*)

Edwards, Blake (William Blake McEdwards) (1922–) Am. film director (*10*; *The Pink Panther*; *S.O.B.*)

Edwards, Cliff ("Ukelele Ike") (1895–

1971) Am. voice actor (Jiminy Cricket)/ singer ("When You Wish upon a Star")

Edwards, Jonathan (1703–1758) Am. theologian/writer (during the Great Awakening)

Edwards, Ralph (Ralph Livingstone Edwards) (1913–) Am. radio/TV host ("This Is Your Life")

Edwards, Turk (Albert Glen Edwards) (1907–1973) Am. football Hall-of-Famer

Edwards, Vince (Vincento Eduardo Zoino) (1928–) Am. actor (TV's "Ben Casey")/singer

Egan, Walter (1948–) Am. rock singer ("Magnet and Steel")

Egbert (died 839) first Eng. king 802–839

Eggar, Samantha (Victoria Louise Samantha Marie Elizabeth Therese Eggar) (1939–) Eng. actress (*The Collector*; *Dr. Dolittle*)

Eggert, Nicole (c. 1972–) Am. actress ("Baywatch" TV series)

Eglevsky, Andre (Andre Yevgenyevich Eglevsky) (1917–1977) Am. ballet dancer

Ehrlichman, John (John Daniel Ehrlichman) (1925–) Am. govt. official/pres. assistant (Nixon)/Watergate participant (18 months in jail for burglary)

Eichhorn, Lisa (1952–) Am. actress (*Cutter's Way*; *Grim Prairie Tales*)

Eichmann, Adolf (Adolf Otto Eichmann) (1906–1962) Ger. Nazi Gestapo leader (tried and executed in Israel for war crimes)

Eiffel, Alexandre (Alexandre-Gustave Eiffel) (1832–1923) Fr. engineer (Eiffel Tower)

Eikenberry, Jill (1947–) Am. actress ("L.A. Law" TV series)

Einstein, Albert (1879–1955) Am. physicist ("E=mc²"; theory of relativity; N—1921)

Eisenhower, Dwight D. (David Dwight Eisenhower; "Ike") (1890–1969) 34th Am. pres. (1953–1961)

Eisenhower, Mamie (Mamie Geneva Doud) (1896–1979) Am. first lady (Dwight D.)

Eisenstaedt, Alfred (1898–) Ger.-Am. photojournalist (*Life*)

Eisenstein, Sergey (Sergey Mikhaylovich Eisenstein) (1898–1948) Russ. film director (*The Battleship Potemkin*)

Eisner, Michael (Michael Dammann Eisner) (1942–) Am. entertainment executive (headed Paramount and Walt Disney)

Ekberg, Anita ("Ice Maiden") (1931–) Swed. actress (*La Dolce Vita*; *War and Peace*)

Ekland, Britt (Britt-Marie Ekland) (1942–) Swed. actress (*The Man with the Golden Gun*)

El Cid (Rodrigo Diaz de Vivar) (c. 1043–1099) Span. mil. leader/national hero of Castile

Elders, Joycelyn (Minnie Lee Jones) (1933–) Am. govt. official (surgeon general)

Eldridge, Florence (Florence McKechnie) (1901–1988) Am. actress (*An Act of Murder*; *Inherit the Wind*)

Eldridge, Roy (David Roy Eldridge; "Little Jazz") (1911–1989) Am. jazz trumpeter

Eleanor of Aquitaine (c. 1122–1204) Eng.-Fr. queen of England (Henry II) and France (Louis VII)

Elfman, Danny (1954–) Am. rock musician (with Oingo Boingo)/film composer (*Beetlejuice*; *Batman*; *Edward Scissorhands*)

Elgar, Sir Edward (Edward William Elgar) (1857–1934) Eng. composer (*Pomp and Circumstance*; *King Olaf*)

El Greco (Doménikos Theotokópoulos) (1541–1614) Span. mannerist painter (studied under Titian)

Elijah (9th century B.C.) Heb. prophet

Eliot, George (Mary Ann Evans) (1819–1880) Eng. novelist (*Adam Bede*; *Silas Marner*; *Middlemarch*)

Eliot, T. S. (Thomas Stearns Eliot) (1888–1965) Eng. poet (*The Waste Land*; N—1948)

Elisha (9th century B.C.) Heb. prophet

Elizabeth (Yelizaveta Petrovna) (1709–1762) Russ. empress 1741–1762

Elizabeth I ("Good Queen Bess"; "The Virgin Queen") (1533–1603) queen of England and Ireland 1558–1603

Elizabeth II (Elizabeth Alexandra Mary) (1926–) queen of England and Northern Ireland 1952– (mother of Charles, Anne, Andrew, and Edward)

Elizondo, Hector (1936–) Am. actor (*Pretty Woman*; *American Gigolo*; *Frankie & Johnny*)

Ellerbee, Linda (Linda Jane Smith) (1944–) Am. newscaster/writer

Elliman, Yvonne (1951–) Am. pop singer ("If I Can't Have You")/actress
Ellington, Duke (Edward Kennedy Ellington) (1899–1974) Am. bandleader/composer ("Satin Doll"; "Mood Indigo")
Elliot, Cass (Cassandra Elliot; born Ellen Naomi Cohen; "Mama Cass") (1941–1974) Am. pop singer (with The Mamas & The Papas; "California Dreamin' ")
Elliot, Denholm (Denholm Mitchell Elliott) (1922–1992) Eng. actor (*Alfie*; *The Boys from Brazil*)
Elliott, Bob (Robert B. Elliot) (1923–) Am. comedian (father of Chris; with Bob & Ray)
Elliott, Chris (1960–) Am. comedian/actor ("Late Night with David Letterman"; "Get a Life" TV series)
Elliott, Joe (1959–) Eng. rock singer (with Def Leppard)
Elliott, Sam (1944–) Am. actor (*Mask*; *Road House*; *Rush*)
Ellis, Bret Easton (1964–) Am. novelist (*Less Than Zero*; *American Psycho*)
Ellis, Havelock (Henry Havelock Ellis) (1859–1939) Eng. psychologist/essayist (*Studies in the Psychology of Sex*)
Ellis, Perry (Perry Edwin Ellis) (1940–1986) Am. fashion designer
Ellison, Harlan (Harlan Jay Ellison) (1934–) Am. science fiction writer (*The City on the Edge of Forever*)/editor (*Dangerous Visions*)
Ellison, Ralph (Ralph Waldo Ellison) (1914–) Am. novelist (*Invisible Man*)
Ellsberg, Daniel (1930–) Am. govt. official/political activist (author of the "Pentagon Papers")
Ellsworth, Lincoln (1880–1951) Am. polar explorer (first to cross both the Arctic and Antarctic by air)
Elmo or **Erasmus** (died c. 303) Ital. saint (patron saint of sailors)
Éluard, Paul (Eugène Grindel) (1895–1952) Fr. poet (*La Rose Publique*)
Elway, John (John Albert Elway) (1960–) Am. football player
Elwes, Cary (1962–) Eng.-Am. actor (*Days of Thunder*; *Glory*)
Ely, Ron (Ronald Pierce) (1938–) Am. actor (TV's Tarzan)
Elytis, Odysseus (Odysseus Elytis Alepoudhelis) (1911–) Gr. poet/essayist (*Six and One Regards for the Sky*; N—1979)
Emerson, Faye (Faye Margaret Emerson) (1917–1983) Am. socialite/actress/game show panelist ("I've Got a Secret" TV series)
Emerson, Keith (1944–) Eng. rock musician (with Emerson, Lake & Palmer)
Emerson, Ralph Waldo ("The Sage of Concord") (1803–1882) Am. poet/essayist (*Self-Reliance*)
Emerson, Roy (1936–) Austral. tennis player (W—1964, 1965)
Empedocles (c. 490–430 B.C.) Gr. philosopher/statesman/poet
Enders, John (John Franklin Enders) (1897–1985) Am. microbiologist (helped develop measles vaccine; N—1954)
Enesco, Georges (or Gheorghe Enescu) (1881–1955) Rom. violinist/composer (*Oedipe*)
Engels, Friedrich (1820–1895) Ger. communist philosopher (Marx's coauthor)
Englehorn, Shirley (Shirley Ruth Englehorn) (1940–) Am. golfer
English, Diane (c. 1948–) Am. TV producer ("Murphy Brown"; "Love & War")
Englund, Robert (1948–) Am. actor (Freddie Krueger in *Nightmare on Elm Street* films)
Ennis, Skinnay (1907–1963) Am. bandleader/singer
Eno, Brian (1948–) Eng. rock composer/musician (formerly with Roxy Music)
Entwistle, John (John Alec Entwistle) (1944–) Eng. rock musician (with The Who)
Enya (Eithne Ni Bhraonain) (c. 1962–) Ir. pop singer/musician ("Orinoco Flow [Sail Away]"; formerly with Clannad)
Ephron, Nora (1941–) Am. novelist/screenwriter (*Heartburn*)/film director (*Sleepless in Seattle*)
Epictetus (c. 55–c. 135) Gr. Stoic philosopher
Epicurus (341–270 B.C.) Gr. philosopher (epicureanism)
Epstein, Brian (1934–1967) Eng. rock group manager (The Beatles)
Epstein, Sir Jacob (1880–1959) Am.-Eng. sculptor (bronze busts of Albert Einstein, Joseph Conrad, etc.)
Equiano, Olaudah (a/k/a Gustavus Vassa) (c. 1745–1801) Afr. slave/autobiographer
Erasmus, Desiderius (Gerhard Gerhards) (c. 1466–1536) Dutch philosopher/scholar (*In Praise of Folly*; *Diatribe on Free Will*)

Erdman, Paul E. (Paul Emil Erdman) (1932–) Can.-Am. writer (*The Billion Dollar Sure Thing*; *The Panic of '89*)

Erhard, Werner (John Paul Rosenberg) (1935–) Am. founder of est

Erickson, Leif (William Wycliffe Anderson) (1911–1986) Am. actor ("The High Chaparral" TV series)

Erik the Red (Erik Thorvaldson) (950–1000) Norw. navigator/explorer (discovered Greenland)

Eriksson, Leif (fl. c. 1000) Norw. explorer (son of Erik the Red; said to have traveled to America [probably landed in Labrador, Newfoundland, and Nova Scotia])

Erlanger, Joseph (1874–1965) Am. physiologist (N—1944)

Ernst, Max (1891–1976) Ger. Dadaist painter/sculptor (helped found the Surrealist group)

Erté (Romain de Tirtoff) (1892–1990) Russ.-Fr. art deco artist/fashion designer

Ertegun, Ahmet (Ahmet Munir Ertegun) (1923–) Turk.-Am. music producer/executive

Erving, Julius (Julius Winfield Erving III; "Dr. J") (1950–) Am. basketball player

Erwin, Stu (Stuart Philip Erwin) (1902–1967) Am. actor ("The Stu Erwin Show" TV series)

Escalante, Jaime (c. 1930–) Am. teacher (subject of the film *Stand and Deliver*)

Esposito, Giancarlo (c. 1958–) Am. actor (*Do the Right Thing*; *Malcolm X*; "Bakersfield, P.D." TV series)

Esposito, Phil (Philip Anthony Esposito) (1942–) Can. hockey player

Essex, David (David Albert Cook) (1947–) Eng. actor/rock singer ("Rock On")

Estefan, Emilio (1953–) Am. pop singer (with wife Gloria in Miami Sound Machine)

Estefan, Gloria (1957–) Cub.-Am. pop singer ("Rhythm Is Gonna Get You"; "Anything for You"; with Miami Sound Machine)

Estevez, Emilio (1962–) Am. actor (son of Martin Sheen, brother of Charlie Sheen; *Stakeout*; *Young Guns*; *St. Elmo's Fire*)

Esther (fl. c. 475 B.C.) Pers. queen

Estrada, Erik (Henry Enrique Estrada) (1949–) Am. actor ("CHiPS" TV series)

Eszterhas, Joe (c. 1944) Am. screenwriter (*Basic Instinct*; *Flashdance*; *Jagged Edge*; *Sliver*)

Etheridge, Melissa (1961–) Am. rock singer ("Similar Features")

Etting, Ruth (1896–1978) Am. singer (played by Doris Day in *Love Me or Leave Me*)

Eubanks, Bob (c. 1937–) Am. game show host ("The Newlywed Game")

Eucken, Rudolf (Rudolf Christoph Eucken) (1846–1926) Ger. philosopher (N—1908)

Euclid (fl. c. 300 B.C.) Gr. mathematician/writer (*Elements*)

Eugénie (Eugénia Maria de Montijo de Guzmán, Comtesse de Teba) (1826–1920) Fr. empress and wife of Napoleon III

Euripides (c. 484–406 B.C.) Gr. playwright (*Medea*; *Electra*; *Orestes*)

Evangelista, Linda (1965–) Can.-Am. model

Evans, Dale (Frances Octavia Smith) (1912–) Am. actress ("The Roy Rogers and Dale Evans Show" TV series)

Evans, Darrell (Darrell Wayne Evans) (1947–) Am. baseball player

Evans, Dwight (Dwight Michael Evans; "Dewey") (1951–) Am. baseball player

Evans, Dame Edith (Edith Mary Evans née Booth) (1888–1976) Eng. actress (*The Importance of Being Earnest*)

Evans, Sir Geraint (Geraint Llewellyn Evans) (1922–) Wel.-Eng. opera singer (baritone)

Evans, Gil (1912–1988) Am. jazz composer/arranger/bandleader

Evans, Harold (Harold Matthew Evans) (1927–) Eng.-Am. journalist/publisher (head of Random House)

Evans, Janet (1971–) Am. swimmer

Evans, Linda (Linda Evanstad) (1942–) Am. actress ("Dynasty" TV series)

Evans, Ray (1915–) Am. lyricist ("Mona Lisa"; "Buttons and Bows"; "Que Sera, Sera")

Evans, Robert or Bob (Robert Shapera) (1930–) Am. actor/film producer (*Chinatown*; *Marathon Man*)

Evans, Rowland, Jr. (1921–) Am. journalist/writer (with Robert Novak, *The Reagan Revolution*)

Evans, Walker (1903–1975) Am. photographer (*Let Us Now Praise Famous Men*, with James Agee)

Everett, Chad (Raymond Lee Cramton or Cranton) (1937–) Am. actor ("Medical Center" TV series)

Everett, Rupert (1959–) Eng. actor (*The

Comfort of Strangers; *Dance with a Stranger*)
Everly, Don (Isaac Donald Everly) (1937–) Am. pop singer (with The Everly Brothers; "Bye Bye Love"; "Wake Up Little Susie")
Everly, Phil (Philip Everly) (1938–) Am. pop singer (with The Everly Brothers)
Evers, Johnny (John Joseph Evers; "The Trojan"; "The Crab") (1883–1947) Am. baseball Hall-of-Famer
Evers, Medgar (Medgar Wiley Evers) (1926–1963) Am. civil rights leader (assassinated)
Evert, Chris (Christine Marie Evert; a/k/a Chris Evert-Lloyd; "The Ice Maiden") (1954–) Am. tennis player (W—1974, 1976, 1981)
Evigan, Greg (Gregory Ralph Evigan) (1953–) Am. actor ("My Two Dads" TV series)
Ewbank, Weeb (Wilbur Charles Ewbank) (1907–) Am. football coach/Hall-of-Famer
Ewell, Tom (Yewell Tompkins) (1909–) Am. actor (*The Seven Year Itch*; *Adam's Rib*; T—1953)
Ewing, Patrick (Patrick Aloysius Ewing) (1962–) Am. basketball player
Ewing, Skip (1964–) Am. country singer ("Burnin' a Hole in My Heart")
Exon, J. James (John James Exon) (1921–) Am. senator
Ezekiel (6th century B.C.) Heb. prophet
Ezekiel, Moses (Moses Jacob Ezekiel) (1844–1917) Am. sculptor (Kentucky's Thomas Jefferson Monument)
Fabares, Shelley (Michele Marie Fabares) (1942–) Am. actress (niece of Nanette Fabray; "The Donna Reed Show," "One Day at a Time," and "Coach" TV series)
Faber, John Eberhard (1822–1879) Am. manufacturer of pencils
Faber, Red (Urban Clarence Faber) (1888–1976) Am. baseball Hall-of-Famer
Fabergé, Peter Carl (1846–1920) Russ. goldsmith (Fabergé eggs)
Fabian (Fabian Anthony Forte) (1943–) Am. actor/singer ("Turn Me Loose")
Fabio (Fabio Lanzone) (c. 1961–) Ital.-Am. male model (romance novel covers)/ actor ("Acapulco H.E.A.T." TV series)/ romance novelist (*Pirate*)
Fabius (Quintus Fabius Maximus Verrucosus) (died 203 B.C.) Roman general
Fabray, Nanette (Ruby Bernadette

Nanette Therese Fabares) (1920–) Am. actress (*The Band Wagon*; "One Day at a Time" TV series); E—1955, 1956; T—1949
Fadiman, Clifton (Clifton Paul Fadiman) (1904–) Am. literary critic/writer (*The Lifetime Reading Plan*)
Fagen, Donald (1948–) Am. pop singer/ musician ("I.G.Y. [What a Beautiful World]"; with Steely Dan)
Fahd (Fahd Ibn Abdul Aziz) (1923–) Saud. Arab. king 1982– (son of Ibn Saud)
Fahey, Jeff (c. 1954–) Am. actor (*White Hunter, Black Heart*; *The Lawnmower Man*)
Fahrenheit, Daniel (Daniel Gabriel Fahrenheit) (1686–1736) Ger. physicist (Fahrenheit scale for measuring temperature)
Fain, Sammy (Samuel Feinberg) (1902–1989) Am. songwriter ("Love Is a Many-Splendored Thing"; "I'll Be Seeing You")
Fairbanks, Charles W. (Charles Warren Fairbanks) (1852–1918) Am. v.p. (T. Roosevelt)
Fairbanks, Chuck (Charles Leo Fairbanks) (1933–) Am. football coach
Fairbanks, Douglas (Douglas Elton Ullman; a/k/a Elton Banks and Elton Thomas; "The Fourth Musketeer") (1883–1939) Am. actor (*Robin Hood* [1922]; founded United Artists Studio)
Fairbanks, Douglas, Jr. (Douglas Elton Fairbanks, Jr.) (1909–) Am. actor (*The Prisoner of Zenda*; *Catherine The Great*)
Fairchild, Morgan (Patsy Ann McClenny) (1950–) Am. actress ("Falcon Crest" TV series)
Faisal (Ibn-Abd-al-Aziz al-Saūd) (c. 1906–1975) Saud. Arab. king 1964–1975
Faith, Adam (Terence Nelhams) (1940–) Eng. rock singer ("What Do You Want")
Faith, Percy (1908–1976) Can.-Am. orchestra leader/composer ("The Theme from a Summer Place")
Faithfull, Marianne (1947–) Am. actress/ rock singer ("As Tears Go By")
Falana, Lola (1939–) Am. actress/singer
Falco (Johann Holzel) (1957–) Aus. rock singer/musician ("Rock Me Amadeus")
Falk, Peter (Peter Michael Falk) (1927–) Am. actor (TV's "Columbo"; *Murder by Death*; *Cookie*; E—1971/72, 1975/76, 1989/90)
Falla, Manuel de (Manuel Maria de Falla y

Matheu) (1876–1946) Span. composer (*La Vida Breve*)

Faludi, Susan (Susan C. Faludi) (1959–) Am. writer (*Backlash*)/journalist (P— 1991)

Falwell, Jerry (Jerry L. Falwell) (1933–) Am. evangelist (founder of Moral Majority, Inc.)

Fame, Herb (Herbert Feemster) (1942–) Am. pop musician (with Peaches & Herb; "Reunited"; "Shake Your Groove Thing")

Fanon, Frantz (Frantz Omar Fanon) (1925–1961) Fr. W. Ind. philosopher (*Black Skin, White Masks*; *The Wretched of the Earth*)

Farentino, James (1938–) Am. actor ("Mary" TV series; *Jesus of Nazareth*)

Fargo, Donna (Yvonne Vaughan) (1945–) Am. country/pop singer ("Funny Face"; "Happiest Girl in the Whole U.S.A.")

Farinelli (Carlo Broschi Farinelli; "Il Ragazzo" [the lad]) (1705–1782) Ital. opera singer (male soprano)

Farley, Chris (c. 1963–) Am. comedian ("Saturday Night Live" TV series)

Farley, Walter (Walter Lorimer Farley) (1915–1989) Am. children's book writer (*Black Stallion* series)

Farmer, Fannie (Fannie Merritt Farmer) (1857–1915) Am. cooking expert/writer (*The Boston Cooking School Cook Book*)

Farmer, Frances (1913–1970) Am. actress (*The Toast of New York*)/autobiographer (*Will There Really Be a Morning?*)

Farmer, James (James Leonard Farmer) (1920–) Am. civil rights activist (founded the Congress of Racial Equality)

Farmer, Philip José (1918–) Am. science fiction writer (*Gods of Riverworld*)

Farnum, Dustin (Dustin Lancy Farnum) (1870–1929) Am. cowboy actor (for whom Dustin Hoffman was named; *The Squaw Man*; *The Virginian*)

Farouk I (1920–1965) Egypt. king 1936–1952

Farr, Jamie (Jameel Joseph Farah) (1934–) Am. actor ("M*A*S*H" TV series)

Farragut, David (David Glasgow Farragut; born James Glasgow Farragut; "Old Salamander") (1801–1870) Am. navy admiral

Farrakhan, Louis (Louis Eugene Walcott) (1933–) Am. civil rights activist (head of the Nation of Islam)

Farrar, Geraldine (1882–1967) Am. opera singer (soprano; appeared frequently with Enrico Caruso)

Farrell, Eileen (1920–) Am. opera singer (soprano)

Farrell, Glenda (1904–1971) Am. actress (*The Mystery of the Wax Museum*; *The Disorderly Orderly*; E—1962/63)

Farrell, James T. (James Thomas Farrell) (1904–1979) Am. novelist (*Studs Lonigan*)

Farrell, Mike (1939–) Am. actor ("M*A*S*H" TV series)

Farrell, Perry (1960–) Am. rock singer (with Jane's Addiction and Porno for Pyros)

Farrell, Suzanne (Roberta Sue Ficker) (1945–) Am. ballerina

Farrow, Mia (Maria de Lourdes Villers Farrow) (1945–) Am. actress (daughter of Maureen O'Sullivan; *Rosemary's Baby*; *Alice*; *Hannah and Her Sisters*)

Fassbinder, Rainer Werner (a/k/a Franz Fassbinder) (1945–1982) Ger. film director (*Fear*; *The Bitter Tears of Petra von Kant*)

Fast, Howard (Howard Melvin Fast; a/k/a E. V. Cunningham and Walter Ericson) (1914–) Am. novelist (*Spartacus*)

Fatimah (c. 616–633) Arab. daughter of Muhammad

Faulkner, William (William Cuthbert Faulkner) (1897–1962) Am. novelist/ short story writer (*The Sound and the Fury*; *Absalom, Absalom!*; N—1949; P— 1955—*A Fable*; P—1963—*The Reivers*)

Fauntroy, Walter E. (1933–) Am. social reformer/congressman

Fauré, Gabriel (Gabriel-Urbain Fauré) (1845–1924) Fr. composer (*Requiem*)

Fausta (Flavia Maximiana Fausta (289–326) Roman empress

Faustino, David (1974–) Am. actor ("Married . . . With Children" TV series)

Fawcett, Farrah (Mary Farrah Leni Fawcett; a/k/a Farrah Fawcett-Majors) (1947–) Am. actress (*The Burning Bed*; *Extremities*; "Charlie's Angels" TV series)

Fawkes, Guy (1570–1606) Eng. conspirator (plotted to blow up the Houses of Parliament)

Faye, Alice (Ann Jeanne Leppert) (1915–) Am. actress (*Alexander's Ragtime Band*; *State Fair*)

Faye, Herbie (1899–1980) Am. actor/

comedian ("The Phil Silvers Show" TV series)

Fazenda, Louise (1895–1962) Am. actress (*No No Nanette*; *The Old Maid*)

Fearing, Kenneth (Kenneth Flexner Fearing) (1902–1961) Am. novelist (*The Big Clock* [filmed as *No Way Out*])/poet

Fears, Tom (Thomas Jesse Fears) (1923–) Am. football Hall-of-Famer

Feiffer, Jules (Jules Ralph Feiffer; "Iconoclast with a Pencil") (1929–) Am. cartoonist (P—1986)/screenwriter (*Carnal Knowledge*)

Feininger, Andreas (Andreas Bernhard Lyonel Feininger) (1906–) Am. photographer/writer (*Basic Color Photography*)

Feinstein, Dianne (Dianne Goldman) (1933–) Am. mayor (San Francisco)/senator

Feinstein, Michael (Michael Jay Cohen) (1956–) Am. cabaret pianist/singer

Feldman, Corey (Corey Scott Feldman) (1971–) Am. actor (*The Lost Boys*; *Stand by Me*)

Feldman, Marty (1933–1982) Eng. comedian/actor (*Young Frankenstein*; *Silent Movie*)/film director (*The Last Remake of Beau Geste*)

Feldon, Barbara (Barbara Hall) (1941–) Am. actress (Agent 99 in "Get Smart" TV series)

Feldshuh, Tovah (Terri Sue Feldshuh) (1952–) Am. actress (*Holocaust*)

Feliciano, José (1945–) P.R. singer/guitarist ("Light My Fire"; G—1968)

Fell, Norman (1924–) Am. actor ("Three's Company" and "The Ropers" TV series)

Feller, Bob (Robert William Andrew Feller; "Rapid Robert"; "Bullet Bob") (1918–) Am. baseball Hall-of-Famer

Fellini, Federico (1920–1993) Ital. film director (*La Strada*; *La Dolce Vita*; *Fellini Satyricon*)

Fender, Freddy (Baldemar G. Huerta) (1937–) Am. country singer ("Before the Next Teardrop Falls"; "Wasted Days and Wasted Nights")

Fender, Leo (Clarence Leo Fender) (1907–1991) Am. electric guitar technology pioneer

Fenn, Sherilyn (c. 1965–) Am. actress ("Twin Peaks" TV series; *Boxing Helena*)

Ferber, Edna (1887–1968) Am. short story writer/novelist (*Giant*; *Show Boat*; *Stage Door*; P—1925—*So Big*)

Ferdinand, Archduke **Francis** or **Franz** (1863–1914) Aus. ruler (his assassination the cause of WWI)

Ferguson, Jay (1943–) Am. pop singer ("Shakedown Cruise")

Ferguson, Maynard (1928–) Can.-Am. jazz trumpeter ("Gonna Fly Now [Theme from Rocky]")

Ferguson, Sarah (Sarah Margaret Ferguson; "Fergie") (1959–) Eng. duchess of York

Ferlinghetti, Lawrence (Lawrence Monsanto Ferling) (1920–) Am. "beat" poet/publisher (*Pictures of the Gone World*)

Fermi, Enrico (1901–1954) Am. physicist (built the first nuclear reactor; created the first manmade atomic reaction and worked on the atomic bomb; N—1938)

Fernandel (Fernand-Joseph-Désiré Contandin) (1903–1971) Fr. actor/comedian (*Don Camillo* films)

Fernandez, Sid (Charles Sidney Fernandez) (1962–) Am. baseball pitcher

Fernandez, Tony (Antonio Octavio Fernandez Castro) (1962–) Dom.-Am. baseball player

Ferrante, Arthur (1921–) Am. pianist (with Louis Teicher; *Exodus*; *Midnight Cowboy*)

Ferrara, Abel (a/k/a Jimmy Laine) (1952–) Am. film director (*King of New York*; *Body Snatchers*; *Bad Lieutenant*)

Ferrare, Christina (1951–) Am. model/talk show host

Ferrari, Enzo (1898–1988) Ital. automobile manufacturer

Ferraro, Geraldine (Geraldine Anne Ferraro) (1935–) Am. politician (first woman to be on the ticket of a major party as Democratic vice-presidential candidate, 1984)

Ferrell, Conchata (Conchata Galen Ferrell; "Chatti") (1943–) Am. actress ("L.A. Law" TV series)

Ferrell, Rick (Richard Benjamin Ferrell) (1905–) Am. baseball Hall-of-Famer

Ferrer, José (José Vincente Ferrer Otero y Cintrón) (1912–1992) Am. actor (*Joan of Arc*; *Moulin Rouge*; O—1950—*Cyrano de Bergerac*; T—1947, 1952)

Ferrer, Mel (Melchior Gaston Ferrer) (1917–) Am. actor ("Falcon Crest" TV series)/film producer (*Wait Until Dark*)

Ferrigno, Lou (1951–) Am. actor (TV's "The Incredible Hulk")

Ferris, George Washington Gale (1859–1896) Am. engineer (Ferris wheel)

Ferry, Bryan (1945–) Eng. rock singer

("Kiss and Tell"; formerly with Roxy Music ["Love Is the Drug"])
Fetchit, Stepin (Lincoln Theodore Monroe Andrew Perry) (1892–1985) Am. actor (*Charlie Chan in Egypt*; *Show Boat*)
Feuerbach, Ludwig (Ludwig Andreas Feuerbach) (1804–1872) Ger. philosopher (studied under Hegel)/writer (*Abalard und Heloise*)
Feynman, Richard (Richard Phillips Feynman) (1918–1988) Am. physicist (worked on the atomic bomb; N—1965)
Fidler, Jimmy (1899–1988) Am. (Hollywood) columnist/radio reporter
Fidrych, Mark (Mark Steven Fidrych; "The Bird"; "Big Bird") (1954–) Am. baseball pitcher
Fiedler, Arthur ("The Potentate of Pop") (1894–1979) Am. orchestra leader/conductor (Boston Pops Orchestra)
Fiedler, Leslie A. (Leslie Aaron Fiedler) (1917–) Am. novelist/critic (*Love and Death in the American Novel*)
Field, Eugene ("Poet of Childhood") (1850–1895) Am. poet (*Little Boy Blue*; *Wynken, Blynken and Nod*)
Field, Marshall (1834–1906) Am. merchant (Marshall Field & Co. department stores)
Field, Marshall III (1893–1956) Am. newspaper publisher (founded *Chicago Sun*)/philanthropist (grandson of Marshall Field)
Field, Rachel (Rachel Lyman Field) (1894–1942) Am. novelist (*All This and Heaven Too*)
Field, Sally (Sally Margaret Field Mahoney) (1946–) Am. actress (stepdaughter of Jock Mahoney; TV's "The Flying Nun"; *Steel Magnolias*; O—1979—*Norma Rae*; O—1984—*Places in the Heart*)
Fielding, Henry (1707–1754) Eng. novelist/playwright (*Tom Jones*; *Tom Thumb*)
Fields, Debbi (Debra Jane Sivyer; a/k/a Mrs. Fields) (1956–) Am. cookie company founder
Fields, Dorothy (1905–1974) Am. lyricist ("On the Sunny Side of the Street"; "The Way You Look Tonight"; "I'm in the Mood for Love")
Fields, Dame Gracie (Grace Stansfield) (1898–1979) Eng. singer/actress (*Holy Matrimony*)
Fields, Kim (1969–) Am. actress ("The

Facts of Life" and "Living Single" TV series)
Fields, Totie (Sophie Feldman) (1930–1978) Am. comedienne
Fields, W. C. (William Claude Dukenfield; a/k/a Charles Bogle, Otis J. Criblecoblis, Cuthbert J. Twilley, Primrose Magoo, Felton J. Satchelstern, Pico J. Steinway, and Mahatma Kane Jeeves) (1879–1946) Am. comedian (*The Bank Dick*; *My Little Chickadee*; *Never Give a Sucker an Even Break*)
Fierstein, Harvey (Harvey Forbes Fierstein) (1954–) Am. actor/playwright (*Torch Song Trilogy*; *Safe Sex*; T—1983)
Fillmore, Abigail (Abigail Powers) (1798–1853) Am. first lady (Millard)
Fillmore, Millard ("The Accidental President") (1800–1874) 13th Am. pres. (1850–1853)
Finch, Jon (Jon Nicholas Finch) (1942–) Eng. actor (*Frenzy*; *Macbeth* [title role])
Finch, Peter (William Peter Mitchell) (1916–1977) Eng. actor (*Sunday, Bloody Sunday*; *The Trials of Oscar Wilde*; O—1976—*Network*)
Fine, Larry (Laurence Feinberg) (1902–1975) Am. comedian (one of The Three Stooges)
Finger, Bill (1917–) Am. cartoonist (with Robert Kane, created Batman)
Fingers, Rollie (Roland Glenn Fingers) (1946–) Am. baseball pitcher
Finkel, Fyrush (c. 1922–) Am. actor (*For Love or Money*; "Picket Fences" TV series)
Finley, Karen (1956–) Am. performance artist
Finley, Martha (a/k/a Martha Farquaharson) (1828–1909) Am. children's book writer (created Elsie Dinsmore)
Finney, Albert (1936–) Eng. film director/actor (*Miller's Crossing*; *Murder on the Orient Express*; *Under the Volcano*)
Finney, Jack (Walter Braden Finney) (1911–) Am. novelist (*Time After Time*; *Invasion of the Body Snatchers*)
Finsterwald, Dow (1929–) Am. golfer
Fiona (Fiona Flanagan) (1961–) Am. rock singer ("Everything You Do [You're Sexing Me]")
Fiorucci, Elio (C) Ital. fashion designer (popular during 1960s)
Firestone, Harvey Samuel (1868–1938) Am. industrialist (founded the Firestone Tire & Rubber Company)
Firpo, Luis (Luis Angel Firpo; "Wild

Bull of the Pampas") (1896–1960) Arg. boxer

Fischbacher, Siegfried (c. 1945–) Am. animal trainer (with Siegfried & Roy)

Fischer, Bobby (Robert James Fischer; "Corduroy Killer"; "Boy Robot"; "Sweatshirt Kid") (1943–) Am. chess player (attained international grand master status at age 15)

Fish, Albert (1870–1936) Am. serial killer (executed)

Fish, Hamilton (1808–1893) Am. Whig senator/secretary of state

Fish, Hamilton, Jr. (1926–) Am. congressman

Fishburne, Larry or **Laurence** (Laurence Fishburne III) (1963–) Am. actor (*School Daze*; *Class Action*; *What's Love Got to Do with It* [as Ike Turner])

Fisher, Amy (Amy Elizabeth Fisher) (1974–) Am. criminal (shot wife of Joey Buttafuoco [her lover], Mary Jo)

Fisher, Brian (Brian Kevin Fisher) (1962–) Am. baseball pitcher

Fisher, Bud (Harry Conway Fisher) (1885–1954) Am. cartoonist (*Mutt 'n' Jeff*)

Fisher, Carrie (Carrie Frances Fisher) (1956–) Am. actress (daughter of Debbie Reynolds and Eddie Fisher; Princess Leia in *Star Wars* films)/writer (*Postcards from the Edge*)

Fisher, Eddie (Edwin Jack Fisher) (1928–) Am. singer ("Dungaree Doll")/actor (*Butterfield 8*; *All About Eve*; father of Carrie and Tricia Leigh)

Fisher, Frances (c. 1953–) Am. actress (*Unforgiven*; companion of Clint Eastwood)

Fisher, Ham (Hammond Edward Fisher) (1900–1955) Am. cartoonist (*Joe Palooka*)

Fisher, M. F. K. (Mary Francis Kennedy Fisher; a/k/a Mary Francis Parrish) (1908–1992) Am. writer (food books; *The Art of Eating*)

Fisher, Terence (Terence R. Fisher) (1904–1980) Eng. film director (*The Phantom of the Opera* [1962]; *The Mummy*)

Fisher, Tricia Leigh (c. 1968–) Am. actress (*Book of Love*)/pop singer ("Empty Beach"; daughter of Eddie Fisher and Connie Stevens)

Fisk, Carlton (Carlton Ernest Fisk; "The Lightning Lad"; "Pudge") (1948–) Am. baseball player

Fitch, John (1743–1798) Am. inventor (steamboat)

Fitzgerald, Barry (William Joseph Shields) (1888–1961) Ir. actor (*Juno and the Paycock*; O—1944—*Going My Way*)

Fitzgerald, Ed (Edward Fitzgerald) (1893–1982) Am. radio host (with wife, Pegeen)

Fitzgerald, Ella ("First Lady of Song") (1918–) Am. jazz singer ("Mack the Knife"; "Baby, It's Cold Outside"; G—1958, 1959, 1960, 1962)

Fitzgerald, F. Scott (Francis Scott Key Fitzgerald) (1896–1940) Am. novelist/short story writer (*The Great Gatsby*; *Tender Is the Night*)

Fitzgerald, Geraldine (1914–) Ir. actress (mother of Michael Lindsay-Hogg; "St. Elsewhere" TV series; *Wuthering Heights*)

Fitzgerald, Pegeen (1910–1989) Am. radio host (with husband, Ed)

Fitzgerald, Zelda (née Sayre) (1900–1948) Am. writer (wife of F. Scott)

Fitzwater, Marlin (Max Marlin Fitzwater) (1942–) Am. govt. official (press secretary)

Flack, Roberta (1939–) Am. soul/pop singer ("Killing Me Softly with His Song"; "The First Time Ever I Saw Your Face"; G—1973)

Flagg, Fannie (Frances Carlton Flagg; born Patricia Neal) (1944–) Am. comedienne ("The New Dick Van Dyke Show" TV series)

Flagg, James Montgomery (1877–1960) Am. painter/illustrator (created Uncle Sam)

Flaherty, Robert (Robert Joseph Flaherty) (1884–1951) Am. documentary filmmaker (*Nanook of the North*; *Man of Aran*)

Flanagan, Father (Edward Joseph Flanagan) (1886–1948) Ir.-Am. priest (founded Boys Town; signature phrase: "There is no such thing as a bad boy")

Flanagan, Fionnula (Fionnula Manon Flanagan) (1941–) Ir.-Am. actress (*Rich Man, Poor Man*; "How the West Was Won" TV series)

Flanery, Sean Patrick (c. 1966–) Am. actor

Flanner, Janet (a/k/a Genet) (1892–1978) Am. journalist ("Letter From Paris" column in the *New Yorker*)

Flatt, Lester (Lester Raymond Flatt) (1914–1979) Am. bluegrass singer/guitarist (with Flatt & Scruggs; "Ballad of Jed Clampett")

Flaubert, Gustave (1821–1880) Fr. novelist (*Madame Bovary*)

Flavor, Flav (William Drayton) (c. 1959–) Am. rapper (with Public Enemy)

Fleetwood, Mick (1942–) Eng. rock musician (with Fleetwood Mac)

Fleischer, Max (1883–1972) Aus.-Am. cartoonist (father of Richard; *Betty Boop*; *Popeye*)

Fleischer, Nat (Nathaniel S. Fleischer; "Mr. Boxing") (1887–1972) Am. boxing expert/journalist (founder/editor of *The Ring* magazine)

Fleischer, Richard (1916–) Am. film director (son of Max; *The Narrow Margin*; *Compulsion*)

Fleiss, Heidi ("Hollywood Madam"; "Madam to the Stars") (c. 1966–) Am. prostitute/madam

Fleming, Sir Alexander (1881–1955) Eng. bacteriologist (discovered penicillin)

Fleming, Ian (Ian Lancaster Fleming) (1908–1964) Eng. suspense novelist (created James Bond; *Casino Royale*; *From Russia, with Love*; *Dr. No*)

Fleming, Peggy (Peggy Gale Fleming) (1948–) Am. figure skater

Fleming, Peter (1955–) Am. tennis player

Fleming, Rhonda (Marilyn Lewis) (1923–) Am. actress (*Spellbound*; *Gunfight at the O.K. Corral*)

Fleming, Victor (1883–1949) Am. film director (*The Wizard of Oz*; O—1939— *Gone with the Wind*)

Fletcher, John Gould (1886–1950) Am. poet/critic (P—1939—*Selected Poems*)

Fletcher, Louise (1934–) Am. actress (*Thieves Like Us*; O—1975—*One Flew Over the Cuckoo's Nest*)

Fletcher, Lucille (1912–) Am. short story writer (*Sorry, Wrong Number*)

Flo and Eddie see Volman, Mark, and Kaylen, Howard

Flon, Suzanne (1918–) Fr. actress (*Moulin Rouge*; *Blackout*)

Flood, Curt (Curtis Charles Flood) (1938–) Am. baseball player (baseball's first "free agent")

Florey, Robert (1900–1979) Am. film director (*The Murders in the Rue Morgue*; *The Beast with Five Fingers*)

Flotow, Baron Friedrich (Friedrich Adolf Ferdinand von Flotow) (1812–1883) Ger. composer (*Martha*)

Flowers, Wayland (Wayland Parrott

Flowers, Jr.) (1939–1987) Am. ventriloquist (*Madame*)/comedian

Floyd, Carlisle (Carlisle Sessions Floyd) (1926–) Am. composer (*Of Mice and Men*; *Wuthering Heights* opera)

Floyd, Pretty Boy (Charles Arthur Floyd) (1904–1934) Am. bank robber/member of the Dillinger gang

Flynn, Errol (Errol Leslie Thomson Flynn) (1909–1959) Tas.-Am. actor (*Captain Blood*; *The Adventures of Robin Hood*)

Flynn, Raymond (Raymond Leo Flynn) (1939–) Am. politician (mayor of Boston)

Flynt, Larry C. (Larry Claxton Flynt) (1942–) Am. porno magazine publisher (*Hustler*)

Foch, Nina (Nina Consuelo Maud Fock) (1924–) Dutch-Am. actress (*An American in Paris*; *The Ten Commandments*)

Fodor, Eugene (1905–1991) Am. editor/publisher (travel books)

Fogelberg, Dan (Daniel Grayling Fogelberg) (1951–) Am. rock singer ("Same Old Lang Syne"; "Leader of the Band")

Fogerty, John (John C. Fogerty) (1945–) Am. rock singer/guitarist ("The Old Man Down the Road"; formerly with Creedence Clearwater Revival, wrote many of their hits ["Proud Mary"; "Bad Moon Rising"])

Fokine, Michel (Mikhail Mikhaylovich Fokine) (1880–1942) Russ.-Am. ballet dancer/choreographer (with Ballet Russe)

Fokker, Anthony (Anthony Herman Gerard Fokker) (1890–1939) Dutch-Am. aircraft designer/builder

Foley, Red (Clyde Julian Foley) (1910–1968) Am. country singer ("Chattanoogie Shoe Shine Boy")

Foley, Thomas S. (Thomas Stephen Foley) (1929–) Am. congressman/speaker of the house

Follett, Ken (Kenneth Martin Follett; a/k/a Myles Symon) (1949–) Wel. suspense writer (*On Wings of Eagles*; *Eye of The Needle*)

Fonda, Bridget (1964–) Am. actress (daughter of Peter; *Single White Female*; *Point of No Return*)

Fonda, Henry (Henry Jaynes Fonda) (1905–1982) Am. actor (father of Peter and Jane; *Twelve Angry Men*; *The Grapes of Wrath*; O—1981—*On Golden Pond*; T—1948)

Fonda, Jane (Jane Seymour Fonda; "Hanoi Jane") (1937–) Am. actress (daughter of Henry; O—1971—*Klute*; O—1978—*Coming Home*)

Fonda, Peter (Peter Henry Fonda) (1939–) Am. actor (son of Henry; father of Bridget; *Easy Rider*)

Fontaine, Frank ("Crazy Guggenheim") (1920–1978) Am. comedian/singer

Fontaine, Joan (Joan de Beauvoir de Havilland; a/k/a Joan Burfield) (1917–) Am. actress (sister of Olivia de Havilland; *Rebecca*; *The Constant Nymph*; O—1941—*Suspicion*)

Fontanne, Lynn (Lillie Louise Fontanne) (1887–1983) Am. actress (*Stage Door Canteen*)

Fonteyn, Dame Margot (Margaret Hookham) (1919–) Eng. ballerina (performed frequently with Nureyev)

Foote, Horton (Albert Horton Foote, Jr.) (1916–) Am. playwright/screenwriter (*The Trip to Bountiful*; *Tender Mercies*)

Foote, Shelby (1916–) Am. historian/novelist (*Love in a Dry Season*)

Forbes, Esther (1891–1967) Am. writer (*Johnny Tremaine*; P—1943—*Paul Revere and the World He Lived In*)

Forbes, Malcolm (Malcolm Stevenson Forbes) (1919–1990) Am. publishing magnate

Ford, Betty (Elizabeth Ann Bloomer) (1918–) Am. first lady (Gerald)/founded substance-abuse clinic

Ford, Edsel (Edsel Bryant Ford) (1893–1943) Am. automobile manufacturer

Ford, Eileen (1922–) Am. modeling agency owner

Ford, Faith (1964–) Am. actress ("Murphy Brown" TV series)

Ford, Ford Madox (Ford Hermann Hueffer) (1873–1939) Eng. novelist (*The Good Soldier*)

Ford, Gerald (Gerald Rudolph Ford, Jr.; born Leslie Lynch King, Jr.) (1913–) 38th Am. pres. (1974–1977)

Ford, Glenn (Gwyllyn Samuel Newton Ford) (1916–) Can.-Am. actor (*The Blackboard Jungle*; *Gilda*)

Ford, Harrison (1942–) Am. actor (*Star Wars* films; *Indiana Jones* films; *Presumed Innocent*; *The Fugitive*)

Ford, Henry (1863–1947) Am. automobile manufacturer (founded the Ford Motor Company)

Ford, John (Sean Aloysius D'Fearna; a/k/a Sean Aloysius O'Feeney, Jack Ford,

Sean O'Feeney; "Pappy"; "Boss"; "Coach") (1895–1973) Am. film director (O—1935—*The Informer*; O—1940—*The Grapes of Wrath*; O—1941—*How Green Was My Valley*; O—1952—*The Quiet Man*)

Ford, Len (Leonard Ford) (1926–1972) Am. football Hall-of-Famer

Ford, Lita (1959–) Am. rock singer/guitarist ("Close My Eyes Forever" [with Ozzy Osbourne]; formerly with The Runaways)

Ford, Paul (Paul Ford Weaver) (1901–1976) Am. actor ("The Phil Silvers Show" TV series; *The Teahouse of the August Moon*)

Ford, Robben (C) Am. jazz guitarist (with The Yellowjackets)

Ford, Tennessee Ernie (Ernest Jennings Ford; "The Ol' Pea-Picker") (1919–1991) Am. country singer ("Ballad of Davy Crockett")

Ford, Whitey (Edward Charles Ford; "The Chairman of the Board") (1926–) Am. baseball Hall-of-Famer

Fordham, Julia (C) Eng. pop singer ("Happy Ever After")

Foreman, George (1948–) Am. boxer/actor ("George" TV series)

Foreman, John (c. 1924–1992) Am. film producer (*WUSA*; *The Effect of Gamma Rays on Man-in-the-Moon Marigolds*; *Prizzi's Honor*)

Forester, C. S. (Cecil Scott Forester) (1899–1966) Eng. novelist (*The African Queen*; *Captain Horatio Hornblower* novels)

Forman, Miloš (a/k/a Tomas Jan) (1932–) Cz.-Am. film director (*Hair*; *Ragtime*; O—1975—*One Flew Over the Cuckoo's Nest*; O—1984—*Amadeus*)

Formby, George (George Booth) (1905–1961) Eng. comedian/actor (*Let George Do It*; *South American George*)

Forrest, Frederic (1936–) Am. actor (*The Rose*; *Music Box*; *Falling Down*)

Forrest, Steve (William Forrest Andrews) (1924–) Am. actor (brother of Dana Andrews; "SWAT" TV series; *The Longest Day*)

Forrestal, James (James Vincent Forrestal) (1892–1949) Am. public official (first defense secretary)

Forster, E. M. (Edward Morgan Forster) (1879–1970) Eng. novelist/short story writer/essayist (*A Room with a View*; *Howard's End*; *A Passage to India*; *Where Angels Fear to Tread*)

Forsyth, Bill (1946–) Scot. film director/writer (*Gregory's Girl*; *Local Hero*)

Forsyth, Frederick (1938–) Eng. thriller writer (*The Day of the Jackal*; *The Odessa File*; *The Dogs of War*)

Forsythe, John (John Lincoln Freund) (1918–) Am. actor ("Dynasty" TV series; *The Trouble with Harry*)

Fortas, Abe (1910–1982) Am. Supreme Court jurist (1965–1969)

Fortmann, Danny (Daniel John Fortmann) (1916–) Am. football Hall-of-Famer

Foss, Lukas (Lukas Fuchs) (1922–) Ger.-Am. composer/pianist/conductor (*Echot*)

Fosse, Bob (Robert Louis Fosse) (1927–1987) Am. dancer/theatrical director/choreographer (*All That Jazz*; O—1972—*Cabaret*)

Fossey, Dian (1932–1985) Am. anthropologist/writer (*Gorillas in the Mist*; murdered)

Foster, Alan Dean (1946–) Am. science fiction writer (*In to the Out Of*; *The Spoils of War*)

Foster, David (1950–) Am. pop composer/musician ("Love Theme from St. Elmo's Fire")

Foster, George (George Arthur Foster; "The Destroyer") (1948–) Am. baseball player

Foster, Hal (Harold Rudolf Foster) (1892–1982) Am. cartoonist (*Tarzan*; *Prince Valiant*)

Foster, Jodie (Alicia Christian Foster) (1962–) Am. actress (*Taxi Driver*; O—1988—*The Accused*; O—1991—*The Silence of the Lambs*)/film director (*Little Man Tate*)

Foster, Meg (1948–) Am. actress (*The Osterman Weekend*; "Cagney & Lacey" TV series)

Foster, Phil (Fivel Feldman) (1914–1985) Am. comedian ("Laverne & Shirley" TV series)

Foster, Rube (George Foster; "The Father of Black Baseball") (1888–1976) Am. baseball Hall-of-Famer

Foster, Stephen (Stephen Collins Foster) (1826–1864) Am. songwriter ("Oh! Susannah"; "My Old Kentucky Home"; "Old Folks at Home"; "Beautiful Dreamer")

Foster, Susanna (Suzanne DeLee Flanders Larson) (1924–) Am. opera singer/actress (*The Phantom of the Opera*)

Foucault, Jean (Jean Bernard Léon Foucault) (1819–1868) Fr. physicist (Foucault's Pendulum shows the rotation of the earth)/inventor (gyroscope)

Foucault, Michel (Michel Paul Foucault) (1926–1984) Fr. philosopher/essayist (*Madness and Civilization*)

Fowles, John (1926–) Eng. novelist (*The Collector*; *The French Lieutenant's Woman*; *The Magus*)

Fox, Fontaine (Fontaine Talbot Fox, Jr.) (1884–1964) Am. cartoonist (*Toonerville Folks*)

Fox, George (1624–1691) Eng. founder of the Quakers (The Society of Friends)

Fox, Michael J. (Michael Andrew Fox) (1961–) Can.-Am. actor ("Family Ties" TV series; *Back to the Future*; *Doc Hollywood*; E—1985/86, 1986/87, 1987/88)

Fox, Nellie (Jacob Nelson Fox) (1927–1975) Am. baseball player

Fox, Samantha (1966–) Eng. pop singer ("Naughty Girls [Need Love Too]")

Fox, Wallace (1898–1958) Am. film director (codirected *The Last of the Mohicans*; Bowery Boys comedies)

Foxx, Jimmie (James Emory Fox; "Double X"; "The Beast"; "The Maryland Strong Boy"; The Right-Handed Babe Ruth") (1907–1967) Am. baseball Hall-of-Famer

Foxx, Redd (John Elroy Sanford) (1922–1991) Am. actor/comedian ("Sanford & Son" TV series)

Foy, Eddie (Edwin Fitzgerald) (1856–1928) Am. vaudeville comedian (father of Eddie, Jr.)

Foy, Eddie, Jr. (Edward Fitzgerald) (1905–1983) Am. entertainer/actor (*The Pajama Game*; *The Farmer Takes a Wife*)

Foyt, A. J. (Anthony Joseph Foyt, Jr.; "Fancy Pants"; "The Houston Hurricane") (1935–) Am. auto racer

Fragonard, Jean (Jean-Honoré Fragonard) (1732–1806) Fr. rococo/neoclassical painter

Frame, Janet (Janet Paterson Frame Clutha) (1924–) N.Z. novelist/autobiographer (*An Angel at My Table*)

Frampton, Peter (Peter Kenneth Frampton) (1950–) Eng.-Am. rock singer/musician ("Show Me the Way"; "I'm in You"; formerly with Humble Pie)

France, Anatole (Jacques-Anatole-François Thibault) (1844–1924) Fr. novelist/poet/critic (*Penguin Island*; N—1921)

Franchi, Sergio (1933–1990) Am. pop singer

Franciosa, Anthony or **Tony** (Anthony George Papaleo) (1928–) Am. actor (TV's "Matt Helm"; *A Hatful of Rain*)

Francis I (1494–1547) Fr. king 1515–1547

Francis II (1544–1560) Fr. king 1559–1560

Francis, Anne ("The Little Queen of Soap Opera") (1930–) Am. actress ("Dallas" and "My Three Sons" TV series)

Francis, Arlene (Arline Francis Kazanjian) (1908–) Am. actress/game show host ("What's My Line?")

Francis, Connie (Concetta Rosa Maria Franconero) (1938–) Am. actress (*Where the Boys Are*)/pop singer ("Who's Sorry Now")

Francis, Cleve (1946–) Am. country singer ("Love Light")

Francis, Dick (Richard Stanley Francis) (1920–) Eng. jockey/mystery novelist (*Bonecrack; High Stakes*)

Francis, Genie (1962–) Am. actress ("General Hospital" soap opera [as Laura])

Francis, Missy (1972–) Am. child actress ("Little House on the Prairie" TV series)

Francis of Assisi, Saint (Francesco di Pietrodi Bernardone) (1181 or 1182–1226) Ital. friar (founded the Franciscan Order)

Francis, Russ (Russell Ross Francis) (1953–) Am. football player

Franciscus, James (James Grover Franciscus) (1934–1991) Am. actor ("Mr. Novak" TV series; *The Greek Tycoon*)

Franck, César Auguste (César Auguste Jean Guillaume Hubert Franck) (1822–1890) Bel.-Fr. composer/organist (*The Accursed Hunter*)

Franck, James (1882–1964) Am. physicist (worked on the atomic bomb; N—1925)

Franco, Francisco (Francisco Paulino Hermenegildo Teódulo Franco Bahamonde) (1892–1975) Span. soldier/dictator

Franco, John (John Anthony Franco) (1961–) Am. baseball pitcher

Franco, Julio (Julio Cesar Robles Franco) (1961–) Am. baseball player

Frank, Anne (1929–1945) Ger.-Dutch-Jew. diarist

Frank, Barney (1940–) Am. congressman

Franken, Al (C) Am. comedian ("Saturday Night Live" TV series)/comedy writer

Frankenheimer, John (John Michael Frankenheimer) (1930–) Am. film director (*52 Pick-Up; The Manchurian Candidate*)

Frankfurter, Felix (1882–1965) Am. Supreme Court jurist (1939–1962)

Franklin, Aretha ("Queen of Soul") (1942–) Am. soul/pop singer ("Respect"; "Freeway of Love")

Franklin, Benjamin (a/k/a Richard Saunders) (1706–1790) Am. writer (*Poor Richard's Almanack*)/statesman/philosopher/scientist/inventor (lightning conductor, bifocal spectacles, Franklin stove)

Franklin, Bonnie (Bonnie Gail Franklin) (1944–) Am. actress ("One Day at a Time" TV series)

Franklin, Miles (Stella Maraia Sarah Miles Franklin; a/k/a Brent of Bin Bin) (1879–1954) Austral. novelist (*My Brilliant Career*)

Frann, Mary (Mary Luecke) (1943–) Am. actress ("Newhart" TV series)

Franz, Arthur (1920–) Am. actor (*The Caine Mutiny; Sands of Iwo Jima*)

Franz, Dennis (1944–) Am. actor ("NYPD Blue" and "Hill Street Blues" TV series)

Franz Ferdinand *see* Ferdinand, Francis Franz

Fraser, Dame Antonia (Antonia Pakenham) (1932–) Eng. novelist/biographer (*Mary, Queen of Scots*)

Fraser, Dawn ("Granny") (1937–) Austral. swimmer

Fratianne, Linda (1960–) Am. figure skater

Fratianno, Jimmy ("The Weasel") (1913–) Am. gangster (highest-ranking Mafia member ever to "turn")

Frawley, William (1887–1966) Am. actor ("I Love Lucy" TV series)

Frayn, Michael (1933–) Eng. journalist/novelist/playwright (*The Tin Men; Noises Off; Sweet Dreams*)

Frazier, Joe (Joseph Frazier; "Smokin' Joe") (1944–) Am. boxer

Frazier, Walt (Walter Frazier, Jr.; "Clyde") (1945–) Am. basketball player

Frears, Stephen (Stephen Arthur Frears) (1941–) Eng. film director (*The Grifters; My Beautiful Laundrette; Sammy and Rosie Get Laid; Hero*)

Frederick I (1657–1713) Ger. king 1710–1713

Frederick II (Frederick the Great) (1712–1786) Ger. king 1740–1786

Frederick III (Friedrich Wilhelm Nikolaus Karl) (1831–1888) Ger. king 1888

Frederick, Pauline (Beatrice Pauline Libbey) (1883–1938) Am. actress (*Madame X*)

Frederick William I (1688–1740) Ger. king 1713–1740

Frederick William II (1744–1797) Ger. king 1786–1797

Frederick William III (1770–1840) Ger. king 1797–1840

Frederick William IV (1795–1861) Ger. king 1840–1861

Freed, Alan (1922–1965) Am. disc jockey/rock 'n' roll pioneer (coined the term "rock 'n' roll")/songwriter ("Sincerely")

Freed, Arthur (Arthur Grossman) (1894–1973) Am. songwriter/film producer (*Gigi; Meet Me in St. Louis; Singin' in the Rain*)

Freeland, Thornton (1898–) Am. film director (*Flying Down to Rio; Brewster's Millions*)

Freeling, Nicolas (1927–) Eng. mystery writer (created Piet Van der Valk; *Love in Amsterdam*)

Freeman, Cynthia (Bea Feinberg) (1915–1988) Am. romance novelist (*Come Pour the Wine; The Last Princess*)

Freeman, Mona (Monica Elizabeth Freeman) (1926–) Am. actress (*The Heiress; Black Beauty*)

Freeman, Morgan (1937–) Am. actor (*Driving Miss Daisy; Unforgiven; Robin Hood: Prince of Thieves*)

Frehley, Ace (Paul Frehley) (1950–) Am. rock guitarist (with Kiss)

Frémont, John C. (John Charles Frémont) (1813–1890) Am. explorer (mapped the Oregon Trail)/soldier/senator/presidential candidate, 1856

French, Daniel (Daniel Chester French) (1850–1931) Am. sculptor (*The Minute Man*)

French, Marilyn (a/k/a Mara Solwoska) (1929–) Am. novelist (*The Women's Room*)

French, Victor (1934–1989) Am. actor ("Little House on the Prairie" TV series)

Freneau, Philip (Philip Morin Freneau; "Poet of the American Revolution") (1752–1832) Am. poet (*American Liberty*)

Freud, Anna (1895–1982) Aus.-Eng. psychoanalyst (daughter of Sigmund; *The Ego and the Mechanisms of Defense*)

Freud, Sigmund (1856–1939) Aus. neurologist/psychiatrist (founder of psychoanalysis)/writer (*The Interpretation of Dreams*)

Frey, Glenn (1948–) Am. rock singer/musician ("You Belong to the City"; "Smuggler's Blues"; formerly with The Eagles)

Frick, Ford C. (Ford Christopher Frick) (1894–1978) Am. baseball Hall-of-Famer (player, pres. of the National League, baseball commissioner)

Fricker, Brenda (C) Ir.-Eng. actress (O—1989—*My Left Foot*)

Frickie, Janie (Janie Fricke) (1947–) Am. country singer ("He's a Heartache [Looking for a Place to Happen]")

Friday, Nancy (1937–) Am. writer (*My Mother/Myself; Jealousy*)

Friedan, Betty (Betty Naomi Goldstein) (1921–) Am. feminist/writer (*The Feminine Mystique*)/founder of NOW

Friedkin, William (1939–) Am. film director (*The Exorcist; To Live and Die in L.A.*; O—1971—*The French Connection*)

Friedman, Bruce J. (Bruce Jay Friedman) (1930–) Am. novelist/short story writer/playwright (*Stern*)/screenwriter (*Doctor Detroit; Splash*)

Friedman, Kinky (Richard Friedman) (1944–) Am. country singer ("Get Your Biscuits in the Oven and Your Buns in Bed")

Friedman, Milton (1912–) Am. economist (N—1976)/presidential adviser (Nixon, Reagan)

Friel, Brian (1929–) Am. playwright/writer (*The Enemy Within; Philadelphia, Here I Come*)

Friels, Colin (C) Austral. actor (*Warm Nights on a Slow Moving Train; Darkman*)

Friml, Rudolf (Charles Rudolf Friml) (1879–1972) Am. composer (*Rose Marie; Indian Love Call*; studied under Dvořák)

Frings, Ketti (Katharine Hartley; a/k/a Anita Kilore) (1909–1981) Am. playwright (P—1958—*Look Homeward, Angel*)/screenwriter (*Come Back, Little Sheba*)

Fripp, Robert (1946–) Eng. rock/avant-garde singer/guitarist (with King Crimson)

Frisch, Frankie (Frank Francis Frisch;

"The Fordham Flash"; "Dutchman") (1898–1973) Am. baseball Hall-of-Famer

Frisch, Max (Max Rudolf Frisch) (1911–) Swi. playwright (*The Firebugs*)/novelist (*Homo Faber*)/architect

Frishberg, Dave (David Lee Frishberg) (1933–) Am. jazz/cabaret pianist/singer ("My Attorney Bernie")

Frizzell, David (1941–) Am. country singer (brother of Lefty; "I'm Gonna Hire a Wino to Decorate Our Home")

Frizzell, Lefty (William Orville Frizzell) (1928–1975) Am. country singer/musician (brother of David; "If You've Got the Money, I've Got the Time")

Fröbe, Gert (Gert Frober) (1913–1988) Ger. actor (*Goldfinger* [title role])

Frobisher, Sir Martin (c. 1535–1594) Eng. soldier/explorer (discovered Frobisher Bay)

Fromm, Erich (1900–1980) Am. philosopher/psychoanalyst (*The Art of Loving*)

Fromme, Squeaky (Lynette Fromme) (1948–) Am. follower of Charles Manson (attempted to assassinate Gerald Ford)

Frost, David (David Paradine Frost) (1939–) Eng. talk show host ("The David Frost Show")

Frost, Robert (Robert Lee Frost) (1874–1963) Am. poet (P—1924—*New Hampshire: A Poem with Notes and Grace Notes*; P—1931—*Collected Poems*; P—1937—*A Further Range*; P—1943—*A Witness Tree*)

Frost, Sadie (C) Eng. actress (*Bram Stoker's Dracula*)

Fry, Christopher (Christopher Fry Harris) (1907–) Eng. playwright (*The Lady's Not for Burning*)/screenwriter (*Ben Hur*; *The Bible*)

Fry, Roger (Roger Eliot Fry) (1866–1934) Eng. art critic/painter

Frye, Northrop (Herman Northrop Frye) (1912–) Am. literary critic (*Anatomy of Criticism*)

Frye, Soleil Moon (1976–) Am. actress (TV's "Punky Brewster")

Fuad I (1868–1936) Egypt. sultan 1917–1922/king 1922–1936

Fuentes, Carlos (1928–) Mex. novelist/short story writer (*The Death of Artemio Cruz*)

Fuentes, Tito (Rigoberto Peat Fuentes) (1944–) Am. baseball player

Fugard, Athol (Athol Harold Fugard) (1932–) S. Afr. playwright/actor/director (*Blood Knot*)

Fulbright, William (James William Fulbright) (1905–) Am. senator/writer (*The Crippled Giant*)

Fulghum, Robert (Robert L. Fulghum) (1937–) Am. writer (*All I Really Need to Know I Learned in Kindergarten*)

Fuller, Alfred Carl (1885–1973) Am. businessman (the Fuller Brush Company)

Fuller, Charles (1939–) Am. playwright (P—1982—*A Soldier's Play*)

Fuller, Loie (Marie Louise Fuller) (1862–1928) Am. dancer (invented serpentine dance)

Fuller, Melville W. III (1833–1910) Am. Supreme Court chief justice (1888–1910)

Fuller, R. Buckminster (Richard Buckminster Fuller) (1895–1983) Am. engineer/inventor (geodesic dome)

Fulton, Eileen (Margaret Elizabeth McLarty) (1934–) Am. actress ("As the World Turns" soap opera)

Fulton, Robert (1765–1815) Am. engineer/inventor (metal-clad submarine, long-distance steamboat)

Funicello, Annette (1942–) Am. actress ("The Mickey Mouse Club" TV series)

Funt, Allen (1914–) Am. TV host ("Candid Camera")

Furie, Sidney J. (1933–) Can. film director (*The Ipcress File*; *Lady Sings the Blues*)

Furillo, Carl (Carl Anthony Furillo; "Skoonj"; "The Reading Rifle") (1922–1989) Am. baseball player

Furlong, Edward (1977–) Am. child actor (*Terminator 2: Judgment Day*; *Home of Our Own*)

Furness, Betty (Elizabeth Mary Furness) (1916–) Am. actress/TV host ("Today")/consumer advocate

Furtwängler, William (1886–1954) Ger. orchestra conductor (Berlin and Vienna Philharmonics)

Fury, Billy (Ronald Wycherly) (1941–1983) Eng. pop singer ("That's Love"; "In Thoughts of You")

Gabel, Martin (1912–1986) Am. actor (*The Front Page*)/game show panelist ("What's My Line?")

Gabin, Jean (Jean-Alexis Gabin Moncorgé) (1904–1976) Fr. actor (*La Grande Illusion*; *Les Miserables*)

Gable, Clark (William Clark Gable; "The

King") (1901–1960) Am. actor (Rhett Butler in *Gone with the Wind*; O— 1931—*It Happened One Night*)

Gabo, Naum (Naum Neemia Pevsner) (1890–1977) Russ. sculptor

Gabor, Eva (1921–) Hung.-Am. actress (sister of Magda and Zsa Zsa; "Green Acres" TV series)

Gabor, Magda (1917–) Hung.-Am. actress (sister of Eva and Zsa Zsa)

Gabor, Zsa Zsa (Sari Gabor) (1916–) Hung.-Am. actress (sister of Magda and Eva; *Public Enemy Number One*; *Moulin Rouge*)

Gabriel, Peter (1950–) Eng. rock singer/ musician ("Sledgehammer"; "Shock the Monkey"; formerly with Genesis)

Gacy, John Wayne (John Wayne Michael Gacy) (1942–) Am. serial killer (33 victims)

Gadda, Carlo (Carlo Emilio Gadda) (1893–1973) Ital. novelist/essayist (*Acquainted with Grief*)

Gaddis, William (William Thomas Gaddis) (1922–) Am. novelist (*JR*; *Carpenter's Gothic*)

Gagarin, Yuri or Yury (Yuri Alekseyovich Gagarin) (1934–1968) Russ. cosmonaut (first man in space, 1961)

Gail, Max (Maxwell Trowbridge Gail, Jr.) (1943–) Am. actor ("Barney Miller" TV series)

Gaines, Ernest J. (1933–) Am. novelist/ short story writer (*The Autobiography of Miss Jane Pittman*)

Gaines, William M. (William Maxwell Gaines) (1922–1992) Am. publisher (*Mad*)

Gainey, Bob (Robert Michael Gainey) (1953–) Can. hockey player

Gainsborough, Thomas (1727–1788) Eng. portrait/landscape painter

Galarraga, Andres (Andres Jose Padovani Galarraga) (1961–) Venez.-Am. baseball player

Galbraith, John Kenneth (1908–) Am. economist/writer (*The Affluent Society*; *The Age of Uncertainty*)

Gale, Zona (1874–1938) Am. novelist/short story writer/playwright (P—1921—*Miss Lulu Bett*)

Galen (Claudius Galen) (129–c. 199) Gr. physician (showed that arteries carry blood)

Galileo (Galileo Galilei) (1564–1642) Ital. mathematician/astronomer/physicist/in-

ventor (telescope; discovered pendulum motion)

Gallagher (c. 1946–) Am. comedian (smashes watermelons with sledgehammers)

Gallagher, Peter (1955–) Am. actor (*sex, lies, and videotape*; *The Player*; *Short Cuts*; *Mother's Boys*)

Gallagher, Rory (1948–) Ir. blues/rock guitarist

Gallico, Paul (Paul William Gallico) (1897–1976) Am. journalist/novelist (*The Poseidon Adventure*)

Galli-Curci, Amelita (née Galli) (1889–1963) Ital.-Am. opera singer (soprano)

Gallo, Ernest (1910–) Am. vintner (brother of Julio)

Gallo, Julio (1911–1993) Am. vintner (brother of Ernest)

Gallup, George (George Horace Gallup) (1901–1984) Am. statistician/pollster (founded the American Institute of Public Opinion)

Galsworthy, John (a/k/a John Sinjohn) (1867–1933) Eng. novelist/playwright (*The Forsyte Saga*; N—1932)

Galway, James (1939–) Ir. classical flute player

Gam, Rita (Rita Eleanor MacKay) (1928–) Am. actress (*Klute*; *No Exit*)

Gambino, Carlo (1902–1976) Ital.-Am. crime boss

Gamow, George (1904–1968) Russ.-Am. cosmologist/physicist (developed the quantum theory of radioactivity)

Gance, Abel (Abel Perethon) (1889–1981) Fr. film director (*Napoléon* [1927]; *J'accuse*)

Gandhi, Indira (Indira Priyadarshini Nehru Gandhi) (1917–1984) Ind. prime minister 1966–1977 (daughter of Jawaharlal Nehru)

Gandhi, Mahatma (Mohandas Karamchand; "Mahatma" means "greatsouled") (1869–1948) Ind. philosopher/ political leader

Gann, Ernest K. (Ernest Kellogg Gann) (1910–1991) Am. adventure novelist (*The High and the Mighty*)

Ganz, Bruno (1941–) Swi.-Ger. actor (*Wings of Desire*; *The Marquise of O*)

Garagiola, Joe (Joseph Henry Garagiola) (1926–) Am. sportscaster

Garbo, Greta (Greta Lovisa Gustafsson) (1905–1990) Swed. actress (*Ninotchka*; *Anna Karenina*; *Queen Christina*)

Garcia, Andy (Andres Arturo Garci-Menendez) (1956–) Cub.-Am. actor (*Internal Affairs*; *Jennifer 8*; *The Godfather, Part III*)

Garcia, Jerry (Jerome John Garcia) (1942–) Am. rock musician (with The Grateful Dead)

García Lorca, Federico (1898–1936) Span. poet/playwright (*Gypsy Ballads*; *Ode to Walt Whitman*)

García Márquez, Gabriel (Gabriel José García Márquez) (1928–) Col. novelist (*One Hundred Years of Solitude*; *Love in the Time of Cholera*; N—1982)

Gardenia, Vincent (Vincent Scognamiglio) (1922–1992) Am. actor (*Bang the Drum Slowly*; *Moonstruck*)

Gardner, Ava (Ava Lavinnia Johnson) (1922–1990) Am. actress (*Mogambo*; *The Barefoot Contessa*)

Gardner, Erle Stanley (a/k/a A. A. Fair, Charles M. Green, Carleton Kendrake, and Charles J. Kenny; "The Fiction Factory") (1889–1970) Am. novelist/detective story writer (created Perry Mason)

Garfield, Allen (Allen Goorwitz) (1939–) Am. actor (*Gable and Lombard*; *The Candidate*)

Garfield, James (James Abram Garfield) (1831–1881) 20th Am. pres. (1881; assassinated by Charles J. Guiteau)

Garfield, John (Julius Garfinkle) (1913–1952) Am. actor (*Body and Soul*; *The Postman Always Rings Twice*)

Garfield, Lucretia (Lucretia Rudolph) (1832–1918) Am. first lady (James)

Garfunkel, Art (Arthur Garfunkel) (1941–) Am. pop singer/songwriter ("I Only Have Eyes for You"; formerly with Simon & Garfunkel)

Gargan, William (1905–1979) Am. actor (TV's "Martin Kane, Private Eye"; *They Knew What They Wanted*)

Garibaldi, Giuseppe ("The Liberator of Italy") (1807–1882) Ital. mil. commander (led the "Red Shirts")

Garland, Beverly (Beverly Lucy Fessenden) (1926–) Am. actress ("My Three Sons" and "Scarecrow and Mrs. King" TV series)

Garland, Hamlin (Hannibal Hamlin Garland) (1860–1940) Am. novelist/short story writer (P—1922—*A Daughter of the Middle Border*)

Garland, Judy (Frances Ethel Milne Gumm) (1922–1969) Am. actress/singer (*The Wizard of Oz*; *Meet Me in St. Louis*; *A Star Is Born*; G—1961)

Garn, Jake (Edwin Jacob Garn) (1932–) Am. senator (and first politician in space, aboard space shuttle *Discovery*)

Garner, Erroll (Erroll Louis Garner) (1921–1977) Am. jazz pianist/songwriter ("Misty")

Garner, James (James Scott Baumgarner) (1928–) Am. actor ("The Rockford Files" TV series; *Murphy's Romance*; E—1976/77)

Garner, John N. (John Nance Garner; "Cactus Jack") (1868–1967) Am. v.p. (F. D. Roosevelt)

Garner, Peggy Ann (1931–1984) Am. child actress (*A Tree Grows in Brooklyn*; *Jane Eyre*)

Garnet, Henry Highland (1815–1882) Am. clergyman/abolitionist/orator

Garnett, Tay (William Taylor Garnett) (1895–1977) Am. film director (*Bataan*; *The Postman Always Rings Twice*)

Garr, Teri (1945–) Am. actress (*Tootsie*; *Mr. Mom*)

Garrett, Leif (1961–) Am. teen idol/pop singer ("I Was Made for Dancin' ")/actor (*The Outsiders*)

Garrett, Pat (Patrick Floyd Garrett) (1850–1908) Am. frontier sheriff (allegedly shot Billy the Kid)

Garrick, David (1717–1779) Eng. actor/theater manager/playwright (*Lethe*)

Garrison, Jim (Jim C. Garrison) (1921–1992) Am. lawyer (investigated the assassination of John F. Kennedy)

Garrison, William Lloyd (1805–1879) Am. abolitionist/journalist (*The Liberator*)

Garroway, Dave (David Cunningham Garroway) (1913–1982) Am. radio/TV host ("Today"; signature phrase: "Peace")

Garson, Greer (1908–) Ir. actress (*Goodbye, Mr. Chips*; *Madame Curie*; O—1942—*Mrs. Miniver*)

Garth, Jennie (1972–) Am. actress ("Beverly Hills, 90210" TV series; Danielle Steel's *Star*)

Garvey, Marcus (Marcus Moziah Garvey; "Emperor of the Kingdom of Africa") (1887–1940) Jam. political leader (led the "Back to Africa" movement)

Garvey, Steve (Steven Patrick Garvey) (1948–) Am. baseball player

Gary, Romain (Romain Kacewgari; a/k/a Emile Ajar) (1914–1980) Fr. novelist (*The Roots of Heaven*)

Gasser, Herbert (Herbert Spencer Gasser) (1888–1963) Am. physiologist (N— 1944)

Gassman, Vittorio (1922–) Ital. actor (A Wedding; Bitter Rice; Anna)

Gastineau, Mark (Marcus D. Gastineau) (1956–) Am. football player

Gateley, Gallagher (1928–) Am. cartoonist (Heathcliff)

Gates, Bill (William Henry Gates) (1955–) Am. computer pioneer (founded Microsoft Corp.)

Gates, David (1940–) Am. pop singer/musician ("Goodbye Girl"; formerly with Bread and Leon Russell)

Gates, Horatio ("The Hero of Saratoga") (c. 1728–1806) Am. Revolutionary general

Gatlin, Larry (Larry Wayne Gatlin) (1948–) Am. country singer/musician (with The Gatlin Brothers; "All the Gold in California")

Gatling, Richard (Richard Jordan Gatling) (1818–1903) Am. inventor (machine gun)

Gatski, Frank (1922–) Am. football Hall-of-Famer

Gaudí, Antonio (Antonio Gaudí y Cornet) (1852–1926) Span. architect

Gauguin, Paul (Eugène-Henri-Paul Gaugin) (1848–1903) Fr. Fauvist painter

Gaultier, Jean-Paul (1952–) Fr. fashion designer (for Madonna, among others)

Gautier, Dick (1931–) Am. comedian/actor ("Get Smart" TV series)

Gautier, Theophile (Pierre Jules Theophile Gautier; "Le Bon Theo") (1811–1872) Fr. novelist/poet (Art for Art's Sake)

Gavilan, Kid (Gerardo González) (1926–) Cub.-Am. boxer

Gavin, John (John Anthony Golenor) (1928–) Am. actor (Psycho; Spartacus; Rich Man, Poor Man)/ambassador

Gay, John (1685–1732) Eng. poet/playwright (The Beggar's Opera)

Gaye, Marvin (Marvin Pentz Gaye) (1939–1984) Am. soul/pop singer ("What's Going On"; "I Heard It Through the Grapevine")

Gaye, Nona (c. 1974–) Am. pop singer (daughter of Marvin)

Gayle, Crystal (Brenda Gail Webb) (1951–) Am. country/pop singer (sister of Loretta Lynn; "Don't It Make My Brown Eyes Blue")

Gaynor, Gloria ("Queen of Disco") (1949–) Am. pop singer ("Never Can Say Goodbye"; "I Will Survive")

Gaynor, Janet (Laura Gainor; "The World's Sweetheart") (1906–1984) Am. actress (Sunrise; Street Angel; O— 1927/28—Seventh Heaven)

Gaynor, Mitzi (Francesca Mitzi Marlene de Charney von Gerber) (1931–) Am. actress (South Pacific; Anything Goes)

Gazzara, Ben (Biagio Anthony Gazzara) (1930–) Am. actor (Anatomy of a Murder; The Strange One)

Geary, Anthony (1947–) Am. actor ("General Hospital" soap opera [as Luke])

Geddes, Norman Bel (Norman Geddes) (1893–1958) Am. architect/stage designer/director/producer

Geer, Will (William Aughe Ghere) (1902–1978) Am. actor ("The Waltons" TV series; Jeremiah Johnson; E—1974/75)

Geffen, David (1944–) Am. entertainment mogul (founded Geffen Records)

Gehrig, Lou (Ludwig Heinrich Gehrig; "The Iron Horse"; "Columbia Lou"; "The Iron Man of Baseball"; "Old Biscuit Pants"; "The Pride of the Yankees"; "Twinkle Toes"; "Larrupin' Lou") (1903–1941) Am. baseball Hall-of-Famer

Gehringer, Charlie (Charles Leonard Gehringer; "The Mechanical Man"; "The Fowlerville Flailer") (1903–1993) Am. baseball Hall-of-Famer

Gehry, Frank (Frank Owen Gehry) (1929–) Am. architect

Geiberger, Al (Allen L. Geiberger) (1937–) Am. golfer

Geiger, Hans (Johannes Hans Wilhelm Geiger) (1882–1945) Ger. physicist (invented the Geiger Counter)

Geils, J. (Jerome Geils) (1946–) Am. rock guitarist (with The J. Geils Band; "Centerfold")

Gein, Ed (1906–1984) Am. murderer (the book and movie Psycho purportedly inspired by him)

Gelbart, Larry (1923–) Am. playwright (City of Angels)

Geldof, Bob ("Saint Bob") (1954–) Ir. rock musician/actor/organizer of Band Aid and Live Aid benefit concerts (formerly with The Boomtown Rats)

Geller, Uri (1946–) Isr. "mentalist" (debunked)

Gell-Mann, Murray (1929–) Am. physicist (discovered quarks; N—1969)

Gems, Pam (1925–) Eng. playwright (Queen Christina)

Genet, Jean (1910–1986) Fr. novelist (Miracle of the Rose; Thief's Journal)/

playwright (*The Maids*; *The Balcony*; *The Blacks*)
Genghis Khan (Temujin) (c. 1162–1227) Mong. mil./political leader
Gennaro, Peter (1924–) Am. dancer/choreographer
Gentry, Bobbie (Roberta Lee Streeter) (1944–) Am. pop singer ("Ode to Billy Joe"; G—1967)
George I (George Louis) (1660–1727) Eng. king 1714–1727
George II (George Augustus) (1683–1760) Eng. king 1727–1760
George III (George William Frederick) (1738–1820) Eng. king 1760–1820
George IV (George Augustus Frederick) (1762–1830) Eng. king 1820–1830
George V (George Frederick Ernest Albert) (1865–1936) Eng. king/emperor of India 1910–1936
George VI (Albert Frederick Arthur George) (1895–1952) Eng. king/emperor of India 1936–1952
George, Bill (William George) (1930–1982) Am. football Hall-of-Famer
George, Gladys (Gladys Clare) (1900–1954) Am. actress (*The Maltese Falcon*; *The Way of All Flesh*)
George, Lynda Day (Lynda Day) (1944–) Am. actress ("Mission: Impossible" TV series)
George, Phyllis (Phyllis Ann George) (1949–) Am. actress/reporter/Miss America 1971
George, Saint (3rd century) patron saint of England/Christian martyr
George, Susan (1950–) Eng. actress (*Straw Dogs*; *The Looking Glass War*)
Gephardt, Richard (Richard Andrew Gephardt) (1941–) Am. congressman
Gerard, Gil (1943–) Am. actor ("The Doctors" and "Buck Rogers of the 25th Century" TV series)
Gerardo (Gerardo Mejia III) (1965–) Ecua.-Am. rapper ("Rico Suave")
Gere, Richard (1949–) Am. actor (*Pretty Woman*; *An Officer and a Gentleman*; *American Gigolo*; *Intersection*)
Géricault, Théodore (Jean-Louis-André-Théodore Géricault) (1791–1824) Fr. "romantic" painter
Gernreich, Rudi (Rudolph Gernreich) (1922–1985) Aus.-Am. fashion designer
Gernsback, Hugo (1884–1967) Am. inventor/science fiction publisher (*Amazing Stories*)/editor (for whom Hugo awards were named)

Geronimo (Indian name Goyathlay: One Who Yawns) (1829–1909) Am. Apache chief
Gerry, Elbridge (Elbridge Thomas Gerry) (1744–1814) Am. v.p. (J. Madison)
Gershwin, George (Jacob Gershowitz; a/k/a Arthur Francis) (1898–1937) Am. composer (brother of Ira; *Rhapsody in Blue*; *Porgy and Bess*)
Gershwin, Ira (Israel Gershowitz) (1896–1983) Am. lyricist (brother of George; "Embraceable You"; "S'Wonderful"; P—1932—*Of Thee I Sing*)
Gertz, Alison (c. 1966–1992) Am. AIDS victim/activist/educator
Gertz, Jami (1965–) Am. actress ("Square Pegs" TV series; *Less Than Zero*; *The Lost Boys*)
Gerulaitis, Vitas (Vitas Kevin Gerulaitis; "The Lithuanian Lion") (1954–) Am. tennis player
Gervin, George ("The Iceman") (1952–) Am. basketball player
Getty, Balthazar (c. 1974–) Am. actor (*Lord of the Flies*)
Getty, Estelle (Estelle Scher) (1923–) Am. actress ("The Golden Girls" TV series; *Stop or My Mom Will Shoot*; E—1987/88)
Getty, J. Paul (Jean Paul Getty) (1892–1976) Am. tycoon/founder of the Getty Museum
Getz, Stan (Stanley Gayetzsky) (1927–1991) Am. jazz saxophonist ("Desafinado")
Ghiberti, Lorenzo ("Father of the Renaissance") (c. 1378–1455) Flor. painter/sculptor
Ghostley, Alice (Allyce Margaret Ghostley) (1926–) Am. actress ("Bewitched" TV series)
Gia (Gia Maria Carangi) (1960–1986) Am. model (subject of *Thing of Beauty: The Tragedy of Supermodel Gia* by Stephen Fried)
Giacometti, Alberto (1901–1966) Swi. sculptor (*Torso*)/painter/lithographer
Giacosa, Giuseppe (1847–1906) Ital. playwright/librettist (*Tosca*; *Madame Butterfly*)
Giaever, Ivar (1929–) Norw.-Am. physicist (N—)
Giambologna see Bologna, Giovanni da
Giancana, Sam ("Moony"; "Momo") (1908–1975) Am. crime boss
Giannini, Giancarlo (1942–) Ital. actor (*Seven Beauties*; *Swept Away*)

Giauque, William (William Francis Giauque) (1895–1982) Can.-Am. chemist (discovered oxygen isotopes; N—1949)

Gibb, Andy (Andrew Roy Gibb) (1958–1988) Eng. pop singer (brother of Barry, Maurice, and Robin; "I Just Want to Be Your Everything"; "An Everlasting Love")

Gibb, Barry (1946–) Eng. pop musician/singer (with The Bee Gees; Saturday Night Fever soundtrack)

Gibb, Cynthia (1963–) Am. actress ("Fame" TV series)

Gibb, Maurice (1949–) Eng. pop musician/singer (with The Bee Gees)

Gibb, Robin (1949–) Eng. pop musician/singer (with The Bee Gees)

Gibbon, Edward (1737–1794) Eng. historian (The Decline and Fall of the Roman Empire)

Gibbons, Leeza (1957–) Am. TV host ("Entertainment Tonight")

Gibbs, Courtney (1966–) Am. actress

Gibbs, Georgia (Fredda Gibbons; "Her Nibs, Miss Gibbs") (1926–) Am. singer ("Tweedle Dee")

Gibbs, Joe (Joe Jackson Gibbs) (1940–) Am. football coach

Gibbs, Josiah (Josiah Willard Gibbs) (1839–1903) Am. physicist (established basic theories for physical chemistry)

Gibbs, Marla (Marla Bradley Gibbs) (1946–) Am. actress ("The Jeffersons" and "227" TV series)

Gibbs, Terri (1954–) Am. country singer ("Somebody's Knockin' ")

Gibran, Kahlil (Jubran Khalil Jubran) (1883–1931) Leb.-Am. poet/essayist/novelist/artist (The Prophet)

Gibson, Althea ("Spider") (1927–) Am. tennis player (W—1957, 1958)

Gibson, Bob (Robert Gibson; "Hoot"; "Old Master") (1935–) Am. baseball Hall-of-Famer

Gibson, Charles (Charles Dana Gibson) (1867–1944) Am. illustrator (created the "Gibson Girl")

Gibson, Debbie (Deborah Ann Gibson) (1970–) Am. pop singer ("Only in My Dreams"; "Lost in Your Eyes")

Gibson, Don (1928–) Am. country singer ("Oh, Lonesome Me")

Gibson, Henry (Henry Bateman) (1935–) Am. comedian/actor ("Rowan & Martin's Laugh-In" TV series)

Gibson, Hoot (Edmund Richard Gibson; "The Smiling Whirlwind") (1892–1962) Am. cowboy actor (Ocean's Eleven; The Taming of the West)

Gibson, Josh (Joshua Gibson; "The Black Babe Ruth"; "The Black Bomber"; "The Babe Ruth of the Negro Leagues") (1911–1947) Am. baseball Hall-of-Famer

Gibson, Kirk (Kirk Harold Gibson; "Gibby") (1957–) Am. baseball player

Gibson, Mel (1956–) Austral. actor (Lethal Weapon films; Mad Max; Hamlet [1990]; Forever Young)

Gide, André (André-Paul-Guillaume Gide) (1869–1951) Fr. novelist (The Immortalist; The Counterfeiters; N—1947)

Gielgud, Sir John (Arthur John Gielgud) (1904–) Eng. actor (Secret Agent; Becket; O—1981—Arthur)

Gifford, Frank (Francis Newton Gifford) (1930–) Am. football Hall-of-Famer/sportscaster

Gifford, Kathie Lee (Kathie Lee Epstein) (1953–) Am. TV host ("Live with Regis & Kathie Lee")

Gift, Roland (1962–) Eng. pop singer (with Fine Young Cannibals; "She Drives Me Crazy")

Gilbert, Cass (1859–1934) Am. architect (Supreme Court building in Washington, DC; New York's Woolworth Building)

Gilbert, Henry F. (Henry Franklin Belknap Gilbert) (1868–1928) Am. composer (Negro Episodes)

Gilbert, John (John Pringle; a/k/a Jack Gilbert) (1895–1936) Am. actor (Flesh and the Devil; Queen Christina)

Gilbert, Melissa (a/k/a/ Melissa Gilbert-Brinkman) (1964–) Am. actress (sister of Sara; "Little House on the Prairie" TV series)

Gilbert, Sara (c. 1975–) Am. actress (sister of Melissa; "Roseanne" TV series)

Gilbert, Sir W. S. (William Schwenk Gilbert) (1836–1911) Eng. lyricist (with Arthur Sullivan; The Mikado; H.M.S. Pinafore)

Gilberto, Astrud (1940–) Braz. singer ("One Note Samba")

Gilbreth, Elizabeth (1908–) Am. novelist (Cheaper by the Dozen)

Gilder, Nick (1951–) Eng.-Can. rock singer/songwriter ("Hot Child in the City")

Giles, Warren C. (Warren Crandall Giles) (1896–1979) Am. National League (baseball) pres./baseball Hall-of-Famer

Gilford, Jack (Jacob Gellman) (1907–1990) Am. actor (*Save the Tiger*; *Catch-22*)

Gill, Brendan (1914–) Am. journalist (*New Yorker*)

Gill, Johnny (1965–) Am. pop singer ("Rub You the Right Way"; formerly with New Edition)

Gill, Vince (Vincent Gill Grant) (1957–) Am. country singer ("I Still Believe in You"; "Pocket Full of Gold")

Gillan, Ian (1945–) Eng. rock singer (with Deep Purple; "Smoke On the Water")

Gillespie, Dizzy (John Birks Gillespie) (1917–1993) Am. jazz (bebop) trumpeter/composer

Gillette, Anita (Anita Lee Luebben) (1936–) Am. actress ("Quincy" TV series)

Gillette, King Camp (1885–1932) Am. businessman/inventor (safety razor, disposable blade)

Gilley, Mickey (Mickey Leroy Gilley) (1936–) Am. country singer/actor (cousin of Jerry Lee Lewis; *Urban Cowboy*)

Gilliam, Terry (Terry Vance Gilliam) (1940–) Am. film director (*Brazil*; *The Adventures of Baron Munchhausen*; *The Fisher King*)

Gilliatt, Penelope (Penelope Ann Gilliat) (1933–1993) Eng. film critic/writer (*Sunday, Bloody Sunday*)

Gilman, Dorothy (a/k/a Dorothy Gilman Butters) (1923–) Am. mystery writer (created Mrs. Pollifax)

Gilmore, Artis (1949–) Am. basketball player

Gingold, Hermione (Hermione Ferdinanda Gingold) (1897–1987) Eng. actress (*Bell, Book and Candle*; *Gigi*)

Gingrich, Newt (Newton Leroy Gingrich) (1943–) Am. congressman

Ginsberg, Allen (1926–) Am. "beat" poet (*Howl*; *Kaddish*)

Ginsburg, Ruth (née Bader) (c. 1933–) Am. feminist/lawyer/Supreme Court jurist (1993–)

Gionfriddo, Al (Albert Francis Gionfriddo) (1922–) Am. baseball player

Giorgione (Giorgione da Castelfranco) (1477–1511) Ital. painter (studied under Giovanni Bellini)

Giotto (Giotto di Bondone) (c. 1267–1337) Flor. painter/sculptor/architect (studied under Cimabue)

Giovanni, Nikki (Yolande Cornelia Gio-

vanni, Jr.) (1943–) Am. poet (*Black Feeling, Black Talk*)

Girardon, François (1628–1715) Fr. sculptor (tomb of Cardinal de Richelieu)

Giraudoux, Jean (Hippolyte-Jean Giraudoux) (1882–1944) Fr. playwright (*Electra*; *Tiger at the Gates*; *The Madwoman of Chaillot*)

Giscard D'Estaing, Valéry (1926–) Fr. pres. 1974–1981

Gish, Annabeth (1971–) Am. actress (*Mystic Pizza*; *Coupe de Ville*; *Shag*)

Gish, Dorothy (Dorothy Elizabeth de Guiche) (1898–1968) Am. actress (*Nell Gwyn*; *Broken Blossoms*)

Gish, Lillian (Lillian Diana de Guiche; a/k/a Dorothy Elizabeth Carter and Baby Lillian; "Carrots"; "First Lady of the Silent Screen") (1893–1993) Am. actress (*The Birth of a Nation*; *Orphans of the Storm*)

Giuliane, Rudy (Rudolph Giuliane) (1944–) Am. attorney/New York City Mayor

Givenchy, Hubert de (Hubert James Taffin de Givenchy) (1927–) Fr. fashion designer

Givens, Robin (1964–) Am. actress ("Head of the Class" TV series; *Harlem Nights*)

Gladstone, William (William Ewart Gladstone; "The Grand Old Man") (1809–1898) Eng. prime minister 1868–1874, 1880–1885, 1886, 1892–1894

Glaser, Donald (Donald Arthur Glaser) (1926–) Am. physicist/inventor (bubble chamber) (N—1960)

Glaser, Paul Michael (Paul Manfred Glaser) (1943–) Am. actor ("Starsky and Hutch" TV series)

Glasgow, Ellen (Ellen Anderson Gholson Glasgow) (1873–1945) Am. novelist (P—1942—*In This Our Life*)

Glaspell, Susan (Susan Keating Glaspell) (1882–1948) Am. novelist/playwright (P—1931—*Alison's House*)

Glass, Carter (1858–1946) Am. senator/govt. official (secretary of the treasury)

Glass, Philip (1937–) Am. composer (*Einstein on the Beach*)

Glazunov, Aleksandr (Aleksandr Konstantinovich Glazunov) (1865–1936) Russ. composer (studied under Rimsky-Korsakov; *Raymonda*)

Gleason, Jackie (Herbert John Clarence Gleason; "The Great One"; "Mr. Saturday Night") (1916–1987) Am. actor ("The

Honeymooners" TV series; T—1960; signature phrase: "How sweet it is")

Gleason, James (1886–1959) Am. actor (*Suddenly*; *Murder on a Honeymoon*)

Glenn, John (John Herschel Glenn, Jr.) (1921–) Am. astronaut (first American to orbit Earth)/senator

Glenn, Scott (Theodore Scott Glenn) (1942–) Am. actor (*The Right Stuff*; *Backdraft*; *The Silence of the Lambs*)

Gless, Sharon (1943–) Am. actress ("Cagney & Lacey" TV series; E—1985/86, 1986/87)

Glière, Reinhold (Reinhold Moritzovich Glière) (1875–1956) Russ. composer (*The Red Poppy* ballet)

Glinka, Mikhail (Mikhail Ivanovich Glinka; "Father of Russian Music") (1804–1857) Russ. composer (*A Life for the Czar*)

Glitter, Gary (Paul Gadd; a/k/a Paul Raven and Paul Monday) (1944–) Eng. rock singer ("Rock and Roll Part 2")

Glover, Crispin (1964–) Am. actor (*River's Edge*; *At Close Range*; *The Doors*)

Glover, Danny (1947–) Am. actor (*Lethal Weapon*; *Grand Canyon*; *Bopha!*)

Gluck, Alma (Reba Fiersohn) (1884–1938) Am. opera singer (soprano)

Gluck, Christoph Willibald (1714–1787) Ger. operatic composer (*Alceste*)

Gluck, Louise (Louise Elisabeth Gluck) (1943–) Am. poet (*The Garden*)

Glyn, Elinor (Elinor Sutherland) (1864–1943) Eng. romance novelist (*Three Weeks*)

Gobel, George (George Leslie Gobel; "Lonesome George") (1919–) Am. actor/comedian ("The George Gobel Show" TV seriesl signature phrase: "Well, I'll be a dirty bird")

Godard, Jean-Luc (a/k/a Hans Lucas) (1930–) Fr. film director (*Breathless*; *Every Man for Himself*; *Contempt*)

Goddard, Paulette (Pauline Marion Goddard Levee; a/k/a Marion Levy) (1911–1990) Am. actress (*Modern Times*; *So Proudly We Hail*)

Goddard, Robert (Robert Hutchings Goddard; "Father of Modern Rocketry"; "Father of American Rocketry") (1882–1945) Am. rocketry pioneer (invented the first liquid-fueled rocket)

Godden, Rumer (Margaret Rumer Godden) (1907–) Eng. novelist (*Black Narcissus*)

Godfrey, Arthur (Arthur Michael Godfrey; "Ole Redhead") (1903–1983) Am. radio/TV host ("Arthur Godfrey and His Friends")

Godiva, Lady (Godgifu) (1010–1067) Eng. social reformer (rode naked through Coventry to get her husband to lower taxes)

Godley, Kevin (1945–) Eng. pop singer/musician ("Cry"; with Godley & Creme; formerly with 10CC)

Godunov, Alexander (Boris Alexander Godunov) (1949–) Am. ballet dancer/actor (*Witness*)

Godunov, Boris (Boris Fyodorovich Godunov) (c. 1551–1605) Russ. czar 1598–1605

Godwin, Gail (1937–) Am. novelist/short story writer (*A Mother and Two Daughters*)

Godwin, William (1756–1836) Eng. novelist/philosopher (father of Mary Shelley; *History of the Commonwealth*)

Goebbels, Joseph (Paul Joseph Goebbels) (1897–1945) Ger. Nazi minister of propaganda

Goeppert-Mayer, Marie (Marie Gertrude Goeppert) (1906–1972) Am. physicist (N—1963)

Goering or **Göring, Hermann** (Hermann Wilhelm Goering) (1893–1946) Ger. Nazi political leader (Hitler's deputy)

Goethals, George (George Washington Goethals) (1858–1928) Am. engineer (Panama Canal)

Goethe, Johann Wolfgang von (1749–1832) Ger. poet (*Faust*)

Goetz, Bernard ("The Subway Vigilante") (1947–) Am. businessman (shot four youths—who he believed were about to rob him—on a New York City subway; convicted of carrying a concealed weapon)

Goffin, Gerry (1939–) Am. pop lyricist (father of Louise; with wife Carole King, "Will You Love Me Tomorrow?"; "The Loco-Motion")

Goffin, Louise (1960–) Am. pop singer (daughter of Carole King and Gerry Goffin; "Remember [Walking in the Sand]")

Gogol, Nikolay (Nikolay Vasilyevich Gogol) (1809–1852) Russ. novelist/short story writer/playwright (*The Inspector-General*)

Golan, Gila (Miriam Goldenburg) (c. 1940–) Pol.-Am. actress (*Ship of Fools*; *Our Man Flint*)

Gold, Andrew (1951–) Am. pop singer/ songwriter (son of Marni Nixon; "Lonely Boy")

Gold, Herbert (1924–) Am. novelist/short story writer (*Therefore Be Bold*)

Gold, Tracey (1969–) Am. actress ("Growing Pains" TV series)

Goldberg, Arthur J. III (Arthur Joseph Goldberg III) (1908–1990) Am. Supreme Court jurist (1962–1965)

Goldberg, Rube (Reuben Lucius Goldberg) (1883–1970) Am. cartoonist (created Boob McNutt; P—1948)

Goldberg, Whoopi (Caryn E. Johnson) (1949–) Am. actress (*The Color Purple*; *Sister Act*; O—1990—*Ghost*)

Goldblum, Jeff (1952–) Am. actor (*The Fly* [1986]; *Jurassic Park*; *The Big Chill*)

Golden, Harry (Harry Lewis Goldhirsch) (1903–1981) Am. writer (*Only in America*; *For 2¢ Plain*)

Golding, Sir William (William Gerald Golding) (1911–1993) Eng. novelist (*Lord of the Flies*; N—1983)

Goldman, Emma (1869–1940) Russ.-Am. political activist/feminist/anarchist

Goldman, William (1931–) Am. writer/ screenwriter (*Butch Cassidy and the Sundance Kid*)

Goldmark, Peter (Peter Carl Goldmark) (1906–1977) Am. inventor (long-playing phonograph record [LP])

Goldsboro, Bobby (1941–) Am. country singer ("Honey")/TV host ("The Bobby Goldsboro Show")

Goldsmith, Jerry (Jerrald Goldsmith) (1929–) Am. film composer (*The Omen*; TV's "Masada"; "Gunsmoke", etc.)

Goldsmith, Oliver ("Noll") (c. 1730–1774) Eng. poet/playwright/novelist (*The Vicar of Wakefield*; *She Stoops to Conquer*)

Goldstein, Joseph L. (Joseph Leonard Goldstein) (1940–) Am. scientist (researched cholesterol; N—1985)

Goldthwait, Bob ("Bobcat") (1962–) Am. comedian (*Police Academy* movies)

Goldwater, Barry (Barry Morris Goldwater) (1909–) Am. senator/presidential candidate, 1964/writer (*The Conscience of a Conservative*; *Why Not Victory?*)

Goldwyn, Samuel (Schmuel Gelbfisz; a/k/a Samuel Goldfish) (1882–1974) Am. movie pioneer/producer

Goldwyn, Tony (c. 1960–) Am. actor (grandson of Samuel; *Ghost*; *The Pelican Brief*)

Golino, Valeria (1966–) Am. actress (*Rain Man*)

Gombell, Minna (a/k/a Winifred Lee and Nancy Carter) (1893–1973) Am. actress (*The Thin Man*; *High Sierra*)

Gombrich, Sir E. H. (Ernst Hans Josef Gombrich) (1909–) Aus.-Eng. art historian/professor/writer (*The Story of Art*)

Gomez, Lefty (Vernon Louis Gomez; "Goofy"; "The Gay Castillion") (1909–1989) Am. baseball Hall-of-Famer

Gompers, Samuel (1850–1924) Am. labor leader (helped found the AF of L)

Gonne, Maud (Maud MacBride Gonne) (1866–1953) Ir. stage actress/artist/ diplomat

Gonzales, Pancho (Richard Alonzo Gonzales; "Gorgo") (1928–) Am. tennis player

Goodall, Jane (1934–) Eng. zoologist (known for work with chimpanzees)

Gooden, Dwight (Dwight Eugene Gooden; "Doc"; "Dr. K") (1964–) Am. baseball pitcher

Goodeve, Grant (1952–) Am. actor ("Eight Is Enough" TV series)

Goodman, Benny (Benjamin David Goodman; "King of Swing") (1909–1986) Am. jazz clarinetist/bandleader ("Let's Dance"; "Avalon")

Goodman, Dody (Dolores Goodman) (1929–) Am. actress ("Mary Hartman, Mary Hartman" TV series)

Goodman, John (1953–) Am. actor ("Roseanne" TV series; *Arachnophobia*; *The Babe*; *Matinee*)

Goodrich, Frances (1891–1984) Am. playwright (P—1956—*The Diary of Anne Frank*)/screenwriter (with Albert Hackett, *The Thin Man*; *Naughty Marietta*)

Goodson, Mark (1915–1992) Am. game show creator/producer (many with William Todman; "The Price Is Right"; "To Tell the Truth")

Goodwin, Kia (1973–) Am. child actress ("227" TV series)

Goodyear, Charles (1800–1860) Am. inventor (vulcanization of rubber)

Goolagong, Evonne (Evonne Fay Goolagong) (1951–) Austral. tennis player (W—1971, 1980)

Goranson, Lecy (Alicia Goranson) (c. 1974–) Am. actress ("Roseanne" TV series)

Gorbachev, Mikhail (Mikhail Sergeyevich

Gorbachev) (1931–) Russ. political leader (N—1990)

Gorbachev, Raisa (Raisa Maksimovna Titorenko) (1934–) Russ. wife of Mikhail Gorbachev

Gorcey, Leo (Leo Bernard Gorcey) (1915–1969) Am. actor (one of the Dead End Kids and the Bowery Boys)

Gordimer, Nadine (1923–) S. Afr. novelist/short story writer (*Burger's Daughter*; *The Conservationist*; *July's People*; N—1991)

Gordon, Bert (Barney Gorodetsky; "The Mad Russian") (1898–1974) Am. radio comedian

Gordon, Dexter (Dexter Keith Gordon) (1923–1990) Am. jazz saxophonist

Gordon, Gale (Charles T. Aldrich, Jr.) (1906–) Am. actor ("The Lucy Show" TV series)

Gordon, Michael (1909–) Am. film director (*Pillow Talk*; *Another Part of the Forest*; *Cyrano de Bergerac*)

Gordon, Ruth (Ruth Gordon Jones) (1896–1985) Am. screenwriter (with Garson Kanin; *Adam's Rib*; *Pat and Mike*)/actress (O—1968—*Rosemary's Baby*)

Gordy, Berry, Jr. (1929–) Am. record producer (founded Motown Records)

Gore, Al (Albert Arnold Gore, Jr.) (1948–) Am. v.p. (Clinton)

Gore, Lesley (1946–) Am. pop singer ("It's My Party"; "You Don't Own Me")

Gore, Tipper (Mary Elizabeth Aitcheson) (1946–) Am. head of the Parents Music Resource Committee (wife of Al)

Goren, Charles H. (Charles Henry Goren) (1901–) Am. bridge (card game) expert/writer (*Winning Bridge Made Easy*)

Gorey, Edward (1925–) Am. writer/illustrator (*Amphigorey*)

Gorgeous George (George Raymond Wagner) (c. 1915–1963) Am. wrestler

Gorgias (a/k/a Gorgias of Leontini) (c. 483–375 B.C.) Gr. philosopher/rhetorician

Gorki or **Gorky, Maxim** or **Maksim** (Aleksey Maksimovich Peshkov) (1868–1936) Russ. writer (*The Lower Depths*)

Gorky, Arshile (Vosdanig Manoog Adoian) (1904–1948) Arm.-Am. painter (*Diary of a Seducer*)

Gorman, Cliff (1936–) Am. actor (*All That Jazz*; *An Unmarried Woman*; Broadway's *Lenny*; T—1972)

Gorme, Eydie (Edith Gormenzano) (1931–) Am. singer ("Blame It on the Bossa Nova"; G—1966)

Gorshin, Frank (Frank John Gorshin) (1934–) Am. actor (The Riddler in "Batman" TV series)

Gortner, Marjoe (Hugh Marjoe Ross Gortner) (1944–) Am. evangelist/actor ("Falcon Crest" TV series)

Gosden, Freeman (Freeman Fisher Gosden) (1899–1982) Am. radio comedian (Amos 'n' Andy)

Gosdin, Vern ("The Voice") (1934–) Am. country singer ("I'm Still Crazy")

Goslin, Goose (Leon Allen Goslin) (1900–1971) Am. baseball Hall-of-Famer

Gossage, Goose (Richard Michael Gossage) (1951–) Am. baseball pitcher

Gossett, Louis or **Lou, Jr.** (1936–) Am. actor (*The Principal*; *A Raisin in the Sun*; O—1982—*An Officer and a Gentleman*)

Gottfried, Brian (1952–) Am. tennis player

Gottfried, Gilbert (C) Am. comedian

Gotti, John ("The Dapper Don"; "The Teflon Don") (c. 1941–) Am. crime boss

Goudge, Elizabeth (1900–1984) Eng. novelist/children's book writer (*Green Dolphin Street*)

Gould, Chester (1900–1985) Am. cartoonist (*Dick Tracy*)

Gould, Elliott (Elliott Goldstein) (1938–) Am. actor (*Bob & Carol & Ted & Alice*; *M*A*S*H*)

Gould, Glenn (Glenn Herbert Gould) (1932–1982) Can. concert pianist

Gould, Harold (1923–) Am. actor ("Rhoda" TV series; *Love and Death*; *Silent Movie*)

Gould, Jay (Jason Gould) (1836–1892) Am. financier/railroad speculator

Gould, Morton (1913–) Am. composer/orchestra conductor

Gould, Stephen Jay (1941–) Am. paleontologist/writer (*The Panda's Thumb*; *The Mismeasure of Man*)

Goulding, Edmund (1891–1959) Am. film director (*Grand Hotel*; *Dark Victory*; *The Old Maid*)

Goulding, Ray (Raymond Walter Goulding) (1922–1990) Eng.-Am. comedian (with Bob & Ray)

Goulet, Robert (Robert Gerard Goulet; born Stanley Applebaum) (1933–) Can. singer/actor (*Gay Purr-ee*; *Camelot*; T—1968)

Gounod, Charles François (1818–1893) Fr. composer (*Faust*; *Romeo and Juliet*)

Gowdy, Curt (Curtis Gowdy) (1919–) Am. sportscaster

Goya (Francisco José de Goya y Lucientes) (1746–1828) Span. painter (*Naked Maja*)

Grable, Betty (Elizabeth Ruth Grable; a/k/a Frances Dean) (1916–1973) Am. actress (*Pin-Up Girl; My Blue Heaven; Call Me Mister*)

Grade, Sir Lew (Lewis Winogradsky; Baron of Elstree) (1906–) Eng. film producer (*The Boys from Brazil; Movie Movie*)

Graf, Steffi (Stefanie Maria Graf; "Grafin") (1969–) Ger. tennis player (W—1988, 1989, 1991, 1992, 1993)

Graham, Bill (Wolfgang Wolodia Grajonca) (1931–1991) Am. rock concert promoter/producer

Graham, Billy (William Franklin Graham) (1918–) Am. evangelist/writer (*Peace with God*)

Graham, Katharine (Katharine Meyer) (1917–) Am. newspaper publisher (*Washington Post*)

Graham, Martha (1894–1991) Am. choreographer/dancer

Graham, Otto (Otto Everett Graham, Jr.; "Automatic Otto") (1921–) Am. football Hall-of-Famer

Graham, Sheilah (Lily Sheil) (1905–1988) Am. (Hollywood) gossip columnist/writer (*Beloved Infidel*)

Graham, Stedman (1951–) Am. businessman/fiancé of Oprah Winfrey

Grahame, Gloria (Gloria Grahame Hallward; a/k/a Gloria Hallward) (1924–1981) Am. actress (*Oklahoma!; Chilly Scenes of Winter;* O—1952—*The Bad and the Beautiful*)

Grahame, Kenneth (1859–1932) Scot. essayist/children's book writer (*The Wind in the Willows*)

Gramm, Lou (1950–) Am. rock singer ("Midnight Blue"; formerly with Foreigner)

Gramm, Phil (William Philip Gramm) (1942–) Am. senator

Grammer, Kelsey (1955–) Am. actor ("Cheers" and "Frasier" TV series)

Granatelli, Andy (Anthony Joseph Granatelli) (1923–) Am. auto racer

Grandmaster Flash (1958–) Am. rapper ("The Message")

Grandy, Fred (Frederick Lawrence Grandy) (1948–) Am. actor ("The Love Boat" TV series)/politician

Grange, Red (Harold Edward Grange; "The Galloping Ghost"; "The Wheaton Ice Man") (1903–1991) Am. football Hall-of-Famer

Granger, Farley (Farley Earle Granger II) (1925–) Am. actor (*Rope; Strangers on a Train*)

Granger, Stewart (James Lablache Stewart) (1913–1993) Eng.-Am. actor (*The Prisoner of Zenda; King Solomon's Mines*)

Grant, Amy ("The First Lady of Contemporary Christian Music") (1960–) Am. pop singer ("Baby Baby"; "Every Heartbeat")

Grant, Bud (Harold Peter Grant) (1927–) Am. football coach

Grant, Cary (Archibald Alexander Leach) (1904–1986) Eng. actor (*North by Northwest; The Awful Truth; Charade; Topper; Bringing Up Baby*)

Grant, Eddy (Edmond Montague Grant) (1948–) Am. rock guitarist/singer ("Electric Avenue")

Grant, Gogi (Myrtle Audrey Arinsberg) (1924–) Am. pop singer ("The Wayward Wind")

Grant, Jennifer (c. 1966–) Am. actress (daughter of Cary Grant and Dyan Cannon; "Beverly Hills, 90210" TV series)

Grant, Julia (Julia Boggs Dent) (1826–1902) Am. first lady (Ulysses S.)

Grant, Kirby (Kirby Grant Horn, Jr.) (1914–1985) Am. actor/bandleader ("Sky King" TV series; *Northwest Territory*)

Grant, Lee (Lyova Haskell Rosenthal) (1927–) Am. actress (mother of Dinah Manoff; O—1975—*Shampoo; Detective Story; Defending Your Life;* E—1965/66)

Grant, Rodney A. (c. 1959–) Am. actor (*Dances with Wolves*)

Grant, Ulysses S. (Ulysses Simpson Grant; born Hiram Ulysses Grant; "The American Caesar"; "Unconditional Surrender Grant"; "The Hero of Appomattox") (1822–1885) Am. mil. leader/18th Am. pres. (1869–1877)

Granville, Bonita (1923–1988) Am. actress (*Hitler's Children; Maid of Salem*)

Granville-Barker, Harley (Harley Granville Granville-Barker) (1877–1946) Eng. playwright/actor/critic (*Prefaces to Shakespeare*)

Grass, Günter (Günter Wilhelm Grass) (1927–) Ger. novelist/poet (*The Tin Drum; Cat and Mouse; Dog Years*)

Grau, Shirley Ann (1929–) Am. writer (P—1965—*The Keepers of the House*)

Grauman, Sid (Sidney Patrick Grauman) (1879–1950) Am. entertainment impresario (built Grauman's Chinese Theater in Hollywood)

Graves, Peter (Peter Aurness) (1925–) Am. actor ("Mission: Impossible" TV series; *Stalag 17*)

Graves, Robert (Robert Ranke Graves) (1895–1985) Eng. poet/writer (*Good-Bye to All That; I, Claudius*)

Gray, Asa (1810–1888) Am. botanist/educator (at Harvard)/writer (*Gray's Manual*)

Gray, Dobie (Leonard Victor Ainsworth, Jr.) (1942–) Am. pop singer ("Drift Away")

Gray, Erin (1952–) Am. actress ("Silver Spoons" TV series)

Gray, Harold (Harold Lincoln Gray) (1894–1968) Am. cartoonist (*Little Orphan Annie*)

Gray, Linda (1940–) Am. actress ("Dallas" TV series)

Gray, Simon (Simon James Holliday Gray) (1936–) Eng. playwright/novelist (*Butley*)

Gray, Spalding (1941–) Am. writer/actor (*Monster in a Box; Swimming to Cambodia*)

Gray, Thomas (1716–1771) Eng. poet (*The Progress of Poesy; Elegy Written in a Country Churchyard*)

Grayson, Kathryn (Zelma Kathryn Hedrick) (1922–) Am. actress/singer (*Kiss Me Kate*)

Graziano, Rocky (Rocco Barbella) (1921–1990) Am. boxer

Greco, Buddy (Armando Greco) (1926–) Am. pop singer/pianist

Greco, José (Costanzo Greco) (1918–) Am. dancer

Greeley, Andrew M. (Andrew Moran Greeley) (1928–) Am. novelist (*Thy Brother's Wife; God Game*)

Greeley, Horace (1811–1872) Am. newspaperman (*New York Tribune*)/politician

Greely, Adolphus (Adolphus Washington Greely) (1844–1935) Am. army general/arctic explorer/writer (*Handbook of Polar Discoveries*)

Green, Al (1946–) Am. soul singer ("Let's Stay Together")

Green, Brian Austin (1973–) Am. actor ("Beverly Hills 90210" TV series)

Green, Hetty (Henrietta Howland Green née Robinson; "The Witch of Wall Street") (1834–1916) Am. financier/investor

Green, Johnny (John W. Green) (1908–1989) Am. bandleader/composer (*Brigadoon; I Cover the Waterfront*)

Green, Mitzi (Elizabeth Keno) (1920–1969) Am. actress (*Tom Sawyer; Little Orphan Annie* [title role])

Green, Paul E. (Paul Eliot Green) (1894–1981) Am. playwright (P—1927—*In Abraham's Bosom*)

Greenaway, Peter (1942–) Eng. film director (*The Belly of an Architect; The Cook, The Thief, His Wife and Her Lover; Prospero's Books*)

Greenberg, Hank (Henry Benjamin Greenberg; "Hammerin' Hank") (1911–1986) Am. baseball Hall-of-Famer

Greene, Bob (Robert Bernard Greene, Jr.) (1947–) Am. journalist/writer (*Billion Dollar Baby; Be True to Your School: A Diary of 1964*)

Greene, Graham (C) Am. actor (*Dances with Wolves*)

Greene, Graham (Henry Graham Greene) (1904–1991) Eng. novelist/playwright/short story writer (*The Third Man; Brighton Rock; The Power and the Glory; Ministry of Fear*)

Greene, Joe (Charles Edward Greene; "Mean Joe Greene") (1946–) Am. football Hall-of-Famer

Greene, Lorne (Lorne Green) (1915–1987) Can. actor ("Bonanza" and "Battlestar Galactica" TV series)

Greene, Shecky (Fred Sheldon Greenfield) (1925–) Am. comedian

Greenspan, Alan (1926–) Am. economist/govt. official (head of the Federal Reserve Board)

Greenstreet, Sydney (Sydney Hughes Greenstreet) (1879–1954) Eng. actor (*The Maltese Falcon; Casablanca*)

Greenwich, Ellie (1940–) Am. pop songwriter (with husband Jeff Barry; "Be My Baby"; "Leader of the Pack"; "Da Do Ron Ron")

Greenwood, Charlotte (Frances Charlotte Greenwood) (1890–1978) Am. actress (*Oklahoma!; Down Argentine Way*)

Greenwood, Lee (1942–) Am. country singer/songwriter/musician ("I.O.U."; "God Bless the USA")

Greer, Germaine (1939–) Austral. feminist/writer (*The Female Eunuch*)

Greer, Jane (Bettejane Greer) (1924–) Am. actress (*Against All Odds; The Prisoner of Zenda*)

Gregg, Forrest (Alvis Forrest Gregg) (1933–) Am. football Hall-of-Famer

Gregory, Cynthia (Cynthia Kathleen Gregory) (1946–) Am. ballerina

Gregory, Dick (Richard Claxton Gregory) (1932–) Am. comedian/political activist/ presidential candidate 1968

Gretchaninoff, Aleksandr (Aleksandr Tikhonovich Grechaninoff) (1864–1956) Russ.-Am. composer (Over the Steppes)

Gretzky, Wayne ("The Great Gretzky"; "The Great One") (1961–) Can. hockey player

Grey, Lady Jane (1537–1554) Eng. queen (for nine days in 1553)

Grey, Jennifer (1960–) Am. actress (daughter of Joel; Dirty Dancing; Ferris Bueller's Day Off)

Grey, Joel (Joel Katz) (1932–) Am. singer/ actor (The Seven Per-Cent Solution; O— 1972—Cabaret)

Grey, Lita (Lillita MacMurray) (1908–) Am. actress/writer (My Life with Chaplin)

Grey, Nan (Eschal Miller) (1918–1993) Am. actress (Three Smart Girls; Sutter's Gold)

Grey, Zane (Pearl Zane Grey) (1875–1939) Am. westerns writer (Riders of the Purple Sage; The Spirit of the Border)

Grieco, Richard (1965–) Am. actor ("21 Jump Street" and "Booker" TV series)

Grieg, Edvard (Edvard Hagerup Grieg) (1843–1907) Norw. composer (Peer Gynt Suite)

Grier, Rosey (Roosevelt Grier) (1932–) Am. football player

Griffey, Ken (George Kenneth Griffey) (1950–) Am. baseball player

Griffin, Alfredo (Alfredo Claudino Baptist Griffin) (1957–) Dom.-Am. baseball player

Griffin, Archie (Archie Mason Griffin) (1954–) Am. football player

Griffin, Merv (Mervyn Edward Griffin) (1925–) Am. TV host/businessman

Griffith, Andy (Andrew Samuel Griffith) (1926–) Am. actor ("Mayberry R.F.D." and "Matlock" TV series)

Griffith, Clark (Clark Calvin Griffith; "The Old Fox") (1869–1955) Am. baseball Hall-of-Famer

Griffith, D. W. (David Llewellyn Wark Griffith; a/k/a Lawrence Griffith, M. Gaston de Trolignac, Granville Warwick, Captain Victor Marier, Marquis de Trolignac, Irene Sinclair, and Roy Sin-

clair) (1874–1948) Am. film pioneer (producer/director; The Birth of a Nation; Intolerance)

Griffith, Emile (Emile Alphonse Griffith) (1938–) Am. boxer

Griffith, Hugh (Hugh Emrys Griffith) (1912–1980) Wel. actor (Exodus; O— 1959—Ben Hur)

Griffith, Melanie (1957–) Am. actress (daughter of Tippi Hedren; Working Girl; A Stranger Among Us; Something Wild; Body Double)

Griffith-Joyner, Florence ("Flo-Jo") (1959–) Am. runner

Griffiths, Trevor (1935–) Eng. playwright (Reds; The Party)

Grimes, Burleigh (Burleigh Arland Grimes; "Ol' Stubblebeard") (1893– 1985) Am. baseball Hall-of-Famer

Grimes, Martha (C) Am. mystery writer (The Deer Leap; The Dirty Duck)

Grimes, Tammy (Tammy Lee Grimes) (1934–) Am. actress (mother of Amanda Plummer; Can't Stop the Music; T—1970)

Grimm, Charlie (Charles John Grimm; "Jolly Cholly") (1898–1983) Am. baseball player/manager

Grimm, Jakob (Jakob Ludwig Carl Grimm) (1785–1863) Ger. philologist/ folklorist (brother of Wilhelm; Grimm's Fairy Tales)

Grimm, Wilhelm (Wilhelm Carl Grimm) (1786–1859) Ger. philologist/folklorist (Grimm's Fairy Tales)

Grinnell, George (George Bird Grinnell) (1849–1938) Am. naturalist/founder of The Audubon Society

Gris, Juan (José Victoriano González) (1887–1927) Span. painter (synthetic cubism style)

Grisham, John (1956–) Am. suspense writer (The Firm; The Pelican Brief)

Grissom, Gus (Virgil Ivan Grissom) (1926– 1967) Am. astronaut (second American in space)

Grizzard, George (George Cooper Grizzard, Jr.) (1928–) Am. actor (Advise and Consent)

Grizzard, Lewis (1946–) Am. humorist/ writer (Don't Bend Over in the Garden, Granny: You Know Them Taters Have Eyes)

Grodin, Charles (1935–) Am. actor (Heaven Can Wait; Catch-22)

Groening, Matt (1954–) Am. cartoonist ("The Simpsons" TV series)

Grofé, Ferde (Ferdinand Rudolf von

Grofé) (1892–1972) Am. composer (*Grand Canyon Suite*)

Groh, David (David Lawrence Groh) (1939–) Am. actor ("Rhoda" TV series)

Gromyko, Andrey (Andrey Andreyevich Gromyko) (1909–1989) Russ. pres. 1985–1989

Gropius, Walter (Walter Adolph Gropius) (1883–1969) Am. architect (Bauhaus founder)

Grosbard, Ulu (1929–) Belg.-Am. film director (*Straight Time*; *The Subject Was Roses*)

Gross, Kevin (Kevin Frank Gross) (1961–) Am. baseball pitcher

Gross, Mary (1953–) Am. comedienne ("Saturday Night Live" TV series)

Gross, Michael (1947–) Am. actor ("Family Ties" TV series)

Gross, Milton (1895–1953) Am. cartoonist (*Gross Exaggerations*; *Nize Baby*; *Hiawatta*)

Grosz, George (George Ehrenfried Grosz) (1893–1959) Ger.-Am. painter/artist

Grove, Lefty (Robert Moses Grove; "Mose") (1900–1975) Am. baseball Hall-of-Famer

Groza, Lou (Louis Groza; "The Toe") (1924–) Am. football Hall-of-Famer

Gruber, Kelly (Kelly Wayne Gruber) (1962–) Am. baseball player

Gruenberg, Louis (1884–1964) Am. composer (*Jack and the Beanstalk*; *The Emperor Jones*)

Grusin, Dave (1934–) Am. film composer (*On Golden Pond*; *Tootsie*; *The Fabulous Baker Boys*)

Guardino, Harry (Harold Vincent Guardino) (1925–) Am. actor (*Dirty Harry*; *The Enforcer*)

Guber, Peter (1939–) Am. film producer (*Tango and Cash*)/executive (head of Sony Pictures)

Gucci, Aldo (1909–1990) Ital. fashion designer

Guccione, Bob (Robert Charles Joseph Edward Sabatini Guccione) (1930–) Am. magazine publisher (*Penthouse*)

Guerrero, Pedro (1956–) Dom.-Am. baseball player

Guest, C. Z. (1922–) Am. socialite/gardening expert/writer (*First Garden*)

Guest, Christopher (1948–) Am. actor (*This Is Spinal Tap*)

Guest, Cornelia ("Deb of the Decade"; "Deb of the Century") (1964–) Am. socialite (daughter of C. Z.)

Guest, Edgar A. (Edgar Albert Guest; "The Poet of the Plain People") (1881–1959) Am. poet/journalist (*A Heap O' Livin'*)

Guest, Judith (Judith Ann Guest) (1936–) Am. novelist (*Ordinary People*)

Guevara, Che (Ernesto Guevara de la Serna) (1928–1967) Arg. guerilla leader/writer (*Guerilla Warfare*)

Guggenheim, Peggy (Marguerite Guggenheim) (1898–1979) Am. art collector/patron

Guidry, Ron (Ronald Ames Guidry; "Louisiana Lightning"; "Gator") (1950–) Am. baseball pitcher

Guillaume, Robert (Robert Peter Williams) (1930 or 1937–) Am. actor ("Benson" [title role] and "Soap" TV series; E—1984/85)

Guillemin, Roger (Roger Charles Louis Guillemin) (1924–) Am. physiologist (N—1977)

Guillen, Ozzie (Oswaldo Jose Guillen Barrios) (1964–) Venez.-Am. baseball player

Guinan, Texas (Mary Louise Cecilia Guinan; "First Lady of the Speakeasies"; "Queen of the Nightclubs") (1884–1933) Am. actress/nightclub hostess (signature phrase: "Hello, sucker")

Guinness, Sir Alec (1914–) Eng. actor (*Kind Hearts and Coronets*; *A Passage to India*; O—1957—*The Bridge on the River Kwai*; T—1964)

Guisewhite, Cathy (Cathy Lee Guisewhite) (1950–) Am. cartoonist (*Cathy*)

Guitar, Bonnie (Bonnie Buckingham) (1924–) Am. pop singer/musician ("Dark Moon")

Guiteau, Charles J. (Charles Julius Guiteau) (c. 1840–1882) Am. lawyer/assassin (executed) of Pres. Garfield

Guitry, Sacha (Alexander Guitry) (1885–1957) Fr. writer/actor/playwright (*The Story of a Cheat*)

Gulager, Clu (1935–) Am. actor ("The Tall Man" and "The Virginian" TV series)

Gumbel, Bryant (Bryant Charles Gumbel) (1948–) Am. sportscaster/TV host ("Today")

Gunn, Moses (1929–1994) Am. actor (*Shaft*)/film director (*Ragtime*)

Gunn, Thom (Thomson William Gunn) (1929–) Eng. poet (*My Sad Captains*)

Gunther, John (1901–1970) Am. journalist/writer (*Inside Europe* and other *Inside* books)

Gutenberg, Beno (1889–1960) Am. seismologist (created the Richter scale with Charles Richter)

Gutenberg, Johannes (Johannes Gensfleisch zur Laden) (between 1390 and 1400–1468) Ger. inventor (printing press)

Guthrie, A. B., Jr. (Alfred Bertram Guthrie) (1901–) Am. novelist (P—1950—*The Way West; The Big Sky*)

Guthrie, Arlo (1947–) Am. folk singer (son of Woody; "Alice's Restaurant")

Guthrie, Janet (1938–) Am. auto racer

Guthrie, Woody (Woodrow Wilson Guthrie) (1912–1967) Am. folk singer/songwriter (father of Arlo; "This Land Is My Land")

Guttenberg, Steve (1958–) Am. actor (*Three Men and a Baby; Diner*)

Guy, Jasmine (1964–) Am. actress ("A Different World" TV series)

Guy, Ray (William Ray Guy) (1949–) Am. football player

Guyon, Joe (Joseph Guyon; "Indian Joe") (1892–1971) Am. football Hall-of-Famer

Guzman, Jose (Jose Alberto Guzman Mirabel) (1963–) P.R.-Am. baseball player

Gwenn, Edmund (1875–1959) Eng. actor (*The Trouble with Harry*; O—1947—*Miracle on 34th Street*)

Gwinnett, Button (c. 1735–1777) Am. Revolutionary leader (signed the Declaration of Independence)

Gwyn, Nell (Eleanor Gwyn or Gwynn or Gwynne) (1650–1687) Eng. actress/comedienne/mistress of Charles II

Gwynn, Tony (Anthony Keith Gwynn) (1960–) Am. baseball player

Gwynne, Fred (1926–1993) Am. actor (Herman Munster in "The Munsters" TV series; "Car 54 Where Are You?" TV series)

Haas, Lukas (1976–) Am. child actor (*Witness; The Wizard of Loneliness*)

Haber, Joyce (Joyce Haber Cramer) (1932–1993) Am. (Hollywood) gossip columnist

Hack, Shelley (1949–) Am. model/actress ("Charlie's Angels" TV series)

Hackett, Albert (1900–) Am. screenwriter (with Frances Goodrich, *The Thin Man, Naughty Marietta*; P—1956—*The Diary of Anne Frank*)

Hackett, Bobby (Robert Leo Hackett) (1915–1976) Am. jazz cornetist

Hackett, Buddy (Leonard Hacker) (1924–) Am. comedian/actor (*The Music Man*)

Hackett, Joan (1934–1983) Am. actress

(*Support Your Local Sheriff; The Terminal Man*)

Hackford, Taylor (1944–) Am. film producer/director (*Everybody's All-American; Mortal Thoughts*)

Hackman, Gene (Eugene Alden Hackman) (1930–) Am. actor (*The Conversation*; O—1971—*The French Connection*; O—1993—*Unforgiven*)

Hadrian (Publius Aelius Hadrianus) (76–138) Roman emperor 117–138

Hafey, Chick (Charles James Hafey) (1903–1973) Am. baseball Hall-of-Famer

Hagar, Sammy (1947–) Am. rock singer ("I Can't Drive 55"; with Van Halen and Montrose)

Hagen, Nina (1955–) Ger. punk singer

Hagen, Uta (1919–) Ger.-Am. actress (*Key Largo; Othello*; T—1951, 1953)

Hagen, Walter (Walter Charles Hagen; "The Haig") (1892–1969) Am. golfer

Hagerty, Julie (1955–) Am. actress (*Airplane!; Lost in America*)

Haggard, Sir H. Rider (Henry Rider Haggard; "The Hag") (1856–1925) Eng. adventure novelist (*King Solomon's Mines*)

Haggard, Merle (Merle Ronald Haggard) (1937–) Am. country singer ("Okie from Muskogee")

Haggerty, Dan (1941–) Am. actor (TV's "Grizzly Adams")

Hagler, Marvin (Marvin Nathaniel Hagler; "Marvelous Marvin") (1954–) Am. boxer

Hagman, Larry (Larry Martin Hageman) (1931–) Am. actor (son of Mary Martin; "I Dream of Jeannie" TV series; J. R. in "Dallas" TV series)

Hahn, Jessica (1959–) Am. entertainer (lover of evangelist Jim Bakker)

Hahn, Otto (1879–1968) Ger. chemist (discovered nuclear fission with Lise Meitner and Fritz Strassman; N—1944)

Haid, Charles (1943–) Am. actor ("Hill Street Blues" TV series)/TV producer ("Cop Rock")

Haig, Alexander (Alexander Meigs Haig, Jr.) (1924–) Am. general/govt. official (secretary of state)

Haile Selassie (Lij Tafari Makonnen; a/k/a Ras [prince] Tafari; "The Lion of Judha") (1891–1975) Eth. emperor 1930–1974

Hailey, Arthur (1920–) Can. novelist (*Airport; Wheels*)

Haim, Corey (1972–) Can.-Am. actor (*The Lost Boys; Lucas* [title role])

Haines, Jesse (Jesse Joseph Haines; "Pop") (1893–1978) Am. baseball Hall-of-Famer

Haines, Randa (1945–) Am. film director (*Children of a Lesser God*; *The Doctor*; *Wrestling Ernest Hemingway*)

Haje, Khrystyne (1968–) Am. actress ("Head of the Class" TV series)

Halas, George (George Stanley Halas; "Papa Bear") (1895–1983) Am. football player/coach/executive

Halberstam, David (1934–) Am. journalist/writer (*The Best and the Brightest*; *The Fifties*; *The Powers That Be*)

Haldeman, H. R. (Harry Robert Haldeman) (1926–1993) Am. politician/ Watergate participant (jailed 1977– 1978)

Hale, Alan (Rufus Alan McKahan) (1892– 1950) Am. actor (father of Alan, Jr.; *The Adventures of Robin Hood*)

Hale, Alan, Jr. (1918–1990) Am. actor ("Casey Jones" and "Gilligan's Island" TV series)

Hale, Barbara (1922–) Am. actress (mother of William Katt; Della Street in TV's "Perry Mason"; E—1958/59)

Hale, George (George Ellery Hale) (1868– 1938) Am. astronomer/inventor (spectroheliograph)

Hale, Jonathan (Jonathan Hatley) (1892– 1966) Am. actor (Mr. Dithers in *Blondie* films)

Hale, Nathan (1755–1776) Am. revolutionary hero (caught behind enemy lines in disguise; hanged for spying)

Haley, Alex (Alexander Palmer Haley) (1921–1992) Am. writer (*Roots*; with Malcolm X, *The Autobiography of Malcolm X*; P—1977 [special citation for *Roots*])

Haley, Bill (William John Clifton Haley, Jr.; "Father of Rock 'n' Roll") (1925– 1981) Am. rock singer ("Rock Around the Clock"; "Shake, Rattle and Roll"; with Bill Haley & The Comets)

Haley, Jack (John Joseph Haley) (1899– 1979) Am. actor (Tin Man in *The Wizard of Oz*)

Haley, Jack, Jr. (John Jack Haley) (1933–) Am. film director/producer (*The Love Machine*; *That's Entertainment*)

Halford, Rob (1951–) Eng. rock singer (with Judas Priest; "Living After Midnight")

Hall, Anthony Michael (1968–) Am. actor (*Sixteen Candles*; *Edward Scissorhands*; *The Breakfast Club*; *Weird Science*)

Hall, Arsenio (a/k/a Chunky A and Chunkston Arthur Hall) (1957–) Am. talk show host

Hall, Daryl (Daryl Franklin Hohl) (1948–) Am. rock singer/musician (with Hall & Oates; "Kiss on My List"; "Out of Touch")

Hall, Deidre (1948–) Am. actress ("Days of Our Lives" and "The Young and the Restless" soap operas)

Hall, Fawn (1959–) Am. secretary (for Oliver North; involved in the Iran-Contra controversy)

Hall, Huntz (Henry Hall) (1920–) Am. actor (one of the Dead End Kids)

Hall, James Norman (1887–1951) Am. novelist/short story writer (with Charles Nordoff, *Mutiny on the Bounty*)

Hall, Jerry ("Tall Hall") (1956–) Am. model/actress

Hall, Juanita (Juanita Long) (1901–1968) Am. actress (Bloody Mary in *South Pacific*)

Hall, Monty (Morton Halparin) (1923–) Am. game show host ("Let's Make a Deal")

Hall, Sir Peter (Peter Reginald Frederick Hall) (1930–) Eng. theatrical director (*Waiting for Godot*)

Hall, Tom T. (1936–) Am. country singer ("I Love")/songwriter ("Harper Valley P.T.A.")

Halley, Edmund (1656–1742) Eng. astronomer (identified Halley's Comet)

Halliwell, Leslie (1928–1989) Eng. film critic/writer (*Halliwell's Filmgoer's Companion*)

Hallström, Lasse (1946–) Swed. film director (*My Life as a Dog*; *What's Eating Gilbert Grape*)

Hals, Frans (between 1581 and 1585–1666) Dutch portrait painter (*Portrait of a Lady*)

Halsey, William (William Frederick Halsey, Jr.; "Bull") (1882–1959) Am. navy admiral

Halsted, William (William Stewart Halsted) (1852–1922) Am. surgery pioneer (considered the father of modern surgery; introduced rubber gloves, performed the first blood transfusion)

Halston (Roy Halston Frowick) (1932– 1990) Am. fashion designer

Ham, Jack (Jack Raphael Ham) (1948–) Am. football Hall-of-Famer

Hamel, Veronica (1943–) Am. actress ("Hill Street Blues" TV series)

Hamer, Rusty (Russell Hamer) (1947–1990) Am. child actor ("The Danny Thomas Show" TV series)
Hamill, Dorothy (Dorothy Stuart Hamill; "Squint") (1956–) Am. figure skater
Hamill, Mark ("Motor Mouth") (1951–) Am. actor (Luke Skywalker in *Star Wars* films)
Hamilton, Alexander (1755–1804) Am. statesman/first treasury secretary/founder of the first political party (Federalists) in America (killed in a duel with Aaron Burr)
Hamilton, Carrie (1963–) Am. actress (daughter of Carol Burnett)
Hamilton, Donald (Donald Bengtsson Hamilton) (1916–) Am. westerns/mystery writer (created Matt Helm)
Hamilton, George (George Stevens Hamilton) (1939–) Am. actor (*Love at First Bite; Once Is Not Enough*)
Hamilton, Linda (1957–) Am. actress (*The Terminator; Children of the Corn*)
Hamilton, Margaret (Margaret Brainard Hamilton) (1902–1985) Am. actress (Wicked Witch of the West in *The Wizard of Oz*)
Hamilton, Scott (1958–) Am. figure skater
Hamlin, Hannibal (1809–1891) Am. v.p. (A. Lincoln)
Hamlin, Harry (Harry Robinson Hamlin) (1951–) Am. actor ("L.A. Law" TV series)
Hamlin, Vincent (1900–1993) Am. cartoonist (created *Alley Oop*)
Hamlisch, Marvin (Marvin Frederick Hamlisch) (1944–) Am. pianist ("The Entertainer")/film songwriter (*The Sting; The Way We Were*; P—1973—*A Chorus Line*; G—1974)
Hammarskjöld, Dag (Dag Hjalmar Agne Carl Hammarskjöld) (1905–1961) Swed. statesman/economist/U.N. secretary-general (N—1961)
Hammer (Stanley Kirk Burrell; a/k/a M.C. Hammer) (1963–) Am. rapper ("U Can't Touch This")
Hammer, Armand (1898–1990) Am. whiskey/cattle/broadcasting tycoon
Hammer, Jan (1948–) Cz.-Am. composer/musician ("Miami Vice Theme"; formerly with Mahavishnu Orchestra)
Hammerstein, Oscar II (Oscar Greeley Clenndenning Hammerstein) (1895–1960) Am. lyricist (*Oklahoma!; Carousel*; P—1944 [special citation for *Okla-*

homa!]; P—1950—*South Pacific*; with Richard Rodgers)
Hammett, Dashiell (Samuel Dashiell Hammett; a/k/a Peter Collinson) (1894–1961) Am. detective story writer (*The Maltese Falcon; The Thin Man*; lived with Lillian Hellman for many years)
Hammon, Jupiter (1720–1800) Afr.-Am. poet (first published Afr.-Am. poet, 1761)
Hammond, Albert (1942–) Eng. pop singer ("It Never Rains in Southern California")
Hammurabi (died 1750 B.C.) Bab. king 1792–1750 B.C.
Hampshire, Susan (1942–) Eng. actress ("The Forsyte Saga" TV series; *David Copperfield*; E—1969/70, 1970/71)
Hampson, Thomas (c. 1955–) Am. opera singer (baritone)
Hampton, Lionel (Lionel Leo Hampton; "King of Vibes") (1913–) Am. bandleader/pianist/drummer
Hampton, Wade (1818–1902) Am. army general/politician
Hamsun, Knut (Knut Pedersen) (1859–1952) Norw. novelist/playwright/poet (*Hunger*; N—1920)
Hancock, Herbie (Herbert Jeffrey Hancock) (1940–) Am. jazz pianist (with Miles Davis)/film composer (*Round Midnight*)
Hancock, John (1737–1793) Am. Revolutionary leader (first signer of the Declaration of Independence)
Hand, Learned (Billings Learned Hand) (1872–1961) Am. jurist/writer (*The Bill of Rights*)
Handel, George Frideric (1685–1759) Eng. composer (*The Messiah; Water Music*)
Handlin, Oscar (1915–) Am. historian (*Boston's Immigrants*; P—1952—*The Uprooted*)
Handy, W. C. (William Christopher Handy; "Father of the Blues") (1873–1958) Am. composer ("St. Louis Blues")
Hanks, Tom (Thomas J. Hanks; a/k/a Thom Hanks) (1956–) Am. actor (*Splash; Big; Sleepless in Seattle; Philadelphia*)
Hanna, William (William Denby Hanna) (1910–) Am. cartoonist/entertainment executive (with Joseph Barbera; created "Tom and Jerry")
Hannah, Daryl (1960–) Am. actress (*Splash; Roxanne; Steel Magnolias*)
Hannah, Page (1964–) Am. actress (sister

of Daryl; "Search for Tomorrow" soap opera; *Shag*)

Hannibal (247–183 B.C.) Carth. general

Hansberry, Lorraine (1930–1965) Am. playwright (*A Raisin in the Sun*)

Hanson, Howard (Howard Harold Hanson) (1896–1981) Am. composer (P—1944—*Symphony No. 4 [Op. 34]*)

Hanson, Marla (C) Am. model/actress (attacked by a slasher)

Harburg, E. Y. (Edgar Yipsel Harburg; "Yip") (1896–1981) Am. lyricist ("Brother, Can You Spare a Dime"; "It's Only a Paper Moon"; "Over the Rainbow")

Hard, Darlene (Darlene R. Hard) (1936–) Am. tennis player

Hardin, Ty (Orson Whipple Hungerford II; a/k/a Ty Hungerford) (1930–) Am. actor ("Bronco" TV series)

Harding, Ann (Dorothy Walton Gatley) (1902–1981) Am. actress (*The Man in the Gray Flannel Suit*; *Holiday*)

Harding, Florence (Florence Kling De Wolfe) (1860–1924) Am. first lady (Warren)

Harding, Warren G. (Warren Gamaliel Harding) (1865–1923) 29th Am. pres. (1921–1923)

Hardison, Kadeem (1965–) Am. actor (*Def by Temptation*)

Hardwicke, Sir Cedric (Cedric Webster Hardwicke) (1893–1964) Eng. actor (*King Solomon's Mines*; *Nell Gwyn*; *Stanley and Livingstone*)

Hardy, Oliver (Oliver Norvell Hardy; a/k/a Babe Hardy; "Ollie") (1892–1957) Am. comedian (with Stan Laurel)

Hardy, Thomas (1840–1928) Eng. novelist/poet (*The Return of the Native*; *Far from the Madding Crowd*; *Tess of the D'Urbervilles*)

Hargitay, Mariska (1964–) Am. actress (daughter of Jayne Mansfield; "Falcon Crest" TV series)

Haring, Keith (1958–1990) Am. pop artist

Harkin, Tom (Thomas R. Harkin) (1939–) Am. senator

Harlan, John Marshall (1899–1971) Am. Supreme Court jurist (1955–1971)

Harlin, Renny (c. 1959–) Finn.-Am. film director (*Cliffhanger*; *Die Hard 2*; *Die Harder*)

Harline, Leigh (1907–1969) Am. composer ("When You Wish upon a Star")

Harlow, Jean (Harlean Carpenter; "Blonde Bombshell"; "The Platinum Blonde") (1911–1937) Am. actress (*Libeled Lady*; *The Public Enemy*; *Platinum Blonde*)

Harmon, Mark (1951–) Am. actor (son of Tom; "St. Elsewhere" TV series; *The Deliberate Stranger*)

Harmon, Tom (Thomas Dudley Harmon; "Old 98") (1919–1990) Am. football player/broadcaster (father of Mark)

Harnick, Sheldon (1924–) Am. lyricist (with Jerry Bock, *Fiddler on the Roof*; P—1960—*Fiorello*)

Harper, Ethel (1904–1979) Am. entertainer (Aunt Jemima in pancake syrup commercials)

Harper, Frances Ellen Watkins (1825–1911) Am. abolitionist

Harper, James (1795–1869) Am. publisher (founder of Harper & Row)

Harper, Jessica (1949–) Am. actress ("It's Garry Shandling's Show" TV series)

Harper, Tess (Tessie Jean Washam) (1950–) Am. actress (*Tender Mercies*; *Crimes of the Heart*)

Harper, Valerie (Valerie Cathryn Harper) (1940–) Am. actress (TV's "Rhoda"; E—1970/71, 1971/72, 1972/73, 1974/75)

Harrelson, Woody (1961–) Am. actor ("Cheers" TV series; *White Men Can't Jump*; *Indecent Proposal*; E—1988/89)

Harrington, Michael (Edward Michael Harrington) (1928–) Am. social scientist/writer (*The Other America*)

Harrington, Pat, Jr. (Daniel Patrick Harrington, Jr.) (1929–) Am. actor ("One Day at a Time" TV series; E—1983/84)

Harris, Barbara (Sandra Markowitz) (1935–) Am. actress (*Nashville*; *Family Plot*; *A Thousand Clowns*; T—1967)

Harris, Bucky (Stanley Raymond Harris) (1896–1977) Am. baseball Hall-of-Famer

Harris, Cliff (1948–) Am. football player

Harris, Ed (1950–) Am. actor (*The Right Stuff*; *Sweet Dreams*; *Glengarry Glen Ross*; *The Firm*)

Harris, Emmylou (1947–) Am. country singer ("Mister Sandman"; "Amarillo"; "Roses on the Snow")

Harris, Franco (1950–) Am. football Hall-of-Famer

Harris, Frank (James Thomas Harris) (1856–1931) Ir. journalist/novelist/autobiographer (*My Life and Loves*)

Harris, Jean (Jean Witt Struven Harris) (1924–) Am. murderess (killed the "Scarsdale Diet Doctor," Herman Tarnower)/prison reformer

Harris, Joel Chandler (1848–1908) Am. journalist/writer (created Uncle Remus)

Harris, Julie (Julia Ann Harris) (1925–) Am. actress (*The Member of the Wedding*; "Knots Landing" TV series; T— 1952, 1956, 1969, 1973, 1977)

Harris, Mel (1957–) Am. actress ("thirtysomething" TV series)

Harris, Neil Patrick (1973–) Am. actor (TV's "Doogie Howser, M.D.")

Harris, Sir Richard (Richard R. St. Johns Harris) (1930–) Ir. actor (*A Man Called Horse*; *Camelot*)

Harris, Roy (Roy Ellsworth Harris) (1898–1979) Am. composer ("When Johnny Comes Marching Home")

Harrison, Anna (Anna Tuthill Symmes) (1775–1864) Am. first lady (William)

Harrison, Benjamin (1833–1901) 23rd Am. pres. (1889–1893)

Harrison, Caroline (Caroline Lavinia Scott) (1832–1892) Am. first lady (Benjamin)

Harrison, George (1943–) Eng. rock singer/musician ("My Sweet Lord"; formerly with The Beatles and The Traveling Wilburys)

Harrison, Gregory (1950–) Am. actor ("Trapper John, M.D." TV series)

Harrison, Jennilee (1959–) Am. actress ("Dallas" TV series)

Harrison, Sir Rex (Reginald Carey Harrison) (1908–1990) Eng. actor (*Dr. Dolittle*; *Unfaithfully Yours*; O—1964—*My Fair Lady*; T—1949, 1957)

Harrison, Wallace (Wallace Kirkman Harrison) (1895–1981) Am. architect (U.N. complex, Lincoln Center)

Harrison, William (William Henry Harrison; "Hero of Tippe-canoe") (1773–1841) 9th Am. pres. (1841)

Harrold, Kathryn (1950–) Am. actress (*Raw Deal*; *Modern Romance*)

Harry, Deborah (Deborah Ann Harry; a/k/a Debbie Harry) (1945–) Am. rock singer ("Heart of Glass"; "Call Me"; "The Tide Is High"; formerly with Blondie)/actress (*Videodrome*)

Harry, Jackee (a/k/a Jackee) (1957–) Am. actress ("227" TV series; E—1986/87)

Hart, Doris (Doris J. Hart) (1925–) Am. tennis player (W—1951)

Hart, Gary (Gary Warren Hartpence)

(1936–) Am. senator/would-be presidential candidate

Hart, Johnny (Johnny Lewis Hart) (1931–) Am. cartoonist (*B.C.*; *The Wizard of Id*)

Hart, Lorenz (Lorenz Milton Hart) (1895–1943) Am. lyricist (with Richard Rodgers; "My Funny Valentine"; "Pal Joey")

Hart, Mary (Mary Johanna Harum) (1950–) Am. TV host ("Entertainment Tonight")

Hart, Moss (Robert Arnold Conrad) (1904–1961) Am. playwright (*The Man Who Came to Dinner*; P—1937—*You Can't Take It with You*)

Hart, William S. (William Surrey Hart) (1862–1946) Am. cowboy actor (*Tumbleweeds*; *The Covered Wagon*)

Hartack, Billy (William John Hartack, Jr.) (1932–) Am. jockey

Harte, Bret (Francis Bret Harte) (1836–1902) Am. novelist/short story writer/poet (*The Luck of Roaring Camp*; *The Outcasts of Poker Flat*)

Hartley, Hal (c. 1959–) Am. film director (*The Unbelievable Truth*; *Trust*)

Hartley, Mariette (1940–) Am. actress ("WIOU" TV series)

Hartley, Marsden (1877–1943) Am. abstract expressionist painter

Hartline, Halden Keffer (1903–1983) Am. physiologist (N—1967)

Hartman, David (David Downs Hartman) (1935–) Am. TV host ("Good Morning, America")

Hartman, Lisa (1956–) Am. actress ("Knots Landing" TV series)

Hartman, Phil (1948–) Am. comedian ("Saturday Night Live" TV series; *CB4*)

Hartnett, Gabby (Charles Leo Hartnett; "Old Tomato Face") (1900–1972) Am. baseball Hall-of-Famer

Harvey, Laurence (Larushka Mischa Skikne) (1928–1973) Lith.-Eng. actor (*The Manchurian Candidate*; *Room at the Top*)

Harvey, Paul (Paul Harvey Aurandt; "Voice of the U.S. Heartland") (1918–) Am. newscaster/journalist

Haskin, Byron (1899–1984) Am. film director (*The War of the Worlds*; *The Naked Jungle*)

Hassam, Childe (Frederick Childe Hassam) (1859–1935) Am. impressionist painter

Hassan II (1929–) Mor. king 1961–

Hasselhoff, David (1952–) Am. actor

("Knight Rider" and "Baywatch" TV series)

Hasso, Signe (Signe Eleanora Cecilia Larssen) (1910–) Swed. actress (*To the Ends of the Earth; The Black Bird*)

Hatch, Orrin (Orrin Grant Hatch) (1934–) Am. senator

Hatcher, Teri (c. 1965–) Am. actress (*Soapdish*; "Lois and Clark: The New Adventures of Superman" TV series)

Hatfield, Hurd (William Rukard Hurd Hatfield) (1918–) Am. actor (*The Picture of Dorian Gray; Joan of Arc*)

Hatfield, Juliana (c. 1967–) Am. rock musician/singer ("My Sister"; with The Blake Babies)

Hatfield, Mark O. (Mark Odom Hatfield) (1922–) Am. senator

Hathaway, Donny (1945–1979) Am. pop singer/musician ("Where Is the Love"; duets with Roberta Flack: "The Closer I Get to You", etc.)

Hathaway, Henry (Henri Leopold de Fiennes) (1898–1985) Am. film director (*Lives of a Bengal Lancer; The Sons of Katie Elder*)

Hatlo, Jimmy (James Cecil Hatlo) (1898–1963) Am. cartoonist (*Little Iodine*)

Hauer, Rutger (1944–) Dutch actor (*Turkish Delight; Bladerunner*)

Hauptmann, Bruno (Bruno Richard Hauptmann) (1899–1936) Am. kidnapper/executed for murder of the Lindbergh baby

Hauser, Wings (c. 1946–) Am. actor (*Tough Guys Don't Dance*)

Havel, Václav (1935–) Cz. poet/playwright/pres. 1989–1992

Havelock, Sir Henry (1795–1857) Eng. army general

Havens, Richie (1941–) Am. folk/rock singer/musician ("Here Comes the Sun")/actor (*Greased Lightning*)

Haver, June (June Stovenour) (1926–) Am. actress (*Look for the Silver Lining; The Girl Next Door*)

Havers, Nigel (1952–) Eng. actor (*A Passage to India*)

Havlicek, John ("Hondo") (1940–) Am. basketball player

Havoc, June (Ellen Evangeline Hovick; "Baby June") (1916–) Am. actress (sister of Gypsy Rose Lee; *Gentleman's Agreement; Can't Stop the Music*)

Hawke, Ethan (1970–) Am. actor (*Alive; Dead Poets Society*)

Hawking, Stephen W. (Stephen William Hawking) (1942–) Eng. scientist/writer (*A Brief History of Time*)

Hawkins, Coleman (1904–1969) Am. jazz saxophonist ("Body and Soul")

Hawkins, Jack (John Edward Hawkins) (1910–1973) Eng. actor (*The Bridge on the River Kwai; A Shot in the Dark*)

Hawkins, Screamin' Jay (Jalacy Hawkins) (1929–) Am. rock/rhythm and blues musician/singer ("Alligator Wine")

Hawkins, Sophie B. (Sophie Ballantine Hawkins) (c. 1967–) Am. pop singer ("Damn I Wish I Was Your Lover")

Hawks, Howard (Howard Winchester Hawks) (1896–1977) Am. film director (*Bringing Up Baby; His Girl Friday*)

Hawn, Goldie (Goldie Jean Studlendgehawn) (1945–) Am. actress ("Rowan & Martin's Laugh-In" TV series; *Death Becomes Her; O—1969—Cactus Flower*)

Hawthorne, Nathaniel (Nathaniel Hawthorne) (1804–1864) Am. novelist/short story writer (*Twice-Told Tales; The Scarlet Letter; The House of the Seven Gables*)

Hay, Ian (John Hay Beith) (1876–1952) Eng. playwright/novelist (*Pip*)

Hayakawa, Sessue (Kintaro Hayakawa) (1889–1973) Jap. actor (*The Bridge on the River Kwai; The Cheat*)

Hayakawa, S. I. (Samuel Ichiye Hayakawa) (1906–1992) Am. senator/educator/writer (*Language in Action*)

Hayden, Melissa (Mildred Herman) (1928–) Can. ballerina

Hayden, Robert (Robert Earl Hayden) (1913–1980) Am. poet (*Heart-Shape in the Dust*)

Hayden, Sterling (Sterling Relyea Walter Hayden; born John Hamilton; "The Most Beautiful Man in the World"; "The Beautiful Blond Viking God") (1916–1986) Am. actor (*Dr. Strangelove; Lord Jim*)

Hayden, Tom (Thomas Emmett Hayden) (1939–) Am. political activist (one of the Chicago 7)

Haydn, Joseph (Franz Joseph Haydn) (1732–1809) Aus. composer (*The Seasons; The Creation*)

Hayes, Billy (c. 1947–) Am. autobiographer (*Midnight Express*)

Hayes, Bob (Robert Hayes; "Bullet Bob"; "The World's Fastest Human") (1942–) Am. runner/football player

Hayes, Elvin (Elvin Ernest Hayes;

"The Big E") (1945–) Am. basketball player

Hayes, Gabby (George Francis Hayes) (1885–1969) Am. cowboy actor (*Wyoming; In Old Santa Fe; Mr. Deeds Goes to Town*)

Hayes, Helen (Helen Hayes Brown; "First Lady of the American Theater") (1900–1993) Am. actress (mother of James MacArthur; *Arrowsmith; A Farewell to Arms*; O—1931/32—*The Sin of Madelon Claudet*; O—1970—*Airport*; E—1952; T—1947, 1958)

Hayes, Isaac ("Black Moses") (1942–) Am. soul/pop singer ("Theme from Shaft")

Hayes, Isaac (Isaac Israel Hayes) (1832–1881) Am. arctic explorer/writer (*Land of Desolation*)

Hayes, Lucy (Lucy Ware Webb) (1831–1889) Am. first lady (Rutherford)

Hayes, Rutherford (Rutherford Birchard Hayes) (1822–1893) 19th Am. pres. (1877–1881)

Hayes, Von (Von Francis Hayes) (1958–) Am. baseball player

Hayes, Woody (Wayne Woodrow Hayes) (1913–1987) Am. football coach

Haymes, Dick (Richard Benjamin Haymes) (1918–1980) Am. singer ("You'll Never Know")/actor (*State Fair*)

Haynes, Elwood (1857–1925) Am. inventor (metal alloys)

Haynes, Marques ("World's Greatest Dribbler") (1926–) Am. basketball player (with The Harlem Globetrotters)

Haynes, Mike (Michael James Haynes) (1953–) Am. football player

Haynie, Sandra (Sandra J. Haynie) (1943–) Am. golfer

Hays, Robert (1947–) Am. actor ("Angie" TV series; *Airplane!*)

Hays, Will (William Harrison Hays) (1879–1954) Am. politician/entertainment executive (developed the "Hays Code")

Hayward, Justin (1946–) Eng. rock singer ("I Dreamed Last Night"; formerly with The Moody Blues)

Hayward, Leland (1902–1971) Am. film producer (*Mister Roberts; The Spirit of St. Louis*)

Hayward, Susan (Edythe Marrener) (1918–1975) Am. actress (*Backstreet*; O—1958—*I Want to Live*)

Hayworth, Rita (Margarita Carmen Cansino; a/k/a Rita Cansino; "The Love Goddess") (1918–1987) Am. actress (*Pal Joey; Blood and Sand; Cover Girl*)

Hazlitt, William (1778–1830) Eng. essayist/literary critic (*Lectures on the English Poets*)

H. D. (Hilda Doolittle) (1886–1961) Am. poet (*Sea Garden*)

Head, Edith (1907–1981) Am. costume designer (*All About Eve; The Heiress; Sabrina; Roman Holiday*)

Headly, Glenne (1955–) Am. actress (*Mortal Thoughts; Dick Tracy*)

Healey, Ed (1894–1978) Am. football Hall-of-Famer

Heaney, Seamus (Seamus Justin Heaney) (1939–) Ir. poet (*Death of a Naturalist*)

Heard, John (1946–) Am. actor (*Betrayed; Beaches; Head Over Heels*)

Hearn, Chick (c. 1917–) Am. sports announcer

Hearn, Lafcadio (Patricio Lafcadio Tessima Carlos Hearn; a/k/a Koisumi Yakumo) (1850–1904) Am. journalist/writer (especially on Japan; *Stray Leaves from Strange Literatures*)

Hearst, Patty (Patricia Campbell Hearst; a/k/a "Tania") (1954–) Am. heiress/kidnap victim (Symbionese Liberation Army)

Hearst, William Randolph (1863–1951) Am. publishing magnate (*San Francisco Examiner, Chicago Examiner, Cosmopolitan, Bazaar*)

Heath, Edward Richard George (1916–) Eng. prime minister 1970–1974

Heatherton, Joey (Davenie Johanna Heatherton) (1944–) Am. actress/dancer/singer

Hecht, Ben (1893–1964) Am. screenwriter (*The Front Page; Twentieth Century; Wuthering Heights*)

Hecht, Chic (1928–) Am. senator/politician

Heck, Barbara (née Ruckle; "Mother of Methodism") (1734–1804) Am. Methodist religious leader

Heckart, Eileen (Anna Eileen Heckart) (1919–) Am. actress (*The Bad Seed*; O—1972—*Butterflies Are Free*)

Heckerling, Amy (1954–) Am. film director (*Fast Times at Ridgemont High; Look Who's Talking*)

Hedren, Tippi (Nathalie Kay Hedren) (1935–) Am. actress (mother of Melanie Griffith; *The Birds; Marnie*)

Heflin, Howell (Howell Thomas Heflin) (1921–) Am. senator

Heflin, Van (Emmett Evan Heflin, Jr.) (1910–1971) Am. actor (*Shane*; *Airport*; O—1942—*Johnny Eager*)

Hefner, Christie (Christine Ann Hefner) (1952–) Am. publisher (pres. of Playboy Enterprises; daughter of Hugh)

Hefner, Hugh (Hugh Marston Hefner) (1926–) Am. magazine publisher (*Playboy*)

Hegel, Georg (Georg Wilhelm Friedrich Hegel) (1770–1831) Ger. philosopher (German Idealism)/writer

Heidegger, Martin (1889–1976) Ger. philosopher (*Being and Time*)

Heiden, Eric (1958–) Am. speed skater

Heidenstam, Verner von (Carl Gustaf Verner von Heidenstam) (1859–1940) Swed. poet/novelist (*Dikter*; N—1916)

Heifetz, Jascha (1901–1987) Russ.-Am. concert violinist

Heilbroner, Robert (Robert Louis Heilbroner) (1919–) Am. economist/writer (*The Worldly Philosophers*)

Heilmann, Harry (Harry Edwin Heilmann; "Slug") (1894–1951) Am. baseball Hall-of-Famer

Hein, Mel (Melvin John Hein) (1909–1992) Am. football Hall-of-Famer

Heine, Heinrich (Harry Heine) (1797–1856) Ger. poet/critic (*Book of Songs*)

Heinlein, Robert A. (Robert Anson Heinlein; a/k/a Anson MacDonald) (1907–1988) Am. science fiction writer (*Stranger in a Strange Land*)

Heiss, Carol (Carol Elizabeth Heiss) (1940–) Am. figure skater

Held, Anna (1873–1918) Am. singer/dancer (in the Ziegfeld Follies)

Helgenberger, Marg (c. 1958–) Am. actress ("China Beach" TV series; E—1989/90)

Hell, Richard (Richard Meyers) (1949–) Am. rock musician/singer (with Richard Hell and The Voidoids; "Blank Generation")

Heller, Joseph (1923–) Am. novelist (*Catch-22*)

Hellman, Lillian (Lillian Florence Hellman) (1905–1984) Am. playwright (*Pentimento*; *The Little Foxes*; *The Children's Hour*; *Watch on the Rhine*)

Helm, Levon (1935–) Am. rock drummer (with The Band)

Helmond, Katharine (1933–) Am. actress ("Soap" and "Who's the Boss?" TV series)

Helms, Jesse (Jesse Alexander Helms, Jr.) (1921–) Am. senator

Helmsley, Leona (Leona Mindy Rosenthal; "The Queen of Mean") (1920–) Am. hotelier (jailed for tax evasion)

Heloïse (c. 1098–1164) Fr. abbess (lover of Pierre Abelard)

Heloise (Heloise Bowles Reese) (1919–1977) Am. columnist ("Hints from Heloise")

Helvétius, Claude-Adrien (1715–1771) Fr. philosopher (developed Sensationalist philosophy)

Hemingway, Ernest (Ernest Miller Hemingway; "Papa") (1899–1961) Am. short story writer/novelist (*For Whom the Bell Tolls*; *The Sun Also Rises*; N—1954; P—1953—*The Old Man and the Sea*)

Hemingway, Margaux (Margot Hemingway) (1955–) Am. model (granddaughter of Ernest)

Hemingway, Mariel (1961–) Am. actress (granddaughter of Ernest; sister of Margaux; "Civil Wars" TV series; *Star 80*)

Hemmings, David (Leslie Edward Hemmings) (1941–) Eng. actor (*Blow-Up*; *Camelot*)

Hemsley, Sherman (1938–) Am. actor ("The Jeffersons" and "Amen" TV series)

Hench, Philip (Philip Showalter Hench) (1896–1965) Am. physician (N—1950)

Henderson, Fletcher (Fletcher Hamilton Henderson; "Smack") (1898–1952) Am. jazz bandleader/pianist

Henderson, Florence (1934–) Am. actress ("The Brady Bunch" TV series; Wesson Oil commercials)

Henderson, Rickey (Rickey Henley Henderson) (1957–) Am. baseball player

Henderson, Skitch (Lyle Russell Cedric Henderson) (1918–) Am. orchestra leader ("The Steve Allen Show" and "The Tonight Show" TV shows)

Hendricks, Thomas A. (Thomas Andrews Hendricks) (1819–1885) Am. v.p. (G. Cleveland)

Hendrix, Jimi (James Marshall Hendricks) (1942–1970) Am. rock guitarist/singer ("Purple Haze"; "Foxy Lady")

Hendrix, Wanda (Dixie Wanda Hendrix) (1928–1981) Am. actress (*The Highwayman*; *Ride the Pink Horse*)

Hendryx, Nona (1944–) Am. pop singer

("Why Should I Cry?"); formerly with LaBelle

Henie, Sonja ("The Golden Girl"; "The Norwegian Doll"; "The Pavlova of the Silver Skates") (1910–1969) Norw. figure skater

Henley, Beth (Elizabeth Becker Henley) (1952–) Am. playwright (P—1981—*Crimes of the Heart*)

Henley, Don (1947–) Am. rock singer/musician ("The End of the Innocence"; "Sunset Grill"; formerly with the Eagles)

Henner, Marilu (1952–) Am. actress ("Taxi" and "Evening Shade" TV series)

Henning, Doug (Douglas James Henning) (1947–) Can. magician

Hennissart, Martha (C) Am. mystery writer (with Mary J. Latis, known as Emma Lathen)

Henreid, Paul (Paul Georg Julius von Hernreid Ritter von Wasel-Waldingau) (1908–1992) Aus. actor (*Casablanca*; *Now, Voyager*)

Henri, Robert (1865–1929) Am. portrait painter/writer (*The Art Spirit*)

Henrich, Tommy (Thomas David Henrich; "Old Reliable") (1913—) Am. baseball player

Henry (Henry Charles Albert David; a/k/a Henry of Wales; "Harry") (1984–) Eng. prince (son of Charles and Diana)

Henry I (c. 1008–1060) Fr. king 1031–1060

Henry I (Henry Beauclerc) (1068–1135) Eng. king 1100–1135

Henry II (1519–1559) Fr. king 1547–1559

Henry II (Curtmantle) (1133–1189) Eng. king 1154–1189

Henry III (1207–1272) Eng. king 1216–1272

Henry III (1551–1589) Fr. king 1574–1589

Henry IV (Henry Bolingbroke) (1366–1413) Eng. king 1399–1413

Henry IV (Henry of Navarre) (1553–1610) Fr. king 1589–1610

Henry V (1387–1422) Eng. king 1413–1422

Henry VI (1421–1471) Eng. king (1422–1461

Henry VII (Henry Tudor) (1457–1509) Eng. king 1485–1509

Henry VIII (1491–1547) Eng. king 1509–1547

Henry, Buck (Buck Henry Zuckerman) (1930–) Am. actor/comedian (occasional "Saturday Night Live" host)/screenwriter (*The Graduate*)/film director (*Heaven Can Wait*)

Henry, Justin (1971–) Am. child actor (*Kramer vs. Kramer*)

Henry, O. (William Sydney Porter) (1862–1910) Am. short story writer (*The Gift of the Magi*; *Cabbages and Kings*; *The Four Million*)

Henry, Patrick (1736–1799) Am. Revolutionary leader/orator (signature phrase: "Give me liberty or give me death")

Henson, Jim (James Maury Henson) (1936–1990) Am. puppeteer (created The Muppets)

Hepburn, Audrey (Audrey Hepburn-Ruston; born Edda van Heemstra Hepburn-Ruston) (1929–1993) Eng.-Am. actress (O—1953—*Roman Holiday*; *Breakfast at Tiffany's*; *Charade*; T—1954)

Hepburn, Katherine (Katherine Houghton Hepburn; "Kate"; "The Great Kate") (1907–) Am. actress (O—1932/33—*Morning Glory*; O—1967—*Guess Who's Coming to Dinner*; O—1968—*The Lion in Winter*; O—1981—*On Golden Pond*)

Hepplewhite, George (died 1786) Eng. neoclassical cabinetmaker/designer

Hepworth, Dame Barbara (Jocelyn Barbara Hepworth) (1903–1975) Eng. abstract sculptor

Heracleitus or **Heraclitus** ("The Weeping Philosopher"; "The Obscure") (c. 540–c. 480 B.C.) Gr. philosopher

Herber, Arnie (Arnold Herber; "Flash") (1910–1969) Am. football Hall-of-Famer

Herbert, Frank (Frank Patrick Herbert) (1920–1986) Am. science fiction writer (*Dune* and sequels)

Herbert, Victor (1859–1924) Am. film composer/conductor (*Babes in Toyland*; *Naughty Marietta*)

Herbert, Zbigniew (1924–) Pol. poet (*A String of Light*)

Herblock (Herbert Lawrence Block) (1909–) Am. political cartoonist (P—1942, 1954, 1979)

Herlihy, James Leo (1927–1993) Am. novelist (*Midnight Cowboy*)

Herman, Babe (Floyd Caves Herman) (1903–1987) Am. baseball Hall-of-Famer

Herman, Billy (William Jennings Bryan Herman) (1909–1992) Am. baseball Hall-of-Famer

Herman, Jerry (Gerald Herman) (1932–) Am. theatrical composer/lyricist (*Hello, Dolly!*; *Mame*)

Herman, Pee Wee (Paul Reubenfeld; a/k/a Paul Reubens) (1952–) Am. actor/comedian (*Pee Wee Herman's Big Adventure*)

Herman, Woody (Woodrow Charles Herman) (1913–1987) Am. jazz bandleader ("Blues in the Night")

Herod the Great (Herod I) (73–4 B.C.) Roman king of Judea 37–4 B.C.

Herodotus ("The Father of History") (c. 484–between 430 and 420 B.C.) Gr. historian

Herriman, George (George Joseph Herriman) (1880–1944) Am. cartoonist (*Krazy Kat*)

Herriot, James (James Alfred Wight) (1916–) Scot. veterinarian/writer (*All Creatures Great and Small*)

Herrmann, Bernard (1911–1975) Am. film composer (*North by Northwest*; *Citizen Kane*; *Vertigo*; *Psycho*)

Herrmann, Edward (1943–) Am. actor (FDR in TV's "Eleanor and Franklin")

Hersey, John (John Richard Hersey) (1914–1993) Am. novelist/journalist (P— 1945—*A Bell for Adano*; *Hiroshima*)

Hershey, Alfred (Alfred Day Hershey) (1908–) Am. biologist/geneticist (N— 1969)

Hershey, Barbara (Barbara Hertzstein; a/k/a Barbara Seagull) (1948–) Am. actress (*Beaches*; *Hannah and Her Sisters*)

Hershey, Milton (Milton Snavely Hershey) (1857–1945) Am. businessman (Hershey Chocolate Co.)

Hershiser, Orel (Orel Leonard Quentin Hershiser) (1958–) Am. baseball pitcher

Hervey, Jason (1972–) Am. actor ("The Wonder Years" TV series)

Herzog, Werner (Werner Herzog Stipetic) (1942–) Ger. film director (*Fitzcarraldo*; *Signs of Life*)

Herzog, Whitey (Dorrel Norman Elvert Herzog; "The White Rat") (1931–) Am. baseball player/manager

Hesiod (fl. c. 800 B.C.) Gr. poet (*Works and Days*; *Theogeny*)

Hess, Dame Myra (1890–1965) Eng. concert pianist

Hess, Rudolf (Walter Richard Rudolf Hess) (1894–) Ger. Nazi leader (convicted of war crimes at Nuremberg; imprisoned for life)

Hesse, Hermann (1877–1962) Ger. novelist/poet (*Siddhartha*; *Steppenwolf*; N—1946)

Hesseman, Howard (1940–) Am. actor ("WKRP in Cincinatti" TV series)

Heston, Charlton (John Charlton Carter) (1924–) Am. actor (*The Ten Commandments*; O—1959—*Ben Hur*)

Hewitt, Bill (William E. Hewitt; "The Off-Side Kid") (1909–1947) Am. football Hall-of-Famer

Hewitt, Don (Don S. Hewitt) (1922–) Am. TV producer (created "60 Minutes")

Hewlett, William (1913–) Am. businessman (with David Packard, founded Hewlett-Packard)

Hexum, Jon-Erik (1957–1984) Am. actor ("Voyagers" TV series; died while playing Russian roulette)

Heydrich, Reinhard (Reinhard Tristan Eugen Heydrich; "The Hangman of Europe") (1904–1942) Ger. Nazi leader

Heyerdahl, Thor (1914–) Norw. explorer/writer (*Kon-Tiki*)

Heyse, Paul (Paul Johann Ludwig von Heyse) (1830–1914) Ger. novelist (*The Fury*; N—1910)

Heyward, Dubose (Edwin Dubose Heyward) (1885–1940) Am. novelist/poet/playwright (*Porgy*)

Heywood, Eddie (1915–1989) Am. jazz pianist/arranger/conductor (*Canadian Sunset*)

Hezekiah (died c. 686 B.C.) king of Judah c. 715–c. 686 B.C.

Hiawatha (orig. Haionhwat'ha: He Makes Rivers) (fl. c. 1570) Am. Onandaga leader

Hibbert, Eleanor (Eleanor Alice Burford Hibbert; a/k/a Victoria Holt, Jean Plaidy, Philippa Carr, Eleanor Burford, Elbur Ford, Kathleen Kellow, and Ellalice Tate) (1906–1993) Eng. romance novelist (*The Devil on Horseback*)

Hickman, Dwayne (Dwyane B. Hickman) (1934–) Am. actor (TV's "Dobie Gillis")

Hickok, Wild Bill (James Butler Hickok) (1837–1876) Am. frontiersman/marshal

Hicks, Catherine (1951–) Am. actress ("Ryan's Hope" soap opera)

Hicks, Edward (1780–1849) Am. painter (*The Peaceable Kingdom*)

Hicks, Granville (1901–1982) Am. Marxist literary critic/writer (*The Great Tradition*)

Hidalgo y Costilla, Miguel ("The Father of Mexican Independence") (1753–1811) Mex. priest/revolutionary leader

Higginbotham, Jay C. (Jay Jack Higginbotham) (1906–1973) Am. jazz trombonist/singer

Higgins, Bertie (Elbert Higgins) (1946–) Am. pop singer/songwriter ("Key Largo" [1982])

Higgins, George V. (George Vincent Higgins) (1939–) Am. lawyer/writer (*Kennedy for the Defense*)

Higgins, Jack (a/k/a Harry Patterson) (1929–) Eng.-Ir. suspense novelist (*The Eagle Has Landed*)

Higgins, Marguerite (1920–1966) Am. journalist/war correspondent (P—1951)

Highsmith, Patricia (1921–) Am. short story writer/suspense novelist (*Strangers on a Train*)

Hightower, Rosella (1920–) Am. ballerina

Hijuelos, Oscar (1951–) Arg.-Am. writer (P—1990—*The Mambo Kings Play Songs of Love*)

Hildebrandt, Johann Lukas von (1668–1745) Aus. architect (developed Baroque style)

Hill, Anita (1956–) Am. law professor (accused Clarence Thomas of sexual harassment)

Hill, Arthur (Arthur Edward Spence Hill) (1922–) Am. actor ("Owen Marshall, Counselor at Law" TV series; T—1963)

Hill, Benny (Alfred Hawthorne Hill) (1925–1992) Eng. comedian ("The Benny Hill Show" TV series)

Hill, Dan (1954–) Am. pop singer/songwriter ("Sometimes When We Touch")

Hill, George Roy (1921–) Am. film director (*Butch Cassidy and the Sundance Kid*; O—1973—*The Sting*)

Hill, Graham (Norman Graham Hill) (1929–1975) Eng. auto racer

Hill, Virginia ("The Flamingo"; "Queen of the Mob") (1916–1966) Am. actress (mistress of gangsters Joe Adonis and Bugsy Siegel)

Hill, Walter (1942–) Am. film director (*The Long Riders*; *48 HRS.*; *Trespass*)

Hillary, Sir Edmund (Edmund Percival Hillary) (1919–) N.Z. explorer/mountaineer (climbed Mt. Everest and traveled to South Pole)

Hiller, Arthur (1923–) Can.-Am. film director (*Love Story*; *The Americanization of Emily*)

Hiller, Dame Wendy (Wendy Margaret Hiller) (1912–) Eng. actress (*Pygmalion*; O—1958—*Separate Tables*)

Hillerman, John (John Benedict Hillerman) (1932–) Am. actor ("Magnum, P.I." TV series; E—1986/87)

Hillier, James (1915–) Can.-Am. physicist/inventor (electron microscope)

Hills, Carla (Carla Anderson Hills) (1934–) Am. govt. official (secretary of HUD; U.S. trade representative)

Hilo Hattie (1901–1979) Am. (Hawaiian) entertainer

Hilton, Conrad (Conrad Nicholson Hilton) (1887–1979) Am. hotelier/autobiographer (*Be My Guest*)

Hilton, James (1900–1954) Eng. novelist (*Lost Horizon*; *Random Harvest*; *Goodbye, Mr. Chips*)

Himes, Chester (Chester Bomar Himes) (1909–1984) Am. novelist (*Cotton Comes to Harlem*)

Himmler, Heinrich (1900–1945) Ger. Nazi leader/head of the Gestapo and the SS

Hinckley, John, Jr. (John Warnock Hinckley, Jr.) (1955–) Am. attempted assassin (shot Pres. Reagan and James Brady)

Hindemith, Paul (1895–1963) Ger. violist/composer (*Sancta Susanna*)

Hindenburg, Paul von (Paul Ludwig Hans Anton von Beneckendorff und von Hindenburg) (1847–1934) Ger. pres. 1925–1932

Hines, Duncan (1880–1959) Am. food critic/writer (*Adventures in Good Eating*)

Hines, Earl "Fatha" (Earl Kenneth Hines) (1905–1983) Am. jazz pianist (with Louis Armstrong)

Hines, Gregory (Gregory Oliver Hines) (1946–) Am. actor/dancer (*White Nights*; *A Rage in Harlem*; *Jelly's Last Jam*)

Hines, Jerome (Jerome Heinz) (1921–) Am. opera singer (basso)

Hingle, Pat (Martin Patterson Hingle) (1923–) Am. actor ("Gunsmoke" TV series; *Bloody Mama*)

Hinkle, Clarke (William Clarke Hinkle) (1912–) Am. football Hall-of-Famer

Hinton, S. E. (Susan Eloise Hinton) (1948–) Am. novelist (*The Outsiders*; *Rumble Fish*; *That Was Then, This Is Now*)

Hippocrates ("The Father of Medicine") (c. 460–c. 377 B.C.) Gr. physician

Hirohito (1901–1989) Jap. emperor 1926–1989

Hirsch, Crazylegs (Elroy Leon Hirsch) (1923–) Am. football Hall-of-Famer

Hirsch, Judd (1935–) Am. actor ("Taxi" and "Dear John" TV series; E— 1980/81, 1982/83; T—1986)
Hirschfield, Al (Albert Hirschfield) (1903–) Am. caricaturist
Hirt, Al (Alois Maxwell Hirt) (1922–) Am. jazz trumpeter ("Java")
Hiss, Alger (1904–) Am. diplomat/ politician/accused spy
Hitchcock, Sir Alfred (Alfred Joseph Hitchcock; "The Master of Suspense") (1899–1980) Eng. film director (Rear Window; North by Northwest; Psycho; Vertigo; Rebecca)
Hitchcock, Robyn (1952–) Eng. rock singer (with The Egyptians)
Hite, Shere (Shirley Diana Gregory) (1942–) Am. sex researcher/writer (The Hite Report)
Hitler, Adolf (1889–1945) Aus. dictator ("führer") of Germany 1933–1945/ writer (Mein Kampf)
Ho, Don (1930–) Am. (Hawaiian) singer ("Tiny Bubbles")
Hoagland, Edward (Edward Murray Hoagland) (1932–) Am. novelist/ journalist/writer (Cat Man)
Hoban, James (c. 1762–1831) Am. architect (designed the White House)
Hoban, Russell (Russell Conwell Hoban) (1925–) Am. children's book writer (The Marzipan Pig; A Birthday for Frances)
Hobart, Garret A. (Garret Augustus Hobart) (1844–1899) Am. v.p. (W. McKinley)
Hobbes, Thomas (1588–1679) Eng. philosopher/writer (Human Nature)
Hobby, Oveta (née) Culp (1905–) Am. politician/newspaper publisher (Houston Post)
Hobson, Laura (Laura Zametkin Hobson) (1900–1986) Am. writer (Gentleman's Agreement)
Ho Chi Minh (Nguyen That Thanh; "Ho Chi Minh"="He who enlightens") (1890–1969) N. Viet. pres. 1945–1969
Hochwalder, Fritz (1911–) Aus. playwright (The Holy Experiment [staged as The Strong Are Lonely])
Hockney, David (1937–) Eng. painter/ artist (developed "new cubism"; Rake's Progress)
Hodges, Gil (Gilbert Raymond Hodge) (1924–1972) Am. baseball player
Hodges, Johnny (John Cornelius Hodges) (1906–1970) Am. jazz saxophonist (with Duke Ellington)

Hodiak, John (1914–1955) Am. actor (Lifeboat; A Bell for Adano)
Hoffa, Jimmy (James Riddle Hoffa) (1913–1975) Am. labor leader (with links to organized crime; probably murdered)
Hoffer, Eric (1902–1983) Am. philosopher/writer (The True Believer)
Hoffman, Abbie (Abbott Hoffman; a/k/a Barry Freed) (1936–1989) Am. political activist (one of the Chicago 7)
Hoffman, Cecil (c. 1963–) Am. actress ("L.A. Law" TV series)
Hoffman, Dustin (Dustin Lee Hoffman; "Little Big Man") (1937–) Am. actor (The Graduate; Marathon Man; O— 1979—Kramer Vs. Kramer; O—1988— Rain Man)
Hoffman, E. T. A. (Ernst Theodor Amadeus Hoffman; born Ernst Theodor Wilhelm Hoffman) (1776–1822) Ger. composer (Aurora)/writer (Fantasy-Pieces)
Hoffman, Malvina (Malvina Cornell Hoffman) (1887–1966) Am. sculptor/writer (Heads and Tales)
Hoffman, Dr. Roald (1937–) Am. chemist (N—1981)
Hoffs, Susanna (1957–) Am. pop singer ("My Side of the Bed"; with The Bangles; "Walk Like an Egyptian")
Hofstadter, Richard (1916–1970) Am. historian (P—1956—The Age of Reform; P—1964—Anti-Intellectualism in American Life)
Hofstadter, Robert (1915–) Pol.-Am. physicist (N—1961)
Hogan, Ben (William Benjamin Hogan; "Bantam Ben"; "The Hawk") (1912–) Am. golfer
Hogan, Hulk (Terry Gene Bollea) (1953–) Am. wrestler/actor
Hogan, Paul (1941–) Austral. actor (Crocodile Dundee [title role])
Hogarth, Burne (1911–) Am. cartoonist (created Tarzan)
Hogarth, William (1697–1764) Eng. painter/engraver (A Rake's Progress)
Holbein, Hans ("The Elder") (1460–1524) Ger. religious painter/sculptor/architect
Holbein, Hans ("The Younger") (c. 1497–1543) Ger. portrait/historical painter
Holbrook, Hal (Harold Rowe Holbrook, Jr.) (1925–) Am. actor ("Designing Women" and "Evening Shade" TV series; E—1970/71; T—1966)
Holden, William (William Franklin Beedle, Jr.; "Golden Holden") (1918–1981)

Am. actor (*Sunset Boulevard*; *Born Yesterday*; O—1953—*Stalag 17*)

Holiday, Billie (Eleanor Gough McKay; "Lady Day" "First Lady of the Blues") (1915–1959) Am. jazz singer ("Strange Fruit"; "Fine and Mellow")/ autobiographer (*Lady Sings the Blues*)

Holland, Brian (1941–) Am. pop songwriter (with brother Eddie and Lamont Dozier, "Heat Wave"; "Stop! In the Name of Love"; "Baby Love")

Holland, Eddie *see* Holland, Brian

Hollander, Xaviera (1943–) Dutch writer (*The Happy Hooker*)

Holley, Robert (Robert William Holley) (1922–1993) Am. chemist (N—1968)

Holliday, Doc (John Henry Holliday) (1851–1887) Am. western lawman (Wyatt Earp's partner)

Holliday, Jennifer (Jennifer Yvette Holliday) (1960–) Am. singer ("And I'm Telling You I'm Not Going" from *Dream Girls*)/stage actress (*Dream Girls*; T—1982)

Holliday, Judy (Judith Tuvim) (1922–1965) Am. actress (*Adam's Rib*; O—1950—*Born Yesterday*; T—1957)

Holliday, Polly (Polly Dean Holliday) (1937–) Am. actress (TV's "Flo"; signature phrase; "Kiss mah grits!")

Holliman, Earl (Anthony Numkena) (1928–) Am. actor ("Police Woman" TV series)

Holloway, Stanley (Stanley Augustus Holloway) (1890–1982) Eng. actor (*My Fair Lady*; *Nicholas Nickleby*)

Holloway, Sterling (Sterling Price Holloway) (1905–1992) Am. actor/voice performer (Walt Disney characters)

Holly, Buddy (Charles Hardin Holley) (1936–1959) Am. rock singer/guitarist/songwriter ("That'll Be the Day"; "Peggy Sue"; with Buddy Holly and The Crickets)

Holm, Celeste (1919–) Am. actress (*All About Eve*; O—1947—*Gentleman's Agreement*)

Holm, Hanya (Johanna Eckert) (1898–) Ger.-Am. dancer/choreographer/modern dance pioneer

Holm, Ian (Ian Holm Cuthbert) (1931–) Eng. actor (*Alien*; *Brazil*; *Chariots of Fire*)

Holman, Nat ("Mister Basketball") (1896–) Am. basketball player/coach

Holmes, Larry (1949–) Am. boxer

Holmes, Oliver Wendell (1809–1894) Am.

poet/novelist (*The Autocrat of the Breakfast Table*)

Holmes, Oliver Wendell, Jr. ("The Great Dissenter") (1841–1935) Am. Supreme Court jurist 1902–1932 (son of Oliver Wendell Holmes)

Holmes, Rupert (1947–) Eng.-Am. pop singer ("Escape [The Piña Colada Song]")

Holst, Gustav (Gustav Theodore Holst; born Gustavus von Holst) (1874–1934) Eng. composer (*The Planets*)

Holt, John (1923–1985) Am. educator/writer (*How Children Fail*)

Holt, Victoria *see* Hibbert, Eleanor

Holyfield, Evander (c. 1963–) Am. boxer

Holzman, Red (William Holzman) (1920–) Am. basketball coach

Homer (9th century B.C.) Gr. epic poet (*The Iliad*; *The Odyssey*)

Homer, Winslow (1836–1910) Am. painter (American landscapes and seascapes)

Honda, Soichiro (1906–) Jap. automobile manufacturer

Honegger, Arthur (1892–1955) Swi.-Fr. composer (*King David* oratorio)

Hood, Darla (Darla Jean Hood) (1931–1979) Am. actress ("Our Gang" TV series)

Hood, Raymond (Raymond Mathewson Hood) (1881–1934) Am. architect (worked on Rockefeller Center)

Hooker, John Lee (1917–) Am. blues/rock guitarist/singer

Hooks, Jan (1957–) Am. actress/comedienne ("Saturday Night Live" and "Designing Women" TV series)

Hooper, Harry (Harry Bartholomew Hooper) (1887–1974) Am. baseball Hall-of-Famer

Hooper, Tobe (1943–) Am. film director (*Poltergeist*; *The Texas Chainsaw Massacre*)

Hoover, Herbert (Herbert Clark Hoover) (1874–1964) 31st Am. pres. (1929–1933)

Hoover, J. Edgar (John Edgar Hoover) (1895–1972) Am. FBI head (1924–1972)

Hoover, William Henry (1849–1932) Am. businessman (developed the vacuum cleaner)

Hope, Anthony (Anthony Hope Hopkins) (1863–1933) Eng. playwright/adventure novelist (*The Prisoner of Zenda*)

Hope, Bob (Leslie Townes Hope) (1903–) Am. comedian (7 *Road* films with Bing Crosby and Dorothy Lamour)

Hopkins, Sir Anthony (1937–) Wel. actor

(*Bram Stoker's Dracula*; *The Lion in Winter*; *84 Charing Cross Road*; *The Remains of the Day*; O—1991—*The Silence of the Lambs*)

Hopkins, Bo (1942–) Am. actor ("The Rockford Files" TV series; *The Wild Bunch*)

Hopkins, Gerard Manley (1844–1889) Eng. poet/writer (*On the Origin of Beauty*)

Hopkins, Johns (1795–1873) Am. financier/philanthropist (namesake of Johns Hopkins University and Hospital)

Hopkins, Lightnin' (Sam Hopkins) (1912–1982) Am. country/blues singer/songwriter ("Baby Please Don't Go")

Hopkins, Miriam (Ellen Miriam Hopkins) (1902–1972) Am. actress (*Becky Sharp*; *Dr. Jekyll and Mr. Hyde*)

Hopkins, Telma (Telma Louise Hopkins) (1948–) Am. singer (with Tony Orlando & Dawn)/actress ("Gimme a Break" TV series)

Hopper, Dennis (1936–) Am. actor (*Blue Velvet*; *Easy Rider*)/film director (*Colors*)

Hopper, De Wolf (William D'Wolf Hopper) (1858–1935) Am. stage/film actor

Hopper, Edward ("Painter of Loneliness") (1882–1967) Am. painter (*Second Story Sunlight*)

Hopper, Hedda (Elda Furry) (1890–1966) Am. (Hollywood) gossip columnist

Horace (Quintus Horatius Flaccus) (65–8 B.C.) Roman poet (*The Carmina*)

Horgan, Paul (1903–) Am. novelist/biographer/historian (P—1955—*Great River: The Rio Grande in North American History*; P—1976—*Lamy of Santa Fe*)

Horne, Lena (Lena Calhoun Horne; a/k/a Helena Horne) (1917–) Am. singer ("Stormy Weather"; G—1981)/actress (*Cabin in the Sky*)

Horne, Marilyn (Marilyn B. Horne) (1934–) Am. opera singer (mezzo-soprano)

Horne, Roy (Roy Uwe Ludwig Horne) (c. 1945–) Am. animal trainer (of Siegfried & Roy)

Hornsby, Bruce (1954–) Am. pop singer/pianist/composer ("The Way It Is"; "Mandolin Rain"; with The Range; G—1986)

Hornsby, Rogers ("The Rajah") (1896–1963) Am. baseball Hall-of-Famer

Hornung, Paul (Paul Vernon Hornung; "The Golden Boy") (1935–) Am. football Hall-of-Famer

Horovitz, Israel (Israel Arthur Horovitz) (1939–) Am. playwright (*Rats*)

Horowitz, Vladimir (1904–1989) Russ.-Am. concert pianist

Horsley, Lee (1955–) Am. actor (TV's "Matt Houston")

Horst (Horst Paul Horst) (1906–) Ger.-Am. fashion photographer

Horton, Edward Everett (1886–1970) Am. actor (*The Merry Widow*; *The Gay Divorcee*)/TV narrator/comedian (TV's "Fractured Fairy Tales")

Horton, Johnny ("The Singing Fisherman") (1927–1960) Am. country singer/guitarist ("The Battle of New Orleans")

Horton, Peter (1953–) Am. actor ("thirtysomething" TV series)

Horton, Robert (Mead Howard Horton, Jr.) (1924–) Am. actor ("Wagon Train" TV series; "As the World Turns" soap opera)

Hosea (8th century B.C.) Heb. prophet

Hoskins, Bob (Robert William Hoskins) (1942–) Eng. actor (*Mona Lisa*; *Who Framed Roger Rabbit?*)

Hotchner, A. E. (Aaron Edward Hotchner) (1920–) Am. writer (*Papa Hemingway*)

Houdini, Harry (Erich Weiss; orig. Erik Weisz) (1874–1926) Am. magician

Hough, Charlie (Charles Oliver Hough) (1948–) Am. baseball pitcher

Houk, Ralph (Ralph George Houk; "The Major") (1919–) Am. baseball player/manager

Houseman, John (Jacques Haussmann) (1902–1988) Am. actor (*Seven Days in May*; O—1973—*The Paper Chase*)

Housman, A. E. (Alfred Edward Housman) (1859–1936) Eng. writer/poet (brother of Laurence; *A Shropshire Lad*)

Housman, Laurence (1865–1959) Eng. novelist/playwright/illustrator (brother of A. E.; *Victoria Regina*)

Houston, Cissy (Emily Drinkard Houston) (1932–) Am. pop/gospel singer (mother of Whitney)

Houston, Ken (Kenneth Ray Houston) (1944–) Am. football Hall-of-Famer

Houston, Sam (Samuel Houston) (1793–1863) Am. (Texas) soldier/statesman/frontiersman

Houston, Thelma (C) Am. pop singer

("Don't Leave Me This Way")/actress ("Norman . . . Is That You?")

Houston, Whitney (1963–) Am. pop singer (daughter of Cissy; "Saving All My Love for You"; "I Will Always Love You"; G— 1985, 1987)/actress (*The Bodyguard*)

Howard, Curly (Jerome Horovitz) (1906–1952) Am. comedian (brother of Moe; one of The Three Stooges)

Howard, Frank (Frank Oliver Howard; "Capital Punishment"; "Hondo") (1936–) Am. baseball player/manager

Howard, Ken (Kenneth Joseph Howard, Jr.) (1944–) Am. actor ("Dynasty" and "The Colbys" TV series)

Howard, Leslie (Leslie Howard Stainer) (1890–1943) Hung.-Eng. actor (*The Scarlet Pimpernel*; *Gone with the Wind*)

Howard, Moe (Moses Horovitz) (1897–1975) Am. comedian (one of The Three Stooges)

Howard, Rance (C) Am. actor (father of Ron Howard; "Gentle Ben" TV series)

Howard, Ron (1954–) Am. actor ("Happy Days" TV series)/film director (*Splash*; *Parenthood*; *Far and Away*; *Cocoon*)

Howard, Shemp (Samuel Horovitz) (1891–1955) Am. comedian (occasional member of The Three Stooges)

Howard, Sidney (Sidney Coe Howard) (1891–1939) Am. playwright (P—1925—*They Knew What They Wanted*)

Howard, Trevor (Trevor Wallace Howard) (1916–1988) Eng. actor (*The Third Man*; *Brief Encounter*; *Sons and Lovers*)

Howe, Elias (1819–1867) Am. inventor (sewing machine)

Howe, Gordie (Gordon Howe; "Blinky") (1928–) Can. hockey player

Howe, Julia (née Ward) (1819–1910) Am. social reformer/writer (*The Battle Hymn of the Republic*)

Howe, Steve (1947–) Eng. rock guitarist (with Yes and Asia)

Howell, C. Thomas (1966–) Am. actor (*Soul Man*; *The Hitcher*)

Howells, William Dean (1837–1920) Am. novelist/editor/poet (*The Rise of Silas Lapham*; *A Modern Instance*)

Howlin' Wolf (Chester Burnette) (1910–1976) Am. country/blues musician/singer ("Sittin' on Top of the World")

Hoyle, Sir Fred (1915–) Eng. astronomer/science fiction writer (*A for Andromeda*; *Man in the Universe*)

Hoyt, Waite (Waite Charles Hoyt;

"Schoolboy") (1899–1984) Am. baseball Hall-of-Famer

Hrabosky, Al (Alan Thomas Hrabosky; "The Mad Hungarian") (1949–) Am. baseball pitcher

Hrbek, Kent (Kent Allen Hrbek; "Buy a Vowel") (1960–) Am. baseball player

Hsien Feng (a/k/a I-chu; Wen Tsung; Hsien Huang-ti) (1831–1861) Chin. emperor 1851–1861

Hubbard, Cal (Robert Calvin Hubbard) (1900–1977) Am. baseball and football Hall-of-Famer

Hubbard, Elbert (Elbert Green Hubbard) (1856–1916) Am. writer (*A Message to Garcia*)/magazine publisher/editor (*The Philistine*)

Hubbard, Kin (Frank McKinney Hubbard) (1868–1930) Am. columnist/caricaturist (created Abe Martin)

Hubbard, L. Ron (Lafayette Ronald Hubbard; a/k/a Elron Elray, Tom Esterbrook, Rene La Fayette, Capt. B. A. Northrop, and Kurt von Rachem) (1911–1986) Am. founder of Scientology and Dianetics/science fiction writer

Hubbell, Carl (Carl Owen Hubbell; "King Carl"; "The Meal Ticket"; "Money") (1903–1988) Am. baseball Hall-of-Famer

Hubble, Edwin (Edwin Powell Hubble) (1889–1953) Am. astronomer (discovered red shift and devised Hubble's Constant)

Hubley, Season (Susan Shelbey Brooks Hubley) (1951–) Am. actress ("Family" TV series)

Hucknall, Mick (1960–) Eng. pop singer ("Holding Back the Years"; with Simply Red)

Hudson, Garth (1937–) Can. rock organist (with The Band)

Hudson, Henry (1575–1611) Eng. navigator/explorer in the New World (namesake of Hudson River)

Hudson, Rock (Roy Scherer, Jr.; adopted name Roy Fitzgerald) (1925–1985) Am. actor (*Pillow Talk*; *Send Me No Flowers*; *Giant*; *Magnificent Obsession*; "McMillan and Wife" TV series)

Huff, Sam (Robert Lee Huff) (1934–) Am. football Hall-of-Famer

Huggins, Charles B. (Charles Brenton Huggins) (1901–) Can.-Am. surgeon/cancer researcher (N—1966)

Huggins, Miller (Miller James Huggins;

"Hug"; "The Mighty Mite") (1879–1929) Am. baseball Hall-of-Famer

Hughes, Charles E. (Charles Evans Hughes) (1862–1948) Am. Supreme Court chief justice (1930–1941)

Hughes, Howard (Howard Robard Hughes, Jr.; "The Billionaire Recluse") (1905–1976) Am. filmmaker/aviator/tycoon

Hughes, John (1950–) Am. screenwriter (*Home Alone*)/film director (*The Breakfast Club*; *Weird Science*)

Hughes, Ken (1922–) Am. film director (*Of Human Bondage*; *Chitty Chitty Bang Bang*)

Hughes, Langston (James Mercer Langston Hughes) (1902–1967) Am. poet/writer (*The Weary Blues*; *The Ways of White Folks*)

Hughes, Ted (Edward James Hughes) (1930–) Eng. poet laureate (*The Hawk in the Rain*)

Hughes, Thomas (1822–1896) Eng. jurist/writer (*Tom Brown's School Days*)

Hugo, Victor (Victor-Marie Hugo) (1802–1885) Fr. poet/novelist/playwright (*Les Miserables*; *The Hunchback of Notre Dame*)

Hulce, Tom (Thomas Hulce) (1953–) Am. actor (*Animal House*; *Amadeus*; *Dominick and Eugene*)

Hull, Bobby (Robert Marvin Hull, Jr.; "The Golden Jet") (1939–) Can. hockey player

Hull, Cordell (1871–1955) Am. statesman/secretary of state (N—1945)

Hull, Isaac ("Old Ironsides") (1773–1843) Am. naval commander

Hull, Josephine (Josephine Sherwood) (1884 or 1886–1957) Am. actress (*Arsenic and Old Lace*; O—1950—*Harvey*)

Hull, Warren (1903–1974) Am. radio/film actor/TV host ("Strike It Rich")

Humboldt, Baron Alexander von (Friedrich Wilhelm Karl Heinrich Alexander von Humboldt) (1769–1859) Ger. naturalist/statesman

Hume, David (1711–1776) Scot. philosopher/historian

Humperdinck, Engelbert (1854–1921) Ger. composer (*Hansel and Gretel*)

Humperdinck, Engelbert (Arnold George Dorsey) (1936–) Eng. pop singer ("Release Me [And Let Me Love Again]")

Humphrey, Hubert H. (Hubert Horatio Humphrey; "The Happy Warrior";

"HHH") (1911–1978) Am. v.p. (L. B. Johnson)/politician/presidential candidate 1968

Hunley, Leann (1955–) Am. actress ("Dynasty" TV series)

Hunt, E. Howard, Jr. (Everette Howard Hunt, Jr.; a/k/a John Baxter, Gordon Davis, Robert Dietrich, and David St. John) (1918–) Am. politician/writer (*Cozumel*; *The Kremlin Conspiracy*)

Hunt, Helen (1963–) Am. actress ("Mad About You" TV series; *The Waterdance*)

Hunt, Holman (William Holman Hunt) (1827–1910) Eng. painter (*The Scapegoat*)

Hunt, Linda (1945–) Am. actress (*She-Devil*; *Popeye*; O—1982—*The Year of Living Dangerously*)

Hunt, Marsha (Marcia Virginia Hunt) (1917–) Am. actress (*Pride and Prejudice*; *Johnny Got His Gun*)

Hunt, Martita (1900–1969) Eng. actress (*Great Expectations*; *Anna Karenina*; T—1949)

Hunt, Richard (Richard Morris Hunt) (1827–1895) Am. architect (Metropolitan Museum of Art)

Hunter, Alberta (a/k/a May Alix, Josephine Beatty, and Helen Roberts) (1895–) Am. blues singer

Hunter, Catfish (James Augustus Hunter) (1946–) Am. baseball Hall-of-Famer

Hunter, Evan (Salvadore Lombino; a/k/a Ed McBain, Hunt Collins, and Richard Marsten) (1926–) Am. novelist (*The Blackboard Jungle*; as Ed McBain, *87th Precinct* thrillers)

Hunter, Holly (1958–) Am. actress (*Broadcast News*; *Raising Arizona*; *The Piano*)

Hunter, Ian (1946–) Eng. rock singer/musician (with Mott the Hoople)

Hunter, Jeffery (Henry Herman McKinnies, Jr.) (1925–1969) Am. radio/film actor (*King of Kings* [as Jesus])

Hunter, Kim (Janet Cole) (1922–) Am. actress (*Stairway to Heaven*; O—1951—*A Streetcar Named Desire*)

Hunter, Rachel (1969–) N.Z. model

Hunter, Ross (Martin Fuss; "Last of the Dream Merchants") (1924 or 1926–) Am. film producer (*Pillow Talk*; *Louisiana Hayride*)

Hunter, Tab (Arthur Andrew Gelien [mother's maiden name]; born Arthur Andrew Kelm) (1931–) Am. actor (*Damn Yankees*; *The Loved One*)

Huntley, Chet (Chester Robert Huntley) (1911–) Am. TV newscaster ("The Huntley-Brinkley Report")

Huppert, Isabelle (1955–) Fr. actress (*Story of Women; The Lacemaker*)

Hurd, Gale Ann (1955–) Am. film producer (*Aliens; The Terminator; The Abyss*)

Hurok, Sol (Solomon Hurok) (1888–1974) Russ.-Am. music impresario (discovered Efrem Zimbalist, Anna Pavlova)

Hurrell, George (1904–1992) Am. fashion/portrait photographer

Hurst, Fannie (1889–1968) Am. novelist (*Back Street; Imitation of Life*)

Hurston, Zora Neale (1903–1960) Am. novelist/short story writer/folklorist (*Their Eyes Were Watching God; Mules and Men*)

Hurt, John (1940–) Eng. actor (*The Elephant Man; Scandal; Midnight Express*)

Hurt, Mary Beth (Mary Beth Supinger) (1948–) Am. actress (*The World According to Garp; Parents; Compromising Positions*)

Hurt, William (1950–) Am. actor (*Children of a Lesser God; The Big Chill; O— 1985—Kiss of the Spider Woman*)

Husky, Ferlin (a/k/a Terry Preston and Simon Crum) (1925–) Am. comedian/singer ("Gone")

Hussein, Abdul ibn (Hussein ibn Talal ibn Abdullah el Hashim; a/k/a Hussein I) (1935–) Jord. king 1953–

Hussein, Saddam ("The Butcher of Baghdad") (1937–) Iraqi dictator/mil. leader/pres. 1979–

Hussey, Olivia (Olivia Osuna) (1951–) Arg.-Eng. actress (*Lost Horizon; Romeo and Juliet*)

Hussey, Ruth (Ruth Carol O'Rourke) (1917–) Am. actress (*The Philadelphia Story; Tennessee Johnson*)

Huston, Anjelica (1951–) Am. actress (daughter of John; *The Addams Family; The Grifters; O—1985—Prizzi's Honor*)

Huston, John (1906–1987) Am. film director (son of Walter; *The Maltese Falcon; O—1948—The Treasure of the Sierra Madre*)

Huston, Walter (Walter Houghston) (1884–1950) Am. actor (*Abraham Lincoln; Dodsworth; O—1948—The Treasure of the Sierra Madre*)

Hutchence, Michael (1960–) Austral. rock singer (with INXS; "Need You Tonight")

Hutchison, Fiona (c. 1961–) Am. actress ("The Guiding Light" soap opera)

Hutchison, Jock (1884–1977) Scot. golfer

Hutson, Don (Donald Montgomery Hutson; "The Alabama Antelope") (1913–) Am. football Hall-of-Famer

Hutton, Barbara ("The Poor Little Rich Girl") (1912–1979) Am. heiress (granddaughter of F. W. Woolworth)

Hutton, Betty (Elizabeth June Thornburg) (1921–) Am. actress/singer/dancer (sister of Marion; *The Miracle of Morgan's Creek*)

Hutton, E. F. (Edward F. Hutton) (1877–1962) Am. banker/business executive (father of Dina Merrill)

Hutton, Ina Ray ("The Blond Bombshell of Swing") (1916–1984) Am. orchestra leader

Hutton, Jim (1934–1979) Am. actor (father of Timothy; TV's "Ellery Queen")

Hutton, Lauren (Mary Laurence Hutton) (1943–) Am. model/actress (*Once Bitten; American Gigolo*)

Hutton, Marion (Marion Thornburg) (1920–1987) Am. singer (sister of Betty; with Glenn Miller's band)

Hutton, Timothy (Timothy James Hutton) (1960–) Am. actor (son of Jim; *The Falcon and the Snowman; O—1980— Ordinary People*)

Huxley, Aldous (Aldous Leonard Huxley) (1894–1963) Eng. novelist/essayist (brother of Julian; *Brave New World*)

Huxley, Sir Julian Sorell (1887–1975) Eng. biologist/writer of scientific books (brother of Aldous)

Huxley, Thomas (Thomas Henry Huxley) (1825–1895) Eng. biologist/philosopher (father of Julius and Aldous; coined the word *agnostic*)

Hwang, David Henry (1957–) Am. playwright (*M. Butterfly*)/actor

Hyams, Peter (1943–) Am. screenwriter/film director (*The Star Chamber; Narrow Margin*)

Hyatt, John (John Wesley Hyatt) (1837–1920) Am. inventor (celluloid)

Hyde-White, Wilfrid (1903–) Eng. actor (*The Third Man; Let's Make Love*)

Hyer, Martha (1929–) Am. actress (*Sabrina; Houseboat; Some Came Running*)

Hyland, Diana (Joan Diana Gentner) (1936–1977) Am. actress ("Eight Is Enough" TV series)

Hynde, Chrissie (Christine Elaine

Hynde) (1951–) Am. rock singer/musician ("Brass in Pocket [I'm Special]"; with The Pretenders)

Iacocca, Lee (Lido Anthony Iacocca) (1924–) Am. automobile executive/autobiographer (*Iacocca*)

Ian, Janis (Janis Eddy Fink) (1950–) Am. pop singer ("At Seventeen"; G—1975)

Ibert, Jacques (Jacques-François-Antoine Ibert) (1890–1962) Fr. composer (*The Little White Donkey*)

Ibn Saud ('Abd al-'Aziz ibn 'Abd ar-Rahmān ibn Faysal ibn Turkī 'Abd Allāh ibn Muhammad Āl Saūd) (1880–1953) Arab. king/founder of Saudi Arabia

Ibsen, Henrik (Henrik Johan Ibsen) (1828–1906) Norw. poet/playwright (*Hedda Gabler*; *A Doll's House*; *Peer Gynt*)

Icahn, Carl (Carl C. Icahn) (1936–) Am. airline executive (TWA)

Ice-T (Tracy Marrow) (c. 1962–) Am. rapper ("Body Count")

Ictinus (a/k/a Iktinos) (5th century B.C.) Gr. architect (with Callicrates, designed the Parthenon)

Idle, Eric (1943–) Eng. comedian/actor (with Monty Python)

Idol, Billy (William Wolfe Broad) (1955–) Eng. rock singer ("Rebel Yell"; "Eyes without a Face"; formerly with Generation X)

Iglesias, Julio (Julio Iglesias de la Cueva) (1943–) Span. singer (with Willie Nelson: "To All the Girls I've Loved Before")

Ignatius of Loyola, Saint (Inigo de Onaz y Loyola) (1491–1556) Span. founder of the Jesuit Order

Iman (Iman Mohamed Abdulmajid; a/k/a Iman Somalia) (1955–) Am. model/actress (*No Way Out*)

Incaviglia, Pete (Peter Joseph Incaviglia) (1964–) Am. baseball player

Ince, Thomas H. (Thomas Harper Ince; a/k/a T. H. Ince; "Rodin of the Shadows") (1882–1924) Am. film producer/director/screenwriter (*Civilization*; *Anna Christie* [1923])

Inge, William (William Motter Inge) (1913–1973) Am. playwright (*Come Back, Little Sheba*; *Bus Stop*; *Splendor in the Grass*; P—1953—*Picnic*)

Ingels, Marty (Martin Ingerman) (1936–) Am. comedian

Ingersoll, Robert G. (Robert Green Ingersoll) (1833–1899) Am. lawyer/orator/writer (*Why I Am an Agnostic*)

Ingram, James (1956–) Am. pop singer ("Just Once"; "I Don't Have the Heart")

Ingram, Luther (1944–) Am. soul singer ("[If Loving You Is Wrong] I Don't Want to Be Right")

Ingram, Rex (Reginald Ingram Montgomery Hitchcock) (1892–1950) Am. film director (*The Prisoner of Zenda*; *The Four Horsemen of the Apocalypse*)

Ingres, Jean (Jean-Auguste-Dominique Ingres) (1780–1867) Fr. classicist painter (*Turkish Bath*)

Innes, Michael (J(ohn). I(nnes). M(ackintosh). Stewart) (1906–) Scot. novelist/scholar/mystery writer (created Inspector Appleby; *Hamlet, Revenge!*)

Inness, George (1825–1894) Am. painter (*Millpond*)

Inouye, Daniel K. (Daniel Ken Inouye) (1924–) Am. lawyer/senator

Iommi, Tony (1948–) Eng. rock guitarist (with Black Sabbath)

Ionesco, Eugene (1912–1994) Fr. playwright (*Rhinoceros*; *Exit the King*; *The Bald Soprano*)

Ireland, Jill (Jill Dorothy Ireland) (1936–1990) Am. actress (*The Mechanic*; *The Evil That Men Do*)

Ireland, John (John Benjamin Ireland) (1914–1992) Can.-Am. actor ("Rawhide" TV series; *All the King's Men*)

Ireland, Kathy (C) Am. model/actress

Irons, Jeremy (Jeremy John Irons) (1948–) Eng. actor ("Brideshead Revisited" TV series; *Dead Ringers*; *Damage*; *M. Butterfly*; O—1990—*Reversal of Fortune*; T—1984)

Irvin, Monte (Monford Merrill Irvin) (1919–) Am. baseball Hall-of-Famer

Irving, Amy (1953–) Am. actress (*Yentl*; *Crossing Delancey*; *Honeysuckle Rose*)

Irving, John (John Winslow Irving) (1942–) Am. novelist (*The World According to Garp*; *The Hotel New Hampshire*)

Irving, Washington (a/k/a Geoffrey Crayon, Jonathan Oldstyle, Launcelot Wagstaffe, and Friar Antonio Agapida) (1783–1859) Am. essayist/biographer/historian (*Rip Van Winkle*; *The Legend of Sleepy Hollow*)

Irwin, Bill (William Mills) (1950–) Am. choreographer/actor/clown

Irwin, Hale (Hale S. Irwin, Jr.) (1945–) Am. golfer

Isaak, Chris (1956–) Am. pop singer/

songwriter/musician ("Wicked Game")/
actor (*The Silence of the Lambs*)
Isabella (Isabella I; "The Catholic") (1451–
1504) Span. queen 1474–1504 (aided
Columbus)
Isaiah (8th century B.C.) Heb. prophet
Isherwood, Christopher (Christopher
William Bradshaw Isherwood) (1904–
1986) Am. novelist/short story writer/
playwright (*Goodbye to Berlin* [filmed as
Cabaret]; *I Am a Camera*; *Mr. Norris
Changes Trains*)
Isley, O'Kelly (1937–1986) Am. pop/soul
musician/singer (with The Isley
Brothers; "It's Your Thing")
Isley, Ronald (1941–) Am. pop/soul
musician/singer (with The Isley
Brothers)
Isley, Rudolph (1939–) Am. pop/soul
musician/singer (with The Isley
Brothers)
Isocrates (436–338 B.C.) Ath. orator/
teacher
Ito, Hirobumi (1841–1909) Jap. statesman/
premier 1885–1888, 1892–1896, 1898,
1900–1901
Iturbi, José (1895–1980) Span. pianist/
conductor
Ivan III (Ivan the Great; Ivan III
Vasilyevich) (1440–1505) grand prince of
Russia 1462–1505
Ivan IV (Ivan the Terrible) (1530–1584)
ruler of Russia 1533–1584
Ivan V (Ivan V Alekseyevich) (1666–1696)
Russ. czar 1682–1689
Ivan VI (Ivan VI Antonovich) (1740–1764)
Russ. czar 1740–1741
Ives, Burl (Burl Icle Ivanhoe) (1909–) Am.
singer/actor (O—1958—*The Big Coun-
try*; *Cat on a Hot Tin Roof* [as Big
Daddy])
Ives, Charles (Charles Edward Ives)
(1874–1954) Am. composer (*Three
Places in New England*; P—1947—
Symphony No. 3)
Ives, James (James Merritt Ivges) (1824–
1895) Am. lithographer/painter/
publisher (with Nathaniel Currier)
Ivey, Judith (1951–) Am. actress (*Compro-
mising Positions*; *In Country*)
Ivory, James (James Francis Ivory) (1928–)
Am. film director (with Ismail Mer-
chant; *A Passage to India*; *A Room with a
View*; *Howard's End*; *The Remains of
the Day*)
Jackee *see* Harry, Jackee
Jackson, Alan (Alan Eugene Jackson)

(1958–) Am. country singer ("Don't
Rock the Jukebox"; "Here in the Real
World")
Jackson, Andrew ("Old Hickory") (1767–
1845) 7th Am. pres. (1829–1837)
Jackson, Anne (1926–) Am. actress (*The
Secret Life of an American Wife*; *Lovers
and Other Strangers*)
Jackson, Bo (Vincent Edward Jackson)
(1962–) Am. athlete (football/baseball)
Jackson, Danny (Danny Lynn Jackson)
(1962–) Am. baseball pitcher
Jackson, Freddie (1956–) Am. soul/pop
singer ("You Are My Lady")
Jackson, Glenda (1936–) Eng. actress
(*Sunday, Bloody Sunday*; O—1970—
Women in Love; O—1973—*A Touch of
Class*)
Jackson, Helen Hunt (Helen Maria Hunt
Jackson née Fiske) (1830–1885) Am.
novelist/poet (*A Century of Dishonor*)
Jackson, Jackie (Sigmund Esco Jackson)
(1951–) Am. pop singer (with The Jack-
sons)
Jackson, Janet (1966–) Am. pop singer
(sister of Michael; "Control"; "Miss You
Much"; "Escapade")/actress (*Poetic Jus-
tice*)
Jackson, Jermaine (Jermaine Lajune Jack-
son) (1954–) Am. pop singer (brother of
Michael; "Let's Get Serious"; with The
Jacksons)
Jackson, Reverend Jesse (Jesse Louis
Jackson) (1941–) Am. politician/civil
rights activist (aide to Martin Luther
King, Jr.; head of the Rainbow Coalition)
Jackson, Joe (Joseph Jefferson Jackson;
"Shoeless Joe") (1888–1951) Am. base-
ball player
Jackson, Joe (1955–) Eng. rock/pop singer/
songwriter ("Steppin' Out")
Jackson, Kate (1948–) Am. actress ("Char-
lie's Angels" and "Scarecrow and Mrs.
King" TV series)
Jackson, La Toya (1956–) Am. pop singer
(sister of Michael; "Heart Don't
Lie")
Jackson, Laura (a/k/a Laura Riding Jack-
son; born Laura Reichenthal) (1901–)
Am. novelist/poet (*Lives of Wives*)
Jackson, Mahalia (1911–1972) Am. gospel
singer ("He's Got the Whole World in
His Hands")
Jackson, Marlon (Marlon David Jackson)
(1957–) Am. pop singer (with The Jack-
sons)
Jackson, Maynard (Maynard Holbrook

Jackson, Jr.) (1938–) Am. govt. official (first Afr.-Am. mayor of Atlanta)

Jackson, Michael (Michael Joseph Jackson; "Jacko"; "The Peter Pan of Pop"; "The King of Pop") (1958–) Am. pop singer ("Bad"; "Thriller"; G—1983)/ songwriter ("We Are the World," with Lionel Richie)

Jackson, Millie (1943–) Am. soul singer ("Hurts So Good"; "Ask Me What You Want")

Jackson, Milt (Milton J. Jackson; "Bags") (1923–) Am. jazz vibraphonist/pianist/ guitarist

Jackson, Phil (1945–) Am. basketball player/coach

Jackson, Rachel (Rachel Donelson Robards) (1767–1828) Am. first lady (Andrew)

Jackson, Rebbie (Maureen Jackson) (1950–) Am. pop singer ("Centipede")

Jackson, Reggie (Reginald Martinez Jackson; "Mr. October") (1946–) Am. baseball player

Jackson, Samuel (Samuel L. Jackson) (C) Am. actor (Jungle Fever; Jurassic Park; National Lampoon's Loaded Weapon I)

Jackson, Shirley (1919–1965) Am. novelist/ short story writer (The Lottery; The Haunting of Hill House)

Jackson, Stonewall (1932–) Am. country singer ("Me and You and a Dog Named Blue")

Jackson, Thomas (Thomas Jonathan Jackson; "Stonewall"; "Invincible Stonewall"; "The Sword of the Confederacy") (1824–1863) Am. Confederate general

Jackson, Tito (Toriano Adaryll Jackson) (1953–) Am. pop singer (with The Jacksons)

Jackson, Victoria (1959–) Am. comedienne/actress ("Saturday Night Live" TV series)

Jacob, Max (Cyprien-Max Jacob) (1876–1944) Fr. poet/painter/writer (Art Poetique)

Jacobi, Derek (Derek George Jacobi) (1938–) Eng. actor ("I, Claudius" [title role] TV series; The Day of the Jackal; T—1985)

Jacobi, Friedrich (Friedrich Heinrich Jacobi) (1743–1819) Ger. novelist/philosopher (developed the "philosophy of feeling")

Jacobi, Lou (Louis Harold Jacobi) (1913–) Can.-Am. actor ("Somerset" TV series; Irma La Douce)

Jacobs, Helen Hull (1908–) Am. tennis player

Jacoby, Brook (Brook Wallace Jacoby) (1959–) Am. baseball player

Jaffe, Rona (1932–) Am. novelist (The Best of Everything; Class Reunion)

Jaffe, Sam (Samuel Jaffe) (1891–1984) Am. actor ("Ben Casey" TV series; The Asphalt Jungle; Lost Horizon)

Jaffe, Stanley (1940–) Am. entertainment executive (head of Paramount)/film producer (Kramer vs. Kramer; Fatal Attraction)

Jagger, Bianca (Bianca Teresa Pérez Morena de Macías) (1945–) Nic.-Eng. actress/socialite

Jagger, Dean (Dean Jeffries) (1903–1991) Am. actor (The Robe; Bad Day at Black Rock; O—1949—Twelve O'Clock High)

Jagger, Jade (1971–) Eng. model (daughter of Bianca and Mick)

Jagger, Mick (Michael Philip Jagger) (1943–) Eng. rock singer (with The Rolling Stones; "Sympathy for the Devil")

Jaglom, Henry (1939–) Am. film director (Someone to Love; Eating; Always)

Jakes, John (1932–) Am. historical novelist (North and South; Love and War)

James I (1566–1625) Eng. king 1603–1625 and Scotland (as James VI) 1567–1625

James II (1633–1701) king of England, Scotland, and Ireland 1685–1688

James, Etta (Jamesetta Hawkins; "Miss Peaches") (1938–) Am. jazz singer ("Tell Mama"; "Pushover")

James, Harry (Harry Haag James) (1916–1983) Am. jazz trumpeter/bandleader ("Sleepy Lagoon"; "I've Heard That Song Before")

James, Henry (Henry James, Jr.) (1843–1916) Am. novelist/short story writer (Daisy Miller; Washington Square; The Bostonians; The Golden Bowl)

James, Jesse (Jesse Woodson James) (1847–1882) Am. outlaw (led the James Gang)

James, John (John James Anderson) (1956–) Am. actor ("Dynasty" TV series)

James, Joni (Joan Carmello Babbo) (1930–) Am. singer ("How Important Can It Be?"; "Why Don't You Believe Me")

James, P. D. (Phyllis Dorothy James White) (1920–) Eng. mystery writer (created Adam Dalgliesh; The Children of Men)

James, Rick (James A. Johnson, Jr.; a/k/a

Moses Johnson) (1952–) Am. pop/disco singer ("Super Freak")/producer

James, Sonny (James Loden; "The Southern Gentleman") (1929–) Am. country singer ("Young Love")

James, Tommy (Thomas Gregory Jackson) (1947–) Am. pop singer (with The Shondells; "Hanky Panky"; "Crimson and Clover")

James, William (1842–1910) Am. philosopher/psychologist (a founder of pragmatism; *Varieties of Religious Experience*; brother of Henry and Alice)

Jan and Dean see Berry, Jan, and Torrence, Dean

Janáček, Leoš (1854–1928) Cz. composer (*Taras Bulba*)

Janeway, Eliot (1913–1993) Am. economist/writer (*Musings on Money: How to Make Dollars out of Sense*)

Janklow, Morton (Morton Lloyd Janklow) (1930–) Am. lawyer/literary agent

Jannings, Emil (Theodor Friedrich Emil Janenz) (1884–1950) Swi.-Am. actor (*Othello*; *Quo Vadis?*; O—1927/28—*The Way of All Flesh*)

Janowitz, Tama (1957–) Am. novelist (*Slaves of New York*)

Janssen, David (David Harold Meyer) (1930–1980) Am. actor (TV's "The Fugitive")

Jardine, Alan (Allan Jardine) (1942–) Am. pop musician (with The Beach Boys)

Jarmusch, Jim (1953–) Am. film director (*Stranger Than Paradise*; *Mystery Train*; *Night on Earth*)

Jarre, Jean-Michel (Jean-Michel Andre Jarre) (1948–) Fr. keyboardist/composer (son of Maurice)

Jarre, Maurice (Maurice Alexis Jarre) (1924–) Fr. composer (father of Jean-Michel; *Lawrence of Arabia*; *Dr. Zhivago*)

Jarreau, Al (1940–) Am. soul/jazz singer ("We're in This Love Together"; "Mornin'"; G—1981)

Jarrell, Randall (1914–1965) Am. poet/writer (*Kipling, Auden & Co.*; *Pictures from an Institution*)

Jarrett, Keith (1945–) Am. jazz pianist/composer (with Miles Davis and Art Blakey)

Jaruzelski, Wojciech (Wojciech Witold Jaruzelski) (1923–) Pol. general/prime minister 1981–1985/pres. 1985–

Jarvik, Dr. Robert Koffler (1946–) Am. physician/inventor (Jarvik-7 artificial heart)

Jaspers, Karl (Karl Theodor Jaspers) (1883–1969) Ger. psychiatrist/existentialist philosopher/writer (*Reason and Existence*)

Jaurès, Jean (Jean-Joseph-Marie-Auguste Jaurès) (1859–1914) Fr. socialist/psychiatrist/writer (*Socialist History of the French Revolution*)

Jaworski, Leon (1905–1982) Am. govt. official/lawyer (prosecuted Nuremberg and Watergate)

Jay, John (1745–1829) Am. jurist (first chief justice of the Supreme Court, 1789–1795)/statesman

Jeans, Isabel (1891–1985) Eng. actress (*Gigi*; *Hard to Get*)

Jeans, Ursula (Ursula McMinn) (1906–1973) Eng. actress (*The Weaker Sex*; *The Life and Death of Colonel Blimp*)

Jeffers, Robinson (John Robinson Jeffers) (1887–1962) Am. poet/playwright (*Medea*; *Roan Stallion*)

Jefferson, Blind Lemon (a/k/a Deacon L. J. Bates) (1897–1930) Am. blues singer/guitarist

Jefferson, Martha (Martha Wayles Skelton) (1748–1782) Am. first lady (Thomas)

Jefferson, Thomas ("The Apostle of Liberty"; "The Sage of Monticello"; "The Philosopher of Democracy") (1743–1826) Am. revolutionary leader/drafter of the Declaration of Independence/3rd Am. pres. (1801–1809)/founder of University of Virginia

Jeffreys, Anne (Anne Jeffreys Carmichael) (1923–) Am. actress ("Topper" TV series; *Dillinger*)

Jekyll, Gertrude (1843–1932) Eng. landscape designer/writer (*Home and Garden*)

Jellicoe, Ann (Patricia Ann Jellicoe) (1927–) Am. playwright/theatrical director (*The Knack*)

Jenkins, Fergie (Ferguson Arthur Jenkins) (1943–) Am. baseball Hall-of-Famer

Jenkins, Hayes Alan (1933–) Am. figure skater

Jenner, Bruce (1949–) Am. decathlete/sportscaster

Jenney, William (William Le Baron Jenney; "Father of the Skyscraper") (1832–1907) Am. architect

Jennings, Hughie (Hughie Ambrose Jennings; "Ee-yah") (1869–1928) Am. baseball Hall-of-Famer

Jennings, Peter (Peter Charles Jennings) (1938–) Am. newscaster

Jennings, Waylon (1937–) Am. country singer ("Goodhearted Woman"; "Mammas Don't Let Your Babies Grow Up to Be Cowboys")

Jens, Salome (1935–) Am. actress (Angel Baby; Savages)

Jensen, Johannes (Johannes Vilhelm Jensen) (1873–1950) Dan. novelist/poet/essayist (The Long Journey; The Fall of the King; N—1944)

Jeremiah (c. 650–c. 570 B.C.) Heb. prophet

Jergens, Adele (Adele Louisa Jergens) (1917–) Am. actress (Show Boat; The Treasure of Monte Cristo)

Jeritza, Maria (Mitzi Jedlicka) (1887–1982) Cz.-Am. opera singer (soprano)

Jeroboam I (died c. 901 B.C.) Isr. king 922–901 B.C.

Jeroboam II (died 741 B.C.) Isr. king 783–741 B.C.

Jerome, Saint (a/k/a Sophronius and Eusebius Hieronymus) (c. 374–419 or 420) Christian scholar/religious writer

Jerome, Jerome K. (Jerome Klapka Jerome) (1859–1927) Eng. playwright/humorist/novelist (Three Men in a Boat)

Jessel, George (George Albert Jessel; "Toastmaster General") (1898–1981) Am. humorist/TV host ("The George Jessel Show")

Jesus Christ (a/k/a Jesus of Nazareth) (c. 6 B.C.–c. 30 A.D.) founder of Christianity (born in Bethlehem)

Jett, Joan (Joan Larkin) (1960–) Am. rock singer/musician ("I Love Rock 'n' Roll"; with The Blackhearts; formerly with The Runaways)

Jewell, Isabell (1913–1972) Am. actress (Lost Horizon; A Tale of Two Cities)

Jewett, Sarah Orne (Theodora Sarah Orne Jewett) (1849–1909) Am. novelist/short story writer (The Country of the Pointed Firs)

Jewison, Norman (Norman Frederick Jewison) (1926–) Can.-Am. film director (Moonstruck; Fiddler on the Roof; Agnes of God)

Jhabvala, Ruth Prawer (1927–) Eng. novelist/short story writer (Heat and Dust; screenwriter [for Merchant Ivory])

Jillette, Penn (1955–) Am. comedian/writer (with Penn & Teller)

Jillian, Ann (Ann Jura Nauseda) (1950–) Am. actress ("It's a Living" TV series)

Jiménez, Juan (Juan Ramón Jiménez) (1881–1958) Span. poet (Diary of a Poet and the Sea; N—1956)

Jimmy the Greek (Jimmy Snyder; born Demetrios George Synodinos) (1919–) Am. sports analyst/columnist

Jinnah, Muhammed Ali (1876–1948) founder/ruler of Pakistan (gov.-general 1947–1948)

Joad, C. E. M. (Cyril Edwin Mitchison Joad) (1891–1953) Eng. philosopher/writer (Commonsense Ethics)

Joan of Arc, Saint ("Maid of Orleans") (1412–1431) Fr. heroine/mil. leader

Joanou, Phil (c. 1962–) Am. film director (U2 Rattle and Hum; State of Grace; Final Analysis)

Jobim, Antonia Carlos (1927–) Braz. musician/songwriter ("Girl from Ipanema"; "Desafinado")

Jobs, Steven (Steven Paul Jobs) (1955–) Am. computer entrepreneur (Apple Computer, Inc., with Steve Wozniak)

Joel (fl. after 516 B.C.) Heb. prophet

Joel, Billy (William Martin Joel) (1949–) Am. pop singer/musician/songwriter ("Just the Way You Are"; "Uptown Girl"; G—1979)

Joffe, Roland (Roland I. V. Joffe) (1945–) Eng. film director (The Killing Fields; The Mission)

Joffrey, Robert (Abdullah Jaffa Bey Khan) (1930–1988) Am. choreographer (Joffrey Ballet)

Johansen, David (a/k/a Buster Poindexter) (1950–) Am. rock singer/entertainer (formerly with The New York Dolls)

John (John Lackland) (1167–1216) Eng. king 1199–1216

John I (John the Posthumous) (1316; lived only 5 days) Fr. king 1316

John II (John the Good) (1319–1364) Fr. king 1350–1364

John XXII (Angelo Giuseppe Roncalli) (1881–1963) Ital. pope

John, Augustus (Augustus Edwin John) (1878–1961) Eng. portrait painter/etcher

John, Elton (Elton Hercules John; born Reginald Kenneth Dwight) (1947–) Eng. pop musician/songwriter ("Crocodile Rock"; "Daniel"; "Bennie and The Jets")

John Paul I (Albino Luciani) (1912–1978) Ital. pope

John Paul II (Karol Jozef Wojtyla) (1920–) Pol. pope

John, Robert (Robert John Pedrick, Jr.) (1946–) Am. pop singer ("Sad Eyes")

John, Tommy (Thomas Edward John, Jr.) (1943–) Am. baseball pitcher

Johns, Glynis (1923–) Eng. actress (Mary Poppins; Under Milk Wood; T—1973)

Johns, Jasper (Jasper Johns, Jr.) (1930–) Am. "pop art" painter/sculptor

Johnson, Andrew ("His Accidency"; "Sir Veto") (1808–1875) 17th Am. pres. (1865–1869)

Johnson, Arte (1934–) Am. comedian ("Rowan & Martin's Laugh-In" TV series; signature phrase: "Verrrry interesting")

Johnson, Ben (Francis Benjamin Johnson) (1918–) Am. actor (Mighty Joe Young; O—1971—The Last Picture Show)

Johnson, Betsey (Betsey Lee Johnson) (1942–) Am. fashion designer

Johnson, Beverly (1951–) Am. model (first Afr.-Am. woman on the cover of Vogue)

Johnson, Brad (c. 1960–) Am. actor (Always; Flight of the Intruder)

Johnson, Bunk (William Geary Johnson) (1879–1949) Am. jazz cornetist/trumpeter

Johnson, Dame Celia (1908–1982) Eng. actress (Brief Encounter; In Which We Serve)

Johnson, Cherie (1975–) Am. actress ("Punky Brewster" TV series)

Johnson, Chic (Harold Ogden Johnson) (1891–1962) Am. vaudeville comedian (with Ole Olsen)

Johnson, Don (Donald Wayne Johnson) (1949–) Am. actor ("Miami Vice" TV series; The Hot Spot; Paradise)

Johnson, Eastman (Jonathan Eastman Johnson) (1824–1906) Am. painter (Old Kentucky Home)

Johnson, Eliza (Eliza McCardle) (1810–1876) Am. first lady (Andrew)

Johnson, Eyvind (Eyvind Olaf Verner Johnson) (1900–1976) Swed. novelist (Novels of Olof; N—1974)

Johnson, Howard (Howard Deering Johnson) (1896–1972) Am. businessman (Howard Johnson restaurants and hotels)

Johnson, Jack (John Arthur Johnson) (1878–1946) Am. boxer (first Afr.-Am. boxer to win the world heavyweight championship)

Johnson, James Weldon (1871–1938) Am. writer/poet/critic/anthologist (The Book of American Negro Poetry)

Johnson, J. J. (James Louis Johnson) (1924–) Am. jazz trombonist/composer

Johnson, John Harold (1918–) Am. magazine publisher (Jet; founded Ebony)

Johnson, Lady Bird (Claudia Alta Taylor) (1912–) Am. first lady (Lyndon Baines)

Johnson, Lyndon Baines (1908–1973) 36th Am. pres. (1963–1968)

Johnson, Magic (Earvin Johnson, Jr.) (1959–) Am. basketball player

Johnson, Michael (1944–) Am. country singer ("Give Me Wings")

Johnson, Nunnally (1897–1977) Am. film director (The Three Faces of Eve)/screenwriter (The Grapes of Wrath)

Johnson, Philip (Philip Cortelyou Johnson) (1906–) Am. architect ("glass house" in Connecticut; New York's AT&T building)

Johnson, Rafer (Rafer Lewis Johnson) (1935–) Am. decathlete/sportscaster

Johnson, Richard M. (Richard Mentor Johnson) (1780–1850) Am. v.p. (M. Van Buren)

Johnson, Van (Charles Van Johnson; "The Voiceless Sinatra") (1916–) Am. actor (The Caine Mutiny; Brigadoon)

Johnson, Virginia (Virginia Eshelman Johnson) (1925–) Am. physician/educator (of [her husband, William] Masters and Johnson; Human Sexual Response)

Johnson, Walter (Walter Perry Johnson; "Big Train"; "Barney"; "Grand Veteran"; "Swede"; "Best Pitcher in Baseball") (1887–1946) Am. baseball Hall-of-Famer

Joliet or Jolliet, Louis (1645–1700) Fr.-Can. explorer in North America (Mississippi River and Gulf of St. Lawrence)

Joliot-Curie, Frédéric (Jean Frédéric Joliot) (1900–1958) Fr. physicist (with wife Irene; N—1935)

Joliot-Curie, Irène (Irène Curie) (1897–1956) Fr. physicist (daughter of Pierre and Marie Curie, N—1935)

Jolson, Al (Asa Yoelson) (1886–1950) Russ.-Am. singer ("Swanee"; "Mammy")/entertainer (The Jazz Singer)

Jones, Allan (1907–1992) Am. singer/actor (father of Jack; Show Boat)

Jones, Anissa (1958–1976) Am. child actress (Buffy in "Family Affair" TV series)

Jones, Bert (Bertram Hays Jones) (1951–) Am. football player

Jones, Bobby (Robert Tyre Jones, Jr.; "King of the Links") (1902–1971) Am. golfer

Jones, Booker T. (1944–) Am. blues singer/bandleader (with Booker T. and The MGs)

Jones, Brian (1943–1969) Eng. rock musician (with The Rolling Stones)

Jones, Buck (Charles Frederick Gebhardt) (1889–1942) Am. cowboy actor (*Riders of the Purple Sage*)

Jones, Carolyn (Carolyn Sue Jones) (1929–1983) Am. actress (Morticia in "The Addams Family" TV series)

Jones, Casey (John Luther Jones) (1863–1900) Am. locomotive engineer (on the "Cannonball Express" that wrecked in Mississippi)

Jones, Chuck (Charles Martin Jones) (1912–) Am. animator (helped create Bugs Bunny, Porky Pig, Daffy Duck)

Jones, Davy (David Jones) (1945–) Eng. actor/pop singer (with The Monkees)

Jones, Deacon (David Jones) (1938–) Am. football Hall-of-Famer

Jones, Dean (Dean Carroll Jones) (1930–) Am. singer/actor (*Under the Yum Yum Tree*; *The Love Bug*; other Disney films)

Jones, Elvin (1927–) Am. jazz drummer

Jones, Etta (1928–) Am. jazz singer (with Earl Hines' orchestra)

Jones, George (George Glen Jones; "The Possum"; "The Crown Prince of Country Music"; "The Rolls Royce of Country Music") (1931–) Am. country singer ("He Stopped Loving Her Today"; "I Don't Need Your Rockin' Chair")

Jones, Grace (1952–) Jam. model/singer ("I'm Not Perfect [But I'm Perfect for You]")/actress (*Vamp*; *A View to a Kill*)

Jones, Grandpa (Louis Marshall Jones) (1913–) Am. country singer/banjo player ("Hee Haw" TV series)

Jones, Howard (1955–) Eng. pop singer/musician/songwriter ("Things Can Only Get Better"; "No One Is to Blame")

Jones, Inigo (1573–1652) Eng. architect (founder of English classical architecture)/stage designer

Jones, Jack (1938–) Am. pop singer ("Wives and Lovers"; "The Impossible Dream [The Quest]"; G—1961, 1963)

Jones, James (1921–1977) Am. novelist (*From Here to Eternity*; *The Thin Red Line*)

Jones, James Earl (1931–) Am. stage (*The Great White Hope*; T—1969, 1987)/

film (*The Hunt for Red October*; *Field of Dreams*)/TV ("Gabriel's Fire"; E—1990/91) actor

Jones, Jennifer (Phyllis Lee Isley) (1919–) Am. actress (*A Farewell to Arms*; O—1943—*The Song of Bernadette*)

Jones, Reverend Jim (James Warren Jones) (1931–1978) Am. leader of the People's Temple in Guyana; led mass suicide

Jones, John Paul (John Paul) (1747–1792) Am. Revolutionary hero/naval commander (signature phrase: "I have not yet begun to fight!")

Jones, John Paul (John Baldwin) (1946–) Eng. rock musician (with Led Zeppelin)

Jones, Mick (1956–) Eng. rock guitarist/songwriter (with The Clash)

Jones, Mick (1944–) Eng. rock keyboardist/songwriter (with Spooky Tooth and Foreigner)

Jones, Parnelli (Rufus Parnell Jones) (1933–) Am. auto racer

Jones, Quincy (Quincy Delight Jones, Jr.) (1933–) Am. orchestra leader/musician/composer/record producer

Jones, Rickie Lee (1954–) Am. pop singer ("Chuck E.'s in Love"; G—1979)

Jones, Shirley (Shirley Mae Jones) (1934–) Am. singer/actress (O—1960—*Elmer Gantry*; "The Partridge Family" TV series)

Jones, Spike (Lindley Armstrong Jones; "King of Corn") (1911–1965) Am. orchestra leader ("All I Want for Christmas [Is My Two Front Teeth]")

Jones, Tom (Thomas Jones Woodward) (1940–) Wel. pop singer ("It's Not Unusual"; "She's a Lady"; G—1965)

Jones, Tommy Lee (1946–) Am. actor (*The Executioner's Song*; *J.F.K.*; *The Fugitive*)

Jong, Erica (Erica Mann Jong) (1942–) Am. poet/novelist (*Fear of Flying*; *Fanny*)

Jonson, Ben (Benjamin Jonson) (1572–1637) Eng. poet/playwright (*Volpone*; *The Alchemist*)

Joplin, Janis (Janis Lyn Joplin; "Pearl") (1943–1970) Am. rock singer ("Me and Bobby McGee")

Joplin, Scott (1868–1917) Am. pianist/composer ("Maple Leaf Rag"; "The Entertainer")

Jordan, Barbara (Barbara Charlene Jordan) (1936–) Am. lawyer/senator

Jordan, Hamilton (William Hamilton McWhorter Jordan; "Ham"; "Hannibal Jerkin") (1944–) Am. politician (chief of staff)

Jordan, Jim (James Edward Jordan) (1896–1988) Am. radio actor (played Fibber McGee)

Jordan, Marian (Marian Driscoll Jordan) (1897–1961) Am. radio actress (played Molly McGee)

Jordan, Michael (Michael Jeffery Jordan; "Air Jordan") (1963–) Am. basketball player

Jordan, Neil (1950–) Ir. writer/film director (*Mona Lisa*; *The Crying Game*)

Jordan, Richard (1938–1993) Am. actor ("The Equalizer" and "Captains and the Kings" TV series)

Jordan, Stanley (1960–) Am. jazz guitarist

Jory, Victor (1902–1982) Can.-Am. actor (*The Miracle Worker*; *Papillon*)

Joséphine (Joséphine de Beauharnais; Marie-Josephe-Rose Tascher de la Pagerie) (1763–1814) Fr. empress (Napoleon)

Joss, Addie (Adrian Joss) (1880–1911) Am. baseball Hall-of-Famer

Jourdan, Louis (Louis Gendre) (1919–) Fr. actor (*Gigi*; *The Paradine Case*)

Joy, Leatrice (Leatrice Joy Zeidler) (1894–1985) Am. actress (*The Ten Commandments*; *The Blue Danube*)

Joyce, James (James Augustine Joyce) (1882–1941) Ir. novelist/short story writer/poet (*Ulysses*; *A Portrait of the Artist As a Young Man*; *Finnegan's Wake*; *Dubliners*)

Joyner, Florence Griffith *see* Griffith-Joyner, Florence

Joyner, Wally (Wallace Keith Joyner) (1962–) Am. baseball player

Joyner-Kersee, Jackie (Jacqueline Joyner-Kersee) (1962–) Am. track and field athlete

Juan Carlos I (1938–) Span. king 1975–

Juarez, Benito (Benito Pablo Juarez; "The Mexican Washington"; "The Second Washington") (1806–1872) Mex. political leader

Judd, Ashley (c. 1967–) Am. actress (daughter of Naomi; "Sisters" TV series; *Ruby in Paradise*)

Judd, Naomi (Diana Ellen Judd) (1946–) Am. country singer (mother of Wynonna and Ashley; with The Judds; "Love Can Build a Bridge"; "Girls Night Out")

Judd, Wynonna (Christina Claire Ciminella; "Wy") (1964–) Am. country singer ("Tell Me Why"; formerly with The Judds)

Julia, Raul (Raul Rafael Carlos Julia y Arcelay) (1940–) P.R.-Am. actor (*Presumed Innocent*; *Kiss of the Spider Woman*; *Romero*; *The Addams Family*)

Juliana (Juliana Louise Emma Marie Wilhelmina) (1909–) Dutch queen 1948–1980 (daughter of Wilhelmina)

Jump, Gordon (1932–) Can.-Am. actor ("WKRP in Cincinnati" TV series)

Jung, Carl (Carl Gustav Jung; "Father of Analytical Psychology") (1875–1961) Swi. psychologist/writer (*Memories, Dreams, Reflections*)

Jurado, Katy (Maria Cristina Jurado Garcia) (1924–) Mex. actress (*Under the Volcano*; *High Noon*; *One-Eyed Jacks*)

Jurgens, Curt (a/k/a Curd Jürgens; born Curt Juergens) (1912–1982) Ger. actor (*I Aim at the Stars*; *The Mephisto Waltz*)

Jurgenson, Sonny (Christian Adolph Jones III) (1934–) Am. football Hall-of-Famer/sportscaster

Juvenal (Decimus Junius Juvenalis; "The Aquinian Sage"; "The Last Poet of Rome") (c. 60–127 or later) Roman poet

Kabalevsky, Dimitry (Dimitry Borisovich Kabalevsky) (1904–1987) Russ. composer (*The Comedians*)

Kabibble, Ish (Merwyn A. Bogue) (1908–) Am. comedian/actor

Kael, Pauline (1919–) Am. film critic/writer

Kafka, Franz (1883–1924) Ger.-Aus. short story writer/novelist (*Metamorphosis*; *The Trial*)

Kahanamoku, Duke (Duke Paoa Kahanamoku; "The Human Fish") (1890–1968) Am. swimmer

Kahlo, Frida (1919–1954) Mex. painter

Kahn, Albert ("Father of Modern Factory Design") (1869–1942) Ger.-Am. architect (factories)

Kahn, Gus (Gustav Gerson Kahn) (1886–1941) Ger.-Am. lyricist ("Memories"; "Ain't We Got Fun"; "Pretty Baby"; "Makin' Whoopee")

Kahn, Louis I (Louis Isadore Kahn) (1901–1974) Russ.-Am. architect (Salk Institute [La Jolla, CA])

Kahn, Madeline (Madeline Gail Kahn) (1942–) Am. actress/comedienne (*Blazing Saddles*; *Young Frankenstein*)

Kalb, Marvin (Marvin Leonard Kalb) (1930–) Am. broadcast journalist ("Meet the Press")

Kalember, Patricia (1954–) Am. actress ("thirtysomething" and "Sisters" TV series)

Kaline, Al (Albert William Kaline) (1934–) Am. baseball Hall-of-Famer

Kallen, Kitty (1922–) Am. singer ("My Coloring Book"; "Little Things Mean a Lot")

Kalmar, Bert (1884–1947) Am. lyricist (with Harry Ruby, "Three Little Words"; "Who's Sorry Now?")

Kamali, Norma (1945–) Am. fashion designer

Kamehameha I (c. 1758–1819) king of Hawaii 1790–1819

Kanaly, Steve (Steven Francis Kanaly) (1946–) Am. actor ("Dallas" TV series)

Kanawa, Dame Kiri te (1944–) N.Z. opera singer (soprano)

Kander, John (1927–) Am. composer/ musician (Cabaret; Funny Lady)

Kandinsky, Wassily (1866–1944) Russ. painter (a pioneer of abstract art)

Kane, Carol (1952–) Am. actress ("Taxi" TV series; The Lemon Sisters; Scrooged; E—1981/82, 1982/83)

Kane, Helen (Helen Schroeder; "The Boop-Boop-A-Doop Girl") (1908–1966) Am. singer ("I Wanna Be Loved by You")/actress (Paramount on Parade)

Kane, Robert (1916–) Am. cartoonist (with Bill Finger, created Batman)

Kanin, Garson (Gershon Labe) (1912–) Am. playwright (Adam's Rib)/film director (Bachelor Mother)/writer (Tracy and Hepburn)

Kant, Immanuel (1724–1804) Ger. philosopher (Critique of Pure Reason)

Kantner, Paul (1942–) Am. rock musician (with Jefferson Airplane)

Kantor, MacKinlay (1904–1977) Am. novelist (P—1956—Andersonville)

Kaplan, Gabe (Gabriel Kaplan) (1945–) Am. actor ("Welcome Back, Kotter" TV series)

Kaplan, Jonathan (1947–) Fr.-Am. film director (The Accused; Love Field)

Karan, Donna (Donna Faske Karan) (1948–) Am. fashion designer

Karina, Anna (Hanne Karin Blarke Bayer) (1940–) Fr.-Dan. actress (Bread and Chocolate; Scheherazade [title role])

Karlen, John (1933–) Am. actor ("Dark Shadows"; "Cagney & Lacey" TV series; E—1985/86)

Karlfeldt, Erik (Erik Axel Karlfeldt) (1864–1931) Swed. poet (Hosthorn; N—1918 [refused]; awarded posthumously in 1931)

Karloff, Boris (William Henry Pratt) (1887–1969) Eng.-Am. actor (Frankenstein; The Mummy)

Karns, Roscoe (1893–1970) Am. actor/ comedian (The Front Page; "Hennessey" TV series)

Karpov, Anatoly (Anatoly Evgenyevich Karpov) (1951–) Russ. chess player

Karras, Alex (Alexander G. Karras; "The Mad Duck"; "Tippy Toes") (1935–) Am. football player/actor

Karsavina, Tamara (Tamara Platonovna Karsavina; "La Tamara") (1885–1978) Eng. ballerina

Karsh, Yousuf (1908–) Arm.-Can. portrait photographer

Kasdan, Lawrence (Lawrence Edward Kasdan) (1949–) Am. film director/ writer (Body Heat; The Accidental Tourist; Grand Canyon)

Kasem, Casey (Kemal Amin) (1933–) Am. TV/radio host ("countdown" programs)

Kasparov, Garri (Garri Kimovich Kasparov) (1963–) Arm. chess player

Kassebaum, Nancy (née) Landon (1932–) Am. senator (daughter of Alf Landon)

Kästner, Erich (Erich Kaestner) (1899–1974) Ger. children's book writer (Emile & the Detectives; Lisa and Lottie [filmed as The Parent Trap])

Katt, William (1951–) Am. actor (son of Barbara Hale; TV's "The Greatest American Hero")

Katzenberg, Jeffrey (c. 1951—) Am. entertainment executive (head of Disney Studios)

Kaufman, Andy (1949–1984) Am. actor/ comedian ("Taxi" TV series)

Kaufman, George S. (George Simon Kaufman; "The Great Collaborator") (1889–1961) Am. journalist/playwright (The Man Who Came to Dinner; P—1932—Of Thee I Sing; P—1937—You Can't Take It with You)

Kaufman, Philip (1936–) Am. film director (The Right Stuff; Henry & June)

Kaukonen, Jorma (1940–) Am. rock guitarist (with Jefferson Airplane and Hot Tuna)

Kavner, Julie (Julie Deborah Kavner) (1951–) Am. actress ("Rhoda" TV series; voice of Marge on "The Simpsons"; Radio Days; Awakenings; E—1977/78)

Kawabata Yasunari (1899–1972) Jap. novelist (Snow Country; N—1968)

Kaye, Danny (Daniel David Kaminsky) (1913–1987) Am. actor (The Secret Life of

Walter Mitty; White Christmas; The Court Jester)
Kaye, Sammy (1910–1987) Am. danceband leader (signature phrase: "Swing and sway with Sammy Kaye")
Kaye, Stubby (1918–) Am. actor/comedian (*Li'l Abner; Guys and Dolls*)
Kaylen, Howard ("Eddie") (1945–) Am. rock singer (with The Turtles and Flo and Eddie)
Kazan, Elia (Elia Kazanjoglous) (1909–) Am. film director (*A Tree Grows in Brooklyn;* O—1947—*Gentleman's Agreement;* O—1954—*On the Waterfront)*
Kazan, Lainie (Lainie Levine) (1942–) Am. singer/actress ("The Paper Chase" TV series)
Kazantzakis, Nikos (1885–1957) Gr. novelist/poet/playwright (*Zorba the Greek; The Last Temptation of Christ)*
Kazin, Alfred (1915–) Am. literary critic/writer (*On Native Grounds)*
Keach, James (James Kech) (c. 1947–) Am. actor (brother of Stacy; *The Long Riders)*
Keach, Stacy (Stacy Walter Kech, Jr.) (1941–) Am. actor (TVs's "Mike Hammer"; *The Long Riders)*
Keane, Bil (1922–) Am. cartoonist (*The Family Circus)*
Keating, H. R. F. (Henry Reymond Fitzwalter Keating) (1926–) Eng. mystery novelist (*Dead on Time; The Bedside Companion to Crime)*
Keaton, Buster (Joseph Francis Keaton; "The Great Stone Face") (1895–1966) Am. comedian/filmmaker (*The General)*
Keaton, Diane (Diane Hall) (1946–) Am. actress (*Radio Days; The Godfather, Part II;* O—1977—*Annie Hall)*
Keaton, Michael (Michael Douglas) (1951–) Am. actor (*Batman; Clean and Sober; Beetlejuice)*
Keats, John (1795–1821) Eng. poet (*Ode on a Grecian Urn)*
Kedrova, Lila (1918–) Russ.-Fr. actress (*Torn Curtain;* O—1964—*Zorba the Greek)*
Keefe, Tim (Timothy John Keith; "Sir Timothy") (1857–1933) Am. baseball Hall-of-Famer
Keel, Howard (Harold Clifford Leek; a/k/a Harold Keel) (1917–) Am. actor ("Dallas" TV series; *Annie Get Your Gun)*

Keeler, Ruby (Ethel Hilda Keeler) (1909–1993) Can.-Am. actress/dancer (*Forty-Second Street; Gold Diggers of 1933)*
Keeler, Willie (William Henry Keeler; "Wee Willie"; "Hit 'Em Where They Ain't") (1872–1923) Am. baseball Hall-of-Famer
Keene, Carolyn (Harriet Stratemeyer Adams; a/k/a Laura Lee Hope and Franklin W. Dixon) (1893–1982) Am. mystery writer (*Nancy Drew* books; daughter of Edward Stratemeyer)
Keeshan, Bob or **Robert** (Robert James Keeshan) (1927–) Am. TV personality (Captain Kangaroo)
Kefauver, Estes (Carey Estes Kefauver) (1903–1963) Am. senator/vicepresidential candidate 1956 (headed commission to investigate organized crime)
Keillor, Garrison (Garrison Edward Keillor) (1942–) Am. humorist/novelist (*Lake Wobegon Days)*/radio personality
Keitel, Harvey (1941–) Am. actor (*Reservoir Dogs; Mean Streets; Bad Lieutenant)*
Keith, Brian (Brian Michael Keith; born Robert A. Keith, Jr.) (1921–) Am. actor ("Family Affair" and "The Westerner" TV series)
Keith, David (David Lemuel Keith) (1954–) Am. actor (*An Officer and a Gentleman)*
Kell, George (George Clyde Kell) (1922–) Am. baseball Hall-of-Famer
Kellaway, Cecil (1891–1973) Eng.-Am. actor (*Hush . . . Hush Sweet Charlotte; Luck of the Irish; Guess Who's Coming to Dinner?)*
Keller, Charlie (Charles Ernest Keller; "King Kong") (1916–) Am. baseball player
Keller, Helen (Helen Adams Keller) (1880–1968) Am. lecturer/essayist/autobiographer (*The Story of My Life)*
Keller, Marthe (1945–) Swi. actress (*Marathon Man; Bobby Deerfield)*
Keller, Mary Page (1961–) Am. actress ("Duet" TV series)
Kellerman, Sally (Sally Claire Kellerman) (1937–) Am. actress ("*M*A*S*H*"; *The Boston Strangler)*
Kelley, David (David E. Kelley) (c. 1956–) Am. TV producer ("L.A. Law" and "Picket Fences" TV series)

Kelley, Deforest (1920–) Am. actor (Dr. McCoy in *Star Trek* TV series and films)
Kelley, Kitty (1942–) Am. "unauthorized" biographer (of Frank Sinatra, Nancy Reagan, Jacqueline Onassis, Elizabeth Taylor)
Kellogg, Will Keith (1860–1951) Am. businessman (invented corn flakes)/philanthropist
Kelly, Colin (Colin P. Kelly) (1915–1941) Am. army pilot/WW II hero
Kelly, Ellsworth (1923–) Am. painter/sculptor
Kelly, Emmett (Emmett Leo Kelly; "Weary Willie") (1898–1979) Am. circus clown
Kelly, Gene (Eugene Curran Kelly) (1912–) Am. singer/actor/dancer (*Singin' in the Rain; An American in Paris; Inherit the Wind*)
Kelly, George (George Lange Kelly; "Highpockets") (1895–1984) Am. baseball Hall-of-Famer
Kelly, Grace (Grace Patricia Kelly; "The Ice Princess") (1929–1982) Am. actress (*High Society; Rear Window;* O—1954—*The Country Girl*)/princess of Monaco
Kelly, Jack (1927–1992) Ir.-Am. actor (brother of Nancy "Kings Row" and "Maverick" TV series)
Kelly, King (Michael Joseph Kelly) (1857–1894) Am. baseball Hall-of-Famer
Kelly, Machine Gun (George R. Kelly) (1897–1954) Am. gangster
Kelly, Moira (C) Am. actress (*The Cutting Edge; Chaplin*)
Kelly, Nancy (1921–) Am. actress (sister of Jack; *Tailspin; The Bad Seed;* T—1955)
Kelly, Patsy (Sarah Veronica Rose Kelly) (1910–1981) Am. actress/comedienne (*Please Don't Eat the Daisies*)
Kelly, Petra (Petra Karin Lehmann) (1947–1992) Ger. socialist politician/activist
Kelly, Shipwreck (Alvin Kelly; "Sailor Kelly") (1885–1952) Am. stuntman/flag pole sitter
Kelly, Walt (Walter Crawford Kelly) (1913–1973) Am. cartoonist (*Pogo*)
Kelsey, Linda (1942–) Am. actress ("Lou Grant" TV series)
Kemble, Fanny (Frances Anne Kemble) (1809–1893) Eng. stage actress
Kemelman, Harry (1908–) Am. mystery writer (created Rabbi David Small; *Friday the Rabbi Slept Late*)

Kemp, Gary (1960–) Eng. rock musician (with Spandau Ballet)/actor (*The Krays;* brother of Martin)
Kemp, Jack (John French Kemp) (1935–) Am. football player/politician
Kemp, Martin (1961–) Eng. rock musician (with Spandau Ballet)/actor (*The Krays;* brother of Gary)
Kempton, Murray (James Murray Kempton) (1918–) Am. columnist (P—1985)/writer (*The Briar Patch*)
Kendall, Edward (Edward Calvin Kendall) (1886–1972) Am. biochemist (isolated thyroxine and cortisone; N—1950)
Kendricks, Eddie (a/k/a Eddie Kendrick) (1939–1992) Am. soul singer ("Keep on Truckin'"; formerly with The Temptations)
Keneally, Thomas (Thomas Michael Keneally) (1935–) Austral. novelist (*Schindler's List*)
Kennedy, Anthony M. (Anthony McLeod Kennedy) (1936–) Am. Supreme Court jurist (1988–)
Kennedy, Arthur (John Arthur Kennedy) (1914–1990) Am. actor (*Death of a Salesman; High Sierra; The Glass Menagerie*)
Kennedy, Burt (1922–) Am. film director (*Support Your Local Sheriff; The Killer Inside Me*)
Kennedy, Caroline *see* Schlossberg, Caroline Kennedy
Kennedy, Edward M. *see* Kennedy, Teddy
Kennedy, George (1925–) Am. actor (*Airport; Lost Horizon;* O—1967—*Cool Hand Luke*)
Kennedy, Jayne (Jayne Harrison) (1951–) Am. actress/TV host ("Speak Up America")
Kennedy, John F. (John Fitzgerald Kennedy; "Jack"; "JFK") (1917–1963) 35th Am. pres. (1961–1963)/writer (P—1957—*Profiles in Courage*)
Kennedy, John, Jr. ("John-John"; "Prince Charming") (1960–) Am. attorney (son of John F.)
Kennedy, Joseph P. (Joseph Patrick Kennedy) (1888–1969) Am. financier/diplomat (father of John F., Robert F., and Teddy)
Kennedy, Joseph P. II (1952–) Am. congressman (son of Robert F.)
Kennedy, Robert F. (Robert Francis Kennedy; "RFK"; "Bobby") (1925–1968) Am. politician/secretary of state/

attorney general (brother of John F. and Teddy)

Kennedy, Rose (Rose Ritzgerald) (1890–) Am. Kennedy family matriarch

Kennedy, Teddy (Edward Moore Kennedy; a/k/a Edward M. Kennedy) (1932–) Am. senator

Kennedy, William (William Joseph Kennedy) (1928–) Am. novelist (P—1984—*Ironweed*)

Kenner, Hugh (William Hugh Kenner) (1923–) Can. literary critic (*Joyce; Beckett*)

Kenny G (Kenneth Gorelick) (1956–) Am. fusion/pop saxophone player ("Silhouette"; "Songbird")

Kenny, Kathryn (1925–) Am. writer (created Trixie Belden)

Kensit, Patsy (c. 1969–) Eng. actress (*Absolute Beginners; Twenty-One*)

Kent, Arthur (c. 1954–) Am. TV journalist

Kent, Rockwell ("RK") (1882–1971) Am. painter/illustrator/writer (*Wilderness*)

Kenton, Stan (Stanley Newcomb Kenton) (1912–1979) Am. orchestra leader ("And Her Tears Flowed Like Wine")

Kepler, Johannes ("The Father of Modern Astronomy") (1571–1630) Ger. astronomer (assistant to Tycho Brahe)

Kern, Jerome (Jerome David Kern) (1885–1945) Am. composer (*Show Boat* and *Swing Time* scores; "Smoke Gets in Your Eyes"; "Ol' Man River")

Kerns, Joanna (1953–) Am. actress ("Growing Pains" TV series)

Kerouac, Jack (Jean-Louis Lebris de Kerouac) (1922–1969) Am. "beat" novelist/poet (*On the Road; Desolation Angels*)

Kerr, Anita (Anita Jean Grob) (1927–) Am. singer

Kerr, Deborah (Deborah Jane Kerr-Trimmer) (1921–) Am. actress (*The King and I; From Here to Eternity; An Affair to Remember*)

Kerr, Graham ("The Galloping Gourmet") (1934–) Eng. chef/TV host

Kerr, Jean (Jean Bridget Kerr née Collins) (1923–) Am. humorist/writer (*Please Don't Eat the Daisies*)

Kerr, Jim (1959–) Eng. rock singer (with Simple Minds; "Don't You [Forget About Me]")

Kerr, Walter (Walter Francis Kerr) (1913–) Am. journalist/playwright/drama critic (*The Silent Clowns*)

Kerrey, Bob (Joseph Robert Kerry) (1943–) Am. senator

Kerrigan, Nancy (1970–) Am. figure skater, subject of controversial attack

Kerry, John F. (John Forbes Kerry) (1943–) Am. senator

Kert, Larry (Frederick Lawrence Kert) (1930–1991) Am. actor/singer

Kershaw, Nik (1958–) Eng. pop singer/musician/songwriter ("Wouldn't It Be Good")

Kershaw, Sammy (1958–) Am. country singer ("Cadillac Style"; "Haunted Heart")

Kerwin, Lance (1960–) Am. actor ("James at 15" TV series)

Kesey, Ken (Kenneth Elton Kesey) (1935–) Am. novelist (*One Flew Over the Cuckoo's Nest*)

Keshishian, Alek (c. 1965–) Am. film director (Madonna's *Truth or Dare; With Honors*)

Kessel, Barney (1923–) Am. jazz guitarist

Ketcham, Hank (Henry King Ketcham) (1920–) Am. cartoonist (*Dennis the Menace*)

Ketchum, Hal (1953–) Am. country singer ("Small Town Saturday Night"; "Hearts Are Gonna Roll")

Kevorkian, Jack ("Doctor Death") (c. 1928–) Am. physician (assists suicides)

Key, Francis Scott (1779–1843) Am. poet (*The Star-Spangled Banner*)/lawyer

Key, Jimmy (James Edward Key) (1961–) Am. baseball pitcher

Key, Ted (Theodore Key) (1912–) Am. cartoonist (*Hazel*)

Keyes, Evelyn (Evelyn Louise Keyes) (1919–) Am. dancer/actress (*Gone with the Wind; The Jolson Story*)

Keyes, Frances Parkinson (née Wheeler) (1885–1970) Am. novelist (*Dinner at Antoine's*)

Keynes, John Maynard, 1st Baron Keynes of Tilton (1883–1946) Eng. economist/writer (*The General Theory of Employment, Interest and Money*)

Khālid (Khālid ibn 'Abd al-'Azīz ibn 'Abd ar-Rahmān āl Saūd) (1913–1982) Saud. Arab. king 1975–1982

Khan, Chaka (Yvette Marie Stevens) (1953–) Am. pop singer ("I Feel for You"; "Through the Fire"; formerly with Rufus)

Khashoggi, Adnan (1935–) Saud. Arab.

businessman (one-time richest man in the world)

Khayyam, Omar (Gheyas Od-din Abu al-Fath) (c. 1048–c. 1131) Pers. poet (*Rubaiyat*)

Khomeini, Ayatollah Ruhollah (Ruhollah Hendi) (1900–1989) Iran. religious leader 1979–1989

Khorana, Har Gobind (1922–) Ind.-Am. chemist (N—1968)

Khrushchev, Nikita (Nikita Sergeyevich Khrushchev; "The Butcher of Budapest") (1894–1971) Russ. premier 1958–1964

Kiam, Victor (Victor Kermit Kiam II) (1926–) Am. businessman (CEO of Remington Products, Inc.)

Kibbee, Guy (Guy Bridges Kibbee) (1882–1956) Am. actor (*Babbitt*; *Lady for a Day*; *Captain Blood*)

Kid Creole (August Darnell) (1951–) Am. singer (with Dr. Buzzard's Original Savannah Band and Kid Creole and the Coconuts)

Kidd, Captain (William Kidd; "The Wizard of the Sea") (c. 1645–1701) Eng. pirate

Kidd, Michael (Milton Greenwald) (1919–) Am. dancer/choreographer

Kidder, Margot (Margaret Ruth Kidder) (1948–) Can. actress (*Superman* [as Lois Lane]; *The Reincarnation of Peter Proud*)

Kidman, Nicole ("Nic") (1967–) Austral. actress (*Dead Calm*; *Far and Away*; *Flirting*; *Malice*)

Kiedis, Anthony (c. 1962–) Am. rock singer (with the Red Hot Chili Peppers)

Kiel, Richard (1939–) Am. actor ("Jaws" in James Bond films; *Silver Streak*)

Kierkegaard, Søren (Søren Aabye Kierkegaard) (1813–1855) Dan. philosopher/writer (*Either/Or*)

Kiesling, Walt (Walter Kiesling) (1903–1962) Am. football player/coach/Hall-of-Famer

Kiley, Richard (Richard Paul Kiley) (1922–) Am. singer/actor (*The Thorn Birds*; *Looking for Mr. Goodbar*; E—1987/88; T—1959, 1966)

Kilgallen, Dorothy (Dorothy Mae Kilgallen) (1913–1965) Am. (New York City) gossip columnist

Killebrew, Harmon (Harmon Clayton Killebrew; "Killer"; "The Brew"; "The King") (1936–) Am. baseball Hall-of-Famer

Killy, Jean-Claude (1943–) Fr. skier

Kilmer, Joyce (Alfred Joyce Kilmer) (1886–1918) Am. poet (*Trees*)

Kilmer, Val (1959–) Am. actor (Jim Morrison in *The Doors*; *Thunderheart*)

Kim, Andy (Andrew Joachim) (1946–) Am. pop singer ("Rock Me Gently")/ songwriter ("Sugar, Sugar")

Kinard, Frank (Frank M. Kinard; "Bruiser") (1914–1985) Am. football Hall-of-Famer

Kiner, Ralph (Ralph McPherran Kiner; "Baseball's Man of the Hour") (1922–) Am. baseball Hall-of-Famer

King, Alan (Irwin Alan Kniberg; a/k/a Earl Knight) (1927–) Am. comedian/actor (*Enemies—A Love Story*)

King, Albert (Albert Nelson) (1923–1992) Am. blues guitarist/singer ("Breaking Up Somebody's Home")

King, B. B. (Blues Boy King; born Riley B. King; "Bassman of the Blues"; "The Beale Street Blues Boy"; "The Blues Boy"; "The Boy from Beale Street"; "King of the Blues") (1925–) Am. blues guitarist/singer ("The Thrill Is Gone")

King, Ben E. (Benjamin Earl Nelson) (1938–) Am. pop singer ("Stand by Me"; formerly with The Moonglows and The Drifters)

King, Billie Jean (née Moffit; "Old Lady"; "Queen of the Courts"; "Tennis Tycoon") (1943–) Am. tennis player (W—1966, 1967, 1968, 1972, 1973, 1975)

King, Carole (Carole Klein) (1942–) Am. pop singer/songwriter (mother of Louise Goffin; "It's Too Late"; "Jazzman"; G—1971)

King, Coretta (née) **Scott** (1927–) Am. lecturer/writer/concert singer (widow of Dr. Martin Luther King, Jr.)

King, Don (Donald King) (1932–) Am. boxing promoter

King, Evelyn "Champagne" (1960–) Am. pop/disco singer ("Shame")

King, Frank O. (1883–1969) Am. cartoonist (*Gasoline Alley*)

King, Henry (1888–1982) Am. film director (*Love Is a Many-Splendored Thing*; *State Fair*; *The Gunfighter*)

King, Larry (Larry Zeiger) (1933–) Am. talk show host

King, Dr./Rev. Martin Luther, Jr. ("The Prince of Peace"; "The Peaceful Warrior") (1929–1968) Am. civil rights advocate ("I have a dream" speech; N—1964)

King, Morgana (1930–) Am. singer/actress (*The Godfather*; *The Godfather, Part II*)

King, Pee Wee (Frank King; born Frank Anthony Kuczynski) (1914–) Am. country bandleader ("Slow Poke")

King, Perry (1948–) Am. actor ("Riptide" TV series; *The Lords of Flatbush*)

King, Stephen (Stephen Edwin King; a/k/a Richard Bachman) (1947–) Am. horror novelist (*Carrie*; *Misery*; *The Shining*; *The Dead Zone*)

King, Wayne ("The Waltz King") (1901–1985) Am. dance-band leader

King, William R. (William Rufus de Vane King) (1786–1853) Am. v.p. (F. Pierce)

Kingman, Dave (David Arthur Kingman; "Big Bird"; "Mr. K") (1948–) Am. baseball player

Kingsley, Ben (Krishna Bhanji) (1943–) Ind.-Eng. actor (*Schindler's List*; O—1982—*Gandhi*)

Kingsley, Sidney (Sidney Kirschner) (1906–) Am. playwright (*Detective Story*; P—1934—*Men in White*)

Kingsolver, Barbara (1955–) Am. writer (*Animal Dreams*; *Pigs in Heaven*)

Kingston, Maxine Hong (1940–) Am. historical novelist (*Woman Warrior*)

Kinison, Sam (1953–1992) Am. comedian (*Back to School*)

Kinmont, Kathleen (c. 1965–) Am. actress ("Renegade" TV series)

Kinnell, Galway (1927–) Am. poet/novelist (*The Book of Nightmares*; P—1983—*Selected Poems*)

Kinsella, Thomas (1928–) Ir. poet (*Wormwood*)

Kinsey, Alfred (Alfred Charles Kinsey) (1894–1956) Am. biologist/sex researcher (*Sexual Behavior in the Human Male*)

Kinski, Klaus (Nikolaus Gunther Nakszynski) (1926–1991) Ger. actor (father of Nastassja; *Fitzcarraldo*; *Aguirre the Wrath of God*)

Kinski, Nastassja (Nastassja Nakszynski; "Nasti") (1960–) Ger. actress (*Paris, Texas*; *Tess*)

Kipling, Rudyard (Joseph Rudyard Kipling) (1865–1936) Eng. novelist/poet/short story writer (*The Jungle Book*; *Gunga Din*; *Captains Courageous*; *Kim*; N—1907)

Kiplinger, W. M. (Willard Monroe Kiplinger) (1891–1967) Am. journalist (founded *The Kiplinger Letter*)

Kirby, Bruno (Bruce Kirby, Jr.) (1949–)

Am. actor (*City Slickers*; *When Harry Met Sally . . .*)

Kirby, Durward (1912–) Am. TV host ("Candid Camera")

Kirchner, Leon (1919–) Am. composer/pianist (P—1967—*Quartet No. 3*)

Kirk, Phyllis (Phyllis Helene Theodora Kirkegaard) (1926–) Am. actress ("The Thin Man" [as Nora Charles] TV series)

Kirkland, Gelsey (1953–) Am. ballerina/writer (*Dancing on My Grave*)

Kirkland, Sally (1944–) Am. actress (*Anna*; *Revenge*; *JFK*)

Kirkpatrick, Jeane (Jeane Duane Jordan) (1926–) Am. ambassador to the U.N.

Kirschner, Don (1934–) Am. TV host ("Don Kirschner's Rock Concert")

Kissinger, Henry (Heinz Alfred Kissinger; "The Drone"; "The Flying Peacemaker"; "Henry the K"; "The Iron Stomach"; "Super Kraut") (1923–) Ger.-Am. politician/political scientist/secretary of state (N—1973)

Kistler, Darci (Darci Anna Kistler) (1964–) Am. ballerina

Kitaen, Tawny (1961–) Am. actress ("The New WKRP in Cincinnati" and "America's Funniest People" TV series)

Kitt, Eartha (Eartha Mae Kitt) (1928–) Am. jazz/pop singer ("Santa Baby")/actress (Catwoman on TV's "Batman")

Kjellin, Alf (a/k/a Christopher Kent) (1920–) Swed. actor (*Madame Bovary*)/film director (*Ship of Fools*)

Klee, Paul (1879–1940) Swi. abstract painter/artist

Klein, Anne (Anne Hannah Klein née Golofski) (1923–1974) Am. fashion designer

Klein, Calvin (Calvin Richard Klein) (1942–) Am. fashion designer

Klein, Chuck (Charles Herbert Klein; "The Hoosier Hammerer") (1904–1958) Am. baseball Hall-of-Famer

Klein, Norma (1938–1989) Am. novelist (*Snapshots*; *American Dream*)

Klein, Robert (1942–) Am. comedian/actor

Kleiser, Randal (1946–) Am. film director (*Grease*; *The Blue Lagoon*)

Kleist, Heinrich von (Bernd Heinrich Wilhelm von Kleist) (1777–1811) Ger. playwright/novelist (*The Marquise of O*)

Klem, Bill (William Joseph Klem; "The Old Arbitrator") (1874–1951) Am. baseball umpire

Klemperer, Otto (1885–1973) Ger. orchestra conductor (Los Angeles Philharmonic, Budapest Opera, London Philharmonic)

Klemperer, Werner (1919–) Ger.-Am. actor ("Hogan's Heroes" [as Colonel Klink] TV series; G—1967/68, 1968/69)

Kliban, B. (Bernard Kliban) (1935–1991) Am. cartoonist (*Cat*)

Klimt, Gustave (1862–1918) Aus. painter (founded the Vienna Sezession school of painting)/muralist

Kline, Franz (Franz Joseph Kline) (1910–1962) Am. abstract expressionist painter

Kline, Kevin (Kevin Delaney Kline) (1947–) Am. actor (*Dave*; O—1988—*A Fish Called Wanda*; *The Big Chill*; T—1981)

Kline, Richard (c. 1950–) Am. comedian

Klopstock, Friedrich (Friedrich Gottlieb Klopstock; "The Birmingham Milton"; "The Creator of Biblical Epic Poetry"; "The German Milton"; "The Milton of Germany") (1724–1803) Ger. poet (*Der Messias*)

Klugh, Earl (1953–) Am. jazz guitarist/pianist

Klugman, Jack (1922–) Am. actor ("The Odd Couple" and "Quincy" TV series; E—1972/73)

Kluszewski, Ted (Theodore Bernard Kluszewski; "Klu"; "The Gentle Giant") (1924–1988) Am. baseball player

Knebel, Fletcher (1911–1993) Am. journalist/writer (*Crossing in Berlin*)

Knepper, Bob (Robert Wesley Knepper) (1954–) Am. baseball pitcher

Knievel, Evel (Robert Craig Knievel; "King of the Daredevils") (1938–) Am. stuntman/daredevil

Knight, Bobby or **Bob** (Robert Montgomery Knight) (1940–) Am. basketball coach

Knight, Damon (1922–) Am. science fiction writer (*Hell's Pavement*; *In Search of Wonder*)

Knight, Eric (1897–1943) Eng. writer (created Lassie)

Knight, Fuzzy (John Forrest Knight) (1901–1976) Am. cowboy actor (*She Done Him Wrong*; *My Little Chickadee*)

Knight, Gladys (Gladys Maria Knight) (1944–) Am. soul/pop singer (with Gladys Knight and The Pips; "Midnight Train to Georgia")

Knight, Jonathan (Jonathan Rashleigh Knight) (1968–) Am. pop musician (brother of Jordan; with New Kids on the Block)

Knight, Jordan (Jordan Nathaniel Marcel Knight) (1970–) Am. pop musician (brother of Jonathan; with New Kids on the Block)

Knight, Philip (1938–) Am. founder of Nike, Inc.

Knight, Shirley (Shirley Enola Knight; a/k/a Shirley Knight Hopkins) (1936–) Am. actress (*Sweet Bird of Youth*; *The Dark at the Top of the Stairs*)

Knight, Ted (Tadeus Wladyslaw Konopka) (1923–1986) Am. actor ("The Mary Tyler Moore Show" TV series; E—1972/73, 1975/76)

Knight, Wayne (c. 1955–) Am. actor (*Basic Instinct*; *Jurassic Park*; "Seinfeld" TV series)

Knopf, Alfred A. (Alfred Abraham Knopf) (1892–1984) Am. publisher (founded Alfred A. Knopf, Inc.)

Knopf, Blanche (née Wolf) (1894–1966) Am. publisher

Knopfler, Mark (1949–) Scot. rock singer/guitarist (with Dire Straits; "Money for Nothing")

Knotts, Don (1924–) Am. comedian ("The Andy Griffith Show" and "Three's Company" TV series; E—1960/61, 1961/62, 1962/63, 1965/66)

Knowles, John (1926–) Am. novelist (*A Separate Peace*)

Knox, John ("The Apostle of Presbytery"; "The Apostle of the Scottish Reformers"; "The Reformer of a Kingdom") (1513–1572) Scot. Protestant reformer

Koch, Ed (Edward Irving Koch) (1924–) Am. politician (mayor of New York City)/congressman

Koch, Howard (a/k/a Joseph Walton) (1902–) Am. playwright/screenwriter (cowrote *Casablanca*; *Sergeant York*)

Kodály, Zoltan (1882–1967) Hung. composer (*Psalmas Hungaricus*)

Koenig, Walter (1938–) Am. actor (Checkov in *Star Trek* TV series and films)

Koestler, Arthur (1905–1983) Hung.-Eng. novelist/essayist (*Darkness at Noon*)

Kohl, Helmut (Helmut Michael Kohl) (1930–) Ger. chancellor 1982–

Kokoschka, Oskar (1886–1980) Aus. expressionist painter/playwright

Kollwitz, Käthe (née Schmidt) (1867–1945) Ger. sculptor/painter/etcher

Kool Moe Dee (Mohandas DeWese) (C) Am. rapper ("Wild, Wild West")

Koontz, Dean (1945–) Am. horror novelist (*Dragon Tears*; *The Eyes of Darkness*)

Koop, C. Everett (Charles Everett Koop) (1916–) Am. surgeon general

Kooper, Al (1944–) Am. rock guitarist/ singer (with Blood, Sweat & Tears and The Blues Project)

Kopell, Bernie (Bernard Morton Kopell) (1933–) Am. actor ("The Love Boat" TV series)

Kopit, Arthur L. (Arthur Lee Kopit) (1937–) Am. playwright (*A Dreambook for Our Time*)

Koppel, Ted (Edward James Koppel) (1940–) Am. newscaster ("Nightline")

Korbut, Olga (1955–) Russ. gymnast

Korda, Sir Alex or **Alexander** (Sandor Laszlo Kellner; a/k/a Sandor Korda and Sursum Corda) (1893–1956) Hung. film director/producer (brother of Zoltán; *That Hamilton Woman*; *Catherine the Great*; *The Third Man*)

Korda, Michael (1919–1973) Am. editor/ writer (son of Alexander; *Charmed Lives*)

Korda, Zoltán (Zoltán Kellner) (1895– 1961) Hung. film director (brother of Alexander; *The Jungle Book*; *Cry, the Beloved Country*)

Koresh, David (Vernon Howell) (1959– 1993) Am. evangelist (Branch Davidians)

Korman, Harvey (Harvey Herschel Korman) (1927–) Am. actor/comedian ("The Carol Burnett Show" TV series; *Young Frankenstein*; *High Anxiety*)

Kornbluth, Cyril M. (1923–1958) Am. science fiction/fantasy writer (with Frederik Pohl, *The Space Merchants*)

Kosar, Bernie (1963–) Am. football player

Kosinski, Jerzy (Jerzy Nikodem Kosinski; a/k/a Joseph Novak) (1933–1991) Pol.- Am. novelist (*The Painted Bird*; *Being There*)

Kostelanetz, Andre (1901–1980) Am. orchestra conductor

Koster, Henry (Hermann Kosterlitz) (1905–) Ger. film director (*The Robe*; *Flower Drum Song*)

Kosygin, Aleksey (Aleksey Nikolayevich Kosygin) (1904–1980) Russ. premier 1964–1980

Kotcheff, Ted (William Theodore Kotcheff) (1931–) Can.-Am. film director (*Fun with Dick and Jane*; *First Blood*; *Switching Channels*)

Kottke, Leo (1945–) Am. blues guitarist/ singer

Kotto, Yaphet (Yaphet Frederick Kotto) (1937–) Am. actor (*Live and Let Die*; *The Running Man*; *I Love You to Death*)

Koufax, Sandy (Sanford Koufax; "The Man with the Golden Arm") (1935–) Am. baseball Hall-of-Famer

Koussevitsky, Serge (Sergey Aleksandrovich Kusevitsky) (1874–1951) Russ.-Am. conductor (taught Leonard Bernstein and Lukas Foss)

Kovacs, Ernie (1919–1962) Am. comedian/ TV host ("Ernie in Kovacsland")

Kovic, Ron (1946–) Am. mil. veteran/ autobiographer (*Born on the Fourth of July*)

Kozak, Harley Jane (Susan Jane Kozack) (C) Am. actress (*Parenthood*; "Harts of the West" TV series)

Kozlowski, Linda (1958–) Am. actress (*Crocodile Dundee*)

Kozol, Jonathan (1936–) Am. educator (*Illiterate America*)

Krafft-Ebing, Baron Richard (Richard von Krafft-Ebing) (1840–1902) Ger. neurologist/psychologist/sex researcher/writer (*Psychopathia Sexualis*)

Kramer, Jack (John Albert Kramer) (1921–) Am. tennis player (W—1947)

Kramer, Stanley (Stanley Earl Kramer) (1913–) Am. film director/producer (*Death of a Salesman*; *High Noon*; *Judgment at Nuremberg*; *Guess Who's Coming to Dinner*)

Kramer, Stepfanie (1956–) Am. actress ("Hunter" TV series)

Kranepool, Ed (Edward Emil Kranepool; "Steady Eddie") (1944–) Am. baseball player

Krantz, Judith (Judith Tarcher) (1928–) Am. novelist (*Scruples*; *Princess Daisy*)

Krasna, Norman (1909–1984) Am. playwright (*Indiscreet*; *Mr. and Mrs. Smith*)/ film director (*Princess O'Rourke*)

Krasner, Lee (Lenore Krassner) (1908– 1984) Am. painter (a founder of abstract expressionism)

Kravis, Henry (1920–) Am. venture capitalist/businessman (leveraged buyout mogul)

Kravitz, Lenny (c. 1964–) Am. pop singer (son of Roxie Roker; "It Ain't Over Til It's Over"; "Let Love Rule")

Kreskin (George Joseph Kresge, Jr.; "The Amazing Kreskin") (1935–) Am. mentalist

Krieger, Robby (1946–) Am. rock musician (with The Doors)
Krishnamurti, Jiddu (1895–1986) Ind. religious philosopher
Kristel, Sylvia (1952–) Dutch actress (*Emmanuel* and sequels)
Kristen, Marta (c. 1945–) Norw.-Am. actress ("Lost in Space" TV series)
Kristofferson, Kris (Kris Carson) (1936–) Am. actor (*The Sailor Who Fell from Grace with the Sea*; *A Star Is Born*)/ singer/songwriter ("Me and Bobby McGee"; "Help Me Make It Through the Night")
Kroc, Ray (Raymond Albert Kroc) (1902–1984) Am. restauranteur (founded McDonald's)
Krock, Arthur ("Gray Eminence") (1887–1974) Am. columnist ("In The Nation"; P—1935, 1938)
Krone, Julie (c. 1963–) Am. jockey (first woman to win a leg [the Belmont] of the Triple Crown)
Kropotkin, Pyotr (Pyotr Alekseyevich Kropotkin) (1842–1921) Russ. revolutionary leader (anarchist)/philosopher
Kruger, Alma (1868–1960) Am. actress ("Dr. Kildare" TV series; *His Girl Friday*)
Krüger, Hardy (Eberhard Krüger) (1928–) Ger. actor (*The One That Got Away*; *Barry Lyndon*)
Kruger, Otto (1885–1974) Am. actor (*Murder, My Sweet*; *Magnificent Obsession*)
Kruk, John (John Martin Kruk) (1961–) Am. baseball player
Krupa, Gene (Eugene Bertram Krupa) (1909–1973) Am. jazz drummer (with Benny Goodman)
Krupp, Alfred ("The Cannon King") (1812–1887) Ger. munitions manufacturer
Kubek, Tony (Anthony Christopher Kubek) (1936–) Am. baseball player/ sportscaster
Kublai Khan (1215–1294) Mongol emperor of China (grandson of Genghis Khan)
Kubler-Ross, Elisabeth (1926–) Am.-Swi. psychiatrist/writer (*On Death and Dying*)
Kubrick, Stanley (1928–) Am. film director (*2001: A Space Odyssey*; *Lolita*; *A Clockwork Orange*; *Dr. Strangelove*)
Kuhn, Bowie (Bowie Kent Kuhn) (1926–) Am. baseball commissioner
Kuhn, Maggie (Margaret E. Kuhn) (1905–) Am. social reformer (founded the Gray Panthers)

Kuhn, Walt (Walter Francis Kuhn) (1877–1949) Am. painter/illustrator/caricaturist (introduced avant-garde style in America)
Kukai (a/k/a Kobo Daishi) (774–835) Jap. priest/founder of Shingon Buddhism
Kulp, Nancy (Nancy Jane Kulp) (1921–1991) Am. actress ("The Beverly Hillbillies" TV series)
Kumin, Maxine (Maxine Winokur Kumin) (1925–) Am. novelist/poet (P—1973— *Up Country*)
Kundera, Milan (1929–) Cz. novelist/short story writer (*The Book of Laughter and Forgetting*; *The Unbearable Lightness of Being*)
Kunitz, Stanley J. (Stanley Jasspon Kunitz; a/k/a Dilly Tante) (1905–) Am. poet (P—1959—*Selected Poems 1928–1958*)
Kunstler, William (William Moses Kunstler) (1919–) Am. civil rights activist/lawyer (defended Lenny Bruce, the Chicago 7, the Black Panthers, etc.)
Kuralt, Charles (Charles Bishop Kuralt) (1934–) Am. newscaster ("On the Road")
Kurosawa, Akira (1910–1992) Jap. film director (*Ran*; *Rashomon*; *Seven Samurai*)
Kurowski, Whitey (George John Kurowski) (1918–) Am. baseball player
Kurtz, Swoosie (1944–) Am. actress ("Sisters" TV series; *Bright Lights, Big City*; *The World According to Garp*)
Kushner, Harold (Harold Samuel Kushner) (1935–) Am. rabbi/writer (*When Bad Things Happen to Good People*)
Kushner, Tony (1957–) Am. playwright (P—1993—*Angels in America*; *Millenium Approaches*)
Kwan, Nancy (Nancy Ka Shen Kwan) (1939–) Chin.-Eng: actress (*The World of Suzie Wong*; *Flower Drum Song*)
Kyd, Thomas (1558–1594) Eng. playwright (*The Spanish Tragedy*)
Kyser, Kay (James King Kern Kyser) (1905–1985) Am. orchestra leader ("Ole Buttermilk Sky")/radio host ("Kay Kyser's Kollege of Musical Knowledge")
Labé, Louise (Louise Chorlin Perrin Labé; "La Belle Cordiere": "The Beautiful Ropemaker") (c. 1524–1566) Fr. poet (*Euvres*)
LaBelle, Patti (Patricia Louise Holt) (1944–) Am. pop singer ("Lady Marmalade"; with Michael McDonald, "On My Own")

La Cava, Gregory (George Gregory La Cava) (1892–1952) Am. film director (*My Man Godfrey*; *Stage Door*)

Laclos, Pierre (Pierre-Ambroise-François Choderlos de Laclos) (1741–1803) Fr. novelist (*Les Liaisons Dangereuses*)

Lacroix, Christian (Christian Marie Marc Lacroix) (1950–) Fr. fashion designer

Ladd, Alan (Alan Wallbridge Ladd, Jr.) (1913–1964) Am. actor (*Shane*; *This Gun for Hire*)

Ladd, Cheryl (Cheryl Jean Stoppelmoor; a/k/a Cherie Moore) (1951–) Am. actress ("Charlie's Angels" TV series)

Ladd, Diane (Diane Rose Ladnier) (1932–) Am. actress (mother of Laura Dern; *Wild at Heart*; *Chinatown*; *Rambling Rose*)

Ladnier, Tommy (1900–1939) Am. jazz cornetist

Laemmle, Carl (1867–1939) Am. film producer (founded Universal Pictures; *The Hunchback of Notre Dame*; *All Quiet on the Western Front*)

La Farge, Oliver (Oliver Hazard Perry La Farge) (1901–1963) Am. anthropologist/writer (P—1930—*Laughing Boy*)

Lafitte or **Laffite, Jean** ("The Pirate of the Gulf") (c. 1780–c. 1826) Fr. pirate

Lafleur, Guy (Guy Damien Lafleur; "The Flower") (1951–) Can. hockey player

La Follette, Robert (Robert Marion La Follette; "Fighting Bob") (1855–1925) Am. senator/presidential candidate 1924

La Fontaine, Jean de (1621–1695) Fr. writer (*Fables*; *Tales*)

Lagerfeld, Karl (1938–) Ger. fashion designer

Lagerkvist, Par (Par Fabian Lagerkvist) (1891–1974) Swed. novelist/playwright/poet (*Barabbas*; N—1951)

Lagerlöf, Selma (Selma Ottiliana Lovisa Lagerlöf) (1858–1940) Swed. novelist/short story writer (*Jerusalem*; N—1909; first woman to win the Nobel in literature)

La Guardia, Fiorello (Fiorello Henry La Guardia; "Little Flower") (1882–1947) Am. (New York City) mayor

La Guma, Alex (1925–1985) S. Afr. novelist/short story writer (*A Walk in the Night*)

Lahr, Bert (Irving Lahrheim) (1895–1967) Am. actor/comedian (Cowardly Lion in *The Wizard of Oz*; *Waiting for Godot*; T—1964)

Lahti, Christine (1950–) Am. actress (*Swing Shift*; *Housekeeping*; *Leaving Normal*; *The Doctor*)

Laine, Cleo (Clementina Dinah Campbell) (1927–) Eng. jazz singer

Laine, Frankie (Frank Paul Lo Vecchio) (1913–) Am. pop singer ("Viva Las Vegas"; "Mule Train")/actor

Laing, R. D. (Ronald David Laing) (1927–1989) Scot. writer/psychiatrist (*The Divided Self*)

Lajoie, Napoleon ("Larry"; "Nap the Nonpareil") (1875–1959) Am. baseball Hall-of-Famer

Lake, Arthur (Arthur Silverlake) (1905–1986) Am. actor (Dagwood Bumstead in *Blondie* films)

Lake, Greg (1948–) Eng. rock bassist (with Emerson, Lake & Palmer)

Lake, Ricki (1968–) Am. actress (in John Waters films)/talk show host ("Ricki")

Lake, Veronica (Constance Frances Marie Ockleman; a/k/a Constance Keane) (1919–1973) Am. actress (*Sullivan's Travels*; *This Gun for Hire*)

LaLanne, Jack (1914–) Am. fitness expert

Lalique, Rene (1860–1945) Fr. art nouveau jeweler/glassmaker

Lalo, Edouard (Edouard-Victor-Antoine Lalo) (1823–1892) Fr. composer (*Fiesque*)

Lamarck, Chevalier de (Jean Baptiste Pierre Antoine de Monet de Lamarck) (1744–1829) Fr. naturalist (forerunner of Darwin's theory of evolution)

Lamarr, Hedy (Hedwig Eva Maria Kiesler; a/k/a Hedy Kiesler) (1913–) Aus. actress (*Ecstasy*; *Algiers*)

Lamas, Fernando (Fernando Alvaro Lamas) (1915–1982) Arg. actor (father of Lorenzo; *Rose Marie*; *The Merry Widow*)

Lamas, Lorenzo (1958–) Am. actor ("Falcon Crest" TV series)

Lamb, Lady Caroline (née Ponsonby) (1785–1828) Eng. novelist (*Glenarvon*)

Lamb, Elia (Charles Lamb) (1775–1834) Eng. essayist (*Essays of Elia*)

Lambeau, Curly (Earl Louis Lambeau) (1898–1965) Am. football Hall-of-Famer

Lambert, Christopher (Christophe Lambert) (1957–) Fr.-Am. actor (*Greystoke: The Legend of Tarzan, Lord of the Apes*; *Highlander*)

Lambert, Jack (John Harold Lambert) (1952–) Am. football Hall-of-Famer

LaMotta, Jake (Jacob LaMotta; "The

Bronx Bull"; "Raging Bull") (1921–) Am. boxer (portrayed by Robert DeNiro in *Raging Bull*)

Lamour, Dorothy (Mary Leta Dorothy Kaumeyer) (1914–) Am. actress (*Road* films with Bob Hope and Bing Crosby)

L'Amour, Louis (Louis Dearborn L'Amour; a/k/a Tex Burns) (1908–1988) Am. westerns writer (*Hondo*; *How the West Was Won*)

Lampedusa, Giusseppe Tomsasi de (1896–1957) Ital. novelist (*The Leopard*)

Lampert, Zohra (1936–) Am. actress (*Splendor in the Grass*)

Lancaster, Burt (Burton Stephen Lancaster) (1913–) Am. actor (*Atlantic City*; *Local Hero*; O—1960—*Elmer Gantry*)

Lanchester, Elsa (Elizabeth Sullivan) (1902–1986) Eng. actress (*The Bride of Frankenstein* [title role])

Land, Edwin (Edwin Herbert Land) (1909–) Am. inventor (instant camera, Polaroid lens, Polaroid Land camera)

Landau, Martin (1925–) Am. actor (*Crimes and Misdemeanors*; *North by Northwest*; "Mission: Impossible" TV series)

Landers, Ann (Esther Pauline Lederer née Friedman; "Eppie") (1918–) Am. advice columnist (twin sister of Abigail Van Buren [Dear Abby])

Landers, Audrey (1959–) Am. actress ("Dallas" TV series)

Landers, Judy (1961–) Am. actress ("Vega$" TV series)

Landis, Jessie Royce (Jessie Royce Medbury) (1904–1972) Am. actress (*North by Northwest*; *To Catch a Thief*)

Landis, John (1950–) Am. film director (*Animal House*; *The Blues Brothers*; *An American Werewolf in London*)

Landis, Judge Kenesaw Mountain (1866–1944) Am. jurist/baseball commissioner and Hall-of-Famer

Lando, Joe (c. 1962–) Am. actor ("Dr. Quinn, Medicine Woman" TV series)

Landon, Alf (Alfred Mossman Landon; "Frugal Alf") (1887–1987) Am. politician/oil executive (father of Nancy Kassebaum)

Landon, Michael (Eugene Maurice Orowitz) (1936–1991) Am. actor ("Bonanza," "Little House on the Prairie," and "Highway to Heaven" TV series)

Landrieu, Moon (Maurice Edwin Landrieu) (1930–) Am. govt. official (secretary of HUD)

Landry, Tom (Thomas Wade Landry; "The Iceberg") (1924–) Am. football coach

Landseer, Sir Edwin Henry (1802–1873) Eng. painter (animals and portraits)

Landsteiner, Karl (1868–1943) Aus.-Am. physician (discovered A, B, M, N, and O blood types; N—1930)

Lane, Abbe (Abigail Francine Lassman) (1932–) Am. singer (with Xavier Cugat)

Lane, Sir Allen (1902–1970) Eng. publisher (founded Penguin Books)

Lane, Burton (Burton Levy) (1912–) Am. film composer (*Royal Wedding*; *On a Clear Day You Can See Forever*)

Lane, Christy (Eleanor Johnston) (1939–) Am. country singer ("One Day at a Time")

Lane, Diane (1965–) Am. actress (*Rumble Fish*; *Streets of Fire*; *The Outsiders*)

Lane, Dick (Richard Lane; "Night Train") (1928–) Am. football Hall-of-Famer

Lang, Fritz (Friedrich Christian Anton Lang) (1890–1976) Aus.-Am. film director (*Metropolis*; *Scarlet Street*; *Rancho Notorious*)

lang, k. d. (Katherine Dawn Lang) (1962–) Am. country singer ("Constant Craving"; G—1992)

Langdon, Harry (Harry Philmore Langdon) (1884–1944) Am. comedian (*Tramp, Tramp, Tramp*; *The Strong Man*)

Langdon, Sue Ane (Sue Ane Lookhoff) (1936–) Am. actress ("Arnie" and "Bachelor Father" TV series)

Lange, Bill (William Alexander Lange; "Little Eva") (1871–1950) Am. baseball player

Lange, Hope (Hope Elise Ross Lange) (1931–) Am. actress (*Peyton Place*; "The Ghost and Mrs. Muir" TV series; E— 1968/69, 1969/70)

Lange, Jessica (1949–) Am. actress (*Frances*; *Sweet Dreams*; *Cape Fear*; *Crimes of the Heart*; O—1982—*Tootsie*)

Lange, Jim (C) Am. game show host ("The Dating Game")

Lange, Ted (1947–) Am. actor ("The Love Boat" TV series)

Langella, Frank (1940–) Am. actor (*Dracula* [1979])

Langer, Jim (James John Langer) (1948–) Am. football Hall-of-Famer

Langer, Susanne K. (Susanne Knauth Langer) (1895–1985) Am. philosopher/writer (*Philosophy in a New Key*)

Langmuir, Irving (1881–1957) Am. chemist (N—1932)

Langtry, Lillie (Emilie Charlotte Le Breton; "The Jersey Lily") (1853–1929) Eng.-Am. stage actress

Lanier, Bob (Robert Jerry Lanier, Jr.; "Bob-A-Dob") (1948–) Am. basketball player

Lanier, Willie (Willie E. Lanier; "Contact") (1945–) Am. football Hall-of-Famer

Lansbury, Angela (Angela Brigid Lansbury) (1925–) Eng.-Am. actress (*Gaslight*; *Bedknobs and Broomsticks*; "Murder, She Wrote" TV series; T—1966, 1969, 1975, 1979)

Lansford, Carney (Carney Ray Lansford) (1957–) Am. baseball player

Lansing, Joi (Joi Wasmansdorf) (1928–1972) Am. actress ("Love That Bob" and "Klondike" TV series)

Lansing, Sherry (Sherry Lee Lansing) (1944–) Am. film executive/producer (*Fatal Attraction*; *The Accused*)

Lansky, Meyer (Maier Suchowljansky) (1902–1983) Russ.-Am. crime boss

Lanson, Snooky (Roy Landman) (1914–1990) Am. pop singer ("It's Almost Tomorrow")/TV host ("Your Hit Parade")

Lantz, Walter (1900–) Am. cartoonist (created Woody Woodpecker)

Lanvin, Jeanne (1867–1946) Fr. fashion designer

Lanza, Mario (Alfredo Arnold Cocozza) (1921–1959) Am. opera singer (tenor; "The Loveliest Night of the Year")

Lao-Tzu or **Lao-Tse** (Li Erh) (6th century B.C.) Chin. philosopher (*Tao Te Ching*)

Lapidus, Ted (1929–) Fr. fashion designer

La Placa, Alison (1960–) Am. actress ("Duet," "Open House," and "The Jackie Thomas Show" TV series)

Lardner, Ring (Ringgold Wilmer Lardner) (1885–1933) Am. humorist/short story writer (*You Know Me, Al*)

Lardner, Ring, Jr. (Ringgold Wilmer Lardner, Jr.) (1915–) Am. screenwriter (son of Ring; *Woman of the Year*; *M*A*S*H*)

Laredo, Ruth (Ruth Meckler) (1937–) Am. concert pianist

Larkin, Philip (Philip Arthur Larkin) (1922–1985) Eng. poet/novelist (*A Girl in Winter*)

Laroccha, Alicia de (1923–) Span. concert pianist

Laroche, Guy (1923–) Fr. fashion designer

La Rochefoucauld, François de (1613–1680) Fr. writer/moralist (*Memoirs*; *Maxims*)

La Rosa, Julius (1930–) Am. singer ("Domani [Tomorrow]")

Larouche, Lyndon (Lyndon Hermyle Larouche, Jr.) (1922–) Am. politician (founded the National Democratic Policy Committee)

Larrieu-Lutz, Francie (1952–) Am. runner

Larroquette, John (1947–) Am. actor ("Night Court" and "The John Larroquette Show" TV series; E—1984/85, 1985/86, 1986/87, 1987/88)

Larsen, Don (Donald James Larsen; "Gooney Bird") (1929–) Am. baseball player (pitched the only perfect game in World Series history)

Larson, Gary (1950–) Am. cartoonist (*The Far Side*)

Larson, John (John Augustus Larson) (1892–1965) Am. psychiatrist/inventor (polygraph)

Larson, Nicolette (1952–) Am. pop singer ("Lotta Love")

La Rue, Lash (Alfred La Rue) (1917–) Am. cowboy actor (*The Fighting Vigilantes*)

Lary, Yale (Robert Yale Lary) (1930–) Am. football Hall-of-Famer

La Salle, Sieur de (René-Robert Cavelier de La Salle) (1643–1687) Fr. explorer (claimed the Louisiana Territory for France)

Lasky, Jesse (Jesse Louis Lasky) (1880–1958) Am. film producer (*The Covered Wagon*; *Beau Geste*)

Lasky, Victor (1918–1990) Am. writer (*J.F.K.: The Man and the Myth*)

Lasorda, Tommy (Thomas Charles Lasorda) (1927–) Am. baseball pitcher/coach

Lasser, Louise (Louise Jane Lasser) (1939–) Am. actress ("Mary Hartman, Mary Hartman" TV series)

Latis, Mary J. (C) Am. mystery writer (with Martha Hennissart, known as Emma Lathen)

La Tour, Georges de (Georges Dumesnil de La Tour) (1593–1652) Fr. painter (*The Mocking of Job*)

Latrobe, Benjamin (Benjamin Henry Latrobe) (1764–1820) Am. architect (worked on the Capitol)

Lattanzi, Matt (c. 1957–) Am. actor (*My Tutor*)

Lattisaw, Stacy (1966–) Am. soul singer ("Love on a Two Way Street")

Lauda, Niki (Nikolaus Andreas von Lauda) (1949–) Aus. auto racer

Lauder, Estee (1908–) Am. cosmetician/businesswoman

Lauder, Sir Harry (Harry MacLennan Lauder; "The Laird of the Halls") (1870–1950) Scot. comedian/singer/songwriter ("Roamin' in the Gloamin'")

Laughlin, Lori (c. 1964–) Am. actress ("Full House" TV series)

Laughlin, Tom (1938–) Am. film director/actor (*Billy Jack* [title role] and sequels)

Laughton, Charles (1899–1962) Eng.-Am. actor (*The Hunchback of Notre Dame*; O—1932/33—*The Private Life of Henry VIII*)/film director (*The Night of the Hunter*)

Lauper, Cyndi (Cynthia Lauper) (1953–) Am. pop singer ("Girls Just Want to Have Fun"; "Time After Time"; G—1984)

Laurel, Stan (Arthur Stanley Jefferson) (1890–1965) Eng.-Am. comedian (with Oliver Hardy)

Lauren, Ralph (Ralph Lifshitz) (1939–) Am. fashion designer

Laurents, Arthur (1918–) Am. playwright (*The Way We Were*; *West Side Story*; *Gypsy*)

Laurie, Piper (Rosetta Jacobs) (1932–) Am. actress (*Carrie*; "Twin Peaks" TV series)

Lavagetto, Cookie (Harry Arthur Lavagetto) (1912–1990) Am. baseball player

Lavelli, Dante (1923–) Am. football Hall-of-Famer

Laver, Rod (Rodney George Laver; "The Rocket") (1938–) Austral. tennis player (W—1961, 1962, 1968, 1969)

Lavin, Linda (1937–) Am. actress (TV's "Alice"; T—1987)

Law, Bonar (Andrew Bonar Law; "The Unknown Prime Minister") (1858–1923) Eng. statesman/prime minister 1922–1923

Law, John Phillip (1937–) Am. actor (*The Russians Are Coming, The Russians Are Coming*; *Barbarella*)

Lawes, Henry (1596–1662) Eng. composer ("Psalms")

Lawford, Sir Peter (Peter Sidney Ernest Aylen Lawford) (1923–1984) Eng. actor (*Royal Wedding*; *Advise and Consent*)

Lawrence, Carol (Carol Maria Laraia) (1934–) Am. actress/singer

Lawrence, D. H. (David Herbert Lawrence) (1885–1930) Eng. short story writer/poet/novelist (*Lady Chatterley's Lover*; *Sons and Lovers*)

Lawrence, Ernest (Ernest Orlando Lawrence) (1901–1958) Am. physicist (N—1939)/inventor (cyclotron)

Lawrence, Florence ("The Biograph Girl"; "The Imp Girl") (1886—1938) Can.-Am. actress (*Salome*; *Anthony and Cleopatra*)

Lawrence, Gertrude (Gertrud Alexandra Dagmar Lawrence-Klasen) (1898–1952) Eng. actress (*The Glass Menagerie*; *Stage Door Canteen*; T—1952)

Lawrence, Joey (1976–) Am. actor ("Blossom" TV series)/singer/teen idol

Lawrence, Marjorie (Marjorie Florence Lawrence) (1907–1979) Austral. opera singer (soprano)

Lawrence of Arabia (Thomas Edward Lawrence; a/k/a T. E. Lawrence, J. H. Ross, and T. E. Shaw) (1888–1935) Eng. soldier/archaeologist/writer (*The Seven Pillars of Wisdom*)

Lawrence, Steve (Sidney Leibowitz) (1935–) Am. pop singer ("Go Away Little Girl")

Lawrence, Sir Thomas ("The Wonderful Boy of Devizes") (1769–1830) Eng. portrait painter

Lawrence, Tracy (1968–) Am. country singer ("Alibi")

Lawrence, Vicki (Vicki Ann Lawrence) (1949–) Am. actress/comedienne ("The Carol Burnett Show")/singer ("The Night the Lights Went Out in Georgia")

Laxness, Halldór (Halldór Kiljan Laxness; born Halldór Kiljan Gudjonsson) (1902–) Icel. poet/playwright/novelist (*The Atom Station*; N—1955)

Layne, Bobby (Robert Lawrence Layne; "The Blond Bomber") (1926–1986) Am. football Hall-of-Famer

Lazar, Swifty (Irving Paul Lazar) (1907–1993) Am. literary agent (hosted annual Oscar party)

Lazarus, Emma (1849–1887) Am. poet (*The New Colossus*, poem at the base of the Statue of Liberty)

Lazarus, Mell (1927–) Am. cartoonist (*Momma*)

Lazenby, George (1939–) Austral. actor (James Bond in *On Her Majesty's Secret Service*)

Lazzeri, Tony (Anthony Michael Lazzeri;

"Poosh 'Em Up") (1903–1946) Am. base-ball player

Leach, Robin (1941–) Eng. TV host ("Lifestyles of the Rich and Famous")

Leachman, Cloris (1926–) Am. actress (*High Anxiety; Young Frankenstein;* O— 1971—*The Last Picture Show*)

Leacock, Stephen (Stephen Butler Leacock) (1869–1944) Can. humorist/writer (*Literary Lapses; Nonsense Novels*)

Leadbelly (Huddie Ledbetter; "King of the 12-String Guitar Players") (1885–1949) Am. blues guitarist/singer ("On Top of Old Smoky")

Leahy, Patrick (Patrick Joseph Leahy) (1940–) Am. senator

Leakey, Louis (Louis Seymour Bazett Leakey) (1903–1972) Eng. anthropologist (discovered human fossils in Tanzania)

Leakey, Mary (Mary Douglas Leakey) (1913–) Eng. anthropologist/archaeologist

Leakey, Richard (Richard Erskine Frere Leakey) (1944–) Eng. anthropologist/archaeologist (son of Louis and Mary)

Lean, Sir David (1908–1991) Eng. film director (O—1957—*The Bridge on the River Kwai;* O—1962—*Lawrence of Arabia*)

Lear, Edward (1812–1888) Eng. painter/poet (*The Owl and the Pussy-Cat*)

Lear, Frances (1923–) Am. magazine publisher/editor (*Lear's*)

Lear, Norman (Norman Milton Lear) (1922–) Am. TV producer ("All in the Family," "Maude," and "The Jeffersons" TV series)

Learned, Michael (1939–) Am. actress ("The Waltons" and "Nurse" TV series; E—1972/73, 1973/74, 1975/76, 1981/82)

Leary, Denis (1958–) Am. comedian/writer (*No Cure for Cancer*)

Leary, Timothy (Timothy Francis Leary) (1920–) Am. political protester/psychologist (signature phrase: "Tune in, turn on, drop out")

Leavitt, Michael D. (1951–) Am. gov. of Utah

Leblanc, Maurice (Maurice-Marie-Emile Leblanc) (1864–1941) Fr. playwright/detective story writer (created Arsène Lupin)

Le Bon, Simon (1958–) Eng. rock singer (with Duran Duran)

Lebowitz, Fran (Frances Ann Lebowitz) (1950–) Am. journalist/humorist

LeBrock, Kelly (1960–) Am. model/actress (*The Woman in Red*)

Le Carré, John (David John Moore Cornwell) (1931–) Eng. spy/spy novelist (*Tinker, Tailor, Soldier, Spy; The Spy Who Came in from the Cold; The Night Manager*)

Le Corbusier (Charles-Édouord Jeanneret) (1887–1965) Swi. architect/city planner

Lederer, William (William Julius Lederer) (1912–) Am. novelist/writer (co-wrote *The Ugly American*)

LeDoux, Chris (1948–) Am. country singer ("Whatcha Gonna Do with a Cowboy")

Lee, Albert (1943–) Eng. blues guitarist (for Jackson Browne, Joe Cocker, Emmylou Harris, etc.)

Lee, Alvin (1944–) Eng. rock singer/guitarist (with Ten Years After)

Lee, Ann ("Mother Ann"; "Ann the Word") (1736–1784) Am. mystic/founder of the American Shaker Society

Lee, Brandon (c. 1964–1993) Am. actor (son of Bruce; killed on the set of *The Crow*)

Lee, Brenda (Brenda Mae Tarpley; "Little Miss Dynamite") (1944–) Am. pop/country singer ("I'm Sorry")

Lee, Bruce (Liu Yuen Kam; "The Little Dragon") (1940–1973) Chin.-Am. martial arts expert/actor (*Enter the Dragon*)

Lee, Canada (Leonard Lionel Cornelius Canegata) (1907–1952) Am. actor (*Cry, The Beloved Country*)

Lee, Christopher (Christopher Frank Carandini Lee) (1922–) Eng. actor (*Dracula; The Mummy*)

Lee, Dickey (Dick Lipscomb) (1941–) Am. country singer/songwriter ("Patches"; "I Saw Linda Yesterday")

Lee, Geddy (1953–) Can. rock musician/singer (with Rush)

Lee, Gypsy Rose (Rose Louise Hovick; "The Queen of Burlesque") (1914–1970) Am. writer (*The G-String Murders*)/nightclub entertainer (striptease artist)

Lee, Harper (Nelle Harper Lee) (1926–) Am. novelist (P—1961—*To Kill a Mockingbird*)

Lee, Johnny (John Lee Harn; "The Urban Cowboy") (1946–) Am. country singer ("Lookin' for Love")

Lee, Joie (C) Am. actress (sister of Spike; *Do the Right Thing*)

Lee, Manfred (Manfred Bennington Lep-

ofsky; with Frederic Dannay, a/k/a Ellery Queen and Barnaby Ross) (1905–
1971) Am. detective story writer
Lee, Michele (Michele Lee Dusiak)
(1942–) Am. actress ("Knots Landing"
TV series)
Lee, Peggy (Norma Delores Egstrom)
(1920–) Am. pop singer ("Fever"; for-
merly with Benny Goodman; G—1969)/
actress (*The Jazz Singer* [1953])
Lee, Pinky (Pincus Leff) (1916–1993)
Am. pop singer/comedian/children's TV
host
Lee, Robert E. (Robert Edward Lee; "The
Bayard of the Confederate Army"; "Un-
cle Robert") (1807–1870) Am. Confeder-
ate general
Lee, Sheryl (c. 1967–) Am. actress ("Twin
Peaks" TV series)
Lee, Spike (Shelton Jackson Lee) (1956–)
Am. actor/film director (*Do the Right
Thing*; *Jungle Fever*; *Malcolm X*; *Crook-
lyn*)
Lee, Stan (1922–) Am. cartoonist (created
Spider-Man)
Lee, Tanith (1947–) Am. science fiction
writer (*Black Unicorn*)
Lee, Tommy (1962–) Am. rock drummer
(with Mötley Crüe)
Lee, Tsung-Dao (1926–) Chin.-Am. physi-
cist (N—1957)
Leeds, Andrea (Antoinette Leeds) (1914–
1984) Am. actress (*Stage Door*; *It Could
Happen to You*)
Leek, Sybil ("The Twentieth-Century
Witch") (c. 1917–1982) Eng. astrologer/
writer
Leemans, Tuffy (Alphonse E. Leemans)
(1915–1979) Am. football Hall-of-Famer
Leeves, Jane (c. 1963–) Eng.-Am. actress
("Throb" and "Frasier" TV series)
Le Fanu, J. S. (Joseph Sheridan Le Fanu)
(1814–1873) Ir. novelist/short story
writer (*Uncle Silas*)
Leflore, Ron (Ronald LeFlore) (1948–)
Am. baseball player
Le Gallienne, Eva (1899–1991) Eng.-Am.
stage actress/director/producer
Léger, Aléxis (Marie-René-Auguste-
Aléxis Saint-Léger; a/k/a St.-John Perse)
(1887–1975) Fr. poet (*Seamarks*)
Léger, Fernand (1881–1955) Fr. painter
(developed "machine art")
Legrand, Michel (Michel Jean Legrand)
(1931–) Fr. film composer (*Summer of
'42*)
Le Guin, Ursula K. (Ursula [née] Kroeber

Le Guin) (1929–) Am. science fiction/
fantasy writer (*Earthsea* trilogy)
Leguizamo, John (c. 1964–) Am. actor
(*Carlito's Way*)/writer (*Mambo Mouth*)
Lehár, Franz (1870–1948) Hung. com-
poser (*The Merry Widow*)
Lehmann, Lilli (1848–1929) Ger. opera
singer (soprano)
Lehmann, Lotte (1888–1976) Ger.-Am.
opera singer (soprano)
Lehmann, Michael (1958–) Am. film di-
rector (*Heathers*; *Hudson Hawk*)
Lehr, Lew (1895–1950) Am. comedian
Leiberman-Cline, Nancy (1958–) Am.
basketball player
Lehrer, Jim (James Charles Lehrer)
(1934–) Am. broadcast journalist ("The
MacNeil-Lehrer Report")
Lehrer, Tom (Thomas Andrew Lehrer)
(1928–) Am. pianist/songwriter/satirist
(*Poisoning Pigeons in the Park*; *The Vati-
can Rag*; *Masochism Tango*)
Leiber, Fritz (a/k/a Francis Lathrop)
(1910–) Am. science fiction writer (*The
Mechanical Bride*; *The Swords of Lan-
khmar*)
Leiber, Jerry (1933–) Am. pop songwriter
(with Mike Stoller, "Yakety Yak"; "Charlie Brown"; "Hound Dog"; "Save the
Last Dance for Me")
Leibman, Ron (1937–) Am. actor (TV's
"Kaz"; *Angels in America*; *Millennium
Approaches*; E—1978/79)
Leibniz, Baron Gottfried Von (Gottfried
Wilhelm Leibniz; "The First of Philoso-
phers"; "A Living Dictionary") (1646–
1716) Ger. philosopher (discovered bi-
nary number system; with Isaac New-
ton, discovered principles of calculus)
Leibovitz, Annie (Anna-Lou Leibovitz)
(1949–) Am. photographer (GAP ads,
rock stars, celebrities)
Leibrandt, Charlie (Charles Louis
Leibrandt, Jr.) (1956–) Am. baseball
pitcher
Leifer, Carol (1956–) Am. comedienne
Leigh, Janet (Jeanette Helen Morrison)
(1927–) Am. actress (mother of Jamie
Lee Curtis; *Psycho*; *Touch of Evil*)
Leigh, Jennifer Jason (1958–) Am. actress
(daughter of Vic Morrow; *Single White
Female*; *Rush*; *Last Exit to Brooklyn*;
Miami Blues)
Leigh, Mitch (Irwins Michnik) (1928–)
Am. composer (*Man of La Mancha*)
Leigh, Vivien (Vivian Mary Hartley)
(1913–1967) Eng. actress (O—1939—

Gone with the Wind; O—1951—*A Streetcar Named Desire*; T—1963)
Leighton, Baron Frederick (Baron Leighton of Stretton) (1830–1896) Eng. painter (*Venus Disrobing for the Bath*)
Leighton, Margaret (1922–1976) Eng. actress (*The Winslow Boy*; *The Go-Between*; T—1957, 1962)
Leinsdorf, Erich (1912–1993) Aus.-Am. conductor (Metropolitan Opera, Boston Symphony)
Leinster, Murray (William F. Jenkins) (1896–1975) Am. science fiction writer (*Monsters and Such*)
Leisure, David (1950–) Am. actor ("Empty Nest" TV series; "Joe Isuzu" [the liar] in Isuzu commercials)
Lelouch, Claude (Claude Barruck Lelouch) (1937–) Fr. film director (*A Man and a Woman; Live for Life*)
Lely, Sir Peter (Pieter Van Der Faes) (1618–1680) Dutch-Eng. portrait painter
Lem, Stanislaw (1921–) Pol. science fiction writer (*Solaris*)
Lemaître, Georges (Georges Henri Lemaître) (1894–1966) Belg. physicist (developed the "big bang" theory)
Le May, Curtis (Curtis Emerson Le May) (1906–) Am. air force chief of staff
Lemieux, Mario (1965–) Can. hockey player
Lemmon, Chris (1954–) Am. actor (son of Jack; "Duet" TV series; *Swing Shift*)
Lemmon, Jack (John Uhler Lemmon III) (1925–) Am. actor (*Some Like It Hot; Glengarry Glen Ross*; O—1955—*Mister Roberts*; O—1973—*Save the Tiger*)
Lemmy (Ian Kilminster) (1945–) Eng. rock musician/singer (with Motorhead)
Lemon, Bob (Robert Granville Lemon) (1920–) Am. baseball Hall-of-Famer
Lemon, Meadowlark (Meadow George Lemon III; "The Clown Prince of Basketball") (1932–) Am. basketball player/actor
Lemond, Greg (Gregory James Lemond; "The Reno Rocket") (1961–) Am. bicyclist
Le Nain, Antoine (1588–1648) Fr. painter (brother of Louis and Mathieu; collaborated with them)
Le Nain, Louis (1593–1648) Fr. painter
Le Nain, Mathieu (1607–1677) Fr. painter
Lenclos, Ninon de (Anne de Lenclos) (1620–1705) Fr. courtesan

Lendl, Ivan (1960–) Cz. tennis player
L'Enfant, Pierre (Pierre Charles L'Enfant) (1754–1825) Fr.-Am. architect/city planner (Washington, DC)
L'Engle, Madeleine (Madeleine L'Engle Camp; born Madeleine Franklin) (1918–) Am. fantasy/children's book writer (*A Wrinkle in Time*)
Lenglen, Suzanne ("The Pavlova of Tennis") (1899–1938) Fr. tennis player
Lenin, Vladimir (a/k/a Nikolay Lenin; born Vladimir Ilich Ulyanov) (1870–1924) Russ. communist political leader 1917–1924 (founder of Bolshevism)
Lennon, Dianne (Dianne Barbara Lennon) (1939–) Am. singer (with The Lennon Sisters; "Sad Movies Make Me Cry")
Lennon, Janet (Janet Elizabeth Lennon) (1946–) Am. singer (with The Lennon Sisters)
Lennon, John (John Winston Lennon) (1940–1980) Eng. rock singer/musician ("Imagine"; "Woman"; formerly with The Beatles)
Lennon, Julian (John Charles Julian Lennon) (1963–) Eng. rock singer/musician (son of John; "Too Late for Goodbyes")
Lennon, Kathy (Kathleen Mary Lennon) (1942–) Am. singer (with The Lennon Sisters)
Lennon, Peggy (Margaret Ann Lennon) (1940–) Am. singer (with The Lennon Sisters)
Lennon, Sean (1975–) Am. musician (son of John Lennon and Yoko Ono)
Lennox, Annie (1954–) Scot. pop/rock singer ("Sweet Dreams"; "Walking on Broken Glass"; "Why"; formerly with The Eurythmics)
Leno, Jay (James Douglas Muir Leno) (1950–) Am. comedian/TV host ("The Tonight Show")
Lenska, Rula (Roza-Maria Lubienska; "The Fair One") (1947–) Eng. actress (commercials)
Lenya, Lotte (Karoline Wilhelmine Blamauer) (1898–1981) Aus. singer/actress (*From Russia, with Love; Semi-Tough*)
Lenz, Kay (1953–) Am. actress ("Rich Man, Poor Man—Book II" TV series)
Leonard, Buck (Walter Fenner Leonard; "The Black Lou Gehrig") (1907–) Am. baseball Hall-of-Famer
Leonard, Elmore (Elmore John Leonard,

Jr.; "Dutch") (1925–) Am. crime novelist/ screenwriter (*52 Pick-Up*; *Glitz*)

Leonard, Robert Sean (c. 1968–) Am. actor (*Dead Poets Society*)

Leonard, Sheldon (Sheldon Leonard Bershad) (1907–) Am. TV producer/director ("The Dick Van Dyke Show" and "I Spy" TV series)/actor (*To Have and Have Not*)

Leonard, Sugar Ray (Ray Charles Leonard) (1956–) Am. boxer

Leoncavallo, Ruggero (1858–1919) Ital. composer/librettist (*Pagliacci*)

Leone, Sergio (1921–1989) Ital. film director (*A Fistful of Dollars*; other "spaghetti westerns")

Leopold, Nathan, Jr. (1904–1971) Am. kidnapper/murderer (with Richard Loeb)

Le Pen, Jean-Marie (1928–) Fr. politician (heads the ultra-conservative French National Front party)

Lermontov, Mikhail (Mikhail Yuryevich Lermontov) (1814–1841) Russ. poet/ novelist (*Hero of Our Time*)

Lerner, Alan Jay (1918–1986) Am. playwright/librettist (with Frederick Loewe; *Brigadoon*; *My Fair Lady*; *Camelot*)

Lerner, Max (1902–1992) Russ.-Am. journalist/editor (*The Nation*)

Leroux, Gaston (1868–1927) Fr. journalist/ playwright/mystery writer (*The Phantom of the Opera*)

Le Roy, Mervyn (1900–1987) Am. film director (*Random Harvest*; *Little Caesar*; *Mister Roberts*)

Lesage, Alain (Alain-René Lesage) (1668–1747) Fr. novelist/playwright (*Gil Blas*)

Le Shan, Eda (Eda Joan Le Shan) (1922–) Am. writer (*The Conspiracy Against Childhood*)

Lesh, Phil (Philip Chapman) (1940–) Am. rock bassist (with The Grateful Dead)

Leslie, Bethel (1929–) Am. actress ("The Doctors" TV series; "Love of Life" soap opera)

Leslie, Joan (Joan Agnes Theresa Sadie Brodel; a/k/a Joan Brodel) (1925–) Am. actress (*Yankee Doodle Dandy*; *Camille*)

Lessing, Doris (Doris May Tayler) (1919–) Eng. novelist/short story writer (*The Golden Notebook*; *The Good Terrorist*)

Lester, Dick (Richard Lester) (1932–) Am. film director (*A Hard Day's Night*; *A Funny Thing Happened on the Way to the Forum*)

Lester, Ketty (Revoyda Frierson) (1938–) Am. actress ("Little House on the Prairie" TV series)/singer ("Love Letters")

Letterman, David (1947–) Am. talk show host

Leucippus (5th century B.C.) Gr. philosopher (taught Democritus)

Leutze, Emanuel (Emanuel Gottlieb Leutze) (1816–1868) Am. painter (*Washington Crossing the Delaware*)

Levant, Oscar (1906–1972) Am. pianist/ composer/wit/writer (*Memoirs of an Amnesiac*)

Levene, Sam (Samuel Levine) (1905–1980) Am. actor (*Crossfire*; *Three Men on a Horse*)

Levertov, Denise (1923–) Eng.-Am. poet/ essayist (*The Jacob's Ladder*; *The Double Image*)

Levesque, René ("René The Red") (1922–1987) Can. premier of Quebec 1976–1985

Levi (1st century A.D.) Heb. son of Jacob

Levi, Primo (1919–1987) Ital.-Jew. novelist/poet/short story writer (*The Periodic Table*)

Levin, Ira (1929–) Am. suspense novelist/ playwright (*Sliver*; *A Kiss Before Dying*; *Rosemary's Baby*; *The Stepford Wives*)

Levin, Meyer (1905–1981) Am. novelist/ journalist/writer (*Compulsion*)

Levine, James (1943–) Am. orchestra conductor (Metropolitan Opera)

Levinson, Barry (1932–) Am. film director/writer ("Homicide" TV series; *Diner*; *Bugsy*; *Avalon*; *O—1988—Rain Man*)

Lévi-Strauss, Claude (Claude Gustave Lévi-Strauss) (1908–) Fr. anthropologist/ writer (*The Savage Mind*)

Lewis, Carl (1961–) Am. track and field athlete

Lewis, C. S. (Clive Staples Lewis; a/k/a N. W. Clerk and Clive Hamilton) (1898–1963) Eng. novelist/essayist (*The Screwtape Letters*; the *Narnia* chronicles)

Lewis, Charlotte (1967–) Am. actress (*The Golden Child*)

Lewis, D. B. Wyndham (Dominic Bevan Wyndham Lewis) (1894–1969) Eng. humorist/essayist/biographer (*The Stuffed Owl*)

Lewis, Dawnn (1960–) Am. actress ("A Different World" TV series)

Lewis, Emmanuel (1971–) Am. child actor ("Webster" TV series)

Lewis, Gary (1946–) Am. rock singer/ bandleader (son of Jerry; "This Diamond Ring"; with Gary Lewis and The Playboys)

Lewis, Huey (Hugh Anthony Cregg III) (1951–) Am. rock/pop singer ("I Want a New Drug"; "The Power of Love"; with Huey Lewis and The News)

Lewis, Jerry (Joseph Levitch) (1926–) Am. comedian (*The Nutty Professor*; *The King of Comedy*)

Lewis, Jerry Lee ("The Killer") (1935–) Am. rock singer/pianist/songwriter (cousin of Jimmy Swaggart and Mickey Gilley; "Whole Lot of Shakin' Going On"; "Great Balls of Fire")

Lewis, Juliette (1973–) Am. actress (*Cape Fear*; *Husbands and Wives*; *What's Eating Gilbert Grape*)

Lewis, Meriwether (1774–1809) Am. explorer of the Pacific Northwest coast (with William Clark)

Lewis, Oscar (1914–1970) Am. anthropologist/writer (*La Vida*)

Lewis, Ramsey (Ramsey Emanuel Lewis, Jr.) (1935–) Am. jazz pianist ("The 'In' Crowd")

Lewis, Richard (1957–) Am. comedian/ actor ("Anything but Love" and "Daddy Dearest" TV series)

Lewis, Shari (Shari Hurwitz) (1934–) Am. ventriloquist/puppeteer (puppet: Lambchop)

Lewis, Sinclair (Harry Sinclair Lewis) (1885–1951) Am. novelist (*Elmer Gantry*; *Babbitt*; N—1930; P—1926— *Arrowsmith* [declined])

Lewis, Ted (Theodore Leopold Friedman) (1892–1971) Am. bandleader/clarinetist

Lewis, Wyndham (Percy Wyndham Lewis) (1884–1957) Am.-Eng. novelist/ painter (*The Apes of God*)

Liadov or **Lyadov, Anatol** or **Anatoly** (Anatoly Konstantinovich Lyadov) (1855– 1914) Russ. composer (studied under Rimsky-Korsakov; *Baba Yaga*)

Liberace (Wladziu Valentino Liberace; a/k/a Walter Busterkeys) (1919–1987) Am. pianist/entertainer

Lichine, David (1910–1972) Russ. ballet dancer

Lichtenstein, Roy (1923–) Am. "pop art" painter

Liddy, G. Gordon (George Gordon Liddy) (1930–) Am. politician/Watergate participant

Liebermann, Max (1847–1935) Ger. painter (founded the Berliner Sezession)

Lifeson, Alex (1953–) Can. rock guitarist (with Rush)

Light, Enoch (Enoch Henry Light) (1907– 1978) Am. orchestra leader (with Enoch Light and The Light Brigade; "I Want to Be Happy Cha Cha")

Light, Judith (Judith Ellen Light) (1949–) Am. actress ("Who's the Boss?" TV series)

Lightfoot, Gordon (Gordon Meredith Lightfoot) (1938–) Can. rock/pop singer ("Sundown"; "Carefree Highway"; "If You Could Read My Mind")

Light-Horse Harry (Henry Lee) (1756– 1818) Am. cavalry commander/gov. of Virginia

Lillie, Beatrice (Constance Sylvia Munston, later Lady Peel) (1898–1989) Eng. comedienne/actress (*Exit Smiling*; *Thoroughly Modern Millie*)

Lilly, Bob (Robert Lewis Lilly) (1939–) Am. football Hall-of-Famer

Limbaugh, Rush (Rush Hudson Limbaugh) (1951–) Am. talk show host/ writer (*The Way Things Ought to Be*)

Limón, José (José Arcadio Limón) (1908– 1972) Mex.-Am. choreographer/dancer

Lincoln, Abraham ("Abe"; "Honest Abe"; "The Great Emancipator") (1809–1865) 16th Am. pres. (1861–1865)

Lincoln, Elmo (Otto Elmo Linkenhelter) (1889–1952) Am. actor (first screen Tarzan)

Lincoln, Mary Todd (Mary Ann Todd) (1818–1882) Am. first lady (Abraham)

Lind, Jenny (Johanna Maria Lind; "The Swedish Nightingale") (1820–1887) Swed. opera singer (soprano)

Lindbergh, Anne (Anne Spencer Morrow) (1906–) Am. writer (*Gift from the Sea*)

Lindbergh, Charles (Charles Augustus Lindbergh; "Lucky Lindy"; "The Lone Eagle") (1902–1974) Am. aviator (first nonstop solo flight across the Atlantic Ocean)/writer (P—1954—*The Spirit of St. Louis*)

Lindblom, Gunnel (1931–) Swed. actress (*Wild Strawberries*; *Scenes from a Marriage*)

Linden, Hal (Harold Lipshitz) (1931–) Am. actor (TV's "Barney Miller"); T—1971

Linder, Kate (1952–) Am. actress ("The Young and the Restless" soap opera)
Lindfors, Viveca (Elsa Viveca Torstendotter) (1920–) Swed. actress (*The Sure Thing*; *No Exit*)
Lindgren, Astrid (1907–) Swed. children's book writer (created Pippi Longstocking)
Lindley, Audra (1918–) Am. actress ("Three's Company" and "The Ropers" TV series)
Lindsay, Howard (1889–1968) Am. actor/playwright (*The Sound of Music*; P—1946—*State of the Union*)
Lindsay, Margaret (Margaret Kies) (1910–1981) Am. actress (*Jezebel*; *Scarlet Street*)
Lindsay, Ted (Robert Blake Theodore Lindsay; "Terrible Ted") (1925–) Can.-Am. hockey player
Lindsay-Hogg, Michael (1940–) Am.-Eng. film director (son of Geraldine Fitzgerald; *Let It Be*)
Lindsey, Mort (1923–) Am. orchestra leader/film and TV composer ("Jeopardy!")
Lindstrom, Freddie (Frederick Charles Lindstrom; "Lindy") (1905–1981) Am. baseball Hall-of-Famer
Linklater, Richard (c. 1961–) Am. film director (*Slacker*; *Dazed and Confused*)
Linkletter, Art (Arthur Gordon Kelley Linkletter) (1912–) Can.-Am. TV personality ("Kids Say the Darndest Things!")
Linnaeus, Carolus (a/k/a Carol von Linné) (1707–1778) Swed. botanist (devised system of classification of plants and animals)
Linn-Baker, Mark (1953–) Am. actor ("Perfect Strangers" TV series)
Liotta, Ray (1954–) Am. actor (*GoodFellas*; *Unlawful Entry*; *Dominick and Eugene*)
Lipchitz, Jacques (Chaim Jacob Lipchitz) (1891–1973) Lat.-Fr.-Am. cubist sculptor
Li Peng (1928–) Chin. premier 1987–
Li Po (a/k/a Li T'ai-Po) (701–762) Chin. poet
Lippi, Fra Lippo or Filippo (1406–1469) Flor. painter (*Life of St. John the Baptist*)
Lippmann, Walter (1889–1974) Am. journalist (P—1962)/writer (*The Good Society*; P—1958 [special citation])
Lipton, Peggy (1947–) Am. actress ("The Mod Squad" and "Twin Peaks" TV series)

Lisi, Virna (Virna Pieralisi) (1937–) Ital. actress (*How to Murder Your Wife*)
Lispector, Clarice (1925–1977) Braz. novelist (*Family Ties*)
Liston, Sonny (Charles Liston) (1932–1971) Am. boxer
Liszt, Franz (Franz Ferencz Liszt) (1811–1886) Hung. composer/pianist (Hungarian rhapsodies)
Lithgow, John (John Arthur Lithgow) (1945–) Am. actor (*Terms of Endearment*; *The World According to Garp*; *Cliffhanger*)
Little Anthony (Anthony Gourdine) (1941–) Am. rock singer ("Tears on My Pillow"; with Little Anthony and The Imperials)
Little, Cleavon (Cleavon Jake Little) (1939–1992) Am. actor (*Blazing Saddles*; "Bagdad Cafe" TV series; T—1970)
Little Eva (Eva Narcissus Boyd) (1945–) Am. pop singer ("The Loco-Motion")
Little, Rich (Richard Caruthers Little) (1938–) Can. comedian/impressionist
Little Richard (Richard Wayne Penniman; "Georgia Peach") (1935–) Am. pop/rock singer ("Tutti-Frutti"; "Long Tall Sally"; "Good Golly, Miss Molly")
Littler, Gene (Eugene Alec Littler; "The Gene Machine"; "Gene the Machine") (1930–) Am. golfer
Litvak, Anatole (Michael Anatol Litwak) (1902–1974) Russ. film director (*The Snake Pit*; *Sorry Wrong Number*)
Livingston, Jay (Jerry Harold Levinson) (1915–) Am. songwriter ("Que Sera, Sera")
Livingstone, David (1813–1873) Scot. explorer/missionary in Africa (named Victoria Falls)
Livingstone, Mary (Sadie Marks) (1908–1983) Am. actress ("The Jack Benny Show" TV series)
Livy (Titus Livius) (59 B.C.–A.D. 17) Roman historian (*The Annals of the Roman People*)
L. L. Cool J (James Todd Smith; "L.L. Cool J." stands for "Ladies Love Cool James") (C) Am. rapper ("Mama Said Knock You Out")
Llewellyn, Richard (Richard David Vivian Llewellyn Lloyd) (1906–1983) Wel. novelist (*How Green Was My Valley*)
Lloyd, Christopher (1938–) Am. actor (*Back to the Future*; *The Addams Family*; E—1981/82, 1982/83)

Lloyd, Emily (Emily Lloyd Pack) (1970–) Eng.-Am. actress (*Wish You Were Here*; *Cookie*; *A River Runs Through It*)

Lloyd, Frank (1888–1960) Am. film director (O—1928/29—*The Divine Lady*; O—1932/33—*Cavalcade*)

Lloyd, Harold (Harold Clayton Lloyd) (1894–1971) Am. actor (*Safety Last*; *The Kid Brother*)

Lloyd George, David (1st Earl Lloyd-George of Dwyfor) (1863–1945) Eng. prime minister 1916–1922

Lo Bianco, Tony (1936–) Am. actor (*Jesus of Nazareth*; "Love of Life" soap opera)

Locane, Amy (1971–) Am. actress (*School Ties*; "Melrose Place" TV series)

Locke, Alain (Alain Leroy Locke) (1886–1954) Am. writer/leader of the Harlem Renaissance (*The New Negro*); first Afr.-Am. Rhodes scholar

Locke, John (1632–1704) Eng. philosopher (*Essay Concerning Human Understanding*)

Locke, Sondra (1947–) Am. actress (*The Gauntlet*; *Every Which Way but Loose*; *The Outlaw Josey Wales*)

Lockhart, June (June Kathleen Lockhart) (1925–) Am. actress ("Lost in Space" and "Lassie" TV series)/film director (*Impulse*)

Locklear, Heather (1961–) Am. actress ("Dynasty" and "Melrose Place" TV series)

Lockridge, Frances (Frances Louise Lockridge) (1896–1963) Am. mystery writer (with husband Richard, created Mr. and Mrs. North; *The Norths Meet Murder*)

Lockridge, Richard (1898–1982) Am. novelist/short story writer/mystery writer (with wife Frances)

Lockwood, Gary (John Gary Yusolfsky) (1937–) Am. actor (*2001: A Space Odyssey*; *Splendor in the Grass*)

Lockwood, Margaret (Margaret Mary Day; a/k/a Margie Day) (1911–1990) Am. actress (*The Lady Vanishes*; *The Slipper and the Rose*)

Loder, John (John Lowe) (1898–) Eng. actor (*Now, Voyager*; *Gentleman Jim*)

Loder, Kurt (C) Am. rock critic (MTV's "This Week in Rock")/writer (*Bat Chain Puller*)

Lodge, Henry Cabot (1850–1924) Am. senator/diplomat/writer (*The Storm Has Many Eyes*)

Loeb, Richard (Richard A. Loeb) (1905–1931) Am. kidnapper/murderer (with Nathan Leopold)

Loeffler, Charles (Charles Martin Tornov Loeffler) (1861–1935) Am. violinist/composer (*Night in the Ukraine*)

Loesser, Frank (Frank Henry Loesser) (1910–1969) Am. songwriter (*Guys and Dolls*; P—1962—*How to Succeed in Business without Really Trying*)

Loew, Marcus (1870–1927) Am. film producer/founder of MGM Studios

Loewe, Frederick (1901–1988) Aus.-Am. composer (*My Fair Lady*; *Camelot*; with Alan Jay Lerner)

Lofgren, Nils ("Lefty") (1951–) Am. rock guitarist (with Bruce Springsteen and Neil Young)

Lofting, Hugh (1886–1947) Eng. children's book writer (created Dr. Dolittle)

Logan, Josh or Joshua (Joshua Lockwood Logan, Jr.) (1908–1988) Am. theatrical/film director/producer (*Annie Get Your Gun*; *Mister Roberts*; P—1950—*South Pacific*)

Loggia, Robert (1930–) Am. actor (*Prizzi's Honor*; *Jagged Edge*; *S.O.B.*)

Loggins, Dave (1947–) Am. pop singer/songwriter (cousin of Kenny; "Please Come to Boston")

Loggins, Kenny (Kenneth Clarke Loggins) (1947–) Am. rock singer/musician ("Footloose"; "I'm Alright"; formerly with Loggins & Messina ["Your Mama Don't Dance"]; G—1980)

Lollobrigida, Gina (Luigina Lollobrigida; a/k/a Diana Loris; "La Lollo") (1927–) Ital. actress (*Solomon and Sheba*; *The Lonely Woman*)

Lom, Herbert (Herbert Charles Angelo Kuchacewicz ze Schluderpacheru) (1917–) Cz. actor (*The Seventh Veil*; *War and Peace*)

Lombard, Carole (Jane Alice Peters; a/k/a Carol Lombard) (1908–1942) Am. actress (*Nothing Sacred*; *My Man Godfrey*; *Twentieth Century*)

Lombard, Karina (c. 1968–) Am. actress (*The Firm*; *Legends of the Fall*)

Lombardi, Vince (Vincent Thomas Lombardi) (1913–1970) Am. football coach/Hall-of-Famer

Lombardo, Guy (Gaetano Alberto Lombardo; "Sweetest Music This Side of Heaven"; "Mr. New Year's Eve") (1902–1977) Am. orchestra leader ("Tennessee Waltz"; "Harbor Lights")

Lonborg, Jim (James Reynold Lonborg;

"Gentleman Jim") (1943–) Am. baseball pitcher

London, Jack (John Griffith Chaney) (1876–1916) Am. novelist (*The Call of the Wild*; *White Fang*)

London, Julie (Julie Peck) (1926–) Am. actress ("Emergency!" TV series)

Long, Huey P. (Huey Pierce Long; "The Kingfish") (1893–1935) Am. gov. of Louisiana/politician (signature phrase: "Every man a king")

Long, Nia (1971–) Am. actress (*Made in America*; "The Guiding Light" soap opera)

Long, Shelley (1949–) Am. actress ("Cheers" TV series; *Night Shift*; *Outrageous Fortune*; E–1982/83)

Longden, Johnny (John Eric Longden) (1907–) Eng.-Am. jockey

Longet, Claudine (Claudine Georgette Longet) (1942–) Fr. actress (*The Party*)

Longfellow, Henry Wadsworth (1807–1882) Am. poet (*The Song of Hiawatha*; *Evangeline*; *The Courtship of Miles Standish*)

Longinus (1st century A.D.) Gr. critic (*On the Sublime*)

Longworth, Alice Roosevelt (Alice Lee Roosevelt; "Princess Alice"; "Washington's Other Monument"; "The Barbed Tongue") (1884–1980) Am. socialite/wit (daughter of Theodore Roosevelt)

Loos, Anita (1893–1981) Am. novelist/screenwriter (*Gentlemen Prefer Blondes*; *The Women*)

Lopat, Ed or **Eddie** (Edmund Walter Lopatynski; "Steady Eddie"; "The Junk Man") (1918–1992) Am. baseball pitcher

Lopez, Al (Alfonso Ramon Lopez) (1908–) Am. baseball Hall-of-Famer

Lopez, Nancy (Nancy Marie Lopez) (1957–) Am. golfer

Lopez, Trini (Trinidad Lopez III) (1937–) Am. singer/bandleader ("If I Had a Hammer")/actor (*The Dirty Dozen*)

Lopokova, Lydia (Lydia Vasilievna Lopokova) (1892–1981) Russ. ballerina

Lord, Jack (John Joseph Patrick Ryan) (1922–) Am. actor ("Hawaii Five-O" TV series)

Lord, Jon (1941–) Eng. rock keyboardist (with Deep Purple)

Lord, Marjorie (1922–) Am. actress (mother of Anne Archer; "The Danny Thomas Show" and "Make Room for Daddy" TV series)

Lords, Traci (Nora Louise Kuzma) (1968–) Am. actress (former porn star; *Cry-Baby*; *Not of This Earth* [1988])

Loren, Sophia (Sofia Villani Scicoloni; a/k/a Sofia Lazzaro) (1934–) Ital. actress (*The Millionairess*; *Marriage Italian Style*; O—1961—*Two Women*)

Lorenz, Konrad (Konrad Zacharias Lorenz) (1903–1989) Aus. ethologist/writer (*On Aggression*; N—1973)

Lorimer, George (George Horace Lorimer) (1867–1937) Am. magazine editor (*Saturday Evening Post*)

Loring, Gloria (Gloria Jean Goff) (1946–) Am. pop singer ("Friends and Lovers")/actress ("Days of Our Lives" soap opera)

Lorne, Marion (Marion Lorne MacDougal) (1888–1968) Am. actress ("Mr. Peepers" and "Bewitched" TV series; E–1967/68)

Lorrain, Claud (Claude Gellée; "Le Lorrain") (1600–1682) Fr. landscape painter

Lorre, Peter (Laszlo Loewenstein) (1904–1964) Am. actor (*The Maltese Falcon*; *M*; *Casablanca*)

Losey, Joseph (Joseph Walton Losey III; a/k/a Victor Hanbury, Joseph Walton, and Andrea Forzano) (1909–1984) Am. film director (*The Servant*; *The Go-Between*)

Lothrop, Harriet (Harriett Mulford Lothrop née Stone; a/k/a Margaret Sidney) (1844–1924) Am. children's book writer (*Five Little Peppers and How They Grew*)

Lott, Ronnie (Ronald Mandel Lott) (1959–) Am. football player

Loudon, Dorothy (1933–) Am. actress/singer (*Annie* on stage; T—1977)

Louganis, Greg (Gregory Efthimios Louganis) (1960–) Am. diver

Louis I (778–840) Fr. king 814–840

Louis II ("Louis the Stammerer") (846–879) Fr. king 877–879

Louis III (863–882) Fr. king 879–882 (with his brother, Carloman)

Louis IV ("Louis from Beyond the Sea") (921–954) Fr. king 936–954

Louis V ("Louis the Sluggard") (967–987) Fr. king 986–987

Louis VI ("Louis the Fat") (1081–1137) Fr. king 1108–1137

Louis VII ("Louis the Young") (c. 1120–1180) Fr. king 1137–1180

Louis VIII ("Louis le Lion" or "Coeur de Lion") (1187–1226) Fr. king 1223–1226

Louis IX ("Saint Louis") (1214–1270) Fr. king 1226–1270
Louis X ("Louis the Stubborn") (1289–1316) Fr. king 1314–1316 (king of Navarre 1305–1316)
Louis XI (1423–1483) Fr. king 1461–1483
Louis XII (1462–1515) Fr. king 1498–1515
Louis XIII (1601–1643) Fr. king 1610–1643
Louis XIV ("The Sun King"; "Louis the Great") (1638–1715) Fr. king 1643–1715
Louis XV ("Louis the Well-Beloved") (1710–1774) Fr. king 1715–1774
Louis XVI (1754–1793) Fr. king 1774–1792
Louis XVII (Louis-Charles) (1785–1795) titular Fr. king 1793–1795
Louis XVIII (Louis-Xavier-Stanislas) (1755–1824) Fr. king 1814–1824
Louis Phillippe ("The Citizen King") (1830–1848) Fr. king 1830–1848
Louis, Joe (Joseph Louis Barrow; "The Brown Bomber"; "Alabam' Assassin"; "Black Beauty"; "The Brown Bludgeon"; "The Brown Behemoth"; "The Brown Embalmer"; "Dark Destroyer") (1914–1981) Am. boxer
Louis-Dreyfuss, Julia (1961–) Am. actress (Elaine on "Seinfeld" TV series)
Louise, Anita (Anita Louise Fremault) (1915–1970) Am. actress (The Story of Louis Pasteur; "My Friend Flicka" TV series)
Louise, Tina (Tina Blacker) (1934–) Am. actress (Ginger on "Gilligan's Island" TV series)
Love, Bessie (Juanita Horton) (1898–1986) Am. actress (Sunday, Bloody Sunday; The Broadway Melody)
Love, Courtney (c. 1966–) Am. rock singer (with Hole)
Love, Darlene (Darlene Wright) (1938–) Am. pop singer (with The Crystals; "He's a Rebel")
Love, Mike (1941–) Am. pop musician/singer (with The Beach Boys)
Lovecraft, H. P. (Howard Phillips Lovecraft) (1890–1937) Am. short story writer (The Shadow Over Innsmouth)
Lovelace, Ada (1815–1852) Eng. mathematician (Lord Byron's daughter)
Lovelace, Linda (Linda Boreman Marciano) (1950–) Am. actress in porn films (Deep Throat)
Loveless, Patty (Patricia Ramey) (1957–) Am. country singer ("Blame It on Your Heart")
Lovelock, James (James Ephraim Love-lock) (1919–) Eng. scientist/theorist (The Ages of Gaia)
Lovett, Lyle (1957–) Am. country singer/musician/actor (The Player; Short Cuts)
Lovitz, Jon (1957–) Am. comedian ("Saturday Night Live" TV series; signature phrase: "That's the ticket!")
Lowe, Chad (1968–) Am. actor (brother of Rob; "Life Goes On" TV series)
Lowe, Chris (1959–) Eng. rock keyboardist (with Pet Shop Boys; "West End Girls")
Lowe, Edmund (Edmund Dante Lowe) (1890–1971) Am. actor (What Price Glory?; In Old Arizona)
Lowe, Nick (1949–) Eng. rock singer/musician ("Cruel to Be Kind"; formerly with Rockpile)
Lowe, Rob (Robert Hepler Lowe) (1963–) Am. actor (About Last Night . . .; The Outsiders; Wayne's World)
Lowell, Amy Lawrence (1874–1925) Am. poet (Patterns; Lilacs; P—1926—What's O'Clock)
Lowell, James Russell (1819–1891) Am. diplomat/poet (Vision of Sir Launfal)
Lowell, Robert (Robert Traill Spence Lowell, Jr.) (1917–1977) Am. poet (P—1947—Lord Weary's Castle)
Lowry, Malcolm (Clarence Malcolm Lowry) (1909–1957) Eng.-Am. novelist (Under the Volcano)
Lowry, Michael (1939–) Am. gov. of Washington
Loy, Myrna (Myrna Williams) (1905–1993) Am. actress (Thin Man films [as Nora Charles]; The Best Years of Our Lives)
Lubin, Arthur (1901–) Am. film director (Buck Privates; The Phantom of the Opera)
Lubitsch, Ernst (1892–1947) Am. film director (Ninotchka; Heaven Can Wait)
Lucas, George (George Walton Lucas, Jr.) (1944–) Am. film director (Star Wars; American Grafitti; Raiders of the Lost Ark)
Lucci, Susan (1949–) Am. actress (Erica Kane on "All My Children" soap opera)
Luce, Clare Booth (Anne Clare Booth) (1903–1987) Am. journalist/playwright (The Women)/politician/ambassador
Luce, Henry R. (Henry Robinson Luce) (1898–1967) Am. magazine editor/publisher (Time, Fortune, Life, Sports Illustrated)
Lucian (c. 120–after 180) Gr. satirist

Luciano, Lucky (a/k/a Charles Luciano and Charles Ross; born Salvatore Lucania) (1896–1962) Am. mobster

Luckinbill, Laurence (Laurence George Luckinbill) (1934–) Am. actor (*The Boys in the Band*; "Secret Storm" soap opera)

Luckman, Sid (Sidney Luckman) (1916–) Am. football Hall-of-Famer

Ludden, Allen (Allen Ellsworth Ludden) (1919–) Am. game show host ("Password")

Ludlum, Robert (a/k/a Jonathan Ryder) (1927–) Am. suspense writer (*The Parsifal Mosaic*; *The Icarus Agenda*)

Ludwig, Christa (1928–) Aus. opera singer (mezzo-soprano)

Luft, Lorna (1952–) Am. singer/actress (daughter of Judy Garland; "Trapper John, M.D." TV series)

Lugosi, Bela (Bela Ferenc Lugosi Blasko; a/k/a Arisztid Olt) (1882–1956) Am. actor (*Dracula*; *The Wolf Man*)

Luhan, Mabel Dodge (née Ganson) (1879–1962) Am. memoirist/patroness of the arts

Lukács, Gyorgy (Gyorgy Szegedy Von Lukács) (1885–1971) Hung. Marxist philosopher/writer (*History and Class Consciousness*)

Lukas, Paul (Pal Lukács) (1887 or 1891–1971) Hung.-Am. actor (*The Lady Vanishes*; O—1943—*Watch on the Rhine*)

Lukather, Steve (1957–) Am. rock guitarist/songwriter (with Toto)

Luke, Keye (1904–1991) Chin.-Am. actor ("Kung Fu" TV series; *The Good Earth*)

Lully, Jean-Baptiste (Giovanni Battista Lulli) (1632–1687) Fr. operatic composer (*Alceste*)

Lulu (Marie McDonald McLaughlin Lawrie) (1948–) Scot. singer/actress (*To Sir with Love*)

Lulu Belle (Myrtle Eleanor Cooper) (1913–) Am. country singer

Lumet, Sidney (1924–) Am. film director (*Dog Day Afternoon*; *Serpico*; *Network*)

Lumière, Louis (1864–1948) Fr. film pioneer (made the first moving picture)

Luna, Barbara (1937–) Am. actress (*The Devil at Four O'Clock*; *Ship of Fools*)

Lunceford, Jimmie (James Melvin Lunceford) (1902–1947) Am. jazz bandleader/saxophonist

Lunch, Lydia (1959–) Am. "no wave" singer (with Teenage Jesus and the Jerks)

Lunden, Joan (Joan Blunden) (1951–) Am. TV host ("Good Morning, America")

Lundgren, Dolph (Hans Lundgren) (1959–) Swed.-Am. actor (*A View to a Kill*; *Universal Soldier*; *Rocky IV*)

Lunt, Alfred (1892–1977) Am. stage actor (*The Guardsman*; *Design for Living*; T—1955)

Lupino, Ida (1918–) Eng. actress (*High Sierra*; *The Adventures of Sherlock Holmes*)

LuPone, Patti (Patti Ann LuPone) (1949–) Am. actress ("Life Goes On" TV series)/stage actress/singer (*Evita* [title role])

Luria, Salvador (Salvador Edward Luria) (1912–) Am. biologist (N—1969)

Lurie, Alison (1926–) Am. novelist (*The War Between the Tates*; P—1985—*Foreign Affairs*)

Lustbader, Eric Van (1946–) Am. horror novelist (*The Miko*; *White Ninja*; *Sirens*)

Luther, Martin (1483–1546) Ger. religious reformer/founder of Lutheranism

Lutoslawski, Witold (1913–) Pol. composer ("Little Suite")

Luxemburg, Rosa ("Red Rosa") (1870–1919) Pol.-Ger. socialist/insurrectionist

Luzinski, Greg (Gregory Michael Luzinski; "The Bull") (1950–) Am. baseball player

Lyle, Sparky (Albert Walter Lyle) (1944–) Am. baseball pitcher

Lyman, Arthur (1934–) Am. musician ("Yellow Bird")

Lyman, Dorothy (1947–) Am. actress ("Mama's Family" TV series; "All My Children" soap opera)

Lyman, Link (William Roy Lyman) (1898–1972) Am. football Hall-of-Famer

Lymon, Frankie (1942–1968) Am. pop singer ("Why Do Fools Fall in Love"; with Frankie Lymon & The Teenagers)

Lyn, Dawn (1963–) Am. child actress ("My Three Sons" TV series)

Lynch, David (David K. Lynch) (1946–) Am. film director (*Blue Velvet*; *The Elephant Man*; *Wild at Heart*)

Lynch, Jennifer (c. 1968–) Am. screenwriter/film director (daughter of David; *Boxing Helena*)

Lynch, Kelly (1959–) Am. actress (*Drugstore Cowboy*; *Three of Hearts*; *Cocktail*)

Lynde, Paul (Paul Edward Lynde) (1926–1982) Am. comedian ("The Paul Lynde Show" TV series)/game show panelist ("Hollywood Squares")

Lyndon, Barré (Alfred Edgar Lyndon) (1896–1972) Eng. playwright/ screenwriter (*The Amazing Dr. Clitterhous*; *The Lodger*)

Lyne, Adrian (1941–) Eng. film director (*Fatal Attraction*; *Flashdance*; *Indecent Proposal*)

Lynley, Carol (Carolyn Lee Jones) (1942–) Am. actress (TV's "Harlow"; *The Poseidon Adventure*)

Lynn, Cheryl (1957–) Am. soul singer ("Got to Be Real")

Lynn, Diana (Dolores Loehr) (1926–1971) Am. actress (*The Miracle of Morgan's Creek*; *My Friend Irma*)

Lynn, Fred (Frederic Michael Lynn) (1952–) Am. baseball player

Lynn, Janet (Janet Lynn Nowicki) (1953–) Am. figure skater

Lynn, Loretta (Loretta Webb; "Coal Miner's Daughter") (1932–) Am. country singer (sister of Crystal Gayle; "Stand by Your Man")

Lynn, Dame Vera (1917–) Eng. singer (popular during WWII)

Lynne, Jeff (1947–) Eng. rock guitarist/ songwriter (with The Electric Light Orchestra; "Don't Bring Me Down")

Lynne, Shelby (Shelby Moorer) (1968–) Am. country singer ("I'll Lie Myself to Sleep"; "Feelin' Kind of Lonely Tonight")

Lynott, Phil (1950–1986) Ir. rock singer (with Thin Lizzy; "The Boys Are Back in Town")

Lyon, Ben (1901–1979) Am. actor (*Hell's Angels*; *Indiscreet*)

Lyon, Sue (1946–) Am. actress (*Lolita* [title role])

Lysander (died 395 B.C.) Spart. mil. leader

Lysias (c. 445–after 380 B.C.) Ath. orator

Lysippus (4th century B.C.) Gr. sculptor

Ma, Yo-Yo (1955–) Fr.-Chin.-Am. cellist

Mabley, Moms (Loretta Mary Aitken) (1894–1975) Am. comedienne/singer ("Abraham, Martin and John")

MacArthur, Charles (Charles Gordon MacArthur) (1895–1956) Am. playwright (father of James; *Twentieth Century*; *The Front Page*)

MacArthur, Douglas (1880–1964) Am. army general/chief of staff

MacArthur, James (1937–) Am. actor (son of Helen Hayes and Charles MacArthur; "Hawaii Five-O" TV series; *The Swiss Family Robinson*)

Macaulay, Thomas Babington (1800–

1859) Eng. historian (*History of England*)

Macchio, Ralph (Ralph George Macchio, Jr.) (1962–) Am. actor (*The Karate Kid*; *My Cousin Vinny*)

MacCorkindale, Simon (1952–) Eng. actor (*Death on the Nile*)

MacDiarmid, Hugh (Christopher Murray Grieve) (1892–1978) Scot. poet/critic (*A Drunk Man Looks at the Thistle*)

MacDonald, Jeanette (Jeanette Anna MacDonald; "The Iron Butterfly") (1901–1965) Am. actress (*Naughty Marietta*; *Rose Marie*)

MacDonald, John D. (John Dann MacDonald) (1916–1986) Am. suspense/ mystery writer (created Travis McGee)

MacDonald, Ross (Kenneth Millar; a/k/a John Ross MacDonald) (1915–1983) Am. detective story writer (created Lew Archer)

MacDowell, Andie (Rose Anderson MacDowell) (1958–) Am. actress/model (*sex, lies, and videotape*; *Green Card*; *Groundhog Day*)

Macenas, Gaius (c. 70–8 B.C.) Rom. statesman/patron of literature

MacGibbon, Harriet (c. 1905–1987) Am. actress ("The Beverly Hillbillies" TV series)

MacGraw, Ali (Alice MacGraw) (1938–) Am. actress (*Love Story*; *Goodbye Columbus*)

MacGregor, Mary (1948–) Am. pop singer ("Torn Between Two Lovers")

Mach, Ernst (1838–1916) Aus. physicist (created the Mach supersonic scale)/ philosopher/educator

Machiavelli, Niccolò (Niccolò di Bernardo dei Machiavelli) (1469–1527) Ital. statesman/philosopher (*The Prince*; *The Art of War*)

MacInnes, Colin (1914–1976) Eng. novelist/essayist (*Absolute Beginners*)

MacInnes, Helen (Helen Clark MacInnes) (1907–1985) Am. suspense writer (*The Salzburg Connection*)

Mack, Connie (Cornelius Alexander McGilicuddy; "The Tall Tactician"; "The Grand Old Man") (1862–1956) Am. baseball Hall-of-Famer

Mack, Connie III (1940–) Am. senator

Mack, Jillie (1960–) Eng. stage actress (*Cats*)

MacKenzie, Sir Alexander Campbell (1847–1935) Eng. violinist/composer ("The Rose of Sharon")

MacKenzie, Sir Compton (Edward Montague Compton MacKenzie) (1883–1972) Eng. literary critic/novelist (*Sinister Street*)

Mackie, Bob (Robert Gordon Mackie) (1940–) Am. fashion designer

MacLachlan, Kyle (1960–) Am. actor (*Blue Velvet*; "Twin Peaks" TV series; *The Doors*)

MacLaine, Shirley (Shirley MacLean Beaty) (1934–) Am. dancer/actress (sister of Warren Beatty; O—1983—*Terms of Endearment*; *The Trouble with Harry*)/writer (*Out on a Limb*)

MacLane, Barton (1900–1969) Am. actor ("I Dream of Jeannie" and "The Outlaws" TV series)

MacLean, Alistair (Alistair Stuart MacLean) (1922–1987) Scot. adventure novelist (*Ice Station Zebra*; *Breakheart Pass*; *Force Ten from Navarone*; *Where Eagles Dare*)

MacLeish, Archibald (1892–1982) Am. poet (P—1933—*Conquistador*; P—1953—*Collected Poems*; P—1959—*J.B.*)

MacLeod, Gavin (1931–) Am. actor ("The Love Boat" TV series)

MacMahon, Aline (Aline Laveen MacMahon) (1899–1991) Am. actress (*Golddiggers of 1933*; *Dragon Seed*)

MacMillan, Harold ("Mac the Knife") (1894–1987) Eng. prime minister 1957–1963

MacMurray, Fred (Frederick Martin MacMurray) (1908–1991) Am. actor ("My Three Sons" TV series; *Double Indemnity*; *The Caine Mutiny*)

MacNee, Patrick (1922–) Eng. actor ("The Avengers" TV series)

MacNeil, Robert (Robert Breckinridge Ware MacNeil) (1931–) Can. newscaster ("The MacNeil Lehrer Report")

MacPhail, Larry (Leland Stanford MacPhail, Sr.) (1890–1975) Am. baseball Hall-of-Famer

MacRae, Gordon (1921–1986) Am. singer/actor (*Oklahoma!*; *Carousel*; father of Meredith)

MacRae, Meredith (1945–) Am. actress (daughter of Gordon; "Petticoat Junction" TV series)

MacRae, Sheila (Sheila Margo Stephens) (1923–) Am. entertainer/singer ("The Jackie Gleason Show" TV series)

Macy, Bill (William Macy Garber) (1922–) Am. actor ("Maude" TV series)

Madden, John (John Earl Madden) (1936–) Am. sportscaster

Maddox, Garry (Garry Lee Maddox; "The Windshield Wiper") (1949–) Am. baseball player

Maddox, Lester (Lester Garfield Maddox) (1915–) Am. gov. of Georgia/segregationist

Madero, Francisco (Francisco Indalécio Madero) (1873–1913) Mex. revolutionist/pres. 1911–1913

Madigan, Amy (1957–) Am. actress (*Twice in a Lifetime*; *Field of Dreams*)

Madison, Dolley (Dorothea Payne Todd) (1768–1849) Am. first lady (James)

Madison, James ("The Father of the Constitution"; "The Sage of Montpelier"; "Jeremy") (1751–1836) 4th Am. pres. (1809–1817)

Madlock, Bill (William Madlock, Jr.; "Mad Dog") (1951–) Am. baseball player

Madonna (Madonna Louise Veronica Ciccone) (1958–) Am. pop singer ("Like a Virgin"; "Material Girl"; "Like a Prayer")/actress (*Body of Evidence*; *A League of Their Own*; *Desperately Seeking Susan*)

Madsen, Virginia (1963–) Am. actress (*The Hot Spot*; *Slam Dance*; *Candy Man*)

Maes, Nicolaes (a/k/a Nicolas Maas) (1634–1693) Dutch painter (studied under Rembrandt)

Maeterlinck, Maurice (Maurice-Polydore-Marie-Bernard Maeterlinck) (1862–1949) Belg. poet/playwright/essayist (*The Blue Bird*; N—1911)

Magellan, Ferdinand (Fernão de Magalhães) (c. 1480–1521) Port. explorer (first to commission a fleet to sail around the world)

Maginot, André (André-Louis-René Maginot) (1877–1932) Fr. govt. official (war minister)

Magnani, Anna (1908–1973) Ital. actress (*Open City*; O—1955—*The Rose Tattoo*)

Magnus (Magnus II Eriksson) (1316–1374) king of Norway (1319–1355) and Sweden (1319–1363)

Magnuson, Ann (C) Am. performance artist/actress

Magritte, René (René-François-Ghislain Magritte) (1898–1967) Belg. surrealist painter (*Pandora's Box*)

Magruder, Jeb (Jeb Stuart Magruder) (1934–) Am. politician/Watergate participant

Mahal, Taj (Henry St. Clair Fredericks) (1942–) Am. blues/rock musician/singer

Maharis, George (1928–) Am. actor ("Route 66" TV series; *Exodus*)

Mahavira (Vardhamana) (c. 599–527 B.C.) Ind. ascetic/founder of Jainism

Mahfouz, Naguib (1911–) Egypt. writer (*Cairo Trilogy*; N—1988)

Mahler, Gustav (1860–1911) Aus. composer (*Das Klagende Lied*)

Mahoney, Jock (Jacques O'Mahoney) (1919–) Am. actor ("Yancy Derringer" TV series; *Tarzan the Magnificent* [title role])

Mahoney, John (1940–) Eng.-Am. actor (*Moonstruck*; *Say Anything . . .*; *Barton Fink*)

Mailer, Norman (Norman Kingsley Mailer) (1923–) Am. journalist/writer (*The Naked and the Dead*; P—1969—*The Armies of the Night*; P—1980—*The Executioner's Song*)

Maillol, Aristide (1861–1944) Fr. sculptor (*The Mediterranean*)

Main, Marjorie (Mary Tomlinson Krebs) (1890–1975) Am. actress (played Ma Kettle in film; *Dead End*)

Mainbocher (Main Rousseau Bocher) (1890–1976) Am. fashion designer

Major, John (1943–) Eng. prime minister 1990–

Majors, Lee (Harvey Lee Yeary II) (1939–) Am. actor ("The Six Million Dollar Man" and "The Fall Guy" TV series)

Makarova, Natalia (Natalia Romanova Makarova; "Giraffe") (1940–) Russ.-Am. ballerina/actress (T—1983)

Makeba, Miriam (Zensi Miriam Makeba) (1932–) S. Afr. folk singer ("Pata Pata")

Mako, Gene (1916–) Am. tennis player

Malamud, Bernard (1914–1986) Am. novelist/short story writer (*The Natural*; P—1967—*The Fixer*)

Malandro, Kristina (c. 1963–) Am. actress ("General Hospital" soap opera)

Malcolm X (Malcolm Little) (1925–1965) Am. civil rights activist/leader of the Nation of Islam

Malden, Karl (Mladen Sekulovich) (1913–) Am. actor ("The Streets of San Francisco" TV series; *On the Waterfront*; O—1951—*A Streetcar Named Desire*)

Malebranche, Nicolas de (1638–1715) Fr. philosopher/scientist/theologian (disciple of Descartes)

Maleska, Eugene T. (c. 1916–1993) Am. crossword puzzle editor (*New York Times*)

Malibran, Maria (Maria Felicita Malibran; born Maria Felicita Garcia) (1808–1836) Span. opera singer (contralto)

Malick, Terence (1943–) Am. screenwriter/film director (*Badlands*; *Days of Heaven*)

Malipiero, Gian Francesco (1882–1973) Ital. composer (*L'Orfeide*)

Malkovich, John (1953–) Am. actor (*Dangerous Liaisons*; *Of Mice and Men*; *Places in the Heart*; *In the Line of Fire*)

Mallarmé, Stephane (1842–1898) Fr. poet (*The Afternoon of a Faun*)

Malle, Louis (1932–) Fr. film director (*My Dinner with Andre*; *Au Revoir les Enfants*; *Damage*)

Malone, Dorothy (Dorothy Eloise Maloney) (1925–) Am. actress (O—1956—*Written on the Wind*; "Peyton Place" TV series)

Malone, Karl ("The Mailman") (1963–) Am. basketball player

Malone, Moses (Moses Eugene Malone) (1955–) Am. basketball player

Malory, Sir Thomas (fl. c. 1470) Eng. writer (*Le Morte d'Arthur*)

Malraux, André (André-Georges Malraux) (1901–1976) Fr. novelist/critic (*Man's Fate*; *Man's Hope*)

Maltbie, Roger (1951–) Am. golfer

Maltin, Leonard (1950–) Am. film critic/writer

Malzberg, Barry N. (Barry Nathaniel Malzberg) (1939–) Am. science fiction writer (*Galaxies*; *The Spread*)

Mamet, David (David Alan Mamet) (1947–) Am. playwright/screenwriter (*The Postman Always Rings Twice*; *American Buffalo*; P—1984—*Glengarry Glen Ross*)

Mamoulian, Rouben (1897–1987) Arm.-Am. film director (*Queen Christina*; *Dr. Jekyll and Mr. Hyde*)

Manchester, Melissa (Melissa Toni Manchester) (1951–) Am. pop singer ("Midnight Blue"; "Don't Cry Out Loud"; G—1982)

Manchester, William (William Raymond Manchester) (1922–) Am. historian/writer (*The Death of a President*)

Mancini, Henry (Enrico Nicola Mancini) (1924–) Am. orchestra leader ("Moon River"; "Days of Wine and Roses")/composer ("The Pink Panther Theme")

Mandel, Howie (1955–) Can. comedian/ actor ("St. Elsewhere" TV series)
Mandel, Johnny (John Alfred Mandel) (1935–) Am. jazz trumpeter and trombonist/conductor
Mandela, Nelson (Nelson Rolihlahia Mandela) (1918–) S. Afr. lawyer/ politician/civil rights leader (organized the African National Congress)
Mandela, Winnie (Nkosikazi Nobandle Nomzano Madikizela) (1936–) S. Afr. civil rights activist
Mandelstam, Osip (Osip Emilyevich Mandelstam) (1891–1938) Russ. poet (*Stone; Tristia*)
Mandlikova, Hana (1963–) Cz. tennis player
Mandrell, Barbara (Barbara Ann Mandrell) (1948–) Am. country singer/ entertainer ("I Was Country When Country Wasn't Cool"; "Sleeping Single in a Double Bed"; with The Mandrell Sisters)
Mandrell, Irlene (1957–) Am. country singer (with The Mandrell Sisters)
Mandrell, Louise (Thelma Louise Mandrell) (1954–) Am. country singer (with The Mandrell Sisters)
Mandylor, Costas (c. 1965–) Am. actor (*Mobsters*)
Manet, Édouard (1832–1883) Fr. painter (a forerunner of impressionism; *Spanish Singer*)
Mangano, Silvana (1930–1989) Ital. actress (*Death in Venice; Bitter Rice*)
Mangione, Chuck (Charles Frank Mangione) (1940–) Am. jazz/pop trumpeter ("Feels So Good")
Mani (a/k/a Manes or Manichaeus) (216–276) Pers. religious leader/founder of Manichaean religion
Manilow, Barry (Barry Alan Pincus) (1946–) Am. pop singer/musician/ songwriter ("Mandy"; "I Write the Songs"; "Copacabana"; G—1978)
Mankiewicz, Herman (Herman Jacob Mankiewicz) (1897–1953) Am. screenwriter (brother of Joseph; *Citizen Kane*)
Mankiewicz, Joseph L. (Joseph Leo Mankiewicz) (1909–1993) Am. film director (O—1949—*A Letter to Three Wives*; O—1950—*All About Eve*)
Manley, Dexter (1959–) Am. football player
Mann, Aimee (C) Am. pop singer (with 'Til Tuesday; "Voices Carry")

Mann, Barry (1939–) Am. pop songwriter ("I Love How You Love Me"; "You've Lost That Lovin' Feeling")
Mann, Delbert (1920–) Am. film director (*That Touch of Mink*; O—1955—*Marty*)
Mann, Heinrich (Heinrich Ludwig Mann) (1871–1950) Ger.-Am. novelist (brother of Thomas; *Small Town Tyrant* [filmed as *The Blue Angel*])
Mann, Herbie (Herbert Jay Solomon) (1930–) Am. jazz flutist ("Hijack")
Mann, Horace (1796–1859) Am. educator/ politician
Mann, Manfred (Michael Lubowitz) (1940–) Eng. rock singer/musician ("Do Wah Diddy Diddy"; "Blinded by the Light"; with Manfred Mann's Earth Band)
Mann, Michael (1943–) Am. TV/film writer/producer/director ("Miami Vice" TV series; *Manhunter; Last of the Mohicans*)
Mann, Thomas (1875–1955) Am. novelist/ essayist (brother of Heinrich; *Death in Venice; The Magic Mountain*; N—1929)
Manne, Shelly (Sheldon Manne) (1920–1984) Am. jazz drummer
Manning, Adelaide (Adelaide Frances Oke Manning) (1891–1959) Eng. mystery writer
Manning, Archie (Elisha Archie Manning III) (1949–) Am. football player
Mannucci, Aldo (Teobaldo Mannucci) (1449–1515) Ital. printer (invented italic type)
Manoff, Dinah (1958–) Am. actress (daughter of Lee Grant; "Soap" and "Empty Nest" TV series)
Manolete (Manuel Laureano Rodríguez y Sánchez) (1917–1947) Span. bullfighter
Man Ray (Emmanuel Rudnitsky) (1890–1976) Am. photographer/founder of Dada
Mansfield, Jayne (Vera Jane Palmer) (1932–1967) Am. actress (mother of Mariska Hargitay; *Will Success Spoil Rock Hunter?*)
Mansfield, Katherine (Katherine Mansfield Beauchamp) (1888–1923) Eng. short story writer (*The Garden Party*)
Manson, Charles (Charles Milles Manson) (1934–) Am. murderer (leader of Manson "family" which killed Sharon Tate, among others)
Mantegna, Andrea (1431–1506) Ital. engraver/painter (*St. George*)
Mantegna, Joe (1947–) Am. actor (*The*

Godfather, Part III; *Suspect*; *House of Games*; *Searching for Bobby Fischer*)
Mantle, Mickey (Mickey Charles Mantle; "The Commerce Comet"; "The Mick") (1931–) Am. baseball Hall-of-Famer
Mantooth, Randolph (1945–) Am. actor ("Emergency!" TV series; "Loving" soap opera)
Mantovani (Annunzio Paolo Mantovani) (1905–1980) Eng.-Ital. orchestra leader ("Misty"; "Greensleeves")
Manush, Heinie (Henry Emmett Manush) (1901–1971) Am. baseball Hall-of-Famer
Manzarek, Ray (1935–) Am. rock musician (with The Doors)
Mao Tse-Tung (1893–1976) Chin. soldier/chairman 1949–1959
Maples, Marla (1963–) Am. model/actress (*Will Rogers' Follies*; Donald Trump's wife)
Mapplethorpe, Robert (1946–1989) Am. photographer
Maranville, Rabbit (Walter James Vincent Maranville) (1891–1954) Am. baseball Hall-of-Famer
Marat, Jean-Paul (1743–1793) Fr. physician/radical politician
Maravich, Pete (Peter Maravich; "Pistol Pete") (1948–1988) Am. basketball player
Marble, Alice (1913–1991) Am. tennis player (W—1939)
Marceau, Marcel (Marceau Mangel) (1923–) Fr. mime
March, Fredric (Ernest Frederick McIntyre Bickel) (1897–1975) Am. actor (*A Star Is Born*; *The Iceman Cometh*; O—1931/32—*Dr. Jekyll and Mr. Hyde*; O—1946—*The Best Years of Our Lives*; T—1947, 1957)
March, Hal (Harold Mendelson) (1920–1970) Am. actor/game show host ("The $64,000 Question")
Marchetti, Gino (1927–) Am. football Hall-of-Famer
Marciano, Rocky (Rocco Francis Marchegiano; "The Brockton Blockbuster"; "Brockton Bull"; "Brockton Bomber"; "Brockton Buster") (1923–1969) Am. boxer
Marconi, Guglielmo (1874–1937) Ital. physicist/inventor (wireless telegraph; VHF electromagnetic waves; N—1909)
Marcos, Ferdinand (Ferdinand Edralin Marcos) (1917–1989) Phil. pres. 1965–1986

Marcos, Imelda (Imelda Romualdez Marcos; "The Iron Butterfly") (1931–) Phil. political leader
Marcovicci, Andrea (1948–) Am. actress/singer
Marcy, William (William Learned Marcy) (1786–1857) Am. senator/Supreme Court jurist (1829–1831)/gov. of New York/govt. official (secretary of war, secretary of state)
Marden, Brice (1938–) Am. abstract painter
Margaret (Margaret Rose) (1930–) Eng. princess
Margo (Maria Marguerita Guadelupe Teresa Estela Boldao y Castilla) (1918–1985) Mex.-Am. dancer/actress (*Viva Zapata!*; *Lost Horizon*)
Margolin, Janet (1943–1994) Am. actress (*The Greatest Story Ever Told*; *David and Lisa*)
Margolin, Stuart (1940–) Am. actor ("The Rockford Files" and "Bret Maverick" TV series; E—1978/79, 1979/80)
Marichal, Juan (Juan Antonio Sanchez Marichal; "Manito"; "The Dominican Dandy") (1937–) Dom.-Am. baseball Hall-of-Famer
Marie (Marie Alexandra Victoria) (1875–1938) Rom. queen 1914–1917
Marie, Teena (Mary Christine Brockert; "Lady T") (1957–) Am. pop singer ("Lovergirl")
Marin, Cheech (Richard Marin) (1946–) Am. comedian (with Tommy Chong; *Born in East L.A.*)
Marin, John (1870–1953) Am. painter (*Lower Manhattan*)
Marinaro, Ed (1951–) Am. actor ("Hill Street Blues" and "Sisters" TV series)
Marino, Dan (Daniel Constantine Marino, Jr.) (1961–) Am. football player
Marion, Francis ("The Swamp Fox") (c. 1732–1795) Am. revolutionary commander/politician
Marion, Marty (Martin Whitford Marion; "Slats"; "Mr. Shortstop"; "The Octopus") (1917–) Am. baseball player/manager
Maris, Roger (Roger Eugene Maras) (1934–1985) Am. baseball player
Marisol (Marisol Escobar) (1930–) Venez.-Am. sculptor
Maritain, Jacques (1882–1973) Fr. philosopher/writer (*The Degrees of Knowledge*)

Marius (Gaius Marius) (c. 157–86 B.C.) Roman general

Markert, Russell (1899–1991) Am. choreographer (for The Rockettes)

Markey, Enid (Enid Virginia Markey) (1890–1981) Am. actress (first screen Jane to Elmo Lincoln's Tarzan)

Markey, Gene (1895–1980) Am. screenwriter (*On the Avenue*; *Baby Face*)

Markham, Beryl (1902–1986) Eng. aviatrix/autobiographer (*West with the Night*)

Markham, Monte (1935–) Am. actor ("The New Perry Mason" and "Baywatch" TV series)

Markham, Pigmeat (Dewey Markham) (1906–1981) Am. comedian ("Rowan & Martin's Laugh-In" TV series)

Markova, Dame Alicia (Lillian Alicia Marks) (1910–) Eng. ballerina (with Ballet Russe)

Marky Mark (Mark Robert Wahlberg) (1971–) Am. rapper (with Marky Mark and The Funky Bunch; "Good Vibrations")

Marley, Bob (Robert Nesta Marley) (1945–1981) Jam. reggae singer ("Roots, Rock, Reggae"; with The Wailers)/songwriter ("I Shot the Sheriff")

Marley, Ziggy (David Marley) (1968–) Jam. reggae singer/guitarist (son of Bob; "Tomorrow People")

Marlowe, Christopher (1564–1593) Eng. poet/playwright (*Dr. Faustus*)

Marquand, John P. (John Phillips Marquand) (1893–1960) Am. novelist (created Mr. Moto; P—1938—*The Late George Apley*)

Marquand, Richard (1938–1987) Eng. film director (*Jagged Edge*; *Eye of the Needle*)

Marquard, Rube (Richard William Marquard; "$11,000 Lemon"; $11,000 Wonder") (1889–1980) Am. baseball Hall-of-Famer

Marquis, Don (Donald Robert Perry Marquis) (1878–1937) Am. humorist/columnist/writer (*The Old Soak*)

Marriot, Steve (1947–1991) Eng. rock guitarist (with Humble Pie and Small Faces)

Marryat, Captain Frederick (1792–1848) Eng. mil. leader/novelist (*Mr. Midshipman Easy*)

Mars, Mick (Bob Deak) (1955–) Am. rock guitarist (with Mötley Crüe)

Marsalis, Branford (1960–) Am. jazz sax

ophonist (brother of Wynton; on "The Tonight Show")

Marsalis, Wynton (1961–) Am. classical trumpeter

Marsden, Gerry (1942–) Eng. rock singer/musician (with Gerry & The Pacemakers)

Marsh, Jean (Jean Lyndsey Tarren Marsh) (1934–) Eng. writer/actress (*Upstairs, Downstairs*; E—1974/75)

Marsh, Mae (Mary Warne Marsh; "The Goldwyn Girl") (1895–1968) Am. actress (*Intolerance*; *The Birth of a Nation*)

Marsh, Dame Ngaio (Edith Ngaio Marsh) (1889–1982) N.Z. mystery writer (created Detective Inspector Roderick Alleyn; *Artists in Crime*; *A Man Lay Dead*)

Marshall, E. G. (Edda Gunnar Marshall) (1910–) Am. actor ("The Defenders" and "The Bold Ones" TV series; E—1961/62, 1962/63)

Marshall, Garry (Garry Kent Marshall) (1934–) Am. TV/film actor/director/writer (brother of Penny; *Beaches*; *Pretty Woman*; *Frankie & Johnny*)

Marshall, George (George Catlett Marshall) (1880–1959) Am. general/govt. official (secretary of defense) (developed the Marshall Plan; N—1953)

Marshall, Herbert (Herbert Brough Falcon Marshall) (1890–1966) Eng.-Am. actor (*Foreign Correspondent*; *Blonde Venus*)

Marshall, John (1755–1835) Am. Supreme Court chief justice (1801–1835)

Marshall, Penny (Carole Penny Marshall) (1942–) Am. actress ("Laverne & Shirley" TV series)/film director (*Awakenings*; *A League of Their Own*)

Marshall, Peter (Ralph Pierre La Cock, Sr.) (1927–) Am. game show host (brother of Joanne Dru; "Hollywood Squares")

Marshall, Thomas R. (Thomas Riley Marshall) (1854–1925) Am. v.p. (W. Wilson)/gov. of Indiana (signature phrase: "What this country really needs is a good five-cent cigar")

Marshall, Thurgood (1908–1993) Am. Supreme Court jurist (1967–1991; first Afr.-Am. member of the Supreme Court)

Marshall, Tully (William Phillips) (1864–1943) Am. actor (*Oliver Twist*; *The Hunchback of Notre Dame*)

Martí, José (José Julián Martí y Pérez) (1853–1895) Cub. poet (*Ismaelillo*)/liberator of Cuba

Martial (Marcus Valerius Martialis) (40–c.

103) Roman poet (*Xenia and Apophoreta*)

Martika (Martika Merrero) (1969–) Am. pop singer ("Toy Soldiers")

Martin, Billy (Alfred Manuel Pesano; "Billy the Kid"; "Casey's Little Bobo"; "The Great Agitator") (1928–1989) Am. baseball player/manager

Martin, Dean (Dino Paul Crocetti) (1917–) Am. singer ("Memories Are Made of This"; "Everybody Loves Somebody")/ actor (*Rio Bravo*; *Some Came Running*)

Martin, Dick (Thomas Richart Martin) (1922–) Am. comedian ("Rowan & Martin's Laugh-In" TV series)

Martin, Don (1931–) Am. cartoonist (*Mad* magazine)

Martin, Frank (1890–1974) Swi. composer (*Der Sturm*)

Martin, Harvey (Harvey Banks Martin) (1950–) Am. football player

Martin, Jared (1943–) Am. actor ("Dallas" TV series)

Martin, Kiel (1944–1991) Am. actor ("Hill Street Blues" TV series)

Martin, Mary (Mary Virginia Martin) (1913–1990) Am. singer/actress (mother of Larry Hagman; played Peter Pan on stage and TV; *South Pacific*; T—1950, 1955, 1960)

Martin, Moon (c. 1950–) Am. pop singer ("Bad Case of Loving You")

Martin, Pamela Sue (1953–) Am. actress ("Dynasty" and "The Nancy Drew Mysteries" TV series)

Martin, Pepper (Johnny Leonard Roosevelt Martin; "The Wild Hoss of the Osage") (1904—1965) Am. baseball player

Martin, Ross (Martin Rosenblatt) (1920–1981) Am. actor ("The Wild, Wild West" TV series)

Martin, Steve (1945–) Am. comedian/ actor (*Roxanne*; *Parenthood*; *L.A. Story*)

Martin, Strother (1919–1980) Am. actor (*Cool Hand Luke*; *The Man Who Shot Liberty Valance*)

Martin, Tony (Alfred Norris, Jr.) (1912–) Am. singer ("There's No Tomorrow")

Martindale, Wink (Winston Conrad Martindale) (1933–) Am. game show host ("Tic Tac Dough")

Martinelli, Elsa (1932–) Ital. actress (*Hatari*; *The Indian Fighter*)

Martinez, A (Adolf Martinez III) (1948–) Am. actor ("Santa Barbara" soap opera and "L.A. Law" TV series)

Martino, Al (Alfred Cini) (1927–) Am.

singer ("Here in My Heart")/actor (*The Godfather*)

Martins, Peter (1946–) Dan. ballet dancer/ choreographer

Martinson, Harry (Harry Edmund Martinson) (1904–1978) Swed. novelist/ poet/playwright/essayist (*The Road*; N—1974)

Marvell, Andrew (1621–1678) Eng. poet (*To His Coy Mistress*)

Marvin, Lee (1924–1987) Am. actor (*Bad Day at Black Rock*; *The Caine Mutiny*; O—1965—*Cat Ballou*)

Marx, Chico (Leonard Marx) (1887–1961) Am. comedian (with The Marx Brothers; *Monkey Business*; *Duck Soup*)

Marx, Groucho (Julius Henry Marx) (1890–1977) Am. comedian (with The Marx Brothers; E—1950)

Marx, Gummo (Milton Marx) (1894–1977) Am. comedian (with The Marx Brothers)

Marx, Harpo (Adolph Arthur Marx; a/k/a Arthur Marx) (1888–1964) Am. comedian (with The Marx Brothers)

Marx, Karl (Karl Heinrich Marx) (1818–1883) Ger. philosopher/founder of communism (wrote *The Communist Manifesto* with Friedrich Engels)

Marx, Richard (1963–) Am. rock/pop singer/songwriter ("Don't Mean Nothing"; "Right Here Waiting")

Marx, Zeppo (Herbert Marx) (1901–1979) Am. comedian (with The Marx Brothers)

Mary I ("Bloody Mary"; Mary Tudor) (1516–1558) queen of England and Ireland 1553–1558

Mary II (1662–1694) queen of England, Scotland, and Ireland 1689–1694

Mary Magdalene (1st century A.D.) Galilean mother of Jesus

Masaccio (Tommaso di Giovanni di Simone Guidi) (1401–1428) Flor. painter (*Madonna and Child with St. Anne*)

Mascagni, Pietro (1863–1945) Ital. composer (*Cavalleria Rusticana*)

Masefield, John (John Edward Masefield) (1878–1967) Eng. poet/playwright/ novelist (*Salt Water Ballads*)

Masekela, Hugh (Hugh Ramapolo Masekela) (1939–) S. Afr. trumpeter/ bandleader ("Grazing in the Grass")

Maserati, Ernesto (1898–1975) Ital. automobile designer/manufacturer

Masina, Giulietta (Giulia Anna Masina) (1920–) Ital. actress (*La Strada*)

Mason, Daniel (Daniel Gregory Mason)

(1873–1953) Am. composer ("Chanticleer Overture")

Mason, Dave (1946–) Eng. rock guitarist/singer (with Traffic)

Mason, Jackie (Yacov Moshe Maza) (1931–) Am. comedian

Mason, James (James Neville Mason) (1909–1984) Eng. actor (*Twenty Thousand Leagues Under the Sea*; *North by Northwest*; *Lolita*; *Odd Man Out*)

Mason, Marsha (1942–) Am. actress (*The Goodbye Girl*; *Cinderella Liberty*; *Only When I Laugh*)

Massasoit (died 1661) Am. Wampanoag chief

Massen, Osa (1915–) Dan.-Am. actress (*Tokyo Rose*; *Deadline at Dawn*)

Massenet, Jules (Jules-Émile-Frédéric Massenet) (1842–1912) Fr. composer (*Le Cid*)

Massey, Ilona (Ilona Hajmassy) (1912–1974) Hung. actress (*Rosalie*; *Love Happy*)

Massey, Raymond (Raymond Hart Massey) (1896–1983) Can.-Am. actor ("Dr. Kildare" TV series; *Abe Lincoln in Illinois*)

Massine, Léonide (Leonid Fedorovich Miassin; "Painter of the Ballet") (1894 or 1896–1979) Russ.-Am. ballet dancer/choreographer (with Ballet Russe)

Massinger, Philip (1583–1640) Eng. playwright (*A New Way to Pay Old Debts*)

Masson, Paul (1859–1940) Am. vintner

Massys, Quentin (last name also spelled Matsys, Messys, Metsys) (c. 1466–1530) Flem. painter (*The Money Changer and His Wife*)

Masters, Edgar Lee (1869–1950) Am. novelist/poet (*Spoon River Anthology*; *Domesday Book*)

Masters, William (William Howell Masters) (1915–) Am. physician/educator (of Masters and [wife Virginia] Johnson; *Human Sexual Response*)

Masterson, Bat (William Barclay Masterson) (1853–1921) Am. frontier marshal (with Wyatt Earp)

Masterson, Mary Stuart (1966–) Am. actress (*Immediate Family*; *Fried Green Tomatoes*; *Benny & Joon*)

Mastroantonio, Mary Elizabeth (1958–) Am. actress (*The Abyss*; *The Color of Money*; *Consenting Adults*)

Mastroianni, Marcello (Marcello Mastroianni) (1924–) Ital. actor (*La Dolce Vita*; *8½*)

Mata Hari (Margaretha Geertruida MacLeod née Zelle) (1876–1917) Dutch dancer/courtesan/spy

Matalin, Mary (c. 1953–) Am. politician/talk show host ("Equal Time")

Maté, Rudy (Rudolph Maté; born Rudolf Matheh) (1899–1964) Aus.-Am. film director (*When Worlds Collide*; *Stella Dallas*)

Materna, Amalia (1844–1918) Aus. opera singer (soprano)

Mather, Cotton (1663–1728) Am. theologist/writer (*Magnalia Christi Americana*)

Mather, Increase (1639–1723) Am. clergyman/theologian (father of Cotton)

Mathers, Jerry (1948–) Am. actor ("Leave It To Beaver" [as Beaver Cleaver] TV series)

Matheson, Richard (Richard Burton Matheson) (1926–) Am. suspense/science fiction writer (*The Incredible Shrinking Man*)

Matheson, Tim (1947–) Am. actor (*Animal House*)

Mathews, Eddie (Edwin Lee Mathews, Jr.) (1931–) Am. baseball Hall-of-Famer

Mathewson, Christy (Christopher Mathewson; "Big Six"; "Matty"; "Husk"; "Matty the Great") (1878–1925) Am. baseball Hall-of-Famer

Mathias, Bob (Robert Bruce Mathias) (1930–) Am. decathlete/congressman

Mathis, Johnny (John Royce Mathis) (1935–) Am. pop singer ("Chances Are")

Mathis, Samantha (1970–) Am. actress (*Pump Up the Volume*; *Super Mario Bros.*)

Matisse, Henri (Henri-Emile-Benoit Matisse) (1869–1954) Fr. Fauvist painter (*Piano Lesson*)/sculptor/stage designer

Matlin, Marlee (1965–) Am. actress (O— 1986—*Children of a Lesser God*)

Matson, Ollie (1930–) Am. football Hall-of-Famer

Mattea, Kathy (1959–) Am. country singer ("Eighteen Wheels and a Dozen Roses")

Matthau, Walter (Walter Matuschanskayasky) (1920–) Am. actor (*The Odd Couple*; *The Sunshine Boys*; O—1966— *The Fortune Cookie*; T—1965)

Matthiessen, Peter (1927–) Am. novelist/nature writer (*The Snow Leopard*; *At Play in the Fields of the Lord*)

Mattingly, Don (Donald Arthur Mattingly) (1961–) Am. baseball player

Mature, Victor (Victor John Mature; "The Hunk"; "Mr. Beefcake") (1915–) Am. actor (*Samson and Delilah*; *After the Fox*)

Maugham, W. Somerset (William Somerset Maugham) (1874–1965) Eng. novelist/short story writer/playwright (*Of Human Bondage*; *The Moon and Sixpence*; *The Razor's Edge*)

Mauldin, Bill (William Henry Mauldin) (1921–) Am. cartoonist (during WWII, drew the G.I.s Willie and Joe; P—1945, 1959)

Maupassant, Guy de (Henri-Rene-Albert-Guy de Maupassant) (1850–1893) Fr. novelist/short story writer (*The Necklace*)

Maupin, Armistead (1944–) Am. novelist/columnist (*Tales of the City* series)

Maurel, Victor (1848–1923) Fr. opera singer (baritone)

Mauriac, François (1885–1970) Fr. novelist/playwright (*The Viper's Tangle*; *A Kiss for the Leper*; N—1952)

Mauriat, Paul (1925–) Fr. orchestra leader ("Love Is Blue")

Maurois, André (Émile-Salomon-Wilhelm Herzog) (1885–1967) Fr. novelist/biographer (*Disraeli*; *Proust*)

Max, Peter (Peter Max Finkelstein) (1937–) Ger.-Am. pop artist

Maximilian (Ferdinand Maximilian Joseph; "The Marionette Emperor") (1832–1867) Aus. archduke/emperor of Mexico 1864–1867

Maxwell, Elsa (1883–1963) Am. journalist/socialite/radio host

Maxwell, Gavin (1914–1969) Scot. writer (*Ring of Bright Water*)

May, Brian (Brian Harold May) (1947–) Eng. rock guitarist (with Queen)

May, Elaine (Elaine Berlin) (1932–) Am. writer/film director (*Ishtar*; *The Heartbreak Kid*; *California Suite*)

May, Phil (Philip William May) (1864–1903) Eng. caricaturist (*Punch*)

Mayall, John (John Brumwell Mayall; "Grandfather of British Rock") (1934–) Eng.-Am. blues singer/musician/bandleader

Mayer, Louis B. (Louis Burt Mayer; born Eliezer Mayer; a/k/a Lazar Mayer; "LB") (1885–1957) Russ.-Am. movie producer/executive

Mayer, Sandy (Alex Mayer) (1952–) Am. tennis player

Mayfield, Curtis (Curtis Lee Mayfield) (1942–) Am. soul/pop singer/songwriter ("Superfly"; formerly with The Impressions)

Maynard, Don (Donald Maynard; "Sunshine") (1937–) Am. football Hall-of-Famer

Mayo, Archie (1891–1968) Am. film director (*The Petrified Forest*; *Bordertown*)

Mayo, Charles (Charles Horace Mayo) (1865–1939) Am. surgeon (cofounder of the Mayo Clinic with brother William)

Mayo, Virginia (Virginia Jones) (1920–) Am. actress (*The Secret Life of Walter Mitty*)

Mayo, William (William James Mayo) (1861–1939) Am. surgeon (cofounder of the Mayo Clinic with brother Charles)

Mayron, Melanie (1952–) Am. actress ("thirtysomething" TV series; *My Blue Heaven*; E—1988/89)

Mays, Willie (Willie Howard Mays, Jr.; "Say Hey"; "Say Hey Kid"; "Amazing Mays"; "Buckduck"; "Willie the Wallop") (1931–) Am. baseball Hall-of-Famer

Maywood, Augusta (Augusta Williams) (1825–1876) Am. ballerina

Mazar, Debi (c. 1965–) Am. actress ("Civil Wars" and "L.A. Law" TV series; *Goodfellas*; *Jungle Fever*; *Money for Nothing*)

Mazursky, Paul (Irwin Mazursky) (1930–) Am. film director/writer (*Scenes from a Mall*; *An Unmarried Woman*; *Down and Out in Beverly Hills*; *Enemies—A Love Story*)

McAdoo, Bob (Robert Allen McAdoo) (1951–) Am. basketball player

McAfee, George (George A. McAfee; "One Play") (1918–) Am. football Hall-of-Famer

McAnally, Mac (1957–) Am. country singer ("Back Where I Come From")

McArdle, Andrea (1963–) Am. child actress (*Annie*)

McAuliffe, Christina (Sharon Christina Corrigan) (1948–1986) Am. school teacher (first non-astronaut in space; died in the space shuttle Challenger explosion)

McBain, Ed *see* Hunter, Evan

McBride, Martina (Martina Mariea Schiff) (1966–) Am. country singer ("The Time Has Come")

McBride, Mary Margaret (Martha Deane) (1899–1976) Am. radio talk show host

McBride, Patricia (1942–) Am. ballerina

McCaffrey, Anne (1926–) Am. science fiction/fantasy writer (*The Dragonriders of Pern*)

McCall, C. W. (William Fries) (1928–) Am. country singer ("Convoy")

McCallister, Lon (Herbert Alonzo McCallister, Jr.) (1923–) Am. actor (*Stage Door Canteen*; *Stella Dallas*)

McCallum, David (1933–) Scot.-Am. actor (Judas in *The Greatest Story Ever Told*; "The Man from U.N.C.L.E." TV series)

McCambridge, Mercedes (Carlota Mercedes Agnes McCambridge) (1918–) Am. actress (*A Farewell to Arms*; *Touch of Evil*; O—1949—*All the King's Men*)

McCarey, Leo (Thomas Leo McCarey) (1898–1969) Am. film producer/director (*Ruggles of Red Gap*; O—1937—*The Awful Truth*; O—1944—*Going My Way*)

McCarthy, Andrew (1962–) Am. actor (*St. Elmo's Fire*; *Pretty in Pink*)

McCarthy, Eugene (Eugene Joseph McCarthy) (1916–) Am. senator/presidential candidate 1968, 1972

McCarthy, Joe (Josephe Vincent McCarthy; "Marse Joe") (1887–1978) Am. baseball manager/Hall-of-Famer

McCarthy, Joseph R. (Joseph Raymond McCarthy) (1908–1957) Am. senator/anticommunist activist (McCarthyism)

McCarthy, Kevin (1914–) Am. actor (brother of Mary; *Invasion of the Body Snatchers* [1956 and 1978]; *Death of a Salesman*)

McCarthy, Mary (Mary Therese McCarthy) (1912–1989) Am. novelist/critic (*The Group*; *Memories of a Catholic Girlhood*)

McCartney, Linda (Linda Louise Eastman) (1942–) Am. rock musician/singer/photographer

McCartney, Paul (James Paul McCartney) (1942–) Eng. rock singer/musician/songwriter ("Live and Let Die"; "My Love"; "Band on the Run"; with Paul McCartney & Wings; former member of The Beatles)

McCarver, Tim (James Timothy McCarver; "Old Second Inning") (1941–) Am. baseball player

McCay, Winsor (Winsor Zenic McKay) (1869–1934) Am. cartoonist (*Little Nemo*)/pioneer of animation

McClanahan, Rue (Eddie-Rue McClanahan) (1936–) Am. actress ("The Golden Girls" TV series; E—1986/87)

McClellan, George B. (George Brinton McClellan) (1826–1885) Am. army general/gov. of New Jersey/presidential candidate 1864

McClintock, Barbara (1902–) Am. geneticist (N—1983)

McClinton, Delbert (1940–) Am. blues singer ("Giving It Up for Your Love"; formerly with The Ron-Dels)

McCloskey, Leigh (C) Am. actor (*Inferno*; "Dallas" TV series)

McClure, Doug (Douglas McClure) (1935–) Am. actor ("The Virginian" TV series; *Beau Geste*)

McClure, S. S. (Samuel Sidney McClure) (1857–1949) Am. magazine editor/publisher (*McClure's*)

McClurg, Edie (1951–) Am. actress/comedienne ("The Hogan Family" TV series)

McCoo, Marilyn (1943–) Am. singer (with Billy Davis, Jr.; "You Don't Have to Be a Star [to Be in My Show]")/TV host ("Solid Gold")

McCord, Kent (Kent McWhirter) (1942–) Am. actor ("Adam 12" TV series)

McCormack, John (John Francis McCormack) (1884–1945) Ir.-Am. opera singer (tenor)

McCormack, Mike (1930–) Am. football Hall-of-Famer

McCormick, Cyrus Hall (1809–1884) Am. inventor (reaper)

McCovey, Willie (Willie Lee McCovey; "Stretch") (1938–) Am. baseball Hall-of-Famer

McCoy, Charlie (1941–) Am. country harmonica player/music director for "Hee Haw" TV series

McCoy, Van (1944–1979) Am. disco musician ("The Hustle")

McCracken, James (James Eugene McCracken) (1926–1988) Am. opera singer (tenor)

McCrae, John (1872–1918) Can. physician/poet (*In Flanders Fields*)

McCrary, Tex (John Reagan McCrary) (1910–) Am. talk show host

McCrea, Joel (1905–1990) Am. actor (*Foreign Correspondent*; *The Palm Beach Story*)

McCullers, Carson (Lula Carson McCullers née Smith) (1917–1967) Am. novelist/short story writer (*The Member of the Wedding*; *The Heart Is a Lonely Hunter*)

McCullough, Colleen (1937–) Austral. novelist (*The Thorn Birds*)

McCullough, David (1933–) Am. writer (*The Johnstown Flood*; *The Great Bridge*; *The Path Between the Seas*; P—1993—*Truman*)

McDaniel, Hattie (1895–1952) Am. actress (O—1939—*Gone with the Wind*; TV's "Beulah")

McDaniel, Mel (1942–) Am. country singer ("Baby's Got Her Blue Jeans On")

McDaniel, Xavier (Xavier Maurice McDaniel; "X-Man") (1963–) Am. basketball player

McDermott, Dylan (c. 1962–) Am. actor (*Steel Magnolias*)

McDonald, Country Joe (1942–) Am. rock singer/bandleader (with Country Joe and the Fish)

McDonald, Harl (1899–1955) Am. composer ("Santa Fe Trail")

McDonald, Michael (1952–) Am. rock singer/musician ("I Keep Forgettin' [Every Time You're Near]"; formerly with Steely Dan and The Doobie Brothers)

McDormand, Frances (1958–) Am. actress (*Blood Simple*; *Mississippi Burning*; *Raising Arizona*)

McDowall, Roddy (Roderick Andrew McDowall) (1928–) Eng. actor (*Planet of the Apes*; *The Greatest Story Ever Told*)/photographer (*Double Exposure* series)

McDowell, Malcolm (Malcolm Taylor) (1943–) Eng. actor (*A Clockwork Orange*; *Voyage of the Damned*)

McDowell, Ronnie (1951–) Am. country singer ("You Made a Wanted Man Out of Me")

McElhenny, Hugh ("King") (1928–) Am. football Hall-of-Famer

McEnroe, John (John Patrick McEnroe, Jr.; "The Brat"; "Superbrat"; "McTantrum") (1959–) Am. tennis player (W—1981, 1983, 1984)

McEntire, Reba ("Queen of Country") (1954–) Am. country singer ("Rumor Has It"; "Whoever's in New England"; "Fancy")

McEwan, Ian (1948–) Eng. short story writer/novelist (*The Comfort of Strangers*)

McFadden, Mary (Mary Josephine McFadden) (1938–) Am. fashion designer

McFarland, Spanky (George Emmett McFarland) (1928–1993) Am. actor ("Our Gang" TV series)

McFarlane, Spanky (Elaine McFarlane) (1942–) Am. pop singer (with Spanky and Our Gang; "Sunday Will Never Be the Same"; "Sunday Morning")

McFerrin, Bobby (1950–) Am. pop/jazz singer/musician ("Don't Worry Be Happy"; G—1988)

McGavin, Darren (1922–) Am. actor (TV's "Kolchak, the Night Stalker")

McGee, Willie (Willie Dean McGee; "ET") (1958–) Am. baseball player

McGillis, Kelly (1958–) Am. actress (*Witness*; *Top Gun*; *The Accused*)

McGinley, Phyllis (1905–1978) Am. poet (P—1961—*Times Three: Selected Verse from Three Decades*)

McGinnis, George (1950–) Am. basketball player

McGinnity, Joe (Joseph Jerome McGinnity; "The Iron Man") (1871–1929) Am. baseball Hall-of-Famer

McGoohan, Patrick (Patrick Joseph McGoohan) (1928–) Am. actor (TV's "The Prisoner")

McGovern, Elizabeth (1961–) Am. actress (*Ordinary People*; *Ragtime*)

McGovern, George (George Stanley McGovern) (1922–) Am. senator/presidential candidate 1972

McGovern, Maureen (Maureen Therese McGovern) (1949–) Am. pop singer ("The Morning After")

McGraw, James (James Herbert McGraw) (1860–1948) Am. publisher/founder of McGraw-Hill

McGraw, John (John Joseph McGraw; "Little Napoleon") (1873–1934) Am. baseball player/manager/Hall-of-Famer

McGraw, Tug (Frank Edwin McGraw) (1944–) Am. baseball pitcher

McGrory, Mary (1918–) Am. journalist (P—1975)

McGuinn, Roger (James McGuinn) (1942–) Am. rock musician (with The Byrds and McGuinn, Clark & Hillman)

McGuire, Al (1931–) Am. basketball coach

McGuire, Christine (1928–) Am. singer (with The McGuire Sisters; "Sincerely")

McGuire, Dorothy (1930–) Am. singer (with The McGuire Sisters)

McGuire, Dorothy (Dorothy Hackett McGuire) (1918–) Am. actress (*A Tree Grows in Brooklyn*; *Gentleman's Agreement*)

McGuire, Phyllis (1931–) Am. singer (with The McGuire Sisters)

M. C. Hammer see Hammer

McHugh, Jimmy (James McHugh) (1894–

1969) Am. songwriter ("I Can't Give You Anything but Love"; "On the Sunny Side of the Street")

McInerney, Jay (1955–) Am. novelist (*Bright Lights, Big City*)

McIntyre, Joe (Joseph Mulrey McIntyre) (1972–) Am. pop musician (with New Kids on the Block)

McIntyre, Vonda N. (Vonda Neel McIntyre) (1948–) Am. science fiction writer (*Star Trek: The Wrath of Khan*)

McKagan, Duff (Michael McKagan) (1965–) Am. rock bassist (with Guns N' Roses)

McKay, Claude (1890–1948) Am. poet/novelist (*Spring in New Hampshire*; *Home to Harlem*; *Banjo*; *Banana Bottom*)

McKay, Gardner (George Cadogan Gardner McKay) (1932–) Am. actor ("Adventures in Paradise" TV series)

McKay, Jim (James Kenneth McManus) (1921–) Am. sportscaster

McKay, John (John Harvey McKay) (1923–) Am. football coach

McKean, Michael (c. 1948–) Am. actor (Lenny in "Laverne & Shirley" TV series; *This Is Spinal Tap*)

McKechnie, Bill (William Boyd McKechnie; "Deacon Bill") (1886–1965) Am. baseball Hall-of-Famer

McKee, Maria (1964–) Am. pop/country singer (with Lone Justice; "I Found Love")

McKellan, Ian (Ian Murray McKellan) (1939–) Eng. actor (*Scandal*; *Plenty*; *The Promise*; T—1981)

McKellar, Danica (Danica Mae McKellar) (1974–) Am. child actress ("The Wonder Years" TV series)

McKenna, Siobhan (Siobhan Giollamhuire Nic Cionnaith) (1923–1986) Ir. actress (*Doctor Zhivago*; *King of Kings*)

McKenzie, Scott (Philip Blondheim) (1939–) Am. pop singer ("San Francisco [Be Sure to Wear Flowers in Your Hair]")

McKeon, Nancy (1966–) Am. actress ("The Facts of Life" TV series)

McKernan, John R., Jr. (John Rettie McKernan, Jr.) (1948–) Am. gov. of Maine

McKim, Charles (Charles Follen McKim) (1847–1909) Am. neoclassical architect (Boston Public Library)

McKinley, Chuck (Charles Robert McKinley) (1941–1986) Am. tennis player (W—1963)

McKinley, Ida (Ida Saxton) (1847–1907) Am. first lady (William)

McKinley, William (1843–1901) 25th Am. pres. (1897–1901)

McKuen, Rod (Rod Marvin McKuen) (1933–) Am. poet (*Come to Me in Silence*; *Lonesome Cities*)/composer (theme song "Jean" from *The Prime of Miss Jean Brodie*)

McLaglen, Victor (1886–1959) Eng.-Am. actor (*Gunga Din*; O—1935—*The Informer*)

McLain, Denny (Dennis Dale McLain; "Sky Wing"; "Sky Young") (1944–) Am. baseball pitcher

McLaren, Malcolm (1946–) Eng. punk music promoter (The Sex Pistols)

McLean, Don (1945–) Am. folk/rock singer/musician ("American Pie"; "Vincent")

McLuhan, Marshall (Herbert Marshall McLuhan) (1911–1980) Can. communications theorist (coined the term *global village*)/educator (*Understanding Media*)

McMahon, Ed (Edward Leo Peter McMahon, Jr.) (1923–) Am. TV host/announcer ("The Tonight Show"; "Star Search"; signature phrase: "Heeere's Johnny!")

McMahon, Jim (James Robert McMahon) (1959–) Am. football player

McManus, George (1884–1954) Am. cartoonist (*Bringing Up Father*)

McMenamy, Kristen (c. 1964–) Am. model

McMillan, Donald (Donald Baxter McMillan) (1874–1970) Am. arctic explorer (with Peary)/writer (*Four Years in the White North*)

McMillan, Terry (1951–) Am. novelist (*Waiting to Exhale*; *Disappearing Acts*)

McMurtry, Larry (Larry Jeff McMurtry) (1936–) Am. novelist (*The Last Picture Show*; *Terms of Endearment*; P—1986—*Lonesome Dove*)

McNair, Barbara (Barbara J. McNair) (1939–) Am. singer/actress (*They Call Me MISTER Tibbs!*)

McNally, Dave (David Arthur McNally; "McLucky") (1942–) Am. baseball pitcher

McNally, Terrence (1939–) Am. playwright (*Frankie and Johnny in the Clair De Lune*; *Last Gasps*)

McNamara, Robert S. (Robert Strange McNamara) (1916–) Am. banker/govt. official (defense secretary)

McNeile, H. C. (Henry Cyril McNeile; a/k/a Sapper) (1888–1937) Eng. mystery writer (created Bulldog Drummond)

McNichol, Jimmy (James Vincent McNichol) (1961–) Am. actor (brother of Kristy; *Smokey Bites the Dust*; "The Fitzpatricks" TV series)

McNichol, Kristy (Christina Ann McNichol) (1962–) Am. actress ("Family" and "Empty Nest" TV series; *Little Darlings*; E—1976/77, 1978/79)

McPartland, Jimmy (James Duigald McPartland) (1907–) Am. jazz cornetist

McPartland, Marian (Mary Margaret McPartland née Turner) (1918–) Am. jazz pianist/composer

McPhatter, Clyde (Clyde Lensley McPhatter) (1933–1972) Am. pop singer (with The Dominoes and The Drifters; "Save the Last Dance for Me"; "Under the Boardwalk")

McPhee, John A. (John Angus McPhee) (1931–) Am. writer (*Encounters with the Archdruid*; *Oranges*; *The Pine Barrens*)

McPherson, Aimee Semple (Aimee Elizabeth Kennedy; "Sister Aimee"; "The World's Most Pulchritudinous Evangelist") (1890–1944) Am. evangelist (founded the International Church of the Foursquare Gospel)

McQueen, Butterfly (Thelma McQueen) (1911–) Am. actress (*Gone With the Wind*; *Mildred Pierce*)

McQueen, Chad (1960–) Am. actor (son of Steve)

McQueen, Steve (Terence Stephen McQueen) (1930–1980) Am. actor (*The Great Escape*; *Bullitt*; *The Getaway*)

McRae, Carmen (1922–) Am. jazz singer

McRaney, Gerald (1947–) Am. actor ("Major Dad" and "Simon & Simon" TV series)

McTiernan, John (C) Am. film director (*Die Hard*; *The Last Action Hero*)

McVie, Christine (Christine Perfect) (1943–) Eng. rock singer ("Got a Hold on Me"; with Fleetwood Mac)

McVie, John (1946–) Eng. rock musician (with Fleetwood Mac)

McWherter, Ned (Ned Ray McWherter) (1930–) Am. gov. of Tennessee

McWhirter, Norris (Norris Dewar McWhirter) (1925–) Eng. editor/writer (*The Guinness Book of World Records*)

McWhirter, Ross (Alan Ross McWhirter) (1925–1975) Eng. editor/writer (*The Guinness Book of World Records*)

Mead, Margaret (Margaret Beteson) (1901–1978) Am. anthropologist/writer (*Coming of Age in Samoa*)

Meadows, Audrey (Audrey Cotter) (1924–) Am. actress (sister of Jayne; "The Honeymooners" TV series; E—1954)

Meadows, Jayne (Jayne Cotter) (1920–) Am. actress ("Medical Center" TV series)/game show panelist ("I've Got a Secret")

Meara, Anne (1929–) Am. comedienne/actress (with Jerry Stiller; mother of Ben Stiller)

Meat Loaf (Marvin Lee Aday) (1947–) Am. rock singer ("Two out of Three Ain't Bad")/actor (*The Rocky Horror Picture Show*)

Medavoy, Mike (1941–) Am. entertainment executive (CEO of TriStar Pictures)

Medeiros, Glenn (1970–) Am. pop singer ("Nothing's Gonna Change My Love for You")

Medici, Lorenzo de' ("The Magnificent") (1449–1492) Flor. poet/statesman/ruler

Medley, Bill (1940–) Am. pop singer (with Jennifer Warnes, "[I've Had] the Time of My Life"; formerly with The Righteous Brothers)

Medtner, Nikolay (Nikolay Karlovich Medtner or Metner) (1880–1951) Russ.-Fr. pianist/composer (fairy tale sonatas)

Medwick, Joe (Joseph Michael Medwick; "Ducky"; "Muscles") (1911–1975) Am. baseball Hall-of-Famer

Meeker, Howie (Howard William Meeker) (1924–) Can. hockey player

Meeker, Ralph (Ralph Rathgeber) (1920–) Am. actor (*Kiss Me Deadly*; *The Dirty Dozen*)

Meese, Edwin (Edwin Meese III) (1931–) Am. politician/govt. official (attorney general)

Mehta, Ved (Ved Parkash Mehta) (1934–) Ind. journalist/novelist (*Mahatma Gandhi and His Apostles*)

Mehta, Zubin (1936–) Ind. orchestra conductor (Los Angeles Philharmonic, New York Philharmonic)

Meinhof, Ulrike (1934–1976) Ger. terrorist (with Andreas Baader)

Meir, Golda (Goldie Mabovitch; a/k/a Goldie Meyerson) (1898–1978) Isr. prime minister 1969–1974

Meisner, Randy (1946–) Am. rock singer/musician ("Hearts on Fire"; formerly with Poco, The Eagles, and The Stone Canyon Band)

Meitner, Lise (1878–1968) Aus. physicist (discovered nuclear fission with Otto Hahn and Fritz Strassmann)

Mekka, Eddie (1952–) Am. actor ("Laverne & Shirley" TV series)

Melanie (Melanie Safka) (1947–) Am. pop singer ("Brand New Key")

Melba, Dame Nellie (Helen Porter Armstrong Mitchell) (1861–1931) Austral. opera singer (soprano)

Melcher, Martin or **Marty** (1915–1968) Am. film producer (Doris Day films)

Melchers, Gari (Julius Gari Melchers) (1860–1932) Am. painter/muralist (Library of Congress' *Peace and War*)

Melchior, Lauritz (Lauritz Lebrecht Hommel) (1890–1973) Dan.-Am. opera singer (tenor)

Mellencamp, John (a/k/a John Cougar and John Cougar Mellencamp) (1951–) Am. rock singer ("Jack & Diane"; "Hurts So Good")/actor (*Falling from Grace*)

Mellon, Andrew (Andrew William Mellon) (1855–1937) Am. industrialist/financier/govt. official (treasury secretary)

Melville, Herman (1819–1891) Am. novelist/short story writer/poet (*Moby Dick*; *Billy Budd*; *Typee*)

Melvin, Harold (C) Am. soul musician/bandleader ("If You Don't Know Me by Now"; with Harold Melvin & The Blue Notes)

Memling, Hans (c. 1430 or 1435–1494) Flem. painter (*Adoration of the Magi*)

Memphis Slim (Peter Chatman) (1915–1988) Am. blues pianist/singer/songwriter ("Every Day [I Have the Blues]")

Menander (342–292 B.C.) Ath. playwright (*Dyscolus*)

Mencius (a/k/a Meng-Tzu; born Meng K'o) (c. 371–289 B.C.) Chin. philosopher/follower of Confucius

Mencken, H. L. (Henry Louis Mencken; "The Sage of Baltimore") (1880–1956) Am. humorist/editor/writer (*Prejudices*)

Mendel, Gregor (Gregor Johann Mendel) (1822–1884) Aus. botanist/scientist (devised early theories about genetics)

Mendelssohn, Felix (Jakob Ludwig Felix Mendelssohn-Bartholdy) (1809–1847) Ger. composer (*A Midsummer Night's Dream*)

Mendes, Sergio (1941–) Braz. bandleader/

pianist ("The Fool on the Hill"; "The Look of Love")

Menendez, Erik (c. 1971–) Am. alleged murderer (of his parents, with brother Lyle)

Menendez, Jose (1944–1989) Am. entertainment executive/murder victim

Menendez, Kitty (1941–1989) Am. wife of Jose Menendez/murder victim

Menendez, Lyle (c. 1968–) Am. alleged murderer (of his parents, with brother Erik)

Menes (a/k/a Mena) (ruled c. 3100 B.C.) Egypt. king

Mengele, Josef ("The Angel of Death") (1911–1979) Ger. Nazi doctor/war criminal

Menjou, Adolphe (Adolphe Jean Menjou) (1890–1963) Am. actor (*Morning Glory*; *Stage Door*)

Menken, Adah (Adah Isaacs Menken; born Adah Bertha Theodore) (c. 1835–1868) Am. actress

Menninger, Karl (Karl Augustus Menninger) (1893–1990) Am. psychiatrist/writer (*Man Against Himself*)

Menotti, Gian Carlo (1911–) Ital. composer (*Amahl and the Night Visitors*; P—1950—*The Consul*; P—1955—*The Saint of Bleecker Street*)

Menuhin, Sir Yehudi (Yehudi Sinai Menuhin) (1916–) Eng.-Am. violinist/conductor

Menzel, Jiří (1938–) Cz. film director (*Closely Watched Trains*)

Mercer, Johnny (John H. Mercer) (1909–1976) Am. lyricist ("Come Rain or Come Shine"; "That Old Black Magic"; "Moon River"; "Days of Wine and Roses")

Mercer, Mabel (1900–1984) Am. singer

Mercer, Marian (Marian E. Mercer) (1935–) Am. actress/singer ("It's a Living" and "St. Elsewhere" TV series)

Merchant, Ismail (1936–) Ind.-Am. film producer (with Merchant-Ivory; *A Room with a View*; *Howard's End*)

Merchant, Natalie (1963–) Am. rock singer (with 10,000 Maniacs)

Merchant, Vivien (Ada Thompson) (1929–1983) Eng. actress (*Alfie*; *Under Milk Wood*)

Mercouri, Melina (Maria Amalia Mercouri) (1923–1994) Gr. actress (*Never on Sunday*; *Once Is Not Enough*)/politician

Mercury, Freddie (Frederick Bulsara)

(1946–1991) Eng. rock singer (with Queen; "Bohemian Rhapsody")
Meredith, Burgess (Oliver Burgess Meredith) (1908–) Am. actor (*The Day of the Locust*; "Batman" TV series)
Meredith, Don ("Dandy Don") (1938–) Am. football player/sportscaster
Meredith, George (1828–1909) Eng. novelist/poet (*The Egoist*)
Mergenthaler, Ottmar (1854–1899) Am. inventor (Linotype machine)
Merimée, Prosper (1803–1870) Fr. novelist (*Carmen*, upon which Bizet based his opera of the same name)
Meriwether, Lee (1935–) Am. Miss America 1955/actress ("Barnaby Jones" TV series)
Merkel, Una (1903–1986) Am. actress (*Destry Rides Again*; *Abraham Lincoln*)
Merman, Ethel (Ethel Agnes Zimmerman) (1908–1984) Am. actress/singer (*Call Me Madam*; on Broadway: *Annie Get Your Gun*; *Anything Goes*; *Gypsy*; T—1951)
Merrick, David (David Margulies; "The Barnum of Broadway Productions") (1912–) Am. theatrical producer (*Oliver!*; *Hello, Dolly*; *Becket*)
Merrill, Dina (Nedenia Hutton Rumbough) (1925–) Am. actress (*The Desk Set*; *The Player*; "The Courtship of Eddie's Father" TV series; daughter of E. F. Hutton and Marjorie Merriweather Post)
Merrill, Gary (Gary Franklin Merrill) (1914–1990) Am. actor (*All About Eve*; *Winged Victory*)
Merrill, James (James Ingram Merrill) (1926–) Am. novelist/playwright/poet (P—1977—*Divine Comedies*)
Merrill, Stephen E. (1946–) Am. gov. of New Hampshire
Merton, Thomas (a/k/a Father Merton Lewis) (1915–1968) Am. monk/poet/essayist/writer (*The Seven Storey Mountain*)
Merwin, W. S. (William Stanley Merwin) (1927–) Am. poet/translator (P—1971—*The Carrier of Ladders*)
Messalina, Valeria (c. 22–48) Roman empress
Messerschmitt, Willy (Wilhelm Messerschmitt) (1898–1978) Ger. aircraft designer/builder
Messiaen, Olivier (1908–1992) Fr. composer/organist (*The Ascension*)

Messick, Dale (Dalia Messick) (1906–) Am. cartoonist (*Brenda Starr, Reporter*)
Messina, Jim (1947–) Am. rock singer/songwriter (with Loggins & Messina and Poco)
Mesta, Perle (née Skirvin) (1889–1975) Am. diplomat/hostess
Meštrović, Ivan (1883–1962) Yug.-Am. sculptor (*Monument to the Unknown Soldiers*)
Metalious, Grace (née de Repentigny) (1924–1964) Am. novelist (*Peyton Place*)
Metcalf, Laurie (1955–) Am. actress (*Internal Affairs*; *Frankie and Johnny*; "Roseanne" TV series)
Metheny, Pat (1955–) Am. jazz guitarist ("This Is Not America")
Methot, Mayo (1904–1951) Am. actress (*Mr. Deeds Goes to Town*)
Metternich, Klemens von (Klemens Wenzel Nepomuk Lothar von Metternich-Winneburg) (1773–1859) Aus. prince 1813–1848
Metzenbaum, Howard (Howard Morton Metzenbaum) (1917–) Am. senator
Meyer, Debbie (Deborah Meyer) (1952–) Am. swimmer
Meyer, Nicholas (1945–) Am. novelist/film director (*The Seven Per-Cent Solution*)
Meyer, Russ (Russell Albion Meyer; "King of the Nudies"; "Mr. X") (1922–) Am. film director (*Vixen*; *Faster, Pussycat! Kill! Kill!*; *Amazon Women on the Moon*)
Meyerbeer, Giacomo (Jakob Liebmann Meyer Beer) (1791–1864) Ger. composer (*Les Huguenots*)
Meyers, Ari (Ariadne Meyers) (1969–) Am. child actress ("Kate & Allie" TV series)
Micah (8th century B.C.) Heb. prophet
Michael, George (Georgios Kyriacos Panayiotou) (1963–) Eng. pop singer/songwriter ("I Want Your Sex"; "Faith"; "Father Figure"; with Wham!, "Wake Me Up Before You Go-Go")
Michaels, Barbara (Barbara Louise Gross Mertz; a/k/a Elizabeth Peters) (1927–) Am. romance novelist (*Patriot's Dream*)
Michaels, Bret (Bret Michael Sychak) (c. 1963–) Am. rock singer (with Poison; "Every Rose Has Its Thorn")
Michaels, Lorne (1944–) Can. TV producer/writer ("Saturday Night Live")

Michelangelo (Michelangelo di Lodovico Buonarotti Simoni) (1475–1564) Ital. painter/sculptor/architect (St. Peter's, Rome)/poet (painted the Sistine Chapel's ceiling)

Michener, James A. (James Albert Michener) (1907–) Am. historical novelist (*Hawaii*; *Alaska*; P—1948—*Tales of the South Pacific*)

Middleton, Thomas (c. 1570–1627) Eng. playwright (*The Changeling*)

Midkiff, Dale (C) Am. actor (*Love Potion #9*; *Pet Sematary*)

Midler, Bette ("The Divine Miss M"; "The Last of the Tacky Ladies") (1945–) Am. singer ("The Rose"; "Wind Beneath My Wings"; G—1973, 1980)/actress (*Ruthless People*; *For the Boys*; *Beaches*)

Mielziner, Jo (1901–1976) Am. stage/film set designer (*Pal Joey*; *Annie Get Your Gun*)

Mifune, Toshiro (1920–) Jap. actor ("Seven Samurai"; *Rashomon*)

Migenes, Julia (a/k/a Julia Migenes-Johnson) (1945–) Am. opera singer/actress

Mikan, George (George Lawrence Mikan, Jr.; "Big Number 99") (1924–) Am. basketball player/executive

Mikita, Stan (Stanley Mikita Gvoth; "Stosh"; "Mouse") (1940–) Can. hockey player

Milano, Alyssa (1972–) Am. actress ("Who's the Boss?" TV series)

Milbanke, Anne (Anne Isabella Milbanke) (1792–1860) Eng. mathematician

Miles, Buddy (George Miles) (1946–) Am. blues drummer (with Jimi Hendrix, The Ink Spots, and Wilson Pickett)

Miles, Sarah (1941–) Eng. actress (*Blow-Up*; *Hope and Glory*)

Miles, Sylvia (1932–) Am. actress (*Wall Street*; *Midnight Cowboy*; *She-Devil*)

Miles, Vera (Vera May Ralston) (1929–) Am. actress (*Psycho*; *The Wrong Man*)

Milestone, Lewis (Levis Milstein) (1895–1980) Am. film director (*Of Mice and Men*; O—1927/28—*Two Arabian Nights*; O—1929/30—*All Quiet on the Western Front*)

Milhaud, Darius (1892–1974) Fr. composer (*Creation of the World* [*La Création du Mond*])

Milius, John (John Frederick Milius) (1944–) Am. film director (*Dillinger*; *Conan the Barbarian*)

Mill, John Stuart (1806–1873) Eng. philosopher/writer (*Utilitarianism*)

Millais, Sir John (John Everett Millais) (1829–1896) Eng. painter (*Pizarro Seizing the Inca of Peru*)

Milland, Ray (Reginald Alfred John Truscott-Jones; a/k/a Reginald Mullane and Spike Milland) (1905–1986) Wel.-Am. actor (*Dial M for Murder*; O—1945—*The Lost Weekend*)

Millay, Edna St. Vincent (a/k/a Nancy Boyd) (1892–1950) Am. poet (P—1923—*The Ballad of the Harp Weaver*; *A Few Figs from Thistles*; *Eight Sonnets in American Poetry, 1922*; *A Miscellany*)

Miller, Ann (Lucille Ann Collier) (1924–) Am. dancer/actress (*Kiss Me Kate*; *On the Town*)

Miller, Arthur (1915–) Am. short story writer/playwright/novelist (*The Crucible*; P—1949—*Death of a Salesman*)

Miller, Bob (1945–) Am. gov. of Nevada

Miller, Cheryl (1964–) Am. baseball player

Miller, Dennis (1953–) Am. comedian/actor ("Saturday Night Live" TV series)/talk show host

Miller, Glenn (1904–1944) Am. bandleader/composer ("Moonlight Serenade"; "Kalamazoo"; "Chattanooga Choo-Choo")

Miller, Henry (Henry John Miller) (1860–1926) Am. writer (*Tropic of Cancer*)

Miller, Jason (John Miller) (1939–) Am. writer (P—1973—*That Championship Season*)

Miller, Joaquin (Cincinnatus Hiner Miller; "The Frontier Poet") (1837–1913) Am. poet/writer/playwright (*Songs of the Sierras*)

Miller, Johnny (John Laurence Miller) (1947–) Am. golfer

Miller, Lara Jill (1967–) Am. child actress ("Gimme a Break" TV series)

Miller, Marilyn (Mary Ellen Reynolds) (1898–1936) Am. dancer/actress (*Till the Clouds Roll By*; *Look for the Silver Lining*)

Miller, Mitch (Mitchell William Miller) (1911–) Am. orchestra leader ("The Yellow Rose of Texas")

Miller, Penelope Ann (1964–) Am. actress (*The Freshman*; *Year of the Comet*; *Awakenings*)

Miller, Roger (Roger Dean Miller) (1936–1992) Am. country singer/musician ("King of the Road")

Miller, Steve (1943–) Am. rock singer/guitarist/songwriter ("The Joker"; "Fly Like an Eagle")

Miller, Walter M., Jr. (Walter Michael Miller, Jr.) (1923–) Am. science fiction writer (*A Canticle for Leibowitz*)

Miller, Zell (1932–) Am. gov. of Georgia

Milles, Carl (Vilhelm Carl Emil Milles; born Vilhelm Carl Emil Andersson) (1875–1955) Swed.-Am. sculptor

Millet, Jean (Jean-Francois Millet; a/k/a Francisque) (1814–1875) Fr. landscape painter

Millett, Kate (Katharine Murray Millett) (1934–) Am. feminist/writer (*Sexual Politics*)

Milligan, Spike (Terence Alan Milligan; a/k/a Spike Ahmaddnagar Milligan) (1918–) Eng. comedian

Millikan, Robert (Robert Andrews Millikan) (1868–1953) Am. physicist (N— 1923)/writer (*The Electron*)

Millner, Wayne (Wayne E. Millner) (1913–1976) Am. football Hall-of-Famer

Mills, Alley (c. 1951–) Am. actress ("The Wonder Years" TV series)

Mills, Donna (Donna Jean Miller) (1943–) Am. actress "Knots Landing" TV series)

Mills, Hayley (Hayley Cathrine Rose Vivien Mills) (1946–) Eng. actress (daughter of John, sister of Juliet; *The Parent Trap*; *Pollyanna*)

Mills, Sir John (John Lewis Ernest Watts Mills) (1908–) Eng. actor (father of Juliet and Hayley; *King Rat*; *The Wrong Box*; O—1970—*Ryan's Daughter*)

Mills, Juliet (Juliet Maryon Mills) (1941–) Eng. actress (sister of Hayley; "Nanny and the Professor" TV series)

Mills, Robert (1781–1855) Am. architect (studied under James Hoban, Benjamin Latrobe, and Thomas Jefferson; the Washington Monument)

Mills, Stephanie (1957–) Am. pop singer ("Never Knew Love Like This Before")/stage actress

Milne, A. A. (Alan Alexander Milne) (1882–1956) Eng. poet/playwright/writer (created Winnie-The-Pooh)

Milner, Martin (Martin Sam Milner) (1927–) Am. actor ("Route 66" and "Adam 12" TV series)

Milnes, Sherill (Sherill Eustace Milnes) (1935–) Am. opera singer (baritone)

Milosz, Czeslaw (1911–) Pol. poet/novelist/essayist (*The Captive Mind*; N—1980)

Milsap, Ronnie (1943–) Am. country singer ("[There's] No Gettin' Over Me")

Milstein, Nathan (1904–1992) Russ.-Am. concert violinist

Milton, John (1608–1674) Eng. poet (*Paradise Lost*)

Mimieux, Yvette (Yvette Carmen Mimieux) (1939–) Am. actress ("Where the Boys Are"; *The Four Horsemen of the Apocalypse*)

Mimms, Garnet (Garrett Mimms) (1933–) Am. pop singer ("Cry Baby"; with The Enchanters)

Mineo, Sal (Salvatore Mineo; "The Switchblade Kid") (1939–1976) Am. actor (*Rebel without a Cause*; *Exodus*)

Miner, Jan (Janice Miner) (1917–) Am. actress ("Madge the manicurist" in TV commercials)

Minetta, Norman (1931–) Am. congressman

Mingo, Norman (1896–1980) Am. cartoonist (*Mad* magazine; created Alfred E. Neuman)

Mingus, Charles ("Jazz's Angry Man") (1922–1979) Am. jazz bassist/composer/bandleader

Minnelli, Liza (Liza May Minnelli) (1946–) Am. show singer/actress (*Arthur*; O—1972—*Cabaret*; daughter of Judy Garland and Vincente Minnelli; T— 1965, 1978)

Minnelli, Vincente (1910–1986) Am. film director (*Meet Me in St. Louis*; *An American in Paris*; *Lust for Life*; O—1958—*Gigi*)

Minnesota Fats (Rudolph Walter Wanderone) (1913–) Am. billiards player

Minogue, Kylie (1968–) Austral. pop singer ("The Loco-Motion")

Minter, Mary Miles (Juliet Reilly) (1902–1984) Am. actress (*Anne of Green Gables*; *The Littlest Rebel*)

Minton, Sherman (1890–1965) Am. Supreme Court jurist (1949–1956)

Miranda, Carmen (Maria de Carmo Miranda de Cunha; "The Brazilian Bombshell") (1909–1955) Port. singer

Miranda, Isa (Inès Isabella Sanpietro) (1905–1982) Ital. actress (*The Night Porter*; *The Seven Deadly Sins*)

Mirisch, Walter (Walter Mortimer Mirisch) (1921–) Am. film producer (*Some Like It Hot*; *Mr. Majestyk*)

Miró, Joan (1893–1983) Span. surrealist painter/artist/stage designer/muralist

Mirren, Helen (1946–) Eng. actress (PBS's "Prime Suspect"; *The Cook, the Thief, His Wife and Her Lover*)
Mishima, Yukio (Hiraoka Kimitake) (1925–1970) Jap. novelist/playwright/essayist (*The Sailor Who Fell from Grace with the Sea*)
Mr. T (Lawrence Tereaud) (1952–) Am. actor ("The A-Team" TV series)
Mistral, Frédéric (1830–1914) Prov. poet (*Mireio; Calendar*; N—1904)
Mistral, Gabriela (Lucila Godoy y Alcayaga) (1889–1957) Chil. poet (*Sonnets of Death; Desolation*; N—1945)
Mitchell, Bobby (Robert C. Mitchell) (1935–) Am. football Hall-of-Famer
Mitchell, Cameron (Cameron Mitzell) (1918–) Am. actor ("The High Chaparral" TV series; *Death of a Salesman*)
Mitchell, George (George John Mitchell) (1933–) Am. senator
Mitchell, Guy (Al Cernik) (1925–) Am. singer ("Singing the Blues")
Mitchell, John (John Newton Mitchell) (1913–) Am. lawyer/Watergate participant (19 months in prison)
Mitchell, Joni (Roberta Joan Anderson) (1943–) Can. pop singer ("Big Yellow Taxi")/songwriter ("Woodstock"; "Both Sides Now")
Mitchell, Kevin (Kevin Darrell Mitchell) (1962–) Am. baseball player
Mitchell, Margaret (Margaret Munnerlyn Mitchell) (1900–1949) Am. novelist (P— 1937—*Gone with the Wind*)
Mitchell, Sasha (c. 1966–) Am. actor (*Spike of Bensonhurst*)
Mitchell, Thomas (1892–1962) Am. actor (*Only Angels Have Wings; Gone with the Wind*; O—1939—*Stagecoach*; E— 1952; T—1953)
Mitchelson, Marvin (Marvin Morris Mitchelson) (1928–) Am. divorce attorney (palimony suits)
Mitchum, Robert (Robert Charles Duran Mitchum) (1917–) Am. actor (*Night of the Hunter; Cape Fear; Farewell My Lovely*)
Mitford, Jessica (Jessica Lucy Mitford; "Queen of the Muckrakers") (1917–) Eng.-Am. writer (*The American Way of Death*)
Mitford, Nancy (Nancy Freeman Mitford) (1904–1973) Eng. writer (*Love in a Cold Climate*)
Mitropoulos, Dimitri (1896–1960) Am. or-chestra conductor (Metropolitan Opera, New York Philharmonic)/composer (*Hedonica*)
Mitterrand, François (François Maurice Marie Mitterrand) (1916–) Fr. pres. 1981–
Mix, Ron (Ronald J. Mix; "The Intellectual Assassin") (1938–) Am. football Hall-of-Famer
Mix, Tom (Thomas Hezikiah Mix) (1880–1940) Am. westerns actor (*Riders of the Purple Sage; Destry Rides Again*)
Miyake, Issey (1938–) Jap. fashion designer
Mize, Johnny (John Robert Mize; "The Big Cat") (1913–1993) Am. baseball Hall-of-Famer
Mizell, Vinegar Bend (Wilmer David Mizell) (1930–) Am. baseball pitcher
Mizner, Addison (1872–1933) Am. architect (brother of Wilson)
Mizner, Wilson (1876–1933) Am. playwright (*The Deep Purple*)/restauranteur (The Brown Derby)
Möbius, August F. (August Ferdinand Möbius) (1790–1868) Ger. mathematician/astronomer (created the Möbius Strip)
Mobley, Mary Ann (1937–) Am. actress/Miss America 1959
Mobutu (Mobutu Sese Seko; born Joseph Désiré Mobutu) (1930–) pres. of Zaïre 1965–
Modigliani, Amedeo (1884–1920) Ital. painter (portraits, nudes)/sculptor
Modine, Matthew (Matthew Avery Modine) (1959–) Am. actor (*Birdy; Full Metal Jacket; Short Cuts*)
Modjeska, Helena (Helena Modrzejewska; born Jadwiga Opio) (1840–1909) Am. stage actress
Moffo, Anna (1934–) Am. opera singer (soprano)
Moiseyev, Igor (Igor Aleksandrovich Moiseyev) (1906–) Russ. ballet dancer/choreographer
Molière (Jean-Baptiste Poquelin) (1622–1673) Fr. playwright/actor (*Le Misanthrope*)
Molinaro, Al (1919–) Am. actor ("Happy Days" TV series)
Molitor, Paul (Paul Leo Molitor) (1956–) Am. baseball player
Moll, Richard (1943–) Am. actor ("Night Court" TV series)
Molnár, Ferenc (1878–1952) Hung.

novelist/playwright (*The Swan; Liliom* [staged/filmed as *Carousel*)

Molotov, Vyacheslav (Vyacheslav Mikhaylovich Skryabin; "Molotov" = "hammer") (1890–1986) Russ. diplomat/political leader

Momaday, N. Scott (Navarre Scott Momaday) (1934–) Am. writer (P—1969— *House Made of Dawn*)

Mondale, Walter F. (Walter Frederick Mondale; "Fritz") (1928–) Am. v.p. (J. Carter)/senator

Mondrian, Piet (Pieter Cornelis Mondriaan) (1872–1944) Dutch-Fr.-Am. painter/artist

Monet, Claude (Claude-Oscar Monet) (1840–1926) Fr. impressionist painter (known for water lily paintings)

Money, Eddie (Edward Mahoney) (1949–) Am. rock singer ("Baby Hold On"; "Two Tickets to Paradise")

Monk, Thelonius (Thelonius Sphere Monk) (1920–1982) Am. jazz pianist (developed "bebop" style; "Well You Needn't"; " 'Round Midnight")

Monroe, Bill (William Smith Monroe; "The Father of Country Music"; "Father of Bluegrass") (1911–) Am. country singer/musician/songwriter ("Blue Moon of Kentucky")

Monroe, Earl (Vernon Earl Monroe; "The Pearl") (1944–) Am. basketball player

Monroe, Elizabeth (Elizabeth Kortright) (1768–1830) Am. first lady (James)

Monroe, James ("The Era-of-Good-Feeling President") (1758–1831) 5th Am. pres. (1817–1825)

Monroe, Marilyn (Norma Jean Mortenson; later Norma Jean Baker) (1926–1962) Am. actress (*Some Like It Hot; The Seven Year Itch; Let's Make Love*)

Monroe, Vaughan (Vaughan Wilton Monroe) (1911–1973) Am. bandleader/singer ("Riders in the Sky"; "Your Show of Shows" TV series)

Montagna, Bartolommeo (c. 1450–1523) Ital. painter (*Madonna and Child*)

Montagu, Ashley (Montague Francis Ashley Montagu; a/k/a Academicus Mentor) (1905–) Eng.-Am. anthropologist/educator/writer (*The Elephant Man*)

Montalban, Ricardo (1920–) Am. actor ("Fantasy Island" TV series; *Star Trek II: The Wrath of Khan*; E—1977/78)

Montale, Eugenio (1896–1981) Ital. poet (*Cuttlefish Bones*; N—1975)

Montana, Bob (1920–1975) Am. cartoonist (*Archie*)

Montana, Joe (Joseph C. Montana, Jr.; "Golden Joe"; "Big Sky") (1956–) Am. football player

Montand, Yves (Ivo Levi) (1921–1991) Ital.-Fr. actor (*On a Clear Day You Can See Forever*)/singer ("Let's Make Love")

Montenegro, Hugo (1925–1981) Am. orchestra leader (*The Good, the Bad and the Ugly*)

Montessori, Maria (1870–1952) Ital. physician/educator (developed teaching method used in Montessori schools)

Monteux, Pierre (1875–1964) Am. orchestra conductor (Boston, Paris, San Francisco, and London symphonies)

Monteverdi or **Monteverde, Claudio** (1567–1643) Ital. composer (*Orfeo; Vespers*)

Montez, Lola (Maria Dolores Eliza Rosanna Gilbert; Baroness Rosenthal; Countess Lansfield) (1818–1861) Am. dancer/mistress of Louis I of Bavaria/writer (*Arts of Beauty*)

Montez, Maria (Maria Antonia Garcia Vidal de Santo Silas; "The Queen of Technicolor") (1918–1951) Span. actress (*Arabian Nights*)

Montezuma II (1466–1520) Aztec emperor of Mexico 1502–1520

Montgomery, Elizabeth (1933–) Am. actress (daughter of Robert; "Bewitched" TV series)

Montgomery, George (George Montgomery Letz) (1916–) Am. actor (*Riders of the Purple Sage; Davy Crockett—Indian Scout* [title role])

Montgomery, Lucy Maud (née MacDonald) (1874–1942) Can. children's book writer (*Anne of Green Gables*)

Montgomery, Robert (Henry Montgomery, Jr.) (1904–1981) Am. actor (*The Lady in the Lake*)/politician (father of Elizabeth)

Montgomery, Wes (John Leslie Montgomery) (1925–1968) Am. jazz guitarist

Montoya, Carlos (1933–1993) Span.-Am. composer/guitarist

Montrose, Ronnie (C) Am. rock guitarist (with Montrose, "Rock Candy"; with Gamma, "Fight to the Finish")

Moody, Dwight (Dwight Lyman Moody) (1837–1899) Am. evangelist

Moody, Ron (Ronald Moodnick) (1924–)

Eng. actor (*Oliver!* [as Fagin]; *David Copperfield*)

Moog, Robert (1934–) Am. inventor (synthesizer)

Moon, Keith (1946–1978) Eng. rock drummer (with The Who)

Moon, Reverend Sun Myung (1920–) Kor. evangelist (established the Unification Church)

Moore, Archie (Archibald Lee Wright; "Ol' Man River"; "The Old Mongoose") (1913–) Am. boxer

Moore, Brian (1921–) Ir.-Can.-Am. novelist (*The Lonely Passion of Judith Hearne*)

Moore, Clayton (1908–) Am. actor (TV's "Lone Ranger")

Moore, Clement C. (Clement Clarke Moore) (1779–1863) Am. scholar/poet (*A Visit from St. Nicholas*)

Moore, Colleen (Kathleen Morrison) (1900–1988) Am. actress (*Ella Cinders*; *The Scarlet Letter*)

Moore, Constance (1919–) Am. singer/actress (*Show Business*)

Moore, Demi (Demetria Guynes) (1962–) Am. actress (*Ghost*; *Indecent Proposal*; *A Few Good Men*)

Moore, Douglas (Douglas Stuart Moore) (1893–1969) Am. composer ("Giants in the Earth"; "The Devil and Daniel Webster")

Moore, Dudley (Dudley Stuart John Moore) (1935–) Eng. musician/actor (*Arthur*; *10*)

Moore, Garry (Thomas Garrison Morfit) (1915–1993) Am. TV host ("The Garry Moore Show")/game show host ("I've Got a Secret")

Moore, G. E. (George Edward Moore) (1873–1958) Eng. philosopher (ideal utilitarianism)

Moore, George (George Augustus Moore) (1852–1933) Ir. novelist/playwright/poet (*Heloise and Abelard*)

Moore, Grace (Mary Willie Grace Moore) (1901–1947) Am. opera singer (soprano)/actress (*One Night of Love*)

Moore, Henry (Henry Spencer Moore; "The Father of the Hole") (1898–1986) Eng. avant-garde sculptor

Moore, Kieron (Kieron O'Hanrahan) (1925–) Ir. actor (*Anna Karenina*; *Mine Own Executioner*)

Moore, Lenny (Leonard Edward Moore) (1933–) Am. football Hall-of-Famer

Moore, Marianne (Marianne Craig Moore) (1887–1972) Am. poet (P— 1952—*Collected Poems*)

Moore, Mary Tyler (1936–) Am. actress (*Ordinary People*; "The Mary Tyler Moore Show" and "The Dick Van Dyke Show" TV series; E—1963/64, 1965/66, 1972/73, 1973/74, 1975/76)

Moore, Melba (Melba Beatrice Hill) (1945–) Am. soul singer ("You Stepped into My Life")

Moore, Michael (c. 1954–) Am. journalist/filmmaker (*Roger and Me*)

Moore, Robin (Robert Lowell Moore, Jr.) (1925–) Am. novelist (*The French Connection*)

Moore, Roger (Roger George Moore) (1927–) Eng. actor (James Bond in films; TV's Simon Templar [The Saint])

Moore, Sam (Samuel Moore) (1935–) Am. soul singer (with Sam & Dave; "Soul Man")

Moore, Sarah Jane (1930–) Am. criminal (attempted to assassinate Gerald Ford)

Moore, Stanford (1913–1982) Am. biochemist (N—1972)

Moore, Terry (Helen Koford) (1929–) Am. actress (*The Sunny Side of the Street*; *Come Back Little Sheba*)

Moore, Victor (Victor Frederick Moore) (1876–1962) Am. actor (*Swing Time*; *Ziegfeld Follies*)

Moorehead, Agnes (Agnes Robinson Moorehead) (1906–1974) Am. actress ("Bewitched" TV series; *Citizen Kane*; *The Magnificent Ambersons*)

Morales, Esai (1962–) Am. actor (*La Bamba*; *Bloodhounds of Broadway*; *Bad Boys*)

Moran, Bugs (George Moran) (1893–1957) Am. (Chicago) crime boss

Moran, Erin (1961–) Am. actress ("Happy Days" TV series)

Moran, Thomas (1837–1926) Eng.-Am. landscape painter

Moranis, Rick (1953–) Can.-Am. comedian/actor (*Honey, I Shrunk the Kids*; *Ghostbusters*; *Spaceballs*)

Morante, Elsa (1916–1985) Ital. novelist/poet (*House of Liars*; *Arturo's Island*)

Moravia, Alberto (Alberto Pincherle) (1907–1990) Ital. novelist/short story writer/essayist/playwright (*Two Women*)

More, Sir Thomas (1478–1535) Eng. poet/statesman/writer (*Utopia*)

Moreau, Jeanne (1928–) Fr. actress (*Diary of a Chambermaid*; *Jules and Jim*)

Moreland, Mantan (1902–1973) Am. actor (*Charlie Chan* films)

Moreno, Rita (Rosita Dolores Alverio; a/k/a Rosita Moreno) (1931–) P.R. actress (*The King and I*; O—1961—*West Side Story*)

Morenz, Howie (Howarth William Morenz; "The Babe Ruth of Hockey"; "Meteor"; "The Stratford Flash"; "The Stratford Streak"; "Hurtling Habitant") (1902–1937) Can. hockey player

Morgan, Dennis (Stanley Morner; a/k/a Richard Stanley) (1910–) Am. opera singer/actor (*My Wild Irish Rose*; "21 Beacon Street" TV series)

Morgan, Frank (Francis Philip Wupperman) (1890–1949) Am. actor (*The Wizard of Oz* [title role])

Morgan, Harry (Harry Bratsburg; a/k/a Henry Morgan) (1915–) Am. actor ("M*A*S*H" TV series; *State Fair*; *High Noon*; E—1979/80)

Morgan, Helen (Helen Riggins) (1900–1941) Am. torch singer (played by Ann Blyth in *The Helen Morgan Story*)

Morgan, Jane (1880–1972) Am. actress ("Our Miss Brooks" TV series)

Morgan, Jane (1920–1974) Am. singer

Morgan, Jaye P. (Mary Margaret Morgan) (1931–) Am. singer ("That's All I Want from You")/game show panelist

Morgan, Joe (Joseph Leonard Morgan) (1943–) Am. baseball Hall-of-Famer

Morgan, J. P. (John Pierpont Morgan) (1837–1913) Am. financier/industrialist (formed the United States Steel Corp.)

Morgan, Julia (1872–1957) Am. architect (Hearst Castle)

Morgan, Lorrie (Loretta Lynn Morgan) (1959–) Am. country singer ("Something in Red"; "Picture of Me [without You]")

Morgan, Marabel (1937–) Am. writer (*The Total Woman*)

Morgenthau, Henry (Henry Morenthau, Jr.) (1891–1967) Am. politician/govt. official (treasury secretary)/writer

Moriarty, Michael (1941–) Am. actor (*Holocaust*; *Bang the Drum Slowly*; *The Last Detail*; "Law & Order" TV series; T—1974)

Morison, Samuel Eliot (1887–1976) Am. historian/writer (P—1942—*Admiral of the Ocean Sea*; P—1960—*John Paul Jones*)

Morisot, Berthe (1841–1895) Fr. impressionist painter (granddaughter of Fragonard)

Morita, Akio (1921–) Jap. businessman (cofounded Sony)

Morita, Pat (Noriyuki Morita) (1930–) Jap.-Am. actor (*The Karate Kid*)

Morley, Christopher (Christopher Darlington Morley; "Kit") (1890–1957) Am. editor/writer (*Parnassus on Wheels*)

Morley, Robert (1908–1992) Eng. actor (*Marie Antoinette*; *Of Human Bondage*)

Moro, Aldo (1916–1978) Ital. prime minister 1974–1976 (kidnapped/murdered by Red Brigade terrorists)

Moroder, Giorgio (1940–) Am. pop music producer (Donna Summer)/film composer (*Midnight Express*)

Morricone, Ennio (a/k/a Leo Nichols and Nicola Piovani) (1928–) Ital.-Am. film composer (*A Fistful of Dollars*; *The Untouchables*; over 300 others)

Morris, Chester (John Chester Brooks Morris) (1901–1970) Am. actor (*The Big House*; *The Great White Hope*; *Boston Blackie* films [title role])

Morris, Garrett (1937–) Am. comedian/actor/singer ("Saturday Night Live" TV series)

Morris, Gary (1948–) Am. country singer (100% Chance of Rain")

Morris, Greg (Gregory Allan Williams) (1934–) Am. actor ("Mission: Impossible" TV series)

Morris, Robert (1931–1992) Am. sculptor

Morris, Wayne (Bertram de Wayne Morris) (1914–1959) Am. actor (*Kid Galahad*; *Lonesome Trail*)

Morris, William (1834–1896) Eng. artist/architect/poet/writer (*News from Nowhere*)

Morris, Willie (1934–) Am. editor/novelist/nonfiction writer (*North Toward Home*)

Morris, Wright (Wright Marion Morris) (1910–) Am. novelist (*Love Among the Cannibals*)

Morrison, Jim (James Douglas Morrison; "The Lizard King") (1943–1971) Am. rock singer/poet (with The Doors)

Morrison, Toni (Chloe Anthony Wofford) (1931–) Am. novelist (*Song of Solomon*; P—1988—*Beloved*; N—1993; first Afr.-Am. woman to win Nobel in literature)

Morrison, Van (George Ivan Morrison) (1945–) Ir.-Am. rock singer/musician ("Brown Eyed Girl"; "Domino"; "Wavelength")

Morrissey (Stephen Morrissey) (1959–) Eng. pop singer (with The Smiths)
Morrissey, Paul (1939–) Am. film director (Andy Warhol movies)
Morrow, Rob (1962–) Am. actor ("Northern Exposure" TV series)
Morrow, Vic (1932–1982) Am. film director/actor (father of Jennifer Jason Leigh; "Combat!" TV series; *The Blackboard Jungle*)
Morse, Robert (Robert Alan Morse) (1931–) Am. actor (*How to Succeed in Business without Really Trying*; played Truman Capote on Broadway; T—1962, 1990)
Morse, Samuel F. B. (Samuel Finley Breese Morse) (1791–1872) Am. artist/inventor (Morse Code, electric telegraph, underwater telegraph cable)
Mortimer, Penelope (Penelope Dimont) (1918–) Eng. novelist (*Johanna*)
Morton, Jelly Roll (Joseph Ferdinand La Menthe Morton) (1885–1941) Am. jazz pianist/composer ("King Porter Stomp"; "Jelly Roll Blues")
Morton, Levi P. (Levi Parsons Morton) (1824–1920) Am. v.p. (B. Harrison)
Morvan, Fab (Fabrice Morvan) (1963–) Ger. entertainer (with Milli Vanilli)
Mosbacher, Georgette (Georgette Paulsin; "Jawsette") (c. 1947–) Am. socialite/cosmetics company executive/writer (*Feminine Force*)
Mosbacher, Robert (Robert Adam Mosbacher) (1927–) Am. oil tycoon/govt. official (Secretary of Commerce)
Mosel, Tad (George Ault Mosel, Jr.) (1922–) Am. playwright (P—1961—*All the Way Home*)
Moser-Proell, Annemarie see Proell, Annemarie
Moses (14th–13th centruy B.C.) Heb. prophet/lawgiver
Moses, Edwin (Edwin Corley Moses) (1955–) Am. hurdler
Moses, Grandma (Anna Mary Robertson) (1860–1961) Am. painter (*Catching the Thanksgiving Turkey*)
Mosley-Braun, Carol (1947–) Am. senator
Moss, Kate (c. 1973–) Eng. "waif" model (Calvin Klein ads with Marky Mark)
Moss, Stirling (Stirling Crauford Moss) (1929–) Eng. auto racer
Most, Donny (1953–) actor ("Happy Days" TV series)
Mostel, Josh (Joshua Mostel) (1957–) Am. actor (son of Zero; "Murphy's Law" TV series)

Mostel, Zero (Samuel Joel Mostel) (1915–1977) Am. actor (*Fiddler on the Roof*; T—1961, 1963, 1965)
Mother Teresa (Agnes Gonxha Bojaxhiu; "Saint of the Gutters") (1910–) Alb. Roman Catholic nun/humanitarian (N—1979)
Motherwell, Robert (Robert Burns Motherwell) (1915–1991) Am. abstract expressionist/"colorfield" painter
Motley, Marion (1920–) Am. football Hall-of-Famer
Motley, Willard (Willard Francis Motley) (1912–1965) Am. novelist (*Knock on Any Door*)
Motta, Dick (John Richard Motta) (1931–) Am. basketball coach
Mountbatten, Louis (Prince Louis Francis Albert Victor Nicholas of Battenberg) (1900–1979) Eng. admiral/statesman
Mouskouri, Nana (1936–) Gr. torch singer
Mowat, Farley (Farley McGill Mowat) (1921–) Can. writer (*A Whale for the Killing*; *Cry Wolf*)
Mowbray, Alan (1893–1969) Eng. actor ("Colonel Flack" TV series; *Peg O' My Heart*)
Moyers, Bill (William Don Moyers) (1934–) Am. press secretary/newscaster/writer (*Bill Moyers' Journal*)
Moyet, Alison (Genevieve Alison-Jane Moyet; "Alf") (1961–) Eng. pop singer ("Invisible"; formerly with Yaz)
Moynihan, Daniel P. (Daniel Patrick Moynihan) (1927–) Am. senator/diplomat/writer
Mozart, Wolfgang Amadeus (Johannes Chrysostomus Wolfgangus Theophilus) (1756–1791) Aus. composer (*The Magic Flute*; *The Marriage of Figaro*; *Don Giovanni*)
Mubarak, Hosni (Muhammad Hosni Mubarak) (1928–) Egypt. pres. 1981–
Mudd, Roger (Roger Harrison Mudd) (1928–) Am. newscaster
Mueller-Stahl, Armin (1920–) Ger. actor (*Music Box*; *Avalon*)
Mugabe, Robert (Robert Gabriel Mugabe) (1924–) Zimbabwean prime minister 1980–1987/pres. 1987–
Muggeridge, Malcolm (1903–1990) Eng. journalist/writer (*Things Past*)
Muhammad (Abū Al-Qāsim Muhammad ibn 'Abd Allāh ibn 'Abd Al-Muttalib ibn Hāshim; "The Apostle of the Sword") (c. 570–632) Arab prophet/founder of Islam
Muhammad, Elijah (Robert Poole; "Mes-

senger of Allah") (1897–1975) Afr.-Am. nationalist religious leader (Nation of Islam)

Muir, Edwin (1887–1959) Scot. poet/critic (*The Labyrinth*; *The Voyage*)

Muir, Gavin (1907–1972) Am. actor (*Nightmare*; *Hitler's Children*)

Muir, John (1838–1914) Am. naturalist/writer (*The Yosemite*)

Muldaur, Diana (Diana Charlton Muldaur) (1943–) Am. actress ("L.A. Law" TV series)

Muldaur, Maria (Maria Grazia Rose Domenica d'Amato) (1943–) Am. pop singer ("Midnight at the Oasis")

Muldowney, Shirley ("Cha-Cha") (1940–) Am. auto racer

Mulford, Clarence E. (Clarence Edward Mulford) (1883–1956) Am. western novelist (created Hopalong Cassidy)

Mulgrew, Kate (Katherine Mulgrew) (1955–) Am. actress ("Ryan's Hope" soap opera)

Mulhare, Edward (1923–) Ir. actor ("The Ghost and Mrs. Muir" and "Knight Rider" TV series)

Mull, Martin (1943–) Am. comedian/actor ("Fernwood 2-Night" and "Mary Hartman, Mary Hartman" TV series)

Muller, Hermann J. (Hermann Joseph Muller) (1890–1967) Am. biologist/geneticist (N—1946)

Müller, Paul (Paul Hermann Müller) (1899–1965) Swi. chemist (invented the pesticide DDT; N—1948)

Mulligan, Gerry (Gerald Joseph Mulligan) (1927–) Am. jazz saxophonist

Mulligan, Richard (1932–) Am. actor ("Soap" and "Empty Nest" TV series; E—1979/80, 1988/89)

Mulloy, Gardnar (1913–) Am. tennis player

Mulroney, Dermot (c. 1964–) Am. actor (*The Thing Called Love*; *Where the Day Takes You*; *Longtime Companion*)

Mulroney, Brian (Martin Brian Mulroney) (1939–) Can. prime minister 1984–1993

Mumford, Lewis (1895–1990) Am. philosopher/writer (*The Pentagon of Power*)

Mumtaz, Mahal (Arjumand Banu Baygam) (1592–1631) Ind. wife of Shah Jahan (the Taj Mahal is her mausoleum)

Mumy, Billy (1954–) Am. child actor ("Lost in Space" TV series)

Münch, Charles (1891–1968) Fr. orchestra conductor (Paris Philharmonic, Boston Symphony)

Munch, Edvard (1863–1944) Norw. painter (of macabre scenes; *The Cry*)

Münchhausen, Baron (Karl Friedrich Hieronymus von Münchhausen) (1720–1797) Ger. soldier/raconteur

Mungo, Van Lingle (1911–1985) Am. baseball pitcher

Muni, Paul (Muni Weisenfreund) (1895–1967) Am. actor (*Scarface* [1932]; *I Am a Fugitive from a Chain Gang*; O—1936—*The Story of Louis Pasteur*; T—1956)

Munsil, Patrice (Patrice Beverly Munsel) (1925–) Am. opera singer (soprano)

Munson, Ona (Ona Wolcott) (1906–1955) Am. actress (*The Shanghai Gesture*; *Gone with the Wind*)

Munson, Thurman (Thurman Lee Munson; "Squatty") (1947–1979) Am. baseball player

Murdoch, Dame Iris (Jean Iris Murdoch) (1919–) Eng. novelist/philosopher (*The Good Apprentice*)

Murdoch, Rupert (Keith Rupert Murdoch) (1931–) Austral.-Am. newspaper publisher (*London Times*; *Chicago Sun-Times*)

Murillo, Bartolome (Bartolome Esteban Murillo; "The Raphael of Seville") (1617–1682) Span. painter (*Ecstasy of St. Diego of Alcala*)

Murphey, Michael (Martin; a/k/a Travis Lewis) (1938–) Am. rock/country singer/songwriter ("Wildfire")

Murphy, Audie (Audie Leon Murphy; "Baby Murphy") (1924–1971) Am. soldier/actor (*The Red Badge of Courage*)

Murphy, Ben (Benjamin Edward Murphy) (1941–) Am. actor ("Alias Smith and Jones" TV series)

Murphy, Calvin (Calvin Jerome Murphy) (1948–) Am. basketball player

Murphy, Eddie (Edward Regan Murphy) (1961–) Am. comedian/actor ("Saturday Night Live" TV series; *Beverly Hills Cop*; *48 HRS.*; *Harlem Nights*)

Murphy, George (George Lloyd Murphy) (1902–1992) Am. actor (*Bataan*)/senator

Murphy, Peter (C) Eng. singer/songwriter ("Cuts You Up"; formerly with Bauhaus)

Murphy, Walter (1952–) Am. jazz pianist/arranger ("A Fifth of Beethoven"; arranger for "The Tonight Show" orchestra)

Murray, Anne (Morna Anne Murray)

(1945–) Can. pop singer ("Snowbird"; "You Needed Me"; G—1978)

Murray, Arthur (Arthur Murray Teichman) (1895–) Am. TV host/dance instructor

Murray, Bill (1950–) Can.-Am. actor/comedian ("Saturday Night Live" TV series; *Groundhog Day*; *Scrooged*; *Ghostbusters*)

Murray, Don (Donald Patrick Murray) (1929–) Am. actor ("Knots Landing" TV series; *The Bachelor Party*)

Murray, Jan (Murray Janowitz or Janofsky) (1917–) Am. comedian/TV host

Murray, Ken (Kenneth Abner Doncourt) (1903–) Am. actor (*The Man Who Shot Liberty Valance*)/TV host (home movies of celebrities on "The Ken Murray Show")

Murray, Mae (Marie Adrienne Koenig) (1889–1965) Am. actress (*The Merry Widow*; *To Have and to Hold*)

Murrow, Edward R. (Edward Roscoe Murrow; born Egbert Roscoe Murrow) (1908–1965) Am. TV newscaster ("See It Now"; "Person to Person")

Musante, Tony (1936–) Am. actor (*The Detective*; *Show Boat*; *Daniel Boone*)

Musberger, Brent (Brent Woody Musberger) (1939–) Am. sportscaster

Musial, Stan (Stanley Frank Musial; "The Man") (1920–) Am. baseball Hall-of-Famer

Music, Lorenzo (1937–) Am. TV producer/actor ("Rhoda" [as Carlton the Doorman] TV series)

Musil, Robert von (1880–1942) Aus.-Ger. novelist (*The Man without Qualities*)

Muskie, Edmund (Edmund Sixtus Muskie) (1914–) Am. senator/presidential candidate 1972

Musset, Alfred de (Louis-Charles-Albert de Musset) (1810–1857) Fr. playwright/poet (*Les Nuits*)

Mussolini, Benito (Benito Amilcare Andrea Mussolini; "Il Duce") (1883–1945) Ital. dictator 1925–1945

Mussorgsky, Modest (Modest Petrovich Mussorgsky) (1839–1881) Russ. composer (*Pictures at an Exhibition*; *Night on Bald Mountain*; *Boris Gudunov*)

Muti, Riccardo (1941–) Ital. conductor (Philadelphia Orchestra)

Mutsuhito (a/k/a Meiji) (1852–1912) Jap. emperor 1867–1912

Muybridge, Eadweard (Edward James

Muggeridge) (1830–1904) Am. photographer/film pioneer

Myers, Mike (1962–) Can. comedian ("Saturday Night Live" TV series; *Wayne's World*)

Myers, Russell (1938–) Am. cartoonist (*Broom Hilda*)

Myerson, Bess (1924–) Am. TV host/columnist/Miss America 1945

Myles, Alannah (c. 1958–) Can. rock singer ("Black Velvet")

Myrdal, Gunnar (Karl Gunnar Myrdal) (1898–1987) Swed. economist/writer (*An American Dilemma*; N—1974)

Myron (fl. c. 480–440 B.C.) Gr. sculptor (*Discus Thrower*)

Nabokov, Vladimir (Vladimir Vladimirovich Nabokov) (1899–1977) Russ.-Am. novelist/poet (*Lolita*)

Nabors, Jim (James Thurston Nabors) (1932–) Am. singer/actor (TV's "Gomer Pyle, U.S.M.C.")

Nader, Ralph ("The People's Lawyer") (1934–) Am. lawyer/consumer advocate/writer (*Unsafe at Any Speed*)

Nagel, Conrad (1896–1970) Austral. actor (*Little Women* [1919]; *Heaven on Earth*)

Nagle, Kel (Kelvin David George Nagle) (1920–) Am. golfer

Nagurski, Bronko (Bronislaw Nagurski) (1908–1990) Can.-Am. football Hall-of-Famer

Nagy, Imre (1896–1958) Hung. communist premier 1953–1955

Naidu, Sarojini (née Chattopadhyay; "The Nightingale of India") (1879–1949) Ind. poet (*The Broken Wing*)

Naipaul, Sir V. S. (Vidiadhar Surajprasad Naipaul) (1932–) W. Ind. novelist/journalist (*A Bend in the River*; *The Middle Passage*)

Nair, Mira (1957–) Ind. film director (*Salaam Bombay*; *Mississippi Masala*)

Naish, J. Carrol (Joseph Patrick Carrol Naish) (1900–1973) Am. actor ("The Adventures of Charlie Chan" TV series; *Sahara*)

Naismith, James (James A. Naismith; "Father of Basketball") (1861–1939) Am. educator/inventor of basketball

Naldi, Nita (Anita Donna Dooley) (1899–1961) Ital.-Am. dancer (Ziegfeld Follies)/actress (*Blood and Sand*)

Namath, Joe (Joseph William Namath; "Broadway Joe") (1943–) Am. football Hall-of-Famer

Nanak (1469–c. 1539) founder of the Indian Sikh faith
Napoleon III (Louis-Napoleon) (1808–1873) Fr. emperor 1852–1870
Naruhito (c. 1960–) Jap. prince (son of Akihito)
Nash, Charles (Charles William Nash) (1864–1948) Am. automobile manufacturer
Nash, Clarence ("Ducky") (1904–1985) Am. voice performer (Donald Duck)
Nash, Graham (1942–) Eng.-Am. pop singer/musician (with Crosby, Stills, Nash & Young)
Nash, Johnny (1940–) Am. reggae/pop singer ("I Can See Clearly Now")
Nash, Ogden (Frederic Ogden Nash) (1902–1971) Am. poet/writer/humorist (Hard Lines; The Bad Parents' Garden of Verse)
Nashe, Thomas (1567–1601) Eng. playwright/satirist (An Anatomie of Absurdities)
Nasser, Gamal Abdel (1918–1970) Egypt. pres. 1956–1958
Nast, Condé (Condé Montrose Nast) (1873–1942) Am. magazine publisher (Vogue, Vanity Fair, House and Garden, Glamour)
Nast, Thomas (1840–1902) Am. cartoonist (created the Republican elephant and the Democratic donkey)
Nastase, Ilie ("Nasty") (1946–) Rom. tennis player
Nathan, George Jean (1882–1958) Am. drama critic
Nathans, Daniel (1928–) Am. biologist (N—1978)
Nation, Carry (Carry Amelia Nation née Moore) (1846–1911) Am. social reformer (temperance advocate)
Natwick, Mildred (1908–) Am. actress ("The Snoop Sisters" TV series; Barefoot in the Park)
Naughton, David (1951–) Am. actor (An American Werewolf in London; "My Sister Sam" TV series; Dr. Pepper commercials)
Navarro, Fats (Theodore Navarro; "Fat Girl") (1923–1950) Am. jazz trumpeter
Navratilova, Martina (1956–) Cz.-Am. tennis player (W—1978, 1979, 1982–1987, 1990)
Nazimova, Alla (Alla Leventon; a/k/a Nazimova) (1878–1945) Russ.-Am. stage actress (The Cherry Orchard; Mourning Becomes Electra)

Neagle, Dame Anna (Florence Marjorie Robertson; a/k/a Marjorie Robertson) (1904–1986) Eng. actress (Nell Gwyn [title role])
Neal, Patricia (Patricia Louise Neal) (1926–) actress (A Face in the Crowd; The Subject Was Roses; O—1963—Hud)
Nealon, Kevin (1953–) Am. comedian/actor ("Saturday Night Live" TV series)
Neame, Ronald (1911–) Eng. film director (The Prime of Miss Jean Brodie; Pygmalion)
Near, Holly (1949–) Am. pop singer/songwriter
Nebuchadnezzar II (c. 630–562 B.C.) Bab. king 605–562 B.C.
Neeson, Liam (1952–) Ir.-Am. actor (Darkman; The Good Mother; Husbands and Wives; Schindler's List)
Nefertiti (1390–1360 B.C.) Egypt. queen c. 1379–1360 B.C.
Neff, Hildegarde (a/k/a Hildegard Knef) (1925–) Eng.-Ger. actress (The Snows of Kilamanjaro)
Negri, Pola (Appolonia Barbara Chalupek) (1897–1987) Am. actress (Forbidden Paradise)
Nehemiah (5th century B.C.) Heb. prophet/Jewish leader
Nehru, Jawaharlal (1889–1964) Ind. prime minister 1947–1964 (father of Indira Gandhi)
Neil, Vince (Vincent Wharton) (1961–) Am. rock singer (with Mötley Crüe; "Dr. Feelgood")
Neill, Sam (Nigel Neill) (1948–) N.Z.-Am. actor (Dead Calm; Jurassic Park; My Brilliant Career)
Neiman, Leroy (1926–) Am. painter (of athletes)
Nelligan, Kate (Patricia Colleen Nelligan) (1951–) Can. actress (Eleni)
Nelson, Baby Face (Lester Nelson Gillis) (1908–1934) Am. bank robber (member of the Dillinger gang)
Nelson, Barry (Robert Haakon Neilson) (1920–) Am. actor ("My Favorite Husband" and "The Hunter" TV series)
Nelson, Byron (John Byron Nelson, Jr.; "Lord Byron") (1912–) Am. golfer
Nelson, Craig T. (1946–) Am. actor ("Coach" TV series)
Nelson, E. Benjamin (1941–) Am. gov. of Nebraska
Nelson, Gunnar (1967–) Am. rock singer

(son of Ricky, brother of Matthew and Tracy; with The Nelsons)

Nelson, Harriet (Peggy Lou Snyder) (1914–) Am. actress/singer (mother of Ricky; "The Adventures of Ozzie and Harriet" TV series)

Nelson, Viscount Horatio (1758–1805) Eng. navy admiral

Nelson, Judd (1959–) Am. actor (*St. Elmo's Fire*; *The Breakfast Club*)

Nelson, Matthew (1967–) Am. rock singer (with The Nelsons)

Nelson, Ozzie (Oswald George Nelson) (1906–1975) Am. bandleader/actor ("The Adventures of Ozzie and Harriet" TV series)

Nelson, Ricky (Eric Hilliard Nelson) (1940–1986) Am. pop singer ("Travelin' Man")/actor (*Rio Bravo*)

Nelson, Tracy (1963–) Am. actress (sister of Gunnar and Matthew; "The Father Dowling Mysteries" TV series)

Nelson, Willie (Willie Hugh Nelson; "Outlaw"; "The Redheaded Stranger") (1933–) Am. country singer/musician/ songwriter ("Always on My Mind"; "On the Road Again")/actor (*Honeysuckle Rose*)

Nemec, Corky (Corin Nemec) (c. 1972–) Am. actor ("Parker Lewis Can't Lose" TV series)

Nemerov, Howard (1920–1991) Am. novelist/short story writer/poet (P— 1978—*Collected Poems*)

Nena (Gabriele Kerner) (1960–) Ger. pop singer ("99 Red Balloons [99 Luftballons]")

Nero (Nero Claudius Caesar Drusus Germanicus; born Lucius Domitius Ahenobarbus) (37–68) Roman emperor 54–68

Nero, Franco (Franco Spartanero) (1941–) Ital. actor (*Camelot*; *Force 10 from Navarone*)

Nero, Peter (Peter Bernard Nierow) (1934–) Am. jazz/pop pianist ("Theme from Summer of '42"; G—1961)

Neruda, Pablo (Neftalí Ricardo Reyes y Basoalto) (1904–1973) Chil. poet (*Toward the Splendid City*; *End of the World*; N—1971)

Nerva, Marcus Cocceius (c. 30–98) Roman emperor 96–98

Nesbitt, Cathleen (Cathleen Mary Nesbitt) (1888–1982) Eng. actress (*An Affair to Remember*; "Upstairs, Downstairs" TV series)

Nesmith, Mike (Michael Nesmith) (1942–) Am. pop musician (with The Monkees)/ filmmaker (*Elephant Parts*)

Ness, Eliot ("The Untouchable") (1903–1957) Am. treasury agent (captured Al Capone)

Nestor (c. 1056–1113) Russ. monk

Nettles, Graig (1944–) Am. baseball player

Nettleton, Lois (Lois June Nettleton) (c. 1929–) Am. actress (*The Best Little Whorehouse in Texas*)

Neumann, Kurt (1908–1958) Ger. film director (*The Fly* [1958]; *The Deerslayer*)

Neuwirth, Bebe (c. 1959–) Am. actress ("Cheers" TV series; *Malice*; E— 1989/90, 1990/91)

Nevelson, BLouise (Louise Berliawsky) (1899–1988) Russ.-Am. painter/sculptor

Nevers, Ernie (Ernest A. Nevers; "Big Dog") (1903–1976) Am. football Hall-of-Famer

Neville, Aaron (1941–) Am. pop singer ("Don't Know Much" duet with Linda Ronstadt; with The Neville Brothers)

Nevin, Ethelbert (Ethelbert Woodbridge Nevin) (1862–1901) Am. composer ("Mighty Lak a Rose")

Nevins, Allan (1890–1971) Am. historian/ biographer/writer (P—1933—*Grover Cleveland*; P—1937—*Hamilton Fish: The Inner History of the Grant Administration*)

Nevsky, Alexander (c. 1220–1263) Russ. soldier/political leader

Newbery, John (1713–1767) Eng. newspaper/children's book publisher (for whom the Newbery Award was named)

Newborn, Phineas, Jr. (1932–1989) Am. jazz pianist

Newcombe, John (John David Newcombe; "Newk") (1943–) Austral. tennis player (W—1967, 1970, 1971)

Newhart, Bob (George Robert Newhart) (1929–) Am. comedian/actor ("Newhart" and "The Bob Newhart Show" TV series; G—1960)

Newhouse, S. I. (Samuel Irving Newhouse) (1895–1979) Am. publisher (owner of the *New Yorker*; Random House)

Newhouser, Hal (Harold Newhouser; "Prince Hal") (1921–) Am. baseball pitcher

Newley, Anthony (Anthony George Newley) (1931–) Eng. singer/actor (*Oliver Twist*; *Dr. Dolittle*)

Newman, Alfred (1901–1970) Am. film composer (*Alexander's Ragtime Band*; *Love Is a Many-Splendored Thing*)

Newman, Barnett (1905–1970) Am. abstract expressionist painter

Newman, Barry (Barry Foster Newman) (1938–) Am. actor (TV's "Petrocelli")

Newman, Edwin (Edwin Harold Newman) (1919–) Am. newscaster/writer

Newman, Laraine (1952–) Am. actress/comedienne ("Saturday Night Live" TV series)

Newman, Nanette (1934–) Eng. actress (*The League of Gentlemen*; *Of Human Bondage*)

Newman, Paul (1925–) Am. actor (*Cat on a Hot Tin Roof*; *The Hustler*; *Cool Hand Luke*; O—1986—*The Color of Money*)

Newman, Randy (1943–) Am. pop singer/musician/songwriter ("Short People")/film composer (*The Natural*; *Avalon*)

Newmar, Julie (Julia Charlene Newmeyer) (1935–) Am. actress (Catwoman in "Batman" TV series)

Newsome, Ozzie (1956–) Am. football player

Newton, Helmut (1920–) Am. fashion photographer

Newton, Huey P. (Huey Percy Newton) (1942–1989) Am. political activist (founded the Black Panther party)

Newton, Sir Isaac (1642–1727) Eng. physicist/mathematician (invented calculus; Newton's law of gravity)

Newton, Juice (Judy Kay Cohen) (1952–) Am. pop/country singer ("Angel of the Morning"; "Queen of Hearts")

Newton, Robert (1905–1956) Eng. actor (*Treasure Island*; *Oliver Twist*)

Newton, Wayne ("Mr. Las Vegas") (1942–) Am. singer ("Danke Schoen"; "Daddy Don't You Walk So Fast")

Newton-John, Olivia (1948–) Eng.-Austral. pop singer ("I Honestly Love You"; "Have You Never Been Mellow"; "Magic"; G—1974)/actress (*Grease*; *Xanadu*)

Nexø, Martin (Martin Anderson Nexø) (1869–1954) Dan. novelist/short story writer (*Pelle the Conqueror*)

Nicholas I (Nikolay Pavlovich) (1796–1855) Russ. czar 1825–1855

Nicholas II (Nikolay Aleksandrovich) (1868–1918) Russ. czar 1894–1917

Nichols, Anne (1891–1966) Am. playwright (*Abie's Irish Rose*)

Nichols, Bobby (Robert Nichols) (1936–) Am. golfer

Nichols, Kid (Charles Augustus Nichols) (1869–1953) Am. baseball Hall-of-Famer

Nichols, Mike (Michael Igor Peschowsky) (1931–) Am. film director (*Who's Afraid of Virginia Woolf?*; *Carnal Knowledge*; *Catch-22*; O—1967—*The Graduate*)

Nichols, Nichelle (1936–) Am. actress (Uhura in "Star Trek" TV series and films)

Nichols, Peter (1927–) Eng. playwright (*A Day in the Death of Joe Egg*)

Nichols, Red (Ernest Loring Nichols) (1905–1965) Am. jazz bandleader/cornetist

Nicholson, Jack (John Nicholson Rose) (1937–) Am. actor (*Five Easy Pieces*; *Chinatown*; *Batman*; O—1975—*One Flew Over the Cuckoo's Nest*; O—1983—*Terms of Endearment*)

Nicklaus, Jack (Jack William Nicklaus; "The Golden Bear"; "Ohio Fats") (1940–) Am. golfer

Nicks, Stevie (Stephanie Nicks) (1948–) Am. rock singer ("Stand Back"; "Edge of Seventeen"; with Fleetwood Mac)

Nicolai, Otto (Carl Otto Ehrenfried Nicolai) (1810–1849) Ger. operatic composer (*The Merry Wives of Windsor*; *Te Deum*)

Nicolet, Jean (1598–1642) Fr. explorer (Lake Michigan, Wisconsin)

Nidetch, Jean (Jean Slutsky) (1923–) Am. founder of Weight Watchers, Inc. (1963)

Niebuhr, Reinhold (1892–1971) Am. philosopher/theologian (*Nature and Destiny of Man*)

Niekro, Joe (Joseph Franklin Niekro) (1944–) Am. baseball pitcher (brother of Phil)

Niekro, Phil (Philip Henry Niekro; "Knucksie") (1939–) Am. baseball pitcher (brother of Joe)

Nielsen, Arthur (Arthur Charles Nielsen) (1897–1980) Am. market researcher (Nielsen ratings)

Nielsen, Asta (1883–1972) Dan. actress (*Hedda Gabler*; *Miss Julie*)

Nielsen, Brigitte (1963–) Dan. actress (*Cobra*; *Red Sonja*)

Nielsen, Leslie (1925–) Can. actor (*Airplane!*; *Naked Gun* movies)

Nielsen, Rick (1946–) Am. rock guitarist (with Cheap Trick)

Nietzsche, Friedrich (Friedrich Wilhelm Nietzsche) (1844–1900) Ger. philosopher/poet (*Thus Spake Zarathustra*; developed the concepts of the "superman" and the "will to power")

Nightingale, Florence ("The Lady with the Lamp") (1820–1910) Eng. pioneer of nursing

Nightingale, Maxine (1952–) Am. pop singer ("Right Back Where We Started From"; "Lead Me On")

Nijinska, Bronislawa (Bronislawa Fominitshna Nijinska) (1891–1972) Russ.-Am. ballerina/choreographer (with Ballet Russe)

Nijinsky, Vaslav (Waslaw Formich Nijinsky) (1890–1950) Russ.-Am. ballet dancer (with Ballet Russe)

Nilsson, Birgit (Fru Bertil Niklasson) (1918–) Swed. opera singer (soprano)

Nilsson, Harry (Harry Edward Nelson III; a/k/a Nilsson) (1941–1994) Am. rock singer/songwriter/musician ("Without You"; G—1969, 1972)

Nilsson, Ulf (1950–) Swed. hockey player

Nimitz, Chester (Chester William Nimitz) (1885–1966) Am. WWII naval commander

Nimoy, Leonard (1931–) Am. actor (Mr. Spock in "Star Trek" TV series and films)/film director (*Three Men and a Baby*)

Nin, Anaïs (1903–1977) Am. novelist/diarist (*The Diaries of Anaïs Nin*; *House of Incest*)

Nitschke, Ray (Raymond E. Nitschke) (1936–) Am. football Hall-of-Famer

Niven, David (James David Graham Niven) (1909–1983) Eng. actor (*The Prisoner of Zenda*; *The Pink Panther*; O—1958—*Separate Tables*)

Niven, Larry (Laurence Von Cott Niven) (1938–) Am. science fiction writer (*A Hole in Space*; *Footfall*; *Ringworld*)

Nixon, Marni (1929–) Am. pop singer (mother of Andrew Gold)

Nixon, Patricia (Thelma Catherine Patricia Ryan; "Pat") (1912–1993) Am. first lady (Richard Milhous)

Nixon, Richard Milhous ("Tricky Dick") (1913–) 37th Am. pres. (1968–1974) (only pres. in U.S. history to resign, after Watergate scandal)/writer (*Six Crises*)

Nixon, Tricia (Patricia Nixon) (1946–) Am. daughter of Richard Nixon

Nizer, Louis (1902–) Am. lawyer (celebrity clients: L.B. Mayer, Quentin Reynolds, etc.)/writer (*My Life in Court*)

Nobel, Alfred (Alfred Bernhard Nobel) (1833–1896) Swed. engineer/industrialist (established Nobel prizes)/inventor (dynamite, nitroglycerin)

Noble, Chelsea (1964–) Am. actress ("Growing Pains" TV series)

Noguchi, Isamu (1904–1988) Jap.-Am. abstract sculptor

Noguchi, Thomas ("The Coroner of the Stars") (1927–) Am. coroner (model for TV's "Quincy")/writer

Nolan, Jeanette (1911–) Am. actress (*Macbeth*; *The Man Who Shot Liberty Valance*)

Nolan, Kathy (Jocelyn Joan Schrum) (1933–) Am. actress ("The Real McCoys" TV series)

Nolan, Lloyd (1902–1985) Am. actor ("Julia" TV series; *Bataan*)

Nolde, Emil (Emil Hansen) (1867–1956) Ger. expressionist painter/artist

Noll, Chuck (Charles Henry Noll) (1932–) Am. football coach

Nolte, Nick (1941–) Am. actor (*The Prince of Tides*; *Down and Out in Beverly Hills*; *48 Hrs.*)

Nomellini, Leo (Leo Joseph Nomellini) (1924–) Am. football Hall-of-Famer

Noone, Jimmie (1895–1944) Am. jazz clarinetist

Noone, Peter (1947–) Am. rock singer/musician/bandleader (with Herman's Hermits)

Nordenskiöld, Baron Adolf (Nils Adolf Erik Nordenskiöld) (1832–1901) Swed. arctic explorer

Nordica, Lillian (Lillian Norton; "The Lily of the North") (1857–1914) Am. opera singer (soprano)

Nordoff, Charles Bernard (1887–1947) Am. writer (with James Norman Hall, *Mutiny on the Bounty*)

Norell, Norman (Norman Levinson) (1900–1972) Am. fashion designer

Noriega, Manuel (Manuel Antonio Morena Noriega) (1934–) Pan. dictator (imprisoned in the U.S. for drug trafficking)

Norman, Greg (1955–) Austral. golfer

Norman, Jessye (1945–) Am. opera singer (soprano)

Norman, Marsha (Marsha Williams Norman) (1947–) Am. playwright (P—1983—'*Night, Mother*)

Normand, Mabel (Mabel Ethelreid Fortescue; a/k/a Muriel Fortescue) (1894–1930) Am. actress (*Tillie's Punctured Romance*)

Norris, Chuck (Carlos Ray) (1939–) Am. actor (*Good Guys Wear Black*; *The Delta Force*)

Norris, Frank (Benjamin Franklin Norris) (1870–1902) Am. novelist (*McTeague*)

Norris, Kathleen (née Thompson) (1880–1966) Am. novelist (*Through a Glass Darkly*)

North, Frederick (1732–1792) Eng. prime minister 1770–1782

North, Jay (1952–) Am. child actor (TV's "Dennis the Menace")

North, Oliver (Oliver Laurence North, Jr.) (1943–) Am. politician/Marines officer

North, Sheree (Dawn Bethel) (1933–) Am. actress ("The Bay City Blues" TV series)

Northrop, John (John Howard Northrop) (1891–1987) Am. biochemist (N—1946)

Northrop, John Knudsen (1895–1981) Am. aircraft designer/manufacturer

Norton, Andre (Alice Mary Norton; a/k/a Andrew North) (1912–) Am. science fiction writer (*Dark Piper*; *Gryphon's Eyrie*)

Norton, Ken (Kenneth Howard Norton) (1945–) Am. boxer

Norton, Mary (1903–1992) Eng. children's writer (*The Borrowers*)

Norton-Taylor, Judy (1958–) Am. actress ("The Waltons" TV series)

Norville, Deborah (1958–) Am. TV newscaster ("Today")

Norvo, Red (Kenneth Norville) (1908–) Am. jazz vibraphonist/xylophonist

Norwood, Eille (Anthony Brett) (1861–1948) Eng. actor (played Sherlock Holmes in 1920s)

Nostradamus (Michel de Nostredame) (1503–1566) Fr. physician/astrologer (*Centuries*)

Novak, Kim (Marilyn Pauline Novak) (1933–) Am. actress (*Vertigo*; *Bell, Book and Candle*; "Falcon Crest" TV series)

Novak, Robert (1931–) Am. journalist/writer (with Rowland Evans, Jr., *The Reagan Revolution*)

Novarro, Ramon (Ramon Samaniegos) (1899–1968) Mex. actor (*Ben Hur* [1925]; *The Prisoner of Zenda*)

Novello, Don (a/k/a Laszlo Toth and Father Guido Sarducci) (1943–) Am. comedian ("Saturday Night Live" TV series)

Novikoff, Lou (Louie Alexander Novikoff; "The Mad Russian"; "Lusty Lou"; "The Clouting Cossak") (1915–1970) Am. baseball player

Novotný, Antonín (1904–1975) Cz. pres. 1957–1968

Nowlan, Phil (a/k/a Frank Phillips) (1888–1940) Am. cartoonist (with Richard Calkins, created Buck Rogers)

Noyce, Phillip (1950–) Austral. film director (*Dead Calm*)

Noyes, Alfred (1880–1958) Eng. poet (*The Highwayman*)

Nugent, Ted (Theodore Anthony Nugent; "Motor City Mad Man") (1948–) Am. rock singer/guitarist ("Cat Scratch Fever")

Numan, Gary (Gary Anthony James Webb) (1958–) Eng. pop singer/musician ("Cars")

Nunn, Sam (Samuel Augustus Nunn, Jr.) (1938–) Am. lawyer/senator

Nunn, Trevor (Trevor Robert Nunn) (1940–) Eng.-Am. theatrical director (*Cats*; *Les Miserables*; *Starlight Express*)

Nureyev, Rudolf (Rudolf Hametovich Nureyev) (1938–1993) Russ.-Eng. ballet dancer/director

Nurmi, Paavo (Paavo Johannes Nurmi; "The Flying Finn"; "The Phantom Finn"; "Peerless Paavo") (1897–1973) Finn. distance runner

Nutt, Reverend Grady (c. 1935–1982) Am. actor ("Hee Haw" TV series)

Nuyen, France (France Denise Nguyen Vannga) (1939–) Chin.-Fr. actress (*South Pacific*)

Nyad, Diana (1949–) Am. swimmer

Nyby, Christian (1913–) Am. film director (*The Thing*; *Operation CIA*)

Nye, Carrie (c. 1937–) Am. actress (*The Seduction of Joe Tynan*)

Nye, Louis (C) Am. comedian ("The Steve Allen Show" and "The Beverly Hillbillies" TV series)

Nyro, Laura (Laura Nigro) (1947–) Am. pop singer ("Up on the Roof")/songwriter ("Stoned Soul Picnic"; "Stoney End")

Oakes, Randi (1951–) Am. actress ("CHiPS" TV series)

Oakie, Jack (Louis Delaney Offield) (1903–1978) Am. actor (*The Great Dictator*)

Oakland, Simon (1922–1983) Am. actor ("Baa Baa Black Sheep" TV series)

Oakley, Annie (Phoebe Anne Oakley Moses or Mozee; "Little Sure Shot"; "America's Sweetheart") (1860–1926) Am. sharpshooter/rodeo performer

Oates, John (John William Oates) (1948–) Am. rock singer (with Hall & Oates)

Oates, Joyce Carol (1938–) Am. novelist/short story writer/poet (*Them; Unholy Loves*)

Oates, Warren (1928–1982) Am. actor (*The Wild Bunch; Bring Me the Head of Alfredo Garcia*)

Oberon, Merle (Estelle Merle O'Brien Thompson) (1911–1979) Eng. actress (*Wuthering Heights; The Divorce of Lady X*)

O'Brian, Hugh (Hugh Charles Krampe) (1925–) Am. actor ("The Life and Legend of Wyatt Earp" TV series)

O'Brien, Conan (1963–) Am. comedian/talk show host

O'Brien, Conor Cruise (a/k/a Donat O'Donnell) (1917–) Ir. historian/diplomat

O'Brien, Edmond (1915–1985) Am. actor (*Seven Days in May*; O—1954—*The Barefoot Contessa*)

O'Brien, Edna (1932–) Ir. novelist/short story writer (*The Country Girl; Johnny I Hardly Knew You*)

O'Brien, Flann (Brian O'Nolan; a/k/a Myles na gCopaleen) (1911–1966) Ir. essayist/novelist/playwright (*At Swim—Two Birds; The Third Policeman*)

O'Brien, Margaret (Angela Maxine O'Brien) (1937–) Am. actress (*Meet Me in St. Louis; Madame Curie*)

O'Brien, Pat (William Joseph Patrick O'Brien, Jr.) (1899–1983) Am. actor (*Knute Rockne—All American* [title role])

O'Brien-Moore, Erin (Annette Erin O'Brien-Moore) (1902–1979) Am. actress ("Peyton Place" TV series)

Ocasek, Ric (Richard Ocasek) (1949–) Am. rock singer/musician ("Emotion in Motion"; formerly with The Cars)

O'Casey, Sean (John Casey or Sean O'Cathasaigh) (1880–1964) Ir. playwright (*Juno and the Paycock*)

Ocean, Billy (Leslie Sebastian Charles) (1950–) Trin.-Am. pop singer ("Caribbean Queen [No More Love on the Run]"; "Get Outta My Dreams, Get into My Car")

Ochoa, Severo (1905–) Span.-Am. bio-chemist (discovered RNA synthesis; N—1959)

Ochs, Adolph (Adolph Simon Ochs; "The Watchdog of Central Park") (1858–1935) Am. newspaper publisher/editor (*New York Times*; signature phrase: "All the news that's fit to print")

Ochs, Phil (Philip David Ochs) (1940–1976) Am. folk singer ("I Ain't Marchin' Anymore")/political activist

Ockham, William of ("Doctor Invincibilis"; "Venerabilis Inceptor") (c. 1285–1349) Eng. philosopher (Ockham's Razor: "entities must not be unnecessarily multiplied")

O'Connell, Arthur (Arthur Joseph O'Connell) (1908–1981) Am. actor ("Mr. Peepers" TV series; *Picnic; Anatomy of a Murder*)

O'Connell, Helen (1920–1993) Am. singer ("Green Eyes"; "Tangerine"; with Jimmy Dorsey, Artie Shaw, Woody Herman, and Glenn Miller)

O'Connor, Carroll (1924–) Am. actor ("All in the Family" [as Archie Bunker] and "In the Heat of the Night" TV series; E—1971/72, 1976/77, 1977/78, 1988/89)

O'Connor, Donald (Donald David Dixon Ronald O'Connor) (1925–) Am. actor (*Singin' in the Rain; The Buster Keaton Story*)

O'Connor, Edwin (Edwin Greene O'Connor) (1918–1968) Am. writer (P—1962—*The Edge of Sadness*)

O'Connor, Flannery (Mary Flannery O'Connor) (1925–1964) Am. novelist/short story writer (*Wise Blood*)

O'Connor, Kevin J. (1964–) Am. actor (*Steel Magnolias; Hero*)

O'Connor, Mark (1961–) Am. country singer ("Restless")

O'Connor, Sandra Day (1930–) Am. jurist (first woman to serve on the Supreme Court; 1981–)

O'Connor, Sinéad (1966–) Ir. pop singer ("Nothing Compares 2 U")

O'Connor, Una (Agnes Teresa McGlade) (1880–1959) Ir. actress (*The Invisible Man; The Bride of Frankenstein*)

Octavia (69–11 B.C.) Roman woman (wife of Marc Antony; mother of Caligula)

O'Day, Anita (Anita Colton) (1919–) Am. jazz singer

Odets, Clifford (1906–1963) Am. playwright (*Waiting for Lefty; Awake and*

Sing!; *The Country Girl*)/film director (*None But the Lonely Heart*)

Odetta (Odetta Holmes Felious Gordon) (1930–) Am. blues/folk singer

O'Donnell, Chris (1970–) Am. actor (*Scent of a Woman*; *The Three Musketeers* [1993])

O'Donnell, Lillian (Lillian Uduardy O'Donnell) (1926–) Am. mystery writer (created Detective Norah Mulcahaney Capretto of the New York Police Department; *The Baby Merchants*)

O'Donnell, Rosie (c. 1961–) Am. comedienne/actress (*A League of Their Own*; *Sleepless in Seattle*)

Oerter, Al (Alfred A. Oerter) (1936–) Am. discus thrower

Oeschger, Joe (Joseph Carl Oeschger) (1892–?) Am. baseball pitcher

O'Faoláin, Seán (Sean Whelan) (1900–) Ir. novelist/short story writer/biographer (*Midsummer Night Madness and Other Stories*)

Offenbach, Jacques (Jacob Offenbach or Jacob Eberscht) (1819–1880) Fr. composer (*Tales of Hoffman*)

O'Flaherty, Liam (1896–1984) Ir. novelist/ short story writer (*The Informer*)

O'Grady, Desmond (Desmond James Bernard O'Grady) (1935–) Ir. poet (*Sing Me Creation*)

Oh, Sadaharu ("Babe Ruth of Japan") (1940–) Jap. baseball player

O'Hair, Madalyn (Madalyn Murray O'Hair née Mays) (1919–) Am. lawyer/ atheist

O'Hara, Frank (1926–1966) Am. poet (*Meditations in an Emergency*)

O'Hara, John (John Henry O'Hara) (1905– 1970) Am. novelist (*Butterfield 8*; *Pal Joey*; *From the Terrace*)

O'Hara, Mary (Mary O'Hara Alsop) (1885– 1980) Am. writer (*My Friend Flicka*)

O'Hara, Maureen (Maureen Fitzsimmons) (1920–) Ir.-Am. actress (*Miracle on 34th Street*; *The Quiet Man*)

O'Herlihy, Dan (Daniel Peter O'Herlihy) (1919–) Ir. actor (*The Adventures of Robinson Crusoe*; *Kidnapped*)

Oistrakh, David (David Fyodorovich Oistrakh) (1908–1974) Russ. concert violinist (father of Igor)

Oistrakh, Igor (Igor Davidovich Oistrakh) (1931–) Russ. concert violinist (son of David)

Okamoto, Ayako (1951–) Jap. golfer

O'Keefe, Dennis (Edward James [or Vance] Flanagan, Jr.; a/k/a Bud Flanagan) (1908–1968) Am. actor ("The Dennis O'Keefe Show" TV series; *Captains Courageous*)

O'Keeffe, Georgia (1887–1986) Am. painter (abstract floral forms, southwestern scenes)

O'Kelly, Seán (Seán Thomas O'Kelly) (1883–1966) Ir. pres. 1945–1959

Olaf or **Olav** (Alexander Edward Christian Frederick) (1903–1991) Norw. king 1957–1991

Olajuwon, Akeem or **Hakeem** ("The Dream") (1963–) Am. basketball player

Oland, Warner (Johan Warner Öhlund) (1880–1938) Swed.-Am. actor (Charlie Chan in 38 films)

Oldfield, Barney (Berna Eli Oldfield) (1878–1946) Am. auto racer

Oldfield, Mike (1953–) Eng. folk/pop musician ("Tubular Bells")

Oldman, Gary (1958–) Eng. actor (*Bram Stoker's Dracula*; *Prick Up Your Ears*; *Sid and Nancy*)

Olds, Ransom Eli (1864–1950) Am. automobile manufacturer (Oldsmobile)

Olin, Ken (1954–) Am. actor ("thirtysomething" TV series)

Olin, Lena (1955–) Swed. actress (*The Unbearable Lightness of Being*; *Enemies— A Love Story*; *Havana*)

Oliphant, Pat (Patrick Bruce Oliphant) (1935–) Am. political cartoonist (P— 1967)

Oliva, Tony (Antonio Lopez Oliva) (1940–) Cub.-Am. baseball player

Oliver, Al (Albert Oliver; "Mr. Scoop") (1946–) Am. baseball player

Oliver, Edna May (Edna May Cox Nutter) (1883–1942) Am. actress (*David Copperfield*; *Little Women*)

Oliver, King (Joseph Oliver) (1885–1938) Am. jazz trumpeter

Oliver, Sy (Melvin James Oliver) (1910– 1988) Am. jazz composer/bandleader

Olivier, Sir Laurence (Laurence Kerr Olivier; "Sir Larry") (1907–1989) Eng. actor (*Wuthering Heights*; *Rebecca*; *Othello*; *Sleuth*; O—1948—*Hamlet*)

Olmedo, Alex (1936–) Am. tennis player (W—1959)

Olmos, Edward James (1947–) Mex.-Am. actor ("Miami Vice" TV series; *Stand and Deliver*; E—1984/85)/film director (*American Me*)

Olmsted or **Olmstead, Frederick** (Frederick Law Olmsted; "Father of American Parks") (1822–1903) Am. landscape architect (Central Park)

Olsen, Merlin (Merlin Jay Olsen) (1940–) Am. football Hall-of-Famer/actor ("Father Murphy" TV series)

Olsen, Ole (John Sigurd Olsen) (1892–1963) Norw.-Am. vaudeville comedian (with Chic Johnson)

Olsen, Tillie (Tillie Lerner) (1913–) Am. novelist (*Silences*)

Onassis, Aristotle (Aristotle Socrates Onassis; "Ari") (1906–1975) Gr. shipping tycoon

Onassis, Jacqueline (Jacqueline Lee Bouvier) (1929–) Am. first lady (John F. Kennedy)/literary editor

O'Neal, Patrick (Patrick Wisdom O'Neal) (1927–) Am. actor (*The Way We Were*; *The Stepford Wives*)

O'Neal, Ryan (Patrick Ryan O'Neal) (1941–) Am. actor (*Paper Moon*; *Love Story*; *Chances Are*)

O'Neal, Shaquille ("Shaq") (1972–) Am. basketball player

O'Neal, Tatum (Tatum Beatrice O'Neal) (1963–) Am. actress (daughter of Ryan; O—1973—*Paper Moon*; *Little Darlings*)

O'Neill, Ed (1946–) Am. actor ("Married . . . With Children" TV series)

O'Neill, Eugene (Eugene Gladstone O'Neill) (1888–1953) Am. playwright (son of James, father of Oona Chaplin; *The Iceman Cometh*; *Mourning Becomes Electra*; N—1936; P—1920—*Beyond the Horizon*; P—1922—*Anna Christie*; P—1928—*Strange Interlude*; P—1957—*A Long Day's Journey into Night*)

O'Neill, James (1849–1920) Am. actor (father of Eugene; *The Count of Monte Cristo* [1913])

O'Neill, Jennifer (1947–) Am. actress (*Rio Lobo*; *Summer of '42*)

O'Neill, Oona *see* Chaplin, Oona

O'Neill, Tip (Thomas Philip O'Neill, Jr.) (1912–1993) Am. speaker of the house/politician/writer (*Man of the House*)

Ono, Yoko (Yoko Ono Cox) (1933–) Jap.-Am. pop singer/artist (mother of Sean Lennon)

Onorati, Peter (C) Am. actor ("Civil Wars" and "Joe's Life" TV series)

Ontkean, Michael (1946–) Can. actor ("Twin Peaks" TV series)

Opel, Wilhelm Von ("The Henry Ford of Germany") (1871–1948) Ger. automobile manufacturer

Ophüls, Marcel (Marcel Oppenheimer; a/k/a Marcel Wall) (1927–) Ger.-Am. film director (*Hotel Terminus*)

Ophüls, Max (Maximilian Oppenheimer; a/k/a Max Opuls) (1902–1957) Ger.-Am. film director (*Lola Montez*)

Oppenheim, E. Phillips (Edward Phillips Oppenheim; "The Prince of Storytellers") (1866–1946) Eng. novelist/thriller writer (*The Double Traitor*; *The Evil Shepherd*)

Oppenheimer, J. Robert (Julius Robert Oppenheimer; "Father of the Atom Bomb") (1904–1967) Am. physicist (headed the Manhattan Project)

Orbach, Jerry (Jerome Orbach) (1935–) Am. actor ("The Law and Harry McGraw" TV series; *Crimes and Misdemeanors*; *Last Exit to Brooklyn*; T—1969)

Orbison, Roy ("The Big O") (1936–1988) Am. rock singer ("Oh, Pretty Woman"; "You Got It"; with The Traveling Wilburys; G—1990)

Orczy, Baroness Emmuska (Emmuska Magdalena Rosalia Marie Josepha Barbara Orczy) (1865–1947) Eng. novelist/playwright (*The Scarlet Pimpernel*)

Orff, Carl (1895–1982) Ger. composer (*Antigone*)

Orlando, Tony (Michael Anthony Orlando Cassevitis) (1944–) Am. pop singer ("Knock Three Times"; with Dawn)

Ormandy, Eugene (Jeno Blau) (1899–1985) Hung.-Am. conductor (Philadelphia Orchestra)

O'Rourke, Heather (1975–1988) Am. child actress (*Poltergeist*)

O'Rourke, P. J. (1947–) Am. humorist/writer (*Give War a Chance*; *Parliament of Whores*)

Orozco, José (José Clemente Orozco) (1883–1949) Mex. muralist (*The Trench*)

Orr, Benjamin (Benjamin Orzechowski) (c. 1952–) Am. rock singer/guitarist ("Stay the Night"; formerly with The Cars)

Orr, Bobby (Robert Gordon Orr; "Bobby Hockey") (1948–) Can. hockey player

Ortega Y Gasset, José (1883–1955) Span. philosopher/writer (*The Revolt of the Masses*)

Orton, Joe (John Kingsley Orton) (1933–1967) Eng. playwright (*Entertaining Mr. Sloan*; *Loot*; *What the Butler Saw*)

Orwell, George (Eric Arthur Blair) (1903–

1950) Eng. novelist/essayist (*Nineteen Eighty-Four*; *Animal Farm*)

Ory, Kid (Edward Ory) (1886–1973) Am. jazz trombone player/bandleader ("Muskrat Ramble")

Orzabal, Roland (Orzabal de la Quintanta) (1961–) Eng. pop musician/singer (with Tears For Fears)

Osborne, Jeffrey (1948–) Am. pop singer ("On the Wings of Love"; formerly with L.T.D.)

Osborne, John (John James Osborne; "The Angry Young Man") (1929–) Eng. playwright (*Look Back in Anger*; *The Entertainer*)

Osbourne, Ozzy (John Michael Osbourne) (1948–) Eng. rock singer ("Crazy Train"; formerly with Black Sabbath)

Osceola (Osceola Nickanochee) (1804–1838) Am. Seminole chief

O'Shea, Milo (1926–) Ir. actor (*Ulysses*; *Romeo and Juliet*; *Barbarella*)

Oslin, K. T. (Kay Toinette Oslin) (1941–) Am. country singer ("80's Ladies")

Osman (1258–c. 1326) founder of the Ottoman Empire

Osmond, Alan (Alan Ralph Osmond) (1949–) Am. pop musician (with The Osmond Brothers)

Osmond, Donny (Donald Clark Osmond) (1957–) Am. pop singer ("Puppy Love"; "Go Away Little Girl")

Osmond, Jay (Jay Wesley Osmond) (1955–) Am. pop musician (with The Osmond Brothers)

Osmond, Jimmy (James Arthur Osmond; "Little Jimmy") (1963–) Am. pop singer (with The Osmond Brothers)

Osmond, Marie (Olive Marie Osmond) (1959–) Am. pop singer ("Paper Roses")

Osmond, Merrill (Merrill Davis Osmond) (1953–) Am. pop musician (with The Osmond Brothers)

Osmond, Wayne (M. Wayne Osmond) (1951–) Am. pop musician (with The Osmond Brothers)

Osterwald, Bibi (Margaret Virginia Osterwald) (1920–) Am. actress ("Bridget Loves Bernie" TV series)

O'Sullivan, Gilbert (Raymond Edward O'Sullivan) (1946–) Ir.-Eng. pop singer ("Alone Again [Naturally]")

O'Sullivan, Maureen (Maureen Paula O'Sullivan) (1911–) Am. actress (mother of Mia Farrow; *The Barretts of Wimpole Street*; *Tarzan the Ape Man*)

Oswald, Gerd (1916–) Ger.-Am. film direc-

tor (*A Kiss Before Dying* [1956]; *Paris Holiday*)

Oswald, Lee Harvey (1939–1963) Am. alleged assassin (John F. Kennedy)

Otis, Carré (1968–) Am. model/actress (*Wild Orchid*)

Otis, Elisha (Elisha Graves Otis) (1811–1861) Am. inventor (passenger elevator)

Otis, Johnny (John Veliotes) (1921–) Ger.-Am. blues singer/bandleader ("Willie and the Hand Jive")

O'Toole, Annette (Annette Toole) (1952–) Am. actress (*48 HRS.*; *Cat People*)

O'Toole, Peter (Peter Seamus O'Toole) (1932–) Ir.-Eng. actor (*Lawrence of Arabia*; *My Favorite Year*)

Ott, Mel (Melvin Thomas Ott; "Master Melvin"; "The Little Giant"; "McGraw's Boy") (1909–1958) Am. baseball Hall-of-Famer

Otto I (Otto The Great) (912–973) Roman emperor/king of Germany 936–973

Otto, Jim (James Otto) (1938–) Am. football Hall-of-Famer

Otto, Nikolaus (Nikolaus August Otto) (1832–1891) Ger. engineer/inventor (internal combustion engine, with E. Langlen)

Ouida (Marie Louise de la Ramee) (1839–1908) Eng. novelist (*Under Two Flags*)

Ouspenskaya, Maria (1876–1949) Russ.-Am. actress (*The Rains Came*; *Dodsworth*)

Outcault, Richard (Richard Felton Outcault) (1863–1928) Am. cartoonist (*Buster Brown*)

Overall, Park (1957–) Am. actress ("Empty Nest" TV series)

Overbury, Sir Thomas (1581–1613) Eng. poet/writer (*Characters*)

Ovid (Publius Ovidius Naso) (43 B.C.–A.D. 17) Roman poet (*Metamorphoses*)

Ovitz, Michael (1947–) Am. talent agent (founded Creative Artists Agency)

Owen, Mickey (Arnold Malcolm Owen) (1916–) Am. baseball player

Owen, Randy (1949–) Am. country singer (with Alabama; "Love in the First Degree")

Owen, Reginald (John Reginald Owen) (1887–1972) Am. actor (*Mrs. Miniver*; *Queen Christina*)

Owen, Seena (Signe Auen) (1894–1966) Am. actress (*Intolerance*; *Queen Kelly*)

Owen, Spike (Spike Dee Owen) (1961–) Am. baseball player

Owen, Steve (Stephen Joseph Owen;

"Stout Steve") (1898–1964) Am. football Hall-of-Famer

Owens, Buck (Alvis Edgar Owens, Jr.) (1929–) Am. country singer ("I've Got a Tiger by the Tail")

Owens, Jesse (James Cleveland Owens; "Buckeye Bullet"; "Brown Bombshell") (1913–1980) Am. track and field athlete

Oxenberg, Catherine (1961–) Eng. actress ("Dynasty" and "Acapulco H.E.A.T." TV series)

Oz, Amos (Amos Klausner) (1939–) Isr. short story writer/novelist (*My Michael; Unto Death*)

Oz, Frank (Frank Richard Oznowicz) (1944–) Am. puppeteer ("Sesame Street"; "The Muppet Show")

Ozawa, Seiji (1935–) Chin.-Am. orchestra conductor (San Francisco and Boston symphonies)

Ozick, Cynthia (1928–) Am. novelist/short story writer (*Levitation; The Cannibal Galaxy; Trust*)

Paar, Jack (Jack Harold Paar) (1918–) Am. TV host (original host of "The Tonight Show"; signature phrase: "I kid you not")

Pacino, Al (Alfredo James Pacino; "The Male Garbo") (1940–) Am. actor (*The Godfather; Dog Day Afternoon*; O— 1993—*Scent of a Woman*; T—1977)

Packard, David (1912–) Am. business executive (cofounded Hewlett-Packard, with William Hewlett)

Packard, Vance (Vance Oakley Packard) (1914–) Am. writer (*The Hidden Persuaders; The Status Seekers*)

Packwood, Bob (Robert William Packwood) (1932–) Am. senator

Pacula, Joanna (1957–) Pol.-Am. actress (*Gorky Park; Husbands and Lovers*)

Paderewski, Ignacy (Ignacy Jan Paderewski) (1860–1941) Pol. pianist/conductor/composer (*Minuet in G*)/statesman

Padgett, Lewis (Henry Kuttner) (1915–1958) Am. science fiction writer

Paganini, Niccolò (1782–1840) Ital. composer/violinist

Page, Alan (Alan Cedric Page) (1945–) Am. football Hall-of-Famer

Page, Geraldine (Geraldine Sue Page; "Gerry") (1924–1987) Am. actress (*Sweet Bird of Youth; Interiors*; O— 1985—*The Trip to Bountiful*)

Page, Jimmy (James Patrick Page) (1944–) Eng. rock guitarist (with Led Zeppelin, The Firm, and The Honeydrippers)

Page, Lawanda (1920–) Am. actress ("Sanford & Son" TV series)

Page, Patti (Clara Ann Fowler; a/k/a Ann Fowler; "The Singing Rage") (1927–) Am. singer ("Allegheny Moon")

Paglia, Camille (1947–) Am. writer (*Sexual Personae*)

Pagnol, Marcel (Marcel Paul Pagnol) (1895–1974) Fr. playwright (*Fanny; Topaze*)/screenwriter/film director (*Jean De Florette*)

Pahlavi, Farah Diba (1938–) Iran. empress

Pahlavi, Mohammad Reza (1919–1980) Iran. shah 1941–1979

Pahlavi, Reza Shah (Reza Khan) (1878–1944) Iran. shah 1925–1941

Paige, Janis (Donna Mae Jaden) (1922–) Am. actress ("Trapper John, M.D." TV series; *Of Human Bondage*)

Paige, Satchel (Leroy Robert Paige; "Black Magic") (1906–1982) Am. baseball Hall-of-Famer

Paine, Thomas (1737–1809) Am. pamphleteer/politician/philosopher (*Common Sense; The Age of Reason*)

Pakula, Alan J. (Alan Jay Pakula) (1928–) Am. film director (*All the President's Men; Sophie's Choice*)

Palade, George (George Emil Palade) (1912–) Am. physiologist (N—1974)

Palance, Jack (Walter Jack Palahniuik) (1919–) Am. actor (*Shane; Sudden Fear*; O—1991—*City Slickers*)

Palestrina (Giovanni Pierluigi da Palestrina) (c. 1525–1594) Ital. composer

Paley, Grace (Grace Goodside Paley) (1922–) Am. short story writer (*Enormous Changes at the Last Minute; Later the Same Day*)

Paley, William (William Samuel Paley) (1901–) Am. entertainment executive (CBS)

Palillo, Ron (Ronald G. Palillo) (1954–) Am. actor ("Welcome Back, Kotter" TV series)

Palin, Michael (Michael Edward Palin) (1943–) Eng. comedian/actor ("Monty Python's Flying Circus"; *A Fish Called Wanda*)

Pallette, Eugene (1889–1954) Am. actor (*My Man Godfrey; The Lady Eve*)

Palmeiro, Rafael (Rafael Corrales) (1964–) Cub.-Am. baseball player

Palmer, Arnold (Arnold Daniel Palmer;

"Arnie"; "The Charger") (1929–) Am. golfer

Palmer, Betsy (Patricia Betsy Hrunek) (1926–) Am. actress ("I've Got a Secret" TV series)

Palmer, Carl (1951–) Eng. rock drummer (with Emerson, Lake & Palmer and Asia)

Palmer, Jim (James Alvin Palmer; "Baby Cakes"; "Cry Old") (1945–) Am. baseball Hall-of-Famer

Palmer, Lilli (Lilli Marie Peiser) (1911–1986) Aus. actress (*Body and Soul; Murders in the Rue Morgue*)

Palmer, Robert (Alan Palmer) (1949–) Eng. rock/pop singer ("Addicted to Love"; "Simply Irresistible"; formerly with The Power Station)

Palmer, Stuart (Stuart Hunter Palmer) (1905–1968) Am. mystery writer/screenwriter

Paltrow, Gwyneth (c. 1972–) Am. actress (daughter of Blythe Danner; *Flesh and Bone*)

Pan, Hermes (Hermes Panagiotopolous) (1905–1990) Am. choreographer (for Fred Astaire)

Panetta, Leon (Leon Edward Panetta)(1938–) Am. congressman/budget director

Pangborn, Franklin (1893–1958) Am. actor (*The Palm Beach Story; Flying Down to Rio*)

Papa Doc *see* Duvalier, Francois

Papandreou, Andreas (Andreas George Papandreou) (1919–) Gr. premier 1981–1989

Papas, Irene (Irene Lelekou) (1926–) Gr. actress (*Zorba the Greek; The Guns of Navarone*)

Papp, Joseph (Joseph Papirofsky) (1921–1991) Am. theatrical producer (*Hair; A Chorus Line; No Place to Be Somebody; That Championship Season*)/founder of the New York Shakespeare Festival

Pardo, Don (1918–) Am. TV announcer

Paré, Michael (1959–) Am. actor (*Eddie and the Cruisers; The Philadelphia Experiment*)

Parillaud, Anna (C) Fr. actress (*La Femme Nikita*)

Paris, Mica (Michelle Warren) (1969–) Eng. pop singer ("My One Temptation")

Parish, Peggy (1927–1988) Am. novelist (*Amelia Bedelia* stories)

Park, Brad (Bradford Douglas Park) (1948–) Can. hockey player

Park, Mungo (1771–1806) Scot. explorer of Africa

Parker, Ace (Clarence Parker) (1913–) Am. football Hall-of-Famer

Parker, Alan (Alan William Parker) (1944–) Eng. film director/writer (*Midnight Express; Fame; Mississippi Burning; The Commitments*)

Parker, Bonnie (1910–1934) Am. outlaw (with Clyde Barrow)

Parker, Charlie (Charles Christopher Parker, Jr.; "Bird"; "Yardbird") (1920–1955) Am. jazz saxophonist

Parker, Dave (David Gene Parker; "The Cobra") (1951–) Am. baseball player

Parker, Dorothy (Dorothy Rothschild; a/k/a Constant Reader; "The Deadly Asp") (1893–1967) Am. short story writer/poet (member of the Algonquin Round Table; *Enough Rope*)

Parker, Eleanor (1922–) Am. actress (*Detective Story; Caged*)

Parker, Fess (Fess Elijah Parker) (1925–) Am. actor ("Daniel Boone" TV series)/singer ("Ballad of Davy Crockett")

Parker, Graham (1950–) Eng. rock singer/songwriter (with Graham Parker and The Rumour; "Wake Up [Next to You]")

Parker, Jameson (1947–) Am. actor ("Simon & Simon" TV series)

Parker, Jim (James Thomas Parker) (1934–) Am. football Hall-of-Famer

Parker, Mary-Louise (C) Am. actress (*Fried Green Tomatoes; Longtime Companion; Mr. Wonderful*)

Parker, Ray, Jr. (1954–) Am. pop singer/musician ("Ghostbusters"; formerly with Raydio)

Parker, Robert B. (Robert Brown Parker) (1932–) Am. detective story writer (created Spenser ["Spenser: For Hire" TV series]; *Perchance to Dream; Stardust*)

Parker, Sarah Jessica (1965–) Am. actress (*L.A. Story; Honeymoon in Vegas;* "Square Pegs" TV series)

Parker, Suzy (Cecilia Anne Renee Parker) (1932–) Am. model/actress (*Ten North Frederick*)

Parker, Colonel Tom (Thomas Andrew Parker; born Andreas Cornelius Van Kuijk) (1910–) Am. rock manager (of Elvis Presley)

Parker-Bowles, Camilla (1947–) Eng. society figure (purported lover of Prince Charles)

Parkins, Barbara (1942–) Can. actress ("Peyton Place" TV series; *Valley of the Dolls*)
Parkinson, Norman (1913–1990) Eng. photographer
Parkman, Francis (1823–1893) Am. historian/writer (*The California and Oregon Trail*)
Parks, Bert (Bert Jacobson) (1914–1992) Am. TV host (Miss America Pageant)
Parks, Gordon (Gordon Alexander Parks) (1912–) Am. film director (*Shaft*)/photographer/novelist (*The Learning Tree*)
Parks, Larry (Samuel Klausman Lawrence Parks) (1914–1975) Am. actor (*The Al Jolson Story* [title role])
Parks, Rosa (Rosa Lee McCauley; "Mother of the Civil Rights Movement") (1913–) Am. civil rights activist (triggered Montgomery bus boycott)
Parks, Van Dyke (1941–) Am. actor/folk-rock musician ("High Coin")
Parlo, Dita (1906–1971) Ger. actress (*La Grande Illusion*)
Parmenides or **Parmenides of Elea** (born c. 515 B.C.) Gr. philosopher (founded the Eleatic School)/poet (*Nature*)
Parmigianino or **Parmigiano** (Girolamo Francesco Mazzola or Mazzuoli) (1503–1540) Ital. mannerist painter
Parnell, Emory (1894–1979) Am. actor (*Call Me Madam*; "The Life of Riley" TV series)
Parnell, Lee Roy (1956–) Am. country singer ("What Kind of Fool Do You Think I Am")
Parnis, Mollie (1905–1992) Am. fashion designer
Parr, Catherine (1512–1548) Eng. wife (sixth and last) of Henry VIII
Parrington, Vernon (Vernon Louis Parrington) (1871–1929) Am. teacher/historian/biographer (P—1928—*Main Currents in American Thought*)
Parrish, Lance (Lance Michael Parrish) (1956–) Am. baseball player
Parrish, Larry (Larry Alton Parrish) (1953–) Am. baseball player
Parrish, Maxfield (Maxfield Frederick Parrish) (1870–1966) Am. painter/illustrator
Parseghian, Ara (Ara Raoul Parseghian) (1923–) Am. football coach
Parsons, Alan (C) Eng. rock musician ("Eye in the Sky"; with The Alan Parsons Project)

Parsons, Estelle (1927–) Am. actress (O—1967—*Bonnie and Clyde*)
Parsons, Gram (Cecil Connor) (1946–1973) Am. country/rock singer (with The Byrds and The Flying Burrito Brothers)
Parsons, Louella (née Oettinger) (1893–1972) Am. (Hollywood) gossip columnist
Parsons, Talcott (1902–1979) Am. sociologist/writer (*The Structure of Social Action*)
Parton, Dolly (Dolly Rebecca Parton) (1946–) Am. country/pop singer ("Islands in the Stream")/actress (*9 to 5*; *Straight Talk*)
Parton, Stella (1949–) Am. country singer (sister of Dolly)
Partridge, Eric (Eric Honeywood Partridge; a/k/a Vigilans; "Word King") (1894–1979) Eng. lexicographer/writer (*A Dictionary of Slang and Unconventional English*)
Pascal, Blaise (1623–1662) Fr. scientist/inventor/philosopher (*Provincial Letters*; *Pensées*)
Pasdar, Adrian (1965–) Am. actor (*Top Gun*; *Near Dark*)
Pasolini, Pier Paolo (1922–1975) Ital. poet/novelist/film director (*The Decameron*; *The Canterbury Tales*)
Pass, Joe (Joseph Anthony Passalaqua) (1929–) Am. jazz guitarist
Pasternak, Boris (Boris Leonidovich Pasternak) (1890–1960) Russ. novelist/poet (*Doctor Zhivago*; N—1958 [declined])
Pasteur, Louis (1822–1895) Fr. chemist/microbiologist (developed pasteurization and inoculation)
Pastorius, Jaco (1951–1987) Am. jazz/rock guitarist (with Weather Report)
Patchen, Kenneth (1911–1972) Am. avant-garde poet/writer (*Memoirs of a Shy Pornographer*)
Pate, Jerry (Jerome Kendrick Pate) (1953–) Am. golfer
Patek, Freddie (Fred Joe Patek; "The Flying Flea") (1944–) Am. baseball player
Pater, Walter (Walter Horatio Pater) (1839–1894) Eng. essayist/critic (*Marius the Epicurean*)
Paterno, Joe (Joseph Vincent Paterno) (1926–) Am. football coach
Patinkin, Mandy (Mandel Patinkin) (1947–) Am. singer/actor (*Sunday in the Park with George*; *Impromptu*; *The Music of Chance*)

Patitz, Tatjana (c. 1966–) Swed.-Am. model/actress (*Rising Sun*)

Paton, Alan (Alan Stewart Paton) (1903–1988) S. Afr. novelist (*Cry, the Beloved Country*)

Patou, Jean (1887–1936) Fr. fashion designer

Patric, Jason (1966–) Am. actor (*After Dark, My Sweet; Rush; The Lost Boys*)

Patrick, John (John Patrick Goggan) (1905–) Am. playwright (P—1954—*Teahouse of the August Moon*)

Patrick, Nigel (Nigel Dennis Wemyss) (1913–1981) Eng. actor (*The Pickwick Papers; Raintree County*)

Patrick, Saint (5th century A.D.) patron saint of Ireland

Patterson, Floyd (1935–) Am. boxer

Patterson, Orlando (Horace Orlando Patterson) (1940–) Jam. novelist/sociologist (*The Sociology of Slavery*)

Patton, George S. (George Smith Patton, Jr.; "Old Blood and Guts") (1885–1945) Am. army general/tank commander/writer (*War as I Knew It*)

Patton, Will (1954–) Am. actor (*No Way Out; Silkwood; After Hours*)

Patty, Budge (1924–) Am. tennis player (W—1950)

Paul I (Pavel Petrovich) (1754–1801) Russ. emperor 1796–1801

Paul, Alexandra (c. 1963–) Am. actress ("Baywatch" TV series)

Paul, Billy (Paul Williams) (1934–) Am. soul singer ("Me and Mrs. Jones")

Paul, Les (Lester William Polfus; a/k/a Hot Rod Red and Rhubarb Red) (1916 or 1923–) Am. guitarist (with Mary Ford; created the solid-body electric guitar)

Paul, Saint (died A.D. 64) Christian missionary/theologian

Paulding, James Kirke (1778–1860) Am. novelist/playwright (*Westward Ho!*)

Pauley, Jane (Margaret Jane Pauley) (1950–) Am. TV newscaster ("Today"; "Real Life with Jane Pauley")

Pauli, Wolfgang (1900–1958) Aus.-Am. physicist (postulated the existence of neutrinos; N—1945)

Pauling, Linus (Linus Carl Pauling) (1901–) Am. chemist (N—1954, 1962)

Paulsen, Pat (Patrick Laton Paulsen) (1927–) Am. comedian ("Rowan & Martin's Laugh-In" TV series)

Pavan, Marisa (Maria Luisa Pierangeli) (1932–) Ital.-Am. actress (sister of Pier Angeli; *The Rose Tattoo*)

Pavarotti, Luciano (1935–) Ital. opera singer (tenor)

Pavlov, Ivan (Ivan Petrovich Pavlov) (1849–1936) Russ. physiologist/psychologist (detected the Pavlovian response; N—1904)

Pavlova, Anna (Anna Pavlovna Pavlova) (1882–1931) Russ. ballerina (with Ballet Russe)

Paxinou, Katina (Katina Constantopoulos) (1900–1973) Gr. actress (*Mourning Becomes Electra*; O—1943—*For Whom the Bell Tolls*)

Paxton, Bill (c. 1955–) Am. actor (*Aliens; Weird Science; One False Move; Boxing Helena*)

Paycheck, Johnny (Donald Eugene Lytle) (1941–) Am. country singer ("Take This Job and Shove It")

Payne, Freda (1945–) Am. big band singer (with Duke Ellington)

Payne, John (John Howard Payne) (1791–1852) Am. actor/playwright/poet (*Clari, The Maid of Milan*)

Pays, Amanda (1959–) Eng.-Am. actress (*Oxford Blues; Off Limits*)

Payson, Joan Whitney (1903–1975) Am. philanthropist/sportswoman

Payton, Walter ("Sweetness") (1954–) Am. football player

Paz, Octavio (1914–) Mex. diplomat/poet/writer (*The Labyrinth of Solitude*; N—1990)

Peaches & Herb see Barker, Francine, and Fame, Herb

Peacock, Thomas (Thomas Love Peacock) (1785–1866) Eng. poet/novelist (*Nightmare Alley*)

Peale, Charles (Charles Wilson Peale) (1741–1827) Am. painter

Peale, Norman Vincent (1898–1993) Am. clergyman/writer (*The Power of Positive Thinking*)

Peale, Rembrandt (1778–1860) Am. portrait painter

Pearl, Minnie (Sarah Ophelia Colley Cannon) (1912–) Am. comedienne/singer ("Hee Haw" TV series)

Pears, Sir Peter (1910–1986) Eng. opera singer (tenor; partnered with Benjamin Britten)

Pearse, Patrick H. (Patrick Henry Pearse) (1879–1916) Ir. revolutionist (led the Irish Republican Brotherhood in Easter Rising [1916]; executed)

Pearson, David (David Gene Pearson) (1934–) Am. auto racer

Pearson, Drew (Andrew Russell Pearson) (1897–1969) Am. newscaster/columnist ("Washington Merry-Go-Round")

Pearson, Lester (Lester Bowles Pearson) (1897–1972) Can. prime minister 1963–1968 (N—1957)

Peart, Neil (1952–) Can. rock drummer (with Rush)

Peary, Robert (Robert Edwin Peary) (1856–1920) Am. explorer (discovered the North Pole)/writer (Northward Over the Great Ice)

Pease, Lute (1869–1963) Am. cartoonist (P—1949)

Pebbles (Perri Alette McKissack) (C) Am. pop singer ("Mercedes Boy")

Peck, Gregory (Eldred Gregory Peck) (1916–) Am. actor (The Yearling; Spellbound; Duel in the Sun; O—1962—To Kill a Mockingbird)

Peck, M. Scott (Morgan Scott Peck) (1936–) Am. psychiatrist/writer (The Road Less Traveled)

Peck, Tony (c. 1956–) Am. actor (son of Gregory)

Peckinpah, Sam (David Samuel Peckinpah; "Bloody Sam") (1925–1985) Am. film director (The Wild Bunch; Straw Dogs)

Peele, Beverly (c. 1974–) Eng. model

Peeples, Nia (1961–) Am. actress ("Fame" TV series)/TV host ("Nina Peeples' Party Machine")

Peerce, Jan (Jacob Pinkus Perelmuth) (1904–1984) Am. opera singer (tenor)

Peete, Calvin (1943–) Am. golfer

Pegler, Westbrook (James Westbrook Pegler; "The Guttersnipe") (1894–1969) Am. journalist (P—1941)

Pei, I. M. (Ieoh Ming Pei) (1917–) Am. architect (East Wing of the National Gallery)

Peirce, Charles (Charles Sanders Peirce; "Father of Pragmatism") (1839–1914) Am. philosopher (pragmatism)/scientist

Pelé (Edson Arantes do Nascimento; "Perola Negra" [The Black Pearl]; "King of Soccer") (1940–) Braz. soccer player

Pell, Claiborne (Claiborne deBorda Pell) (1918–) Am. business executive/senator

Pena, Alejandro (Alejandro Pena Vasquez) (1959–) Dom.-Am. baseball pitcher

Pena, Elizabeth (1960–) Am. actress (La Bamba; Jacob's Ladder)

Peña, Tony (Antonio Francesco Padilla Padilla) (1957–) Dom.-Am. baseball player

Penderecki, Krzysztof (1933–) Pol. conductor/composer (St. Luke's Passion)

Pendergrass, Teddy (Theodore D. Pendergrass; "Teddy Bear") (1950–) Am. soul/pop singer ("Close the Door"; formerly with The Blue Notes)

Pendleton, Terry (Terry Lee Pendleton) (1960–) Am. baseball player

Penn, Arthur (Arthur Hiller Penn) (1922–) Am. film director (Bonnie and Clyde; The Miracle Worker)

Penn, Christopher or Chris (1967–) Am. actor (brother of Sean; Mobsters; Reservoir Dogs; True Romance)

Penn, Sean (1960–) Am. actor (Colors; Fast Times at Ridgemont High; State of Grace)/film director (The Indian Runner)

Penn, Sir William (1621–1670) Eng. naval commander/founder of Pennsylvania

Penney, Alexandra (C) Am. writer (How to Keep Your Man Monogamous)

Penney, J. C. (James Cash Penney) (1875–1971) Am. merchant (founded J. C. Penney Co.)/philanthropist

Pennock, Herb (Herbert Jefferis Pennock; "The Knight of Kennett Square") (1894–1948) Am. baseball Hall-of-Famer

Penny, Joe (1956–) Am. actor (Jake in "Jake and the Fatman" TV series)

Peppard, George (1928–) Am. actor (TV's "Banacek"; Breakfast at Tiffany's)

Pepper, Art (Arthur Edward Pepper) (1925–1982) Am. jazz saxophonist

Pepys, Samuel (1633–1703) Eng. naval officer/diarist (Memoirs of the Royal Navy)

Percy, Sir Henry ("Hotspur") (1364–1403) Eng. soldier/nobleman

Percy, Walker (1916–1990) Am. novelist (The Moviegoer; Love in the Ruins)

Perelman, S. J. (Sidney Joseph Perelman) (1904–1979) Am. humorist (Under the Spreading Atrophy; The Rising Gorge)

Peres, Shimon (Shimon Persky) (1923–) Pol. prime minister of Israel 1984–1986

Peretti, Elsa (1940–) Am. jewelry designer

Peretz, I. L. (Isaac Leib Peretz) (1852–1915) Pol.-Jew. poet/short story writer/playwright (The Golden Chain; The Hunchback)

Perez, Rosie (c. 1966–) Am. dancer/choreographer/actress (Do the Right Thing; Untamed Heart; White Men Can't Jump)

Pérez de Cuellar, Javier (1920–) Peruv.

diplomat (secretary general of the U.N.)

Pergolesi, Giovanni (Giovanni Battista Pergolesi) (1710–1736) Ital. composer (*Stabat Mater*)

Pericles (c. 495–429 B.C.) Ath. statesman/general

Perkins, Anthony (1932–1992) Am. actor (*Mahogany*; *Psycho*; *Fear Strikes Out*)

Perkins, Carl (Carl Lee Perkins) (1932–) Am. rock/country singer ("Blue Suede Shoes")

Perkins, Elizabeth (1961–) Am. actress (*He Said, She Said*; *Avalon*; *Big*)

Perkins, Marlin (Richard Marlin Perkins) (1902–1986) Am. TV host ("Wild Kingdom")

Perkins, Maxwell (Maxwell Evarts Perkins) (1884–1947) Am. literary editor (worked with F. Scott Fitzgerald, Ernest Hemingway, Thomas Wolfe, etc.)

Perlman, Itzhak (1945–) Isr.-Am. concert violinist

Perlman, Rhea (1948–) Am. actress ("Cheers" TV series; E—1983/84, 1984/85, 1985/86, 1988/89)

Perlman, Ron (1950–) Am. actor (Vincent, the Beast, in "Beauty and the Beast" TV series)

Perón, Evita or **Eva** (Maria Eva Duarte Perón née Ibarguren) (1919–1952) Arg. political leader/singer

Perón, Juan (Juan Domingo Perón Sosa) (1895–1974) Arg. pres./dictator 1946–1955, 1973–1974

Perot, H. Ross (Henry Ross Perot; born Henry Ray Perot) (1930–) Am. businessman/presidential candidate 1992

Perrault, Charles (1628–1703) Fr. fairy tale writer (*Cinderella*; *Puss in Boots*; *Sleeping Beauty*)

Perrine, Valerie (1943–) Am. actress (*Slaughterhouse Five*; *Lenny*)

Perry, Antoinette (Mary Antoinette Perry) (1888–1946) Am. theatrical director/actress (namesake of the Tony awards)

Perry, Gaylord (Gaylord Jackson Perry; "The Ancient Mariner"; "The Spitball Pitcher"; "Gaylord the Greaser") (1938–) Am. baseball pitcher

Perry, Joe (Fletcher Perry; "The Jet") (1927–) Am. football Hall-of-Famer

Perry, Luke (Coy Luke Perry III) (1966–) Am. actor ("Beverly Hills, 90210" TV series; *Buffy the Vampire Slayer*; *Eight Seconds*)

Perry, Matthew Calbraith (1794–1858)

Am. naval commander (brother of Oliver Hazard)

Perry, Oliver Hazard (1785–1819) Am. naval commander

Perry, Steve (1949–) Am. rock singer ("Oh Sherrie"; "Foolish Heart"; formerly with Journey)

Perry, William ("Refrigerator") (1962–) Am. football player

Pershing, John (John Joseph Pershing; "Black Jack") (1860–1948) Am. general (P—1932—*My Experiences in the World War*)

Persius (Aulus Persius Flaccus) (34–62) Roman poet/satirist

Perugino (Pietro di Cristoforo Vannucci) (c. 1450–1523) Ital. painter (*Vision of St. Bernard*)

Pesci, Joe (1943–) Am. actor (*Home Alone*; *J.F.K.*; *My Cousin Vinnie*; O—1990—*GoodFellas*)

Pescow, Donna (Donna Gail Pescow) (1954–) Am. actress ("Out of This World" and "Angie" TV series)

Pesky, Johnny (John Michael Paveskovich) (1919–) Am. baseball player

Pétain, Philippe (Henri-Philippe Pétain) (1856–1951) Fr. mil. leader/premier (aided the Nazis; convicted of treason)

Peter (a/k/a Simon Peter; born Simeon or Simon) (died c. A.D. 64) Christian apostle (leader of the twelve apostles)

Peter I (Pyotr Alekseyevich; Peter the Great) (1672–1725) Russ. czar 1682–1725

Peter II (Pyotr Alekseyevich) (1715–1730) Russ. czar 1727–1730

Peter III (Pyotr Fyodorovich) (1728–1762) Russ. czar 1762

Peter, Paul & Mary *see* Yarrow, Peter; Stookey, Paul; and Travers, Mary

Peters, Bernadette (Bernadette Lazzaro) (1948–) Am. singer/stage actress (*Sunday in the Park with George*; *Into the Woods*; T—1986)

Peters, Brock (Brock Fisher) (1927–) Am. singer/actor (*To Kill a Mockingbird*; *Carmen Jones*)

Peters, Jean (Elizabeth Jean Peters) (1926–) Am. actress (*Three Coins in a Fountain*; *Viva Zapata!*)

Peters, Jon (1947–) Am. film producer (*Batman*)/entertainment executive

Peterson, Oscar (Oscar Emmanuel Peterson) (1925–) Can. jazz pianist

Petit, Roland (1924–) Fr. ballet dancer/choreographer

Petra, Yvon (1916–) Fr. tennis player (W—1946)

Petrarch (Francesco Petrarca; born Francesco Petracco) (1304–1374) Ital. poet (*On Solitude*)

Petri, Elio (1929–1982) Ital. film director (*Investigation of a Citizen Above Suspicion*)

Petrie, Sir Flinders (William Matthew Flinders Petrie) (1853–1942) Eng. archaeologist/Egyptologist

Petronius, Gaius ("Judge of Elegance") (died A.D. 66) Roman writer (*Satyricon*)

Pettiford, Oscar (1922–1960) Am. jazz bassist/composer

Pettit, Bob (Robert E. Lee Pettit, Jr.) (1932–) Am. basketball player

Petty, Lee (1937–) Am. auto racer

Petty, Lori (c. 1963–) Am. actress (*Point Break; A League of Their Own*)

Petty, Richard (Richard Lee Petty; "King of the Road") (1937–) Am. auto racer

Petty, Tom (1953–) Am. rock singer/musician ("Don't Do Me Like That"; "Free Fallin' "; with Tom Petty and The Heartbreakers and The Traveling Wilburys)

Pfeiffer, Michelle (1957–) Am. actress (*Frankie and Johnny; Dangerous Liaisons; Batman Returns; The Fabulous Baker Boys; The Age of Innocence*)

Pflug, Jo Ann (C) Am. actress (*M*A*S*H*; "The Fall Guy" TV series)

Phaedrus (5th century B.C.) Gr. philosopher

Phaedrus (c. 15 B.C.–c. A.D. 50) Roman fabulist

Phelps, Babe (Ernest Gordon Phelps; "The Blimp"; "The Grounded Blimp") (1908–1992) Am. baseball player

Phelps, Richard ("Digger") (1941–) Am. basketball coach

Phidias (fl. c. 490–430 B.C.) Gr. sculptor

Philbin, Regis (1931–) Am. TV host ("Live with Regis & Kathie Lee")

Philby, Kim (Harold Adrian Russell Philby) (1912–) Eng. intelligence officer/spy (for Russia)

Philip, Duke of Edinburgh (1921–) Gr. husband of Queen Elizabeth

Philip (1st century B.C.–1st century A.D.) Christian apostle

Philip I (1052–1108) Fr. king 1059–1108

Philip II ("Philip Augustus") (1165–1223) Fr. king 1179–1223

Philip III ("Philip the Bold") (1245–1285) Fr. king 1270–1285

Philip IV ("Philip the Fair") (1268–1314) Fr. king 1285–1314

Philip V ("Philip the Tall") (1294–1322) Fr. king 1316–1322

Philip VI (1293–1350) Fr. king 1328–1350

Philips, Emo (C) Am. comedian

Phillips, Chynna (1968–) Am. pop singer (daughter of John and Michelle; with Wilson Phillips)

Phillips, David Graham (a/k/a John Graham) (1867–1911) Am. social reformer (women's rights)/journalist/novelist (*The Great God Success*)

Phillips, Esther (Esther Mae Jones; "Little Esther") (1935–1984) Am. blues singer ("Release Me")

Phillips, John (1935–) Am. rock singer/musician (with The Mamas & The Papas; "Monday Monday")

Phillips, Julia (1944–) Am. film producer (*The Sting*)/writer (*You'll Never Eat Lunch in This Town Again*)

Phillips, Julianne (1960–) Am. model/actress ("Sisters" TV series)

Phillips, Lou Diamond (Lou Upchurch) (1962–) Phil.-Am. actor (*Stand and Deliver; Young Guns; La Bamba*)

Phillips, Mackenzie (Laura Mackenzie Phillips) (1959–) Am. actress (daughter of John; "One Day at a Time" TV series)

Phillips, Michelle (Holly Michelle Gilliam) (1944–) Am. actress ("Knots Landing" TV series)/pop singer (with The Mamas & The Papas)

Phillips, Stone (1954–) Am. TV journalist

Phillips, Wendell (1811–1884) Am. abolitionist/civil rights activist (pres. of the Anti-Slavery Society)

Phillpotts, Eden (a/k/a Harrington Hext) (1862–1960) Eng. novelist/playwright (*Children of the Mists; The Farmer's Wife*)

Philostratus (Flavius Philostratus; "The Athenian") (c. 170–c. 245) Gr. writer (*Lives of the Sophists*)

Phiz (Hablot Knight Browne) (1815–1882) Eng. illustrator (of Dickens novels)/caricaturist

Phoenix, Leaf (Joaquin Phoenix) (1974–) Am. actor (brother of River; *Russkies; Even Cowgirls Get the Blues*)

Phoenix, Rain (c. 1972–) Am. actress (sister of River and Leaf)

Phoenix, River (1970–1993) Am. actor (*Dogfight; My Own Private Idaho; Stand by Me*)

Phrynicus (fl. c. 420 B.C.) Ath. playwright (*Capture of Miletus*)

Phyfe, Duncan (Duncan Fife) (1768–1854) Am. neoclassical furniture designer/manufacturer

Piaf, Edith (Edith Giovanna Gassion; "Piaf" is French slang for "sparrow"; "The Kid") (1915–1963) Fr. singer/songwriter ("La Vie En Rose")

Piaget, Jean (1896–1980) Swi. psychologist (*The Psychology of the Child*)

Piatigorsky, Gregor (1903–1976) Russ.-Am. concert cellist

Picasso, Pablo (Pablo Ruiz y Picasso) (1881–1973) Span. painter (*Guernica*)/sculptor/artist

Picasso, Paloma (1949–) Fr. fashion designer (daughter of Pablo)

Piccolo, Brian (Louis Brian Piccolo) (1943–1970) Am. football player

Pickens, Slim (Louis Bert Lindley, Jr.) (1919–1983) Am. actor (*Dr. Strangelove*; "Hee Haw" TV series)

Pickens, T. Boone (Thomas Boone Pickens) (1928–) Am. oil executive

Pickett, Wilson ("The Wicked Pickett") (1941–) Am. soul singer ("In the Midnight Hour"; "Sugar Sugar")/songwriter ("You're So Fine")

Pickford, Mary (Gladys Mary Smith; "America's Sweetheart") (1893–1979) Can.-Am. actress (*Rebecca of Sunnybrook Farm*; O—1928/29—*Coquette*)

Picon, Molly (Molly Pyekoon) (1898–1992) Am. actress ("Somerset" TV series)

Pidgeon, Walter (Walter David Pidgeon) (1897–1984) Can.-Am. actor (*How Green Was My Valley*; *Mrs. Miniver*)

Pierce, David Hyde (c. 1959–) Am. actor (*Sleepless in Seattle*; *Little Man Tate*; "Frasier" TV series)

Pierce, Franklin (1804–1869) 14th Am. pres. (1853–1857)

Pierce, Jane (Jane Mears Appleton) (1806–1863) Am. first lady (Franklin)

Pierce, Webb (1921–1991) Am. country singer/musician ("I Ain't Never")

Piercy, Marge (1936–) Am. poet/novelist (*Going Down Fast*; *The High Cost of Living*)

Pierne, Gabriel (Henri-Constant-Gabriel Pierne) (1863–1937) Fr. conductor/composer (*Salome*)

Piersall, Jimmy (James Anthony Piersall; "The Waterbury Wizard") (1929–) Am. baseball player

Pierson, Kate (1948–) Am. rock singer (with The B-52s; "Love Shack"; "Rock Lobster")

Pihos, Pete (Peter L. Pihos; "Big Dog") (1923–) Am. football Hall-of-Famer

Pike, Zebulon (Zebulon Montgomery Pike) (1779–1813) Am. explorer (discovered Pike's Peak)

Pilate, Pontius (died after A.D. 36) Roman ruler of Judea 26–c. 36 (ordered the crucifixion of Christ)

Pilatus, Rob (1965–) Ger. entertainer (with Milli Vanilli)

Pilbeam, Nova (1919–) Eng. actress (*Young and Innocent*; *The Man Who Knew Too Much*)

Pilcher, Rosamunde (Jane Fraser) (1924–) Eng. writer (*The Shell Seekers*)

Pileggi, Nicholas (1933–) Am. writer (*GoodFellas*)

Pincay, Laffit, Jr. ("Panama") (1946–) Pan. jockey

Pinchot, Bronson (Bronson Alcott Pinchot) (1959–) Am. actor ("Perfect Strangers" and "The Trouble with Larry" TV series)

Pinchot, Gifford (1865–1946) Am. gov. of Pennsylvania/conservationist (coined the word *conservation*)/writer (*A Primer of Forestry*)

Pinckney, Charles (Charles Cotesworth Pinckney) (1757–1824) Am. politician/diplomat (reported on the "XYZ Affair")

Pincus, Gregory (Gregory Goodwin Pincus) (1903–1967) Am. biologist/inventor (birth-control pill)

Pindar (c. 522–438 B.C.) Gr. lyric poet (*Odes of Victory*)

Pinella, Lou (Louis Victor Pinella; "Piney"; "Sweet Lou") (1943–) Am. baseball player/manager

Pinero, Sir Arthur Wing (1855–1934) Eng. playwright/actor/essayist (*The Second Mrs. Tanqueray*)

Pinkerton, Allan ("The Eye") (1819–1884) Scot.-Am. detective (signature phrase: "We never sleep")/autobiographer (*Thirty Years a Detective*)

Pinochet, Augusto (Augusto Pinochet Ugarte) (1915–) Chil. pres. 1974–1990

Pinter, Harold (a/k/a David Baron) (1930–) Eng. playwright/screenwriter (*The Birthday Party*; *The Dumb Waiter*; *Betrayal*)

Pinza, Ezio (Fortunato Ezio Pinza) (1892–1957) Ital. opera singer (basso)/actor (T—1950)

Pious, Minerva (1909–1979) Am. radio comedienne (with Fred Allen)

Piozzi, Hester (Hester Lynch Piozzi née Salusbury; a/k/a Mrs. Thrale) (1741–1821) Eng. biographer (of Samuel Johnson)

Piper, William Thomas ("The Henry Ford of Aviation") (1881–1970) Am. airplane manufacturer (Piper Cub)

Pippen, Scottie (1965–) Am. basketball player

Pirandello, Luigi (1867–1936) Ital. novelist/playwright (*The Rules of the Game; Six Characters in Search of an Author*; N—1934)

Piscopo, Joe (Joseph Charles Piscopo) (1951–) Am. comedian ("Saturday Night Live" TV series; *Sidekicks; Dead Heat*)

Pisistratus or Peisistratus (c. 612–527 B.C.) Ath. tyrant 561 B.C.; 556–555 B.C.; 546–527 B.C.

Pissarro, Camille (1830–1903) Fr. pointillist/impressionist painter

Piston, Walter (Walter Hamor Piston, Jr.) (1894–1976) Am. composer (P—1948—*Symphony No. 3*; P—1961—*Symphony No. 7*)

Pitcher, Molly (Mary Ludwig Hays McCauley née Ludwig) (1754–1832) Am. Revolutionary heroine (carried water to wounded soldiers in battle)

Pitkin, Walter (Walter Broughton Pitkin) (1878–1953) Am. psychologist/editor/journalist/writer (*Life Begins at Forty*)

Pitman, Sir Isaac (1813–1897) Eng. educator/inventor of shorthand

Pitney, Gene (1941–) Am. pop singer ("Only Love Can Break a Heart")/songwriter ("He's a Rebel"; "Hello Mary Lou")

Pitt, Brad (William Bradley Pitt) (1964–) Am. actor (*Thelma & Louise; A River Runs Through It; Kalifornia*)

Pitt, William ("The Great Commoner"; "The Elder Pitt") (1708–1778) Eng. statesman/war minister

Pitt, William ("The Younger") (1759–1806) Eng. prime minister 1783–1801, 1804–1806

Pitts, ZaSu (Eliza Susan Pitts) (1898–1963) Am. actress (*Greed*; "The Gale Storm Show" TV series)

Pius X, Saint (Giuseppe Melchiorre Sarto) (1835–1914) Ital. pope

Pius XI (Ambrogio Damiano Achille Ratti) (1857–1939) Ital. pope

Pius XII (Eugenio Pacelli) (1876–1958) Ital. pope

Pizarro, Francisco (c. 1475–1541) Span. explorer/conqueror of Peru

Pizzetti, Ildebrando (1880–1968) Ital. composer (*I Pastore*)

Place, Mary Kay (1947–) Am. actress (*The Big Chill; Baby Boom; Private Benjamin*; E—1976/77)

Plain, Belva (1919–) Am. novelist (*Blessings; Evergreen; Tapestry*)

Planck, Max (Max Karl Ernst Ludwig Planck) (1858–1947) Ger. physicist (N—1918; devised Planck's Constant and developed quantum theory; N—1918)

Plank, Eddie (Edward Stewart Plank; "Gettysburg Eddie") (1875–1926) Am. baseball Hall-of-Famer

Plant, Robert (Robert Anthony Plant) (1947–) Eng. rock singer ("Stairway to Heaven"; formerly with Led Zeppelin and The Honeydrippers)

Plante, Jacques (Joseph Jacques Omer Plante; "Jake the Snake") (1929–1986) Can. hockey player

Plath, Sylvia (a/k/a Victoria Lucas) (1932–1963) Am. poet/writer (*The Bell Jar*; P—1982—*The Collected Poems*)

Plato (c. 428–347 or 348 B.C.) Gr. philosopher (*The Republic; Parmenides; Apologia*)

Plato, Dana (1964–) Am. actress ("Diff'rent Strokes" TV series)

Plautus (Titus Maccius Plautus) (c. 254–184 B.C.) Roman playwright (*Epidicus*)

Player, Gary (Gary Jim Player) (1935–) S. Afr. golfer

Pleasence, Donald (1919–) Eng. actor (*The Caretaker; The Great Escape; Fantastic Voyage*)

Plekhanov, Georgy (Georgy Valentinovich Plekhanov; "The Father of Russian Marxism") (1857–1918) Russ. Marxist philosopher/historian/writer (*Fundamental Problems of Marxism*)

Pleshette, Suzanne (1937–) Am. actress ("The Bob Newhart Show" TV series)

Plimpton, George (George Ames Plimpton) (1927–) Am. TV host/writer/editor (*Paris Review*)

Plimpton, Martha (1970–) Am. actress (daughter of David Carradine; *Running on Empty; The Mosquito Coast; Parenthood*)

Pliny the Elder (Gaius Plinius Secundus) (23–79) Roman scholar (*Historia Naturalis*)

Pliny the Younger (Gaius Plinius Caecilius Secundus) (61 or 62–113) Roman letter-writer (nephew of Pliny the Elder)

Plisetskaya, Maya (Maya Mikhailovna Plisetskaya) (1925–) Russ. ballerina/choreographer (*Anna Karenina*)

Plotinus (205–270) Roman neoplatonist philosopher (*Enneads*)

Plowright, Joan (Joan Anne Plowright) (1929–) Eng. actress (*Drowning by Numbers*; *Enchanted April*; *The Entertainer*; T—1961)

Plumb, Eve (1957–) Am. actress ("The Brady Bunch" TV series)

Plumb, Sir J. H. (John Harold Plumb) (1911–) Eng. historian

Plummer, Amanda (1957–) Am. actress (daughter of Christopher Plummer and Tammy Grimes; *Agnes of God*; *The World According to Garp*)

Plummer, Christopher (Arthur Christopher Orme) (1927–) Can.-Am. actor (*The Sound of Music*; *The Man Who Would Be King*; T—1974)

Plunkett, Jim (James William Plunkett, Jr.) (1947–) Am. football player

Plutarch (c. 46–after 119) Gr. biographer (*Parallel Lives*; *Moralia*)

Pocahontas (Indian name Matoaka) (c. 1595–1617) Am. Indian princess (daughter of Powhatan)

Podhoretz, Norman (1930–) Am. editor/critic/essayist (*The Present Danger*)

Poe, Edgar Allen (1809–1849) Am. short story writer/poet (*The Raven*; *The Murders in the Rue Morgue*; *The Purloined Letter*; *The Fall of the House of Usher*; *Annabel Lee*)

Pohl, Frederik (1919–) Am. science fiction writer (*Gateway*; *The Space Merchants*)

Poincaré, Raymond (Raymond Nicholas Landry Poincaré) (1860–1934) Fr. premier/pres. 1913–1920

Pointer, Anita (1948–) Am. pop singer (with The Pointer Sisters; "Fire"; "He's So Shy"; "Slow Hand")

Pointer, Bonnie (1951–) Am. pop singer (with The Pointer Sisters)

Pointer, June (1954–) Am. pop singer (with The Pointer Sisters)

Pointer, Ruth (1946–) Am. pop singer (with The Pointer Sisters)

Poitier, Sidney (1924–) Am. actor (*The Blackboard Jungle*; *To Sir with Love*; O—1963—*Lilies of the Field*)

Polanski, Roman (1933–) Pol.-Fr. film director (*Chinatown*; *Repulsion*; *Rosemary's Baby*)

Polk, James Knox ("The First Dark Horse"; "Young Hickory") (1795–1849) 11th Am. pres. (1845–1849)

Pollack, Sydney (1934–) Am. film director (*The Way We Were*; *The Firm*; O—1985—*Out of Africa*)

Pollan, Tracy (1960–) Am. actress ("Family Ties" TV series; *A Stranger Among Us*)

Pollard, Fritz (Frederic Douglass Pollard) (1894–1986) Am. football player/coach (first Afr.-Am. coach in the NFL)

Pollard, Michael J. (Michael J. Pollack) (1939–) Am. actor (*Bonnie and Clyde*)

Pollock, Jackson (Paul Jackson Pollock; "Jack the Dripper") (1912–1956) Am. abstract painter

Polo, Marco (1254–1324) Ven. explorer/diplomat

Pol Pot (a/k/a Saloth Sar; Tol Saut; Pol Porth) (1928–) Cambod. prime minister 1975–1979

Polybius (c. 200–c. 118 B.C.) Gr. historian of the Roman world

Polyclitus or **Polycleitus** (5th century B.C.) Gr. sculptor/architect

Polycrates (died c. 522 B.C.) Gr. tyrant of Samos

Pompadour, Madame de (Jeanne-Antoinette Poisson) (1721–1764) Fr. mistress of Louis XV

Pompey the Great (Gaius Pompeius Magnus) (106–48 B.C.) Roman general/statesman

Pompidou, Georges (Georges-Jean-Raymond Pompidou) (1911–1974) Fr. pres. 1969–1974

Ponchielli, Amilcare (1834–1886) Ital. composer (*La Gioconda*)

Pons, Lily (Alice-Joséphine Pons) (1904–1976) Fr.-Am. opera singer (soprano)

Ponselle, Rosa (Rosa Melba Ponzillo) (1897–1981) Am. opera singer (soprano)

Pontecorvo, Gillo (Gilberto Pontecorvo) (1919–) Ital. film director (*The Battle of Algiers*; *Burn!*)

Ponti, Carlo (1910–) Ital. film producer (*La Strada*; *War and Peace*)

Pontiac (c. 1720–1769) Am. Ottawa chief

Pontoppidan, Henrik (1857–1943) Dan. novelist (*The Promised Land*; N—1917)

Pontormo, Jacopo da (a/k/a Jacopo Carrucci) (1494–1557) Ital. painter (studied under Da Vinci and Andrea del Sarto; *Adam And Eve Driven from Paradise*)

Ponty, Jean-Luc (1942–) Fr. jazz/rock violinist (with Mahavishnu Orchestra and Frank Zappa)

Poole, Ernest Cook (1880–1950) Am. journalist/novelist (*The Harbor*; P— 1917—*His Family*)

Pop, Iggy (James Newell Osterberg; "Iggy Stooge") (1947–) Am. punk/rock singer ("Candy"; with The Stooges)

Pope, Alexander (1688–1744) Eng. poet/satirist (*An Essay on Man*; *The Rape of the Lock*)

Popper, Sir Karl (Karl Raimund Popper) (1902–) Aus.-Eng. philosopher (*The Poverty Of Historicism*)

Porizkova, Paulina (1965–) Pol. model/actress (*Her Alibi*)

Porsche, Ferdinand (1875–1951) Aus. automobile designer (Volkswagen and Porsche cars)

Porter, Cole (Cole Albert Porter) (1891–1964) Am. composer ("Anything Goes;"; "Kiss Me Kate"; "Night and Day")

Porter, Darrell (Darrell Ray Porter) (1952–) Am. baseball player

Porter, Edwin (Edwin Stanton Porter) (1870–1941) Am. film director/pioneer (editing)

Porter, Eleanor (née Hodgman) (1868–1920) Am. novelist (*Pollyanna*)

Porter, Hal (Harold Porter) (1911–1984) Austral. short story writer/playwright/novelist/poet (*The Extra*; *The Paper Chase*)

Porter, Katherine Anne (Katherine Anne Maria Veronica Callista Russell Porter) (1890–1980) Am. novelist/short story writer (*Pale Horse, Pale Rider*; *Ship of Fools*; P—1966—*Collected Stories of Katherine Anne Porter*)

Porter, Quincy (William Quincy Porter) (1897–1966) Am. composer (P—1954—*Suite in C Minor*)

Porter, Sylvia (Sylvia Field Porter née Feldman) (1913–1991) Am. journalist/writer (*Sylvia Porter's Money Book*)

Post, Emily (née Price) (1872–1960) Am. etiquette expert/columnist

Post, Marjorie Merriweather (1887–1973) Am. financier (founded General Foods; mother of Dina Merrill)

Post, Markie (1950–) Am. actress ("Night Court" TV series)

Poston, Tom (1927–) Am. actor ("Mork &

Mindy" and "Newhart" TV series; E— 1958/59)

Potok, Chaim (1929–) Am. novelist (*My Name Is Asher Lev*; *The Chosen*)

Potter, Beatrix (Helen Beatrix Potter) (1866–1943) Eng. children's book writer/illustrator (*The Tale of Peter Rabbit*)

Potter, Dennis (Dennis Christopher George Potter) (1935–) Eng. writer/playwright (*The Singing Detective*)

Potts, Annie (1952–) Am. actress ("Designing Women" and "Love & War" TV series)

Potvin, Denis (Denis Charles Potvin; "Bear") (1953–) Can. hockey player

Poulenc, Francis (Francis-Jean-Marcel Poulenc) (1899–1963) Fr. pianist/composer (*Dialogues des Carmélites*)

Pound, Ezra (Ezra Loomis Pound) (1885–1972) Am. poet (*Cantos*)

Poundstone, Paula (1959–) Am. comedienne ("The Paula Poundstone Show" TV series)

Poussin, Nicolas (1594–1665) Fr. painter (*The Assumption of the Virgin*)

Povich, Maury (1939–) Am. talk show/TV host ("A Current Affair")

Powell, Adam Clayton, Jr. ("The Voice of Harlem") (1908–1972) Am. politician

Powell, Anthony (Anthony Dymoke Powell) (1905–) Eng. novelist (*A Dance to the Music of Time*)

Powell, Boog (John Wesley Powell) (1941–) Am. baseball player

Powell, Bud (Earl Powell) (1924–1966) Am. jazz pianist/pioneer of modern jazz

Powell, Colin (Colin Luther Powell) (1937–) Am. army general (first Afr.-Am. chairman of the Joint Chiefs of Staff)

Powell, Dick (Richard Ewing Powell) (1904–1963) Am. singer/actor (*Murder, My Sweet*; *The Day of the Locust*)

Powell, Eleanor (Eleanor Torrey Powell; "The World's Greatest Female Tap Dancer") (1910–1982) Am. dancer/actress (*Broadway Melody*; *Thousands Cheer*)

Powell, Jane (Suzanne Burce) (1929–) Am. actress ("Growing Pains" TV series; *Seven Brides for Seven Brothers*)

Powell, Lewis F., Jr. (1907–) Am. Supreme Court jurist (1972–1987)

Powell, Michael (Michael Latham Powell; "Mickey") (1905–1990) Eng. film director (*The Red Shoes*; *One of Our Aircraft Is Missing*)

Powell, William (William Horatio Powell) (1892–1984) Am. actor (*The Thin Man* films; *My Man Godfrey*)

Power, Tyrone (Frederick Tyrone Edmond Power, Jr.) (1913–1958) Ir.-Am. actor (*Witness for the Prosecution*)

Powers, Francis Gary (1929–1977) Am. pilot/spy (shot down by Russia while on a reconnaisance mission)

Powers, Hiram (1805–1873) Am. neoclassical sculptor

Powers, Stefanie (Stefania Zofia Federkiewicz) (1942–) Am. actress ("Hart to Hart" TV series)

Powhatan (c. 1550–1618) Am. Indian chief (father of Pocahontas)

Prado, Perez (Damaso Perez Prado; "The King of Mambo") (1916–1989) Cub. bandleader/organist ("Cherry Pink and Apple Blossom White")

Prater, Dave (David Prater) (1937–1988) Am. soul singer (with Sam & Dave; "Soul Man")

Praxiteles (fl. 370–330 B.C.) Ath. sculptor (*Dionysius*)

Preminger, Otto (Otto Ludwig Preminger) (1905–1986) Aus.-Am. film producer/director (*Laura; Anatomy of a Murder; Exodus; Advise and Consent*)

Prendergast, Maurice (Maurice Brazil Prendergast) (1859–1924) Am. pointillist painter (*Umbrellas in the Rain*)

Prentiss, Paula (Paula Ragusa) (1939–) Am. actress ("He and She" TV series; *The World of Henry Orient*)

Presley, Elvis (Elvis Aron Presley; "Elvis the Pelvis"; "The King"; "King of Rock 'n' Roll") (1935–1977) Am. rock singer ("Heartbreak Hotel"; "Don't Be Cruel"; "Hound Dog"; "Love Me Tender")/actor (*Viva Las Vegas; Jailhouse Rock*)

Presley, Lisa Marie (1968–) Am. rock singer (daughter of Elvis and Priscilla)

Presley, Priscilla (Priscilla Ann Beaulieu; born Priscilla Ann Wagner) (1945–) Am. actress ("Dallas" TV series)

Presnell, Harve (George Harve Presnell II) (1933–) Am. opera singer/actor (*Paint Your Wagon; The Unsinkable Molly Brown*)

Press, Irina (Irina Natanova Press) (1939–) Russ. runner

Preston, Billy (William Everett Preston) (1946–) Am. blues singer/musician ("Nothing from Nothing")

Preston, Kelly (1963–) Am. actress (*Run*)

Preston, Robert (Robert Preston Mes-

servey) (1918–1987) Am. actor (*The Music Man; S.O.B.*; T—1958, 1967)

Prévert, Jacques (1900–1977) Fr. poet/screenwriter (*Les Enfants du Paradis*)

Previn, André (Andre George Previn; born Andreas Ludwig Priwin) (1929–) Am. film conductor/composer/pianist

Previn, Dory (Dory Langdon) (1925–) Am. pop singer/film lyricist (*Valley of the Dolls; Irma La Douce*)

Price, Anthony (1928–) Eng. novelist (*Here Be Monsters; October Men*)

Price, Leontyne (Mary Leontyne Price) (1927–) Am. opera singer (soprano)

Price, Ray (Ray Noble Price; "The Cherokee Cowboy") (1926–) Am. country singer ("For the Good Times")

Price, Reynolds (Edward Reynolds Price) (1933–) Am. novelist/short story writer/poet (*A Long and Happy Life*)

Price, Vincent ("Master of Menace") (1911–1993) Am. actor (*Laura; The Abominable Dr. Phibes*)

Pride, Charley (Charley Frank Pride; "Country Charley"; "The Pride of Country Music") (1934–) Am. country singer ("Kiss an Angel Good Mornin' ")

Priestley, Jason (1969–) Can.-Am. actor ("Beverly Hills, 90210" TV series)

Priestley, J. B. (John Boynton Priestley) (1894–1984) Eng. novelist/playwright/essayist (*The Good Companions; Literature and Western Man*)

Prima, Louis (1911–1978) Am. trumpet player/singer/composer/bandleader ("Wonderland by Night")

Prince (Prince Rogers Nelson; "His Royal Badness") (1958–) Am. actor (*Purple Rain*)/rock singer/musician/songwriter ("Little Red Corvette"; "Let's Go Crazy")

Prince, Hal (Harold Smith Prince) (1928–) Am. theatrical producer/director (*Fiddler on the Roof; West Side Story; Damn Yankees*)

Principal, Victoria (1945–) Am. actress ("Dallas" TV series)

Prine, John (1946–) Am. country/folk singer/songwriter ("Hello in There")

Pringle, Aileen (Aileen Bisbee) (1895–) Am. actress (*Three Weeks; His Hour*)

Prinze, Freddie (Freddie Preutzel) (1954–1977) Am. comedian/actor ("Chico and the Man" TV series)

Prior, Matthew (1664–1721) Eng. diplomat/poet/writer (*Country Mouse and the City Mouse*)

Pritchett, Sir V. S. (Victor Sawdon Pritchett) (1900–) Eng. novelist/short story writer (*Midnight Oil*)

Prochnow, Jurgen (1941–) Ger. actor (*Das Boot*; *Dune*)

Proclus (c. 410–485) Gr. neoplatonist philosopher (studied under Plutarch; *The Nature of Evil*)

Proell, Annemarie (a/k/a Annemarie Moser-Proell) (1953–) Aus. skier

Prokofiev, Sergey (Sergey Sergeyevich Prokofiev) (1891–1953) Russ. composer (*Peter and the Wolf*)

Protagorus (c. 485–410 B.C.) Gr. philosopher (signature phrase: "Man is the measure of all things")

Proust, Marcel (1871–1922) Fr. novelist (*Remembrance of Things Past*)

Provine, Dorothy (Dorothy Michele Provine) (1937–) Am. singer/actress ("The Alaskans" and "The Roaring Twenties" TV series)

Prowse, Juliet (1937–) Eng.-Am. dancer

Proxmire, William (Edward William Proxmire) (1915–) Am. senator

Prudhomme, Paul (1941–) Am. chef/TV host/writer (*Paul Prudhomme's Louisiana Kitchen*)

Prudhomme, Sully (Rene-François-Armand Prudhomme) (1839–1907) Fr. poet (*La Justice*; N—1901)

Pruitt, Greg (Gregory Donald Pruitt) (1951–) Am. football player

Pryor, Rain (1969–) Am. actress (daughter of Richard; "Head of the Class" TV series)

Pryor, Richard (Richard Franklin Lennox Thomas Pryor III) (1940–) Am. comedian (*Stir Crazy*; *Silver Streak*)

Pucci, Emilio (Marchese Emilio Pucci di Barsento) (1914–1992) Ital. fashion designer (pop art prints)

Puccini, Giacomo (Giacomo Antonio Domenico Michele Secondo Maria Puccini) (1858–1924) Ital. opera composer (*Tosca*; *La Bohème*; *Madama Butterfly*)

Puck, Wolfgang (1949–) Am. chef

Puckett, Gary (1942–) Am. rock singer/guitarist ("Young Girl"; with Gary Puckett and The Union Gap)

Puckett, Kirby (1961–) Am. baseball player

Puente, Tito ("El Rey"; "The King of Latin Music") (1923–) Am. jazz percussionist/bandleader

Puig, Manuel (1932–1990) Arg. writer (*Kiss of the Spider Woman*)

Pulitzer, Joseph (1847–1911) Am. journalist (established the Pulitzer prizes)

Pulitzer, Peter (Herbert Peter Pulitzer, Jr.) (1930–) Am. publisher (grandson of Joseph, ex-husband of Roxanne)

Pulitzer, Roxanne (1951–) Am. writer (*Twins*; *Facade*)

Pulliam, Keshia Knight (1979–) Am. child actress ("The Cosby Show" TV series)

Pullman, Bill (c. 1954–) Am. actor (*Ruthless People*; *Malice*; *Sleepless in Seattle*)

Purcell, Edward Mills (1912–) Am. physicist (discovered nuclear magnetic resonance with Felix Bloch; N—1952)

Purcell, Henry (c. 1659–1695) Eng. composer (*Dido and Aeneas*)

Purdy, James (1923–) Am. novelist/short story writer (*Color of Darkness*)

Purl, Linda (1955–) Am. actress ("Happy Days" and "Matlock" TV series)

Purviance, Edna (1894–1958) Am. actress (Chaplin films)

Pushkin, Aleksandr (Aleksandr Sergeyevich Pushkin) (1799–1837) Russ. poet/novelist/playwright (*Boris Godunov*)

Putnam, George (George Palmer Putnam) (1814–1872) Am. publisher (G.P. Putnam & Son)

Putnam, Israel (1718–1790) Am. revolutionary army general (cousin of Rufus)

Putnam, Rufus (1738–1824) Am. revolutionary army general/pioneer (cousin of Israel)

P'u Yi or P'ui, Henry (a/k/a Hsuan-t'ung; K'ang-te) (1906–1967) Chin. emperor 1908–1912

Puzo, Mario (1920–) Am. novelist (*The Godfather*)

Pyle, Denver (1920–) Am. actor ("The Dukes of Hazzard" TV series; *Bonnie and Clyde*)

Pyle, Ernie (Ernest Taylor Pyle) (1900–1945) Am. journalist/war correspondent (P—1944)

Pym, Barbara (Barbara Mary Pym Crampton) (1913–1980) Eng. novelist (*Excellent Women*)

Pynchon, Thomas (1937–) Am. novelist (*Gravity's Rainbow*)

Pyrrhus (c. 319–272 B.C.) Gr. king of Epirus

Pythagoras ("The Samian Sage") (c. 580–c. 500 B.C.) Gr. philosopher/mathematician (may have coined the word *philosophy*)

Qaddafi, Muammar (Muammar Muhammad al-Qaddafi; also spelled Khadafy,

Gaddafi, Quaddafi; "The Spider of Tripoli") (1942–) Lib. mil./political leader 1969–

Quaid, Dennis (Dennis William Quaid) (1953–) Am. actor (brother of Randy; *The Big Easy*; *Postcards from the Edge*)

Quaid, Randy (1950–) Am. actor (*Parents*; *LBJ: The Early Years*)

Quant, Mary (1934–)Eng. "mod" fashion designer (popularized the miniskirt)

Quasimodo, Salvatore (1901–1968) Ital. poet (*Day After Day*; N—1959)

Quatro, Suzi (Suzi Soul) (1950–) Am. actress ("Happy Days" TV series)/rock singer ("Stumblin' In")

Quayle, Sir Anthony (John Anthony Quayle) (1913–1989) Eng. actor (*Anne of the Thousand Days*; *Hamlet*)

Quayle, Dan (James Danforth Quayle) (1947–) Am. v.p. (G. Bush)/senator

Quayle, Marilyn (1949–) Am. wife of Dan

Queen, Ellery *see* Lee, Manfred, and Dannay, Fred

Queen Latifah (Dana Owens; "Latifah"- "beautiful and sensitive") (c. 1970–) Am. rapper ("Nature of a Sista' ")/actress (*Juice*; *Jungle Fever*; "Living Single" TV series)

Quennell, Peter (Peter Courtney Quennell) (1905–) Eng. poet/biographer/ literary critic (*Byron in Italy*)

Quindlen, Anna (1952–) Am. journalist (P—1992)/novelist

Quinlan, Kathleen (1954–) Am. actress (*Lifeguard*; *I Never Promised You a Rose Garden*; *The Doors*)

Quinn, Aidan (1959–) Am. actor (*Benny & Joon*; *Desperately Seeking Susan*; *Avalon*; *Blink*)

Quinn, Anthony (Anthony Rudolph Oaxaca Quinn) (1915–) Ir.-Mex. actor (O— 1952—*Viva Zapata!*; O—1956—*Lust for Life*)

Quinn, Martha (1959–) Am. "veejay" (MTV)

Quintilian (Marcus Fabius Quintilianus) (c. 35–c. 99) Roman rhetorician/teacher

Quisenberry, Dan (Daniel Raymond Quisenberry; "Quiz") (1953–) Am. baseball pitcher

Quisling, Vidkun (Vidkun Abraham Lauritz Jonsson Quisling) (1887–1945) Norw. politician/traitor (collaborated in the Nazi conquest of Norway)

Quivers, Robin (c. 1950–) Am. radio personality (Howard Stern's sidekick)

Rabb, Ellis (1930–) Am. stage actor/ director/producer

Rabbitt, Eddie (Edward Thomas Rabbitt) (1941–) Am. country singer ("I Love a Rainy Night"; "Drivin' My Life Away")

Rabe, David (David William Rabe) (1940–) Am. playwright (*I'm Dancing as Fast as I Can*; *Hurlyburly*; *Sticks and Bones*)

Rabelais, François (a/k/a Alcofribas Nasier) (c. 1483–1553) Fr. physician/ scholar/writer (*Gargantua and Pantagruel*)

Rabi, Isidor (Isidor Isaac Rabi) (1898– 1988) Am. physicist (worked on the atomic bomb; helped develop microwave radar; N—1944)

Rabin, Itzhak (1922–) Isr. prime minister 1974–1977

Rachel (born 1753 B.C.) Heb. wife of Jacob

Rachins, Alan (1947–) Am. actor ("L.A. Law" TV series)

Rachmaninoff, Sergey (Sergey Vasileyevich Rachmaninoff) (1873–1943) Russ. composer (*Prelude in C Sharp Minor*)/pianist/conductor

Racine, Jean (Jean Baptiste Racine) (1639–1699) Fr. playwright (*Britannicus*; *Andromaque*)

Radbourn, Old Hoss (Charles Gardner Radbourn) (1854–1897) Am. baseball Hall-of-Famer

Radcliffe, Ann (née Ward) (1764–1823) Eng. novelist (*The Mysteries of Udolpho*)

Radner, Gilda (1946–1989) Am. comedienne ("Saturday Night Live" TV series)

Radziwill, Lee (Carolyn Lee Bouvier) (1933–) Am. writer/socialite (sister of Jacqueline Onassis)

Rae, Charlotte (Charlotte Rae Lubotsky) (1926–) Am. actress ("Diff'rent Strokes" and "The Facts of Life" TV series)

Rae, John (1813–1893) Scot. explorer (Canadian arctic coast)

Raeburn, Sir Henry ("The Scottish Reynolds") (1756–1823) Scot. portrait painter

Rafelson, Bob (Robert Rafelson) (1934–) Am. film director (*The Postman Always Rings Twice* [1981]; *Five Easy Pieces*)

Rafferty, Gerry (1945–) Scot. rock/pop singer ("Baker Street"; "Right Down the Line")

Raffin, Deborah (1953–) Am. actress (*Once Is Not Enough*)

Raft, George (George Ranft) (1895–1980) Am. actor (*Scarface* [1932]; *Each Dawn I Die*; *Stage Door Canteen*)

Rafsanjani, Hojatolislam Hashemi (1934–) Iran. pres. 1989–

Ragland, Rags (John Lee Morgan Beauregard Ragland) (1905–1946) Am. boxer/comedian

Raimi, Sam (1959–) Am. screenwriter/film director (*Darkman*; *Army of Darkness*)

Rainer, Luise (1909–) Aus.-Am. actress (O—1936—*The Great Ziegfeld*; O—1937—*The Good Earth*)

Raines, Ella (Ella Wallace Raubes) (1921–1988) Am. actress (*Phantom Lady*; *Hail the Conquering Hero*)

Rainey, Ma (Gertrude Malissa Nix Rainey née Pridgett) (1886–1939) Am. blues singer (taught Bessie Smith)

Rainier III (Louis Henri Maxence Bertrand de Grimaldi) (1923–) ruler (prince) of Monaco 1949–

Rains, Claude (William Claude Rains) (1889–1967) Eng. actor (*Now, Voyager*; *Mr. Skeffington*; *Notorious*; *Casablanca*; T—1951)

Rainwater, L. James (Leo James Rainwater) (1917–1986) Am. physicist (worked on the Manhattan Project; N—1975)

Raitt, Bonnie (Bonnie Lynn Raitt) (1949–) Am. country/pop singer (daughter of John; "Nick of Time"; "Something to Talk About"; G—1989, 1991)

Raitt, John (John Emmett Raitt) (1917–) Am. actor/singer ("The Buick Circus Hour" TV series)

Raleigh, Sir Walter (1554–1618) Eng. navigator/historian/courtier

Ralph, Jessie (Jessie Ralph Chambers) (1864–1944) Am. actress (*David Copperfield*; *Captain Blood*)

Ralston, Dennis (Richard Dennis Ralston) (1942–) Am. tennis player

Ralston, Esther ("The American Venus") (1902–) Am. actress (*Tin Pan Alley*; *Black Beauty*)

Ralston, Jobyna (1901–1967) Am. actress (with Harold Lloyd; *Wings*)

Ralston, Vera (Vera Helena Hruba) (1919–) Cz.-Am. actress (*Wyoming*)

Rambeau, Marjorie (1889–1970) Am. actress (*Tugboat Annie Sails Again*; *Primrose Path*)

Rambo, Dack (Norman J. Rambo) (1941–) Am. actor (twin brother of Dirk; "Dallas" TV series)

Rambo, Dirk (Orman Rambo) (1941–1967) Am. actor ("The New Loretta Young Show" TV series)

Ramirez, Raul (1953–) Mex. tennis player

Ramirez, Richard ("The Night Stalker") (1960–) Am. serial killer

Ramis, Harold (1944–) Am. writer/film director (*Caddyshack*; *Ghostbusters*; *Groundhog Day*)

Ramone, Dee Dee (Douglas Colvin) (1952–) Am. rock bassist (with The Ramones)

Ramone, Joey (Jeffrey Hyman) (1952–) Am. rock singer (with The Ramones; "Blitzkrieg Bop"; "Sheena Is a Punk Rocker")

Ramone, Johnny (John Cummings) (1951–) Am. rock guitarist (with The Ramones)

Rampal, Jean-Pierre (Jean-Pierre Louis Rampal) (1922–) Fr. flute player

Rampling, Charlotte (1945–) Eng.-Am. actress (*The Night Porter*; *Angel Heart*)

Rand, Ayn (1905–1982) Russ.-Am. philosopher/novelist (*The Fountainhead*; *Atlas Shrugged*)

Rand, Sally (Helen Gould Beck) (1904–1979) Am. fan dancer/entertainer

Randall, Tony (Anthony Leonard Rosenberg) (1920–) Am. actor (Felix Unger in "The Odd Couple" TV series; E—1974/75)

Randi, James (Randall James Hamilton Zwinge; "The Amazing Randi") (1928–) Can. magician/debunker of mysticism and mystics

Randolph, Amanda (1902–1967) Am. actress ("The Danny Thomas Show" TV series)

Randolph, A. Philip (Asa Philip Randolph) (1889–1979) Am. labor leader/social reformer

Randolph, Boots (Homer Louis Randolph III) (1927–) Am. country saxophonist ("Yakety Sax")

Randolph, Willie (Willie Larry Randolph, Jr.) (1954–) Am. baseball player

Rankin, Judy (Judith Rankin née Torluemke) (1945–) Am. golfer

Ranks, Shabba (Rawlston Fernando Gordon; a/k/a Jamaican DJ Don) (1966–) Am. reggae singer ("Slow and Sexy")

Ransom, John (John Crowe Ransom) (1888–1974) Am. poet/critic (*Chills and Fever*)

Raphael (Raffaello or Raffael or Raffaelo

Sanzio) (1483–1520) Ital. architect/ painter (*Vision of a Knight*)

Raphael, Sally Jessy (1943–) Am. talk show host

Raphaelson, Samson (1896–1983) Am. playwright (*The Jazz Singer*)

Rappaport, David (1951–1990) Eng. dwarf actor ("L.A. Law" TV series)

Rapper, Irving (1898–) Am. film director (*Now, Voyager*; *Marjorie Morningstar*)

Rasche, David (1944–) Am. actor (TV's "Sledge Hammer!"; "Nurses" TV series)

Raschi, Vic (Victor John Raschi; "The Springfield Rifle") (1919–) Am. baseball pitcher

Rashad, Ahmad (Bobby Moore) (1949–) Am. football player/sportscaster

Rashad, Phylicia (Phylicia Ayers-Allen) (1948–) Am. actress ("The Cosby Show" TV series)

Rasmussen, Knud (Knud Johan Viktor Rasmussen) (1879–1933) Dan. explorer/ writer (*Across Arctic America*)

Rasputin (Grigory Yefimovich Rasputin; born Grigory Yefimovich Novykh; "The Mad Monk") (1872–1916) Russ. mystic

Rathbone, Basil (Philip St. John Basil Rathbone) (1892–1967) Eng. actor (Sherlock Holmes in film; *The Mark of Zorro*; T—1948)

Rather, Dan (Daniel Irvin Rather) (1931–) Am. TV newscaster ("60 Minutes"; "48 Hours")

Rattigan, Sir Terence (Terence Mervyn Rattigan) (1911–1977) Eng. playwright (*Separate Tables*)/screenwriter (*Goodbye, Mr. Chips*)

Ratzenberger, John (John Dezso Ratzenberger) (1947–) Am. actor ("Cheers" TV series)

Rauschenberg, Robert (Milton Rauschenberg) (1925–) Am. pop artist

Ravel, Maurice (Joseph-Maurice Ravel) (1875–1937) Fr. composer (*Bolero*)

Raven, Eddy (Edward Garvin Futch) (1945–) Am. country singer ("I'm Gonna Get You")

Rawlings, Marjorie (née) Kinnan (1896–1953) Am. novelist (*Cross Creek*; P—1939—*The Yearling*)

Rawls, Lou (Louis Allen Rawls) (1935–) Am. blues/pop singer ("You'll Never Find Another Love Like Mine")

Ray, Aldo (Aldo da Re) (1926–1991) Am. actor (*The Marrying Kind*; *The Naked and the Dead*)

Ray, Dixy Lee (1914–1993) Am. politician/ marine biologist

Ray, James Earl (1928–) Am. assassin (Martin Luther King, Jr.)

Ray, Johnnie (John Alvin Ray; "The Prince of Wails") (1927–1990) Am. pop singer

Ray, Nicholas (Raymond Nicholas Kienzle) (1911–1979) Am. film director (*Rebel without a Cause*; *You Can't Go Home Again*)

Ray, Satyajit (1921–1992) Ind. filmmaker (*Apu* film trilogy)

Rayburn, Gene (Eugene Rubessa) (1917–) Am. game show host ("Match Game")

Rayburn, Sam (Samuel Taliaferro Rayburn; "Mr. Democrat") (1882–1961) Am. politician (speaker of the house)

Raye, Martha (Margaret Theresa Yvonne O'Reed) (1916–) Am. actress ("Alice" TV series; denture commercials)

Raymond, Alex (Alexander Gillespie Raymond) (1909–1956) Am. cartoonist (*Flash Gordon*; *Jungle Jim*)

Raymond, Gene (Raymond Guion) (1908–) Am. actor (*Mr. and Mrs. Smith*; *Flying Down to Rio*)

Raymond, Henry Jarvis (1820–1869) Am. publisher/editor (*New York Times*, which he also founded)

Rea, Chris (1951–) Eng. rock singer ("Fool If You Think It's Over")

Rea, Stephen (c. 1949–) Ir. actor (*The Crying Game*; *Bad Behaviour*)

Read, Sir Herbert (1893–1968) Eng. literary/art critic/poet (*The Tenth Muse*; *Art Now*)

Reagan, Nancy (Anne Frances Robbins Davis; "Marie Antoinette"; "First Mannequin") (1923–) Am. first lady (Ronald)

Reagan, Ron (1958–) Am. talk show host ("Front Page"; son of Ronald and Nancy)

Reagan, Ronald (Ronald Wilson Reagan; "Dutch"; "The Great Communicator") (1911–) Am. actor/40th Am. pres. (1981–1988)

Reardon, Jeff (Jeffrey James Reardon; "The Terminator") (1955–) Am. baseball pitcher

Reason, Rex (a/k/a Bart Roberts) (1928–) Am. actor (*Salome*; *Thundering Jets*)

Reasoner, Harry (1923–1991) Am. TV newscaster

Reber, Grote (1911–) Am. astronomer (created the first radio telescope)

Récamier, Jeanne (Jeanne-Françoise-

Julie-Adélaïde Récamier née Bernard) (1777–1849) Fr. society figure/wit
Red Cloud (Indian name: Mahpiua Luta) (1822–1909) Am. Indian (Oglala, Sioux, Cheyenne) chief
Redbeard see Barbarossa
Redding, Otis (1941–1967) Am. blues singer ("[Sittin' on] The Dock of the Bay")
Reddy, Helen ("Queen of Housewife Rock") (1941–) Austral. pop singer ("I Am Woman"; "Delta Dawn"; "Angie Baby"; G—1972)
Redenbacher, Orville (1907–) Am. manufacturer/popcorn pitchman
Redford, Robert (Charles Robert Redford, Jr.) (1937–) Am. actor (*The Way We Were*; *The Sting*)/film director (*A River Runs Through It*; O—1980—*Ordinary People*)
Redgrave, Lynn (Lynn Rachel Redgrave) (1943–) Eng. actress (daughter of Michael, sister of Vanessa; *Georgy Girl*)
Redgrave, Sir Michael (Michael Scudamore Redgrave) (1908–1985) Eng. actor (*The Loneliness of the Long Distance Runner*)
Redgrave, Vanessa (1937–) Eng. actress (*Howard's End*; *Blow-Up*; O—1977—*Julia*)/documentarist (*The Palestinians*)/political activist
Redon, Odilon (1840–1916) Fr. symbolist painter/engraver/lithographer
Redus, Gary (Gary Eugene Redus) (1956–) Am. baseball player
Reed, Alaina (1946–) Am. actress ("227" and "Sesame Street" TV series)
Reed, Sir Carol (1906–1976) Eng. film director (*The Third Man*; O—1968—*Oliver!*)
Reed, Donna (Donna Belle Mullenger) (1921–1986) Am. actress (*Shadow of the Thin Man*; O—1953—*From Here to Eternity*)
Reed, Ishmael (Ishmael Scott Reed) (1938–) Am. novelist/poet (*Mumbo Jumbo*)
Reed, Jerry (Jerry Reed Hubbard; "Guitar Man"; "The Alabama Wild Man") (1937–) Am. country singer/guitarist ("Amos Moses")
Reed, John (John Silas Reed) (1887–1920) Am. poet/journalist (*Ten Days That Shook the World*)
Reed, Lou (Louis Firbank) (1942–) Am. rock singer/musician/songwriter ("Walk

on the Wild Side"; formerly with Velvet Underground)
Reed, Oliver (Robert Oliver Reed) (1938–) Eng. actor (*Oliver!*; *The Damned*)
Reed, Pamela (1949–) Am. actress (*The Long Riders*; *The Right Stuff*)
Reed, Rex (Rex Taylor Reed) (1938–) Am. film critic/writer
Reed, Robert (John Robert Rietz) (1932–1992) Am. actor ("The Brady Bunch" TV series)
Reed, Shanna (c. 1956–) Am. actress ("Major Dad" TV series)
Reed, Walter (1851–1902) Am. army surgeon (found that yellow fever is transmitted by mosquitoes)
Reed, Willis (Willis Reed, Jr.) (1942–) Am. basketball player/coach
Reese, Della (Delloreese Patricia Early) (1932–) Am. jazz singer ("Don't You Know")/actress ("Chico and the Man" TV series)
Reese, Mason (1965–) Am. child actor (Underwood Deviled Ham commercials)
Reese, Pee Wee (Harold Henry Reese; "The Champ"; "The Little Colonel") (1918–) Am. baseball Hall-of-Famer
Reeve, Christopher (1952–) Am. actor (*Superman*; *Deathtrap*; *Switching Channels*)
Reeves, Del (Franklin Delano Reeves) (1934–) Am. country singer ("Girl on the Billboard")
Reeves, George (George Brewer) (1914–1959) Am. actor ("The Adventures of Superman" TV series)
Reeves, Jim (James Travis Reeves; "Gentleman Jim") (1924–1964) Am. country singer ("He'll Have to Go")
Reeves, Keanu (1964–) Am. actor (*My Own Private Idaho*; *Bill and Ted's Excellent Adventure*; *Bram Stoker's Dracula*)
Reeves, Martha (1941–) Am. pop singer ("Heat Wave"; "Dancing in the Street"; "Nowhere to Run"; with Martha and The Vandellas)
Reeves, Steve (1926–) Am. bodybuilder/actor (*The Last Days of Pompeii*)
Regan, Donald (Donald Thomas Regan) (1918–) Am. govt. official (chief of staff and treasury secretary)
Reger, Max (Johann Baptist Joseph Maximillian Reger) (1873–1916) Ger. composer (*Sonata in F Sharp Minor*)
Rehnquist, William (William Hubbs

Rehnquist) (1924–) Am. Supreme Court chief justice (1986–)

Rehoboam (10th century B.C.) king of Judah c. 934–917 B.C.

Reid, Mayne (Thomas Mayne Reid) (1818–1883) Ir. writer (*The Scalp Hunters; The Rifle Rangers*)

Reid, Tim (1944–) Am. comedian/actor ("WKRP in Cincinnati" TV series)

Reid, Wallace (William Wallace Reed) (1890–1923) Am. actor (*The Birth of a Nation; To Have and to Hold*)

Reid, Whitelaw (1837–1912) Am. journalist (editor of *New York Tribune*)/diplomat

Reilly, Charles Nelson (1931–) Am. comedian/game show panelist ("Match Game")

Reiner, Carl (1922–) Am. film director/actor (father of Rob; *Oh God; It's a Mad, Mad, Mad, Mad World;* E—1956, 1957)

Reiner, Fritz (1888–1963) Hung.-Am. orchestra conductor (Metropolitan Opera; Chicago Symphony)

Reiner, Rob (Robert Reiner) (1945–) Am. actor ("All in the Family" TV series; E—1977/78)/film director (*When Harry Met Sally . . .*)

Reinhardt, Django (Jean-Baptiste Reinhardt) (1910–1953) Bel.-Fr. jazz guitarist (with Duke Ellington)

Reinhardt, Max (Maximilian Goldmann) (1873–1943) Aus. theatrical producer/filmmaker (*A Midsummer Night's Dream*)

Reinhold, Judge (Edward Ernest Reinhold) (1956–) Am. actor (*Beverly Hills Cop; Fast Times at Ridgemont High; Ruthless People*)

Reinking, Ann (Ann H. Reinking) (1949–) Am. dancer/actress (*All That Jazz*)

Reiser, Paul (C) Am. actor ("Mad About You" and "My Two Dads" TV series)

Reiser, Pete (Harold Patrick Reiser; "Pistol Pete"; "Ye Childe Harold") (1919–1981) Am. baseball player

Reitman, Ivan (1946–) Can. film director (*Ghostbusters; Stripes; Dave*)

Relph, Michael (1915–) Eng. film director/producer (*The League of Gentlemen; Man In The Moon*)

Remarque, Erich Maria (Erich Paul Remark) (1898–1970) Ger. journalist/novelist (*All Quiet on the Western Front*)

Rembrandt (Rembrandt Harmensz [or Harmenszoon] Van Rijn [or Van Ryn])

(1606–1669) Dutch painter (*The Anatomy Lesson*)

Remick, Lee (Lee Ann Remick) (1935–1991) Am. actress (*Anatomy of a Murder; Days of Wine and Roses*)

Remington, Frederic ("The Rembrandt of the West") (1861–1909) Am. painter/illustrator/sculptor (western themes)

Remsen, Ira (1846–1927) Am. chemist (discovered saccharin)

Renaldo, Duncan (Renault Renaldo Duncan; "The Cisco Kid") (1904–1980) Am. cowboy actor ("The Cisco Kid" in films)

Renault, Louis ("France's Henry Ford") (1877–1944) Fr. automobile manufacturer

Rendell, Ruth (née Grasemann; a/k/a Barbara Vine) (1930–) Eng. crime novelist (*Talking to Strange Men; Speaker of Mandarin*)

Reni, Guido (1575–1642) Ital. painter (*The Glory of St. Dominic*)

Rennie, Michael (Eric Alexander Rennie) (1909–1971) Eng. actor (*The Day the Earth Stood Still; The Divorce of Lady X*)

Reno, Janet (1938–) Am. govt. official (first female attorney general)

Renoir, Jean (1894–1979) Fr. film director (*La Grande Illusion; The Rules of the Game; La Bete Humaine;* son of Pierre Auguste)

Renoir, Pierre Auguste (a/k/a Auguste Renoir) (1841–1919) Fr. impressionist painter

Renwick, James (1818–1895) Am. architect (the Smithsonian)

Resnais, Alain (1922–) Fr. film director (*Hiroshima, Mon Amour; Last Year at Marienbad*)

Resnik, Regina (1924–) Am. opera singer (mezzo-soprano)

Respighi, Ottorino (1879–1936) Ital. composer (*Lucrezia; The Fountains of Rome*)

Reston, James (James Barrett Reston) (1909–) Am. writer/journalist (P—1945; P—1957)

Retton, Mary Lou (1968–) Am. gymnast

Reuben, David (David Robert Reuben) (1933–) Am. psychiatrist/writer (*Everything You Always Wanted to Know About Sex but Were Afraid to Ask*)

Reuschel, Rick (Rickey Eugene Reuschel) (1949–) Am. baseball pitcher

Reuter, Baron Paul von (Paul Julius von

Reuter; born Israel Beer Josaphat) (1816–1899) Ger.-Eng. journalist

Revere, Anne (1903–1972) Am. actress (*The Song of Bernadette*; *Gentleman's Agreement*; O—1945—*National Velvet*)

Revere, Paul (1735–1818) Am. revolutionary hero ("The British are coming, the British are coming")

Revere, Paul (1942–) Am. rock singer ("Indian Reservation"; with Paul Revere & The Raiders)

Reville, Alma (1900–1982) Eng. screenwriter (Hitchcock films)

Revson, Charles (1906–1975) Am. cosmetics executive (founded Revlon)

Rexroth, Kenneth (1905–1982) Am. poet (*The Phoenix and the Tortoise*)

Rey, Alvino (Alvin McGurney) (1911–) Am. orchestra leader ("The King Family Show" TV series)

Rey, Fernando (Fernando Casado Arambillet Veiga) (1912–) Span. actor (*The French Connection*; *The Discreet Charm of the Bourgeoisie*)

Reymont, Wladyslaw (Wladyslaw Stanislaw Reymont or Rejment) (1867–1925) Pol. novelist (*The Peasants*; N—1924)

Reynolds, Adeline De Walt (1862–1961) Am. actress (*Going My Way*; *A Tree Grows in Brooklyn*)

Reynolds, Allie (Allie Pierce Reynolds; "The Chief"; "Superchief") (1915–) Am. baseball pitcher

Reynolds, Burt (Burton Leon Reynolds, Jr.) (1936–) Am. actor ("Evening Shade" TV series; *Sharkey's Machine*; *Semi-Tough*; *Deliverance*; E—1990/91)

Reynolds, Debbie (Mary Frances Reynolds) (1932–) Am. singer/actress (mother of Carrie Fisher; *The Unsinkable Molly Brown*)

Reynolds, Sir Joshua (1723–1792) Eng. portrait painter

Rhee, Syngman (1875–1965) 1st pres. of the Republic of Korea (1948–1960)

Rhoden, Rick (Richard Alan Rhoden) (1953–) Am. baseball pitcher

Rhodes, Cecil (Cecil John Rhodes) (1853–1902) Eng. financier/Am. colonial administrator (established Rhodes scholarships)

Rhodes, Hari (1932–) Am. actor ("Daktari" and "The Bold Ones" TV series)

Rhodes, Zandra (1940–) Eng. fashion designer

Rhue, Madlyn (Madeleine Roche) (1934–)

Am. actress (*It's a Mad, Mad, Mad, Mad World*)

Rhys, Jean (Ella Gwendolyn Rees Williams) (1894–1979) Eng. novelist/short story writer (*Wide Sargasso Sea*)

Rhys-Davies, John (1944–) Eng. actor (*Raiders of the Lost Ark*; *Victor/Victoria*)

Ribbentrop, Joachim Von (Joachim Ribbentrop; "The Traveling Salesman of National Socialism"; "The Second Bismark") (1893–1946) Ger. Nazi diplomat (executed for war crimes)

Ribera, José De ("Lo Spagnoletto" [The Little Spaniard]) (1588–1652) Span. painter/etcher (*Portrait of a Bearded Woman*)

Ricci, Christina (c. 1980–) Am. child actress (*The Addams Family*; *Addams Family Values*)

Ricci, Nina (Marie Nielli) (1883–1970) Fr. fashion designer

Rice, Anne (born Howard Allen O'Brien [parents wanted a boy]) (1941–) Am. novelist (*The Vampire Lestat*; *The Witching Hour*; *Queen of the Damned*)

Rice, Craig (Georgiana Ann Randolph) (1908–1957) Am. detective story writer (*My Kingdom for a Hearse*)

Rice, Donna (1958–) Am. model (involved with Gary Hart)

Rice, Elmer (Elmer Leopold Reizenstein) (1892–1967) Am. playwright (P—1929—*Street Scene*)

Rice, Grantland (Henry Grantland Rice) (1880–1954) Am. sportscaster/journalist

Rice, Jerry (Jerry Lee Rice) (1962–) Am. football player

Rice, Jim (James Edward Rice) (1953–) Am. baseball player

Rich, Adam (1968–) Am. actor ("Eight Is Enough" TV series)

Rich, Adrienne (Adrienne Cecile Rich) (1929–) Am. poet (*Of Woman Born*)

Rich, Buddy (Bernard Rich) (1917–1987) Am. jazz drummer (with Tommy Dorsey)

Rich, Charlie (Charles Allan Rich; "The Silver Fox") (1932–) Am. pop/country singer ("Behind Closed Doors"; "The Most Beautiful Girl")

Rich, Irene (Irene Luther) (1891–1988) Am. film/radio actress ("Dear John" radio show)

Richard I (Richard the Lion-Hearted) (1157–1199) Eng. king 1189–1199

Richard II (1367–1400) Eng. king 1377–1399
Richard III (1452–1485) Eng. king 1483–1485
Richard, Cliff (Harry Rodger Webb) (1940–) Eng. pop singer ("Devil Woman"; "We Don't Talk Anymore")
Richard, Maurice (Maurice Joseph Henri Richard; "Rocket") (1921–) Can. hockey player
Richards, Ann (Ann Willis Richards) (1933–) Am. gov. of Texas 1990–
Richards, I. A. (Ivor Armstrong Richards) (1893–1979) Eng. critic/scholar/poet (Principles of Literary Criticism)
Richards, Keith (Keith Richard) (1943–) Eng. rock guitarist/songwriter (with The Rolling Stones)
Richards, Michael (c. 1949–) Am. comedian/actor (Kramer in "Seinfeld" TV series)
Richards, Theodore (Theodore William Richards) (1868–1928) Am. chemist (N—1914)
Richardson, Henry (Henry Hobson Richardson) (1838–1886) Am. architect (Chicago's Marshall Field building)
Richardson, Joely (c. 1965–) Eng. actress (daughter of Tony Richardson and Vanessa Redgrave; Drowning by Numbers; Shining Through; I'll Do Anything)
Richardson, Miranda (1958–) Eng. actress (Dance with a Stranger; Enchanted April; Damage; The Crying Game)
Richardson, Natasha (1963–) Eng. actress (daughter of Tony Richardson and Vanessa Redgrave; The Handmaid's Tale; Patty Hearst)
Richardson, Patricia (c. 1952–) Am. actress ("Home Improvement" TV series)
Richardson, Sir Ralph (Ralph David Richardson; "The Duke of Dark Corners") (1902–1983) Eng. actor (The Heiress; Richard III)
Richardson, Samuel (1689–1761) Eng. novelist (Clarissa Harlowe)
Richardson, Tony (Cecil Antonio Richardson) (1928–1991) Eng. stage/film director (father of Natasha; O—1963—Tom Jones)
Richelieu, Cardinal De (Armand-Jean du Plessis; "Eminence Rouge" [or "Red Eminence"]) (1585–1642) Fr. statesman
Richie, Lionel (Lionel Brockman Richie) (1949–) Am. pop singer ("Truly"; "Hello"; "Say You, Say Me"; formerly with The Commodores; G—1982)

Richler, Mordecai (1931–) Can. novelist (The Apprenticeship of Duddy Kravitz)
Richman, Jonathan (1951–) Am. pop singer (with The Modern Lovers; "Roadrunner")
Richter, Burton (1931–) Am. physicist (N—1976)
Richter, Charles (Charles Francis Richter) (1900–1985) Am. seismologist (with Beno Gutenberg, created the Richter Scale)
Richter, Conrad (Conrad Michael Richter) (1890–1968) Am. novelist/short story writer (P—1951—The Town)
Richter, Jean Paul (Johann Paul Friedrich Richter; a/k/a Jean Paul) (1763–1825) Ger. novelist (Titan)
Rickenbacker, Eddie (Edward Vernon Rickenbacher; "Captain Eddie") (1890–1973) Am. aviator/WWII hero
Rickey, Branch (Wesley Branch Rickey; "The Mahatma") (1881–1965) Am. baseball Hall-of-Famer
Rickles, Don ("Mr. Warmth") (1926–) Am. comedian ("Daddy Dearest" TV series with Richard Lewis)
Rickman, Alan (C) Eng. actor (Die Hard; Truly, Madly, Deeply; Bob Roberts)
Rickover, Hyman (Hyman George Rickover; "Father of the Atomic Submarine") (1900–1986) Am. admiral (developed the first nuclear-powered submarine)
Riddle, Nelson (Nelson Smock Riddle) (1921–1985) Am. orchestra leader/composer (Lisbon Antigua)
Ride, Sally (Sally Kristen Ride) (1951–) Am. astronaut (first American woman in space)
Ridgeley, Andrew (1963–) Eng. pop guitarist/singer (with Wham!)
Riding Jackson, Laura see Jackson, Laura
Riefenstahl, Leni (Helene Berta Amalie Riefenstahl) (1902–) Ger. filmmaker (Triumph of the Will; Olympiad)
Riegert, Peter (1947–) Am. actor (Animal House; Local Hero; The Object of Beauty)
Riessen, Marty (Martin Clare Riessen) (1941–) Am. tennis player
Rigby, Cathy (1952–) Am. gymnast
Rigg, Diana (Enid Diana Elizabeth Rigg) (1938–) Eng. actress ("The Avengers" TV series; host of TV's "Mystery")
Riggs, Bobby (Robert Larimore Riggs; "The Happy Hustler") (1918–) Am. tennis player (W—1939)

Rigney, Bill (William Joseph Rigney; "The Cricket"; "Specs") (1918–) Am. baseball player/manager

Riis, Jacob (Jacob August Riis) (1849–1914) Am. journalist/social reformer/writer (*How the Other Half Lives*)

Riley, James (James Whitcomb Riley; "The Hoosier Poet") (1849–1916) Am. journalist/poet (*The Old Swimmin' Hole*)

Riley, Jeannie C. (Jeanne Carolyn Stephenson) (1945–) Am. country singer ("Harper Valley P.T.A.")

Riley, Jeannine (1939–) Am. actress ("Petticoat Junction" and "Hee Haw" TV series)

Riley, Pat (Patrick James Riley) (1945–) Am. basketball coach

Rilke, Rainer Maria (1875–1926) Ger. poet (*Divine Elegies; Book of Hours*)

Rimbaud, Arthur (Jean-Nicolas-Arthur Rimbaud) (1854–1891) Fr. poet (*A Season in Hell*)

Rimsky-Korsakov, Nikolay (Nikolay Andreyevich Rimsky-Korsakov) (1844–1908) Russ. composer (*Scheherazade; The Snow Maiden; Capriccio Espagnol*)

Rinehart, Mary (née) Roberts (1876–1958) Am. playwright/mystery novelist (*The Circular Staircase*)

Ringling, Charles (Charles Rüngeling) (1863–1926) Am. circus owner (brother of John)

Ringling, John (John Rüngeling) (1866–1936) Am. circus owner (brother of Charles)

Ringo, Jim (James Ringo) (1932–) Am. football Hall-of-Famer

Ringwald, Molly (1968–) Am. actress (*Pretty in Pink; The Breakfast Club*)

Riperton, Minnie (1947–1979) Am. pop singer ("Lovin' You")

Ripken, Billy (William Oliver Ripken) (1964–) Am. baseball player

Ripken, Cal (Calvin Edwin Ripken, Jr.) (1960–) Am. baseball player

Ripley, Robert (Robert Leroy Ripley) (1893–1949) Am. cartoonist (*Believe It or Not!*)

Rippy, Rodney Allen (1968–) Am. child actor (Burger King Whopper commercials)

Riskin, Robert (1897–1955) Am. screenwriter/playwright (*It Happened One Night; Mr. Deeds Goes to Town*)

Ritchard, Cyril (Cyril Trimnell-Richard) (1896–1977) Austral.-Eng. stage/film actor (*Blackmail*)

Ritchie, Michael (1938–) Am. film director (*The Candidate; The Golden Child; Diggstown*)

Ritenour, Lee ("Captain Fingers") (1952–) Am. jazz/rock guitarist (with Fourplay)

Ritt, Martin (1914–1990) Am. film director (*Norma Rae; The Long Hot Summer; Hud; Stanley and Iris*)

Ritter, John (Jonathan Southworth Ritter) (1948–) Am. actor (son of Tex; "Three's Company" TV series; *Hero at Large; Skin Deep*; E—1983/84)

Ritter, Tex (Woodward Maurice Nederland Ritter; "America's Most Beloved Cowboy") (1905–1974) Am. actor (father of John; *Song of the Gringo*)/singer ("I've Got Spurs That Jingle, Jangle, Jingle")

Ritter, Thelma (Thelma Adele Ritter) (1905–1969) Am. comedienne (*All About Eve; Rear Window*; T—1958)

Ritz, Al (Al Joachim) (1901–1965) Am. comedian (with The Ritz Brothers)

Ritz, Harry (Herschel Joachim) (1906–1986) Am. comedian (with The Ritz Brothers)

Ritz, Jim (James Joachim) (1903–1985) Am. comedian (with The Ritz Brothers)

Riva, Emmanuelle (1932–) Fr. actress (*Hiroshima, Mon Amour*)

Rivera, Chita (Dolores Conchita Figueroa del Rivero) (1933–) Am. actress/dancer (*Sweet Charity; Kiss of the Spider Woman*; T—1984, 1993)

Rivera, Diego (Diego Maria Conceptión Juan Nepomuseno Estanislao de la Rivera y Barrientos Acosta y Rodríguez; "The Painter for Millionaires") (1886–1957) Mex. muralist

Rivera, Geraldo (Geraldo Miguel Rivera; "Rock 'n' Roll Newsman") (1943–) Am. talk show host

Rivera, José (José Eustacio Rivera) (1889–1928) Col. novelist/poet (*The Vortex*)

Rivers, Joan (Joan Alexandra Molinsky) (1933–) Am. comedienne/talk show host (signature phrase: "Can we talk?")

Rivers, Johnny (John Ramistella) (1942–) Am. rock singer/musician ("Memphis"; "Baby I Need Your Lovin'")

Rivers, Larry (Yitzroch Loiza Grossberg) (1923–) Am. abstract expressionist painter/sculptor

Rivers, Mickey (John Milton Rivers; "Mick the Quick"; "Mickey Mouth"; "The Weatherman") (1948–) Am. baseball player

Rixey, Eppa ("Eppa Jephtha"; "The Eiffel Tower of Culpepper") (1891–1963) Am. baseball Hall-of-Famer

Roach, Hal (Hal E. Roach) (1892–1992) Am. film producer (*Safety Last*; *Of Mice and Men* [1939])

Roach, Max (Maxwell Lemuel Roach) (1924–) Am. jazz drummer

Robards, Jason (Jason Nelson Robards, Jr.) (1922–) Am. stage actor (*The Iceman Cometh*; *Long Day's Journey Into Night*)/film actor (*Melvin and Howard*; O—1976—*All the President's Men*; O—1977—*Julia*; T—1959)

Robbe-Grillet, Alain (1922–) Fr. novelist/critic/filmmaker (*Last Year at Marienbad*; *In the Labyrinth*)

Robbins, Harold (Harold Rubins; a/k/a Francis Kane) (1916–) Am. novelist (*The Dream Merchants*; *The Carpetbaggers*)

Robbins, Jerome (Jerome Rabinowitz) (1918–) Am. theatrical director/choreographer (O—1961—*West Side Story*)

Robbins, Marty (Martin David Robinson) (1925–1982) Am. country singer ("El Paso")

Robbins, Tim (1958–) Am. actor (*Bull Durham*; *The Hudsucker Proxy*; *The Player*)/film director (*Bob Roberts*)

Robbins, Tom (1936–) Am. novelist (*Even Cowgirls Get the Blues*; *Skinny Legs and All*)

Roberts, Barbara (1936–) Am. gov. of Oregon

Roberts, Sir Charles G. D. (Charles George Douglas Roberts) (1860–1943) Can. poet/writer (*Red Fox*; *In Divers Tones*)

Roberts, Cokie (Corinne Boggs Roberts) (1943–) Am. newscaster (daughter of Hale Boggs)

Roberts, Elizabeth Madox (1886–1941) Am. novelist/poet (*My Heart and My Flesh*)

Roberts, Eric (1956–) Am. actor (brother of Julia; *Star 80*; *Runaway Train*; *King of the Gypsies*)

Roberts, Julia (Julia Fiona Roberts) (1967–) Am. actress (*Pretty Woman*; *Steel Magnolias*; *Mystic Pizza*; *The Pelican Brief*)

Roberts, Kenneth (Kenneth Lewis Roberts) (1885–1957) Am. historical novelist (*Northwest Passage*; P—1957—(special citation)

Roberts, Oral (Granville Oral Roberts) (1918–) Am. evangelist/faith healer

Roberts, Pat (1936–) Am. congressman

Roberts, Pernell (1930–) Am. actor ("Bonanza" and "Trapper John, M.D." TV series)

Roberts, Rachel (1927–1980) Wel. actress (*This Sporting Life*; *Murder on the Orient Express*)

Roberts, Robin (Robin Evan Roberts) (1926–) Am. baseball Hall-of-Famer

Roberts, Tanya (1955–) Am. actress ("Charlie's Angels" TV series)

Roberts, Tony (1939–) Am. actor (*Serpico*; *Radio Days*)

Robertson, Cliff (Clifford Parker Robertson III) (1925–) Am. actor (*PT-109*; *The Naked and the Dead*; O—1968—*Charly*)

Robertson, Oscar (Oscar Palmer Robertson; "Big O") (1938–) Am. basketball player

Robertson, Pat (Marion Gordon Robertson) (1930–) Am. evangelist ("The 700 Club" TV show)/presidential candidate

Robertson, Robbie (Jaime Robbie Robertson) (1944–) Can. rock singer/musician/songwriter ("Somewhere Down the Crazy River"; formerly with The Band)

Robeson, Paul (Paul Bustill Robeson) (1898–1976) Am. stage actor/singer (*Show Boat*; *Othello*; *The Emperor Jones*)

Robespierre, Maximilien (Maximilien-François-Marie-Isidore de Robespierre; "The Incorruptible") (1758–1794) Fr. revolutionary leader

Robin, Dany (1927–) Fr. actress (*Topaz*; *Napoleon*)

Robinson, Bartlett (c. 1912–1986) Am. actor (radio's Perry Mason)

Robinson, Bill (Luther Robinson; "Bojangles") (1878–1949) Am. tap dancer

Robinson, Brooks (Brooks Calbert Robinson, Jr.; "Vacuum Cleaner"; "The Hoover") (1937–) Am. baseball Hall-of-Famer

Robinson, David (David Maurice Robinson; "The Admiral") (1965–) Am. basketball player

Robinson, Edward G. (Emanuel Goldenberg) (1893–1973) Rum.-Am. actor (*Little Caesar*; *Double Indemnity*)

Robinson, Edwin Arlington (1869–1935) Am. poet (P—1922—*Collected Poems*; P—1925—*The Man Who Died Twice*; P—1928—*Tristram*)

Robinson, Frank ("Robby") (1935–) Am. baseball Hall-of-Famer

Robinson, Holly (1965–) Am. actress ("21 Jump Street" TV series)

Robinson, Jackie (Jack Roosevelt Robinson) (1919–1972) Am. baseball Hall-of-Famer (first Afr.-Am. player in the major leagues)

Robinson, Smokey (William Robinson, Jr.) (1940–) Am. soul singer ("Shop Around"; formerly with The Miracles)

Robinson, Sugar Ray (Walker Smith) (1920–1989) Am. boxer

Robinson, Wilbert ("Uncle Robbie"; "Grapefruit") (1864–1934) Am. baseball Hall-of-Famer

Robson, Dame Flora (Flora McKenzie Robson) (1902–1984) Eng. actress (Black Narcissus; Saratoga Trunk)

Robson, May (Mary Jeanette Robison) (1858–1942) Am. actress (Lady for a Day; Little Orphan Annie)

Robustelli, Andy (Andrew Robustelli) (1930–) Am. football Hall-of-Famer

Rochambeau, Comte De (Jean-Baptiste-Donatien de Vimeur) (1725–1807) Fr. army general/marshal

Rock, Chris (1967–) Am. comedian ("Saturday Night Live" TV series; CB4)

Rockefeller, John D. IV (John Davison Rockefeller IV; "Jay") (1937–) Am. senator

Rockefeller, Nelson (Nelson Aldrich Rockefeller) (1908–1979) Am. v.p. (G. Ford)/gov. of New York

Rockne, Knute (Knute Kenneth Rockne; "The Great Man"; "The Rock of Notre Dame") (1888–1931) Am. football player/coach

Rockwell, George Lincoln (1918–1967) Am. Nazi leader

Rockwell, Norman (Norman Percival Rockwell) (1894–1978) Am. painter/illustrator (Saturday Evening Post covers)

Roddenberry, Gene (Eugene Wesley Roddenberry) (1931–1991) Am. TV producer (created "Star Trek")

Roddick, Anita (1943–) Eng. businesswoman (founded The Body Shop)

Rodgers, Bill (William Henry Rodgers) (1947–) Am. distance runner

Rodgers, Jimmie (James Charles Rodgers; "America's Blue Yodeler"; "The Singing Brakeman"; "The Father of Country Music"; "The Yodeling Cowboy"; "The Blue Yodeler"; "Little Jimmie Rodgers") (1897–1933) Am. country singer/songwriter ("Honeycomb")

Rodgers, Nile (1952–) Am. pop musician (with Chic)/producer (David Bowie, etc.)

Rodgers, Paul (1949–) Eng. rock singer (with Free and Bad Company; "Can't Get Enough")

Rodgers, Richard (1902–1979) Am. composer (The King and I; The Sound of Music; P—1950—South Pacific)

Rodin, Auguste (François-Auguste-René Rodin) (1840–1917) Fr. sculptor (The Thinker)

Rodnina, Irina (1949–) Russ. ice skater

Rodriguez, Johnny (1951—) Am. country singer ("You Always Come Back [to Hurting Me])

Roe, Tommy (1942–) Am. pop musician/singer ("Sheila")

Roeg, Nicolas (Nicolas Jack Roeg) (1928–) Eng. film director (The Man Who Fell to Earth; Whore)

Roehm, Carolyne (1951–) Am. fashion designer

Roentgen, Wilhelm (William Conrad Roentgen or Röntgen) (1845–1923) Ger. physicist (discovered X-rays; N—1901)

Roethke, Theodore (Theodore Huebner Roethke) (1908–1963) Am. poet (P—1954—The Waking)

Rogers, Buddy (Charles Rogers) (1904–) Am. actor (Wings; Abie's Irish Rose)

Rogers, Fred (Fred McFeely Rogers; "Mr. Rogers") (1928–) Am. TV host ("Mr. Rogers' Neighborhood")

Rogers, Ginger (Virginia Katherine McMath) (1911–) Am. actress (numerous films with Fred Astaire [Top Hat; Swing Time]; O—1940—Kitty Foyle)

Rogers, Kenny (Kenneth Ray Rogers) (1938–) Am. country singer ("Lady"; "You Decorated My Life")/actor (The Gambler; Coward of the County)

Rogers, Mimi (1956–) Am. actress (The Rapture; Desperate Hours)

Rogers, Rosemary (a/k/a Marina Mayson) (1932–) Am. romance novelist (Sweet Savage Love)

Rogers, Roy (Leonard Slye; "King of the Cowboys"; "Hollywood's Straightest Straight-Shooter") (1911–) Am. westerns actor/singer (with Sons of the Pioneers)/restauranteur

Rogers, Shorty (Milton M. Rogers) (1924–) Am. jazz trumpet player

Rogers, Tristan (1946–) Am. actor ("General Hospital" soap opera)

Rogers, Wayne (1933–) Am. actor ("M*A*S*H" and "House Calls" TV series)

Rogers, Will (William Penn Adair Rogers; "The Cowboy Philosopher") (1879–1935) Am. actor (*State Fair*)/humorist/columnist/writer (*Will Rogers's Political Follies*)

Roget, Peter (Peter Mark Roget) (1779–1869) Eng. physician/scholar (created *Roget's Thesaurus*)

Rohmer, Eric (Jean-Marie Maurice Scherer; a/k/a Gilbert Cordier) (1920–) Fr. writer/filmmaker (*The Marquise of O*)

Rohmer, Sax (Arthur Sarsfield Ward) (1886–1959) Eng. novelist (created Fu Manchu)

Roker, Roxie (1929–) Am. actress ("The Jeffersons" TV series; mother of Lenny Kravitz)

Roland, Gilbert (Luis Antonio Damaso De Alonso) (1905–) Mex.-Am. actor (*She Done Him Wrong*; *Camille*)

Rolfe, Red (Robert Abial Robinson) (1908–1969) Am. baseball player

Rolland, Romain (a/k/a Saint Just) (1866–1944) Fr. novelist/playwright/essayist (*Jean-Christophe*; N—1915)

Rolle, Esther (1933–) Am. actress ("Maude" and "Good Times" TV series)

Rollin, Betty (1936–) Am. writer (*First, You Cry*; *Last Wish*)

Rollins, Howard, Jr. (1950–) Am. actor ("In the Heat of the Night" TV series; *Ragtime*)

Rollins, Sonny (Theodore Walter Rollins) (1929–) Am. jazz saxophonist

Romains, Jules (Louis-Henri-Jean Farigoule) (1885–1972) Fr. novelist/essayist/playwright (*The Boys in the Back Room*)

Roman, Ruth (1924–) Am. actress (*Strangers on a Train*)

Romanoff, Mike (Harry F. Gerguson; posed as Prince Michael Alexandrovich Dmitri Obolensky Romanoff, a member of the Romanov dynasty; "Prince Mike") (1890–1971) Am. (Hollywood) restauranteur/personality

Romanov, Mikhail or Michael (dates of birth and death unknown) Russ. czar 1613–1645

Rombauer, Irma S. (Irma von Starkloff Rombauer) (c. 1876–1962) Am. cookbook writer (*The Joy of Cooking*)

Romberg, Sigmund (1887–1951) Hung.-Am. composer ("Stout Hearted Men"; "Blue Heaven")

Romer, Roy (1928–) Am. gov. of Colorado

Romero, Cesar (Caesar Julius Romero) (1907–1994) Am. actor (grandson of José Martí; "Batman" [as the Joker] and "Falcon Crest" TV series)

Romero, George (George Andrew Romero) (1939–) Am. horror film director (*Night of the Living Dead*; *Creep Show*; *The Dark Half*)

Rommel, Erwin (Erwin Johannes-Eugen Rommel; "The Desert Fox") (1891–1944) Ger. army general

Romney, George (1734–1802) Eng. portrait painter (*Death of General Wolfe*)

Ronsard, Pierre de ("Prince of Poets") (1524–1585) Fr. poet (*La Franciade*)

Ronstadt, Linda (Linda Maria Ronstadt) (1946–) Am. pop singer ("You're No Good"; "Blue Bayou"; G—1976)

Rooker, Michael (1956–) Am. actor (*Henry: Portrait of a Serial Killer*; *Cliffhanger*)

Rooney, Andy (Andrew Aitken Rooney) (1919–) Am. humorist/writer/TV pundit

Rooney, Art (Arthur Joseph Rooney) (1901–) Am. football executive/Hall-of-Famer

Rooney, Mickey (Joe Yule, Jr.) (1920–) Am. actor (*Boys Town*; *National Velvet*; *The Black Stallion*)

Roosevelt, Alice (Alice Hathaway Lee) (1861–1884) Am. first lady (Theodore)

Roosevelt, Eleanor (Anna Eleanor Roosevelt; "The First Lady of the World") (1884–1962) Am. first lady (Franklin Delano)/writer/diplomat/humanitarian

Roosevelt, Franklin Delano ("FDR") (1882–1945) 32nd Am. pres. (1933–1945)

Roosevelt, Kermit (1889–1943) Am. son of Theodore Roosevelt

Roosevelt, Theodore ("Teddy"; "The Rough Rider"; "The Bull Moose"; "Patron Saint of Dry Sundays") (1858–1919) 26th Am. pres. (1901–1909; N—1906)

Root, Charlie (Charles Henry Root; "Chinski") (1899–1970) Am. baseball pitcher

Root, Elihu (1845–1937) Am. lawyer/statesman/diplomat (N—1912)/govt. official (secretary of war)/writer (*Military and Colonial Policy of the United States*)

Root, John (John Wellborn Root) (1850–1891) Am. architect (Montauk building)

Rorem, Ned (1923–) Am. composer (stud-

ied under Virgil Thomson and Aaron Copland; P—1976—*Air Music*)
Rose, Axl (William Bailey; a/k/a W. Axl Rose) (1960–) Am. rock singer (with Guns N' Roses; "Sweet Child O' Mine")
Rose, Billy (William Samuel Rosenberg) (1899–1966) Am. theatrical entrepreneur/composer ("Barney Google"; "It's Only a Paper Moon"; "Me and My Shadow")
Rose, Jamie (1959–) Am. actress ("Falcon Crest" and "St. Elsewhere" TV series)
Rose Marie (Rose Maria Mazzetta) (1925–) Am. actress ("The Dick Van Dyke Show" TV series)/game show panelist ("Hollywood Squares")
Rose, Pete (Peter Edward Rose; "Charlie Hustle") (1941–) Am. baseball player
Rose, William (1918–) Am. screenwriter (*Guess Who's Coming to Dinner?*; *The Flim-Flam Man*)
Rosenberg, Alan (c. 1951–) Am. actor ("Civil Wars" and "L.A. Law" TV series)
Rosenberg, Ethel (née Greenglass) (1915–1953) Am. accused spy (convicted and executed with her husband Julius for selling atomic secrets to Russia during WWII)
Rosenberg, Julius (1918–1953) Am. spy/traitor (with wife Ethel)
Rosenberg, Stuart (1925–) Am. film director (*Cool Hand Luke*; *The Drowning Pool*)
Rosenbloom, Maxie (Max Rosenbloom; "Slapsie Maxie") (1903–1976) Am. boxer/actor (*Nothing Sacred*)
Rosenquist, James (James Albert Rosenquist) (1933–) Am. "pop art" painter
Ross, Betsy (Elizabeth Ross née Griscom) (1752–1836) Am. seamstress/patriot (made the first American flag)
Ross, Diana (Diane Earle) (1944–) Am. pop singer/actress ("Theme from Mahogany"; "Love Hangover"; formerly with The Supremes)
Ross, Harold (Harold Wallace Ross) (1892–1951) Am. founder/editor of the *New Yorker*
Ross, Herbert (1927–) Am. choreographer (*Carmen Jones*; *Funny Girl*)/film director (*Play It Again, Sam*; *The Goodbye Girl*)
Ross, Katharine (1942–) Am. actress (*The Graduate*; *Butch Cassidy and the Sundance Kid*)
Ross, Marion (1928–) Am. actress ("Happy Days" TV series)

Ross, Nellie (née) **Tayloe** (1876–1977) Am. politician (first woman to be a state gov. [Wyoming])
Rossellini, Isabella (1952–) Ital. model/actress (daughter of Ingrid Bergman and Roberto Rossellini; *Blue Velvet*; *Wild at Heart*)
Rossellini, Roberto (1906–1977) Ital. film director/producer (*Stromboli*; *Open City*)
Rossen, Robert (1908–1966) Am. screenwriter/film director (*Body and Soul*; *All the King's Men*)
Rossetti, Christina (Christina Georgina Rossetti) (1830–1894) Eng. poet (sister of Dante Gabriel; *Goblin Market*)
Rossetti, Dante Gabriel (Gabriel Charles Dante Rossetti) (1828–1882) Eng. pre-Raphaelite painter/poet (love sonnets)
Rossini, Gioacchino Antonio (1792–1868) Ital. composer (*The William Tell Overture*; *The Barber of Seville*)
Rossner, Judith (1935–) Am. novelist (*Looking for Mr. Goodbar*)
Rostand, Edmond (Edmond-Eugène-Alexis Rostand) (1868–1918) Fr. playwright (*Cyrano de Bergerac*)
Rosten, Leo (Leo Calvin Rosten; a/k/a Leonard Q. Ross) (1908–) Am. humorist/political scientist/teacher (*The Education of H*Y*M*A*N K*A*P*L*A*N*)
Rostenkowski, Dan (Daniel David Rostenkowski) (1928–) Am. congressman
Rostropovich, Mstislav (Mstislav Leopoldovich Rostropovich) (1927–) Russ.-Am. cellist/orchestra conductor
Roswitha (a/k/a Hrosvita or Hrotsvitha) (c. 935–1000) Ger. poet/playwright/historian
Rota, Nino (1911–1979) Ital. film composer (*The Godfather*; Fellini films)
Roth, David Lee (1955–) Am. rock singer ("Just a Gigolo"; formerly with Van Halen)
Roth, Henry (1906–) Am. short story writer/novelist (*Call It Sleep*)
Roth, Lillian (Lillian Rutstein) (1910–1980) Am. actress (*The Love Parade*; *Animal Crackers*)/autobiographer (*I'll Cry Tomorrow*)
Roth, Philip (Philip Milton Roth) (1933–) Am. novelist/short story writer (*Goodbye Columbus*; *Portnoy's Complaint*)
Rothko, Mark (Marcus Rothkovich) (1903–1970) Russ.-Am. abstract expressionist painter (*Baptismal Scene*)

Rotten, Johnny (John Lydon) (1958–) Eng. punk singer/musician (formerly with The Sex Pistols; currently with P.I.L. [Public Image Ltd.])

Rouault, Georges (Georges-Henri Rouault) (1871–1958) Fr. expressionist painter/printmaker/glazier

Roundtree, Richard (1937–) Am. actor ("Shaft" [title role])

Rourke, Mickey (Philip Andre Rourke, Jr.) (1950–) Am. actor (*Barfly*; *Diner*; *9½ Weeks*)

Rouse, Charlie (1924–1988) Am. jazz saxophonist

Roush, Edd (Edd J. Roush; "Eddie") (1893–1988) Am. baseball Hall-of-Famer

Rousseau, Henri (Henri-Julien-Felix Rousseau; "Le Douanier") (1844–1910) Fr. painter (*The Sleeping Gypsy*; *The Hungry Lion*)

Rousseau, Jean-Jacques (1712–1778) Fr. philosopher/writer (*The Social Contract*)

Rousseau, Theodore (Pierre-Etienne-Theodore Rousseau) (1812–1867) Fr. painter (*Descent of the Cattle*)

Roussel, Albert (Albert-Charles-Paul Marie Roussel) (1869–1937) Fr. composer (studied under D'Indy; taught Satie and Varèse)

Rowan, Dan (Dan Hale Rowan) (1922–1987) Am. comedian ("Rowan & Martin's Laugh-In" TV series)

Rowe, Nicholas (1674–1718) Eng. poet laureate/playwright (*Lady Jane Grey*)

Rowlands, Gena (Virginia Cathryn Rowlands) (1934–) Am. actress (*A Woman Under the Influence*; *Gloria*)

Rowlandson, Thomas (1756–1827) Eng. caricaturist (*Tours of Dr. Syntax*)

Rowse, A. L. (Alfred Leslie Rowse) (1903–) Eng. poet/writer/historian (*The Elizabethan Age*)

Royal, Billy Joe (1942–) Am. country singer ("Down in the Boondocks"; "I Knew You When")

Royce, Josiah (1855–1916) Am. pragmatist philosopher (*The World and the Individual*; *The Problem of Christianity*)

Royko, Mike (1932–) Am. journalist (*P—* 1972)

Royle, Selena (1904–1983) Am. radio/film actress (*Joan of Arc*)/writer (*A Gringa's Guide to Mexican Cooking*)

Rozelle, Pete (Alvin Ray Rozelle; "The Boy Commissioner"; "St. Peter") (1926–) Am. NFL commissioner/football Hall-of-Famer

Rozsa, Miklos (1907–) Hung.-Am. film composer (*Ben Hur* [1959]; *Spellbound*; *A Double Life*)

Ruark, Robert (Robert Chester Ruark) (1915–1965) Am. novelist/journalist (*Something of Value*; *The Old Man & the Boy*)

Rubens, Alma (Alma Smith) (1897–1931) Am. actress (*Intolerance*; *Show Boat*)

Rubens, Peter Paul (1577–1640) Flem. Baroque painter (*Rape of the Sabines*)

Rubik, Erno (1944–) Hung. architect/inventor (Rubik's Cube)

Rubinstein, Artur or Arthur ("The Playboy of the Piano") (1887–1982) Pol.-Am. concert pianist

Rubinstein, Helena (1870–1965) Pol.-Am. cosmetician/businesswoman

Ruby, Harry (Harry Rubinstein) (1895–1974) Am. songwriter (with Bert Halmar, "Three Little Words")

Ruby, Jack (Jacob Rubinstein) (1911–1967) Am. nightclub owner/assassin of Lee Harvey Oswald

Rudman, Warren (Warren Bruce Rudman) (1930–) Am. senator

Rudner, Rita (1956–) Am. comedienne/actress (*Peter's Friends*)

Rudolph, Alan (1943–) Am. screenwriter/film director (*Choose Me*; *Mortal Thoughts*)

Rudolph, Wilma (Wilma Glodean Rudolph; "Skeeter") (1940–) Am. sprinter

Ruehl, Mercedes (c. 1953–) Am. actress (*Married to the Mob*; O—1991—*The Fisher King*; *Lost in Yonkers*; T—1991)

Ruffin, David (Davis Eli Ruffin) (1941–1991) Am. soul singer ("Walk Away from Love"; formerly with The Temptations)

Ruffing, Red (Charles Herbert Ruffing) (1904–1986) Am. baseball player

Ruffo, Titta (Ruffo Cafiero Titta; "The Caruso of Baritones") (1887–1953) Ital.-Am. opera singer (baritone)

Ruggles, Charlie (Charles Ruggles) (1886–1970) Am. actor (brother of Wesley; *Ruggles of Red Gap*)

Ruggles, Wesley (1889–1972) Am. film director (*Sing You Sinners*; *Silk Stockings*; *Cimarron*)

Ruisdael or Ruysdael, Jacob Van (1628 or 1629–1682) Dutch landscape painter

Rukeyser, Louis (Louis Richard Rukeyser) (1933–) Am. business TV commentator ("Wall Street Week")

Rukeyser, Muriel (1913–1980) Am. poet (*Theory of Flight*)

Rule, Elton (Elton H. Rule) (1917–) Am. entertainment executive (head of ABC)

Ruman, Sig (Sigfried Rumann) (1884–1967) Ger. actor (*A Night at the Opera*; *Ninotchka*)

Rundgren, Todd (1948–) Am. rock musician/singer ("Hello It's Me"; "Can We Still Be Friends"; formerly with Nazz and Utopia)

Runyan, Paul (Paul Scott Runyan; "Little Poison") (1908–) Am. golfer

Runyon, Damon (Alfred Damon Runyon; "The Prose Laureate of the Semi-Literate") (1884–1946) Am. journalist/short story writer (*Guys and Dolls*)/screenwriter (*Lady for a Day*)

Rupp, Adolph (Adolph Frederick Rupp; "The Baron") (1901–1977) Am. basketball coach

Ruppert, Jacob (1867–1939) Am. brewer/baseball team owner (New York Yankees)

Rush, Barbara (1930–) Am. actress (*Come Blow Your Horn*; *When Worlds Collide*)

Rushdie, Salman (Salman Ahmed Rushdie) (1947–) Ind.-Eng. novelist (*The Satanic Verses*; under a death sentence from the Ayatollah Khomeini)

Rushen, Patrice (Patrice Louise Rushen) (1954–) Am. jazz/soul singer ("Forget-Me-Nots")

Rushing, Jimmy ("Mr. Five by Five") (1903–1972) Am. jazz/blues singer (with Count Basie, Eddie Condon, and Benny Goodman)

Rusie, Amos (Amos Wilson Rusie; "The Hoosier Thunderbolt") (1871–1942) Am. baseball Hall-of-Famer

Rusk, Dean (David Dean Rusk) (1909–) Am. govt. official (secretary of state)

Ruskin, John (1819–1900) Eng. writer/art critic (*Modern Painters*)

Russell, Bertrand (Bertrand Arthur William Russell) (1872–1970) Eng. mathematician/philosopher/writer (*History of Western Philosophy*; N—1950)

Russell, Bill (William Felton Russell; "Number 6") (1934–) Am. basketball player

Russell, Bobby (1941–1992) Am. country/pop singer/songwriter ("The Night the Lights Went Out in Georgia"; "Little Green Apples"; "Honey")

Russell, Harold (1914–) Can. mil. officer/actor (O—1946–*The Best Years of Our Lives*)

Russell, Jane (Ernestine Jane Geraldine Russell) (1921–) Am. actress (*The Paleface*; *Gentlemen Prefer Blondes*; *Rio Bravo*)

Russell, Ken (Henry Kenneth Alfred Russell) (1927–) Eng. film director (*Women in Love*; *Tommy*; *Lisztomania*; *Altered States*)

Russell, Kurt (Kurt Von Vogel Russell) (1947–) Am. actor (*Tango and Cash*; *Swing Shift*; *Backdraft*)

Russell, Leon (Hank Wilson; a/k/a Russell Bridges and Hank Wilson) (1941–) Am. rock singer ("Lady Blue")/songwriter ("This Masquerade")

Russell, Lillian (Helen Louise Leonard; "The American Beauty") (1861–1922) Am. singer/entertainer

Russell, Nipsey (1924–) Am. comedian

Russell, Pee Wee (Charles Ellsworth Russell) (1906–1969) Am. jazz clarinetist

Russell, Rosalind (1908–1976) Am. actress (*His Girl Friday*; *Mourning Becomes Electra*; *Picnic*; *Auntie Mame*; T—1953)

Russell, Theresa (Theresa Paup) (1957–) Am. actress (*Whore*; *Black Widow*)

Russo, Rene (1954–) Am. model/actress (*In the Line of Fire*; *Lethal Weapon 3*; *One Good Cop*)

Rustin, Bayard ("Mr. March") (1910–1987) Am. civil rights activist (worked with Martin Luther King, Jr.)

Ruth, Babe (George Herman Ruth; "The Sultan of Swat"; "The Bambino"; "The Home Run King") (1895–1948) Am. baseball Hall-of-Famer

Rutherford, Ann (Theresa Ann Rutherford) (1917–) Can.-Am. actress (*The Secret Life of Walter Mitty*; *The Oregon Trail*)

Rutherford, Johnny (John Sherman Rutherford III) (1938–) Am. auto racer

Rutherford, Kelly (c. 1969–) Am. actress ("Homefront" and "The Adventures of Brisco County, Jr." TV series)

Rutherford, Dame Margaret (Margaret Taylor Rutherford) (1892–1972) Eng. actress (*Blithe Spirit*; O—1963—*The VIPs*)

Rutherford, Mike (1950–) Eng. rock bass-

ist (with Genesis and Mike + The Mechanics ["Living Years"])
Rutledge, Wiley (Wiley Blount Rutledge, Jr.) (1894–1949) Am. Supreme Court jurist 1943–1949
Ruttan, Susan (1950–) Am. actress ("L.A. Law" TV series)
Ryan, Cornelius (Cornelius John Ryan) (1920–1974) Ir.-Am. journalist/novelist (*A Bridge Too Far*)
Ryan, Elizabeth (1892–1979) Am. tennis player
Ryan, Irene (Irene Noblette) (1903–1973) Am. actress ("The Beverly Hillbillies" TV series)
Ryan, Meg (1962–) Am. actress (*When Harry Met Sally . . .*; *Sleepless in Seattle*; *Prelude to a Kiss*)
Ryan, Nolan (Lynn Nolan Ryan, Jr.; "The Ryan Express") (1947–) Am. baseball pitcher
Ryan, Paddy (1853–1901) Am. boxer
Ryan, Peggy (Margaret O'Rene Ryan) (1924–) Am. actress (*Bowery to Broadway*; *The Grapes of Wrath*)
Ryan, Robert (Robert Bushnell Ryan) (1903–1973) Am. actor (*The Wild Bunch*; *Crossfire*; *God's Little Acre*)
Rydell, Bobby (Robert Lewis Ridarelli) (1942–) Am. pop singer ("Wild One")/ actor (*Bye Bye Birdie*)
Rydell, Mark (1934–) Am. film director (*On Golden Pond*; *For the Boys*; *Intersection*)
Ryder, Albert Pinkham (1847–1917) Am. painter (*The Flying Dutchman*)
Ryder, Mitch (William S. Levise, Jr.) (1945–) Am. rock singer ("Jenny Take a Ride!"; with Mitch Ryder and The Detroit Wheels)
Ryder, Winona (Winona Laura Horowitz) (1971–) Am. actress (*Heathers*; *Bram Stoker's Dracula*; *Edward Scissorhands*; *The Age of Innocence*)
Ryskind, Morrie (1895–1985) Am. playwright (P—1932—*Of Thee I Sing*)/ screenwriter (Marx Brothers films; *My Man Godfrey*; *Penny Serenade*)
Ryun, Jim (James Ronald Ryun; "Stork in Shorts") (1947–) Am. runner (former mile record-holder)
Saarinen, Eero (1910–1961) Am. architect (MIT auditorium and chapel)
Saarinen, Eliel (Gottlieb Eliel Saarinen) (1873–1950) Finn.-Am. architect (performance halls, Berkshire Music Center; father of Eero)/writer (*Search for Form*)

Sabatini, Gabriela ("Pearl of the Pampas") (1970–) Arg. tennis player
Sabatini, Rafael (1875–1950) Ital. novelist (*Captain Blood*)
Sabato, Antonio, Jr. (c. 1971–) Am. actor ("General Hospital" soap opera)
Sábato, Ernesto (1911–) Arg. novelist/ essayist (*On Heroes and Tombs*)
Saberhagen, Bret (Bret William Saberhagen) (1964–) Am. baseball pitcher
Sabin, Albert (Albert Bruce Sabin) (1906–1993) Am. microbiologist (developed oral polio vaccine)
Sabu (Sabu Dastagir) (1924–1963) Ind. actor (*The Jungle Book*; *Elephant Boy*)
Sacajawea or **Sacagawea** (Sacajawea: Bird Woman) (c. 1786–1812) Am. Indian guide (for Lewis and Clark)
Sacco, Nicola (1891–1927) Am. anarchist (with Bartolomeo Vanzetti; executed for treason)
Sachs, Nelly (Nelly Leonie Sachs) (1891–1970) Ger. poet (*In the Dwellings of Death*; N—1966)
Sackler, Howard (Howard Oliver Sackler) (1929–1982) Am. playwright (P—1969—*The Great White Hope*)
Sackville-West, Victoria (Victoria Mary Sackville-West; "Vita") (1892–1962) Eng. novelist/poet (*All Passion Spent*)
Sadat, Anwar (Muhammad Anwar Al-Sadat) (1918–1981) Egypt. soldier/pres. 1970–1981 (N—1978)
Sade (Helen Folasade Adu) (1959–) Niger. pop singer ("Smooth Operator"; "The Sweetest Taboo"; G—1985)
Safer, Morley (1931–) Can.-Am. newscaster ("60 Minutes")
Safire, William (William L. Safire) (1929–) Am. writer (*On Language*)/journalist (P—1978)
Sagal, Katey (1956–) Am. actress ("Married . . . With Children" TV series)
Sagan, Dr. Carl (Carl Edward Sagan) (1934–) Am. astronomer/scientist/writer (P—1978—*The Dragons of Eden*; created TV series "Cosmos")
Sagan, Françoise (Françoise Quoirez) (1935–) Fr. novelist/playwright (*Bonjour Tristesse*)
Sagebrecht, Marianne (1945–) Ger. actress (*Bagdad Cafe*; *Sugarbaby*)
Sager, Carole Bayer (1946–) Am. pop songwriter ("Midnight Blue"; "Nobody Does It Better"; "A Groovy Kind of Love")

Saget, Bob (1956–) Am. talk show host ("America's Funniest Home Videos")/ actor ("Full House" TV series)

Sahl, Mort (Morton Lyon Sahl) (1927–) Can. comedian

Saint, Eva Marie (1924–) Am. actress (*North by Northwest*; O—1954—*On the Waterfront*)

St. Clair, Mal (Malcolm St. Clair) (1897–1952) Am. film director (*Gentlemen Prefer Blondes*; *The Trouble with Wives*)

St. Cyr, Lili (Marie Van Schaak) (1917–) Am. dancer/lingerie designer

Sainte-Marie, Buffy (Beverly Sainte-Marie) (1941–) Can.-Am. folk singer ("Mister Can't You See")/songwriter ("Until It's Time for You to Go"; "Up Where We Belong")

Saint-Exupéry, Antoine de (Andre-Marie-Roger de Saint-Exupéry) (1900–1944) Fr. novelist/essayist (*The Little Prince*)

Saint-Gaudens, Augustus (1848–1907) Ir.-Am. sculptor (*Lincoln* in Chicago's Lincoln Park)

Saint James, Susan (Susan Jane Miller) (1946–) Am. actress ("McMillan and Wife" TV series; E—1968/69)

St. John, Betta (Betty Streidler) (1930–) Am. actress (*The Robe*; *Tarzan the Magnificent*)

St. John, Jill (Jill Oppenheim) (1940–) Am. actress (*Diamonds Are Forever*; *Tony Rome*)

St. Johns, Adela (née) Rogers (1894–1988) Am. writer/journalist

St. Laurent, Yves (Henri Donat Mathieu) (1936–) Fr. fashion designer

Saint-Saëns, Camille (Charles Camille Saint-Saëns) (1835–1921) Fr. composer (*Danse Macabre*)

Sajak, Pat (Pat Sadjak) (1947–) Am. game show host ("Wheel of Fortune")

Sakharov, Andrei (Andrei Dmitriyevich Sakharov; "The Father of the Soviet Hydrogen Bomb") (1921–1989) Russ. physicist (N—1975)

Saki (H[ector]. H[ugh]. Munro) (1870–1916) Scot. writer (*Beasts and Super-Beasts*)

Saks, Gene (Jean Michael Saks) (1921–) Am. theatrical/film director (*Brighton Beach Memoirs*; *Mame*; *Cactus Flower*)

Saladin (Saladin Yusuf ibn Ayyub) (1138–1193) Syr. commander/vizier in Egypt (1169)/sultan of Egypt and Syria

Salant, Richard S. (1914–1993) Am. entertainment executive (CBS/NBC)

Salazar, António (António de Oliveira Salazar) (1889–1970) Port. dictator 1932–1968

Saldana, Theresa (c. 1955–) Am. actress (*I Wanna Hold Your Hand*; "The Commish" TV series; stalking victim)

Salerno-Sonnenberg, Nadja (1961–) Ital. concert violinist

Sales, Soupy (Milton Hines) (1926–) Am. comedian

Salinger, J. D. (Jerome David Salinger) (1919–) Am. novelist/short story writer (*The Catcher in the Rye*; *Franny and Zooey*)

Salinger, Pierre (Pierre Emil George Salinger) (1925–) Am. politician/newscaster/journalist

Salisbury, Harrison (Harrison Evans Salisbury) (1908–1993) Am. journalist (P—1955)/writer (*The 900 Days*; *The Long March*)

Salk, Jonas (Jonas Edward Salk) (1914–) Am. physician (discovered polio vaccine)

Sallust (Gaius Sallustius Crispus) (86–34 B.C.) Roman historian/statesman

Salonga, Lea (c. 1971–) Am. actress (Broadway's *Miss Saigon*; T—1991)/ singer ("A Whole New World" from *Aladdin*)

Salten, Felix (Siegmund Salzmann) (1869–1945) Hung. novelist (*Bambi*)

Sam & Dave see Moore, Sam, and Prater, Dave

Sambora, Richie (1959–) Am. rock guitarist (with Bon Jovi)

Samms, Emma (Emma Samuelson) (1960–) Eng. actress ("Dynasty" TV series and "General Hospital" soap opera)

Sample, Joe (1939–) Am. jazz musician (with The Crusaders)

Samples, Alvin "Junior" (1926–1983) Am. comedian ("Hee Haw" TV series)

Sampras, Pete ("Sweet Pete") (1971–) Gr.-Am. tennis player (W—1993)

Sampson, Will (1935–1987) Am. actor (*One Flew Over the Cuckoo's Nest*)

Sam the Sham (Sam Samudio; born Domingo Samudio) (1940–) Am. rock musician/singer (with Sam the Sham and The Pharaohs; "Wooly Bully")

Sanborn, David (1945–) Am. jazz/pop saxophone player ("Bang Bang"; formerly with Stevie Wonder and Paul Butterfield)

Sand, George (Amandine-Aurore-Lucile

Dudevant née Dupin) (1804–1876) Fr. novelist (*The Haunted Pool*; *He and She*)

Sand, Paul (Pablo Sanchez) (1944–) Am. actor ("Gimme a Break" TV series; "Wholly Moses")

Sanda, Dominique (Dominique Varaigne) (1948–) Fr. actress (*The Garden of the Finzi-Continis*; *Damnation Alley*)

Sandberg, Ryne (Ryne Dee Sandberg) (1959–) Am. baseball player

Sandburg, Carl (Carl August Sandburg) (1878–1967) Am. writer/poet (P—1919 —*Cornhuskers*; P—1940—*Abraham Lincoln: The War Years*; P—1951— *Complete Poems*)

Sande, Earl (1898–1968) Am. jockey (rode Man o' War)/horse trainer

Sanders, George (1906–1972) Russ.-Eng. actor (*The Moon and Sixpence*; O— 1950—*All About Eve*)

Sanders, "Colonel" Harland (Harland David Sanders) (1890–1980) Am. fast food merchant (Kentucky Fried Chicken)

Sanders, Lawrence (1920–) Am. suspense novelist (*The First Deadly Sin*; *The Anderson Tapes*)

Sandford, Tiny (Stanley J. Sandford) (1894–1961) Am. actor (Laurel & Hardy films)

Sandler, Adam (c. 1966–) Am. comedian ("Saturday Night Live" TV series)

Sandoz, Mari (Marie Susette Sandoz) (1896–1966) Am. biographer/historical writer (*The Battle of Little Big Horn*)

Sandrich, Mark (1900–1945) Am. film director (*Top Hat*; *The Gay Divorcee*; *Shall We Dance?*)

Sands, Diana (Diana Patricia Sands) (1934–1973) Am. actress (*A Raisin in the Sun*; *Ensign Pulver*)

Sands, Julian (1958–) Eng.-Am. actor (*Warlock*; *Arachnophobia*; *Impromptu*; *Boxing Helena*)

Sands, Tommy (Thomas Adrian Sands) (1937–) Am. singer ("Teen-Age Crush")/ actor (*Babes in Toyland*)

Sandy, Gary (1943–) Am. actor ("WKRP in Cincinnati" TV series)

Sanford, Isabel (Isabel Gwendolyn Sanford) (1917–) Am. actress (Louise in "The Jeffersons" TV series; E— 1980/81)

Sang, Samantha (Cheryl Gray) (1953–) Am. pop singer ("Emotion")

Sangallo, Giuliano da (c. 1445–1516) Flor. architect/sculptor (assisted Raphael)

Sanger, Margaret (Margaret Louise Sanger née Higgins) (1879–1966) Am. birth-control advocate

San Giacomo, Laura (c. 1962–) Am. actress (*sex, lies, and videotape*; *Under Suspicion*)

Sanguillen, Manny (Manuel Dejesus Magan Sanguillen) (1944–) Pan.-Am. baseball player

San Martín, José de (José Francisco de San Martín) (1778–1850) Arg. mil./ political leader

Sansom, Art (1920–) Am. cartoonist (*The Born Loser*)

Santa Anna, Antonio de (Antonio López de Santa Anna) (1794–1876) Mex. revolutionary leader/political ruler

Santana, Carlos (a/k/a Devadip ["The light of the lamp supreme"] Carlos Santana) (1947–) Mex.-Am. rock musician ("Black Magic Woman"; "She's Not There"; with Santana)

Santana, Rafael (Rafael Francisco Santana de la Cruz) (1958–) Dom.-Am. baseball player

Santayana, George (1863–1952) Span.-Am. philosopher/poet (*The Sense of Beauty*)

Santiago, Benito (Benito Rivera) (1965–) P.R.-Am. baseball player

Santiago, Saundra (1957–) Am. actress ("Miami Vice" TV series)

Saperstein, Abe (Abraham Saperstein) (1903–1966) Eng.-Am. basketball promoter (formed the Harlem Globetrotters)

Sapho *see* Scudéry, Madeleine de

Sappho or Psappho ("The Tenth Muse") (fl. c. 610–c. 580 B.C.) Gr. lyric poet

Sarandon, Chris (1942–) Am. actor (*Dog Day Afternoon*; *Slaves of New York*)

Sarandon, Susan (Susan Abigail Tomaling) (1946–) Am. actress (*Atlantic City*; *Thelma and Louise*; *White Palace*)

Sarazen, Gene (Eugene Saraceni) (1901–) Am. golfer

Sargent, Dick (Richard Cox) (1933–) Am. actor ("Bewitched" TV series)

Sargent, John Singer (1856–1925) Am. portrait painter (*Madame X*)

Sargent, Joseph (Giuseppe Danielle Sargente) (1925–) Am. film director (*The Taking of Pelham One Two Three*)

Sargeson, Frank (1903–1982) N.Z.

novelist/playwright (*Conversations with My Uncle*)

Sargon (died 705 B.C.) Assyr. king 721–705 B.C.

Saroyan, Aram (1943–) Am. novelist (son of William; *The Romantic*)

Saroyan, William (a/k/a Sirak Goryan) (1908–1981) Am. novelist/short story writer/playwright (*The Human Comedy*; P—1940—*The Time of Your Life* [refused])

Sarrazin, Michael (Jacques Michel Andres Sarrazin) (1940–) Can. actor (*The Flim-Flam Man*; *They Shoot Horses, Don't They?*)

Sarris, Andrew (1928–) Am. film critic/columnist

Sarto, Andrea del (Andrea Domenico d'Agnolodi Francisco; "Andrew the Faultless") (1486–1530) Ital. painter (*Madonna of the Harpies*)

Sarton, May (1912–) Am. poet (*Encounter in April*)

Sartre, Jean-Paul (1905–1980) Fr. playwright/philosopher (*Nausea*; *Being and Nothingness*; *No Exit*; N—1964 [declined])

Sassoon, Vidal (1928–) Eng. hair care expert

Satie, Erik (Erik-Alfred-Leslie Satie) (1866–1925) Fr. composer (*Socrate*)

Sato, Eisaku (1901–1975) Jap. prime minister 1964–1972 (N—1974)

Saul (11th century B.C.) Isr. king c. 1020–1000 B.C.

Savage, Fred (Fred A. Savage) (1976–) Am. child actor ("The Wonder Years" TV series)

Savalas, Telly (Aristotle Savalas) (1926–1994) Am. actor (TV's "Kojak"; signature phrase: "Who loves ya, baby?"; E—1973/74)

Saviano, Josh (C) Am. child actor ("The Wonder Years" TV series)

Savitch, Jessica (Jessica Beth Savitch) (1948–1983) Am. newscaster

Savitt, Dick (1927–) Am. tennis player (W—1951)

Savonarola, Fra Girolamo (1452–1498) Ital. (Ferraran) monk/reformer

Sawchuk, Terry (Terrance Gordon Sawchuk; "Ukey") (1929–1970) Can. hockey player

Sawyer, Diane (Diane K. Sawyer) (1945–) Am. newscaster ("60 Minutes"; "Prime Time Live")

Sawyer, Forrest (c. 1951–) Am. TV journalist

Sax, Steve (Stephen Louis Sax) (1960–) Am. baseball player

Saxon, John (Carmine Orrico) (1935–) Am. actor ("Falcon Crest" TV series; *The Electric Horseman*)

Sayer, Leo (Gerard Hugh Sayer) (1948–) Eng. pop singer ("When I Need You")

Sayers, Dorothy L. (Dorothy Leigh Sayers) (1893–1957) Eng. detective story writer (created Lord Peter Wimsey)

Sayers, Gale (Gale Eugene Sayers; "Magic") (1940–) Am. football Hall-of-Famer

Sayles, John (John T. Sayles) (1950–) Am. film director (*Matewan*; *The Brother from Another Planet*; *City of Hope*; *Passion Fish*)

Scacchi, Greta (1960–) Ital.-Am. actress (*Presumed Innocent*; *White Mischief*)

Scaggs, Boz (William Royce Scaggs) (1944–) Am. rock/pop singer ("Lowdown"; "Jojo")

Scala, Gia (Giovanna Scoglio) (1934–1972) Ital. actress (*The Guns of Navarone*; *I Aim at the Stars*)

Scales, Prunella (Prunella Margaret Rumney West Illingworth) (c. 1938–) Eng. actress ("Fawlty Towers" TV series)

Scalia, Antonin (1936–) Am. Supreme Court jurist (1986–)

Scalia, Jack (1951–) Am. actor ("Dallas" TV series)

Scarlatti, Alessandro (Pietro Alessandro Gaspare Scarlatti) (1660–1725) Ital. opera composer (*Gli Equivoci Nel Sembiante*)

Scarlatti, Domenico (Giuseppe Domenico Scarlatti) (1685–1757) Ital. composer (sonatas, cantatas)

Scarwid, Diana (1955–) Am. actress (*Inside Moves*; *Mommie Dearest*; *Silkwood*)

Scavullo, Francesco (1929–) Am. fashion photographer

Schact, Al (Alexander Schact; "The Clown Prince of Baseball") (1892–1984) Am. baseball pitcher

Schaeffer, Rebecca (1968–1989) Am. actress (*Scenes from the Class Struggle in Beverly Hills*; "My Sister Sam" TV series; murdered by a stalker)

Schaffner, Franklin (Franklin James Schaffner) (1920–1989) Am. film director (*Planet of the Apes*; O—1970—*Patton*)

Schalk, Ray (Raymond William Schalk; "Cracker") (1892–1970) Am. baseball Hall-of-Famer

Schally, Andrew (Andrew Victor Schally) (1926–) Am. biochemist (discovered hormones; N—1977)

Schary, Dore (Isidore Schary) (1905–1980) Am. film producer/writer (*Boys Town*)

Schatzberg, Jerry (1927–) Am. film director (*The Seduction of Joe Tynan*; *Honeysuckle Rose*)

Schayes, Dolph (Adolph Schayes) (1928–) Am. basketball player

Scheider, Roy (Roy Richard Scheider) (1932–) Am. actor (*Marathon Man*; *Klute*; *All That Jazz*)

Schell, Maria (Maria Margarethe Schell) (1926–) Aus. actress (sister of Maximilian; *The Brothers Karamazov*)

Schell, Maximilian (Maximilian Konrad Schell) (1930–) Aus.-Am. actor (*Julia*; O—1961—*Judgment at Nuremberg*)

Schepisi, Fred (1936–) Austral.-Am. screenwriter (*The Russia House*; *Mr. Baseball*)

Schiaparelli, Elsa (1890–1973) Fr. fashion designer (grandmother of Marisa Berenson)

Schiff, Dorothy (1903–1989) Am. newspaper publisher (*New York Post*)

Schiffer, Claudia (1970–) Ger. model

Schifrin, Lalo (Boris Claudio Schifrin) (1932–) Arg. pianist/composer/conductor/film composer (*Bullitt*; *Dirty Harry*)

Schildkraut, Joseph (1895–1964) Aus. actor (*The Diary of Anne Frank*; O—1937—*The Life of Emile Zola*)

Schiller, Friedrich von (Johann Christoph Friedrich von Schiller) (1759–1805) Ger. poet/playwright/historian (*Wilhelm Tell*)

Schipa, Tito (1889–1965) Ital. opera singer (tenor)

Schirra, Wally (Walter Marty Schirra, Jr.) (1923–) Am. astronaut

Schlafly, Phyllis (Phyllis Stewart Schlafly; "The Sweetheart of the Silent Majority") (1924–) Am. anti-feminist politician/lawyer/columnist/writer (*A Choice, Not an Echo*)

Schlesinger, Arthur M. (Arthur Meier Schlesinger, Jr.) (1888–1965) Am. historian (P—1946—*The Age of Jackson*; P—1966—*A Thousand Days*)

Schlesinger, John (John Richard Schle-

singer) (1926–) Eng. film director (*Sunday, Bloody Sunday*; *Marathon Man*; O—1969—*Midnight Cowboy*)

Schliemann, Heinrich (1822–1890) Ger. archaeologist (discovered the ruins of Troy)

Schlossberg, Caroline Kennedy (1957–) Am. socialite (daughter of Pres. John F. Kennedy and Jaqueline Onassis)

Schmeling, Max (Maximilian Schmeling; "The Black Uhlan") (1905–) Ger. boxer

Schmidt, Benno C., Jr. (Benno Charles Schmidt, Jr.) (1942–) Am. educator (pres. of Yale 1986–1992)

Schmidt, Helmut (1918–1992) Ger. chancellor 1974–1982

Schmidt, Joe (Joseph Paul Schmidt) (1932–) Am. football Hall-of-Famer

Schmidt, Mike (Michael Jack Schmidt) (1949–) Am. baseball player

Schmitt, Florent (1870–1958) Fr. composer (studied under Massenet and Fauré; *La Tragedie de Salome*)

Schnabel, Artur ("The High Priest of Intellectual Musicianship") (1882–1951) Aus. concert pianist

Schnabel, Julian (1951–) Am. painter

Schneider, John (1954–) Am. country singer/actor ("The Dukes of Hazzard" TV series)

Schneider, Maria (1952–) Fr. actress (*Last Tango in Paris*)

Schneider, Romy (Rosemarie Albach-Retty) (1938–1982) Aus. actress (*Good Neighbor Sam*; *What's New, Pussycat?*)

Schneider, Tawny (1956–) Am. newscaster/Miss America 1976

Schöenberg, Arnold (Arnold Franz Walter Schönberg) (1874–1951) Aus.-Am. composer (*Verklärte Nacht*)

Scholz, Tom (1947–) Am. rock guitarist (with Boston; "More Than a Feeling")

Schon, Neal (1954–) Am. rock guitarist (with Santana, Journey, and Bad English)

Schoolcraft, Henry Rowe (1793–1864) Am. explorer (Lake Superior)/ethnologist

Schopenhauer, Arthur ("The Philosopher of Disenchantment") (1788–1860) Ger. philosopher (*The World as Will and Idea*)

Schorr, Friedrich (1888–1953) Hung. opera singer (baritone)

Schrader, Paul (1946–) Am. screenwriter (*Taxi Driver*; *Raging Bull*)/film director (*American Gigolo*; *Patty Hearst*; *Light Sleeper*)

Schreiber, Avery (1935–) Am. actor/comedian (Doritos commercials; "My Mother the Car" TV series)
Schroder, Ricky (1970–) Am. actor ("Silver Spoons" TV series)
Schroeder, Barbet (1941–) Iran.-Fr. film director (*Reversal of Fortune*; *Barfly*)
Schroeder, Patricia (Patricia Scott Schroeder; "Patsy") (1940–) Am. congresswoman
Schroeder, Ted (Frederick Rudolph Schroeder, Jr.) (1921–) Am. tennis player (W—1949)
Schubert, Franz (Franz Peter Schubert) (1797–1828) Aus. composer (*Unfinished Symphony*)
Schulberg, Budd (Budd Wilson Schulberg) (1914–) Am. novelist/short story writer (*What Makes Sammy Run?*)/screenwriter (*On the Waterfront*)
Schuller, Robert (Robert Harold Schuller) (1926–) Am. evangelist/author
Schultz, Dutch (Arthur Flegenheimer; "The Dutchman") (1902–1935) Am. mobster
Schulz, Charles M. (Charles Monroe Schulz) (1922–) Am. cartoonist (*Peanuts*)
Schumacher, Joel (1939–) Am. film director (*St. Elmo's Fire*; *The Lost Boys*; *Dying Young*)
Schumann, Robert (Robert Alexander Schumann) (1810–1856) Ger. composer (*Carnaval*)
Schuster, Max (Max Lincoln Schuster) (1897–1970) Aus.-Am. publisher (co-founded Simon & Schuster)
Schütz, Heinrich (a/k/a Henricus Sagitarius) (1585–1672) Ger. composer (*Psalmen Davids*)
Schuyler, James (James Marcus Schuyler) (1923–) Am. poet/novelist/playwright (P—1981—*The Morning of the Poem*)
Schwartz, Arthur (1900–1984) Am. theatrical composer (*Thank Your Lucky Stars*; *The Bandwagon*)
Schwartz, Delmore (1913–1966) Am. poet (*In Dreams Begin Responsibility*)
Schwarzenegger, Arnold (Arnold Alois Schwarzenegger; "The Austrian Oak") (1947–) Aus.-Am bodybuilder/actor (*The Terminator*; *The Last Action Hero*)
Schwarzkopf, Elisabeth (1915–) Ger. opera singer (soprano)
Schwarzkopf, Norman (H. Norman Schwarzkopf; "Stormin' Norman") (1934–) Am. army general (commanded "Desert Storm" forces)

Schweitzer, Albert (1875–1965) Fr.-Ger. philosopher/humanitarian/writer (*The Quest of the Historical Jesus*; N—1952)
Schwinger, Julian (Julian Seymour Schwinger) (1918–) Am. physicist (N—1965)
Schygulla, Hanna (1943–) Pol. actress (Fassbinder films)
Scialfa, Patti (1956–) Am. singer (with Bruce Springsteen's band)
Sciorra, Annabella (c. 1964–) Am. actress (*Jungle Fever*; *The Hand That Rocks the Cradle*)
Scofield, Paul (David Paul Scofield) (1922–) Eng. actor (O—1966—*A Man for All Seasons*; T—1962)
Scoggins, Tracy (1958–) Am. actress ("Dynasty" TV series)
Scola, Ettore (1931–) Ital. screenwriter/film director (*Down and Dirty*; *A Special Day*)
Scolari, Peter (1954–) Am. actor ("Newhart" and "Family Album" TV series)
Scopes, John Thomas (1900–1970) Am. educator (taught evolution in public school; the Scopes monkey trial)
Scorsese, Martin (1942–) Am. film director (*Taxi Driver*; *Mean Streets*; *Raging Bull*; *Goodfellas*)
Scott, Bon (1946–1980) Scot. rock singer (with AC/DC; "Highway to Hell")
Scott, Debralee (1953–) Am. actress ("Welcome Back, Kotter" TV series)
Scott, Dred (c. 1795–1858) Am. slave (petition for freedom denied by the U.S. Supreme Court)
Scott, George C. (George Campbell Scott) (1927–) Am. actor (*Anatomy of a Murder*; *Dr. Strangelove*; O—1970—*Patton* [refused])
Scott, Gordon (Gordon M. Werschkul) (1927–) Am. actor (Tarzan in fifties films)
Scott, Hazel (Hazel Dorothy Scott) (1920–1981) Am. jazz singer/pianist
Scott, Lizabeth (Lizabeth Virginia Scott; born Emma Matzo) (1922–) Am. actress (*You Came Along*; *The Strange Love of Martha Ivers*)
Scott, Martha (Martha Ellen Scott) (1914–) Am. stage/film actress (*Our Town*; *The Turning Point*)
Scott, Randolph (Randolph Crane Scott) (1898 or 1903–1987) Am. actor (*The Last of the Mohicans*; *Rebecca of Sunnybrook Farm*)
Scott, Ridley (1939–) Eng. film director

(brother of Tony; *Alien*; *Blade Runner*; *Thelma and Louise*)

Scott, Tony (1944–) Eng.-Am. film director (brother of Ridley; *Days of Thunder*; *True Romance*)

Scott, Sir Walter (a/k/a Chrystal Croftangry, Captain Cuthbert Clutterbuck, Peter Pattieson, and Jedediah Cleishbotham; "The Border Minstrel"; "Father of the Historical Novel") (1771–1832) Scot. novelist/poet/historian/biographer (*Ivanhoe*; *Kenilworth*)

Scott, Willard (Willard Herman Scott, Jr.) (1934–) Am. TV weatherman ("Today")

Scott, Winfield ("Old Fuss and Feathers") (1786–1866) Am. army general/presidential candidate 1852

Scott-Heron, Gil (1949–) Am. novelist/poet (*This Revolution Will Not Be Televised*)/musician ("Johannesburg")

Scotti, Antonio (1866–1936) Ital. opera singer (baritone)

Scotto, Renata (1935–) Ital. opera singer (soprano)

Scourby, Alexander (1913–1985) Am. actor (*The Big Heat*; narrator of TV's "Victory at Sea")

Scowcroft, Brent (1925–) Am. air force officer/politician (national security advisor to Pres. Bush)

Scriabin or **Skryabin, Aleksandr** (Aleksandr Nikolayevich Scriabin) (1872–1915) Russ. pianist/composer (*The Poem of Ecstasy*)

Scribner, Charles (Charles Scrivener) (1821–1871) Am. publisher

Scripps, Ellen (Ellen Browning Scripps) (1836–1932) Am. newspaper publisher/philanthropist (founded Scripps College)

Scripps, E. W. (Edward Wyllis Scripps) (1854–1926) Am. newspaper publisher (formed United Press)

Scruggs, Earl (Earl Eugene Scruggs) (1924–) Am. country banjo player (with Flatt & Scruggs; "Ballad of Jed Clampett")

Scudéry, Madeleine de (a/k/a Sapho) (1607–1701) Fr. poet/novelist (*Almahide, or the Slave as Queen*)

Scully, Vin (Vincent Edward Scully; "Mr. Dodger") (1927–) Am. sportscaster

Seaborg, Glenn T. (Glenn Theodore Seaborg) (1912–) Am. chemist (discovered many radioactive isotopes; N—1951)

Seagal, Steven (1950–) Am. actor (*Under Siege*; *Out for Justice*)

Seals, Dan (1948–) Am. pop/country singer/musician (brother of Jim; "I'd Really Love to See You Tonight"; with England Dan & John Ford Coley)

Seals, Jim (James Seals) (1941–) Am. pop singer/musician ("Summer Breeze"; with Seals and Crofts)

Searle, Ronald (Ronald William Fordham Searle) (1920–) Eng. illustrator/humorist (*The Big Fat Cat Book*)

Seaton, George (George Stenius) (1911–1979) Am. film director/writer (*The Country Girl*; *Miracle on 34th Street*)

Seaver, Tom (George Thomas Seaver; "Tom Terrific"; "The Franchise") (1944–) Am. baseball player/sportscaster

Sebastian, John (John B. Sebastian; a/k/a John Benson) (1944–) Am. rock singer/musician ("Welcome Back"; formerly with The Lovin' Spoonful)

Seberg, Jean (Jean Dorothy Seberg) (1938–1979) Am. actress (*Breathless*; *Bonjour Tristesse*)

Secada, Jon (c. 1961–) Cub.-Am. singer ("Just Another Day")

Sedaka, Neil (1939–) Am. pop singer ("Breaking Up Is Hard to Do"; "Laughter in the Rain")

Sedgwick, Edie (1943–1971) Am. entertainer (protégée of Andy Warhol)

Sedgwick, Kyra (c. 1965–) Am. actress (*Mr. & Mrs. Bridge*; *Singles*; *Born on the Fourth of July*)

Seeger, Pete (Peter R. Seeger) (1919–) Am. folk singer/songwriter ("If I Had a Hammer"; "Where Have All the Flowers Gone")

Seeley, Blossom (1892–1974) Am. jazz singer

Seferis, George (Georgios Stylianou Seferiades) (1900–1971) Gr. poet (*Turning Point*; N—1963)

Segal, Erich (Erich Wolf Segal) (1937–) Am. novelist (*Love Story*)

Segal, George (1934–) Am. actor (*Who's Afraid of Virginia Woolf?*; *Fun with Dick and Jane*)

Segar, E. C. (Elzie Crisler Segar) (1894–1938) Am. cartoonist (*Popeye*)

Seger, Bob (Robert Clark Seger) (1945–) Am. rock singer ("Night Moves"; "Like a Rock"; with The Silver Bullet Band)

Segovia, Andrés (1893–1987) Span. classical guitarist

Segrè, Emilio (Emilio Gino Segrè) (1905–
1989) Am. physicist (with Owen Chamberlain; N—1959)

Seidelman, Susan (1952–) Am. film director (*Smithereens*; *Desperately Seeking
Susan*; *She-Devil*)

Seifert, Jaroslav (1901–1986) Cz.
journalist/poet (*Put Out the Lights*; N—
1984)

Seinfeld, Jerry (1954–) Am. comedian/
actor ("Seinfeld" TV series)/writer
(*SeinLanguage*)

Seixas, Vic (Elias Victor Seixas) (1923–)
Am. tennis player (W—1953)

Selby, Hubert, Jr. (1928–) Am. novelist
(*Last Exit to Brooklyn*)

Seles, Monica ("Little Miss Grunt")
(1973–) Yug. tennis player

Sellars, Peter (1957–) Am. theatrical director (*The Marriage of Figaro*; *Don
Giovanni*)

Sellecca, Connie (Concetta Sellechia)
(1955–) Am. actress ("Hotel" and "P.S. I
Luv You" TV series)

Selleck, Tom ("Clark Gable of the '80s")
(1945–) Am. actor ("Magnum, P.I." TV
series; *Three Men and a Baby*; *Quigley
Down Under*; *Mr. Baseball*; E—1983/84)

Sellers, Peter (Peter Richard Henry
Sellers) (1925–1980) Eng. actor (*Pink
Panther* films; *Dr. Strangelove*; *Being
There*)

Selznick, David O. (David Oliver Selz-
nick) (1902–1965) Am. film producer
(*Gone with the Wind*; *Rebecca*; *King
Kong*; *Anna Karenina*)

Sendak, Maurice (Maurice Bernard
Sendak) (1928–) Am. children's book
writer/illustrator (*Where the Wild
Things Are*)

Seneca (Seneca Lucius Annaeus; "The
Younger") (c. 4 B.C.–A.D. 65) Roman
statesman/playwright/philosopher (*Phae-
dra*; *Agamemnon*; *Medea*)

Senghor, Léopold Sédar (1906–) Sen.
statesman/poet (*Chants D'Ombre*)

Sennett, Mack (Michael [or Mikall] Sin-
nott; "The King of Comedy") (1880–
1960) Am. film producer/director (*Keystone Kops* films)

Serious, Yahoo (Greg Pead) (c. 1954–)
Austral. actor (*Young Einstein*)

Serkin, Rudolf (1903–1991) Aus.-Am. concert pianist

Serlin, Oscar (1901–1971) Am. theatrical
director/producer

Serling, Rod (1924–1975) Am. TV writer/
host ("The Twilight Zone")

Serra, Father Junipero (Miguel Jose
Serra) (1713–1784) Span. missionary in
Mexico and California

Service, Robert W. (Robert William Service; "The Canadian Kipling") (1874–
1958) Can. writer/poet (*Songs of a Sour-
dough*)

Sesshu ("Sesshu" = "Snow Boat"; a/k/a
Toyo) (1420–1506) Jap. Zen priest/
painter

Sessions, Roger (Roger Huntington Ses-
sions) (1896–1985) Am. composer (*Black
Maskers* suite; P—1982—*Concerto for
Orchestra*)

Sessions, William S. (1930–) Am. former
head of the FBI

Seton, Anya (Anya Chase Seton) (1916–
1990) Am. historical novelist (daughter
of Ernest; *My Theodosia*)

Seton, Ernest (Ernest Thompson Seton;
born Ernest Thompson) (1860–1946)
Am. writer/illustrator (*Wild Animals I
Have Known*)

Seton, Mother (Elizabeth Ann Seton née
Bailey) (1774–1821) Am. religious
leader/saint

Setzer, Brian (1960–) Am. rockabilly
singer/musician (with The Stray Cats)

Seurat, Georges (Georges-Pierre Seurat)
(1859–1891) Fr. painter (founded poin-
tillism and neo-impressionism)

Seuss, Dr. (Theodor Seuss Geisel; a/k/a
Theo LeSieg) (1904–1991) Am. children's book writer/illustrator (*Green
Eggs and Ham*; *The Cat in the Hat*; *How
the Grinch Stole Christmas*)

Sevareid, Eric (Arnold Eric Sevareid)
(1912–1992) Am. newscaster

Severinson, Doc (Carl H. Severinson)
(1927–) Am. trumpet player/bandleader
(with "The Tonight Show" band)

Seville, David (Ross Seville Bagdasarian)
(1919–1972) Am. entertainer (created
The Chipmunks)

Sewall, Samuel (1652–1730) Am.
statesman/jurist (presided over the
Salem witch trials)

Seward, William Henry ("The Abolitionist of Abolitionists"; "The Sage of Au-
burn") (1801–1872) Am. secretary of
state (purchased Alaska from Russia in
1867)

Sewell, Anna (1820–1878) Eng. novelist
(*Black Beauty*)

Sewell, Joe (Joseph Wheeler Sewell) (1898–1990) Am. baseball Hall-of-Famer

Sexton, Anne (née Harvey) (1928–1974) Am. poet (P—1967—*Live or Die*)

Seymour, Anne (Anne Seymour Eckert) (1909–1988) Am. actress (*All the King's Men*; *Desire Under the Elms*)

Seymour, Jane (Joyce Penelope Wilhelmina Frankenberg) (1951–) Eng. actress (*East of Eden*; "Dr. Quinn, Medicine Woman" TV series)

Seymour, Stephanie (1968–) Am. model

Shackelford, Ted (1946–) Am. actor ("Dallas" and "Knots Landing" TV series)

Shaffer, Anthony (Anthony Joshua Shaffer) (1926–) Eng. playwright/screenwriter (twin brother of Peter; *Evil Under the Sun*)

Shaffer, Paul (1949–) Can.-Am. comedian/orchestra leader ("Late Night with David Letterman" TV series)

Shaffer, Peter (Peter Levin Shaffer) (1926–) Eng. playwright (twin brother of Anthony; *Amadeus*; *Equus*)

Shahn, Ben (Benjamin Shahn) (1898–1969) Lith.-Am. painter/muralist/illustrator

Shakespeare, William ("The Bard of Avon") (1564–1616) Eng. poet/playwright (*Hamlet*; *Macbeth*; *Much Ado About Nothing*; *King Lear*)

Shakur, Tupac (a/k/a 2Pac Shakur) Am. "gangsta" rapper ("Keep Ya Head Up")/actor (*Juice*; *Poetic Justice*)

Shalala, Donna E. (Donna Edna Shalala) (1941–) Am. political scientist/educator

Shalit, Gene (1932–) Am. film critic/writer

Shamir, Yitzhak (Yitzhak Yernitsky) (1915–) Pol. prime minister of Israel 1986–1988

Shandling, Garry (1949–) Am. comedian ("It's Garry Shandling's Show" and "The Larry Sanders Show" TV series)

Shankar, Ravi (1920–) Ind. sitarist/film composer (*Apu* trilogy)

Shanley, John Patrick (1950–) Am. screenwriter/film director (*Joe versus the Volcano*; *Moonstruck*)

Shannon, Del (Charles Westover) (1939–1990) Am. rock singer ("Runaway")

Shapiro, Jacob (a/k/a Jake Gurrah) (1897–1947) Am. mobster (Lepke Buchalter's partner in Murder, Inc.)

Shapiro, Karl (Karl Jay Shapiro) (1913–) Am. critic/educator/poet (P—1945—*V-Letter and Other Poems*)

Sharif, Omar (Michael Shalhoub; a/k/a Omar El-Sharif) (1932–) Egypt. actor (*Doctor Zhivago*; *Lawrence of Arabia*)

Sharkey, Ray (1952–1993) Am. actor (*Scenes from the Class Struggle in Beverly Hills*; *The Idolmaker*; "Wiseguy" TV series)

Sharpton, Reverend Al (1954–) Am. political activist

Shatner, William (1931–) Can.-Am. actor (Captain Kirk in *Star Trek* TV series and films)/novelist (*TekWar* series)

Shaud, Grant (1961–) Am. actor ("Murphy Brown" TV series)

Shaver, Helen (1952–) Can. actress (*The Color of Money*; *The Osterman Weekend*)

Shaw, Artie (Abraham Isaac Arshawsy) (1910–) Am. bandleader/clarinetist ("Stardust"; "Begin the Beguine")

Shaw, George Bernard (1856–1950) Ir.-Eng. playwright/critic (*Pygmalion* [filmed/staged as *My Fair Lady*]; *Man and Superman*; *Androcles and the Lion*; *Saint Joan*; *Arms and the Man*; N—1925)

Shaw, Irwin (1912–1984) Am. novelist (*Rich Man, Poor Man*; *The Young Lions*)/screenwriter (*Desire Under the Elms*)

Shaw, Robert (1927–1978) Eng. actor (*The Sting*; *Jaws*; *A Man for All Seasons*)

Shawn, Dick (Richard Schulefand) (1928–1987) Am. comedian (*It's a Mad, Mad, Mad, Mad World*)

Shawn, Ted (Edwin Myers Shawn) (1891–1972) Am. dancer/choreographer

Shawn, Wallace (1943–) Am. playwright (*My Dinner with Andre*)/actor (*Manhattan*)

Shawn, William (1907–1992) Am. magazine editor (*New Yorker*)

Shearer, Moira (Moira Shearer King) (1926–) Scot. ballerina/actress (*The Red Shoes*; *Tales of Hoffman*)

Shearer, Norma (Edith Norma Shearer; "First Lady of the Screen"; "The First Lady of Hollywood") (1900–1983) Can.-Am. actress (*Romeo and Juliet*; *Marie Antoinette*; O—1929/30—*The Divorcee*)

Shearing, George (George Albert Shearing) (1919–) Eng.-Am. jazz pianist/composer ("Lullaby of Birdland")

Sheed, Wilfrid (Wilfrid John Joseph Sheed) (1930–) Am. journalist/writer (*Frank and Maisie*)

Sheedy, Ally (Alexandra Sheedy) (1962–)

Am. actress (*The Breakfast Club*; *St. Elmo's Fire*)

Sheehy, Gail (Gail Henion Sheehy) (1937–) Am. journalist/writer (*The Silent Passage*; *Passages*)

Sheen, Charlie (Carlos Irwin Estevez) (1965–) Am. actor (son of Martin, brother of Emilio Estevez; *Hot Shots*; *Wall Street*)

Sheen, Fulton (Fulton John Sheen) (1895–1979) Am. Catholic bishop

Sheen, Martin (Ramón Estevez) (1940–) Am. actor (father of Charlie Sheen and Emilio Estevez; *Apocalypse Now*)

Sheila E. (Sheila Escovedo) (1959–) Am. percussionist/singer ("The Glamourous Life"; toured with Prince and Lionel Richie)

Sheldon, Sidney (1917–) Am. novelist (*The Other Side of Midnight*; *Rage of Angels*; *Windmills of the Gods*)/screenwriter

Shelley, Mary (Mary Wollstonecraft Shelley née Godwin) (1797–1851) Eng. novelist (daughter of William Godwin; *Frankenstein*)

Shelley, Percy Bysshe (1792–1822) Eng. poet (*Prometheus Unbound*)

Shelton, Ricky Van (1952–) Am. country singer ("Somebody Lied")

Shelton, Ron (1945–) Am. screenwriter/film director (*Bull Durham*; *White Men Can't Jump*)

Shepard, Alan, Jr. (Alan Bartlett Shepard, Jr.) (1923–) Am. astronaut

Shepard, Ernest (Ernest Howard Shepard) (1879–1976) Eng. illustrator (*Winnie the Pooh*)

Shepard, Sam (Samuel Shepard Rogers) (1943–) Am. actor/playwright (*Fool for Love*; *True West*; P—1979—*Buried Child*)/screenwriter (*Paris, Texas*)

Shepherd, Cybill (Cybill Lynne Shepherd) (1949–) Am. model/actress (*The Last Picture Show*; "Moonlighting" TV series)

Sheppard, T. G. (William Browder; "The Good Shepard") (1942–) Am. country singer ("I Loved 'Em Every One")

Sheridan, Ann (Clara Lou Sheridan; "The Oomph Girl") (1915–1967) Am. actress (*King's Row*; "Another World" soap opera)

Sheridan, Nicollette (1963–) Am. actress ("Knots Landing" TV series)

Sheridan, Richard (Richard Brinsley Sheridan) (1751–1816) Ir. politician/playwright (*The School for Scandal*)

Sherman, Allan (Allan Copelon) (1924–1973) Am. comedian (created "I've Got a Secret")

Sherman, Bobby (1943–) Am. pop singer ("Julie, Do Ya Love Me")/actor ("Here Come the Brides" TV series)

Sherman, James S. (James Schoolcraft Sherman) (1855–1912) Am. v.p. (W. Taft)

Sherman, William Tecumseh (1820–1891) Am. army commander (Sherman's March to the sea; signature phrase: "War is hell")

Sherwood, Robert E. (Robert Emmet Sherwood) (1896–1955) Am. playwright (P—1936—*Idiot's Delight*; P—1939—*Abe Lincoln in Illinois*; P—1941—*There Shall Be No Night*; P—1949—*Roosevelt and Hopkins*)

Shevardnadze, Eduard (Eduard Amvrosiyevich Shevardnadze) (1928–) Russ. statesman

Shields, Brooke (Christa Brooke Camille Shields; "Brookie") (1965–) Am. actress (*Endless Love*; *The Blue Lagoon*; *Pretty Baby*)

Shih-Huang-Ti (259–210 B.C.) Chin. emperor 221–210 B.C. (built the Great Wall of China)

Shilts, Randy (1951–1994) Am. writer (*And the Band Played On*; *The Mayor of Castro Street*)

Shire, Talia (Talia Rose Coppola; a/k/a Talia Shire Schwartzman) (1946–) Am. actress (sister of Francis Ford Coppola; *Rocky* and *Godfather* films)

Shirer, William L. (William Lawrence Shirer) (1904–1993) Am. journalist/historian (*The Rise and Fall of the Third Reich*)

Shirley, Anne (Dawn Evelyeen Paris) (1918–1993) Am. actress (*Anne of Green Gables*; *Stella Dallas*)

Shocked, Michelle (Karen Michelle Johnson) (C) Am. folk singer ("Anchorage")

Shockley, William (c. 1964–) Am. actor ("Dr. Quinn, Medicine Woman" TV series)

Shoemaker, Willie (William Lee Shoemaker; "Shoe") (1931–) Am. jockey

Sholokhov, Mikhail (Mikhail Aleksandrovich Sholokhov) (1905–1984) Russ. novelist (*And Quiet Flows the Don*; N—1965)

Shor, Toots (Bernard Shor) (1905–1977) Am. restauranteur

Shore, Dinah (Frances Rose Shore; "Fannie") (1917–1994) Am. pop singer/talk show host

Shore, Eddie (Edward William Shore) (1902–1985) Can. hockey player

Shore, Pauly (c. 1968–) Am. comedian/actor (*Son-in-Law*)/MTV host

Short, Bobby (Robert Waltrip Short) (1924–) Am. cabaret singer/pianist

Short, Martin (1950–) Can. comedian/actor ("Saturday Night Live" TV series; *Innerspace*; *Father of the Bride*)

Shorter, Wayne (1933–) Am. jazz saxophonist (with Art Blakey and Miles Davis)

Shostakovich, Dmitri (Dmitri Dmitryevich Shostakovich) (1906–1975) Russ. composer (*First Symphony*)

Show, Grant (c. 1961–) Am. actor ("Melrose Place" TV series)

Shrimpton, Jean (Jean Rosemary Shrimpton; "The Shrimp") (1942–) Eng. model/hotelier

Shriner, Herb (1918–1970) Am. comedian ("The Herb Shriner Show" TV series)

Shriner, Kin (1953–) Am. actor (son of Herb; "General Hospital" soap opera)

Shriner, Wil (1953–) Am. comedian

Shriver, Maria (Maria Owings Shriver) (1955–) Am. newscaster

Shriver, Pam (Pamela Howard Shriver) (1962–) Am. tennis player

Shubert, Jacob J. (1880–1963) Russ.-Am. theatrical producer (brother of Lee and Samuel)

Shubert, Lee (Levi Szemanski) (1875–1953) Russ.-Am. theatrical producer

Shubert, Samuel S. (1876–1905) Russ.-Am. theatrical producer

Shue, Andrew (c. 1967–) Am. actor (brother of Elisabeth; "Melrose Place" TV series)

Shue, Elisabeth (1963–) Am. actress (*Adventures in Babysitting*; *Cocktail*; *Soapdish*)

Shula, Don (Donald Francis Shula) (1930–) Am. football coach

Shulman, Max (1919–1988) Am. novelist/playwright/humorist (*Barefoot Boy with Cheek*)

Shultz, George P. (George Pratt Shultz) (1920–) Am. economist/politician (secretary of state/treasury/labor)

Shuster, Joe (Joseph Shuster) (1914–1992) Am. cartoonist (*Superman*, with Jerry Siegel)

Shute, Denny (Herman Densmore Shute) (1904–1974) Am. golfer

Shute, Nevil (Nevil Shute Norway) (1899–1960) Eng. novelist (*On the Beach*)

Sibelius, Jean (Jean Julius Christian Sibelius; born Johan Julius Christian Sibelius) (1865–1957) Finn. composer (*Finlandia*)

Siddons, Sarah (née) **Kemble** (1755–1831) Eng. actress

Sidney, Sir Phillip (1554–1586) Eng. soldier/politician/poet (*Astrophil and Stella*)

Sidney, Sylvia (Sophia Kosow) (1910–) Am. actress (*Sabotage*; *Madame Butterfly*)

Siegel, Bugsy (Benjamin Siegel) (1906–1947) Am. mobster

Siegel, Don (Donald Siegel) (1912–) Am. film director (*Dirty Harry*; *Invasion of the Body Snatchers*)

Siegel, Jerry (1914–) Am. cartoonist (*Superman*, with Joe Shuster)

Siegfried & Roy *see* Fischbacher, Siegfried, and Horne, Roy

Siegmeister, Elie (1909–) Am. composer (*Ozark Set*)

Sienkiewicz, Henryk (Henryk Adam Aleksandr Pius Sienkiewicz; a/k/a Litwos) (1846–1916) Pol. novelist (*Quo Vadis?*; N—1905)

Sierra, Ruben (Ruben Angel Garcia) (1965–) P.R.-Am. baseball player

Signoret, Simone (Simone-Henriette-Charlotte Kaminker) (1921–1985) Ger.-Fr. actress (*Ship of Fools*; *Diabolique*; O—1959—*Room at the Top*)

Sikes, Cynthia (1954–) Am. actress ("St. Elsewhere" TV series)

Sikorsky, Igor Ivan (1889–1972) Russ.-Am. aircraft/helicopter designer/manufacturer/inventor (cabin biplane [jet forerunner])

Silkwood, Karen (Karen Gay Silkwood) (1946–1974) Am. atomic worker/union activist (possibly murdered)

Sillanpaa, Frans Eemil (1888–1964) Finn. novelist/short story writer (*Meek Heritage*; N—1939)

Silliphant, Stirling (Stirling Dale Silliphant) (1918–) Am. screenwriter (*In the Heat of the Night*; *The Poseidon Adventure*)

Sillitoe, Alan (1928–) Eng. novelist/poet (*The Loneliness of the Long Distance Runner*)

Sills, Beverly (Belle Silverman; "Bubbles") (1929–) Am. opera singer (soprano)

Silone, Ignazio (Secondo Tranquilli)

(1900–1978) Ital. novelist (*Bread and Wine*)

Silver, Joel (c. 1952–) Am. film producer (*48 Hrs.*; *Lethal Weapon*; *Demolition Man*)

Silver, Ron (Ron Zimelman) (1946–) Am. actor (*Enemies—A Love Story*; *Reversal of Fortune*; T—1988)

Silverberg, Robert (1935–) Am. science fiction writer (*Epoch*; *Capricorn Games*)

Silverheels, Jay (Harold Jay Smith) (1919–1980) Can. actor (Tonto in "The Lone Ranger" TV series)

Silverman, Fred (1937–) Am. entertainment executive

Silverman, Sime (1873–1933) Am. magazine publisher (founded *Variety*; coined the term *disc jockey*)

Silvers, Phil (Philip Silversmith) (1911–1985) Am. comedian/actor (Sgt. Bilko on "The Phil Silvers Show" TV series; E—1955; T—1952, 1972)

Silverstein, Shel (Shelby Silverstein) (1932–) Am. songwriter/writer (*A Light in the Attic*)

Simak, Clifford D. (1904–) Am. science fiction writer (*Cemetery World*)

Simenon, Georges (Georges Joseph Christian Sim) (1903–1989) Fr. detective story writer (created Inspector Maigret)

Simic, Charles (1938–) Am. poet (P—1990—*The World Doesn't End*)

Simmons, Al (Aloys Szymanski; "Bucketfoot Al"; "The Duke of Milwaukee") (1902–1956) Am. baseball Hall-of-Famer

Simmons, Gene (Gene Klein) (1949–) Am. rock musician (with Kiss)

Simmons, Jean (Jean Merilyn Simmons) (1929–) Eng. actress (*Hamlet*; *Elmer Gantry*)

Simmons, Richard ("The Clown Prince of Fitness"; "The Pied Piper of Pounds") (1948–) Am. exercise expert

Simms, Ginny (Virginia E. Sims) (1916–) Am. singer (with Kay Kyser's band)

Simon, Carly (1945–) Am. pop singer/songwriter ("Anticipation"; "You Belong to Me"; "You're So Vain"; G—1971)

Simon, Claude (Claude Eugene Henri Simon) (1913–) Fr. novelist (*The Palace*; N—1985)

Simon, John (John Ivan Simon; "The Critic You Love to Hate") (1925–) Am. film critic (*Esquire* and *New York* magazines)

Simon, Neil (Marvin Neil Simon; "Doc") (1927–) Am. playwright (*The Odd Couple*; *Barefoot in the Park*; P—1991—*Lost in Yonkers*)

Simon, Norton (c. 1907–1993) Am. industrialist/art collector/museum founder

Simon, Paul (Paul Martin Simon) (1928–) Am. writer/educator/senator

Simon, Paul (Paul Frederick Simon) (1942–) Am. singer/musician/songwriter ("50 Ways to Leave Your Lover"; "Slip Slidin' Away"; formerly with Simon & Garfunkel; G—1975)

Simon, Richard (Richard Leo Simon) (1899–1960) Am. publisher (father of Carly; co-founded Simon & Schuster)

Simon, Simone (1910–) Fr. actress (*Cat People*; *The Human Beast*)

Simone, Nina (Eunice Kathleen Waymon) (1933–) Am. jazz singer/pianist ("I Loves You, Porgy")

Simonetta (1922–) Ital. fashion designer

Simonides (a/k/a Simonides of Ceos) (c. 556–c. 478 B.C.) Gr. lyric poet

Simpson, Adele (Adele Smithline) (1903–) Am. fashion designer

Simpson, Don (1945–) Am. film producer (*Days of Thunder*)

Simpson, Louis (Louis Aston Marantz Simpson) (1923–) Am. poet (P—1964—*At the End of the Open Road*)

Simpson, O. J. (Orenthal James Simpson; "Juice") (1947–) Am. football Hall-of-Famer

Simpson, Valerie (1946–) Am. pop singer (with Ashford & Simpson)

Sims, Zoot (John Haley Sims) (1925–1985) Am. jazz saxophone/clarinet player

Sinatra, Frank (Francis Albert Sinatra; "Ol' Blue Eyes"; "The Chairman of the Board") (1915–) Am. singer ("Love and Marriage"; "All the Way"; "Strangers in the Night"; G—1959, 1965, 1966)/actor (O—1953—*From Here to Eternity*)

Sinatra, Frank, Jr. (Francis Albert Sinatra, Jr.) (1944–) Am. orchestra leader (for his father)

Sinatra, Nancy (Nancy Sandra Sinatra) (1940–) Am. pop singer (daughter of Frank; "These Boots Are Made for Walkin' ")

Sinclair, Upton (Upton Beall Sinclair; a/k/a Clarke Fitch, Frederick Garrison, and Arthur Stirling) (1878–1968) Am. novelist/nonfiction writer (*The Jungle*; P—1943—*Dragon's Teeth*)

Singer, Isaac Bashevis (a/k/a Isaac War-shofsky) (1904–) Pol.-Am. novelist/short story writer/journalist (*The Magician of Lublin*; N—1978)

Singer, Isaac Merrit (1811–1875) Am. inventor (sewing machine)

Singer, Israel (Israel Joshua Singer) (1893–1944) Am. novelist/playwright/journalist (brother of Isaac Bashevis; *Blood Harvest*)

Singer, Lori (1962–) Am. actress (*Footloose*; *The Falcon and the Snowman*)

Singleton, John (c. 1968–) Am. film director (*Boyz N the Hood*; *Poetic Justice*)

Singleton, Penny (Mariana Dorothy Agnes Letitia McNulty) (1908–) Am. actress (*Blondie*; *After the Thin Man*)

Singleton, Zutty (Arthur James Singleton) (1898–1975) Am. jazz drummer

Sirhan Sirhan (Sirhan Bishara Sirhan) (1945–) Pal.-Am. assassin (of senator R. F. Kennedy)

Sirica, John (John Joseph Sirica) (1904–1992) Am. jurist (Watergate)

Sirk, Douglas (Detlef Sierck) (1900–1987) Dan. film director (*Magnificent Obsession*; *Written on the Wind*)

Siskel, Gene (Eugene Karl Siskel) (1946–) Am. film critic (with Richard Ebert)

Sisler, George (George Harold Sisler; "The Perfect Ballplayer"; "Gorgeous George") (1893–1973) Am. baseball Hall-of-Famer

Sisley, Alfred (1839–1899) Eng.-Fr. landscape painter

Sitting Bull (Indian name: Tatanka Zyotake) (c. 1831–1890) Am. Sioux leader

Sitwell, Dame Edith (1887–1964) Eng. poet/novelist (*Façade*)

Sixx, Nikki (Frank Ferrano) (1958–) Am. rock musician (with Mötley Crüe)

Sjöwall, Maj (1935–) Swed. poet/mystery writer (created Chief Inspector Martin Beck of the Swedish National Police; *The Terrorists*)

Skaggs, Ricky (1954–) Am. country singer/guitarist ("Crying My Heart Out over You")

Skelton, Red (Richard Bernard Skelton) (1913–) Am. comedian/actor ("The Red Skelton Show" TV series; created Clem Kaddidlehopper, Freddie the Freeloader, and Willie Lump-Lump; E—1951)

Skerritt, Tom (Thomas Roy Skerritt)

(1933–) Am. actor ("Picket Fences" TV series; *The Turning Point*; *Alien*)

Skidmore, Louis (1897–1962) Am. architect (helped construct Oak Ridge, Tennessee)

Skinner, B. F. (Burrhus Frederic Skinner) (1904–1990) Am. psychologist/writer (*Walden Two*)

Skinner, Cornelia Otis (1901–1979) Am. actress (daughter of Otis; *The Swimmer*)

Skye, Ione (Ione Skye Leitch) (1971–) Am. actress (daughter of Donovan; *River's Edge*; *Say Anything . . .*; *Gas Food Lodging*)

Slash (Saul Hudson) (1965–) Am. rock guitarist (with Guns N' Roses)

Slater, Christian (Christian Hawkins) (1969–) Am. actor (*Heathers*; *Pump Up the Volume*; *Kuffs*; *Untamed Heart*)

Slater, Helen (1963–) Am. actress (*Supergirl*; *Ruthless People*)

Slatkin, Leonard (1944–) Am. orchestra conductor

Slaughter, Enos (Enos Bradsher Slaughter; "Country") (1916–) Am. baseball Hall-of-Famer

Slaughter, Frank (Frank Gill Slaughter; a/k/a C. V. Terry) (1908–) Am. novelist (*Plague Ship*; *Doctors' Wives*)

Slayton, Deke (Donald Kent Slayton) (1924–1993) Am. astronaut

Sledge, Percy (1940–)Am. pop singer ("When a Man Loves a Woman")

Slesar, Henry (1927–) Am. suspense writer (for Alfred Hitchcock)

Slezak, Erika (1946–) Am. actress ("One Life to Live" soap opera)

Slick, Grace (Grace Barnett Wing) (1939–) Am. rock singer (with Jefferson Airplane)

Sloan, John (John French Sloan) (1871–1951) Am. painter (*Wake of the Ferry*)

Sloane, Everett (1909–1965) Am. actor (*Citizen Kane*; *The Lady from Shanghai*)

Smetana, Bedřich (Bedřich Frederick Smetana) (1824–1884) Cz. composer (*The Bartered Bride*)

Smirnoff, Yakov (Yakov Pokhis) (1951–) Russ.-Am. comedian

Smith, Alexis (Gladys Smith) (1921–1993) Can.-Am. actress ("Dallas" TV series; *The Turning Point*; T—1972)

Smith, Anna Nicole (c. 1967–) Am. model (Guess advertisements)

Smith, Bessie (Elizabeth Smith; "Empress of the Blues"; "Empress of Jazz")

(1894–1937) Am. blues singer/ songwriter ("Back Water Blues")

Smith, Betty (Betty Wehner) (1904–1972) Am. novelist/playwright (*A Tree Grows in Brooklyn*)

Smith, Bob (Robert E. Smith; "Buffalo Bob") (1917–) Am. entertainer/TV host (created "The Howdy Doody Show")

Smith, Bob (Robert Holbrook Smith; "Dr. Bob") (1879–1950) Am. founder of Alcoholics Anonymous (with Bill Wilson)

Smith, Bubba (Charles Aaron Smith) (1945–) Am. football player/actor

Smith, Carl (1927–) Am. country singer (father of Carlene Carter; "Loose Talk")

Smith, Sir C. Aubrey (Charles Aubrey Smith) (1863–1948) Eng. actor (*Lives of a Bengal Lancer*; *Rebecca*)

Smith, Cordwainer (Paul Myron Anthony Linebarger) (1913–1966) Am. science fiction writer (*Space Lords*; *You Will Never Be the Same*)

Smith, Cotter (1949–) Am. actor ("L.A. Law" TV series; *Lady Beware*)

Smith, Curt (1961–) Eng. pop musician/ singer (with Tears For Fears)

Smith, Dodie (Dorothy Gladys Smith; a/k/a C. L. Anthony) (1896–) Eng. playwright/novelist (*The Hundred and One Dalmations*)

Smith, E. E. (Edward Elmer Smith; a/k/a E. E. Doc Smith) (1890–1965) Am. science fiction writer (*Galactic Patrol*; *The Skylark of Space*)

Smith, H. Allen (Harry Allen Smith) (1907–1976) Am. humorist

Smith, Horton ("The Joplin Ghost") (1908–1963) Am. golfer

Smith, Howard K. (Howard Kingsbury Smith) (1914–) Am. newscaster

Smith, Jabbo (1908–1991) Am. jazz trumpet player

Smith, Jaclyn (Jaclyn Ellen Smith) (1947–) Am. actress ("Charlie's Angels" TV series)/K-Mart clothing pitchwoman

Smith, Jedediah (Jedediah Strong Smith) (1799–1831) Am. explorer/frontiersman

Smith, Jeff (Jeffrey Alan Smith; "The Frugal Gourmet") (1958–) Am. chef/writer

Smith, Joe (1902–1937) Am. jazz trumpet player

Smith, Joseph (1805–1844) Am. founder of the Mormon Church

Smith, Kate (Kathryn Elizabeth Smith) (1909–1986) Am. entertainer/singer ("God Bless America")

Smith, Keely (Dorothy Jacqueline Keely) (1932–) Am. jazz/pop singer

Smith, Liz (Mary Elizabeth Smith) (1923–) Am. (New York) gossip columnist

Smith, Dame Maggie (Margaret Natalie Smith) (1934–) Eng. actress (O— 1969—*The Prime of Miss Jean Brodie*; O—1978—*California Suite*; T—1990)

Smith, Margaret (née **Chase**) (1897–) Am. senator

Smith, Merriman ("Smitty") (1913–1970) Am. journalist (P—1964)

Smith, Ozzie (Osborne Earl Smith; "The Wizard of Oz"; "The Wizard of Ozzie") (1954–) Am. baseball player

Smith, Patti (Patti Lee Smith) (1946–) Am. "new wave" singer/songwriter ("Because the Night")

Smith, Pinetop (Clarence Smith) (1904– 1929) Am. jazz pianist

Smith, Red (Walter Wellesley Smith) (1905–1982) Am. sports columnist (P— 1976)

Smith, Rex (1956–) Am. singer ("You Take My Breath Away")/actor (*The Pirates of Penzance*)

Smith, Robert (1957–) Eng. rock singer (with The Cure)

Smith, Robyn (Robyn Caroline Smith) (1944–) Am. jockey

Smith, Roger (1932–) Am. actor ("Father Knows Best" and "77 Sunset Strip" TV series)

Smith, Sammi (1941–) Am. country singer ("Help Me Make It Through the Night")

Smith, Scott (c. 1966–) Am. novelist (*A Simple Plan*)

Smith, Stan (Stanley Roger Smith) (1946–) Am. tennis player (W—1972)

Smith, Stevie (Florence Margaret Smith) (1902–1971) Eng. novelist/poet (*Novel on Yellow Paper*)

Smith, Sydney (1887–1935) Am. cartoonist (*The Gumps*)

Smith, Thorne (1892–1934) Am. humorist/ novelist (*Topper*)

Smith, Will (Willard Smith) (1968–) Am. actor ("Fresh Prince of Bel Air" TV series)/rapper (with D. J. Jazzy Jeff and The Fresh Prince)

Smith, Willie (William Henry Joseph Berthel Bonaparte Bertholoff) (1897– 1973) Am. jazz pianist

Smithers, Jan (1949–) Am. actress ("WKRP in Cincinnati" TV series)

Smits, Jimmy (1955–) Am. actor ("L.A. Law" TV series; E—1989/90)

Smothers, Dick (Richard Smothers) (1939–) Am. comedian (with The Smothers Brothers)

Smothers, Tommy (Thomas Bolyn Smothers III) (1937–) Am. comedian (with The Smothers Brothers)

Smuts, Jan C. (Jan Christian Smuts) (1870–1950) S. Afr. statesman/soldier/ prime minister 1919–1924

Smyth, Patty (1957–) Am. rock singer ("Sometimes Love Just Ain't Enough"; formerly with Scandal)

Snead, Sam (Samuel Jackson Snead; "Slammin' Sam"; "Swinging Sam") (1912–) Am. golfer

Sneed, Ed (Edgar Sneed) (1944–) Am. golfer

Snider, Duke (Edwin Donald Snider; "The Duke of Flatbush"; "The Silver Fox") (1926–) Am. baseball Hall-of-Famer

Snipes, Wesley (1962–) Am. actor (*Jungle Fever*; *Passenger 57*; *Rising Sun*)

Snodgrass, W. D. (William DeWitt Snodgrass; a/k/a S.S. Gardens) (1926–) Am. poet (P—1960—*Heart's Needle*)

Snodgrass, Carrie (Caroline Snodgrass) (1946–) Am. actress (*Diary of a Mad Housewife*)

Snoop Doggy Dogg (Calvin Broadus) (c. 1972–) Am. rapper

Snow, Sir C. P. (Charles Percy Snow) (1905–1980) Eng. scientist/novelist (*Strangers and Brothers* series)

Snow, Hank (Clarence Eugene Snow; "The Singing Ranger"; "The Yodeling Ranger") (1914–) Am. country singer ("I'm Moving On")

Snow, Phoebe (Phoebe Laub Snow) (1952–) Am. pop singer ("Poetry Man")

Snowden, 1st Earl of (Antony Charles Robert Armstrong-Jones; "The Royal Black Sheep") (1930–) Eng. photographer

Snyder, Gary (Gary Sherman Snyder) (1930–) Am. poet/essayist (P—1975—*Turtle Island*)

Snyder, Tom (1936–) Am. newscaster/TV and radio host

Snyder, Zilpha Keatley (1927–) Am. science fiction/fantasy writer (*Black & Blue Magic*; *The Egypt Game*)

Socrates (c. 470–399 B.C.) Gr. philosopher (the Socratic method)

Soderbergh, Steven (1963–) Am. film director (*sex, lies, and videotape*; *Kafka*; *King of the Hill*)

Solomon (10th century B.C.) Isr. king

Solon (c. 630–c. 560 B.C.) Ath. statesman (one of the Seven Wise Men of Greece)

Solow, Robert (Robert Merton Solow) (1924–) Am. economist/educator (N—1987)

Solti, Sir Georg (1912–) Hung.-Eng. orchestra conductor (Chicago Symphony)

Solzhenitsyn, Aleksandr I. (Aleksandr Isayevich Solzhenitsyn) (1918–) Russ. novelist (*The Gulag Archipelago*; *The Cancer Ward*; N—1970)

Somers, Brett (1927–) Am. actress ("The Odd Couple" TV series)

Somers, Suzanne (Suzanne Marie Mahoney) (1946–) Am. actress ("Three's Company" TV series)/writer

Somerville, E. O. (Edith Anna Oeone Somerville) (1858–1949) Ir. novelist (with Martin Ross, *The Real Charlotte*)

Sommer, Elke (Elke Schletz) (1940–) Ger.-Am. actress (*The Prize*; *A Shot in the Dark*)

Somoza, Anastasio (Anastasio Somoza García; "Tacho") (1896–1956) Nic. pres. 1936–1947 (father of Anastasio Somoza de Bayle)

Somoza de Bayle, Anastasio (1925–1980) Nic. political leader 1963–1979 (overthrown by the Sandinistas)

Sondergaard, Gale (Edith Holm Sondergaard) (1899–1985) Am. actress (*Anna and the King of Siam*; O—1936—*Anthony Adverse*)

Sondheim, Stephen (Stephen Joshua Sondheim) (1930–) Am. composer (*A Little Night Music*; P—1985—*Sunday in the Park with George*)

Son of Sam see Berkowitz, David

Sontag, Susan (1933–) Am. novelist/short story writer/philosopher (*Illness as Metaphor*)

Soo, Jack (Carl or Goro Suzuki) (1917–1979) Jap.-Am. actor ("Barney Miller" TV series)

Sophocles (c. 496–406 B.C.) Gr. playwright (*Oedipus Rex*; *Electra*; *Antigone*)

Soren, Tabitha (c. 1967–) Am. TV journalist (for MTV)

Sorvino, Paul (1939–) Am. actor (*Cruising*; *GoodFellas*; "Law & Order" TV series)

Sothern, Ann (Harriette Lake) (1909–)

Am. comedienne/actress (*A Letter to Three Wives*; *The Whales of August*)

Soul, David (David Solberg) (1943–) Am. actor ("Starsky and Hutch" TV series)

Sousa, John Philip ("The March King") (1854–1932) Am. composer ("Stars and Stripes Forever")

Souter, David H. (1939–) Am. Supreme Court jurist (1990–)

Souther, J. D. (John David Souther) (1945–) Am. country singer ("You're Only Lonely")

Southey, Robert (1774–1843) Eng. poet (*The Battle of Blenheim*)

Soyinka, Wole (Akinwande Oluwole Soyinka) (1934–) Niger. poet/essayist/ playwright (*The Road*; *The Strong Breed*; N—1986)

Spacek, Sissy (Mary Elizabeth Spacek) (1949–) Am. actress (*Badlands*; *Carrie*; O—1980—*Coal Miner's Daughter*)

Spacey, Kevin (1959–) Am. actor (*Working Girl*; *Henry & June*; *Consenting Adults*)

Spader, James (1960–) Am. actor (*sex, lies, and videotape*; *White Palace*; *True Colors*; *Storyville*)

Spahn, Warren (Warren Edward Spahn; "The Invincible One"; "Hook"; "Spahny") (1921–) Am. baseball Hall-of-Famer

Spanier, Muggsy (Francis Joseph Spanier) (1906–1967) Am. jazz cornetist/ bandleader

Spano, Vincent (1962–) Am. actor (*City of Hope*; *Rumble Fish*; *Alive*)

Spark, Muriel (Muriel Sarah Camberg) (1918–) Eng. novelist/poet (*The Prime of Miss Jean Brodie*; *Memento Mori*)

Sparks, Ned (Edward A. Sparkman) (1883–1957) Can. actor (*Forty-Second Street*; *Lady for a Day*)

Spartacus (died 71 B.C.) Roman slave/ insurrectionist

Spassky, Boris (Boris Vasiliyevich Spassky) (1937–) Russ. chess player

Speaker, Tris (Tristram E. Speaker; "The Gray Eagle"; "Spoke") (1888–1958) Am. baseball Hall-of-Famer

Spears, Billie Jo (1937–) Am. country singer ("Blanket on the Ground")

Specter, Arlen (1930–) Am. senator

Spector, Phil (Philip Harvey Spector) (1940–) Am. record producer

Spector, Ronnie (Veronica Bennett) (1947–) Am. pop singer (with The Ronettes; "Be My Baby")

Speer, Albert (1905–1981) Ger. architect/ Nazi govt. official/writer (*Inside the Third Reich*)

Spelling, Aaron (1928–) Am. TV producer/ writer (father of Tori; "Beverly Hills, 90210," "Charlie's Angels," "The Love Boat," "Fantasy Island" TV series)

Spelling, Tori (c. 1973–) Am. actress (daughter of Aaron; "Beverly Hills, 90210" TV series)

Spencer, Diana (Diana Frances Spencer) (1961–) Eng. princess of Wales

Spencer, John (1946–) Am. actor ("L.A. Law" TV series)

Spender, Sir Stephen (Stephen Harold Spender) (1909–) Eng. poet (*Trial of a Judge*)

Spengler, Oswald (1880–1936) Ger. philosopher/writer (*The Decline of the West*)

Spenser, Edmund (1552–1599) Eng. writer/poet (*The Faerie Queen*)

Sperber, Wendie Jo (C) Am. actress ("Bosom Buddies" TV series)

Sperry, Elmer (Elmer Ambrose Sperry) (1860–1930) Am. inventor (gyroscopic compass and stabilizer)

Spheeris, Penelope (1945–) Am. film director (*The Decline of Western Civilization*; *Wayne's World*)

Spiegel, Sam (a/k/a S. P. Eagle) (1901–1985) Aus.-Am. film producer (*The African Queen*; *The Bridge on the River Kwai*; *On the Waterfront*)

Spielberg, Steven (1947–) Am. film writer/ producer/director (*Close Encounters of the Third Kind*; *E.T.: The Extra-Terrestrial*; *Jurassic Park*; *Raiders of the Lost Ark*; *Schindler's List*)

Spillane, Mickey (Frank Morrison Spillane) (1918–) Am. detective story writer (created Mike Hammer; *I, The Jury*; *Kiss Me Deadly*)

Spingarn, Arthur (Arthur Barnett Spingarn) (1878–1971) Am. civil rights advocate/pres. of the NAACP (brother of Joel)

Spingarn, Joel E. (Joel Elias Spingarn) (1875–1939) Am. writer/critic (*Creative Criticism*; founder of the NAACP)

Spinks, Leon (1953–) Am. boxer

Spinks, Michael (1956–) Am. boxer

Spinoza, Baruch (1632–1677) Dutch philosopher (*Ethics*)

Spitteler, Carl (Karl Friedrich Georg Spitteler; a/k/a Carl Felix) (1845–1924) Swi.

poet/novelist (*Prometheus and Epi-metheus*; N—1919)

Spitz, Mark (Mark Andrew Spitz; "The King of Amateur Swimming") (1950–) Am. swimmer

Spock, Benjamin (Benjamin McLane Spock; a/k/a Dr. Spock) (1903–) Am. pediatrician/child-care expert/writer

Spode, Josiah (1754–1827) Eng. potter (developed bone china)

Spottiswoode, Roger (1945–) Can.-Am. screenwriter/film director (*Turner and Hooch*; *Stop or My Mom Will Shoot*)

Springfield, Dusty (Mary Isobel Catherine O'Brien) (1939–) Eng. pop singer ("You Don't Have to Say You Love Me")

Springfield, Rick (Richard Springfield) (1949–) Austral.-Am. rock singer ("Jessie's Girl")/actor ("General Hospital" soap opera; *Hard to Hold*)

Springsteen, Bruce ("The Boss") (1949–) Am. rock singer/guitarist/songwriter ("Born in the U.S.A."; "Glory Days"; "I'm on Fire"; "Tunnel of Love"; with The E Street Band)

Sprouse, Stephen (1953–) Am. fashion designer

Spruance, Raymond (Raymond Ames Spruance) (1886–1969) Am. navy admiral/ambassador

Spyri, Johanna (née Heusser) (1827–1901) Swi. children's book writer (*Heidi*)

Squier, Billy (1950–) Am. rock singer ("The Stroke"; "Everybody Wants You")

Stabler, Kenny or **Ken** (Kenneth Michael Stabler; "The Snake") (1945–) Am. football player

Stack, Robert (Robert Langford Modini) (1919–) Am. actor (*The Untouchables* [as Eliot Ness] and "Unsolved Mysteries" TV series; E—1959/60)

Staël, Madame de (Anne Louise Germaine de Staël née Necker; Baronne de Staël-Holstein) (1766–1817) Fr. writer/society figure

Stafford, Jean (1915–1979) Am. novelist/short story writer (*The Mountain Lion*; P—1970—*Collected Stories*)

Stafford, Jim (James Wayne Stafford) (1944–) Am. rock singer ("Spiders & Snakes")

Stafford, Jo (1918–) Am. singer ("Suddenly There's a Valley")

Stagg, Amos Alonzo ("The Grand Old Man of American Football") (1862–1965) Am. football player/coach

Stahl, John M. (1886–1950) Am. film director (*Imitation of Life*; *Magnificent Obsession*)

Stahl, Lesley (Lesley Rene Stahl) (1941–) Am. TV newscaster ("60 Minutes")

Stalin, Joseph (Iosif Vissarionovich Dzhugashvili) (1879–1953) Russ. dictator 1924–1953

Stallings, Laurence (Laurence Tucker Stallings, Jr.) (1894–1968) Am. playwright (with Maxwell Anderson, *What Price Glory?*; *The Big Parade*)

Stallone, Sylvester (Sylvester Enzio Stallone; "Sly"; "The Italian Stallion") (1946–) Am. actor/film director (*Rocky* and *Rambo* films; *Cliffhanger*; *Demolition Man*)

Stamos, John (1963–) Am. actor ("Full House" TV series)

Stamp, Terence (1938–) Eng. actor (*Billy Budd* [title role]; *Far from the Madding Crowd*)

Stampley, Joe (Joseph Ronald Stampley) (1943–) Am. country singer ("Too Much on My Heart")

Stander, Lionel (Lionel Jay Stander) (1908–) Am. actor (*A Star Is Born* [1937]; "Hart to Hart" TV series)

Standish, Miles or **Myles** ("The Hero of New England"; "Little Indian Fighter") (c. 1584–1656) Am. Plymouth Colony leader

Stanford, Leland (Amasa Leland Stanford) (1824–1893) Am. university founder/railroad builder/politician

Stang, Arnold (1925–) Am. actor (Milton Berle's sidekick)

Stanky, Eddie (Edward Raymond Stanky; "The Brat"; "Muggsy"; (1916–) Am. baseball player/manager

Stanislavsky, Konstantin (Konstantin Sergeyevich Alekseyev) (1863–1938) Russ. theatrical actor/acting teacher (the Stanislavsky method)/director/producer/writer (*An Actor Prepares*)

Stanley, Sir Henry Morton (John Rowlands) (1841–1904) Eng. explorer/journalist/writer (*How I Found Livingstone in Darkest Africa*)

Stanley, Kim (Patricia Kimberley Reid) (1921–) Am. actress (*The Right Stuff*; *Seance on a Wet Afternoon*)

Stansfield, Lisa (1966–) Eng. pop singer ("All Around the World")

Stanley, Paul (Paul Stanley Eisen) (1952–) Am. rock singer/musician (with Kiss)

Stanton, Elizabeth (née) **Cady** (1815–1902) Am. suffragist

Stanton, Harry Dean (a/k/a Dean Stanton) (1926–) Am. actor (*Repo Man*; *Alien*; *Wild at Heart*)

Stanwyck, Barbara (Ruby Stevens) (1907–1990) Am. actress (*The Lady Eve*; *Double Indemnity*; E–1960/61, 1965/66)

Stapleton, Jean (Jeanne Murray) (1923–) Am. actress (Edith Bunker in "All in the Family" TV series; E—1970/71, 1971/72, 1977/78)

Stapleton, Maureen (Lois Maureen Stapleton) (1925–) Am. actress (*Interiors*; *Queen of the Stardust Ballroom*; O—1981—*Reds*; T–1971)

Stargell, Willie (Wilver Dornel Stargell; "Pops") (1941–) Am. baseball Hall-of-Famer

Starkweather, Charles ("The Nebraska Fiend") (1940–1959) Am. mass murderer (nine people)

Starr, Bart (Bryan Bart Starr) (1934–) Am. football Hall-of-Famer

Starr, Belle (Myra Belle Starr née Shirley; "Bandit Queen"; "Lady Desperado"; "The Female Robin Hood") (1848–1889) Am. western outlaw (hid Jesse James; rustled cattle)

Starr, Kay (Kathryn or Katherine Stark or Starks) (1922–) Am. singer ("Rock and Roll Waltz"; "Wheel of Fortune")

Starr, Ringo (Richard Starkey) (1940–) Eng. rock musician ("It Don't Come Easy"; formerly with The Beatles)

Staub, Rusty (Daniel Joseph Staub; "Le Grand Orange") (1944–) Am. baseball player

Staubach, Roger (Roger Thomas Staubach; "The Artful Dodger") (1942–) Am. football Hall-of-Famer

Stautner, Ernie (Ernest Stautner) (1925–) Am. football Hall-of-Famer

Stead, Christina (Christina Ellen Stead) (1902–1983) Austral. novelist (*The Man Who Loved Children*; *For Love Alone*)

Steadman, Alison (1946–) Eng. actress (*Shirley Valentine*; "The Singing Detective" TV series)

Steel, Danielle (Danielle Fernande Schuelein-Steel) (1947–) Am. romance novelist (*Palomino*; *Secrets*)

Steel, Dawn (Dawn Spielberg) (1947–) Am. entertainment executive (Paramount and Columbia studios)/writer (*They Can Kill You . . . But They Can't Eat You*)

Steele, Sir Richard (a/k/a Isaac Bick-

erstaff) (1672–1729) Eng. playwright/essayist (*The Conscious Lovers*)

Steen, Jan (c. 1626–1679) Dutch painter (*The Feast of St. Nicholas*)

Steenburgen, Mary (1953–) Am. actress (O—1980—*Melvin and Howard*; *Ragtime*; *Parenthood*)

Steffens, Lincoln (Joseph Lincoln Steffens; "King of the Muckrakers") (1866–1936) Am. writer/editor (*The Shame of the Cities*)

Stegner, Wallace (Wallace Earle Stegner) (1909–1993) Am. writer (P—1972—*Angle of Repose*)

Steichen, Edward (Edouard Jean Steichen) (1879–1973) Am. portrait photographer/autobiographer (*A Life in Photography*)

Steiger, Rod (Rodney Stephen Steiger) (1925–) Am. actor (*On the Waterfront*; O—1967—*In The Heat of the Night*)

Stein, Gertrude (1874–1946) Am. writer (*Three Lives*; *The Autobiography of Alice B. Toklas*; signature phrase: "A rose is a rose is a rose")

Stein, Joseph (1912–) Am. playwright (*Fiddler on the Roof*)

Steinbeck, John (John Ernst Steinbeck) (1902–1968) Am. novelist/short story writer (*Tortilla Flat*; *Cannery Row*; *East of Eden*; N—1962; P—1940—*The Grapes of Wrath*)

Steinberg, Saul (1914–) Rom.-Am. artist (drawings)

Steinberger, Jack (1921–) Ger.-Am. physician (N—1988)

Steinbrenner, George (George Michael Steinbrenner III; "The Principal Owner"; "Patton in Pinstripes") (1930–) Am. baseball manager

Steinem, Gloria (Gloria Marie Steinem) (1934–) Am. feminist/writer/lecturer/founder of NOW and *Ms.* magazine

Steiner, George (Francis George Steiner) (1929–) Am. writer (*The Death of Tragedy*; *Language and Silence*)

Steiner, Max (Maximilian Raoul Steiner) (1888–1971) Aus.-Am. film composer (*Gone With the Wind*; *Now, Voyager*)

Stella, Frank (Frank Philip Stella) (1936–) Am. painter ("black" paintings)

Sten, Anna (Anjuschka Stenski Sujakevitch; "Goldwyn's Folly") (1908–1993) Russ. actress (*Nana* [title role])

Stendhal (Marie-Henri Beyle) (1783–1842) Fr. novelist (*The Charterhouse of Parma*; *The Red and the Black*)

Stengel, Casey (Charles Dillon Stengel; "The Old Professor") (1889–1975) Am. baseball Hall-of-Famer

Stephanie (Stephanie Marie Elisabeth Grimaldi) (1965–) Monacan princess/entertainer

Stephanopoulos, George (1961–) Am. political adviser (Clinton)

Stephen (c. 1097–1154) Eng. king 1135–1154 (son of Adela)

Sterling, Jan (Jane Sterling Adriance) (1923–) Am. actress (*Ace in the Hole*; *The High and the Mighty*)

Sterling, Robert (William John Hart) (1917–) Am. actor (*Only Angels Have Wings*; "Topper" TV series)

Stern, Daniel (1957–) Am. actor (*Home Alone*; *City Slickers*)

Stern, Howard (1954–) Am. "shock" disc jockey/TV host/writer (*Private Parts*)

Stern, Isaac (1920–) Russ.-Am. concert violinist

Stern, Otto (1888–1969) Ger.-Am. physicist (N—1943)

Sterne, Laurence (a/k/a Mister Yorick) (1713–1768) Eng. novelist (*Tristram Shandy*)

Stevens, Andrew (1955–) Am. actor (son of Stella; "Dallas" TV series)

Stevens, April (Carol Lo Tempio) (1936–) Am. pop singer ("Deep Purple"; sister of Nino Tempo, with whom she sang)

Stevens, Cat (Steven Demetre Georgiou; a/k/a Yusef Islam) (1947–) Eng. rock singer ("Peace Train"; "Morning Has Broken")

Stevens, Connie (Concetta Rosalie Ann Ingolia) (1938–) Am. actress/singer ("Kookie, Kookie [Lend Me Your Comb]")/actress ("Hawaiian Eye" TV series; mother of Tricia Leigh Fisher)

Stevens, Craig (Gail Hughes Shekles, Jr.) (1918–) Am. actor (TV's "Peter Gunn")

Stevens, Fisher (1963–) Am. actor (*Short Circuit*; *Mystery Date*; "Key West" TV series)

Stevens, George (George Cooper Stevens) (1904–1975) Am. film director (*Woman of the Year*; *Gunga Din*; O—1951—*A Place in the Sun*; O—1956—*Giant*)

Stevens, Inger (Inger Stensland) (1934–1970) Swed. actress ("The Farmer's Daughter" TV series; *Madigan*)

Stevens, John Paul III (1920–) Am. Supreme Court jurist (1975–)

Stevens, Ray (Harold Ray Ragsdale) (1939–) Am. pop singer ("Everything Is Beautiful"; "The Streak"; G—1970)

Stevens, Stella (Estelle Eggleston) (1936–) Am. actress (mother of Andrew; "Santa Barbara" soap opera; *The Nutty Professor*)

Stevens, Thaddeus (1792–1868) Am. lawyer/politician/abolitionist

Stevens, Wallace (1879–1955) Am. poet (P—1955—*Collected Poems*)

Stevenson, Adlai (Adlai Ewing Stevenson; "Egghead") (1835–1914) Am. v.p. (G. Cleveland)/politician

Stevenson, Adlai (Adlai Ewing Stevenson) (1900–1965) Am. politician (grandson of above; presidential candidate 1952, 1956)/writer (*Call to Greatness*)

Stevenson, McLean (1929–) Am. actor ("M*A*S*H" TV series)

Stevenson, Parker (Richard Stevenson Parker) (1952–) Am. actor ("The Hardy Boys Mysteries" and "Melrose Place" TV series)

Stevenson, Robert Louis (Robert Louis Balfour Stevenson) (1850–1894) Scot. novelist/poet/essayist (*Kidnapped*; *Treasure Island*; *The Strange Case of Dr. Jekyll and Mr. Hyde*)

Stewart, Al (1945–) Scot. rock singer/songwriter ("Year of the Cat"; "Time Passages")

Stewart, Catherine Mary (1959–) Am. actress (*The Last Starfighter*; *Mischief*)

Stewart, Dave (1952–) Eng. rock musician (with The Eurythmics)

Stewart, Donald Ogden (a/k/a Gilbert Holland) (1894–1980) Am. novelist/playwright/screenwriter (*The Philadelphia Story*; *Holiday*)

Stewart, Dugald (1753–1828) Scot. philosopher ("commonsense" philosophy)

Stewart, Jackie (John Young Stewart) (1939–) Scot. auto racer

Stewart, James (James Maitland Stewart; "Jimmy") (1908–) Am. actor (*It's a Wonderful Life*; *Rear Window*; *Vertigo*; *Mr. Smith Goes to Washington*; O—1940—*The Philadelphia Story*)

Stewart, Martha (1942–) Am. lifestyle expert/writer (*Martha Stewart's Guide to Good Living*)

Stewart, Potter (1915–1985) Am. Supreme Court jurist (1958–1981)

Stewart, Rod (Roderick David Stewart) (1945–) Scot. rock/pop singer ("Maggie May"; "Da Ya Think I'm Sexy?";

"Downtown Train"; formerly with Faces)

Stieglitz, Alfred ("Father of Modern Photography") (1864–1946) Am. photographer/editor (*Camera Work*)

Stiers, David Ogden (1942–) Am. actor ("M*A*S*H" TV series)

Stigers, Curtis (c. 1966–) Am. rock singer/saxophonist ("I Wonder Why")

Stiller, Ben (1965–) Am. comedian/actor (son of Jerry Stiller and Anne Meara; "The Ben Stiller Show" TV series)

Stiller, Jerry (Gerald Stiller) (1926–) Am. comedian/actor (with Anne Meara)

Stills, Stephen (1945–) Am. rock singer/guitarist ("Love the One You're With"; formerly with Buffalo Springfield and Crosby, Stills & Nash)

Sting (Gordon Matthew Sumner) (1951–) Eng. pop singer/musician ("If You Love Somebody Set Them Free"; formerly with The Police; G—1987)/actor (*The Bride*)

Stipe, Michael (1960–) Am. rock singer (with REM, "Losing My Religion")

Stitt, Sonny (Edward Stitt) (1924–1982) Am. jazz saxophonist

Stockman, David (David Allen Stockman) (1946–) Am. govt. official/writer (*The Triumph of Politics*)

Stockton, John (1962–) Am. basketball player

Stockwell, Dean (Robert Dean Stockwell) (1936–) Am. actor ("Quantum Leap" TV series; *Sons and Lovers*; *Blue Velvet*)

Stockwell, Guy (1936–) Am. actor (*Beau Geste*; *Anchors Aweigh*)

Stoker, Bram (Abraham Stoker) (1847–1912) Ir. writer (*Dracula*)

Stokowski, Leopold (Leopold Boleslawawicz Antoni Stanislaw Stokowski) (1882–1977) Am. orchestra conductor (featured in *Fantasia*)

Stoller, Mike (1933–) Am. pop songwriter (with Jerry Leiber, "Yakety Yak"; "Charlie Brown"; "Hound Dog")

Stoltz, Eric (1961–) Am. actor (*Mask*; *Say Anything . . .*; *The Waterdance*; *Killing Zoe*)

Stone, Doug (Doug Brooks) (1956–) Am. country singer ("I Thought It Was You")

Stone, Edward (Edward Durell Stone) (1902–1978) Am. architect (John F. Kennedy Center for the Performing Arts)

Stone, Harlan Fiske (1872–1946) Am. attorney general/Supreme Court chief justice (1941–1946)

Stone, I. F. (Isidor Feinstein Stone) (1907–1989) Am. journalist

Stone, Irving (Irving Tennenbaum) (1903–1989) Am. biographer/novelist (*Lust for Life*; *The Agony and the Ecstasy*)

Stone, Lewis (1879–1953) Am. actor (*Treasure Island*; *The Prisoner of Zenda*)

Stone, Lucy (a/k/a Mrs. Stone) (1818–1893) Am. suffragist

Stone, Milburn (Hugh Milburn Stone) (1904–1980) Am. actor ("Gunsmoke" TV series; E—1967/68)

Stone, Oliver (William Oliver Stone) (1946–) Am. film director (O—1986—*Platoon*; *Wall Street*; O—1989—*Born on the Fourth of July*; *JFK*)

Stone, Sharon (1958–) Am. actress (*Basic Instinct*; *Sliver*; *Total Recall*; *Intersection*)

Stone, Sly (Sylvester Stewart) (1943–) Am. rock/pop singer/musician ("Everyday People"; with Sly & The Family Stone)

Stookey, Paul (Noel Paul Stookey) (1937–) Am. pop singer/musician ("Wedding Song [There Is Love]"; formerly with Peter, Paul & Mary)

Stoppard, Tom (Thomas Straussler) (1937–) Cz.-Eng. playwright (*Rosencrantz and Guildenstern Are Dead*)

Storch, Larry (Lawrence Samuel Storch) (1923–) Am. comedian/actor ("F Troop" TV series)

Storm, Gale (Josephine Owaisca Cottle) (1922–) Am. actress ("My Little Margie" TV series)/singer ("I Hear You Knocking")

Stout, Rex (Rex Todhunter Stout) (1886–1975) Am. detective story writer (created Nero Wolfe; *Too Many Cooks*)

Stowe, Harriet Beecher (Harriet Elizabeth Beecher) (1811–1896) Am. novelist (daughter of Lyman Beecher; *Uncle Tom's Cabin*)

Stowe, Madeleine (1958–) Am. actress (*Unlawful Entry*; *The Last of the Mohicans*; *Short Cuts*; *Bad Girls*)

Strabo (64 or 63 B.C.–A.D. 24) Gr. geographer

Strachey, Lytton (Giles Lytton Strachey) (1880–1932) Eng. biographer/historian (*Queen Victoria*; *Eminent Victorians*)

Stradivari, Antonio (a/k/a Antonius Stradivarius) (1644–1737) Ital. violin maker

Stradlin, Izzy (Jeff Isabelle) (1967–) Am. rock guitarist (with Guns N' Roses)

Straight, Beatrice (Beatrice Whitney

Straight) (1916–) Am. actress (O—1976—*Network*)

Strait, George (1952–) Am. country singer ("You Look So Good in Love")

Strand, Mark (1934–) Can.-Am. poet (*The Story of Our Lives*)

Strand, Paul (1890–1976) Am. photographer/documentarist

Strange, Curtis (1955–) Am. golfer

Strasberg, Lee (Israel Strassberg) (1901–1982) Am. actor/drama teacher (father of Susan; "method" acting)

Strasberg, Susan (Susan Elizabeth Strasberg) (1938–) Am. actress (daughter of Lee; *Picnic*)

Strassman, Marcia (1948–) Am. actress ("Welcome Back, Kotter" TV series)

Stratemeyer, Edward L. (1862–1930) Am. writer (*Tom Swift*, the *Hardy Boys*, the *Bobbsey Twins*, and *Nancy Drew* books under numerous pseudonyms; father of Carolyn Keene)

Stratton, Dorothy (Dorothy Hoogstratten) (1960–1980) Can.-Am. *Playboy* centerfold/actress (murdered by her estranged husband; subject of the film *Star 80*)

Straub, Peter (Peter Francis Straub) (1943–) Am. horror novelist (*Koko*; *Floating Dragon*; *Ghost Story*)

Straus, Oscar (1870–1954) Aus.-Fr. composer (*The Chocolate Soldier*)

Strauss, Johann (Johann Baptist Strauss; "The Father of the Waltz") (1804–1849) Aus. composer (*The Blue Danube*; *Tales from the Vienna Woods*)

Strauss, Levi (1829–1902) Am. manufacturer (introduced denim jeans)

Strauss, Peter (1942–) Am. actor (*Rich Man, Poor Man*)

Strauss, Richard (Richard Georg Strauss) (1864–1949) Ger. composer (*Thus Spake Zarathustra*; *Der Rosenkavalier*)

Stravinsky, Igor (Igor Fyodorovich Stravinsky) (1882–1971) Am. composer (*Petrushka*; *The Firebird*)

Strawberry, Darryl (Darryl Eugene Strawberry) (1962–) Am. baseball player

Strayhorn, Billy (William Thomas Strayhorn) (1915–1967) Am. jazz pianist/composer ("Lush Life"; "Take the 'A' Train")

Streep, Meryl (Mary Louise Streep) (1949–) Am. actress (*The Deer Hunter*; *The French Lieutenant's Woman*; O—1979—*Kramer vs. Kramer*; O—1982—*Sophie's Choice*)

Streeter, Edward (1892–1976) Am. novelist (*Father of the Bride*)

Streisand, Barbra (Barbara Joan Streisand) (1942–) Am. actress (*The Way We Were*; O—1968—*Funny Girl*)/film director (*The Prince of Tides*)/singer ("People"; "Woman in Love"; "You Don't Bring Me Flowers" [with Neil Diamond]; G—1963, 1964, 1965, 1977, 1986)

Strieber, Whitley (1945–) Am. horror novelist (*The Hunger*; *The Wolfen*; *Warday*)

Strindberg, August (Johan August Strindberg) (1849–1912) Swed. playwright/novelist/poet (*The Creditors*; *The Father*; *Miss Julie*)

Stringbean (David Akeman) (1915–1973) Am. country banjo player/comedian ("Hee Haw" TV series)

Stritch, Elaine (1925–) Am. singer/actress (*A Farewell to Arms*)

Strong, Ken (Kenneth E. Strong) (1906–1978) Am. football Hall-of-Famer

Stroud, Robert ("The Birdman of Alcatraz") (1890–1963) Am. murderer/ornithologist

Strudwick, Shepperd (a/k/a John Shepperd) (1907–1983) Am. actor (*The Loves of Edgar Allan Poe*; *Joan of Arc*)

Strummer, Joe (John Mellors) (1952–) Eng. rock guitarist/singer (with The Clash; "Train in Vain")

Strunk, Jud (Justin Strunk, Jr.) (1936–1981) Am. singer/comedian ("Rowan & Martin's Laugh-In" TV series)

Struthers, Sally (Sally Anne Struthers) (1948–) Am. actress ("All in the Family" TV series; E—1971/72)

Stuart, Chad (1943–) Eng. pop singer (with Chad and Jeremy)

Stuart, Dick (Richard Lee Stuart; "Dr. Strangelove") (1932–) Am. baseball player

Stuart, Gilbert (Gilbert Charles Stuart) (1755–1828) Am. painter (portrait head of George Washington)

Stuart, J. E. B. (James Ewell Brown Stuart; "Jeb") (1833–1864) Am. Civil War brigadier general

Stuart, Marty (John Marty Stuart) (1958–) Am. country singer ("Tempted")

Stubbs, George (1724–1806) Eng. painter (horses)

Sturgeon, Theodore (Theodore Hamilton Sturgeon; born Edward Hamilton Waldo) (1918–1985) Am. science fiction writer (*The Golden Helix*; *More Than Human*)/TV scriptwriter ("Star Trek")

Sturges, John (John Eliot Sturges) (1911–1992) Am. film director (*Gunfight at the OK Corral*; *Bad Day at Black Rock*)

Sturges, Preston (Edmund Preston Biden) (1898–1959) Am. playwright/film director (*The Palm Beach Story*; *The Great McGinty*; *The Miracle of Morgan's Creek*)

Stuyvesant, Peter (Petrus Stuyvesant) (c. 1610–1672) early Am. administrator

Stydahar, Joe (Joseph Leo Stydahar; "Jumbo Joe") (1912–1977) Am. football Hall-of-Famer

Styne, Jule (Julius Kerwin Stein) (1905–) Am. composer ("Funny Girl"; "Three Coins in the Fountain"; with Sammy Cahn)

Styron, William (William Clark Styron, Jr.) (1925–) Am. novelist (*Lie Down in Darkness*; P—1968—*The Confessions of Nat Turner*; *Sophie's Choice*)

Suggs, Louise (1923–) Am. golfer

Sukarno (Kusnasosro) (1901–1970) Indon. pres. 1949–1967

Sullavan, Margaret (Margaret Brooke Sullavan) (1911–1960) Am. actress (*The Good Fairy*; *Back Street*)

Sullivan, Anne (1866–1936) Am. teacher of Helen Keller

Sullivan, Sir Arthur (Arthur Seymour Sullivan) (1842–1900) Am. composer (with W. S. Gilbert; *H. M. S. Pinafore*; *The Mikado*)

Sullivan, Barry (Patrick Francis Barry Sullivan) (1912–) Am. actor ("The Tall Man" TV series; *The Great Gatsby*)

Sullivan, Ed (Edward Vincent Sullivan) (1902–1974) Am. TV host ("The Ed Sullivan Show"; signature phrase: "We have a really big show")

Sullivan, Frank (Francis John Sullivan) (1892–1976) Am. columnist/humorist (created Mr. Arbuthnot)

Sullivan, John L. (John Lawrence Sullivan; "The Great John"; "The Boston Strong Boy") (1858–1918) Am. boxer

Sullivan, Kathleen (1954–) Am. newscaster

Sullivan, Louis (Louis Henry Sullivan) (1856–1924) Am. architect (Chicago's Auditorium building)

Sullivan, Pat (1887–1933) Austral.-Am. animator/cartoonist (*Felix the Cat*)

Sullivan, Susan (1944–) Am. actress ("Falcon Crest" TV series; Tylenol commercials)

Sully, Thomas (1783–1872) Am. portrait painter

Sumac, Yma (Emperatriz Chavarri Yma Sumac) (1922–) Peruv. singer

Summer, Cree (1970–) Am. actress ("A Different World" TV series)

Summer, Donna (Ladonna Andrea Gaines) (1948–) Am. disco/pop singer ("Love to Love You Baby"; "Hot Stuff"; "She Works Hard for the Money")

Summerall, Pat (George Summerall; "The Gary Cooper of Sportscasters") (1931–) Am. sportscaster

Summers, Andy (Andrew Somers) (1942–) Eng. rock guitarist (with The Police)

Summerville, Slim (George J. Summerville) (1892–1946) Am. actor (*All Quiet on the Western Front*; *King of the Rodeo*)

Sumner, Charles (1811–1874) Am. senator/abolitionist

Sundance Kid, The (Harry Longabaugh) (died 1909) Am. western outlaw

Sunday, Billy (William Ashley Sunday; "The Huckster of the Tabernacle") (1863–1935) Am. evangelist

Sununu, John H. (John Henry Sununu) (1939–) Am. politician (gov. of New Hampshire; member of Bush administration)

Sun Yat-Sen (Sun Wen; a/k/a Sun I-Hsein and Sun Chung-shan) (1866–1925) Chin. statesman/revolutionary leader

Susann, Jacqueline (1921–1974) Am. novelist (*Valley of the Dolls*; *Once Is Not Enough*)

Susskind, David (David Howard Susskind) (1920–1987) Am. TV host/producer ("Philco TV Playhouse")

Sutherland, Donald (Donald McNichol Sutherland) (1934–) Can.-Am. actor (*M*A*S*H*; *Ordinary People*; *Klute*)

Sutherland, Dame Joan (1926–) Austral. opera singer (soprano)

Sutherland, Kiefer (1966–) Am. actor (son of Donald; *Flatliners*; *The Lost Boys*)

Sutter, John (John Augustus Sutter; born Johann August Suter) (1803–1880) Am. pioneer (founded a colony at Sacramento, CA)

Sutton, Don (Donald Howard Sutton) (1945–) Am. baseball pitcher

Sutton, Grady (1908–) Am. actor (*The Bank Dick*; *My Man Godfrey*)

Sutton, Hal (Hal Evan Sutton) (1958–) Am. golfer

Sutton, Willie (William Francis Sutton;

"Willie the Actor") (1901–1980) Am. bank robber/writer (*Where the Money Was*)

Svenson, Bo (1941–) Am. actor (*North Dallas Forty*; *Heartbreak Ridge*)

Swaggart, Jimmy (Jimmy Lee Swaggart) (1935–) Am. evangelist (cousin of Jerry Lee Lewis; involved in prostitution scandals)

Swann, Lynn (Lynn Curtis Swann) (1952–) Am. football player

Swanson, Gloria (Gloria Mae Josephine Svensson; a/k/a Gloria Mae) (1899–1983) Am. actress (*Queen Kelly*; *Sunset Boulevard*)

Swarthout, Gladys (1904–1969) Am. opera singer/actress

Swayze, John Cameron (1906–) Am. newscaster

Swayze, Patrick ("Buddy") (1952–) Am. actor (*Dirty Dancing*; *Ghost*; *City of Joy*)

Sweet, Blanche (Daphne Wayne) (1895–1986) Am. actress (*Anna Christie*; *Tess of the D'Urbervilles*)

Sweet, Dolph (Adolphus Jean Sweet) (1920–1985) Am. actor ("Gimme a Break" TV series; "Another World" soap opera)

Swenson, Inga (1932–) Am. actress ("Benson" TV series)

Swift, Jonathan (a/k/a Isaac Bickerstaff) (1667–1745) Eng. poet/political satirist (*Gulliver's Travels*)

Swinburne, Algernon (Algernon Charles Swinburne) (1837–1909) Eng. poet (*Atalanta in Calydon*)

Swing, Raymond Gram ("The Best-Known Voice in the World") (1887–1968) Am. radio commentator

Swit, Loretta (1937–) Am. actress ("M*A*S*H" TV series; E—1979/80, 1981/82)

Switzer, Carl (1926–1959) Am. child actor ("Our Gang" [as Alfalfa] TV series)

Swoboda, Ron (Ronald Alan Swoboda; "Rocky") (1944–) Am. baseball player

Swope, Herbert (Herbert Bayard Swope) (1882–1958) Am. journalist (P—1917)/writer (*Inside the German Empire*)

Sylvia (Sylvia Kirby Allen) (1956–) Am. country singer ("Nobody")

Sylvie (Louise Sylvain) (1883–1970) Fr. actress (*The Adulteress*; *The Shameless Old Lady*)

Syms, Sylvia (1918–1992) Am. singer ("I Could Have Danced All Night")

Synge, John (John Millington Synge) (1871–1909) Ir. playwright (*The Playboy of the Western World*; *Riders to the Sea*)

Szell, George (Georg Szell) (1897–1970) Hung.-Am. orchestra conductor (Cleveland Symphony)

Szymanowski, Karol (Karol Maciej Szymanowski) (1882–1937) Pol. composer (*Stabat Mater*)

Tabackin, Lew (1940–) Am. jazz saxophonist (with Toshiko Akiyoshi)

Tacitus (Cornelius Tacitus) (c. 56–c. 120) Roman historian/orator (*Germania*)

Taft, Helen (Helen Herron; "Nellie") (1861–1943) Am. first lady (William)

Taft, William (William Howard Taft) (1857–1930) 27th Am. pres. (1909–1913)/Supreme Court chief justice (1921–1930)

Tagore, Sir Rabindranath (Rabindrath Thakur) (1861–1941) Ind. poet (*Chitra*)/playwright (*Mukta Dhara*)/novelist (*Gora*; N—1913)

Taine, Hippolyte (Hippolyte-Adolphe Taine) (1828–1893) Fr. philosopher/critic/historian (*History of English Literature*)

Taisho (a/k/a Yoshihito) (1879–1926) Jap. emperor 1912–1926

Tai Thai ("The Elvis of Vietnam") (c. 1968–) Viet.-Am. actor (*The Waterdance*; *Killing Zoe*; *Heaven and Earth*)

Takei, George (1940–) Am. actor (Sulu in *Star Trek* TV series and films)

Talbot, Lyle (Lysle Henderson) (1904–1987) Am. actor ("The Bob Cummings Show" and "Ozzie and Harriet" TV series)

Talese, Gay (1932–) Am. writer (*Thy Neighbor's Wife*)

Tallchief, Maria (Elizabeth Marie Tallchief) (1925–) Am. ballerina (founded the Chicago City Ballet)

Talley, Nedra (1947–) Am. pop singer (with The Ronettes)

Talleyrand (Charles Maurice de Talleyrand-Perigord, Prince de Benevent) (1754–1838) Fr. statesman/diplomat

Talmadge, Constance (1898–1973) Am. actress (sister of Norma; *Intolerance*)

Talmadge, Norma (1893–1957) Am. actress (*Camille*; *A Tale of Two Cities* [1911])

Tamblyn, Russ (1934–) Am. dancer/actor (*West Side Story*; *Seven Brides for Seven Brothers*)

Tambo, Oliver (1917–1993) S. Afr. political activist (head of the ANC)

Tamerlane (a/k/a Tamburlaine; Timur; Timur Lenk [Timur the Lame]; "The Prince of Destruction") (1336–1405) Turk. Mongol ruler

Tamiroff, Akim (1899–1972) Am. actor (*For Whom the Bell Tolls*; *The Way of All Flesh*)

Tan, Amy (1952–) Chin.-Am. novelist (*The Joy Luck Club*; *The Kitchen God's Wife*)

Tanana, Frank (Frank Darryl Tanana) (1953–) Am. baseball pitcher

Tandy, Jessica (1909–) Eng.-Am. actress (*Cocoon*; *Fried Green Tomatoes*; O— 1989—*Driving Miss Daisy*; T—1948, 1978, 1983)

Taney, Roger B. (Roger Brooke Taney; "King Coody") (1777–1864) Am. Supreme Court chief justice (1836–1864)

Tanguy, Yves (1900–1955) Fr.-Am. surrealist painter

Tanner, Roscoe (Leonard Roscoe Tanner III; "Cannonball Kid") (1951–) Am. tennis player

Tarantino, Quentin (1963–) Am. film director (*Reservoir Dogs*; *Pulp Fiction*; *True Romance*)

Tarbell, Ida (Ida Minerva Tarbell) (1857–1944) Am. journalist/biographer (*The History of the Standard Oil Company*)

Tarkanian, Jerry ("Tark the Shark") (1930–) Am. basketball coach

Tarkenton, Fran (Francis Asbury Tarkenton; "The Scrambler") (1940–) Am. football Hall-of-Famer/sportscaster

Tarkington, Booth (Newton Booth Tarkington) (1869–1946) Am. novelist/playwright (P—1919—*The Magnificent Ambersons*; P—1922—*Alice Adams*)

Tarkovsky, Andre (1932–1986) Russ. film director (*Solaris*; *Stalker*; *The Sacrifice*)

Tarnower, Herman ("The Scarsdale Diet Doctor") (1910–1980) Am. physician/dietician (murdered by his lover Jean Harris)

Tartikoff, Brandon (1949–) Am. entertainment executive

Tartt, Donna (c. 1964–) Am. novelist (*The Secret History*)

Tashman, Lilyan (Lillian Tashman) (1899–1934) Am. actress (*Frankie and Johnny* [1933]; *No No Nanette*)

Tasman, Abel Janszoon (c. 1603–1659) Dutch explorer (discovered Tasmania, New Zealand, Tonga, and Fiji)

Tate, Allen (John Orley Allen Tate) (1899–

1979) Am. poet/critic/biographer (*Stonewall Jackson*)

Tate, Sharon (1943–1969) Am. actress (*Valley of the Dolls*; murdered by followers of Charles Manson)

Tati, Jacques (Jacques Tatischeff) (1908–1982) Fr. actor (*Mon Oncle*; *Mr. Hulot's Holiday*)

Tatum, Art (Arthur Tatum) (1910–1956) Am. jazz pianist

Tatum, Goose (Reese Tatum; "The Clown Prince of Basketball") (1921–1967) Am. basketball player (with the Harlem Globetrotters)

Taupin, Bernie (1950–) Eng. lyricist (with Elton John)

Taurog, Norman (1899–1981) Am. film director (*Boys Town*; O—1930/31—*Skippy*)

Tavernier, Bertrand (1941–) Fr. film director ('*Round Midnight*; *Coup De Terchon*)

Tayback, Vic (Victor Tabback) (1929–1990) Am. actor ("*Alice*" TV series)

Taylor, A. J. P. (Alan John Percivale Taylor) (1906–1990) Eng. historian/journalist (*The Origins of the Second World War*)

Taylor, Andy (1961–) Eng. rock guitarist (with Duran Duran and The Power Station)

Taylor, Billy (William Edward Taylor) (1921–) Am. jazz pianist

Taylor, Charley (1942–) Am. football Hall-of-Famer

Taylor, Deems (Joseph Deems Taylor) (1885–1966) Am. composer ("The Siren Song")/writer (*The Well Tempered Listener*)

Taylor, Elizabeth (Elizabeth Rosemond Taylor; "Liz") (1932–) Am. actress (*National Velvet*; *Cat on a Hot Tin Roof*; O—1960—*Butterfield 8*; O—1966—*Who's Afraid of Virginia Woolf?*; *Cleopatra*)

Taylor, Estelle (Estelle Boylan) (1899–1958) Am. actress (*Don Juan*; *Cimarron*)

Taylor, James (James Vernon Taylor; "Sweet Baby James") (1948–) Am. rock singer/songwriter/musician ("Fire and Rain"; "You've Got a Friend"; "Handy Man"; G—1971, 1977)

Taylor, Jim (James Taylor) (1935–) Am. football Hall-of-Famer

Taylor, Lawrence (Lawrence Julius Taylor) (1959–) Am. football player

Taylor, Lili (c. 1967–) Am. actress (*Dogfight*; *Mystic Pizza*; *Household Saints*)

Taylor, Mick (1948–) Eng. rock guitarist (with The Rolling Stones)

Taylor, Niki (c. 1974–) Am. model

Taylor, Paul (Paul Belville Taylor, Jr.) (1930–) Am. dancer/choreographer

Taylor, Peter (Peter Matthew Hillsman Taylor) (1917–) Am. writer (P—1987—A *Summons to Memphis*)

Taylor, Rip (1934–) Am. comedian ("The Gong Show" TV series)

Taylor, Robert (Spangler Arlington Brugh; "The Man with the Perfect Profile") (1911–1969) Am. actor (*Magnificent Obsession*; "Death Valley Days" TV series)

Taylor, Rod (Rodney Stuart Taylor; a/k/a Rodney Taylor) (1929–) Austral.-Am. actor (*The Time Machine*; *Billy the Kid*; *The Birds*; "Falcon Crest" TV series)

Taylor, Tom (1817–1880) Eng. playwright (*Our American Cousin*)

Taylor, William Desmond (William Cunningham Deane Tanner) (1877–1922) Ir.-Am. film director (*Huckleberry Finn*; *Tom Sawyer*)

Taylor, Zachary ("Old Rough and Ready") (1784–1850) 12th Am. pres. (1849–1850)

Taylor-Young, Leigh (1944–) Am. actress (*I Love You, Alice B. Toklas*; *Soylent Green*)

Tchaikovsky, Peter Ilyich (a/k/a Pyotr Ilich Tchaikovsky) (1840–1893) Russ. composer (*Swan Lake*; *The Nutcracker Suite*; *The Sleeping Beauty*)

Teagarden, Jack (Weldon John Teagarden; "Big T") (1905–1964) Am. jazz trombonist/bandleader

Tearle, Conway (Frederick Levy) (1878–1938) Am. actor (half brother of Godfrey; *Vanity Fair*)

Tearle, Sir Godfrey (1884–1953) Eng. actor (*One of Our Aircraft Is Missing*; *The Thirty-Nine Steps*)

Teasdale, Sara (Sara Trevor Teasdale) (1884–1933) Am. poet (P—1918—*Love Songs*)

Teasdale, Verree (1904–1987) Am. actress (*Roman Scandals*; *A Midsummer Night's Dream*)

Tebaldi, Renata (1922–) Ital. opera singer (soprano)

Teicher, Louis (1924–) Am. pianist (with Arthur Ferrante; for film; *Exodus*; *Midnight Cowboy*)

Teilhard de Chardin, Pierre (Marie-Joseph-Pierre Teilhard de Chardin) (1881–1955) Fr. theologian

Tekulve, Kent (Kenton Charles Tekulve; "The Book End"; "Mr. Bones") (1947–) Am. baseball pitcher

Telemann, Georg (Georg Philipp Telemann) (1681–1767) Ger. composer

Teller (uses only one name) (1948—) Am. comedian/writer (with Penn & Teller)

Teller, Edward ("Father of the Hydrogen Bomb") (1908–) Am. physicist (worked on the Manhattan Project and the Strategic Defense Initiative, a/k/a Star Wars; with Igor Kurchatov, invented the hydrogen bomb)

Tempest, Dame Marie (Marie Susan Etherington) (1864–1942) Eng. stage actress

Temple, Shirley (Shirley Janet Temple; a/k/a Shirley Temple-Black) (1928–) Am. child actress (*Curly Top*; *The Little Princess*)/diplomat

Templeton, Garry (Garry Lewis Templeton; "Jump Steady"; "Tempy") (1956–) Am. baseball player

Tempo, Nino (Antonio Lo Tempio) (1935–) Am. pop singer ("Deep Purple"; brother of April Stevens, with whom he sang)

Tennant, Emma (1937–1988) Eng. novelist (*The Bad Sister*)

Tennant, Kylie (1912–) Austral. novelist (*Tiburon*)

Tennant, Neil (1954–) Eng. rock singer (with The Pet Shop Boys; "West End Girls")

Tennant, Victoria (1950–) Eng. actress (*All of Me*; *L.A. Story*)

Tenniel, Sir John (1820–1914) Eng. illustrator/cartoonist (*Punch* magazine)

Tennille, Toni (Cathryn Antoinette Tennille) (1943–) Am. pop singer/entertainer (with The Captain & Tennille; "Love Will Keep Us Together")

Tennyson, Alfred Lord (1809–1892) Eng. poet (*The Charge of the Light Brigade*; *Idylls of the King*)

Tenuta, Judy (C) Am. comedienne

Terborch, Gerard (a/k/a Gerard Ter Borch) (1617–1681) Dutch painter (*The Reading Lesson*)

Terence (Publius Terentius Afer) (186 or 185–159 B.C.) Roman playwright (*The Woman from Andros*)

Terhune, Albert (Albert Payson Terhune) (1872–1942) Am. writer (*Lad: A Dog*)

Terkel, Studs (Studs Louis Terkel) (1912–) Am. interviewer/writer (*Working*; *The Great Divide*; P—1985—*The Good War*)/broadcaster

Terranova, Ciro ("The Artichoke King") (1891–1938) Am. Mafia boss

Terrell, Mary Church (1863–1954) Am.

civil rights activist/writer (*A Colored Woman in a White World*)

Terrell, Tammi (1946–1970) Am. soul/pop singer (duets with Marvin Gaye; "Your Precious Love")

Terry, Bill (William Harold Terry; "Memphis Bill") (1896–1989) Am. baseball Hall-of-Famer

Terry, Dame Ellen (Ellen Alicia Terry) (1847–1928) Eng. stage actress

Terry, Lucy (c. 1730–1821) Am. poet

Terry-Thomas (Thomas Terry Hoar-Stevens; a/k/a Thomas Terry) (1911–1990) Eng. actor (*How to Murder Your Wife*; *It's a Mad, Mad, Mad, Mad World*)

Tertullian (Quintus Septimius Florens Tertullianus) (c. 155–after 220) Latin church father/ecclesiastical writer (*Apologeticum*)

Tesh, John (1952–) Am. TV host ("Entertainment Tonight")

Tesla, Nikola (1856–1943) Am. electrician/inventor (induction motor)

Testaverde, Vinny ("Miami Nice") (1963–) Am. football player

Tetrazzini, Luisa (1871–1940) Ital. opera singer (soprano)

Tewes, Lauren (1953–) Am. actress ("The Love Boat" TV series)

Tex, Joe (Joseph Arrington, Jr.; a/k/a Joseph Hazziez) (1933–1982) Am. blues singer/songwriter ("I Gotcha")

Tey, Josephine (Elizabeth Mackintosh; a/k/a Gordon Daviot) (1897–1952) Scot. novelist (*The Daughter of Time*)

Thackeray, William Makepeace (a/k/a Michael Angelo Titmarsh, Charles James Yellowplush, George Savage Fitzboodle, Jeames, Mr. Brown, and Theophile Wagstaff) (1811–1863) Am. novelist (*Barry Lyndon*; *Vanity Fair*)

Thalberg, Irving (Irving Grant Thalberg; "The Boy Wonder") (1899–1936) Am. film producer (*Grand Hotel*; *Mutiny on the Bounty*)

Thales (a/k/a Thales of Miletus) (c. 624–c. 546 B.C.) Gr. philosopher (one of the Seven Wise Men of Greece)

Thant, U (1909–1974) Bur. statesman/United Nations secretary general

Tharp, Twyla (1941–) Am. dancer/choreographer (jazz ballets)

Thatcher, Margaret (Margaret Hilda Roberts; "Iron Lady"; "Maggie") (1925–) Eng. politician/prime minister 1979–1991/writer (*The Downing Street Years*)

Thatcher, Torin (Torin Herbert Erskine Thatcher) (1905–1981) Eng. actor (*Witness for the Prosecution*; *Great Expectations*)

Themistocles (524–462 B.C.) Ath. statesman/mil. leader

Theocritus (c. 310–250 B.C.) Gr. poet (*Idyls*)

Theodore I (Fyodor I Ivanovich) (1557–1598) Russ. czar 1584–1598

Theodore II (Fyodor II Borisovich) (1589–1605) Russ. czar 1605

Theodore III (Fyodor III Alekseyevich) (1661–1682) Russ. czar 1676–1682

Theodosius The Great (347–395) Roman general/emperor 379–395

Theroux, Paul (Paul Edward Theroux) (1941–) Am. novelist/travel writer (*The Mosquito Coast*)

Thespis (6th century B.C.) Gr. poet/dramatist (the word *thespian* comes from his name)

Thicke, Alan (1947–) Can.-Am. actor ("Growing Pains" TV series)/talk show host ("Thicke of the Night")

Thigpen, Bobby (Robert Thomas Thigpen) (1963–) Am. baseball pitcher

Thomas, B. J. (Billy Joe Thomas) (1942–) Am. country singer ("Raindrops Keep Fallin' on My Head"; "Hooked on a Feeling")

Thomas, Clarence (1948–) Am. Supreme Court jurist (1991–)

Thomas, Danny (Amos Muzyad Yakhoob) (1914–1991) Am. comedian/actor (father of Marlo; "Make Room for Daddy" and "The Danny Thomas Show" TV series; E—1954)

Thomas, Dave (R. David Thomas) (1932–) Am. restauranteur (founded Wendy's fast food)

Thomas, Debi (1967–) Am. figure skater

Thomas, Dylan (Dylan Marlais Thomas) (1914–1953) Wel. poet (*A Child's Christmas in Wales*; *Under Milk Wood*)

Thomas, Heather (1957–) Am. actress ("The Fall Guy" TV series)

Thomas, Henry (1972–) Am. child actor (*E.T.: The Extra-Terrestrial*)

Thomas, Jay (c. 1949–) Am. disc jockey/actor ("Love and War" TV series)

Thomas, Kurt (1956–) Am. gymnast

Thomas, Lowell (Lowell Jackson Thomas) (1892–1981) Am. newscaster/writer (*With Lawrence in Arabia*)

Thomas, Marlo (Margaret Julia Thomas) (1938–) Am. actress (daughter of Danny; TV's "That Girl")

Thomas, Michael Tilson (1944–) Am. orchestra conductor

Thomas, Norman (Norman Mattoon Thomas) (1884–1968) Am. politician/socialist (helped found the ACLU)

Thomas, Philip Michael (1949–) Am. actor ("Miami Vice" TV series)

Thomas, Richard (Richard Earl Thomas) (1951–) Am. actor (John-Boy in "The Waltons" TV series; E—1972/73)

Thomas, Seth (1785–1859) Am. clock manufacturer

Thompson, David (David O'Neil Thompson) (1954–) Am. basketball player

Thompson, Dorothy ("The Contemporary Cassandra") (1894–1961) Am. journalist/writer (The Courage To Be Happy)

Thompson, Emma (1959–) Eng. actress (Peter's Friends; Much Ado About Nothing; The Remains of the Day; O— 1993—Howard's End)

Thompson, Hunter S. (Hunter Stockton Thompson; a/k/a Sebastian Owl) (1939–) Am. "gonzo" journalist/writer (Hell's Angels; Fear and Loathing in Las Vegas)

Thompson, Jim (1906–1977) Am. novelist (The Grifters; After Dark, My Sweet)

Thompson, Lea (1961–) Am. actress (Casual Sex?; The Wizard of Loneliness; Back to the Future films)

Thompson, Milt (Milton Bernard Thompson) (1959–) Am. baseball player

Thompson, Randall (1899–1984) Am. composer (Festival of Freedom)

Thompson, Robby (Robert Randall Thompson) (1962–) Am. baseball player

Thompson, Sada (Sada Carolyn Thompson) (1929–) Am. actress ("Family" TV series; E—1977/78; T—1972)

Thompson, Tommy (Thomas George Thompson) (1941–) Am. gov. of Wisconsin

Thomson, Bobby (Robert Brown Thomson; "The Staten Island Scot"; "The Shot Heard Round the World") (1923–) Am. baseball player

Thomson, Virgil (Virgil Garnett Thomson) (1897–1989) Am. composer (P—1949—Louisiana Story)/music critic

Thoreau, Henry David (David Henry Thoreau; "The Concord Rebel"; "The Sage of Walden Pond"; "The Poet Naturalist") (1817–1862) Am. poet/essayist (Walden; Civil Disobedience)

Thornburgh, Richard (1932–) Am. govt. official (attorney general)

Thorndike, Dame Sybil (Agnes Sybil Thorndike) (1882–1976) Eng. stage/film actress (Nicholas Nickleby)

Thorne-Smith, Courtney (C) Am. actress ("Melrose Place" TV series)

Thorogood, George (1951–) Am. rock singer/musician (with The Destroyers; "Willie and the Hand Jive")

Thorpe, Jim (James Francis Thorpe) (1888–1953) Am. football Hall-of-Famer

Thrale, Mrs. (Hester Lynch Thrale; a/k/a Hester Thrale Piozzi; born Hester Salusbury) (1741–1821) Eng. writer (Anecdotes of the Late Samuel Johnson)

Throckmorton, Cleon (1897–1965) Am. fashion designer

Throneberry, Marv (Marvin Eugene Throneberry; "Marvelous Marv"; "Born to Be a Met") (1933–) Am. baseball player

Thucydides (c. 455–400 B.C.) Gr. historian (History of the Peloponnesian War)

Thulin, Ingrid (1929–) Swed. actress (Cries and Whispers; The Damned)

Thurber, James (James Grover Thurber) (1894–1961) Am. essayist/short story writer/humorist (The Secret Life of Walter Mitty)

Thurman, Uma (Uma Karuna Thurman) (1970–) Am. actress (Dangerous Liaisons; Jennifer 8; Mad Dog and Glory; Even Cowgirls Get the Blues)

Thurmond, Strom (James Strom Thurmond) (1902–) Am. lawyer/senator

Thurow, Lester (Lester Carl Thurow) (1938–) Am. economist/educator

Tiant, Luis (Luis Clemente Tiant Vega) (1940–) Cub.-Am. baseball pitcher

Tiberius (Tiberius Claudius Nero Caesar Augustus) (42 B.C.–A.D. 37) Roman emperor 14–37

Tickner, Charlie (Charles Tickner) (1953–) Am. figure skater

Ticknor, George (1791–1871) Am. historian/scholar/writer (History of Spanish Literature)

Ticotin, Rachel (1958–) Am. actress (Total Recall; Raging Bull; Fort Apache, the Bronx)

Tieck, Ludwig (Johann Ludwig Tieck) (1773–1853) Ger. writer (Puss in Boots)

Tiegs, Cheryl (1947–) Am. model

Tiepolo, Giovanni (Giovanni Battista Tiepolo) (1696–1770) Ital. painter (Adoration of the Magi)

Tierney, Gene (Gene Eliza Taylor

Tierney) (1920–1991) Am. actress (*Laura*; *Leave Her to Heaven*)
Tiffany (Tiffany Renee Darwish) (1971–) Am. pop singer ("I Think We're Alone Now")
Tiffany, Charles (Charles Lewis Tiffany) (1812–1902) Am. jeweler (founded Tiffany & Co.)
Tiffany, Louis (Louis Comfort Tiffany) (1848–1933) Am. designer/glassmaker/painter
Tiffin, Pamela (Pamela Kimberley Tiffin Wonso) (1942–) Am. actress (*State Fair*; *The Pleasure Seekers*)
Tikaram, Tanita (1969–) Ger.-Eng. pop singer ("Twist in My Sobriety")
Tilbrook, Glenn (1957–) Eng. rock singer/musician/songwriter (with Squeeze and Difford & Tilbrook)
Tilden, Bill (William Tatem Tilden II; "Big Bill"; "Court Jouster") (1893–1953) Am. tennis player
Tildy, Zoltán (1889–1961) Hung. premier 1945/pres. 1946–1948
Tillich, Paul (Paul Johannes Tillich) (1886–1965) Am. theologian/philosopher/writer (*Systematic Theology*)
Tillis, Mel (Lonnie Melvin Tillis) (1932–) Am. country singer ("I Ain't Never"; "Good Woman Blues")
Tillis, Pam (1957–) Am. country singer (daughter of Mel)
Tillstrom, Burr (1917–1985) Am. puppeteer (created Kukla and Ollie of "Kukla, Fran & Ollie")
Tilly, Jennifer (1958–) Can.-Am. actress (sister of Meg; *Made in America*; *Shadow of the Wolf*)
Tilly, Meg (1960–) Can.-Am. actress (*Agnes of God*; *The Big Chill*; *Leaving Normal*)
Tilton, Charlene (1958–) Am. actress ("Dallas" TV series)
Timerman, Jacobo (1923–) Arg. newspaper publisher (founded *La Opinión*)
Tinker, Grant (Grant Almerin Tinker) (1926–) Am. TV executive (pres. of MTM Enterprises)
Tinker, Joe (Joseph Bert Tinker) (1880–1948) Am. baseball Hall-of-Famer
Tintoretto (Jacopo Robusti) (1518–1594) Ital. mannerist painter (*Christ and the Adulteress*)
Tiny Tim (Herbert David Khaury) (1922–) Am. novelty singer ("Tip-Toe Thru' the Tulips with Me")
Tiomkin, Dmitri (1899–1979) Russ.-Am. film composer (*Lost Horizon*; *High Noon*; *Giant*)
Tippin, Aaron ("Tip"; "Little Tip") (1958–) Am. country singer ("There Ain't Nothing Wrong with the Radio")
Titian (Tiziano Vecelli or Vechelio) (1488 or 1490–1576) Ital. painter (studied under Giovanni Bellini; *Pietá*)
Tito (Josip Broz) (1892–1980) Yug. pres. 1953–1980
Tittle, Y. A. (Yelberton Abraham Tittle; "YAT") (1926–) Am. football Hall-of-Famer
Titus (Titus Flavius Sabinus Vespasianus) (39–81) Roman emperor 79–81
Tjader, Cal (1925–1982) Am. jazz musician
Tobias, Andy (Andrew Previn Tobias) (1947–) Am. financial columnist/writer (*The Only Investment Guide You'll Ever Need*)
Tobias, George (1901–1980) Am. actor (*The Glenn Miller Story*; "Bewitched" TV series)
Toch, Ernst (1887–1964) Am. composer (P—1956—*Symphony No. 3*)
Tocqueville, Count Alexis de (Alexis-Charles Henri Clerel de Tocqueville) (1805–1859) Fr. historian/philosopher (*Democracy in America*)
Todd, Ann (1909–1993) Eng. actress (*The Seventh Veil*; *The Paradine Case*)
Todd, Mike or Michael (Avrom Hirsch Goldbogen) (1909–1958) Am. film producer (*Around the World in Eighty Days*; *Oklahoma!*)
Todd, Richard (Richard Andrew Palethorpe-Todd) (1919–) Eng. actor (*Robin Hood* [1952]; *The Hasty Heart*)
Todd, Thelma ("Hot Toddy"; "The Ice Cream Blonde") (1905–1935) Am. actress (*Monkey Business*; *The Maltese Falcon*)
Todman, Bill (William Selden Todman) (1916–1979) Am. game show producer (with Mark Goodson)
Toffler, Alvin (1928–) Am. writer (*Future Shock*)
Tognazzi, Ugo (1922–1990) Ital. actor (*La Cage Aux Folles*)
Tojo, Hideki (Hideki Eiki Tojo) (1884–1948) Jap. statesman/soldier/prime minister 1941–1944
Tokyo Rose (Iva Ikuko Toguri d'Aquino) (1916–) Am. World War II propagandist/traitor (pardoned)
Toler, Sidney (1874–1947) Am. actor (Charlie Chan in 22 films)

Tolkein, J. R. R. (John Ronald Reuel Tolkein) (1892–1973) Eng. fantasy novelist (*The Hobbit*; *The Lord of the Rings*)

Tolstoy, Count **Leo** (Lev Nikolayevich Tolstoy) (1828–1910) Russ. novelist/ philosopher (*War and Peace*; *Anna Karenina*)

Tomba, Alberto ("Tomba La Bomba") (1966–) Ital. skier

Tomei, Marisa (1964–) Am. actress ("As the World Turns" soap opera; *Untamed Heart*; O—1993—*My Cousin Vinny*)

Tomita, Tamlyn (c. 1966–) Am. actress (*Come See the Paradise*; *The Joy Luck Club*)

Tomjanovich, Rudy (1948–) Am. basketball player

Tomlin, Lily (Mary Jean Tomlin) (1939–) Am. comedienne/actress (*The Search for Intelligent Life in the Universe*; *All of Me*; *Big Business*; *9 to 5*; T—1986)

Tomlinson, David (1917–) Scot. actor (*Mary Poppins*; *Tom Jones*)

Tommasini, Vincenzo (1878–1950) Ital. composer (*Poema Erotico*)

Tompkins, Daniel D. (1774–1825) Am. v.p. (J. Monroe)

Tone, Franchot (Stanislas Pascal Franchot Tone) (1905–1968) Am. actor (*Phantom Lady*; *The Lives of a Bengal Lancer*; *Mutiny on the Bounty*)

Tone Lōc (Anthony Smith; "Antonio Loco") (c. 1966–) Am. rapper ("Funky Cold Medina"; "Wild Thing")

Tong, Sammee (1901–1964) Am. actor ("Bachelor Father" TV series)

Toomer, Jean (1894–1967) Am. poet/writer (during the Harlem Renaissance; *Cane*)

Toomey, Regis (1902–) Am. actor (*The Big Sleep*; "Petticoat Junction" TV series)

Topol (Chaim Topol; a/k/a Haym Topol) (1935–) Isr. actor (*Fiddler on the Roof* [as Tevye])

Torgeson, Earl (Clifford Earl Torgeson; "The Earl of Snohomish") (1924–1990) Am. baseball player

Tork, Peter (Peter Torkelson) (1944–) Am. pop musician (with The Monkees)

Torme, Mel (Melvin Howard Torme; "The Velvet Fog") (1925–) Am. singer

Torn, Rip (Elmore Rual Torn, Jr.) (1931–) Am. actor (*Cross Creek*; *Sweet Bird of Youth*)

Torre, Joe (Joseph Paul Torre) (1940–) Am. baseball player/manager

Torrence, Dean (1940–) Am. pop singer (with Jan and Dean; "Surf City")

Toscanini, Arturo (1867–1957) Ital. orchestra conductor (Metropolitan Opera, many symphonies)

Tosh, Peter (Winston Hubert MacIntosh) (1944–1987) Jam. reggae musician/ singer ("[You Got to Walk and] Don't Look Back")

Totter, Audrey (1918–) Am. actress (*The Lady in the Lake*; "Medical Center" TV series)

Toulouse-Lautrec, Henri de (Henri-Marie-Raymond de Toulouse-Lautrec-Monfa) (1864–1901) Fr. painter (*At the Moulin Rouge*)

Tower, John (John Goodwin Tower) (1925–) Am. senator

Towne, Robert (a/k/a P. H. Vazak) (1936–) Am. screenwriter/film producer/ director (*The Last Detail*; *Chinatown*; *Shampoo*)

Townsend, Robert (1957–) Am. actor/film director (*Hollywood Shuffle*; *The Five Heartbeats*; *The Meteor Man*)

Townshend, Pete (Peter Dennis Blandford Townshend; "Towser") (1945–) Eng. rock guitarist/singer ("Let My Love Open the Door"; formerly with The Who)

Toynbee, Arnold (Arnold Joseph Toynbee) (1889–1975) Eng. historian (*A Study of History*)

Trabert, Tony (Marion Anthony Trabert) (1930–) Am. tennis player (W—1955)

Tracy, Lee (William Lee Tracy) (1898–1968) Am. actor (TV's "Martin Kane, Private Eye")

Tracy, Spencer (Spencer Bonaventure Tracy) (1900–1967) Am. actor (*Adam's Rib*; *Woman of the Year*; O—1937—*Captains Courageous*; O—1938—*Boys Town*)

Trafton, George (1896–1971) Am. football Hall-of-Famer

Trajan (Marcus Ulpius Traianus) (53–117) Roman emperor 98–117

Traubel, Helen (1903–1972) Am. opera singer (soprano)

Travanti, Daniel J. (Daniel John Travanti) (1940–) Am. actor ("Hill Street Blues" TV series; E—1980/81, 1981/82)

Traven, B. (Berwick Traven Torsvan; a/k/a Ret Marut) (1890–1969) Ger.-Am. novelist (*The Treasure of the Sierra Madre*)

Travers, Mary (Mary Allin Travers) (1936–) Am. pop singer (with Peter, Paul & Mary)

Travers, P. L. (Pamely Lyndon Travers)

(1906–) Austral. writer (created Mary Poppins)

Travers, Pat (1954–) Am. blues/rock singer/musician ("Is This Love")

Travis, Merle (1917–) Am. country singer/songwriter ("Divorce Me C.O.D.")

Travis, Nancy (C) Am. actress (*Internal Affairs*; *Three Men and a Baby*; *The Vanishing*)

Travis, Randy (Randy Bruce Traywick) (1959–) Am. country singer/musician ("Forever and Ever, Amen")

Travolta, John (John Joseph Travolta) (1954–) Am. actor (*Saturday Night Fever*; "Welcome Back, Kotter" TV series)

Traynor, Pie (Harold Joseph Traynor) (1899–1972) Am. baseball Hall-of-Famer

Treacher, Arthur (Arthur Treacher Veary) (1894–1975) Eng. actor (*Thank You Jeeves*)/restauranteur (fast food fish and chips)

Trebek, Alex (1940–) Can.-Am. game show host ("Jeopardy!")

Tree, Sir **Herbert Draper Beerbohm** (Herbert Draper Beerbohm) (1853–1917) Eng. actor/producer/playwright (half-brother of Max Beerbohm)

Trevino, Lee (Lee Buck Trevino; "Supermex") (1939–) Am. golfer

Trevor, Claire (Claire Wemlinger) (1909–) Am. actress (*Stagecoach*; *The High and the Mighty*; O—1948—*Key Largo*)

Trigere, Pauline (1912–) Am. fashion designer

Trillin, Calvin (Calvin Marshall Trillin; "Bud") (1935–) Am. columnist (for *New Yorker*)/writer (*Alice, Let's Eat*)

Trilling, Lionel (1905–1975) Am. literary critic (*The Liberal Imagination*)

Trillo, Manny (Jesus Manuel Marcado Marcano; "Indio") (1950–) Venez.-Am. baseball player

Trintignant, Jean-Louis (Jean-Louis Xavier Trintignant) (1930–) Fr. actor (*And God Created Woman*; *Z*)

Trippi, Charlie (Charles L. Trippi; "The Scintillating Sicilian"; "Triple Threat Trippi") (1922–) Am. football Hall-of-Famer

Tripplehorn, Jeanne (c. 1963–) Am. actress (*Basic Instinct*; *The Firm*)

Tritt, Travis (James Travis Tritt) (1963–) Am. country singer ("T-R-O-U-B-L-E")

Trollope, Anthony (1815–1882) Eng. novelist (*The Warden*; *Barchester Towers*)

Trollope, Frances (née Milton) (1780–

1863) Eng. novelist/travel writer (mother of Anthony; *Domestic Manners of the Americans*)

Trotsky, Leon (Lev Davidovich Bronstein) (1879–1940) Russ. revolutionary/founder of the Red Army

Trower, Robin (1945–) Eng. rock guitarist/bandleader (with Procul Harum)

Troyanos, Tatiana (1938–1993) Am. opera singer (mezzo-soprano)

Trudeau, Garry (Garretson Beckman Trudeau) (1948–) Am. cartoonist (*Doonesbury*; P—1975)

Trudeau, Pierre (Pierre Elliott Trudeau) (1919–) Can. prime minister 1969–1979, 1980–1984

Truex, Ernest (1889–1973) Am. actor ("Mr. Peepers" TV series; *The Adventures of Marco Polo*)

Truffaut, François (1932–1984) Fr. film director (*Day for Night*; *The 400 Blows*; *Jules and Jim*)

Trujillo Molina, Rafael (Rafael Leonidas Trujillo Molina) (1891–1961) Dom. pres. 1930–1938, 1942–1952

Truman, Bess (Elizabeth Virginia Wallace; "The Boss") (1885–1982) Am. first lady (Harry S.)

Truman, Harry S ("The Man from Missouri"; "Give 'Em Hell Harry"; "The Man from Independence") (1884–1972) 33rd Am. pres. (1945–1953)

Trumbo, Dalton (James Dalton Trumbo) (1905–1976) Am. novelist (*Johnny Got His Gun*)/screenwriter (*Exodus*; *Spartacus*)

Trumbull, John (1756–1843) Am. painter (*The Signing of the Declaration of Independence*)

Trump, Donald (Donald John Trump) (1946–) Am. business executive/financier/writer (*The Art of the Deal*)

Trump, Ivana (Ivana Winkelmayr) (1949–) Am. hotelier/lecturer/novelist

Truth, Sojourner (Isabella; Isabella Van Wagener) (c. 1797–1883) Am. abolitionist/ex-slave

Tryon, Thomas (1926–1991) Am. writer (*All That Glitters*; *The Wings of the Morning*)

Tschirky, Oscar (Oscar Michel Tschirky; "Oscar of the Waldorf") (1866–1950) Am. maitre d'hotel

Tsongas, Paul (1940–) Am. senator

Tubb, Ernest ("The Texas Troubador") (1914–1984) Am. country singer ("I'm Walking the Floor over You")

Tubman, Harriet (Araminta Tubman; "Moses of Her People") (c. 1820–1913) Am. abolitionist (freed slaves via the "underground railroad")

Tuchman, Barbara W. (Barbara Wertheim Tuchman) (1911–1989) Am. historian/writer (P—1963—*The Guns of August*; P—1972—*Stilwell and the American Experience in China 1911–1945*; *A Distant Mirror*)

Tucker, Forrest (Forrest Meredith Tucker) (1919–1986) Am. actor ("F Troop" TV series; *Sands of Iwo Jima*)

Tucker, Jim Guy (1943–) Am. gov. of Arkansas

Tucker, Michael (1944–) Am. actor ("L.A. Law" TV series)

Tucker, Sophie (Sophia Kalish; "Last of the Red Hot Mamas") (1884–1966) Am. actress/singer/entertainer

Tucker, Tanya (Tanya Denise Tucker) (1958–) Am. country singer ("Lizzie and the Rainman"; "Just Another Love"; "Strong Enough to Bend")

Tucker, Tommy ("Little Tommy Tucker") (1908–1989) Am. jazz bandleader ("I Don't Want to Set the World on Fire")

Tudor, Antony (William Cook) (1908–1987) Eng. ballet dancer/choreographer

Tufts, Sonny (Bowen Charleston Tufts III) (1911–1970) Am. actor (*The Virginian*)

Tull, Jethro (1674–1741) Eng. inventor (machine seed drill)

Tune, Tommy (Thomas James Tune) (1939–) Am. theatrical director/choreographer (*The Will Rogers Follies*; *Grand Hotel*; *Nine*; T—1983)

Tung Chih or **Tung Chi** (a/k/a Tsai-ch'un; Mu Tsug; I Huang-ti) (1856–1875) Chin. emperor 1862–1875

Tunnell, Em (Emlen Tunnell) (1925–1975) Am. football Hall-of-Famer

Tunney, Gene (James Joseph Tunney; "The Fighting Marine") (1898–1978) Am. boxer

Turco, Paige (C) Am. actress ("All My Children" soap opera; *Teenage Mutant Ninja Turtles II*)

Turcotte, Ron (Ronald Turcotte) (1950–) Can. jockey

Turgenev, Ivan (Ivan Sergeyevich Turgenev) (1818–1883) Russ. novelist (*Fathers and Sons*; *A Month in the Country*)

Turina, Joaquín (1882–1949) Span. composer (*Margot*)

Turing, Alan (Alan Mathison Turing) (1912–1954) Eng. mathematician/computer pioneer (the Turing machine)

Turlington, Christy ("Turlie") (1968–) Am. model

Turner, Big Joe (1911–1985) Am. blues/big band singer ("Shake, Rattle and Roll"; formerly with Duke Ellington and Count Basie)

Turner, Bulldog (Clyde Turner) (1919–) Am. football Hall-of-Famer

Turner, Ike (1931–) Am. soul/rock musician ("Proud Mary")

Turner, Janine (Janine Gauntt) (1962–) Am. actress ("Northern Exposure" TV series)

Turner, J. M. W. (Joseph Mallord William Turner) (1775–1851) Eng. painter (*Calais Pier*)

Turner, Kathleen (1954–) Am. actress (*Body Heat*; *The War of the Roses*; *Cloak and Dagger*; *Romancing the Stone*)

Turner, Lana (Julia Jean Mildred Frances Turner; "The Sweater Girl") (1920–) Am. actress (*Peyton Place*; *Imitation of Life*)

Turner, Nat (1800–1831) Am. slave insurrectionist/autobiographer (*The Confessions of Nat Turner*)

Turner, Ted (Robert Edward Turner III; "The Mouth of the South"; "Terrible Ted"; "Captain Outrageous"; "The Steinbrenner of the South") (1938–) Am. broadcasting (cable TV) mogul/baseball team owner

Turner, Tina (Annie Mae Bullock) (1938–) Am. pop/rock singer ("What's Love Got to Do with It"; "Private Dancer"; G—1984)

Turow, Scott (1949–) Am. novelist (*Presumed Innocent*; *The Burden of Proof*)

Turpin, Ben (1869–1940) Am. actor (*The Love Parade*; *Romeo and Juliet*)

Turturro, John (1957–) Am. actor (*Do the Right Thing*; *Barton Fink*; *Jungle Fever*; *Miller's Crossing*)/director (*Mac*)

Tushingham, Rita (1940–) Eng. actress (*A Taste of Honey*; *Doctor Zhivago*)

Tussaud, Madame (Marie Grosholtz Tussaud) (1760–1850) Swi. wax modeler

Tutankhamen (Tutankhaten; "King Tut") (c. 1370–1352 B.C.) Egypt. king 1361–1352 B.C.

Tuttle, Lurene (1906–1986) Am. actress ("Life with Father" and "Julia" TV series)

Tutu, Desmond (Desmond Mpilo Tutu) (1931–) S. Afr. bishop (N—1984)

Tutuola, Amos (1920–) Niger. novelist (*My Life in the Bush of Ghosts*)

Twain, Mark (Samuel Langhorne Clemens; "The People's Author") (1835–1910) Am. humorist/lecturer/ newspaperman (*A Connecticut Yankee in King Arthur's Court*; *The Adventures of Tom Sawyer*; *Adventures of Huckleberry Finn*)

Tweed, Shannon (1957–) Am. actress ("Days of Our Lives" soap opera; *Twisted Justice*)

Tweed, William Marcy ("Boss Tweed") (1823–1878) Am. politician/head of Tammany Hall

Twiggy (Lesley Lawson née Hornby; "Sticks") (1949–) Eng. model/actress (*Madame Sousatzka*)

Twilley, Dwight (1951–) Am. country singer ("I'm on Fire"; "Girls")

Twitty, Conway (Harold Lloyd Jenkins; "The High Priest of Country Music") (1933–1993) Am. country singer ("Hello Darlin' ")

Tyler, Anne (1941–) Am. writer (*The Accidental Tourist*; P—1989—*Breathing Lessons*)

Tyler, Bonnie (Gaynor Hopkins) (1953–) Am. rock singer ("It's a Heartache"; "Total Eclipse of the Heart")

Tyler, John ("His Accidency") (1790–1862) 10th Am. pres. (1841–1845)

Tyler, Julia (Julia Gardiner) (1820–1889) Am. first lady (John)

Tyler, Letitia (Letitia Christian) (1790–1842) Am. first lady (John)

Tyler, Liv (1977–) Am. model (daughter of Bebe Buell and Steven Tyler)

Tyler, Steven (1948–) Am. rock singer (father of Liv; with Aerosmith)

Tylo, Hunter (c. 1962–) Am. actress ("The Bold and the Beautiful" soap opera)

Tynan, Kenneth (Kenneth Peacock Tynan) (1927–1980) Eng. drama critic

Tyner, McCoy (1938–) Am. jazz pianist/ composer (with John Coltrane and Ike & Tina Turner)

Typhoid Mary (Mary Mallon) (c. 1870–1938) Am. cook/typhoid carrier

Tyra (c. 1974–) Am. model/actress ("The Fresh Prince of Bel-Air" TV series)

Tyre, Nedra (1921–) Am. mystery writer (*Mouse in Eternity*)

Tyson, Cicely (1933–) Am. actress (*The Au-*

tobiography of Miss Jane Pittman; *Sounder*)

Tyson, Mike (Mike G. Tyson; "Iron Mike") (1966–) Am. boxer

Uccello, Paolo (Paolo di Dono) (1397–1475) Flor. painter (*St. George and the Dragon*)

Udall, Morris or Mo K. (Morris King Udall) (1922–) Am. lawyer/congressman

Ueberroth, Peter (Peter Victor Ueberroth) (1937–) Am. baseball commissioner

Uecker, Bob (Robert George Uecker; "Mr. Baseball") (1935–) Am. baseball player/ comedian/actor ("Mr. Belvedere" TV series)

Uggams, Leslie (Leslie Marian Crayne) (1943–) Am. singer/actress (*Roots*; T—1968)

Uhnak, Dorothy (1930–) Am. policewoman/mystery writer (*Law and Order*)

Ullman, Tracey (1959–) Eng. comedienne ("The Tracey Ullman Show")/actress (*I Love You to Death*)

Ullmann, Liv (Liv Johanne Ullmann) (1938–) Norw. writer/actress (*Autumn Sonata*; *Cries and Whispers*)

Ulric, Lenore (Lenore Ulrich) (1892–1970) Am. actress (*Camille*)

Umeki, Miyoshi (1929–) Jap.-Am. actress (O—1957—*Sayonara*; "The Courtship of Eddie's Father" TV series)

Uncas (c. 1588–c. 1683) Am. Mohican Indian chief

Underwood, Blair (1964–) Am. actor ("L.A. Law" TV series)

Undset, Sigrid (1882–1949) Norw. novelist (*Kristin Lavransdatter*; N—1928)

Ungaro, Emanuel (Emanuel Matteotti Ungaro) (1933–) Fr. fashion designer

Unitas, Johnny (John Constantine Unitas) (1933–) Am. football Hall-of-Famer

Unseld, Wes (Wesley Sissel Unseld) (1946–) Am. basketball player

Unser, Al (1939–) Am. auto racer (father of Al, Jr.; brother of Bobby)

Unser, Al, Jr. ("Little Al") (1962–) Am. auto racer

Unser, Bobby (Robert William Unser) (1934–) Am. auto racer

Untermeyer, Louis (1885–1977) Am. poet/ writer/editor/anthologist (*A Treasury of Great Humor*)

Updike, John (John Hoyer Updike) (1932–) Am. novelist/short story writer (*The Witches of Eastwick*; P—1982—

Rabbit Is Rich; P—1991—*Rabbit at Rest*)

Upjohn, Richard (1802–1878) Am. architect (New York's Trinity Church)

Upshaw, Gene (Eugene Upshaw) (1945–) Am. football Hall-of-Famer

Ure, Mary (1933–1975) Scot. actress (*Look Back in Anger*; *Sons and Lovers*)

Ure, Midge (James Ure) (1953–) Scot.-Eng. rock guitarist/singer (with Ultravox)

Urey, Harold (Harold Clayton Urey) (1893–1981) Am. chemist (discovered deuterium; N—1934)

Urich, Robert (1946–) Am. actor ("Vega$," "Spenser: For Hire," and "It Had To Be You" TV series)

Uris, Leon (Leon Marcus Uris) (1924–) Am. novelist (*QB VII*; *Exodus*; *Topaz*)

Ustinov, Sir Peter (Peter Alexander Ustinov) (1921–) Eng. actor (O—1960—*Spartacus*; O—1964—*Topkapi*)

Utley, Garrick (Clifton Garrick Utley) (1939–) Am. newscaster

Utrillo, Maurice (1883–1955) Fr. painter (Montmartre street scenes)

Vaccaro, Brenda (Brenda Buell Vaccaro) (1939–) Am. actress (*Midnight Cowboy*; *Once Is Not Enough*)

Vadim, Roger (Roger Vadim Plemiannikov) (1927–) Fr. film director (*Barbarella*; *And God Created Woman*)

Vai, Steve (1960–) Am. rock guitarist (with Frank Zappa and Whitesnake)

Valdivia, Pedro de (c. 1498–1553) Span. soldier/conquerer of Chile

Vale, Jerry (Genaro Louis Vitaliano) (1931–) Am. singer ("You Don't Know Me")

Valens (c. 328–378) Roman emperor 364–378

Valens, Ritchie (Richard Valenzuela) (1941–1959) Am. rock singer ("La Bamba")

Valenti, Jack (Jack Joseph Valenti) (1921–) Am. film executive (pres. of the MPAA)

Valentine, Karen (1947–) Am. actress ("Room 222" TV series; E—1969/70)

Valentino (Valentino Garavani) (1932–) Ital. fashion designer

Valentino, Rudolph (Rodolfo Alfonzo Raffaelo Pierre Filibert Guglielmi di Valentina d'Antonguolla; "The Great Lover") (1895–1926) Am. actor (*Blood and Sand*; *The Sheik*)

Valenzuela, Fernando (Fernand Anguamea Anguamea; "El Toro"; "Tortilla Flats") (1960–) Mex.-Am. baseball pitcher

Valerian (Publius Licinius Valerianus) (died 260) Roman emperor 253–260

Valéry, Paul (Ambrose-Paul-Toussaint-Jules Valéry) (1871–1945) Fr. poet (*The Graveyard by the Sea*)

Vallee, Rudy (Hubert Prior Vallee; "The Vagabond Lover") (1901–1986) Am. singer/actor (*The Palm Beach Story*; *I Remember Mama*)

Vallely, Tannis (1975–) Am. child actress ("Head of the Class" TV series)

Valletta, Amber (c. 1973–) Am. model

Valli, Alida (Alida Maria von Altenburger; a/k/a Valli) (1921–) Ital. actress (*The Third Man*; *The Cassandra Crossing*)

Valli, Frankie (Frank Castelluccio) (1937–) Am. pop singer ("Can't Take My Eyes Off You"; "My Eyes Adored You"; formerly with The Four Seasons)

Vallone, Raf (Raffaele Vallone) (1916–) Ital. actor (*Bitter Rice*; *The Greek Tycoon*)

Van, Bobby (Robert Stein King) (1930–1980) Am. singer/dancer/actor (*Lost Horizon*)

Van Allen, James Alfred (1914–) Am. physicist (discovered the Van Allen radiation belts)

Van Ark, Joan (1943–) Am. actress ("Knots Landing" TV series)

Van Brocklin, Norm (Norman Mack Van Brocklin; "The Dutchman"; "Stormin' Norman") (1926–1983) Am. football Hall-of-Famer

Van Buren, Abigail (Pauline Esther Friedman Phillips; "Popo") (1918–) Am. advice columnist ("Dear Abby"; twin sister of Ann Landers)

Van Buren, Hannah (Hannah Hoes) (1783–1819) Am. wife of Martin Van Buren (died before he entered office)

Van Buren, Martin ("The Little Magician"; "Kinderhook Fox"; "Martin Van Ruin"; "The Panic of 1837"; "Whiskey Van") (1782–1862) 8th Am. pres. (1837–1841)

Van Buren, Steve (Steve W. Van Buren) (1920–) Am. football Hall-of-Famer

Vance, Cyrus (Cyrus Roberts Vance) (1917–) Am. statesman/govt. official (secretary of state)

Vance, Dazzy (Clarence Arthur Vance; "The Dazzler") (1891–1961) Am. baseball Hall-of-Famer

Vance, Vivian (Vivian Roberta Jones) (between 1903 and 1912–1979) Am. actress ("I Love Lucy" TV series; E—1953)

Van Cleef, Lee (1925–1989) Am. actor (*The Good, the Bad and the Ugly*; *For a Few Dollars More*)

Van Damme, Jean-Claude (Jean-Claude Van Varenberg; a/k/a Frank Cujo; "Muscles from Brussels") (1961–) Belg. martial arts expert/actor (*Cyborg*; *Lionheart*; *Universal Soldier*; *Hard Target*)

Vanderbilt, Amy (1908–1974) Am. journalist/etiquette expert

Vanderbilt, Cornelius ("The Commodore") (1794—1877) Am. entrepreneur (steamboat business; one-time richest man in the U.S.)

Vanderbilt, Gloria (Gloria Laura Morgan Cooper) (1924–) Am. fashion designer/ autobiographer

Vander Meer, Johnny (John Samuel Vander Meer; "The Dutch Master"; "Double No-Hit") (1914–) Am. baseball pitcher (only pitcher in history to pitch two consecutive no-hit games)

Van Der Meer, Simon (1925–) Dutch physicist (N—1984)

Van Devere, Trish (Patricia Dressel) (1943–) Am. actress (*Movie Movie*; *Where's Poppa?*)

Van Dine, S. S. (Willard Huntington Wright) (1888–1939) Am. detective story writer (created Philo Vance)

Van Doren, Mamie (Joan Lucille Olander) (1933–) Am. actress (*Teacher's Pet*; *Ain't Misbehavin'*)

Vandross, Luther (1951–) Am. soul/pop singer ("Here and Now"; "Power of Love/Love Power")

Vandyck, Sir Anthony (1599–1641) Flem. painter (studied under Rubens; *Samson and Delilah*; *Cupid and Psyche*)

Van Dyke, Dick (1925–) Am. actor/ comedian (brother of Jerry; "The Dick Van Dyke Show" TV series; E— 1963/64, 1964/65, 1965/66)

Van Dyke, Jerry (1932–) Am. actor (brother of Dick; "My Mother, the Car" and "Coach" TV series)

Van Dyke, W. S. (William S. Van Dyke II; "Woody"; "One-Take Van Dyke") (1889–1943) Am. film director (*The Thin Man*; *Trader Horn*)

Van Eyck, Hubert (a/k/a Huybrecht Van Eyck) (c. 1370–1426) Flem. painter (brother of Jan)

Van Eyck, Jan (before 1395–1441) Flem. painter (*Annunciation*)

Van Fleet, Jo (1919–) Am. actress (*The Rose Tattoo*; O—1955—*East of Eden*)

Vangelis (Evangelos Papathanassiu) (1943–) Gr. musician/composer (*Chariots of Fire*)

Van Gogh, Vincent (Vincent Wilhelm Van Gogh) (1853–1890) Dutch painter (*Sunflowers*)

Van Halen, Alex (1955–) Am. rock drummer (with Van Halen; brother of Eddie)

Van Halen, Eddie (1957–) Am. rock guitarist (with Van Halen; "Jump")

Van Heusen, Jimmy (Edward Chester Babcock) (1913–1990) Am. composer ("All the Way"; "Love and Marriage"; "High Hopes"; "Call Me Irresponsible")

Vanilla Ice (Robert Van Winkle) (1968–) Am. rapper ("Ice Ice Baby")

Vanity (Denise Matthews) (C) Can.-Am. pop singer ("Pretty Mess")/actress (*52 Pick-Up*; *Action Jackson*)

Vannelli, Gino (1952–) Can. pop/rock singer ("I Just Wanna Stop"; "Living Inside Myself")

Vanocur, Sander (Sander Vinocur) (1928–) Am. radio/TV newscaster

Van Patten, Dick (Richard Vincent Van Patten) (1928–) Am. actor (brother of Joyce; "Eight Is Enough" TV series)

Van Patten, Joyce (Joyce Benigna Van Patten) (1934–) Am. actress ("The Danny Kaye Show" TV series)

Van Peebles, Mario (1957–) Am. actor/film director (son of Melvin; *Posse*; *New Jack City*)

Van Peebles, Melvin (Melvin Peebles) (1932–) Am. film director (*The Watermelon Man*)

Van Ryn, John (John William Van Ryn) (1906–) Am. tennis player

Van Sant, Gus (Gus Van Sant, Jr.) (1952–) Am. film director (*Drugstore Cowboy*; *My Own Private Idaho*; *Even Cowgirls Get the Blues*)

Van Slyke, Helen (Helen Lenore Vogt Van Slyke) (1919–1979) Am. novelist (*Sisters and Strangers*)

Van Vechten, Carl (1880–1964) Am. novelist (*Nigger Heaven*)/photographer/ drama critic

Van Vogt, A. E. (Alfred Elton Van Vogt) (1912–) Can. science fiction/short story writer (*The Voyage of the Space Beagle*; *Slan*; *The Weapon Shops of Isher*)

Vanwarmer, Randy (Randall Van Wormer) (1955–) Am. country singer/musician ("Just When I Needed You Most")

Van Zant, Ronnie (1949–1977) Am. rock singer (with Lynyrd Skynyrd; "Free Bird")

Vanzetti, Bartolomeo (1888–1927) Am. anarchist (with Nicola Sacco)

Vare, Glenda (Glenda Collett née Vare) (1903–1989) Am. golfer

Varèse, Edgard (Edgar Victor Achille Charles Varèse) (1883–1965) Fr.-Am. composer (*Hyperprism*)

Vargas Llosa, Mario (Jorge Maria Pedro Vargas Llosa) (1936–) Peruv. novelist (*Conversations in the Cathedral*; *Aunt Julia and the Scriptwriter*)

Varney, Jim (1946–) Am. comedian ("Fernwood 2-Night" TV series; "Hey, Vern" commercials; *The Beverly Hillbillies*)

Varsi, Diane (Diane Marie Antonia Varsi) (1938–1992) Am. actress (*Peyton Place*; *Ten North Frederick*)

Vasari, Giorgio (1511–1574) Ital. mannerist painter/architect (Uffizi Palace)

Vasily III (Vasily Ivanovich) (1479–1533) Russ. grand prince 1505–1533

Vasily IV (Vasily Shuysky) (1552–1612) Russ. czar 1606–1610

Vaughan, Arky (Joseph Floyd Vaughan) (1912–1952) Am. baseball Hall-of-Famer

Vaughan, Sarah (Sarah Lois Vaughan; "Sassy"; "The Divine One") (1924–1990) Am. jazz singer ("Make Yourself Comfortable")

Vaughan, Stevie Ray (1955–1990) Am. rock guitarist (with Stevie Ray Vaughn & Double Trouble)

Vaughan Williams, Ralph (1872–1959) Eng. composer ("Fantasia On Greensleeves")

Vaughn, Billy (Richard Vaughn) (1919–1991) Am. orchestra leader ("Melody of Love")

Vaughn, Robert (Robert Francis Vaughn) (1932–) Am. actor (Napoleon Solo in "The Man from U.N.C.L.E." TV series; E—1977/78)

Vedder, Eddie (c. 1965–) Am. rock singer (with Pearl Jam)

Vee, Bobby (Robert Thomas Velline) (1943–) Am. pop singer ("Take Good Care of My Baby"; "Come Back When You Grow Up")

Veeck, Bill (William Louis Veeck; "Short Shirt Bill"; "The Clown Prince of Baseball") (1914–) Am. baseball promoter

Vega, Lope de (Lope Félix de Vega Carpio; "The Phoenix") (1562–1635) Span. poet/playwright (*The Star of Seville*; *The Golden Fleece*)

Vega, Suzanne (1959–) Am. folk/pop singer/musician ("Luka")

Veidt, Conrad (Hans Walter Conrad Weidt) (1893–1943) Ger. actor (*The Cabinet of Dr. Caligari*; *Casablanca*)

Velázquez, Diego (Diego Rodriguez de Silva Velázquez de Cuéllar) (1599–1660) Span. painter

Velez, Lupe (Maria Guadeloupe Velez de Villalobos; "Firecracker") (1908–1944) Am. actress (*Mexican Spitfire*; *The Squaw Man*)

Vendela (c. 1967–) Swed.-Am. model

Ventura, Lino (Angelo Borrini) (1919–1987) Ital. boxer/actor (*The Valachi Papers*)

Vera, Billy (William McCord, Jr.) (1944–) Am. rock singer/songwriter/musician ("At This Moment"; with The Beaters)

Verdi, Giuseppe (Giuseppe Fortunino Francesco Verdi) (1813–1901) Ital. opera composer (*Aida*; *Rigoletto*; *La Traviata*)

Verdon, Gwen (Gwyneth Evelyn Verdon) (1925–) Am. dancer/actress (*Damn Yankees*; *The Farmer Takes a Wife*; T—1956, 1958, 1959)

Verdugo, Elena (1926–) Span.-Am. actress ("Marcus Welby, M.D." TV series)

Vereen, Ben (Benjamin Augustus Vereen) (1946–) Am. actor/dancer ("Webster" TV series; *Roots*; T—1973)

Verhoeven, Paul (1938–) Dutch-Am. film director (*The Fourth Man*; *Total Recall*; *Robocop*; *Spetters*)

Verlaine, Paul (Paul Marie Verlaine) (1884–1896) Fr. poet (*Romances Sans Paroles*)

Vermeer, Jan (a/k/a Jan van der Meer) (1632–1675) Dutch painter (*Young Woman with Water Jug*)

Verne, Jules ("The Father of Science Fiction") (1828–1905) Fr. fantasy/science fiction writer (*Twenty Thousand Leagues Under the Sea*; *Journey to the Center of the Earth*; *Around the World in Eighty Days*)

Veronese, Paolo (Paolo Caliari; "Painter of Pageants") (1528–1588) Ital. painter (*Mars and Venus*)

Verrocchio, Andrea Del (Andrea di Michele di Francesco Cione) (1435–1488) Flor. painter (*Baptism of Christ; David*; studied under Fra Lippo Lippi; taught da Vinci and Perugino)/sculptor

Versace, Gianni (1946–) Ital.-Am. fashion designer

Vesey, Denmark (1767–1822) Am. slave insurrectionist

Vespucci, Amerigo (1454–1512) Ital. navigator/explorer (America named for him)

Vicious, Sid (John Simon Ritchie) (1957–1979) Eng. punk musician (with The Sex Pistols)

Vickers, Jon (1926–) Can. opera singer (tenor)

Vickers, Martha (Martha MacVicar) (1925–1971) Am. actress (*The Big Sleep*)

Victoria (Alexandrina Victoria) (1819–1901) queen of England and Ireland 1837–1901

Vidal, Gore (Eugene Luther Vidal, Jr.; a/k/a Edgar Box) (1925–) Am. novelist/playwright/essayist/short story writer (*Myra Breckenridge; Williwaw; The Best Man*)

Vidor, King (King Louis Wallis Vidor) (1894–1982) Am. film director (*The Fountainhead; The Big Parade*)

Vieira, Meredith (c. 1954–) Am. newscaster ("60 Minutes")

Vigoda, Abe (1921–) Am. actor ("Barney Miller" TV series)

Vila, Bob (Robert Joseph Vila) (1946–) Am. TV host ("This Old House"; "Vila's Home Again")

Vilas, Guillermo ("Young Bull of the Pampas") (1952–) Arg. tennis player

Villa, Pancho (Francisco Villa; born Doroteo Arango; "The Puma"; "The Tiger of the North") (1878–1923) Mex. bandit/revolutionary

Villa-Lobos, Heitor (1887–1959) Braz. composer ("Dawn in a Tropical Forest")

Villard, Oswald (Oswald Garrison Villard) (1872–1949) Am. editor/journalist (*The Nation*)

Villechaize, Hervé (Hervé Jean Pierre Villechaize) (1943–1993) Fr. actor ("Fantasy Island" TV series)

Villella, Edward (Edward Joseph Villella) (1936–) Am. ballet dancer

Villon, François (François de Montcorbier) (1431–after 1463) Fr. poet (*Petit Testament*)

Villon, Jacques (Gaston Duchamp) (1875–

1963) Fr. painter (brother of Marcel Duchamp)

Vincent, Gene (Vincent Eugene Craddock) (1935–1971) Am. rock singer ("Be-Bop-A-Lula"; with The Blue Caps)

Vincent, Jan-Michael (a/k/a Michael Vincent) (1944–) Am. actor ("Airwolf" TV series; *White Line Fever*)

Vinson, Fred M. (Fred Moore Vinson) (1890–1953) Am. Supreme Court chief justice (1946–1953)

Vinton, Bobby (Stanley Robert Vintulla; "The Polish Prince") (1935–) Am. pop singer ("Roses Are Red [My Love]"; "Blue Velvet")

Viorst, Judith (Judith Stahl Viorst) (1931–) Am. poet/writer (*People and Other Aggravations*)

Virgil (Publius Vergilius Maro) (70–19 B.C.) Roman poet (*Aeneid*)

Virgil, Ozzie (Osvaldo Jose Lopez Virgil) (1956–) Am. baseball player

Visconti, Luchino (1906–1976) Ital. film director (*The Damned; The Leopard; Death in Venice*)

Vitale, Dick (Richard Vitale) (1940–) Am. basketball coach/sportscaster

Vitali, Giovanni (Giovanni Battista Vitali) (1632–1692) Ital. composer (*Artifici Musicali*)

Vittadini, Adrienne (c. 1945–) Am. fashion designer

Vivaldi, Antonio (Antonio Lucio Vivaldi; "The Red Priest") (1678–1741) Ital. composer (*The Four Seasons*)

Vlaminck, Maurice de (1876–1958) Fr. Fauvist/expressionist painter

Voight, Jon (1938–) Am. actor (*Midnight Cowboy; Deliverance;* O—1978—*Coming Home*)

Voinovich, George (George Victor Voinovich) (1936–) Am. gov. of Ohio

Vollenweider, Andreas (1953–) Swi. harpist

Volman, Mark ("Flo") (1944–) Am. rock guitarist/singer (with The Turtles and Flo and Eddie)

Volta, Alessandro (Alesssandro Giuseppe Antonio Anastasio Volta) (1745–1827) Ital. physicist/inventor (electrophorus)

Voltaire (Jean François Marie Arouet) (1694–1778) Fr. philosopher/writer/poet (*Candide*)

Von Bulow, Claus (Claus Cecil Borberg) (1926–) Aus.-Am. businessman/accused attempted murderer (of wife Sunny)

Von Bulow, Sunny (Martha Sharp Crawford) (1932–) Am. socialite
Von Daniken, Erich (1935–) Swi. writer (*Chariots of the Gods?*)
Von Furstenberg, Diane (Diane Halfin Von Furstenberg) (1946–) Belg.-Am. fashion designer
Von Goethe, Johann Wolfgang *see* Goethe, Johann Wolfgang Von
Vonnegut, Kurt, Jr. (1922–) Am. novelist/essayist (*Cat's Cradle; Slaughterhouse Five; Breakfast of Champions*)
Von Stade, Frederica ("Flicka") (1945–) Am. opera singer (mezzo-soprano)
Von Sternberg, Josef (Jonas Sternberg) (1894–1969) Aus.-Am. director (*The Blue Angel; Blonde Venus; Morocco*)
Von Stroheim, Erich (Erich Oswald Stroheim) (1885–1957) Aus.-Am. film director/actor (*Greed; Sunset Boulevard*)
Von Sydow, Max (Max Carl Adolf Von Sydow) (1929–) Swed. actor (*The Exorcist; The Seventh Seal; The Greatest Story Ever Told*)
Von Trapp, Maria (Maria Augusta Von Trapp) (1905–) Aus.-Am. musician (*The Sound of Music* is her life story)
Von Zell, Harry (Harry R. Von Zell; "Giggles") (1906–1981) Am. TV/radio announcer (with Burns & Allen)
Vreeland, Diana (Diana Dalziel Vreeland) (1903–1989) Am. magazine editor (*Vogue*)
Vuckovich, Pete (Peter Dennis Vuckovich) (1952–) Am. baseball player
Vuillard, Edouard (Jean-Edouard Vuillard) (1868–1940) Fr. intimist painter/muralist
Wace (c. 1100–after 1174) Norman poet (*Roman de Brut*)
Waddell, Rube (George Edward Waddell) (1876–1914) Am. baseball Hall-of-Famer
Wade, Virginia (Sarah Virginia Wade; "Our Ginny"; "Ginny Fizz") (1945–) Am. tennis player (W—1977)
Wadkins, Lanny (Jerry Lanny Wadkins) (1949–) Am. golfer
Waggoner, Lyle (Lyle Wesley Waggoner) (1935–) Am. actor ("Wonder Woman" and "The Carol Burnett Show" TV series)
Wägner, Elin (Elin Matilda Elisabeth Wägner) (1882–1949) Swed. novelist/journalist (*Asa-Hanna*)
Wagner, Honus (Johannes Peter Wagner;

"The Flying Dutchman") (1874–1955) Am. baseball Hall-of-Famer
Wagner, Jack (1959–) Am. pop singer ("All I Need")/actor ("General Hospital" soap opera)
Wagner, Jane (1935–) Am. comedy writer (*The Incredible Shrinking Woman*)
Wagner, Katie (C) Am. actress (daughter of Robert)
Wagner, Lindsay (Lindsay Jean Wagner) (1949–) Am. actress (TV's "The Bionic Woman"; E—1976/77)
Wagner, Richard (Wilhelm Richard Wagner) (1813–1883) Ger. composer (*Lohengrin; Tristan und Isolde; The Ring*)
Wagner, Robert (Robert John Wagner; "RJ") (1930–) Am. actor ("Hart to Hart" and "It Takes a Thief" TV series)
Wagoner, Porter ("The Thin Man from West Plains") (1927–) Am. country singer/composer ("Misery Loves Company")
Wahl, Ken (1953–) Am. actor (TV's "Wiseguy")
Wahlberg, Donny (Donald E. Walhberg, Jr.) (1969–) Am. pop musician (with New Kids on the Block)
Wahlöö, Per (1926–1975) Swed. mystery writer (with wife Maj Sjöwall)
Waihee, John (John David Waihee) (1946–) Am. gov. of Hawaii
Wainwright, Loudon III (1946–) Am. folk singer/musician ("Dead Skunk")
Waite, John (1955–) Eng. rock singer ("Missing You"; with The Babys and Bad English)
Waite, Morrison R. (1816–1888) Am. Supreme Court chief justice (1874–1888)
Waite, Ralph (1928–) Am. actor ("The Waltons" TV series)
Waite, Terry (1939–) Eng. hostage/autobiographer
Waits, Tom (1949–) Am. singer ("Heartattack and Vine")/songwriter ("Downtown Train")/actor (*Ironweed*)
Waitz, Greta (1953–) Norw. marathon runner
Wajda, Andrzej (1926–) Pol. film director (*Man of Marble*)
Wakeman, Rick (1949–) Eng. rock keyboardist (with The Strawbs and Yes)
Walcott, Derek (Derek Alton Walcott) (1930–) W. Ind. playwright/poet (*In a Green Night; O Babylon!*; N—1992)
Walcott, Jersey Joe (Arnold Raymond Cream) (1914–1994) Am. boxer

Wald, Jerry (Jerome Irving Wald) (1911–1962) Am. film producer (*Mildred Pierce; Johnny Belinda*)

Waldheim, Kurt (1918–) Aus. pres. 1986–/U.N. official

Walesa, Lech ("The Man of Iron") (1943–) Pol. pres. 1990– (N—1983; led solidarity movement)

Walgreen, Charles Rudolph ("Father of the Modern Drugstore") (1873–1939) Am. merchant (Walgreen's Drugstores)

Walken, Christopher (Ronald Walken) (1943–) Am. actor (*The Dead Zone; Biloxi Blues;* O—1978—*The Deer Hunter*)

Walker, Alice (Alice Malsenior Walker) (1944–) Am. short story writer/novelist/poet (P—1983—*The Color Purple*)

Walker, Ally (C) Am. actress (*Universal Soldier;* "Moon Over Miami" TV series)

Walker, Bree (c. 1954–) Am. newscaster

Walker, Clint (Norman Walker) (1927–) Am. actor ("Cheyenne" and "Kodiak" TV series)

Walker, Dixie (Fred Walker; "The People's Cherce") (1910–1982) Am. baseball player (brother of Harry)

Walker, Doak (Ewell Doak Walker, Jr.; "Doaker"; "Dauntless Doak"; "All-American Mustang"; "Dynamic Doak"; "Little Man in Pro Football") (1927–) Am. football Hall-of-Famer

Walker, Harry (Harold William Walker; "The Hat") (1918–) Am. baseball player/manager (brother of Dixie)

Walker, Herschel (1962–) Am. football player

Walker, Jerry Jeff (Paul Crosby) (1942–) Am. country singer

Walker, Jimmie (James Carter Walker) (1949–) Am. comedian ("Good Times" TV series; signature phrase: "Dy-no-mite!")

Walker, Junior (Autry de Walt II) (1942–) Am. rock musician ("Shotgun"; with The Allstars)

Walker, Marcy (c. 1962–) Am. actress ("Santa Barbara" soap opera)

Walker, Margaret (Margaret Abigail Walker) (1915–) Am. poet/novelist (*For My People; Jubilee*)

Walker, Mickey (Edward Patrick Walker; "The Toy Bulldog") (1901–1981) Am. boxer

Walker, Mort (Mortimer Walker Addison) (1923–) Am. cartoonist (*Beetle Bailey*)

Walker, Nancy (Ann Myrtle Swoyer Barto) (1921–1992) Am. comedienne/actress

("The Mary Tyler Moore Show" and "Rhoda" TV series)

Walker, Robert (Robert Hudson Walker) (1914–1951) Am. actor (*Till the Clouds Roll By; The Song of Bernadette; Strangers on a Train*)

Walker, T-Bone (Aaron Thibeaux Walker; "Daddy of the Blues") (1910–1975) Am. blues singer/musician/songwriter ("Stormy Monday")

Wallace, Bobby (Roderick John Wallace; "Rhody") (1873–1960) Am. baseball Hall-of-Famer

Wallace, Dewitt (William Roy Dewitt Wallace) (1889–1981) Am. publisher/cofounder of *Reader's Digest*

Wallace, George (George Corley Wallace) (1919–) Am. gov. of Alabama (presidential candidate 1968 and 1972)

Wallace, Henry A. (Henry Agard Wallace) (1888–1965) Am. v.p. (F. D. Roosevelt)

Wallace, Irving (Irving Wallechinsky) (1916–1990) Am. writer/novelist (*The Fan Club; The Word; The Prize; The Book of Lists*)

Wallace, Lew (Lewis Wallace) (1827–1905) Am. general/novelist (*Ben Hur*)

Wallace, Lila Bell (Lila Bell Acheson) (1889–1981) Am. publisher/cofounder of *Reader's Digest*

Wallace, Lurleen Burns (Lurleen Burns) (1926–1968) Am. govt. official (first woman gov. of Alabama)

Wallace, Mike (Myron Leon Wallace) (1918–) Am. newscaster ("60 Minutes")

Wallach, Eli (1915–) Am. actor (*The Magnificent Seven; The Good, the Bad and the Ugly*)

Wallenberg, Raoul (1912–1947?) Swed. diplomat (imprisoned by the Soviets in 1945 for his attempts to save Jews; possibly died in prison)

Wallenda, Karl (1905–1978) Ger.-Am. circus performer ("The Flying Wallendas")

Wallenstein, Alfred (Alfred Franz Wallenstein) (1898–1983) Am. orchestra conductor/cellist

Waller, Fats (Thomas Wright Waller) (1904–1943) Am. jazz pianist/composer ("Ain't Misbehavin'"; "Honeysuckle Rose")

Waller, Robert James (c. 1939–) Am. novelist (*The Bridges of Madison County; Slow Waltz in Cedar Bend*)

Wallis, Hal B. (Hal Brent Wallis) (1898–1986) Am. film producer (*Little Caesar; Casablanca; The Maltese Falcon*)

Walpole, Horace (Horatio Walpole, 4th Earl of Oxford) (1717–1797) Eng. writer/historian (*Castle of Otranto*)

Walpole, Sir Hugh (Hugh Seymour Walpole) (1884–1941) Eng. novelist (*Mr. Perrin and Mr. Traill*)

Walpole, Sir Robert (1676–1745) Eng. statesman (considered England's first prime minister)

Walsh, Ed (Edward Augustine Walsh; "The Big Moose"; "Big Ed") (1881–1959) Am. baseball Hall-of-Famer

Walsh, Joe (1947–) Am. rock singer/guitarist/songwriter ("Life's Been Good"; "A Life of Illusion"; formerly with The James Gang and The Eagles)

Walsh, M. Emmet (Michael Emmet Walsh) (1935–) Am. actor (*Blood Simple*; *Clean and Sober*)

Walsh, Raoul (1887–1980) Am. film director (*High Sierra*; *What Price Glory?*)

Walsh, Stella (Stanislawa Walasiewicz) (1911–1980) Pol.-Am. track and field athlete

Walter, Bruno (Bruno Walter Schlesinger) (1876–1962) Ger.-Am. orchestra conductor (Metropolitan Opera; New York Philharmonic)

Walter, Jessica (1940–) Am. actress (*Play Misty for Me*; "Love of Life" soap opera)

Walters, Barbara (1931–) Am. TV interviewer/newscaster ("Today"; "60 Minutes")

Walters, Bucky (William Henry Walters) (1909–1991) Am. baseball player

Walton, Bill (William Theodore Walton) (1952–) Am. basketball player

Walton, Izaak (1593–1683) Eng. writer (*The Compleat Angler*)

Walton, Sam (Samuel Moore Walton; "Mountain Man") (1918–1992) Am. businessman/entrepreneur (Wal-Mart stores)

Walton, Sir William (William Turner Walton) (1902–1983) Eng. composer (*Troilus and Cressida*)

Wambaugh, Joseph (Joseph Aloysius Wambaugh, Jr.) (1937–) Am. policeman/police novelist (*The Choir Boys*; *The Onion Field*)

Wanamaker, Sam (1919–1994) Am. film director (*The Spy Who Came in from the Cold*; *Those Magnificent Men in Their Flying Machines*)

Waner, Lloyd (Lloyd James Waner; "Little Poison") (1906–1982) Am. baseball Hall-of-Famer (brother of Paul)

Waner, Paul (Paul Glee Waner; "Big Poison") (1903–1965) Am. baseball Hall-of-Famer (brother of Lloyd)

Wang, An (1920–1990) Chin.-Am. physicist/businessman (founded Wang Labs)

Wang, Wayne (1949–) Chin. film director (*Eat a Bowl of Tea*; *The Joy Luck Club*)

Wanger, Walter (Walter Feuchtwanger) (1894–1968) Am. film producer (*Queen Christina*; *The Coconuts*)

Wapner, Joseph (Joseph A. Wapner) (1919–) Am. judge ("The People's Court" TV series)

Ward, Anita (1957–) Am. disco singer ("Ring My Bell")

Ward, Artemus (Charles Farrar Browne [orig. Brown]) (1834–1867) Am. humorist (*Vanity Fair*)

Ward, Burt (Herbert John Gervis, Jr.) (1945–) Am. actor (Robin in TV's "Batman")

Ward, Fred (1943–) Am. actor (*The Right Stuff*; *Henry & June*; *Miami Blues*)

Ward, Jay (1931–1989) Am. cartoonist (*Bullwinkle*)

Ward, Montgomery (Aaron Montgomery Ward) (1843–1913) Am. merchant

Ward, Rachel (1957–) Eng.-Am. actress (*The Thorn Birds*; *After Dark, My Sweet*; *Dead Men Don't Wear Plaid*)

Ward, Robert (1917–) Am. composer (P—1962—*The Crucible*)

Ward, Sela (1956–) Am. actress ("Sisters" TV series)

Warden, Jack (Jack Warden Lebzetter) (1920–) Am. actor ("Crazy Like a Fox" TV series)

Warfield, Marsha (1955–) Am. actress ("Night Court" TV series)/talk show host

Warfield, Paul (Paul Dryden Warfield; "Mr. Unemotional") (1942–) Am. football Hall-of-Famer

Warfield, Wallis (Bessie Wallis Warfield; married name Simpson; "Wally") (1896–1986) Duchess of Windsor

Warhol, Andy (Andrew Warhola) (1926–1987) Am. artist/filmmaker (*Kitchen*; *Bad*; founded *Interview* magazine)

Wariner, Steve (1954–) Am. country singer ("All Roads Lead to You")

Waring, Fred (Frederic Malcolm Waring; "The Man Who Taught America to Sing") (1900–1984) Am. orchestra leader/inventor (Waring blender)

Warneke, Lon (Lonnie Warneke; "The Arkansas Hummingbird") (1909–1976) Am. baseball pitcher

Warner, H. B. (Henry Byron Warner-Lickford) (1876–1958) Eng. actor (*Lost Horizon*; *King of Kings*)

Warner, Jack L. (Jack Leonard Warner; born Jack Eichelbaum) (1892–1978) Am. film producer (one of the Warner Brothers; *My Fair Lady*)

Warner, John (John William Warner) (1927–) Am. senator

Warner, Malcolm Jamal (1970–) Am. actor ("The Cosby Show" TV series)

Warner, Pop (Glenn Scobey Warner) (1871–1954) Am. football coach

Warner, Sylvia Townsend (1893–1978) Eng. novelist/poet/short story writer (*The Corner That Held Them*)

Warnes, Jennifer (1947–) Am. pop singer ("Right Time of the Night"; with Joe Cocker, "Up Where We Belong"; with Bill Medley, "[I've Had] The Time of My Life" from *Dirty Dancing*)

Warren, Earl (1891–1974) Am. attorney general/Supreme Court chief justice (1953–1969)

Warren, Harry (1893–1981) Am. songwriter ("Lullaby of Broadway"; "Shuffle Off to Buffalo"; "You Must Have Been a Beautiful Baby")

Warren, Jennifer (1941–) Am. actress (*Ice Castles*)

Warren, Leonard (Leonard Vaarenov) (1911–1960) Am. opera singer (baritone)

Warren, Lesley Ann (1946–) Am. actress (*Choose Me*; *Clue*; *Life Stinks*)

Warren, Robert Penn (1905–1989) Am. novelist/poet (P—1947—*All the King's Men*; P—1958—*Promises: Poems 1954–1956*; P—1979—*Now and Then: Poems 1976–1978*)

Warrick, Ruth (1915–) Am. actress (*Citizen Kane*; *Journey into Fear*; "All My Children" soap opera)

Warwick, Dionne (Marie Dionne Warwick) (1940–) Am. pop singer ("Then Came You"; "Walk on By"; G—1968, 1970, 1979)

Washburn, Bryant (1889–1963) Am. actor (*Sutter's Gold*; *The Wizard of Oz*)

Washington, Booker T. (Booker Taliaferro Washington) (1856–1915) Am. educator/writer (*Up from Slavery*)

Washington, Denzel (Denzel Washington, Jr.) (1954–) Am. actor (*Malcolm X* [title role]; O—1989—*Glory*; *Philadelphia*; *The Pelican Brief*)

Washington, Dinah (Ruth Lee Jones; "Queen of the Blues") (1924–1963) Am. pianist/blues singer ("What a Diff'rence a Day Makes")

Washington, George ("The Father of His Country") (1732–1799) 1st Am. pres. (1789–1797)

Washington, Grover, Jr. (1943–) Am. saxophonist/pop singer (with Bill Withers, "Just the Two of Us")

Washington, Martha (Martha Dandridge Custis) (1732–1802) Am. first lady (George)

Wasserstein, Wendy (1950–) Am. playwright (P—1989—*The Heidi Chronicles*)

Waterfield, Bob (Robert Stanton Waterfield; "Rifle") (1920–1983) Am. football Hall-of-Famer

Waters, Ethel (1896–1977) Am. singer ("Heat Wave")/actress (*The Member of the Wedding*)

Waters, John (1946–) Am. film director (*Cry-Baby*; *Lust in the Dust*; *Polyester*; *Serial Mom*)

Waters, Maxine (1938–) Am. congresswoman

Waters, Muddy (McKinley Morganfield) (1915–1983) Am. blues singer ("I've Got My Mojo Working"; "Honey Bee")

Waters, Roger (George Roger Waters) (1943–) Eng. rock musician/singer (with Pink Floyd)

Waterston, Sam (Samuel Atkinson Waterston) (1940–) Am. actor ("I'll Fly Away" TV series; *Crimes and Misdemeanors*)

Watley, Jody (1959–) Am. pop singer ("Looking for a New Love"; "Real Love"; formerly with Shalamar; G—1987)

Watrous, Bill (1939–) Am. jazz trombonist

Watson, Bobs (Robert Watson) (1931–) Am. child actor (*On Borrowed Time*; *Boys Town*)

Watson, Doc (Arthel Lane Watson) (1923–) Am. country guitarist/entertainer

Watson, James (James Dewey Watson) (1928–) Am. biologist (discovered DNA with Francis Crick; N—1962)

Watson, Lucile (1879–1962) Can. actress (*The Razor's Edge*; *Watch on the Rhine*)

Watson, Tom (Thomas Sturges Watson) (1949–) Am. golfer

Watt, James (1736–1819) Scot. engineer/inventor (condensing steam engine, copying machine)

Watt, James (James Gaius Watt) (1938–)

Am. lawyer/govt. official (secretary of the interior)

Watteau, Antoine (Jean-Antoine Watteau) (1684–1721) Fr. rococo painter

Watterson, Bill (1958–) Am. cartoonist (*Calvin & Hobbes*)

Wattleton, Faye (Alyce Faye Wattleton) (1943–) Am. head of Planned Parenthood/lecturer

Watts, Alan (Alan Witson Watts) (1915–1973) Am. lecturer/philosopher/writer (*Spirit of Zen*)

Watts, Andre (1946–) Am. concert pianist

Watts, Charlie (Charles Robert Watts) (1941–) Eng. rock musician (with The Rolling Stones)

Watts, Isaac (1674–1748) Eng. theologian/writer (*Psalms of David*)

Waugh, Alec (Alexander Raban Waugh) (1898–1981) Eng. novelist (*Loom of Youth*)/travel writer (*Island in the Sun*; brother of Evelyn)

Waugh, Auberon (Auberon Alexander Waugh) (1939–) Eng. novelist/journalist (son of Evelyn; *The Foxglove Saga*)

Waugh, Evelyn (Evelyn Arthur St. John Waugh) (1903–1966) Eng. novelist (*The Loved One*; *Brideshead Revisited*; brother of Alec)

Waugh, Hillary (Hillary Baldwin Waugh) (1920–) Am. detective story writer/novelist (*Madman at My Door*)

Waxman, Franz (Franz Wachsmann) (1906–1967) Ger.-Am. film composer (*Sunset Boulevard*; *A Place in the Sun*)

Waxman, Henry (1939–) Am. congressman

Wayans, Damon (1960–) Am. actor (brother of Keenen Ivory; "In Living Color" TV series)

Wayans, Keenen Ivory (1958–) Am. actor ("In Living Color" TV series; *I'm Gonna Git You Sucka*)

Waybill, Fee (John Waldo) (1950–) Am. rock singer (with The Tubes)

Wayne, David (Wayne James McMeekan) (1914–) Am. actor (*Adam's Rib*; *How to Marry a Millionaire*; T—1954)

Wayne, John (Marion Michael Morrison; a/k/a Duke Morrison; "The Duke") (1907–1979) Am. actor (*The Quiet Man*; *The Shootist*; *Rio Bravo*; *The Searchers*; O—1969—*True Grit*)

Weatherford, Teddy (1903–1945) Am. jazz pianist

Weathers, Carl (C) Am. actor (*Rocky*; *Action Jackson*)

Weaver, Dennis (1924–) Am. actor ("Gunsmoke" and "McCloud" TV series; E—1958/59)

Weaver, Doodles (Winstead Sheffield Glendening Dixon Weaver) (1911–1983) Am. comedian (with Spike Jones' band)

Weaver, Earl (Earl Sidney Weaver; "The Earl of Baltimore") (1930–) Am. baseball manager

Weaver, Fritz (Fritz William Weaver) (1926–) Am. actor (*Holocaust*; *Marathon Man*; T—1970)

Weaver, Sigourney (Susan Weaver) (1949–) Am. actress (niece of Doodles; *Alien* films; *Ghostbusters*; *Working Girl*)

Webb, Beatrice (Martha Beatrice Potter) (1858–1943) Eng. socialist writer (*Life and Labour of the People in England*)/autobiographer (*My Apprenticeship*)

Webb, Chick (William Webb) (1909–1939) Am. jazz drummer/bandleader

Webb, Chloe (C) Am. actress (*Sid and Nancy*)

Webb, Clifton (Webb Parmalle [or Parmelee] Hollenbeck) (1891–1966) Am. actor (*Laura*; *The Razor's Edge*)

Webb, Jack (Jack Randolph Webb; a/k/a John Farr and Tex Grady) (1920–1982) Am. actor/writer ("Dragnet" [as Sgt. Joe Friday] TV series; signature phrase: "Just the facts, ma'am")

Webb, James R. (1909–1974) Am. short story writer/screenwriter (*How the West Was Won*; *Cape Fear*; *The Big Country*)

Webb, Jimmy (Jimmy Layne Webb) (1946–) Am. songwriter/musician ("Up, Up and Away"; "By the Time I Get to Phoenix")

Webber, Andrew Lloyd (1948–) Eng. theatrical composer (*Phantom of the Opera*; *Cats*; *Evita*; *Jesus Christ Superstar*)

Weber, Carl von (Carl Maria Friedrich Ernst von Weber) (1786–1826) Ger. composer (*Invitation to the Dance*)

Weber, Max (1864–1920) Ger. sociologist/historian (*The Protestant Ethic and the Spirit of Capitalism*)

Webster, Daniel ("Defender of the Constitution") (1782–1852) Am. lawyer/govt. official (secretary of state)

Webster, Noah (1758–1843) Am. lexicographer/writer (*An American Dictionary of the English Language*)

Webster, William (William Hedgcock Webster) (1924–) Am. govt. official (head of the CIA and FBI)

Wedgwood, Josiah (1730–1795) Eng. potter/inventor (jasperware; pyrometer)

Weegee (Arthur Felig) (1899–1968) Aus.-Am. photographer (city people)

Weems, Mason (Mason Locke Weems; a/k/a Parson Weems) (1759–1825) Am. clergyman/biographer (*Benjamin Franklin*)

Weidman, Jerome (1913–) Am. novelist/short story writer/playwright (P—1960—*Fiorello*)

Weil, Simone (1909–1943) Fr. philosopher/mystic (*Oppression and Liberty*)

Weill, Kurt (Kurt Julian Weill) (1900–1950) Ger.-Am. composer (*The Threepenny Opera*)

Weinberger, Caspar (Caspar Willard Weinberger; "Cap the Knife") (1917–) Am. govt. official (defense secretary)

Weinmeister, Arnie (Arnold Weinmeister) (1923–) Am. football Hall-of-Famer

Weir, Bob (Robert Hall) (1947–) Am. rock guitarist/singer (with The Grateful Dead)

Weir, Peter (Peter Lindsay Weir) (1944–) Austral. film director (*Witness*; *Gallipolli*; *Dead Poets Society*; *Green Card*)

Weisberg, Tim (1943–) Am. pop/jazz flute player ("Power of Gold")

Weiss, Peter (Peter Ulrich Weiss) (1916–1982) Ger. playwright (*Marat/Sade*)/novelist (*Vanishing Point*)

Weissmuller, Johnny (Peter John Weissmuller) (1904–1984) Am. swimmer/actor (*Jungle Jim*; *Tarzan and the Amazons*)

Weizmann, Chaim (Chaim Azriel Weizmann) (1874–1952) Russ. chemist/1st pres. of Israel 1949–1952

Welch, Bob (1946–) Am. rock singer/musician ("Sentimental Lady"; formerly with Fleetwood Mac)

Welch, Lenny (1938–) Am. pop singer ("Since I Fell for You")

Welch, Raquel (Raquel Tejada) (1940–) Am. actress (*One Million Years B.C.*; *Myra Breckenridge*)

Weld, Tuesday (Susan Kerr Weld) (1943–) Am. actress (*The Cincinnati Kid*; *A Safe Place*; *Author! Author!*)

Weldon, Fay (1931–) Eng. writer/novelist (*The Life and Loves of a She Devil*; *Leader of the Band*)

Welk, Lawrence ("The King of Champagne Music"; "Mr. Music-Maker") (1903–1992) Am. bandleader/accordionist/TV host (theme song: "I'm Forever Blowing Bubbles")

Weller, Peter (1947–) Am. actor (*Robocop*; *Naked Lunch*; *Leviathan*)

Welles, Orson (George Orson Welles; "The Boy Genius") (1915–1985) Am. film director/actor (*Citizen Kane*; *Touch of Evil*; *The Magnificent Ambersons*)

Welles, Sumner (1892–1961) Am. diplomat (developed the Good Neighbor Policy)

Wellington, Duke of (Arthur Wellesley; born Arthur Wesley; "The Iron Duke") (1769–1852) Ir.-Eng. general/prime minister 1828–1830

Wellman, William (William Augustus Wellman; "Wild Bill") (1896–1975) Am. film director (*Nothing Sacred*; *Public Enemy*)

Wells, H. G. (Herbert George Wells; a/k/a Reginald Bliss) (1866–1946) Eng. novelist/journalist (*The War of the Worlds*; *The Time Machine*)

Wells, Ida (Ida Bell Wells; a/k/a Ida Wells-Barnett) (1862–1931) Am. social reformer (led antilynching campaigns)

Wells, Kitty (Muriel Deason Wright; "Queen of Country Music") (1918–) Am. country singer ("Heartbreak, U.S.A.")

Wells, Mary (1943–1992) Am. gospel/blues/pop singer ("Two Lovers"; "My Guy")

Welty, Eudora (1909–) Am. novelist/short story writer (P—1973—*The Optimist's Daughter*; *One Writer's Beginnings*)

Wen, Ming-Na (c. 1969–) Chin.-Am. actress (*The Joy Luck Club*)

Wenders, Wim (Wilhelm Ernst Wenders) (1945–) Ger. film director (*Wings of Desire*; *Paris, Texas*)

Wendt, George (1947–) Am. actor ("Cheers" TV series)

Wenner, Jann (1946–) Am. magazine editor (*Rolling Stone*)

Wenonah (dates of birth and death unknown) Am. Indian woman (mother of Hiawatha)

Werfel, Franz (1890–1945) Ger. novelist/poet/playwright (*The Song of Bernadette*)

Werner, Oskar (Oskar Josef Schliessmayer) (1922–1984) Aus. actor (*Fahrenheit 451*; *Jules and Jim*)

Werner, Tom (c. 1950–) Am. TV producer (with Marcy Carsey, "The Cosby Show"; "Roseanne"; "Grace Under Fire")

Wertmuller, Lina (Arcangela Felice Assunta Wertmuller Von Elgg Spanol Von Brauchich) (1928–) Ital. film director (*Swept Away*; *Seven Beauties*)

Wesley, Charles (1707–1788) Eng. hymn writer ("Hark, the Herald Angels Sing")

Wesley, John (1703–1791) Eng. founder of Methodism

West, Adam (William Anderson) (1929–) Am. actor (TV's "Batman")

West, Alvy (1915–) Am. orchestra leader

West, Anthony (Anthony Panther West) (1914–1987) Eng. novelist/critic (son of Rebecca West and H. G. Wells)

West, Benjamin (1738–1820) Am. painter (*Christ Healing the Sick*)

West, Dottie (Dorothy Marie Marsh) (1932–1991) Am. country singer (with Kenny Rogers, "What Are We Doin' in Love")

West, Jerry (Jerome Allen West; "Mr. Clutch"; "Zeke from Cabin Creek") (1938–) Am. basketball player

West, Jessamyn (Mary Jessamyn West) (1902–1984) Am. writer (*Double Discovery: A Journey*)

West, Mae (1892–1980) Am. actress (*She Done Him Wrong; Diamond Lil; My Little Chickadee*)

West, Morris L. (Morris Langlo West) (1916–) Austral. novelist (*The Shoes of the Fisherman*)

West, Nathanael (Nathan Wallenstein Weinstein) (1903–1940) Am. novelist (*The Day of the Locust; Miss Lonely Hearts*)

West, Dame Rebecca (Cicely Isabel Fairfield Andrews) (1892–1983) Eng. journalist/novelist/critic (*The Return of a Soldier; The Fountain Overflows*)

West, Shelly (1958–) Am. country singer (daughter of Dottie; "Jose Cuervo")

Westheimer, Dr. Ruth (Karola Ruth Siegel) (1928 or 1929–) Am. sex therapist/radio talk show host

Westinghouse, George (1846–1914) Am. inventor (railroad air brakes, railroad signals)/businessman

Westlake, Donald E. (Donald Edwin Edmund Westlake; a/k/a Richard Stark and Tucker Cole) (1933–) Am. mystery writer (*God Save the Mark*)

Westman, Nydia (1902–1970) Am. actress (*The Cat and the Canary; Little Women*)

Westmoreland, William (William Childs Westmoreland) (1914–) Am. army general/chief of staff

Weston, Edward (1886–1958) Am. photographer

Weston, Paul (Paul Wetstein) (1912–) Am. musician/composer   ("Nevertheless")

Westover, Russ (Russell Channing Westover) (1886–1966) Am. cartoonist (*Tillie the Toiler*)

Westwood, Vivienne (1941–) Eng. punk fashion designer

Wettig, Patricia (1951–) Am. actress ("thirtysomething" TV series; E—1987/88, 1989/90, 1990/91)

Wetton, John (1949–) Eng. rock bassist/singer (with Uriah Heep, Roxy Music, and Asia)

Weyden, Rogier Van Der (a/k/a Roger de La Pasture) (c. 1400–1464) Flem. painter (*Christ on the Cross*)

Weymouth, Tina (Martina Weymouth) (1950–) Am. rock musician (with The Talking Heads)

Whale, James (1886–1957) Eng. film director (*Frankenstein; The Invisible Man; The Bride of Frankenstein*)

Whalley-Kilmer, Joanne (Joanne Whalley) (1964–) Eng.-Am. actress (*Scandal*)

Wharton, Edith (Edith Newbold Wharton née Jones) (1862–1937) Am. novelist/short story writer (*Ethan Frome*; P—1921—*The Age of Innocence*)

Wheat, Zack (Zachary Davis Wheat; "Buck") (1886–1972) Am. baseball Hall-of-Famer

Wheatley, Phillis (c. 1753–1784) Am. poet (first Afr.-Am. woman to have poetry published)

Wheaton, Wil (1972–) Am. actor (*Stand by Me; Toy Soldiers;* "Star Trek: The Next Generation" TV series)

Wheeler, William A. (William Almon Wheeler) (1819–1887) Am. v.p. (R. B. Hayes)

Whelan, Jill (1966–) Am. child actress ("The Love Boat" TV series)

Whelan, Tim (1893–1957) Am. film director (*The Divorce of Lady X; Tramp Tramp Tramp*)

Whelchel, Lisa (1963–) Am. actress ("The Facts of Life" TV series)

Whistler, James McNeill (James Abbott McNeill Whistler) (1834–1903) Am. etcher/painter (*Portrait of the Artist's Mother*)

Whitaker, Forest (1961–) Am. actor (*The Color of Money; The Crying Game; Consenting Adults*)

White, Antonia (1899–1980) Eng. journalist/novelist (*Frost in May*)

White, Barry (1944–) Am. soul/pop

singer/bandleader ("Can't Get Enough of Your Love, Babe"; with Love Unlimited Orchestra)

White, Betty (Betty Marion White) (1922–) Am. actress ("The Mary Tyler Moore Show" and "The Golden Girls" TV series; E—1974/75, 1975/76, 1985/86)

White, Byron (Byron Raymond White; "Whizzer") (1917–) Am. Supreme Court jurist (1962–1993)

White, E. B. (Elwyn Brooks White) (1899–1985) Am. novelist/essayist/humorist (*Charlotte's Web*; *Stuart Little*; *One Man's Meat*)

White, Edward D. (Edward Douglass White) (1845–1921) Am. Supreme Court chief justice (1910–1921)

White, Jaleel (1976–) Am. actor ("Family Matters" TV series)

White, Jesse (Jesse Marc Weidenfeld) (1919–) Am. actor (the "lonely Maytag repairman" in TV commercials)

White, Josh (1908–1969) Am. folksinger ("Sometimes I Feel Like a Motherless Child")

White, Karyn (1965–) Am. pop singer ("Romantic"; "Way You Love Me")

White, Maurice (1941–) Am. pop singer (with Earth, Wind & Fire)

White, Patrick (Patrick Victor Martindale White) (1912–1990) Austral. novelist (*The Tree of Man*; *The Eye of the Storm*; N—1973)

White, Pearl (Pearl Fay White; "Queen of Silent Serials") (1897–1938) Am. actress (*The Perils of Pauline*)

White, Randy (Randy Lee White) (1953–) Am. football player

White, Stanford ("The Builder") (1853–1906) Am. architect (Madison Square Garden)

White, T. H. (Terence Hanbury White) (1906–1964) Eng. writer (*The Once and Future King*)

White, Theodore (Theodore Harold White) (1915–1986) Am. journalist/writer (P—1962—*The Making of the President 1960*)

White, Vanna (Vanna Marie White) (1957–) Am. game show personality (letter-turner on "Wheel of Fortune")

White, William Allen ("The Sage of Emporia") (1868–1944) Am. journalist (P—1923)/writer (P—1947—*The Autobiography of William Allen White*)

Whitehead, Alfred North (1861–1947)

Eng. philosopher/mathematician (with Bertrand Russell, *Principia Mathematica*)

Whitehead, William (1715–1785) Eng. poet laureate (*The Roman Father*)

Whiteman, Paul ("Pops"; "King of Jazz") (1890–1967) Am. jazz bandleader

Whiting, Margaret ("Madcap Maggie") (1924–) Am. singer ("A Tree in the Meadow")

Whitley, Keith (1955–1989) Am. country singer ("Don't Close Your Eyes")

Whitman, Charles ("The Tower Murderer") (1942–1966) Am. mass murderer (killed 18 people and injured 30 others with a rifle from a tower on a Texas college campus)

Whitman, Slim (Otis Whitman, Jr.) (1924–) Am. country singer/musician ("Indian Love Call")

Whitman, Stuart (Stuart Maxwell Whitman) (1926–) Am. actor (*Ten North Frederick*; *Those Magnificent Men in Their Flying Machines*)

Whitman, Walt (Walter Whiteman) (1819–1892) Am. poet (*Leaves of Grass*)

Whitney, Cornelius Vanderbilt (1899–1992) Am. businessman (with Juan Trippe, founded Pan Am Airways)/government official/racehorse breeder

Whitney, Eli (1765–1825) Am. inventor (cotton gin)

Whitney, Gertrude (née) **Vanderbilt** (a/k/a L. J. Webb) (1875–1942) Am. sculptor/museum founder

Whitney, Grace Lee (1930–) Am. singer/actress ("Star Trek" TV series)

Whitney, Phyllis A. (Phyllis Ayame Whitney) (1903–) Am. mystery writer/children's book writer/novelist (*Black Amber*)

Whittaker, Charles E. (1901–1973) Am. Supreme Court jurist (1957–1962)

Whittier, John Greenleaf ("The Poet Laureate of New England"; "The Puritan Poet") (1807–1892) Am. politician/poet (*Snow-Bound*; *The Tent on the Beach*)

Whitty, Dame May (1865–1948) Eng. actress (*The Lady Vanishes*; *Mrs. Miniver*)

Whitworth, Kathy (Kathrynne Ann Whitworth) (1939–) Am. golfer

Wicker, Ireene Seaton ("Lady with a Thousand Voices"; "The Singing Lady") (1905–1987) Am. radio/TV personality

Widmark, Richard ("Young Man with a Sneer") (1914–) Am. actor (*Murder on*

the Orient Express; *Madigan*; *Judgment at Nuremberg*)
Wiedlin, Jane (1958–) Am. pop guitarist (with The Go-Go's)/singer ("Rush Hour")
Wiesel, Elie (Eliezer Wiesel) (1928–) Rom.-Am. novelist/essayist (*Night*; N—1986)
Wiesenthal, Simon (1908–) Aus. Nazi hunter/war crimes investigator
Wiest, Dianne (1948–) Am. actress (*Radio Days*; *Parenthood*; O—1986—*Hannah and Her Sisters*)
Wiggin, Kate (Kate Douglas Smith Wiggin) (1856–1923) Am. children's book writer (*Rebecca of Sunnybrook Farm*)
Wilberforce, William (1759–1833) Eng. abolitionist/philanthropist/politician
Wilbur, Richard (Richard Purdy Wilbur) (1921–) Am. poet (P—1957—*Things of This World*; P—1989—*New and Collected Poems*)
Wilde, Cornel (Cornelius Louis Wilde) (1915–1989) Am. actor (*The Naked Prey*; *The Greatest Show on Earth*)
Wilde, Kim (Kim Smith) (1960–) Eng. pop singer ("You Keep Me Hangin' On"; "Kids in America")
Wilde, Oscar (Oscar Fingal O'Flahertie Wills Wilde) (1854–1900) Ir. poet/playwright/novelist (*The Importance of Being Earnest*; *The Picture of Dorian Gray*)
Wilder, Billy (Samuel Wilder) (1906–) Aus.-Am. film director/writer (*Sunset Boulevard*; O—1945—*The Lost Weekend*; O—1960—*The Apartment*)
Wilder, Gene (Jerome Silberman) (1933–) Am. comedian/actor (*Blazing Saddles*; *Young Frankenstein*; *Funny About Love*)
Wilder, Laura Ingalls (Laura Elizabeth Ingalls) (1867–1957) Am. children's book writer (*Little House on the Prairie*)
Wilder, L. Douglas (1931–) Am. gov. of Virginia
Wilder, Robert (Robert Ingersoll Wilder) (1901–1974) Am. novelist/screenwriter (*Written on the Wind*)
Wilder, Thornton (Thornton Niven Wilder) (1897–1975) Am. novelist/playwright (*The Matchmaker* [staged/filmed as *Hello, Dolly!*]; P—1928—*The Bridge of San Luis Rey*; P—1938—*Our Town*; P—1943—*The Skin of Our Teeth*)
Wilding, Michael (1912–1979) Eng. actor (*In Which We Serve*; *Stage Fright*)

Wilhelm, Hoyt (James Hoyt Wilhelm) (1923–) Am. baseball Hall-of-Famer
Wilhelmina (Wilhelmina Helena Pauline Maria) (1880–1962) Dutch queen 1890–1948
Wilkes, Jamaal (Jackson Keith Wilkes) (1953–) Am. basketball player
Will, George (George Frederick Will) (1941–) Am. columnist (*Newsweek*)/political commentator (P—1977)/writer (*The Pursuit of Happiness and Other Sobering Thoughts*; *Men at Work*)
Willard, Frank Henry (1893–1958) Am. cartoonist (created Moon Mullins, Lady Plushbottom, and Mushmouth)
Willard, Jess (1883–1968) Am. boxer
William (William Arthur Philip Louis; "Wills") (1981–) Eng. prince (son of Charles and Diana)
William I (1797–1888) Ger. emperor/king 1861–1888
William I ("William the Conqueror") (c. 1028–1087) Eng. king 1066–1087
William II (1859–1941) Ger. emperor/king 1888–1918
William II (William Rufus) (c. 1056–1100) Eng. king 1087–1100
William III (1662–1694) king of England, Scotland, and Ireland 1689–1702
William IV ("The Sailor King"; "Silly Billy") (1765–1837) king of England, Ireland, and Hanover 1830–1837
Williams, Andy (Howard Andrew Williams) (1928–) Am. singer ("Butterfly"; "Can't Get Used to Losing You")
Williams, Anson (Anson William Heimlick) (1949–) Am. actor ("Happy Days" TV series)
Williams, Bill (William Katt) (1916–) Am. actor ("The Adventures of Kit Carson" TV series)
Williams, Billy Dee (1937–) Am. actor (*Brian's Song*; *Star Wars*; *Lady Sings the Blues*)
Williams, Cara (Bernice Kamiat) (1925–) Am. radio/TV comedienne ("Rhoda" TV series)
Williams, Cindy (Cynthia Jane Williams) (1947–) Am. actress ("Laverne & Shirley" TV series)
Williams, Cootie (Charles Melvin Williams) (1908–1985) Am. jazz trumpeter
Williams, Cynda (c. 1966–) Am. actress (*One False Move*)
Williams, Deniece (Deniece Chandler) (1951–) Am. pop singer ("Too Much, Too

Little, Too Late"; "Let's Hear It for the Boy")
Williams, Don ("The Gentle Giant") (1939–) Am. country singer ("Back in My Younger Days")
Williams, Emlyn (George Emlyn Williams) (1905–1987) Wel. actor/director/playwright (*The Citadel*)
Williams, Esther (Esther Jane Williams; "Hollywood's Mermaid"; "The Queen of the Surf") (1923–) Am. swimmer/actress (*Take Me Out to the Ball Game*; *Dangerous When Wet*)
Williams, Gus (1953–) Am. basketball player
Williams, Guy (Armando Catalano) (1924–) Am. actor (Zorro in the Disney TV series and films)
Williams, Hank (Hiram Hank Williams; "The Drifting Cowboy"; "The Hillbilly Shakespeare") (1923–1953) Am. country singer ("Your Cheatin' Heart"; "I'm So Lonesome I Could Cry")
Williams, Hank, Jr. (Randall Hank Williams; "Bocephus") (1949–) Am. country singer ("Eleven Roses"; "Honky Tonkin' ")
Williams, JoBeth (Margaret JoBeth Williams) (1953–) Am. actress (*The Big Chill*; *American Dreamer*)
Williams, Joe (Joseph Goreed) (1918–) Am. jazz singer
Williams, John (John Towner Williams; a/k/a Johnny Williams) (1932–) Am. film composer (*Star Wars*; *E.T.: The Extraterrestrial*; *Jaws*; *Jurassic Park*)
Williams, Kimberly (c. 1971–) Am. actress (*Father of the Bride*; *Indian Summer*)
Williams, Montel (c. 1957–) Am. talk show host
Williams, Paul (Paul Hamilton Williams) (1940–) Am. pianist/songwriter ("Rainy Days & Mondays"; "We've Only Just Begun")
Williams, Robin (1952–) Am. comedian/actor ("Mork & Mindy" TV series; *Awakenings*; *The World According to Garp*; *Good Morning Vietnam*)
Williams, Roger (Louis Weertz) (1926–) Am. pianist/composer ("Autumn Leaves")
Williams, Ted (Theodore Samuel Williams; "The Splendid Splinter"; "The Thumper"; "Mr. Ballgame"; "The Kid") (1918–) Am. baseball Hall-of-Famer
Williams, Tennessee (Thomas Lanier Williams) (1911–1983) Am. playwright (*The Glass Menagerie*; *Sweet Bird of Youth*; P—1948—*A Streetcar Named Desire*; P—1955—*Cat on a Hot Tin Roof*)
Williams, Treat (Richard Treat Williams) (1951–) Am. actor (*Prince of the City*; *Once Upon a Time in America*)
Williams, Vanessa (1963–) Am. pop singer ("Dreamin' ")/Miss America 1984 (resigned)
Williams, Wendy O. (Wendy Orlean Williams) (1946–) Am. rock singer (with The Plasmatics)
Williamson, Jack (John Stewart Williamson) (1908–) Am. science fiction writer (*Firechild*; *The Humanoids*)
Williamson, Marianne (c. 1953–) Am. spiritualist/writer (*A Return to Love*; *A Woman's Worth*)
Williamson, Nicol (1938–) Scot. actor (*The Reckoning*; *The Seven Per-Cent Solution*)
Willis, Bill (William Willis) (1921–) Am. football Hall-of-Famer
Willis, Bruce (Bruce Walter [or Walter Bruce] Willis; "Bruno") (1955–) Am. actor (*Die Hard*; *Hudson Hawk*; *The Last Boy Scout*; "Moonlighting" TV series; E—1986/87)
Willis, Kelly (c. 1968–) Am. country singer ("Baby, Take a Piece of My Heart")
Willkie, Wendell (Wendell Lewis Willkie) (1892–1944) Am. businessman/politician/presidential candidate 1940/writer (*One World*)
Wills, Bob (James Robert Wills; "King of Western Swing") (1905–1975) Am. country singer/songwriter ("San Antonio Rose")
Wills, Chill (1903–1978) Am. actor (*Giant*; *The Alamo*)
Wills, Helen (Helen Newington Wills; a/k/a Helen Wills Moody; "Little Miss Poker Face"; "Queen Helen"; "The Princess"; "The Queen of Courts") (1905–) Am. tennis player
Wills, Maury (Maurice Morning Wills) (1932–) Am. baseball player
Willson, Meredith (Robert Meredith Reiniger) (1902–1984) Am. songwriter/conductor (*The Music Man*)
Wilson, Sir Angus (Frank Johnstone-Wilson) (1913–) Eng. novelist/short story writer (*Hemlock and After*)
Wilson, Ann (1951–) Am. rock singer (with Heart; also, with Mike Reno, "Almost

Paradise ... Love Theme from *Foot-loose*"; sister of Nancy)
Wilson, August (1945–) Am. playwright (*Ma Rainey's Black Bottom*; P—1987—*Fences*; P—1990—*The Piano Lesson*; *Joe Turner's Come and Gone*)
Wilson, Bill (William Griffith Wilson; "Bill W.") (1895–1971) Am. founder of Alcoholics Anonymous (with Bob Smith)
Wilson, Brian (Brian Douglas Wilson) (1942–) Am. pop singer/musician/songwriter (with The Beach Boys)
Wilson, Carl (Carl Dean Wilson) (1946–) Am. pop musician/singer (with The Beach Boys)
Wilson, Carnie (c. 1968–) Am. pop singer (with Wilson Phillips; daughter of Brian, sister of Wendy)
Wilson, Cindy (1957–) Am. rock singer (with The B-52s; "Love Shack"; "Rock Lobster")
Wilson, Colin (Colin Henry Wilson) (1931–) Eng. critic/novelist (*The Outsider*)
Wilson, Demond (1946–) Am. actor ("Sanford & Son" TV series)
Wilson, Dennis (1944–1983) Am. pop musician/singer (with The Beach Boys)
Wilson, Don (Donald Harlow Wilson) (1900–1982) Am. radio/TV announcer (with Jack Benny)
Wilson, Dooley (Arthur Wilson) (1894–1953) Am. pianist/actor (Sam in *Casablanca*)
Wilson, Earl (Harvey Earl Wilson) (1907–1987) Am. gossip columnist (*That's Earl, Brother*)
Wilson, Edmund ("Bunny") (1895–1972) Am. novelist/short story writer/critic/poet (*Axel's Castle*)/editor (*Vanity Fair*)
Wilson, Ellen (Ellen Louise Axson) (1860–1914) Am. first lady (Woodrow)
Wilson, Flip (Clerow Wilson) (1933–) Am. comedian (created Geraldine; "The Flip Wilson Show" TV series; signature phrase: "The devil made me do it")
Wilson, Gahan (1930–) Am. writer/cartoonist (for the *New Yorker* and *Playboy*)
Wilson, Hack (Lewis Robert Wilson; "The Million-Dollar Baby from the 5 & 10 Cent Store") (1900–1948) Am. baseball Hall-of-Famer
Wilson, Harry Leon (1867–1939) Am. novelist/playwright (*Ruggles of Red Gap*)
Wilson, Henry (1812–1875) Am. v.p. (U.S. Grant)/senator

Wilson, Jackie ("Mr. Excitement") (1932–1984) Am. pop singer ("Lonely Teardrops")
Wilson, Lanford (1937–) Am. playwright (P—1980—*Talley's Folly*; *Burn This*)
Wilson, Larry (Lawrence Frank Wilson; "Wildcat") (1938–) Am. football Hall-of-Famer
Wilson, Margaret (1882–1973) Am. novelist (P—1924—*The Able McLaughlins*)
Wilson, Marie (Katherine Elizabeth White) (1916–1972) Am. actress ("My Friend Irma" TV series; *Boy Meets Girl*)
Wilson, Mary (1944–) Am. pop singer (with The Supremes)
Wilson, Mookie (William Hayward Wilson) (1956–) Am. baseball player
Wilson, Nancy (1954–) Am. rock singer ("These Dreams")/guitarist (with Heart; sister of Ann)
Wilson, Nancy (1937–) Am. jazz singer ("Can't Take My Eyes off You")
Wilson, Pete (Peter Barton Wilson) (1933–) Am. gov. of California
Wilson, Shanice (1973–) Am. pop singer ("I Love Your Smile")
Wilson, Sloan (1920–) Am. novelist (*The Man in the Gray Flannel Suit*)
Wilson, Wendy (1969–) Am. pop singer (with Wilson Phillips; daughter of Brian; sister of Carnie)
Wilson, Woodrow (Thomas Woodrow Wilson) (1856–1924) 28th Am. pres. (1913–1921; N—1919)
Wimmer, Brian (c. 1960–) Am. actor ("China Beach" TV series)
Winchell, Paul (1922–) Am. ventriloquist (dummies' names: Jerry Mahoney, Knucklehead Smith)
Winchell, Walter (Walter Winchel) (1897–1972) Am. (New York) gossip columnist/broadcaster
Winchester, Oliver Fisher (1810–1880) Am. rifle manufacturer
Winding, Kai (Kai Chresten Winding) (1922–1983) Am. jazz trombonist/composer
Windom, William (1923–) Am. actor ("Murder, She Wrote" TV series; E—1969/70)
Winfield, Dave (David Mark Winfield; "The $25 Million Man") (1951–) Am. baseball player
Winfield, Paul (1940–) Am. actor (*Sounder*; "Julia" TV series)
Winfrey, Oprah (Oprah Gail Winfrey)

(1954–) Am. talk show host/actress (*The Color Purple*)

Wingate, Sir Reginald (Francis Reginald Wingate, Baronet) (1861–1953) Eng. army general

Winger, Debra (Mary Debra Winger) (1955–) Am. actress (*An Officer and a Gentleman; Urban Cowboy; Terms of Endearment; A Dangerous Woman*)

Winkler, Henry (Henry Franklin Winkler) (1945–) Am. actor ("Happy Days" [as The Fonz] TV series)

Winner, Michael (Michael Robert Winner) (1935–) Eng. film director (*Death Wish; The Mechanic; The Stone Killer*)

Winninger, Charles (Karl Winninger) (1884–1969) Am. actor (*Nothing Sacred; Destry Rides Again; Show Boat*)

Winningham, Mare (1959–) Am. actress (*Hard Promises; Turner and Hooch; St. Elmo's Fire*)

Winter, Alex (Alexander Winter) (1965–) Eng.-Am. actor (*The Lost Boys; Bill and Ted's Excellent Adventure*)

Winter, Edgar (Edgar Holand Winter) (1946–) Am. rock singer/musician (with The Edgar Winter Group and White Trash; "Frankenstein")

Winter, Johnny (John Dawson Winter III) (1944–) Am. blues guitarist/producer (Muddy Waters)

Winters, Jonathan (Jonathan Harshman Winters III) (1925–) Am. comedian ("Mork & Mindy" TV series; E— 1990/91)

Winters, Shelley (Shirley Schrift) (1922–) Am. actress (*A Double Life; A Place in the Sun*; O—1959—*The Diary of Anne Frank*; O—1965—*A Patch of Blue*)

Winthrop, John (1588–1649) Am. Puritan leader/gov. of Massachusetts

Wintour, Anna (1949–) Am. magazine editor (*Vogue*)

Winwood, Estelle (Estelle Goodwin; "Cow Eyes") (1883–1984) Eng. stage/actress (*The Swan; The Misfits*)

Winwood, Steve (Stevie Winwood) (1948–) Eng. rock singer/musician ("Higher Love"; "Roll with It"; formerly with The Spencer Davis Group, Blind Faith, and Traffic; G—1986)

Wise, Robert (Robert Earl Wise) (1914–) Am. film director/producer (O—1961—*West Side Story*; O—1965—*The Sound of Music*)

Wister, Owen (1860–1938) Am. westerns writer (*The Virginian*)

Withers, Bill (1938–) Am. pop singer/songwriter ("Lean on Me")

Withers, Jane (1926–) Am. actress (*Giant; The Farmer Takes a Wife*)

Witherspoon, Cora (1890–1957) Am. actress (*Libeled Lady; The Bank Dick*)

Witherspoon, Reese (c. 1976–) Am. actress (*Jack the Bear; The Man in the Moon*)

Witkin, Joel-Peter (c. 1940–) Am. fine-art photographer

Witt, Katarina (1965–) Ger. figure skater

Wittgenstein, Ludwig (Ludwig Josef Johan Wittgenstein) (1889–1951) Eng. philosopher (*Philosophical Investigations*)

Wodehouse, Sir P. G. (Pelham Grenville Wodehouse) (1881–1975) Eng.-Am. writer/humorist (created Jeeves; *Anything Goes*)

Wojciechowicz, Alex (Alexander Wojciechowicz; "Wojie") (1915–1992) Am. football Hall-of-Famer

Wolf, Christa (1929–) Ger. writer (*The Divided Heaven*)

Wolf, Naomi (1963–) Am. feminist writer (*The Beauty Myth*)

Wolf, Peter (Peter Blankenfield) (1946–) Am. rock singer (with The J. Geils Band; "Centerfold")

Wolfe, Thomas (Thomas Clayton Wolfe) (1900–1938) Am. novelist (*Look Homeward, Angel; You Can't Go Home Again*)

Wolfe, Tom (Thomas Kennerly Wolfe, Jr.) (1931–) Am. journalist/novelist (*The Bonfire of the Vanities; The Right Stuff; The Electric Kool-Aid Acid Test*)

Wolff, Tobias (1945–) Am. writer (*This Boy's Life: A Memoir*)

Wolfman Jack (Robert Smith) (1938–) Am. disc jockey/TV host ("Midnight Special")

Wollstonecraft, Mary (Mary Goodwin née Wollstonecraft) (1759–1797) Eng. feminist writer (mother of Mary Shelley)

Wolsey, Thomas (c. 1475–1530) Eng. cardinal/chancellor 1515–1529

Womack, Bobby ("The Preacher") (1944–) Am. soul/pop singer ("Lookin' for a Love")

Wonder, Stevie (Steveland Judkins Morris) (1950–) Am. pop singer ("You Are the Sunshine of My Life"; "Superstition"; "Sir Duke"; "I Just Called to Say I Love You"; G–1973, 1974, 1976)

Wong, Anna May (Wong Liu Tsong) (1907–1961) Chin.-Am. actress (*The Thief of Baghdad*; *Shanghai Express*)

Woo, John (c. 1943–) Chin.-Am. film director (*The Killer*; *Hard Boiled*; *Hard Target*)

Wood, Danny (1969–) Am. pop musician (with New Kids on the Block)

Wood, Grant (Grant De Volsen Wood) (1892–1942) Am. painter (*American Gothic*)

Wood, Lana (1946–) Am. actress ("Peyton Place" TV series)

Wood, Natalie (Natasha Nicholas Gurdin) (1938–1981) Am. actress (*Miracle on 34th Street*; *Rebel without a Cause*; *Splendor in the Grass*)

Wood, Peggy (Margaret Wood) (1892–1978) Am. opera singer/actress (TV's "Mama")

Wood, Ron (Ronald Wood) (1946–) Eng. rock guitarist (with The Rolling Stones)

Wood, Sam (Samuel Grosvenor Wood; a/k/a Chad Applegate) (1883–1949) Am. film director (*Goodbye, Mr. Chips*; *Madame X*)

Woodard, Alfre (1953–) Am. actress ("St. Elsewhere" TV series; *Miss Firecracker*; *Passion Fish*; *Bopha!*; *Crooklyn*; E— 1983–84)

Wooden, John (John Robert Wooden; "The India Rubber Man") (1910–) Am. basketball coach

Woods, James (1947–) Am. actor (*The Onion Field*; *Salvador*; *Citizen Cohn*)

Woodward, Bob (Robert Upshur Woodward) (1943–) Am. journalist (Watergate)/writer (with Carl Bernstein, *All the President's Men*)

Woodward, Edward (1930–) Eng. actor (TV's "The Equalizer")

Woodward, Joanne (Joanne Gignilliat Woodward) (1930–) Am. actress (*The Long Hot Summer*; *Mr. and Mrs. Bridge*; O—1957—*The Three Faces of Eve*)

Woolery, Chuck (c. 1943–) Am. TV host ("Love Connection")

Wooley, Sheb (Shelby F. Wooley; a/k/a Ben Colder) (1921–) Am. country/pop singer ("Purple People Eater")/actor ("Rawhide" TV series)

Woolf, Virginia (Adeline Virginia Woolf née Stephen) (1882–1941) Eng. novelist (*A Room of One's Own*; *To the Lighthouse*; *Orlando*)

Woollcott, Alexander (Alexander Humphreys Woollcott; "The Town Crier") (1887–1943) Am. journalist/critic/writer (*While Rome Burns*; *The Story of Irving Berlin*)

Woolley, Monty (Edgar Montillion Woolley; "Mr. Beard") (1888–1963) Am. actor (*The Man Who Came to Dinner*; *The Pied Piper*)

Woolrich, Cornell (a/k/a George Hopley and William Irish) (1903–1968) Am. suspense novelist/short story writer (*Rear Window*; *Phantom Lady*)

Woolworth, F. W. (Frank Winfield Woolworth) (1852–1919) Am. merchant (five-and-ten-cent stores)

Wopat, Tom (1951–) Am. country singer/actor ("The Dukes of Hazzard" TV series)

Wordsworth, William ("The Poet of Nature") (1770–1850) Eng. poet (*Tintern Abbey*)

Worley, Jo Anne (1937–) Am. comedienne ("Rowan & Martin's Laugh-In" TV series)

Woronov, Mary (c. 1943–) Am. actress (*Eating Raoul*; *Scenes from the Class Struggle in Beverly Hills*)

Worsley, Gump (Lorne John Worsley) (1929–) Can. hockey player

Worth, Charles (Charles Frederick Worth) (1825–1895) Eng. fashion designer

Worth, Irene (1916–) Eng. stage/film actress (*Death Trap*; *Nicholas and Alexandra*; T—1965, 1976)

Wouk, Herman (1915–) Am. novelist (*Marjorie Morningstar*; *The Winds of War*; P—1952—*The Caine Mutiny*)

Wozencraft, Kim (C) Am. writer (*Rush*; *Notes from the Country Club*)

Wozniak, Steve ("Rocky Raccoon Clark") (1950–) Am. computer entrepreneur (Apple Computer, Inc., with Steven Jobs)

Wray, Fay (1907–) Can.-Am. actress (*King Kong*; *The Wedding March*)

Wren, Sir Christopher (1632–1723) Eng. architect (St. Paul's Cathedral in London)

Wren, P. C. (Percival Christopher Wren) (1885–1941) Eng. adventure novelist (*Beau Geste*)

Wright, Amy (1950–) Am. actress (*The Accidental Tourist*; *Miss Firecracker*)

Wright, Frank Lloyd (c. 1867–1959) Am. architect ("Fallingwater" house; Guggenheim Museum)

Wright, Gary (1943–) Am. rock singer/ musician ("Dream Weaver"; formerly with Spooky Tooth)

Wright, Harry (William Henry Wright) (1835–1895) Am. baseball Hall-of-Famer

Wright, Michelle (1961—) Can.-Am. country singer ("Take It Like a Man")

Wright, Mickey (Mary Kathryn Wright) (1935–) Am. golfer

Wright, Orville (1871–1948) Am. aviation pioneer (with Wilbur, the Wright Brothers; invented the airplane)

Wright, Richard (Richard Nathaniel Wright) (1908–1960) Am. novelist (Native Son; Black Boy)

Wright, Robin (c. 1966–) Am. actress (The Princess Bride; Toys; The Playboys)

Wright, Steven (1955–) Am. comedian

Wright, Teresa (Muriel Teresa Wright) (1918–) Am. actress (The Little Foxes; Pride of the Yankees; O—1942—Mrs. Miniver)

Wright, Wilbur (1867–1912) Am. aviation pioneer (with Orville, the Wright Brothers; invented the airplane)

Wrigley, William, Jr. (1861–1932) Am. chewing gum manufacturer

Wyatt, Jane (Jane Waddington Wyatt) (1911–) Am. actress ("Father Knows Best" TV series; Lost Horizon; None but the Lonely Heart; E—1957, 1958/59, 1959/60)

Wyeth, Andrew (Andrew Newell Wyeth) (1917–) Am. painter (Christina's World; Helga Pictures)

Wyeth, Jamie (James Browning Wyeth) (1946–) Am. artist (son of Andrew)

Wyeth, N. C. (Newell Convers Wyeth) (1882–1945) Am. artist/illustrator (father of Andrew)

Wyler, Gretchen (Gretchen Patricia Wienecke) (1932–) Am. stage actress (Sweet Charity)

Wyler, William (1902–1981) Ger.-Am. film director (O—1942—Mrs. Miniver; O—1946—The Best Years of Our Lives; O—1959—Ben Hur)

Wyman, Bill (William George Wyman) (1941–) Eng. rock musician (with The Rolling Stones)

Wyman, Jane (Sarah Jane Fulks; a/k/a Jane Durrell) (1914–) Am. actress (The Lost Weekend; Magnificent Obsession; O—1948—Johnny Belinda)

Wyndham, John (John Wyndham Parkes Lucas Benyon Harris) (1903–1969) Eng. science fiction writer (The Day of The Triffids; The Midwich Cuckoos [filmed as Village of the Damned])

Wynette, Tammy (Virginia Wynette Pugh; "Heroine of Heartbreak"; "The First Lady of Country Music") (1942–) Am. country singer ("Stand by Your Man"; "D-I-V-O-R-C-E")

Wynn, Early ("Gus") (1920–) Am. baseball Hall-of-Famer

Wynn, Ed (Isaiah Edwin Leopold; "The Perfect Fool") (1886–1966) Am. comedian (father of Keenan)/actor (The Diary of Anne Frank; E—1949)

Wynn, Keenan (Francis Xavier Aloysius Keenan Wynn) (1916–1986) Am. actor (son of Ed; Dr. Strangelove; "Dallas" TV series)

Wynter, Dana (Dagmar Spencer-Marcus) (1930–) Eng. actress (Invasion of the Body Snatchers [1956]; Airport)

Xanthippe (5th century B.C.) Gr. wife of Socrates

Xenocrates (396–314 B.C.) Gr. philosopher (studied under Plato)

Xenophanes (c. 560–c. 478 B.C.) Gr. philosopher (Anabasis)

Xenophon (c. 431–c. 352 B.C.) Gr. historian (disciple of Socrates)

Xerxes (a/k/a Xerxes The Great) (c. 519–465 B.C.) Pers. king 486–465 B.C.

Yamagata Prince Aritomo (1838–1922) Jap. general/premier 1889–1891, 1898–1900

Yankovic, Al (Alfred Matthew Yankovic; "Weird Al") (1959–) Am. comedian/ musician ("Eat It")

Yanni (Yiannis Chryssolmalis) (1954–) Gr.-Am. "new age" musician

Yarborough, Cale (William Caleb Yarborough) (1939–) Am. auto racer

Yarbrough, Glenn (1930–) Am. folk/ country singer/musician ("Baby the Rain Must Fall"; formerly with The Limeliters)

Yarrow, Peter (1938–) Am. pop singer/ musician (with Peter, Paul & Mary)/song-writer ("Torn Between Two Lovers")

Yastrzemski, Carl (Carl Michael Yastrzemski; "Yaz") (1939–) Am. baseball Hall-of-Famer

Yawkey, Tom (Thomas Austin Yawkey) (1903–1976) Am. baseball Hall-of-Famer

Yeager, Chuck (Charles Elwood Yeager) (1923–) Am. aviator (first to break the sound barrier)

Yearwood, Trisha (Patricia Yearwood) (1964–) Am. country singer ("You Done Me Wrong [and That Ain't Right]")

Yeats, William Butler (1865–1939) Ir. poet/playwright (*The Wild Swans at Coole*; *The Tower*; N—1923)

Yeltsin, Boris (Boris Nikolayevich Yeltsin) (1921–) Russ. pres. 1991–

Yerby, Frank (Frank Garvin Yerby) (1916–1992) Am. novelist (first best-selling Afr.-Am. author; *The Foxes of Harrow*; *Vixen*)

Yevtushenko, Yevgeny (Yevgeny Aleksandrovich Yevtushenko) (1933–) Russ. poet (*Babi Yar*)

Yoakam, Dwight (1956–) Am. country/pop singer/guitarist ("If There Was a Way", "I Sang Dixie")

York, Dick (Richard Allen York) (1928–1992) Am. actor ("Bewitched" TV series)

York, Michael (Michael York-Johnson) (1942–) Eng. actor (*Cabaret*; *Logan's Run*; *The Three Musketeers*)

York, Sergeant (Alvin Cullum York) (1887–1964) Am. soldier/WWI hero/autobiographer (*Sergeant York*)

York, Susannah (Susannah Yolande Fletcher) (1941–) Eng. actress (*A Man for All Seasons*; *They Shoot Horses, Don't They?*)

Yorkin, Bud (Alan David Yorkin) (1926–) Am. film director (*Divorce American Style*; *Come Blow Your Horn*)

Yothers, Tina (1973–) Am. actress ("Family Ties" TV series)

Youmans, Vincent (Vincent Millie Youmans) (1898–1946) Am. composer (*No No Nanette*; *Tea for Two*)

Young, Alan (Angus Young) (1919–) Am. comedian/actor ("The Alan Young Show" and "Mr. Ed" TV series; E–1950)

Young, Andrew (Andrew Jackson Young, Jr.) (1932–) Am. ambassador/govt. official (mayor of Atlanta)

Young, Angus (1959–) Scot.-Austral. rock guitarist (with AC/DC)

Young, Brigham ("The Lion of the Lord") (1801–1877) Am. Mormon leader

Young, Burt (1940–) Am. actor (*Rocky* films)

Young, Carleton (1907–1971) Am. actor (*Sergeant Rutledge*)

Young, Chic (Murat Bernard Young) (1901–1973) Am. cartoonist (*Blondie*)

Young, Clara Kimball (1890–1960) Am.

actress (*Beau Brummell*; *The Little Minister*)

Young, Cy (Denton True Young; "Cy" is short for "Cyclone") (1867–1955) Am. baseball Hall-of-Famer (namesake of the Cy Young award for pitchers)

Young, Faron ("The Singing Sheriff") (1932–) Am. country singer/songwriter ("Live Fast, Love Hard, Die Young"; "Hello Walls")

Young, Gig (Byron Elsworth Barr; a/k/a Bryant Fleming) (1917–1978) Am. actor (*That Touch of Mink*; O—1969—*They Shoot Horses, Don't They?*)

Young, Jesse Colin (Perry Miller) (1944–) Am. country/pop singer ("Songbird")

Young, Leigh Taylor see Taylor-Young, Leigh

Young, Lester (Lester Willis Young; "Pres") (1909–1959) Am. jazz saxophonist (with Count Basie and Billie Holiday)

Young, Loretta (Gretchen Michaela Young) (1913–) Am. actress (sister of Sally Blane; *A Night to Remember*; *Call of the Wild*; O—1947—*The Farmer's Daughter*; E—1954, 1956, 1958/59)

Young, Neil (1945–) Can.-Am. rock singer ("Heart of Gold"; formerly with Crosby, Stills, Nash & Young and Buffalo Springfield)

Young, Paul (1956–) Eng. rock singer/musician ("Everytime You Go Away")

Young, Robert (Robert George Young) (1907–) Am. actor (TV's "Marcus Welby, M.D."; E—1956, 1957, 1969/70)

Young, Roland (Roland Keith Young) (1887–1953) Eng. actor (*Topper* and sequels)

Young, Sean (1959–) Am. actress (*Blade Runner*; *A Kiss Before Dying*; *No Way Out*)

Young, Sheila (1950–) Am. speed skater

Young, Steve (c. 1963–) Am. football player

Young, Terence (1915–) Eng.-Am. film director (*Dr. No*; *From Russia, with Love*; *Wait Until Dark*)

Young, Victor (1900–1956) Am. film composer (*Around the World in Eighty Days*)

Youngblood, Jack (Herbert Jackson Youngblood III) (1950–) Am. football player

Youngman, Henny (Henry Youngman) (1906–) Am. comedian/actor (signature phrase: "Take my wife . . . please")

Young MC (Marvin Young) (1967–) Am. rapper ("Bust a Move")
Youngs, Ross (Royce Middlebrook Youngs; "Pep") (1897–1927) Am. baseball Hall-of-Famer
Yount, Robin (Robin R. Yount) (1955–) Am. baseball player
Yourcenar, Marguerite (Margaret de Crayencour) (1903–1987) Belg.-Fr.-Am. novelist (*Memoirs of Hadrian*)
Zadora, Pia (Pia Schipani) (1955–) Am. singer/actress (*Butterfly*)
Zahn, Paula (1956–) Am. TV host
Zander, Robin (1952–) Am. rock singer (with Cheap Trick; "The Flame")
Zangwill, Israel (1864–1926) Eng. writer (*Children of the Ghetto*)
Zanuck, Darryl F. (Darryl Francis Zanuck) (1902–1979) Am. film producer (*The Grapes of Wrath*; *Gentleman's Agreement*)/cofounder of 20th-Century Fox Studios
Zapata, Emiliano (1879–1919) Mex. revolutionary leader (with Pancho Villa)
Zappa, Dweezil (1969–) Am. actor/rock musician (son of Frank)
Zappa, Frank (Francis Vincent Zappa, Jr.) (1940–1993) Am. rock singer/musician/songwriter ("Valley Girl"; "Don't Eat the Yellow Snow"; leader of The Mothers of Invention; father of Moon Unit and Dweezil)
Zappa, Moon Unit (1967–) Am. actress (daughter of Frank)
Zarathustra *see* Zoroaster
Zatopek, Emil ("Iron Man") (1922–) Cz. runner
Zatureuska, Marya (1902–1982) Am. poet (P—1938—*Cold Morning Sky*)
Zechariah (fl. c. 520 B.C.) Heb. prophet
Zeffirelli, Franco (Gianfranco Zeffirelli Corisi) (1923–) Ital. film director (*The Taming of the Shrew*; *Romeo and Juliet*; *La Traviata*; *Hamlet* [1990])
Zelazny, Roger (1937–) Am. science fiction writer (*A Dark Traveling*)
Zemeckis, Robert (1952–) Am. film director (*Back to the Future*; *Romancing the Stone*; *Who Framed Roger Rabbit?*)
Zenger, John Peter (1697–1746) Am. printer/journalist (founded the *New York Weekly Journal*)
Zeno (a/k/a Zeno of Citium) (c. 335–c. 263 B.C.) Gr. philosopher (founder of Stoicism)
Zeppelin, Count Ferdinand Von (1838–

1917) Ger. dirigible balloon designer/builder
Zetterling, Mai (Mai Elisabeth Zetterling) (1925–) Swed.-Eng. stage actress (*Knock on Wood*)
Zevon, Warren (1947–) Am. rock singer ("Werewolves of London")/songwriter ("Poor Poor Pitiful Me")
Zhao Ziyang (1919–) Chin. premier 1980–1987
Ziegfeld, Florenz ("Flo") (1869–1932) Am. theatrical producer (Ziegfeld Follies)
Ziering, Ian (1966–) Am. actor ("Beverly Hills, 90210" TV series)
Zimbalist, Efrem (Efren Alexandrovich Zimbalist) (1890–1985) Russ.-Am. violinist/composer (*Landava*; father of Efrem, Jr.)
Zimbalist, Efrem, Jr. (between 1913 and 1923–) Am. actor ("The FBI" and "77 Sunset Strip" TV series; son of Efrem)
Zimbalist, Stephanie (1956–) Am. actress (daughter of Efrem, Jr.; "Remington Steele" TV series)
Zimmer, Don (Donald William Zimmer; "Buffalo Head") (1931–) Am. baseball player/manager
Zimmer, Norma (Norma Beatrice Larsen; Lawrence Welk's "Champagne Lady") (C) Am. singer
Zindel, Paul (1936–) Am. playwright/novelist (P—1971—*The Effect of Gamma Rays on Man-in-the-Moon Marigolds*)
Zinnemann, Fred (1907–) Am. film director (*High Noon*; O—1953—*From Here to Eternity*; O—1966—*A Man for All Seasons*)
Zmed, Adrian (1954–) Am. actor ("T. J. Hooker" TV series)
Zoeller, Fuzzy (Frank Urban Zoeller, Jr.) (1951–) Am. golfer
Zog I (Ahmed Bey Zogu) (1895–1961) Alb. king 1928–1939
Zola, Émile (Émile-Édouard-Charles-Antoine Zola) (1840–1902) Fr. writer/critic (*L' Assommoir*; *Nana*; *Germinal*)
Zorina, Vera (Eva Brigitta Hartwig) (1917–) Ger.-Am. ballerina (with Ballet Russe)/actress (*I Was an Adventuress*)
Zoroaster (a/k/a Zarathustra) (c. 628–551 B.C.) Pers. founder of Zoroastrianism
Zucker, David (1947–) Am. screenwriter/film director (brother of Jerry)
Zucker, Jerry (1950–) Am. film producer/director (*Ruthless People*)

Zuckmayer, Carl (1896–1977) Ger. playwright (*The Captain from Köpenick*)/ screenwriter (*The Blue Angel*)

Zuckerman, Pinchas (1948–) Isr.-Am. violinist (protégé of Isaac Stern)/conductor

Zukor, Adolph (1873–1976) Am. movie producer (*The Sheik*; *The Ten Commandments*)/founder of Famous Players Film Co.

Zumwalt, Elmo (Elmo Russell Zumwalt, Jr.) (1920–) Am. naval officer

Zuniga, Daphne (1963–) Am. actress (*The Sure Thing*; *Gross Anatomy*; *Vision Quest*; "Melrose Place" TV series)

Zurbaran, Francisco de (1598–1664) Span. painter (religious subjects)

Zweig, Stefan (1881–1942) Aus. writer (*Three Masters*; *Beware of Pity*)

INDEX OF
FIRST NAMES

☆

Each first name included here is followed by an alphabetical list of surname entries together with a general occupational category reference for quick identification:

Arts/Ent.—arts and entertainment. Includes film and stage actors/ actresses, directors, writers, musicians, artists, fashion designers, architects and cartoonists.

Business—includes entrepreneurs, manufacturers, merchants and industrialists.

Govt./Mil.—government and the military. Includes politicians, military leaders, social reformers, political activists and royalty.

Misc.—people who do not fit in any other category.

Pion./Exp.—pioneers and explorers.

Rel./Phil.—religion and philosophy.

Sci/Inv.—science and invention.

Sports—includes players, team owners and officials.

★ In the case of different people with identical names, separate entries are included only if they are not in the same occupational category.

★ A separate entry is included for each alternate first-name spelling.

A
  Martinez (arts/ent.)
A. A.
  Milne (arts/ent.)
A. B.
  Dick (sci./inv.)
  Guthrie, Jr. (arts/ent.)

A. E.
  Hotchner (arts/ent.)
  Housman (arts/ent.)
  Van Vogt (arts/ent.)
A. J.
  Ayer (rel./phil.)
  Cronin (arts/ent.)

  Foyt (sports)
A. J. P.
  Taylor (arts/ent.)
A. L.
  Rowse (arts/ent.)
A. PHILIP
  Randolph (misc.)

AARON
Burr (govt./mil.)
Copland (arts/ent.)
Neville (arts/ent.)
Spelling (arts/ent.)
Tippin (arts/ent.)
ABBE
Lane (arts/ent.)
ABBIE
Hoffman (govt./mil.)
ABBY
Dalton (arts/ent.)
ABDUL
Ibn Hussein (govt./mil.)
ABE
Burrows (arts/ent.)
Fortas (govt./mil.)
Saperstein (sports)
Vigoda (arts/ent.)
ABEL
Ferrara (arts/ent.)
Gance (arts/ent.)
Janszoon Tasman (pion./
exp.)
ABIGAIL
Adams (govt./mil.)
Fillmore (govt./mil.)
Van Buren (arts/ent.)
ABNER
Doubleday (misc.)
ABRAHAM
Lincoln (govt./mil.)
ACE
Frehley (arts/ent.)
Parker (sports)
ADA
Lovelace (sci./inv.)
ADAH
Menken (arts/ent.)
ADAM
Ant (arts/ent.)
Baldwin (arts/ent.)
Faith (arts/ent.)
Clayton Powell, Jr.
(govt./mil.)
Rich (arts/ent.)
Sandler (arts/ent.)
Smith (misc.)
West (arts/ent.)
ADDIE
Joss (sports)
ADDISON
Mizner (arts/ent.)
ADELA
St. Johns (arts/ent.)
ADELAIDE
Manning (arts/ent.)

ADELE
Astaire (arts/ent.)
Jergens (arts/ent.)
Simpson (arts/ent.)
ADELINE
De Walt Reynolds (arts/
ent.)
ADELLE
Davis (arts/ent.)
ADLAI
Stevenson (govt./mil.)
ADNAN
Khashoggi (business)
ADOLF
Von Baeyer (sci./inv.)
Eichmann (govt./mil.)
Hitler (govt./mil.)
Nordenskiöld (pion./
exp.)
ADOLPH
Ochs (business)
Rupp (sports)
Zukor (arts/ent.)
ADOLPHE
Menjou (arts/ent.)
ADOLPHUS
Greely (pion./exp.)
ADRIAN
Boult (arts/ent.)
Dantley (sports)
Lyne (arts/ent.)
Pasdar (arts/ent.)
Zmed (arts/ent.)
ADRIEN
Arpel (arts/ent.)
ADRIENNE
Barbeau (arts/ent.)
Corri (arts/ent.)
Rich (arts/ent.)
Vittadini (arts/ent.)
AGATHA
Christie (arts/ent.)
AGNES
De Mille (arts/ent.)
Moorehead (arts/ent.)
AHMAD
Rashad (sports)
AHMET
Ertegun (business)
AIDAN
Quinn (arts/ent.)
AILEEN
Pringle (arts/ent.)
AIMÉ
Césaire (arts/ent.)
AIMEE
Mann (arts/ent.)

Semple McPherson
(rel./phil.)
AKEEM
Olajuwon (sports)
AKIM
Tamiroff (arts/ent.)
AKIO
Morita (business)
AKIRA
Kurosawa (arts/ent.)
AL
Capone (misc.)
Capp (arts/ent.)
Cohn (arts/ent.)
Dark (sports)
Di Meola (arts/ent.)
Franken (arts/ent.)
Geiberger (sports)
Gionfriddo (sports)
Gore (govt./mil.)
Green (arts/ent.)
Hirschfield (arts/ent.)
Hirt (arts/ent.)
Hrabosky (sports)
Jarreau (arts/ent.)
Jolson (arts/ent.)
Kaline (sports)
Kooper (arts/ent.)
Lopez (sports)
Martino (arts/ent.)
McGuire (sports)
Molinaro (arts/ent.)
Oerter (sports)
Oliver (sports)
Pacino (arts/ent.)
Ritz (arts/ent.)
Schacht (sports)
Sharpton (govt./mil.)
Simmons (sports)
Stewart (arts/ent.)
Unser (sports)
Unser, Jr. (sports)
Yankovic (arts/ent.)
ALAIN
Delon (arts/ent.)
Lesage (arts/ent.)
Locke (arts/ent.)
Resnais (arts/ent.)
Robbe-Grillet (arts/ent.)
ALAINA
Reed (arts/ent.)
ALAN
Alda (arts/ent.)
Arkin (arts/ent.)
Ashby (sports)
Ayckbourn (arts/ent.)
Bates (arts/ent.)

Bergman (arts/ent.)
Cranston (govt./mil.)
Dershowitz (misc.)
Dean Foster (arts/ent.)
Freed (arts/ent.)
Greenspan (govt./mil.)
Hale (arts/ent.)
Hale, Jr. (arts/ent.)
Jackson (arts/ent.)
Jardine (arts/ent.)
King (arts/ent.)
Ladd (arts/ent.)
Jay Lerner (arts/ent.)
Mowbray (arts/ent.)
Osmond (arts/ent.)
Page (sports)
J. Pakula (arts/ent.)
Parker (arts/ent.)
Parsons (arts/ent.)
Paton (arts/ent.)
Rachins (arts/ent.)
Rickman (arts/ent.)
Rosenberg (arts/ent.)
Rudolph (arts/ent.)
Shepard, Jr. (pion./exp.)
Sillitoe (arts/ent.)
Thicke (arts/ent.)
Turing (sci./inv.)
Watts (rel./phil.)
Young (arts/ent.)
ALANNAH
Myles (arts/ent.)
ALBAN
Berg (arts/ent.)
ALBEN
W. Barkley (govt./
mil.)
ALBERT
Anastasia (misc.)
Brooks (arts/ent.)
Camus (arts/ent.)
Cuyp (arts/ent.)
Einstein (sci./inv.)
Finney (arts/ent.)
Fish (misc.)
Hackett (arts/ent.)
Hammond (arts/ent.)
Kahn (arts/ent.)
King (arts/ent.)
Lee (arts/ent.)
Roussel (arts/ent.)
Pinkham Ryder (arts/
ent.)
Sabin (sci./inv.)
Speer (govt./mil.)
Schweitzer (rel./phil.)
Terhune (arts/ent.)

ALBERTA
Hunter (arts/ent.)
ALBERTO
Giacometti (arts/ent.)
Moravia (arts/ent.)
Tomba (sports)
ALBRECHT
Altdorfer (arts/ent.)
Dürer (arts/ent.)
ALDO
Ciccolini (arts/ent.)
Gucci (arts/ent.)
Mannucci (sci./inv.)
Moro (govt./mil.)
Ray (arts/ent.)
ALDOUS
Huxley (arts/ent.)
ALEC
Baldwin (arts/ent.)
Guinness (arts/ent.)
Waugh (arts/ent.)
ALEISTER
Crowley (misc.)
ALEJANDRO
Pena (sports)
ALEK
Keshishian (arts/ent.)
ALEKSANDR
Archipenko (arts/ent.)
Borodin (arts/ent.)
Glazunov (arts/ent.)
Gretchaninoff (arts/ent.)
Pushkin (arts/ent.)
Scriabin (arts/ent.)
I. Solzhenitsyn (arts/
ent.)
ALEKSEY
Kosygin (govt./mil.)
ALESSANDRO
Scarlatti (arts/ent.)
Volta (sci./inv.)
ALEX
Comfort (arts/ent.)
Cord (arts/ent.)
Cox (arts/ent.)
Haley (arts/ent.)
Karras (sports)
Korda (arts/ent.)
La Guma (arts/ent.)
Lifeson (arts/ent.)
Olmedo (sports)
Raymond (arts/ent.)
Trebek (arts/ent.)
Van Halen (arts/ent.)
Winter (arts/ent.)
Wojciechowicz
(sports)

ALEXANDER
Graham Bell (sci./inv.)
Calder (arts/ent.)
Fleming (sci./inv.)
Godunov (arts/ent.)
Haig (govt./mil.)
Hamilton (govt./mil.)
Von Humboldt (misc.)
Korda (arts/ent.)
Campbell MacKenzie
(arts/ent.)
Nevsky (govt./mil.)
Pope (arts/ent.)
Scourby (arts/ent.)
Woollcott (arts/ent.)
Danilova (arts/ent.)
ALEXANDRA
Paul (arts/ent.)
Penney (arts/ent.)
ALEXANDRE
Dumas (arts/ent.)
Eiffel (sci./inv.)
ALEXIS, ALÉXIS
Léger (arts/ent.)
Smith (arts/ent.)
Tocqueville (rel./phil.)
ALF
Kjellin (arts/ent.)
Landon (business)
ALFIE
Bass (arts/ent.)
ALFONSE
D'Amato (govt./mil.)
ALFRE
Woodard (arts/ent.)
ALFRED
Adler (sci./inv.)
Bester (arts/ent.)
Binet (sci./inv.)
Döblin (arts/ent.)
Drake (arts/ent.)
Dreyfus (govt./mil.)
Eisenstaedt (arts/ent.)
Carl Fuller (business)
Hershey (sci./inv.)
Hitchcock (arts/ent.)
Kazin (arts/ent.)
Kinsey (sci./inv.)
A. Knopf (business)
Krupp (business)
Lunt (arts/ent.)
De Musset (arts/ent.)
Newman (arts/ent.)
Nobel (misc.)
Noyes (arts/ent.)
Sisley (arts/ent.)
Stieglitz (arts/ent.)

Tennyson (arts/ent.)
Wallenstein (arts/ent.)
Whitehead (sci./inv.)
ALFREDO
Griffin (sports)
ALGER
Hiss (govt./mil.)
ALGERNON
Blackwood (arts/ent.)
Swinburne (arts/ent.)
ALI
MacGraw (arts/ent.)
ALICE
Adams (arts/ent.)
Brady (arts/ent.)
Cooper (arts/ent.)
Faye (arts/ent.)
Ghostley (arts/ent.)
Roosevelt Longworth
(misc.)
Marble (sports)
Roosevelt (govt./mil.)
Walker (arts/ent.)
ALICIA
Alonso (arts/ent.)
De Laroccha (arts/
ent.)
Markova (arts/ent.)
ALIDA
Valli (arts/ent.)
ALINE
MacMahon (arts/ent.)
ALISON
Arngrim (arts/ent.)
Gertz (misc.)
La Placa (arts/ent.)
Lurie (arts/ent.)
Moyet (arts/ent.)
Steadman (arts/ent.)
ALISTAIR
Cooke (arts/ent.)
MacLean (arts/ent.)
ALLA
Nazimova (arts/ent.)
ALLAN
Arkush (arts/ent.)
Bloom (misc.)
Dwan (arts/ent.)
Jones (arts/ent.)
Nevins (arts/ent.)
Pinkerton (misc.)
Sherman (arts/ent.)
ALLEN
Curnow (arts/ent.)
Drury (arts/ent.)
Funt (arts/ent.)
Garfield (arts/ent.)

Ginsberg (arts/ent.)
Lane (business)
Ludden (arts/ent.)
Tate (arts/ent.)
ALLEY
Mills (arts/ent.)
ALLIE
Reynolds (sports)
ALLY
Sheedy (arts/ent.)
Walker (arts/ent.)
ALLYCE
Beasley (arts/ent.)
ALMA
Gluck (arts/ent.)
Kruger (arts/ent.)
Reville (arts/ent.)
Rubens (arts/ent.)
ALPHONSE
Daudet (arts/ent.)
ALTHEA
Gibson (sports)
ALVAR
Aalto (misc.)
ALVIN
Ailey (arts/ent.)
Dark (sports)
Lee (arts/ent.)
Samples (arts/ent.)
Toffler (arts/ent.)
ALVINO
Rey (arts/ent.)
ALVY
West (arts/ent.)
ALYSSA
Milano (arts/ent.)
AMALIA
Materna (arts/ent.)
AMANDA
Bearse (arts/ent.)
Blake (arts/ent.)
Donohoe (arts/ent.)
Pays (arts/ent.)
Plummer (arts/ent.)
Randolph (arts/ent.)
AMBER
Valletta (arts/ent.)
AMBROSE
Bierce (arts/ent.)
Burnside (govt./
mil.)
AMEDEO
Modigliani (arts/ent.)
AMELIA
Earhart (misc.)
AMELITA
Galli-Curci (arts/ent.)

AMERIGO
Vespucci (pion./exp.)
AMI
Dolenz (arts/ent.)
AMILCARE
Ponchielli (arts/ent.)
AMOS
Oz (arts/ent.)
Rusie (sports)
Alonzo Stagg (sports)
Tutuola (arts/ent.)
AMY
Alcott (sports)
Fisher (misc.)
Grant (arts/ent.)
Heckerling (arts/ent.)
Irving (arts/ent.)
Locane (arts/ent.)
Lowell (arts/ent.)
Madigan (arts/ent.)
Tan (arts/ent.)
Vanderbilt (arts/ent.)
Wright (arts/ent.)
AN
Wang (business)
ANA
Alicia (arts/ent.)
ANAÏS
Nin (arts/ent.)
ANASTASIO
Somoza (govt./mil.)
Somoza De Bayle
(govt./mil.)
ANATOL
Liadov or Lyadov (arts/
ent.)
ANATOLE
France (arts/ent.)
Litvak (arts/ent.)
ANATOLY
Karpov (misc.)
Liadov or Lyadov (arts/
ent.)
ANDERS
Celsius (sci./inv.)
ANDIE
MacDowell (arts/ent.)
ANDRAE
Crouch (arts/ent.)
ANDRE, ANDRÉ
Agassi (sports)
Ampère (sci./inv.)
Bazin (arts/ent.)
Breton (arts/ent.)
Chénier (arts/ent.)
Gustav Citröen
(business)

Courrèges (arts/ent.)
Derain (arts/ent.)
Eglevsky (arts/ent.)
Gide (arts/ent.)
Kostelanetz (arts/ent.)
Maginot (govt./mil.)
Malraux (arts/ent.)
Maurois (arts/ent.)
Norton (arts/ent.)
Previn (arts/ent.)
Tarkovsky (arts/ent.)
Watts (arts/ent.)
ANDREA
Castagno (arts/ent.)
Doria (govt./mil.)
Leeds (arts/ent.)
Mantegna (arts/ent.)
Marcovicci (arts/ent.)
McArdle (arts/ent.)
Del Sarto (arts/ent.)
Verrocchio (arts/ent.)
ANDREAS
Baader (misc.)
Feininger (arts/ent.)
Papandreou (govt./mil.)
Vollenweider (arts/
ent.)
ANDREI
Sakharov (sci./inv.)
ANDRES, ANDRÉS
Galarraga (sports)
Segovia (arts/ent.)
ANDREW
Carnegie (business)
"Dice" Clay (arts/ent.)
Gold (arts/ent.)
M. Greeley (arts/ent.)
Jackson (govt./mil.)
Johnson (govt./mil.)
Marvell (arts/ent.)
McCarthy (arts/ent.)
Mellon (business)
Ridgeley (arts/ent.)
Sarris (arts/ent.)
Schally (sci./inv.)
Shue (arts/ent.)
Stevens (arts/ent.)
Lloyd Webber (arts/
ent.)
Wyeth (arts/ent.)
Young (govt./mil.)
ANDREY
Gromyko (govt./mil.)
ANDRZEJ
Wajda (arts/ent.)
ANDY
Allanson (sports)

Bell (arts/ent.)
Clyde (arts/ent.)
Devine (arts/ent.)
Garcia (arts/ent.)
Gibb (arts/ent.)
Granatelli (sports)
Griffith (arts/ent.)
Kaufman (arts/ent.)
Kim (arts/ent.)
Robustelli (sports)
Rooney (arts/ent.)
Summers (arts/ent.)
Taylor (arts/ent.)
Tobias (business)
Warhol (arts/ent.)
Williams (arts/ent.)
ANGEL
Cordero, Jr. (sports)
ANGELA
Baddeley (arts/ent.)
Bassett (arts/ent.)
Bofill (arts/ent.)
Carter (arts/ent.)
Cartwright (arts/ent.)
Davis (govt./mil.)
Lansbury (arts/ent.)
ANGELICA
Catalani (arts/ent.)
ANGIE
Dickinson (arts/ent.)
ANGUS
Wilson (arts/ent.)
Young (arts/ent.)
ANISSA
Jones (arts/ent.)
ANITA
Baker (arts/ent.)
Björk (arts/ent.)
Brookner (arts/ent.)
Bryant (arts/ent.)
Desai (arts/ent.)
Ekberg (arts/ent.)
Gillette (arts/ent.)
Hill (misc.)
Kerr (arts/ent.)
Loos (arts/ent.)
Louise (arts/ent.)
O'Day (arts/ent.)
Pointer (arts/ent.)
Roddick (business)
Ward (arts/ent.)
ANJELICA
Huston (arts/ent.)
ANN
Beattie (arts/ent.)
Blyth (arts/ent.)
B. Davis (arts/ent.)

Dvorak (arts/ent.)
Harding (arts/ent.)
Jellicoe (arts/ent.)
Jillian (arts/ent.)
Landers (arts/ent.)
Lee (rel./phil.)
Magnuson (arts/ent.)
Miller (arts/ent.)
Radcliffe (arts/ent.)
Reinking (arts/ent.)
Richards (govt./mil.)
Rutherford (arts/ent.)
Sheridan (arts/ent.)
Sothern (arts/ent.)
Todd (arts/ent.)
Wilson (arts/ent.)
ANNA
Akhmatova (arts/ent.)
Maria Alberghetti (arts/
ent.)
Freud (misc.)
Harrison (govt./mil.)
Held (arts/ent.)
Karina (arts/ent.)
Magnani (arts/ent.)
Moffo (arts/ent.)
Neagle (arts/ent.)
Parillaud (arts/ent.)
Pavlova (arts/ent.)
Quindlen (arts/ent.)
Sewell (arts/ent.)
Nicole Smith (arts/ent.)
Sten (arts/ent.)
Wintour (business)
May Wong (arts/ent.)
ANNABELLA
Sciorra (arts/ent.)
ANNABETH
Gish (arts/ent.)
ANNE
Archer (arts/ent.)
Bancroft (arts/ent.)
Baxter (arts/ent.)
Boleyn (govt./mil.)
Bradstreet (arts/ent.)
Brontë (arts/ent.)
Francis (arts/ent.)
Frank (arts/ent.)
Jackson (arts/ent.)
Jeffreys (arts/ent.)
Klein (arts/ent.)
Lindbergh (arts/ent.)
McCaffrey (arts/ent.)
Meara (arts/ent.)
Milbanke (sci./inv.)
Murray (arts/ent.)
Nichols (arts/ent.)

Revere (arts/ent.)
Rice (arts/ent.)
Sexton (arts/ent.)
Seymour (arts/ent.)
Shirley (arts/ent.)
Sullivan (misc.)
Tyler (arts/ent.)
ANNEMARIE
Proell (sports)
ANNETTE
Bening (arts/ent.)
Funicello (arts/ent.)
O'Toole (arts/ent.)
ANNIE
Jump Cannon (sci./
inv.)
Dillard (arts/ent.)
Leibovitz (arts/ent.)
Lennox (arts/ent.)
Oakley (misc.)
Potts (arts/ent.)
ANOUK
Aimée (arts/ent.)
ANSEL
Adams (arts/ent.)
ANSON
Williams (arts/ent.)
ANTHONY
Andrews (arts/ent.)
Asquith (arts/ent.)
Boucher (arts/ent.)
Burgess (arts/ent.)
Berkeley Cox (arts/
ent.)
Eden (govt./mil.)
Edwards (arts/ent.)
Fokker (arts/ent.)
Franciosa (arts/ent.)
Geary (arts/ent.)
Michael Hall (arts/ent.)
Hope (arts/ent.)
Hopkins (arts/ent.)
M. Kennedy (govt./
mil.)
Kiedis (arts/ent.)
Newley (arts/ent.)
Perkins (arts/ent.)
Powell (arts/ent.)
Price (arts/ent.)
Quayle (arts/ent.)
Quinn (arts/ent.)
Shaffer (arts/ent.)
Trollope (arts/ent.)
Vandyck (arts/ent.)
West (arts/ent.)
ANTOINE
Le Nain (arts/ent.)

De Saint-Exupéry (arts/
ent.)
Watteau (arts/ent.)
ANTOINETTE
Perry (arts/ent.)
ANTON
Bruckner (arts/ent.)
Chekhov (arts/ent.)
Von Webern (arts/ent.)
ANTONIA
Fraser (arts/ent.)
White (arts/ent.)
ANTONIN, ANTONÍN
Artaud (arts/ent.)
Dvořák (arts/ent.)
Novotny (govt./mil.)
Scalia (govt./mil.)
ANTONIO, ANTÓNIO
Banderas (arts/ent.)
Canova (arts/ent.)
Correggio (arts/ent.)
Gaudí (arts/ent.)
Carlos Jobim
(sports)
Sabato, Jr. (arts/ent.)
Salazar (govt./mil.)
de Santa Anna (govt./
mil.)
Scotti (arts/ent.)
Stradivari (arts/ent.)
Vivaldi (arts/ent.)
ANTONY
Tudor (arts/ent.)
ANWAR
Sadat (govt./mil.)
ANYA
Seton (arts/ent.)
APHRA
Behn (arts/ent.)
APRIL
Stevens (arts/ent.)
ARA
Parseghian (sports)
ARAM
Avakian (arts/ent.)
Saroyan (arts/ent.)
ARCHIBALD
Cox (govt./mil.)
MacLeish (arts/ent.)
ARCHIE
Bell (arts/ent.)
Bleyer (arts/ent.)
Campbell (arts/ent.)
Griffin (sports)
Manning (sports)
Mayo (arts/ent.)
Moore (rel./phil.)

ARETHA
Franklin (arts/ent.)
ARI
Meyers (arts/ent.)
ARIEL
Durant (arts/ent.)
ARISTIDE
Briand (govt./mil.)
Maillol (arts/ent.)
ARISTOTLE
Onassis (business)
ARKY
Vaughan (sports)
ARLEN
Specter (govt./mil.)
ARLENE
Dahl (arts/ent.)
Francis (arts/ent.)
ARLO
Guthrie (arts/ent.)
ARMAND
Assante (arts/ent.)
Hammer (business)
ARMIN
Mueller-Stahl (arts/ent.)
ARMISTEAD
Maupin (arts/ent.)
ARMY
Archerd (arts/ent.)
ARNA
Bontemps (arts/ent.)
ARNIE
Herber (sports)
Weinmeister (sports)
ARNOLD
Bax (arts/ent.)
Bennett (arts/ent.)
Palmer (sports)
Schoenberg (arts/ent.)
Schwarzenegger (arts/
ent.)
Stang (arts/ent.)
Toynbee (arts/ent.)
ARRIGO
Boito (arts/ent.)
ARSENIO
Hall (arts/ent.)
ARSHILE
Gorky (arts/ent.)
ART
Acord (arts/ent.)
Blakey (arts/ent.)
Buchwald (arts/ent.)
Carney (arts/ent.)
Donovan (sports)
Garfunkel (arts/ent.)
Linkletter (arts/ent.)

Pepper (arts/ent.)
Rooney (sports)
Sansom (arts/ent.)
Tatum (arts/ent.)
ARTE
  Johnson (arts/ent.)
ARTEMUS
  Ward (arts/ent.)
ARTHUR
  Ashe (sports)
  Baer (arts/ent.)
  James Balfour (govt./
    mil.)
  Bliss (arts/ent.)
  C. Clarke (arts/ent.)
  Compton (sci./inv.)
  Conan Doyle (arts/ent.)
  Ferrante (arts/ent.)
  Fiedler (arts/ent.)
  Franz (arts/ent.)
  Freed (arts/ent.)
  Godfrey (arts/ent.)
  J. Goldberg III (govt./
    mil.)
  Hailey (arts/ent.)
  Hill (arts/ent.)
  Hiller (arts/ent.)
  Honegger (arts/ent.)
  Kennedy (arts/ent.)
  Kent (arts/ent.)
  Kober (arts/ent.)
  Koestler (arts/ent.)
  L. Kopit (arts/ent.)
  Krock (arts/ent.)
  Lake (arts/ent.)
  Laurents (arts/ent.)
  Lubin (arts/ent.)
  Lyman (arts/ent.)
  Miller (arts/ent.)
  Murray (arts/ent.)
  Nielsen (misc.)
  O'Connell (arts/ent.)
  Penn (arts/ent.)
  Wing Pinero (arts/ent.)
  Rimbaud (arts/ent.)
  Rubinstein (arts/ent.)
  M. Schlesinger (arts/
    ent.)
  Schopenhauer (rel./
    phil.)
  Schwartz (arts/ent.)
  Spingarn (govt./mil.)
  Sullivan (arts/ent.)
  Treacher (arts/ent.)
ARTIE
  Auerbach (arts/ent.)
  Shaw (arts/ent.)

ARTIS
  Gilmore (sports)
ARTUR
  Rubinstein (arts/ent.)
  Schnabel (arts/ent.)
ARTURO
  Toscanini (arts/ent.)
ASA
  Gray (sci./inv.)
ASHER
  Durand (arts/ent.)
ASHLEY
  Judd (arts/ent.)
  Montagu (sci./inv.)
ASTA
  Nielsen (arts/ent.)
ASTRID
  Lindgren (arts/ent.)
ASTRUD
  Gilberto (arts/ent.)
ATHOL
  Fugard (arts/ent.)
AUBERON
  Waugh (arts/ent.)
AUBREY
  Beardsley (arts/ent.)
AUDIE
  Murphy (arts/ent.)
AUDRA
  Lindley (arts/ent.)
AUDREY
  Hepburn (arts/ent.)
  Landers (arts/ent.)
  Meadows (arts/ent.)
  Totter (arts/ent.)
AUGUST
  Derleth (arts/ent.)
  F. Möbius (sci./inv.)
  Strindberg (arts/ent.)
  Wilson (arts/ent.)
AUGUSTA
  Maywood (arts/ent.)
AUGUSTE
  Comte (rel./phil.)
  Rodin (arts/ent.)
AUGUSTO
  Pinochet (govt./mil.)
AUGUSTUS
  John (arts/ent.)
  Saint-Gaudens (arts/
    ent.)
AVA
  Gardner (arts/ent.)
AVERY
  Brooks (arts/ent.)
  Brundage (sports)
  Schreiber (arts/ent.)

AXL
  Rose (arts/ent.)
AYAKO
  Okamoto (sports)
AYN
  Rand (arts/ent.)
AZZEDINE
  Alaïa (arts/ent.)
B.
  Kliban (arts/ent.)
  Traven (arts/ent.)
B. B.
  King (arts/ent.)
B. F.
  Skinner (arts/ent.)
B. J.
  Thomas (arts/ent.)
BABE
  Adams (sports)
  Didrikson (sports)
  Herman (sports)
  Phelps (sports)
  Ruth (sports)
BABY FACE
  Nelson (misc.)
BALTASAR
  Gracián (rel./phil.)
BALTHAZAR
  Getty (arts/ent.)
BARBARA
  Jo Allen (arts/ent.)
  Anderson (arts/ent.)
  Bach (arts/ent.)
  Bain (arts/ent.)
  Barrie (arts/ent.)
  Baxley (arts/ent.)
  Bel Geddes (arts/ent.)
  Billingsley (arts/ent.)
  Bosson (arts/ent.)
  Boxer (govt./mil.)
  Taylor Bradford (arts/
    ent.)
  Britton (arts/ent.)
  Bush (govt./mil.)
  Carrera (arts/ent.)
  Cartland (arts/ent.)
  Eden (arts/ent.)
  Feldon (arts/ent.)
  Hale (arts/ent.)
  Harris (arts/ent.)
  Heck (rel./phil.)
  Hepworth (arts/ent.)
  Hershey (arts/ent.)
  Hutton (misc.)
  Jordan (govt./mil.)
  Kingsolver (arts/ent.)
  Luna (arts/ent.)

Mandrell (arts/ent.)
McClintock (sci./inv.)
McNair (arts/ent.)
Michaels (arts/ent.)
Parkins (arts/ent.)
Pym (arts/ent.)
Roberts (govt./mil.)
Rush (arts/ent.)
Stanwyck (arts/ent.)
Tuchman (arts/ent.)
Walters (arts/ent.)

BARBET
Schroeder (arts/ent.)

BARBI
Benton (arts/ent.)

BARBRA
Streisand (arts/ent.)

BARNETT
Newman (arts/ent.)

BARNEY
Frank (govt./mil.)
Kessel (arts/ent.)
Oldfield (sports)

BARRÉ
Lyndon (arts/ent.)

BARRY
Bostwick (arts/ent.)
Corbin (arts/ent.)
Diller (arts/ent.)
Fitzgerald (arts/ent.)
Gibb (arts/ent.)
Goldwater (govt./mil.)
Levinson (arts/ent.)
N. Malzberg (arts/ent.)
Manilow (arts/ent.)
Mann (arts/ent.)
Nelson (arts/ent.)
Newman (arts/ent.)
Sullivan (arts/ent.)
White (arts/ent.)

BART
Braverman (arts/ent.)
Starr (sports)

BARTLETT
Robinson (arts/ent.)

BARTOLOME
Murillo (arts/ent.)

BARTOLOMEO
Vanzetti (govt./mil.)

BARTOLOMEU
Dias (pion./exp.)

BARTOLOMMEO
Montagna (arts/ent.)

BARTON
MacLane (arts/ent.)

BARUCH
Spinoza (rel./phil.)

BASIL
Dearden (arts/ent.)
Rathbone (arts/ent.)

BAT
Masterson (misc.)

BAYARD
Rustin (govt./mil.)

BEA
Arthur (arts/ent.)
Benaderet (arts/ent.)

BEAR
Bryant (sports)

BEATRICE
Lillie (arts/ent.)
Straight (arts/ent.)
Webb (arts/ent.)

BEATRIX
Potter (arts/ent.)

BEAU
Bridges (arts/ent.)
Brummell (misc.)

BEBE
Daniels (arts/ent.)
Neuwirth (arts/ent.)

BEDŘICH
Smetana (arts/ent.)

BELA, BÉLA
Bartók (arts/ent.)
Lugosi (arts/ent.)

BELINDA
Carlisle (arts/ent.)

BELLA
Abzug (govt./mil.)

BELLE
Starr (misc.)

BELVA
Plain (arts/ent.)

BEN
Blue (arts/ent.)
Bova (arts/ent.)
Bradlee (arts/ent.)
Gazzara (arts/ent.)
Hecht (arts/ent.)
Hogan (sports)
Johnson (arts/ent.)
Jonson (arts/ent.)
E. King (arts/ent.)
Kingsley (arts/ent.)
Lyon (arts/ent.)
Murphy (arts/ent.)
Shahn (arts/ent.)
Stiller (arts/ent.)
Turpin (arts/ent.)
Vereen (arts/ent.)

BENAZIR
Bhutto (govt./mil.)

BENEDICT
Arnold (govt./mil.)

BENITO
Juarez (govt./mil.)
Mussolini (govt./mil.)
Santiago (sports)

BENJAMIN
Banneker (sci./inv.)
Britten (arts/ent.)
Cardozo (govt./mil.)
Disraeli (govt./mil.)
Franklin (arts/ent.)
Harrison (govt./mil.)
Latrobe (arts/ent.)
Orr (arts/ent.)
Spock (misc.)
West (arts/ent.)

BENNETT
Cerf (arts/ent.)

BENNO
C. Schmidt (misc.)

BENNY
Carter (arts/ent.)
Goodman (arts/ent.)
Hill (arts/ent.)

BENO
Gutenberg (sci./inv.)

BENVENUTO
Cellini (arts/ent.)

BERENICE
Abbott (arts/ent.)

BERKE
Breathed (arts/ent.)

BERNADETTE
Peters (arts/ent.)

BERNADINE
Dohrn (govt./mil.)

BERNARD
M. Baruch (govt./mil.)
Blier (arts/ent.)
Goetz (misc.)
Herrmann (arts/ent.)
Malamud (arts/ent.)

BERNARDO
Bertolucci (arts/ent.)

BERNIE
Kopell (arts/ent.)
Kosar (sports)
Taupin (arts/ent.)

BERRY
Gordy, Jr. (arts/ent.)

BERT
Blyleven (sports)
Campaneris (sports)
Convy (arts/ent.)
Gordon (arts/ent.)

Jones (sports)
Kalmar (arts/ent.)
Lahr (arts/ent.)
Parks (arts/ent.)
BERTHE
Morisot (arts/ent.)
BERTIE
Higgins (arts/ent.)
BERTOLT
Brecht (arts/ent.)
BERTRAND
Blier (arts/ent.)
Russell (sci./inv.)
Tavernier (arts/ent.)
BERYL
Bainbridge (arts/ent.)
Markham (misc.)
BESS
Armstrong (arts/ent.)
Myerson (arts/ent.)
Truman (govt./mil.)
BESSIE
Love (arts/ent.)
Smith (arts/ent.)
BETH
Henley (arts/ent.)
BETHEL
Leslie (arts/ent.)
BETSEY
Johnson (arts/ent.)
BETSY
Blair (arts/ent.)
Drake (arts/ent.)
Palmer (arts/ent.)
Ross (misc.)
BETTA
St. John (arts/ent.)
BETTE
Davis (arts/ent.)
Midler (arts/ent.)
BETTY
Buckley (arts/ent.)
Carter (arts/ent.)
Comden (arts/ent.)
Ford (govt./mil.)
Friedan (arts/ent.)
Furness (arts/ent.)
Grable (arts/ent.)
Hutton (arts/ent.)
Rollin (arts/ent.)
Smith (arts/ent.)
White (arts/ent.)
BEULAH
Bondi (arts/ent.)
BEVERLY
Cleary (arts/ent.)
D'Angelo (arts/ent.)

Garland (arts/ent.)
Johnson (arts/ent.)
Peele (arts/ent.)
Sills (arts/ent.)
BIANCA
Jagger (arts/ent.)
BIBI
Andersson (arts/ent.)
Osterwald (arts/ent.)
BIG BILL
Broonzy (arts/ent.)
BIG JOE
Turner (arts/ent.)
BIL
Baird (arts/ent.)
Keane (arts/ent.)
BILL
Anderson (arts/ent.)
Bergey (sports)
Bevens (sports)
Bixby (arts/ent.)
Blass (arts/ent.)
Bradley (govt./mil.)
Campbell (arts/ent.)
Clinton (govt./mil.)
Conti (arts/ent.)
Cosby (arts/ent.)
Cullen (arts/ent.)
Daily (arts/ent.)
Dana (arts/ent.)
Dickey (sports)
Dudley (sports)
Finger (arts/ent.)
Forsyth (arts/ent.)
Gates (sci./inv.)
George (sports)
Graham (arts/ent.)
Haley (arts/ent.)
Hewitt (sports)
Hickock (govt./mil.)
Irwin (arts/ent.)
Klem (sports)
Lange (sports)
Macy (arts/ent.)
Madlock (sports)
Mauldin (arts/ent.)
Mazeroski (sports)
McKechnie (sports)
Medley (arts/ent.)
Monroe (arts/ent.)
Moyers (arts/ent.)
Murray (arts/ent.)
Paxton (arts/ent.)
Pullman (arts/ent.)
Rigney (sports)
Robinson (arts/ent.)
Rodgers (sports)

Russell (sports)
Terry (sports)
Tilden (sports)
Todman (arts/ent.)
Veeck (sports)
Walton (sports)
Watrous (arts/ent.)
Watterson (arts/ent.)
Williams (arts/ent.)
Willis (sports)
Wilson (misc.)
Withers (arts/ent.)
Wyman (arts/ent.)
BILLIE
Burke (arts/ent.)
Holiday (arts/ent.)
King (sports)
BILLIE JO
Spears (arts/ent.)
BILLY
Baldwin (arts/ent.)
Barty (arts/ent.)
Benedict (arts/ent.)
Butterfield (arts/ent.)
Carter (misc.)
Casper (sports)
Cobham (arts/ent.)
Conn (sports)
Crystal (arts/ent.)
Ray Cyrus (arts/ent.)
Davis, Jr. (arts/ent.)
De Wolfe (arts/ent.)
Dean (arts/ent.)
Debeck (arts/ent.)
Eckstine (arts/ent.)
Fury (arts/ent.)
Graham (rel./phil.)
Hartack (sports)
Hayes (arts/ent.)
Herman (sports)
Idol (arts/ent.)
Joel (arts/ent.)
Martin (sports)
Mumy (arts/ent.)
Ocean (arts/ent.)
Paul (arts/ent.)
Preston (arts/ent.)
Ripken (sports)
Rose (arts/ent.)
Royal (arts/ent.)
Squier (arts/ent.)
Strayhorn (arts/ent.)
Sunday (rel./phil.)
Taylor (arts/ent.)
Vaughn (arts/ent.)
Vera (arts/ent.)
Wilder (arts/ent.)

Dee Williams (arts/
ent.)
BING
Crosby (arts/ent.)
BINNIE
Barnes (arts/ent.)
BIRGIT
Nilsson (arts/ent.)
BIX
Beiderbecke (arts/ent.)
BJORN
Borg (sports)
BJØRNSON
Bjørnstjerne (arts/ent.)
BLAIR
Brown (arts/ent.)
Underwood (arts/ent.)
BLAISE
Cendrars (arts/ent.)
Pascal (sci./inv.)
BLAKE
Edwards (arts/ent.)
BLANCHE
Knopf (business)
Sweet (arts/ent.)
BLIND LEMON
Jefferson (arts/ent.)
BLOSSOM
Dearie (arts/ent.)
Seeley (arts/ent.)
BLYTHE
Danner (arts/ent.)
BO
Derek (arts/ent.)
Diddley (arts/ent.)
Hopkins (arts/ent.)
Jackson (sports)
Svenson (arts/ent.)
BOB
Barker (arts/ent.)
Brenly (sports)
Costas (arts/ent.)
Cousy (sports)
Crane (arts/ent.)
Crosby (arts/ent.)
Cummings (arts/ent.)
Denver (arts/ent.)
Dole (govt./mil.)
Dylan (arts/ent.)
Elliott (arts/ent.)
Eubanks (arts/ent.)
Feller (sports)
Fosse (arts/ent.)
Gainey (sports)
Geldof (arts/ent.)
Gibson (sports)
Goldthwait (arts/ent.)

Greene (arts/ent.)
Guccione (business)
Hayes (sports)
Hope (arts/ent.)
Hoskins (arts/ent.)
Keeshan (arts/ent.)
Kerrey (govt./mil.)
Knepper (sports)
Lanier (sports)
Lemon (sports)
Lilly (sports)
Mackie (arts/ent.)
Marley (arts/ent.)
Mathias (sports)
McAdoo (sports)
Miller (govt./mil.)
Montana (arts/ent.)
Newhart (arts/ent.)
Packwood (govt./
mil.)
Pettit (sports)
Rafelson (arts/ent.)
Saget (arts/ent.)
Seger (arts/ent.)
Smith (arts/ent.)
Smith (misc.)
Uecker (sports)
Vila (arts/ent.)
Waterfield (sports)
Weir (arts/ent.)
Welch (arts/ent.)
Wills (arts/ent.)
Woodward (arts/ent.)
BOBBIE
Gentry (arts/ent.)
BOBBY
Allison (sports)
Bare (arts/ent.)
Bell (sports)
Bland (arts/ent.)
Bonilla (sports)
Brown (arts/ent.)
Caldwell (arts/ent.)
Clarke (sports)
Darin (arts/ent.)
Day (arts/ent.)
Doerr (sports)
Driscoll (arts/ent.)
Fischer (misc.)
Goldsboro (arts/ent.)
Hackett (arts/ent.)
Hull (sports)
Jones (sports)
Knight (sports)
Layne (sports)
McFerrin (arts/ent.)
Mitchell (sports)

Nichols (sports)
Orr (sports)
Riggs (sports)
Russell (arts/ent.)
Rydell (arts/ent.)
Sherman (arts/ent.)
Short (arts/ent.)
Thigpen (sports)
Thomson (sports)
Unser (sports)
Van (arts/ent.)
Vee (arts/ent.)
Vinton (arts/ent.)
Wallace (sports)
Womack (arts/ent.)
BOBS
Watson (arts/ent.)
BON
Scott (arts/ent.)
BONAR
Law (govt./mil.)
BONITA
Granville (arts/ent.)
BONNIE
Bartlett (arts/ent.)
Bedelia (arts/ent.)
Bramlett (arts/ent.)
Franklin (arts/ent.)
Guitar (arts/ent.)
Parker (misc.)
Pointer (arts/ent.)
Raitt (arts/ent.)
Tyler (arts/ent.)
BONO
Vox (arts/ent.)
BOOG
Powell (sports)
BOOKER
Jones (arts/ent.)
T. Washington (arts/
ent.)
BOOTH
Tarkington (arts/ent.)
BOOTS
Randolph (arts/ent.)
BORIS
Becker (sports)
Godunov (govt./mil.)
Karloff (arts/ent.)
Pasternak (arts/ent.)
Spassky (misc.)
Yeltsin (govt./mil.)
BOSLEY
Crowther (arts/ent.)
BOUTROS
Boutros-Ghali (govt./
mil.)

BOWIE
  Kuhn (sports)
BOZ
  Scaggs (arts/ent.)
BRAD
  Anderson (arts/ent.)
  Davis (arts/ent.)
  Dourif (arts/ent.)
  Johnson (arts/ent.)
  Park (arts/ent.)
  Pitt (arts/ent.)
BRADFORD
  Dillman (arts/ent.)
BRAM
  Stoker (arts/ent.)
BRANCH
  Rickey (sports)
BRANDON
  Cruz (arts/ent.)
  De Wilde (arts/ent.)
  Lee (arts/ent.)
  Tartikoff (business)
BRANFORD
  Marsalis (arts/ent.)
BRANWELL
  Brontë (arts/ent.)
BRAXTON
  Bragg (govt./mil.)
BREE
  Walker (arts/ent.)
BRENDA
  Fricker (arts/ent.)
  Lee (arts/ent.)
  Vaccaro (arts/ent.)
BRENDAN
  Behan (arts/ent.)
  Gill (arts/ent.)
BRENT
  Musberger (sports)
  Scowcroft (govt./
    mil.)
BRET
  Easton Ellis (arts/ent.)
  Harte (arts/ent.)
  Michaels (arts/ent.)
  Saberhagen (sports)
BRETT
  Butler (arts/ent.)
  Butler (sports)
  Somers (arts/ent.)
BRIAN
  Aherne (arts/ent.)
  Aldiss (arts/ent.)
  Boitano (sports)
  Bosworth (sports)
  Dennehy (arts/ent.)
  Depalma (arts/ent.)

Donlevy (arts/ent.)
Eno (arts/ent.)
Epstein (arts/ent.)
Friel (arts/ent.)
Gottfried (sports)
Austin Green (arts/ent.)
Holland (arts/ent.)
Jones (arts/ent.)
Keith (arts/ent.)
May (arts/ent.)
Moore (sports)
Mulroney (govt./mil.)
Piccolo (sports)
Setzer (arts/ent.)
Wilson (arts/ent.)
Wimmer (arts/ent.)
BRICE
  Marden (arts/ent.)
BRIDGET
  Fonda (arts/ent.)
BRIGHAM
  Young (rel./phil.)
BRIGID
  Brophy (arts/ent.)
BRIGITTE
  Bardot (arts/ent.)
  Nielsen (arts/ent.)
BRITT
  Ekland (arts/ent.)
BROCK
  Peters (arts/ent.)
BRODERICK
  Crawford (arts/ent.)
BRONISLAWA
  Nijinska (arts/ent.)
BRONKO
  Nagurski (sports)
BRONSON
  Alcott (arts/ent.)
  Pinchot (arts/ent.)
BROOK
  Benton (arts/ent.)
  Jacoby (sports)
BROOKE
  Adams (arts/ent.)
  Astor (misc.)
  Shields (arts/ent.)
BROOKS
  Atkinson (arts/ent.)
  Robinson (sports)
BRUCE
  Beresford (arts/ent.)
  Boxleitner (arts/ent.)
  Cabot (arts/ent.)
  Campbell (arts/ent.)
  Davison (arts/ent.)
  Dern (arts/ent.)

Dickinson (arts/ent.)
J. Friedman (arts/ent.)
Hornsby (arts/ent.)
Jenner (sports)
Lee (arts/ent.)
Springsteen (arts/ent.)
Willis (arts/ent.)
BRUNO
  Bettelheim (misc.)
  Ganz (arts/ent.)
  Hauptmann (misc.)
  Kirby (arts/ent.)
  Walter (arts/ent.)
BRYAN
  Adams (arts/ent.)
  Brown (arts/ent.)
  Ferry (arts/ent.)
BRYANT
  Gumbel (sports)
  Washburn (arts/ent.)
BUBBA
  Smith (sports)
BUCK
  Henry (arts/ent.)
  Jones (arts/ent.)
  Leonard (sports)
  Owens (arts/ent.)
BUCKY
  Dent (sports)
  Harris (sports)
  Walters (sports)
BUD
  Abbott (arts/ent.)
  Collyer (arts/ent.)
  Cort (arts/ent.)
  Fisher (arts/ent.)
  Grant (sports)
  Powell (arts/ent.)
  Yorkin (arts/ent.)
BUDD
  Schulberg (arts/ent.)
BUDDY
  Bell (sports)
  Bolden (arts/ent.)
  De Franco (arts/ent.)
  Desylva (arts/ent.)
  Ebsen (arts/ent.)
  Greco (arts/ent.)
  Hackett (arts/ent.)
  Holly (arts/ent.)
  Miles (arts/ent.)
  Rich (arts/ent.)
  Rogers (arts/ent.)
BUDGE
  Patty (sports)
BUFFY
  Sainte-Marie (arts/ent.)

BUGS
Moran (misc.)
BUGSY
Siegel (misc.)
BULLDOG
Turner (sports)
BUNK
Johnson (arts/ent.)
BUNNY
Berigan (arts/ent.)
Debarge (arts/ent.)
BURGESS
Meredith (arts/ent.)
BURL
Ives (arts/ent.)
BURLEIGH
Grimes (sports)
BURNE
Hogarth (arts/ent.)
BURR
Tillstrom (arts/ent.)
BURT
Bacharach (arts/ent.)
Kennedy (arts/ent.)
Lancaster (arts/ent.)
Reynolds (arts/ent.)
Ward (arts/ent.)
Young (arts/ent.)
BURTON
Lane (arts/ent.)
Richter (sci./inv.)
BUSBY
Berkeley (arts/ent.)
BUSTER
Crabbe (arts/ent.)
Keaton (arts/ent.)
BUTCH
Cassidy (misc.)
BUTTERFLY
McQueen (arts/ent.)
BUTTON
Gwinnett (govt./mil.)
BUZZ
Aldrin (pion./exp.)
BYRON
Allen (arts/ent.)
Haskin (arts/ent.)
Nelson (sports)
White (govt./mil.)
C.
Day Lewis (arts/ent.)
C. C.
Beck (arts/ent.)
C. E. M.
Joad (rel./phil.)
C. P.
Snow (arts/ent.)

C. S.
Forester (arts/ent.)
Lewis (arts/ent.)
C. W.
McCall (arts/ent.)
C. Z.
Guest (misc.)
C. AUBREY
Smith (arts/ent.)
C. EVERETT
Koop (govt./mil.)
C. THOMAS
Howell (arts/ent.)
CAB
Calloway (arts/ent.)
CAL
Hubbard (sports)
Ripken (sports)
Tjader (arts/ent.)
CALE
Yarborough (sports)
CALEB
Cushing (govt./mil.)
CALVIN
Coolidge (govt./mil.)
Klein (arts/ent.)
Murphy (sports)
Peete (sports)
Trillin (arts/ent.)
CAMERON
Crowe (arts/ent.)
Mitchell (arts/ent.)
CAMILLA
Parker-Bowles (misc.)
CAMILLE
Paglia (arts/ent.)
Pissarro (arts/ent.)
Saint-Saëns (arts/ent.)
CAMILO
Cela (arts/ent.)
CANADA
Lee (arts/ent.)
CANDICE
Bergen (arts/ent.)
CANDY
Clark (arts/ent.)
Cummings (sports)
CANNONBALL
Adderley (arts/ent.)
CAP
Anson (sports)
CARA
Williams (arts/ent.)
CARL
Albert (govt./mil.)
Bernstein (arts/ent.)
Betz (arts/ent.)

Cori (sci./inv.)
Dreyer (arts/ent.)
Furillo (sports)
Hubbell (sports)
Icahn (business)
Jung (sci./inv.)
Laemmle (arts/ent.)
Lewis (sports)
Milles (arts/ent.)
Orff (arts/ent.)
Palmer (arts/ent.)
Perkins (arts/ent.)
Reiner (arts/ent.)
Sagan (sci./inv.)
Sandburg (arts/ent.)
Smith (arts/ent.)
Spitteler (arts/ent.)
Switzer (arts/ent.)
Van Vechten (arts/ent.)
Weathers (arts/ent.)
Von Weber (arts/ent.)
Wilson (arts/ent.)
Yastrzemski (sports)
Zuckmayer (arts/ent.)
CARLA
Hills (govt./mil.)
CARLENE
Carter (arts/ent.)
CARLETON
Young (arts/ent.)
CARLISLE
Floyd (arts/ent.)
CARLO
Collodi (arts/ent.)
Gadda (arts/ent.)
Gambino (misc.)
Ponti (arts/ent.)
CARLOS
Castaneda (arts/ent.)
Chávez (arts/ent.)
Fuentes (arts/ent.)
Montoya (arts/ent.)
Santana (arts/ent.)
CARLTON
Fisk (sports)
CARLY
Simon (arts/ent.)
CARMEN
Appice (arts/ent.)
Basilio (sports)
Cavallaro (arts/ent.)
McRae (arts/ent.)
Miranda (arts/ent.)
CARMINE
Coppola (arts/ent.)
CARNEY
Lansford (sports)

CARNIE
Wilson (arts/ent.)
CAROL
Alt (arts/ent.)
Burnett (arts/ent.)
Channing (arts/ent.)
Heiss (sports)
Kane (arts/ent.)
Lawrence (arts/ent.)
Leifer (arts/ent.)
Lynley (arts/ent.)
Mosley-Braun (govt./
mil.)
Reed (arts/ent.)
CAROLE
King (arts/ent.)
Lombard (arts/ent.)
Bayer Sager (arts/
ent.)
CAROLINE
Harrison (govt./mil.)
Lamb (arts/ent.)
Kennedy Schlossberg
(misc.)
CAROLUS
Linnaeus (sci./inv.)
CAROLYN
Jones (arts/ent.)
Keene (arts/ent.)
CAROLYNE
Roehm (arts/ent.)
CARRÉ
Otis (arts/ent.)
CARRIE
Fisher (arts/ent.)
Hamilton (arts/ent.)
Nye (arts/ent.)
Snodgress (arts/ent.)
CARROLL
Baker (arts/ent.)
Ballard (arts/ent.)
O'Connor (arts/ent.)
CARRY
Nation (misc.)
CARSON
McCullers (arts/ent.)
CARTER
Glass (govt./mil.)
CARY
Elwes (arts/ent.)
Grant (arts/ent.)
CARYL
Chessman (misc.)
CASEY
Jones (misc.)
Kasem (arts/ent.)
Stengel (sports)

CASPAR
Weinberger (govt./mil.)
CASS
Canfield (business)
Elliot (arts/ent.)
Gilbert (arts/ent.)
CAT
Stevens (arts/ent.)
CATFISH
Hunter (sports)
CATHERINE
Bach (arts/ent.)
Deneuve (arts/ent.)
Hicks (arts/ent.)
Oxenberg (arts/ent.)
Parr (misc.)
Mary Stewart (arts/ent.)
CATHLEEN
Nesbitt (arts/ent.)
CATHRYN
Damon (arts/ent.)
CATHY
Lee Crosby (arts/ent.)
Dennis (arts/ent.)
Guisewhite (arts/ent.)
Rigby (sports)
CATLIN
Adams (arts/ent.)
CECIL
Beaton (arts/ent.)
B. De Mille (arts/ent.)
Hoffman (arts/ent.)
Kellaway (arts/ent.)
Rhodes (govt./mil.)
CECILIA
Bartoli (arts/ent.)
CEDRIC
Hardwicke (arts/
ent.)
CELESTE
Holm (arts/ent.)
CELIA
Johnson (arts/ent.)
CELINE
Dion (arts/ent.)
CESAR, CÉSAR
Chavez (govt./mil.)
Auguste Franck (arts/
ent.)
Romero (arts/ent.)
CESARE
Borgia (govt./mil.)
CHAD
Everett (arts/ent.)
Lowe (arts/ent.)
McQueen (arts/ent.)
Stuart (arts/ent.)

CHAIM
Potok (arts/ent.)
Weizmann (govt./mil.)
CHAKA
Khan (arts/ent.)
CHARLENE
Tilton (arts/ent.)
CHARLES
Addams (arts/ent.)
Atlas (sports)
Aznavour (arts/ent.)
Barkley (sports)
Barton (arts/ent.)
Baudelaire (arts/ent.)
Berlitz (misc.)
Herbert Best (sci./inv.)
Bickford (arts/ent.)
Boyer (arts/ent.)
Bronson (arts/ent.)
Brush (sci./inv.)
Bukowski (arts/ent.)
Bulfinch (arts/ent.)
Burchfield (arts/ent.)
Butterworth (arts/ent.)
Chesnutt (arts/ent.)
Coburn (arts/ent.)
W. Colson (govt./mil.)
Crichton (arts/ent.)
Curtis (govt./mil.)
Darwin (sci./inv.)
G. Dawes (govt./mil.)
De Gaulle (govt./mil.)
Dickens (arts/ent.)
Durning (arts/ent.)
Eames (arts/ent.)
W. Fairbanks (govt./mil.)
Fuller (arts/ent.)
Gibson (arts/ent.)
Goodyear (sci./inv.)
H. Goren (misc.)
François Gounod (arts/
ent.)
Grodin (arts/ent.)
J. Guiteau (misc.)
Haid (arts/ent.)
B. Huggins (sci./inv.)
E. Hughes (govt./mil.)
Ives (arts/ent.)
Kuralt (arts/ent.)
Laughton (arts/ent.)
Lindbergh (arts/ent.)
Loeffler (arts/ent.)
MacArthur (arts/ent.)
Manson (misc.)
Mayo (sci./inv.)
McKim (arts/ent.)
Merz (arts/ent.)

Mingus (arts/ent.)
Münch (arts/ent.)
Nash (business)
Bernard Nordoff (arts/
ent.)
Peale (arts/ent.)
Peirce (rel./phil.)
Perrault (arts/ent.)
Pinckney (govt./mil.)
Nelson Reilly (arts/ent.)
Revson (business)
Richter (sci./inv.)
Ringling (arts/ent.)
Roberts (arts/ent.)
M. Schulz (arts/ent.)
Scribner (business)
Simic (arts/ent.)
Starkweather (misc.)
Sumner (govt./mil.)
Tiffany (arts/ent.)
Rudolph Walgreen
(business)
Wesley (arts/ent.)
Whitman (misc.)
E. Whittaker (govt./
mil.)
Winninger (arts/ent.)
Worth (arts/ent.)
CHARLEY
Pride (arts/ent.)
Taylor (sports)
CHARLIE
Barnet (arts/ent.)
Byrd (arts/ent.)
Chaplin (arts/ent.)
Christian (arts/ent.)
Comiskey (sports)
Daniels (arts/ent.)
Gehringer (sports)
Grimm (sports)
Hough (sports)
Keller (sports)
Leibrandt (sports)
McCoy (arts/ent.)
Parker (arts/ent.)
Rich (arts/ent.)
Root (sports)
Rouse (arts/ent.)
Ruggles (arts/ent.)
Sheen (arts/ent.)
Tickner (sports)
Trippi (sports)
Watts (arts/ent.)
CHARLOTTE
Armstrong (arts/ent.)
Brontë (arts/ent.)
Caffey (arts/ent.)

Greenwood (arts/ent.)
Lewis (arts/ent.)
Rae (arts/ent.)
Rampling (arts/ent.)
CHARLTON
Heston (arts/ent.)
CHASTITY
Bono (arts/ent.)
CHE
Guevara (govt./
mil.)
CHEECH
Marin (arts/ent.)
CHELSEA
Clinton (misc.)
Noble (arts/ent.)
CHERIE
Currie (arts/ent.)
Johnson (arts/ent.)
CHERYL
Ladd (arts/ent.)
Lynn (arts/ent.)
Tiegs (arts/ent.)
CHESTER
Arthur (govt./mil.)
Conklin (arts/ent.)
Gould (arts/ent.)
Himes (arts/ent.)
Morris (arts/ent.)
Nimitz (govt./mil.)
CHET
Atkins (arts/ent.)
Baker (arts/ent.)
Huntley (arts/ent.)
CHEVY
Chase (arts/ent.)
CHI
Coltrane (arts/ent.)
CHIC
Hecht (govt./mil.)
Johnson (arts/ent.)
Young (arts/ent.)
CHICK
Corea (arts/ent.)
Hafey (sports)
Hearn (sports)
Webb (arts/ent.)
CHICO
Marx (arts/ent.)
CHIEF
Bender (sports)
CHILDE
Hassam (arts/ent.)
CHILI
Davis (sports)
CHILL
Wills (arts/ent.)

CHINUA
Achebe (arts/ent.)
CHITA
Rivera (arts/ent.)
CHLOE
Webb (arts/ent.)
CHRIS
Columbus (arts/ent.)
Deburgh (arts/ent.)
Difford (arts/ent.)
Elliott (arts/ent.)
Evert (sports)
Farley (arts/ent.)
Isaak (arts/ent.)
LeDoux (arts/ent.)
Lemmon (arts/ent.)
Lowe (arts/ent.)
O'Donnell (arts/ent.)
Penn (arts/ent.)
Rea (arts/ent.)
Rock (arts/ent.)
Sarandon (arts/ent.)
CHRISSIE
Hynde (arts/ent.)
CHRISTA
Ludwig (arts/ent.)
McAuliffe (misc.)
Wolfe (arts/ent.)
CHRISTIAAN
Barnard (sci./inv.)
CHRISTIAN
Anfinsen (sci./inv.)
Dior (arts/ent.)
Doppler (sci./inv.)
Lacroix (arts/ent.)
Nyby (arts/ent.)
Slater (arts/ent.)
CHRISTIE
Brinkley (arts/ent.)
Hefner (business)
CHRISTINA
Applegate (arts/ent.)
Ferrare (arts/ent.)
Ricci (arts/ent.)
Rossetti (arts/ent.)
Stead (arts/ent.)
CHRISTINE
Lahti (arts/ent.)
McGuire (arts/ent.)
McVie (arts/ent.)
CHRISTOPH
Willibald Gluck (arts/
ent.)
CHRISTOPHER
Atkins (arts/ent.)
Cerf (arts/ent.)
Columbus (pion./exp.)

Cross (arts/ent.)
Fry (arts/ent.)
Guest (arts/ent.)
Isherwood (arts/ent.)
Lambert (arts/ent.)
Lee (arts/ent.)
Lloyd (arts/ent.)
Marlowe (arts/ent.)
Morley (arts/ent.)
Penn (arts/ent.)
Plummer (arts/ent.)
Reeve (arts/ent.)
Walken (arts/ent.)
Wren (arts/ent.)
CHRISTY
Mathewson (sports)
Turlington (arts/ent.)
CHUBBY
Checker (arts/ent.)
CHUCK
Barris (arts/ent.)
Bednarik (sports)
Berry (arts/ent.)
Connors (arts/ent.)
Daly (sports)
Fairbanks (sports)
Jones (arts/ent.)
Klein (sports)
Mangione (arts/ent.)
McKinley (sports)
Noll (sports)
Norris (arts/ent.)
Woolery (arts/ent.)
Yeager (misc.)
CHYNNA
Phillips (arts/ent.)
CICELY
Courtneidge (arts/ent.)
Tyson (arts/ent.)
CILLA
Black (arts/ent.)
CINDY
Crawford (arts/ent.)
Williams (arts/ent.)
Wilson (arts/ent.)
CIRO
Terranova (misc.)
CISSY
Houston (arts/ent.)
CLAIBORNE
Pell (govt./mil.)
CLAIRE
Bloom (arts/ent.)
Chennault (govt./mil.)
Trevor (arts/ent.)
CLANCY
Brown (arts/ent.)

CLARA
Barton (misc.)
Bow (arts/ent.)
Kimball Young (arts/ent.)
CLARE
Booth Luce (arts/ent.)
CLARENCE
Badger (arts/ent.)
Birdseye (business)
Brown (arts/ent.)
Clemons (arts/ent.)
Darrow (misc.)
Day (arts/ent.)
E. Mulford (arts/ent.)
Nash (arts/ent.)
Thomas (govt./mil.)
CLARICE
Lispector (arts/ent.)
CLARK
Gable (arts/ent.)
Griffith (sports)
CLARKE
Hinkle (sports)
CLAUD
Lorrain (arts/ent.)
CLAUDE
Binyon (arts/ent.)
Bolling (arts/ent.)
Brown (arts/ent.)
Chabrol (arts/ent.)
Dauphin (arts/ent.)
Debussy (arts/ent.)
Lelouch (arts/ent.)
Lévi-Strauss (sci./inv.)
McKay (arts/ent.)
Monet (arts/ent.)
Rains (arts/ent.)
Simon (arts/ent.)
CLAUDE-ADRIEN
Helvétius (rel./phil.)
CLAUDETTE
Colbert (arts/ent.)
CLAUDIA
Cardinale (arts/ent.)
Schiffer (arts/ent.)
CLAUDINE
Longet (arts/ent.)
CLAUDIO
Abbado (arts/ent.)
Arrau (arts/ent.)
Monteverdi or
Monteverde (arts/ent.)
CLAUS
Von Bulow (misc.)
CLAYTON
Moore (arts/ent.)

CLEAVON
Little (arts/ent.)
CLEM
Bevans (arts/ent.)
CLEMENS
Brentano (arts/ent.)
CLEMENT, CLÉMENT
Ader (sci./inv.)
Attlee (govt./mil.)
C. Moore (arts/ent.)
CLEO
Laine (arts/ent.)
CLEON
Throckmorton (arts/ent.)
CLETE
Boyer (sports)
CLEVE
Francis (arts/ent.)
CLEVELAND
Amory (arts/ent.)
CLIFF
Arquette (arts/ent.)
Battles (sports)
Deyoung (arts/ent.)
Edwards (arts/ent.)
Gorman (arts/ent.)
Harris (sports)
Richard (arts/ent.)
Robertson (arts/ent.)
CLIFFORD
Odets (arts/ent.)
D. Simak (arts/ent.)
CLIFTON
Davis (arts/ent.)
Fadiman (arts/ent.)
Webb (arts/ent.)
CLINT
Black (arts/ent.)
Eastwood (arts/ent.)
Walker (arts/ent.)
CLINTON
Davisson (sci./inv.)
Barker (arts/ent.)
CLIVE
Barnes (arts/ent.)
Bell (arts/ent.)
Brook (arts/ent.)
Cussler (arts/ent.)
Donner (arts/ent.)
CLORIS
Leachman (arts/ent.)
CLU
Gulager (arts/ent.)
CLYDE
Barrow (misc.)
Drexler (sports)

McPhatter (arts/ent.)
Coco
Chanel (arts/ent.)
Cokie
Roberts (arts/ent.)
Cole
Porter (arts/ent.)
Coleman
Hawkins (arts/ent.)
Colin
Blakely (arts/ent.)
Clive (arts/ent.)
Friels (arts/ent.)
Kelly (govt./mil.)
MacInnes (arts/ent.)
Powell (govt./mil.)
Wilson (arts/ent.)
Colleen
Dewhurst (arts/ent.)
McCullough (arts/
ent.)
Moore (arts/ent.)
Compton
Bennett (arts/ent.)
MacKenzie (arts/ent.)
Con
Conrad (arts/ent.)
Conan
O'Brien (arts/ent.)
Conchata
Ferrell (arts/ent.)
Condé
Nast (business)
Connee
Boswell (arts/ent.)
Connie
Chung (arts/ent.)
Francis (arts/ent.)
Mack (sports)
Mack III (govt./mil.)
Sellecca (arts/ent.)
Stevens (arts/ent.)
Conor
O'Brien (arts/ent.)
Conrad
Aiken (arts/ent.)
Bain (arts/ent.)
Hilton (business)
Nagel (arts/ent.)
Richter (arts/ent.)
Veidt (arts/ent.)
Constance
Bennett (arts/ent.)
Collier (arts/ent.)
Cummings (arts/ent.)
Moore (arts/ent.)
Talmadge (arts/ent.)

Constantin
Brancusi (arts/ent.)
Constantine
P. Cavafy (arts/ent.)
Conway
Tearle (arts/ent.)
Twitty (arts/ent.)
Cookie
Lavagetto (sports)
Cootie
Williams (arts/ent.)
Cora
Baird (arts/ent.)
Witherspoon (arts/
ent.)
Coral
Browne (arts/ent.)
Corazon
Aquino (govt./mil.)
Corbin
Bernsen (arts/ent.)
Cordell
Hull (govt./mil.)
Cordwainer
Smith (arts/ent.)
Coretta
King (arts/ent.)
Corey
Feldman (arts/ent.)
Haim (arts/ent.)
Corky
Nemec (arts/ent.)
Cornel
Wilde (arts/ent.)
Cornelia
Otis Skinner (arts/
ent.)
Cornelius
Ryan (arts/ent.)
Tacitus (arts/ent.)
Vanderbilt (business)
Vanderbilt Whitney
(business)
Cornell
Woolrich (arts/ent.)
Costas
Mandylor (arts/ent.)
Cotter
Smith (arts/ent.)
Cotton
Mather (rel./phil.)
Count
Basie (arts/ent.)
Countee
Cullen (arts/ent.)
Country Joe
McDonald (arts/ent.)

Courteney
Cox (arts/ent.)
Courtney
Gibbs (arts/ent.)
Love (arts/ent.)
Thorne-Smith (arts/ent.)
Cozy
Cole (arts/ent.)
Craig
Claiborne (arts/ent.)
T. Nelson (arts/ent.)
Rice (arts/ent.)
Stevens (arts/ent.)
Crash
Corrigan (arts/ent.)
Craddock (arts/ent.)
Crazylegs
Hirsch (sports)
Cree
Summer (arts/ent.)
Crispin
Glover (arts/ent.)
Crispus
Attucks (govt./mil.)
Cristóbal
Balenciaga (arts/ent.)
Cristy
Lane (arts/ents.)
Crystal
Bernard (arts/ent.)
Gayle (arts/ent.)
Curley
Culp (sports)
Curly
Howard (arts/ent.)
Lambeau (sports)
Curt
Flood (sports)
Gowdy (sports)
Jurgens (arts/ent.)
Smith (arts/ent.)
Curtis
Le May (govt./mil.)
Mayfield (arts/ent.)
Stigers (arts/ent.)
Strange (sports)
Cy
Coleman (arts/ent.)
Young (sports)
Cybill
Shepherd (arts/ent.)
Cyd
Charisse (arts/ent.)
Cynda
Williams (arts/ent.)
Cyndi
Lauper (arts/ent.)

CYNTHIA
Freeman (arts/ent.)
Gibb (arts/ent.)
Gregory (arts/ent.)
Ozick (arts/ent.)
Sikes (arts/ent.)
CYRANO
De Bergerac (govt./mil.)
CYRIL
Henry Coles (arts/ent.)
Cusack (arts/ent.)
Delevanti (arts/ent.)
M. Kornbluth (arts/ent.)
Ritchard (arts/ent.)
CYRUS
H. K. Curtis (business)
Hall McCormick (sci./
inv.)
Vance (govt./mil.)
CZESLAW
Milosz (arts/ent.)
D. B.
Wyndham Lewis (arts/
ent.)
D. H.
Lawrence (arts/ent.)
D. W.
Griffith (arts/ent.)
DABNEY
Coleman (arts/ent.)
DACK
Rambo (arts/ent.)
DAG
Hammarskjöld (govt./
mil.)
DAISY
Ashford (arts/ent.)
DALE
Bumpers (govt./mil.)
Carnegie (arts/ent.)
Evans (arts/ent.)
Messick (arts/ent.)
Midkiff (arts/ent.)
DALTON
Trumbo (arts/ent.)
DAMON
Knight (arts/ent.)
Runyon (arts/ent.)
Wayans (arts/ent.)
DAN
Aykroyd (arts/ent.)
Blocker (arts/ent.)
Brouthers (sports)
Dailey (arts/ent.)
Devine (sports)
Duryea (arts/ent.)
Fogelberg (arts/ent.)

Haggerty (arts/ent.)
Hill (arts/ent.)
Marino (sports)
O'Herlihy (arts/ent.)
Quisenberry (sports)
Rather (arts/ent.)
Rostenkowski (govt./
mil.)
Rowan (arts/ent.)
DANA
Andrews (arts/ent.)
Carvey (arts/ent.)
Delany (arts/ent.)
Plato (arts/ent.)
Wynter (arts/ent.)
DANICA
McKellar (arts/ent.)
DANIEL
Boone (pion./exp.)
Boorstin (arts/ent.)
Burnham (arts/ent.)
Day-Lewis (arts/ent.)
Ellsberg (govt./mil.)
Fahrenheit (sci./inv.)
French (arts/ent.)
K. Inouye (govt./mil.)
Mason (arts/ent.)
Moynihan (govt./mil.)
Nathans (sci./inv.)
Stern (arts/ent.)
D. Tompkins (govt./mil.)
J. Travanti (arts/ent.)
Webster (govt./mil.)
DANIELLE
Brisebois (arts/ent.)
Darrieux (arts/ent.)
Steel (arts/ent.)
DANNY
Aiello (arts/ent.)
Bonaduce (arts/ent.)
Cox (sports)
Darwin (sports)
Devito (arts/ent.)
Elfman (arts/ent.)
Fortmann (sports)
Glover (arts/ent.)
Jackson (sports)
Kaye (arts/ent.)
Thomas (arts/ent.)
Wood (arts/ent.)
DANTE
Lavelli (sports)
Rossetti (arts/ent.)
DANY
Robin (arts/ent.)
DAPHNE
Dumaurier (arts/ent.)

Zuniga (arts/ent.)
DARCI
Kistler (arts/ent.)
DARIO
Argento (arts/ent.)
DARIUS
Milhaud (arts/ent.)
DARLA
Hood (arts/ent.)
DARLEEN
Carr (arts/ent.)
DARLENE
Hard (sports)
Love (arts/ent.)
DARRELL
Evans (sports)
Porter (sports)
DARREN
McGavin (arts/ent.)
DARRYL
Dawkins (sports)
Strawberry (sports)
F. Zanuck (arts/ent.)
DARYL
Dragon (arts/ent.)
Hall (arts/ent.)
Hannah (arts/ent.)
DASH
Crofts (arts/ent.)
DASHIELL
Hammett (arts/ent.)
DAVE
Barry (arts/ent.)
Bing (sports)
Brubeck (arts/ent.)
Casper (sports)
Clark (arts/ent.)
Concepcion (sports)
Coulier (arts/ent.)
Debusschere (sports)
Dravecky (sports)
Edmunds (arts/ent.)
Frischberg (arts/ent.)
Garroway (arts/ent.)
Grusin (arts/ent.)
Kingman (sports)
Loggins (arts/ent.)
Mason (arts/ent.)
McNally (sports)
Parker (sports)
Prater (arts/ent.)
Stewart (arts/ent.)
Thomas (business)
Winfield (sports)
DAVID
Belasco (arts/ent.)
Bellamy (arts/ent.)

Ben-Gurion (govt./mil.)
Berkowitz (misc.)
Birney (arts/ent.)
Bowie (arts/ent.)
Brenner (arts/ent.)
Brinkley (arts/ent.)
Byrne (arts/ent.)
Carradine (arts/ent.)
Caruso (arts/ent.)
Cassidy (arts/ent.)
Charret (arts/ent.)
Allan Coe (arts/ent.)
Copperfield (arts/ent.)
Cronenberg (arts/ent.)
Crosby (arts/ent.)
Diamond (arts/ent.)
Dinkins (govt./mil.)
Duchovny (arts/ent.)
Essex (arts/ent.)
Farragut (govt./mil.)
Faustino (arts/ent.)
Foster (arts/ent.)
Frizzell (arts/ent.)
Frost (arts/ent.)
Garrick (arts/ent.)
Gates (arts/ent.)
Geffen (arts/ent.)
Groh (arts/ent.)
Halberstam (arts/ent.)
Hartman (arts/ent.)
Hasselhoff (arts/ent.)
Hemmings (arts/ent.)
Hockney (arts/ent.)
Hume (rel./phil.)
Henry Hwang (arts/
  ent.)
Janssen (arts/ent.)
Johansen (arts/ent.)
Keith (arts/ent.)
Kelley (arts/ent.)
Koresh (rel./phil.)
Lean (arts/ent.)
Leisure (arts/ent.)
Letterman (arts/ent.)
Lichine (arts/ent.)
Livingstone (pion./
  exp.)
Lloyd George (govt./
  mil.)
Lynch (arts/ent.)
Mamet (arts/ent.)
McCallum (arts/ent.)
McCullough (arts/ent.)
Merrick (arts/ent.)
Naughton (arts/ent.)
Niven (arts/ent.)
Oistrakh (arts/ent.)

Packard (business)
Pearson (sports)
Graham Phillips (arts/
  ent.)
Rabe (arts/ent.)
Rappaport (arts/ent.)
Rasche (arts/ent.)
Reuben (arts/ent.)
Robinson (sports)
Lee Roth (arts/ent.)
Ruffin (arts/ent.)
Sanborn (arts/ent.)
O. Selznick (arts/ent.)
Seville (arts/ent.)
Soul (arts/ent.)
H. Souter (govt./mil.)
Ogden Stiers (arts/ent.)
Stockman (govt./mil.)
Susskind (arts/ent.)
Thompson (sports)
Tomlinson (arts/ent.)
Wayne (arts/ent.)
Zucker (arts/ent.)
DAVIS
Dresser (arts/ent.)
DAVY
Crockett (pion./exp.)
Jones (arts/ent.)
DAWN
Addams (arts/ent.)
Fraser (sports)
Lyn (arts/ent.)
Steel (arts/ent.)
DAWNN
Lewis (arts/ent.)
DAYTON
Allen (arts/ent.)
DAZZY
Vance (sports)
DEACON
Jones (sports)
DEAN
Acheson (govt./mil.)
Cain (arts/ent.)
Jagger (arts/ent.)
Jones (arts/ent.)
Koontz (arts/ent.)
Martin (arts/ent.)
Rusk (govt./mil.)
Stockwell (arts/ent.)
Torrence (arts/ent.)
DEANNA
Durbin (arts/ent.)
DEBBE
Dunning (arts/ent.)
DEBBI
Fields (business)

DEBBIE
Allen (arts/ent.)
Gibson (arts/ent.)
Meyer (sports)
Reynolds (arts/ent.)
DEBBY
Boone (arts/ent.)
DEBI
Mazar (arts/ent.)
Thomas (sports)
DEBORAH
Allen (arts/ent.)
Harry (arts/ent.)
Kerr (arts/ent.)
Norville (arts/ent.)
Raffin (arts/ent.)
DEBRA
Winger (arts/ent.)
DEBRALEE
Scott (arts/ent.)
DEE
Alexander Brown (arts/
  ent.)
DEE DEE
Ramone (arts/ent.)
DEEMS
Taylor (arts/ent.)
DEFOREST
Kelley (arts/ent.)
DEIDRE
Hall (arts/ent.)
DEKE
Slayton (pion./exp.)
DEL
Reeves (arts/ent.)
Shannon (arts/ent.)
DELANEY
Bramlett (arts/ent.)
DELBERT
Mann (arts/ent.)
McClinton (arts/ent.)
DELLA
Reese (arts/ent.)
DELMER
Daves (arts/ent.)
DELMORE
Schwartz (arts/ent.)
DELTA
Burke (arts/ent.)
DEMI
Moore (arts/ent.)
DEMOND
Wilson (arts/ent.)
DENHOLM
Elliot (arts/ent.)
DENIECE
Williams (arts/ent.)

DENIS
  Diderot (rel./phil.)
  Leary (arts/ent.)
  Potvin (sports)
DENISE
  Levertov (arts/ent.)
DENMARK
  Vesey (misc.)
DENNIS
  De Concini (govt./mil.)
  Dugan (arts/ent.)
  Franz (arts/ent.)
  Hopper (arts/ent.)
  Miller (arts/ent.)
  Morgan (arts/ent.)
  O'Keefe (arts/ent.)
  Potter (arts/ent.)
  Quaid (arts/ent.)
  Ralston (sports)
  Weaver (arts/ent.)
  Wilson (arts/ent.)
DENNY
  McLain (sports)
  Shute (sports)
DENVER
  Pyle (arts/ent.)
DENZEL
  Washington (arts/
    ent.)
DEREK
  Bok (misc.)
  Jacobi (arts/ent.)
  Walcott (arts/ent.)
DERMOT
  Mulroney (arts/ent.)
DESI
  Arnaz (arts/ent.)
  Arnaz, Jr. (arts/ent.)
DESIDERIUS
  Erasmus (rel./phil.)
DESMOND
  O'Grady (arts/ent.)
  Tutu (govt./mil.)
DE WITT
  Clinton (govt./mil.)
DEWITT
  Wallace (business)
DEXTER
  Gordon (arts/ent.)
  Manley (sports)
DIAHANN
  Carroll (arts/ent.)
DIAN
  Fossey (arts/ent.)
DIANA
  Canova (arts/ent.)
  Dors (arts/ent.)

Hyland (arts/ent.)
Lynn (arts/ent.)
Muldaur (arts/ent.)
Nyad (sports)
Rigg (arts/ent.)
Ross (arts/ent.)
Sands (arts/ent.)
Scarwid (arts/ent.)
Spencer (govt./mil.)
Vreeland (business)
DIANE
  Arbus (arts/ent.)
  Baker (arts/ent.)
  Cilento (arts/ent.)
  English (arts/ent.)
  Keaton (arts/ent.)
  Ladd (arts/ent.)
  Lane (arts/ent.)
  Sawyer (arts/ent.)
  Varsi (arts/ent.)
  Von Furstenberg (arts/
    ent.)
DIANNE
  Feinstein (govt./mil.)
  Lennon (arts/ent.)
  Wiest (arts/ent.)
DICK
  Butkus (sports)
  Button (sports)
  Cavett (arts/ent.)
  Clark (arts/ent.)
  Francis (arts/ent.)
  Gautier (arts/ent.)
  Gregory (arts/ent.)
  Haymes (arts/ent.)
  Lane (sports)
  Lester (arts/ent.)
  Martin (arts/ent.)
  Motta (sports)
  Powell (arts/ent.)
  Sargent (arts/ent.)
  Savitt (sports)
  Shawn (arts/ent.)
  Smothers (arts/ent.)
  Stuart (sports)
  Van Dyke (arts/ent.)
  Van Patten (arts/
    ent.)
  Vitale (sports)
  York (arts/ent.)
DICKEY
  Betts (arts/ent.)
  Lee (arts/ent.)
DIDERIK
  Buxtehude (arts/ent.)
DIDI
  Conn (arts/ent.)

DIEGO
  Rivera (arts/ent.)
  Velázquez (arts/ent.)
DIETRICH
  Bonhoeffer (rel./phil.)
DIK
  Browne (arts/ent.)
DIMITRI
  Mitropoulos (arts/ent.)
DIMITRY
  Kabalevsky (arts/ent.)
DINA
  Merrill (arts/ent.)
DINAH
  Manoff (arts/ent.)
  Shore (arts/ent.)
  Washington (arts/ent.)
DINO
  De Laurentiis (arts/ent.)
DIONNE
  Warwick (arts/ent.)
DIRK
  Benedict (arts/ent.)
  Bogarde (arts/ent.)
  Rambo (arts/ent.)
DITA
  Parlo (arts/ent.)
DIXIE
  Carter (arts/ent.)
  Dunbar (arts/ent.)
  Walker (sports)
DIXY
  Lee Ray (govt./mil.)
DIZZY
  Dean (sports)
  Gillespie (arts/ent.)
DJANGO
  Reinhardt (arts/ent.)
DJUNA
  Barnes (arts/ent.)
DMITRI
  Shostakovich (arts/ent.)
  Tiomkin (arts/ent.)
DOAK
  Walker (sports)
DOBIE
  Gray (arts/ent.)
DOC
  Holliday (misc.)
  Severinson (arts/ent.)
  Watson (arts/ent.)
DODIE
  Smith (arts/ent.)
DODY
  Goodman (arts/ent.)
DOLF
  Camilli (sports)

DOLLEY
Madison (govt./mil.)
DOLLY
Parton (arts/ent.)
DOLORES
Costello (arts/ent.)
Del Rio (arts/ent.)
DOLPH
Lundgren (arts/ent.)
Schayes (sports)
Sweet (arts/ent.)
DOM
Deluise (arts/ent.)
DOMENICO
Scarlatti (arts/ent.)
DOMINICK
Dunne (arts/ent.)
DOMINIQUE
Sanda (arts/ent.)
DON
Adams (arts/ent.)
Ameche (arts/ent.)
Baylor (sports)
Bluth (arts/ent.)
Budge (sports)
Defore (arts/ent.)
Delillo (arts/ent.)
Drysdale (sports)
Everly (arts/ent.)
Gibson (arts/ent.)
Henley (arts/ent.)
Hewitt (arts/ent.)
Ho (arts/ent.)
Hutson (sports)
Johnson (arts/ent.)
King (sports)
Kirshner (arts/ent.)
Knotts (arts/ent.)
Larsen (sports)
Marquis (arts/ent.)
Martin (arts/ent.)
Mattingly (sports)
Maynard (sports)
McLean (arts/ent.)
Meredith (sports)
Murray (arts/ent.)
Novello (arts/ent.)
Pardo (arts/ent.)
Rickles (arts/ent.)
Shula (sports)
Siegel (arts/ent.)
Simpson (arts/ent.)
Sutton (sports)
Williams (arts/ent.)
Wilson (arts/ent.)
Zimmer (sports)

DONA
Drake (arts/ent.)
DONALD
Barthelme (arts/ent.)
Crisp (arts/ent.)
Wills Douglas
(business)
Fagen (arts/ent.)
Glaser (sci./inv.)
Hamilton (arts/ent.)
McMillan (pion./exp.)
O'Connor (arts/ent.)
Pleasence (arts/ent.)
Regan (govt./mil.)
Ogden Stewart (arts/ent.)
Sutherland (arts/ent.)
Trump (business)
E. Westlake (arts/ent.)
DONNA
Dixon (arts/ent.)
Fargo (arts/ent.)
Karan (arts/ent.)
Mills (arts/ent.)
Pescow (arts/ent.)
Reed (arts/ent.)
Rice (arts/ent.)
E. Shalala (misc.)
Summer (arts/ent.)
Tartt (arts/ent.)
DONNY
Hathaway (arts/ent.)
Most (arts/ent.)
Osmond (arts/ent.)
Wahlberg (arts/ent.)
DOODLES
Weaver (arts/ent.)
DOOLEY
Wilson (arts/ent.)
DORE
Schary (arts/ent.)
DORIS
Day (arts/ent.)
Duke (misc.)
Hart (sports)
Lessing (arts/ent.)
DOROTHEA
Dix (misc.)
DOROTHY
Arzner (arts/ent.)
Collins (arts/ent.)
Dandridge (arts/ent.)
Dix (arts/ent.)
Fields (arts/ent.)
Gilman (arts/ent.)
Gish (arts/ent.)
Hamill (sports)

Kilgallen (arts/ent.)
Lamour (arts/ent.)
Loudon (arts/ent.)
Lyman (arts/ent.)
Malone (arts/ent.)
McGuire (arts/ent.)
McGuire (arts/ent.)
Parker (arts/ent.)
Provine (arts/ent.)
L. Sayers (arts/ent.)
Schiff (business)
Stratten (arts/ent.)
Thompson (arts/ent.)
Uhnak (arts/ent.)
DORSEY
Burnette (arts/ent.)
DORY
Previn (arts/ent.)
DOTTIE
West (arts/ent.)
DOUG
Atkins (sports)
Decinces (sports)
Drabek (sports)
Henning (arts/ent.)
McClure (arts/ent.)
Stone (arts/ent.)
DOUGLAS
Dumbrille (arts/ent.)
Fairbanks (arts/ent.)
Fairbanks, Jr. (arts/ent.)
MacArthur (govt./mil.)
Moore (arts/ent.)
Sirk (arts/ent.)
DOW
Finsterwald (sports)
DOYLE
Alexander (sports)
DOYLY
Carte (arts/ent.)
DRED
Scott (misc.)
DREW
Barrymore (arts/ent.)
Pearson (arts/ent.)
DUANE
Allman (arts/ent.)
Eddy (arts/ent.)
DUBOSE
Heyward (arts/ent.)
DUDLEY
Moore (arts/ent.)
DUFF
McKagan (arts/ent.)
DUGALD
Stewart (rel./phil.)

DUKE
Ellington (arts/ent.)
Kahanamoku (sports)
Snider (sports)
DUNCAN
Hines (arts/ent.)
Phyfe (arts/ent.)
Renaldo (arts/ent.)
DURWARD
Kirby (arts/ent.)
DUSTIN
Farnum (arts/ent.)
Hoffman (arts/ent.)
DUSTY
Baker (sports)
Springfield (arts/
ent.)
DUTCH
Clark (sports)
Schultz (misc.)
DWAYNE
Hickman (arts/ent.)
DWEEZIL
Zappa (arts/ent.)
DWIGHT
D. Eisenhower (govt./
mil.)
Evans (sports)
Gooden (sports)
Moody (rel./phil.)
Twilley (arts/ent.)
Yoakam (arts/ent.)
DYAN
Cannon (arts/ent.)
DYLAN
McDermott (arts/ent.)
Thomas (arts/ent.)
E.
Biggs (arts/ent.)
E. B.
White (arts/ent.)
E. C.
Bentley (arts/ent.)
Segar (arts/ent.)
E. E.
Cummings (arts/ent.)
Smith (arts/ent.)
E. F.
Hutton (business)
E. G.
Marshall (arts/ent.)
E. H.
Gombrich (misc.)
E. L.
Doctorow (arts/ent.)
E. M.
Forster (arts/ent.)

E. O.
Somerville (arts/ent.)
E. T. A.
Hoffman (arts/ent.)
E. W.
Scripps (business)
E. Y.
Harburg (arts/ent.)
E. BENJAMIN
Nelson (govt./mil.)
E. HOWARD
Hunt, Jr. (arts/ent.)
E. PHILLIPS
Oppenheim (arts/ent.)
EADWEARD
Muybridge (arts/ent.)
EAMON
De Valera (govt./mil.)
EARL
Averill (sports)
Derr Biggers (arts/ent.)
Blackwell, Jr. (arts/ent.)
Browder (govt./mil.)
Butz (govt./mil.)
Campbell (sports)
Thomas Conley (arts/
ent.)
Hines (arts/ent.)
Holliman (arts/ent.)
Klugh (arts/ent.)
Monroe (sports)
Sande (sports)
Scruggs (arts/ent.)
Torgeson (sports)
Warren (govt./mil.)
Weaver (sports)
Wilson (arts/ent.)
EARLE
Combs (sports)
EARLY
Wynn (sports)
EARTHA
Kitt (arts/ent.)
EASTMAN
Johnson (arts/ent.)
ED
Ames (arts/ent.)
Asner (arts/ent.)
Barrow (sports)
Begley (arts/ent.)
Begley, Jr. (arts/ent.)
Bradley (arts/ent.)
Delahanty (sports)
Fitzgerald (arts/ent.)
Gein (misc.)
Harris (arts/ent.)
Healey (sports)

Koch (govt./mil.)
Kranepool (sports)
Lopat (sports)
Marinaro (arts/ent.)
McMahon (arts/ent.)
O'Neill (arts/ent.)
Sneed (sports)
Sullivan (arts/ent.)
Walsh (sports)
Wynn (arts/ent.)
EDA
Le Shan (arts/ent.)
EDD
Byrnes (arts/ent.)
Roush (sports)
EDDIE
Acuff (arts/ent.)
Albert (arts/ent.)
Anderson (arts/ent.)
Arcaro (sports)
Bracken (arts/ent.)
Cantor (arts/ent.)
Cline (arts/ent.)
Cochran (arts/ent.)
Collins (sports)
Condon (arts/ent.)
Duchin (arts/ent.)
Fisher (arts/ent.)
Foy (arts/ent.)
Foy, Jr. (arts/ent.)
Heywood (arts/ent.)
Holland (arts/ent.)
Kendricks (arts/ent.)
Lopat (sports)
Mathews (sports)
Mekka (arts/ent.)
Money (arts/ent.)
Murphy (arts/ent.)
Plank (sports)
Rabbitt (arts/ent.)
Rickenbacker (govt./
mil.)
Shore (sports)
Stanley (sports)
Van Halen (arts/ent.)
Vedder (arts/ent.)
EDDY
Arnold (arts/ent.)
Duchin (arts/ent.)
Grant (arts/ent.)
Raven (arts/ent.)
EDEN
Phillpotts (arts/ent.)
EDGAR
Bergen (arts/ent.)
Rice Burroughs (arts/
ent.)

Cayce (misc.)
Degas (arts/ent.)
A. Guest (arts/ent.)
Lee Masters (arts/
ent.)
Poe (arts/ent.)
Wallace (arts/ent.)
Winter (arts/ent.)
EDGARD
Varèse (arts/ent.)
EDIE
Adams (arts/ent.)
Brickell (arts/ent.)
McClurg (arts/ent.)
Sedgwick (arts/ent.)
EDITH
Evans (arts/ent.)
Head (arts/ent.)
Piaf (arts/ent.)
Sitwell (arts/ent.)
Wharton (arts/ent.)
EDMOND
O'Brien (arts/ent.)
Rostand (arts/ent.)
EDMUND
Crispin (arts/ent.)
Goulding (arts/ent.)
Gwenn (arts/ent.)
Halley (sci./inv.)
Hillary (pion./exp.)
Lowe (arts/ent.)
Muskie (govt./mil.)
Spenser (arts/ent.)
Wilson (arts/ent.)
EDNA
Best (arts/ent.)
Buchanan (arts/ent.)
Ferber (arts/ent.)
St. Vincent Millay (arts/
ent.)
O'Brien (arts/ent.)
Oliver (arts/ent.)
Purviance (arts/ent.)
EDO
De Waart (arts/ent.)
EDOUARD, ÉDOUARD
Detaille (arts/ent.)
Lalo (arts/ent.)
Manet (arts/ent.)
Vuillard (arts/ent.)
EDSEL
Ford (business)
EDUARD
Beneš (govt./mil.)
Shevardnadze (govt./
mil.)

EDVARD
Grieg (arts/ent.)
Munch (arts/ent.)
EDWARD
Abbey (sci./inv.)
Albee (arts/ent.)
Arnold (arts/ent.)
Bellamy (arts/ent.)
Bulwer-Lytton (arts/
ent.)
Coley Burne-Jones
(arts/ent.)
Dmytryk (arts/ent.)
Elgar (arts/ent.)
Furlong (arts/ent.)
Gibbon (arts/ent.)
Gorey (arts/ent.)
Richard George Heath
(govt./mil.)
Herrmann (arts/ent.)
Hicks (arts/ent.)
Hoagland (arts/ent.)
Hopper (arts/ent.)
Everett Horton (arts/
ent.)
Kendall (sci./inv.)
Lear (arts/ent.)
Mulhare (arts/ent.)
R. Murrow (arts/ent.)
Olmos (arts/ent.)
Mills Purcell (sci./inv.)
G. Robinson (arts/ent.)
Steichen (arts/ent.)
Stone (arts/ent.)
L. Stratemeyer (arts/
ent.)
Streeter (arts/ent.)
Teller (sci./inv.)
Villella (arts/ent.)
Weston (arts/ent.)
D. White (govt./mil.)
Woodward (arts/ent.)
EDWIN
Abbey (arts/ent.)
Armstrong (sci./inv.)
Booth (arts/ent.)
Hubble (sci./inv.)
Land (sci./inv.)
Henry Landseer (arts/
ent.)
Meese (govt./mil.)
Moses (sports)
Muir (arts/ent.)
Newman (arts/ent.)
O'Connor (arts/ent.)
Porter (arts/ent.)

Arlington Robinson
(arts/ent.)
EERO
Saarinen (arts/ent.)
EFREM
Zimbalist (arts/ent.)
Zimbalist, Jr. (arts/ent.)
EILEEN
Brennan (arts/ent.)
Farrell (arts/ent.)
Ford (business)
Fulton (arts/ent.)
Heckart (arts/ent.)
EILLE
Norwood (arts/ent.)
EISAKU
Sato (govt./mil.)
EL
Brendel (arts/ent.)
Cid (govt./mil.)
Cordobés (sports)
Debarge (arts/ent.)
ELAINE
May (arts/ent.)
Stritch (arts/ent.)
ELAYNE
Boosler (arts/ent.)
ELBERT
Hubbard (arts/ent.)
ELBRIDGE
Gerry (govt./mil.)
ELDRIDGE
Cleaver (govt./mil.)
ELEANOR
Hibbert (arts/ent.)
Parker (arts/ent.)
Porter (arts/ent.)
Powell (arts/ent.)
Roosevelt (govt./mil.)
ELENA
Verdugo (arts/ent.)
ELEONORA
Duse (arts/ent.)
ELGIN
Baylor (sports)
ELI
Wallach (arts/ent.)
Whitney (sci./inv.)
ELIA
Kazan (arts/ent.)
Lamb (arts/ent.)
ELIAS
Canetti (arts/ent.)
Howe (sci./inv.)
ELIE
Ducommun (arts/ent.)

Siegmeister (arts/ent.)
Wiesel (arts/ent.)
ELIEL
Saarinen (arts/ent.)
ELIHU
Root (govt./mil.)
ELIJAH
Muhammad (rel./phil.)
ELIN
Wägner (arts/ent.)
ELINOR
Glyn (arts/ent.)
ELIO
Fiorucci (arts/ent.)
Petri (arts/ent.)
ELIOT
Janeway (misc.)
Ness (govt./mil.)
ELISABETH
Kubler-Ross (sci./inv.)
Schwarzkopf (arts/ent.)
Shue (arts/ent.)
ELISHA
Cook, Jr. (arts/ent.)
Otis (sci./inv.)
ELIZA
Johnson (govt./mil.)
ELIZABETH
Allan (arts/ent.)
Arden (business)
Ashley (arts/ent.)
Bishop (arts/ent.)
Barrett Browning (arts/ent.)
Daly (arts/ent.)
Dole (govt./mil.)
Gilbreth (arts/ent.)
Goudge (arts/ent.)
McGovern (arts/ent.)
Monroe (govt./mil.)
Montgomery (arts/ent.)
Pena (arts/ent.)
Perkins (arts/ent.)
Madox Roberts (arts/ent.)
Ryan (sports)
Stanton (govt./mil.)
Taylor (arts/ent.)
ELKE
Sommer (arts/ent.)
ELLA
Fitzgerald (arts/ent.)
Raines (arts/ent.)
ELLEN
Arthur (govt./mil.)
Barkin (arts/ent.)

Burstyn (arts/ent.)
Corby (arts/ent.)
Drew (arts/ent.)
Glasgow (arts/ent.)
Scripps (business)
Terry (arts/ent.)
Wilson (govt./mil.)
ELLIOT
Easton (arts/ent.)
ELLIOTT
Gould (arts/ent.)
ELLIS
Burks (sports)
Rabb (arts/ent.)
ELLSWORTH
Kelly (arts/ent.)
ELMER
Bernstein (arts/ent.)
Rice (arts/ent.)
Sperry (sci./inv.)
ELMO
Lincoln (arts/ent.)
Zumwalt (govt./mil.)
ELMORE
Leonard (arts/ent.)
ELSA
Lanchester (arts/ent.)
Martinelli (arts/ent.)
Maxwell (arts/ent.)
Morante (arts/ent.)
Peretti (arts/ent.)
Schiaparelli (arts/ent.)
ELTON
John (arts/ent.)
Rule (business)
ELVIN
Bishop (arts/ent.)
Hayes (sports)
Jones (arts/ent.)
ELVIS
Costello (arts/ent.)
Presley (arts/ent.)
ELWOOD
Haynes (sci./inv.)
ELY
Culbertson (arts/ent.)
EM
Tunnell (sports)
EMANUEL
Ax (arts/ent.)
Leutze (arts/ent.)
Ungaro (arts/ent.)
EMIL
Jannings (arts/ent.)
Nolde (arts/ent.)

Zatopek (sports)
EMILE, ÉMILE
Berliner (sci./inv.)
Griffith (sports)
Zola (arts/ent.)
EMILIANO
Zapata (govt./mil.)
EMILIO
Estefan (arts/ent.)
Estevez (arts/ent.)
Pucci (arts/ent.)
Segrè (sci./inv.)
EMILY
Brontë (arts/ent.)
Dickinson (arts/ent.)
Harris (misc.)
Lloyd (arts/ent.)
Post (arts/ent.)
EMLYN
Williams (arts/ent.)
EMMA
Calvé (arts/ent.)
Goldman (misc.)
Lazarus (arts/ent.)
Samms (arts/ent.)
Tennant (arts/ent.)
Thompson (arts/ent.)
EMMANUEL
Lewis (arts/ent.)
EMMANUELLE
Riva (arts/ent.)
EMMETT
Kelly (arts/ent.)
EMMUSKA
Orczy (arts/ent.)
EMMYLOU
Harris (arts/ent.)
EMO
Philips (arts/ent.)
EMORY
Parnell (arts/ent.)
ENGELBERT
Humperdinck (arts/ent.)
ENID
Bagnold (arts/ent.)
Blyton (arts/ent.)
Markey (arts/ent.)
ENNIO
Morricone (arts/ent.)
ENOCH
Light (arts/ent.)
ENOS
Slaughter (sports)
ENRICO
Caruso (arts/ent.)
Fermi (sci./inv.)

ENZO
Ferrari (business)
EPPA
Rixey (sports)
ERIC
Ambler (arts/ent.)
Bogosian (arts/ent.)
Burdon (arts/ent.)
Carmen (arts/ent.)
Clapton (arts/ent.)
Heiden (sports)
Hoffer (rel./phil.)
Idle (arts/ent.)
Knight (arts/ent.)
Van Lustbader (arts/
ent.)
Partridge (arts/ent.)
Roberts (arts/ent.)
Rohmer (arts/ent.)
Sevareid (arts/ent.)
Stoltz (arts/ent.)
ERICA
Jong (arts/ent.)
ERICH
Fromm (misc.)
Kästner (arts/ent.)
Leinsdorf (arts/ent.)
Maria Remarque (arts/
ent.)
Segal (arts/ent.)
Von Daniken (arts/ent.)
Von Stroheim (arts/ent.)
ERIK
Estrada (arts/ent.)
Karlfeldt (arts/ent.)
Menendez (misc.)
Satie (arts/ent.)
ERIKA
Alexander (arts/ent.)
Slezak (arts/ent.)
ERIN
Gray (arts/ent.)
Moran (arts/ent.)
O'Brien-Moore (arts/
ent.)
ERLE
Stanley Gardner (arts/
ent.)
ERMA
Bombeck (arts/ent.)
ERNEST
Ansermet (arts/ent.)
Ball (arts/ent.)
Bloch (arts/ent.)
Borgnine (arts/ent.)
J. Gaines (arts/ent.)
Gallo (misc.)

K. Gann (arts/ent.)
Hemingway (arts/
ent.)
Lawrence (sci./inv.)
Cook Poole (arts/ent.)
Seton (arts/ent.)
Shepard (arts/ent.)
Truex (arts/ent.)
Tubb (arts/ent.)
ERNESTINE
Carey (arts/ent.)
ERNESTO
Maserati (business)
Sábato (arts/ent.)
ERNIE
Banks (sports)
Bushmiller (arts/ent.)
Kovacs (arts/ent.)
Nevers (sports)
Pyle (arts/ent.)
Stautner (sports)
ERNO
Rubik (arts/ent.)
ERNST
Bloch (rel./phil.)
Lubitsch (arts/ent.)
Mach (sci./inv.)
Toch (arts/ent.)
ERROL
Flynn (arts/ent.)
ERROLL
Garner (arts/ent.)
ERSKINE
Caldwell (arts/ent.)
ERWIN
Rommel (arts/ent.)
ESAI
Morales (arts/ent.)
ESTEE
Lauder (business)
ESTELLE
Getty (arts/ent.)
Parsons (arts/ent.)
Taylor (arts/ent.)
Winwood (arts/ent.)
ESTES
Kefauver (govt./mil.)
ESTHER
Forbes (arts/ent.)
Phillips (arts/ent.)
Ralston (arts/ent.)
Rolle (arts/ent.)
Williams (arts/ent.)
ETHAN
Allen (govt./mil.)
Coen (arts/ent.)
Hawke (arts/ent.)

ETHEL
Barrymore (arts/ent.)
Harper (arts/ent.)
Merman (arts/ent.)
Rosenberg (govt./mil.)
Waters (arts/ent.)
ETHELBERT
Nevin (arts/ent.)
ETTA
James (arts/ent.)
Jones (arts/ent.)
ETTORE
Bugatti (business)
Scola (arts/ent.)
EUBIE
Blake (arts/ent.)
EUDORA
Welty (arts/ent.)
EUGENE, EUGÈNE
Burdick (arts/ent.)
V. Debs (govt./mil.)
Delacroix (arts/ent.)
Field (arts/ent.)
Fodor (arts/ent.)
Ionesco (govt./mil.)
T. Maleska (arts/ent.)
McCarthy (govt./mil.)
O'Neill (arts/ent.)
Ormandy (arts/ent.)
Pallette (arts/ent.)
EUGENIO
Montale (arts/ent.)
EVA
Bartok (arts/ent.)
Braun (misc.)
Gabor (arts/ent.)
Le Gallienne (arts/ent.)
Marie Saint (arts/ent.)
Perón (govt./mil.)
EVAN
S. Connell, Jr. (arts/
ent.)
Dando (arts/ent.)
Hunter (arts/ent.)
EVANDER
Holyfield (sports)
EVE
Arden (arts/ent.)
Curie (arts/ent.)
Plumb (arts/ent.)
EVEL
Knievel (misc.)
EVELYN
Ankers (arts/ent.)
Keyes (arts/ent.)
King (arts/ent.)
Waugh (arts/ent.)

EVERETT
Sloane (arts/ent.)
EVITA
Perón (govt./mil.)
EVONNE
Goolagong (sports)
EWA
Aulin (arts/ent.)
EWELL
Blackwell (sports)
EYDIE
Gorme (arts/ent.)
EYVIND
Johnson (arts/ent.)
EZIO
Pinza (arts/ent.)
EZRA
Cornell (business)
Pound (arts/ent.)
EZZARD
Charles (sports)
F. I.
Dupont (business)
F. W.
De Klerk (govt./
    mil.)
Woolworth (business)
F. LEE
Bailey (misc.)
F. MURRAY
Abraham (arts/ent.)
F. SCOTT
Fitzgerald (arts/ent.)
FAB
Morvan (arts/ent.)
FAITH
Daniels (arts/ent.)
Ford (arts/ent.)
FANNIE
Farmer (arts/ent.)
Flagg (arts/ent.)
Hurst (arts/ent.)
FANNY
Abington (arts/ent.)
Brice (arts/ent.)
Burney (arts/ent.)
Kemble (arts/ent.)
FARAH
Diba Pahlavi (govt./
    mil.)
FARLEY
Granger (arts/ent.)
Mowat (arts/ent.)
FARON
Young (arts/ent.)
FARRAH
Fawcett (arts/ent.)

FATS
Domino (arts/ent.)
Navarro (arts/ent.)
Waller (arts/ent.)
FATTY
Arbuckle (arts/ent.)
FAWN
Hall (misc.)
FAY
Bainter (arts/ent.)
Crocker (sports)
Weldon (arts/ent.)
Wray (arts/ent.)
FAYE
Dunaway (arts/ent.)
Emerson (misc.)
Wattleton (misc.)
FEDERICO
Fellini (arts/ent.)
García Lorca (arts/ent.)
FEE
Waybill (arts/ent.)
FELIX
Bloch (sci./inv.)
Frankfurter (govt./
    mil.)
Mendelssohn (arts/ent.)
Salten (arts/ent.)
FERDE
Grofé (arts/ent.)
FERDINAND
Magellan (pion./exp.)
Marcos (govt./mil.)
Porsche (business)
Von Zeppelin (sci./inv.)
FERENC
Molnár (arts/ent.)
FERGIE
Jenkins (sports)
FERLIN
Husky (arts/ent.)
FERNAND
Léger (arts/ent.)
FERNANDO
Lamas (arts/ent.)
Rey (arts/ent.)
Valenzuela (sports)
FERRUCCIO
Busoni (arts/ent.)
FESS
Parker (arts/ent.)
FIDEL
Castro (govt./mil.)
FILIPPO
Brunelleschi or
    Brunellescho (arts/
    ent.)

Lippi (arts/ent.)
FINLEY
Peter Dunne (arts/ent.)
FIONA
Hutchison (arts/ent.)
FIONNULA
Flanagan (arts/ent.)
FIORELLO
La Guardia (govt./mil.)
FISHER
Stevens (arts/ent.)
FLANN
O'Brien (arts/ent.)
FLANNERY
O'Connor (arts/ent.)
FLETCHER
Christian (misc.)
Henderson (arts/ent.)
Knebel (arts/ent.)
FLINDERS
Petrie (sci./inv.)
FLIP
Wilson (arts/ent.)
FLO
Ziegfeld (arts/ent.)
FLORA
Robson (arts/ent.)
FLORENCE
Ballard (arts/ent.)
Chadwick (sports)
Eldridge (arts/ent.)
Griffith-Joyner (sports)
Harding (govt./mil.)
Henderson (arts/ent.)
Lawrence (arts/ent.)
Nightingale (misc.)
FLORENT
Schmitt (arts/ent.)
FLOYD
Cramer (arts/ent.)
Patterson (sports)
FONTAINE
Fox (arts/ent.)
FORD
Madox Brown (arts/
    ent.)
Madox Ford (arts/ent.)
C. Frick (sports)
FOREST
Whitaker (arts/ent.)
Compton (arts/ent.)
FORREST
Gregg (sports)
Sawyer (arts/ent.)
Tucker (arts/ent.)
FOSTER
Brooks (arts/ent.)

FRAN
Allison (arts/ent.)
Lebowitz (arts/ent.)
Tarkenton (sports)
FRANCE
Nuyen (arts/ent.)
FRANCES
Hodgson Burnett (arts/
ent.)
Cleveland (govt./mil.)
Dee (arts/ent.)
Farmer (arts/ent.)
Fisher (arts/ent.)
Goodrich (arts/ent.)
Ellen Watkins Harper
(govt./mil.)
Parkinson Keyes (arts/
ent.)
Lear (business)
Lockridge (arts/ent.)
McDormand (arts/ent.)
Trollope (arts/ent.)
FRANCESCA
Cabrini (misc.)
Cuzzoni (arts/ent.)
FRANCESCO
Borromini (arts/ent.)
Scavullo (arts/ent.)
FRANCHOT
Tone (arts/ent.)
FRANCIE
Larrieu-Lutz (sports)
FRANCINE
Barker (arts/ent.)
FRANCIS
Bacon (arts/ent.)
Bacon (rel./phil.)
Beaufort (govt./mil.)
X. Bushman (arts/ent.)
Ford Coppola (arts/ent.)
Crick (sci./inv.)
Drake (pion./exp.)
Ferdinand (govt./mil.)
Scott Key (arts/ent.)
Marion (govt./mil.)
Parkman (arts/ent.)
Poulenc (arts/ent.)
Gary Powers (govt./mil.)
FRANCISCO
De Coronado (pion./
exp.)
Franco (govt./mil.)
Madero (govt./mil.)
Pizarro (pion./exp.)
Zurbaran (arts/ent.)
FRANCO
Corelli (arts/ent.)

Harris (sports)
Nero (arts/ent.)
Zeffirelli (arts/ent.)
FRANÇOIS
Boucher (arts/ent.)
Couperin (arts/ent.)
Duvalier (govt./mil.)
Girardon (arts/ent.)
De La Rochefoucauld
(arts/ent.)
De Malherbe (arts/ent.)
Mauriac (arts/ent.)
Mitterrand (govt./mil.)
Rabelais (sci./inv.)
Truffaut (arts/ent.)
Villon (arts/ent.)
FRANÇOISE
Sagan (arts/ent.)
FRANK
Baker (sports)
Borman (pion./exp.)
Borzage (arts/ent.)
Capra (arts/ent.)
Chance (sports)
Conroy (arts/ent.)
Costello (misc.)
Duveneck (arts/ent.)
Fontaine (arts/ent.)
Gatski (sports)
Gehry (arts/ent.)
Gifford (sports)
Gorshin (arts/ent.)
Harris (arts/ent.)
Herbert (arts/ent.)
Howard (sports)
Kinard (sports)
O. King (arts/ent.)
Langella (arts/ent.)
Lloyd (arts/ent.)
Loesser (arts/ent.)
Martin (arts/ent.)
Morgan (arts/ent.)
Norris (arts/ent.)
O'Hara (arts/ent.)
Oz (arts/ent.)
Robinson (sports)
Sargeson (arts/ent.)
Sinatra (arts/ent.)
Sinatra, Jr. (arts/ent.)
Slaughter (arts/ent.)
Stella (arts/ent.)
Sullivan (arts/ent.)
Tanana (sports)
Henry Willard (arts/
ent.)
Lloyd Wright (arts/ent.)
Yerby (arts/ent.)

Zappa (arts/ent.)
FRANKIE
Avalon (arts/ent.)
Crosetti (sports)
Frisch (sports)
Laine (arts/ent.)
Lymon (arts/ent.)
Valli (arts/ent.)
FRANKLIN
P. Adams (arts/ent.)
Pangborn (arts/ent.)
Pierce (govt./mil.)
Delano Roosevelt
(govt./mil.)
Schaffner (arts/ent.)
FRANS
Hals (arts/ent.)
Eemil Sillanpaa (arts/
ent.)
FRANTZ
Fanon (rel./phil.)
FRANZ
Boas (sci./inv.)
Ferdinand (govt./mil.)
Kafka (arts/ent.)
Kline (arts/ent.)
Lehár (arts/ent.)
Liszt (arts/ent.)
Schubert (arts/ent.)
Waxman (arts/ent.)
Werfel (arts/ent.)
FRED
Allen (arts/ent.)
Astaire (arts/ent.)
Biletnikoff (sports)
Dannay (arts/ent.)
Dryer (arts/ent.)
Ebb (arts/ent.)
Grandy (arts/ent.)
Gwynne (arts/ent.)
Hoyle (arts/ent.)
Lynn (sports)
MacMurray (arts/ent.)
Rogers (arts/ent.)
Savage (arts/ent.)
Schipesi (arts/ent.)
Silverman (business)
M. Vinson (govt./mil.)
Ward (arts/ent.)
Waring (arts/ent.)
Zinnemann (arts/ent.)
FREDA
Payne (arts/ent.)
FREDDIE
Bartholomew (arts/ent.)
Jackson (arts/ent.)
Lindstrom (sports)

Mercury (arts/ent.)
Patek (sports)
Prinze (arts/ent.)
FREDDY
Cannon (arts/ent.)
Fender (arts/ent.)
FREDERIC, FRÉDÉRIC
Bartholdi (arts/ent.)
Chopin (arts/ent.)
Forrest (arts/ent.)
Joliot-Curie (sci./inv.)
Mistral (arts/ent.)
Remington (arts/ent.)
FREDERICA
Von Stade (arts/ent.)
FREDERICK
Church (arts/ent.)
Delius (arts/ent.)
Douglass (govt./mil.)
Forsyth (arts/ent.)
Leighton (arts/ent.)
Loewe (arts/ent.)
Marryat (govt./mil.)
North (govt./mil.)
Olmsted or Olmstead
(misc.)
FREDERIK
Pohl (arts/ent.)
FREDRIC
Brown (arts/ent.)
March (arts/ent.)
FREDRIK
Bajer (arts/ent.)
FREEMAN
Crofts (arts/ent.)
Gosden (arts/ent.)
FRIDA
Kahlo (arts/ent.)
FRIEDRICH
Dürrenmatt (arts/ent.)
Engels (rel./phil.)
Flotow (arts/ent.)
Jacobi (arts/ent.)
Klopstock (arts/ent.)
Nietzsche (rel./phil.)
Von Schiller (arts/
ent.)
Schorr (arts/ent.)
FRITZ
Hochwalder (arts/ent.)
Lang (arts/ent.)
Leiber (arts/ent.)
Pollard (sports)
Reiner (arts/ent.)
Weaver (arts/ent.)
FULGENCIO
Batista (govt./mil.)

FULTON
Sheen (rel./phil.)
FUZZY
Knight (arts/ent.)
Zoeller (sports)
FYODOR
Chaliapin (arts/ent.)
Dostoyevsky (arts/ent.)
FYVUSH
Finkel (arts/ent.)
G. E.
Moore (rel./phil.)
G. K.
Chesterton (arts/ent.)
G. GORDON
Liddy (govt./mil.)
G. WILSON
Knight (arts/ent.)
GABBY
Hartnett (sports)
Hayes (arts/ent.)
GABE
Kaplan (arts/ent.)
GABRIEL
Byrne (arts/ent.)
Dell (arts/ent.)
Fauré (arts/ent.)
García Márquez (arts/
ent.)
Pierne (arts/ent.)
GABRIELA
Mistral (arts/ent.)
Sabatini (sports)
GABRIELLE
Anwar (arts/ent.)
Carteris (arts/ent.)
GAETANO
Donizetti (arts/ent.)
GAHAN
Wilson (arts/ent.)
GAIL
Borden (sci./inv.)
Godwin (arts/ent.)
Sheehy (arts/ent.)
GAIUS
Valerius Catullus (arts/
ent.)
Macenas (govt./mil.)
Petronius (arts/ent.)
GALE
Gordon (arts/ent.)
Ann Hurd (arts/ent.)
Sayers (sports)
Sondergaard (arts/ent.)
Storm (arts/ent.)
GALLAGHER
Gateley (arts/ent.)

GALWAY
Kinnell (arts/ent.)
GAMAL
Abdel Nasser (govt./
mil.)
GAMALIEL
Bailey (arts/ent.)
GARDNAR
Mulloy (sports)
GARDNER
McKay (arts/ent.)
GARI
Melchers (arts/ent.)
GARNET
Mimms (arts/ent.)
GARRET
A. Hobart (govt./
mil.)
GARRETT
Morris (arts/ent.)
GARRI
Kasparov (misc.)
GARRICK
Utley (arts/ent.)
GARRISON
Keillor (arts/ent.)
GARRY
Maddox (sports)
Marshall (arts/ent.)
Moore (arts/ent.)
Shandling (arts/ent.)
Templeton (sports)
Trudeau (arts/ent.)
GARSON
Kanin (arts/ent.)
GARTH
Brooks (arts/ent.)
Hudson (arts/ent.)
GARY
"U.S." Bonds (arts/ent.)
Burghoff (arts/ent.)
Busey (arts/ent.)
Cole (arts/ent.)
Coleman (arts/ent.)
Collins (arts/ent.)
Cooper (arts/ent.)
Glitter (arts/ent.)
Hart (govt./mil.)
Kemp (arts/ent.)
Larson (arts/ent.)
Lewis (arts/ent.)
Lockwood (arts/ent.)
Merrill (arts/ent.)
Morris (arts/ent.)
Numan (arts/ent.)
Oldman (arts/ent.)
Player (sports)

Puckett (arts/ent.)
Redus (sports)
Sandy (arts/ent.)
Snyder (arts/ent.)
Wright (arts/ent.)
GASTON
Leroux (arts/ent.)
GATO
Barbieri (arts/ent.)
GAVIN
MacLeod (arts/ent.)
Maxwell (arts/ent.)
Muir (arts/ent.)
GAY
Brewer (sports)
Talese (arts/ent.)
GAYLORD
Perry (sports)
GEDDY
Lee (arts/ent.)
GEENA
Davis (arts/ent.)
GEEZER
Butler (arts/ent.)
GELSEY
Kirkland (arts/ent.)
GENA
Rowlands (arts/ent.)
GENE
Autry (arts/ent.)
Barry (arts/ent.)
Chandler (arts/ent.)
Hackman (arts/ent.)
Kelly (arts/ent.)
Krupa (arts/ent.)
Littler (sports)
Mako (sports)
Markey (arts/ent.)
Pitney (arts/ent.)
Rayburn (arts/ent.)
Raymond (arts/ent.)
Roddenberry (arts/
ent.)
Saks (arts/ent.)
Sarazen (sports)
Shalit (arts/ent.)
Simmons (arts/ent.)
Siskel (arts/ent.)
Tierney (arts/ent.)
Tunney (sports)
Upshaw (sports)
Vincent (arts/ent.)
Wilder (arts/ent.)
GENEVIÉVE
Bujold (arts/ent.)
GENIE
Francis (arts/ent.)

GENTILE
Bellini (arts/ent.)
GEOFFREY
Beene (arts/ent.)
Chaucer (arts/ent.)
GEORG
Sanford Brown (arts/
ent.)
Hegel (rel./phil.)
Solti (arts/ent.)
Telemann (arts/ent.)
GEORGE
Abbott (arts/ent.)
Ade (arts/ent.)
Allen (sports)
Antheil (arts/ent.)
Arliss (arts/ent.)
Baker (arts/ent.)
Balanchine (arts/ent.)
Barnard (arts/ent.)
Beadle (sci./inv.)
Benson (arts/ent.)
Bingham (arts/ent.)
Blanda (sports)
Brent (arts/ent.)
Brett (sports)
Burns (arts/ent.)
Bush (govt./mil.)
Washington Cable (arts/
ent.)
Carlin (arts/ent.)
Carver (sci./inv.)
Catlin (arts/ent.)
W. Chadwick (arts/ent.)
Chakiris (arts/ent.)
Clinton (arts/ent.)
Clinton (govt./mil.)
M. Cohan (arts/ent.)
Connor (sports)
Cukor (arts/ent.)
A. Custer (govt./mil.)
M. Dallas (govt./mil.)
Dewey (govt./mil.)
Dzundza (arts/ent.)
Eastman (sci./inv.)
Eliot (arts/ent.)
Washington Gale Ferris
(sci./inv.)
Foreman (sports)
Formby (arts/ent.)
Foster (sports)
Fox (rel./phil.)
Gallup (misc.)
Gamow (sci./inv.)
Gershwin (arts/ent.)
Gervin (sports)
Gobel (arts/ent.)

Goethals (sci./inv.)
Grinnell (misc.)
Grizzard (arts/ent.)
Grosz (arts/ent.)
Halas (sports)
Hale (sci./inv.)
Hamilton (arts/ent.)
Frideric Handel (arts/
ent.)
Harrison (arts/ent.)
Hepplewhite (arts/ent.)
Herriman (arts/ent.)
V. Higgins (M)
Hill (arts/ent.)
Hurrell (arts/ent.)
Inness (arts/ent.)
Jessel (arts/ent.)
Jones (arts/ent.)
S. Kaufman (arts/ent.)
Kell (sports)
Kelly (sports)
Kennedy (arts/ent.)
Lazenby (arts/ent.)
Lewes (rel./phil.)
Lorimer (arts/ent.)
Lucas (arts/ent.)
Maharis (arts/ent.)
Marshall (govt./mil.)
McAfee (sports)
B. McClellan (govt./
mil.)
McGinnis (sports)
McGovern (govt./mil.)
McManus (arts/ent.)
Meredith (arts/ent.)
Michael (arts/ent.)
Mikan (sports)
Mitchell (govt./mil.)
Montgomery (arts/ent.)
Moore (arts/ent.)
Murphy (arts/ent.)
Musso (sports)
Jean Nathan (arts/ent.)
Orwell (arts/ent.)
Palade (sci./inv.)
S. Patton (govt./mil.)
Peppard (arts/ent.)
Plimpton (arts/ent.)
Putnam (business)
Raft (arts/ent.)
Reeves (arts/ent.)
Lincoln Rockwell
(misc.)
Romero (arts/ent.)
Romney (arts/ent.)
Sand (arts/ent.)
Sanders (arts/ent.)

Santayana (arts/ent.)
C. Scott (arts/ent.)
Seaton (arts/ent.)
Seferis (arts/ent.)
Bernard Shaw (arts/
ent.)
Shearing (arts/ent.)
P. Shultz (govt./mil.)
Sisler (sports)
Steinbrenner (sports)
Steiner (arts/ent.)
Stephanopoulos (govt./
mil.)
Stevens (arts/ent.)
Strait (arts/ent.)
Stubbs (arts/ent.)
Szell (arts/ent.)
Takei (arts/ent.)
Thorogood (arts/ent.)
Ticknor (misc.)
Tobias (arts/ent.)
Trafton (sports)
Voinovich (govt./mil.)
Wallace (govt./mil.)
Washington (govt./mil.)
Wendt (arts/ent.)
Westinghouse (sci./inv.)
Will (arts/ent.)
GEORGES
Bataille (arts/ent.)
Bernanos (arts/ent.)
Bizet (arts/ent.)
Braque (arts/ent.)
Clemenceau (govt./mil.)
Enesco (arts/ent.)
De La Tour (arts/ent.)
Lemaître (sci./inv.)
Pompidou (govt./mil.)
Rouault (arts/ent.)
Seurat (arts/ent.)
Simenon (arts/ent.)
GEORGETTE
Mosbacher (arts/ent.)
GEORGIA
Brown (arts/ent.)
Gibbs (arts/ent.)
O'Keeffe (arts/ent.)
GEORGIANA
Barrymore (arts/ent.)
GEORGIO
Bassani (arts/ent.)
Plekhanov (rel./phil.)
GERAINT
Evans (arts/ent.)
GERALD
Edelman (sci./inv.)
Ford (govt./mil.)

McRaney (arts/ent.)
GERALDINE
Brooks (arts/ent.)
Chaplin (arts/ent.)
Farrar (arts/ent.)
Ferraro (govt./mil.)
Fitzgerald (arts/
ent.)
Page (arts/ent.)
GERALDO
Rivera (arts/ent.)
GERARD, GÉRARD
David (arts/ent.)
Depardieu (arts/ent.)
Manley Hopkins (arts/
ent.)
Terborch (arts/ent.)
GERD
Oswald (arts/ent.)
GERMAINE
Greer (arts/ent.)
GERRY
Cooney (sports)
Goffin (arts/ent.)
Marsden (arts/ent.)
Mulligan (arts/ent.)
Rafferty (arts/ent.)
GERT
Fröbe (arts/ent.)
GERTRUDE
Astor (arts/ent.)
Berg (arts/ent.)
Ederle (sports)
Jekyll (misc.)
Lawrence (arts/ent.)
Stein (arts/ent.)
Vanderbilt Whitney
(misc.)
GERTY
Cori (sci./inv.)
GIA
Scala (arts/ent.)
GIACOMO
Casanova (misc.)
Meyerbeer (arts/ent.)
Puccini (arts/ent.)
GIAN
Bernini (arts/ent.)
Francesco Malipiero
(arts/ent.)
Carlo Menotti (arts/
ent.)
GIANCARLO
Esposito (arts/ent.)
Giannini (arts/ent.)
GIANNI
Versace (arts/ent.)

GIFFORD
Pinchot (govt./mil.)
GIG
Young (arts/ent.)
GIL
Evans (arts/ent.)
Gerard (arts/ent.)
Hodges (sports)
Scott-Heron (arts/ent.)
GILBERT
Anderson (arts/ent.)
Gottfried (arts/ent.)
O'Sullivan (arts/ent.)
Roland (arts/ent.)
Stuart (arts/ent.)
GILDA
Radner (arts/ent.)
GILLIAN
Armstrong (arts/ent.)
GILLO
Pontecorvo (arts/ent.)
GINA
Lollobrigida (arts/ent.)
GINGER
Baker (arts/ent.)
Rogers (arts/ent.)
GINNY
Simms (arts/ent.)
GINO
Marchetti (sports)
Vannelli (arts/ent.)
GIOACCHINO
Rossini (arts/ent.)
GIORGIO
Armani (arts/ent.)
De Chirico (arts/ent.)
Moroder (arts/ent.)
Vasari (arts/ent.)
GIOVANNI
Bellini (arts/ent.)
Lorenzo Bernini (arts/
ent.)
Boccaccio (arts/ent.)
Bologna (arts/ent.)
Cimabue (arts/ent.)
Pergolesi (arts/ent.)
Tiepolo (arts/ent.)
Vitali (arts/ent.)
GIROLAMO
Savonarola (rel./phil.)
GIULIANO
Da Sangallo (arts/
ent.)
GIULIETTA
Masina (arts/ent.)
GIUSEPPE
De Luca (arts/ent.)

Garibaldi (govt./mil.)
Giacosa (arts/ent.)
Verdi (arts/ent.)
GLADYS
Cooper (arts/ent.)
George (arts/ent.)
Knight (arts/ent.)
Swarthout (arts/ent.)
GLEN
Campbell (arts/ent.)
GLENDA
Farrell (arts/ent.)
Jackson (arts/ent.)
Vare (sports)
GLENN
Close (arts/ent.)
Cunningham (sports)
Curtiss (sci./inv.)
Ford (arts/ent.)
Frey (arts/ent.)
Gould (arts/ent.)
Medeiros (arts/ent.)
Miller (arts/ent.)
T. Seaborg (sci./inv.)
Tilbrook (arts/ent.)
Yarbrough (arts/ent.)
GLENNE
Headly (arts/ent.)
GLORIA
De Haven (arts/ent.)
Estefan (arts/ent.)
Gaynor (arts/ent.)
Grahame (arts/ent.)
Loring (arts/ent.)
Steinem (misc.)
Swanson (arts/ent.)
Vanderbilt (arts/
ent.)
GLYN
E. Daniel (I)
GLYNIS
Johns (arts/ent.)
GODFREY
Cambridge (arts/ent.)
Tearle (arts/ent.)
GOGI
Grant (arts/ent.)
GOLDA
Meir (govt./mil.)
GOLDIE
Hawn (arts/ent.)
GOODMAN
Ace (arts/ent.)
GOOSE
Goslin (sports)
Gossage (sports)
Tatum (sports)

GORDIE
Howe (sports)
GORDON
Dickson (arts/ent.)
Jump (arts/ent.)
Lightfoot (arts/ent.)
MacRae (arts/ent.)
Parks (arts/ent.)
Scott (arts/ent.)
GORE
Vidal (arts/ent.)
GOTTFRIED
Von Leibniz (rel./phil.)
GOTTLIEB
Daimler (business)
GOWER
Champion (arts/ent.)
GRACE
Bumbry (arts/ent.)
Coolidge (govt./mil.)
Jones (arts/ent.)
Kelly (arts/ent.)
Metalious (arts/ent.)
Moore (arts/ent.)
Paley (arts/ent.)
Slick (arts/ent.)
Lee Whitney (arts/
ent.)
GRACIE
Allen (arts/ent.)
Fields (arts/ent.)
GRADY
Nutt (arts/ent.)
Sutton (arts/ent.)
GRAHAM
Chapman (arts/ent.)
Greene (arts/ent.)
Hill (sports)
Kerr (arts/ent.)
Nash (arts/ent.)
Parker (arts/ent.)
GRAIG
Nettles (sports)
GRAM
Parsons (arts/ent.)
GRANDMA
Moses (arts/ent.)
GRANDPA
Jones (arts/ent.)
GRANT
Goodeve (arts/ent.)
Shaud (arts/ent.)
Show (arts/ent.)
Tinker (arts/ent.)
Wood (arts/ent.)
GRANTLAND
Rice (sports)

GRANVILLE
Hicks (arts/ent.)
GRAZIA
Deledda (arts/ent.)
GREER
Garson (arts/ent.)
GREG
Brock (sports)
Evigan (arts/ent.)
Lake (arts/ent.)
Lemond (sports)
Louganis (sports)
Luzinski (sports)
Morris (arts/ent.)
Norman (sports)
Pruitt (sports)
GREGG
Allman (arts/ent.)
GREGOR
Mendel (sci./inv.)
Piatigorsky (arts/ent.)
GREGORY
Corso (arts/ent.)
Harrison (arts/ent.)
Hines (arts/ent.)
La Cava (arts/ent.)
Peck (arts/ent.)
Pincus (sci./inv.)
GRETA
Garbo (arts/ent.)
Scacchi (arts/ent.)
Waitz (sports)
GRETCHEN
Wyler (arts/ent.)
GRIFFIN
Dunne (arts/ent.)
GROTE
Reber (sci./inv.)
GROUCHO
Marx (arts/ent.)
GROVER
Cleveland Alexander
(sports)
Cleveland (govt./mil.)
Washington, Jr. (arts/
ent.)
GUGLIELMO
Marconi (sci./inv.)
GUIDO
Reni (arts/ent.)
GUILLAUME
Apolinnaire (arts/ent.)
GUILLERMO
Vilas (sports)
GUISSEPPE
De Lampedusa (arts/
ent.)

GUMMO
Marx (arts/ent.)
GUMP
Worsley (sports)
GUNNAR
Myrdal (arts/ent.)
Nelson (arts/ent.)
GUNNEL
Lindblom (arts/
ent.)
GÜNTER
Grass (arts/ent.)
GUS
Grissom (pion./exp.)
Kahn (arts/ent.)
Van Sant (arts/ent.)
Williams (sports)
GUSTAV
Holst (arts/ent.)
Mahler (arts/ent.)
GUSTAVE
Courbet (arts/ent.)
Doré (arts/ent.)
Flaubert (arts/ent.)
Klimt (arts/ent.)
GUTZON
Borglum (arts/ent.)
GUY
De Maupassant (arts/
ent.)
Fawkes (misc.)
Kibbee (arts/ent.)
Lafleur (sports)
Laroche (arts/ent.)
Lombardo (arts/ent.)
Mitchell (arts/ent.)
Stockwell (arts/ent.)
Williams (arts/ent.)
GWEN
Verdon (arts/ent.)
GWENDOLYN
Brooks (arts/ent.)
GWYNETH
Paltrow (arts/ent.)
GYORGY
Lukacs (rel./phil.)
GYPSY ROSE
Lee (arts/ent.)
H. B.
Warner (arts/ent.)
H. C.
Bailey (arts/ent.)
McNeile (arts/ent.)
H. G.
Wells (arts/ent.)
H. L.
Mencken (arts/ent.)

H. P.
Lovecraft (arts/ent.)
H. R.
Haldeman (govt./mil.)
H. R. F.
Keating (arts/ent.)
H. ALLEN
Smith (arts/ent.)
H. RAP
Brown (govt./mil.)
H. RIDER
Haggard (arts/ent.)
H. ROSS
Perot (business)
HACK
Wilson (sports)
HAFEZ
Assad (govt./mil.)
HAL
Ashby (arts/ent.)
Chase (sports)
David (arts/ent.)
Foster (arts/ent.)
Holbrook (arts/ent.)
Hartley (arts/ent.)
Ketchum (arts/ent.)
Linden (arts/ent.)
March (arts/ent.)
Newhouser (sports)
Porter (arts/ent.)
Prince (arts/ent.)
Roach (arts/ent.)
Sutton (sports)
B. Wallis (arts/ent.)
HALDEN
Keffer Hartline (sci./
inv.)
HALE
Irwin (sports)
HALLDÓR
Laxness (arts/ent.)
HALLE
Berry (arts/ent.)
HAM
Fisher (arts/ent.)
HAMILTON
Fish (govt./mil.)
Fish, Jr. (govt./mil.)
Jordan (govt./mil.)
HAMLIN
Garland (arts/ent.)
HANA
Mandlikova (sports)
HANK
Aaron (sports)
Ballard (arts/ent.)
Bauer (sports)

Greenberg (sports)
Ketcham (arts/ent.)
Ketchum (arts/ent.)
Snow (arts/ent.)
Williams (arts/ent.)
Williams, Jr. (arts/ent.)
HANNA
Schygulla (arts/ent.)
HANNAH
Arendt (rel./phil.)
Cowley (arts/ent.)
Van Buren (govt./mil.)
HANNIBAL
Hamlin (govt./mil.)
HANS
Christian Andersen
(arts/ent.)
Berger (sci./inv.)
Christian Branner (arts/
ent.)
Conreid (arts/ent.)
Geiger (sci./inv.)
Holbein (arts/ent.)
Memling (arts/ent.)
HANYA
Holm (arts/ent.)
HAPPY
Chandler (sports)
HAR
Gobind Khorana (sci./
inv.)
HARDIE
Albright (arts/ent.)
HARDY
Krüger (arts/ent.)
HARI
Rhodes (arts/ent.)
HARL
McDonald (arts/ent.)
HARLAN
Ellison (arts/ent.)
Fiske Stone (govt./mil.)
HARLAND
Sanders (business)
HARLEY
Granville-Barker (arts/
ent.)
Jane Kozak (arts/ent.)
HARMON
Killebrew (sports)
HAROLD
Arlen (arts/ent.)
Evans (business)
Gould (arts/ent.)
Gray (arts/ent.)
Kushner (arts/ent.)
Lloyd (arts/ent.)

MacMillan (govt./
  mil.)
Melvin (arts/ent.)
Pinter (arts/ent.)
Ramis (arts/ent.)
Robbins (arts/ent.)
Ross (business)
Russell (arts/ent.)
Urey (sci./inv.)
HARPER
Lee (arts/ent.)
HARPO
Marx (arts/ent.)
HARRIET
Lothrop (arts/ent.)
MacGibbon (arts/ent.)
Nelson (arts/ent.)
Beecher Stowe (arts/
  ent.)
Tubman (misc.)
HARRISON
Ford (arts/ent.)
Salisbury (arts/ent.)
HARRY
Anderson (arts/ent.)
Armstrong (arts/ent.)
Belafonte (arts/ent.)
A. Blackmun (govt./mil.)
Blackstone (arts/ent.)
Blackstone, Jr. (arts/
  ent.)
Blyth (arts/ent.)
Brecheer (sports)
Carey (arts/ent.)
Carey, Jr. (arts/ent.)
Casey (arts/ent.)
Chandler (business)
Chapin (arts/ent.)
Cohn (arts/ent.)
Connick (arts/ent.)
Coveleski (sports)
Golden (arts/ent.)
Guardino (arts/ent.)
Hamlin (arts/ent.)
Heilmann (sports)
Hooper (sports)
Houdini (arts/ent.)
James (arts/ent.)
Kemelman (arts/ent.)
Langdon (arts/ent.)
Lauder (arts/ent.)
Martinson (arts/ent.)
Morgan (arts/ent.)
Nilsson (arts/ent.)
Reasoner (arts/ent.)
Ritz (arts/ent.)
Ruby (arts/ent.)

Dean Stanton (arts/
  ent.)
S Truman (govt./mil.)
Von Zell (arts/ent.)
Walker (sports)
Warren (arts/ent.)
Leon Wilson (arts/ent.)
Wright (sports)
HART
Bochner (arts/ent.)
Crane (arts/ent.)
HARTLEY
Coleridge (arts/ent.)
HARVE
Presnell (arts/ent.)
HARVEY
Fierstein (arts/ent.)
Samuel Firestone
  (business)
Keitel (arts/ent.)
Korman (arts/ent.)
Martin (sports)
HASHEMI
Rafsanjani (govt./
  mil.)
HATTIE
Caraway (govt./mil.)
Carnegie (arts/ent.)
McDaniel (arts/ent.)
HAVELOCK
Ellis (misc.)
HAYDEN
Carruth (arts/ent.)
HAYES
Alan Jenkins (sports)
HAYLEY
Mills (arts/ent.)
HAZEL
Scott (arts/ent.)
HEATHER
Angel (arts/ent.)
Locklear (arts/ent.)
O'Rourke (arts/ent.)
Thomas (arts/ent.)
HECTOR
Babenco (arts/ent.)
Berlioz (arts/ent.)
Elizondo (arts/ent.)
HEDDA
Hopper (arts/ent.)
HEDY
Lamarr (arts/ent.)
HEIDI
Bohay (arts/ent.)
Fleiss (misc.)
HEINIE
Manush (sports)

HEINRICH
Böll (arts/ent.)
Brüning (govt./mil.)
Heine (arts/ent.)
Himmler (govt./mil.)
Von Kleist (arts/ent.)
Mann (arts/ent.)
Schliemann (sci./inv.)
Schütz (arts/ent.)
HEITOR
Villa-Lobos (arts/ent.)
HELEN
Broderick (arts/ent.)
Gurley Brown (arts/
  ent.)
Cornelius (arts/ent.)
Douglas (arts/ent.)
Hayes (arts/ent.)
Hunt (arts/ent.)
Hunt Jackson (arts/ent.)
Hull Jacobs (sports)
Kane (arts/ent.)
Keller (arts/ent.)
MacInnes (arts/ent.)
Mirren (arts/ent.)
Morgan (arts/ent.)
O'Connell (arts/ent.)
Reddy (arts/ent.)
Shaver (arts/ent.)
Slater (arts/ent.)
Taft (govt./mil.)
Traubel (arts/ent.)
Van Slyke (arts/ent.)
Wills (sports)
HELENA
Bonham Carter (arts/
  ent.)
Modjeska (arts/ent.)
Rubinstein (business)
HELENE
Costello (arts/ent.)
HELMUT
Berger (arts/ent.)
Dantine (arts/ent.)
Kohl (govt./mil.)
Newton (arts/ent.)
Schmidt (govt./mil.)
HENNY
Youngman (arts/ent.)
HENRI
Bergson (rel./phil.)
Cartier-Bresson (arts/
  ent.)
Matisse (arts/ent.)
Rousseau (arts/ent.)
De Toulouse-Lautrec
  (arts/ent.)

HORTENSE
Calisher (arts/ent.)
HORTON
Foote (arts/ent.)
Smith (sports)
HOSNI
Mubarak (govt./mil.)
HOWARD
Bellamy (arts/ent.)
Cosell (sports)
Da Silva (arts/ent.)
Dietz (arts/ent.)
Duff (arts/ent.)
Fast (arts/ent.)
Hanson (arts/ent.)
Hawks (arts/ent.)
Hesseman (arts/ent.)
Hughes (arts/ent.)
Johnson (business)
Jones (arts/ent.)
Kaylen (arts/ent.)
Keel (arts/ent.)
Koch (arts/ent.)
Lindsay (arts/ent.)
Metzenbaum (govt./
    mil.)
Nemerov (arts/ent.)
Rollins, Jr. (arts/ent.)
Sackler (arts/ent.)
K. Smith (arts/ent.)
Stern (arts/ent.)
HOWELL
Heflin (govt./mil.)
HOWIE
Mandel (arts/ent.)
Meeker (sports)
Morenz (sports)
HOYT
Axton (arts/ent.)
Wilhelm (sports)
HUBERT
De Givenchy (arts/ent.)
H. Humphrey (govt./
    mil.)
Selby, Jr. (arts/ent.)
Van Eyck (arts/ent.)
HUBIE
Brooks (sports)
HUEY
Lewis (arts/ent.)
P. Long (govt./mil.)
P. Newton (govt./mil.)
HUGH
Brackenridge (arts/ent.)
Capet (govt./mil.)
Downs (arts/ent.)
Duffy (sports)

Griffith (arts/ent.)
Hefner (business)
Kenner (arts/ent.)
Lofting (arts/ent.)
MacDiarmid (arts/ent.)
Masekela (arts/ent.)
McElhenny (sports)
O'Brian (arts/ent.)
Walpole (arts/ent.)
HUGHIE
Jennings (sports)
HUGO
Ball (arts/ent.)
Black (govt./mil.)
Gernsback (arts/ent.)
Montenegro (arts/ent.)
Wolf (arts/ent.)
HULK
Hogan (sports)
HUME
Cronyn (arts/ent.)
HUMPHREY
Bogart (arts/ent.)
Gilbert (pion./exp.)
HUNTER
S. Thompson (arts/
    ent.)
Tylo (arts/ent.)
HUNTZ
Hall (arts/ent.)
HURD
Hatfield (arts/ent.)
HYMAN
Rickover (govt./mil.)
I. A.
Richards (arts/ent.)
I. F.
Stone (arts/ent.)
I. L.
Peretz (arts/ent.)
I. M.
Pei (arts/ent.)
IAN
Anderson (arts/ent.)
Ballantine (arts/ent.)
Bannen (arts/ent.)
Carmichael (arts/ent.)
Charleson (arts/ent.)
Dury (arts/ent.)
Fleming (arts/ent.)
Gillan (arts/ent.)
Hay (arts/ent.)
Holm (arts/ent.)
Hunter (arts/ent.)
McEwan (arts/ent.)
McKellan (arts/ent.)
Ziering (arts/ent.)

IDA
Lupino (arts/ent.)
McKinley (govt./mil.)
Tarbell (arts/ent.)
Wells (govt./mil.)
IDI
Amin (govt./mil.)
IGGY
Pop (arts/ent.)
IGNACY
Paderewski (arts/ent.)
IGNAZZIO
Silone (arts/ent.)
IGOR
Moiseyev (arts/ent.)
Oistrakh (arts/ent.)
Ivan Sikorsky (business)
Stravinsky (arts/ent.)
IKE
Turner (arts/ent.)
ILDEBRANDO
Pizzetti (arts/ent.)
ILIE
Nastase (sports)
ILKA
Chase (arts/ent.)
ILONA
Massey (arts/ent.)
IMAMU
Amiri Baraka (arts/ent.)
IMELDA
Marcos (govt./mil.)
IMMANUEL
Kant (rel./phil.)
IMOGEN
Cunningham (arts/ent.)
IMOGENE
Coca (arts/ent.)
IMRE
Nagy (govt./mil.)
INA
Balin (arts/ent.)
Claire (arts/ent.)
Coolbrith (arts/ent.)
Ray Hutton (arts/ent.)
INCREASE
Mather (rel./phil.)
INDIRA
Gandhi (govt./mil.)
INGA
Swenson (arts/ent.)
INGEMAR
Stenmark (sports)
INGER
Stevens (arts/ent.)
INGMAR
Bergman (arts/ent.)

INGRID
Bergman (arts/ent.)
Thulin (arts/ent.)
INIGO
Jones (arts/ent.)
ION
Antonescu (govt./mil.)
IONE
Skye (arts/ent.)
IRA
Gershwin (arts/ent.)
Levin (arts/ent.)
Remsen (sci./inv.)
IREENE
Seaton Wicker (arts/
ent.)
IRENE, IRÈNE
Cara (arts/ent.)
Castle (arts/ent.)
Dunne (arts/ent.)
Joliot-Curie (sci./inv.)
Papas (arts/ent.)
Rich (arts/ent.)
Ryan (arts/ent.)
Worth (arts/ent.)
IRINA
Press (sports)
Rodnina (sports)
IRIS
Adrian (arts/ent.)
Murdoch (arts/ent.)
IRLENE
Mandrell (arts/ent.)
IRMA
S. Rombauer (arts/ent.)
IRVIN
S. Cobb (arts/ent.)
IRVING
Berlin (arts/ent.)
Langmuir (sci./inv.)
Rapper (arts/ent.)
Stone (arts/ent.)
Thalberg (arts/ent.)
Wallace (arts/ent.)
IRWIN
Allen (arts/ent.)
Corey (arts/ent.)
Shaw (arts/ent.)
ISA
Miranda (arts/ent.)
ISAAC
Albéniz (arts/ent.)
Asimov (arts/ent.)
Hayes (arts/ent.)
Hayes (pion./exp.)
Hull (govt./mil.)
Newton (sci./inv.)

Pitman (misc.)
Bashevis Singer (arts/
ent.)
Merrit Singer (sci./inv.)
Stern (arts/ent.)
ISABEL
Jeans (arts/ent.)
Jewell (arts/ent.)
Sanford (arts/ent.)
ISABELLA
Rossellini (arts/ent.)
ISABELLE
Adjani (arts/ent.)
Allende (arts/ent.)
Huppert (arts/ent.)
ISADORA
Duncan (arts/ent.)
ISAIAH
Berlin (rel./phil.)
ISAK
Dineson (arts/ent.)
ISAMU
Noguchi (arts/ent.)
ISH
Kabibble (arts/ent.)
ISHMAEL
Reed (arts/ent.)
ISIDOR
Rabi (sci./inv.)
ISMAIL
Merchant (arts/ent.)
ISRAEL
Horovitz (arts/ent.)
Putnam (govt./mil.)
Singer (arts/ent.)
Zangwill (arts/ent.)
ISSEY
Miyake (arts/ent.)
ITALO
Calvino (arts/ent.)
ITZHAK
Perlman (arts/ent.)
Rabin (govt./mil.)
IVAN
Boesky (business)
Bunin (arts/ent.)
Dixon (arts/ent.)
Lendl (sports)
Meštrović (arts/
ent.)
Pavlov (sci./inv.)
Reitman (arts/ent.)
Turgenev (arts/ent.)
IVANA
Trump (business)
IVAR
Giaever (sci./inv.)

IVO
Andŕic (arts/ent.)
IVY
Compton-Burnett (arts/
ent.)
IZAAK
Walton (arts/ent.)
IZZY
Stradlin (arts/ent.)
J. B.
Priestley (arts/ent.)
J. C.
Penney (business)
J. D.
Salinger (arts/ent.)
Souther (arts/ent.)
J. E. B.
Stuart (govt./mil.)
J. G.
Ballard (arts/ent.)
J. H.
Plumb (arts/ent.)
J. J.
Cale (arts/ent.)
Johnson (arts/ent.)
J. M.
Barrie (arts/ent.)
J. M. W.
Turner (arts/ent.)
J. P.
Donleavy (arts/ent.)
Morgan (business)
J. R. R.
Tolkein (arts/ent.)
J. S.
Le Fanu (arts/ent.)
J. CARROL
Naish (arts/ent.)
J. DANFORTH
Quayle (govt./mil.)
J. EDGAR
Hoover (govt./mil.)
J. JAMES
Exon (govt./mil.)
J. PAUL
Getty (business)
J. ROBERT
Oppenheimer (sci./
inv.)
J. WILLIAM
Fulbright (govt./mil.)
JABBO
Smith (arts/ent.)
JACINTO
Benavente (arts/ent.)
JACK
Albertson (arts/ent.)

Farmer (govt./mil.)
T. Farrell (arts/ent.)
Montgomery Flagg
(arts/ent.)
Forrestal (govt./mil.)
Franciscus (arts/ent.)
Franck (sci./inv.)
Galway (arts/ent.)
Garfield (govt./mil.)
Garner (arts/ent.)
Gleason (arts/ent.)
Norman Hall (arts/
ent.)
Harper (business)
Herlihy (arts/ent.)
Herriot (arts/ent.)
Hillier (sci./inv.)
Hilton (arts/ent.)
Hoban (arts/ent.)
Ingram (arts/ent.)
Ives (arts/ent.)
Ivory (arts/ent.)
Weldon Johnson (arts/
ent.)
Jones (arts/ent.)
Earl Jones (arts/ent.)
Joyce (arts/ent.)
Keach (arts/ent.)
Levine (arts/ent.)
Lovelock (sci./inv.)
Lowell (arts/ent.)
MacArthur (arts/ent.)
Madison (govt./mil.)
Mason (arts/ent.)
McCracken (arts/ent.)
McGraw (business)
Merrill (arts/ent.)
A. Michener (arts/ent.)
Monroe (govt./mil.)
Naismith (misc.)
O'Neill (arts/ent.)
Kirke Paulding (arts/
ent.)
Knox Polk (govt./mil.)
Purdy (arts/ent.)
Randi (arts/ent.)
Earl Ray (misc.)
Renwick (arts/ent.)
Reston (arts/ent.)
Riley (arts/ent.)
Rosenquist (arts/ent.)
Schuyler (arts/ent.)
G. Sherman (govt./mil.)
Spader (arts/ent.)
Stewart (arts/ent.)
Taylor (arts/ent.)
Thurber (arts/ent.)

Alfred Van Allen (sci./
inv.)
Watson (sci./inv.)
Watt (govt./mil.)
Watt (sci./inv.)
R. Webb (arts/ent.)
Whale (arts/ent.)
McNeill Whistler (arts/
ent.)
Woods (arts/ent.)
JAMESON
Parker (arts/ent.)
JAMI
Gertz (arts/ent.)
JAMIE
Lee Curtis (arts/ent.)
Farr (arts/ent.)
Rose (arts/ent.)
Wyeth (arts/ent.)
JAN
Berry (arts/ent.)
Clayton (arts/ent.)
Hammer (arts/ent.)
Hooks (arts/ent.)
Miner (arts/ent.)
Murray (arts/ent.)
Peerce (arts/ent.)
Smithers (arts/ent.)
C. Smuts (govt./mil.)
Steen (arts/ent.)
Sterling (arts/ent.)
Van Eyck (arts/ent.)
Vermeer (arts/ent.)
JAN-MICHAEL
Vincent (arts/ent.)
JANE
Ace (arts/ent.)
Addams (govt./mil.)
Alexander (arts/ent.)
Austen (arts/ent.)
Birkin (arts/ent.)
Brody (arts/ent.)
Campion (arts/ent.)
Curtin (arts/ent.)
Darwell (arts/ent.)
Fonda (arts/ent.)
Goodall (sci./inv.)
Greer (arts/ent.)
Grey (govt./mil.)
Morgan (arts/ent.)
Pauley (arts/ent.)
Pierce (govt./mil.)
Powell (arts/ent.)
Russell (arts/ent.)
Seymour (arts/ent.)
Wagner (arts/ent.)
Wiedlin (arts/ent.)

Withers (arts/ent.)
Wyatt (arts/ent.)
Wyman (arts/ent.)
JANET
Dailey (arts/ent.)
Evans (arts/ent.)
Flanner (arts/ent.)
Frame (arts/ent.)
Gaynor (arts/ent.)
Guthrie (sports)
Jackson (arts/ent.)
Leigh (arts/ent.)
Lennon (arts/ent.)
Lynn (sports)
Margolin (arts/
ent.)
Reno (govt./mil.)
JANIE
Frickie (arts/ent.)
JANINE
Turner (arts/ent.)
JANIS
Ian (arts/ent.)
Joplin (arts/ent.)
Paige (arts/ent.)
JANN
Wenner (business)
JARED
Martin (arts/ent.)
JAROSLAV
Seifert (arts/ent.)
JASCHA
Heifetz (arts/ent.)
JASMINE
Guy (arts/ent.)
JASON
Bateman (arts/ent.)
Hervey (arts/ent.)
Miller (arts/ent.)
Patric (arts/ent.)
Priestley (arts/ent.)
Robards (arts/ent.)
JASPER
Johns (arts/ent.)
JAVIER
Pérez De Cuellar
(govt./mil.)
JAWAHARLAL
Nehru (govt./mil.)
JAY
Ferguson (arts/ent.)
Gould (business)
C. Higginbotham (arts/
ent.)
Leno (arts/ent.)
Livingston (arts/ent.)
McInerney (arts/ent.)

North (arts/ent.)
Osmond (arts/ent.)
Silverheels (arts/ent.)
Thomas (arts/ent.)
Ward (arts/ent.)
JAYE
P. Morgan (arts/ent.)
JAYNE
Kennedy (arts/ent.)
Mansfield (arts/ent.)
Meadows (arts/ent.)
JEAN
Anouilh (arts/ent.)
Arp (arts/ent.)
Arthur (arts/ent.)
Auel (arts/ent.)
Beliveau (sports)
Bodin (rel./phil.)
De Brunhoff (arts/ent.)
Cocteau (arts/ent.)
Corot (arts/ent.)
Dubuffet (arts/ent.)
Bernard Leon Foucault
(sci./inv.)
Fragonard (arts/ent.)
Gabin (arts/ent.)
Genet (arts/ent.)
Giraudoux (arts/ent.)
Harlow (arts/ent.)
Harris (misc.)
Ingres (arts/ent.)
Jaurès (govt./mil.)
Kerr (arts/ent.)
De La Fontaine (arts/
ent.)
Lafitte or Laffite (misc.)
Marsh (arts/ent.)
Millet (arts/ent.)
Nicolet (pion./exp.)
Nidetch (business)
Patou (arts/ent.)
Peters (arts/ent.)
Piaget (misc.)
Racine (arts/ent.)
Renoir (arts/ent.)
Rhys (arts/ent.)
Paul Richter (arts/
ent.)
Seberg (arts/ent.)
Shrimpton (arts/ent.)
Sibelius (arts/ent.)
Simmons (arts/ent.)
Stafford (arts/ent.)
Stapleton (arts/ent.)
Toomer (arts/ent.)
JEAN-BAPTISTE
Lully (arts/ent.)

JEAN-BAPTISTE-SIMÉON
Chardin (arts/ent.)
JEAN-CLAUDE
Killy (sports)
Van Damme (arts/ent.)
JEAN-FRANÇOIS
Champollion (sci./inv.)
JEAN-JACQUES
Rousseau (rel./phil.)
JEAN-LOUIS
Barrault (arts/ent.)
Trintignant (arts/ent.)
JEAN-LUC
Godard (arts/ent.)
Ponty (arts/ent.)
JEAN-MARIE
Le Pen (govt./mil.)
JEAN-MICHEL
Jarre (arts/ent.)
JEAN-PAUL
Belmondo (arts/ent.)
Gaultier (arts/ent.)
Marat (govt./mil.)
Sartre (rel./phil.)
JEAN-PIERRE
Aumont (arts/ent.)
Rampal (arts/ent.)
JEANE
Dixon (arts/ent.)
Kirkpatrick (govt./mil.)
JEANETTE
MacDonald (arts/ent.)
Nolan (arts/ent.)
JEANNE
Bécu Barry (misc.)
Crain (arts/ent.)
Lanvin (arts/ent.)
Moreau (arts/ent.)
Récamier (misc.)
Tripplehorn (arts/
ent.)
JEANNIE
C. Riley (arts/ent.)
JEANNINE
Riley (arts/ent.)
JEB
Magruder (govt./
mil.)
JEDEDIAH
Smith (pion./exp.)
JEFF
Barry (arts/ent.)
Beck (arts/ent.)
Bridges (arts/ent.)
Conaway (arts/ent.)
Daniels (arts/ent.)
Fahey (arts/ent.)

Goldblum (arts/ent.)
Lynne (arts/ent.)
Reardon (sports)
Smith (arts/ent.)
JEFFERSON
Davis (govt./mil.)
JEFFREY
Amherst (govt./mil.)
Howard Archer (arts/
ent.)
Dahmer (misc.)
Hunter (arts/ent.)
Katzenberg (arts/ent.)
Osborne (arts/ent.)
JELLYBEAN
Benitez (arts/ent.)
JELLY ROLL
Morton (arts/ent.)
JENNIE
Garth (arts/ent.)
JENNIFER
Bartlett (arts/ent.)
Beals (arts/ent.)
Capriati (sports)
Connelly (arts/ent.)
Grant (arts/ent.)
Grey (arts/ent.)
Holliday (arts/ent.)
Jones (arts/ent.)
Jason Leigh (arts/ent.)
Lynch (arts/ent.)
O'Neill (arts/ent.)
Tilly (arts/ent.)
Warnes (arts/ent.)
Warren (arts/ent.)
JENNILEE
Harrison (arts/ent.)
JENNY
Agutter (arts/ent.)
Dolly (arts/ent.)
Lind (arts/ent.)
JERE
Burns (arts/ent.)
JEREMY
Bentham (rel./phil.)
Brett (arts/ent.)
Clyde (arts/ent.)
Irons (arts/ent.)
JERILYN
Britz (sports)
JERMAINE
Jackson (arts/ent.)
JEROME
Hines (arts/ent.)
K. Jerome (arts/ent.)
Kern (arts/ent.)
Robbins (arts/ent.)

Weidman (arts/ent.)
JERRY
Bock (arts/ent.)
Brown (govt./mil.)
Bruckheimer (arts/ent.)
Butler (arts/ent.)
Clower (arts/ent.)
Colonna (arts/ent.)
Falwell (rel./phil.)
Garcia (arts/ent.)
Goldsmith (arts/ent.)
Hall (arts/ent.)
Herman (arts/ent.)
Leiber (arts/ent.)
Lewis (arts/ent.)
Lee Lewis (arts/ent.)
Mathers (arts/ent.)
Orbach (arts/ent.)
Pate (sports)
Reed (arts/ent.)
Rice (sports)
Schatzberg (arts/ent.)
Seinfeld (arts/ent.)
Siegel (arts/ent.)
Stiller (arts/ent.)
Tarkanian (sports)
Vale (arts/ent.)
Van Dyke (arts/ent.)
Wald (arts/ent.)
Jeff Walker (arts/ent.)
West (sports)
Zucker (arts/ent.)
JERSEY JOE
Walcott (sports)
JERZY
Kosinski (arts/ent.)
JESS
Willard (sports)
JESSAMYN
West (arts/ent.)
JESSE
Barfield (arts/ent.)
Burkett (sports)
Haines (sports)
Helms (govt./mil.)
Jackson (govt./mil.)
James (misc.)
Lasky (arts/ent.)
Owens (sports)
Stuart (arts/ent.)
White (arts/ent.)
Colin Young (arts/ent.)
JESSI
Colter (arts/ent.)
JESSICA
Hahn (misc.)

Harper (arts/ent.)
Lange (arts/ent.)
Mitford (arts/ent.)
Savitch (arts/ent.)
Tandy (arts/ent.)
Walter (arts/ent.)
JESSIE
Royce Landis (arts/ent.)
Ralph (arts/ent.)
JESSYE
Norman (arts/ent.)
JETHRO
Tull (sci./inv.)
JILL
Clayburgh (arts/ent.)
Eikenberry (arts/ent.)
Ireland (arts/ent.)
St. John (arts/ent.)
Whelan (arts/ent.)
JILLIE
Mack (arts/ent.)
JIM
Backus (arts/ent.)
Bakker (rel./phil.)
Bannon (arts/ent.)
Belushi (arts/ent.)
Bishop (arts/ent.)
Bouton (sports)
Bowie (govt./mil.)
Braddock (sports)
Brady (misc.)
Ed Brown (arts/ent.)
Brown (sports)
Bunning (sports)
Capaldi (arts/ent.)
Carrey (arts/ent.)
Carroll (arts/ent.)
Clark (sports)
Croce (arts/ent.)
Davis (arts/ent.)
Garrison (misc.)
Henson (arts/ent.)
Hutton (arts/ent.)
Jarmusch (arts/ent.)
Jones (arts/ent.)
Jordan (arts/ent.)
Kerr (arts/ent.)
Lange (arts/ent.)
Langer (sports)
Lehrer (arts/ent.)
Lonborg (sports)
McKay (sports)
McMahon (sports)
Messina (arts/ent.)
Morrison (arts/ent.)
Nabors (arts/ent.)
Otto (sports)

Palmer (sports)
Parker (sports)
Plunkett (sports)
Reeves (arts/ent.)
Rice (sports)
Ringo (sports)
Ritz (arts/ent.)
Ryun (sports)
Seals (arts/ent.)
Stafford (arts/ent.)
Taylor (sports)
Thompson (arts/ent.)
Thorpe (sports)
Guy Tucker (govt./mil.)
Varney (arts/ent.)
JIMI
Hendrix (arts/ent.)
JIMMIE
Foxx (sports)
Lunceford (arts/ent.)
Noone (arts/ent.)
Rodgers (arts/ent.)
Walker (arts/ent.)
JIMMY
Baio (arts/ent.)
Blanton (arts/ent.)
Breslin (sports)
Buffett (arts/ent.)
Carter (govt./mil.)
Cliff (arts/ent.)
Connors (sports)
Dean (arts/ent.)
Dickens (arts/ent.)
Dorsey (arts/ent.)
Durante (arts/ent.)
Fidler (arts/ent.)
Fratianno (misc.)
Hatlo (arts/ent.)
Hoffa (govt./mil.)
Key (sports)
McHugh (arts/ent.)
McNichol (arts/ent.)
McPartland (arts/ent.)
Osmond (arts/ent.)
Page (arts/ent.)
Piersall (sports)
Rushing (arts/ent.)
Smits (arts/ent.)
Snyder (Jimmy the Greek) (sports)
Swaggart (rel./phil.)
Van Heusen (arts/ent.)
Webb (arts/ent.)
JIŘÍ
Menzel (arts/ent.)
JO
Davidson (arts/ent.)

Mielziner (arts/ent.)
Ann Pflug (arts/ent.)
Stafford (arts/ent.)
Van Fleet (arts/ent.)
Worley (arts/ent.)

JOACHIM
Von Ribbentrop (govt./ mil.)

JOAN
Aiken (arts/ent.)
Armatrading (arts/ent.)
Baez (arts/ent.)
Bennett (arts/ent.)
Benoit (sports)
Blondell (arts/ent.)
Caulfield (arts/ent.)
Chen (arts/ent.)
Collins (arts/ent.)
Crawford (arts/ent.)
Cusack (arts/ent.)
Davis (arts/ent.)
Didion (arts/ent.)
Fontaine (arts/ent.)
Hackett (arts/ent.)
Jett (arts/ent.)
Leslie (arts/ent.)
Lunden (arts/ent.)
Miró (arts/ent.)
Whitney Payson (misc.)
Plowright (arts/ent.)
Rivers (arts/ent.)
Sutherland (arts/ent.)
Van Ark (arts/ent.)

JOANNA
Barnes (arts/ent.)
Cassidy (arts/ent.)
Kerns (arts/ent.)
Pacula (arts/ent.)

JOANNE
Gunderson Carner (sports)
Dru (arts/ent.)
Whalley-Kilmer (arts/ ent.)
Woodward (arts/ent.)

JOAQUIN, JOAQUÍN
Miller (arts/ent.)
Turina (arts/ent.)

JOBETH
Williams (arts/ent.)

JOBYNA
Ralston (arts/ent.)

JOCK
Hutchison (sports)
Mahoney (arts/ent.)

JOCKO
Conlan (sports)

JODIE
Foster (arts/ent.)

JODY
Davis (sports)
Watley (arts/ent.)

JOE
Adonis (misc.)
Don Baker (arts/ent.)
E. Brown (arts/ent.)
Cocker (arts/ent.)
Cronin (sports)
Dallesandro (arts/ent.)
Diffie (arts/ent.)
DiMaggio (sports)
Elliott (arts/ent.)
Eszterhas (arts/ent.)
Frazier (sports)
Garagiola (sports)
Gibbs (sports)
Greene (sports)
Guyon (sports)
Jackson (arts/ent.)
Jackson (sports)
Lando (arts/ent.)
Louis (sports)
Mantegna (arts/ent.)
McCarthy (sports)
McGinnity (sports)
McIntyre (arts/ent.)
Medwick (sports)
Montana (sports)
Morgan (sports)
Namath (sports)
Niekro (sports)
Oeschger (sports)
Orton (arts/ent.)
Pass (arts/ent.)
Paterno (sports)
Penny (arts/ent.)
Perry (sports)
Pesci (arts/ent.)
Piscopo (arts/ent.)
Sample (arts/ent.)
Schmidt (sports)
Sewell (sports)
Shuster (arts/ent.)
Smith (arts/ent.)
Stampley (arts/ent.)
Strummer (arts/ent.)
Stydahar (sports)
Tex (arts/ent.)
Tinker (sports)
Torre (sports)
Walsh (arts/ent.)
Williams (arts/ent.)

JOEL
Coen (arts/ent.)

Grey (arts/ent.)
Chandler Harris (arts/ ent.)
McCrea (arts/ent.)
Schumacher (arts/ ent.)
Silver (arts/ent.)
E. Spingarn (arts/ent.)

JOEL-PETER
Witkin (arts/ent.)

JOEY
Adams (arts/ent.)
Bishop (arts/ent.)
Buttafuoco (misc.)
Dee (arts/ent.)
Heatherton (arts/ent.)
Lawrence (arts/ent.)
Ramone (arts/ent.)

JOHANN
Sebastian Bach (arts/ ent.)
Lukas Von Hildebrandt (arts/ent.)
Strauss (arts/ent.)
Von Goethe (arts/ent.)

JOHANNA
Spyri (arts/ent.)

JOHANNES
Brahms (arts/ent.)
Gutenberg (sci./inv.)
Jensen (arts/ent.)
Kepler (sci./inv.)

JOHN
Abbott (arts/ent.)
Acton (arts/ent.)
Adams (govt./mil.)
Quincy Adams (govt./ mil.)
Alden (pion./exp.)
Anderson (arts/ent.)
Archer (arts/ent.)
Ashbery (arts/ent.)
Astin (arts/ent.)
Jacob Astor (business)
Audubon (misc.)
Avildsen (arts/ent.)
Badham (arts/ent.)
Logie Baird (sci./inv.)
Ball (arts/ent.)
Barbirolli (arts/ent.)
Bardeen (sci./inv.)
Barry (arts/ent.)
Barrymore (arts/ent.)
Barrymore, Jr. (arts/ent.)
Barth (arts/ent.)
Bartlett (arts/ent.)
Beal (arts/ent.)

Northrop (sci./inv.)
Knudsen Northrop
  (business)
O'Hara (arts/ent.)
Oates (arts/ent.)
Osborne (arts/ent.)
Patrick (arts/ent.)
Payne (arts/ent.)
Pershing (govt./mil.)
Phillips (arts/ent.)
Prine (arts/ent.)
Rae (pion./exp.)
Raitt (arts/ent.)
Ransom (arts/ent.)
Ratzenberger (arts/ent.)
Reed (arts/ent.)
Rhys-Davies (arts/ent.)
Ringling (arts/ent.)
Ritter (arts/ent.)
D. Rockefeller IV
  (govt./mil.)
Root (arts/ent.)
Ruskin (arts/ent.)
Singer Sargent (arts/
  ent.)
Saxon (arts/ent.)
Sayles (arts/ent.)
Schlesinger (arts/ent.)
Schneider (arts/ent.)
Thomas Scopes (misc.)
Sebastian (arts/ent.)
Patrick Shanley (arts/
  ent.)
Simon (arts/ent.)
Singleton (arts/ent.)
Sirica (govt./mil.)
Sloan (arts/ent.)
Philip Sousa (arts/ent.)
Spencer (arts/ent.)
M. Stahl (arts/ent.)
Stamos (arts/ent.)
Steinbeck (arts/ent.)
Paul Stevens III (govt./
  mil.)
Stockton (sports)
Sturges (arts/ent.)
L. Sullivan (sports)
H. Sununu (govt./mil.)
Sutter (pion./exp.)
Cameron Swayze (arts/
  ent.)
Synge (arts/ent.)
Tenniel (arts/ent.)
Tesh (arts/ent.)
Tower (govt./mil.)
Travolta (arts/ent.)
Trumbull (arts/ent.)

Turturro (arts/ent.)
Tyler (govt./mil.)
Updike (arts/ent.)
Van Ryn (sports)
Waihee (govt./mil.)
Waite (arts/ent.)
Warner (govt./mil.)
Waters (arts/ent.)
Wayne (arts/ent.)
Wesley (rel./phil.)
Wetton (arts/ent.)
Greenleaf Whittier
  (arts/ent.)
Williams (arts/ent.)
Winthrop (govt./mil.)
Woo (arts/ent.)
Wooden (sports)
Wyndham (arts/ent.)
Peter Zenger (arts/ent.)
JOHNNIE
Ray (arts/ent.)
JOHNNY
Ace (arts/ent.)
Appleseed (pion./exp.)
Bench (sports)
Bond (arts/ent.)
Burke (arts/ent.)
Burnette (arts/ent.)
Carson (arts/ent.)
Cash (arts/ent.)
Depp (arts/ent.)
Duncan (arts/ent.)
Evers (sports)
Gill (arts/ent.)
Green (arts/ent.)
Hart (arts/ent.)
Hodges (arts/ent.)
Horton (arts/ent.)
Lee (arts/ent.)
Longden (sports)
Mandel (arts/ent.)
Mathis (arts/ent.)
Mercer (arts/ent.)
Miller (sports)
Mize (sports)
Otis (arts/ent.)
Paycheck (arts/ent.)
Pesky (sports)
Ramone (arts/ent.)
Rivers (arts/ent.)
Rodriguez (arts/ent.)
Rotten (arts/ent.)
Rutherford (sports)
Unitas (sports)
Vander Meer (sports)
Weissmuller (arts/ent.)
Winter (arts/ent.)

Hopkins (business)
JOI
Lansing (arts/ent.)
JOIE
Lee (arts/ent.)
JON
Anderson (arts/ent.)
Bauman (arts/ent.)
Bon Jovi (arts/ent.)
Cryer (arts/ent.)
Finch (arts/ent.)
Lord (arts/ent.)
Lovitz (arts/ent.)
Peters (arts/ent.)
Secada (arts/ent.)
Vickers (arts/ent.)
Voight (arts/ent.)
JON-ERIK
Hexum (arts/ent.)
JONAS
Salk (sci./inv.)
JONATHAN
Demme (arts/ent.)
Edwards (rel./phil.)
Hale (arts/ent.)
Kaplan (arts/ent.)
Knight (arts/ent.)
Kozol (arts/ent.)
Richman (arts/ent.)
Swift (arts/ent.)
Winters (arts/ent.)
JONI
James (arts/ent.)
Mitchell (arts/ent.)
JORDAN
Knight (arts/ent.)
JORGE
Amado (arts/ent.)
Luis Borges (arts/ent.)
JORMA
Kaukonen (arts/ent.)
JOSE, JOSÉ
Canseco (sports)
Carreras (arts/ent.)
Napoléon Duarte (govt./
  mil.)
Feliciano (arts/ent.)
Ferrer (arts/ent.)
Greco (arts/ent.)
Guzman (sports)
Iturbi (arts/ent.)
Limón (arts/ent.)
Martí (arts/ent.)
Menendez (arts/ent.)
Orozco (arts/ent.)
Ortega y Gasset (rel./
  phil.)

Ribera (arts/ent.)
Rivera (arts/ent.)
De San Martín (govt./
mil.)
JOSEF
Albers (arts/ent.)
Mengele (govt./mil.)
Von Sternberg (arts/
ent.)
JOSEPH
Addison (arts/ent.)
Alioto (govt./mil.)
W. Alsop (arts/ent.)
Barbera (arts/ent.)
R. Biden (govt./mil.)
Bologna (arts/ent.)
Bonanno (misc.)
Bottoms (arts/ent.)
Brodsky (arts/ent.)
Califano (misc.)
Campbell (arts/ent.)
Conrad (arts/ent.)
Cotten (arts/ent.)
Erlanger (sci./inv.)
Goebbels (govt./mil.)
L. Goldstein (sci./inv.)
Haydn (arts/ent.)
Heller (arts/ent.)
P. Kennedy (business)
P. Kennedy II (govt./
mil.)
Krutch (arts/ent.)
Losey (arts/ent.)
L. Mankiewicz (arts/
ent.)
R. McCarthy (govt./
mil.)
Papp (arts/ent.)
Pulitzer (arts/ent.)
Sargent (arts/ent.)
Schildkraut (arts/ent.)
Smith (rel./phil.)
Stalin (govt./mil.)
Stein (arts/ent.)
Wambaugh (arts/ent.)
Wapner (arts/ent.)
JOSEPHINE
Baker (arts/ent.)
Hull (arts/ent.)
Tey (arts/ent.)
JOSH
Billings (arts/ent.)
Gibson (sports)
Logan (arts/ent.)
Mostel (arts/ent.)
Saviano (arts/ent.)
White (arts/ent.)

JOSHUA
Logan (arts/ent.)
Reynolds (arts/ent.)
JOSIAH
Bartlett (govt./mil.)
Gibbs (sci./inv.)
Royce (rel./phil.)
Spode (arts/ent.)
Wedgwood (misc.)
JOSIP
Broz (govt./mil.)
JOSS
Ackland (arts/ent.)
JOY
Adamson (arts/ent.)
JOYCE
Brothers (misc.)
Cary (arts/ent.)
Dewitt (arts/ent.)
Haber (arts/ent.)
Kilmer (arts/ent.)
Carol Oates (arts/ent.)
Van Patten (arts/ent.)
JUAN
Batista De Anza (pion./
exp.)
Cabrillo (pion./exp.)
Gris (arts/ent.)
Jiménez (arts/ent.)
Marichal (sports)
Perón (govt./mil.)
JUANITA
Hall (arts/ent.)
JUBAL
Early (govt./mil.)
JUD
Strunk (arts/ent.)
JUDD
Hirsch (arts/ent.)
Nelson (arts/ent.)
JUDGE
Reinhold (arts/ent.)
JUDITH
Anderson (arts/ent.)
Crist (arts/ent.)
Dench (arts/ent.)
Guest (arts/ent.)
Ivey (arts/ent.)
Krantz (arts/ent.)
Light (arts/ent.)
Rossner (arts/ent.)
Viorst (arts/ent.)
Wright (arts/ent.)
JUDY
Blume (arts/ent.)
Canova (arts/ent.)
Carne (arts/ent.)

Chicago (arts/ent.)
Collins (arts/ent.)
Davis (arts/ent.)
Garland (arts/ent.)
Holliday (arts/ent.)
Landers (arts/ent.)
Norton-Taylor (arts/
ent.)
Rankin (sports)
Tenuta (arts/ent.)
JUICE
Newton (arts/ent.)
JULE
Styne (arts/ent.)
JULES
Dassin (arts/ent.)
Feiffer (arts/ent.)
Massenet (arts/ent.)
Romains (arts/ent.)
Verne (arts/ent.)
JULIA
Child (arts/ent.)
Duffy (arts/ent.)
Fordham (arts/ent.)
Grant (govt./mil.)
Howe (arts/ent.)
Louis-Dreyfuss (arts/
ent.)
Migenes (arts/ent.)
Morgan (arts/ent.)
Phillips (arts/ent.)
Roberts (arts/ent.)
Tyler (govt./mil.)
JULIAN
Bond (govt./mil.)
Bream (arts/ent.)
Sorell Huxley (sci./inv.)
Lennon (arts/ent.)
Sands (arts/ent.)
Schnabel (arts/ent.)
Schwinger (sci./inv.)
JULIANNE
Phillips (arts/ent.)
JULIE
Adams (arts/ent.)
Andrews (arts/ent.)
Bishop (arts/ent.)
Brown (arts/ent.)
Christie (arts/ent.)
Hagerty (arts/ent.)
Harris (arts/ent.)
Kavner (arts/ent.)
Krone (sports)
London (arts/ent.)
Newmar (arts/ent.)
JULIEN
Duvivier (arts/ent.)

JULIET
Mills (arts/ent.)
Prowse (arts/ent.)
JULIETTE
Lewis (arts/ent.)
JULIO
Cortázar (arts/ent.)
Franco (sports)
Gallo (misc.)
Iglesias (arts/ent.)
JULIUS
Axelrod (sci./inv.)
Caesar (govt./mil.)
Erving (sports)
La Rosa (arts/ent.)
Rosenberg (govt./mil.)
JUNE
Allyson (arts/ent.)
Carter (arts/ent.)
Christy (arts/ent.)
Collyer (arts/ent.)
Haver (arts/ent.)
Havoc (arts/ent.)
Lockhart (arts/ent.)
Pointer (arts/ent.)
JUNIOR
Durkin (arts/ent.)
Walker (arts/ent.)
JUNIPERO
Serra (rel./phil.)
JUPITER
Hammon (arts/ent.)
JURGEN
Prochnow (arts/ent.)
JÜSSI
Björling or Bjoerling
(arts/ent.)
JUSTIN
Hayward (arts/ent.)
Henry (arts/ent.)
JUSTINE
Bateman (arts/ent.)
K. D.
Lang (arts/ent.)
K. T.
Oslin (arts/ent.)
KADEEM
Hardison (arts/ent.)
KAHLIL
Gibran (arts/ent.)
KAI
Winding (arts/ent.)
KAMI
Cotler (arts/ent.)
KAREEM
Abdul-Jabbar
(sports)

KAREL
Čapek (arts/ent.)
KAREN
Akers (arts/ent.)
Allen (arts/ent.)
Black (arts/ent.)
Carpenter (arts/ent.)
Duffy (arts/ent.)
Finley (arts/ent.)
Silkwood (misc.)
Valentine (arts/ent.)
KARINA
Lombard (arts/ent.)
KARL
Baedeker (arts/ent.)
Barth (rel./phil.)
Friedrich Benz
(business)
Carstens (govt./mil.)
Czerny (arts/ent.)
Jaspers (rel./phil.)
Lagerfeld (arts/ent.)
Landsteiner (sci./inv.)
Malden (arts/ent.)
Malone (sports)
Marx (rel./phil.)
Menninger (sci./inv.)
Popper (rel./phil.)
Shapiro (arts/ent.)
Wallenda (arts/ent.)
KARLA
Bonoff (arts/ent.)
Devito (arts/ent.)
KAROL
Szymanowski (arts/ent.)
KARYN
White (arts/ent.)
KATARINA
Witt (sports)
KATE
Bush (arts/ent.)
Capshaw (arts/ent.)
Chopin (arts/ent.)
Jackson (arts/ent.)
Linder (arts/ent.)
Millett (arts/ent.)
Moss (arts/ent.)
Mulgrew (arts/ent.)
Nelligan (arts/ent.)
Pierson (arts/ent.)
Smith (arts/ent.)
Wiggin (arts/ent.)
KATEY
Sagal (arts/ent.)
KATHARINE
Cornell (arts/ent.)
Graham (business)

Helmond (arts/ent.)
Ross (arts/ent.)
KÄTHE
Kollwitz (arts/ent.)
KATHERINE
Dunham (arts/ent.)
Hepburn (arts/ent.)
Mansfield (arts/ent.)
Anne Porter (arts/ent.)
KATHIE
Lee Gifford (arts/ent.)
KATHLEEN
Battle (arts/ent.)
Kinmont (arts/ent.)
Norris (arts/ent.)
Quinlan (arts/ent.)
Sullivan (arts/ent.)
Turner (arts/ent.)
KATHRYN
Bigelow (arts/ent.)
Forbes (arts/ent.)
Grayson (arts/ent.)
Harrold (arts/ent.)
Kenny (arts/ent.)
KATHY
Baker (arts/ent.)
Bates (arts/ent.)
Ireland (arts/ent.)
Lennon (arts/ent.)
Mattea (arts/ent.)
Nolan (arts/ent.)
Whitworth (sports)
KATIE
Couric (arts/ent.)
Wagner (arts/ent.)
KATINA
Paxinou (arts/ent.)
KATY
Jurado (arts/ent.)
KAY
Boyle (arts/ent.)
Kyser (arts/ent.)
Lenz (arts/ent.)
Starr (arts/ent.)
KAYE
Ballard (arts/ent.)
KEANU
Reeves (arts/ent.)
KEEFE
Brasselle (arts/ent.)
KEELY
Smith (arts/ent.)
KEENAN
Wynn (arts/ent.)
KEENEN
Ivory Wayans (arts/
ent.)

KEIR
Dullea (arts/ent.)
KEITH
Carradine (arts/ent.)
Emerson (arts/ent.)
Haring (arts/ent.)
Jarrett (arts/ent.)
Moon (arts/ent.)
Richards (arts/ent.)
Whitley (arts/ent.)
KEL
Nagle (sports)
KELLY
Gruber (sports)
Lebrock (arts/ent.)
Lynch (arts/ent.)
McGillis (arts/ent.)
Preston (arts/ent.)
Rutherford (arts/ent.)
Willis (arts/ent.)
KELSEY
Grammer (arts/ent.)
KEMAL
Atatürk (govt./mil.)
KEN
Annakin (arts/ent.)
Berry (arts/ent.)
Curtis (arts/ent.)
Follett (arts/ent.)
Griffey (sports)
Houston (sports)
Howard (arts/ent.)
Hughes (arts/ent.)
Kesey (arts/ent.)
Murray (arts/ent.)
Norton (sports)
Olin (arts/ent.)
Russell (arts/ent.)
Stabler (sports)
Strong (sports)
Wahl (arts/ent.)
KENESAW
Mountain Landis
(sports)
KENNETH
Anger (arts/ent.)
Branagh (arts/ent.)
Fearing (arts/ent.)
Grahame (arts/ent.)
Patchen (arts/ent.)
Rexroth (arts/ent.)
Roberts (arts/ent.)
Tynan (arts/ent.)
KENNY
Loggins (arts/ent.)
Rogers (arts/ent.)
Stabler (sports)

KENT
Hrbek (sports)
McCord (arts/ent.)
Tekulve (sports)
KERMIT
Roosevelt (misc.)
KESHIA
Knight Pulliam (arts/
ent.)
KETTI
Frings (arts/ent.)
KETTY
Lester (arts/ent.)
KEVIN
Anderson (arts/ent.)
Bacon (arts/ent.)
Costner (arts/ent.)
Cronin (arts/ent.)
Curran (sports)
Dillon (arts/ent.)
Dobson (arts/ent.)
Godley (arts/ent.)
Gross (sports)
Kline (arts/ent.)
McCarthy (arts/ent.)
Mitchell (sports)
Nealon (arts/ent.)
J. O'Connor (arts/ent.)
Spacey (arts/ent.)
KEYE
Luke (arts/ent.)
KEYES
Beech (arts/ent.)
KHIGH
Dheigh (arts/ent.)
KHRYSTYNE
Haje (arts/ent.)
KIA
Goodwin (arts/ent.)
KID
Creole (arts/ent.)
Gavilan (sports)
Nichols (sports)
Ory (arts/ent.)
KIEFER
Sutherland (arts/ent.)
KIEL
Martin (arts/ent.)
KIERON
Moore (arts/ent.)
KIKI
Cuyler (sports)
Dee (arts/ent.)
KIM
Alexis (arts/ent.)
Basinger (arts/ent.)
Campbell (govt./mil.)

Carnes (arts/ent.)
Cattrall (arts/ent.)
Darby (arts/ent.)
Fields (arts/ent.)
Hunter (arts/ent.)
Novak (arts/ent.)
Philby (govt./mil.)
Stanley (arts/ent.)
Wilde (arts/ent.)
Wozencraft (arts/ent.)
KIMBERLY
Williams (arts/ent.)
KIN
Hubbard (arts/ent.)
Shriner (arts/ent.)
KING
Camp Gillette
(business)
Kelly (sports)
Oliver (arts/ent.)
Vidor (arts/ent.)
KINGSLEY
Amis (arts/ent.)
KINKY
Friedman (arts/ent.)
KIRBY
Grant (arts/ent.)
Puckett (sports)
KIRI
Te Kanawa (arts/ent.)
KIRK
Cameron (arts/ent.)
Douglas (arts/ent.)
Gibson (sports)
KIRSTIE
Alley (arts/ent.)
KIT
Carson (pion./exp.)
KITTY
Carlisle (arts/ent.)
Carruthers (sports)
Dukakis (arts/ent.)
Kallen (arts/ent.)
Kelley (arts/ent.)
Menendez (misc.)
Wells (arts/ent.)
KIX
Brooks (arts/ent.)
KLAUS
Barbie (govt./mil.)
Brandauer (arts/ent.)
Kinski (arts/ent.)
KLEMENS
Von Metternich (govt./
mil.)
KNUD
Rasmussen (pion./exp.)

KNUT
Hamsun (arts/ent.)
KNUTE
Rockne (sports)
KŌBŌ
Abe (arts/ent.)
KONRAD
Adenauer (govt./mil.)
Lorenz (sci./inv.)
KONSTANTIN
Chernenko (govt./mil.)
Stanislavsky (arts/ent.)
KRIS
Kristofferson (arts/ent.)
KRISTEN
McMenamy (arts/ent.)
KRISTINA
Malandro (arts/ent.)
KRISTY
McNichol (arts/ent.)
KRZYSZTOF
Penderecki (arts/ent.)
KURT
Cobain (arts/ent.)
Loder (arts/ent.)
Neumann (arts/ent.)
Russell (arts/ent.)
Thomas (sports)
Vonnegut, Jr. (arts/ent.)
Waldheim (govt./mil.)
Weill (arts/ent.)
KURTIS
Blow (arts/ent.)
KYLE
MacLachlan (arts/ent.)
KYLIE
Minogue (arts/ent.)
Tennant (arts/ent.)
KYRA
Sedgwick (arts/ent.)
L. L.
Bean (business)
L. DOUGLAS
Wilder (govt./mil.)
L. FRANK
Baum (arts/ent.)
L. JAMES
Rainwater (sci./inv.)
L. RON
Hubbard (rel./phil.)
L. SPRAGUE
De Camp (arts/ent.)
LACY
J. Dalton (arts/ent.)
LADY BIRD
Johnson (govt./mil.)

LAFCADIO
Hearn (arts/ent.)
LAFFIT
Pincay, Jr. (sports)
LAINIE
Kazan (arts/ent.)
LAIRD
Cregar (arts/ent.)
LALO
Schifrin (arts/ent.)
LAMONT
Dozier (arts/ent.)
LANA
Turner (arts/ent.)
Wood (arts/ent.)
LANCE
Alworth (sports)
Kerwin (arts/ent.)
Parrish (sports)
LANCELOT
Brown (misc.)
LANFORD
Wilson (arts/ent.)
LANGSTON
Hughes (arts/ent.)
LANNY
Wadkins (sports)
LARA
Flynn Boyle (arts/ent.)
Jill Miller (arts/ent.)
LARAINE
Day (arts/ent.)
Newman (arts/ent.)
LARRY
Bird (sports)
Bowa (sports)
Csonka (sports)
Drake (arts/ent.)
Fine (arts/ent.)
Fishburne (arts/ent.)
C. Flynt (misc.)
Gatlin (arts/ent.)
Gelbart (arts/ent.)
Hagman (arts/ent.)
Holmes (sports)
Kert (arts/ent.)
King (arts/ent.)
MacPhail (sports)
McMurtry (arts/ent.)
Niven (arts/ent.)
Parks (arts/ent.)
Parrish (sports)
Rivers (arts/ent.)
Storch (arts/ent.)
Wilson (sports)
LASH
La Rue (arts/ent.)

LASSE
Hallström (arts/ent.)
LA TOYA
Jackson (arts/ent.)
LAURA
Ashley (arts/ent.)
Branigan (arts/ent.)
Dern (arts/ent.)
Hobson (arts/ent.)
Jackson (arts/ent.)
Nyro (arts/ent.)
San Giacomo (arts/ent.)
Ingalls Wilder (arts/ent.)
LAUREN
Bacall (arts/ent.)
Hutton (arts/ent.)
Tewes (arts/ent.)
LAURENCE
Fishburne (arts/ent.)
Harvey (arts/ent.)
Housman (arts/ent.)
Luckinbill (arts/ent.)
Olivier (arts/ent.)
Stallings (arts/ent.)
Sterne (arts/ent.)
LAURIE
Anderson (arts/ent.)
Metcalf (arts/ent.)
LAURITZ
Melchior (arts/ent.)
LAVERN
Baker (arts/ent.)
LAVERNE
Andrews (arts/ent.)
LAWANDA
Page (arts/ent.)
LAWRENCE
Block (arts/ent.)
Durrell (arts/ent.)
Ferlinghetti (arts/ent.)
Kasdan (arts/ent.)
Sanders (arts/ent.)
Taylor (sports)
Welk (arts/ent.)
LAWTON
Chiles (govt./mil.)
LEA
Salonga (arts/ent.)
Thompson (arts/ent.)
LEAF
Phoenix (arts/ent.)
LEANN
Hunley (arts/ent.)
LEARNED
Hand (govt./mil.)

LEATRICE
Joy (arts/ent.)
LECH
Walesa (govt./mil.)
LECY
Goranson (arts/ent.)
LEE
Aaker (arts/ent.)
J. Cobb (arts/ent.)
De Forest (sci./inv.)
Dorsey (arts/ent.)
Grant (arts/ent.)
Greenwood (arts/ent.)
Horsley (arts/ent.)
Iacocca (business)
Krasner (arts/ent.)
Majors (arts/ent.)
Marvin (arts/ent.)
Meriwether (arts/ent.)
Harvey Oswald (misc.)
Petty (sports)
Radziwill (misc.)
Remick (arts/ent.)
Ritenour (arts/ent.)
Shubert (business)
Strasberg (arts/ent.)
Tracy (arts/ent.)
Trevino (sports)
Van Cleef (arts/ent.)
LEE ROY
Parnell (arts/ent.)
LEEZA
Gibbons (arts/ent.)
LEFTY
Frizzell (arts/ent.)
Gomez (sports)
Grove (sports)
LEGS
Diamond (misc.)
LEIF
Erickson (arts/ent.)
Eriksson (pion./exp.)
Garrett (arts/ent.)
LEIGH
Harline (arts/ent.)
McCloskey (arts/ent.)
Taylor-Young (arts/ent.)
LELAND
Hayward (arts/ent.)
Stanford (misc.)
LEN
Dawson (sports)
Deighton (arts/ent.)
Ford (sports)
LENA
Horne (arts/ent.)
Olin (arts/ent.)

LENI
Riefenstahl (arts/ent.)
LENNY
Bruce (arts/ent.)
Dykstra (sports)
Kravitz (arts/ent.)
Moore (sports)
Welch (arts/ent.)
LENORE
Ulric (arts/ent.)
LEO, LÉO
Baekeland (sci./inv.)
Buscaglia (arts/ent.)
Carrillo (arts/ent.)
G. Carroll (arts/ent.)
Delibes (arts/ent.)
Durocher (sports)
Fender (arts/ent.)
Gorcey (arts/ent.)
Kottke (arts/ent.)
McCarey (arts/ent.)
Nomellini (sports)
Rosten (arts/ent.)
Sayer (arts/ent.)
Tolstoy (arts/ent.)
LEON, LÉON
Ames (arts/ent.)
Bakst (arts/ent.)
Cadore (sports)
Edel (arts/ent.)
Jaworski (govt./
mil.)
Kirchner (arts/ent.)
Panetta (govt./mil.)
Russell (arts/ent.)
Spinks (sports)
Trotsky (govt./mil.)
Uris (arts/ent.)
LEONA
Helmsley (business)
LEONARD
Bernstein (arts/ent.)
Cohen (arts/ent.)
DiCaprio (arts/ent.)
Maltin (arts/ent.)
Nimoy (arts/ent.)
Slatkin (arts/ent.)
Warren (arts/ent.)
LEONARDO
Da Vinci (arts/ent.)
LEONID
Andreyev (arts/ent.)
Brezhnev (govt./mil.)
LÉONIDE
Massine (arts/ent.)
LEONTYNE
Price (arts/ent.)

LEOPOLD, LÉOPOLD
Sédar Senghor (govt./
mil.)
Stokowski (arts/ent.)
LEOPOLDO
Lugones (arts/ent.)
LEORA
Dana (arts/ent.)
LEOŠ
Janáček (arts/ent.)
LEPKE
Buchalter (misc.)
LEROY
Anderson (arts/ent.)
Neiman (arts/ent.)
LES
Aspin (govt./mil.)
Baxter (arts/ent.)
Brown (arts/ent.)
Dudek (arts/ent.)
Paul (arts/ent.)
LESLEY
Gore (arts/ent.)
Stahl (arts/ent.)
Ann Warren (arts/ent.)
LESLEY-ANNE
Down (arts/ent.)
LESLIE
Caron (arts/ent.)
Charteris (arts/ent.)
A. Fiedler (arts/ent.)
Halliwell (arts/ent.)
Howard (arts/ent.)
Nielsen (arts/ent.)
Uggams (arts/ent.)
LESTER
Del Rey (arts/ent.)
Flatt (arts/ent.)
Maddox (govt./mil.)
Pearson (govt./mil.)
Thurow (misc.)
Young (arts/ent.)
LETITIA
Baldridge (misc.)
Tyler (govt./mil.)
LEVAR
Burton (arts/ent.)
LEVI
P. Morton (govt./mil.)
Strauss (business)
LEVON
Helm (arts/ent.)
LEW
Ayres (arts/ent.)
Burdette (sports)
Grade (arts/ent.)
Lehr (arts/ent.)

Tabackin (arts/ent.)
Wallace (arts/ent.)
LEWIS
Carroll (arts/ent.)
Grizzard (arts/ent.)
Milestone (arts/ent.)
Mumford (rel./phil.)
Padgett (arts/ent.)
F. Powell, Jr. (govt./mil.)
Stone (arts/ent.)
LEX
Barker (arts/ent.)
LIAM
Neeson (arts/ent.)
O'Flaherty (arts/ent.)
LICIA
Albanese (arts/ent.)
LIGHTNIN'
Hopkins (arts/ent.)
LIL
Dagover (arts/ent.)
LILA
Kedrova (arts/ent.)
Bell Wallace (business)
LILI
Damita (arts/ent.)
St. Cyr (arts/ent.)
Taylor (arts/ent.)
LILLI
Lehmann (arts/ent.)
Palmer (arts/ent.)
LILLIAN
Gish (arts/ent.)
Hellman (arts/ent.)
Nordica (arts/ent.)
O'Donnell (arts/ent.)
Roth (arts/ent.)
Russell (arts/ent.)
LILLIE
Langtry (arts/ent.)
LILY
Pons (arts/ent.)
Tomlin (arts/ent.)
LILYAN
Tashman (arts/ent.)
LINA
Basquette (arts/ent.)
Wertmuller (arts/ent.)
LINCOLN
Ellsworth (pion./exp.)
Steffens (arts/ent.)
LINDA
Blair (arts/ent.)
Christian (arts/ent.)
Dano (arts/ent.)
Darnell (arts/ent.)
Ellerbee (arts/ent.)

Evangelista (arts/ent.)
Evans (arts/ent.)
Fratianne (sports)
Gray (arts/ent.)
Hamilton (arts/ent.)
Hunt (arts/ent.)
Kelsey (arts/ent.)
Kozlowski (arts/ent.)
Lavin (arts/ent.)
Lovelace (arts/ent.)
McCartney (arts/ent.)
Purl (arts/ent.)
Ronstadt (arts/ent.)
LINDSAY
Anderson (arts/ent.)
Crouse (arts/ent.)
Wagner (arts/ent.)
Buckingham (arts/ent.)
LINK
Lyman (sports)
LINO
Ventura (arts/ent.)
LINUS
Pauling (sci./inv.)
LIONEL
Atwill (arts/ent.)
Barrymore (arts/ent.)
Hampton (arts/ent.)
Richie (arts/ent.)
Stander (arts/ent.)
Trilling (arts/ent.)
LIPPO
Lippi (arts/ent.)
LISA
Bonet (arts/ent.)
Eichhorn (arts/ent.)
Hartman (arts/ent.)
Marie Presley (arts/ent.)
Stansfield (arts/ent.)
Whelchel (arts/ent.)
LISE
Meitner (sci./inv.)
LITA
Ford (arts/ent.)
Grey (arts/ent.)
LIV
Tyler (arts/ent.)
Ullmann (arts/ent.)
LIZ
Claiborne (arts/ent.)
Smith (arts/ent.)
LIZA
Minnelli (arts/ent.)
LIZABETH
Scott (arts/ent.)
LIZZIE
Borden (arts/ent.)

Borden (misc.)
LLOYD
Bentsen (govt./mil.)
Bochner (arts/ent.)
Bridges (arts/ent.)
Cole (arts/ent.)
C. Douglas (arts/ent.)
Nolan (arts/ent.)
Waner (sports)
LODOVICO
Ariosto (arts/ent.)
LOIE
Fuller (arts/ent.)
LOIS
Nettleton (arts/ent.)
LOL
Creme (arts/ent.)
LOLA
Albright (arts/ent.)
Falana (arts/ent.)
Montez (arts/ent.)
LOLITA
Davidovich (arts/ent.)
LON
Chaney (arts/ent.)
Chaney, Jr. (arts/ent.)
McCallister (arts/ent.)
Warneke (sports)
LONG JOHN
Baldry (arts/ent.)
LONI
Anderson (arts/ent.)
LONNIE
Donegan (arts/ent.)
LOPE
De Vega (arts/ent.)
LORENZ
Hart (arts/ent.)
LORENZO
Ghiberti (arts/ent.)
Lamas (arts/ent.)
De' Medici (govt./
mil.)
Music (arts/ent.)
LORETTA
Lynn (arts/ent.)
Swit (arts/ent.)
Young (arts/ent.)
LORI
Laughlin (arts/ent.)
Petty (arts/ent.)
Singer (arts/ent.)
LORNA
Luft (arts/ent.)
LORNE
Greene (arts/ent.)
Michaels (arts/ent.)

LORRAINE
Bracco (arts/ent.)
Hansberry (arts/ent.)
LORRIE
Morgan (arts/ent.)
LOTTE
Lehmann (arts/ent.)
Lenya (arts/ent.)
LOU
Boudreau (sports)
Brock (sports)
Christie (arts/ent.)
Costello (arts/ent.)
Ferrigno (arts/ent.)
Gehrig (sports)
Gramm (arts/ent.)
Groza (sports)
Jacobi (arts/ent.)
Novikoff (sports)
Diamond Phillips (arts/
ent.)
Piniella (sports)
Rawls (arts/ent.)
Reed (arts/ent.)
LOUDON
Wainwright III (arts/
ent.)
LOUELLA
Parsons (arts/ent.)
LOUIE
Anderson (arts/ent.)
LOUIS
Agassiz (sci./inv.)
Aragon (arts/ent.)
Armstrong (arts/ent.)
Auchincloss (arts/ent.)
Bellson (arts/ent.)
Braille (misc.)
Brandeis (govt./mil.)
Bromfield (arts/ent.)
Calhern (arts/ent.)
Chevrolet (business)
Daguerre (arts/ent.)
David (arts/ent.)
Farrakhan (govt./mil.)
Gossett (arts/ent.)
Gruenberg (arts/ent.)
Joliet or Jolliet (pion./
exp.)
Jourdan (arts/ent.)
I. Kahn (arts/ent.)
L'Amour (arts/ent.)
Le Nain (arts/ent.)
Leakey (sci./inv.)
Lumière (arts/ent.)
Malle (arts/ent.)
B. Mayer (arts/ent.)

Mountbatten (govt./
mil.)
Nizer (misc.)
Nye (arts/ent.)
Pasteur (sci./inv.)
Prima (arts/ent.)
Renault (business)
Rukeyser (business)
Simpson (arts/ent.)
Skidmore (arts/ent.)
Sullivan (arts/ent.)
Teicher (arts/ent.)
Tiffany (arts/ent.)
Untermeyer (arts/ent.)
LOUISA
May Alcott (arts/ent.)
LOUISE
Adams (govt./mil.)
Beavers (arts/ent.)
Bogan (arts/ent.)
Brooks (arts/ent.)
Brough (sports)
Fazenda (arts/ent.)
Fletcher (arts/ent.)
Gluck (arts/ent.)
Goffin (arts/ent.)
Labé (arts/ent.)
Lasser (arts/ent.)
Mandrell (arts/ent.)
Nevelson (arts/ent.)
Suggs (sports)
LOWELL
Thomas (arts/ent.)
LUANA
Anders (arts/ent.)
LUC
Besson (arts/ent.)
LUCA
Della Robbia (arts/ent.)
LUCHINO
Visconti (arts/ent.)
LUCIANO
Pavarotti (arts/ent.)
LUCIE
Arnaz (arts/ent.)
Duff-Gordon (arts/
ent.)
LUCILE
Watson (arts/ent.)
LUCILLE
Ball (arts/ent.)
Fletcher (arts/ent.)
LUCINDA
Childs (arts/ent.)
LUCIUS
Quinctius Cincinnatus
(govt./mil.)

LUCKY
Luciano (arts/ent.)
LUCRETIA
Garfield (govt./mil.)
LUCREZIA
Borgia (govt./mil.)
Bori (arts/ent.)
LUCY
Hayes (govt./mil.)
Montgomery (arts/ent.)
Stone (govt./mil.)
Terry (arts/ent.)
LUDOVICO
Ariosto (arts/ent.)
LUDWIG
Van Beethoven (arts/
ent.)
Bemelmans (arts/ent.)
Feuerbach (rel./phil.)
Tieck (arts/ent.)
Wittgenstein (rel./phil.)
LUIGI
Cherubini (arts/ent.)
Pirandello (arts/ent.)
LUIS
Alvarez (sci./inv.)
Aparicio (sports)
Buñuel (arts/ent.)
Firpo (sports)
Tiant (sports)
LUISA
Tetrazzini (arts/ent.)
LUISE
Rainer (arts/ent.)
LUKAS
Foss (arts/ent.)
Haas (arts/ent.)
LUKE
Appling (sports)
Askew (arts/ent.)
Perry (arts/ent.)
LUPE
Velez (arts/ent.)
LURENE
Tuttle (arts/ent.)
LURLEEN
Burns Wallace (govt./
mil.)
LUTE
Pease (arts/ent.)
LUTHER
Adler (arts/ent.)
Ingram (arts/ent.)
Vandross (arts/ent.)
LYDIA
Lopokova (arts/ent.)
Lunch (arts/ent.)

LYLE
Alzado (sports)
Bettger (arts/ent.)
Lovett (arts/ent.)
Menendez (misc.)
Talbot (arts/ent.)
Waggoner (arts/ent.)
LYMAN
Beecher (rel./phil.)
Bostock (sports)
LYNDA
Carter (arts/ent.)
Day George (arts/ent.)
LYNDON
Johnson (govt./mil.)
Larouche (govt./mil.)
LYNN
Anderson (arts/ent.)
Bari (arts/ent.)
Fontanne (arts/ent.)
Redgrave (arts/ent.)
Swann (sports)
LYTTON
Strachey (arts/ent.)
M. F. K.
Fisher (arts/ent.)
M. EMMET
Walsh (arts/ent.)
M. SCOTT
Peck (arts/ent.)
MA
Barker (misc.)
Rainey (arts/ent.)
MABEL
Dodge Luhan (arts/ent.)
Mercer (arts/ent.)
Normand (arts/ent.)
MAC
Davis (arts/ent.)
McAnally (arts/ent.)
MACAULAY
Culkin (arts/ent.)
MACDONALD
Carey (arts/ent.)
MACHINE GUN
Kelly (misc.)
MACK
Sennett (arts/ent.)
MACKENZIE
Phillips (arts/ent.)
MACKINLAY
Kantor (arts/ent.)
MADALYN
O'Hair (misc.)
MADELEINE
Carroll (arts/ent.)
L'Engle (arts/ent.)

De Scudéry (arts/ent.)
Stowe (arts/ent.)
MADELINE
Kahn (arts/ent.)
MADLYN
Rhue (arts/ent.)
MAE
Busch (arts/ent.)
Clarke (arts/ent.)
Marsh (arts/ent.)
Murray (arts/ent.)
West (arts/ent.)
MAGDA
Gabor (arts/ent.)
MAGGIE
Kuhn (govt./mil.)
Smith (arts/ent.)
MAGIC
Johnson (sports)
MAHAL
Mumtaz (govt./mil.)
MAHALIA
Jackson (arts/ent.)
MAI
Zetterling (arts/ent.)
MAJ
Sjöwall (arts/ent.)
MAJEL
Barrett (arts/ent.)
MAKSIM
Gorki or Gorky (arts/
ent.)
MAL
St. Clair (arts/ent.)
MALCOLM
Baldridge (govt./mil.)
Bradbury (arts/ent.)
Forbes (business)
Lowry (arts/ent.)
McDowell (arts/ent.)
McLaren (arts/ent.)
Muggeridge (arts/ent.)
Jamal Warner (arts/
ent.)
MALVINA
Hoffman (arts/ent.)
MAMIE
Eisenhower (govt./mil.)
Van Doren (arts/ent.)
MANDY
Patinkin (arts/ent.)
MANFRED
Lee (arts/ent.)
Mann (arts/ent.)
MANNY
Sanguillen (sports)
Trillo (sports)

MANTAN
Moreland (arts/ent.)
MANUEL
De Falla (arts/ent.)
Noriega (govt./mil.)
Puig (arts/ent.)
MARABEL
Morgan (arts/ent.)
MARC
Allégret (arts/ent.)
Almond (arts/ent.)
Antony (govt./mil.)
Blitzstein (arts/ent.)
Bolan (arts/ent.)
Chagall (arts/ent.)
Cohn (arts/ent.)
Connelly (arts/ent.)
MARCEL
Breuer (arts/ent.)
Camus (arts/ent.)
Duchamp (arts/ent.)
Marceau (arts/ent.)
Ophüls (arts/ent.)
Pagnol (arts/ent.)
Proust (arts/ent.)
MARCELLO
Mastroianni (arts/ent.)
MARCIA
Strassman (arts/ent.)
MARCO
Polo (pion./exp.)
MARCUS
Aurelius (govt./mil.)
Junius Brutus (govt./
mil.)
Tullius Cicero (arts/ent.)
Garvey (govt./mil.)
Loew (business)
Cocceius Nerva (govt./
mil.)
MARCY
Carsey (arts/ent.)
Walker (arts/ent.)
MARE
Winningham (arts/ent.)
MARG
Helgenberger (arts/ent.)
MARGARET
Atwood (arts/ent.)
Bourke-White (arts/ent.)
Cavendish (arts/ent.)
Court (sports)
Drabble (arts/ent.)
Dumont (arts/ent.)
Hamilton (arts/ent.)
Leighton (arts/ent.)
Lindsay (arts/ent.)

Lockwood (arts/ent.)
Mead (sci./inv.)
Mitchell (arts/ent.)
O'Brien (arts/ent.)
Rutherford (arts/ent.)
Sanger (misc.)
Chase Smith (govt./mil.)
Sullavan (arts/ent.)
Thatcher (govt./mil.)
Walker (arts/ent.)
Whiting (arts/ent.)
Wilson (arts/ent.)
MARGAUX
Hemingway (arts/ent.)
MARGE
Champion (arts/ent.)
Piercy (arts/ent.)
MARGERY
Allingham (arts/ent.)
MARGOT
Asquith (misc.)
Fonteyn (arts/ent.)
Kidder (arts/ent.)
MARGUERITE
Churchill (arts/ent.)
Duras (arts/ent.)
Higgins (arts/ent.)
Yourcenar (arts/ent.)
MARI
Sandoz (arts/ent.)
MARIA
Alonso (arts/ent.)
Bueno (sports)
Callas (arts/ent.)
Jeritza (arts/ent.)
Malibran (arts/ent.)
McKee (arts/ent.)
Montessori (misc.)
Montez (arts/ent.)
Muldaur (arts/ent.)
Ouspenskaya (arts/ent.)
Schell (arts/ent.)
Schneider (arts/ent.)
Shriver (arts/ent.)
Tallchief (arts/ent.)
Von Trapp (arts/ent.)
MARIAH
Carey (arts/ent.)
MARIAN
Anderson (arts/ent.)
Jordan (arts/ent.)
McPartland (arts/ent.)
Mercer (arts/ent.)
MARIANNE
Faithfull (arts/ent.)
Moore (arts/ent.)
Sagebrecht (arts/ent.)

Williamson (arts/ent.)
MARIANO
Duncan (sports)
MARIE
Antoinette (M)
Corelli (arts/ent.)
Curie (sci./inv.)
Dressler (arts/ent.)
Goeppert-Mayer (sci./inv.)
Osmond (arts/ent.)
Tempest (arts/ent.)
Wilson (arts/ent.)
MARIEL
Hemingway (arts/ent.)
MARIETTE
Hartley (arts/ent.)
MARILU
Henner (arts/ent.)
MARILYN
Bergman (arts/ent.)
Chambers (arts/ent.)
French (arts/ent.)
Horne (arts/ent.)
McCoo (arts/ent.)
Miller (arts/ent.)
Monroe (arts/ent.)
Quayle (govt./mil.)
MARIO
Andretti (sports)
Cuomo (govt./mil.)
Lanza (arts/ent.)
Lemieux (sports)
Puzo (arts/ent.)
Van Peebles (arts/ent.)
Vargas Llosa (arts/ent.)
MARION
Bradley (arts/ent.)
Davies (arts/ent.)
Hutton (arts/ent.)
Lorne (arts/ent.)
Motley (sports)
Ross (arts/ent.)
MARISA
Berenson (arts/ent.)
Pavan (arts/ent.)
Tomei (arts/ent.)
MARISKA
Hargitay (arts/ent.)
MARJOE
Gortner (arts/ent.)
MARJORIE
H. Buell (arts/ent.)
Lawrence (arts/ent.)
Lord (arts/ent.)
Main (arts/ent.)

Meriweather Post (business)
Rambeau (arts/ent.)
Rawlings (arts/ent.)
MARK
David Chapman (misc.)
Chesnutt (arts/ent.)
Collie (arts/ent.)
Debarge (arts/ent.)
Fidrych (arts/ent.)
Gastineau (sports)
Goodson (arts/ent.)
Hamill (arts/ent.)
Harmon (arts/ent.)
O. Hatfield (govt./mil.)
Knopfler (arts/ent.)
Linn-Baker (arts/ent.)
O'Connor (arts/ent.)
Rothko (arts/ent.)
Rydell (arts/ent.)
Sandrich (arts/ent.)
Spitz (sports)
Strand (arts/ent.)
Twain (arts/ent.)
Volman (arts/ent.)
MARKIE
Post (arts/ent.)
MARLA
Gibbs (arts/ent.)
Hanson (arts/ent.)
Maples (arts/ent.)
MARLEE
Matlin (arts/ent.)
MARLENE
Dietrich (arts/ent.)
MARLIN
Fitzwater (govt./mil.)
Perkins (arts/ent.)
MARLO
Thomas (arts/ent.)
MARLON
Brando (arts/ent.)
Jackson (arts/ent.)
MARNI
Nixon (arts/ent.)
MARQUES
Haynes (sports)
MARQUIS
Childs (arts/ent.)
Desade (arts/ent.)
MARSDEN
Hartley (arts/ent.)
MARSHA
Hunt (arts/ent.)
Mason (arts/ent.)
Norman (arts/ent.)
Warfield (arts/ent.)

MARSHALL
Crenshaw (arts/ent.)
Field (business)
Field III (business)
McLuhan (arts/ent.)
MARTA
Kristen (arts/ent.)
MARTHA
Boswell (arts/ent.)
Clarke (arts/ent.)
Coolidge (arts/ent.)
Davis (arts/ent.)
Finley (arts/ent.)
Graham (arts/ent.)
Grimes (arts/ent.)
Hennissart (arts/ent.)
Hyer (arts/ent.)
Jefferson (govt./mil.)
Plimpton (arts/ent.)
Quinn (arts/ent.)
Raye (arts/ent.)
Reeves (arts/ent.)
Scott (arts/ent.)
Stewart (arts/ent.)
Vickers (arts/ent.)
Washington (govt./mil.)
MARTHE
Keller (arts/ent.)
MARTIN
Agronsky (arts/ent.)
Amis (arts/ent.)
Balsam (arts/ent.)
Beck (arts/ent.)
Bormann (govt./mil.)
Brest (arts/ent.)
Buber (rel./phil.)
Delany (govt./mil.)
Frobisher (pion./exp.)
Gabel (arts/ent.)
Heidegger (rel./phil.)
Kemp (arts/ent.)
Luther King, Jr. (govt./
mil.)
Landau (arts/ent.)
Luther (rel./phil.)
Melcher (arts/ent.)
Milner (arts/ent.)
Mull (arts/ent.)
Nexo (arts/ent.)
Ritt (arts/ent.)
Scorsese (arts/ent.)
Sheen (arts/ent.)
Short (arts/ent.)
Van Buren (govt./mil.)
MARTINA
Arroyo (arts/ent.)
McBride (arts/ent.)

Navratilova (sports)
MARTITA
Hunt (arts/ent.)
MARTY
Balin (arts/ent.)
Brown (arts/ent.)
Feldman (arts/ent.)
Ingels (arts/ent.)
Marion (sports)
Melcher (arts/ent.)
Riessen (sports)
Robbins (arts/ent.)
Stuart (arts/ent.)
MARV
Throneberry (sports)
MARVIN
Chomsky (arts/ent.)
Gaye (arts/ent.)
Hagler (sports)
Hamlisch (arts/ent.)
Kalb (arts/ent.)
Mitchelson (misc.)
MARY
Kay Wagner Ash
(business)
Astor (arts/ent.)
McCleod Bethune
(govt./mil.)
J. Blige (arts/ent.)
Cassatt (arts/ent.)
Chase (arts/ent.)
Higgins Clark (arts/ent.)
Crosby (arts/ent.)
Decker (sports)
Elizabeth Dodge (arts/
ent.)
Baker Eddy (rel./phil.)
Frann (arts/ent.)
Gross (arts/ent.)
Hart (arts/ent.)
Beth Hurt (arts/ent.)
Page Keller (arts/ent.)
J. Latis (arts/ent.)
Leakey (sci./inv.)
Todd Lincoln (govt./
mil.)
Livingstone (arts/ent.)
MacGregor (arts/ent.)
Magdalene (rel./phil.)
Martin (arts/ent.)
Stuart Masterson (arts/
ent.)
Matalin (govt./mil.)
Elizabeth Mastro-
antonio (arts/ent.)
Margaret McBride
(arts/ent.)

McCarthy (arts/ent.)
McFadden (arts/ent.)
McGrory (arts/ent.)
Miles Minter (arts/ent.)
Ann Mobley (arts/ent.)
Tyler Moore (arts/ent.)
Norton (arts/ent.)
O'Hara (arts/ent.)
Pickford (arts/ent.)
Kay Place (arts/ent.)
Quant (arts/ent.)
Lou Retton (sports)
Roberts Rinehart (arts/
ent.)
Shelley (arts/ent.)
Steenburgen (arts/ent.)
Church Terrell (govt./
mil.)
Travers (arts/ent.)
Ure (arts/ent.)
Wells (arts/ent.)
Wilson (arts/ent.)
Wollstonecraft (arts/
ent.)
Woronov (arts/ent.)
MARY JO
Buttafuoco (misc.)
MARY-LOUISE
Parker (arts/ent.)
MARY-CHAPIN
Carpenter (arts/ent.)
MARYA
Zatureuska (arts/ent.)
MARYAM
D'Abo (arts/ent.)
MASON
Reese (arts/ent.)
Weems (rel./phil.)
MATHIEU
Le Nain (arts/ent.)
MATT
Biondi (sports)
Dillon (arts/ent.)
Groening (arts/ent.)
Lattanzi (arts/ent.)
MATTEO
Bandello (arts/ent.)
Boiardo (arts/ent.)
MATTHEW
Arnold (arts/ent.)
Brady (arts/ent.)
Broderick (arts/ent.)
Modine (arts/ent.)
Nelson (arts/ent.)
Calbraith Perry (govt./
mil.)
Prior (arts/ent.)

MAUD
Adams (arts/ent.)
Gonne (arts/ent.)
MAUDE
Adams (arts/ent.)
MAUREEN
Connolly (sports)
McGovern (arts/ent.)
O'Hara (arts/ent.)
O'Sullivan (arts/ent.)
Stapleton (arts/ent.)
MAURICE
Béjart (arts/ent.)
Chevalier (arts/ent.)
Gibb (arts/ent.)
Jarre (arts/ent.)
Leblanc (arts/ent.)
Maeterlinck (arts/ent.)
Prendergast (arts/ent.)
Ravel (arts/ent.)
Richard (sports)
Sendak (arts/ent.)
Utrillo (arts/ent.)
De Vlaminck (arts/ent.)
White (arts/ent.)
MAURY
Povich (arts/ent.)
Wills (sports)
MAX
Abramowitz (arts/ent.)
Ascoli (arts/ent.)
Baer (sports)
Baer, Jr. (arts/ent.)
Beckmann (arts/ent.)
Beerbohm (arts/ent.)
Brand (arts/ent.)
Bruch (arts/ent.)
Carey (sports)
Delbrück (sci./inv.)
Eastman (arts/ent.)
Ernst (arts/ent.)
Fleischer (arts/ent.)
Frisch (arts/ent.)
Gail (arts/ent.)
Jacob (arts/ent.)
Lerner (arts/ent.)
Liebermann (arts/ent.)
Ophüls (arts/ent.)
Planck (sci./inv.)
Reger (arts/ent.)
Reinhardt (arts/ent.)
Roach (arts/ent.)
Schmeling (sports)
Schuster (business)
Shulman (arts/ent.)
Steiner (arts/ent.)
Von Sydow (arts/ent.)

Weber (arts/ent.)
Weber (misc.)
MAXENE
Andrews (arts/ent.)
MAXFIELD
Parrish (arts/ent.)
MAXIE
Rosenbloom (sports)
MAXIM
Gorki or Gorky (arts/
ent.)
MAXIMILIAN
Schell (arts/ent.)
MAXIMILIEN
Robespierre (govt./
mil.)
MAXINE
Hong Kingston (arts/
ent.)
Winokur Kumin (arts/
ent.)
Nightingale (arts/ent.)
Waters (govt./mil.)
MAXWELL
Anderson (arts/ent.)
Bodenheim (arts/ent.)
Caulfield (arts/ent.)
Perkins (business)
MAY
Britt (arts/ent.)
Robson (arts/ent.)
Sarton (arts/ent.)
Whitty (arts/ent.)
MAYA
Angelou (arts/ent.)
Plisetskaya (arts/ent.)
MAYIM
Bialik (arts/ent.)
MAYNARD
Ferguson (arts/ent.)
Jackson (govt./mil.)
MAYNE
Reid (arts/ent.)
MAYO
Methot (arts/ent.)
McCoy
Tyner (arts/ent.)
McLEAN
Stevenson (arts/ent.)
MEADOWLARK
Lemon (sports)
MEDGAR
Evers (govt./mil.)
MEG
Foster (arts/ent.)
Ryan (arts/ent.)
Tilly (arts/ent.)

MEL
Allen (sports)
Blanc (arts/ent.)
Brooks (arts/ent.)
Ferrer (arts/ent.)
Gibson (arts/ent.)
Harris (arts/ent.)
Hein (sports)
McDaniel (arts/ent.)
Ott (sports)
Tillis (arts/ent.)
Torme (arts/ent.)
MELANIE
Griffith (arts/ent.)
Mayron (arts/ent.)
MELBA
Moore (arts/ent.)
MELINA
Mercouri (arts/ent.)
MELINDA
Dillon (arts/ent.)
MELISSA
Sue Anderson (arts/ent.)
Etheridge (arts/ent.)
Gilbert (arts/ent.)
Hayden (arts/ent.)
Manchester (arts/ent.)
MELL
Lazarus (arts/ent.)
MELVIL
Dewey (misc.)
MELVILLE
Cooper (arts/ent.)
Fuller (govt./mil.)
MELVIN
Belli (misc.)
Calvin (sci./inv.)
Van Peebles (arts/ent.)
MELVYN
Douglas (arts/ent.)
MENACHEM
Begin (govt./mil.)
MERCE
Cunningham (arts/ent.)
MERCEDES
McCambridge (arts/
ent.)
Ruehl (arts/ent.)
MEREDITH
Baxter-Birney (arts/ent.)
MacRae (arts/ent.)
Vieira (arts/ent.)
Willson (arts/ent.)
MERIE
Earle (arts/ent.)
MERIWETHER
Lewis (pion./exp.)

MERLE
Haggard (arts/ent.)
Oberon (arts/ent.)
Travis (arts/ent.)
MERLIN
Olsen (sports)
MERRILL
Osmond (arts/ent.)
MERRIMAN
Smith (arts/ent.)
MERV
Griffin (arts/ent.)
MERVYN
Le Roy (arts/ent.)
MERYL
Streep (arts/ent.)
MEYER
Lansky (misc.)
Levin (arts/ent.)
MIA
Farrow (arts/ent.)
MICA
Paris (arts/ent.)
MICHAEL
Anderson (arts/ent.)
Anthony (arts/ent.)
Apted (arts/ent.)
Balfe (arts/ent.)
Biehn (arts/ent.)
Bolton (arts/ent.)
Caine (arts/ent.)
Chiklis (arts/ent.)
Cimino (arts/ent.)
Collins (pion./exp.)
Connors (arts/ent.)
Crawford (arts/ent.)
Crichton (arts/ent.)
Cristofer (arts/ent.)
Curtiz (arts/ent.)
Damian (arts/ent.)
Ellis Debakey (sci./inv.)
Douglas (arts/ent.)
Dukakis (govt./mil.)
Eisner (arts/ent.)
Feinstein (arts/ent.)
J. Fox (arts/ent.)
Frayn (arts/ent.)
Gordon (arts/ent.)
Gross (arts/ent.)
Harrington (arts/ent.)
Hutchence (arts/ent.)
Innes (arts/ent.)
Jackson (arts/ent.)
Johnson (arts/ent.)
Jordan (sports)
Keaton (arts/ent.)
Kidd (arts/ent.)

Korda (arts/ent.)
Landon (arts/ent.)
Learned (arts/ent.)
O. Leavitt (govt./mil.)
Lehmann (arts/ent.)
Lindsay-Hogg (arts/
ent.)
Lowry (govt./mil.)
Mann (arts/ent.)
McDonald (arts/ent.)
McKean (arts/ent.)
Moore (arts/ent.)
Moriarty (arts/ent.)
Martin Murphey (arts/
ent.)
Ontkean (arts/ent.)
Ovitz (arts/ent.)
Palin (arts/ent.)
Paré (arts/ent.)
J. Pollard (arts/ent.)
Powell (arts/ent.)
Redgrave (arts/ent.)
Relph (arts/ent.)
Rennie (arts/ent.)
Richards (arts/ent.)
Ritchie (arts/ent.)
Rooker (arts/ent.)
Sarrazin (arts/ent.)
Spinks (sports)
Stipe (arts/ent.)
Tilson Thomas (arts/
ent.)
Todd (arts/ent.)
Tucker (arts/ent.)
Wilding (arts/ent.)
Winner (arts/ent.)
York (arts/ent.)
MICHEL
Fokine (arts/ent.)
Foucault (rel./phil.)
Legrand (arts/ent.)
MICHELANGELO
Antonioni (arts/ent.)
MICHELE
Lee (arts/ent.)
MICHELLE
Pfeiffer (arts/ent.)
Phillips (arts/ent.)
Shocked (arts/ent.)
Wright (arts/ent.)
MICK
Fleetwood (arts/ent.)
Hucknall (arts/ent.)
Jagger (arts/ent.)
Jones (arts/ent.)
Mars (arts/ent.)
Taylor (arts/ent.)

MICKEY
Cochrane (sports)
Cohen (misc.)
Dolenz (arts/ent.)
Gilley (arts/ent.)
Mantle (sports)
Owen (sports)
Rivers (sports)
Rooney (arts/ent.)
Rourke (arts/ent.)
Spillane (arts/ent.)
Walker (sports)
Wright (sports)
MIDGE
Ure (arts/ent.)
MIGNON
Eberhart (arts/ent.)
MIGUEL
Angel Asturias (arts/
ent.)
De Cervantes (arts/
ent.)
Covarrubias (arts/ent.)
Delibes (arts/ent.)
Hidalgo y Costilla
(govt./mil.)
MIKE
Bloomfield (arts/ent.)
Boddicker (sports)
Bossy (sports)
Connors (arts/ent.)
Ditka (sports)
Douglas (arts/ent.)
Farrell (arts/ent.)
Haynes (sports)
Love (arts/ent.)
McCormack (sports)
Medavoy (business)
Myers (arts/ent.)
Nesmith (arts/ent.)
Nichols (arts/ent.)
Oldfield (arts/ent.)
Romanoff (misc.)
Royko (arts/ent.)
Rutherford (arts/ent.)
Schmidt (sports)
Stoller (arts/ent.)
Todd (arts/ent.)
Tyson (sports)
Wallace (arts/ent.)
MIKHAIL
Baryshnikov (arts/
ent.)
Glinka (arts/ent.)
Gorbachev (govt./mil.)
Lermontov (arts/ent.)
Romanov (govt./mil.)

Sholokhov (arts/ent.)
MIKLOS
Rozsa (arts/ent.)
MILAN
Kundera (arts/ent.)
MILBURN
Stone (arts/ent.)
MILDRED
Dunnock (arts/ent.)
Natwick (arts/ent.)
MILES
Davis (arts/ent.)
Franklin (arts/ent.)
Standish (govt./mil.)
MILLARD
Fillmore (govt./
mil.)
MILLER
Huggins (sports)
MILLIE
Jackson (arts/ent.)
MILO
O'Shea (arts/ent.)
MILOŠ
Forman (arts/ent.)
MILT
Jackson (arts/ent.)
Thompson (sports)
MILTON
Ager (arts/ent.)
Berle (arts/ent.)
Caniff (arts/ent.)
Delugg (arts/ent.)
Friedman (misc.)
Gross (arts/ent.)
S. Hershey (business)
MIMI
Benzell (arts/ent.)
Rogers (arts/ent.)
MINDY
Cohn (arts/ent.)
MINERVA
Pious (arts/ent.)
MING-NA
Wen (arts/ent.)
MINNA
Gombell (arts/ent.)
MINNIE
Pearl (arts/ent.)
Riperton (arts/ent.)
MINTA
Durfee (arts/ent.)
MIRA
Nair (arts/ent.)
MIRANDA
Richardson (arts/
ent.)

MIRIAM
Hopkins (arts/ent.)
Makeba (arts/ent.)
MISSY
Francis (arts/ent.)
MITCH
Leigh (arts/ent.)
Miller (arts/ent.)
Ryder (arts/ent.)
MITZI
Gaynor (arts/ent.)
Green (arts/ent.)
MIYOSHI
Umeki (arts/ent.)
MO
Udall (govt./mil.)
MODEST
Mussorgsky (arts/ent.)
MOE
Bandy (arts/ent.)
Berg (sports)
Drabowsky (sports)
Howard (arts/ent.)
MOHAMMAD
Reza Pahlavi (govt./
mil.)
MOIRA
Kelly (arts/ent.)
Shearer (arts/ent.)
MOLLIE
Parnis (arts/ent.)
MOLLY
Picon (arts/ent.)
Pitcher (misc.)
Ringwald (arts/ent.)
MOMS
Mabley (arts/ent.)
MONA
Freeman (arts/ent.)
MONICA
Seles (sports)
MONTE
Irvin (sports)
Markham (arts/ent.)
MONTEL
Williams (arts/ent.)
MONTGOMERY
Clift (arts/ent.)
Ward (business)
MONTY
Hall (arts/ent.)
Woolley (arts/ent.)
MOOKIE
Wilson (sports)
MOON
Landrieu (govt./mil.)
Martin (arts/ent.)

MOON UNIT
Zappa (arts/ent.)
MORDECAI
Richler (arts/ent.)
MOREY
Amsterdam (arts/ent.)
MORGAN
Brittany (arts/ent.)
Conway (arts/ent.)
Fairchild (arts/ent.)
Freeman (arts/ent.)
MORGANA
King (arts/ent.)
MORLEY
Safer (arts/ent.)
MORRIE
Ryskind (arts/ent.)
MORRIS
Albert (arts/ent.)
Carnovsky (arts/ent.)
Day (arts/ent.)
Udall (govt./mil.)
L. West (arts/ent.)
MORRISON
R. Waite (govt./mil.)
MORT
Cooper (sports)
Drucker (arts/ent.)
Lindsey (arts/ent.)
Sahl (arts/ent.)
Walker (arts/ent.)
MORTIMER
Adler (rel./phil.)
MORTON
Da Costa (arts/ent.)
Downey, Jr. (arts/ent.)
Gould (arts/ent.)
Janklow (business)
MOSE
Allison (arts/ent.)
MOSES
Ezekiel (arts/ent.)
Gunn (arts/ent.)
Malone (sports)
MOSHE
Dayan (govt./mil.)
MOSS
Hart (arts/ent.)
MSTISLAV
Rostropovich (arts/
ent.)
MUAMMAR
Qaddafi (govt./mil.)
MUDDY
Waters (arts/ent.)
MUGGSY
Spanier (arts/ent.)

MUHAMMED
Ali (sports)
Ali Jinnah (govt./mil.)
MUNGO
Park (pion./exp.)
MURIEL
Rukeyser (arts/ent.)
Spark (arts/ent.)
MURRAY
Gell-Mann (sci./inv.)
Kempton (arts/ent.)
Leinster (arts/ent.)
MYLES
Standish (govt./mil.)
MYRA
Hess (arts/ent.)
MYRNA
Loy (arts/ent.)
MYRON
Cohen (arts/ent.)
N. C.
Wyeth (arts/ent.)
N. SCOTT
Momaday (arts/ent.)
NACIO
Herb Brown (arts/ent.)
NADIA
Boulanger (arts/ent.)
Comaneci (sports)
NADINE
Conner (arts/ent.)
Gordimer (arts/ent.)
NADJA
Salerno-Sonnenberg
(arts/ent.)
NAGUIB
Mahfouz (arts/ent.)
NAN
Grey (arts/ent.)
NANA
Mouskouri (arts/ent.)
NANCY
Allen (arts/ent.)
Astor (govt./mil.)
Dussault (arts/ent.)
Friday (arts/ent.)
Kassebaum (govt./
mil.)
Kelly (arts/ent.)
Kulp (arts/ent.)
Kwan (arts/ent.)
Lopez (sports)
McKeon (arts/ent.)
Mitford (arts/ent.)
Reagan (govt./mil.)
Sinatra (arts/ent.)
Travis (arts/ent.)

Walker (arts/ent.)
Wilson (arts/ent.)
NANETTE
Fabray (arts/ent.)
Newman (arts/ent.)
NAOMI
Campbell (arts/ent.)
Judd (arts/ent.)
NAPOLEON, NAPOLÉON
Bonaparte (govt./mil.)
Lajoie (sports)
NASTASSJA
Kinski (arts/ent.)
NAT
"King" Cole (arts/ent.)
Fleischer (sports)
Holman (sports)
Turner (misc.)
NATALIA
Makarova (arts/ent.)
NATALIE
Cole (arts/ent.)
Merchant (arts/ent.)
Wood (arts/ent.)
NATASHA
Richardson (arts/ent.)
NATHAN
Hale (govt./mil.)
Leopold (misc.)
Milstein (arts/ent.)
NATHANAEL
West (arts/ent.)
NATHANIEL
Bacon (govt./mil.)
Benchley (arts/ent.)
Currier (arts/ent.)
Hawthorne (arts/ent.)
NAUM
Gabo (arts/ent.)
NEAL
Schon (arts/ent.)
NED
Beatty (arts/ent.)
Buntline (arts/ent.)
Rorem (arts/ent.)
Sparks (arts/ent.)
NEDRA
Talley (arts/ent.)
Tyre (arts/ent.)
NEIL
Armstrong (pion./exp.)
Diamond (arts/ent.)
Patrick Harris (arts/ent.)
Jordan (arts/ent.)
Peart (arts/ent.)
Sedaka (arts/ent.)
Simon (arts/ent.)

Tennant (arts/ent.)
Young (arts/ent.)
NELL
Carter (arts/ent.)
Gwyn (arts/ent.)
NELLA
Walker (arts/ent.)
NELLIE
Bly (arts/ent.)
Fox (arts/ent.)
Melba (arts/ent.)
Tayloe Ross (govt./mil.)
NELLY
Sachs (arts/ent.)
NELSON
Aldrich (govt./mil.)
Algren (arts/ent.)
Demille (arts/ent.)
Doubleday (business)
Eddy (arts/ent.)
Mandela (govt./mil.)
Riddle (arts/ent.)
Rockefeller (govt./mil.)
NENEH
Cherry (arts/ent.)
NESTOR
Almendros (arts/ent.)
NEVIL
Shute (arts/ent.)
NEVILLE
Brand (arts/ent.)
Chamberlain (govt./
mil.)
NEWT
Gingrich (govt./mil.)
NGAIO
Marsh (arts/ent.)
NIA
Long (arts/ent.)
Peeples (arts/ent.)
NICCOLO, NICCOLÒ
Machiavelli (rel./phil.)
Paganini (arts/ent.)
NICHELLE
Nichols (arts/ent.)
NICHOLAS
Biddle (business)
Brady (govt./mil.)
Meyer (arts/ent.)
Pileggi (arts/ent.)
Ray (arts/ent.)
Rowe (arts/ent.)
NICK
Adams (arts/ent.)
Gilder (arts/ent.)
Lowe (arts/ent.)
Nolte (arts/ent.)

NICKOLAS
Ashford (arts/ent.)
NICOL
Williamson (arts/ent.)
NICOLA
Sacco (govt./mil.)
NICOLAE
Ceauşescu (govt./
   mil.)
NICOLAES
Maes (arts/ent.)
NICOLAS
Cage (arts/ent.)
Freeling (arts/ent.)
De Malebranche (rel./
   phil.)
Poussin (arts/ent.)
Roeg (arts/ent.)
NICOLAUS
Copernicus (sci./inv.)
NICOLE
Eggert (arts/ent.)
Kidman (arts/ent.)
NICOLETTE
Larson (arts/ent.)
NICOLLETTE
Sheridan (arts/ent.)
NICOLÒ
Amati (arts/ent.)
NIELS
Bohr (sci./inv.)
NIGEL
Bruce (arts/ent.)
Davenport (arts/ent.)
Havers (arts/ent.)
Patrick (arts/ent.)
NIK
Kershaw (arts/ent.)
NIKI
Lauda (sports)
Taylor (arts/ent.)
NIKITA
Khrushchev (govt./
   mil.)
NIKKI
Giovanni (arts/ent.)
Sixx (arts/ent.)
NIKOLA
Tesla (sci./inv.)
NIKOLAUS
Otto (sci./inv.)
NIKOLAY
Bukharin (govt./mil.)
Gogol (arts/ent.)
Medtner (arts/ent.)
Rimsky-Korsakov (arts/
   ent.)

NIKOS
Kazantzakis (arts/ent.)
NILE
Rodgers (arts/ent.)
NILS
Lofgren (arts/ent.)
NINA
Foch (arts/ent.)
Hagen (arts/ent.)
Ricci (arts/ent.)
Simone (arts/ent.)
NINO
Rota (arts/ent.)
Tempo (arts/ent.)
NINON
De Lenclos (misc.)
NIPSEY
Russell (arts/ent.)
NITA
Naldi (arts/ent.)
Talbot (arts/ent.)
NIVEN
Busch (arts/ent.)
NOAH
Beery (arts/ent.)
Beery, Jr. (arts/ent.)
Webster (arts/ent.)
Chomsky (arts/ent.)
NOËL
Coward (arts/ent.)
NOLAN
Ryan (sports)
NONA
Gaye (arts/ent.)
Hendryx (arts/ent.)
NORA
Bayes (arts/ent.)
Dunn (arts/ent.)
Ephron (arts/ent.)
NORM
Cash (sports)
Crosby (arts/ent.)
Van Brocklin (sports)
NORMA
Kamali (arts/ent.)
Klein (arts/ent.)
Shearer (arts/ent.)
Talmadge (arts/ent.)
Zimmer (arts/ent.)
NORMAN
Angell (arts/ent.)
Cousins (arts/ent.)
Dello Joio (arts/ent.)
Douglas (arts/ent.)
Fell (arts/ent.)
Bel Geddes (arts/ent.)
Jewison (arts/ent.)

Krasna (arts/ent.)
Lear (arts/ent.)
Mailer (arts/ent.)
Minetta (govt./mil.)
Mingo (arts/ent.)
Norell (arts/ent.)
Parkinson (arts/ent.)
Vincent Peale (arts/ent.)
Podhoretz (arts/ent.)
Rockwell (arts/ent.)
Schwarzkopf (govt./
   mil.)
Taurog (arts/ent.)
Thomas (govt./mil.)
NORRIS
McWhirter (arts/ent.)
NORTHROP
Frye (arts/ent.)
NORTON
Simon (business)
NOVA
Pilbeam (arts/ent.)
NUNNALLY
Johnson (arts/ent.)
NYDIA
Westman (arts/ent.)
O.
Henry (arts/ent.)
O. J.
Simpson (sports)
OCTAVIO
Paz (arts/ent.)
ODILON
Redon (arts/ent.)
ODYSSEUS
Elytis (arts/ent.)
OGDEN
Nash (arts/ent.)
OIL CAN
Boyd (sports)
O'KELLY
Isley (arts/ent.)
OLAUDAH
Equiano (misc.)
OLD HOSS
Radbourn (sports)
OLE
Olsen (arts/ent.)
OLEG
Cassini (arts/ent.)
OLETA
Adams (arts/ent.)
OLGA
Baclanova (arts/ent.)
Korbut (sports)
OLIN
Dutra (sports)

OLIVER
Cromwell (govt./mil.)
Goldsmith (arts/ent.)
Hardy (arts/ent.)
Wendell Holmes (arts/
ent.)
Wendell Holmes (govt./
mil.)
La Farge (sci./inv.)
North (govt./mil.)
Hazard Perry (govt./
mil.)
Reed (arts/ent.)
Stone (arts/ent.)
Tambo (govt./mil.)
Fisher Winchester
(business)

OLIVIA
D'abo (arts/ent.)
De Havilland (arts/
ent.)
Hussey (arts/ent.)
Newton-John (arts/
ent.)

OLIVIER
Messiaen (arts/ent.)

OLLIE
Matson (sports)

OLYMPIA
Dukakis (arts/ent.)

OMAR
Bradley (govt./mil.)
Khayyam (arts/ent.)
Sharif (arts/ent.)

ONA
Munson (arts/ent.)

OONA
Chaplin (arts/ent.)

OPRAH
Winfrey (arts/ent.)

ORAL
Roberts (rel./phil.)

OREL
Hershiser (sports)

ORLANDO
Cepeda (sports)
Patterson (arts/ent.)

ORNETTE
Coleman (arts/ent.)

ORRIN
Hatch (govt./mil.)

ORSON
Bean (arts/ent.)
Scott Card (arts/ent.)
Welles (arts/ent.)

ORVILLE
Redenbacher (business)

Wright (sci./inv.)

OSA
Massen (arts/ent.)

OSCAR
Charleston (sports)
De La Renta (arts/ent.)
Hammerstein II (arts/
ent.)
Handlin (arts/ent.)
Hijuelos (arts/ent.)
Homolka (arts/ent.)
Levant (arts/ent.)
Lewis (sci./inv.)
Peterson (arts/ent.)
Pettiford (arts/ent.)
Robertson (sports)
Serlin (arts/ent.)
Straus (arts/ent.)
Tschirky (business)
Wilde (arts/ent.)

OSIP
Mandelstam (arts/ent.)

OSKAR
Kokoschka (arts/ent.)
Werner (arts/ent.)

OSSIE
Davis (arts/ent.)

OSWALD
Spengler (rel./phil.)
Villard (arts/ent.)

OTHMAR
Ammann (arts/ent.)

OTIS
Chandler (business)
Redding (arts/ent.)

OTTMAR
Mergenthaler (sci./inv.)

OTTO
Bismarck (govt./mil.)
Dix (arts/ent.)
Graham (sports)
Hahn (sci./inv.)
Klemperer (arts/ent.)
Kruger (arts/ent.)
Nicolai (arts/ent.)
Preminger (arts/ent.)
Stern (sci./inv.)

OTTORINO
Respighi (arts/ent.)

OVETA
Culp Hobby (business)

OVID
Demaris (arts/ent.)

OWEN
Chamberlain (sci./inv.)
Davis (arts/ent.)
Wister (arts/ent.)

OZZIE
Guillen (sports)
Nelson (arts/ent.)
Newsome (sports)
Smith (sports)
Virgil (sports)

OZZY
Osbourne (arts/ent.)

P. C.
Wren (arts/ent.)

P. D.
James (arts/ent.)

P. G.
Wodehouse (arts/ent.)

P. J.
O'Rourke (arts/ent.)

P. L.
Travers (arts/ent.)

P. T.
Barnum (arts/ent.)

PAAVO
Nurmi (sports)

PABLO
Casals (arts/ent.)
Neruda (arts/ent.)
Picasso (arts/ent.)

PACO
Delucia (arts/ent.)

PADDY
Chayefsky or
Chayevsky (arts/
ent.)
Driscoll (sports)
Ryan (sports)

PAGE
Hannah (arts/ent.)

PAIGE
Turco (arts/ent.)

PALOMA
Picasso (arts/ent.)

PAM
Dawber (arts/ent.)
Gems (arts/ent.)
Shriver (sports)
Tillis (arts/ent.)

PAMELA
Anderson (arts/ent.)
Britton (arts/ent.)
Sue Martin (arts/ent.)
Reed (arts/ent.)
Tiffin (arts/ent.)

PANCHO
Gonzales (sports)
Villa (misc.)

PAOLO
Uccello (arts/ent.)
Veronese (arts/ent.)

PAPPY
Boyington (misc.)
PAR
Lagerkvist (arts/ent.)
PARK
Overall (arts/ent.)
PARKER
Stevenson (arts/ent.)
Baer (arts/ent.)
PARNELLI
Jones (sports)
PAT
Benatar (arts/ent.)
Boone (arts/ent.)
Buchanan (govt./mil.)
Buttram (arts/ent.)
Cash (sports)
Conroy (arts/ent.)
Garrett (misc.)
Harrington, Jr. (arts/
ent.)
Hingle (arts/ent.)
Metheny (arts/ent.)
Morita (arts/ent.)
O'Brien (arts/ent.)
Oliphant (arts/ent.)
Paulsen (arts/ent.)
Riley (sports)
Roberts (govt./mil.)
Robertson (rel./phil.)
Sajak (arts/ent.)
Sullivan (arts/ent.)
Summerall (sports)
Travers (arts/ent.)
PATRICE
Munsil (arts/ent.)
Rushen (arts/ent.)
PATRICIA
Arquette (arts/ent.)
D. Cornwell (arts/
ent.)
Highsmith (arts/ent.)
Kalember (arts/ent.)
McBride (arts/ent.)
Neal (arts/ent.)
Nixon (govt./mil.)
Richardson (arts/ent.)
Schroeder (govt./mil.)
Wettig (arts/ent.)
PATRICK
Bergin (arts/ent.)
Dempsey (arts/ent.)
Dennis (arts/ent.)
Duffy (arts/ent.)
Ewing (sports)
Henry (govt./mil.)
Leahy (govt./mil.)

MacNee (arts/ent.)
McGoohan (arts/ent.)
O'Neal (arts/ent.)
H. Pearse (misc.)
Swayze (arts/ent.)
White (arts/ent.)
PATSY
Cline (arts/ent.)
Kelly (arts/ent.)
Kensit (arts/ent.)
PATTI
Austin (arts/ent.)
Davis (arts/ent.)
Labelle (arts/ent.)
Lupone (arts/ent.)
Page (arts/ent.)
Scialfa (arts/ent.)
Smith (arts/ent.)
PATTY
Andrews (arts/ent.)
Duke-Astin (arts/ent.)
Hearst (misc.)
Loveless (arts/ent.)
Smyth (arts/ent.)
PAUL
Anka (arts/ent.)
Bartel (arts/ent.)
Bowles (arts/ent.)
Brown (sports)
Butterfield (arts/ent.)
Carrack (arts/ent.)
Cézanne (arts/ent.)
Claudel (arts/ent.)
Creston (arts/ent.)
Delaroche (arts/ent.)
Desmond (arts/ent.)
Douglas (arts/ent.)
Dukas (arts/ent.)
Dunbar (arts/ent.)
Éluard (arts/ent.)
E. Erdman (arts/ent.)
Ford (arts/ent.)
Gallico (arts/ent.)
Gauguin (arts/ent.)
Michael Glaser (arts/
ent.)
E. Green (arts/ent.)
Harvey (arts/ent.)
Henreid (arts/ent.)
Heyse (arts/ent.)
Hindemith (arts/ent.)
Von Hindenburg (govt./
mil.)
Hogan (arts/ent.)
Horgan (arts/ent.)
Hornung (sports)
Kantner (arts/ent.)

Klee (arts/ent.)
Lukas (arts/ent.)
Lynde (arts/ent.)
Masson (misc.)
Mauriat (arts/ent.)
Mazursky (arts/ent.)
McCartney (arts/ent.)
Molitor (sports)
Morrissey (arts/ent.)
Müller (sci./inv.)
Muni (arts/ent.)
Newman (arts/ent.)
Prudhomme (arts/ent.)
Reiser (arts/ent.)
Von Reuter (arts/ent.)
Revere (arts/ent.)
Revere (govt./mil.)
Robeson (arts/ent.)
Rodgers (arts/ent.)
Runyan (sports)
Sand (arts/ent.)
Schrader (arts/ent.)
Scofield (arts/ent.)
Shaffer (arts/ent.)
Simon (arts/ent.)
Simon (govt./mil.)
Sorvino (arts/ent.)
Stanley (arts/ent.)
Stookey (arts/ent.)
Strand (arts/ent.)
Taylor (arts/ent.)
Theroux (arts/ent.)
Tillich (rel./phil.)
Tsongas (govt./mil.)
Valery (arts/ent.)
Verhoeven (arts/ent.)
Verlaine (arts/ent.)
Waner (sports)
Warfield (sports)
Weston (arts/ent.)
Whiteman (arts/ent.)
Williams (arts/ent.)
Winchell (arts/ent.)
Winfield (arts/ent.)
Young (arts/ent.)
Zindel (arts/ent.)
PAULA
Abdul (arts/ent.)
Poundstone (arts/ent.)
Prentiss (arts/ent.)
Zahn (arts/ent.)
PAULETTE
Goddard (arts/ent.)
PAULINA
Porizkova (arts/ent.)
PAULINE
Betz (sports)

Collins (arts/ent.)
Frederick (arts/ent.)
Kael (arts/ent.)
Trigere (arts/ent.)
PAULY
Shore (arts/ent.)
PEABO
Bryson (arts/ent.)
PEARL
Bailey (arts/ent.)
S. Buck (arts/ent.)
White (arts/ent.)
PEDRO
Almodóvar (arts/ent.)
Armendariz (arts/ent.)
Cabral (pion./exp.)
Guerrero (sports)
De Valdivia (govt./mil.)
PEE WEE
Herman (arts/ent.)
King (arts/ent.)
Reese (sports)
Russell (arts/ent.)
PEGEEN
Fitzgerald (arts/ent.)
PEGGIE
Castle (arts/ent.)
PEGGY
Ashcroft (arts/ent.)
Cass (arts/ent.)
Dow (arts/ent.)
Fleming (sports)
Ann Garner (arts/ent.)
Guggenheim (misc.)
Lee (arts/ent.)
Lennon (arts/ent.)
Lipton (arts/ent.)
Parish (arts/ent.)
Ryan (arts/ent.)
Wood (arts/ent.)
PENELOPE
Gilliatt (arts/ent.)
Ann Miller (arts/ent.)
Mortimer (arts/ent.)
Spheeris (arts/ent.)
PENN
Jillette (arts/ent.)
PENNY
Marshall (arts/ent.)
Singleton (arts/ent.)
PEPPER
Martin (sports)
PER
Wahlöö (arts/ent.)
PERCY
Adlon (arts/ent.)
Bridgman (sci./inv.)

Faith (arts/ent.)
Bysshe Shelley (arts/ent.)
Sledge (arts/ent.)
PEREZ
Prado (arts/ent.)
PERLE
Mesta (misc.)
PERNELL
Roberts (arts/ent.)
PERRY
Como (arts/ent.)
Ellis (arts/ent.)
Farrell (arts/ent.)
King (arts/ent.)
PERSIS
Khambatta (arts/ent.)
PETE
Browning (sports)
Incaviglia (sports)
Maravich (sports)
Pihos (sports)
Reiser (sports)
Rose (sports)
Rozelle (sports)
Sampras (sports)
Seeger (arts/ent.)
Townshend (arts/ent.)
Vuckovich (sports)
Wilson (govt./mil.)
PETER
Allen (arts/ent.)
Arno (arts/ent.)
Benchley (arts/ent.)
Bogdanovich (arts/ent.)
Bonerz (arts/ent.)
Boyle (arts/ent.)
Brook (arts/ent.)
Cetera (arts/ent.)
Coyote (arts/ent.)
Criss (arts/ent.)
Cushing (arts/ent.)
Davies (arts/ent.)
Debye (sci./inv.)
Deluise (arts/ent.)
Devries (arts/ent.)
Duchin (arts/ent.)
Carl Fabergé (arts/ent.)
Falk (arts/ent.)
Finch (arts/ent.)
Fleming (sports)
Fonda (arts/ent.)
Frampton (arts/ent.)
Gabriel (arts/ent.)
Gallagher (arts/ent.)
Gennaro (arts/ent.)
Goldmark (sci./inv.)

Graves (arts/ent.)
Greenaway (arts/ent.)
Guber (arts/ent.)
Hall (arts/ent.)
Horton (arts/ent.)
Hyams (arts/ent.)
Jennings (arts/ent.)
Lawford (arts/ent.)
Lely (arts/ent.)
Lorre (arts/ent.)
Marshall (arts/ent.)
Martins (arts/ent.)
Matthiessen (arts/ent.)
Max (arts/ent.)
Murphy (arts/ent.)
Nero (arts/ent.)
Nichols (arts/ent.)
Noone (arts/ent.)
Onorati (arts/ent.)
O'Toole (arts/ent.)
Pears (arts/ent.)
Pulitzer (business)
Quennell (arts/ent.)
Riegert (arts/ent.)
Roget (arts/ent.)
Rubens (arts/ent.)
Scolari (arts/ent.)
Sellars (arts/ent.)
Sellers (arts/ent.)
Shaffer (arts/ent.)
Straub (arts/ent.)
Strauss (arts/ent.)
Stuyvesant (govt./mil.)
Taylor (arts/ent.)
Ilyich Tchaikovsky (arts/ent.)
Tork (arts/ent.)
Tosh (arts/ent.)
Ueberroth (sports)
Ustinov (arts/ent.)
Weir (arts/ent.)
Weiss (arts/ent.)
Weller (arts/ent.)
Wolf (arts/ent.)
Yarrow (arts/ent.)
PETRA
Kelly (govt./mil.)
PETULA
Clark (arts/ent.)
PHIL
Collins (arts/ent.)
Donahue (arts/ent.)
Esposito (sports)
Everly (arts/ent.)
Foster (arts/ent.)
Gramm (govt./mil.)
Hartman (arts/ent.)

Joanou (arts/ent.)
Lesh (arts/ent.)
Lynott (arts/ent.)
May (arts/ent.)
Niekro (sports)
Nowlan (arts/ent.)
Ochs (arts/ent.)
Silvers (arts/ent.)
Spector (arts/ent.)
PHILIP
Ahn (arts/ent.)
W. Anderson (sci./
inv.)
Bailey (arts/ent.)
Barry (arts/ent.)
Bosco (arts/ent.)
K. Dick (arts/ent.)
Dunne (arts/ent.)
José Farmer (arts/ent.)
Freneau (arts/ent.)
Glass (arts/ent.)
Hench (sci./inv.)
Johnson (arts/ent.)
Kaufman (arts/ent.)
Larkin (arts/ent.)
Massinger (arts/ent.)
Roth (arts/ent.)
Michael Thomas (arts/
ent.)
PHILIPPE
Pétain (govt./mil.)
PHILLIP
Noyce (arts/ent.)
Sidney (govt./mil.)
PHILLIPE
De Broca (arts/ent.)
PHILLIS
Wheatley (arts/ent.)
PHINEAS
Newborn (arts/ent.)
PHOEBE
Cary (arts/ent.)
Cates (arts/ent.)
Snow (arts/ent.)
PHYLICIA
Rashad (arts/ent.)
PHYLLIS
Brooks (arts/ent.)
Diller (arts/ent.)
George (arts/ent.)
Kirk (arts/ent.)
McGinley (arts/ent.)
McGuire (arts/ent.)
Schlafly (govt./mil.)
A. Whitney (arts/ent.)
PIA
Zadora (arts/ent.)

PIE
Traynor (sports)
PIER
Angeli (arts/ent.)
Paolo Pasolini (arts/ent.)
PIERCE
Brosnan (arts/ent.)
PIERRE
Abélard (rel./phil.)
Balmain (arts/ent.)
Beauregard (govt./mil.)
Bonnard (arts/ent.)
Boulez (arts/ent.)
Boulle (arts/ent.)
Cardin (arts/ent.)
Corneille (arts/ent.)
Culliford (arts/ent.)
Curie (sci./inv.)
L'Enfant (arts/ent.)
Laclos (arts/ent.)
Monteux (arts/ent.)
Auguste Renoir (arts/
ent.)
De Ronsard (arts/ent.)
Salinger (govt./mil.)
Teilhard de Chardin
(rel./phil.)
Trudeau (govt./mil.)
PIET
Mondrian (arts/ent.)
PIETER
Botha (govt./mil.)
Bruegel (arts/ent.)
PIETRO
Mascagni (arts/ent.)
PIGMEAT
Markham (arts/ent.)
PINCHAS
Zukerman (arts/ent.)
PINETOP
Smith (arts/ent.)
PINKY
Lee (arts/ent.)
PIPER
Laurie (arts/ent.)
PLÁCIDO
Domingo (arts/ent.)
POLA
Negri (arts/ent.)
POLLY
Bergen (arts/ent.)
Draper (arts/ent.)
Holliday (arts/ent.)
PONCE
De León (pion./exp.)
PONTIUS
Pilate (govt./mil.)

POP
Warner (sports)
PORFIRIO
Díaz (govt./mil.)
Rubirosa (misc.)
PORTER
Wagoner (arts/ent.)
POTTER
Stewart (govt./mil.)
POUL
Anderson (arts/ent.)
POWERS
Boothe (arts/ent.)
PRESTON
Sturges (arts/ent.)
PRIMO
Carnera (sports)
Levi (arts/ent.)
PRISCILLA
Barnes (arts/ent.)
Presley (arts/ent.)
PROSPER
Merimée (arts/ent.)
PRUNELLA
Scales (arts/ent.)
PYOTR
Kropotkin (govt./
mil.)
QUENTIN
Crisp (arts/ent.)
Massys (arts/ent.)
Tarantino (arts/ent.)
QUINCY
Jones (arts/ent.)
Porter (arts/ent.)
QUINN
Cummings (arts/ent.)
R.
Crumb (arts/ent.)
R. D.
Laing (misc.)
R. BUCKMINSTER
Fuller (sci./inv.)
RABBIT
Maranville (sports)
RABINDRANATH
Tagore (arts/ent.)
RACHEL
Carson (sci./inv.)
Field (arts/ent.)
Hunter (arts/ent.)
Jackson (govt./mil.)
Roberts (arts/ent.)
Ticotin (arts/ent.)
Ward (arts/ent.)
RAE
Dawn Chong (arts/ent.)

RAF
Vallone (arts/ent.)
RAFAEL
Palmeiro (sports)
Sabatini (arts/ent.)
Santana (sports)
Trujillo Molina (govt./
mil.)
RAFER
Johnson (sports)
RAGS
Ragland (arts/ent.)
RAIN
Phoenix (arts/ent.)
Pryor (arts/ent.)
RAINER
Werner Fassbinder
(arts/ent.)
Maria Rilke (arts/ent.)
RAISA
Gorbachev (govt./mil.)
RALPH
Abernathy (govt./mil.)
Bakshi (arts/ent.)
Bellamy (arts/ent.)
Branca (sports)
Bunche (govt./mil.)
Edwards (arts/ent.)
Ellison (arts/ent.)
Waldo Emerson (arts/
ent.)
Houk (sports)
Kiner (sports)
Lauren (arts/ent.)
Macchio (arts/ent.)
Meeker (arts/ent.)
Nader (govt./mil.)
Richardson (arts/ent.)
Vaughan Williams (arts/
ent.)
Waite (arts/ent.)
RAMON
Novarro (arts/ent.)
RAMSEY
Clark (govt./mil.)
Lewis (arts/ent.)
RANCE
Howard (arts/ent.)
RANDA
Haines (arts/ent.)
RANDAL
Kleiser (arts/ent.)
RANDALL
Jarrell (arts/ent.)
Thompson (arts/ent.)
RANDI
Oakes (arts/ent.)

RANDOLPH
Mantooth (arts/ent.)
Scott (arts/ent.)
RANDY
Debarge (arts/ent.)
Meisner (arts/ent.)
Newman (arts/ent.)
Owen (arts/ent.)
Quaid (arts/ent.)
Shilts (arts/ent.)
Travis (arts/ent.)
Vanwarmer (arts/ent.)
White (sports)
RANSOM
Olds (business)
RAOUL
Dufy (arts/ent.)
Wallenberg (govt./mil.)
Walsh (arts/ent.)
RAQUEL
Welch (arts/ent.)
RAUL
Julia (arts/ent.)
Ramirez (sports)
RAVI
Shankar (arts/ent.)
RAY
Anthony (arts/ent.)
Stannard Baker (arts/
ent.)
Bloch (arts/ent.)
Bolger (arts/ent.)
Bradbury (arts/ent.)
Charles (arts/ent.)
Conniff (arts/ent.)
Dandridge (sports)
Danton (arts/ent.)
Davies (arts/ent.)
Eberle (arts/ent.)
Evans (arts/ent.)
Goulding (arts/ent.)
Guy (sports)
Kroc (business)
Liotta (arts/ent.)
Manzarek (arts/ent.)
Milland (arts/ent.)
Nitschke (sports)
Parker, Jr. (arts/ent.)
Price (arts/ent.)
Schalk (sports)
Sharkey (arts/ent.)
Stevens (arts/ent.)
RAYMOND
Berry (sports)
Burr (arts/ent.)
Carver (arts/ent.)
Chandler (arts/ent.)

Flynn (govt./mil.)
Hood (arts/ent.)
Massey (arts/ent.)
Poincaré (govt./mil.)
Spruance (govt./mil.)
Gram Swing (arts/ent.)
RAZZY
Bailey (arts/ent.)
REBA
McEntire (arts/ent.)
REBBIE
Jackson (arts/ent.)
REBECCA
De Mornay (arts/ent.)
Schaeffer (arts/ent.)
West (arts/ent.)
RED
Allen (arts/ent.)
Auerbach (sports)
Barber (sports)
Buttons (arts/ent.)
Faber (sports)
Foley (arts/ent.)
Grange (sports)
Holzman (sports)
Nichols (arts/ent.)
Norvo (arts/ent.)
Rolfe (sports)
Ruffing (sports)
Skelton (arts/ent.)
Smith (sports)
REDD
Foxx (arts/ent.)
REESE
Witherspoon (arts/
ent.)
REGGIE
Jackson (sports)
REGINA
Resnik (arts/ent.)
REGINALD
Beckwith (arts/ent.)
Denny (arts/ent.)
Owen (arts/ent.)
Wingate (govt./mil.)
REGINE
Crespin (arts/ent.)
REGIS
Philbin (arts/ent.)
Toomey (arts/ent.)
REINHARD
Heydrich (govt./mil.)
REINHOLD
Glière (arts/ent.)
Niebuhr (rel./phil.)
REMBRANDT
Peale (arts/ent.)

RENATA
Scotto (arts/ent.)
Tebaldi (arts/ent.)
RENATO
Dulbecco (sci./inv.)
RENE, RENÉ
Auberjonois (arts/ent.)
Clair (arts/ent.)
Clément (arts/ent.)
Descartes (rel./phil.)
Dubos (sci./inv.)
Lalique (arts/ent.)
Levesque (govt./mil.)
Magritte (arts/ent.)
Russo (arts/ent.)
RENÉE
Adorée (arts/ent.)
RENNY
Harlin (arts/ent.)
REX
Allen (arts/ent.)
Allen, Jr. (arts/ent.)
Bell (arts/ent.)
Harrison (arts/ent.)
Ingram (arts/ent.)
Reason (arts/ent.)
Reed (arts/ent.)
Smith (arts/ent.)
Stout (arts/ent.)
REYNOLDS
Price (arts/ent.)
REZA
Shah Pahlavi (govt./mil.)
RHEA
Perlman (arts/ent.)
RHONDA
Fleming (arts/ent.)
RIC
Ocasek (arts/ent.)
RICARDO
Cortez (arts/ent.)
Montalban (arts/ent.)
RICCARDO
Muti (arts/ent.)
RICH
Little (arts/ent.)
RICHARD
Adams (arts/ent.)
Dean Anderson (arts/ent.)
Arlen (arts/ent.)
Armour (arts/ent.)
Attenborough (arts/ent.)
Avedon (arts/ent.)
Bach (arts/ent.)
Barthelmess (arts/ent.)
Basehart (arts/ent.)

Belzer (arts/ent.)
Benjamin (arts/ent.)
Branson (business)
Brautigan (arts/ent.)
Brooks (arts/ent.)
Burton (arts/ent.)
Francis Burton (pion./exp.)
Byrd (pion./exp.)
Calkins (arts/ent.)
Carpenter (arts/ent.)
Castellano (arts/ent.)
Chamberlain (arts/ent.)
B. Cheney (govt./mil.)
Clayderman (arts/ent.)
Condon (arts/ent.)
Crenna (arts/ent.)
Daley (govt./mil.)
Henry Dana (arts/ent.)
Darman (govt./mil.)
Dawson (arts/ent.)
Denning (arts/ent.)
Donner (arts/ent.)
Dreyfuss (arts/ent.)
Dysart (arts/ent.)
Eberhart (arts/ent.)
Feynman (sci./inv.)
Fleischer (arts/ent.)
Gatling (sci./inv.)
Gephardt (govt./mil.)
Gere (arts/ent.)
Grieco (arts/ent.)
Harris (arts/ent.)
Hell (arts/ent.)
Hofstadter (arts/ent.)
Hunt (arts/ent.)
Johnson (govt./mil.)
Jordan (arts/ent.)
Kiel (arts/ent.)
Kiley (arts/ent.)
Kline (arts/ent.)
Krafft-Ebing (sci./inv.)
Leakey (sci./inv.)
Lewis (arts/ent.)
Linklater (arts/ent.)
Llewellyn (arts/ent.)
Lockridge (arts/ent.)
Loeb (misc.)
Marquand (arts/ent.)
Marx (arts/ent.)
Matheson (arts/ent.)
Moll (arts/ent.)
Mulligan (arts/ent.)
Milhous Nixon (govt./mil.)
Outcault (arts/ent.)
Petty (sports)

Phelps (sports)
Pryor (arts/ent.)
Ramirez (misc.)
Rodgers (arts/ent.)
Roundtree (arts/ent.)
S. Salant (arts/ent.)
Sheridan (arts/ent.)
Simmons (misc.)
Simon (business)
Steele (arts/ent.)
Strauss (arts/ent.)
Thomas (arts/ent.)
Thornburgh (govt./mil.)
Todd (arts/ent.)
Upjohn (arts/ent.)
Wagner (arts/ent.)
Widmark (arts/ent.)
Wilbur (arts/ent.)
Wright (arts/ent.)
RICHIE
Havens (arts/ent.)
Sambora (arts/ent.)
RICK
Aguilera (sports)
Astley (arts/ent.)
Barry (sports)
Cerone (sports)
Danko (arts/ent.)
Dees (arts/ent.)
Derringer (arts/ent.)
Ferrell (sports)
James (arts/ent.)
Moranis (arts/ent.)
Nielsen (arts/ent.)
Reuschel (sports)
Rhoden (sports)
Springfield (arts/ent.)
Wakeman (arts/ent.)
RICKEY
Henderson (sports)
RICKI
Lake (arts/ent.)
RICKIE
Lee Jones (arts/ent.)
RICKY
Nelson (arts/ent.)
Schroder (arts/ent.)
Van Shelton (arts/ent.)
Skaggs (arts/ent.)
RIDDICK
Bowe (sports)
RIDLEY
Scott (arts/ent.)
RING
Lardner (arts/ent.)
Lardner, Jr. (arts/ent.)

RINGO
  Starr (arts/ent.)
RIP
  Taylor (arts/ent.)
  Torn (arts/ent.)
RITA
  Mae Brown (arts/ent.)
  Coolidge (arts/ent.)
  Gam (arts/ent.)
  Hayworth (arts/ent.)
  Moreno (arts/ent.)
  Rudner (arts/ent.)
  Tushingham (arts/ent.)
RITCHIE
  Blackmore (arts/ent.)
  Valens (arts/ent.)
RIVER
  Phoenix (arts/ent.)
ROALD
  Amundsen (pion./exp.)
  Dahl (arts/ent.)
  Hoffman (sci./inv.)
ROB
  Camiletti (arts/ent.)
  Deer (sports)
  Halford (arts/ent.)
  Lowe (arts/ent.)
  Morrow (arts/ent.)
  Pilatus (arts/ent.)
  Reiner (arts/ent.)
ROBBEN
  Ford (arts/ent.)
ROBBIE
  Dupree (arts/ent.)
  Robertson (arts/ent.)
ROBBY
  Benson (arts/ent.)
  Krieger (arts/ent.)
  Thompson (sports)
ROBERT
  Adam (arts/ent.)
  Aitken (arts/ent.)
  Alda (arts/ent.)
  Aldrich (arts/ent.)
  Altman (arts/ent.)
  Anderson (arts/ent.)
  Benchley (arts/ent.)
  Benton (arts/ent.)
  Blake (arts/ent.)
  Bloch (arts/ent.)
  Bly (arts/ent.)
  Bolt (arts/ent.)
  Bork (govt./mil.)
  Bresson (arts/ent.)
  Bridges (arts/ent.)
  Browning (arts/ent.)
  Bunsen (sci./inv.)

Burns (arts/ent.)
Campin (arts/ent.)
Coles (arts/ent.)
Conrad (arts/ent.)
Cray (arts/ent.)
Culp (arts/ent.)
Cummings (arts/ent.)
Davi (arts/ent.)
De Niro (arts/ent.)
Donat (arts/ent.)
Downey, Jr. (arts/ent.)
Duvall (arts/ent.)
Englund (arts/ent.)
Evans (arts/ent.)
Joseph Flaherty (arts/
  ent.)
Florey (arts/ent.)
Fripp (arts/ent.)
Frost (arts/ent.)
Fulghum (arts/ent.)
Fulton (sci./inv.)
Goddard (sci./inv.)
Goulet (arts/ent.)
Graves (arts/ent.)
Guillaume (arts/ent.)
Hayden (arts/ent.)
Hays (arts/ent.)
Heilbroner (arts/ent.)
A. Heinlein (arts/ent.)
Henri (arts/ent.)
Hofstadter (sci./inv.)
Holley (sci./inv.)
Horton (arts/ent.)
G. Ingersoll (M)
Koffler Jarvik (sci./inv.)
Joffrey (arts/ent.)
John (arts/ent.)
Kane (arts/ent.)
Keeshan (arts/ent.)
F. Kennedy (govt./mil.)
Klein (arts/ent.)
La Follette (govt./mil.)
E. Lee (govt./mil.)
Sean Leonard (arts/ent.)
Loggia (arts/ent.)
Lowell (arts/ent.)
Ludlum (arts/ent.)
MacNeil (arts/ent.)
Mapplethorpe (arts/
  ent.)
S. McNamara (govt./
  mil.)
Merrill (arts/ent.)
Millikan (sci./inv.)
Mills (arts/ent.)
Mitchum (arts/ent.)
Montgomery (arts/ent.)

Moog (sci./inv.)
Morley (arts/ent.)
Morris (arts/ent.)
Morse (arts/ent.)
Mosbacher (business)
Motherwell (arts/ent.)
Mugabe (govt./mil.)
Von Musil (arts/ent.)
Newton (arts/ent.)
Novak (arts/ent.)
Palmer (arts/ent.)
B. Parker (arts/ent.)
Peary (pion./exp.)
Plant (arts/ent.)
Preston (arts/ent.)
Rauschenberg (arts/
  ent.)
Redford (arts/ent.)
Reed (arts/ent.)
Ripley (arts/ent.)
Riskin (arts/ent.)
Rossen (arts/ent.)
Ruark (arts/ent.)
Ryan (arts/ent.)
Schuller (rel./phil.)
Schumann (arts/ent.)
W. Service (arts/ent.)
Shaw (arts/ent.)
E. Sherwood (arts/ent.)
Silverberg (arts/ent.)
Smith (arts/ent.)
Solow (misc.)
Southey (arts/ent.)
Stack (arts/ent.)
Sterling (arts/ent.)
Louis Stevenson (arts/
  ent.)
Stroud (misc.)
Taylor (arts/ent.)
Towne (arts/ent.)
Townsend (arts/ent.)
Urich (arts/ent.)
Vaughn (arts/ent.)
Wagner (arts/ent.)
Walker (arts/ent.)
James Waller (arts/ent.)
Walpole (govt./mil.)
Ward (arts/ent.)
Penn Warren (arts/ent.)
Wilder (arts/ent.)
Wise (arts/ent.)
Young (arts/ent.)
Zemeckis (arts/ent.)
ROBERTA
  Flack (arts/ent.)
ROBERTO
  Clemente (sports)

Duran (sports)
Rossellini (arts/ent.)
ROBERTSON
Davies (arts/ent.)
ROBIN
Cook (arts/ent.)
Gibb (arts/ent.)
Givens (arts/ent.)
Leach (arts/ent.)
Moore (arts/ent.)
Quivers (arts/ent.)
Roberts (sports)
Trower (arts/ent.)
Williams (arts/ent.)
Wright (arts/ent.)
Yount (sports)
Zander (arts/ent.)
ROBINSON
Jeffers (arts/ent.)
ROBYN
Hitchcock (arts/ent.)
Smith (sports)
ROCK
Hudson (arts/ent.)
ROCKWELL
Kent (arts/ent.)
ROCKY
Graziano (arts/ent.)
Marciano (sports)
ROD
Carew (sports)
Laver (sports)
McKuen (arts/ent.)
Serling (arts/ent.)
Steiger (arts/ent.)
Stewart (arts/ent.)
Taylor (arts/ent.)
RODDY
McDowall (arts/ent.)
RODNEY
Crowell (arts/ent.)
Dangerfield (arts/ent.)
A. Grant (arts/ent.)
King (misc.)
Allen Rippy (arts/ent.)
ROGER
Bacon (sci./inv.)
Baldwin (govt./mil.)
Bannister (sports)
Bresnahan (sports)
Clemens (sports)
Corman (arts/ent.)
Craig (sports)
Daltrey (arts/ent.)
Donaldson (arts/ent.)
Ebert (arts/ent.)
Fry (arts/ent.)

Guillemin (sci./inv.)
Maltbie (sports)
Maris (sports)
McGuinn (arts/ent.)
Miller (arts/ent.)
Moore (arts/ent.)
Mudd (arts/ent.)
Sessions (arts/ent.)
Smith (arts/ent.)
Spottiswoode (arts/ent.)
Staubach (sports)
B. Taney (govt./mil.)
Vadim (arts/ent.)
Waters (arts/ent.)
Williams (arts/ent.)
Zelazny (arts/ent.)
ROGERS
Hornsby (sports)
ROGIER
Van Der Weyden (arts/ent.)
ROLAND
Gift (arts/ent.)
Joffe (arts/ent.)
Orzabal (arts/ent.)
Petit (arts/ent.)
Young (arts/ent.)
ROLLIE
Fingers (sports)
ROMAIN
Gary (arts/ent.)
Rolland (arts/ent.)
ROMAN
Polanski (arts/ent.)
ROMY
Schneider (arts/ent.)
RON
Darling (sports)
Ely (arts/ent.)
Guidry (sports)
Howard (arts/ent.)
Kovic (arts/ent.)
Leflore (sports)
Leibman (arts/ent.)
Mix (sports)
Moody (arts/ent.)
Palillo (arts/ent.)
Perlman (arts/ent.)
Reagan (arts/ent.)
Shelton (arts/ent.)
Silver (arts/ent.)
Swoboda (sports)
Turcotte (sports)
Wood (arts/ent.)
RONA
Barrett (arts/ent.)
Jaffe (arts/ent.)

RONALD
Colman (arts/ent.)
Isley (arts/ent.)
Neame (arts/ent.)
Reagan (govt./mil.)
Searle (arts/ent.)
RONEE
Blakley (arts/ent.)
RONNIE
Burns (arts/ent.)
James Dio (arts/ent.)
Dove (arts/ent.)
Dunn (arts/ent.)
Lott (sports)
McDowell (arts/ent.)
Milsap (arts/ent.)
Montrose (arts/ent.)
Spector (arts/ent.)
Van Zant (arts/ent.)
RONNY
Cox (arts/ent.)
ROONE
Arledge (arts/ent.)
ROOSEVELT
Brown (sports)
RORY
Calhoun (arts/ent.)
Gallagher (arts/ent.)
ROSA
Bonheur (arts/ent.)
Luxemburg (govt./mil.)
Parks (govt./mil.)
Ponselle (arts/ent.)
ROSALIND
Russell (arts/ent.)
ROSALYNN
Carter (govt./mil.)
ROSAMUNDE
Pilcher (arts/ent.)
ROSANNA
Arquette (arts/ent.)
ROSANNE
Cash (arts/ent.)
ROSCOE
Ates (arts/ent.)
Lee Browne (arts/ent.)
Conkling (govt./mil.)
Karns (arts/ent.)
Tanner (sports)
ROSE
Kennedy (misc.)
ROSEANNE
Arnold (arts/ent.)
ROSELLA
Hightower (arts/ent.)
ROSEMARY
Casals (sports)

Clooney (arts/ent.)
De Camp (arts/ent.)
Rogers (arts/ent.)
ROSEY
Grier (sports)
ROSIE
Dolly (arts/ent.)
O'Donnell (arts/ent.)
Perez (arts/ent.)
ROSS
Hunter (arts/ent.)
MacDonald (arts/ent.)
Martin (arts/ent.)
McWhirter (arts/ent.)
Perot (business)
Youngs (sports)
ROSSANO
Brazzi (arts/ent.)
ROUBEN
Mamoulian (arts/ent.)
ROWLAND
Evans, Jr. (arts/ent.)
ROXANNE
Pulitzer (arts/ent.)
ROXIE
Roker (arts/ent.)
ROY
Acuff (arts/ent.)
Bean (govt./mil.)
Buchanan (arts/ent.)
Campanella (sports)
Clark (arts/ent.)
Eldridge (arts/ent.)
Emerson (sports)
Harris (arts/ent.)
Horne (arts/ent.)
Lichtenstein (arts/ent.)
Orbison (arts/ent.)
Rogers (arts/ent.)
Romer (govt./mil.)
Scheider (arts/ent.)
ROYAL
Dano (arts/ent.)
ROZ
Chast (arts/ent.)
RUBE
Foster (sports)
Goldberg (arts/ent.)
Marquard (sports)
Waddell (sports)
RUBEN, RUBÉN
Blades (arts/ent.)
Darío (arts/ent.)
Sierra (sports)
RUBY
Dee (arts/ent.)
Keeler (arts/ent.)

RUDI
Gernreich (arts/ent.)
RUDOLF
Bing (arts/ent.)
Eucken (rel./phil.)
Friml (arts/ent.)
Hess (govt./mil.)
Nureyev (arts/ent.)
Serkin (arts/ent.)
RUDOLPH
Diesel (sci./inv.)
Dirks (arts/ent.)
Isley (arts/ent.)
Valentino (arts/ent.)
RUDY
Giuliani (govt./mil.)
Maté (arts/ent.)
Tomjanovich (sports)
Vallee (arts/ent.)
RUDYARD
Kipling (arts/ent.)
RUE
McClanahan (arts/ent.)
RUFUS
Putnam (govt./mil.)
RUGGERO
Leoncavallo (arts/ent.)
RUHOLLAH
Khomeini (govt./mil.)
RULA
Lenska (arts/ent.)
RUMER
Godden (arts/ent.)
RUPERT
Brooke (arts/ent.)
Davies (arts/ent.)
Everett (arts/ent.)
Holmes (arts/ent.)
Murdoch (business)
RUSH
Limbaugh (arts/ent.)
RUSS
Columbo (arts/ent.)
Francis (sports)
Meyer (arts/ent.)
Tamblyn (arts/ent.)
Westover (arts/ent.)
RUSSEL
M. Crouse (arts/ent.)
RUSSELL
Baker (arts/ent.)
Banks (arts/ent.)
Hoban (arts/ent.)
Markert (arts/ent.)
Myers (arts/ent.)
RUSTY
Draper (arts/ent.)

Hamer (arts/ent.)
Staub (sports)
RUTGER
Hauer (arts/ent.)
RUTH
Buzzi (arts/ent.)
Chatterton (arts/ent.)
Etting (arts/ent.)
Ginsburg (govt./mil.)
Gordon (arts/ent.)
Hussey (arts/ent.)
Prawer Jhabvala (arts/
ent.)
Laredo (arts/ent.)
Pointer (arts/ent.)
Rendell (arts/ent.)
Roman (arts/ent.)
Warrick (arts/ent.)
Westheimer (misc.)
RUTHERFORD
B. Hayes (govt./mil.)
RY
Cooder (arts/ent.)
RYAN
O'Neal (arts/ent.)
RYNE
Sandberg (sports)
S. E.
Hinton (arts/ent.)
S. I.
Hayakawa (govt./mil.)
Newhouse (business)
S. J.
Perelman (arts/ent.)
S. N.
Behrman (arts/ent.)
S. S.
McClure (arts/ent.)
Van Dine (arts/ent.)
SACHA
Guitry (arts/ent.)
SADA
Thompson (arts/ent.)
SADAHARU
Oh (sports)
SADDAM
Hussein (govt./mil.)
SADIE
Thompson (arts/ent.)
SAL
Mineo (arts/ent.)
SALLY
Benson (arts/ent.)
Blane (arts/ent.)
Field (arts/ent.)
Kellerman (arts/ent.)
Kirkland (arts/ent.)

Rand (arts/ent.)
Jessy Raphael (arts/ent.)
Ride (pion./exp.)
Struthers (arts/ent.)
SALMAN
Rushdie (arts/ent.)
SALMON
P. Chase (govt./mil.)
SALOME
Jens (arts/ent.)
SALVADOR
Allende (govt./mil.)
Dali (arts/ent.)
Luria (sci./inv.)
SALVATORE
Quasimodo (arts/ent.)
SAM
Bottoms (arts/ent.)
Cooke (arts/ent.)
Crawford (sports)
Donaldson (arts/ent.)
Elliott (arts/ent.)
Giancana (misc.)
Houston (govt./mil.)
Huff (sports)
Jaffe (arts/ent.)
Kinison (arts/ent.)
Levene (arts/ent.)
McDowell (sports)
Moore (arts/ent.)
Neill (arts/ent.)
Nunn (arts/ent.)
Peckinpah (arts/ent.)
Raimi (arts/ent.)
Rayburn (govt./mil.)
Samudio (arts/ent.)
Shepard (arts/ent.)
Snead (sports)
Spiegel (arts/ent.)
Walton (business)
Wanamaker (arts/ent.)
Waterston (arts/ent.)
Wood (arts/ent.)
SAMANTHA
Eggar (arts/ent.)
Fox (arts/ent.)
Mathis (arts/ent.)
Sang (arts/ent.)
SAMMEE
Tong (arts/ent.)
SAMMI
Davis (arts/ent.)
Smith (arts/ent.)
SAMMY
Baugh (sports)
Cahn (arts/ent.)
Davis, Jr. (arts/ent.)

Fain (arts/ent.)
Hagar (arts/ent.)
Kaye (arts/ent.)
Kershaw (arts/ent.)
SAMSON
Raphaelson (arts/ent.)
SAMUEL
Adams (govt./mil.)
Barber (arts/ent.)
Beckett (arts/ent.)
Butler (arts/ent.)
Butler (arts/ent.)
De Champlain (pion./
exp.)
Chase (govt./mil.)
Taylor Coleridge (arts/
ent.)
Colt (sci./inv.)
Delany (arts/ent.)
Duesenberg (business)
Goldwyn (arts/ent.)
Gompers (govt./mil.)
L. Jackson (arts/ent.)
Morison (arts/ent.)
F. B. Morse (sci./inv.)
Pepys (govt./mil.)
Richardson (arts/ent.)
Sewall (govt./mil.)
S. Shubert (govt./mil.)
SANDER
Vanocur (arts/ent.)
SANDRA
Bernhard (arts/ent.)
Bullock (arts/ent.)
Dee (arts/ent.)
Haynie (sports)
Day O'Connor (govt./
mil.)
SANDRO
Botticelli (arts/ent.)
SANDY
Dennis (arts/ent.)
Duncan (arts/ent.)
Koufax (sports)
Mayer (sports)
SARA
Gilbert (arts/ent.)
Teasdale (arts/ent.)
SARAH
Adams (arts/ent.)
Bernhardt (arts/ent.)
Caldwell (arts/ent.)
Ferguson (govt./mil.)
Orne Jewett (arts/ent.)
Miles (arts/ent.)
Jane Moore (misc.)
Jessica Parker (arts/ent.)

Siddons (arts/ent.)
Vaughan (arts/ent.)
SAROJINI
Naidu (arts/ent.)
SASHA
Mitchell (arts/ent.)
SATCHEL
Paige (sports)
SATYAJIT
Ray (arts/ent.)
SAUL
Bellow (arts/ent.)
Steinberg (arts/ent.)
SAUNDRA
Santiago (arts/ent.)
SAX
Rohmer (arts/ent.)
SCATMAN
Crothers (arts/ent.)
SCHUYLER
Colfax (govt./mil.)
SCOTT
Baio (arts/ent.)
Bakula (arts/ent.)
Carpenter (pion./exp.)
Glenn (arts/ent.)
Hamilton (sports)
Joplin (arts/ent.)
McKenzie (arts/ent.)
Smith (arts/ent.)
Turow (arts/ent.)
SCOTTY
Beckett (arts/ent.)
SCREAMIN' JAY
Hawkins (arts/ent.)
SEAMUS
Heaney (arts/ent.)
SEAN, SEÁN
Astin (arts/ent.)
Connery (arts/ent.)
Patrick Flanery (arts/
ent.)
Lennon (arts/ent.)
O'Casey (arts/ent.)
O'Faoláin (arts/ent.)
O'Kelly (govt./mil.)
Penn (arts/ent.)
Young (arts/ent.)
SEASON
Hubley (arts/ent.)
SEBASTIAN
Brant (arts/ent.)
Cabot (arts/ent.)
Cabot (pion./exp.)
Coe (sports)
SEENA
Owen (arts/ent.)

SEIJI
Ozawa (arts/ent.)
SELA
Ward (arts/ent.)
SELENA
Royle (arts/ent.)
SELMA
Lagerlöf (arts/ent.)
SERGE
Koussevitsky (arts/ent.)
SERGEY
Diaghilev (arts/ent.)
Eisenstein (arts/ent.)
Prokofiev (arts/ent.)
Rachmaninoff (arts/ent.)
SERGIO
Franchi (arts/ent.)
Leone (arts/ent.)
Mendes (arts/ent.)
SESSUE
Hayakawa (arts/ent.)
SETH
Thomas (business)
SEVE
Ballesteros (sports)
SEVERN
Darden (arts/ent.)
SEVERO
Ochoa (sci./inv.)
SEYMOUR
Cray (sci./inv.)
SHABBA
Ranks (arts/ent.)
SHANA
Alexander (arts/ent.)
SHANICE
Wilson (arts/ent.)
SHANNA
Reed (arts/ent.)
SHANNEN
Doherty (arts/ent.)
SHANNON
Tweed (arts/ent.)
SHAQUILLE
O'Neal (sports)
SHARI
Belafonte-Harper (arts/
ent.)
Lewis (arts/ent.)
SHARON
Gless (arts/ent.)
Stone (arts/ent.)
Tate (arts/ent.)
SHAUN
Cassidy (arts/ent.)
SHAWON
Dunston (sports)

SHEB
Wooley (arts/ent.)
SHECKY
Greene (arts/ent.)
SHEENA
Easton (arts/ent.)
SHEILA
MacRae (arts/ent.)
Young (sports)
SHEILAH
Graham (arts/ent.)
SHEL
Silverstein (arts/ent.)
SHELAGH
Delaney (arts/ent.)
SHELBY
Foote (arts/ent.)
Lynne (arts/ent.)
SHELDON
Harnick (arts/ent.)
Leonard (arts/ent.)
SHELLEY
Berman (arts/ent.)
Duvall (arts/ent.)
Fabares (arts/ent.)
Hack (arts/ent.)
Long (arts/ent.)
Winters (arts/ent.)
SHELLY
Manne (arts/ent.)
West (arts/ent.)
SHEMP
Howard (arts/ent.)
SHEPPERD
Strudwick (arts/ent.)
SHERE
Hite (arts/ent.)
SHEREE
North (arts/ent.)
SHERILL
Milnes (arts/ent.)
SHERILYN
Fenn (arts/ent.)
SHERMAN
Adams (govt./mil.)
Hemsley (arts/ent.)
Minton (govt./mil.)
SHERRY
Lansing (arts/ent.)
SHERWOOD
Anderson (arts/ent.)
SHERYL
Lee (arts/ent.)
SHIMON
Peres (govt./mil.)
SHIPWRECK
Kelly (misc.)

SHIRL
Conway (arts/ent.)
SHIRLEY
Bassey (arts/ent.)
Booth (arts/ent.)
Chisolm (govt./mil.)
Englehorn (sports)
Ann Grau (arts/ent.)
Jackson (arts/ent.)
Jones (arts/ent.)
Knight (arts/ent.)
MacLaine (arts/ent.)
Muldowney (sports)
Temple (arts/ent.)
SHMUEL
Agnon (arts/ent.)
SHOLEM
Asch (arts/ent.)
SHOLOM
Aleichem (arts/ent.)
SHORTY
Rogers (arts/ent.)
SIAN
Phillips (arts/ent.)
SID
Abel (sports)
Bream (sports)
Caesar (arts/ent.)
Catlett (arts/ent.)
Fernandez (sports)
Grauman (arts/ent.)
Luckman (sports)
Vicious (arts/ent.)
SIDNEY
Bechet (arts/ent.)
Blackmer (arts/ent.)
J. Furie (arts/ent.)
Howard (arts/ent.)
Kingsley (arts/ent.)
Lumet (arts/ent.)
Poitier (arts/ent.)
Sheldon (arts/ent.)
Toler (arts/ent.)
SIEGFRIED
Fischbacher (arts/ent.)
SIG
Arno (arts/ent.)
Ruman (arts/ent.)
SIGMUND
Freud (sci./inv.)
Romberg (arts/ent.)
SIGNE
Hasso (arts/ent.)
SIGOURNEY
Weaver (arts/ent.)
SIGRID
Undset (arts/ent.)

SILAS
Deane (govt./mil.)
SILVANA
Mangano (arts/ent.)
SIME
Silverman (business)
SIMON
Bolívar (govt./mil.)
Gray (arts/ent.)
Lebon (arts/ent.)
MacCorkindale (arts/ent.)
Oakland (arts/ent.)
Van Der Meer (sci./inv.)
Wiesenthal (misc.)
SIMONE
De Beauvoir (arts/ent.)
Signoret (arts/ent.)
Simon (arts/ent.)
Weil (rel./phil.)
SINCLAIR
Lewis (arts/ent.)
SINEAD, SINÉAD
Cusack (arts/ent.)
O'Connor (arts/ent.)
SIOBHAN
McKenna (arts/ent.)
SISSELA
Bok (arts/ent.)
SISSY
Spacek (arts/ent.)
SKEETER
Davis (arts/ent.)
SKINNAY
Ennis (arts/ent.)
SKIP
Ewing (arts/ent.)
SKITCH
Henderson (arts/ent.)
SLIM
Pickens (arts/ent.)
Summerville (arts/ent.)
Whitman (arts/ent.)
SLOAN
Wilson (arts/ent.)
SLY
Stone (arts/ent.)
SMOKEY
Robinson (arts/ent.)
SNOOKY
Lanson (arts/ent.)
SOFIA
Coppola (arts/ent.)
SOICHIRO
Honda (business)
SOJOURNER
Truth (misc.)

SOL
Hurok (arts/ent.)
SOLEIL
Moon Frye (arts/ent.)
SOLOMON
Burke (arts/ent.)
SOMERSET
Maugham (arts/ent.)
SONDRA
Locke (arts/ent.)
SONIA
Braga (arts/ent.)
SONJA
Henie (sports)
SONNY
Bono (arts/ent.)
James (arts/ent.)
Jurgenson (sports)
Liston (sports)
Rollins (arts/ent.)
Stitt (arts/ent.)
Tufts (arts/ent.)
SOPHIA
Loren (arts/ent.)
SOPHIE
B. Hawkins (arts/ent.)
Tucker (arts/ent.)
SOREN
Kierkegaard (rel./phil.)
SOUPY
Sales (arts/ent.)
SPADE
Cooley (arts/ent.)
SPALDING
Gray (arts/ent.)
SPANKY
McFarland (arts/ent.)
McFarlane (arts/ent.)
SPARKY
Anderson (sports)
Lyle (sports)
SPENCER
Davis (arts/ent.)
Dryden (arts/ent.)
Tracy (arts/ent.)
SPIKE
Jones (arts/ent.)
Lee (arts/ent.)
Milligan (arts/ent.)
Owen (sports)
SPIRO
T. Agnew (govt./mil.)
SPOTTISWOODE
Aitken (arts/ent.)
SPUD
Chandler (sports)

SQUEAKY
Fromme (misc.)
STACY
Keach (arts/ent.)
Lattisaw (arts/ent.)
STAN
Coveleski (sports)
Getz (arts/ent.)
Kenton (arts/ent.)
Laurel (arts/ent.)
Lee (arts/ent.)
Mikita (sports)
Musial (sports)
Smith (sports)
STANFORD
Moore (sci./inv.)
White (arts/ent.)
STANISLAW
Lem (arts/ent.)
STANLEY
Andrews (arts/ent.)
Baldwin (govt./mil.)
Clarke (arts/ent.)
Donen (arts/ent.)
Holloway (arts/ent.)
Jaffe (arts/ent.)
Jordan (arts/ent.)
Kramer (arts/ent.)
Kubrick (arts/ent.)
Kunitz (arts/ent.)
STEDMAN
Graham (business)
STEFAN
Edberg (sports)
Zweig (arts/ent.)
STEFANIE
Powers (arts/ent.)
Graf (sports)
STELLA
Adler (arts/ent.)
Parton (arts/ent.)
Stevens (arts/ent.)
Walsh (sports)
STEPFANIE
Kramer (arts/ent.)
STEPHANE, STÉPHANE
Audran (arts/ent.)
Mallarmé (arts/ent.)
STEPHANIE
Beacham (arts/ent.)
Mills (arts/ent.)
Seymour (arts/ent.)
Zimbalist (arts/ent.)
STEPHEN
Austin (govt./mil.)
Baldwin (arts/ent.)
Vincent Benét (arts/ent.)

Bishop (arts/ent.)
J. Cannell (arts/ent.)
Crane (arts/ent.)
A. Douglas (govt./mil.)
Foster (arts/ent.)
Frears (arts/ent.)
Jay Gould (sci./inv.)
W. Hawking (sci./inv.)
King (arts/ent.)
Leacock (arts/ent.)
E. Merrill (govt./mil.)
Rea (arts/ent.)
Sondheim (arts/ent.)
Spender (arts/ent.)
Sprouse (arts/ent.)
Stills (arts/ent.)
STEPIN
Fetchit (arts/ent.)
STERLING
Hayden (arts/ent.)
Holloway (arts/ent.)
STEVE
Allen (arts/ent.)
Bedrosian (sports)
Biko (govt./mil.)
Blass (sports)
Brodie (sports)
Buscemi (arts/ent.)
Carlton (sports)
Cauthen (sports)
Ditko (arts/ent.)
Earle (arts/ent.)
Forrest (arts/ent.)
Garvey (sports)
Guttenberg (arts/ent.)
Howe (arts/ent.)
Kanaly (arts/ent.)
Lawrence (arts/ent.)
Lukather (arts/ent.)
Marriot (arts/ent.)
Martin (arts/ent.)
McQueen (arts/ent.)
Miller (arts/ent.)
Owen (sports)
Perry (arts/ent.)
Reeves (arts/ent.)
Sax (sports)
Vai (arts/ent.)
Van Buren (sports)
Wariner (arts/ent.)
Winwood (arts/ent.)
Wozniak (business)
Young (sports)
STEVEN
Bauer (arts/ent.)
Bochco (arts/ent.)
Jobs (business)

Seagal (arts/ent.)
Soderbergh (arts/ent.)
Spielberg (arts/ent.)
Tyler (arts/ent.)
Wright (arts/ent.)
STEVIE
Nicks (arts/ent.)
Smith (arts/ent.)
Ray Vaughan (arts/ent.)
Wonder (arts/ent.)
STEWART
Copeland (arts/ent.)
Granger (arts/ent.)
STIRLING
Moss (sports)
Silliphant (arts/ent.)
STOCKARD
Channing (arts/ent.)
STOKELY
Carmichael (govt./mil.)
STONE
Phillips (arts/ent.)
STONEWALL
Jackson (arts/ent.)
STROM
Thurmond (govt./mil.)
STROTHER
Martin (arts/ent.)
STU
Erwin (arts/ent.)
STUART
Margolin (arts/ent.)
Palmer (arts/ent.)
Rosenberg (arts/ent.)
Whitman (arts/ent.)
STUBBY
Kaye (arts/ent.)
STUDS
Terkel (arts/ent.)
SUDIE
Bond (arts/ent.)
SUE
Ane Langdon (arts/ent.)
Lyon (arts/ent.)
SUGAR RAY
Leonard (sports)
Robinson (sports)
SULLY
Prudhomme (arts/ent.)
SUMNER
Welles (govt./mil.)
SUN
Myung Moon (arts/ent.)
SUNNY
Von Bulow (misc.)
SUSAN
Anspach (arts/ent.)

B. Anthony (govt./mil.)
Anton (arts/ent.)
Blakely (arts/ent.)
Clark (arts/ent.)
Dey (arts/ent.)
Faludi (arts/ent.)
George (arts/ent.)
Glaspell (arts/ent.)
Hampshire (arts/ent.)
Hayward (arts/ent.)
Lucci (arts/ent.)
Ruttan (arts/ent.)
Saint James (arts/ent.)
Sarandon (arts/ent.)
Seidelman (arts/ent.)
Sontag (arts/ent.)
Strasberg (arts/ent.)
Sullivan (arts/ent.)
SUSANNA
Foster (arts/ent.)
Hoffs (arts/ent.)
SUSANNAH
York (arts/ent.)
SUSANNE
K. Langer (rel./phil.)
SUSIE
Maxwell Berning
(sports)
SUZANNE
Farrell (arts/ent.)
Flon (arts/ent.)
Lenglen (sports)
Pleshette (arts/ent.)
Somers (arts/ent.)
Vega (arts/ent.)
SUZI
Quatro (arts/ent.)
SUZY
Bogguss (arts/ent.)
Chaffee (sports)
Parker (arts/ent.)
SWIFTY
Lazar (arts/ent.)
SWOOSIE
Kurtz (arts/ent.)
SY
Oliver (arts/ent.)
SYBIL
Danning (arts/ent.)
Leek (misc.)
Thorndike (arts/ent.)
SYD
Barrett (arts/ent.)
SYDNEY
Biddle Barrows (misc.)
Greenstreet (arts/
ent.)

Pollack (arts/ent.)
Smith (arts/ent.)
SYLVESTER
Stallone (arts/ent.)
SYLVIA
Kristel (arts/ent.)
Miles (arts/ent.)
Plath (arts/ent.)
Porter (arts/ent.)
Sidney (arts/ent.)
Syms (arts/ent.)
Townsend Warner (arts/ent.)
SYNGMAN
Rhee (govt./mil.)
T. B.
Macaulay (arts/ent.)
T. G.
Sheppard (arts/ent.)
T. H.
White (arts/ent.)
T. S.
Eliot (arts/ent.)
T. BOONE
Pickens (business)
T-BONE
Burnett (arts/ent.)
Walker (arts/ent.)
T. GRAHAM
Brown (arts/ent.)
TAB
Hunter (arts/ent.)
TABITHA
Soren (arts/ent.)
TAD
Mosel (arts/ent.)
TAI
Babilonia (sports)
Thai (arts/ent.)
TAJ
Mahal (arts/ent.)
TAKEO
Miki (govt./mil.)
TALCOTT
Parsons (misc.)
TALIA
Shire (arts/ent.)
TALLULAH
Bankhead (arts/ent.)
TAMA
Janowitz (arts/ent.)
TAMARA
Karsavina (arts/ent.)
TAMMI
Terrell (arts/ent.)
TAMMY
Faye Bakker (rel./phil.)

Grimes (arts/ent.)
Wynette (arts/ent.)
TANITA
Tikaram (arts/ent.)
TANITH
Lee (arts/ent.)
TANNIS
Vallely (arts/ent.)
TANYA
Roberts (arts/ent.)
Tucker (arts/ent.)
TATIANA
Troyanos (arts/ent.)
TATJANA
Patitz (arts/ent.)
TATUM
O'Neal (arts/ent.)
TAWNY
Schneider (arts/ent.)
Kitaen (arts/ent.)
TAY
Garnett (arts/ent.)
TAYLOR
Caldwell (arts/ent.)
Dayne (arts/ent.)
Hackford (arts/ent.)
TED
Bessell (arts/ent.)
Bundy (misc.)
Cassidy (arts/ent.)
Danson (arts/ent.)
Hughes (arts/ent.)
Key (arts/ent.)
Kluszewski (sports)
Knight (arts/ent.)
Koppel (arts/ent.)
Kotcheff (arts/ent.)
Lange (arts/ent.)
Lapidus (arts/ent.)
Lewis (arts/ent.)
Lindsay (sports)
Nugent (arts/ent.)
Schroeder (sports)
Shackelford (arts/ent.)
Shawn (arts/ent.)
Turner (business)
Williams (sports)
TEDDY
Kennedy (govt./mil.)
Pendergrass (arts/ent.)
Weatherford (arts/ent.)
TEENA
Marie (arts/ent.)
TELLY
Savalas (arts/ent.)
TELMA
Hopkins (arts/ent.)

TEMPESTT
Bledsoe (arts/ent.)
TENLEY
Albright (sports)
TENNESSEE
Williams (arts/ent.)
TENNESSEE ERNIE
Ford (arts/ent.)
TERENCE
Alexander (arts/ent.)
Trent D'Arby (arts/ent.)
Fisher (arts/ent.)
Malick (arts/ent.)
Rattigan (arts/ent.)
Stamp (arts/ent.)
Young (arts/ent.)
TERESA
Brewer (arts/ent.)
Wright (arts/ent.)
TERI
Austin (arts/ent.)
Copley (arts/ent.)
Garr (arts/ent.)
Hatcher (arts/ent.)
TERRENCE
McNally (arts/ent.)
TERRI
Gibbs (arts/ent.)
TERRY
Bradshaw (sports)
Gilliam (arts/ent.)
MacMillan (arts/ent.)
McMillan (arts/ent.)
Moore (arts/ent.)
Pendleton (sports)
Sawchuk (sports)
Southern (arts/ent.)
Waite (misc.)
TESS
Harper (arts/ent.)
TEX
Avery (arts/ent.)
Beneke (arts/ent.)
McCrary (arts/ent.)
Ritter (arts/ent.)
TEXAS
Guinan (arts/ent.)
THADDEUS
Stevens (govt./mil.)
THEDA
Bara (arts/ent.)
THELMA
Houston (arts/ent.)
Ritter (arts/ent.)
Todd (arts/ent.)
THELONIUS
Monk (arts/ent.)

THEODORE, THÉODORE
Bikel (arts/ent.)
Dreiser (arts/ent.)
Dubois (arts/ent.)
Géricault (arts/ent.)
Richards (sci./inv.)
Roethke (arts/ent.)
Roosevelt (govt./mil.)
Rousseau (arts/ent.)
Sturgeon (arts/ent.)
White (arts/ent.)
THEOPHILE
Gautier (arts/ent.)
THERESA
Russell (arts/ent.)
Saldana (arts/ent.)
THOM
Gunn (arts/ent.)
THOMAS
Aquinas (rel./phil.)
Augustine Arne (arts/
ent.)
À Becket (rel./phil.)
Beecham (arts/ent.)
Hart Benton (arts/ent.)
Hart Benton (govt./mil.)
Berger (arts/ent.)
Bulfinch (arts/ent.)
Campion (arts/ent.)
Carew (arts/ent.)
Carlyle (arts/ent.)
Chatterton (arts/ent.)
Chippendale (arts/ent.)
Cole (arts/ent.)
Costain (arts/ent.)
Cromwell (govt./mil.)
De Quincey (arts/ent.)
Robert Dewar
(business)
E. Dewey (govt./mil.)
Dolby (arts/ent.)
Eakins (arts/ent.)
Edison (sci./inv.)
S. Foley (govt./mil.)
Gainsborough (arts/
ent.)
Gray (arts/ent.)
Hampson (arts/ent.)
Hardy (arts/ent.)
A. Hendricks (govt./
mil.)
Hobbes (rel./phil.)
Hughes (arts/ent.)
Huxley (rel./phil.)
H. Ince (arts/ent.)
Jackson (govt./mil.)
Jefferson (govt./mil.)

Keneally (arts/ent.)
Kinsella (arts/ent.)
Kyd (arts/ent.)
Lawrence (arts/ent.)
Malory (arts/ent.)
Mann (arts/ent.)
R. Marshall (govt./mil.)
Merton (arts/ent.)
Middleton (arts/ent.)
Mitchell (arts/ent.)
Moran (arts/ent.)
More (arts/ent.)
Nashe (arts/ent.)
Nast (arts/ent.)
Noguchi (misc.)
Overbury (arts/ent.)
Paine (rel./phil.)
Peacock (arts/ent.)
Pynchon (arts/ent.)
Rowlandson (arts/ent.)
Sully (arts/ent.)
Tryon (arts/ent.)
Wolfe (arts/ent.)
Wolsey (govt./mil.)
THOR
Heyerdahl (pion./exp.)
THORNE
Smith (arts/ent.)
THORNTON
Waldo Burgess (arts/
ent.)
Freeland (arts/ent.)
Wilder (arts/ent.)
THREE-FINGER
Brown (misc.)
Brown (sports)
THURGOOD
Marshall (govt./mil.)
THURMAN
Munson (sports)
TIA
Carrere (arts/ent.)
TIFFANY
Chin (sports)
TIGE
Andrews (arts/ent.)
TILLIE
Olsen (arts/ent.)
TIM
Allen (arts/ent.)
Burton (arts/ent.)
Conway (arts/ent.)
Curry (arts/ent.)
Keefe (sports)
Matheson (arts/ent.)
McCarver (sports)
Reid (arts/ent.)

Robbins (arts/ent.)
Weisberg (arts/ent.)
Whelan (arts/ent.)
TIMOTHY
Chow (misc.)
Bottoms (arts/ent.)
Busfield (arts/ent.)
Dalton (arts/ent.)
Daly (arts/ent.)
Hutton (arts/ent.)
Leary (govt./mil.)
TINA
Louise (arts/ent.)
Turner (arts/ent.)
Weymouth (arts/ent.)
Yothers (arts/ent.)
TINY
Sandford (arts/ent.)
TIP
O'Neill (govt./mil.)
TIPPER
Gore (govt./mil.)
TIPPI
Hedren (arts/ent.)
TITO
Fuentes (sports)
Jackson (arts/ent.)
Puente (arts/ent.)
Schipa (arts/ent.)
TITTA
Ruffo (arts/ent.)
TOBE
Hooper (arts/ent.)
TOBIAS
Wolff (arts/ent.)
TOD
Browning (arts/ent.)
TODD
Bridges (arts/ent.)
Rundgren (arts/ent.)
TOE
Blake (sports)
TOM
Arnold (arts/ent.)
Berenger (arts/ent.)
Bosley (arts/ent.)
Bradley (govt./mil.)
Brokaw (arts/ent.)
Browning (sports)
Clancy (arts/ent.)
Conti (arts/ent.)
Cruise (arts/ent.)
Ewell (arts/ent.)
Fears (sports)
T. Hall (arts/ent.)
Hanks (arts/ent.)
Harkin (govt./mil.)

Harmon (sports)
Hayden (govt./mil.)
Hulce (arts/ent.)
Jones (arts/ent.)
Landry (sports)
Laughlin (arts/ent.)
Lehrer (arts/ent.)
Mix (arts/ent.)
Parker (arts/ent.)
Petty (arts/ent.)
Poston (arts/ent.)
Robbins (arts/ent.)
Scholz (arts/ent.)
Seaver (sports)
Selleck (arts/ent.)
Skerritt (arts/ent.)
Snyder (arts/ent.)
Stoppard (arts/ent.)
Taylor (arts/ent.)
Waits (arts/ent.)
Watson (sports)
Werner (arts/ent.)
Wolfe (arts/ent.)
Wopat (arts/ent.)
Yawkey (sports)
TOMMY
Bolt (sports)
Chong (arts/ent.)
Connolly (sports)
Davis (sports)
Dorsey (arts/ent.)
Henrich (sports)
James (arts/ent.)
John (sports)
Lee Jones (arts/ent.)
Ladnier (arts/ent.)
Lasorda (sports)
Lee (arts/ent.)
Roe (arts/ent.)
Sands (arts/ent.)
Smothers (arts/ent.)
Thompson (govt./mil.)
Tucker (arts/ent.)
Tune (arts/ent.)
TONI
Basil (arts/ent.)
Braxton (arts/ent.)
Morrison (arts/ent.)
Tennille (arts/ent.)
TONY
Armas (sports)
Banks (arts/ent.)
Bennett (arts/ent.)
Bill (arts/ent.)
Canadeo (sports)
Curtis (arts/ent.)
Danza (arts/ent.)

Dorsett (sports)
Fernandez (sports)
Franciosa (arts/ent.)
Goldwyn (arts/ent.)
Gwynn (sports)
Iommi (arts/ent.)
Kubek (sports)
Kushner (arts/ent.)
Lazzeri (sports)
Lo Bianco (arts/ent.)
Martin (arts/ent.)
Musante (arts/ent.)
Oliva (sports)
Orlando (arts/ent.)
Peck (arts/ent.)
Pena (sports)
Randall (arts/ent.)
Richardson (arts/ent.)
Roberts (arts/ent.)
Scott (arts/ent.)
Trabert (sports)
TOOTS
Shor (misc.)
TORI
Amos (arts/ent.)
Spelling (arts/ent.)
TORIN
Thatcher (arts/ent.)
TOSHIKO
Akiyoshi (arts/ent.)
TOSHIRO
Mifune (arts/ent.)
TOTIE
Fields (arts/ent.)
TOVAH
Feldshuh (arts/ent.)
TRACEY
Gold (arts/ent.)
Ullman (arts/ent.)
TRACI
Lords (arts/ent.)
TRACY
Austin (sports)
Caulkins (sports)
Chapman (arts/ent.)
Lawrence (arts/ent.)
Nelson (arts/ent.)
Pollan (arts/ent.)
Scoggins (arts/ent.)
TRAVIS
Tritt (arts/ent.)
TREAT
Williams (arts/ent.)
TREVOR
Bardette (arts/ent.)
Griffiths (arts/ent.)
Howard (arts/ent.)

Nunn (govt./mil.)
TRICIA
Leigh Fisher (arts/ent.)
Nixon (arts/ent.)
TRINI
Lopez (arts/ent.)
TRIS
Speaker (sports)
TRISH
Van Devere (arts/ent.)
TRISHA
Yearwood (arts/ent.)
TRISTAM
Coffin (arts/ent.)
TRISTAN
Rogers (arts/ent.)
TROY
Donahue (arts/ent.)
TRUMAN
Capote (arts/ent.)
TSUNG-DAO
Lee (sci./inv.)
TUESDAY
Weld (arts/ent.)
TUFFY
Leemans (sports)
TUG
McGraw (sports)
TULLY
Marshall (arts/ent.)
TUPAC
Shakur (arts/ent.)
TURHAN
Bey (arts/ent.)
TURK
Edwards (sports)
TUTTI
Camarata (arts/ent.)
TWYLA
Tharp (arts/ent.)
TY
Cobb (sports)
Hardin (arts/ent.)
TYCHO
Brahe (sci./inv.)
TYNE
Daly (arts/ent.)
TYRONE
Power (arts/ent.)
U
Thant (govt./mil.)
UGO
Tognazzi (arts/ent.)
ULF
Nilsson (sports)
ULRIKE
Meinhoff (misc.)

ULU
Grosbard (arts/ent.)
ULYSSES
S. Grant (govt./
mil.)
UMA
Thurman (arts/ent.)
UMBERTO
Eco (arts/ent.)
UNA
Merkel (arts/ent.)
O'Connor (arts/ent.)
UPTON
Sinclair (arts/ent.)
URI
Geller (misc.)
URSULA
Andress (arts/ent.)
Jeans (arts/ent.)
K. Le Guin (arts/ent.)
UTA
Hagen (arts/ent.)
V. C.
Andrews (arts/ent.)
V. S.
Naipaul (arts/ent.)
Pritchett (arts/ent.)
VÁCLAV
Havel (govt./mil.)
VAL
Bisoglio (arts/ent.)
Kilmer (arts/ent.)
VALENTINA
Cortesa or Cortese
(arts/ent.)
VALERIA
Golino (arts/ent.)
Messalina (govt./mil.)
VALERIE
Bertinelli (arts/ent.)
Harper (arts/ent.)
Perrine (arts/ent.)
Simpson (arts/ent.)
VALÉRY
Giscard D'Estaing
(govt./mil.)
VAN
Brooks (arts/ent.)
Cliburn (arts/ent.)
Heflin (arts/ent.)
Johnson (arts/ent.)
McCoy (arts/ent.)
Morrison (arts/ent.)
Lingle Mungo (sports)
VANCE
Colvig (arts/ent.)
Packard (arts/ent.)

VAN DYKE
Parks (arts/ent.)
VANESSA
Bell (arts/ent.)
Redgrave (arts/ent.)
Williams (arts/ent.)
VANNA
White (arts/ent.)
VANNEVAR
Bush (sci./inv.)
VASCO
Núñez De Balboa
(pion./exp.)
Da Gama (pion./exp.)
VASLAV
Nijinsky (arts/ent.)
VAUGHAN
Monroe (arts/ent.)
VED
Mehta (arts/ent.)
VEDA
Borg (arts/ent.)
VENYAMIN
Kaverin (arts/ent.)
VERA
Brittain (arts/ent.)
Caspary (arts/ent.)
Lynn (arts/ent.)
Miles (arts/ent.)
Ralston (arts/ent.)
Zorina (arts/ent.)
VERN
Gosdin (arts/ent.)
VERNER
Von Heidenstam (arts/
ent.)
VERNON
Castle (arts/ent.)
Dalhart (arts/ent.)
Duke (arts/ent.)
Parrington (arts/
ent.)
VERONICA
Cartwright (arts/ent.)
Hamel (arts/ent.)
Lake (arts/ent.)
VERREE
Teasdale (arts/ent.)
VET
Boswell (arts/ent.)
VIC
Damone (arts/ent.)
Dana (arts/ent.)
Morrow (arts/ent.)
Raschi (sports)
Seixas (sports)
Tayback (arts/ent.)

VICENTE
Aleixandre (arts/ent.)
Blasco Ibañez (arts/ent.)
VICKI
Baum (arts/ent.)
Lawrence (arts/ent.)
VICTOR
Borge (arts/ent.)
Buono (arts/ent.)
Canning (arts/ent.)
Cousin (rel./phil.)
Fleming (arts/ent.)
French (arts/ent.)
Herbert (arts/ent.)
Hugo (arts/ent.)
Jory (arts/ent.)
Kiam (business)
Lasky (arts/ent.)
Mature (arts/ent.)
Maurel (arts/ent.)
McLaglen (arts/ent.)
Moore (arts/ent.)
Young (arts/ent.)
VICTORIA
Jackson (arts/ent.)
Principal (arts/ent.)
Sackville-West (arts/
ent.)
Tennant (arts/ent.)
VIDA
Blue (sports)
VIDAL
Sassoon (business)
VIDKUN
Quisling (govt./mil.)
VIKKI
Carr (arts/ent.)
VILMA
Banky (arts/ent.)
VIN
Scully (sports)
VINCE
Coleman (sports)
Edwards (arts/ent.)
Gill (arts/ent.)
Lombardi (sports)
Neil (arts/ent.)
VINCENT
Bugliosi (misc.)
Canby (arts/ent.)
D'Indy (arts/ent.)
D'Onofrio (arts/ent.)
Du Vigneaud (sci./inv.)
Gardenia (arts/ent.)
Hamlin (arts/ent.)
Price (arts/ent.)
Spano (arts/ent.)

Van Gogh (arts/ent.)
Youmans (arts/ent.)
VINCENTE
Minnelli (arts/ent.)
VINCENZO
Bellini (arts/ent.)
Tommasini (arts/
ent.)
VINEGAR BEND
Mizell (sports)
VINNY
Testaverde (sports)
VIRGIL
Thomson (arts/ent.)
VIRGINIA
Bruce (arts/ent.)
Dare (misc.)
Hill (misc.)
Johnson (sci./inv.)
Madsen (arts/ent.)
Mayo (arts/ent.)
Wade (sports)
Woolf (arts/ent.)
VIRNA
Lisi (arts/ent.)
VITAS
Gerulaitis (sports)
VITTORE
Carpaccio (arts/ent.)
VITTORIO
De Sica (arts/ent.)
Gassman (arts/ent.)
VITUS
Bering (pion./exp.)
VIVECA
Lindfors (arts/ent.)
VIVIAN
Vance (arts/ent.)
VIVIEN
Leigh (arts/ent.)
Merchant (arts/ent.)
VIVIENNE
Westwood (arts/ent.)
VLADIMIR
Ashkenazy (arts/ent.)
Horowitz (arts/ent.)
Lenin (govt./mil.)
Nabokov (arts/ent.)
VON
Hayes (sports)
VONDA
N. McIntyre (arts/ent.)
VYACHESLAV
Molotov (govt./mil.)
W. C.
Fields (arts/ent.)
Handy (arts/ent.)

W. D.
Snodgrass (arts/
ent.)
W. E. B.
Dubois (govt./mil.)
W. H.
Auden (arts/ent.)
W. M.
Kiplinger (arts/ent.)
W. R.
Burnett (arts/ent.)
W. S.
Gilbert (arts/ent.)
Merwin (arts/ent.)
Van Dyke (arts/ent.)
W. W.
Jacobs (arts/ent.)
WADE
Boggs (sports)
Hampton (govt./mil.)
WAITE
Hoyt (sports)
WALKER
Cooper (sports)
Evans (arts/ent.)
Percy (arts/ent.)
WALLACE
Beery (arts/ent.)
Hume Carothers (sci./
inv.)
Fox (arts/ent.)
Harrison (arts/ent.)
Reid (arts/ent.)
Stegner (arts/ent.)
Stevens (arts/ent.)
WALLIS
Warfield (govt./mil.)
WALLY
Backman (sports)
Cox (arts/ent.)
Joyner (sports)
Schirra (pion./exp.)
Shawn (arts/ent.)
WALT
Disney (arts/ent.)
Frazier (sports)
Kelly (arts/ent.)
Kiesling (sports)
Kuhn (arts/ent.)
Whitman (arts/ent.)
WALTER
Alston (sports)
Hubert Annenberg
(business)
Becker (arts/ent.)
Brattain (sci./inv.)
Brennan (arts/ent.)

Chauncey Camp
(sports)
Carlos (arts/ent.)
Chrysler (business)
Clark (arts/ent.)
Cronkite (arts/ent.)
Damrosch (arts/ent.)
De La Mare (arts/ent.)
D. Edmonds (arts/ent.)
Egan (arts/ent.)
Farley (arts/ent.)
E. Fauntroy (govt./mil.)
Gropius (arts/ent.)
Hagen (sports)
Hill (arts/ent.)
Huston (arts/ent.)
Johnson (sports)
Kerr (arts/ent.)
Koenig (arts/ent.)
Lantz (arts/ent.)
Lippmann (arts/ent.)
Matthau (arts/ent.)
D. Miller (govt./mil.)
Mirisch (arts/ent.)
F. Mondale (govt./mil.)
Murphy (arts/ent.)
Pater (arts/ent.)
Payton (sports)
Pidgeon (arts/ent.)
Piston (arts/ent.)
Pitkin (arts/ent.)
Raleigh (pion./exp.)
Reed (sci./inv.)
Scott (arts/ent.)
Wanger (arts/ent.)
Winchell (arts/ent.)
WANDA
Hendrix (arts/ent.)
WARD
Bond (arts/ent.)
WARNER
Baxter (arts/ent.)
Oland (arts/ent.)
WARREN
Beatty (arts/ent.)
E. Burger (govt./mil.)
Christopher (govt./mil.)
C. Giles (sports)
Harding (govt./mil.)
Hull (arts/ent.)
Oates (arts/ent.)
Rudman (govt./mil.)
Spahn (sports)
Zevon (arts/ent.)
WASHINGTON
Allston (arts/ent.)
Irving (arts/ent.)

WASSILY
Kandinsky (arts/ent.)
WAYLAND
Flowers (arts/ent.)
WAYLON
Jennings (arts/ent.)
WAYNE
Gretzky (sports)
King (arts/ent.)
Knight (arts/ent.)
Millner (sports)
Morris (arts/ent.)
Newton (arts/ent.)
Osmond (arts/ent.)
Rogers (arts/ent.)
Shorter (arts/ent.)
Wang (arts/ent.)
WEBB
Pierce (arts/ent.)
WEEB
Ewbank (sports)
WENDELL
Berry (arts/ent.)
Corey (arts/ent.)
Phillips (govt./mil.)
Willkie (govt./mil.)
WENDIE
Jo Sperber (arts/ent.)
WENDY
Barrie (arts/ent.)
Hiller (arts/ent.)
Wasserstein (arts/ent.)
O. Williams (arts/ent.)
Wilson (arts/ent.)
WERNER
Erhard (rel./phil.)
Herzog (arts/ent.)
Klemperer (arts/ent.)
WERNHER
Von Braun (sci./inv.)
WES
Craven (arts/ent.)
Montgomery (arts/ent.)
Unseld (sports)
WESLEY
Addy (arts/ent.)
Ruggles (arts/ent.)
Snipes (arts/ent.)
WESTBROOK
Pegler (arts/ent.)
WHIT
Bissell (arts/ent.)
WHITELAW
Reid (business)
WHITEY
Ford (sports)
Herzog (sports)

Kurowski (sports)
WHITLEY
Strieber (arts/ent.)
WHITNEY
Houston (arts/ent.)
WHITTAKER
Chambers (arts/ent.)
WHOOPI
Goldberg (arts/ent.)
WIL
Shriner (arts/ent.)
Wheaton (arts/ent.)
WILBERT
Robinson (sports)
WILBUR
Wright (sci./inv.)
WILEY
Rutledge (govt./mil.)
WILFORD
Brimley (arts/ent.)
WILFRID
Hyde-White (arts/ent.)
Sheed (arts/ent.)
WILHELM
Grimm (arts/ent.)
Von Opel (business)
Roentgen (sci./inv.)
WILKIE
Collins (arts/ent.)
WILL
Clark (sports)
Cuppy (arts/ent.)
Durant (arts/ent.)
Geer (arts/ent.)
Hays (govt./mil.)
Keith Kellogg (business)
Patton (arts/ent.)
Rogers (arts/ent.)
Sampson (arts/ent.)
Smith (arts/ent.)
WILLA
Cather (arts/ent.)
WILLARD
Motley (arts/ent.)
Scott (arts/ent.)
WILLEM
Barents (pion./exp.)
Dafoe (arts/ent.)
De Kooning (arts/ent.)
WILLIAM
Ainsworth (arts/ent.)
Maxwell Aitken (arts/ent.)
Baldwin (arts/ent.)
Bateson (sci./inv.)
Beebe (pion./exp.)
Bendix (arts/ent.)

Rose Benét (arts/ent.)
Blake (arts/ent.)
Peter Blatty (arts/ent.)
Bligh (govt./mil.)
Boeing (business)
Boyd (arts/ent.)
Bradford (govt./mil.)
J. Brennan, Jr. (govt./mil.)
Brewster (govt./mil.)
Wells Brown (arts/ent.)
Jennings Bryan (govt./mil.)
Cullen Bryant (arts/ent.)
F. Buckley, Jr. (arts/ent.)
S. Burroughs (arts/ent.)
Byrd (arts/ent.)
Byrd (govt./mil.)
Casey (govt./mil.)
Caxton (arts/ent.)
Clark (pion./exp.)
Conrad (arts/ent.)
Demarest (arts/ent.)
Desmond (arts/ent.)
Devane (arts/ent.)
O. Douglas (govt./mil.)
Faulkner (arts/ent.)
Frawley (arts/ent.)
Friedkin (arts/ent.)
Furtwängler (arts/ent.)
Gaddis (arts/ent.)
M. Gaines (business)
Gargan (arts/ent.)
Lloyd Garrison (arts/ent.)
Giauque (sci./inv.)
Gladstone (govt./mil.)
Godwin (arts/ent.)
Golding (arts/ent.)
Goldman (arts/ent.)
Halsey (govt./mil.)
Halsted (sci./inv.)
Hanna (arts/ent.)
Harris (misc.)
Harrison (govt./mil.)
S. Hart (arts/ent.)
Hazlitt (arts/ent.)
Randolph Hearst (business)
Hewlett (business)
Hogarth (arts/ent.)
Holden (arts/ent.)
Henry Hoover (business)
Dean Howells (arts/ent.)
Hurt (arts/ent.)

Inge (arts/ent.)
James (rel./phil.)
Jenney (arts/ent.)
Katt (arts/ent.)
Kennedy (arts/ent.)
R. King (govt./mil.)
Kunstler (govt./mil.)
Lederer (arts/ent.)
Manchester (arts/ent.)
Marcy (govt./mil.)
Masters (misc.)
Mayo (sci./inv.)
McKinley (govt./mil.)
Morris (arts/ent.)
Paley (business)
Penn (govt./mil.)
Perry (sports)
Thomas Piper
  (business)
Pitt (govt./mil.)
Powell (arts/ent.)
Proxmire (govt./mil.)
Rehnquist (govt./mil.)
Rose (arts/ent.)
Safire (arts/ent.)
Saroyan (arts/ent.)
Sessions (govt./mil.)
Henry Seward (govt./
  mil.)
Shakespeare (arts/ent.)
Shatner (arts/ent.)
Shawn (business)
Tecumseh Sherman
  (govt./mil.)
L. Shirer (arts/ent.)
Shockley (arts/ent.)
Stapleton (arts/ent.)
Styron (arts/ent.)
Taft (govt./mil.)
Desmond Taylor (arts/
  ent.)
Makepeace Thackeray
  (arts/ent.)
Marcy Tweed (govt./
  mil.)
Walton (arts/ent.)
Webster (govt./mil.)
Wellman (arts/ent.)
Westmoreland (govt./
  mil.)
A. Wheeler (govt./mil.)
Allen White (arts/ent.)
Whitehead (arts/ent.)
Wilberforce (govt./
  mil.)
Windom (arts/ent.)
Wordsworth (arts/ent.)

Wrigley, Jr. (business)
Wyler (arts/ent.)
Butler Yeats (arts/ent.)
WILLIE
  Aames (arts/ent.)
  Brown (sports)
  Davis (sports)
  Dixon (arts/ent.)
  Keeler (sports)
  Lanier (sports)
  Mays (sports)
  McCovey (sports)
  McGee (sports)
  Morris (arts/ent.)
  Nelson (arts/ent.)
  Randolph (sports)
  Shoemaker (sports)
  Smith (arts/ent.)
  Stargell (sports)
  Sutton (misc.)
WILLIS
  Reed (sports)
WILLY
  Brandt (govt./mil.)
  Messerschmitt
    (business)
WILMA
  Rudolph (sports)
WILSON
  Mizner (arts/ent.)
  Pickett (arts/ent.)
WILT
  Chamberlain (sports)
WIM
  Wenders (arts/ent.)
WINFIELD
  Scott (govt./mil.)
WINGS
  Hauser (arts/ent.)
WINK
  Martindale (arts/ent.)
WINNIE
  Mandela (govt./mil.)
WINONA
  Ryder (arts/ent.)
WINSLOW
  Homer (arts/ent.)
WINSOR
  McCay (arts/ent.)
WINSTON
  Churchill (govt./mil.)
WITOLD
  Lutoslawski (arts/ent.)
WLADYSLAW
  Reymont (arts/ent.)
WOJCIECH
  Jaruzelski (govt./mil.)

WOLE
  Soyinka (arts/ent.)
WOLFGANG
  Mozart (arts/ent.)
  Pauli (sci./inv.)
  Puck (arts/ent.)
WOODROW
  Wilson (govt./mil.)
WOODY
  Allen (arts/ent.)
  Guthrie (arts/ent.)
  Harrelson (arts/ent.)
  Hayes (sports)
  Herman (arts/ent.)
WRIGHT
  Morris (arts/ent.)
WRONG WAY
  Corrigan (misc.)
WYATT
  Earp (govt./mil.)
WYNDHAM
  Lewis (arts/ent.)
WYNONNA
  Judd (arts/ent.)
WYNTON
  Marsalis (arts/ent.)
XAVIER
  Cugat (arts/ent.)
  McDaniel (sports)
XAVIERA
  Hollander (arts/ent.)
Y. A.
  Tittle (sports)
YAHOO
  Serious (arts/ent.)
YAKOV
  Smirnoff (arts/ent.)
YALE
  Lary (sports)
YANCY
  Butler (arts/ent.)
YAPHET
  Kotto (arts/ent.)
YASIR
  Arafat (govt./mil.)
YASSER
  Arafat (govt./mil.)
YEHUDI
  Menuhin (arts/ent.)
YEVGENY
  Yevtushenko (arts/ent.)
YITZHAK
  Shamir (govt./mil.)
YMA
  Sumac (arts/ent.)
YO-YO
  Ma (arts/ent.)

YOGI
Berra (sports)
YOKO
Ono (arts/ent.)
YOUSUF
Karsh (arts/ent.)
YUKIO
Mishima (arts/ent.)
YUL
Brynner (arts/ent.)
YURI
Andropov (govt./mil.)
Gagarin (pion./exp.)
YURY
Gagarin (pion./exp.)
YVES
Allégret (arts/ent.)
Montand (arts/ent.)
St. Laurent (arts/ent.)
Tanguy (arts/ent.)
YVETTE
Mimieux (arts/ent.)
YVON
Petra (sports)
YVONNE
De Carlo (arts/ent.)

Elliman (arts/ent.)
ZACHARY
Taylor (govt./mil.)
ZACK
Wheat (sports)
ZANDRA
Rhodes (arts/ent.)
ZANE
Grey (arts/ent.)
ZASU
Pitts (arts/ent.)
ZBIGNIEW
Brzezinski (govt./mil.)
Herbert (arts/ent.)
ZEBULON
Pike (pion./exp.)
ZELDA
Fitzgerald (arts/ent.)
ZELL
Miller (govt./mil.)
ZEPPO
Marx (arts/ent.)
ZERO
Mostel (arts/ent.)
ZIGGY
Marley (arts/ent.)

ZILPHA
Keatley Snyder (arts/
ent.)
ZOE, ZOË
Akins (arts/ent.)
Caldwell (arts/ent.)
ZOHRA
Lampert (arts/ent.)
ZOLTÁN
Kodály (arts/ent.)
Korda (arts/ent.)
Tildy (govt./mil.)
ZONA
Gale (arts/ent.)
ZOOT
Sims (arts/ent.)
ZORA
Neale Hurston (arts/
ent.)
ZSA ZSA
Gabor (arts/ent.)
ZUBIN
Mehta (arts/ent.)
ZUTTY
Singleton (arts/ent.)

INDEX OF NICKNAMES

☆

Of course, famous people in all fields tend to pick up nicknames from their admirers—and detractors—as their fame spreads. While hundreds of nicknames are included in the individual entries in this volume, here are some of the more well-known nicknames you might encounter and the respective real names. See the last name entries for more biographical details.

ABE
Abraham Lincoln
ACCIDENTAL PRESIDENT, THE
John Quincy Adams
ADMIRAL, THE
David Robinson
AIR JORDAN
Michael Jordan
ALABAM' ASSASSIN
Joe Louis
ALABAMA ANTELOPE, THE
Don Hutson
ALABAMA WILD MAN, THE
Jerry Reed
ALF
Alison Moyet
ALL-AMERICAN MUSTANG
Doak Walker
AMAZIN' AMAZON
Margaret Court Smith
AMAZING KRESKIN, THE
Kreskin
AMAZING MAYS
Willie Mays
AMAZING RANDI, THE
James Randi
AMBLING ALP, THE
Primo Carnera

AMERICA'S MOST BELOVED COWBOY
Tex Ritter
AMERICA'S SWEETHEART
Mary Pickford
AMERICAN BEAUTY, THE
Lillian Russell
AMERICAN VENUS, THE
Esther Ralston
ANGEL OF DEATH, THE
Joseph Mengele
ANGEL OF THE BATTLEFIELD
Clara Barton
ANGELIC DOCTOR
Thomas Aquinas
ANGRY YOUNG MAN
Kingsley Amis
ANIMAL
Dick Butkus
ANN THE WORD
Ann Lee
ANNE OF THE THOUSAND DAYS
Anne Boleyn
ANTONIO LOCO
Tone Lōc
APOSTLE OF PRESBYTERY, THE
John Knox

APOSTLE OF THE SCOTTISH REFORMERS, THE
John Knox
AQUINIAN SAGE, THE
Juvenal
ARI
Aristotle Onassis
ARKANSAS HUMMINGBIRD, THE
Lon Warneke
ARNIE
Arnold Palmer
ARRIBA
Roberto Clemente
ARTFUL DODGER, THE
Roger Staubach
ATHENIAN, THE
Philostratus
ATLAS OF INDEPENDENCE, THE
John Adams
ATTICUS
Joseph Addison
AUSTRIAN OAK, THE
Arnold Schwarzenegger
AUTOCRAT OF THE AISLE, THE
Brooks Atkinson
AUTOMATIC OTTO
Otto Graham

341

BABE RUTH OF HOCKEY,
THE
Howie Morenz
BABE RUTH OF JAPAN
Sadaharu Oh
BABE RUTH OF THE
NEGRO LEAGUES, THE
Josh Gibson
BABY JUNE
June Havoc
BABY SNOOKS
Fanny Brice
BACHELOR PRESIDENT,
THE
James Buchanan
BAD HENRY
Hank Aaron
BAGEL BOY
Rob Camilletti
BAGS
Milt Jackson
BAMBI
Lance Alworth
BAMBINO, THE
Babe Ruth
BANANA NOSE
Eddie Arcaro
BANTAM BEN
Ben Hogan
BARD OF AVON, THE
William Shakespeare
BARD OF THE
BOULEVARD
John Carradine
BARNEY
Walter Johnson
BARNUM OF BROADWAY
PRODUCTIONS, THE
David Merrick
BARON, THE
Adolph Rupp
BASSMAN OF THE BLUES
B. B. King
BATTLING BELLA
Bella Abzug
BEALE STREET BLUES
BOY, THE
B. B. King
BEAR
Denis Potvin
BEAR, THE
James Brady
BEAST, THE
Jimmie Foxx
BELLE OF AMHERST, THE
Emily Dickinson

BEST-KNOWN VOICE IN
THE WORLD, THE
Raymond Gram Swing
BEST PITCHER IN
BASEBALL
Walter Johnson
BETTY
Lauren Bacall
BIG A
Eddie Arcaro
BIG AL
Al Capone
BIG BILL
Bill Tilden
BIG CAT, THE
Johnny Mize
BIG D
Don Drysdale
BIG DADDY
Idi Amin
BIG DAN
Dan Brouthers
BIG DIPPER, THE
Wilt Chamberlain
BIG DOG
Ernie Nevers
Pete Pihos
BIG E, THE
Elvin Hayes
BIG ED
Ed Delahanty
BIG ED
Ed Walsh
BIG MOMMA
Joanne Gunderson
Carner
BIG NUMBER 99
George Mikan
BIG O
Oscar Robertson
BIG O, THE
Roy Orbison
BIG POISON
Paul Waner
BIG SIX
Christy Mathewson
BIG SKY
Joe Montana
BIG T
Jack Teagarden
BIG TRAIN
Walter Johnson
BIRD
Charlie Parker
BLACK BABE RUTH, THE
Josh Gibson

BLACK BEAUTY
Joe Louis
BLACK BOMBER, THE
Josh Gibson
BLACK JACK
John Pershing
BLACK LOU GEHRIG,
THE
Buck Leonard
BLACK MIKE
Mickey Cochrane
BLACK MOSES
Isaac Hayes
BLACK PEARL, THE
(PEROLA NEGRA)
Pelé
BLACK RHINO, THE
John Belushi
BLACK UHLAN, THE
Max Schmeling
BLINKY
Gordie Howe
BLOND BOMBER, THE
Bobby Layne
BLOND BOMBSHELL OF
SWING
Ina Ray Hutton
BLONDE BOMBSHELL
Jean Harlow
BLOODY MARY
Mary I
BLOODY SAM
Sam Peckinpah
BLUES BOY, THE
B. B. King
BOB-A-DOB
Bob Lanier
BOBBY HOCKEY
Bobby Orr
BOBCAT
Bob Goldthwait
BOCEPHUS
Hank Williams, Jr.
BOGIE
Humphrey Bogart
BOJANGLES
Bill Robinson
BONZO
John Bonham
BOOP-BOOP-A-DOOP
GIRL, THE
Helen Kane
BOOTNOSE
Sid Abel
BORDER MINSTREL, THE
Walter Scott

Boss
 Mike Bossy
Boss, The
 Bruce Springsteen
 Bess Truman
**Boston Strong Boy,
 The**
 John L. Sullivan
Boy Commissioner, The
 Pete Rozelle
**Boy from Beale
 Street, The**
 B.B. King
Boy Robot
 Bobby Fischer
Boy Wonder, The
 Irving Thalberg
Boz
 Brian Bosworth
Boz
 Charles Dickens
Brat, The
 John McEnroe
Brazilian Bombshell
 Sonia Braga
**Brazilian Bombshell,
 The**
 Carmen Miranda
Broadway Joe
 Joe Namath
**Brockton
 Blockbuster, The**
 Rocky Marciano
Brockton Bomber
 Rocky Marciano
Brockton Bull
 Rocky Marciano
Brockton Buster
 Rocky Marciano
Bronco Billy
 Gilbert Anderson
Bronx Bull, The
 Jake LaMotta
**Brown Behemoth,
 The**
 Joe Louis
Brown Bomber, The
 Joe Louis
Brown Bombshell
 Jesse Owens
Bruiser
 Frank Kinard
Bruno
 Bruce Willis
Bubbles
 Beverly Sills

Bucketfoot Al
 Al Simmons
Buckeye Bullet
 Jesse Owens
Bud
 Calvin Trillin
Buddy
 Marlon Brando
 Patrick Swayze
Buffalo Bob
 Bob Smith
Buffalo, The
 Dave Debusschere
Bugs
 Arthur Baer
 Bugs Moran
Bull
 William Halsey
Bull, The
 Greg Luzinski
Bulldog
 Jim Bouton
Bullet, The
 Bill Dudley
Bullet Bill
 Bill Dudley
Bullet Bob
 Bob Hayes
Bunny
 Edmund Wilson
**Butcher of Baghdad,
 The**
 Saddam Hussein
Butcher of Lyon, The
 Klaus Barbie
Cactus Jack
 John N. Garner
**California Comet,
 The**
 Don Budge
Campy
 Roy Campanella
 Bert Campaneris
Candy Man, The
 John Candelaria
Cannonball Kid
 Roscoe Tanner
Cap the Knife
 Caspar Weinberger
Capability Brown
 Lancelot Brown
Captain Fingers
 Lee Ritenour
**Car Park Golfer,
 The**
 Seve Ballesteros

**Caruso of Baritones,
 The**
 Titta Ruffo
Cassius The Brashest
 Muhammad Ali
Catholic, The
 Isabella
Censor, The
 Cato
Cha-Cha
 Shirley Muldowney
**Chairman of the
 Board, The**
 Whitey Ford
 Frank Sinatra
Champagne Lady
 Norma Zimmer
Charger, The
 Arnold Palmer
Charlie
 Oscar Charleston
Charlie Hustle
 Pete Rose
Chatti
 Conchata Ferrell
Cherokee Cowboy, The
 Ray Price
Cinderella Man
 Jim Braddock
Cisco Kid, The
 Duncan Renaldo
**Clark Gable of the
 80s**
 Tom Selleck
**Clown Prince of
 Basketball, The**
 Meadowlark Lemon
 Goose Tatum
**Clown Prince of
 Fitness, The**
 Richard Simmons
Clyde
 Walt Frazier
**Coal Miner's
 Daughter**
 Loretta Lynn
Cobra, The
 Dave Parker
Cocky
 Eddie Collins
Colby Jack
 Jack Coombs
Columbia Lou
 Lou Gehrig
Comet
 Willie Davis

COMMERCE COMET, THE
Mickey Mantle
COMMONER, THE
William Jennings
Bryan
COMMY
Charlie Comiskey
CONTACT
Willie Lanier
COOZ
Bob Cousy
CORDUROY KILLER
Bobby Fischer
CORY
Corazon Aquino
COUNTRY
Enos Slaughter
COUNTRY CHARLEY
Charley Pride
COURT JOUSTER
Bill Tilden
COUSIN ED
Ed Barrow
COW EYES
Estelle Winwood
CRAB, THE
Jesse Burkett
Johnny Evers
CRACKER
Ray Schalk
CRAZY GUGGENHEIM
Frank Fontaine
CRITIC YOU LOVE TO
HATE, THE
John Simon
CROWN PRINCE OF
COUNTRY MUSIC, THE
George Jones
DADDY OF THE BLUES
T-Bone Walker
DANDY DON
Don Meredith
DAPPER DON, THE
John Gotti
DARK DESTROYER
Joe Louis
DAUNTLESS DOAK
Doak Walker
DAZZLER, THE
Dazzy Vance
DEACON BILL
Bill McKechnie
DEFENDER OF THE
CONSTITUTION
Daniel Webster
DESERT FOX, THE
Erwin Rommell

DESTROYER, THE
George Foster
DEWEY
Dwight Evans
DIGGER
Richard Phelps
DIVINE MISS M, THE
Bette Midler
DIVINE ONE, THE
Sarah Vaughan
DIVINE SARAH, THE
Sarah Bernhardt
DIZZY
Benjamin Disraeli
DOAKER
Doak Walker
DOC
Neil Simon
Dwight Gooden
DR. BOB
Bob Smith
DR. HUG
Leo Buscaglia
DR. J
Julius Erving
DR. K
Dwight Gooden
DR. LOVE
Leo Buscaglia
DOLLAR BILL
Bill Bradley
DOMINICAN DANDY,
THE
Juan Marichal
DOUBLE D
Don Drysdale
DOUBLE NO-HIT
Johnny Vander Meer
DOUBLE X
Jimmie Foxx
THE DREAM
Akeem Olojuwon
DRIFTING COWBOY,
THE
Hank Williams
DRONE, THE
Henry Kissinger
DUCKY
Joe Medwick
Clarence Nash
DUKE OF DARK
CORNERS, THE
Ralph Richardson
DUKE OF TRALEE, THE
Roger Bresnahan
DUKE, THE
John Wayne

DUTCH
Elmore Leonard
Ronald Reagan
DUTCH MASTER, THE
Johnny Vander Meer
DUTCHMAN
Frankie Frisch
DUTCHMAN, THE
Dutch Schultz
Norm Van Brocklin
DYNAMIC DOAK
Doak Walker
EARL OF SNOHOMISH
Earl Averill
EDDIE
Edd Roush
EE-YAH
Hughie Jennings
EIFFEL TOWER OF
CULPEPPER, THE
Eppa Rixey
EL DORADO
Francisco de Coronado
EL LIBERTADOR
Simon Bolívar
EL REY
Tito Puente
EL TORO
Fernando Valenzuela
ELDER, THE
Cato
$11,000 LEMON
Rube Marquard
$11,000 WONDER
Rube Marquard
EMINENCE ROUGE (OR
RED EMINENCE)
Cardinal de Richelieu
EMPRESS OF THE BLUES
Bessie Smith
ENFORCER, THE
Dick Butkus
EPPA JEPHTHA
Eppa Rixey
EPPIE
Ann Landers
EYE, THE
Allan Pinkerton
FABULOUS MR. B,
THE
Billy Eckstine
FAIR ONE, THE
Rula Lenska
FANCY PANTS
A.J. Foyt
FANNIE
Dinah Shore

FAT GIRL
Fats Navarro
FATHER OF AMERICAN FOOTBALL
Walter Chauncey Camp
FATHER OF AMERICAN PARKS
Frederick Olmsted
FATHER OF ANALYTICAL PSYCHOLOGY
Carl Jung
FATHER OF BASEBALL, THE
Abner Doubleday
FATHER OF BASKETBALL
James Naismith
FATHER OF BLACK BASEBALL, THE
Rube Foster
FATHER OF BLUEGRASS
Bill Monroe
FATHER OF COUNTRY MUSIC, THE
Bill Monroe
Jimmie Rodgers
FATHER OF FRENCH TRAGEDY
Pierre Corneille
FATHER OF GENETICS, THE
William Bateson
FATHER OF HIS COUNTRY, THE
George Washington
FATHER OF HISTORY, THE
Herodotus
FATHER OF ITALIAN PAINTING
Giovanni Cimabue
FATHER OF MEDICINE, THE
Hippocrates
FATHER OF MEXICAN INDEPENDENCE, THE
Miguel Hidalgo y Costilla
FATHER OF MODERN ASTRONOMY, THE
Johannes Kepler
FATHER OF MODERN PHOTOGRAPHY
Alfred Stieglitz
FATHER OF MODERN ROCKETRY
Robert Goddard

FATHER OF PEACE
Andrea Doria
FATHER OF PRAGMATISM
Charles Peirce
FATHER OF RADIO
Lee De Forest
FATHER OF ROCK 'N' ROLL
Bill Haley
FATHER OF RUSSIAN MARXISM, THE
Georgy Plekhanov
FATHER OF RUSSIAN MUSIC
Mikhail Glinka
FATHER OF THE AMERICAN REVOLUTION
Samuel Adams
FATHER OF THE ATOM BOMB
J. Robert Oppenheim
FATHER OF THE ATOMIC SUBMARINE
Hyman Rickover
FATHER OF THE BLUES
W. C. Handy
FATHER OF THE CONSTITUTION, THE
James Madison
FATHER OF THE HOLE, THE
Henry Moore
FATHER OF THE HYDROGEN BOMB
Edward Teller
FATHER OF THE MODERN DRUGSTORE
Charles Rudolph Walgreen
FATHER OF THE RENAISSANCE
Lorenzo Ghiberti
FATHER OF THE SKYSCRAPER
William Jenney
FATHER OF THE WALTZ, THE
Johann Strauss
FATHER OF TRAGEDY, THE
Aeschylus
FDR
Franklin Delano Roosevelt
FERGIE
Sarah Ferguson

FIGHTING BOB
Robert La Follette
FIGHTING MARINE, THE
Gene Tunney
FIRST LADY OF CONTEMPORARY CHRISTIAN MUSIC, THE
Amy Grant
FIRST LADY OF COUNTRY MUSIC, THE
Tammy Wynette
FIRST LADY OF SONG
Ella Fitzgerald
FIRST LADY OF THE AMERICAN THEATER
Ethel Barrymore
Katharine Cornell
Helen Hayes
FIRST LADY OF THE SCREEN
Norma Shearer
FIRST LADY OF THE SILENT SCREEN
Lillian Gish
FIRST LADY OF THE SPEAKEASIES
Texas Guinan
FIRST LADY OF THE WORLD, THE
Eleanor Roosevelt
FIRST OF PHILOSOPHERS, THE
Gottfried von Leibniz
FLAMINGO, THE
Virginia Hill
FLASH
Arnie Herber
FLICKA
Frederica Von Stade
FLO
Florenz Ziegfeld
FLO-JO
Florence Griffith-Joyner
FLOWER, THE
Guy Lafleur
FLYING DUTCHMAN, THE
Honus Wagner
FLYING FINN, THE
Paavo Nurmi
FLYING PEACEMAKER, THE
Henry Kissinger
FLYING SCOT, THE
Jim Clark

FORDHAM FLASH, THE
Frankie Frisch
FOUNDER OF SCIENCE FICTION, THE
Jules Verne
FPA
Franklin Pierce Adams
FRANCHISE, THE
Kareem Abdul-Jabbar
Lou Brock
Tom Seaver
FRENCH HENRY FORD, THE
André Citroën
FRITZ
Walter F. Mondale
FRONTIER POET, THE
Joaquin Miller
FROSTY
Dyan Cannon
FRUGAL GOURMET, THE
Jeff Smith
GALLOPING GHOST, THE
Red Grange
GALLOPING GOURMET, THE
Graham Kerr
GARY COOPER OF SPORTSCASTERS, THE
Pat Summerall
GATOR
Ron Guidry
GAY CASTILLION, THE
Lefty Gomez
GENE MACHINE, THE
Gene Littler
GENE THE MACHINE
Gene Littler
GENIUS OF SOUL, THE
Ray Charles
GENTLEMAN JIM
James J. Corbett
GENTLEMAN JOHNNY
John Burgoyne
GEORGIA PEACH
Little Richard
GEORGIA PEACH, THE
Ty Cobb
GERRY
Geraldine Page
GETTYSBURG EDDIE
Eddie Plank
GI's GENERAL, THE
Omar Bradley
GIBBY
Kirk Gibson

GINNY FIZZ
Virginia Wade
GOLDEN BEAR, THE
Jack Nicklaus
GOLDEN BOY, THE
Paul Hornung
GOLDEN GIRL, THE
Sonja Henie
GOLDEN JET, THE
Bobby Hull
GOLDEN JOE
Joe Montana
GOOFY
Lefty Gomez
GORGEOUS GEORGE
George Sisler
GORGO
Pancho Gonzales
GRAFIN
Steffi Graf
GRAND OLD MAN OF AMERICAN FOOTBALL, THE
Amos Alonzo Stagg
GRAND VETERAN
Walter Johnson
GRANDFATHER OF BRITISH ROCK
John Mayall
GRANNY
Dawn Fraser
GRAPEFRUIT
Wilbert Robinson
GREAT BEAST, THE
Aleister Crowley
GREAT COLLABORATOR, THE
George S. Kaufman
GREAT COMMUNICATOR, THE
Ronald Reagan
GREAT COMPROMISER, THE
Henry Clay
GREAT DISSENTER, THE
Oliver Wendell Holmes
GREAT EMANCIPATOR, THE
Abraham Lincoln
GREAT GRETZKY, THE
Wayne Gretzky
GREAT GUNDY, THE
Joanne Gunderson Carner
GREAT JOHN, THE
John L. Sullivan

GREAT KATE, THE
Katherine Hepburn
GREAT LOVER, THE
Rudolph Valentino
GREAT MAGICIAN, THE
Walter Scott
GREAT ONE, THE
Jackie Gleason
Wayne Gretzky
GREAT PACIFICATOR, THE
Henry Clay
GREAT PROFILE, THE
John Barrymore
GREAT STONE FACE, THE
Buster Keaton
GREAT WHITE HOPE, THE
Gerry Cooney
GREATEST, THE
Muhammad Ali
GREY GHOST OF GONZAGA, THE
Tony Canadeo
GUITAR MAN
Jerry Reed
GUS
Early Wynn
HAIG, THE
Walter Hagen
HAM
Hamilton Jordan
HAMMER
Mike Ditka
HAMMER, THE
Hank Aaron
HAMMERIN' HANK
Hank Greenberg
HANDS
Johnny Bench
HANDS OF STONE
Roberto Duran
HANGMAN OF EUROPE, THE
Reinhard Heydrich
HANNIBAL JERKIN
Hamilton Jordan
HANOI JANE
Jane Fonda
HAPPY HUSTLER, THE
Bobby Riggs
HAPPY JACK
Jack Chesbro
HAPPY WARRIOR, THE
Hubert H. Humphrey
HARRY
Prince Henry

HAWK
Ralph Branca
Tony Dorsett
HAWK, THE
Ezzard Charles
Ben Hogan
**HENRY FORD OF
AVIATION, THE**
William Thomas Piper
**HENRY FORD OF
GERMANY, THE**
Wilhelm Von Opel
HENRY THE K
Henry Kissinger
HER NIBS, MISS GIBBS
Georgia Gibbs
HHH
Hubert H. Humphrey
**HIGH PRIEST OF
COUNTRY MUSIC, THE**
Conway Twitty
**HILLBILLY SHAKESPEARE,
THE**
Hank Williams
HIS ROYAL BADNESS
Prince
HOLLYWOOD MADAM
Heidi Fleiss
HOMICIDE HANK
Henry Armstrong
HONDO
John Havlicek
HONEST ABE
Abraham Lincoln
HOOK
Warren Spahn
HOOKS
Ray Dandridge
HOOSIER POET, THE
James Riley
**HOOSIER THUNDERBOLT,
THE**
Amos Rusie
HOOT
Bob Gibson
HOT TODDY
Thelma Todd
HOTSPUR
Henry Percy
**HOUDINI OF THE
HARDWOOD, THE**
Bob Cousy
HUG
Miller Huggins
**HUMAN BUZZSAW,
THE**
Henry Armstrong

**HUNGARIAN RHAPSODY,
THE**
Vilma Banky
HURRICANE HENRY
Henry Armstrong
HURTLING HABITANT
Howie Morenz
HUSK
Frank Chance
Christy Mathewson
ICE CREAM
George Allen
ICE MAIDEN
Anita Ekberg
ICE MAIDEN, THE
Chris Evert
ICE MAN, THE
Jerry Butler
ICEMAN, THE
George Gervin
**ICONOCLAST WITH A
PENCIL**
Jules Feiffer
IGGY STOOGE
Iggy Pop
IKE
Dwight D. Eisenhower
IL DUCE
Benito Mussolini
**INCOMPARABLE MAX,
THE**
Max Beerbohm
INCORRUPTIBLE, THE
Maximilien Robespierre
**INDIA RUBBER MAN,
THE**
John Wooden
INDIAN JOE
Joe Guyon
INDIO
Manny Trillo
**INTELLECTUAL ASSASSIN,
THE**
Ron Mix
**INTELLECTUAL OF
BASEBALL, THE**
Moe Berg
INVINCIBLE ONE, THE
Warren Spahn
IRON BUTTERFLY, THE
Imelda Marcos
IRON CHANCELLOR, THE
Otto von Bismarck
IRON DUKE, THE
Duke of Wellington
IRON HORSE, THE
Lou Gehrig

IRON LADY
Margaret Thatcher
IRON MAN
Emil Zatopek
**IRON MAN OF BASEBALL,
THE**
Lou Gehrig
IRON MIKE
Mike Tyson
IRON STOMACH, THE
Henry Kissinger
IT GIRL, THE
Clara Bow
IZZIE
Eddie Cantor
JACK
John F. Kennedy
JACK THE DRIPPER
Jackson Pollock
JAKE THE SNAKE
Jacques Plante
JAY
John D. Rockefeller IV
JAZZ'S ANGRY MAN
Charles Mingus
JEB
J. E. B. Stuart
JERSEY LILY, THE
Lillie Langtry
JET, THE
Joe Perry
JEWISH COWBOY, THE
James Caan
JFK
John F. Kennedy
JIMMY
James Stewart
JIMMY THE GREEK
Jimmy Snyder
JOE BANANAS
Joseph Bonanno
JOLTIN' JOE
Joe DiMaggio
JOPLIN GHOST, THE
Horton Smith
JUICE
O. J. Simpson
JUMBO JOE
Joe Stydahar
JUMP STEADY
Garry Templeton
JUNK MAN, THE
Ed Lopat
KANSAS IRONMAN, THE
Glenn Cunningham
KATE
Katherine Hepburn

KC
  Harry Casey
KENTUCKY COLONEL,
  THE
  Earle Combs
KID, THE
  Steve Cauthen
  Edith Piaf
  Ted Williams
KILLER
  Harmon Killebrew
KILLER, THE
  Jerry Lee Lewis
KING
  Hugh McElhenny
KING, THE
  Clark Gable
  Elvis Presley
KING CARL
  Carl Hubbell
KING OF CHAMPAGNE
  MUSIC, THE
  Lawrence Welk
KING OF COMEDY, THE
  Mack Sennett
KING OF CORN
  Spike Jones
KING OF COUNTRY
  MUSIC
  Roy Acuff
KING OF GOSPEL
  MUSIC
  James Cleveland
KING OF HI DE HO
  Cab Calloway
KING OF JAZZ
  Paul Whiteman
KING OF LATIN MUSIC,
  THE
  Tito Puente
KING OF LITTLE MEN
  Eddie Arcaro
KING OF MAMBO, THE
  Perez Prado
KING OF POP, THE
  Michael Jackson
KING OF SWING
  Benny Goodman
KING OF THE BLUES
  B.B. King
KING OF THE COWBOYS
  Roy Rogers
KING OF THE
  DAREDEVILS
  Evel Knievel
KING OF THE LINKS
  Bobby Jones

KING OF THE
  NUDIES
  Russ Meyer
KING OF THE PULP
  WRITERS
  Max Brand
KING OF THE STAKES
  RIDERS
  Eddie Arcaro
KING OF THE WILD
  FRONTIER
  Davy Crockett
KING OF TORTS, THE
  Melvin Belli
KING OF THE 12-STRING
  GUITAR PLAYERS
  Leadbelly
KING OF VIBES
  Lionel Hampton
KING TUT
  Tutankhamen
KINGFISH, THE
  Huey P. Long
KISSIN' JIM
  Jim Folsom, Jr.
KIT
  Christopher Morley
KLU
  Ted Kluszewski
KNIGHT OF KENNETT
  SQUARE, THE
  Herb Pennock
KNUCKSIE
  Phil Niekro
LA LOLLO
  Gina Lollobrigida
LA TAMARA
  Tamara Karsavina
LADY DAY
  Billie Holiday
LADY LINDY
  Amelia Earhart
LADY T
  Teena Marie
LADY WITH A THOUSAND
  VOICES
  Ireene Seaton Wicker
LADY WITH THE LAMP,
  THE
  Florence Nightingale
LAIRD OF THE HALLS,
  THE
  Harry Lauder
LARRUPIN' LOU
  Lou Gehrig
LARRY
  Napoleon Lajoie

LAST OF THE DREAM
  MERCHANTS
  Ross Hunter
LAST OF THE ROMANS,
  THE
  Cassius
LAST POET OF ROME,
  THE
  Juvenal
LB
  Louis B. Mayer
LE GRAND
  François Couperin
LE GROS BILL
  Jean Beliveau
LEFTY
  Steve Carlton
  Nils Lofgren
LINDY
  Freddie Lindstrom
LIP, THE
  Leo Durocher
LITTLE AL
  Al Unser, Jr.
LITTLE BIG MAN
  Dustin Hoffman
LITTLE COLONEL,
  THE
  Pee Wee Reese
LITTLE DRAGON, THE
  Bruce Lee
LITTLE ESTHER
  Esther Phillips
LITTLE FLOWER
  Fiorello La Guardia
LITTLE GIANT
  Stephen A. Douglas
LITTLE JAZZ
  Roy Eldridge
LITTLE JIMMIE RODGERS
  Jimmie Rodgers
LITTLE JIMMY
  Jimmy Osmond
LITTLE LOOIE
  Luis Aparicio
LITTLE MAN IN PRO
  FOOTBALL
  Doak Walker
LITTLE MARY
  Mary Decker
LITTLE MISS DYNAMITE
  Brenda Lee
LITTLE MISS GRUNT
  Monica Seles
LITTLE MISS POKER
  FACE
  Helen Wills

LITTLE MO
Maureen Connolly
LITTLE NAPOLEON
John McGraw
LITTLE POISON
Paul Runyan
Lloyd Waner
LITTLE QUEEN OF SOAP
OPERA, THE
Anne Francis
LITTLE SURE SHOT
Annie Oakley
LITTLE TOMMY
TUCKER
Tommy Tucker
LITTLE TRAMP, THE
Charlie Chaplin
LIVING DICTIONARY, A
Gottfried von Leibniz
LIZ
Elizabeth Taylor
LIZARD KING, THE
Jim Morrison
LO SPAGNOLETTO (THE
LITTLE SPANIARD)
José de Ribera
LONE EAGLE, THE
Charles Lindbergh
LONESOME GEORGE
George Gobel
LORD BYRON
Byron Nelson
LOUISIANA LIGHTNING
Ron Guidry
LOUISVILLE LIP, THE
Muhammad Ali
LOVABLE LUSH, THE
Foster Brooks
LOVE GODDESS, THE
Rita Hayworth
LUCKY LINDY
Charles Lindbergh
MAC
Malcolm Baldridge
Macaulay Culkin
MAD DOG
Bill Madlock
MAD DUCK, THE
Alex Karras
MAD HUNGARIAN, THE
Al Hrabosky
MAD MONK, THE
Rasputin
MAD RUSSIAN, THE
Bert Gordon
MADAM TO THE STARS
Heidi Fleiss

MADCAP MAGGIE
Margaret Whiting
MAESTRO OF MAYHEM,
THE
Dick Butkus
MAGGIE
Margaret Thatcher
MAGIC
Magic (Earvin) Johnson
Gale Sayers
MAGNIFICENT, THE
Lorenzo de' Medici
MAHATMA, THE
Branch Rickey
MAID OF ORLEANS
Joan of Arc
MAILMAN, THE
Karl Malone
MALE GARBO, THE
Al Pacino
MAMA CASS
Cass Elliot
MAN, THE
Bear Bryant
Stan Musial
MAN IN BLACK, THE
Johnny Cash
MAN OF A THOUSAND
FACES
Lon Chaney
MAN OF A THOUSAND
MOVES, THE
Elgin Baylor
MAN OF IRON, THE
Lech Walesa
MAN WHO TAUGHT
AMERICA TO SING,
THE
Fred Waring
MAN WITH THE PERFECT
PROFILE, THE
Robert Taylor
MANASSA MAULER, THE
Jack Dempsey
MANITO
Juan Marichal
MARCH KING, THE
John Philip Sousa
MARVELOUS MARVIN
Marvin Hagler
MARYLAND STRONG BOY,
THE
Jimmie Foxx
MASTER MELVIN
Mel Ott
MASTER OF FLEMALLE
Robert Campin

MASTER OF MENACE
Vincent Price
MASTER OF MERODE
Robert Campin
MASTER OF SUSPENSE,
THE
Alfred Hitchcock
MASTER, THE
Eddie Arcaro
MATTY THE GREAT
Christy Mathewson
MAYFLOWER MADAM,
THE
Sidney Biddle Barrows
MEAL TICKET, THE
Carl Hubbell
MECHANICAL MAN, THE
Charlie Gehringer
MEMPHIS BILL
Bill Terry
MERRY MADCAP, THE
Max Baer
METEOR
Howie Morenz
MEXICAN WASHINGTON,
THE
Benito Juarez
MIAMI NICE
Vinny Testaverde
MICKEY
Michael Powell
MIGHTY MITE, THE
Miller Huggins
MISHA
Mikhail Baryshnikov
MISS PEACHES
Etta James
MR. B
George Balanchine
MISTER BASKETBALL
Nat Holman
MR. BOXING
Nat Fleischer
MR. CLUTCH
Jerry West
MR. COUNTRY ROCK
Crash Craddock
MISTER COWBOY
Rex Allen
MR. DEMOCRAT
Sam Rayburn
MR. EXCITEMENT
Jackie Wilson
MR. FIVE BY FIVE
Jimmy Rushing
MR. GUITAR
Chet Atkins

MR. KNICKERBOCKER
Bill Bradley
MR. LINCOLN'S CAMERAMAN
Matthew Brady
MR. MARCH
Bayard Rustin
MR. MUSIC-MAKER
Lawrence Welk
MR. NEW YEAR'S EVE
Guy Lombardo
MR. OCTOBER
Reggie Jackson
MR. SATURDAY NIGHT
Jackie Gleason
MR. SCOOP
Al Oliver
MR. TELEVISION
Milton Berle
MR. UNEMOTIONAL
Paul Warfield
MONEY
Carl Hubbell
MOSE
Lefty Grove
MOSES OF HER PEOPLE
Harriet Tubman
MOTHER OF THE CIVIL RIGHTS MOVEMENT
Rosa Parks
MOTOR CITY MAD MAN
Ted Nugent
MOTOR MOUTH
Mark Hamill
MOUSE
Stan Mikita
MOUTH OF THE SOUTH, THE
Ted Turner
MULLETHEAD
George Brett
MUSCLES
Joe Medwick
MUSCLES FROM BRUSSELS
Jean-Claude Van Damme
NAILS
Lenny Dykstra
NAP THE NONPAREIL
Napoleon Lajoie
NASTI
Nastassja Kinski
NASTY
Ilie Nastase
NELLIE
Helen Taft

NEW SULTAN OF SWAT, THE
Hank Aaron
NEWK
John Newcombe
NIGHT STALKER, THE
Richard Ramirez
NIGHT TRAIN
Dick Lane
NIGHTINGALE OF INDIA, THE
Sarojini Naidu
NORWEGIAN DOLL, THE
Sonja Henie
NUMBER 6
Bill Russell
OBSCURE, THE
Heracleitus
OFF-SIDE KID, THE
Bill Hewitt
OHIO FATS
Jack Nicklaus
OL' BLUE EYES
Frank Sinatra
OL' MAN RIVER
Archie Moore
OL' PEA PICKER, THE
Tennessee Ernie Ford
OL' SCHNOZZOLA
Jimmy Durante
OL' STUBBLEBEARD
Burleigh Grimes
OLD 98
Tom Harmon
OLD ACHES AND PAINS
Luke Appling
OLD ARBITRATOR, THE
Bill Klem
OLD BISCUIT PANTS
Lou Gehrig
OLD BLOOD AND GUTS
George S. Patton
OLD BROWN OF OSAWATOMIE
John Brown
OLD FUSS AND FEATHERS
Winfield Scott
OLD HICKORY
Andrew Jackson
OLD IRONSIDES
Isaac Hull
OLD LADY
Billie Jean King

OLD LOW-AND-AWAY
Grover Cleveland Alexander
OLD MAN
Connie Mack
OLD MAN ELOQUENT
John Quincy Adams
OLD MONGOOSE, THE
Archie Moore
OLD PETE
Grover Cleveland Alexander
OLD PROFESSOR, THE
Casey Stengel
OLD ROMAN, THE
Charlie Comiskey
OLD ROUGH AND READY
Zachary Taylor
OLD SALAMANDER
David Farragut
OLD TOMATO FACE
Gabby Hartnett
OLE REDHEAD
Arthur Godfrey
OLLIE
Oliver Hardy
ONE PLAY
George McAfee
ONLY LAW WEST OF THE PECOS, THE
Roy Bean
OOMPH GIRL, THE
Ann Sheridan
OSCAR OF THE WALDORF
Oscar Tschirky
OUR GINNY
Virginia Wade
OZARK IKE
Terry Bradshaw
PADDLES
Dick Butkus
PANAMA
Laffit Pincay, Jr.
PAPA
Ernest Hemingway
PAPA BEAR
George Halas
PAPA DOC
Francois Duvalier
PAPPY
John Ford
PAT
Patricia Nixon
PAVLOVA OF THE SILVER SKATES, THE
Sonja Henie

PEACEFUL WARRIOR,
THE
Martin Luther King, Jr.
PEARL
Janis Joplin
PEARL OF THE PAMPAS
Gabriela Sabatini
PEARL, THE
Earl Monroe
PEARLIE MAY
Pearl Bailey
PEERLESS LEADER, THE
Frank Chance
PEERLESS PAAVO
Paavo Nurmi
PEOPLE'S ATTORNEY,
THE
Louis Brandeis
PEOPLE'S AUTHOR, THE
Mark Twain
PEP
Ross Youngs
PEROLA NEGRA (THE
BLACK PEARL)
Pelé
PETE
Grover Cleveland
Alexander
PETER PAN OF POP, THE
Michael Jackson
PHANTOM FINN, THE
Paavo Nurmi
PHILADELPHIA LADY,
THE
Marian Anderson
PHOENIX, THE
Lope de Vega
PIED PIPER OF POUNDS,
THE
Richard Simmons
PINEAPPLE KING, THE
James Drummond
Dole
PINEY
Lou Piniella
PISTOL PETE
Pete Maravich
PITTSBURGH KID, THE
Billy Conn
PLATINUM BLONDE, THE
Jean Harlow
POET OF THE AMERICAN
REVOLUTION
Philip Freneau
POET OF THE CHICAGO
SLUMS
Nelson Algren

POET OF THE PLAIN
PEOPLE, THE
Edgar A. Guest
POLISH PRINCE, THE
Bobby Vinton
PONDEROUS PRIMO
Primo Carnera
POOR LITTLE RICH GIRL,
THE
Barbara Hutton
POP
Cap Anson
Jesse Haines
POPO
Abigail Van Buren
POPS
Louis Armstrong
Willie Stargell
Paul Whiteman
POTENTATE OF POP, THE
Arthur Fiedler
PREACHER, THE
Bobby Womack
PREEM, THE
Primo Carnera
PRES
Lester Young
PRIDE OF THE YANKEES,
THE
Lou Gehrig
PRINCE CHARMING
John F. Kennedy, Jr.
PRINCE HAL
Hal Newhouser
PRINCE MIKE
Mike Romanoff
PRINCE OF DARKNESS,
THE
Johnny Carson
PRINCE OF PEACE, THE
Andrew Carnegie
Martin Luther King, Jr.
PRINCE OF PESSIMISM
Chuck Daly
PRINCESS, THE
Helen Wills
PROPHET OF SILHOUETTE
Cristóbal Balenciaga
PROSE LAUREATE OF
THE SEMI-LITERATE,
THE
Damon Runyon
PUBLIC ENEMY NUMBER
ONE
John Dillinger
PUBLICOLA
John Quincy Adams

PUDGE
Carlton Fisk
PUFFIN
Anthony Asquith
QUEEN HELEN
Helen Wills
QUEEN OF BURLESQUE,
THE
Gypsy Rose Lee
QUEEN OF COUNTRY
MUSIC
Kitty Wells
QUEEN OF COURTS
Helen Wills
QUEEN OF CRIME
Agatha Christie
QUEEN OF DISCO
Gloria Gaynor
QUEEN OF HOUSEWIFE
ROCK
Helen Reddy
QUEEN OF MEAN, THE
Leona Helmsley
QUEEN OF ROMANCE,
THE
Barbara Cartland
QUEEN OF SILENT
SERIALS
Pearl White
QUEEN OF SOUL
Aretha Franklin
QUEEN OF
TECHNICOLOR, THE
Maria Montez
QUEEN OF THE BLUES
Dinah Washington
QUEEN OF THE
COURTS
Billie Jean King
QUEEN OF THE HORROR
MOVIES
Evelyn Ankers
QUEEN OF THE
MUCKRAKERS
Jessica Mitford
QUIZ
Dan Quisenberry
RAGIN' CAJUN, THE
James Carville
RAGING BULL
Jake LaMotta
RAJAH, THE
Rogers Hornsby
RANDY ANDY
Prince Andrew
RAPID ROBERT
Bob Feller

RED PRIEST, THE
Antonio Vivaldi
REFORMER OF A
KINGDOM, THE
John Knox
REFRIGERATOR
William Perry
RENO ROCKET, THE
Greg Lemond
RFK
Robert F. Kennedy
RHODY
Bobby Wallace
RHUMBA KING
Xavier Cugat
RIFLE
Bob Waterfield
RIGHT-HANDED BABE
RUTH, THE
Jimmie Foxx
RJ
Robert Wagner
RK
Rockwell Kent
ROBBY
Frank Robinson
ROCK 'N' ROLL
NEWSMAN
Geraldo Rivera
ROCKET
Maurice Richard
ROCKET, THE
Rod Laver
ROCKY
Ron Swoboda
ROCKY RACCOON CLARK
Steve Wozniak
ROLLS ROYCE OF
COUNTRY MUSIC, THE
George Jones
ROSIE
Roseanne Arnold
RYAN EXPRESS, THE
Nolan Ryan
SAGE OF BALTIMORE,
THE
H.L. Mencken
SAGE OF EMPORIA, THE
William Allen White
SAGE OF MONTICELLO,
THE
Thomas Jefferson
SAINT BOB
Bob Geldof
SAINT OF THE
GUTTERS
Mother Teresa

SATCHMO
Louis Armstrong
SAY HEY
Willie Mays
SCARFACE
Al Capone
SCARFACE AL
Al Capone
SCHNOZ, THE
Jimmy Durante
SCOOPS
Max Carey
SCOURGE OF AMERICAN
LIBERALISM
William F. Buckley, Jr.
SCOURGE OF GOD
Attila The Hun
SCRAMBLER, THE
Fran Tarkenton
SCREAMER, THE
Evelyn Ankers
SENTIMENTAL
GENTLEMAN OF SWING
Tommy Dorsey
SHAQ
Shaquille O'Neal
SHERIFF, THE
Faron Young
SHOE
Willie Shoemaker
SHOELESS JOE
Joe Jackson
SHRIMP, THE
Jean Shrimpton
SILENT CAL
Calvin Coolidge
SILVER FOX, THE
Charlie Rich
Duke Snider
SINGER'S SINGER, THE
Tony Bennett
SINGING BRAKEMAN,
THE
Jimmie Rodgers
SINGING COWBOY, THE
Gene Autry
SINGING FISHERMAN,
THE
Johnny Horton
SINGING HOBO, THE
Boxcar Willie
SINGING LADY, THE
Ireene Seaton Wicker
SINGING RAGE, THE
Patti Page
SIR LARRY
Laurence Olivier

SIR TIMOTHY
Tim Keefe
SISTER AIMEE
Aimee Semple
McPherson
SKEETER
Wilma Rudolph
SKOONJ
Carl Furillo
SLAMMIN' SAM
Sam Snead
SLINGIN' SAM
Sammy Baugh
SLUG
Harry Heilmann
SLY
Sylvester Stallone
SMACK
Fletcher Henderson
SMILING WHIRLWIND,
THE
Hoot Gibson
SMOKIN' JOE
Joe Frazier
SMOKY MOUNTAIN BOY,
THE
Roy Acuff
SNAKE, THE
Ken Stabler
SON OF SAM
David Berkowitz
SOUL BROTHER NUMBER
ONE
James Brown
SOUTHERN GENTLEMAN,
THE
Sonny James
SPAHNY
Warren Spahn
SPIDER
Althea Gibson
SPLENDID SPLINTER, THE
Ted Williams
SPRINGFIELD RIFLE, THE
Vic Raschi
SQUATTY
Thurman Munson
SQUINT
Dorothy Hamill
STEADY EDDIE
Ed Lopat
STEVEREENO
Steve Allen
STONEWALL
Thomas Jackson
STORK IN SHORTS
Jim Ryun

STORMIN' NORMAN
  Norm Cash
  Norman Schwarzkopf
  Norm Van Brocklin
STOSH
  Stan Mikita
STOUT STEVE
  Steve Owen
STRATFORD FLASH, THE
  Howie Morenz
STRATFORD STREAK,
THE
  Howie Morenz
STRETCH
  Willie McCovey
SUBWAY VIGILANTE, THE
  Bernhard Goetz
SULTAN OF SWAT, THE
  Babe Ruth
SUNSHINE
  Don Maynard
SUPERBRAT
  John McEnroe
SUPERCHIEF
  Allie Reynolds
SUPERMEX
  Lee Trevino
SWEATER GIRL, THE
  Lana Turner
SWEDE
  Walter Johnson
SWEDISH NIGHTINGALE,
THE
  Jenny Lind
SWEET BABY JAMES
  James Taylor
SWEET LOU
  Lou Piniella
SWEETEST MUSIC THIS
SIDE OF HEAVEN
  Guy Lombardo
SWEETNESS
  Walter Payton
SWINGING SAM
  Sam Snead
SWITCHBLADE KID, THE
  Sal Mineo
TALL HALL
  Jerry Hall
TALL TACTICIAN, THE
  Connie Mack
TARK THE SHARK
  Jerry Tarkanian
TD
  Tony Dorsett
TEDDY
  Theodore Roosevelt

TEDDY BALLGAME
  Ted Williams
TEDDY BEAR
  Teddy Pendergrass
TEFLON DON, THE
  John Gotti
TEMPY
  Garry Templeton
TENNESSEE PLOWBOY,
THE
  Eddy Arnold
TENNIS TYCOON
  Billie Jean King
TENTH MUSE, THE
  Sappho
TERMINATOR, THE
  Jeff Reardon
TEXAS COWBOY
  Sammy Baugh
TEXAS TROUBADOR, THE
  Ernest Tubb
THUMPER, THE
  Ted Williams
TIPPY TOES
  Alex Karras
TOE, THE
  Lou Groza
TOM TERRIFIC
  Tom Seaver
TOMBA LA BOMBA
  Alberto Tomba
TOOTS
  Tutti Camarata
TOY BULLDOG, THE
  Mickey Walker
TRANE
  John Coltrane
TRIPLE THREAT TRIPPI
  Charlie Trippi
TROJAN, THE
  Johnny Evers
TRU
  Truman Capote
TWINKLE TOES
  Lou Gehrig
UKELELE IKE
  Cliff Edwards
UKEY
  Terry Sawchuk
UNCLE ESEK
  Josh Billings
UNCLE MILTIE
  Milton Berle
UNCLE ROBBIE
  Wilbert Robinson
UNCLE WALTER
  Walter Cronkite

UNTOUCHABLE, THE
  Eliot Ness
VACUUM CLEANER
  Brooks Robinson
VAGABOND LOVER, THE
  Rudy Vallee
VAST VENETIAN, THE
  Primo Carnera
VELVET FOG, THE
  Mel Torme
VIRGIN QUEEN, THE
  Elizabeth I
VOICE OF HARLEM, THE
  Adam Clayton Powell,
  Jr.
VOICE OF THE U.S.
HEARTLAND
  Paul Harvey
VOICELESS SINATRA,
THE
  Van Johnson
WAHOO SAM
  Sam Crawford
WALTZ KING, THE
  Wayne King
WATCHDOG OF CENTRAL
PARK, THE
  Adolph Ochs
WEARY WILLIE
  Emmett Kelly
WEE WILLIE
  Willie Keeler
WEIRD AL
  Al Yankovic
WEST COAST
  Julie Brown
WHEATON ICE MAN, THE
  Red Grange
WHIZZER
  Byron White
WICKED PICKETT, THE
  Wilson Pickett
WILD BILL
  William Wellman
WILD BULL OF THE
PAMPAS
  Luis Firpo
WILDCAT
  Larry Wilson
WILLIE THE WALLOP
  Willie Mays
WILLS
  Prince William
WILT THE STILT
  Wilt Chamberlain
WINNIE
  Winston Churchill

FAMOUS MARRIAGES

☆

Celebrities, like everyone else, tend to marry within their own class. And, like everyone else's marriages, theirs sometimes don't last very long (witness the marriage of Michelle Phillips and Dennis Hopper, which lasted a grand total of *eight days*, or the union of Ethel Merman and Ernest Borgnine: three weeks). The following chapter lists famous people who have married other famous people. It does not purport to be a complete record of each individual's nuptials, but is limited to noted and/or notorious personalities.

Abdul, Paula
  Emilio Estevez
Adams, Edie
  Ernie Kovacs
Addy, Wesley
  Celeste Holm
Adrian
  Janet Gaynor
Aherne, Brian
  Joan Fontaine
Aimée, Anouk
  Albert Finney
Aitken, Maria
  Nigel Davenport
Prince Albert
  Queen Victoria
Albert, Eddie
  Margo
Allégret, Yves
  Simone Signoret
Allen, Gracie
  George Burns
Allen, Nancy
  Brian DePalma
Allen, Peter
  Liza Minnelli
Allen, Steve
  Jayne Meadows
Allen, Woody
  Louise Lasser
Alley, Kirstie
  Parker Stevenson
Allman, Gregg
  Cher

Allyson, June
  Dick Powell
Anderson, Loni
  Burt Reynolds
Anderson, Robert
  Teresa Wright
Andress, Ursula
  John Derek
  Blake Edwards
Andrews, Julie
  Blake Edwards
Angeli, Pier
  Vic Damone
Ann-Margret
  Roger Smith
Arbuckle, Fatty
  Minta Durfee
Archer, John
  Marjorie Lord
Arkin, Alan
  Barbara Luna
Arnaz, Desi
  Lucille Ball
Arnaz, Lucie
  Laurence Luckinbill
Arnold, Tom
  Roseanne Barr
  (Arnold)
Arthur, Bea
  Gene Saks
Asherson, Renée
  Robert Donat
Ashford, Nickolas
  Valerie Simpson

Ashley, Elizabeth
  James Farentino
  George Peppard
Astaire, Fred
  Robyn Smith
Astin, John
  Patty Duke
Audran, Stéphane
  Claude Chabrol
  Jean-Louis Trintignant
Aumont, Jean-Pierre
  Maria Montez
  Marisa Pavan
Aykroyd, Dan
  Donna Dixon
Ayres, Lew
  Ginger Rogers
Bacall, Lauren
  Humphrey Bogart
  Jason Robards (Jr.)
Bach, Barbara
  Ringo Starr
Bacharach, Burt
  Angie Dickinson
  Carole Bayer
  Sager
Bacon, Kevin
  Kyra Sedgwick
Bailey, Pearl
  Louis Bellson
Bain, Barbara
  Martin Landau
Balanchine, George
  Maria Tallchief

Vera Zorina
Baldwin, Alec
    Kim Basinger
Ball, Lucille
    Desi Arnaz
Balsam, Martin
    Joyce Van Patten
Bancroft, Anne
    Mel Brooks
Barbeau, Adrienne
    John Carpenter
Bardot, Brigitte
    Roger Vadim
Barker, Lex
    Arlene Dahl
    Lana Turner
Barkin, Ellen
    Gabriel Byrne
Barr, Roseanne
(Roseanne Arnold)
    Tom Arnold
Barry, John
    Jane Birkin
Barrymore, John
    Dolores Costello
Barrymore, John, Jr.
    Cara Williams
Bartel, Paul
    Mary Woronov
Bartok, Eva
    Curt Jurgens
Basinger, Kim
    Alec Baldwin
Bauer, Steven
    Melanie Griffith
Baxter, Anne
    John Hodiak
Baxter, Meredith
    David Birney
Bean, Orson
    Alley Mills
Beatty, Warren
    Annette Bening
Beery, Wallace
    Gloria Swanson
Begley, Ed
    Martha Raye
Bell, Clive
    Vanessa Bell
Bell, Rex
    Clara Bow
Bell, Vanessa
    Clive Bell
Bellson, Louis
    Pearl Bailey
Bening, Annette
    Warren Beatty

Benjamin, Richard
    Paula Prentiss
Bennett, Constance
    Gilbert Roland
Bennett, Jill
    John Osborne
Bennett, Joan
    Gene Markey
    Walter Wanger
Benny, Jack
    Mary Livingstone
Benson, Robby
    Karla Devito
Bergen, Candice
    Louis Malle
Bergerac, Jacques
    Dorothy Malone
    Ginger Rogers
Bergman, Ingrid
    Roberto Rossellini
Bernsen, Corbin
    Amanda Pays
Bernstein, Carl
    Nora Ephron
Bertinelli, Valerie
    Eddie Van Halen
Best, Edna
    Herbert Marshall
Bigelow, Kathryn
    James Cameron
Birkin, Jane
    John Barry
Birney, David
    Meredith Baxter
Black, Clint
    Lisa Hartman
Blair, Betsy
    Gene Kelly
Blakely, Colin
    Margaret Whiting
Blondell, Joan
    Dick Powell
    Mike Todd
Bloom, Claire
    Philip Roth
    Rod Steiger
Bochco, Steven
    Barbara Bosson
Bogart, Humphrey
    Lauren Bacall
    Mayo Methot
Bolt, Robert
    Sarah Miles
Bonet, Lisa
    Lenny Kravitz
Bono, Sonny
    Cher

Borgnine, Ernest
    Katy Jurado
    Ethel Merman
Bosson, Barbara
    Steven Bochco
Bourke-White,
Margaret
    Erskine Caldwell
Bow, Clara
    Rex Bell
Bowie, David
    Iman
Bracco, Lorraine
    Harvey Keitel
    Edward James Olmos
Branagh, Kenneth
    Emma Thompson
Brent, George
    Ruth Chatterton
    Ann Sheridan
Brice, Fanny
    Billy Rose
Brickell, Edie
    Paul Simon
Brinkley, Christie
    Billy Joel
Britt, May
    Sammy Davis, Jr.
Brolin, James
    Jan Smithers
Bronson, Charles
    Jill Ireland
Brooks, Geraldine
    Budd Schulberg
Brooks, Mel
    Anne Bancroft
Brooks, Richard
    Jean Simmons
Brown, Bobby
    Whitney Houston
Brown, Bryan
    Rachel Ward
Brown, Georg Sanford
    Tyne Daly
Browne, Coral
    Vincent Price
Browning, Elizabeth
Barrett
    Robert Browning
Bruce, Virginia
    John Gilbert
Burke, Billie
    Florenz Ziegfeld
Burke, Delta
    Gerald McRaney
Burns, George
    Gracie Allen

Burton, Richard
  Elizabeth Taylor
Busch, Niven
  Teresa Wright
Byrne, Gabriel
  Ellen Barkin
Cabot, Bruce
  Adrienne Ames
Cain, James M.
  Aileen Pringle
Caldwell, Erskine
  Margaret Bourke-
  White
Calhern, Louis
  Ilka Chase
Cameron, James
  Kathryn Bigelow
  Gale Anne Hurd
Cameron, Kirk
  Chelsea Noble
Cannon, Dyan
  Cary Grant
Carlisle, Kitty
  Moss Hart
Carmichael, Stokely
  Miriam Makeba
Carne, Judy
  Burt Reynolds
Caron, Leslie
  Peter Hall
Carpenter, John
  Adrienne Barbeau
Carroll, Diahann
  Vic Damone
Carroll, Madeleine
  Sterling Hayden
Carson, Jack
  Lola Albright
Carter, Carlene
  Nick Lowe
Carter, Dixie
  Hal Holbrook
Carter, June
  Johnny Cash
  Carl Smith
Caruso, David
  Rachel Ticotin
Carville, James
  Mary Matalin
Cash, Johnny
  June Carter
Cash, Rosanne
  Rodney Crowell
Cassavetes, John
  Gena Rowlands
Cassidy, David
  Kay Lenz

Cassidy, Jack
  Shirley Jones
Cassini, Oleg
  Gene Tierney
Cates, Phoebe
  Kevin Kline
Caulfield, Maxwell
  Juliet Mills
Cerf, Bennett
  Sylvia Sidney
Chabrol, Claude
  Stéphane Audran
Champion, Gower
  Marge Champion
Chaplin, Charlie
  Oona (O'Neill) Chaplin
  Paulette Goddard
  Lita Grey
  Mildred Harris
Charisse, Cyd
  Tony Martin
Charo
  Xavier Cugat
Chase, Ilka
  Louis Calhern
Chatterton, Ruth
  George Brent
Cher
  Gregg Allman
  Sonny Bono
Chong, Rae Dawn
  C. Thomas Howell
Christian, Linda
  Tyrone Power
Chung, Connie
  Maury Povich
Cilento, Diane
  Sean Connery
Clair, Ina
  John Gilbert
Clayburgh, Jill
  David Rabe
Clooney, Rosemary
  José Ferrer
Cloutier, Suzanne
  Peter Ustinov
Cobain, Kurt
  Courtney Love
Cody, Lew
  Mabel Normand
Collins, Gary
  Mary Ann Mobley
Collins, Joan
  Anthony Newley
Collyer, June
  Stu Erwin
Colman, Ronald

  Benita Hume
Colter, Jessi
  Duane Eddy
  Waylon Jennings
Connery, Sean
  Diane Cilento
Coogan, Jackie
  Betty Grable
Coolidge, Rita
  Kris Kristofferson
Costello, Dolores
  John Barrymore
Crawford, Cindy
  Richard Gere
Crawford, Joan
  Douglas Fairbanks, Jr.
  Franchot Tone
Cronyn, Hume
  Jessica Tandy
Crosby, Bing
  Dixie Lee
Crouse, Lindsay
  David Mamet
Crowe, Cameron
  Nancy Wilson
Crowell, Rodney
  Rosanne Cash
Cruise, Tom
  Nicole Kidman
  Mimi Rogers
Cugat, Xavier
  Charo
  Abbe Lane
Curtis, Jamie Lee
  Christopher Guest
Curtis, Tony
  Janet Leigh
Cusack, Sinead
  Jeremy Irons
Dahl, Arlene
  Lex Barker
  Fernando Lamas
Dahl, Roald
  Patricia Neal
Daly, Tyne
  Georg Sanford
  Brown
Damita, Lili
  Errol Flynn
Damone, Vic
  Pier Angeli
  Diahann Caroll
Darin, Bobby
  Sandra Dee
Dassin, Jules
  Melina Mercouri
Davenport, Nigel

Maria Aitken
Davis, Bette
Gary Merrill
Davis, Billy Jr.
Marilyn McCoo
Davis, Geena
Jeff Goldblum
Renny Harlin
Davis, Judy
Colin Friels
Davis, Miles
Cicely Tyson
Davis, Ossie
Ruby Dee
Davis, Sammy, Jr.
May Britt
Dawber, Pam
Mark Harmon
Day, Doris
Martin Melcher
DeBarge, James
Janet Jackson
Dee, Frances
Joel McCrea
Dee, Ruby
Ossie Davis
Dee, Sandra
Bobby Darin
De Haven, Gloria
John Payne
De Laurentiis, Dino
Silvana Mangano
De Lorean, John
Christina Ferrare
Dempsey, Jack
Estelle Taylor
Dennis, Sandy
Gerry Mulligan
DePalma, Brian
Nancy Allen
Derek, Bo
John Derek
Derek, John
Ursula Andress
Bo Derek
Linda Evans
Dern, Bruce
Diane Ladd
Devito, Danny
Rhea Perlman
Devito, Karla
Robby Benson
Dewhurst, Colleen
George C. Scott
Dickinson, Angie
Burt Bacharach
Didion, Joan

John Gregory Dunne
Dillman, Bradford
Suzy Parker
DiMaggio, Joe
Marilyn Monroe
Dixon, Donna
Dan Aykroyd
Dole, Bob
Elizabeth Dole
Donahue, Phil
Marlo Thomas
Donahue, Troy
Suzanne Pleshette
Donat, Robert
Renée Asherson
Donen, Stanley
Yvette Mimieux
Douglas, Helen
Melvyn Douglas
Douglas, Paul
Jan Sterling
Douglas, Shirley
Donald Sutherland
Down, Lesley-Anne
William Friedkin
Dragon, Daryl
Toni Tennille
Drake, Betsy
Cary Grant
Dru, Joanne
Dick Haymes
John Ireland
Duff, Howard
Ida Lupino
Dukakis, Michael
Kitty Dukakis
Duke, Doris
Porfirio Rubirosa
Duke, Patty
John Astin
Dunaway, Faye
Peter Wolf
Dunne, John Gregory
Joan Didion
Durfee, Minta
Fatty Arbuckle
Eddy, Duane
Jessi Colter
Edward VIII
Wallis Warfield
Edwards, Blake
Ursula Andress
Julie Andrews
Eikenberry, Jill
Michael Tucker
Ekland, Britt
Peter Sellers

Eldridge, Florence
Fredric March
Elliott, Sam
Katherine Ross
Emerson, Faye
Skitch Henderson
Ephron, Nora
Carl Bernstein
Nicholas Pileggi
Erickson, Leif
Francis Farmer
Erwin, Stu
June Collyer
Estevez, Emilio
Paula Abdul
Evans, Dale
Roy Rogers
Evans, Linda
John Derek
Evans, Robert
Phyllis George
Ali MacGraw
Camilla Sparv
Fabares, Shelley
Mike Farrell
Fairbanks, Douglas
Mary Pickford
Fairbanks, Douglas, Jr.
Joan Crawford
Farentino, James
Elizabeth Ashley
Michele Lee
Farmer, Francis
Leif Erickson
Farr, Felicia
Jack Lemmon
Farrell, Mike
Shelley Fabares
Farrow, Mia
Andre Previn
Frank Sinatra
Fawcett, Farrah
Lee Majors
Faye, Alice
Phil Harris
Tony Martin
Fellini, Federico
Giulietta Masina
Ferrare, Christina
John De Lorean
Ferrer, José
Rosemary Clooney
Uta Hagen
Ferrer, Mel
Audrey Hepburn
Field, Betty

Elmer Rice
Finney, Albert
Anouk Aimee
Fisher, Carrie
Paul Simon
Fisher, Eddie
Debbie Reynolds
Connie Stevens
Elizabeth Taylor
Fitzgerald, F. Scott
Zelda Fitzgerald
Fitzgerald, Zelda
F. Scott Fitzgerald
Flynn, Errol
Lili Damita
Fonda, Henry
Margaret Sullavan
Fonda, Jane
Tom Hayden
Ted Turner
Roger Vadim
Fontaine, Joan
Brian Aherne
Fontanne, Lynn
Alfred Lunt
Ford, Glenn
Eleanor Powell
Fosse, Bob
Gwen Verdon
Elena Verdugo
Fox, Michael J.
Tracy Pollan
Franciosa, Anthony
Shelley Winters
Francis, Arlene
Martin Gabel
Frankenthaler,
Helen
Robert Motherwell
Fraser, Antonia
Harold Pinter
Friedkin, William
Lesley-Anne Down
Jeanne Moreau
Friels, Colin
Judy Davis
Furness, Betty
Johnny Green
Gabel, Martin
Arlene Francis
Gable, Clark
Carole Lombard
Gabor, Magda and Zsa
Zsa
George Sanders
Gam, Rita
Sidney Lumet

Gardner, Ava
Mickey Rooney
Artie Shaw
Frank Sinatra
Garland, Judy
Vincente Minnelli
Gary, Romain
Jean Seberg
Gassman, Vittorio
Shelley Winters
Gavin, John
Constance Towers
Gaynor, Janet
Adrian
George, Phyllis
Robert Evans
George, Susan
Simon MacCorkindale
Gerard, Gil
Connie Sellecca
Gere, Richard
Cindy Crawford
Gilliat, Penelope
John Osborne
Gish, Annabeth
John Goodman
Givens, Robin
Mike Tyson
Godard, Jean-Luc
Anna Karina
Goddard, Paulette
Charlie Chaplin
Burgess Meredith
Erich Maria Remarque
Goffin, Gerry
Carole King
Goldblum, Jeff
Geena Davis
Goodman, John
Annabeth Gish
Gordon, Ruth
Garson Kanin
Gorme, Eydie
Steve Lawrence
Gould, Elliott
Barbra Streisand
Goulet, Robert
Carol Lawrence
Grable, Betty
Jackie Coogan
Harry James
Grahame, Gloria
Nicholas Ray
Granger, Farley
Shelley Winters
Granger, Stewart
Jean Simmons

Grant, Cary
Dyan Cannon
Betsy Drake
Barbara Hutton
Green, Johnny
Betty Furness
Greer, Jane
Rudy Vallee
Grey, Nan
Frankie Lane
Griffith, Melanie
Steven Bauer
Don Johnson
Grimes, Tammy
Christopher
Plummer
Guest, Christopher
Jamie Lee Curtis
Hagen, Uta
José Ferrer
Haley, Jack, Jr.
Liza Minelli
Hall, Fawn
Danny Sugarman
Hall, Jerry
Mick Jagger
Hall, Peter
Leslie Caron
Hamlin, Harry
Nicollette Sheridan
Harlon, Renny
Geena Davis
Harmon, Mark
Pam Dawber
Harris, Ed
Amy Madigan
Harris, Mel
Cotter Smith
Harris, Mildred
Charlie Chaplin
Harris, Phil
Alice Faye
Harris, Richard
Ann Turkel
Harrison, Rex
Kay Kendall
Lilli Palmer
Rachel Roberts
Hart, Moss
Kitty Carlisle
Hartman, Lisa
Clint Black
Harvey, Laurence
Margaret Leighton
Haver, June
Fred MacMurray
Hawkes, Jacquetta

J. B. Priestley
Hawkins, Jack
Jessica Tandy
Hayden, Sterling
Madeleine
Carroll
Hayden, Tom
Jane Fonda
Hayes, Helen
Charles MacArthur
Haymes, Dick
Joanne Dru
Rita Hayworth
Hayward, Leland
Margaret Sullavan
Hayward, Louis
Ida Lupino
Hayworth, Rita
Dick Haymes
Orson Welles
Headly, Glenne
John Malkovich
Heard, John
Margot Kidder
Held, Anna
Florenz Ziegfeld
Helenberger, Marg
Alan Rosenberg
Hellman, Lillian
Arthur Kober
Hemmings, David
Gayle Hunnicutt
Henderson, Skitch
Faye Emerson
Hendrix, Wanda
Audie Murphy
Hepburn, Audrey
Mel Ferrer
Hilton, Conrad, Jr.
Elizabeth Taylor
Hitchcock, Alfred
Alma Reville
Hodiak, John
Anne Baxter
Hogan, Paul
Linda Kozlowski
Holbrook, Hal
Dixie Carter
Holm, Celeste
Wesley Addy
Hopkins, John
Shirley Knight
Hopkins, Miriam
Anatole Litvak
Hopper, Dennis
Michelle Phillips
Hopper, De Wolf

Hedda Hopper
Horton, Peter
Michelle Pfeiffer
Houston, Whitney
Bobby Brown
Howell, C. Thomas
Rae Dawn Chong
Hughes, Howard
Terry Moore
Jean Peters
Hughes, Ted
Sylvia Plath
Hunnicutt, Gayle
David Hemmings
Hunter, Jeffrey
Barbara Rush
Hunter, Rachel
Rod Stewart
Hurd, Gale Anne
James Cameron
Hurt, Mary Beth
Paul Schrader
William Hurt
Hurt, William
Mary Beth Hurt
Huston, John
Evelyn Keyes
Hutton, Barbara
Cary Grant
Porfirio Rubirosa
Hutton, E. F.
Marjorie Meriweather
Post
Hutton, Timothy
Debra Winger
Hyer, Martha
Hal B. Wallis
Hynde, Chrissie
Jim Kerr
Iman
David Bowie
Ingels, Marty
Shirley Jones
Ireland, Jill
Charles Bronson
David McCallum
Ireland, John
Joanne Dru
Irons, Jeremy
Sinead Cusack
Irving, Amy
Steven Spielberg
Jackson, Anne
Eli Wallach
Jackson, Janet
James DeBarge
Jagger, Bianca

Mick Jagger
Jagger, Mick
Jerry Hall
Bianca Jagger
James, Harry
Betty Grable
Jarre, Jean-Michel
Charlotte Rampling
Jeanmaire, Zizi
Roland Petit
Jeans, Isabel
Claude Rains
Jeffreys, Anne
Robert Sterling
Jennings, Waylon
Jessi Colter
Jens, Salome
Ralph Meeker
Jessel, George
Norma Talmadge
Joel, Billy
Christie Brinkley
Johnson, Don
Melanie Griffith
Jolson, Al
Ruby Keeler
Jones, George
Tammy Wynette
Jones, Jack
Jill St. John
Jones, Jennifer
David O. Selznick
Norton Simon
Robert Walker
Jones, Quincy
Peggy Lipton
Jones, Shirley
Jack Cassidy
Marty Ingels
Joy, Leatrice
John Gilbert
Jurado, Katy
Ernest Borgnine
Jurgens, Curt
Eva Bartok
Kahlo, Frida
Diego Rivera
Kanin, Garson
Ruth Gordon
Karina, Anna
Jean-Luc Godard
Kazan, Elia
Barbara Loden
Keach, James
Jane Seymour
Keeler, Ruby
Al Jolson

Keitel, Harvey
  Lorraine Bracco
Kelley, David
  Michelle Pfeiffer
Kelly, Gene
  Betsy Blair
Kelly, Grace
  Rainier III
Kelly, Nancy
  Edmond O'Brien
Kendall, Kay
  Rex Harrison
Kendall, Suzy
  Dudley Moore
Kennedy, John F.
  Jacqueline (Bouvier)
  Kennedy-Onassis
Kennedy-Onassis,
Jacqueline
  John F. Kennedy
  Aristotle Onassis
Kerr, Jean
  Walter Kerr
Kerr, Jim
  Chrissie Hynde
Kerr, Walter
  Jean Kerr
Keyes, Evelyn
  John Huston
  Artie Shaw
Kidder, Margot
  John Heard
Kidman, Nicole
  Tom Cruise
Kilmer, Val
  Joanne Whalley-
  Kilmer
King, Billie Jean
  Larry King
King, Carole
  Gerry Goffin
King, Larry
  Billie Jean King
Kinmont, Kathleen
  Lorenzo Lamas
Kline, Kevin
  Phoebe Cates
Klugman, Jack
  Brett Somers
Knight, Shirley
  John Hopkins
Knopf, Alfred
  Blanche Knopf
Korda, Alexander
  Merle Oberon
Kostelanetz, Andre
  Lily Pons

Kovacs, Ernie
  Edie Adams
Kozlowski, Linda
  Paul Hogan
Krasner, Lee
  Jackson Pollock
Kravitz, Lenny
  Lisa Bonet
Kristofferson, Kris
  Rita Coolidge
Ladd, Diane
  Bruce Dern
Laine, Frankie
  Nan Grey
Lamarr, Hedy
  John Loder
  Gene Markey
Lamas, Fernando
  Arlene Dahl
  Esther Williams
Lamas, Lorenzo
  Kathleen Kinmont
Lambert, Christopher
  Diane Lane
Lanchester, Elsa
  Charles Laughton
Landau, Martin
  Barbara Bain
Lane, Abbe
  Xavier Cugat
Lane, Diane
  Christopher Lambert
Lange, Hope
  Don Murray
  Alan J. Pakula
Lasser, Louise
  Woody Allen
Lattanzi, Matt
  Olivia Newton-John
Laughton, Charles
  Elsa Lanchester
Lavin, Linda
  Ron Leibman
Lawrence, Carole
  Robert Goulet
Lawrence, Steve
  Eydie Gorme
Lawrence, Vicki
  Bobby Russell
Lean, David
  Ann Todd
Le Brock, Kelly
  Steven Seagal
Lee, Dixie
  Bing Crosby
Lee, Michele
  James Farentino

Lee, Tommy
  Heather Locklear
Leibman, Ron
  Linda Lavin
  Jessica Walter
Leigh, Janet
  Tony Curtis
Leigh, Mike
  Alison Steadman
Leigh, Vivien
  Laurence Olivier
Leighton, Margaret
  Laurence Harvey
  Michael Wilding
Lemmon, Jack
  Felicia Farr
Lennon, John
  Yoko Ono
Lenya, Lotte
  Kurt Weill
Lenz, Kay
  David Cassidy
Lewis, Sinclair
  Dorothy
  Thompson
Lindfors, Viveca
  Don Siegel
Lindsay, Howard
  Dorothy Stickney
Lipton, Peggy
  Quincy Jones
Litvak, Anatole
  Miriam Hopkins
Livingstone, Mary
  Jack Benny
Locklear, Heather
  Tommy Lee
Lockwood, Gary
  Stephanie Powers
Loden, Barbara
  Elia Kazan
Loder, John
  Hedy Lamarr
Lombard, Carole
  Clark Gable
  William Powell
London, Julie
  Jack Webb
Lord Byron
  Anne Milbanke
Lord, Marjorie
  John Archer
Loren, Sophia
  Carlo Ponti
Loring, Gloria
  Alan Thicke
Love, Courtney

Price, Leontyne
William Warfield
Price, Vincent
Coral Browne
Priestley, J. B.
Jacquetta Hawkes
Prima, Louis
Keely Smith
Pringle, Aileen
James M. Cain
Quaid, Dennis
Meg Ryan
Rabe, David
Jill Clayburgh
Radner, Gilda
Gene Wilder
Rainer, Luise
Clifford Odets
Rainier III
Grace Kelly
Rains, Claude
Isabel Jeans
Rampling, Charlotte
Jean-Michel
Jarre
Rashad, Ahmad
Phylicia Rashad
Ray, Nicholas
Gloria Grahame
Raye, Martha
Ed Begley
Billy Rose
Raymond, Gene
Jeanette MacDonald
Reagan, Nancy
Ronald Reagan
Reagan, Ronald
Nancy Reagan
Jane Wyman
Redgrave, Vanessa
Tony Richardson
Reiner, Rob
Penny Marshall
Remarque, Erich Maria
Paulette Goddard
Reville, Alma
Alfred Hitchcock
Reynolds, Burt
Loni Anderson
Judy Carne
Reynolds, Debbie
Eddie Fisher
Rice, Elmer
Betty Field
Richardson, Tony
Vanessa Redgrave
Riskin, Robert

Fay Wray
Rivera, Diego
Frida Kahlo
Robards, Jason (Jr.)
Lauren Bacall
Roberts, Julia
Lyle Lovett
Roberts, Rachel
Rex Harrison
Robertson, Cliff
Dina Merrill
Roeg, Nicolas
Theresa Russell
Rogers, Buddy
Mary Pickford
Rogers, Ginger
Lew Ayres
Jacques Bergerac
Rogers, Mimi
Tom Cruise
Rogers, Roy
Dale Evans
Roland, Gilbert
Constance Bennett
Rooney, Mickey
Ava Gardner
Martha Vickers
Rose, Billy
Fanny Brice
Martha Raye
Rosenberg, Allen
Marg Helgenberger
Ross, Katharine
Sam Elliott
Rossellini, Isabella
Martin Scorsese
Rossellini, Roberto
Ingrid Bergman
Roth, Philip
Claire Bloom
Rourke, Mickey
Carré Otis
Rowlands, Gena
John Cassavetes
Ruberis, Alma
Ricardo Cortez
Rubirosa, Porfirio
Danielle Darrieux
Doris Duke
Barbara Hutton
Rush, Barbara
Jeffrey Hunter
Russell, Bobby
Vicki Lawrence
Russell, Theresa
Nicolas Roeg
Ryan, Meg

Dennis Quaid
Sager, Carole
Bayer
Burt Bacharach
St. John, Jill
Jack Jones
Robert Wagner
Saks, Gene
Bea Arthur
Sanders, George
Magda and Zsa Zsa
Gabor
Sands, Tommy
Nancy Sinatra
Sarandon, Chris
Susan Sarandon
Sarandon, Susan
Chris Sarandon
Sawyer, Diane
Mike Nichols
Schrader, Paul
Mary Beth Hurt
Schulberg, Budd
Geraldine Brooks
Schwarzenegger, Arnold
Maria Shriver
Scialfa, Patti
Bruce Springsteen
Scorsese, Martin
Isabella Rossellini
Scott, George C.
Colleen Dewhurst
Trish Van Devere
Scott, Gordon
Vera Miles
Seagal, Steven
Kelly Le Brock
Seberg, Jean
Romain Gary
Sedgwick, Kyra
Kevin Bacon
Seeley, Blossom
Rube Marquard
Sellecca, Connie
Gil Gerard
John Tesh
Selleck, Tom
Jillie Mack
Sellers, Peter
Britt Ekland
Selznick, David O.
Jennifer Jones
Seymour, Jane
James Keach
Shaw, Artie
Ava Gardner

David Lean
Todd, Mike
Joan Blondell
Elizabeth Taylor
Tone, Franchot
Joan Crawford
Jean Wallace
Torn, Rip
Geraldine Page
Towers, Constance
John Gavin
Travolta, John
Kelly Preston
Trintignant, Jean-Louis
Stéphane Audran
Trudeau, Garry
Jane Pauley
Trump, Donald
Marla Maples
Ivana Trump
Tucker, Michael
Jill Eikenberry
Turkel, Ann
Richard Harris
Turner, Ike
Tina Turner
Turner, Lana
Lex Barker
Artie Shaw
Turner, Ted
Jane Fonda
Turner, Tina
Ike Turner
Tyson, Cicely
Miles Davis
Tyson, Mike
Robin Givens
Ure, Mary
John Osborne
Robert Shaw
Ustinov, Peter
Suzanne Cloutier
Vadim, Roger
Brigitte Bardot
Jane Fonda
Vanderbilt, Gloria
Sidney Lumet
Van Devere, Trish
George C. Scott
Van Halen, Eddie
Valerie Bertinelli
Van Patten, Joyce
Martin Balsam
Velez, Lupe
Johnny Weissmuller

Verdon, Gwen
Bob Fosse
Verdugo, Elena
Bob Fosse
Vickers, Martha
Mickey Rooney
Queen Victoria
Prince Albert
Wagner, Robert
Jill St. John
Natalie Wood
Walker, Robert
Jennifer Jones
Wallace, George
Lurleen Burns Wallace
Wallace, Jean
Franchot Tone
Cornel Wilde
Wallach, Eli
Anne Jackson
Wallis, Hal B.
Louise Fazenda
Martha Hyer
Walter, Jessica
Ron Leibman
Wanger, Walter
Joan Bennett
Ward, Rachel
Bryan Brown
Warfield, Wallis
Edward VIII
Warfield, William
Leontyne Price
Warner, John
Elizabeth Taylor
Webb, Jack
Julie London
Weill, Kurt
Lotte Lenya
Weissmuller, Johnny
Lupe Velez
Weld, Tuesday
Dudley Moore
Pinchas Zukerman
Welles, Orson
Rita Hayworth
Wells, H. G.
Rebecca West
West, Rebecca
H. G. Wells
Weston, Paul
Jo Stafford
Wettig, Patricia
Ken Olin
Whalley-Kilmer,

Joanne
Val Kilmer
White, Betty
Allen Ludden
Whiting, Margaret
Colin Blakely
Whitley, Keith
Lorrie Morgan
Wilde, Cornel
Jean Wallace
Wilder, Gene
Gilda Radner
Wilding, Michael
Margaret Leighton
Elizabeth Taylor
Williams, Cara
John Barrymore, Jr.
Williams, Esther
Fernando Lamas
Willis, Bruce
Demi Moore
Wilson, Nancy
Cameron Crowe
Winger, Debra
Timothy Hutton
Winters, Shelley
Anthony Franciosa
Vittorio Gassmann
Farley Granger
Wolf, Peter
Faye Dunaway
Wood, Natalie
Robert Wagner
Woodward, Joanne
Paul Newman
Woronov, Mary
Paul Bartel
Wray, Fay
Robert Riskin
Wright, Teresa
Robert Anderson
Niven Busch
Wyler, William
Margaret Sullavan
Wyman, Jane
Ronald Reagan
Wynette, Tammy
George Jones
Young, Gig
Elizabeth Montgomery
Ziegfeld, Florenz
Billie Burke
Anna Held
Zukerman, Pinchas
Tuesday Weld

SELECTED
BIBLIOGRAPHY

☆

In addition to the works listed below, innumerable copies of *Star, National Enquirer, Globe, Vanity Fair, Esquire, People Weekly, Entertainment Weekly, GQ, Rolling Stone, Movieline, Premiere*, and *Details* were used as references.

Benét, William Rose, and Kate Siepmann, eds. 1987. *Benét's Reader's Encyclopedia, 3rd Edition.* New York: Harper & Row.

Biracree, Tom. 1993. *The Country Music Almanac.* New York: Prentice Hall.

Blackwell, Earl. 1991. *Earl Blackwell's Entertainment Celebrity Register.* New York: Visible Ink Press.

Bland, Alexander and John Percival. 1984. *Men Dancing.* New York: Macmillan Publishing Co.

Bronough, Robert Brett. 1981. *The Celebrity Birthday Book.* Middle Village, NY: Jonathan David Publishers.

Brooks, Tim. 1987. *The Complete Directory to Prime Time TV Shows 1946–Present.* New York: Ballantine Books.

Carruth, Gordon, and Eugene Erlich. 1988. *Facts and Dates of American Sports.* New York: Harper & Row.

Cross, Milton, and David Ewen. 1969. *Milton Cross Encyclopedia of the Great Composers and Their Music.* New York: Doubleday & Co.

Cummings, Paul. 1971. *A Dictionary of Contemporary American Artists.* New York: St. Martin's Press.

De Mille, Agnes. 1963. *The Book of the Dance.* Golden Press.

Dickson, Paul. 1991. *Baseball's Greatest Quotations.* New York: Edward Burlingame Books.

Digaetani, John Louis. 1986. *An Invitation to the Opera.* New York: Doubleday & Co.

Ewen, David. 1959. *The Complete Book of 20th Century Music.* New York: Prentice Hall.

Fargis, Paul, and Sheree Bykofsky, eds. 1989. *The New York Public Library Desk Reference.* New York: The Stonesong Press/Webster's New World.

Flint, Country Joe, and Judy Nelson, 1993. *The Insider's Country Music Handbook.* Salt Lake City, UT: Gibbs-Smith Publisher.

Halas, John, and David Rider. 1976. *The Great Movie Cartoon Parade.* New York: Bounty Books.

Halliwell, Leslie. 1988. *Halliwell Filmgoer's Companion, 9th Edition.* New York: Charles Scribner's Sons.

Herbert, Ian, ed. 1981. *Who's Who in the Theatre.* Detroit: Gale Research Company.

Hoffman, Mark S., ed. 1991. *The World Almanac and Book of Facts.* New York: World Almanac Publications.

Inman, David. 1991. *The TV Encyclopedia.* New York: Perigee Books.

367

James, Bill, ed. 1988. *The Great American Baseball Stat Book.* New York: Villard Books.

Johnson, Otto, ed. 1993. *The 1993 Information Please Almanac.* Boston: Houghton-Mifflin.

Kaplan, Mike, ed. 1989. *Variety Who's Who in Show Business.* New York: R. R. Bowker.

Karney, Robin, ed. 1993. *The Hollywood Who's Who.* New York: The Continuum Publishing Co.

Katz, Ephraim. 1979. *The Film Encyclopedia.* New York: Perigree Books.

Keating, H. R. F. 1989. *The Bedside Companion to Crime.* New York: Mysterious Press.

Kenin, Richard, and Justin Wintle, eds. 1978. *The Dictionary of Biographical Quotations.* New York: Alfred A. Knopf.

Lane, Hana Umlauf, ed. 1980. *The World Almanac Book of Who.* New York: World Almanac Publications.

Levine, Michael. 1986. *The New Address Book.* New York: Perigree Books.

———. 1989. *The Music Address Book.* New York: Perennial Library.

Lucaire, Ed. 1991. *The Celebrity Almanac.* New York: Prentice Hall.

Magnusson, Magnus, ed. 1990. *Cambridge Biographical Dictionary.* Cambridge, England: Press Syndicate of the University of Cambridge.

Marks, Frederick M., ed. 1992. *Who's Who in America 1992–1993.* New Providence, NJ: Marquis Who's Who.

Mason, Wiley, and Damien Bona. 1993. *Inside Oscar.* New York: Ballantine Books.

McHenry, Robert, ed. 1980. *Famous American Women.* Springfield, MA: Merriam-Webster.

———. 1988. *Webster's New Biographical Dictionary.* Springfield, MA: Merriam-Webster.

McWhirter, Ross, and Norris McWhirter. 1981. *Guinnes Book of World Records.* New York: Sterling Publishing Co.

Monaco, James, and the Editors of Baseline. 1991. *The Encyclopedia of Film.* New York: Perigree Books.

O'Donnell, Owen, ed. 1990. *Contemporary Theatre, Film and Television.* Detroit: Gale Research.

Pareles, John, and Patricia Romanowski, eds. 1983. *The Rolling Stone Encyclopedia of Rock & Roll.* New York: Rolling Stone Press/Summit Books.

Phillips, Louis, and Burnham Holmes. 1994. *Yogi, Babe and Magic: The Complete Book of Sports Nicknames.* New York: Prentice Hall.

Reichler, Joseph L., ed. 1990. *The Baseball Encyclopedia.* New York: Macmillan Publishing Co.

Robertson, Patrick. 1989. *Movie Clips.* London, England: Guinness Superlatives Ltd.

Rosenbaum, Robert A., Eleanor M. Gates, and Wesley F. Strombeck, eds. 1993. *The New American Desk Encyclopedia.* New York: Signet.

Salzman, Jack, ed. 1986. *The Cambridge Handbook of American Literature.* New York: Cambridge University Press.

Sennett, Ted. 1976. *The Old Time Radio Book.* New York: Pyramid Books.

Singer, Michael. 1989. *Film Directors.* Los Angeles: Lone Eagle Publishing Co.

Steinbrunner, Chris, and Otto Penzler, eds. 1976. *Encyclopedia of Mystery and Detection.* New York: McGraw-Hill.

Stetler, Susan L., ed. 1989. *Almanac of Famous People.* Detroit: Gale Research.

Tobler, Josh, ed. 1991. *Who's Who In Rock & Roll.* New York: Crescent Books.

Upshall, Michael, ed. 1990. *The Hutchinson Paperback Dictionary of Biography.* London, England: Arrow Books Ltd.

Vernoff, Edward and Rima Shore. 1987. *The International Dictionary of 20th-Century Biography.* New York: NAL.

Wallechinsky, David, and Amy Wallace. 1993. *The Book of Lists: The '90s Edition.* Boston: Little Brown and Co.

Weiner, Ed, and the Editors of TV Guide. 1992. *The TV Guide TV Book.* New York: Harper Perennial.

Whitburn, Joel. 1987. *Top Pop 1955–1986.* Menomonee Falls, WI: Record Research.

———. 1992. *The Billboard Book of Top 40 Hits.* Menomonee Falls, WI: Record Research.

———. 1993. *Top Pop Albums 1955–1992.* Menomonee Falls, WI: Record Research.

Wynne-Davies, Marion, ed. 1990. *The Bloomsbury Guide to English Literature.* New York: Prentice Hall.

York, William. 1982. *Who's Who in Rock Music.* New York: Charles Scribner's Sons.

SUBJECT INDEX

☆

The following lists are intended as a sort of "reverse dictionary" for the reader who wants to find out who is behind a significant achievement, discovery, invention, or award, but doesn't know the individual's name. A complete listing of American presidents follows. Also provided are complete listings of winners of the Nobel peace and literature prizes and Pulitzer Prize winners in fiction and non-fiction, with selected lists for winners in poetry and drama. Additional subject categories are geographic and scientific discoveries, scientific and technological inventions, and creators of architectural landmarks. After you have found the name you are looking for, see the last names section for further biographical details. (For the Nobel and Pulitzer winners, only names marked with an asterisk (*) are included in this volume; the complete list is provided for the reader's convenience.)

AMERICAN PRESIDENTS

Number	President (Party)	Vice-President (Party)	Term
1	George Washington (Federalist)	John Adams (Federalist)	4/30/1789–3/3/1797
2	John Adams (Federalist)	Thomas Jefferson (Federalist)	3/4/1797–3/3/1801
3	Thomas Jefferson (Democratic-Republican)	Aaron Burr (Democratic-Republican)	3/4/1801–3/3/1805
		George Clinton (Democratic-Republican)	3/4/1805–3/3/1809
4	James Madison (Democratic-Republican)	George Clinton (Democratic-Republican)	3/4/1809–3/3/1813
		Elbridge Gerry (Democratic-Republican)	3/4/1813–3/3/1817
5	James Monroe (Democratic-Republican)	Daniel D. Tompkins (Democratic-Republican)	3/4/1817–3/3/1825
6	John Quincy Adams (Democratic-Republican)	John C. Calhoun (Democratic-Republican)	3/4/1825–3/3/1829
7	Andrew Jackson (Democratic-Republican)	John C. Calhoun (Democratic-Republican)	3/4/1829–3/3/1833
		Martin Van Buren (Democratic-Republican)	3/4/1833–3/3/1837

Number	President (Party)	Vice-President (Party)	Term
8	Martin Van Buren (Democrat)	Richard M. Johnson (Democrat)	3/4/1837–3/3/1841
9	William Henry Harrison (Whig)	John Tylor (Whig)	3/4/1841–4/4/1841
10	John Tyler (Whig)		4/6/1841–3/3/1845
11	James Knoll Polk (Democrat)	George M. Dallas (Democrat)	3/4/1845–3/3/1849
12	Zachary Taylor (Whig)	Millard Fillmore (Whig)	3/4/1850–7/9/1850
13	Millard Fillmore (Whig)		7/10/1850–3/3/1853
14	Franklin Pierce (Democrat)	William R. King (Democrat)	3/4/1853–3/3/1857
15	James Buchanan (Democrat)	John C. Breckinridge (Democrat)	3/4/1857–3/3/1861
16	Abraham Lincoln (Republican)	Hannibal Hamlin (Republican)	3/4/1861–3/3/1865
		Andrew Johnson (Republican)	3/4/1865–4/15/1865
17	Andrew Johnson (National Union Party)		4/15/1865–3/3/1869
18	Ulysses S. Grant (Republican)	Schuyler Colfax (Republican)	3/4/1869–3/3/1873
		Henry Wilson (Republican)	3/4/1873–3/3/1877
19	Rutherford B. Hayes (Republican)	William A. Wheeler (Republican)	3/4/1877–3/3/1881
20	James Garfield (Republican)	Chester A. Arthur (Republican)	3/4/1881–9/19/1881
21	Chester A. Arthur (Republican)		9/20/1881–3/3/1885
22	Grover Cleveland (Democrat)	Thomas Hendricks (Democrat)	3/4/1885–3/3/1889
23	Benjamin Harrison (Republican)	Levi P. Morton (Republican)	3/4/1889–3/3/1893
24	Grover Cleveland (Democrat)	Adlai Stevenson (Democrat)	3/4/1893–3/3/1897
25	William McKinley (Republican)	Garret H. Hobart (Republican)	3/4/1897–3/3/1901
		Theodore Roosevelt (Republican)	3/4/1901–9/14/1901
26	Theodore Roosevelt (Republican)		9/14/1901–3/3/1905
		Charles W. Fairbanks (Republican)	3/4/1905–3/3/1909
27	William H. Taft (Republican)	James S. Sherman (Republican)	3/4/1909–3/3/1913
28	Woodrow Wilson (Democrat)	Thomas R. Marshall (Democrat)	3/4/1913–3/3/1921
29	Warren G. Harding (Republican)	Calvin Coolidge (Republican)	3/4/1921–8/2/1923
30	Calvin Coolidge (Republican)		8/3/1923–3/3/1925
		Charles G. Dawes (Republican)	3/4/1925–3/3/1929
31	Herbert Hoover (Republican)	Charles Curtis (Republican)	3/4/1929–3/3/1933
32	Franklin D. Roosevelt (Democrat)	John Nance Garner (Democrat)	3/4/1933–1/20/1941
		Henry A. Wallace (Democrat)	1/20/1941–1/20/1945
		Harry S Truman (Democrat)	1/20/1945–4/12/1945
33	Harry S Truman (Democrat)		4/12/1945–1/20/1949
		Alben W. Barkley (Democrat)	1/20/1949–1/20/1953
34	Dwight D. Eisenhower (Republican)	Richard Nixon (Republican)	1/20/1953–1/20/1961
35	John F. Kennedy (Democrat)	Lyndon Johnson (Democrat)	1/20/1961–11/22/1963
36	Lyndon Johnson (Democrat)		11/22/1963–1/20/1965
		Hubert Humphrey (Democrat)	1/20/1965–1/20/1969
37	Richard Nixon (Republican)	Spiro Agnew (Republican)	1/20/1969–1/20/1973
		Gerald Ford (Republican)	1/20/1973–8/9/1974
38	Gerald Ford (Republican)	Nelson Rockefeller (Republican)	8/9/1974–1/20/1977
39	Jimmy Carter (Democrat)	Walter Mondale (Democrat)	1/20/1977–1/20/1981
40	Ronald Reagan (Republican)	George Bush (Republican)	1/20/1981–1/20/1989
41	George Bush (Republican)	Dan Quayle (Republican)	1/20/1989–1/20/1993
42	Bill Clinton (Democrat)	Al Gore (Democrat)	1/20/1993–

NOBEL PRIZE WINNERS

LITERATURE

Year	Winner	Year	Winner	Year	Winner
1901	Sully Prudhomme*	1933	Ivan Bunin*	1966	Shmuel Agnon*
1902	Theodore Mommsen	1934	Luigi Pirandello*		Nelly Sachs*
1903	Bjørnstjerne Bjørnson*	1935	no prize	1967	Miguel Angel Asturias*
1904	Frédéric Mistral*	1936	Eugene O'Neill*	1968	Kawabata Yasunari*
1905	Henryk Sienkiewicz*	1937	Roger Martin du Gard	1969	Samuel Beckett*
1906	Giosuc Carducci	1938	Pearl S. Buck*	1970	Aleksandr I.
1907	Rudyard Kipling*	1939	Frans Eemil Sillanpaa*		Solzhenitsyn*
1908	Rudolf Eucken*	1940–43	no prize	1971	Pablo Neruda*
1909	Selma Lagerlöf*	1944	Johannes Jensen*	1972	Heinrich Böll*
1910	Paul Heyse*	1945	Gabriela Mistral*	1973	Patrrick White*
1911	Maurice Maeterlink*	1946	Hermann Hesse*	1974	Eyvind Johnson*
1912	Gerhart Hauptmann	1947	André Gide*		Harry Martinson*
1913	Rabindranath Tagore*	1948	t.s. eliot*	1975	Eugenio Montale*
1914	no prize	1949	William Faulkner*	1976	Saul Bellow*
1915	Romain Rolland*	1950	Bertrand Russell*	1977	Vicente Aleixandre
1916	Verner von Heidenstam*	1951	Par Lagerkvist*	1978	Isaac Bashevis Singer*
1917	Henrik Pontoppidan*	1952	François Mauriac*	1979	Odysseus Elytis*
1918	no prize	1953	Winston Churchill*	1980	Czeslaw Milosz*
1919	Carl Spitteler*	1954	Ernest Hemingway*	1981	Elias Canetti*
1920	Knut Hamsun*	1955	Halldór Laxness*	1982	Gabriel García
1921	Anatole France*	1956	Juan Jiménez*		Márquez*
1922	Jacinto Benavente*	1957	Albert Camus*	1983	William Golding*
1923	William Butler Yeats*	1958	Boris Pasternak	1984	Jaroslav Seifert*
1924	Wladyslaw Reymont*		(declined)*	1985	Claude Simon*
1925	George Bernard Shaw*	1959	Salvatore Quasimodo*	1986	Wole Soyinka*
1926	Grazia Deledda*	1960	Saint-John Perse	1987	Joseph Brodsky*
1927	Henri Bergson*	1961	Ivo Andríc*	1988	Naguib Mahfouz*
1928	Sigrid Undset*	1962	John Steinbeck*	1989	Camilo Cela*
1929	Thomas Mann*	1963	George Seferis*	1990	Octavio Paz*
1930	Sinclair Lewis*	1964	Jean-Paul Sartre	1991	Nadine Gordimer*
1931	Erik A. Karlfeldt		(declined)*	1992	Derek Walcott*
1932	John Galsworthy*	1965	Mikhail Sholokhov*	1993	Toni Morrison*

PEACE

Year	Winner	Year	Winner	Year	Winner
1901	Jean H. Cunant Frederic Passy	1910	Permanent International Peace Bureau	1926	Aristide Briand* Gustav Stresemann
1902	Elie Ducommun* Charles A. Gobat	1911	Tobias M. C. Asser Alfred H. Fried	1927	Ferdinand E. Buisson Ludwig Quidde
1903	Sir William R. Cremer	1912	Elihu Root*	1928	no prize
1904	Institute of International Law	1913	Henri La Fontaine	1929	Frank B. Kellogg
		1914–16	no prize	1930	Nathan Soderblom
1905	Baroness Bertha von Suttner	1917	International Red Cross	1931	Jane Addams* Nicholas Murray Butler
		1918	no prize		
1906	Theodore Roosevelt*	1919	Woodrow Wilson*	1932	no prize
1907	Ernesto T. Moncta Louis Renault	1920	Leon V. A. Bourgeois	1933	Norman Angell*
		1921	Karl H. Branting Christian L. Lange	1934	Arthur Henderson
1908	Klas P. Arnoldson Fredrik Bajer*	1922	Fridtjof Nansen	1935	Carl von Ossietzky
1909	Auguste M. F. Beemaert Paul H. B. B. d'Estournelles de Constant	1923–24	no prize	1936	Carlos de Saavedra Lamas
		1925	Sir J. Austen Chamberlain Charles G. Dawes*	1937	Viscount Cecil of Chelwood

Year	Winner	Year	Winner	Year	Winner
1938	Nansen International Office for Refugees	1960	Albert J. Luthuli	1979	Mother Teresa*
		1961	Daag Hammarskjöld*	1980	Adolfo Perez Esquivel
		1962	Linus Pauling*	1981	Office of U.N. High
1939–43	no prize	1963	International Red Cross;		Commissioner for
1944	International Red Cross		League of Red Cross		Refugees
1945	Cordell Hull*		Societies	1982	Alva Myrdal
1946	Emily G. Balch	1964	Martin Luther King, Jr.*		Alfonso Garcia Robles
	John R. Mott	1965	UNICEF	1983	Lech Walesa*
1947	Friends Service Council	1966–67	no prize	1984	Desmond Tutu*
	American Friends	1968	Rene Cassin	1985	International Physicians
	Service Com.	1969	International Labor		for the Prevention of
1948	no prize		Organization		Nuclear War
1949	Lord John Boyd Orr of	1970	Norman E. Borlaug	1986	Elie Wiesel*
	Brechin Mearns	1971	Willie Brandt*		Oscar Arias Sanchez
1950	Ralph Bunche*	1972	no prize	1988	U.N. Peacekeeping
1951	Leon Jouhaux	1973	Henry Kissinger*		Forces
1952	Albert Schweitzer*		Le Duc Tho (declined)	1989	Dalai Lama*
1953	George Marshall*	1974	Hisaku Sato*	1990	Mikhail Gorbachev*
1954	Office of the U.N. High		Sean McBride	1991	Daw Aung San Suu Kyi
	Commissioner for	1975	Andrei Sakharov*	1992	Rigoberta Menchu
	Refugees	1976	Mairead Corrigan	1993	F. W. de Klerk*
1955–56	no prize		Betty Williams		Nelson Mandela*
1957	Lester Pearson*	1977	Amnesty International		
1958	Georges Pire	1978	Menachem Begin*		
1959	Philip J. Noel-Baker		Anwar Sadat*		

PULITZER PRIZE WINNERS

FICTION

Year	Winner	Title	Year	Winner	Title
1918	Ernest Cook Poole*	His Family	1940	John Steinbeck*	The Grapes of Wrath
1919	Booth Tarkington*	The Magnificent Ambersons	1941	no prize	
			1942	Ellen Glasgow*	In This Our Life
1920	no prize		1943	Upton Sinclair*	Dragon's Teeth
1921	Edith Wharton*	The Age of Innocence	1944	Martin Flavin	Journey in the Dark
1922	Booth Tarkington*	Alice Adams	1945	John Hersey*	A Bell for Adano
1923	Willa Cather*	One of Ours	1946	no prize	
1924	Margaret Wilson*	The Able McLaughlins	1947	Robert Penn Warren*	All the King's Men
1925	Edna Ferber*	So Big	1948	James A. Michener*	Tales of the South Pacific
1926	Sinclair Lewis*	Arrowsmith (declined)	1949	James Gould Cozzens*	Guard of Honor
1927	Louis Bromfield*	Early Autumn			
1928	Thornton Wilder*	The Bridge of San Luis Rey	1950	A. B. Guthrie, Jr.*	The Way West
			1951	Conrad Richter*	The Town
1929	Julia M. Peterkin	Scarlet Sister Mary	1952	Herman Wouk*	The Caine Mutiny
1930	Oliver La Farge*	Laughing Boy	1953	Ernest Hemingway*	The Old Man and the Sea
1931	Margaret Ayer Barnes	Years of Grace			
			1954	no prize	
1932	Pearl S. Buck*	The Good Earth	1955	William Faulkner*	A Fable
1933	T. S. Stribling	The Store	1956	MacKinlay Kantor*	Andersonville
1934	Caroline Miller	Lamb in His Bosom	1957	no prize	
1935	Josephine W. Johnson	Now in November	1958	James Agee*	A Death in the Family
1936	Harold L. Davis	Honey in the Horn	1959	Robert Lewis Taylor	The Travels of Jaimie McPheeters
1937	Margaret Mitchell*	Gone with the Wind			
1938	John P. Marquand*	The Late George Apley	1960	Allen Drury*	Advise and Consent
			1961	Harper Lee*	To Kill a Mockingbird
1939	Marjorie Kinnan Rawlings*	The Yearling	1962	Edwin O'Connor*	The Edge of Sadness
			1963	William Faulkner*	The Reivers

GENERAL NONFICTION

AMERICAN POETRY

Year	Winner	Title	Year	Winner	Title
1922	Edwin Arlington Robinson	Collected Poems	1955	Wallace Stevens	Collected Poems
1923	Edna St. Vincent Millay	The Ballad of the Harp Weaver	1956	Elizabeth Bishop	Poems, North and South
1924	Robert Frost	New Hampshire: A Poem with Notes and Grace Notes	1957	Richard Wilbur	Things of This World
			1958	Robert Penn Warren	Promises: Poems 1954–1956
1925	Edwin Arlington Robinson	The Man Who Died Twice	1959	Stanley J. Kunitz	Selected Poems 1928–1958
1926	Amy Lawrence Lowell	What's O'Clock	1960	W. D. Snodgrass	Heart's Needle
			1961	Phyllis McGinley	Times Three: Selected Verse from Three Decades
1928	Edwin Arlington Robinson	Tristram			
1929	Stephen Vincent Benèt	John Brown's Body	1964	Louis Simpson	At the End of the Open Road
1930	Conrad Aiken	Selected Poems	1965	John Berryman	Dream Songs
1931	Robert Frost	Collected Poems	1966	Richard Eberhart	Selected Poems
1933	Archibald MacLeish	Conquistador	1967	Anne Sexton	Live or Die
1936	Tristam Coffin	Strange Holiness	1971	W. S. Merwin	The Carrier of Ladders
1937	Robert Frost	A Further Range			
1938	Marya Zatureuska	Cold Morning Sky	1973	Maxine Winokur Kumin	Up Country
1939	John Gould Fletcher	Selected Poems	1975	Gary Snyder	Turtle Island
1942	William Rose Benét	The Dust Which Is God	1976	John Ashbery	Self-Portrait in a Convex Mirror
1943	Robert Frost	A Witness Tree	1977	James Merrill	Divine Comedies
1944	Stephen Vincent Benét	Western Star	1978	Howard Nemerov	Collected Poems
			1979	Robert Penn Warren	Now and Then: Poems 1976–1978
1945	Karl Shapiro	V-Letter and Other Poems	1981	James Schuyler	The Morning of the Poem
1947	Robert Lowell	Lord Weary's Castle			
1948	W. H. Auden	The Age of Anxiety	1982	Sylvia Plath	The Collected Poems
1950	Gwendolyn Brooks	Annie Allen	1983	Galway Kinnell	Selected Poems
1951	Carl Sandburg	Complete Poems	1989	Richard Wilbur	New and Collected Poems
1952	Marianne Moore	Collected Poems			
1953	Archibald MacLeish	Collected Poems	1990	Charles Simic	The World Doesn't End
1954	Theodore Roethke	The Waking			

DRAMA

Year	Winner	Title	Year	Winner	Title
1920	Eugene O'Neill	Beyond the Horizon	1936	Robert E. Sherwood	Idiot's Delight
1921	Zona Gale	Miss Lulu Bett	1937	Moss Hart and George S. Kaufman	You Can't Take It with You
1922	Eugene O'Neill	Anna Christie			
1923	Owen Davis	Icebound	1938	Thornton Wilder	Our Town
1925	Sidney Howard	They Knew What They Wanted	1939	Robert E. Sherwood	Abe Lincoln in Illinois
1927	Paul E. Green	In Abraham's Bosom	1940	William Saroyan	The Time of Your Life (refused)
1928	Eugene O'Neill	Strange Interlude			
1929	Elmer Rice	Street Scene	1941	Robert E. Sherwood	There Shall Be No Night
1930	Marc Connelly	The Green Pastures			
1931	Susan Glaspell	Alison's House	1943	Thornton Wilder	The Skin of Our Teeth
1932	Ira Gershwin, George S. Kaufman, and Morrie Ryskind	Of Thee I Sing	1945	Mary Chase	Harvey
			1946	Russel M. Crouse and Howard Lindsay	State of the Union
1933	Maxwell Anderson	Both Your Houses			
1934	Sidney Kingsley	Men in White	1948	Tennessee Williams	A Streetcar Named Desire
1935	Zoë Akins	The Old Maid			

Year	Winner	Title	Year	Winner	Title
1949	Arthur Miller	Death of a Salesman	1971	Paul Zindel	The Effect of Gamma
1950	Oscar II Hammerstein, Josh Logan, and Richard Rodgers	South Pacific			Rays on Man-in-the-Moon Marigolds
			1973	Jason Miller	That Championship Season
1953	William Inge	Picnic	1975	Edward Albee	Seascape
1954	John Patrick	Teahouse of the August Moon	1976	Marvin Hamlisch	A Chorus Line
			1977	Michael Cristofer	The Shadow Box
1955	Tennessee Williams	Cat on a Hot Tin Roof	1979	Sam Shepard	Buried Child
			1980	Lanford Wilson	Talley's Folly
1956	Frances Goodrich and Albert Hackett	The Diary of Anne Frank	1981	Beth Henley	Crimes of the Heart
			1982	Charles Fuller	A Soldier's Play
1957	Eugene O'Neill	A Long Day's Journey into Night	1983	Marsha Norman	'Night, Mother
			1984	David Mamet	Glengarry Glen Ross
1958	Ketti Frings	Look Homeward, Angel	1985	Stephen Sondheim	Sunday in the Park with George
1959	Archibaald MacLeish	J.B.	1986		
1960	George Abbott, Jerry Bock, Sheldon Harnick, and Jerome Weidman	Fiorello	1987	August Wilson	Fences
			1988		
			1989	Wendy Wasserstein	The Heidi Chronicles
			1990	August Wilson	The Piano Lesson
1961	Tad Mosel	All the Way Home	1991	Neil Simon	Lost in Yonkers
1962	Abe Burrows and Frank Loesser	How to Succeed in Business without Really Trying	1992		
			1993	Tony Kushner	Angels in America: Millennium Approaches
1967	Edward Albee	A Delicate Balance			
1969	Howard Sackler	The Great White Hope			

FIRSTS IN SCIENCE AND EXPLORATION

Achievement	Person	Achievement	Person
American to orbit Earth	John Glenn	moving picture	Louis Lumière
analog computer	Vannevar Bush	multi-stage rocket designed by	Robert Godard
blood transfusion	William Halsted		
break the sound barrier	Chuck Yeager	non-astronaut in space	Christa McAuliffe
commission a fleet to sail around the world	Ferdinand Magellan	nonstop solo flight across the Atlantic	Charles Lindbergh
cross Arctic and Antarctic by air	Lincoln Ellsworth	nuclear-powered submarine developed by	Hyman Rickover
diesel engine	Rudolph Diesel	nuclear reactor built by	Enrico Fermi
Englishman to sail around the world	Francis Drake	politician in space	Jake Garn
European to reach North America	John Cabot	sail around the Cape of Good Hope	Bartolomeu Dias
human artificial heart transplant by	Michael Ellis Debakey	solo flight across the Atlantic	Charles Lindbergh
human-heart transplant by	Christiaan Barnard	solo flight from Hawaii to mainland America	Amelia Earhart
liquid-fueled rocket launched by	Robert Godard	synthesize penicillin	Vincent Du Vigneaud
man in space	Yuri Gagarin	voyage from Europe to Asia via Africa	Vasco Da Gama
man on the moon	Neil Armstrong		
man to reach South Pole	Roald Amundsen		

FIRSTS FOR WOMEN

GEOGRAPHICAL DISCOVERIES

SCIENTIFIC DISCOVERIES AND DEVELOPMENTS

Discovery	Person	Discovery	Person
theory of evolution	Charles Darwin	X-rays	Wilhelm Roentgen
theory of relativity	Albert Einstein	yellow fever	
theory of gravity	Isaac Newton	transmitted by	
Van Allen radiation		mosquitoes	Walter Reed
belts	James Alfred Van Allen		

SIGNIFICANT INVENTIONS

Invention	Person	Invention	Person
AC (alternating current)	Nikola Tesla (with	double convex	Johannes Kepler
motor	Galileo Ferraris)	microscope	
airplane	Orville and Wilbur	dubbing systems (for	
	Wright	film)	Lee De Forest
alkaline battery	Thomas Edison	dynamic tension	
analog computer	Vannevar Bush	(bodybuilding	
arc light	Charles Brush	method)	Charles Atlas
Archimedian screw (for	Archimedes	dynamite	Alfred Nobel
raising water)		electric telegraph	Samuel F. B. Morse
artificial heart	Robert Jarvik	electron microscope	James Hillier
atomic bomb	J. R. Oppenheimer (with	evaporated milk	Gail Borden
	Arthur Compton,	Fahrenheit scale (for	
	Enrico Fermi, and	measuring	
	Leo Szilard)	temperature)	Daniel Fahrenheit
atomic reaction	Enrico Fermi (and team)	Ferris wheel	George Washington
(manmade)			Gale Ferris
automatic revolver	Samuel Colt	FM (frequency	
baseball	Abner Doubleday	modulation)	Edwin Armstrong
basketball	James Naismith	Franklin stove	Benjamin Franklin
Beaufort's scale (wind	Francis Beaufort	Geiger Counter	Hans Geiger
scale)		geodesic dome	R. Buckminster Fuller
bifocal lenses	Benjamin Franklin	gyroscope	Jean Foucault
birth-control pill	Gregory Pincus (with	gyroscopic compass	Elmer Sperry
	Min Chuch Chang,	gyroscopic stabilizer	Elmer Sperry
	John Rock, and Carl	hydraulic press	Blaise Pascal
	Djerassi)	hydrogen bomb	Edward Teller (with
Bowie knife	Jim Bowie		Igor Kurchatov)
Braille	Louis Braille	hydroplane	Glenn Curtiss
bubble chamber	Donald Glaser	incandescent lamp	Thomas Edison
Bunsen burner	Robert Bunsen	induction motor	Nicola Tesla
Bunsen cell	Robert Bunsen	instant camera	Edwin Land
cabin biplane	Igor Sikorsky	internal combustion	Nikolaus Otto and
camera blimp	Lee De Forest	engine	Eugene Langlen
carburetor	Gottlieb Daimler	italic type	Aldo Mannucci
celluloid	John Hyatt	Jarvik-7 artificial heart	Robert Koffler Jarvis
Celsius temperature		jasperware	Josiah Wedgwood
scale	Anders Celsius	Kodak camera	George Eastman
color television	John Baird Logie	light bulb (carbon	Thomas Edison (with
condensing steam		filament)	J. W. Swan)
engine	James Watt	lightning conductor	Benjamin Franklin
copying machine	James Watt	Linotype machine	Ottman Mergenthaler
corn flakes	Will Keith Kellogg	liquid-fuel rocket	Robert Goddard
cotton gin	Eli Whitney	long-playing	
cyclotron	Ernest Lawrence	phonograph record	
daguerrotype	Louis Daguerre	(LP)	Peter Goldmark
dehydrating food	Clarence Birdseye	Mach supersonic scale	Ernst Mach
denim jeans	Levi Strauss	machine gun	Richard Gatling
Dewey Decimal System	Melvil Dewey	mass production	Eli Whitney
diesel engine	Rudolph Diesel	metal alloys	Elwood Haynes
disposable razor blade	King Camp Gillette	microphone	Clément Ader and
			Thomas Edison

Invention	Person	Invention	Person
mimeograph	A. B. Dick	sewing machine	
mini-skirt	André Courrèges (credited)	(improved)	Isaac Merrit Singer
		shorthand	Isaac Pitman
Morse Code	Samuel F. B. Morse	sower (machine seed	
nitroglycerine	Alfred Nobel	drill)	Jethro Tull
nylon	Wallace Hume Carothers	steamboat	John Fitch
		steamboat, long-distance	Robert Fulton
passenger elevator	Elisha Otis	stock ticker	Thomas Edison
phonograph	Thomas Edison	submarine, metal-clad	Robert Fulton
phonograph record	Émile Berliner	sundial	Anaximander (possible)
Polaroid Land Camera	Edwin Land	synthesizer	Robert Moog
polygraph	John Larson	syringe	Blaise Pascal
printing press	Johannes Gutenberg	telephone	Alexander Graham Bell
pyrometer	Josiah Wedgwood	telescope (astronomical)	Galileo
quick-freezing food		television	John Logie Baird (with
(frozen food)	Clarence Birdseye		C. F. Jenkins and
radio telescope	Grote Reber		D. Mihaly)
railroad signals/air		transistor	John Bardeen, Walter
brakes	George Westinghouse		Brattain, and William
reaper	Cyrus Hall McCormick		Shockley
reflecting telescope	Isaac Newton	underwater telegraph	
Richter scale	Charles Richter and Beno Gutenberg	cable	Samuel F. B. Morse
		VHF electromagnetic	
roll film	George Eastman	waves	Guglielmo Marconi
Rubik's Cube	Erno Rubik	visual display tubes	James Bryce
safety razor	King Camp Gillette	wireless telegraph	Guglielmo Marconi
sewing machine	Elias Howe		

ARCHITECTURAL LANDMARKS

Landmark	Architect	Landmark	Architect
AT&T building, NYC	Philip Johnson	Marshall Field building,	
Auditorium Building,		Chicago	Henry Richardson
Chicago	Louis Sullivan	Metropolitan Museum	Richard Hunt
Avery Fisher Hall,		MIT auditorium, chapel	Eero Saarinen
Lincoln Center	Max Abramowitz	Pan Am Building, New	
Boston Public Library	Charles McKim	York City	Walter Gropius
Capitol, Washington DC	Charles Bulfinch	Parthenon	Callicrates and Ictinus
Central Park	Frederick Olmsted	Rockefeller Center	Raymond Hood
East Wing, National		St. Paul's Cathedral,	
Gallery	I. M. Pei	London	Christopher Wren
Empire State Building	Shreve, Lamb, and Harmon	St. Peter's, Rome	Michelangelo
		Salk Institute, La Jolla,	
Falling Water House,		CA	Louis I. Kahn
Bear Run, PA	Frank Lloyd Wright	Smithsonian	James Renwick
Flatiron Building, New		Supreme Court	Cass Gilbert
York City	Daniel Burnham	Trinity Church, Boston	Henry Richardson
George Washington	Othmar Hermann	Trinity Church, NYC	Richard Upjohn
Bridge	Ammann	Uffizi Palace	Giorgio Vasari
Glass House	Philip Johnson	UNESCO headquarters,	
Golden Gate Bridge	Othmar Hermann Ammann	Paris	Marcel Breuer
		Union Station,	
Guggenheim Museum	Frank Lloyd Wright	Washington DC	Daniel Burnham
Hearst Castle, San		United Nations complex	Wallace Harrison
Simeon, CA	Julia Morgan	Washington, DC	Pierre L'Enfant
Kennedy Center	Edward Stone	Washington Monument	Robert Mills
Lincoln Center	Wallace Harrison	White House	James Hoban
Lincoln Memorial	Henry Bacon	Woolworth Bldg., NYC	Cass Gilbert
Madison Square Garden	Stanford White		